Encyclopedia of

World Environmental History

Encyclopedia of

World Environmental History

Shepard Krech III
J. R. McNeill
Carolyn Merchant
Editors

Volume 1 A–E

A Berkshire Reference Work

Routledge
New York London

Published in 2004 by

Routledge
29 West 35th Street
New York, NY 10001
www.routledge-ny.com

Published in Great Britain by
Routledge
11 New Fetter Lane
London EC4P 4EE
www.routledge.co.uk

Routledge is an imprint of the Taylor and Francis Group.
A Berkshire Reference Work
314 Main Street, Suite 12
Great Barrington, MA 01230
berkshirepublishing.com

10 9 8 7 6 5 4 3 2 1

Library of Congress Cataloging-in-Publication Data

ISBN 0-415-93732-9 (set)
ISBN 0-415-93733-7 (vol. 1)
ISBN 0-415-93734-5 (vol. 2)
ISBN 0-415-93735-3 (vol. 3)

Encyclopedia of world environmental history / Shepard Krech III, J.R. McNeill,
Carolyn Merchant, editors.
        p. cm.
Includes bibliographical references and index.
    ISBN 0-415-93732-9 (set : acid-free paper) — ISBN 0-415-93733-7 (v. 1 :
acid-free paper) — ISBN 0-415-93734-5 (v. 2 : acid-free paper) — ISBN 0-415-
93735-3 (v. 3 : acid-free paper)
    1. Human ecology—Encyclopedias. 2. Human beings—Effect of environment
on—Encyclopedias. 3. Nature—Effect of human beings on—Encyclopedias.
I. Krech, Shepard, 1944– II. McNeill, John Robert. III. Merchant, Carolyn.
    GF10.E63 2003
    304.2′03—dc21
                                                                2003008288

Printed in the United States of America on acid-free paper.

CONTENTS

EDITORIAL BOARD

Introduction

The *Encyclopedia of World Environmental History* offers a dynamic view of human interaction with the environment from the deep past to the present, encompassing the entire globe. Its three volumes comprise concise overviews of hundreds of topics, events, people, natural resources, and aspects of human culture and natural history, together with wide-ranging lists for further reading and hundreds of sidebars, photographs, and maps. This unique work is the product of a global community of scholars who include founders of the field of environmental history as well as prominent scholars in related fields.

A Global Endeavor

The logic of pursuing environmental history on the global scale is straightforward. Many processes of environmental change unfold without reference to borders or to our usual mental maps. In the centuries after Columbus, the prickly pear cactus spread from its Mexican home to South Africa, Morocco, Spain, Australia, and dozens of other lands. The European rabbit was another global conquistador, colonizing parts of every continent except Antarctica. The ongoing accumulation of carbon dioxide in the atmosphere, sulfur dioxide moving with the winds to fall as acid rain far from its point of origin, the overharvesting of the sea's richest fishing grounds, salt accumulation in irrigated lands, the late-nineteenth-century establishment of national parks, and the late-twentieth-century emergence of popular environmentalism—these and many processes like them were global, or nearly global, in scale.

At the same time, of course, some aspects of environmental history are national or regional in scope. When the United States created its Environmental Protection Agency in 1970, its jurisdiction was explicitly national. The desiccation of the Aral Sea, under way since 1960, is a regional affair, involving and affecting what are now several countries and populations in Central Asia. The poisoning of Minamata Bay, in Japan, with methyl mercury in the 1950s was a local matter at first, but became a national affair through lawsuits and political wrangling. Ultimately rather few subjects in environmental history are truly local, because as the naturalist John Muir noted, in nature everything is always hitched to everything else. The *Encyclopedia of World Environmental History* tries to take into account the fact that the arenas in which the events of environmental history have been played out are of various sizes and are often overlapping.

In seeking to take into account the range of environments on Earth, the *Encyclopedia* also aims to put human history into its broadest context. This is one of the signal contributions environmental history can make. Human struggles have always occurred within the framework of the natural world, and that framework has, always and everywhere, been in flux—sometimes rapid, sometimes slow. Wildlife, soils, climate, and disease are just some of the hundreds of factors in the natural world that have always constrained and conditioned the human experience. For its part, human action has increasingly affected the natural world and its evolution. Human society coevolves with nature; human history unfolds within a broad natural context even as it helps shape that context.

The emergence of environmental history as field of scholarship is part of a broad shift in the way we understand our environment. Centuries ago, at least in most cultures, the stars and the planets were thought to be immutable fixtures of the heavens. The Earth too was generally understood as everlasting, and life on Earth, even if in some versions created all of a piece, consisted of a fixed number of species which had been there from the start and would remain until the finish. But since the 1830s geologists have offered a picture of Earth's history that is truly historical. Biologists since the 1860s have increasingly agreed that life on Earth is always in flux, that species come and go. More recently astronomers and cosmologists have concluded that the universe itself is not timeless but instead historical: It is perhaps 13 to 14 billion years old, still expanding, and the stars, galaxies, and planets within it come and go. Increasingly, static or even equilibrium models of how everything works have given way to dynamic, historical models. The field of environmental history chronicles and analyses the dynamics of life on Earth.

World environmental history not only considers the whole world, it is also a worldwide undertaking. Although it was in the United States that historians first began to refer to themselves as environmental historians and first formed an organization explicitly devoted to environmental history, scholars elsewhere had long been interested in the same sorts of questions, historical geographers foremost among them. Indeed, drawing a distinction between the interests and methods of historical geographers and those of environmental historians is difficult. Nevertheless, from roughly the 1980s scholars choosing to call themselves environmental historians have set to work around the world. In Europe the most active communities developed in Germany, Sweden, Finland, Spain, and Britain. In Africa, where political and economic instability are huge obstacles to scholarly work, environmental historians have emerged since the mid-1980s, especially in South Africa, but in East Africa too. India has had a particularly active group of environmental historians since about 1985, as has Australia, and, more recently, New Zealand. Since 1990 or so a small but determined group of environmental historians has emerged in Latin America, mainly in Brazil and Mexico. By and large, environmental history has few practitioners in Russia, China, Japan, or the Arab world, although foreigners have explored environmental-history themes quite successfully for China and Japan. There are signs, moreover, that these pioneering efforts are attracting followers and inspiring new research.

If it comes to pass that environmental historians in those areas catch up to their colleagues in India, Germany, or the United States, then one day we shall have a richer, deeper command of the world's environmental history. That day is some way off. In the meantime, this *Encyclopedia* offers a comprehensive, up-to-date, in-depth, worldwide vision of environmental history, on every scale from local to global. In a few entries, it even ventures into space.

Chronicling Scholarship in Environmental History

The formation of the American Society for Environmental History in 1977 marked the birth of environmental history as a formal discipline, but its roots reach back to Plato in ancient Greece and Laozi in ancient China. In nineteenth-century North America, George Perkins Marsh's *Man and Nature* (1864) documented the destructive effects of human action on the land from the days of the ancient civilizations of the Mediterranean world. Marsh called for the restoration of forests, soils, and rivers through human cooperation with nature. Almost a century later, *Man's Role in Changing the Face of the Earth* (1956), edited by the geographer William L. Thomas, again offered a comprehensive history of environmental change from prehistory to the present. Samuel P. Hays showed how the conservation movement of the early twentieth century attempted reforestation and rangeland restoration in his book *Conservation and the Gospel of Efficiency* (1959), while Roderick Nash wrote on the evolution of attitudes toward wilderness in his *Wilderness and the American Mind*, first published in 1967. That same year, Clarence Glacken published a monumental account of the history of human attitudes toward nature from ancient times to the eighteenth century in *Traces on the Rhodean Shore*. William McNeill added to the discussion with *Plagues and Peoples* (1976), an analysis of the role of microbes and human disease in shaping history.

Since the 1970s an explosion of scholarship on United States environmental history has taken place. Historians of the U.S. West and Middle West have been especially active, and a considerable literature has developed, with the scholars William Cronon, Patricia Limerick, Vera Norwood, Donald Pisani, Stephen J. Pyne, Richard White, and Donald Worster being among the most widely read. Building on the early work of Avery O. Craven and Lewis Cecil Gray, scholarship on slavery and agriculture in the South has been carried out by Albert Cowdrey, Jack Temple Kirby, Timothy Silver, Mart A. Stewart, and most recently by Dianne D. Glave and Elizabeth Blum. Foundational work on the environment of the Northeast includes that of William Cronon, John T. Cumbler, Calvin Martin, Carolyn Merchant, Theodore Steinberg, and Alan S. Taylor, while the urban environment and its problems has been the focus of study by Robert Gottlieb, Suellen Hoy, Andrew Hurley, Martin Melosi, Adam Rome, and Joel Tarr. New directions in the field include the roles of women in environmental and conservation history, the history of environmental justice, and the responses of minorities to environmental change.

In Europe, historians of the Annales School (a group of French historians who published in the journal *Annales*) examined environmental changes in Europe, such as forest clearing and wetland drainage in response to population fluctuations. Emmanuel LeRoy Ladurie, Marc Bloch, and Fernand Braudel were especially concerned with the environments of France and the Mediterranean world and the ways in which population, disease, poverty, and resources interacted. In England, historians such as W. G. Hoskins, Joan Thirsk, Jerome Blum, Eric Hobsbawm, and B. H. Slicher Van Bath examined how the English and northern European landscapes changed with the spread of grazing and the three-field system of agriculture. Joseph Needham's multivolume *Science and Civilization in China* (1954–2000) is an important starting point for an environmental history of China, while Anil Agarwal and Sunita Narain's *The State of India's Environment* (1985) and Richard P. Tucker and John F. Richards's *Global Deforestation and the Nineteenth-Century World Economy* (1983) are launching points for an environmental history of South and Southeast Asia. Finally, *The Earth As Transformed by Human Action* (1990), a comprehensive environmental history of the world over the past three hundred years, edited by B. L. Turner II and others, followed in the tradition of the works by George Perkins Marsh and William L. Thomas. In a mere three decades the field of environmental history has grown exponentially and spread over the world. These volumes are an effort to synthesize that work and array it in an accessible manner.

Perspectives and Approaches

Environmental history encompasses a variety of approaches to analyzing human interactions with the natural world. By viewing physical and biological processes as integral parts of history, the natural world becomes a subject for historical investigation. Mammals, birds, plants, bacteria, and viruses constitute biotic actors that play important roles in the unfolding of history. Abiotic constituents and processes—climatic change, soil composition, hydraulic forces, and atmospheric compounds, for example—are also im-

portant in the eyes of environmental historians. In the human realm, economic systems, population sizes, consumption patterns, political institutions, attitudes toward race and gender, and ideas about nature affect our interaction with natural systems.

Cultural perspectives on nature vary widely around the globe. Indigenous peoples, Eastern philosophers, nineteenth-century Romantics, and environmental scientists all had or have differing views of what nature is and how the natural world arose. People have used stories, myths, dance, art, photography, and religion to express their perceptions of nature as a gift of the gods or a collection of resources to be used for human benefit, and to craft guidelines for ethical behavior. A narrative approach sets up overarching story lines of progress in subduing and controlling nature or of the loss of pristine nature and the decline in species and environmental quality. Whatever the approach, the complexity and unpredictability of nature and human societies are inescapable themes in environmental history. Environmental history is thus of growing interest and value to many other disciplines, to policy makers, restoration ecologists, and a variety of cultures and societies around the world.

Environmental History and the History of Science

Environmental history draws on numerous sciences and their histories. Ecology, botany, zoology, bacteriology, medicine, geology, physics, and chemistry all bear directly on environmental history. Perhaps the most fundamental and encompassing science is ecology. Climate, rainfall, and average annual temperatures set limits to the vegetation and related animal life in a given region. Soil types may vary greatly over short distances, as may water availability. Depending on the array of conditions present, the region will either be attractive for human settlement attractive or challenging. A given culture's extraction of such resources as plant and animal foods, pelts, fuels, and minerals for trade affects local ecological conditions and hence the potential for continued settlement or the necessity of migration. The science of ecology therefore aids environmental historians in interpreting the ways a culture interacts with the land and surrounding peoples. But environmental historians are also aware that ecology as a science continues to evolve and that the history of ecology is relevant to how environmental history is written. Ecological concepts such as plant succession, biodiversity, the balance of nature, and the unpredictability of weather are reassessed and modified over the years, influencing the way environmental history is written and revised.

Equally important for environmental historians is the history of disease and medicine. Whether a population is susceptible or immune to an introduced disease is critical to the success both of colonizers and indigenous populations. Much of world environmental history can be interpreted in the light of epidemics of diseases such as smallpox, measles, bubonic plague, tuberculosis, influenza, and viruses that European colonizers brought to the New World. Outbreaks of cholera and yellow fever associated with contaminated or stagnant water and black and brown lung diseases associated with the mining and manufacturing industries are also influential disease patterns in environmental history. Knowing the history of epidemiology, virology, and toxicology can therefore be critical to the way environmental historians interpret their subject matter.

Another way to approach environmental history is through the history of the environmental and earth sciences. How a culture understands geology, climatology, and mineralogy influenced the ways in which it extracts minerals, processes them, and attaches importance to them—and that understanding changes with time. Whether a society uses coal, iron, gold, or silicon as a resource depends not only on their availability but also on how they are conceptualized at a given historical moment and how they fit into a society's material infrastructure and interpretation of nature. For example, whether it is acceptable to mine for metals may depend on whether metals are thought of as living or dead, as well as the technologies available to extract and process them and the importance of metal products to material culture and personal wealth.

Finally, the histories of physics, biology, and chemistry help environmental historians understand the ways a society thinks about the natural world. Newtonian mechanics, Darwinian evolution, thermodynamics, atomic theory, and the periodic table of elements are frameworks both for technological development and for aesthetic, ethical, and religious appreciation of the natural order and humanity's place within it. All branches of the history of science, then, are integral parts of world environmental history.

Environmental History and Gender

Gender is important to environmental history because the nature of male and female interactions with the natural world has changed over time and differs from culture to culture. Gathering, hunting, fishing, and horticulture—all activities that affect environmental quality and resource availability—often have sex-specific components. In some cultures men are primarily responsible for hunting larger game animals while women may participate in hunting smaller animals and in meat processing. In some cultures women are primarily responsible for gathering and shifting horticulture, using digging tools, while in others men may assume responsibility for horticulture and for settled agriculture when large draft animals are used in plowing. Fishing likewise is often differentiated along gender lines, with men setting nets and weirs or fishing from boats and women gathering shellfish or fishing with hooks and lines.

The ways in which such gendered production systems use, exploit, or conserve resources is relevant to the production systems' sustainability over time and their adaptability to new environments. Environmental historians study them on a case-by-case basis. For example, during the period of European colonization, agricultural systems in which men used draft animals and plows in large fields for grain production and women worked in vegetable and herb gardens, tended poultry, and processed food spread rapidly around the temperate regions of the globe, supplanting indigenous systems based on gathering, hunting, fishing, and horticulture. While the colonizing systems may have been more efficient than the indigenous systems in exploiting soils and forests for subsistence and profit, they may also have wasted resources—at least initially, until resource degradation stimulated agricultural improvement and forest conservation. Of interest to environmental historians is the interaction between women and men in traditional systems and between cultures during colonization. Environmental historians ask whether any generalizations can be made or patterns discerned regarding the roles of the sexes in conserving or exploiting resources.

Environmental historians are also interested in the ways women and men responded to the need for resource conservation and environmental improvement during the era of industrialization at the beginning of the nineteenth century and the era of environmentalism at the end of the twentieth century. Women played major roles in lobbying for the conservation of forests, parks, and wildlife, often seeing themselves at odds with the interests and activities of men, which they perceived as exploitative and wasteful. Similarly, women also challenged the men of their communities to clean up polluted air and water and to institute street cleaning and garbage collection. During the environmental movement of the 1970s and subsequent decades, which was sparked in large part by Rachel Carson's 1962 book *Silent Spring*, women pressed for wilderness preservation, clean air and water legislation, pesticide controls, and the cleanup of toxic landfills and chemical incinerators. Women around the world became leaders in conservation, environmental, and antitoxic movements both in industrialized and developing nations, from the local to the international level.

A third issue is the relationship between gender and metaphor in depicting nature in myth, religion, science, literature, and art. Whether nature is viewed as created and directed by a male god, a goddess, female nature acting through God's direction, a raven, a grandmother spider, or a set of gender-neutral processes can be relevant to the ways in which it is used. Nature may be viewed as a mother to be revered, a virgin to raped, or a witch who brings bad harvests and human ailments. Such images of nature can influence human ethical behavior and ritual practice. Some rituals may encourage the conservation of resources while others may have little practical consequence but may nevertheless set up a framework of reverence and respect for the natural world. Conversely, rituals may encourage exploitation and waste. Analyzing the gendered meanings found within a given culture's icons and narratives can thus provide clues to attitudes that may reinforce particular practices or provide inspiration for changing those practices.

Environmental History and Anthropology

For well over a century anthropologists have posed many of the same questions as environmental historians. As their discipline took shape in the nineteenth century, a number of anthropologists were concerned with the relationship between humans and the environment; specifically, the determining or constraining influence of geography, environment, or climate on human society and culture. Their arguments (now discredited) suggested that extremes in climate or latitude, or barrenness of land, hindered the development of culture and mental disposition, while temperate climates were believed to favor the development of what theorists perceived as human capacity.

Nineteenth-century anthropology was swept along by evolutionism, which brought to the discipline a continuing focus on human adaptations in different environments. At first, evolutionary interest centered on grand unilineal schemes—evolution of the family, religion, or human society. Reaction to these speculative designs was sharp at the beginning of the twentieth century, which saw the beginning of an era of anti-evolutionist (and anti-environmental-determinist) fervor, but in the 1930s and 1940s anthropologists returned to evolution with greatly lowered sights in a succession of fields called cultural evolution, cultural ecology, ecological anthropology, and historical ecology. Their theories about the static or dynamic relationship between humans and the environment tended to be grounded in specific historical and cultural contexts and have been important for the unfolding relationship between anthropology and environmental history.

Cultural Evolution and Cultural Ecology

Cultural evolution and cultural ecology, premised on the theory that humans adapt to natural and social environments by cultural means, were popular fields in anthropology for decades. Anthropologists explored the relationship between technology, population, control of energy, and social complexity. Many considered technology and the instruments and modes of production as well as certain natural characteristics (for example, the environmental circumscription of societies with expanding populations) important determinants of culture and human behavior. A modified geographical determinism linked these schemes to those of the nineteenth century, but it was almost always tempered by the interplay of environment and technology. The focus almost always remained on human society, however, not on the environment, although clearly evolution played out in unfolding relationships between human societies and their environments.

Ecological Anthropology and Historical Ecology

In the 1960s, anthropological interest in the human-environmental relationship matured as ecological anthropology, which explores the application in human societies of the concepts of ecosystem, ecological niche, habitat, and adaptation, came into its own. The most famous work of ecological anthropology suggested that ritual was the regulatory mechanism balancing the ratio of human and pig populations to the carrying capacity of the land in New Guinea. Others works explored the adaptations and human-land relations of hunter-gatherers, pastoralists, or agriculturalists under changing circumstances (including the encroaching presence of global economic systems). The challenges of applying the concepts of function, adaptation, and system at both the level of the individual and the group have been constant in both ecology and anthropology.

The most recent iteration of the anthropological interest in human-environment relations is historical ecology, defined as the study of ecosystems of the past through change in landscapes. For many of its proponents, historical ecology emerged not merely because scholars wished to understand past human-environment relationships but also out of a desire to guide humanity to a sustainable future.

Anthropological Archaeology

The commitment of anthropological archaeologists to exploring ecological and evolutionary questions has remained particularly constant through the years. Many have been deeply influenced by cultural ecology; others focus on individual decision making and still others on more systemic processes in environmental change (insofar as either is revealed in the archaeological record).

Recent archaeological contributions to our understanding of the impact of humans on ancient environments around the world have been substantial. They include studies of the impact of predation, fire, increases in population size and density, the domestication of plants and animals, urbanism, intensification of production, and crowd diseases. A growing number of archaeologists are interested in large-scale histories of past societies. For example, they have investigated the impact of climatic fluctuation or volcanic eruptions in the American West, the impact of farming in the Mediterranean, the connections, if any, between the demand for trees, deforestation, and human population dispersal. When people migrate they transport their landscapes (both mental models and physical icons) with them, and anthropological archaeologists are increasingly interested in the impact of such movements and changes.

Social and Cultural Anthropology

Social and cultural anthropologists contribute to environmental history through ethnography and historical analysis. Their interests are remarkably varied. Some study indigenous peoples' extensive knowledge of the natural world, made sense of culturally and organized in taxonomies that both overlap with and depart significantly from Western scientific schemes. Others focus on the cultural construction of nature, the demo-graphic and environmental impact of epidemic disease, anthropogenic landscapes, the impacts of pastoralism and agrarianism, long-term adaptations and the possibilities of sustainability, the cultural construction of environmental values, the ethnography of environmentalism, the politics of environmental issues, and environmental justice. It is a varied and rapidly expanding field, one no doubt enhanced by the realization that the relationship between humans and the environment will present some of the most critical challenges of the twenty-first century.

Environmental History and Natural History

The links between natural history—the descriptive, systematic and, ultimately, scientific study of the natural world—and environmental history are varied. In the West, the roots of the discipline of natural history can be traced to Aristotle and to certain early-modern thinkers, whose taxonomies reflected the importance of the perceived relationship between the natural world and humans. Not surprisingly, ideas about the natural world reflected thoughts about human emotions, aesthetics, morality, society, and culture. In the sixteenth through eighteenth centuries, a period of Western expansion of geographical and descriptive knowledge of the natural world through exploration and the return of specimens to cabinets of curiosities, more detached perspectives on nature entered natural history even as religious explanations of nature remained essentially intact.

In some ways the eighteenth century was a high point for natural history. During that century significant works of natural description and classification (by Linneaus, Buffon, and others) were published, governments sponsored the study of natural history, botanical decoration and illustration became popular, people celebrated arcadian harmony, a benign, holistic relationship between man and nature was posited, and there was a significant rise in concern for the environment.

In the nineteenth century natural history's emphasis on morphological study of life forms continued but theoretical energy shifted to newly emergent disciplines, all of which were increasingly (after mid-century) affected by evolutionary thought. By the early twentieth century biology, physiology, ecology, and other fields of scientific inquiry had pushed natural history aside, relegating it in the minds of many to an antiquarian pursuit confined to museums. Many regarded ecology in particular as the new natural history.

Yet natural history continued, both as a descriptive and taxonomic pursuit and in the nature essays of such writers as John Burroughs, John Muir, Aldo Leopold, and many others whose humanist, aesthetic, or spiritual awe mediated their experience of nature as much as did science. It may be in the nature essay, traceable to the eighteenth-century British clergyman and naturalist Gilbert White, that natural history has seen its most consistent overlap with environmental history. Today's nature writers continue to stress the importance of combining in their narratives close descriptive, systematic knowledge of the natural world with empathy and reflection.

But natural history remains highly visible to the public not just in natural-history essays but through the existence of major museums whose names proclaim dedication to assemblages of facts about the natural world, to scientific description and taxonomy. The outgrowth of cabinets of curiosities, museums of natural history emerged in the eighteenth century and proliferated in the nineteenth. Today they educate millions of visitors in the Western world about the natural world and, increasingly, about environmental history.

Content and Types of Articles

The *Encyclopedia of World Environmental History* contains 520 articles arranged from A to Z with numerous cross references. It provides coverage of the following general topics:

Arts, Literature, and Architecture
Biomes, Climate, and Natural Events
Economic Systems
Energy Sources
Eras and Civilizations, Ancient
Exploitation and Processes
Key Concepts and Philosophies
Law and Regulation
Nations and Regions, Modern
Nonliving Resources
Organizations
People
Places and Events
Plant and Animal Resources
Religion
Sociocultural Resources
Technology and Science

Some of the articles are general, focusing on a region of the world or a period of time; others are shorter and cover specific environmental issues or organizations; still others are brief accounts of an individual or a species in relation to environmental history. In order to keep the *Encyclopedia* within reasonable page and volume limits, we have excluded living environmentalists from our coverage.

Additional Content

The *Encyclopedia* is enriched by 20 maps, 111 photographs, and 115 sidebars, which provide supplemental information not in the articles themselves. Eight maps, which appear together in the front matter of each volume, identify the nations of each major region of the world. The other twelve maps accompany articles on such topics as oil or tropical forests and show the distribution of resources or processes around the world. The photographs enhance the articles by showing artwork, historical figures, plants, animals, and minerals, environmental phenomena, and more. The sidebars provide additional information and include:

- Extracts from historical documents, including quotations from environmental scientists, brief descriptions of environmental events, and firsthand accounts by explorers, settlers, and early travelers.
- Extracts from ethnographic accounts that provide firsthand descriptions of the ways that indigenous peoples used their environments and of treaties made between settlers and indigenous peoples.
- Extracts from environmental literature, poetry, and religious traditions that influence the ways people respond to the environment, both positively and negatively.

In short, the *Encyclopedia of World Environmental History* is an indispensable, up-to-date, in-depth guide to the multitude of issues environmental history addresses. We believe it will prove to be the authoritative reference on environmental history, and we hope it will inspire today's as well as the next generation of scholars, as well as students and environmentally aware citizens across the globe.

Shepard Krech III, J. R. McNeill, and Carolyn Merchant

Acknowledgments

Creating an encyclopedia requires the combined talents, good will, and breadth of knowledge of hundreds of people. It depends on the relationships between ideas, fields of study, and the research of hundreds, even thousands, of people working over decades, and even over centuries. The *Encyclopedia of World Environmental History* is the creation of a global network of scholars, led by editors Shepard Krech III, J. R. McNeill, and Carolyn Merchant, working with the project directors and editorial team at Berkshire Publishing Group of Great Barrington, Massachusetts.

Editor J. R. McNeill deserves particular thanks both for ensuring that the project was as global as we could make it and for his prompt and cogent responses to hundreds of queries. We had talked to J. R. McNeill about the project before it was begun with Routledge, and he was frank about the difficulties involved in trying to cover the world—a task he had just completed in his *Something New Under the Sun: An Environmental History of the 20th Century.* "But," he said, "that doesn't mean you shouldn't try."

We were also extremely fortunate to have Carolyn Merchant and Shepard Krech III as editors. The editorial guidance and wide knowledge of U.S. historian Carolyn Merchant was a huge help, and her calm belied the fact that she was also serving as president of the American Society of Environmental History during the period we were working on the *Encyclopedia.* Shepard Krech III understood the importance of this project right away, introduced us to Carolyn, and was instrumental in setting up our first editorial meeting. Throughout the project he provided the perspective of an anthropologist, something we welcome in any multidisciplinary project and particularly in this one.

Our editorial advisory board—Carole Crumley, Mark Elvin, Susan Flader, Don Fowler, Margaretta Lovell, Jim McCann, Cheryl Oakes, Vera Norwood, Emily Russell, Doug Weiner, Verena Winiwarter, and John Wirth—provided invaluable suggestions and an international perspective. We want especially to acknowledge the contribution—as editorial board member and author—of John Wirth, whose sudden death in 2002 was a great loss to the community of environmental historians. Cheryl Oakes's suggestions of potential authors were especially helpful and Verena Winiwarter, president of the European Society of Environmental History, was a great help in working with our many European contributors.

At Berkshire Publishing, project coordinator Elizabeth Eno ably steered both articles and authors and cheerfully faced the daily challenge of finding a way to cover the whole wide world. Associate editor Marcy Ross and copy editors Mike Nichols, Francesca Forrest, Stephen Sanborn, and Peter Donovan took responsibility for ensuring that articles were consistent and clear, while Berkshire's resident anthropologist, David Levinson, provided invaluable advice throughout the course of the project.

The *Encyclopedia's* origins at Berkshire Publishing go back to 1993, when I was managing editor for the *Encyclopedia of U.S. Foreign Relations* and looking for an author for an article on the environment and U.S. foreign policy. I was intrigued by the field of environmental history and followed its gradual development over the next few years, as we founded Berkshire and developed other major global references, including the *Encyclopedia of Modern Asia* (Scribners 2002). The idea planted in 1993 finally sprang to life six years later, as this *Encyclopedia of World Environmental History,* during a meeting with Sylvia Miller, the new publisher at Routledge in New York. To my surprise and delight she responded with instant enthusiasm when I mentioned environmental history as a possible topic for an encyclopedia. Sylvia, too, deserves special thanks for her continued support and commitment. Others at Routledge who have played an important role in bringing this project to completion are Marie-Claire Antoine, Elizabeth Sheehan, and Michael Aneiro.

We are also grateful to the National Humanities Center in North Carolina for their role in funding fellowships in the ecological humanities. These fellowships brought both Shepard Krech and Carolyn Merchant to the NHC in March 2001 and facilitated two meetings of the editors with the Berkshire Publishing team.

Our contributors include old friends and colleagues (including Kurk Dorsey, the long-ago author of the article for *U.S. Foreign Relations*), and through this project we have made many new friends, whose thoughtful writing and enthusiasm for the environmental history has been an inspiration. Some of our authors did much more than write; they also suggested other contributors and gave advice on editorial matters related to their area of expertise. Those who deserve special credit in this respect are William Kovarick, Stuart McCook, and Martin Reuss. We also want to acknowledge the support and practical assistance given by several people who did not write articles: William Cronon, Samuel Hays, and Jeffrey Stine.

Late in the project, we sent out an e-mail asking for suggestions for short quotations that could accompany articles. We received an enthusiastic response, and readers will see selections offered by Phil Cafaro, Neil Clayton, William Forbes, Choyun Hsu, Richard Jones, Linda Lear, Peter Matthews, Wesley Mott, Vera Norwood, Gene Robinson, Mikko Saikku, Mark Stoll, Abby Van Slyck, and Robert Wojtowicz.

While the *Encyclopedia of World Environmental History* offers the most comprehensive coverage of the history of human interaction with the natural world, it is far from being the last word on the subject. The editors and Berkshire Publishing welcome corrections and suggestions for further work in this area, and can be contacted at the website listed below.

Karen Christensen
Berkshire Publishing Group LLC
www.berkshirepublishing.com

List of Entries

Environmental Education
Environmental Ethics
Environmental Impact Statement
Environmental Justice
Environmental Narratives
Environmental Philosophy
Environmental Politics
Environmental Protection Agency
Environmental Regulation
Environmentalism
Estuaries
Ethnobotany
Eucalyptus
Europe, Ancient
Europe, Medieval
European Starling
Evolution and the Spread of Humans
Exotic Species
Exploration
Extinction

Fascism
Fertilizers
Fiber Crops
Fire
Fishing
Floods
Fodder Crops
Food Chain
Ford, Henry
Forests, Temperate
Forests, Tropical
France
Free Trade
Fresh Air Fund
Friends of the Earth

Gaia Theory
Gandhi, Mohandas K.
Ganges River
Gardens and Gardening
Genetically Modified Food
Geothermal Energy
Germany
Glaciers
Glen Canyon
Global Warming
Goats
Gold
Grains
Grapes

Grasslands
Great Auk
Great Lakes and St. Lawrence River
Green Building
Green Parties
Green Revolution
Green Urbanism
Greenbelt Movement
Greenpeace
Grinnell, George Bird
Guano

Haber, Fritz
Hamilton, Alice
Hardin, Garrett
Heavy Metals
Herring Gull
Himalayas
Hinduism
Honeybee
Hornaday, William T.
Horse
House Sparrow
Huang River
Hudson River
Hudson River School
Hungary
Hunting and Fishing
Hunting and Gathering

Ice Ages
Ickes, Harold
India
India, Ancient—Indus Valley
Indigenous Peoples
Indus River
Industrial Health and Safety
Industrial Revolution
Insects
International Law
International Union for the Conservation of Nature
International Whaling Commission
Intertropical Convergence Zone
Iron
Irrigation
Islam
Italy
Ivory-billed Woodpecker
Izaak Walton League of America

Jainism
Japan

Contributor List

Ackland, Len
University of Colorado, Boulder
Media

Adams, Carol J.
Richardson, Texas
Animal Rights

Adelson, Jon
Environmental Justice

Adshead, S. A. M.
University of Canterbury
Salt

Aftandilian, David
Chicago, Illinois
Bear

Agnoletti, Mauro
University of Florence, Italy
Forests, Temperate

Alagona, Peter S.
University of California, Los Angeles
Lake Victoria

Applegate, Roger D.
Kansas Department of Wildlife and Parks
Wild Turkey

Armiero, Marco
Istituto di Storia Economica del Mezzogiorno
Italy

Armitage, Kevin C.
University of Kansas
Dewey, John
Seton, Ernest T.

Arnebeck, Bob
Thousand Island Park, New York
Beaver

Ayres, Ed
Worldwatch Institute
Biophilia

Bale, John
Keele University
Sports

Balee, William
Tulane University
Ecology, Historical

Banerjee, Tirtho
Centre for Science and Environment, New Delhi, India
Ecotourism
Ganges River

Barrow. Jr., Mark V.
Virginia Tech University
Audubon, John James
Hornaday, William T.

Bartolome, James W.
Grasslands
Ranching
Succession

Bassett, Thomas J.
University of Illinois
Bush Meat

Bates, Albert K.
Global Village Institute for Appropriate Technology
Utopianism

Beach, Hugh
Uppsala University
Caribou

Beach, Timothy
Georgetown University
Soil
Terracing and Field Ridging

Beatley, Timothy
University of Virginia, Charlottesville
Green Urbanism

Bedell, Rebecca
Wellesley College
Landscape Art, American

Beinart, William
St. Antony's College, University of Oxford
Africa, Southern
Communal Areas Management Programme for
Indigenous Resources (CAMPFIRE)
South Africa

Bendik-Keymer, Jeremy
Colorado College
Sacred Places

Bennett, Judith A.
University of Otago
Oceania

Berg, Peter
Planet Drum Foundation
Bioregionalism

Bergad, Laird W.
Graduate Center, City University of New York
Sugar and Sugarcane

Berry, Brian
University of Texas, Dallas
Urbanization

Bescoby, David
University of East Anglia
Europe, Medieval

Black, Brian
Pennsylvania State University
Nuclear Power
Sprawl
Suburbanization

Blockstein, David
Takona Park, Maryland
Passenger Pigeon

Bourke, R. M.
Australia National University
Sweet Potato

Brimblecombe, Peter
University of East Anglia
Acid Rain

Broadway, Michael J.
Northern Michigan University
Meat Processing

Brondizio, Eduardo
University of Indiana
Ecology, Cultural

Brooking, Tom
University of Otago, New Zealand
New Zealand

Brosnan, Kathleen A.
University of Houston
Tourism
United States - Southwest

Bunin, Lisa J.
University of California, Santa Cruz
Greenpeace

Burger, Joanna
Rutgers University
Oil Spills

Cafaro, Philip
Colorado State University
Thoreau, Henry David

Caffrey, Patrick
Washington and Jefferson College
Mao Zedong

Cain, Louis P.
Loyola University, Chicago & Northwestern
University
Endangered Species Act
Snail Darter

Camino, Alejandro
Mountain Formum
Peru

Campbell, Gary
Michigan Technological University
Silver

Campbell, Gwyn
University of Avignon, France
Madagascar

Carey, Mark
University of California, Davis
Avalanches
Glaciers
Mountaineering

Carey, Ryan
University of Texas, Austin
Brower, David
League of Conservation Voters
National Wildlife Federation
Natural Resources Defense Council

Castro, Jose Esteban
University of Oxford
Argentina
Commodification
Marx, Karl
Rio de la Plata River
Socialism and Communism
Southern Cone

Cernea, Michael
George Washington University
Resettlement

Chouvy, Pierre-Arnaud
Courbevoie, France
Drug Production and Trade

Christensen, Karen
Berkshire Publishing Group
Green Parties

Christian, David
San Diego State University
Asia, Central - Ancient

Church, Chris
United Kingdom Community Development
Foundation
Friends of the Earth

Cioc, Mark
University of California, Santa Cruz
Germany
Rhine River
Rivers

Clark, Robert P.
George Mason University
Migration

Clayton, Neil
University of Otago
Weeds

Cleary, David
Nature Conservancy
Amazon River

Coates, Peter
University of Bristol
Exotic Species
Trans-Alaska Pipeline
Zebra Mussel

Cohen, Mark N.
State University of New York, Plattsburgh
Nutrition and Diet

Collins, Robert O.
University of California, Santa Barbara
Nile Valley (Aswan Dam)

Conte, Christopher A.
Utah State University
Africa, East

Crane, Jeff
University of Missouri
Dams, Reservoirs, and Artificial Lakes

Crosby, Alfred W.
University of Texas, Austin
Ecological Imperialism
Exploration

Cumbler, John
University of Louisville
United States - Northeast

Dameron Hager, Irene
Ohio State University
Great Lakes and St. Lawrence River

Daneel, Marthinus L.
Boston University
Association of African Earthkeeping Churches
Chimurenga

Davis, Diana K.
University of Texas, Austin
Middle East

de Boer, K. Lauren
EarthLight: Journal of Spiritual Ecology
Ecology, Spiritual

Delcourt, Hazel
University of Tennessee
North America - East

Delcourt, Paul
University of Tennessee
North America - East

DeLong, Carol Ann
Victor Valley College
Sierra Nevada Mountains

Dendy, David
Okanagan University College
Grains

Dickson, D. Bruce
Texas A&M University
Domestication, Plant and Animal
Horse
Pleistocene Overkill

Dicum, Gregory
Coffee

Diehl, Michael W.
Desert Archaeology, Inc.
North America - Southwest

DiMaria, Salvatore
Montgomery College
Biological Corridors

Dix, Andreas
University of Bonn
Phylloxera

Dodgen, Randall
Sonoma State University
Huang River

Dorsey, Kurk
University of New Hampshire
International Whaling Commission
Whale

Doughty, Robin
University of Texas, Austin
Birds

Draper, Malcom
University of Natal
Millennialism

Drummond, Jose
Universidade Federal Fluminense, Brazil
Brazil

Dwivedi, O. P.
University of Guelph
Chipko

Eaton, Heather
Saint Paul University
Ecofeminism

Egan, Michael
Washington State University
Dubos, Rene

Enstad, Craig
Boston University
Lake Chad

Eubanks, Mary W.
Duke University
Genetically Modified Food

Evans, Sterling
Humboldt State University
Central America
Fiber Crops
Mexico

Evenden, Matt
University of British Columbia
Canada

Evered, Kyle T.
Illinois State University
Balkans
Volga River

Feare, Chris J
Haslemere, Surrey, United Kingdom
European Starling

Feldman, James W.
University of Wisconsin, Madison
Rodale, J. I.

Fiege, Mark
Colorado State University
Irrigation

Fischer-Kowalski, Marina
University of Vienna
Ecology, Social

Fischman, Robert L.
University of Indiana
Law - Biological Conservation

Fisher, R. Colin
University of San Diego
Eastman, Charles

Flader, Susan
University of Missouri
Leopold, Aldo

Flippen, Brooks
Southeastern Oklahoma State University
Chesapeake Bay
Council on Environmental Quality

Forbes, William
University of North Texas
Korea

Ford, Richard
University of Michigan
Ethnobotany

Fortmann, Louise
University of California, Berkeley
Law - Land Use and Property Rights

Fougeres, Dorian
University of California, Berkeley
Law - Land Use and Property Rights

Fowler, Don D.
University of Nevada, Reno
Glen Canyon
North America - Great Basin and Columbia Plateau

Franceschetti, Donald R.
University of Memphis
Cosmology
Edison, Thomas Alva
Ford, Henry
Industrial Revolution
Linnaeus, Carolus
Spinoza

Frey, Bertram C.
Environmental Protection Agency
Environmental Regulation

Friend, Milton
Salton Sea Science Office
Salton Sea

Fuentes, Agustin
University of Notre Dame
Primates

Furtado, Junia
Belo Horizonte, Brazil
Diamonds
Gold

Gade, Daniel
University of Vermont
Andes

Galaty, John G.
McGill University
Pastoralism

Galter, Hannes D.
Institute of Ancient History, University of Graz
Mesopotamia

Garza, Roberto
University of Houston, Downtown
Droughts

Gibb, Steven
Risk Policy Report
Environmental Defense

Giles-Vernick, Tamara
City University of New York
Africa, Central

Glantz, Michael
National Center for Atmospheric Research, Boulder, CO
Aral Sea
El Nino and La Nina

Gordon, Robert B.
Yale University
Copper
Iron

Goto, Seiko
University of Manitoba
Landscape Art, Japanese

Grundmann, Reiner
Aston University, Birmingham, UK
Montreal Protocol

Guillet, David
Catholic University of America
Spain and Portugal

Haddad, Brent M.
University of California, Santa Cruz
Water

Hall, C. Michael
University of Otago
Greenbelt Movement
Murray River
Parks and Recreation

Hall, Marcus
Swiss Federal Research Institute
Ecological Restoration
Italy

Hamed, Safei-Eldin A.
Texas Tech University
Islam

Hammerl, Christa
Central Institute for Meteorology and Geodynamics
Earthquakes

Hammond, Debora
Sonoma State University
Ecopsychology

Haney, Alan
University of Wisconsin
Ecosystems

Harding, Stephan
Schumacher College, Devon, UK
Ecology, Deep

Harms, Robert
Yale University
Congo (Zaire) River

Harper, Krista
Smith College
Danube River
Hungary

Harper, Lila Marz
Central Washington University
Bird, Isabella

Harrison, Gary
University of New Mexico
Romanticism

Hasenoehrl, Ute
Wissenschaftszentrum Berlin für Sozialforschung
Bahro, Rudolf
Steiner, Rudolf

Haught, Jack
Georgetown University
Catholicism
Ecology, Christian

Hausdoerffer, John
Washington State University
Jefferson, Thomas

Hawks, John
University of Wisconsin, Madison
Evolution and the Spread of Humans

Hay, Peter
University of Tasmania
Environmental Philosophy

Hayes, Denis
Bullitt Foundation
Earth Day

Headland, Thomas N.
Summer Institute of Linguistics & University of Texas, Arlington
Pristine Myth

Heiman, Michael K.
Dickinson College
Capitalism
Toxicity
Tragedy of the Commons

Herrmann, Bernd
Georg August Universitaet
Microorganisms

Hill, Jen
University of Nevada, Reno
Bailey, Florence Merriam

Hineline, Mark L.
University of California, San Diego
Coral and Coral Reefs
Estuaries

Hirt, Paul
Washington State University
North America - Northwest Coast

Hodges, Richard
University of East Anglia
Europe, Medieval

Holm, Poul
University of Southern Denmark
Fishing
Oceans and Seas

Hoppe, Kirk Arden
University of Illinois, Chicago
Nile Perch

Hsu, Cho-yun
University of Pittsburgh
China, Ancient

Huba, Mikulas
Slovak Academy of Science
Slovakia

Hughes, J. Donald
University of Denver
Aristotle
Egypt, Ancient
Lucretius
Mediterranean Basin
Theophrastus

Huntsinger, Lynn
University of California, Berkeley
Grasslands
Ranching
Succession

Hurley, Andrew
University of Missouri, St. Louis
Mississippi and Missouri Rivers

Hutcheson, Michael R.
Landmark College
Agroecology and Agroforestry
British Empire
White, Gilbert

Hutton, Drew
Queensland University of Technology
Australian Conservation Foundation

Hyson, Jeffrey
Saint Joseph's University
Zoos

Ingram, David S.
Cambridge University
Diseases, Plant

Irvine, Sandy
City of Sunderland College
Brundtland Commission
Club of Rome
Consumer Movement
International Union for the Conservation of Nature
Nongovernmental Organizations
Soil Association
United Nations, Environment Programme
World Wildlife Fund

Isenberg, Andrew C.
Princeton University
Bison

Ives, Jack D.
Carleton University
Mountains

Jacoby, Karl
Brown University
Conservation

Jarvis, Kimberly A.
Colby College
Landscape Art, European
Manifest Destiny
Nature Photography
Nixon, Richard

Jelecek, Leos
Charles University
Czechia

Jones, Errol D.
Boise State University
Chavez, Cesar
Mendes, Chico

Jones, Richard A.
East Dulwich, London, UK
Black Fly
Darwin, Charles
Honeybee
Insects
Silk and Silkworm

Jordan, Peter
OSI Vienna
Poland

Jordan, William
New Academy for Nature and Culture
Ecological Restoration

Josephson, Paul
Colby College
Stalin, Joseph

Joyner, Chris
Georgetown University
Antarctica
Ice Ages

Jundt, Thomas
Brown University
Keep America Beautiful

Kates, James
Jefferson, Wisconsin
Reforestation

Kaufman, Polly Welts
University of Southern Maine
Douglas, Marjorie Stoneman
Women and Conservation

Keeling, Arn
University of British Columbia
Dioxins
Mackenzie River

Kheel, Marti
Feminists for Animal Rights
Vegetarianism

Kidwell, Clara Sue
University of Oklahoma
Religion, American Indian

Klubock, Thomas Miller
State University of New York, Stonybrook
Chile

Knapp, Gregory
University of Texas, Austin
Ecuador

Kovarik, William
Radford University
Industrial Health and Safety
Law - Toxic Waste

Krech III, Shepard
Brown University
Beaver
Catlin, George
Dodo
Traditional Environmental Knowledge

Kumar, Satish
Schumacher College, Devon, UK
Hinduism
Jainism
Schumacher, E. F.

Lachman, Charles
University of Oregon
Landscape Art, Chinese

Lajus, Dmitry L.
St. Petersburg, Russia
Tilapia

Lajus, Julia A.
Institute for the History of Science and Technology
Cod
Lamprey
Tilapia

Lamb, Peter J.
University of Oklahoma
Intertropical Convergence Zone

Larabee, Ann
Michigan State University
Bhopal Disaster

Latorre, Juan Garcia
Association for Landscape Research in Arid Zones
Deserts

Leaf, Murray J.
University of Texas, Dallas
Agribusiness
Boserup, Ester
Green Revolution
Himalayas
Rice

Lear, Linda
George Washington University
Carson, Rachel

Lenzi, Laura
University of Florence
Forests, Temperate

Levinson, David
Berkshire Publishing Group
Gandhi, Mohandas K.

Lewis, James G.
Falls Church, Virginia
Cotton
Hudson River School
Ickes, Harold
Marsh, George Perkins
Marshall, Robert
Philippines
Pinchot, Gifford
Roosevelt, Theodore
Ruckleshaus, William D.
Schurz, Carl
United States - Overview
United States - South

Lide, James
History Associates Incorporated
Chang River
Oceania, Ancient
Scandinavia
Yellow Sea

Liese, Walter
University of Hamburg
Bamboo

Liu, Keshun
Monsanto
Soybeans

Lourandos, Harry
University of Queensland, Australia
Australia, Aboriginal

Lovelock, James
European Communities Information Office
Gaia Theory

Lowther, Peter E.
Field Museum, Chicago
Brown-Headed Cowbird

Luttinger, Nina
TransFair USA, Oakland, CA
Coffee

Macfarlane, Alan
University of Cambridge
Tea

Madison, Mark
National Conservation Training Center
Malthus, Thomas
United States Fish and Wildlife Service

Magoc, Chris
Mercyhurst College
Environmental Narratives

Mannion, A. M.
University of Reading
Europe, Ancient
Fodder Crops
Manioc
Pesticides
Root Crops

Marsh, Kevin R.
Boise State University
North America - Northwest Coast

Matthews, P. J.
National Museum of Ethnology, Osaka, Japan
Taro

McCann, James C.
Boston University
Africa - Overview

McClain, W. Russ
The Nature Conservancy
Logging
Northern Spotted Owl

McCook, Stuart
University of Guelph
Cacao
Caribbean Coastlands
Colombia
Orinoco River
Venezuela

McMurry Edwards, Linda O.
North Carolina State University
Carver, George Washington

McNeill, J. R.
Georgetown University
Biological Exchanges
Black Sea
Mediterranean Sea
Midgley, Thomas
Population, Human

McNeill, William H.
University of Chicago
Potato

Medland, Vicki L.
University of Wisconsin, Green Bay
Biodiversity
Ecological Simplicity
Endangered Species
Food Chain
Shrimp

Mehta, Lyla
University of Sussex
Narmada Dam Project

Melosi, Martin V.
University of Houston
Waste Management

Meltzer, David J.
Southern Methodist University
North America - Plains

Mendelsohn, Betsy
University of Virginia
von Humboldt, Alexander

Merchant, Carolyn
University of California, Berkeley
Introduction
Eden
Richards, Ellen Swallow
Scientific Revolution

Miller, James
Queen's University
Laozi

Miller, Kristine
University of Minnesota
Landscape Architecture

Mitchell, Paul
Bexhill, UK
Mining

Moberg, Mark
University of Southern Alabama
Caribbean

Montevecchi, W. A.
Memorial University of Newfoundland
Great Auk

Moratto, Michael J.
California State University, Fresno
North America - California

Motavalli, Jim
E: The Environmental Magazine
Automobile

Mukherjee, Anup
Jabalpur (MP), India
Asia, Southeast - Ancient

Murphy, Raymond
University of Ottawa
Weather Events, Extreme

Nelson, Michael P.
University of Wisconsin, Stevens Point
Animism
Environmental Ethics

Nicholson, Sharon E.
Florida State University
Desertification

Norwood, Vera
University of New Mexico
Nature

Obringer, Frederic
Centre d'Etudes sur la Chine Moderne et
Contemporaine
Medicinal Plants

Oelschlaeger, Max
Northern Arizona University
Wilderness

Okonta, Ike
St. Peter's College, Oxford University
Niger Delta

Oliver, Paul
University of Huddersfield
Buddhism
Confucianism
Mencius

Oosthoek, K. Jan
Universitaet Goettingen
Albedo Effect
Dutch Elm Disease

O'Sullivan, Robin K.
University of Southern Maine
Appalachian Mountain Club
Clamshell Alliance
Defenders of Wildlife
Nature Conservancy
Public Interest Research Groups
Wilderness Society

Paavola, Jouni
University of East Anglia
Izaak Walton League
Law - Water and Air Pollution

Parkin, Sara
Forum for the Future
Kelly, Petra

Pawson, Eric
University of Canterbury
New Zealand

Perlin, John
Santa Barbara, California
Wood

Pfister, Christian
University of Bern
Climate
Switzerland

Philippon, Daniel J.
University of Minnesota, Twin Cities
Wright, Mabel Osgood

Pierotti, Raymond
University of Kansas
Diseases, Animal
Herring Gull

Pimentel, David
Cornell University
Fertilizers

Plumwood, Val
University of Sydney
Plato

Possehl, Gregory L.
University of Pennsylvania
India, Ancient - Indus Valley
Indus River

Price, Jennifer
University of California, Los Angeles
Audubon Society

Price, Steven J.
University of Wisconsin, Green Bay
Sea Turtle

Pritchard, Sara B.
Massachusetts Institute of Technology
Rhone River

Pyne, Stephen J.
Arizona State University
Fire

Quivik, Fred L.
St. Paul, Minnesota
Smelters
Tailings

Raby, Peter
University of Cambridge
Wallace, A. R.

Randolph, Kirby
University of Pennsylvania
Fresh Air Fund

Rangarajan, Mahesh
Cornell University
India

Reiger, John
Ohio University, Chillicothe
Boone and Crockett Club

Reuss, Martin
United States Army Corps of Engineers
Floods

Richardson, Cynthia Watkins
University of Maine, Orono
Environmental Education

Richter, Jr., Daniel D.
Duke University
Salinization

Ringer, Greg
University of Oregon
Asia, Southeast - Insular
Asia, Southeast - Mainland

Robinson, Gene
James Madison University
Asbestos

Roe, Emery
Mills College
Development Narratives

Rose-Redwood, Reuben Skye
Pennsylvania State University
Goats

Rosier, Paul
Villanova University
Land Tenure

Rowley, William D.
University of Nevada, Reno
Clements, Frederic
United States Forest Service

Ryser, Rudolph C.
Center for World Indigenous Studies
Indigenous Peoples

Saikku, Mikko
Renvall Institute, University of Helsinki
House Sparrow
Ivory-billed Woodpecker

Salwasser, Harold
Oregon State University
Pathway Hypothesis

Sandweiss, Dan
University of Maine, Orono
Peru, Coastal

Sax, Boria
Mercy College
Dogs
Sheep

Scarce, Rik
Michigan State University
Earth First!

Scheiber, Harry N.
University of California, Berkeley
Law of the Sea

Schernewski, Gerald
Baltic Sea Research Institute Warnemünde
Baltic Region
Baltic Sea

Schrepfer, Susan
Rutgers University
Redwoods

Segerstahl, Boris
University of Oulu
Mayak

Sellmann, James D.
University of Guam
Taoism

Shallat, Todd
Boise State University
Army Corps of Engineers

Silver, Tim
Appalachian State University
Appalachian Mountains
White-tailed Deer

Simberloff, Dan
University of Tennessee
Extinction

Simmons, I.G.
University of Durham
Hunting and Gathering

Slovic, Scott
University of Nevada, Reno
Nature Writing

Smil, Vaclav
University of Manitoba
Coal
Dung
Geothermal Energy
Haber, Fritz
Natural Gas
Oil
Solar Energy
Water Energy
Wind Energy

Smyntyna, Olena V.
Odessa I.I. Mechnikov National University
Ukraine

Sneddon, Chris
Dartmouth College
Development

Snyder, Helen A.
Portal, Arizona
California Condor

Sowards, Adam M.
Shoreline Community College
Douglas, William O.

Spalding, Mark D.
University of Cambirdge
Mangroves

Spence, Mark
Knox College
Grinnell, George Bird

Stanfield, Michael Edward
University of San Francisco
Rubber Tree

Staudenmaier, Peter
Institute for Social Ecology
Fascism

Steltenkamp, Michael F.
Wheeling Jesuit University
Black Elk

Sterling, Keir B.
United States Army Combined Arms Support
Command
Civilian Conservation Corps
Hamilton, Alice
Roosevelt, Franklin Delano
Sierra Club

Stewart, Mart A.
Western Washington University
Agent Orange
Defoliation
Gardens and Gardening

Stiner, Mary C.
University of Arizona
Hunting and Fishing
Scavenging

Stoll, Mark
Texas Tech University
Judaism
Muir, John
Preservationism
Protestantism

Stoll, Steven
Yale University
National Park Service

Stradling, David
University of Cincinnati
Air Pollution

Tarr, Joel A.
Carnegie Mellon University
Water Pollution

Taylor III, Jospeh E.
National Humanities Center
Columbia River
Salmon
Sturgeon

Teisch, Jessica B.
University of California, Berkeley
Elephants
Hardin, Garrett
Hudson River
Tiger
Tobacco
Yam

Tilley, Helen
Princeton University
Colonialism and Imperialism

Torgerson, Douglas
Trent University
Environmentalism

Totman, Conrad
Yale University
Japan
Japan, Ancient
Tanaka, Shozo

Townsend, Patricia K.
Amherst, New York
Papua New Guinea
Pig
White Jr., Lynn
World Bank

Tucker, Jonathan B.
Monterey Institute of International Studies
Biological Weapons

Tucker, Richard P.
University of Michigan
War

Tuxill, John
New York Botanical Garden and Yale University
Comanagement

Tyrrell, Ian
University of New South Wales
Australia
Eucalyptus

Ubelaker, Douglas H.
Smithsonian Institution
Diseases, Human

Uriarte, R.
Universidad del Pais Vasco
Heavy Metals

Vallve, Frederic
Georgetown University
Bolivia
Guano

Van Dam, Petra J. E. M.
Vrije Universiteit, Amsterdam
Peat
Rabbits

Van Slyck, Abigail A.
Connecticut College
Summer Camps

van Zon, Henk
State University of Groningen
Netherlands

Vasey, Daniel E.
Divine Word College
Agriculture

Vasseur, Liette
University of Moncton
Commission for Environmental Cooperation
Global Warming

Vaughn, Jacqueline
Northern Arizona University
Wise-Use Movement

Vermeer, Eduard
University of Leiden
China

Vileisis, Ann
Port Orford, Oregon
Wetlands

Vrtis, George
Georgetown University
Colorado River
Rocky Mountains

Walker, Brett L.
Montana State University
Shinto

Walters, Bradley B.
Mount Allison University
Environmental Politics

Warhurst, Alyson
Warwick University
Mining

Washington, Sylvia Hood
Northwestern University
Africa, Western
Space Exploration
Technology
Transport Systems
United States - Midwest

Watson, Fiona
University of Stirling
United Kingdom and Ireland

Watts, Michael
University of Calfornia, Berkeley
Niger Delta

Webb, Jr., James L. A.
Colby College
Camels
Sahara
Sahel

Weiner, Douglas R.
University of Arizona
Asia, Central
Lake Baikal
Russia and the Soviet Union

Weiss, Edith Brown
Georgetown University Law Center
International Law

Wester, Barbara L.
U.S. Environmental Protection Agency
Environmental Impact Statement
Environmental Protection Agency

Whited, Tamara
Indiana University of Pennsylvania
France

Whitehead, Neil
University of Wisconsin, Madison
Amazonia, Ancient

Williams, Brett
American University
Environmental Justice

Williams, Charles E.
Clarion University of Pennsylvania
Circumpolar Regions
Prickly Pear
Taiga
Tundra

Williams, Larry E.
University of California, Davis
Grapes

Williams, Michael
Oriel College
Deforestation
Forests, Tropical

Wills, John
University of Essex
Nuclear Weapons and Testing

Wilson, Alex
Environmental Building News
Green Building

Wilson, Robert M.
University of British Columbia
Johnson, Lyndon

Winiwarter, Verena
University of Vienna
Austria
Ozone Depletion
Ozone, Tropospheric

Winiwarter, Wilfried
Ozone, Tropospheric

Wirth, John
Stanford University
Free Trade

Wood, Michael
Univeristy of Aberdeen
Mapping and Surveying

Worster, Donald
University of Kansas
Dust Bowl
Powell, John Wesley

Worthy, Trevor H.
Museum of New Zealand Te Papa Tongarewa
Moa

Wynn, Graeme
University of British Columbia
Canada

Yaryan, William
University of California, Santa Cruz
White, Laura Lyon

Zug, George R.
Smithsonian Museum
Reptiles

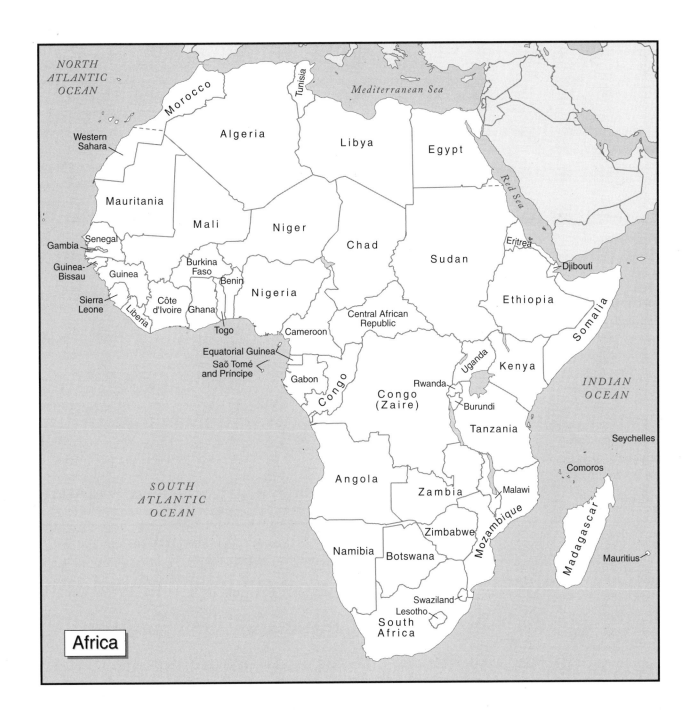

NORTH
ATLANTIC
OCEAN

Mediterranean Sea

Morocco

Tunisia

Algeria

Libya

Egypt

Western
Sahara

Red Sea

Mauritania

Mali

Niger

Chad

Sudan

Eritrea

Gambia
Senegal

Guinea-
Bissau
Guinea

Burkina
Faso

Benin

Nigeria

Central African
Republic

Djibouti

Ethiopia

Somalia

Sierra
Leone

Liberia

Côte
d'Ivoire
Ghana

Togo

Cameroon

Equatorial Guinea

Saõ Tomé
and Príncipe

Gabon

Congo

Uganda

Kenya

INDIAN
OCEAN

Congo
(Zaire)

Rwanda

Burundi

SOUTH
ATLANTIC
OCEAN

Tanzania

Seychelles

Comoros

Angola

Zambia

Malawi

Mozambique

Madagascar

Zimbabwe

Namibia

Botswana

Mauritius

Swaziland

Lesotho

South
Africa

Africa

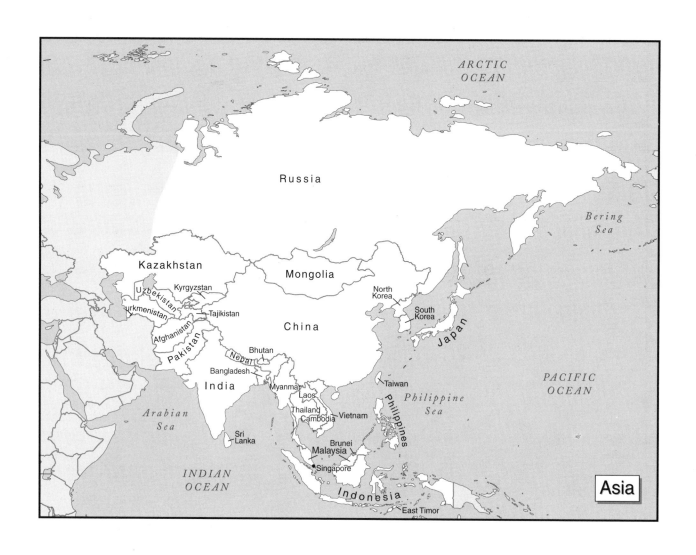

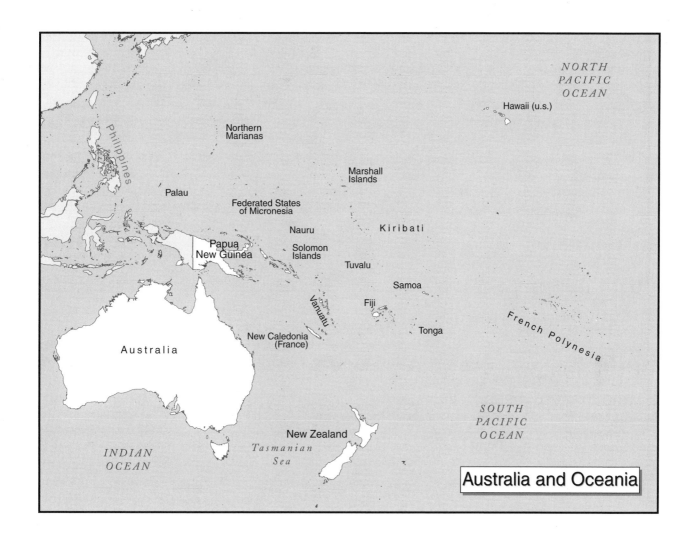

NORTH
PACIFIC
OCEAN

Hawaii (u.s.)

Philippines

Northern
Marianas

Marshall
Islands

Palau

Federated States
of Micronesia

Kiribati

Nauru

Papua
New Guinea

Solomon
Islands

Tuvalu

Vanuatu

Fiji

Samoa

Tonga

French Polynesia

New Caledonia
(France)

Australia

SOUTH
PACIFIC
OCEAN

INDIAN
OCEAN

New Zealand

Tasmanian
Sea

Australia and Oceania

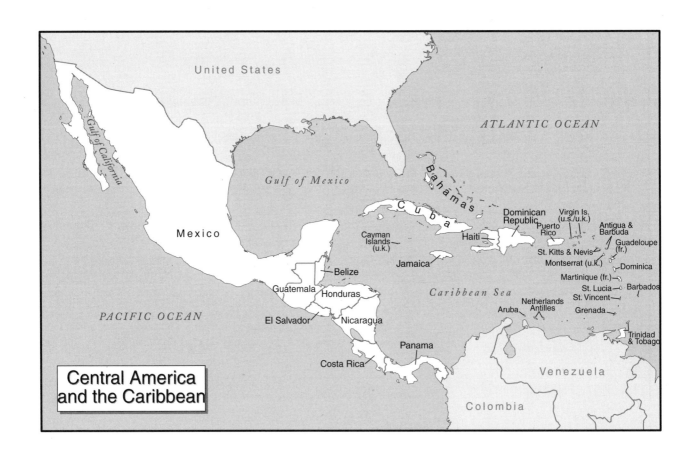

Central America and the Caribbean

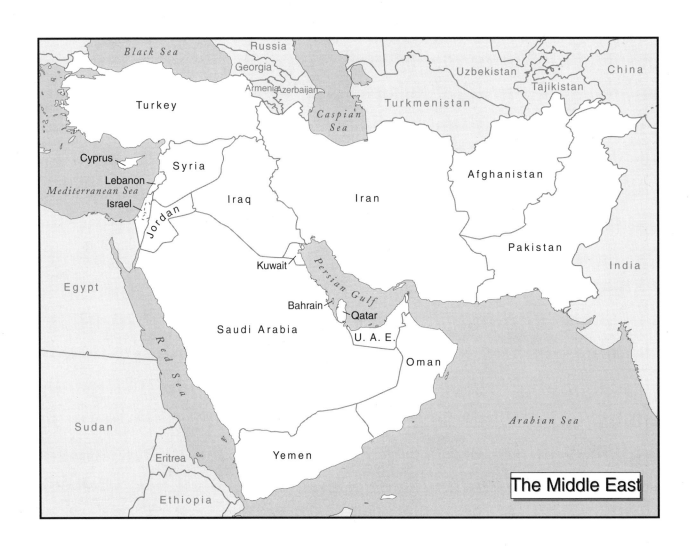

The Middle East

ARCTIC OCEAN

Greenland

Iceland

Alaska (u.s.)

Baffin Bay

Hudson Bay

Canada

PACIFIC OCEAN

United States

ATLANTIC OCEAN

Gulf of California

Gulf of Mexico

Cuba

Dominican Republic

Mexico

Jamaica

Haiti

North America

A

Acid Rain

Rain is naturally acidic. This can be because of the presence of weakly acidic carbon dioxide in the atmosphere (typically yielding a pH close to 5.6) and strong acids that arise from volcanic activities, emissions from the sea, or lightning. Human activities have added to this acidification. Acid rain is most readily formed from the sulfur dioxide emitted from fossil fuel combustion. Its effects are often felt in rural areas far from sources and it can be distinguished from the more general issue of air pollution and air pollution history that typically focuses on industrial or urban environments. It has also meant that its impacts are often on ecosystems rather than human health, thus invoking broader environmental issues rather than narrow and pragmatic concerns over public health. The impact of combustion processes, the recognition of acidification, and the policy responses to a complex issue thus form an important aspect of environmental history.

Early Observations

The diarist John Evelyn wrote the first treatise on air pollution, *Fumifugium* (1661), where he sought a broad explanation of the corrosive effects of coal-burning. Evelyn saw plants, materials, and health damaged, and even dew became contaminated by air pollutants (although he viewed the damage as coming from toxins rather than acids). He observed long-range transport from the Great Fire of London and argued that smoke from English moor burning drifted to France where it injured grapes. Widespread plant damage from vol-

canic emissions was recognized from the eighteenth century in locations very remote from fossil-fuel burning. The eruptions of Laki in Iceland (1783) may have had widespread effects on European agriculture and perhaps even human health.

Remote observations of black rain in Scotland and Scandinavia were made in the late nineteenth century. The term *moorgrime* was used to describe the black industrial soot that accumulated in the fleeces of upland sheep. Some of the most significant early work came from Norway. The geologist Waldemar Brøgger, who became Rector of the Royal University of Christiania, noted there were deposits of soot on the snowfields of Norway. His patriotic colleague Amund Helland reported on the loss of fish stocks from the 1890s, possibly because of acidification. This early work took on a modern character in Knut Dahl's studies of the effect of water acidity on salmon-trout in the 1920s and Haakon Torgersen's restocking experiments of the 1930s. The trout reintroduced in acidic streams preferred streams to which lime had been added to reduce the acidity.

Beginnings of Rainfall Analysis

Although there was an early awareness of dissolved salts in rain, it was not until the early nineteenth century that more sophisticated chemical techniques were used for the analysis of rainwater. Chemists such as the German Justus von Leibig focused interest on the role of rainwater in delivering nutrients to plants. Over time this developed, most notably through work by his student Angus Smith, into a concern about the role of combustion contaminants in rainfall. Smith was the

United Kindgom's first government scientist and recognized the importance of acids in rain. There was a parallel interest in the effect of this contamination of English drinking water in the late 1860s.

An understanding of the use of artificial fertilizers required a lengthy study at the fledgling agricultural station at Rothamsted, England. It established the annual flux of nitrate brought to the ground by rain in the second half of the nineteenth century. The deposit gauges at Rothamsted left a record that spans more than a century and hints at a notable increase in nitrate and sulfate. This agricultural interest in rainfall spread to United States, Europe, and New Zealand. In Japan the arrival of German chemists encouraged studies of rainfall composition, with nitrate and ammonia analyses beginning in Komaba, Tokyo in 1883. Such work continued almost to the mid-twentieth century and the subsequent acid rain debate reestablished some of these earliest sites.

Industrial Smoke

The widespread damage to vegetation by the alkali industry, which produced caustic soda in nineteenth-century England, led to the Alkali Acts (1863) that were influential in allowing governments to sense how pollution might be controlled. Angus Smith as Alkali Inspector implemented a scientifically based form of emission control. The damage from these industries was most often cause by gases they emitted rather than the acids formed during long-range transport. Scientific studies of smelter smoke in Germany and the United States gave new understanding of acidification. The best known may be the U.S. Bureau of Mines' extensive study (1915) of the Selby, California smelter emissions mentioned by Jack London in *John Barleycorn*: "Out of the Oakland Estuary . . . and the Carquinez Straits off the Selby Smelter were smoking."

Smelter smoke drifted across jurisdictional borders, which introduced the notion of transboundary pollutants to modern debate. One of the most important cases concerned the Trail smelter in British Columbia, which damaged agriculture in the Columbia River valley along a thirty-mile stretch from the international boundary to Kettle Falls, Washington. After periods of legal debate from 1928 to 1931 and later 1935 to 1941, farmers in the area received some compensation. These proceedings recognized both the need and the difficulties in addressing transnational pollution problems, which became so general to the acid rain debate fifty years later.

It was not until after World War II that there was a renewed interest in the broader concerns of atmospheric chemistry. New studies of rainfall chemistry, most notably with the work of Hans Egner and Erik Erikkson from the late 1940s, stimulated the growth of the European Air Chemistry Network. In the United Kingdom, Eville Gorham realized that precipitation was contributing acids to high-altitude lake and bog water tarns, while in the United States, the virtual founder of modern atmospheric chemistry, Christian Junge, measured the composition of precipitation across the country in the 1950s.

The monitoring programs in Sweden became important in triggering public and political interest in acid rain. A three-minute television feature showing the high levels of sulfur dioxide experienced in Stockholm was broadcast on 2 December 1966. This short piece was widely seen by politicians such as Valfrid Paulsson, who became Director General of the Swedish Environmental Protection Agency, formed in July 1967. The agency quickly recognized the local and global problems of sulfur. However, the real shift in interest from urban air pollution to acid rain was induced through an article by Svante Odén, "The acidification of precipitation" in the newspaper *Dagens Nyheter* on 27 October 1967. This raised the specter of widespread ecological damage. Odén's work drew upon an extensive body of both chemical and biological information that had accumulated from studies since the 1950s. This suddenly shifted the emphasis away from urban sulfur dioxide to regional sulfuric acid deposition, with pH values less than 4.0 in annual rainfall in some areas. Sweden with its thin soil cover was seen as particularly vulnerable, and the government realized it would have to act and reduce emissions, but also encourage other nations to recognize the problem.

Sweden hosted the 1972 U.N. Conference on the Human Environment in Stockholm. The meeting represented a milestone in environmental diplomacy, and Sweden used it to raise the need to control the long-range transport of air pollutants. The eventual outcome was the development of a set of guiding principles that included the idea that states had the responsibility to ensure that their activities did not damage the environment of other states. The concerns were not welcomed by the industrialized nations burning huge quantities of coal, but the Organisation for Economic Co-operation and Development F(OECD) was able to establish a cooperative program to measure the long-range transport of air pollutants (LRTAP). Norway once again played a vital part by establishing its program on the effects of acid rain on forests and fish.

In 1979 LRTAP drafted a convention on the long-range transport of air pollutants. The convention had not come into force by 1982 when Sweden hosted the Stockholm Conference on Acidification to try and get agreement. Germany, with its widespread forest damage, soon joined, but Britain proved much more reluctant. However, the issue received a much greater degree of public attention and acid rain became very much the environmental issue of the 1980s.

In the eastern United States there was parallel alarm at the acidification of lakes and effects on ecosystems. This led to the formation of the National Acid Precipitation Assessment Program (NAPAP) in 1980, an interagency task force under the auspices of the Council on Environmental Quality. It coordinated long-term monitoring of precipitation. In the same year the MAP3S (Multistate Atmospheric Power Production Pollution Study) program was initiated by the U.S. Department of Energy. By the early 1990s, NAPAP had produced a series of reports: *Acidic Deposition: State of Science and Technology*. The program was reauthorized through the 1990 Clean Air Act Amendments and examined trends in emissions, deposition, and effects, to evaluate the expected benefits of the 1990 legislation.

The research programs that developed out of political interest in acid rain examined a wide range of problems. Vegetation damage proved to be a complex issue. Gaseous pollutants seemed to be intercepted by foliage, but it became increasingly evident that ozone was a culprit. Magnesium and aluminum were mobilized by acid rain. In Sweden there was evidence that the acidification of groundwater had increased the concentrations of toxic metals such as copper and cadmium. Although the concentrations typically remained below levels of human health concern, there was the potential for the acid water to leach further toxic metals from water-supply pipes. In urban areas, acid rain combined with sulfur dioxide increased the rate of damage to buildings, most notably those of calcareous stone.

Gradually the countries of Europe and North America had seen that joint action was necessary. Although public interest was high through the 1980s it gradually shifted to other issues such as the greenhouse effect and the ozone hole. It may have been that there was a sense that the problems had been solved, or that the attention span of the media was short. However, industrial changes and fuel shifts had meant that in many countries the emissions of sulfur were in decline from the early 1970s, even before legislative pressures. There was a substantial rise in the nitrogen-to-sulfur ratio in rainfall from many parts of Europe and North America because of declining sulfur emissions and increasing nitrogen from large combustion sources and the automobile. A different atmospheric chemistry (nitric acid, unlike sulfuric acid, is formed through homogeneous processes) shifted the spatial distribution of the acids deposited in rain. The declining sulfate deposition caused some crops in England and Germany to show signs of sulfur deficiency. Rainfall acidity did not show quite the expected improvements. Calcium, once abundant in the atmosphere, had started to decline, possibly because of a decline in road and industrial dusts. Thus there was less alkaline material to neutralize acidity.

Acid rain was not abolished, but there is evidence of a reduced deposition of acidic contaminants in some areas. Ecosystems have different sensitivities to acidic inputs, so the impact is often described in terms of the critical load that the ecosystem can bear. In the 1990s there was an improvement, with fewer locations in Britain exceeding the critical load. Nevertheless, despite continuing reductions, some 50 percent of grasslands, heathlands, and deciduous woodlands will continue to exceed their critical load as late as 2010. Salmon and trout catches have begun to increase in some Norwegian rivers. In North America improvements are also seen, but these are not always evenly spread. The situation at the millennium was improving but much has yet to be done.

On a global scale the geography of acid rain has changed. Sulfur emissions have increased rapidly in the industrializing world, most importantly on the Asia-Pacific rim. Here vast quantities of coal are now burnt and research and regulation must now confront a novel acid rain problem. Entirely new ecosystems will be threatened by acidic deposition. The chemistry of these regions is different because of the presence of alkaline dust and the combustion products of extensive forest fires that became widely observed in the 1990s. The greater extension of acid rain into the tropics, where soils are often deeply weathered, makes available new routes for mobilizing metals. These emerging problems have required new initiatives such as the development of an acid precipitation monitoring network in East Asia from the Toyama meeting of 1993. China, which grew most rapidly as an emitter of sulfur dioxide in the last decades of the twentieth century, is rapidly shifting its fuel base. The transition from high-sulfur solid fuels to cleaner liquid and gaseous ones may occur rapidly there, reducing the future impact of acid rain in East Asia.

The history of acid rain reminds us of the difficulties in creating environmental legislation, which so often has to break new ground. Early acts had to confront the notion that the release of toxic byproducts was a necessary part of industrial activity. In the twentieth century, environmental diplomacy grew with an awareness that many problems did not respect national boundaries. Both air pollution and acid rain have declined in many industrial countries, but it is not clear whether this is an outcome of legislation, of preexisting pressures for industrial change, or fuel shifts. The acid rain problem has moved to industrializing nations, but even here there are already hints of changing patterns of combustion.

Peter Brimblecombe

See also Air Pollution, Coal

Further Reading

Brimblecombe, P. (1987). *The big smoke*. London: Methuen.

Gould, R. (1985). *Going sour*. Boston: Birkhauser.

Jago, L. (2002). *The northern lights*. London: Penguin Books.

Lundgren, L. J. (1998). *Acid rain on the agenda*. Lund, Sweden: Lund University Press.

Park, C.C. (1987). *Acid rain: Reality and rhetoric*. London: Methuen.

Wirth, J. D. (2000). *Smelter smoke in North America: The politics of transborder Pollution*. Lawrence: University Press of Kansas.

Africa—Overview

The African environment and its history are the product, like all regional environmental systems, of the dynamic interaction of a distinctive physical geography, human action, and climatic systems. Cambridge historian John Illife posits this environmental struggle as the key theme in Africa's history, observing that "Africans have been and are the frontiersmen who have colonized an especially hostile region of the world on behalf of the entire human race." (Illife 1995, 1).

Despite mythic narratives of pristine nature, wildlife, and Edenic innocence, Africa's landscapes and environmental history is fundamentally anthropogenic (that is, modified by humans). Human activities that have affected the physical environment include agriculture, pastoralism, and resource extraction; the general patterns of population growth and movement have also had significant impact. These human actions respond, in turn, to changes in climate and environment brought on by local geographical nuance and global patterns of climate such as the El Niño Southern Oscillation (ENSO; temperature oscillation in the Pacific Ocean), the Hadley Circulation (movement of warm equatorial air toward the poles and cold polar air toward the equator), and the Intertropical Convergence Zone (ITCZ; the phenomenon of rainy seasons that follow prevailing winds).

Africa's Geomorphology and Climate

Africa's geomorphology is extremely ancient, forming the center of the original landmass of Gondwanaland. Its geological history at its core is between 3 billion and 500 million years old; its topography includes relatively few major mountain regions. Its soils are old and generally poor in nutrients, though its land has substantial wealth in minerals. East Africa, in contrast to the continent's other regions, has experienced faulting and the action of volcanoes that produced highlands, the Great Rift Valley, and a set of lakes that have sustained a distinctive population of freshwater ecosystems. East Africa's geological processes over time have also preserved significant evidence of prehistoric human activity and strong evidence that humankind originated in Africa and subsequently migrated across the globe.

Africa's geomorphology and its localized effects on climate have created a number of centers of endemism (locally distinctive species of flora and fauna). These include the Ethiopian highlands, the Western Cape region of South Africa, Tanzania's Usambara Mountains, the Congolia rain forest in central Africa, and the Great Lakes ecosystems in the Great Rift Valley of eastern central Africa. Patterns of climate also create local phenomena such as rainfall shadows (well-watered southern slopes of mountains adjacent to dried northern slopes). Moreover, West Africa's rain forests are distinctive globally because of their comparatively low levels of endemism, a result of the particular effects of climate described below.

Africa's climate and local patterns of weather derive from its position astride the equator and the global circulation of wind, sea temperature, and currents. The limiting factor on Africa's patterns of human settlement and agricultural and pastoral activity has largely been rainfall (rather than temperature, as in more temperate zones). Rainfall is bimodal; that is, moisture concentrates in a few months of the year, followed by a protracted dry season.

The primary force driving Africa's climate is the opposing circulation of winds north and south of the equator that migrate north and south, following the movement of the sun into and out of the Northern and Southern Hemispheres. Rainfall follows the lines of latitude where the two circulation zones meet, generally producing wet summers and dry winters across most of the continent (the ITCZ phenomenon mentioned earlier). The long-term patterns of north-south movement define the wet and dry seasons in most of Africa, and the fluctuation and inconsistencies from year to year produce the periods of drought that have historically affected Africa, especially West Africa's Sahel (the semiarid region bordering the Sahara), the northern highlands of Ethiopia and Eritrea, and many areas of southern Africa. The frequency and location of African droughts in turn seems to be correlated with El Niño Southern Oscillation (ENSO) events in the Western Hemisphere.

A familiar sight in Africa, a baobab tree spreads over a dirt road. COURTESY MARY CORINNE LOWENSTEIN.

Climate Changes

Using historical accounts, core samples taken from lake beds, and global climate modeling techniques, climatologists have been able to reconstruct evidence for several climate epochs in the Sahel from 800 to 1600 CE, during which time a succession of empires dominated the region's political and economic life. According to this evidence the period from 800 to 1300 was relatively wet, followed by a drier period from 1300 to 1450, after which another a wetter period took hold until the late eighteenth century. These general patterns contained within them annual cycles that also varied considerably from year to year. It was those fluctuations from good, timely rains to drought or flooding that prompted farmers to engage in strategies of risk management and habits of migration. The historical distribution of moisture had specific effects on the rise and decline of Sahelian empire systems by restricting or expanding the range of horsed warriors, the availability of the wood fuel needed by iron smiths, and the frontiers of agriculture and pastoral economies.

Over the long-term geological time frame, Africa's climate has been more often dry than wet and more often warmer than cooler. In that long-term perspective, the Sahara may have encroached as far south as the Kalahari along arid corridors through a truncated central African forest. Many African species of arboreal fauna, such as hyraxes, squirrels, and monkeys, actually descended from ancestors forced to survive on the ground as tree cover diminished in past epochs. The lack of endemism in West Africa's Upper Guinea forest, in contrast with other world rain forests, is probably a product of this long-term effect. Indeed, related species of flora and fauna in the Upper Guinea forest cover a wide swath of territory, a distinctive feature of West Africa's forest zones. Within the last few millennia, however, there have also been wetter periods, including one in which the Sahara was a pastoral grassland that supported cattle, game, and human settlement. This period ended somewhere in the middle of the third millennium BCE (c. 2300 BCE).

Human Adaptation to Africa's Climate

These long-term fluctuations helped shape the evolution of social institutions and economic strategies among farmers, pastoralists, and hunters. Africa's agricultural systems, for example, have been highly mobile historically, using swidden (slash-and-burn) systems that maximized nutrients in poor soils. They developed drought-resistant cereals and rotational pulse

The plains of Tanzania. COURTESY MARY CORINNE LOWENSTEIN.

crops in a way finely tuned to the arrival of summer rains followed by a long dry season. Most livestock economies in Africa chose to follow the seasonal ebb and flow of moisture and pasture rather than stockpiling their animals' food supply (as is more common in temperate zones). Pastoral peoples synchronized their movements to coincide with the seasonal grazing needs of their livestock (cattle, camels, sheep, and goats) or their wild prey (wildebeest, gazelle, and various ungulates). Hadendowa, camel-herding pastoralists in eastern Sudan, planted sorghum in moist riverine soils at the end of the dry season and then retreated with their animals to wet-season pastures until the harvest was ready eight months later.

Farmers in the Sahel, in Zambia, and in many other areas of the continent practiced shifting cultivation that required vast amounts of land, but maximized scarce soil nutrients by shifting cultivation between plots and allowing them to lie fallow for periods of five to fifteen years. Farmers and pastoralists also used fire systematically to control aspects of their local environment. Fire can help humans to clear fallowed or harvested fields, raise phosphorus and pH levels in the soil, control insect pests such as ticks, and stimulate the growth of new pasture grasses. In addition to fire originating with humans, fire from lightning strikes also shaped the landscape's vegetative cover over time.

Floral and Faunal Endemism and Domestication

Africa's living landscapes historically have been dynamic blends of endemism and exotic plants and animals brought by humans in trade, in migration, and by accident. Endemism usually results when localized ecologies promote the development of biodiversity.

Food Crops

Africa is poorly endowed with the wild species from which farmers could develop domestic food crops. Of the world's fifty-six heaviest-seeded wild grass species, Africa is home to only four, while the Fertile Crescent has thirty-three. Nevertheless, Africa's pattern of bimodal climate encouraged its gatherers (probably mostly women) over time to develop two major types of cereal crops—sorghums and millets—and an indigenous type of rice. Sorghum and millet shared characteristics of long maturity and resistance to drought. Variants of these two cereal crops along with fruits and local varieties of yams (in forested areas) made up the vast majority of Africans' carbohydrate calories prior to 1500. Unlike sorghum and millet, Africa's rice cultivation had a somewhat restricted geography along the west coast and later in parts of Tanzania.

The Ethiopia and Eritrea region in the Horn of Africa was an exception to Africa's general poverty in crop endemism. Gatherers and farmers in the highlands there developed a number of food crops from local wild species, including teff, eleusine (finger millet), and niger seed. In all, twenty-four types of grains and oil seeds are endemic to that region, with distinctive cultivars of wheat, barley, sorghum, and millet also developed by farmers there as an offshoot of the eastern Mediterranean agrarian system.

Over the last millennium, however, African farmers have adopted a new set of exotic food crops, cash crops, and plant species that originated off the continent but which its farmers have embraced and made their own. These crops include cultigens from the New World such as maize (corn), cassava (manioc), potatoes, peppers, and many types of pulses (leguminous crops such as beans or peas). From Asia they have adopted bananas (plantain), Asian rice, and sugarcane. These crops (especially maize and cassava) now make up the bulk of Africa's current food supply. Exotic tree species such as eucalyptus, wattle, and Asian teak also appeared as economically valuable.

Domesticated Animals

In the area of domesticated animals Africa's food supply and economies also faced severe challenges over the long sweep of history. Ironically, of the fifty-one large mammal species in sub-Saharan Africa, none has been commercially domesticated. Of the fourteen major domesticated species of livestock in the world, only one (the donkey) has its wild ancestor in Africa. This is doubly ironic given that fact that Africa is home to a fascinating variety of large mammals now protected within its national parks, conservation areas, and private game areas: elephants, rhinoceros, ungulates, large cats, and wildebeest. Africa's population of large mammals is approximately 1.5 million, the great-

est assemblage of large wild mammals on earth. Interestingly, none of these creatures has ever been successfully domesticated (as opposed to the taming of individuals). A combination of factors such as diet, growth rate, failure of captive breeding, and herding behavior seems to account for the lack of success. Ecologist Jared Diamond points out that failure in any one of these areas makes a species impossible as a candidate for commercial or household domestication.

Like their key modern food crops, Africans have had to adopt exotic domestic species from which they have developed elaborate cultures and economies of husbandry. Depending on the ecology of a given area, the species mix of Africa's domestic livestock can vary. Cattle are the most widespread, comprising the livestock base of herding people such as the Fulani of West Africa, the Masai of East Africa, the Nuer of the Nile Valley, the Herero of Angola, and the Nguni of South Africa. They also make up a critical part of the farm economy in the highlands of Ethiopia and Eritrea, where ox plows are the basis for agriculture. Camels are the basis for the domestic economy in lowland cultures in the Horn of Africa, the lower Nile, and on the fringes of the Sahara because of their ability to turn poor water sources and desert pasture into sweet milk, meat, and transport. Small ruminants—sheep and goats, or both—and poultry fill in the edges of most African pastoral systems. Many farm economies also depend on animals (mainly donkeys and camels) as beast of burden and for transportation. Horses were historically important for empires that utilized cavalry to dominate their neighbors, especially at the southern edge of West Africa's Sahel (the Mali, Songhay, and Hausa) on the Ethiopian and Eritrean highlands (the Oromo), and the South African highveld (the Griqua and Afrikaaners).

Africa's Human Population Growth

Africa's human population is an essential element of the continent's environmental history. Humans' ability to manage and change soils, vegetation, and biodiversity is fundamentally tied to the concentration of labor at particular points in time and space. The effects of population density on local economies have long been the subject of controversy. The Malthusian view is that increased population density strains food supply, while the perspective of Boserup is that population pressure on land raises its efficiency by intensifying labor and stimulating technological change. Africa's history provides evidence for both arguments.

Technology

Technology—the combination of tools, knowledge, and experience—has been a major element in the human population's effects on Africa's landscapes. Iron tools, produced locally or obtained in regional trade, were in wide use in Africa in the last millennium and in many places well before that. Iron-tipped plows, which made preparing fields more efficient, had long been in use in Ethiopia and Eritrea and the lower Nile Valley, but appeared in eastern and southern Africa only in the late nineteenth and twentieth centuries. In most areas of Africa, preindustrial economies depended directly on human labor (including the use of fire) for economic activity, and the distribution of labor on land and the effect of migration has been one of the most significant factors in determining the human impact on landscapes.

It is beyond doubt that Africa's population has grown overall through time, but it is the localized rate of growth, decline, age structure, morbidity, and fertility rates at particular times that most matter to Africa's environmental history. In the last third of the twentieth century Africa had the world's highest rates of population growth and fertility, over 4 percent growth in some areas (such as the Great Lakes region in East Africa), and maintained an overall rate of almost 3 percent over most of the continent. The rate began to subside somewhat by the beginning of the twenty-first century but remains among the world's highest.

Urbanization

While Africa has historically been the least urbanized of the major continents, it now has the world's highest rate of urbanization. Its urban environmental footprint includes "halos" of settlements around its cities. Africa's urban population doubles roughly every twelve years, and 90 percent of newly established households in sub-Saharan Africa are located in the peri-urban halos. These zones lie outside of formal urban infrastructure and therefore have a very different environmental footprint than the older colonial cities established in the late nineteenth and early twentieth centuries.

Disease

An additional environmental factor that has affected human settlement patterns as well as farm and livestock economies has been the distribution of and response to disease organisms. Over the course of their history Africans have structured their economies and social institutions around endemic disease, such as malaria, onchocirciasis (river blindness), shistosomiasis (bilharzia), trypanosomiasis (sleeping sickness), and relapsing fever. These diseases are often seasonal and often result in morbidity rather than mortality, affecting efficiency of labor rather than simply lowering population growth. Other diseases have arrived from outside or cropped up mysteriously and have caused sharp, unexpected crises. These include rinderpest, smallpox, influenza, and, most recently, HIV/AIDS, Ebola, and Lassa fever. Some diseases have profoundly shaped human settlement, such as trypanosomiasis, which restricted domestic animals to areas with less than 1,000 millimeters of annual rainfall (in other words, zones where the tsetse fly, which transmits trypanosomiasis, had no habitat). HIV/AIDS, which first struck Africa in the mid-1980s, is largely a sexually transmitted disease that has hit hardest in Africa's young-adult populations, threatening a crisis in the industrial workforce and educated classes in coming decades.

Africa in the Twenty-First Century

Over the course of the twentieth century Africa's human and physical landscapes have undergone rapid transformations brought on by colonialism, the impact of a globalizing economy, and an accelerating movement of exotic biological influences (both accidental and intentional). A number of trends have emerged in the past two or three decades that suggest the nature of Africa's place in the world of the twenty-first century. Each of these has environmental implications, though some of them are manifestations of long-term trends and others are surprising new developments.

Several of the environmental threats that appear in Africa today are products of its colonial past, such as economies based on the extraction of primary resources such as minerals, forests products, and cash crops. Economic structures and global forces often supersede efforts at conservation beyond a few instances of ecotourism and tourist income derived from conservation areas and national parks. International agencies and African government ministries have made broad claims of massive deforestation in Africa. More recent research suggests that such claims are exaggerated and based less on fact than on "degradation narratives" that blame African farmers, herders, and refugees for the problems. Some problems of environmental degradation, such as desertification, are more the result of global climate patterns than local farm practice.

Political instability in places such as Sierra Leone, Liberia, and central Africa (Rwanda, Congo) has produced refugee populations that disrupt the environmental resources of the areas in which they settle, causing localized deforestation or water pollution. The conflict that produces refugees also allows the illegal and destructive extraction of diamonds and other minerals that might otherwise fuel wider national development.

Above all, the increasing scarcity of clean water supplies in urban areas and in water-stressed regions such as southern Africa place Africa's political and economic well being in the balance. Elaborate hydroelectric projects control water flows, inundate local lands, and concentrate control of water and power in the hands of the powerful, though they also offer tempting benefits in irrigation, electrification of low-income areas, and a basis for needed industrial expansion. By the mid-1990s such projects included the Lesotho Highlands project (Lesotho), the Epupa Falls Dam (Namibia), Cabora Bassa Dam (Mozambique), Kariba Dam (Zambia and Zimbabwe), Kafue Dam (Zambia), Grand Inga Dam (Congo), and the Batoka Dam (Zimbabwe). Longer-term implications of such water control tend to favor South Africa's industrial sector and urban residents over rural peoples. In the twenty-first century water will be power in southern Africa, and the struggles over it will play themselves out decisively at local, regional, and national levels.

A number of issues on Africa's horizon are related to population and demographic trends. The alarming population growth rates from the 1960s to 1980s have moderated somewhat, perhaps indicating the demographic transition (a decline in fertility rates accompanying economic growth) that some demographers have predicted. Yet, Africa's population is also extraordinarily young, with the majority of the population in many countries under the age of sixteen. The question remains whether Africa's growing population will lead to a Malthusian future of food crises, social conflict, and political instability or to Boserup's vision of technological innovation in food production and resource management.

Dependence on Maize

Two particular trends are worth observing in this regard. The first falls in the area of food production. Since 1960 Africa has slowly but steadily increased its dependency on maize in its food supply. In the past ten years that trickle has become a flood as countries have adopted hybrid and improved maize as the primary staple of their agricultural economies and national food supply, displacing historical African food grains like sorghum, millet, and local varieties of rice. In southern Africa, for example, maize has become the most important staple food, accounting for well over 50 percent of calories in local diets. In Malawi, maize occupies 90 percent of cultivated land and 54 percent of Malawians's total calories. Zambia has the world's highest percentage of maize consumption in the national diet (58 percent). In South Africa, maize comprises 60 percent of all land planted in cereals and 40 percent of all calories consumed. Of the twenty countries in the world with the highest percentage of maize consumption in national diets, thirteen are in Africa. Even Ethiopia, one of the world centers of historical crop biodiversity, now produces more maize than any other crop.

Some economists have seen maize domination as Africa's Green Revolution. Others point to maize's darker side as an agricultural crop. It is highly vulnerable to drought, it stores poorly in tropical settings, hybrid maize is dependent on nitrogen fertilizer, and its world market price has declined by approximately 50 percent in real terms since 1961. Moreover, for many African farmers maize is a subsistence crop, grown for its low labor requirements and quick yield during the hungry season that precedes the main harvest. It is not only the symbol of poverty but its reality as well. On big commercial farms in South Africa and Zimbabwe maize is an industrial crop grown to economies of scale with tractors, fertilizer, and hybrid seed. For small farmers it is a crop of desperation that marks their loss of labor to male migration, disease (notably HIV/AIDS), and lack of capital.

The Impact of HIV/AIDS

The most significant environmental crisis facing African in the twenty-first century is the demographic effect of HIV/AIDS, whose mortality and morbidity will take its greatest toll between the ages of late adolescence and middle age, decimating the heart of the agricultural and industrial labor force. In some countries the disease will double or triple under-five child mortality rates by the year 2010. The loss of labor to death and morbidity will force households and even nations to adopt increasingly short time frames when deciding how to allocate resources. In other words, conservation plans for water, forest cover, urban infrastructure planning and so forth will be made for short-term gain, leaving environmental resources under threat.

The future of African environmental resources is very much in the balance as local imperatives and global forces drive decisions and actions regarding wildlife preservation, agricultural development, and the emergence of cities as the engines of economic and cultural life. Africa's countries, regions, and entire ecosystems will respond to global efforts at preservation, but will also have to endure market forces for extraction, migration, and exploitation.

James C. McCann

See also British Empire; Chipko; Congo (Zaire) River; Egypt, Ancient; Lake Chad; Lake Victoria; Madagascar; Niger Delta; Nile Valley (Aswan Dam); Sahara; Sahel

Further Reading

Adams, J., & McShane, T. (1996). *The myth of wild Africa: Conservation without illusion.* Berkeley and Los Angeles: University of California Press.

Anderson, D., & Grove, R. (1987). *Conservation in Africa: People, policies and practice.* Cambridge, UK: Cambridge University Press.

Beinart W., & Coates, P. (1995). *Environment and history: The taming of nature in the USA and South Africa.* London: Routledge.

Bonner, R. (1994). *At the hand of man: Peril and hope for Africa's wildlife.* New York: Vintage.

Brooks, G. (1993). *Landlords and strangers: Ecology, society, and trade in West Africa* Boulder, CO: Westview Press.

Carruthers, J. (1995). *The Kruger National Park: A social and political history.* Pietermaritzburg, South Africa: University of Natal Press.

Collins, R. (1990). *The waters of the Nile: Hydropolitics and the Jonglei Canal, 1900–1988.* Oxford, UK: Oxford University Press.

Fairhead, J., & Leach, M. (1996). *Misreading the African landscape: Society and ecology in a forest-savanna mosaic.* Cambridge, UK: Cambridge University Press.

Ford, J. (1971). *The Role of Trypanosomiasis in African ecology.* Oxford, UK: Oxford University Press.

Giblin, J. (1990). Trypanosomiasis control in African history. *Journal of African History, 31,* 59–80.

Giblin, J. (1993). *The politics of environmental control in northeastern Tanzania, 1840–1940.* Philadelphia: University of Pennsylvania Press.

Harms, R. (1987). *Games against nature: An eco-cultural history of the Nunu of equatorial Africa.* Cambridge, UK: Cambridge University Press.

Iliffe, J. (1989). The origins of population growth. *Journal of African History, 30,* 165–169.

Iliffe, J. (1995). *Africa: History of a continent.* Cambridge, UK: Cambridge University Press.

Johnson, D. (1989). Political ecology in the Upper Nile. *Journal of African History, 30,* 463–486.

Kjekshus, H. (1996). *Ecology control and economic development in East African history.* Athens: Ohio University Press.

Koponen, J. (1988). *People and production in late precolonial Tanzania: History and structures.* Helsinki, Finland: Scandinavian Institute of African Studies.

Leach, M., & Mearns, R. (1996). *The lie of the land: Challenging received wisdom in African environmental change and policy.* Portsmouth, NH, and Oxford, UK: James Currey and Heinemann.

Lyons, M. (1992). *The colonial disease: A social history of sleeping sickness in northern Zaire, 1900–1940.* Cambridge, UK: Cambridge University Press.

MacKenzie, J. M. (1988). *The empire of nature: Hunting, conservation, and British imperialism.* Manchester, UK: Manchester University Press.

Maddox, G., Giblin, J., & Kimambo, I. (1996). *Custodians of the land: Ecology and culture in the history of Tanzania.* Athens: Ohio University Press.

Mandala, E. (1990). *Work and control in a peasant economy: A history of the lower Tchiri Valley in Malawi, 1859–1960.* Madison: University of Wisconsin Press.

McCann, J. C. (1990). Agriculture and African history. *Journal of African History, 31,* 121–134.

McCann, J. C. (1995). *People of the plow: An agricultural history of Ethiopia.* Madison: University of Wisconsin Press.

McCann, J. C. (1999). *Green land, brown land, black land: An environmental history of Africa.* Portsmouth, NH, and Oxford, UK: Heinemann.

Moore, H., & Vaughn, M. (1993). *Cutting Down Trees.* Portsmouth, NH: Heinemann.

Nicholson, S. (1979). The methodology of historical climate reconstruction and its application to Africa. *Journal of African History, 20,* 31–49.

Steinhart, E. (1989). Hunters, poachers, and gamekeepers: Towards a social history of hunting in colonial Kenya. *Journal of African History, 30,* 247–264.

Sutton, J. (1984). Irrigation and soil conservation in African agricultural history. *Journal of African History, 25,* 25–41.

Tosh, J. (1978). Lango agriculture during the early colonial period. *Journal of African History, 19,* 415–439.

Turshen, M. (1984). *The political ecology of disease in Tanzania.* New Brunswick, NJ: Rutgers University Press.

Vaughan, M. (1989). *Story of an African famine: Gender and famine in twentieth-century Malawi.* Oxford, UK: Oxford University Press.

Vaughan, M. (1991). *Curing their ills.* Stanford, CA: Stanford University Press.

Webb, J. L. A. (1995). *Desert frontier: Ecological and economic change along the Western Sahel, 1600–1850.* Madison: University of Wisconsin Press.

Africa, Central

Central Africa encompasses a huge expanse of territory, over 7.7 million square kilometers stretching from just south of the Sahara desert in the north to the Kalahari Desert in the south. Central Africa's environment is marked by several features: two major river basins, the Congo and the Zambezi; a vast equatorial rain forest; and two savannas bordering that forest, one in the north and one in the south. The rain forest is one of the world's largest, extending over 2 million square kilometers from southern Cameroon and the Central African Republic throughout the Congo River basin to below the mouth of the Congo River. The northern savanna stretches from the edge of the Sahara desert through much of Cameroon, the Central African Republic, and Sudan; the southern savanna extends from south of the mouth of the Congo to the Kalahari Desert.

Biological Diversity and Early History to 1400

Central Africa boasts great diversity in its ecological forms plant and animal life, and mineral endowments. Among the rain forest's ecological forms are monodominant (single-species) forest with very tall trees and scant understory; montane forest; semi-deciduous mixed forest of prized mahoganies, ebony, and the edible bush mango; dense forest with tangled understories on marshy soil; and raffia palm forest in flooded areas. The central African forest contains more than seven thousand species of flowering plants. Rainfall is generally very high, topping 1,800 millimeters annually in some locations. Animal populations include such charismatic species as elephants, bongo antelope, sitatunga (an aquatic antelope), forest buffalo, gorillas, and leopards. Gold and diamond deposits are found in some parts of the forest as well. The southern savanna is also varied; there are well-watered woodlands with highly fertile soils, semiarid zones prone to

drought and food shortages, and highlands in Zimbabwe veined with rich gold reserves. The northern savanna ranges from open grasslands and dry forests, interspersed with lush gallery forests (forests that grow along waterways in areas otherwise devoid of forests), to more arid, scrubby zones closer to the Sahara desert. Elephants, lions, now-dwindling populations of rhinos, and baboons are among the savanna mammalian populations.

Biological diversity in central Africa is the result of long-term natural and human processes, and ecologists are only beginning to understand the complex interrelations between the forest, climatic and seasonal changes, wildlife, and people. Storms, landslides, flooding, and the migration and feeding of such mammals as elephants have crucial effects on ecological forms, as well as on the plant life in central Africa. And although most of central Africa has never been densely populated, its people have long interacted with and fundamentally shaped its diverse ecological features by hunting, trapping, gathering, farming, fishing, mining, and logging. Human beings have lived in and exploited central African environments since very early times. About eight thousand years ago, Sudanic peoples living in the northern savannas began to cultivate the first domesticated cereals in Africa (sorghum and millet), and they number among the first farmers in the tropics. While it took over four thousand years for these farmers to begin intensive cultivation, some scholars have hypothesized that they effectively transformed the region's dry woodlands into open grasslands. During this same period, some of these people acquired domesticated animals, including cattle, sheep, and dogs.

Human habitation in the rainforest has not been dated, but by the end of the last millennium BCE, forest inhabitants had developed a variety of ways of exploiting their diverse environment: They farmed bananas, yams and other crops, hunted elephants and other game, raised animals, and gathered fruits, leaves, honey, medicinal plants, and building materials. They thus helped to influence the forest's composition by clearing lands, dispersing seeds, and encouraging particular plants to flourish. This history of cultivation is closely tied to the expansion of the Bantu-speaking peoples, a two thousand-year process in which people, the Bantu language family, agriculture, and iron-making techniques expanded from West Africa through the equatorial rain forest and into the southern savannas, eastern Africa, and southern Africa. This process most likely ended sometime between 500 and

1000 CE. The introduction of iron products throughout central Africa in farming regions caused populations to grow rapidly and to alter the social relationships that supported their environmental practices. By 1000 CE, the hunter-gatherer peoples living in the forest developed associations with Bantu-speaking agriculturalists, assuming primary responsibility for supplying forest products such as meat, honey, and fruits in exchange for iron implements and cultivated foods such as bananas, introduced from Southeast Asia or India.

Initially, the original hunter-gatherers of the southern savanna acquired Bantu speakers' techniques of farming and animal husbandry very gradually. The process of technological and linguistic change accelerated dramatically between 400 and 1400 CE, when people began to farm and herd more intensively, forge iron, and adopt the languages of Bantu speakers.

Global Connections and Environmental Change, 1400–1900

After 1400, some parts of central Africa encountered outside traders and experienced significant environmental, economic, political, and social change. The southwestern savanna was profoundly affected by the Portuguese, and later other Europeans, who arrived on the west coast of central Africa to acquire gold and silver but subsequently shifted to a trade in slaves for plantations and mines in the Americas. Importantly, the Portuguese introduced cassava (*Manihot esculenta*) from the Americas to Africa, and cultivation of the tuber spread throughout central Africa over the next six centuries. Historian Joseph Miller has argued that southwest central Africa's vulnerability to intermittent drought and food shortages fundamentally shaped its engagement with the Atlantic slave trade. Drought and famine drove people to concentrate in fertile, well-watered areas, which eventually produced considerable shortages in arable, well-watered land, but some political leaders in these areas were able to centralize power in their own hands. Over the next four centuries, these rulers, their kin, and their successors, seeking to increase their power and to profit from a trade in weapons and luxury goods with European slave traders, expanded their slave raiding into the southern savanna's interior. Periodic drought and food dearth could also aggravate slave raiding, Miller has argued, because people enslaved during times of ecological crisis suffered more ill health and higher death rates than those captured in better times, and their increased

death rates intensified American demand for more captives.

The nineteenth century brought considerable upheaval to central Africa. During this century, equatorial Africa found itself increasingly incorporated into a global economy, a process fueled partly by an industrializing Europe, which needed African raw materials to produce its textiles, steel, and other products. Africans in the Congo river basin forest took advantage of these opportunities, forming their own trading networks to exchange manioc, palm oil and wine, slaves, and ivory for such imports as firearms, beads and, cloth. Not all parts of the Congo basin were evenly affected by this international trade, and some forest peoples, though they engaged in small-scale, lively local trading, did not participate in long-distance trading caravans through the forest. Elsewhere, in the southern savanna, Africans shifted from sending slaves overseas in the Atlantic trade to keeping them to produce wax, ivory, rubber, and other valued resources for a trade with European merchants. The northern savanna saw the development of slave and ivory raiding empires linked to the Nile river basin.

Generally, this burgeoning central African trade was based upon intensive environmental exploitation, and in many regions competition for valued resources sparked warfare, slave raiding, and flight among central Africans. Elephant populations dwindled, overhunted to meet the Europeans' insatiable demands for ivory. Increasing populations and competition for valuable resources precipitated forest clearing for agriculture. In the northern savanna, contact with a trans-Saharan slave and ivory trade precipitated the creation of large, concentrated trading posts and introduced new diseases—smallpox, syphilis, and measles—that became endemic among central Africans.

The Twentieth Century and Colonial Rule

European colonial rule introduced new ways of exploiting the forest, but also continued older ones. In the late nineteenth century, central Africa became the focus of Belgian, French, British, and German dreams of commercial exploitation and immense wealth. Several European powers coped with limited finances, relatively sparse and intractable central African populations, and the enormous difficulties of communication and transportation in central Africa by delegating the responsibility for "developing" this wealth to private concessionary companies. Paying a fixed yearly rent and additional fees, these commercial enterprises held monopolies on valuable resources. They were supposed to build roads, customs posts, and telegraph lines in their concessions, but most did nothing. Instead, they sent armed guards into villages to conscript Africans to harvest rubber from trees and vines for months at a time, hunt for ivory and animal skins, gather copal (a tree resin), tropical oils, and other products. Many companies, though they kidnapped, beat, cheated, and stole from workers, did not prosper, but others, such as that of the Belgian king Leopold II (1835–1909), known as the Congo Independent State (1885–1908), reaped enormous wealth. Nevertheless, the changes that these companies wrought on central African environments were significant: They depleted the savannas and forests of rubber-producing trees and vines, and they exhausted the once-copious elephant and game populations. Widespread recruitment of laborers also helped to spread infectious diseases throughout central Africa. Epidemics of trypanosomiasis, or sleeping sickness, swept through much of central Africa in the early twentieth century, prompting a French medical service campaign to control them.

Even after European states put an end to the concessionary system, colonizers still welcomed the activities of companies that would "develop" central Africa's riches. Companies (and, at times, colonial administrators) avidly pushed cash cropping, diamond and gold mining, and logging, and the environmental consequences of these activities were considerable: Farmers cleared more forest to expand cultivation, and hunters and trappers stepped up their activities to feed workers in the diamond camps and logging centers. Mining lay waste to forests and highlands, caused rivers to dry up during the dry season and to flood during the rainy season, and water pumps polluted these waters with oil and other chemicals. Elsewhere, large-scale colonial development projects transformed landscapes irrevocably. One of the most dramatic development interventions was the 1955–1959 construction of the Kariba hydroelectric dam—one of the world's largest—on what is now the Zambia-Zimbabwe border (formerly Northern Rhodesia and Southern Rhodesia). Supplying electricity to the Copperbelt in present-day Zambia as well as to parts of present-day Zimbabwe, the dam created a huge reservoir, Kariba Lake, and displaced fifty thousand people and significant numbers of wildlife from the area.

Postcolonial Dilemmas

Following independence from colonial powers in the early 1960s, central African states have maintained an equivocal relationship with the environment. On the one hand, environmental exploitation has continued to be at the foundation of their economies, a crucial source of export earnings. Hence, cash cropping, mining, logging, and other activities of the colonial era continued. Some states initiated large-scale development projects with finances from multi- and bilateral aid organizations that cleared wider expanses of forest and woodland and encouraged mechanized commercial agriculture. While much of central Africa is not highly urbanized, cities such as Brazzaville, Kinshasa, and Douala experienced rapid growth and have helped to redirect rural resources toward feeding, housing, and supplying the needs of growing urban populations.

On the other hand, there have been considerable efforts to protect central Africa's environment and resources. Colonial powers once took some measures to protect game and forests, creating hunting reserves and parks and implementing hunting permits for different classes of hunters. But in the 1980s and 1990s, many African states revived, built upon, or expanded on colonial measures, partly because conservation could earn much-needed tourism revenues, but also because states were under pressure from the World Bank to implement conservation programs as one condition for receiving loans. Conservation, however, has not been universally popular among ordinary Africans, who resent limits placed on where, what species, and how they can hunt, trap, fish, and gather. Others dislike the fact that conservation interventions limit mining, logging, and other activities within protected areas, thus reducing access to jobs, salaries, and consumer goods. Some central Africans, however, have found the small-scale development activities and provision of some services and jobs that go along with conservation projects a real boon.

Still, the twin demands of development and conservation pose a serious dilemma for central African states and their citizens. For many impoverished central African states and people, cash comes most readily through forms of environmental exploitation that are not always sustainable. Yet depleting central Africa of its valued resources and lands would also pose real losses as well. Balancing those twin demands will remain a critical problem in central Africa in the coming decades.

Tamara Giles-Vernick

Further Reading

Bailey, R.C., Head, G., Jenike, M., Owen, B., Rechtman, R., and Zechenter, E. (1989). "Hunting and gathering in tropical rain forests: Is it possible?" *American Anthropologist, 91* (March), 59–82.

Birmingham, D., & Martin, P. M. (Eds.). (1983). *History of central Africa* (Vols. 1 & 2). New York and London: Longman. Vols. 1 and 2.

Birmingham, D., & Martin, P. M. (Eds.). (1997). *History of central Africa* (Vol. 3). New York and London: Longman.

Burnham, P. (1980). *Opportunity and constraint in a savanna society: The Gbaya of Meiganga.* London: Academic Press.

Burnham, P. (1996). *The politics of cultural difference in northern Cameroon.* Edinburgh, UK.: Edinburgh University Press for the International African Institute.

Coquery-Vidrovitch, C. (1972). *Le Congo au temps des grands compagnies concessionnaires.* Paris: Mouton.

Cordell, D. D. (1985). *Dar al-Kuti and the last years of the trans-Saharan trade.* Madison: University of Wisconsin Press.

Giles-Vernick, T. (2002). *Cutting the vines of the past: Environmental histories of the equatorial rain forest.* Charlottesville: University Press of Virginia.

Harms, R. (1987). *Games against nature: An eco-cultural history of the Nunu* Cambridge, UK: Cambridge University Press.

Headrick, R. (1994). *Colonialism, health and illness in French Equatorial Africa, 1885–1935.* (D. Headrick, Ed.). Atlanta, GA: African Studies Association.

Hoschschild, A. (1998). *King Leopold's Ghost.* New York: Houghton Mifflin.

Miller, J. C. (1982). The significance of drought, disease and famine in the agriculturally marginal zones of western central Africa. *Journal of African History, 23,* 17–61.

Richards, P. W. (1996). *The tropical rain forest: An ecological study* (2nd ed.). New York: Cambridge University Press.

Vansina, J. (1990). *Paths in the rainforests: Toward a history of political tradition in equatorial Africa.* Madison: University of Wisconsin Press.

Africa, East

East Africa contains a broad environmental diversity that is attributable to the historical idiosyncrasies and interactions of humankind and nature. Given the evidence for the evolution of *Homo sapiens* in eastern Africa, the interactive processes involving culture and nature have likely been occurring for over 300,000 years. Until recently, however, historical analyses of ancient East Africa have stressed stasis rather than dynamism, preferring to see Africans struggling with nature for their very survival or living with it in harmony. Neither characterization is apt.

Geography and Climate

Defining East Africa with the political boundaries of the contemporary countries of Uganda, Kenya, Tanzania, Rwanda, and Burundi, its total area is 1.7 million square kilometers (Tanzania 886,034, Kenya 566,966, Uganda 199,548, Rwanda 24,949, and Burundi 25,648). This area contains an extraordinary range of environments, the majority shaped to some extent by land-use patterns that incorporated some combination of hunting, agriculture, and pastoralism. Geologically, most of East Africa's landmass, aside from its coastal plain, consists of a raised plateau cut by rifts that contain basins and lakes. Highlands—uplifted granitic massifs, escarpments, and volcanoes—that formed through complex tectonic movements and volcanism surround the rift valleys in dramatic contrast. Uplifted granitic massifs are mountain massifs formed by tectonic forces. They consist principally of metamorphic rock, principally granite. Escarpments are the walls of the massifs and East African valleys, in this case, the Great Rift Valley. Volcanoes are volcanoes, ex. Kilimanjaro, Mt. Kenya, Mt. Elgon, Mt. Meru and many others. East Africa's rainfall patterns are highly variable as well. The region's equatorial location and proximity to the Indian Ocean expose it twice annually to the abundant moisture that accompanies the passage of a tropical low-pressure zone, the Intertropical Convergence Zone (ITCZ). Not all the moisture reaches the mainland, however. Coastal winds, the speed of the ITCZ's passage, geographical features on the mainland, and the rain shadow effect of Madagascar all limit rainfall distribution, creating a more generally arid climate than at comparable latitudes in West Africa. In East Africa, weather generally comes onshore in the form of a seasonal monsoon pattern. When it encounters the cooler highlands rainfall covers the southern and southeastern slopes and diminishes as it moves west northwest. Thus one finds mountains were annual rainfall varies on one massif from say 2000 mm on it southern and eastern slopes to 1000 on its northern and western slopes. One also finds very localized rain shadow effects. Further variability results from sea surface temperature oscillations that precipitate El

Niño and La Niña climatological events. As a result, climate has been broadly stable over the long term, but annual weather patterns can diverge wildly.

Making a Living

Given East Africa's capricious weather, East Africa's premodern environmental history has been characterized by the development of complex production and exchange systems to facilitate survival under almost any environmental circumstances. The gradual transformation in food ways (a cultural term that denotes the production and consumption patters of agricultural societies) constituted the most significant development in East Africa's environmental history before the first millennium CE. During the past two or three millennia, farming and herding supplanted foraging as the dominant feature on East Africa's varied landscape. Two separate husbandry traditions dominated the process. The most recent involved the introduction—into the fertile and well-watered lakes region of Uganda and western Tanzania some two thousand years ago—of a root-crop complex (agricultural production system based on root crops [ex. taro and yams]) that had evolved in central Africa. A more ancient tradition extends back some three thousand years and concerns the spread southward—from Sudan and Ethiopia—of livestock herding and grain cultivation into the Central Rift Valley highlands. Both traditions involved complex transformations in autochthonous (a common anthropological term meaning the earliest know inhabitants of a place [syn. aboriginal]) ideologies, languages, social organization, and technologies, whose nature and environmental initial effects remain only partially understood. Fortunately, archeologists and historical linguists have shed more light on the subsequent dynamics of technological and environmental change.

Pastoralists

In highland Kenya and Tanzania, where most elevations range between 1,500 and 3,000 meters, variations in rainfall and elevation created an ecological mosaic in which montane (relating to the biogeographic zone of moist, cool upland slopes below the timberline dominated by large coniferous trees) forest, rich savanna pasture, and fertile volcanic hills intersected. The environmental variety led to opportunities for numerous husbandry innovations. In drier reaches, pastoralism became the preferred means of subsistence. One of the most distinctive pastoral groups was the Sirikwa (twelfth to eighteenth century), the ancestors of today's Nilotic-speaking peoples who now occupy western Kenya's Rift Valley highlands. The archeological remnants of these ancient herding communities lay scattered across the landscape in the form of thousands of saucer-like depressions, each about 10 meters wide. The depressions housed Sirikwa cattle, whose owners lived in attached structures facing outward from the cattle enclosure. The Sirikwa were neither the first nor the last pastoral society to occupy these grazing lands, but their adaptations represent part of a long East African pastoralist tradition that combined the milk production of their humped zebu cattle with the meat provided from sheep and goats. Furthermore, the demonstrated mobility (moving several times a generation) of the Sirikwa and the defensive posture of their dwellings suggest that they had learned that productivity of pastures fluctuates in response to climate and to human and animal population levels.

Under conditions of extreme drought, famine, disease, and marauding neighbors threatened herding communities. Therefore, East African pastoralists rarely relied on their herds alone. Nineteenth-century European observers reported extensive grain farming by pastoralists along the margins of the Rift Valley highlands where mountain streams discharged into the arid plains. Archeological remains suggest that this pattern is centuries old. One striking example is evident at Engaruka, an isolated village at the base of the Rift Valley's western escarpment in northern Tanzania. Researchers have uncovered a complex of irrigation furrows and terraces dating to the twelfth and thirteenth centuries. Whereas some East African pastoralists clearly learned to farm themselves, others forged social relations with their neighbors who occupied East Africa's wetter montane environments where geography allowed for the possibility of rain-fed agriculture.

Farmers

As pastoralists adapted their economy to the highland savannas, a horticultural tradition took hold around two thousand years ago on the forested hills of the Lake Victoria basin. This early agricultural transformation coincided with the incorporation into autochthonous societies of a new cultural complex that included root crops like yams, a new language (the ancestor of the Bantu languages now spoken across much of the region), new pottery styles, sedentary communities,

Zebras approach a water source in Tanzania. COURTESY MARY CORINNE LOWENSTEIN.

and eventually iron working. As the cultural and agricultural complex moved eastward, it drew from its origins in the Great Lakes of the Rift Valley a proclivity to seek out places that offered abundant moisture and forest resources. However, when agricultural societies encountered new environments such as lake shores, ocean coasts, and volcanic mountains, they fine-tuned their farming systems accordingly, creating a variety of adaptations. Successful farming ultimately led to population growth. Of course, environmental transformation, sometimes large in scale, accompanied the process. For example, the accumulation of evidence from linguistics, archeology, and paleoecology (a branch of ecology concerned with the characteristics of ancient environments) has revealed a pattern of large-scale deforestation and subsequent ecological change in the interlacustrine (common term in geography meaning interlaces) highlands beginning about two thousand years ago, a process tied closely to the industrial demands of iron working. Similar circumstances, although perhaps smaller in scale, undoubtedly accompanied agriculture's fluorescence (blooming, blossoming, condition or period of blossoming) in other locales.

As demographic change brought herders and farmers into closer contact during the second millennium CE, the lines between pastoralism and agriculture sometimes became blurred. In some places pastoralists shifted completely into farming, whereas others with a herding tradition switched expertly back and forth between horticulture and herding as the climate allowed. In the Interlacustrine Zone, where farmers had introduced and refined what became a highly successful farming system, immigrant herders introduced new notions of political power and prestige associated with cattle ownership. The result was the polarization of the two production complexes, where those with access to cattle garnered the social prestige necessary to form a ruling class and, in some cases, viable states.

Globalization and the Coast, 1000–1800 CE

After the East African agricultural revolution reached the Indian Ocean coastal region at the end of the first millennium CE, its practitioners adapted to the coastal environment. In the early stages of their transformation, coastal villagers remained in many ways tied to their history of agricultural innovation, turning to the ocean simply to gather their subsistence during the dry seasons. However, by the middle of the second millennium CE, coastal settlements stretching from the Lamu archipelago in northern Kenya to Kilwa in southern Tanzania shared a language, Kiswahili, and a maritime economy that sharply differentiated them from other East Africans. They had become expert boat builders and fishers whose skills enabled them to efficiently harvest the biologically rich offshore reefs. Coastal peoples also became international traders, receiving the ships and cargoes that the seasonal northeast monsoon winds brought from the Red Sea, the Persian Gulf, and India. In order to enhance business, some of the foreigners settled permanently in the growing coastal port towns, intermarried with the Swahili (language and cultural zone of the East African coastal littoral) families, and introduced Islam. As trade expanded, foreign demand grew for eastern and southern Africa's raw materials such as gold, slaves, ivory, and timber. With these commodities, Swahili merchants purchased the luxury items and manufactured goods that increased the wealth, architectural splendor, and prestige of the coastal towns well into the nineteenth century. By the beginning of the nineteenth century the Swahili coast (East Africa) was dotted with the urban landscapes.

As the commodity trade shows, the relationship between East Africa and Asia had ramifications far beyond the coastal region. The pattern was not exclusively extractive, however. For example, the introduction of bananas from the East Indies revolutionized agriculture across Africa's equatorial regions, helping to precipitate unprecedented population increases. In the 1600s the scope of East Africa's ties to far-flung environments grew when East Africans gained access to American crops such as maize, manioc, and potatoes, crops that in many places have come to dominate farming regimes in modern times.

The internationalization of East Africa's coastal region therefore touched in profound ways both the coastal and the interior environments. As trade continued to flourish into the eighteenth and nineteenth centuries, the negative ramifications of East Africa's incorporation into the world economy became all too apparent. As it had in western and central Africa in previous centuries, a burgeoning slave trade began to decimate the productive capacity of communities in the interior.

The Colonial Era and Beyond

In the decades before European colonization, East Africa experienced a series of ecological disasters that decimated human and animal populations. The violence and dislocation of the nineteenth century slave trade had reduced the resiliency of farming and herding systems, creating populations of refugees seeking protection. When drought and disease combined with the regional violence, the agricultural environment fell apart. Terraces and irrigation systems collapsed in the highlands while tsetse fly infested bush vegetation encroached on abandoned lowland gardens and pastures. In the 1880s and 1890s, colonial armies from Germany, Britain, and Belgium entered the devastated countryside and installed a new authoritarian state systems whose policy dictated a complete reorientation of production systems along European lines. As a result, African production systems experience yet another set of shocks. In places like Kenya's "white highlands," European settlers claimed the finest highland pastures in order to produce livestock and agricultural commodities like coffee and tea. Kenya's government forced the aggrieved pastoralists onto crowded reserves. On other huge swaths of alienated land, European plantation companies produced commodities like cotton, sisal, and tobacco. Where African farmers remained on their land, colonially-introduced tax burdens forced them either to produce exportable commodities or to labor on settler farms; either way they had to procure cash.

In the 1930s, colonial governments drew upon very preliminary scientific research to conclude that Africans farmers and herders had precipitated an ecological crisis, manifest in deforestation and soil erosion. As an antidote, colonial governments introduced conservation programs in their forestry and agricultural services. Sustained yield forestry systems, developed in

Europe, failed miserably in their tropical setting. Not only did the delineation of forest reserves displace many Africans, the system of forest exploitation devastated irreplaceable forest ecosystems. After World War II, colonial governments across East Africa forced highland farmers to build terraces, plant hedge lines, and take other onerous soil erosion control measures. The program encountered stiff resistance, which helped to foster a vocal anti-colonial sentiment.

The legacy of colonial environmental policy has found its way into contemporary conservation and development programs now operating on East Africa agricultural landscapes. Development organizations still place a premium on soil and forest conservation, but they now seek more democratic means to achieve their ends. Since the 1980s, East Africa's highland forests have attracted the attention of conservation biologists, who seek to study the evolutionary processes of forest plants and animals and to preserve their great biological diversity. Whether either group will succeed remains an open question.

Christopher A. Conte

Further Reading

Anderson, D. (1988). Cultivating pastoralists: Ecology and economy among the Il Chamus of Baringo, 1840–1980. In D. Johnson & D. Anderson (Eds.), *The ecology of survival: Case studies from northeast African history* (pp. 241–260). Boulder, CO: Westview Press.

Anderson, D., & Grove, R. (1987). *Conservation in Africa: People, policies and practice.* Cambridge, UK: Cambridge University Press.

Ehret, C. (2000). *An African classical age: Eastern and southern Africa in world history, 1000 B.C. to A.D. 400.* Charlottesville: University of Virginia Press.

Ehret, C., & Posnansky, M. (Eds.). (1982). *The archaeological and linguistic reconstruction of African history.* Berkeley and Los Angeles: University of California Press.

Johnson, D. H., & Anderson, D. M. (Eds.). (1989). *The ecology of survival: Case studies from northeast African history.* Boulder, CO: Westview Press.

Lovett, J. C., & Wasser, S. K. (Eds.). (1993). *Biogeography and ecology of the rain forests of eastern Africa.* Cambridge, UK: Cambridge University Press.

McClanahan, T. R., & Young, T. P. (Eds.). (1996). *East African ecosystems and their conservation.* Oxford, UK: Oxford University Press.

Nicholson, S. (1996). Environmental change within the historical period. In W. M. Adams, A. S. Goudie, &

A. R. Orme (Eds.), *The physical geography of Africa* (pp. 60–87). Oxford, UK: Oxford University Press.

Nurse, D., & Spear, T. (1985). *The Swahili: Reconstructing the history and language of an African society, 800–1500*. Philadelphia: University of Pennsylvania Press.

Pouwells, R. (1987). *Horn and crescent: Cultural change and traditional Islam on the East African coast, 800–1900*. Cambridge, UK: Cambridge University Press.

Robertshaw, P. (1990). *Early pastoralists of south-western Kenya*. Nairobi, Kenya: British Institute of Eastern Africa.

Schmidt, P. (1994). Historical ecology and landscape transformation in eastern equatorial Africa. In C. Crumley (Ed.), *Historical ecology: Cultural knowledge and changing landscapes* (pp. 99–126). Santa Fe, NM: School of American Research Press.

Schmidt, P. (1997). *Iron technology in east Africa: Symbolism, science, and archaeology*. Bloomington: Indiana University Press.

Schoenbrun, D. L. (1998). *A green place, a good place: Agrarian change, gender, and social identity in the Great Lakes region to the 15th century*. Portsmouth, NH: Heinemann.

Sutton, J. E. G. (Ed.). (1989). The history of African agricultural technology and field systems [Special issue]. *Azania, 24*.

Sutton, J. E. G. (1990). *A thousand years of East Africa*. Nairobi, Kenya: British Institute in eastern Africa.

Sutton, J. E. G. (1994–1995). The growth of farming communities in Africa from the equator southwards [Special issue]. *Azania, 29–30*.

Vansina, J. (1990). *Paths in the rainforest*. Madison: University of Wisconsin Press.

Vansina, J. (1994–1995). A slow revolution: Farming in subequatorial Africa. *Azania, 29–30*, 15–26.

Africa, Southern

Southern Africa, comprising the present states of South Africa, Namibia, Botswana, Lesotho, Swaziland, Zimbabwe, Zambia, Malawi, and Mozambique, is roughly half the size of the United States including Alaska. Climatic and ecological conditions vary greatly. On the east coast, facing the Indian Ocean, and in the central highlands, which rear above 1,000 meters, rainfall exceeds 500 mm a year. In much of the western half of the sub-continent, however, precipitation is far less. Some of the world's great arid lands, such as the Namib (Namibia), the Kalahari (Botswana), and the Karoo (South Africa) are situated here. Most of the region experiences summer storm rainfall. In the north, around the Zambezi Valley, the climate is tropical; in the far south, a more temperate, Mediterranean climate prevails.

Pre-Colonial Settlement

Environment played a key role in the peopling of southern Africa. Settlement by hunter-gatherers, using stone tools, dates back perhaps 50,000 years. Partly on account of its varied ecology, the region was home to particularly diverse wildlife, and antelopes were especially plentiful. About 2,500 years ago, Bantu-speaking Africans dispersed through the region: they worked iron, made pottery, kept cattle, and grew sorghum and millet. This was no sudden invasion, and earlier settlements were sometimes absorbed. Because they relied on rainfall for crops, these Africans did not move into the more arid western parts of the subcontinent. Thus protected, hunter-gatherers survived as recognizably different communities until the colonial era. Those who became known as the Khoikhoi adopted cattle, herding them to scarce water sources and seasonal pastures.

African social and economic systems were shaped by relatively open frontiers and small populations. Settlement was dispersed, and wealth and power lay in controlling people and livestock. A major African achievement, John Iliffe maintains (1995), was to gain control of one of the most difficult environments on behalf of mankind. However, a number of centralized political units developed, such as Great Zimbabwe (c. 1200 to 1500 CE). It amassed large cattle herds, conquered its neighbors, carried on trade as far away as the coast, and was the first to exploit the area's rich gold deposits. Such systems were hard to sustain, and by the early nineteenth century, on the eve of colonization, few large kingdoms remained. The recently formed Zulu state, with perhaps 250,000 people, was the most powerful of these.

Africans changed the landscape of southern Africa. They burnt pastures to renew them for spring rains, cleared woodland for settlement and agriculture, and exploited timber for fuel. They hunted for food and skins, and to protect their livestock. Southern Africa shared in the Columbian exchange with the Americas, and introduced crops such as corn (maize)—a staple by the early twentieth century—which greatly enhanced agricultural productivity. But African economies had limited environmental impact; they depended largely on local produce, renewable natural products, long agricultural fallow periods, and a limited range of crafts. Tsetse flies, which carry trypanosomiasis, a disease fatal to cattle, restricted the build up of livestock numbers in many tropical and lowland zones to the north of the Limpopo River.

Colonialism and Environmental Transformations

Colonial intrusions began when Portuguese arrived on the Mozambican coast in the sixteenth century and Dutch arrived at Cape Town in the seventeenth. By chance the Dutch found themselves in some of the best terrain for European settlement, and faced only the Khoisan people, who could not resist the firearms or diseases of the intruders. Settlers followed game, water sources, and grazing routes into the semi-arid interior; in the nineteenth century they went beyond it, to the high veldt. They mastered this hostile environment and introduced new breeds, such as merino sheep, that vastly increased their wealth and capacity to invest. Unlike the settlers of North America and Australia, they were constrained to a greater extent by indigenous Africans as they moved eastwards and northwards; the tsetse and malaria belts also hampered their progress.

Colonization transformed southern Africa's environments, as was widely recognized in the twentieth century: commercial grazing exhausted pastures; the limited indigenous timber, as in western Zimbabwe, was felled for railway sleepers, mine props, and flooring; some of the world's largest forest plantations, planted with exotic pine and eucalypts, spread along the northern Natal coast and through the Drakensberg watershed. Monocultural cash crops, such as sugar along the subtropical east coast, corn on the high veld, and citrus in irrigated valleys, displaced significant amounts of indigenous vegetation. Earth dams, boreholes and irrigation projects burgeoned in an attempt to tap southern Africa's water resources: the Zambezi projects of Kariba (Zimbabwe and Zambia, 1950s) and Cahora Bassa (Mozambique, 1970s), as well as South Africa's Orange (now Gariep) River Scheme were major undertakings. Much of the region's reticulated water was funneled towards irrigation and industrial use, producing stark inequality in access to tapped water. Yet control over the most fundamental natural resource has also made it possible to provide for the region's rapidly growing cities.

Mining accelerated southern African economic growth starting in the late nineteenth century. Exploitation of diamonds in Kimberley and later Botswana, gold on the Witwatersrand and in Zimbabwe, and copper in Zambia all created urban enclaves and transport routes that demanded raw materials. Energy needs were largely met by coal—the second most important mining sector after gold—which was also used to generate electricity for industries and cities. Lacking oil, and threatened by apartheid-era embargoes, South Africa built the largest oil from coal plant in the world. While cheap coal does pollute, it has brought a degree of energy self-sufficiency in key economic sectors.

African populations grew dramatically throughout the region in the twentieth century, and by the 1960s, annual population growth of over 3 percent was the norm. The black population of South Africa itself increased from 3.5 million in 1904 to about 30 million (of 40 million total) in 1996. Growth in southern Africa as a whole, with perhaps 100 million people at the end of the century, may have been even faster. Old systems of peasant and small-holder production, dependent on sparse settlement and long fallow periods, put natural resources under acute pressure in rural areas, especially because the amount of land in black African hands had diminished in some countries. While acute famine was largely conquered, except where violent conflict erupted, malnutrition and diseases of poverty became widespread. The percentage of people living off the land diminished sharply, and in some countries over half the population became urban. This was increasingly visible in the growth of large, unserviced, informal, dense settlements that placed new environmental strains on urban hinterlands.

Although rapid economic development and population growth has placed natural resources under great strain, southern Africa was at the forefront of conservation initiatives in the twentieth century. British colonial governments, and the settler states of South Africa and Zimbabwe, carved out wildlife reserves where hunting and settlement were prohibited. These reserves are now key sites for preservation and tourism. The same authorities also tried to reshape African settlements and peasant economies in such a way as to develop sustainable agricultural practices. Such interventions were often met with hostility by rural people because they were seen, as attempts to undermine local control over natural resources. In a number of countries, these conflicts fed into anti-colonial struggles, and they remain an important feature of rural politics in the region.

William Beinart

Further Reading

African environments: Past and present. (2000). Special issue of *Journal of Southern African Studies, 26*(4).

Connah, G. (1987). *African civilizations: Precolonial cities and states in tropical Africa, an archaeological perspective.* Cambridge, UK: Cambridge University Press.

Iliffe, J. (1995). *Africans: The history of a continent.* Cambridge, UK: Cambridge University Press.

McCann, J. (1999). *Green land, brown land, black land: An environmental history of Africa, 1800–1990.* Oxford: James Currey.

Beinart, W., & Coates, P. (1995). *Environment and history: The taming of nature in the USA and South Africa.* London: Routledge.

Ramphele, M. (Ed.). (1991). *Restoring the land: Environment and change in post-apartheid South Africa.* London: Panos.

Moyo, S., O'Keefe, P., & Sill, M. (1993). *The southern African environment: Profiles of the SADC countries.* London: Earthscan.

Africa, Western

Studying the environmental history of ancient western Africa (3000 BCE–700 CE) is necessary in order to understand how sustainable communities evolved, and any such study would be incomplete without considering the geological history of the African continent.

Geological History

Africa was originally part of the ancient supercontinent Gondwanaland, which also included contemporary Antarctica, South America, and Australia, as well as the Indian subcontinent. Gondwanaland then underwent orogenic geological transformations (occurrences that usually occur when the oceanic and continental plates meet each other) that produced massive mountain ranges running southwest to northeast. These placations were eventually eroded by denudation to produce peneplains (nearly flat surfaces that represent an advanced stage of erosion), the largest of which are found in Africa. Africa itself has not undergone appreciable plication since the pre-Cambrian era. Africa's physical geography was further shaped by erosion extending through all geological eras.

These changes resulted, primarily during the Quaternary period, in alternating humid and semi-arid climates. Periods of abundant rain increased the percentage of land suitable for human habitation, while arid periods made the Sahara into a climatic break between the Mediterranean and the tropical worlds that included western Africa. The Sahara limited the penetration of Mediterranean influences in architecture, craft, and especially agriculture into the tropical regions of ancient western Africa.

Geological transformations over 5 billion years produced the mineral resources of ancient western Africa—iron, copper, and gold. Gold was deposited in part by Pre-Cambrian volcanism that produced granitic intrusions, and it was largely gold that motivated the trans-Saharan trade between West and North Africans. The gold trade was also motivated by the lack of salt in most of ancient western Africa.

Life Zones of Ancient Western Africa

Ancient western Africa, also referred to as the Sudan region, lies south of the Sahara and extends west to the Atlantic Ocean, comprising the Chad and Niger Basins, the Niger River, Lake Volta, and the Fouta Djallon Highland. Today West Africa consists of the republics of Mauritania, Mali, Niger, Chad, Senegal, Gambia, Guinea Bissau, Guinea, Sierra Leone, Liberia, Ivory Coast, Burkina Faso, Ghana, Togo, Benin (formerly Dahomey), Nigeria, and Cameroon. Western Africa is characterized by three major life zones (geographical regions characterized by distinctive terrain, climate, and natural vegetation): coastal, forest, and the Sudan Savanna. Each of these zones yielded natural resources that were important in the emergence of the three famous ancient western African empires of Ghana, Mali, and Songhai (3000 BCE–700 CE).

The coastal zone extends from the Atlantic Ocean, to twenty to eighty miles inland, and the ancient peoples inhabiting it included the Jola, Pepel, and Serer peoples of Senegambia and the Sherboro and Bulom of Sierra Leone. These people engaged in salt production for trade or consumption, and salt, along with gold, was an important trading commodity in Africa. The coastal inhabitants were initially nomadic, surviving by fishing, hunting, and gathering. They began radically transforming their environment when they learned the art of cultivation and entered the Iron Age (c. 11 CE).

The forest zone is an area of tall trees and dense undergrowth stretching approximately three thousand miles from Sierra Leone to Cameroon. Its ancient inhabitants included the Mende, Kru, Asante, Fon Yoruba,

Edo, and Ibo peoples, who fall into two groups: the Gulf forest people near the gulf coast of Guinea, and the western forest people near the Atlantic. This region was settled prior to 1000 CE, and the original inhabitants had a subsistence economy until the Neolithic revolution. After learning how to make polished stone tools, they began to clear land, cultivate the soil, and domesticate animals. The Guinea forest people cultivated white and yellow yams, while the western forest people grew rice. Eventually plantain, bananas, and larger varieties of yam spread to this region from Asia.

Forest zone people were among the first in ancient western Africa to produce food surpluses for trade, once they entered the Iron Age around 11 CE and began clearing forest. Iron was used extensively in this zone, and archaeologists have found Iron Age settlements here as far apart as Senegambia and modern-day southern Ghana. They have also found ancient bronze works at Igbo-Ukwu in eastern Nigeria. Most of the iron ore in this region lay at the surface and was first mined using open-cast methods.

The Sudan savanna zone, characterized by tall savanna grasses and open woodland, covers vast fertile plains between the Sahara and Africa's tropical deserts. This was the most hospitable part of ancient West Africa for agriculture and the domestication of animals such as cattle, sheep, goats, and fowl. It also contains considerable gold resources, particularly in the Wangara mines of upper Senegal, the upper Niger River, Bonduku, and the area known as Elmina. Most of the gold in this region was alluvial and mined by panning. The Sudan also had abundant iron ore but lacked salt reserves. Early inhabitants of this area included the Wolof, Tukulor, Fulani, Soninke, Malinke, Songhai, and Hausa peoples. Early inhabitants of this area cultivated Guinea corn, millet, and rice. In the upper Niger, the Mandingo and Hausa peoples cultivated rice easily because they had developed heavy hoes for cultivating and ridging their crops. Their knowledge and expertise with iron protected their early empires and trade interests with North Africa.

The Rise of Ancient Ghana, Mali, and Songhai Empires

Abundant natural resources—especially gold and iron ores—in the Sudan region led to the rise of the ancient empires of Ghana, Mali, and Songhai, and to the emergence of trans-Saharan trade. All three empires employed one or more of four primary trans-Saharan trade routes. The items transported along the first two routes were gold, salt, and horses, while the third carried a mixture of items including gold, salt, shells, skins, ivory, cloth, and kola nuts. The fourth route was primarily a slave-trading route supplying the Arabs through Tripoli and Benghazi. The most important exports to North Africa were gold, slaves (especially eunuchs), hides, ivory, ostrich feathers, kola nuts, gum and manufactured goods.

Environmental Problems

The abundance of natural resources in western Africa is reflected by its geographical names: the Gold Coast, Ivory Coast, and Slave Coast. The Gold Coast refers to a region rich in gold ore that encompasses both current and ancient Ghana. The Slave Coast was the center of slave traffic between the sixteenth and nineteenth centuries, and was located between the Benin (now in Nigeria) and Volta rivers. The Slave Coast region—Nigeria in particular—is now exploited for petroleum, causing devastating environmental degradation. An investigation conducted by the Nigerian Environmental Society in 1985 revealed that between 1970 and 1983, offshore and on-shore oil spillage amounted to 1,711,354 barrels.

Commercial logging has been part of the Ghanaian economy since the colonial era, and the country now faces the consequences of rapidly increasing deforestation. Pressures on the forests mounted with the initiation of the Economic Recovery Program in 1981 and with increased European demand. Since 1981, deforestation in Ghana has proceeded at two percent per year, and only 25 percent of the original forests remain. Timber is Ghana's third most important export commodity after cocoa and minerals.

Ghana has rich mineral resources, including gold, bauxite, manganese, limestone, diamonds, and salt. Gold now accounts for 80 percent of the country's total mineral exports, and Ghana is second only to South Africa in gold production in Africa. There are over 500 legal small-scale mines in Ghana; their operations are haphazard, leading to preventable environmental problems such as ground- and surface-water contamination.

West Africa continues to attract international trade, including illegal trade in waste products. Many West African countries became favorite targets of international waste traders in the 1980s because they had weak environmental laws and limited state control over the customs officers who approved import shipments. These countries, like many others on the continent, felt compelled to accept toxic and hazardous wastes because of the economic devastation wrought by war, poverty, and famine. By 1990 over half of the countries in the continent had been approached to accept hazardous waste imports.

Sylvia Hood Washington

Further Reading

Alagoa, E. J. (1988). Introduction. In E. J. Alagoa & N. Newnan (Eds.), *The early history of the Niger Delta.* Hamburg, Germany: Helmut Buske Verlag.

Diarra, S. (1981). Historical geography: Physical aspects. In J. Ki-Zerbo (Ed.), *General history of Africa, I* (pp. 316–332). Berkeley: University of California.

Harris, J. E. (1998). *Africans and their history* (2nd ed.). New York: Penguin Books.

July, R. W. (1970). *A history of the African people.* New York: Charles Scribners and Sons.

Mabogunje, A. L. (1981). Historical geography: Economic aspects. In J. Ki-Zerbo (Ed.), *General history of Africa, I* (pp. 333–347). Berkeley: University of California.

McIntosh, R. J. (1998). *Peoples of the middle Niger: The island of gold.* Oxford, UK: Blackwell Publishers.

Okyere, V. (2000). *Ghana: A historical survey.* Accra, Ghana: Vinojab Publications.

Oliver, R., & Fagan, B. M. (1975). *Africa in the iron age, c. 500 B.C. to A.D. 1400.* Cambridge, UK: Cambridge University Press.

Stride, G. T., & Ifeka, C. (1971). *Peoples and empires of West Africa. West Africa in history 1000–1800.* Nairobi, Kenya: Thomas Nelson and Sons.

Agent Orange

Agent Orange is a 1:1 mixture of two herbicides, 2,4-D and 2,4,5-T, that became the chemical defoliant used most often by U.S. forces in South Vietnam during the Vietnam War. Forests sprayed by Agent Orange began to die by dropping their leaves within two to four months. Both of the constituent herbicides of Agent Orange had been used in the United States in much different and tightly regulated conditions as defoliants in cotton and soybean production (to make the leaves fall off the plants just before the crops were harvested). Agent Orange and other herbicides were shipped to Vietnam in color-coded drums; their names—Agent Orange, Agent Blue, Agent White, Agent Purple, and

so on—came from a 10-centimeter band painted around the 55-gallon (208-liter) drums they were shipped in. During Operation Ranch Hand about 10 percent of the land area of Vietnam was sprayed with 41 million liters of Agent Orange between 1965 and 1970. Operation Ranch Hand targets were mainly in South Vietnam: on forest areas (86 percent) to strip them of cover for opposing forces and on rice fields and other agricultural areas (14 percent) to destroy potential food supplies for the enemy. Agent Orange was sprayed from specially outfitted Fairchild UC–123 airplanes and then, after April 1969, UC–123Ks, which applied about 11 liters per .4 hectare during low-flying aerial runs over target areas.

The environmental effects of Agent Orange have been profound and persistent. About 14 percent of the woody vegetation of southern Vietnam was attacked by herbicides. Coastal mangrove forests were targeted in several places in the Mekong Delta and south of Saigon, and significant portions of different kinds of wetland mangrove forests were destroyed. Although populations of brackish-water shrimp increased because food supplies of detritus were increased by the defoliation of wetland forests, the increase in detritus and in water temperature in exposed wetlands adversely affected other wetlands organisms. In general, the destruction of coastal mangrove forests also destroyed nurseries for marine organisms, and this contributed to the reduction of marine resources. The flow of water and nutrients in these areas was also affected by the chemical destruction of mangrove forests. Secondary tree species and tenacious grasses such as *Pennisetum polystachon* and *Imperata cylindrica* have invaded areas of inland forest that lost their canopies because of applications of Agent Orange. Agent Orange also destroyed animal habitats, contributed to soil erosion, and in general transformed biologically rich forests into exhausted remnants of themselves.

Health Effects

Research that might establish precisely the effects of Agent Orange on inland and wetland ecosystems—deforestation caused by defoliants as distinct from deforestation caused by logging, government resettlement schemes, or shrimp farming—will be difficult to complete. But research on the long-term effects of Agent Orange on humans is another matter. An impurity created in the production of 2,4,5-T, TCDD (tetrachlorodibenzo-para-dioxin, commonly known as dioxin) is an especially dangerous form of dioxin that is toxic to humans even in small quantities and has been linked to several forms of cancer, type 2 diabetes, disorders of the nervous, immune, and endocrine systems, and a range of birth defects in the children of people exposed to dioxin. Heavy monsoon rains and powerful tides have purged many defoliated watersheds of most dioxin, but in some places, especially around air bases where Agent Orange was stored and used and at about fifty sites identified to date where unintended dumping of Agent Orange occurred, toxic concentrations of Agent Orange can still be found. It has also worked its way into the food chain in these locales, where it is stored in the fatty tissue of fish and ducks. People living near these dioxin "hot spots" have a higher incidence of the kinds of health problems caused by dioxin contamination. A recent study of forty-three people living around Bien Hoa, the headquarters of Operation Ranch Hand after 1966, have yielded blood tests that show dioxin levels up to 206 times higher than the normal level. The average contamination level of this group, in a "hot spot" not far from Ho Chi Minh City (the former Saigon) thirty years after Operation Ranch Hand, was thirty-three times higher than the average level in Vietnam. A study of residents of the A Luoi Valley, around the Ho Chi Minh Trail in central Vietnam, was conducted by Hatfield Consultants and the 10–80 Committee (established by the Vietnamese government in 1980 to study the long-term health consequences of defoliant spraying). That study has also shown high blood and tissue levels of dioxin. Young people as well as old showed relatively high concentrations of dioxin, suggesting that the food chain was significantly contaminated. The Vietnamese government estimates that as many as 1 million Vietnamese people across three generations are victims of Agent Orange spraying.

Political Issues

Operation Ranch Hand and the persistence of dioxin in several environments in Vietnam have become multidimensional political issues. First of all, the use of chemicals by the United States to wage environmental warfare on opposing forces in Vietnam, Cambodia, and Laos provoked responses that led to several international conferences and protocols in the 1970s condemning environmental warfare. Years of litigation against companies that manufactured Agent Orange, several scientific studies on the effects of dioxin on human health, and lobbying with the Veterans Administration (VA) yielded a cash settlement and an agree-

ment by the VA to compensate American veterans of the war for several ailments that are linked to Agent Orange exposure. By 1998 about six thousand had qualified for Agent Orange-related compensation.

The U.S. government has resisted requests by the Vietnamese government for compensation or assistance to Vietnamese victims of Agent Orange or for assistance in the expensive research that is required to analyze dioxin concentrations. However, scientists from the United States, Vietnam, and eleven other counties met in a landmark meeting in Hanoi in March 2002 and established a framework for mutual assistance in understanding the health and environmental effects of dioxin. In July 2002 international delegates met in Stockholm, Sweden, to study the long-term consequences of the Vietnam War and produced a "Declaration on the Long-Term Consequences of War in Cambodia, Laos and Vietnam." This declaration calls for assistance to victims of the war from those "directly or indirectly involved in the reduction and use of the weapons at issue." The use of Agent Orange by American forces in Vietnam, then, has had an enduring legacy that continues to victimize and to provoke discussion and efforts to alleviate the suffering it has caused.

Mart A. Stewart

Further Reading

Cecil, P. F. (1986). *Herbicidal warfare: The Ranch Hand project in Vietnam.* New York: Praeger.

Dreyfuss, R. (2000, January/February). Apocalypse still. *Mother Jones*, 42–51, 91.

Dwernychuk, L. W., et al. (2002). Dioxin reservoirs in southern Vietnam: A legacy of Agent Orange. *Chemosphere, 47*(2), 117–137.

Hatfield Consultants & 10–80 Committee. (1998). *Preliminary assessment of environmental impacts related to spraying of Agent Orange herbicide during the Vietnam War.* West Vancouver, Canada: Hatfield Consultants.

Hatfield Consultants & 10–80 Committee. (2000). *Development of impact mitigation strategies related to the use of Agent Orange in the Aluoi Valley, Vietnam.* West Vancouver, Canada: Hatfield Consultants.

Westing, A. H., Boi, P. H., Quy, V., Lang, B. T., & Dwernychuck, L. W. (2002). *Long-term consequences of the Vietnam War*: Ecosystems. Retrieved December 19, 2002, http://www.nnn.se/vietnam/environ.htm

Agribusiness

Agribusiness is business engaged in processing and transporting agricultural products after they leave the farm as well as in producing and distributing all inputs to farms that do not originate on them. So defined, agribusiness involves three distinct systems and types of institutions with three distinct historical bases. The first is farmer-based agribusiness, which arises as a natural outgrowth of the operation of large numbers of small farms by relatively autonomous owner-producers, usually family groups, for their own benefit. The second is elite agribusiness, which rests on the use of government power to limit access to farmland or farm resources to members of a social elite and, when engaged in farm production, commonly involves absentee ownership and unfree (e.g. serfdom, conscripted labor, slavery, etc.) labor. The third is industrial agribusiness, which arises as a consequence of industrialization and the greatly accelerated process of societal economic specialization to which it has given rise.

Farmer-Based Agribusiness

In systems of farming based on small-scale farms whose operators have either actual ownership or de facto rights of disposal of their land, incentives lead the farmer-owners to invest in themselves by investing in the productivity of their land. Such systems have comprised the most productive and usually dominant type of agricultural production in Africa, southern Asia, southeastern Asia, and the Far East, where the rural population consistently makes up 70–80 percent of the population. It still characterizes much of the farming in Europe, particularly in the mountainous regions, and is the dominant mode of agriculture in Japan. In America and Canada it characterizes almost all of the smaller farms, whereas larger farms are increasingly owned by corporations. In Latin America peasants operating subsistence-oriented family farms are common, but power lies with elite agribusiness.

Small-scale private farming consistently gives rise to systems of commerce and trade that utilize two major organizational forms: regional fairs and membership associations. Regional fairs are periodic gatherings in specific and fixed places at specific and fixed times where local producers come together with itinerant brokers and dealers in manufactured or craft goods. Small fairs often feed into larger ones, and larger ones cycle around the country in a regular manner, aggregating goods into ever-larger flows. In the United States, such fairs persist as county and state fairs and also as periodic local roundups and the like that commonly include auctions and entertainments.

In places as diverse as Nigeria and India, traditional fairs continue their ancient cycles in full vigor. A few, such as the Pushkar fair held annually in Rajasthan, India, have even become widely recognized tourist attractions.

Modern membership associations include producers associations, self-regulatory bodies, and cooperatives, usually formed with legislative and legal support. These are ubiquitous in North America and Europe and increasingly important in developing countries. In the United States the legislative framework dates mainly from the New Deal. Organizations include cotton ginning cooperatives, rural electric cooperatives, rural telephone companies, state dairy associations, irrigation associations, federal agencies such as the Reconstruction Finance Corporation and the Rural Electrification Administration, and parastatals (bodies established by government and sometimes exercising some governmental power, but functioning autonomously and usually economically self-supporting), including the Tennessee Valley Authority. In some countries of the former Soviet Union, former collective farms have been reorganized as cooperatives. In Japan the land reforms accompanying demilitarization after World War II established a comprehensive farmer cooperative in every municipality (cho). Membership is mandatory and ties every farmer into a wide variety of interrelated services from granting credit to establishing product brands, grading, and marketing. In India, village-level credit societies were a major support of the Green Revolution—a major change in agricultural technologies worldwide that occurred from the 1960s through the 1980s, revolving around the spread of new high-yielding varieties of major food crops. Regional milk cooperatives have been the basis of a subsequent "white revolution," and many sugar mills are farmer-run cooperatives.

Although such organizations are aimed more often at cost reduction for their members than at profit maximization for themselves, the total amount of economic activity they account for is enormous.

Elite Agribusiness

Elite agribusiness depends on government or military force to maintain either direct control over land and those who actually farm it or monopolistic or monopsonistic (market condition in which there is one buyer and many sellers) advantages in the markets for agricultural commodities. In such systems neither those who control the land nor those who actually work it have an incentive to invest in its productivity, and rural poverty and social instability are common. Historical examples include the trading monopolies of Egyptian princes and Babylonian priests, the estates of the Roman senatorial class based on land and slaves taken by conquest, European serfdom, New World plantation slavery, and colonial trading monopolies. Modern examples are the persistence of large absentee landholdings of many thousands of acres with at best semifree tenant farmers in Pakistan, the latifundia (large estates) of Latin America, United Fruit in Honduras and Guatemala, and the Rimbunan Hiajau logging company in Malaysia. They also include government-established marketing boards that act as monopsony buyers and monopoly traders of cotton, cocoa, coffee, tea, sugar, and other important commodities throughout the underdeveloped tropics and manufacturers of fertilizer, agrochemicals, and sometimes agricultural equipment who enjoy monopoly licenses.

Industrial Agribusiness

Industrial agribusiness grows out of the increasingly specialized system of modern industrial production rather than either of the major historical systems of farm production. Ancient forms of large-scale production, such as factory spinning and weaving, wine making, and oil pressing, were essentially farm technologies scaled up and sometimes streamlined. The technologies of industrial agribusiness, by contrast, cannot exist on farms because farms cannot have the infrastructure they require. The transition to this system of production began in the early nineteenth century with the application of steam power to cotton ginning and cloth manufacture. This in turn allowed transformation of the processes themselves, and this cycle has been accelerating ever since.

Industrial agribusiness is now dominant in the production of fertilizers, herbicides and pesticides, farm equipment, veterinary supplies and, increasingly, hybridized and bioengineered seed. In food processing and distribution, the longer and more complex the chain of steps between the farmer and the final consumer, the more completely it is dominated by large-scale industrial agribusiness.

Recent Trends

In the last fifty years the most prominent trend worldwide has been the disproportionately rapid growth of industrial agribusiness. Although this has been largely

TABLE 1.
INDICATORS OF AGRICULTURAL CHANGE IN THE UNITED STATES, 1900–1999

Indicator	1900	1999
Rural population as percentage of total population	54.39	20.99
Number of farms	5,740,000	1,911,859
Land in farms (of at least 404 hectares)	841,202	931,795
Farm share of U.S. employment (%)	37–40	2.6
Farm cash receipts ($ billions)	5.2	191.7
Agricultural exports ($ millions)	949	49,102
Share of farms producing 50% of agricultural sales	17	2

Source: Data compiled from Goodloe (n.d.); U.S. Census Bureau (2000, 2002).

rooted in the United States, Australia, and the European Union, its effects have been global. It has two major dimensions: the movement of work other than immediate farm production off the farms and the concentration of industrial agribusiness itself in fewer and fewer increasingly larger firms. (See table 1.)

The most comprehensive change that these statistics reflect is the enormous increase in specialization and differentiation among agriculturally related occupations. This underlies the great decrease in the proportion of the population directly engaged in farm production as well as the corresponding increase in total agricultural production. Great increase in specialization is also reflected in the way the decline in farm employment so greatly exceeds the decline in rural population generally, even though many agriculturally related jobs are no longer rural and many rural jobs are no longer agricultural.

By 1997, 19 million Americans were employed in occupations classified as agriculturally related, whereas only about 3 million were in direct farm production. Virtually all this off-farm employment is agribusiness, and most of it is industrial. The largest categories are agricultural processing and marketing (over 3 million people), textiles (about 1.5 million), and agricultural wholesale and retail (more than 15 million).

The shift of production activities from farms to agribusinesses has been accompanied by increasing industrial concentration, both on the farm and off. Whereas 17 percent of American farms produced 50 percent of all agricultural sales in 1900, only 2 percent did so in 1997. These farms were much larger and more often either directly owned by large firms or closely tied to them by contractual relationships. In 1997, 32 percent of all U.S. production was contractual, and the proportion went up to 44 percent for farms classified by the United States Department of Agriculture as "very large."

Concentration in industry is measured by the proportion of total production in the hands of the largest three, four, or five firms. In the United States between 1980 and 1997, the proportion of total hog production controlled by the top four firms increased from 34 percent to 54 percent. In cattle slaughter it increased from 36 percent to 78 percent. In flour milling it increased from 33 percent to 62 percent and in soybean milling from 54 percent to 83 percent. Moreover, the same firms consistently recur in the different areas, most prominently ADM, Cargill, and Conagra.

In seed production, four-firm concentration in the United States now ranges from 36 percent for wheat to 87 percent for cotton, with the dominant companies consistently being DuPont, Pioneer, Monsanto, Novartis, and Dow. All except Novartis are based in the United States.

Agribusiness, Globalization, and the Environment

The rapid growth of industrial agribusiness raises the possibility that powerful firms can use their resources to obtain the kind of exploitive control historically associated with elite agribusinesses. Although a few commentators leap from specific—and thus far relatively isolated—problems to theories of vast international conspiracies, most recognize that the growth of agribusiness thus far responds to real needs and presents the possibilities of real benefits, and that the problems with it are more technical as well as more resolvable.

The expansion of industrial agribusiness was greatly stimulated by the worldwide Green Revolution, even though the core Green Revolution technologies were produced on a not-for-profit basis by governments, universities, and philanthropic foundations. The Green Revolution varieties of plants were designed to be more responsive to fertilizer, herbicides, and pesticides. The bulk of these inputs were provided commercially by industrial agribusiness. Between 1958 and 1988, world fertilizer consumption increased from 25 million metric tons to a peak of 145 million. In 1989 it fell back to 121 million metric tons because of the collapse of the Soviet Union, but by 1995 it had recovered to about 133 million metric tons. Of this total, 76.3 million metric tons were consumed in developing countries. Herbicide and insecticide consumption has followed a similar pattern. The consequence has been that although food production has been able to outpace population growth, it has been accompanied by rapidly increasing environmental pollution.

The agencies that have promoted the Green Revolution now recognize that the movement is unsustainable on the original basis. Agricultural production will have to continue to increase, but it will also have to become much less reliant on these inputs. The way to do this seems to be through biotechnology, the creation of modified crop varieties and other organisms by incorporating genetic material from other species in their genetic makeup.

However, biotechnology, too, poses threats. Some threats are similar to those of Green Revolution technologies, and some are different. The former revolve mainly around further environmental pollution and threats to biodiversity (biological diversity as indicated by the number of species of plants and animals). The latter revolve mainly around biopiracy.

Biopiracy occurs when someone obtains a patent on a cultivar (an organism originating under cultivation) or other biological material that either occurs naturally or occurs as part of the common cultural heritage in some place. An instance of particular importance to farmers in India was the acquisition of an American patent by a Texas firm (owned indirectly by the family of the earl of Lichtenstein) on *basmati* rice, an ancient type widely grown throughout southern Asia. Although the patent application had been narrowly framed to cover a Texas version called "Texmati," the grantee attempted to assert that the patent gave worldwide control of the name *basmati* as well. American imports of *basmati* from India are worth $300 million a year. In a similar instance the European Patent Office granted a patent to the U.S. Department of Agriculture and the multinational firm W. R. Grace for a method to use the oil of the Indian *neem* tree for fungicidal purposes, although such uses are common knowledge in India. Although these patents have been overturned, others have been taken out on the plants turmeric and quinoa. Monsanto owns patents on genetically engineered corn and soybean varieties, among other things.

On land, the most widely recognized threat by industrial agribusiness to biodiversity is the rapid mechanized destruction of the world's remaining rain forests, but another kind of threat emerges from biotechnology. This is most dramatically illustrated by Monsanto's "terminator" technology.

In part to respond to concerns that transgenic (taking genes from one species and placed in the DNA of another, different species) genes put into its own plants would get loose among the surrounding plant populations, Monsanto proposed to include in its seeds a gene that would cause all seeds from the plants produced from them to be sterile. When this technology was introduced in India, protests were widespread and intense. The main reason was that people feared that the gene would be spread by pollen to other crops of the same type and sterilize them. Their fear was not groundless. Such spread had already occurred with Monsanto's Starlink maize, which incorporated a gene to produce *Bacillus thuringiensis* (Bt) toxin as a biological insecticide. It had been approved only for use as a fodder but ended up in foodstuffs. Monsanto has now said it will not introduce the technology, at least temporarily.

The increasing domination of agricultural production by a combination of peasant farmer and industrial agribusiness, to the exclusion of elite agribusiness, would be both natural and desirable. Yet, the abuses that have accompanied the recent growth of the latter point to an important need. The agencies that have been designed to regulate commerce and protect consumers and the environment within countries must be coordinated to provide comparable regulation and protection across them.

Murray J. Leaf

Further Reading

Brush, S. (2001). Overview of the use of genetically modified organisms and pesticides in agriculture. *Indiana Journal of Global Legal Studies 9*, 51, 135.

Cernea, M. (Ed.). (1991). *Putting people first: Sociological variables in rural development*. New York: Oxford University Press.

Goodloe, C. (n.d.). *Where have all the oats and horses gone? Changes in U.S. agriculture over the 20th century*. Washington, DC: Office of the Chief Economist, U.S. Department of Agriculture.

Gruhn, P., Goletti, F., & Roy, R. N. (Eds.). (1995). *Proceedings of the IFPRI/FAO Workshop on Plant Nutrient Management, Food Security, and Sustainable Agriculture: The future through 2020*. Viterbo, Italy: Markets and Structural Studies Division, International Food Policy Research Institute and Land and Water Development Division, United Nations Food and Agriculture Organization.

Leaf, M. J. (1998). *Pragmatism and development: The prospect for pluralism in the Third World*. New York: Bergen and Garvey.

MacDonald, J. M. (2000). *Concentration in agribusiness*. Retrieved September 12, 2002, from http://www.usda.gov/oce/waob/oc2000/speeches/macdonald.txt

U.S. Census Bureau. (2000). *Detailed tables*. Retrieved July 31, 2002, from http://www.census.gov/population/www/censusdata/hiscendata.html

U.S. Census Bureau. (2002). *Selected historical decennial census population and housing counts*. Retrieved July 31, 2002, from http://www.census.gov/population/www/censusdata/hiscendata.html

Agriculture

Agriculture comprises *cultivation* and *herding*, human management of populations of plants and animals, respectively, to produce food and fiber. Foragers have practiced some cultivation, using techniques such as burning fields, irrigation, and planting, and influenced animal movements and breeding. Agriculture, however, takes these practices to the point where both environments and the plants and animals in question are significantly modified. Agriculture is often defined as food production based on domesticated plants, with or without domesticated animals. Systems based on domesticated animals alone may be included, but are alternatively distinguished as *pastoralism*.

The accepted criteria of domestication are morphological changes resulting from human control of plant and animal reproduction. Modification of plants and animals is almost unavoidable under human management. For example, harvesting selects for seeds that stay longer on the plant. Maize (corn) is an extreme case. It has been so altered that it requires human assistance to disperse, the seeds clinging tightly to the mature ears.

Environmental Impact: Preindustrial and Industrial Agriculture Compared

Agriculture inevitably alters natural ecosystems and has environmental impact. Even grazing on natural grasslands favors some plant and animal populations over others. Conversion of wild areas to farmland reduces the habitat of many species. Erosion of soil by wind and water has degraded or destroyed vast areas that grew food several millennia ago. Such damage, slight in some locations, increases with slope, sand or silt content of soils, degree of tillage, and reduction of ground cover. Ancient irrigation left some low-lying soils too alkaline or salty for most plants.

Some modern trends increase environmental impact, and it is important to determine how much of this is avoidable. Specialization in a limited number of varieties of many major crops threatens genetic diversity. Seed banks have been proposed, though some dispute their adequacy. In some places the use of tractors has increased tillage and accelerated erosion. Reduced tillage methods, often substituting chemical for mechanical weed control, are one remedy. In some temperate regions, heavy use of chemical fertilizers has replaced the growing of *cover crops* that once provided winter ground cover. A partial remedy is to leave crop residues on the ground all winter.

Pollution from agriculture is increasing. Excess nutrients from agricultural fields contaminate water systems. Chemical fertilizers are not solely to blame, though high application rates aggravate the problem. Concentration of livestock has turned manure from a valuable fertilizer to a potential pollutant if it is not contained. Direct threats to the health of humans and ecosystems led to the widespread banning of DDT and other insecticides that persist in the environment. Some shorter-lived but toxic pesticides and herbicides continue to be used. Increasing resistance in pests and some weeds, and the destruction of beneficial organisms that help control pests, threaten to erase many of the previous gains achieved with these agents. Consequently, there is much interest in *integrated pest management* and *integrated weed management*, in which chemicals are used selectively and with restraint.

Agriculture increasingly depends upon nonrenewable resources. Fossil fuels power machinery and enter into every major industrial input, adding to global warming, though agriculture directly accounts for only about 5 to 10 percent of fossil fuel use in industrialized countries. Powerful pumps draw down aquifers by exceeding natural recharge from precipitation. A well-known example is the steady fall of the water table in the Ogallala Aquifer of the North American plains. Among the elements in chemical fertilizers, only nitrogen is renewable, because it naturally cycles among air, crops, and soil; the other elements come from mineral deposits. Reserves of most are enormous, phosphorus being the notable exception, and estimates of how long deposits will last range from less than a century to several millennia.

Much present-day agriculture is unsustainable. Whether technology and the prevailing economy will head off the destruction of vast areas and still feed billions is a key question regarding the future.

From Foraging to Agriculture

Transitions to agriculture probably began with efforts to increase the yields of wild plants, not expressly to make them dependent on human care. Humans and certain plants became increasingly mutually dependent in a self-reinforcing process that David Rindos (1984) calls *coevolutionary*. The actors who initiated it did not understand the transformation it would eventually bring. Rindos argues that the process was unintentional for a long time, but some scholars feel that some deliberate selection occurred fairly early.

Agriculture is a Holocene epoch phenomenon. It arose independently, involving different species or races of plants, in widely separate locations. The earliest domesticated wheat and barley in Southwest Asia are dated to about 9250 BCE, a few hundred years after the abrupt warming at the start of the Holocene. Sheep, goat, and cattle domestication followed a millennium or more after that elsewhere in the region. Domesticated rice in the Yangtze Valley and millet in northern China date from the early seventh millennium BCE, well into the Holocene. These locations were also where pigs, chickens, and later on in the Yangtze, water buffalo were domesticated. Other crops were domesticated around 3500–2500 BCE in central Mexico (maize, amaranth, and squash), the central Andes (quinoa), and eastern North America (marsh elder, squash, goosefoot, and sunflower). There are earlier dates for domesticated squash from Mexico and a bean variety from Peru, but not in association with other staple-food domesticates. In several other places independent transitions to agriculture occurred well before the Christian era, but dates are uncertain because the evidence is poorly preserved, particularly in the case of root crops. Such locations include the Amazon Basin (manioc, peanut), the Sudan region of Africa (millets, sorghum), the West African forest (yams), and Southeast Asia and New Guinea (taro, yams, banana, and sugarcane).

If agriculture readily and independently arose in several locations from foraging, a logical question is why it did not happen earlier. The species that were domesticated had survived the Pleistocene epoch, though because of prevailing cold and aridity, many occupied smaller ranges than in the Holocene. Ice core

The Sacred Digging Stick

Although often ignored in modern, scientific analysis of farming, religious rituals have always been an important element of planting and harvesting in farming communities around the world. The following example is of the Tikopia of the South Pacific.

The next morning everyone of the yam group had to be awake long before dawn, for this was the day of planting. I was told "the yam is planted in the night"—a statement too near truth for my comfort. The reason given was that "the yam should be hidden in the woods" before people stirred in the villages, so that the paths might not be contaminated by ordinary affairs. It was said that this was the command and practice of the Atua i Kafika, though no express utterance to this effect was known.

On each occasion I came over from my house in Faea soon after four a.m. When the people of the household had been roused from sleep one man was sent off first with the *koso tapu*, the sacred digging stick, a piece of wood some seven feet long, pointed at both ends, one of which was ornamented by some roughly cut notches.

This implement is one of the most intensely sacred articles in the island. Through its association with the yam, the vegetable foodstuff of primary significance, this digging stick has become as it were the prototype of all instruments of cultivation, the material symbol of agriculture. Like all other objects in this particular context it is regarded as the property, even the embodiment, of the Atua i Kafika, and therefore must be handled with extreme care, and only by persons authorised by the Ariki and at the appropriate time. No woman, for instance, would dare to touch it, nor is it probably ever seen by them. It is kept normally at the far end of the Kafika temple, and the custom is to hang a few kava leaves over it in token of its unique value and importance. As the implement decays it is replaced by a fresh one, but as its use is ritual, not practical, it lasts for many years without attention. The stick employed in 1928–9 was very frail, so much so that the Ariki, in handing it over to the man who was appointed to carry it, gave the caution "That one has become aged; go carefully lest you stumble in the path." The bearer, out of deference to his sacred burden, had a clean white strip of bark-cloth wound as an extra cincture round his waist and a bundle of scented leaves stuck in the back of his girdle. The significance of these in ritual matters has already been explained. The sanctity of the *koso* required also that its bearer should precede the rest of the working party and go alone. Soon after he had disappeared in the darkness another man was dispatched with the *fakaora*, a basket containing food from the oven of the day before to provide the offerings in the cultivation, and following him went a youth with the little kit of seed yams. All these articles were *tapu*, hence their bearers had to proceed apart from the crowd so that they were not contaminated . . . .

As the sky was brightening before the dawn the party reached the mara, to which they had been preceded by the bearer of the koso tapu and his comrades. Immediately the work began. They all sharpened the ordinary digging sticks which they brought with them, or hastily cut fresh ones from shrubs on the border of the clearing. The bearer of the sacred implement stood alone and silent at the far end of the field; he had held communication with noone since leaving the house in Uta. The Ariki put on his ritual necklet of coconut frond, and the black pani stripe was drawn down his forehead.

Source: Firth, Raymond. (1940). *The Work of the Gods in Tikopia*. London: The London School of Economics and Political Science, pp. 123–124.

get milk ... locally

Our Family Farms

of Western Massachusetts

This slogan is on a coaster distributed by an organization that supports local farming in a region where farming has declined and tourism is now the dominant economic sector.

readings and other paleoclimatic proxies indicate that Pleistocene climates were over twice as variable as Holocene climates. Peter Richerson, Robert Boyd, and Robert L. Bettinger (2001) argue that Holocene climatic stability was essential for agriculture. Other suggested reasons include prior global population growth, increased sedentism (permanence of settlement), and social change.

By 1500 CE, agriculture had spread across all of Africa except the extreme south, almost all of Europe, Asia south of Siberia, most Pacific islands, South America down to central Chile and the northern Argentinean plains, and North America up to the lower Colorado river valley, southern Utah, the Missouri valley, the central Great Lakes, and central New England. Australia was nonagricultural, though the aborigines cultivated some plants. During the colonial era agriculture reached nearly all the remaining areas except where it was not practicable.

Agricultural Intensification

Intensification is doing more to get more. Occasionally a new crop, variety, or breed, or a more efficient method raises yields without burdening the farmer, but usually increased inputs are required. Most inputs, such as weeding and fertilizing, bring quick returns but must be repeated for continuing benefit. Some scholars argue that *labor efficiency*, i.e., the yield from a given expenditure of effort, steadily declines as preindustrial systems become more intensive. Others disagree. One

exception is the effect of investment in durable improvements, such as field drainage: the initial cost is high, but a small continuing effort maintains increased yields indefinitely, and labor efficiency may improve as a result.

Increased demand drives intensification. Population growth is historically the greatest source of increased demand. Prestige production, for consumption at feasts and for display, has often been a factor, as much as doubling demand in some communities. Consumption well above nutritional requirements, especially of meat and dairy products, is particularly prevalent in modern industrial countries.

Agricultural intensity may in turn affect population. One controversy in historical demography and economic history concerns the possible stimulation of population growth by technical innovations, introduced crops, or large capital improvements in agriculture. Proposed connections variously include improved nutrition, earlier marriage, and incentives to migrate.

Increasing one agricultural input tends to stimulate further intensification, for both economic and ecological reasons. Capital improvements encourage further inputs to maximize returns and repay the investment. Ordinarily one factor at a time limits plant growth and yields. It may be warmth, moisture, or a specific plant nutrient, such as nitrogen, potassium, or phosphorus. If enough is supplied to remove the limitation, some other factor becomes limiting and worth supplying. Thus, where scant soil moisture supports only slow growth, fertilizers would probably not significantly raise yields; with irrigation, however, fertilization becomes effective.

Growing populations have fed themselves through both intensification and expansion of agriculture. In some places cultivation began in mostly *extensive* forms, i.e., comparatively less intensive ones, often in which long fallow periods alternated with one or two seasons of cultivation. The fallows helped maintain soil fertility without the use of fertilizers. Shortening fallows often required more frequent cultivation and weeding and the adoption of methods for maintaining soil fertility. Elsewhere, cultivation began in at least moderately intensive forms, in small, particularly suitable patches, and later spread.

Zonal and Regional Comparisons

Agriculture evolved in distinct ways in different climatic zones. Discussion is for the moment confined to *preindustrial* agriculture, that is, without inputs from modern industry.

Dry Lands

Farming in arid and semi-arid climates evolved around the need to provide moisture. The same is partly true of Mediterranean climates, where winters are mild and wet, and summers are hot and dry. Methods were often strikingly parallel in widely separated places.

The classification of climates as semi-arid is partly based on their precipitation being barely sufficient to support rain-fed cultivation. Widely adopted moisture-conserving, or *dry farming*, techniques include the wide spacing of plants to reduce transpiration and mulching with crop residues, volcanic ash, and other materials to reduce evaporation. Where draft animals are available, land is sometimes fallowed for a year, shallow tillage being used to create a layer of dust that conserves moisture for the next crop. The intensity of dry farming tends to be moderate. Because moisture ordinarily limits crop growth, there is no reason for long fallows and fertilization tends to be unrewarding. However, animal manures have been used along with dry farming methods in the Mediterranean since the classical era, often where grain crops had ample moisture in the early growing season but were limited by drought as they ripened.

High groundwater areas and seepage zones have long been exploited. Gardens excavated to a level where roots reach moist soil just above the water table are reported in a few places in the Arabian and Sahara deserts and in Peru's coastal desert, where they were particularly prevalent when the Spanish arrived.

Throughout arid and semi-arid regions of Africa, Southwest Asia, and the Americas similar methods of exploiting floodwaters were evident in early agriculture and persist in some places. In *decrue* cultivation, crops are planted as slowly receding floodwaters uncover moist soils. In the right situations yields are excellent and sustainable with little effort. The deep alluvial soils are often highly fertile, and each year's deposit of silt provides an increment of plant nutrients. Weed growth is slow to start. Another strategy is to exploit runoff from brief rains, generally by some means of diversion. Designs vary with topography, but parallels exist among far-flung locations. A simple method is to take advantage of natural or human-made depressions to concentrate scarce rainwater.

True irrigation can be simple and small scale, or entail prodigious engineering works to move water long distances. Arguably the most awe-inspiring examples were fourteenth- and fifteenth-century Incan systems of tunnels, aqueducts, and canals spanning the high Andes. Irrigation may involve continuous diversion from rivers and lakes or the lifting of water from them or from wells. Preindustrial methods, mostly using containers or vacuum or "pull" pumps, can only lift water about seven meters. One solution is to bore tunnels horizontally into mountains to reach water-bearing strata—an ancient technique still used from Iran to North Africa.

Some distinctive regional systems or technologies emerged. Sand dunes trap scarce rainfall, and planting around their bases is done from North Africa into parts of central Asia. Around the Mediterranean, there is an emphasis on grapevines, olives, and other deep-rooted perennials that tap receding soil moisture during the long, dry summers. The mainstay of ancient Egyptian agriculture was a large-scale elaboration of *decrue* cultivation. Before 3000 BCE the Egyptians began building levees across the Nile floodplain. During the third millennium BCE they created a continuous system of flat-bottomed basins, through which the annual floods were led in turn. This allowed control of the rate of flood recession and more complete use of the water.

The Tropics

Adaptations of agriculture to tropical environments are often parallel, though there are also distinct regional or local practices and systems.

An important climatic factor is the amount and duration of the annual rains. Where frequent rains last nearly all year, excess water percolating downward through the soil leaches nutrients. Dense forests suggest fertility, but most of the nutrients are retained in the biomass. Dead vegetation quickly decomposes, releasing nutrients that root systems quickly take up. As rainfall decreases, the natural cover becomes open forest, bush or thorn scrub, and grassland or savanna, containing progressively fewer nutrients in its biomass, but usually more in the soils, which are not so highly leached.

Systems incorporating long fallow periods are common in the tropics. A widespread form of extensive cultivation is known as *slash-and-burn*. Cultivators cut undergrowth, then trees, and burn the cut vegetation once it dries. The first crop benefits from nutrients in the ashes and decaying slash. The plot is abandoned after one to three crops, before invading weeds and lowered yields make the effort unrewarding. A fallow of five years to several decades passes before a new cycle begins. Where fallows are under five years old or where disturbance or frequent dry season burning prevents woody regrowth, the dominant vegetation remains grass. Grass, however, retains smaller amounts of nutrients than forest does. Where the soil is infertile, because of leaching or unfavorable parent material, grass fallow systems are hard to maintain, and grass invasion sometimes results in the abandonment of cultivation. Where soil is more fertile, grass fallow systems become more attractive, particularly where long dry seasons slow woody regrowth.

Permanent cultivation systems are varied. On a few soils, adequate yields continue for many years even though no soil amendments are used. Tree crops, alone or with interspersed annuals, appear to give more sustainable yields, possibly because their deep root systems efficiently cycle nutrients. In most locations, however, something must be done to maintain fertility: vegetation from bordering areas, along with weeds and residues from the previous crop, may be dug into mounds or ridges where the crop grows. Animal manures are widely used where available, as is human excrement in a few places, mostly in Southeast Asia. The African savannas historically supported systems that combined grazing with manure-supported cultivation. *Wet* systems take advantage of nutrients made available in the accompanying water or by alternating waterlogging and drying. Asian paddy fields are one example. Pre-colonial Pacific islanders grew taro, a root crop, in shallow pond-fields or on low beds surrounded by water, and many still do. A technique of fairly widespread pre-colonial distribution in the Americas, also reported in parts of New Guinea and Africa, was cultivation on high beds raised with the help of mud and organic sediments from surrounding ditches.

Early agriculture and developmental sequences are not generally well known in the tropics. The islands of Polynesia and eastern Melanesia are a partial exception. Between 2000 BCE and 500 CE settlers moved eastward, bringing agriculture with them. Archaeological evidence indicates that they employed slash-and-burn methods across the island interiors, though they probably also cultivated tree crops along the beaches. As populations grew, short-fallow systems and wet taro cultivation began to supply the most food, although slash-and-burn cultivation often continued in hilly areas.

Humid Temperate Climates

In East Asia, eastern North America, and Europe agricultural evolution diverged early on, despite some climatic similarities. A crucial difference lay in the integration of grazing animals into agricultural systems.

Pre-colonial eastern North America lacked domesticated grazing animals. Foraging continued to be important long after native plants were domesticated. Much of the cultivation appears to have been in small, easily cultivated plots in river floodplains. Maize was introduced from Mexico before the Christian era, but was unimportant until about 800 CE. From then until 1500 rapid population growth and agricultural expansion took place from the Mississippi Valley to the Atlantic seaboard. Colonial-era descriptions are mostly of slash-and-burn cultivation, but archaeology has revealed signs of tillage suggesting earlier, more intensive systems, particularly in the Mississippi Valley, before introduced diseases caused depopulation.

Agriculture spread fairly rapidly on the Asian mainland from the Yangtze Valley and the northern interior of China. Rice cultivation reached Japan around 300–400 BCE, though there was some earlier cultivation of native plants by a population that remained mostly reliant on foraging. In China, Korea, and Japan, grazing animals—oxen, water buffalo, and horses—were mostly used for draft and transport (horses). Pigs and poultry, which graze little, provided most meat, and dairying was rare. When iron-shod plows became available in China, during the Han dynasty (206 BCE–220 CE) in the north, but later in the south, use of draft animals increased. Large-scale use of draft animals occurred no earlier than the fourth or fifth centuries CE in Japan.

Since pasture requirements were modest, and because cultivation tended to be moderately to highly intensive, farms were generally small. The earliest relevant Chinese documents, from the Han dynasty, indicate an average farm size of three to five hectares. Subsequent variation was not wide, despite population swings, until the fifteenth century. Thereafter, the average size fell below three hectares by the nineteenth century. In seventeenth-century Japan, a household of five was allotted about a hectare of paddy fields and an unspecified area for other crops, pasture, and other purposes.

Writers of the Han dynasty described the use of various fertilizers and the planting of one or more crops each year, though these methods were not yet universal. Particularly intensive methods emerged throughout much of the region in the second millennium CE, as average farm sizes shrank further. Every possible fertilizer, including human excrement and vegetation from uncultivated hillsides, was collected and used on cropland. Two or three crops a year were grown as the growing season allowed—facilitated, in the case of rice, by transplanting seedlings from nurseries. Fallows became uncommon. In dry areas of China and in certain hilly areas of China and Japan, slash-and-burn methods persisted into the twentieth century.

Agriculture spread to Europe from Southwest Asia, reaching the eastern Aegean before 8000 BCE, the Danube basin circa 6400 BCE, the northern plains in the mid and late fifth millennium BCE, and southern Scandinavia and the British Isles a few centuries later. Throughout the forests north of the Alps and the Carpathians early cultivation was on small, widely scattered plots. Numerous cattle and sheep grazed the forest undergrowth and interspersed meadows.

Fields replaced much of the forest over succeeding millennia. Field marks and some models of yoked oxen indicate plowing was known by the late fourth millennium BCE or earlier, and evidence of manure use is almost as old. Wet areas, or meadows, were typically used to produce hay for winter fodder. Depopulation and agricultural contraction occurred during the late Roman Empire and following the Black Death, with growth and expansion at other times. Evidence of large numbers of livestock and particular agricultural practices suggest that animal manures supported either permanent cultivation or the alternation of a year or two of cultivation with a year or so of fallow, systems well known later, during the Middle Ages.

Farms in medieval Europe were generally 10 to 20 hectares in size, with regional and local variation and some shrinkage during the high Middle Ages. Holdings of comparable size or larger were probably standard in earlier periods, given the numbers of grazing animals and indications that cattle ownership had long been a major source of prestige.

Industrial Agriculture

Industrial agriculture is that which is supported by an industrial system that supplies machinery to save labor, chemical fertilizers to raise yields, and a variety of chemicals to control weeds, pests, and diseases. Like modern industry, industrial agriculture uses large amounts of energy, largely substituting that for human and animal effort. It has also come to rely heavily on modern scientific research, although applications of science and of industrial inputs are not always dependent upon one another.

The 1830s marked the first substantial use of industrial machinery and inputs in agriculture. Horse- or oxen-pulled reapers were first marketed in Scotland and the United States, and the inexpensive iron of the industrial revolution made them and later machines affordable. Chemical fertilizers in early use in England included sodium nitrate from natural deposits in Chile and ammonium sulfate, a byproduct of coal gas and coke manufacture.

For decades chemical fertilizers were most widely adopted in Western Europe, while mechanization was more prevalent in North America, trends influenced by the high prices of land in the former and of labor in the latter. Steam tractors were in use in the nineteenth century, but only gasoline tractors seriously competed with draft animals. That was after 1910 in the United States, Canada, Australia, and Great Britain, and in the 1930s in the Soviet Union. In Japan and parts of Europe, small farm size meant that the adoption of tractors lagged behind the use of chemical fertilizers between the world wars. In less developed regions, both trends essentially began after World War II and are still far from universal.

The impact of pesticides on the cultivation of major field crops was small until after World War II. The insecticide lead arsenate was in fairly widespread use after 1867, as were several fungicides on fruit by the late nineteenth century. DDT and organophosphate insecticides, developed during World War II, were very widely adopted during the 1950s and 1960s, and in many developing nations their adoption outpaced that of other industrial inputs. In developed countries herbicides have now largely replaced hand and mechanical weed controls, but their use was slight until 2, 4-D was released in 1944.

Mechanization greatly increased labor efficiency. To plow what a large tractor can in a day, a team of oxen needs weeks. Mobile machines exist for most basic tasks of cultivation, except that most weed suppression is now accomplished with chemical herbicides. Though the United States is a net exporter of farm commodities, its farms are highly mechanized and less than 2 percent of the workforce is employed on farms or in direct support. Even including employment in ancillary industries producing agricultural machinery, chemicals, and other inputs, would not likely raise the proportion to 5 percent. In most historic preindustrial economies at least 70 percent of the workforce was employed in agriculture.

Industrial agriculture has boosted yields. Force pumps, which can tap water deep underground, have made possible a large extension of irrigated farmland. Chemical control of diseases and pests has reduced losses, at least in the short term. The increased yields obtained through the use of chemical fertilizers are also obtainable with manure and other amendments long used in preindustrial agriculture. However, chemical fertilizers increase the potential supply of amendments, allowing high application rates to be more common. The plant nutrient that is most often limiting is nitrogen. Biological *nitrogen fixation*, by which microorganisms in the soil and in association with the roots of legumes, such as beans, makes atmospheric nitrogen available to crops, is crucial to preindustrial agricultural systems. Modern scientific breeding has created high-yielding crop varieties that respond to levels of available nitrogen that biological nitrogen fixation cannot provide.

Daniel E. Vasey

See also Capitalism; Cereals; Chavez, Cesar; Cotton; Deforestation; Diseases, Plant; Domestication, Animal and Plant; Droughts; Fertilizers; Fiber Crops; Fodder Crops; Genetically Modified Foods; Grapes; Green Revolution; Irrigation; Land Tenure; Peat; Potato; Rice; Root Crops; Soil; Soybeans; Sugar and Sugarcane; Terracing/Field Ridging; Tobacco; Weeds

Further Reading

Boserup, E. (1965). *The conditions of agricultural growth.* Chicago: Aldine.

Farrington, I. (Ed.). (1985). *Prehistoric intensive agriculture in the tropics* (British Archaeological Reports, International Series, No. 232). Oxford, UK: British Archaeological Reports.

Grigg, D. B. (1995). *An introduction to agricultural geography* (2nd ed.). London: Routledge.

Kirch, P. V. (1994). *The wet and the dry: Irrigation and agricultural intensification in polynesia.* Chicago: University of Chicago Press.

Kirch, P. V., & Hunt, T. L. (Eds.). (1997). *Historical ecology in the pacific islands: Prehistoric environmental and landscape change.* New Haven, CT: Yale University Press.

Nabhan, G. P. (1989). *Enduring seeds.* New York: North Point Press.

Opie, J. (2000). *Ogallala: Water for a dry land.* Lincoln: University of Nebraska Press.

Pimentel, D., & Pimentel, M. (Eds.). (1996). *Food, energy, and society.* Boulder: University Press of Colorado.

Richerson, P. J., Boyd, R., & Bettinger, R. L. (2001). Was agriculture impossible during the Pleistocene but mandatory during the Holocene? A climate change hypothesis. *American Antiquity, 66*(3), 387–411.

Rindos, D. (1984). *The origins of agriculture: An evolutionary perspective.* Orlando, FL: Academic Press.

Ruthenberg, H. (1971). *Farming systems in the tropics.* London: Clarendon

Smith, B. (1999). *The emergence of agriculture.* New York: W. H. Freeman.

Vasey, D. E. (1992). *An ecological history of agriculture, 10,000 B.C.–A.D. 10,000.* Ames: Iowa State University Press.

Agroecology and Agroforestry

Often used synonymously with "sustainable agriculture," agroecology is an approach to food production that seeks long-term ecological and economic sustainability by using farming techniques sensitive to the local ecosystem. Because of the variety of ecosystems in the world, proponents of agroecology often emphasize that broad solutions to agricultural challenges are not possible: "Adopting an ecological approach to agriculture means a shift toward dealing with unique circumstances and a simultaneous shift away from general formula solutions applied over a broad range of conditions" (Soule & Piper 1992, 80).

However, there is a core of common agroecological principles, including maintaining the nutrient and resource base; conserving soil, water, and energy; managing, rather than attempting to eliminate, weeds and pests; and applying only naturally occurring materials, especially those produced on-site. These principles all serve the overarching goal of providing human food while still assuring the long-term viability of the ecosystem.

The main planting techniques of agroecology include growing two or more crops sequentially on the same land (crop rotation), growing two or more crops simultaneously on the same land (intercropping), and planting a second annual on land supporting another crop nearing maturity (overlap cropping). One of the most widely studied of these planting techniques is the maize/bean/squash intercropping which originated in the Amerindian culture of Mexico and is still common throughout Latin America. In the 1970s, "an average of 80% of the bean crop in many Latin American countries [was] grown in association with other crops" (Gliessman 1997, 147). Field studies and demonstration experiments have shown that these planting techniques reduce the need for chemical fertilization and

Selections from *An Agricultural Testament* by Sir Albert Howard on the Indore Process

The Raw Materials Needed

1. *Vegetable Wastes.* In temperate countries like Great Britain these include—straw, chaff, damaged hay and clover, hedge and bank trimmings, weeds including sea—and water-weeds, prunings, hop-vine and hop-string, potato haulm, market-garden residues including those of the greenhouse, bracken, fallen leaves, sawdust, and wood shavings. A limited amount of other vegetable material like the husks of cotton seed, cacao, and ground nuts as well as banana stalks are also available near some of the large cities.

2. *Animal Residues.* The animal residues ordinarily available all over the world are much the same—the urine and dung of live stock, the droppings of poultry, kitchen waste including bones. Where no live stock is kept and animal residues are not available, substitutes such as dried blood, slaughter-house refuse, powdered hoof and horn, fish manure, and so forth can be employed. The waste products of the animal in some form or another are essential if real humus is to be made for the two following reasons.

3. *Bases for Neutralizing Excessive Acidity.* In the manufacture of humus the fermenting mixture soon becomes acid in reaction. This acidity must be neutralized, otherwise the work of the microorganisms cannot proceed at the requisite speed. A base is therefore necessary. Where the carbonates of calcium or potassium are available in the form of powdered chalk or limestone, or wood ashes, these materials either alone, together, or mixed with earth, provide a convenient base for maintaining the general reaction within the optimum range (pH 7.0 to 8.0) needed by the microorganisms which break down cellulose. Where wood ashes, limestone, or chalk are not available, earth can be used by itself. Slaked lime can also be employed, but it is not so suitable as the carbonate. Quicklime is much too fierce a base.

4. *Water and Air.* Water is needed during the whole of the period during which humus is being made. Abundant aeration is also essential during the early stages. If too much water is used the aeration of the mass is impeded, the fermentation stops and may soon become anaerobic too soon. If too little water is employed the activities of the micro-organisms slow down and then cease. The ideal condition is for the moisture content of the mass to be maintained at about half saturation during the early stages, as near as possible to the condition of a pressed-out sponge. Simple as all this sounds, it is by no means easy in practice simultaneously to maintain the moisture content and the aeration of a compost heap so that the micro-organisms can carry out their work effectively. The tendency almost everywhere is to get the mass too sodden.

Source: Howard, Sir Albert. (1943). *An Agricultural Testament.* New York and London: Oxford University Press.

---

pest control, thus minimizing species elimination and long-term chemical sequestration in the ecosystem.

Historical antecedents to agroecology can be found in diverse sources, from the *Eclogues* of the Roman poet Virgil to the farming practices of Mayan civilization to the traditional northern European practice of pannage, allowing pigs to forage in woodlands. The modern agroecology movement, however, has historical roots in the early twentieth century. In the United States, Liberty Hyde Bailey (1858–1984), a founder of the Cornell University College of Agriculture and Life Sciences, argued in such works as *The Holy Earth* (1915) that living in harmony with natural processes was the first requirement of successful farming. Like the organic farming movement, modern agroecology is also partly based on British researcher Sir Albert Howard's (1873–1947) "Indore Process" of composting experiments in India in the 1920s and 1930s.

Although some proponents are critical of the Western scientific mindset, modern agroecology generally values ecological field studies as a basis for determining suitable crops, understanding species interaction, and providing techniques suited to the local physical environment. As a result, the scientific basis of agroecology has expanded along with the spread of environmental field studies since the 1960s and 1970s. This emphasis on ecosystem-specific scientific investigation distinguishes agroecology somewhat from some other alternative agricultural movements, such as "organic agriculture" (or in continental Europe, "biological agriculture"), which in the past has emphasized both broad-scale techniques (such as the use of seaweed for fertilizer) and inherent "spiritual" values. In addition to its scientific basis, however, the "whole systems" approach of agroecology does emphasize ethical goals such as maximizing human and animal health, maintaining indigenous knowledge, and strengthening rural communities.

Agroecology is intended to be an alternative to industrial agriculture, which relies on chemical fertilizers and pesticides to eliminate elements of the ecosystem such as weeds and herbivorous insects. This proscription against chemical inputs has been a source of disagreement with engineers of the "green revolution," which uses chemical applications and irrigation to equalize ecosystems. Faced with the food demands of a rapidly increasing world population, some identified with agroecology have urged minimizing rather than completely avoiding the use of chemicals, William Albrecht's "eco-agriculture" being one example. One of the major challenges to agroecology, therefore, is to demonstrate that long-term yields per unit of cultivated land are equal to the task of feeding the world's population.

Agroforestry

Agroforestry applies the same goal of long-term ecosystem sustainability to the use and maintenance of woodland. As the name indicates, agroforestry is an approach to land use that includes trees native to the local ecosystem as a component of agriculture. This was common practice throughout the world before the advent of large-scale monoculture farming, and is still routine in a number of tropical locations. For example, legume shade trees are often integrated into coffee plantations in Central America, and Nigerian farmers use "alley cropping," growing annual crops in lanes between woody hedges.

There are a variety of basic agroforestry schemes. The least labor- or capital-intensive is simply maintaining existing woodlands as buffers between farms. Intercropping—growing trees and annual crops concurrently on the same land—is a variation of the agroecology technique, and is commonly used in Southeast Asia to provide a single source for food and firewood. Agroforestry can also play a role in animal production, by planting trees in pastures, or opening existing woods to grazing.

There are many benefits of successful agroforestry. As with other forms of polyculture, agroforestry allows the creation of microsites within the ecosystem, maintains the biodiversity of the ecosystem, and enhances resistance to disease and pests. Because trees develop deeper root systems than annual crops, they can often draw on deeper groundwater supplies, an important advantage in times of drought. Trees also deter soil erosion in several ways: they can act as a windbreak, their root system holds the soil, and the canopy lessens the impact of rain on the soil, the last extremely important in monsoon zones. In hot, dry climates, the canopy of certain tree species can reduce evaporation of surface soil moisture. In addition to such ecological benefits, agroforestry can also enhance the financial sustainability of the farm by providing additional products to use on-site or to sell, including timber, firewood, and material for tools, food, and fodder. Some authorities see agroforestry as a viable approach primarily for developing countries (Floyd 2002); however, there is a growing agroforestry movement in developed nations as well.

Michael R. Hutcheson

Further Reading

Allen, P. (Ed.). (1993). *Food for the future: Conditions and contradictions of sustainability*. New York: Wiley-Interscience.

Altieri, M. (1995). *Agroecology: The science of sustainable agriculture* (2nd ed.). Boulder, CO: Westview Press.

Boeringa, R. (Ed.). (1980). Alternative methods of agriculture: Description, evaluation and recommendations for research [Special issue]. *Agriculture and Environment*, 5.

Floyd, D. W. (2002). *Forest sustainability: The history, the challenge, the promise*. Durham, NC: Forest History Society.

Gliessman, S. R. (1997). *Agroecology: Ecological processes in sustainable agriculture*. Boca Raton, FL: Lewis Press.

Jarvis, P. G. (Ed.) (1991). *Agroforestry: Principles and practice*. Amsterdam: Elsevier.

Kiley-Worthington, M. (1993). *Eco-agriculture: Food first farming*. London: Souvenir Press.

Nair, P. K. R. (1993). *An introduction to agroforestry*. Dordrecht, Netherlands: Kluwer Scientific Press.

Soule, J. D. & Piper, J. K. (1992). *Farming in nature's image: An ecological approach to agriculture*. Washington, DC: Island Press.

Vasey, D. E. (1992). *An ecological history of agriculture, 10,000 BC–AD 10,000*. Ames: Iowa State University Press.

Air Pollution

Air pollution comes in many forms. Essentially any substance held in the atmosphere can be a pollutant if it occurs in harmful or undesirable concentrations for lengthy periods of time. Even natural occurrences, such as volcanoes and forest fires, can cause serious air pollution. In the late twentieth century, forest fires, not always with natural causes, sent irritating clouds of smoke thousands of miles away, especially in North America, Southeast Asia, and the Amazon basin in South America. Suspended soil, in the form of dust and sand storms, again often with human causes, can also cause problems in communities near sites of wind erosion and desertification. Throughout history, however, the most common air pollutants have been the result of fuel combustion—particularly from the burning of dung, wood, coal, and petroleum products. These pollutants include carbon dioxide, sulfur dioxide, nitrous oxides, and particulate matter (soot). But other pollutants have also caused problems, including toxic substances, especially lead, mercury, and other heavy metals. Some of these pollutants, such as sulfuric acid, created when sulfurous emissions mix with water vapor in the atmosphere, have wreaked havoc on the health of people and ecosystems in some parts of the world for over a hundred years. Still, additional pollutants can be harmless in small quantities but can pose serious threats when produced in larger amounts, a development that researchers are still studying in relationship to carbon dioxide and other "greenhouse gases" and ozone, a key ingredient in urban smog.

A distinction must be made between indoor air pollution and outdoor air pollution. Often these categories contain the very same pollutants, many of which are much more dangerous when found in unventilated indoor spaces. This is particularly true of products of combustion, including carbon monoxide, which can be deadly when it builds up inside residences. Other indoor pollutants include allergens, dust, and tobacco smoke, all of which can harm human health. People in certain occupations, including lead workers and miners, have also been exposed to harmful concentrations of pollution. Although indoor air pollution became an important issue in the late twentieth century with the development of tightly sealed buildings with year-round temperature control, it actually has a long history. Early cave dwellers apparently suffered from indoor air pollution as their fires blackened cave walls and human lungs alike. By the nineteenth century, residents of coal-burning cities faced the consequences of smoky open hearths and dusty, sooty coal, raising public health concerns about the consequences of people living in small, poorly ventilated apartments, especially in densely populated cities.

As with other environmental problems, worsening air pollution around the globe has been closely related to two other important trends—urbanization and industrialization. Of course, humanity has been emitting substances into the air since the acquisition of fire, but air pollution occurs only when concentrations of noxious emissions reach undesirable or harmful levels, a rare occurrence in sparsely populated, rural societies. Thus, as societies moved into larger and larger cities, particularly those with considerable industrial combustion, more and more people around the globe found themselves living with worsening air quality. In more recent decades, however, the most developed nations have also seen a new trend in the amelioration of certain types of air pollution, even while other problems have continued to deepen.

Air Pollution as an Urban Problem

Air pollution has a surprisingly long history, most of it related to the development of cities. In 61 CE the rhetorician Lucius Annaeus Seneca left Rome on the advice of his physician. The foul air and odors of the city, Seneca tells us, had made him ill, and the fresh air of the countryside improved his health. Seneca's story reveals the long connection between air pollution and human health and the long conception of foul odors as important threatening pollutants. Around 200 CE, the Jewish Mishnah, a collection of oral interpretations of the Bible, also makes reference to air pollution, creating rules for the control of offensive smoke by prescrib-

> As we watch the sun go down, evening after evening, through the smog across the poisoned waters of our native earth, we must ask ourselves seriously whether we really wish some future universal historian on another planet to say about us: "With all their genius and with all their skill, they ran out of foresight and air and food and water and ideas," or, "They went on playing politics until their world collapsed around them."
>
> —United Nations Secretary General U Thant, from a 1970 speech.

ing set distances between polluters and the rest of a village's population.

Medieval cities suffered from stenches caused by rotting organic material (including dead animals), accumulated sewage, and fetid waters. Indeed, cities with insufficient sewage systems still suffer from such problems, with dire consequences for human health. In addition to foul odors, medieval London suffered from smoke pollution, which grew especially offensive due to the city's size and Londoners' heavy use of coal. The foul air drew the attention of the government as early as the thirteenth century, and the pollution was still poor enough in 1661 for Londoner John Evelyn to plead for action in *Fumifugium, or, The Inconveniencie of the Aer and Smoak of London Dissipated*, one of the earliest tracts to lay out the problems associated with urban air pollution. The problem persisted, and by the early twentieth century, London's thick air had helped that city create a new word—*smog*—a combination of the same *smoke* and *fog* that mingled above the city.

Some cities are at a distinct natural disadvantage when it comes to air pollution. Los Angeles, Mexico City, and Santiago, Chile, for instance, all suffer from extremely poor air quality not just because their large populations are dependent on combustion for transportation and production. Each of these cities, and many others around the globe, find their air trapped at certain times of the year by nearby mountain ranges, and they suffer from frequent temperature inversions that hold pollutants close to the ground where they accumulate until the weather breaks. These inversions have been particularly dangerous for at-risk populations—those with respiratory or cardiac diseases. Famous for its modern smog problem, Los Angeles has received comment about its pollution since 1542, when Spanish explorer Juan Rodriguez Cabrillo called the area the "Bay of Smokes" due to the lingering Native American campfire smoke. Since becoming an automobile city, Los Angeles has also suffered due to its abundant sunshine—a key factor in creating photochemical smog there and in other sun-drenched cities, such as Phoenix and Cairo. With its propensity for heavy, humid air, London, too, faced disadvantages as pollution-embedded fogs lingered over the city for weeks at a time, periodically turning deadly, as in 1873, 1880, 1892, and 1952. The latter episode caused perhaps four thousand deaths over five days.

Beyond combustion for heating and cooking, transportation within large cities has also caused considerable air pollution. Horse-reliant cities experienced pollution problems, not just from the accumulation of organic wastes on streets, but also from the creation of airborne dusts of pulverized manure. Steam locomotives and steamships posed greater problems, emitting particularly dense smoke. Locomotive smoke proved so offensive in its concentration around terminals, usually near the heart of cities, that some large cities forced the electrification of railroads to permanently alleviate the problem. Some railroads turned to electrification to solve the problem of underground pollution, as Paris constructed its Quai D'Orsay Terminal (1897–1900) and New York City built its Pennsylvania Station (1904–1910) with subterranean and subaqueous rail approaches, neither of which could work with trains emitting coal smoke and consuming oxygen in the tunnels.

In the twentieth century, automobiles and diesel trucks have been significant contributors to urban air pollution, plaguing most large cities in the world by the twenty-first century. As automobiles gained in popularity in the prosperous 1920s in North America and Europe, a new type of air pollution hung over many cities—brown, acidic smog. By the 1940s this new air pollution plagued Los Angeles in particular, gaining the attention of Cal Tech scientist Arie Haagen-Smit. In the late 1940s Haagen-Smit developed the theory of photochemical smog, attributing the acidic cloud above Los Angeles to the unburned gasoline that

Damage from Acid Rain in Seventeenth Century London

English diarist John Evelyn wrote the first general English-language work on air pollution in 1661. He opened his treatise, with the following letter to the king.

TO

THE KINGS MOST SACRED

MAJESTY.

Sir,

It was one day, as I was Walking in Your MAJESTIES Palace, at WHITE-HALL (where I have sometimes the honour to refresh my self with the Sight of Your Illustrious Presence, which is the Joy of Your Peoples hearts) that a presumptuous Smoake issuing from one or two Tunnels neer Northumberland-House, and not far from Scotland-yard, did so invade the Court; that all the Rooms, Galleries, and Places about it were fill'd and infested with it; and that to such a degree, as Men could hardly discern one another for the Clowd, and none could support, without manifest Inconveniency. It was not this which did first suggest to me what I had long since conceived against this pernicious Accident, upon frequent observation; But it was this alone, and the trouble that it must needs procure to Your Sacred Majesty, as well as hazzard to Your Health, which kindled this Indignation of mine, against it, and was the occasion of what it has produc'd in these Papers.

Your Majesty who is a Lover of noble Buildings, Gardens, Pictures, and all Royal Magnificences, must needs desire to be freed from this prodigious annoyance; and, which is so great an Enemy to their Lustre and Beauty, that where it once enters there can nothing remain long in its native Splendor and Perfection: Nor must here forget that Illustrious and divine Princesse, Your Majesties only Sister, the now Dutchesse of Orleans, who at her Highnesse late being in this City, did in my hearing, complain of the Effects of this Smoake both in her Breast and Lungs, whilst She was in Your Majesties Palace. I cannot but greatly apprehend, that Your Majesty (who has been so long accustom'd to the excellent Aer of other Countries) may be as much offended at it, in that regard also, especially since the Evil is so Epidemicall; indangering as well the Health of Your Subjects, as it sullies the Glory of this Your Imperial Seat.

Sir, I prepare in this short Discourse, an expedient how this pernicious Nuisance may be reformed; and offer at another also, by which the Aer may not only be freed from the present Inconveniency; but (that remov'd) to render not only Your Majesties Palace, but the whole City likewise, one of the sweetest, and most delicious Habitations in the World; and this, with little or no expence; but by improving those Plantations which Your Majesty so laudably affects, in the moyst, depressed and Marshy Grounds about the Town, to the Culture and production of such things, as upon every gentle emission through the Aer, should so perfume the adjacent places with their breath; as if, by a certain charm, or innocent Magick, they were transferred to that part of Arabia, which is therefore styl'd the Happy, because it is amongst the Gums and precious spices. Those who take notice of the Sent of the Orange-flowers from the Rivage of Genöa, and St.Pietro dell'Arena; the Blossomes of the Rosemary from the Coasts of Spain many Leagues off at Sea; or the manifest, and odoriferous wasts which flow from Fontenay and Vaugirard, even to Paris in the season of Roses, with the contrary Effects of those less pleasing smells from other accidents, will easily consent to

Continues

Continued

what I suggest: And, I am able to enumerate a Catalogue of native Plants, and such as are familiar to our Country and Clime, whose redolent and agreeable Emissions would even ravish our senses, as well as perfectly improve and meliorate the Aer about London; and that, without the least prejudice to the Owners and Proprietors of the Land to be employ'd about it. But because I have treated of this more at large in another curious and noble subject, which I am preparing to present to Your Majesty, as God shall afford me Leasure to finish it, and that I give a Touch of it in this Discourse, I will enlarge my Addresses no farther, then to beg pardon for this Presumption of

SIR,

Your Majesties ever Loyal, most obedient

Subject, and Servant.

J. EVELYN.

Source: Evelyn, John. (1661). *Fumifugium: Or the Inconveniencie of the AER and SMOAK of LONDON Dissipated together with some REMEDIES humbly Porposed by J. E. Esq; to His Sacred MAJESTIE, and to the Parliament now Assembled.* London: W. Godbid for Gabriel Bedel, and Thomas Collins.

spilled at filling stations and passed through engines unburned. Although this understanding of automobile smog gained acceptance by the mid-1950s, not until the 1970s, after many more cities became enveloped by smog, did the U.S. government take effective action to force changes in automobile technology, including the adoption of catalytic converters to consume pollutants before they passed out tailpipes. Meanwhile, in developing nations older technologies remained in use, and as the middle class expanded in Asia and Latin America particularly, car ownership also expanded rapidly. By the late twentieth century auto smog plagued Mexico City; Buenos Aires, Argentina; Bangkok, Thailand; New Delhi, India; and numerous other cities around the world.

Automobiles also have a history of contributing a particularly dangerous pollutant to urban atmospheres—lead. In the early 1920s American engineer Thomas Midgely developed tetraethyl lead as an additive to gasoline to reduce engine knocking and to increase power. Unfortunately, the ethyl fuels that gained in popularity soon thereafter created a serious environmental threat as automobiles spewed toxic lead exhaust. In the 1950s and 1960s citizens living in cities where cars burned ethyl fuels lived in a highly polluted environment. In the United States, where large cars

were particularly popular, essentially all urban dwellers were lead poisoned until the Environmental Protection Agency forced automobile manufacturers to phase out leaded gasoline in the 1970s, and by the 1980s the American population saw a dramatic decrease in blood lead levels. Despite the long-understood dangers of lead poisoning, not until 2000 did the European Union ban leaded gasoline, and it is still sold in Latin America, Asia, and Africa. By the 1990s urban children in Africa faced a number of lead-related health problems, including retardation of growth and development.

Air Pollution as an Industrial Problem

Although the concentration of great numbers of people in cities has caused a host of air pollution problems, these problems are more various and intractable when urbanization has been accompanied by industrialization. Although very large residential cities, such as ancient Rome and medieval London, could experience polluted air, beginning in the mid-1800s industrial cities generated air pollution on a scale never before seen. The burning of huge quantities of fuel, mostly coal, first in large textile mills and later in iron/steel plants, made these cities infamous for their thick, unhealthful air. First among these was Manchester, England,

II 26 TRAFFIC PARALYSIS DUE TO GREAT SMOG IN LONDON

Photo shows a bus inspector leading a London bus through the
dense smog with a burning torch in the East End of London.
6/1/56 Credit: Topical Press, London, England.

This 1956 photograph illustrates the dense smog with which
Londoners were forced to contend. COURTESY TOPICAL PRESS, LONDON,
ENGLAND.

known by the 1850s as the "workshop of the world"
because of the high concentration of textile manufacturers and their steam engines; but dense smoke also
made it the "chimney of the world." In 1868 a visitor to
Pittsburgh, already an important iron-manufacturing
city, peered down from a hill at the shifting smoke and
open flames in the valley and called the place "hell
with the lid taken off."

Polluting industries have not always been located in
cities. Indeed, demand for wood fuel or proximity to
ores often kept heavily polluting industries in the
countryside. Early iron smelting generally took place
near forests, for instance, moving to cities only when
coal and coke replaced wood as the major source of fuel
in the smelting process. As early as 1727 Swedish botanist Carl Von Linne noted damage to vegetation caused
by fumes coming from the smelting plant in Falum, outside Stockholm. By the late 1800s, as the Industrial Revolution greatly increased the demand for metals, farmers around smelters complained about crop damages
they assumed were caused by industrial emissions. Indeed, by the 1890s sulfuric emissions in places such as

Sudbury, Canada, and Ashio, Japan, led to farmer protests and at least some progress in abating the pollution.

Clearly rural industrial pollution posed threats to
agriculture and natural environments, but in large cities
industries could produce especially dangerous air pollution, causing both chronic and acute human health effects. By the beginning of the twentieth century, industrial concentration had created entire regions of heavy
pollution, including Germany's Ruhr Valley, Japan's
Hanshin region, and the American industrial Midwest.
Episodic concentrations of pollutants caused killing
smog. In late 1930 the Meuse Valley, Belgium, suffered
under a pall of toxic pollution that caused the death of
sixty-three residents. Eighteen years later, Donora,
Pennsylvania, suffered a similar episode, in which the
accumulation of a zinc smelter's acidic emissions
caused the death of twenty residents of that small city,
while almost half of the other residents felt ill from the
pollution. More common than these deadly episodes,
however, was the near-constant drag on health caused
by irritating particulates and other emissions. Residents
of industrial cities around the world have faced greater
incidences of asthma, bronchitis, and other lung ailments and have tended to suffer higher death rates due
to lung and heart diseases.

Nonhuman species have suffered, too, particularly
vegetation in and around cities. By the late 1800s some
industrial areas, including Butte, Montana, became famous for their "moonscape" environments, too toxic to
support any significant vegetation. Buildings and monuments suffered damage, too. Limestone and marble
are particularly susceptible to the ravages of acidic pollution, and many of the world's most precious architectural gems are threatened by air pollution, including the
Acropolis in Athens and the pyramids south of Cairo.
The fading features on Europe's monuments speak to
the breadth of acidic pollution's consequences.

Industrial areas also face the specter of escaped
toxic gases. In 1950 twenty-two people died in Poza
Rica, Mexico, as the result of a sulfide gas leak at a
natural gas facility. In 1984 India experienced the most
extreme industrial accident in history, when a cloud
of methyl-isocyanate escaped from a Union Carbide
facility in Bhopal, killing perhaps three thousand people and injuring thousands of others. Two years later
a nuclear reactor at Chernobyl in the Soviet Union
leaked radioactive gases that eventually spread around
the Northern Hemisphere. Local residents suffered
with radiation sickness and higher disease and birth
defect rates, although efforts to cover up the extent

of the damage may prevent a full accounting of the consequences of this nuclear disaster.

The Control of Air Pollution

Cultural and political differences around the globe have led to distinct environmental movements and regulatory responses to many environmental threats. But one universal feature of extreme air pollution problems—that they are deadly to human beings—has led to some conformity in the control of air pollution across national borders.

The principle of doing no harm to a neighbor's property has guided air pollution control efforts through most of history. Ancient Hebrew law and Roman codes, for example, prohibited the burning of materials in such a manner or such a place as would cause harm to others. This principle became established in British common law, which held that "nuisances" must be abated when damage appears.

Enforcing the principle of doing no harm was very difficult in densely populated regions and in industrializing societies, but even before the environmental movement of the late twentieth century some people did demand better air quality, or at least the cessation of damages caused by air pollution. For instance, after convening commissions to study England's smoke problem in 1285 and 1288, the British government banned the use of coal in London in 1306, although clearly the law was widely ignored. More successful efforts to control air pollution in Britain would await the passage of the Alkali Act in 1863, which focused on damaging acidic emissions. Other types of air pollution did not receive effective attention until after London's killing smog of 1952, an event that sparked the passage of the Clean Air Act of 1956.

In the United States an antismoke movement in the early 1900s forced the creation of air quality regulations and some improvements, but as in Britain, real progress would await late twentieth-century legislation. Most important, the 1970 Clean Air Act for the first time set national air quality goals, with the Environmental Protection Agency taking responsibility for the oversight of automobile and factory emissions. A major amendment to the Clean Air Act in 1990 required even further improvements. In several key pollution areas, including particulates and heavy metals, the United States and other developed nations have seen remarkable improvements since the early 1970s.

The internationalization of environmental concern and a growing understanding of the health conse-quences of air pollution led to reforms in many industrial nations, including Japan, which passed a law to control soot and smoke in 1962, and Taiwan, which passed its landmark Air Pollution Control Act in 1975. Eastern Europe, with archaic technology and weak economies, struggled to catch up to Western Europe in both economic attainment and environmental cleanliness in the 1990s. In 1991 Czechoslovakia took an important step in passing its Clean Air Act, part of an earnest effort to abate a terrible smoke problem. Also in 1991 Poland created a State Environmental Policy, setting targets for the reduction of a number of air pollutants.

Trends within the most developed nations suggest further improvements in air quality as other nations achieve greater economic success and stability. Some of this improvement comes not only through effective government regulation, demanded by a wealthier population seeking improved health and environmental amenities, but also through some common consequences of economic development. The most developed nations witnessed dramatic fuel changes in the last half of the twentieth century, with use of coal giving way to greater use of electricity and natural gas, both of which significantly reduced particulate pollution. At the same time, myriad technological developments in all aspects of production greatly improved efficiency, allowing greater economic growth at lower environmental costs. Perhaps most important, however, has been the illusion of decreased air pollution caused by "deindustrialization." Beginning as early as the 1950s in Britain and the United States, many industrial nations began to see industrial production shift to less developed nations. This far-reaching trend has brought significant air quality improvements in cities that no longer support great heavy industry, such as Pittsburgh, Buffalo, Manchester, and Glasgow, but at the cost of declining air quality in areas of industrial growth, including southern China and northern Mexico. In one sign that the problem remained serious, in 1997 the World Health Organization estimated that air pollution killed 400,000 people annually around the world.

Regional Air Pollution

Although much of the globe's air pollution is produced in cities, it doesn't all stay there. Indeed, high smoke-stacks, constructed to abate local pollution, have long contributed to the creation of regional problems. Most important among these is the development of acidic precipitation, commonly called "acid rain." Although it became a major concern only in the 1980s, particularly in central and northern Europe and the United States and Canada, acidic pollution has plagued coal-burning nations for more than a century. Indeed, British chemist Robert Angus Smith first connected plant deaths with acids created by the sulfuric pollutants of Manchester in 1852. Acid precipitation from smelter smoke caused both intranational and international disputes, including most famously the Trail Smelter conflict of the 1930s, in which U.S. citizens complained about crop damage caused by a massive Canadian zinc and lead smelter. This conflict resulted in an international agreement that established the "polluter pays" principle, but it also established the right of polluters to continue damaging the environment.

Unfortunately, acid precipitation research remained largely ignored until after a rapid growth in fossil-fuel consumption in the 1950s and 1960s led to broader and more obvious damage to forests and crops. In 1967 Swedish scientist Svante Oden published the first widely discussed research connecting acid rain to forest, stream, lake, and crop damage. By the 1970s researchers connected damaged forests, acidified lakes, and dwindling fish populations to acid rain, created aloft as sulfur and nitrogen oxides turned to acid and fell back to Earth, sometimes at great distances from their sources. By the 1980s forest death in Germany forced government action in that nation, even as countries that imported most of their pollution, including Scandinavian nations (downwind from central Europe and Russia) and Canada (downwind from the United States), pleaded for an international solution. In the United States acid rain became one of the most important environmental issues of the 1980s as northern lakes, many of them in popular recreation areas, rapidly became too acidic to support fish life. President Ronald Reagan, whose antienvironmentalist positions helped reenergize the environmental movement, stalled efforts to force a solution to the acid rain problem, a solution that would require coal-fired plants in the American Midwest to dramatically cut sulfur emissions. After Reagan's delays, however, the new Clean Air Act in 1990 forced a reduction in sulfur emissions.

Although acid rain has affected North America and Europe primarily, since 1970 some Latin American and Asian nations have increased fossil-fuel consumption dramatically. For example, China, with large stores of coal and a political interest in rapid economic development, leaped to the ranks of the world's great polluters in the 1980s, and its very high production of sulfur emissions bodes poorly for China's forests, crops, and lakes, as well as those of its neighbors, including Japan and Taiwan.

Global Air Pollution

The first indication that human activity might be capable of creating truly global environmental change came in 1957, when Columbia University scientists determined that strontium 90, a radioactive isotope created by nuclear explosions, could be found in every human on Earth. The isotope, which mimicked calcium and entered human bones, posed a significant health threat, particularly to children who consumed contaminated milk. Fear over the consequences of global radioactive pollution through nuclear testing led to one of the most important international agreements designed to protect the environment—the 1963 Nuclear Test Ban Treaty, which ended aboveground testing by the Soviet Union and the United States, immediately diminishing the fear of universal radioactive poisoning.

In 1974 scientists suggested the possibility of another global threat—the destruction of the ozone layer by human-made chemicals. Sherwood Roland and Mario Molina theorized that chemicals like chlorofluorocarbons (CFCs) could destroy individual ozone molecules, even those in the stratosphere responsible for reducing the ultraviolet light reaching the Earth's surface. By the mid-1980s growing evidence of ozone depletion, and the creation of an "ozone hole" over Antarctica, convinced governments to act swiftly. A weakened ozone layer posed threats to all life on Earth, including human beings, whom scientists predicted would suffer growing numbers of skin cancers from increased ultraviolet exposure. Working through the U.N. Environmental Programme, the nations that led in the consumption of CFCs created in 1987 the Montreal protocol, which required immediate and dramatic decreases in CFC production. Used as propellants in aerosol cans and as a coolant (Freon is a CFC), CFCs had gained wide use in industrialized nations, causing considerable objection to their ban from some corporations. Still, substitutes were readily found without the huge expenses that the regulation opponents claimed would come from the ban. Unfortunately, CFCs already produced continue to damage the ozone layer and will continue to do so for decades to come.

Global threats from strontium 90 and CFCs may have been diminished, but the threat from global warming due to increased emissions of carbon dioxide and other gases has yet to gain the same type of urgent attention. As early as 1896, Swedish scientist Svante Arrhenius predicted that rising atmospheric carbon dioxide concentrations, the consequence of industrial coal burning, would trap increasing amounts of heat on the Earth. Arrhenius predicted global warming should coal consumption continue to rise at such remarkable rates. Arrhenius's theory, though, remained just that until the late twentieth century, when better instruments could trace both the actual rise in global temperatures and the concomitant rise in atmospheric carbon dioxide. Although doubts about both the causes and consequences of global warming remained, in the 1990s the U.N. sponsored research and gathered data. Disagreements persisted, but most climate specialists agreed that continued warming would cause ocean levels to rise as the polar ice caps melted, endangering coastal and island communities around the globe. In addition, scientists predicted changing climate patterns, with some areas become much drier, others wetter, and most areas experiencing greater weather extremes, including more intense storms and longer droughts. In 1997 the U.N. convened the Conference on Climate Change in Kyoto, Japan. With both European and American support, the conference established the need for developed nations to control emissions of greenhouse gases, particularly carbon dioxide. Shortly after the creation of the Kyoto protocol, President George W. Bush's administration removed its support of the agreement, even while Europe proceeded in efforts to reduce greenhouse emissions.

David Stradling

See also Acid Rain; Automobile

Further Reading

Brimblecombe, P. (1987). *The big smoke: A history of air pollution in London since medieval times.* New York: Methuen.

Clapp, B. W. (1994). *An environmental history of Britain since the Industrial Revolution.* London: Longman.

Dewey, S. H. (2000). *Don't breathe the air: Air pollution and U. S. environmental politics, 1945–1970.* College Station: Texas A&M University Press.

McCormick, J. (1997). *Acid Earth: The politics of acid pollution.* London: Earthscan.

McNeill, J. R. (2000). *Something new under the sun: An environmental history of the twentieth-century world.* New York: W. W. Norton.

Mosley, S. (2001). *The chimney of the world: A history of smoke pollution in Victorian and Edwardian Manchester.* Cambridge, UK: White Horse Press.

Stradling, D. (1999). *Smokestacks and progressives: Environmentalists, engineers, and air quality in America, 1881–1951.* Baltimore: Johns Hopkins University Press.

Wirth, J. D. (2000). *Smelter smoke in North America: The politics of transborder pollution.* Lawrence: University Press of Kansas.

Alaska Pipeline *See* Trans-Alaska Pipeline

Albedo Effect

Albedo refers to the whiteness or reflectivity of a surface, measured as the ratio between the amount of light reflected and the amount absorbed by an object, and it is expressed either as a number between 0 and 1 or as a percentage. The average albedo of the Earth is 0.34, which means that 34 percent of light received from the sun is reflected back into space. The remaining sunlight is absorbed by the ground and raises the average surface temperature of the Earth to 15° C. A change in the albedo of the Earth's surface results in a temperature change. This influence of the albedo on the Earth's surface temperature is called the albedo effect.

Albedo varies around the Earth according to the texture and color of the surface material. Snow and clouds have a high albedo, and it is estimated that about half the Earth's albedo is due to reflection of sunlight by clouds and snow. Vegetation and the oceans have a low albedo, and absorb a large fraction of the light received. The albedo of water changes according to the angle at which light falls upon its surface. In general, bare land and deserts have a higher albedo than grassland or forest. Albedo also changes with latitude and is low in the equatorial zone of the Earth, which can be explained by the extensive ocean surfaces, tropical rain forests, and the absence of persistent cloud blankets. At lower latitudes, albedo increases steadily polewards, reaching maximum values over snow-covered polar regions.

For millennia, humans have been transforming the Earth's surface by clearing forests, overgrazing, irrigation, and more recently, by expanding urban development. These activities are changing the albedo of the Earth's surface over large areas. The albedo of urban areas is generally lower than the surrounding landscape, which explains why cities are normally warmer. The warmer air above cities has a tendency to rise (through convective heating), which leads to increased cloud formation. Albedos of low-latitude cities are higher than those at mid-latitudes because of the use of light colored materials and paint to increase reflectivity.

The reduction of forest cover at lower latitudes and its replacement by grassland or desert causes changes in precipitation patterns. Deforestation increases albedo, causing lower surface temperatures. This suppresses convection, encouraging prevailing downward motion of air, which leads to lower precipitation and more frequent drought. The 1970s and 1980s drought in the Sahel has partly been attributed to this phenomenon.

At higher latitudes increased albedo due to human activity could lead to a cooling of the climate, or cancel out some effects of global warming caused by an increase of greenhouse gases. In this model, drier conditions and continuing deforestation will further increase the area of bare ground, thus enhancing cooling. In addition this cooling might increase the size of glaciers and ice caps, which will reflect still more sunlight, further cooling the planet. How albedo change in different parts of the world will affect the global climate in the future is still uncertain and is the subject of ongoing research and debate.

K. Jan Oosthoek

Further Reading

Barry, R. G., & Carleton, A. M. (2001). *Synoptic and dynamic climatology*. London: Routledge.

Coppin, P. A. (1977). *The albedo of natural surfaces*. Bedford Park, S. Australia: Flinder Institute for Atmospheric and Marine Sciences, Flinders University of South Australia.

Gorniz, V., & Henderson-Sellers, A. (1984). Possible climatic impacts of land cover transformations, with particular emphasis on tropical deforestation. *Climatic Change, 6*, 231–256.

Oke, T. R. (1987). *Boundary layer climates*. London: Methuen.

Roesch, A. C. (2000). *Assessment of the land surface scheme in climate models with focus on surface albedo and snow cover*. Zürich, Switzerland: Geographisches Institut ETH.

Alps *See* Austria, France; Italy; Mountaineering; Switzerland

Amazon River

In geological terms the Amazon River is young, having assumed its current form around 4 million years ago when tectonic plate shifts in the Earth raised the Andes Mountains to the point where they blocked off the Amazon's original westward drainage into the Pacific Ocean, creating an enormous lake in the heart of the South American landmass. Around 2 million years ago a new channel developed, draining east into the Atlantic Ocean, and the Amazon River basin assumed something like its present form. The climatic fluctuations of the Quaternary period over the last million years then periodically altered Amazonian geography. Lower sea levels and temperatures during ice ages projected the Amazon's estuary 320 kilometers into the Atlantic from its present position, where it flowed into the ocean through a network of high and narrow drainage channels. The Amazon River during ice ages was thus quite unlike the modern Amazon. Its large delta, broad main channel, and meandering flow are temporary and will alter again in the next ice age.

Pollen cores from lake sediments, carbon isotope analysis of soils, marine cores from the Amazon delta, and ice cores from the Andes all suggest that the climate of the Amazon has been unstable, fluctuating between wet and dry periods since the end of the last ice age around thirteen thousand years ago. The high levels of biodiversity (biological diversity as indicated by numbers of species of animals and plants) in the Amazon, by some ways of measuring the most elevated on the planet, may have been even higher during the early Holocene epoch, around eight thousand years ago, when mean temperatures were some 5° C lower, the Andean snowline about .6 kilometers lower, and cold-adapted montane (relating to the biogeographic zone of moist, cool upland slopes below the timberline dominated by large coniferous trees) tree species found at lower elevations in the western Amazon, giving what is now steamy jungle something of the look and feel of a temperate forest.

This climatic instability led biogeographers concerned with the origins of Amazonian biodiversity to formulate the Pleistocene refuge theory, which domi-

Seasons in the Amazon Basin

The following account describes the seasonal adjustments made by the Tukano Indians of the northwest Amazon.

During the two "dry" seasons, ihíbo (October–December, February and March), the Indian communities are perched on high banks, in many places clayey and sources of ceramic clay. Access is difficult; the steep, often slippery slopes are hard to manage unless the people have troubled to provide wooden steps or a handrail. At the height of the June, or great, rains, the flood reaches to the clearing, and the river is brought close. A community with its plantations is then an island, the low-lying country a vast lake.

The Cubeo are more pleased with low water than with high. High water, to be sure, does not threaten cultivations, which are always on high ground, and flooding facilitates river travel, yielding shorter routes over ordinarily sinuous turnings of the river. But the seasons of high water (ilákoro) (May-August and January) bring relative scarcity even though bitter manioc is an unfailing crop. Fish and game are then most difficult to catch. At the bottom of low water, fish are scarce but game, drawn to the dwindling streams, is now abundant. The peak seasons, when game and fish are both abundant, are after the beginning of the rains, when the rivers are filling in November, and at the conclusion of the rains in July, when the rivers have begun to fall off. The Cubeo render ihíbo as summer and ilákoro as winter. They also refer to seasons as kwaíno (falling river) and as edávaiya (growing river).

Thus, while the Cubeo normally do not experience famine or, for that matter, serious deprivation at any season, the periods of glut are short, one falling roughly between October and December, and the other a minor dry season between February and April. During these seasons fish need only be scooped out of the drying streams, game—tapir, peccary, deer, capybara, and paca—crowds the river banks, and the manioc yield is at its peak. These are favorable seasons for ceremony—initiation into the ancestral cult, fish dances, deer dances, mourning rites, and the most frequent round of drinking parties. The seasons, however, lack abruptness. The rains increase and then decrease. Neither economic nor ceremonial life need be precisely geared to a season.

Source: Goldman, Irving. (1963). *The Cubeo: Indians of the Northwest Amazon.* Urbana: University of Illinois Press, p. 50.

nated models of Pleistocene (100,000 to 10,000 before present) Amazonian environmental history until the 1990s. This theory asserted that the Amazon was dry, even arid, during much of the Pleistocene epoch, when savanna was the dominant vegetation type and forest retreated into islands scattered through the drainage basin, which served as species reservoirs. When forest expanded during wetter periods, species moved over a wider area, only to be isolated again as forest retracted. The repetition of this process was believed to lie behind high biodiversity. More recently the scientific consensus has been that Pleistocene refuge theory is mistaken and that Amazonian biodiversity is better explained by a combination of high levels of natural disturbance, the presence of river barriers, and the stability of forest ecosystems over time.

Human Colonization

Precisely when human colonization of the Amazon began is unknown. The earliest reliable radiocarbon dates are from 11,500 years ago, but the earliest sites, coastal and riverine by definition, have been destroyed by changing sea levels and river courses. Most specialists accept early penetration by humans at around fifteen thousand years ago or even earlier. Some genetic and linguistic evidence suggests a human presence as long ago as twenty thousand years, but this is controversial. The archeological record suggests that human impacts on Amazonian ecosystems were more intense and longer lasting than previously thought. By the late prehistoric period few parts of the Amazon had not been occupied at least sporadically, and sophisticated cultures had evolved in both floodplain and upland areas. Lifeways (ways of living) were complex: Agriculture was supplemented by gathering, especially of palm products; large patches of fertile artificial soils were created throughout the basin; and aquatic and marine ecosystems were intensively exploited. Population densities were lower than in Andean and Central America, but total populations were probably comparable to either.

The consequence was considerable human impact on ecosystems even before the arrival of Europeans. Forest burning was probably sufficient to cause greater seasonality and local drops in rainfall in the late prehistoric period, and at least one complex prehistoric culture, the Marajoara, may well have collapsed through over exploitation of its natural resource base. The arrival of Europeans and the colonial experience paradoxically reduced human impacts on the floodplain through the destruction or enslavement of the indigenous population. Much of the floodplain, which had been an intensively exploited landscape in the sixteenth century, was reclaimed by forest. Much less is known about environmental change in upland areas during the colonial period, but it is likely that there was a similar advance in forest cover. The greater productivity brought by metal tools was counterbalanced by the severe long-term decline of the indigenous population. It is one of the great ironies of Amazonian history that these young forests were construed by early European science as primeval and as uninhabited rather than depopulated.

Rubber Boom

Not until the rubber boom of the late nineteenth century did new influxes of population into both floodlands and uplands push the Amazon's population back up to late prehistoric levels. The environmental impacts were far reaching; colonization cut back forest on a large scale for the first time through slash-and-burn agriculture and ranching, driven by the demands of rapidly growing urban centers. Belém and Manaus, Brazil, and Iquitos, Peru, had populations over 100,000 in 1900—the first time that the Amazon basin had included cities of such size; Belém and Manaus would both have populations well over 1 million a century later.

The environmental impacts of the rubber boom subsided with its rapid collapse after 1912 as plantation rubber from southeastern Asia, originally cultivated from purloined Amazonian seedlings, pushed wild rubber out of world markets. Colonization of the Amazon stopped and then reversed, with many parts of the basin again reverting to secondary forest. Not until the 1960s did national societies renew their penetration of the Amazon, this time with far more dramatic environmental consequences.

Beginning in the late 1960s the construction of a network of highways linked the Amazon to the national hinterlands of the states that divided the basin between them and funneled millions of migrants into the region. Road building was on the largest scale in Brazil, where it had the most far-reaching consequences, but all Amazonian countries passed through a similar cycle of frontier development. The consequences were largely disastrous. Some 12 percent of the Amazon's forest cover was removed by the end of the twentieth century, replaced largely by low-productivity ranches and subsistence smallholdings. Many ranches lasted less than a generation before declining pasture quality forced their abandonment. The destruction was concentrated largely in the uplands; for once the floodplain was much less affected by colonization.

Although deforestation rates declined from their peak in the 1980s, there is evidence of regional climate change in some parts of the Amazon basin linked to forest clearance, with declines in rainfall and greater seasonality. This will be permanent. The long-term effect of global warming will be to increase drought stress and make many parts of the Amazon more flammable. Local and global climate change may feed into each other, to the detriment of forest cover and biodiversity. On the other hand, the basin's enormous size and the resilience of its ecosystems may buffer human influences. It is a gamble whose outcome will be clearer by 2100.

David Cleary

See also Brazil; Peru; South America; Tropical Forests

Further Reading

Bates, H. (1863). *The naturalist on the River Amazon*. London: John Murray.

Cleary, D. (2001). Towards an environmental history of the Amazon: From prehistory to the nineteenth century. *Latin American Research Review, 36*(2), 65–96.

Dean, W. (1987). *Brazil and the struggle for rubber*. Cambridge, UK: Cambridge University Press.

Medina, J. (Ed.). (1988). *The discovery of the Amazon*. New York: Dover.

Meggers, B. (1991). *Amazonia: Man and culture in a counterfeit paradise*. Washington, DC: Smithsonian Institution Press.

Moran, E. (1993). *Through Amazonian eyes: The human ecology of Amazonian populations*. Iowa City: Iowa University Press.

Roosevelt, A. (1991). *Moundbuilders of the Amazon*. San Diego, CA: Academic Press.

Schmink, M., & Wood, C. (1984). *Frontier expansion in Amazonia*. Gainesville: Florida University Press.

Amazonia, Ancient

As the largest tropical rain forest on the planet, Amazonia holds a unique place in both world environmental history and the imagination of South America. A vast region that extends through present-day Brazil and seven other South American nations (Colombia, Ecuador, French Guiana, Guyana, Peru, Surinam, and Venezuela) it symbolically stands for the dominance of nature over humans and as a source of still-unknown plants and animals. But in fact Amazonia has been an intensively managed, human-made environment for many hundreds of years. The current perception of Amazonia as one of the last wildernesses reflects not the rain forest's pristine nature, but rather the erasure of its human population through the violence of the colonial conquest of the native population.

Conventionally, the Amazon River basin is considered, at a minimum, to comprise 96 million hectares; the Amazon River itself is the largest (by volume) in the world, being nearly 160 kilometers wide at its mouth. The civilizations that arose there were functionally isolated from the rest of the world, and this has meant that evidence for these past civilizations has emerged only slowly, given the absence of stone-building and the sheer scale of the Amazon as a context for research.

Any definition of Amazonia as an ecological, cultural, or political unit therefore tends to proceed more by a process of exclusion than by reference to broad uniformities in the Amazonian environment because such uniformities are illusory. The definition of Amazonia employed here reflects the conventions established in Steward's *Handbook of South American Indians* (1946–1963) and carried over into current anthropological usages, whereby Amazonia is understood to comprise the whole of the Amazon River drainage system, including the right-bank tributaries of the Orinoco, to which the Amazon River has two connections: one permanent (via the Casiquiare Canal) and one seasonal (via the flooding of the upland savannas between the Rio Branco and the Essequibo River). This latter connection effectively unites the Atlantic coastal region of the Guianas with the Amazon River basin, giving rise to the designation "Guayana" or "Guianas" (in Steward's *Handbook*) for this area encircled by the Atlantic, Orinoco, and Amazon, which can then be considered as a subregion of Amazonia, as defined earlier. Steward (1946–1963, III, 885) also hypothesized that Guiana was a center of dispersal for the "tropical forest-complex" of agriculture of the manioc plant—a tuber whose pulp became a staple of the regional diet—although this view was later challenged.

However, it should be noted that these conventions in the geographical criteria for the delimitation of regions were connected to a wider classificatory scheme in the *Handbook*. In an attempt to give some analytical shape to the mass of ethnological, historical, and archaeological information that the *Handbook* brought together, these contrasting geographical zones were also thought to delineate cultural regions. As Robert Lowie put it in his introductory essay to Volume III of the *Handbook*, "The Tropical Forest complex is marked off from the higher Andean civilizations by lacking architectural and metallurgical refinements, yet outranks cultures with the hunting-gathering economy" (Lowie 1948, 1). Accordingly, the Andean and Colombian-Venezuelan regions, fitting their status as the locale of the Incan empire and other gold-working chiefdoms of the Circum-Caribbean and Colombia sierras, were assigned "advanced" sociocultural status on the basis of cultural traits, such as hierarchical organization, metalworking, burial practices, and so forth. Because these cultures lay outside the agriculturally poor region of the tropical forests of Amazonia, their complex and large-scale character was accepted as a logical result of an environment conducive to the development of human civilization.

A "Counterfeit Paradise"

In the Amazonian region, any evidence of advanced civilizations was rejected by archaeologists and historians as the exaggeration of an unreliable historical record or as a result of extraneous origins, the result of cultural diffusion from the Colombian or Andean regions. The evidence was dismissed because of the assumption that the Amazon region was ecologically unfavorable to human settlement on a large scale, despite its dense vegetation and variety of fauna—it was a "counterfeit paradise" (Meggers 1992). The evidence for this was taken to be the poverty of soils away from the flood plain deposits, the small scale of contemporary indigenous societies, and the absence of major archaeological sites, except in the case of the mound builders of Marajó Island at the mouth of the Amazon. The presence of this sophisticated culture was "explained" as having resulted from a down-river migration from a more complex center in the Peruvian or Colombian Andes. The apparent decline of this cultural complex, almost from the point of its establishment on Marajó, was then taken as "proof" that higher sociocultural forms could not sustain themselves in the lowland tropics where manioc agriculture was practiced. In contrast, other experts championed the idea of the Amazon basin as a cradle of migration across the rest of the continent, a view supported by a significant proportion of recent research.

Whether or not Amazonia was, or is, in fact a "counterfeit paradise," therefore, remains at the heart of scholarly dispute. Because there have been insufficient archaeological data to resolve this dispute, historians and ethnographers have added their voices to the debates on native ecology and agriculture, demography, and population levels. The eventual outcomes of such research are of profound significance in answering questions not just about human-environmental relationships, but also about the place of Amazonia in the overall development of New World society and culture.

Early Settlement

It transpires that human occupation of Amazonia is much more ancient and more extensive there than had once been assumed. By about 9000 BCE two lithic (using stone tools) traditions had become widespread in Amazonia. (These stone implements included arrowheads and edged cutting tools for processing animal game and grindstones for preparing maize.) By 5000 BCE two more practices had emerged. First, there is evidence that by 2000 BCE groups on the Atlantic coast were using domesticated plants, with maize use emerging in the Minas Gerais region by about 1500 BCE. Second, current research indicates that occupation of the lower Amazon began around 10,000 BCE, and there has been a dramatic discovery of ceramics from around 6000 BCE in a site along the lower Amazon,

making this the earliest example of pottery in the Americas.

Close examination of this early period in northeastern Amazonia, along the Guiana coastal region, illustrates the close relationship between agricultural adaptation to a complex environment and a resultant development of appropriate lithic technologies. Transitions from gathering to the horticulture of certain plants, particularly the *ite* palm (*Mauritia flexuosa*) and the *mora* tree (*Mora excelsa*), as well as other utilitarian species, are directly reflected in the development of the lithic repertoire. Although these subsistence techniques are theorized as being ancestral to the emergence of tropical forest horticulture in the region, the developmental analogies are probably stronger with the *sambaqui* (shell-mound) peoples of coastal Brazil than with the occupants of the tropical forests because their horticultural and foraging repertoires are quite distinct. This suggests that progressive adaptation to the complexities of the Amazonian environment was a process repeated across the whole region.

Various ancient societies also practiced relatively intensive forms of agriculture, evidenced by widespread landscape modification throughout Amazonia. In fact, it has been argued that the landscape of Amazonia, as it is seen today and as it has been for the last 350 years or so, is the historical product of a return to a semiwilderness, consequent on the colonial depopulation of the native inhabitants. Moreover, the current evidence for the existence of prehistoric roads and causeways in both the llanos (prairies) of Bolivia, Colombia, and Venezuela and in the heart of Amazonia itself indicates that these landscape modifications were related to the presence of large and complex societies.

For example, recently investigated systems of extensive ridged fields and agricultural mounds along the Atlantic coast of the Guianas underline how limited knowledge of the "tropical forest" region really is. The presence of complex agricultural techniques to deal with the low-lying, swampy conditions in this region, as well as the use of intensive farming practices from at least 700 CE, shows how complex adaptations were made to a variety of Amazonian environments. Thus archaeological evidence also fits well with the historical sources that report both significant population and a complex agricultural repertoire among the indigenous groups.

Soil Holds Clues

Apart from this physical manipulation of the landscape, research interest in ancient Amazonia has focused on anthropic or anthropogenic soils (that is, soils whose formation is directly related to human activity)—or at least on trying to assess what kind of soils in Amazonia may have been generated through human activities, how widespread they actually are, and to what extent such soils were intentionally fomented. The banks of the main channel of the Amazon as well as of many of its tributaries are replete with black earth sites, illustrating both the continuity and antiquity of human presence. The use of such sites for agricultural purposes thus illustrates both sophisticated knowledge of soil properties and systems of agricultural management that were stable over many generations.

These kinds of soils, particularly *terra preta* (black earth), which is black anthropogenic soil with enhanced fertility due to high levels of soil organic matter and nutrients, are common throughout Amazonia. (The valuable soil has been created either through direct agricultural fertilization or as a consequence of intense human settlement—human waste materials enrich the soil with nitrogen.) The historical evidence shows that there was no one-to-one relationship between the presence of agriculturally favorable soils and the past existence of complex polity or an extensive cultural repertoire. This investigation of anthropogenic soils by scientists seems to provide evidence that human occupation of an area was not dependent on conducive environmental conditions. However, archaeological investigation of the many well-documented *terra preta* deposits along the main Amazon channel, as well as along its tributaries, is still in the early stages.

Agriculture and Diet

The addition of maize to modes of subsistence that previously centered on palms and manioc, as well as the systematic exploitation of other food plants, has also been the subject of study. However, interest in the advent of maize cultivation results from seeing maize use as a token of social and cultural complexity—given its easy storage and high nutritional value—and so evidence of its use in Amazonia, where the use of manioc varieties is predominant in the historic and ethnographic reports of aboriginal horticulture, is especially significant. However, this apparent predominance of manioc agriculture in ethnographic and historical materials about Amazonia may result from the way in which manioc use increased over the last five hundred years as a result of indigenous access to steel tools via trade with the Europeans. The use of steel axes would

have permitted much greater clearance of forest for the forest of manioc, a root that must be dug from the earth, than would have the use of stone axes. As a result, and also stimulated by European trading interest in manioc flour, there were distinct advantages for domestic groups in opting out of the systems of intensive agricultural production that sustain large civilizations. Consequently the dietary use of manioc, as opposed to maize, may well have increased substantially during the historic period.

Basic Questions Remain

The nature of these transformations over the last five hundred years is critical to an understanding of ancient Amazonia, but the sheer size of the region and the lack of sociocultural continuity between past and present society and culture, as a result of colonial depopulation, make comprehensive study of the environmental history of the region especially challenging. Many of the basic questions of Amazonian prehistory remain open, not least of which are those of the scale and longevity of human occupation. It seems likely that ethnography and history, as much as archaeology, will continue to play a role in the discussion of human adaptations to the Amazonian environment. Work in progress that emphasizes ethnoarchaeological techniques, systematic survey, and interpretation of historical records, as well as the deployment of new technical resources, such as geophysical survey, seems well positioned to do justice to the complexity of Amazonian antiquity.

As these techniques are deployed and the database grows, it already seems likely that issues of human environmental adaptation will be cast in a different framework than that which produced the idea of Amazonia as some kind of false paradise whose apparent botanical bounty belied the actual poverty of its soils for human usages. Already much of the work there tends to suggest that Amazonia is too complex an environment, and its human adaptations too various, to be adequately characterized as either utterly unfavorable or uniformly conducive to human settlement. The very uncertainties about the definition of an Amazonian region, discussed earlier, reflect the fact that the conceptualization of Amazonia as a homogeneous entity is in itself flawed. As debates about models of the Amazonian environment are replaced with actual investigation of human adaptations through time, researchers will be in a far better position to appreciate the variety and complexity of human adaptation to both the challenges and the potential of the Amazon basin proper, as well as of the surrounding regions.

Neil L. Whitehead

See also Amazon River; Brazil

Further Reading

Acuña, C. de. (1859). A new discovery of the great river of the Amazons. In C. R. Markham (Ed.), *Expeditions into the valley of the Amazons* (pp. 44–142). London: Hakluyt Society.

Denevan, W. (2002). *Cultivated landscapes of native Amazonia and the Andes.* New York: Oxford University Press.

Lowie, R. (1948). The tropical forests: An introduction. In J. Steward (Ed.), *Handbook of South American Indians: Vol. 3. The tropical forest tribes* (pp. 1–57). Washington, DC: U.S. Government Printing Office.

Meggers, B. (1992). Amazonia: Real or counterfeit paradise? *The Review of Archaeology, 13*(2), 25–40.

Posey, D., & Balée, W. (Eds.). (1989). Resource management in Amazonia: Indigenous and folk strategies. In *Advances in economic botany (7).* New York: New York Botanical Garden.

Roosevelt, A. C. (1980). *Parmana: Prehistoric maize and manioc subsistence along the Amazon and Orinoco.* New York: Academic Press.

Roosevelt, A. C. (1991). *Moundbuilders of the Amazon: Geophysical archaeology on Marajó Island, Brazil.* New York: Academic Press.

Steward, J. H. (Ed.). (1946–1963). *Handbook of South American Indians* (Vols. 1–6). Washington, DC: U.S. Government Printing Office.

Whitehead, N. L. (1994). The ancient Amerindian polities of the lower Orinoco, Amazon and Guayana coast: A preliminary analysis of their passage from antiquity to extinction. In A. C. Roosevelt (Ed.), *Amazonian Indians from prehistory to the present: Anthropological perspectives* (pp. 33–54). Tucson: University of Arizona Press.

Whitehead, N. L. (1996). Searching for paradise? Recent research in Amazonian archaeology. *Journal of Archaeological Research, 4*(3), 241–264.

Andes

The environmental history of the Andes has unfolded in the context of a spectacular natural diversity and notable cultural achievement. The Andes form a complex of mountain ranges in western South America that extend 7,000 kilometers from Venezuela to Tierra del Fuego. Few people have lived in the southern Andes, where conditions make it difficult to sustain human life. In contrast, the portion of the Andean Highlands that lie within tropical latitudes have fertile valleys and sharply telescoped vertical habitats that have favored agricultural diversification over short distances.

Prehistoric Andean peoples domesticated a wide range of plants, of which the potato is the best known, permitting a sedentary form of life that goes back to at least 4000 BCE. The consolidation of local societies into larger polities started around 1000 BCE. At a much later time, the Inca Empire (c. 1100–1532 CE) absorbed people of different cultures into an intricately organized state apparatus based on sustainable farming and the raising of llamas and alpacas. At different periods, pre-Colombian peoples constructed earthworks that dramatically reshaped certain landscapes. Stone bench terraces on steep slopes enabled crops to be irrigated with little loss of soil to erosion. Elsewhere, systems of artificial ridges made it possible to grow crops in swampy terrain. In 1532 the Spaniards conquered the Inca empire and introduced most of the inventory of European crops, animals, technology, religion, and political organization. Native people of the Andes long resisted wholesale absorption into Spanish culture. To this day, the highland peasantry reflects a mixed heritage of indigenous and introduced folkways.

The Andes manifest both continuity and discontinuity from their pre-Colombian past. Highland deforestation is the most visible human impact, but the bulk of the tree cover had already been removed by or in the Inca period. Colonizing Spaniards stripped most remaining woodland to meet the increased demand for firewood and house timbers and to accommodate the grazing needs of cattle, sheep, goats, and equines. The fortuitous introduction of eucalyptus after 1860 provided an alternative wood supply, although plantations of exotic species have created vulnerable monocultures of one kind of tree that also have taken massive quantities of water out of the soil.

The contemporary Andean landscape must be seen as a product of human interventions in the past, not as a simple response to biophysical factors. Desertification, especially severe in Bolivia, reflects overgrazing, not climatic change. Soil erosion and water pollution are not recent, but are of growing severity. Unrestrained cultivation of steep slopes and negative effects of mining on streams continue to take their toll on land

Machu Picchu, an ancient scholarly city of the Incas, in the Andes Mountains of Peru.

and water quality. An environmental consciousness emerged in the latter part of the twentieth century that was largely inspired by the movement in industrialized countries. Local and international advocacy groups formulated conservation agendas, promulgated correctives to counter past abuses, passed laws, and established natural areas to preserve what is left of a greatly diminished flora and fauna.

Daniel W. Gade

Further Reading

Gade, D. W. (1999). *Nature and culture in the Andes*. Madison: University of Wisconsin Press.

Animal Rights

"Animal rights" is both a philosophical argument—that nonhuman animals have inherent value as individuals and thus have the moral right not to be used, abused, or killed—and a general term for the movement to end the exploitation of other animals by human beings (who tend to forget that they too are animals). The necessity for animal rights arises from the conception of species as a fundamental ethical demarcation. Though culture arises from nature, and humans are animals, a distorted conceptual view imposes a division, a conceptual dualism, that separates human beings from animals and culture from nature. The ethical hierarchy that posits human beings as superior and permits abuse and enslavement of nonhuman animals has precipitated the movement known as "animal rights."

While the term *animal rights* is relatively recent, over the centuries some individuals have protested the mistreatment of nonhuman animals. Recently, the animal rights movement has successfully introduced the term "speciesism" into common usage. According to Peter Singer, "speciesism," coined by Richard Ryder in 1970, is "a prejudice or attitude of bias in favor of the interests of members of one's own species and against those of members of other species" (Singer 1990, 6). If differences between humans and nonhumans are arbitrary, it is posited, then the institutions that arise from these arbitrary demarcations are unjustifiable. Thus, those who become convinced that speciesism, like sexism and racism, must be challenged become involved with the animal rights movement.

The animal rights movement challenges the use of nonhuman animals for food (namely, flesh foods, dairy products, eggs, and honey, as well as hunting and fishing), clothing (including silk, wool, and leather), entertainment (circuses and zoos), and for experimentation (medical research and product safety testing).

Concern for nonhuman animals can be traced back to the Asian concept of *ahimsa*—nonharming. Main Asian religions, such as Jainism, Buddhism, Taoism, and Hinduism, are rooted in an ancient religious tradition that proposed nonviolent relationships with the world, including other beings. In addition to *ahimsa*, other early religious reasons for not harming animals included belief in the transmigration of souls. For religions whose sacred texts include the Book of Genesis, a vegan diet is pronounced as the appropriate food for human beings in Genesis 1:29; the much-contested "dominion" granted in Genesis 1:26 is dominion within a vegan world.

The animal rights debate often focuses on what distinguishes human beings from other animals. It is argued that humans alone were made in God's image. However, Darwinism showed clearly that humans, like nonhumans, are descended from animals.

What capacities do humans and nonhumans share? At one time it was proposed that humans were the only tool-using animals. Then it was discovered that other animals use tools as well. Further, the emphasis on tool use was perceived as an example of how the methodology for determining differences between species is based on humanocentric standards such as manipulation by *hands*. Such standards eliminate from consideration beings that have no hands, such as marine mammals like dolphins.

It has been proposed that no other animals have the reasoning capacity that humans do. To that, Jeremy Bentham responded, "The question is not, Can they *reason*? nor Can they *talk*? but, Can they *suffer*?" (Singer 1990, 7).

Historically, animal rights arguments often arise within the context of widening human rights, for instance, in Britain of the 1790s, when support of the French Revolution, anti-slavery activism, and animal rights were seen to be interconnected. Again, in the 1890s and the following decade, in both Great Britain and the United States, connections were made among pacifist, temperance, suffragist, vegetarian, antivivisection, and trade union activists. In the 1960s in the United States, the anti-war, civil rights, and women's liberation movements paved the way for the animal rights/animal liberation movement.

Animal Rights Is Not a New Idea

As the following excerpt—written more than a century ago—makes clear, concerns about animals (and even about the appropriate language to use when describing them) have been expressed long before the present day.

Something must here be said on the important subject of nomenclature. It is to be feared that the ill-treatment of animals is largely due—or at any rate the difficulty of amending that treatment is largely increased—by the common use of such terms as "brute-beast," "live-stock," etc., which implicitly deny to the lower races that intelligent individuality which is most undoubtedly possessed by them. It was long ago remarked by Bentham, in his "Introduction to Principles of Morals and Legislation," that, whereas human beings are styled *persons*, "other animals, on account of their interests having been neglected by the insensibility of the ancient jurists, stand degraded into the class of *things*;" and Schopenhauer also has commented on the mischievous absurdity of the idiom which applies the neuter pronoun "it" to such highly organized primates as the dog and the ape.

A word of protest is needed also against such an expression as "dumb animals," which, though often cited as "an immense exhortation to pity," has in reality a tendency to influence ordinary people in quite the contrary direction, inasmuch as if fosters the idea of an impassable barrier between mankind and their dependents. It is convenient to us men to be deaf to the entreaties of the victims of our injustice; and, by a sort of grim irony, we therefore assume that it is *they* who are afflicted by some organic incapacity—they are "dumb animals," forsooth! Although a moment's consideration must prove that they have innumerable ways, often quite human in variety and suggestiveness, of uttering their thoughts and emotions. Even the term "animals," as applied to the lower races, is incorrect, and not wholly unobjectionable, since it ignores the fact that *man* is an animal no less than they.

Source: Salt, Henry S. (1980). *Animals' Rights Considered in Relation to Social Progress*. Clarks Summit, PA: Society for Animal Rights, 17–19. (Originally published 1892)

By the 1980s, with the founding of Feminists for Animal Rights, it was recognized that the issue was not that species is like race or sex in being an oppressive ideology, but that all these oppressions are interconnected. For instance, Western cultures have equated women, children, people of color, nonhumans, and "the natural" with each other and with the body—which was devalued, if not repudiated.

Many women have an ethical history that is rooted in culturally prescribed practices of caring. Part of this history is an active concern about nonhumans. Josephine Donovan suggests that the eighteenth-century emphasis on sentiment, associated with the appearance of numerous women writers, paved the intellectual way for the appearance of animal rights in the nineteenth century. Yet, historically animal rights were articulated in the West as a part of the liberal Enlightenment commitment to rights, and Western animal rights theorists have been mainly men. Women have composed the majority in most animal welfare groups, yet animal advocacy has often been belittled because of this association with women. For example, in the seventeenth century, Spinoza argued that opposing animal exploitation was "womanish." During the nineteenth century, when most antivivisectionists were women, the movement was called "illogical" and "emotional."

The relationship between environmental activism and animal rights is vexed. From an environmental perspective, hunting animals for food is often viewed as "natural" and the consumption of hunted animals is *the* acceptable way of consuming animal flesh. However, this deflects attention from the principal method of obtaining animal bodies, that is, by enslaving nonhumans. Consequently, the demands each individual animal places on the environment—the food they need, the manure they produce, the water they require and that is needed to maintain the crops that feeds them—disappear as well—and with them, a common ground that links environmentalists and animal rights activists.

The animal rights debate is essentially about relationships. How should we relate to other beings, hierarchically or equally? Some propose that humans do sense their connectedness with other beings, yet continue to defend themselves against this knowledge because it would require change and change demands effort. Animal rights discussions, therefore, bear the burden not only of education about speciesism, but of helping a worldview motivate itself sufficiently to allow for self-transformation.

Carol J. Adams

Further Reading

Adams, C. J. (1994). *Neither man nor beast: Feminism and the defense of animals.* New York: Continuum.

Donovan, J., & Adams, C. J. (Eds.). (1995). *Beyond animal rights: A feminist caring ethic for the treatment of animals.* New York: Continuum.

Dunayer, J. (2001). *Animal equality: Language and liberation.* Derwood, MD: Ryce Publishing.

Mason, J. (1997). *An unnatural order: Why we are destroying the planet and each other.* New York: Continuum.

Noske, B. (1997). *Beyond boundaries: Humans and animals.* Montreal, Canada: Black Rose.

Regan, T. (1983). *The case for animal rights.* Berkeley: University of California Press.

Regan, T., & Singer, P. (Eds.). (1976). *Animal rights and human obligations.* Englewood Cliffs, NJ: Prentice-Hall, Inc.

Salt, H. S. (1980) *Animals' rights considered in relation to social progress.* Preface by P. Singer. Clarks Summit, PA: Society for Animal Rights, Inc. (Original work published in 1892)

Singer, P. (1990). *Animal liberation* (2nd ed.). New York: New York Review Book.

Wise, S. (2000). *Rattling the cage: Toward legal rights for animals.* Cambridge, MA: Perseus Books.

Animism

Animism can be defined as the belief either that all natural things and phenomena are alive, or that they possess an innate soul or spirit. Religious traditions ranging from various aboriginal belief systems to con- temporary paganism are premised upon such assumptions. Such a worldview contrasts with other belief systems that posit that soul or spirit resides only outside nature or within certain exceptionally designated beings (e.g., humans), or is merely an extension of an external deity.

Historical Presence of Animism

Various forms of animism have found their way into the natural philosophies of numerous environmental thinkers throughout history. Whether in reaction to the reductionist approaches to nature of Renaissance thinkers, or to the perceived anthropocentrism of Christianity, a thread of animism—sometimes known as "vitalism," "organicism," or "paganism"—has repeatedly woven its way into the fabric of the Western worldview.

For example, the English philosopher Henry More (1614–1687) believed in an *anima mundi* or "a Soul of the World, or Spirit of Nature." Along with his colleague John Ray, and in opposition to "Atomick Theists" such as French philosopher René Descartes, More argued for the existence of a more than mechanical organizational presence in all plants and animals. He believed there was a force comprising "a substance incorporeal but without sense and animadversion, pervading the whole matter of the universe, and exercising a plastical power therein" (1925). The thought of the English naturalist and parson Gilbert White (1720–1793) is also often felt to contain animistic elements.

The English poet William Blake (1757–1827) famously coupled the belief that nature is inspirited with a reaction against a reductionist view of nature. His poem "Mock On" is a blunt rebuke of the atomism of Democritus, Rousseau, and Voltaire, while his poem "Earth's Answer" animates the angry Earth herself to reject "starry jealousy" and "the father of ancient men" (Christianity) and its inherent reductionism (1994). Expanding on his belief that life attached to more than what are typically regarded as living, Blake also asserted that "Everything that lives is holy."

This British animism made its way to America. Oscillating between transcendent and immanent concepts of spirit or divinity, U.S. naturalist and writer Henry David Thoreau (1817–1862) fought scientific reductionism even as he found himself embedded within it. Commenting on an encounter with phosphorescent wood while camping in 1857, Thoreau (1972) "rejoiced in that light as if it had been a fellow creature." For a moment Thoreau confesses to believing "that the woods were not tenantless, but chock-full of honest spirits as good as myself any day. . . ." Deeply attracted to Amerindian animistic traditions, Thoreau believed that their life with and beliefs about nature gave Indians a more accurate rendering of natural workings than that delivered by Western science.

Late in his life, American naturalist John Burroughs (1837–1921) came to view nature as "a huge organism pulsing with life, real and potential," and as "a living joy, something to love." Burroughs professed to seeking to overthrow the "physico-chemical explanation of life and consciousness," and to "transmute and spiritualize science."

Contemporary environmental philosophies such as deep ecology, or even scientific theories such as the Gaia hypothesis, are often regarded as sympathetic to animistic beliefs. Moreover, perhaps because of a desire to embrace a religious tradition consistent with one's worldview, animistic nature religions such as paganism are attracting many new adherents from among the ecologically minded.

Environmental Relevance of Animism

Given that values and a sense of right and wrong—or a system of ethics—flow from and are consistent with a specific worldview, an animistic worldview clearly has moral implications. The possession of soul or spirit is believed to endow its possessor with intrinsic or sacred value, or value in and of itself. The religion scholar Graham Harvey (1997, 133) suggests that the contemporary pagan "world view is one in which everything that lives deserves honor and rights not normally given to other-than-human life."

Contrasting this sense of value with that emanating from non-animistic traditions helps one to understand this position. Those systems that do not posit soul or spirit within natural entities and phenomena need either to find some other way to establish intrinsic value, or be viable only within a framework attributing greater or lesser amounts of instrumental, utilitarian, or use value. As environmental historian Donald Worster (1994, 29) put it, those belief systems "denying to non-human entities a soul or indwelling spirit . . . helped reduce man's perception of nature to the status of mechanical contrivance." Harvey (1997, 171) intimates the practical dimension of an animistic paganism. Pagans act "as if" the story they tell is true: as if their deities exist, as if magic works, and as if nature is worth celebrating. In doing so, they might find that the intuition or hypothesis fits; things do work this

way and life is enhanced by this approach. Acting as if everything is alive and related tends to lead away from an obsession with deities and towards an interest in a wider diversity of other-than-human persons.

The specific environmental actions that animists might engage in cannot necessarily be glimpsed through an understanding of their belief that nature is inspirited. Animistic environmental ethics, however, will at least begin with a broad assumption about what constitutes the category of "living things" and an enlarged sense of moral inclusiveness.

Michael P. Nelson

Further Reading

Albanese, C. L. (1990). *Nature religion in America: From the Algonkian Indians to the new age.* Chicago: University of Chicago Press.

Blake, W. (1994). *William Blake: A selection of his finest poems.* Oxford, UK: Oxford University Press.

Blake, W. (1972). Vala or the four zoas. In G. Keynes (Ed.). (1972). *Blake: Complete writings.* Oxford, UK: Oxford University Press. (Original work published 1795)

Burroughs, J. (1904–1913). *The writings of John Burroughs* (17 vols.). Boston: Riverby Edition.

Glacken, C. (1967). *Traces on the Rhodian shore: Nature and culture in western thought from ancient times to the end of the eighteenth century.* Berkelely: University of California Press.

Harvey, G. (1997). *Contemporary paganism: Listening people speaking earth.* New York: New York University Press.

Hayden, H. C. (1950). *The counter-renaissance.* New York: Charles Scribner's Sons.

More, H. (1925). *The philosophical writings of Henry More.* MacKinnon, F. (Ed.). New York: Oxford University Press.

Thoreau, H. D. (1972). *The Maine woods.* Moldenhauer, J. J. (Ed.). Princeton, NJ: Princeton University Press.

White, G. (1788). *The natural history of Selborne.* Allen, G. (Ed.). Hertfordshire, UK: Wadsworth Classics.

Worster, D. (1994). *Nature's economy: A history of ecological ideas* (2nd ed.). Cambridge, UK: Cambridge University Press.

Antarctica

Antarctica is the continent of superlatives. It is the coldest, windiest, highest, driest, and remotest place on

Earth. The most southerly among the seven continents and the fifth largest, Antarctica covers 14.2 million square kilometers—about the size of the United States and Mexico combined. The continent is circular in shape except for the Antarctic Peninsula, which juts out toward the tip of South America, and two major embayments, the Ross and Weddell Seas.

Glaciology and Geology

The massive Antarctic ice sheet overlays 98 percent of the continent and averages 2,000 meters in thickness. Only areas of the northern peninsula and the southern dry valleys are ice free. With a volume of about 30 billion cubic kilometers of water, the vast Antarctic polar ice cap contains 75 percent of the world's freshwater and 90 percent of its ice. The ice sheet is pliable and flows out like a huge glacier from a high ice-domed central plateau. This enormous ice sheet conceals the geology of the continent, which is divided into two unequal portions. The larger portion, eastern Antarctica, consists of one huge rock mass, whereas the smaller portion, western Antarctica, resembles an archipelago of mountainous islands fused together by ice. Several metallic minerals, such as chromium, copper, tin, gold, lead, zinc, and uranium, are found in the Transantarctic Mountains in the peninsula region, albeit in trace amounts. Larger deposits of iron and coal are present but not in commercially recoverable quantities. No petroleum or natural gas has been discovered on Antarctica or in its circumpolar continental shelf.

Climate

Antarctica's extreme climate makes the continent a vast crystal desert. The lowest temperature ever recorded, −58.3°C, was measured at Russia's Vostok Station in July 1983, although summer temperatures can climb to 15° C on the Antarctic Peninsula. Cold, dense air blowing down from the interior polar plateau generates turbulent winds up to 160 kilometers per hour and can create blizzard-like conditions. Still, little precipitation falls in Antarctica, an average of less than 50 millimeters each year. This produces an intriguing natural paradox: Antarctica's polar ice accounts for three-fourths of the world's freshwater resources, yet, the continent receives less precipitation than the Sahara Desert, making it the driest place on the planet.

Life Forms

The harsh climate in Antarctica produces a distinctive terrestrial ecosystem. There are eight hundred species of land vegetation, most of which are lichens. Mosses, molds, liverworts, yeasts, fungi, bacteria, and algae are also found. No herbs, shrubs, grasses, or trees exist on the continent. Animal life on Antarctica is even more scanty and primitive. No vertebrates are indigenous to the continent—there are no mammals, reptiles, or amphibians. Most animals are protozoans and arthropods, such as mites and fleas.

In southern polar seas, however, a remarkably rich biosystem thrives. Most significant among Antarctic marine life is krill, a small shrimp-like crustacean. Krill serves as the basic food for fish, whales, seals, and seabirds in the Antarctic. Among fish in southern circumpolar seas, Antarctic cod and the Pantagonian toothfish are most heavily exploited. Weddell, crabeater, leopard, and elephant seals inhabit Antarctic waters, as do porpoises, dolphins, whales, and squid. Land areas in Antarctica support huge numbers of seabirds, including albatrosses, petrels, skuas, cormorants, and terns. Most numerous are emperor and Adelie penguins, which account for 65 percent of the 200 million birds in the region.

History

Antarctica was long ignored, except by adventurers such as Robert F. Scott, Ernest Shackleton, Roald Amundsen, and Richard E. Byrd, who explored the region in the early twentieth century. Between 1908 and 1942, seven nations (Argentina, Australia, Chile, France, New Zealand, Norway, and the United Kingdom) decreed national sovereignty over pie-shaped sectors of the continent. None of these territorial claims, however, is recognized as lawful by any other state. During the International Geophysical Year (IGY) of 1957–1958, twelve nations (the seven claimants plus Belgium, Japan, South Africa, Soviet Union, and the United States) established more than fifty stations on the continent for cooperative scientific study. This IGY experience became the impetus for the special legal regime that today governs activities in the region.

Population and Government

No indigenous people inhabit Antarctica. Humans who live there are scientists and support personnel, although at the height of the scientific season they number fewer than five thousand. As many as fourteen thousand shipborne tourists now visit the continent annually, however. Antarctica's unique and largely pristine environment means that it can be used as a scientific laboratory platform for measuring and monitoring global processes, especially world climate change, ozone depletion, atmospheric current flow, and ocean current circulation. Science remains the principal endeavor on the continent. Such scientific research is administered by national programs and coordinated internationally through a special governance system.

The core legal agreement is the Antarctic Treaty, signed by the twelve IGY nations in 1959. Today forty-five nations are members. This treaty makes the continent a demilitarized zone preserved for scientific research. Although the treaty neither denies nor accepts the national claims to sovereignty in Antarctica, it does prohibit the establishment of military bases, conduct of military maneuvers, testing of any weapons (including nuclear weapons), or disposal of radioactive wastes in the area. The treaty strongly encourages freedom of scientific investigation and the exchange of scientific personnel between contracting parties.

Environmental concerns have driven the development of new international legal rules since the Antarctic Treaty went into force in 1961. A special measure was adopted in 1964 to foster conservation of plants and animal life on the continent. There followed in 1972 a convention to conserve and protect Antarctic seals, and in 1980 came a special agreement for the conservation of Antarctic marine living resources, specifically to control commercial harvests of krill and finfish in circumpolar seas. A treaty to regulate development of Antarctic mineral resources was negotiated during the 1980s but disintegrated in 1989, mainly because of political opposition from environmental groups. During the late 1980s and early 1990s anxiety arose among environmentalists over increasing pollution on the frozen continent. Although the threats of mineral development and increasing tourism to the Antarctic were aggravating, the real concern was the increasing amounts of garbage, sewage, and chemical wastes generated by scientists and support personnel in forty scientific stations. These wastes were not being disposed of by being returned to their original continents. Rather, they were being buried in landfills, stored in metal barrels, incinerated in the open air, or dumped into circumpolar waters. To foreclose the possibility of mineral development, but also to address these pollution concerns, a special environmental protection protocol to the Antarctic Treaty was agreed to in 1991. That protocol provides for comprehensive regulation over activities affecting the Antarctic environment. This protocol, which became binding on Antarctic Treaty governments in 1998, establishes principles for conducting human activities in the Antarctic and integrates various recommendations, codes of conduct, and guidelines into a coherent, obligatory legal whole. Significantly, the protocol bans mineral development, which includes drilling for oil and natural gas, onshore or offshore. Five annexes accompany the protocol. These set procedures for environmental-impact assessment, restate the need to conserve Antarctic fauna and flora, set standards for waste disposal and waste management, fix rules to prevent pollution from ships in Antarctic waters, and expand the Antarctic protected area system. Although this protocol and its annexes contribute much to environmental protection and resource conservation in the polar south, the treaty system will continue to evolve to deal with new Antarctic environmental concerns, such as increasing tourism, land-based pollution, and global warming.

Christopher C. Joyner

Further Reading

Berkman, P. A. (2001). *Science into policy: Global lessons from Antarctica*. New York: Academic Press.

Heacox, K. (1998). *Antarctica: The last continent*. Washington, DC: National Geographic Society.

Joyner, C. C. (1998). *Governing the frozen commons: The Antarctic regime and environmental protection*. Columbia: University of South Carolina Press.

McGonigal, D., Woodworth, L., & Hillary, E. (2001). *Antarctica and the Arctic: The complete encyclopedia*. Toronto, Canada: Firefly Books.

Appalachian Mountain Club

The Appalachian Mountain Club (AMC) is a conservation and recreation organization in the United States. The AMC's mission is to promote the protection, enjoyment, and wise use of mountains, rivers, and trails in the Northeast. The three pillars of the AMC are conservation, education, and recreation. The AMC hopes to increase recreational access to rivers and parks and recruits volunteers to build and maintain trails throughout the northeastern United States. It also manages a hut system for hikers.

In 1876, thirty-four outdoor enthusiasts met in Boston and formed the Appalachian Mountain Club as an organization devoted to exploration and scientific investigation of remote areas. Members mapped the White Mountains in New Hampshire and actively supported the Weeks Act, which was passed by Congress in 1911 and created White Mountain National Forest.

The AMC hut system began in 1888 when members proposed construction of huts modeled after European alpine huts as shelters for hikers. The first hut was built at Madison Spring, a day hike from the summit of New Hampshire's Mount Washington. Wooden bunks provided sleeping accommodations for a dozen guests, and the hut was a convenient base for scientific exploration of the mountains. AMC volunteers subsequently built a network of huts throughout the Appalachian region. The Appalachian Mountains stretch from Maine to Georgia and encompass the popular 3,400-kilometer Appalachian Trail.

Joseph B. Dodge (1898–1973), who ran the AMC hut system for thirty years beginning in 1928, oversaw a rise in the popularity of outdoor recreation among middle-class Americans who found themselves with more leisure time. Dodge helped organize the first ski race in Tuckerman Ravine in the White Mountains, and he encouraged the growth of downhill skiing in the area. By the 1940s, AMC huts were a regular destination for summer hikers in New England. In the 1950s, the huts often filled up beyond capacity with eager hikers.

As lightweight camping gear was being developed, the word *backpacker* was coined. Improved roads made access to the mountain trails easier for city dwellers. The AMC began to concentrate more on building and maintaining trails and educating the public about low-impact hiking practices. The AMC operation grew rapidly and became a leader in New England recreation. A hundred years after its inception, the AMC hut system had become so popular that a sophisticated reservation system was required to process the thousands of annual requests for lodging, education programs, and guided hikes.

The AMC's activism increased in the 1960s, when it supported the creation of Cape Cod National Seashore and passage of the 1964 Wilderness Act. In the 1970s, the AMC successfully helped block a four-lane interstate highway through New Hampshire's Franconia Notch. In the 1980s, the AMC argued for increased protection of New England's Northern Forest from logging and development. In the 1990s, the AMC achieved increases in funding that helped lead a national effort to permanently fund the Land and Water Conservation Fund (LWCF). The LWCF provides money to federal, state, and local governments to purchase land, water, and wetlands and conserve them for the benefit of the public.

The AMC advocacy campaigns focus on threatened forests and parks, air quality, river safety and stewardship, and trail preservation. Current priorities are the Northern Forest of New England; the Highland region of New York, New Jersey, Pennsylvania, and Connecticut; and the White Mountain National Forest. The AMC's conservation efforts strive to develop stewardship in the threatened mountain and river ecosystems of the Appalachian Mountain region.

In the 1990s, the AMC began to draw fire for its activism from elected officials in timber-dependent towns surrounding the White Mountains. Critics protested that the AMC was earning a profit from its huts on national forest lands and then using the profit to advocate protection of other public lands. The AMC was involved in efforts to place stricter environmental regulations on hydroelectric dams and to purchase large tracts of unspoiled land that were threatened by the logging industry. Opponents who supported the timber industry challenged the U.S. Forest Service's issuance of permits for the AMC's huts, which help bring millions of dollars in tourist spending to the White Mountains each year. The AMC retained its right to operate the huts but has faced criticism in recent years for attempting to expand the system into other areas of the Appalachian region.

The AMC continues to struggle with finding a balance between its recreation and conservation interests. The organization attempts to attract hikers while also minimizing their impact on the environment. The AMC provides waste management and safe water sources in heavily traveled sections of the forest. Use of all the facilities continues to increase, contributing to overcrowding in the backcountry. Overnight fees for the huts must cover the costs of septic and water systems, although 75 percent of the people who use the facilities are day hikers who do not pay fees.

The AMC now has over ninety-four thousand members and publishes *AMC Outdoors* magazine. The AMC maintains twelve local chapters in Maine, New Hampshire, Massachusetts, Connecticut, Rhode Island, New York, New Jersey, Pennsylvania, and Washington, D.C. The organization is supported by membership fees and donations.

Robin O'Sullivan

Further Reading

Hut and bothered. (1995, August). *Backpacker*, 13.

Shaw, R. (2000, March 18). Appalachian Mountain conservation group offers training, fun in wild. *Environmental News Network*. Sun Valley, Idaho: Knight Ridder/Tribune Business News.

Stewart, C., & Torrey, M. (Eds.). (1988). *A century of hospitality in high places*. Littleton, NH: Appalachian Mountain Club.

Trouble above the treeline. (1997, November/December). *E Magazine: The Environmental Magazine*, 24–25.

Appalachian Mountains

The Appalachian Mountains stretch from the coasts of Newfoundland and Labrador to northern Alabama, covering 1,600 miles and fifteen degrees of latitude. The basic contours of the range developed 500 million years ago, giving the Appalachians distinction as the continent's oldest mountains. With rainfall that often exceeds 70 inches per year, the Appalachians are home to the most extensive and diverse forests in eastern North America.

Indian people probably migrated into the Appalachians eight thousand years ago. The region's Indian population included the maritime Beothuk people of Newfoundland, the hunting and gathering Micmacs of northern New England, and the farming people of the eastern woodlands, notably the Iroquois confederacy in upstate New York and the Cherokees of the southern highlands. The natives altered the mountain environment in subtle, but important, ways. They used fire to clear agricultural fields, open the woods for travel, and encourage the growth of mast-bearing oaks and American chestnut.

Hernando de Soto was the first European to traverse the Appalachians in 1540. White settlement spread slowly, due in part to fierce resistance by native people. In the first decades of the nineteenth century, rampant land speculation, the discovery of gold in Georgia, and government removal of the southern Indians led to rapid population growth. More than subsistence farmers, white settlers sold surplus crops, cattle, and hogs to merchants in the emerging cities along the Atlantic coast. Such practices led to increased erosion, and Appalachian hardwood forests suffered damage from free-roaming livestock.

The most extensive and potentially devastating alterations in the Appalachian environment have occurred in the last 100 years. By 1910, a growing network of railroads and the burgeoning steel industry created an insatiable demand for coal. Steel companies in Pennsylvania and Ohio developed vast mining operations in Virginia, West Virginia, and Kentucky along the Allegheny and Cumberland Plateaus. The coal industry also took a toll on the region's forests as companies cut nearby trees for mine timber and construction.

Lumbermen, too, followed railroads into mountain forests. By the 1890s, the forests of Maine, New York, and Pennsylvania had been largely depleted, forcing the industry to move south. Between 1914 and 1918, lumber companies removed more timber from the southern Appalachians than in all the years before 1900. Rapid deforestation from lumbering and mining greatly increased erosion and flooding. Cutover regions became susceptible to devastating forest fires. Beginning in 1904, an exotic fungus introduced from Asia spread throughout the Appalachians, killing American chestnut trees by the thousands. The blight and salvage logging by lumber companies eventually reduced the once-majestic tree to little more than a forest shrub.

The mining and logging industries also created within Appalachia a colonial economy that supplied raw materials to urban centers and made local people dependent on urban capital.

In 1898, Gifford Pinchot and Carl Alwin Schenck established a forestry school on a 120,000-acre forested tract near Asheville, North Carolina and the southern Appalachians became the birthplace of modern American forestry. The nationwide growth of the conservation movement led to the setting aside of national forests throughout the range and by 1940, the United States Forest Service became the single largest landowner in southern Appalachia.

The establishment of Great Smoky Mountains National Park, the building of the Blue Ridge Parkway, and the creation of a host of state parks fostered a post-World War II boom in automobile travel. During the last half of the twentieth century, much of Appalachia began a pronounced shift from agriculture and extractive industries toward an economy based on tourism. The change brought new environmental problems. Air pollution and acid deposition—resulting from automobile traffic and emissions from coal-fired power plants in the Ohio Valley—currently threaten the remaining high elevation forests. Ozone levels in the

Great Smoky Mountains routinely exceed those in the nation's largest cities. State and federal governments have thus far been slow to respond and the Appalachian forest remains an environment at risk.

Timothy Silver

Further Reading

Brooks, M. (1965). *The Appalachians*. Boston: Houghton Mifflin.

Silver, T. (2003). *Mount Mitchell and the Black Mountains: An environmental history of the highest peaks in eastern America*. Chapel Hill: University of North Carolina Press.

Weidensaul, S. (1994). *Mountains of the heart: A natural history of the Appalachians*. Golden, CO: Fulcrum Publishing.

Williams, J. A. (2002). *Appalachia: A history*. Chapel Hill: University of North Carolina Press.

Aral Sea

In 1960, the Aral Sea was the fourth-largest inland body of water in the world. By 2000 it had all but disappeared. The Aral Sea in central Asia is a terminal sea, meaning that it has no outlets to the open ocean. The Aral Sea is located in the territories of the former Soviet Union. After the breakup of the Soviet Union into independent republics, the sea has fallen within the borders of two newly independent states, Kazakhstan and Uzbekistan. Water in central Asia is a scarce commodity, and the Aral Sea is sandwiched between two deserts, the Kara Kum and the Kyzyl Kum. It is filled primarily by water from the Aral Sea's basin by two major rivers, the Amu Dar'ya and the Syr Dar'ya, which begin in the Pamir Mountains and the Hindu Kush, respectively. The Amu Dar'ya (*dar'ya* means river in Kyrgyz, Uzbek, Turkmen, Uighur, and Persian) also forms a border between Afghanistan and Tajikistan. The river then flows through Turkmenistan and Uzbekistan through Karakalpakstan, a so-called autonomous region within Uzbekistan, ending its journey at the sea. The Syr Dar'ya starts in the Hindu Kush and flows through Kyrgyzstan, and then through Uzbekistan and Kazakhstan. It is half the size of the mighty Amu Dar'ya and flows into the northern part of the Aral Sea, into what is now known as the Little Aral.

Problems and Issues

For millennia, the water of these rivers has been used by major civilizations in and around the region for a variety of life-sustaining purposes. Today, the rivers are overused by the large and expanding populations in the region. Given the increasing demands for water all along the course of the rivers, very little water reaches the sea in amounts sufficient enough to replenish it. For all intents and purposes, the sea has dried out. It did so in a forty-year period, beginning about 1960. It was then that policy makers in the Soviet Union decided to sharply increase cotton production in central Asia. The Soviet Union was already producing cotton on about 4 million hectares of irrigated land. The goal of the Soviet leaders was to increase the area of desert to be irrigated to over 7 million hectares. Such an expansion would require a sharp increase in water diversions. Central Asian climate is perfect for cotton production: low rainfall and abundant sunshine. Water could be taken from the two rivers and put on the fertile but dry desert sands. Fertilizers and pesticides could be used to increase production and yields. The cotton was to be used by textile mills in other parts of the Soviet Union for domestic use and for export, as well as in the production of ammunitions and rocket fuel.

Too much water was being withdrawn from the rivers, to the extent that stream flow of the Syr Dar'ya failed to reach the sea by the late 1970s, and stream flow from the Amu Dar'ya failed to reach the sea by the late 1980s. Since then, water has reached the sea in some years, but not enough to balance out the demands of evaporation. In the meantime, the level of the sea, from evaporative losses, dropped more than 17 meters (from 53 meters above sea level to 36 meters). As a result, the sea became divided into a northern and a southern part, the Little Aral and the Big Aral, respectively. A dam was built to prevent a further decline in the level of the Little Aral. The level of the Big Aral continues to drop. It is deep on its western edge, whereas the eastern half is relatively shallow and is shrinking at a rapid rate.

As the seabed became exposed to the air currents, dust storms began to appear. In the mid-1970s, Soviet cosmonauts captured central Asian dust storms on film. Since then, these storms have increased in number and frequency. The dust is a mix of sand and toxic chemicals that had been returned to the rivers in drainage water from the irrigated fields. The dust in the air has had adverse affects on human health, as well as on croplands a few hundred kilometers downwind of the increasingly exposed desiccated seabeds. Human health in the region deteriorated sharply as a result of contaminated air and surface and ground waters. The health statistics for people in the region, especially the minority Karakalpak, were considerably worse than those in all other parts of the Soviet Union. The food supply too was contaminated. For example, the sea supported a thriving fishing industry with a fleet of fishing vessels and fish processing and canning plants. This industry employed about 60,000 people in its heyday (before 1970). Today, few fish remain in the sea, the salinity level of which now rivals that of the open ocean, a tenfold increase from 1960. As the sea continues to drop, it will eventually break up into about twelve saline ponds in the midst of two deserts.

Potential Solutions

The World Bank, among several other international governmental and nongovernmental organizations, has suggested various potential ways to improve the environmental quality of the region, especially water supply, as well as sorely needed human health conditions. In the mid-1990s, the proposal from the World Bank was to save the delta of the Amu Dar'ya and to sacrifice the sea, using it as a receptacle for heavily contaminated irrigation drainage water. Various proposals have been made to make the use of water more efficient in the basin, as well as to seek other crops to grow in place of water-consuming cotton.

It is easy to see that the cause of the demise of the Aral is primarily human. While it appears to have begun in 1960 as a result of decisions made in the Soviet Politburo, the story of its demise really started in 1908 when Russian geographer Berg suggested that the water in the sea was of little value to the Russian Empire, if it was left to evaporate without having been of use to human settlements. In 1927, another Soviet scientist, Tzinzerling, warned the government of what might happen to the sea if too much water was diverted from the two rivers to be used for irrigating desert lands. His calculations showed how the sea level would drop in tandem with increased stream flow diversions. At the height of the Cold War, the Soviet Union tended toward a view was that nature was to be exploited to the fullest extent. Bringing water to a desert was a normal thing to do. In the late 1970s, Soviet studies showed in a cost-benefit analysis that the value of a unit of water placed on the land was 100 times more valuable than if that same amount were to

be used to keep some commercial fish stocks alive. These studies show that there was an awareness that the fate of the sea was determined by Soviet politics, and that the politics was based on the perception that an unexploited Aral Sea was a worthless body of water. They did not take into account such externalities as the affect that the sea had on regional climate. Since the sea has declined, some studies have shown that in the region the summers have gotten hotter and the winters colder.

Soviet leaders called for plans to divert large volumes of water from the country's northward-flowing rivers away from the Arctic and toward the arid parts of Soviet Central Asia. The proposed redirection was very controversial within the Soviet Union and especially among Soviet geographers, many of whom opposed in their own way (given the totalitarian nature of the Soviet regime) the river flow reversal idea.

When Mikhail Gorbachev became the head of the Communist Party and the Soviet government, he pursued a policy of *glasnost* or openness. As a result of this openness, the world's environmentalists were able to talk to Soviet citizens directly about the situation in the Aral Sea basin. In the mid-1980s, the international community as well as Soviet citizens learned for the first time the sad state of the Aral Sea and the sad state of affairs in central Asia. When the Soviet Union broke up in December 1991, the central Asian republics (Turkmenistan, Uzbekistan, Tajikistan, and Kyrgyzstan) plus Kazakhstan found themselves without Russian Federation assistance in coping with or resolving what came to be known as the Aral crisis.

Despite words from the leaders of these newly independent countries in support of "saving the Aral Sea," their actions show little concern for returning the sea to any of its previous levels or of saving what remains. It appears that the inhabitants near the sea have given up hope that their political leaders will save it. Poems and plays have begun to appear that lament the disappearance of the sea. Culturally, the people are getting ready for an object of nature that will soon disappear. Meanwhile, the economies are trying to diversify in order to reduce dependence on cotton production for a variety of reasons, few of which are environmental: fertilizers and pesticides are costly, cotton sales have to compete in the international marketplace but the quality of the area's cotton is not the highest, soils have become increasingly salinized, leading to lower yields and eventual land abandonment, and so on. In order to restore the sea by allowing river water to flow into the sea, very large reductions in diversions would have to be made over several decades, crippling local and national economies. Afghanistan has been involved in political turmoil and in war since the overthrow of the Afghan king in the early 1970s. With the overthrow of the Taliban in late 2001, it is likely that the new Afghan regime will be in a position to request (maybe demand) a share of water from the Amu Dar'ya. While it is estimated that Afghan territory makes up 17 percent of the Aral basin, it uses about 1.5 cubic kilometers of water each year out of an estimated 70 cubic kilometers flowing in the Amu Dar'ya. It is likely that Afghanistan authorities will seek something on the order of 10 cubic kilometers from the river, which will put tremendous pressures on the downstream states, especially Uzbekistan and Karakalpakstan in its lowest reaches.

There are very few countries that highlight their environmental disasters by putting them on postage stamps for the world to see. The Soviet Union is one of those countries, producing stamps that commemorated a few of its human-induced disasters such as the nuclear accident at Chernobyl and the drying out of the Aral Sea.

The Aral Sea as it existed through much of the 1900s is dead, but the rivers and their deltas are not. The rivers still support life in the form of water resources for food, fiber, energy, and natural ecosystems. There appears to be the political will to save them. However, it will take resources from the international donor organizations to provide the way.

Michael H. Glantz

Further Reading

Boisson de Chazournes, L. (1998). Elements of a legal strategy for managing international watercourse: The Aral Sea Basin. In S. Salman (Ed.) *International Watercourses: Enhancing cooperation and managing conflict: Proceedings of a World Bank seminar, 141*, 65–76.

Glantz, M. H. (Ed.). (1999). *Creeping environmental problems and sustainable development in the Aral Sea Basin.* Cambridge, UK: Cambridge University Press.

Glantz, M. H. & R. Figueroa (1998). Does the Aral Sea merit world heritage status? *Global Environmental Change, 7*(4), 357–380.

Gleason, G. (1997). *The Central Asian states: Discovering independence.* Boulder, CO: Westview Press.

Micklin. P.P. (1992). *The water management crisis in Soviet Central Asia.* (No. 905). Pittsburgh, PA: University of Pittsburgh, Center for Russian and East European Studies.

Franklin Institute (2002, June). *Water, climate, and development issues in the Amudarya Basin.* Philadelphia, PA: Franklin Institute.

Glantz, M. H., & Vinogradov, S., 1996. Transboundary water resources in the former Soviet Union: Between conflict and cooperation. *Natural Resources Journal, 36*(2), 393–415.

Weinthal, E. (2002). *State making and environmental cooperation: Linking domestic and international politics in Central Asia.* Cambridge, MA: MIT Press.

Argentina

(2002 est. pop. 36 million)

Located in the southernmost part of South America, covering an area of 2.8 million square kilometers, Argentina is the eighth-largest country in the world. Taking into account that the country has territorial claims over the British-administered Falkland (Malvinas) Islands, the Georgias, Orcadas, and Sandwich Islands, and over part of Antarctica, the total area covered would be 3.8 million square kilometers. Although it became independent from Spain in 1816, the Argentinean state was consolidated only in the 1880s. After that, the country entered a phase of sustained economic development and became integrated into the world economy as a key exporter of foodstuffs (especially cereals and beef) and raw materials. Argentina received over 6 million European immigrants between 1870 and 1930, a period when the economy became one of the fastest growing in the world and enjoyed scientific and cultural development. It was during this time that Florentino Ameghino (1854–1911) made important contributions to evolutionary biology, zoology, geology, physical anthropology, and cultural history with his detailed study and classification of over nine thousand extinct animals. His titles include *Contribution to the Knowledge of Argentina's Fossil Mammals* (1880), *The Age of Man in the Rio de la Plata* (1881), *Phylogeny* (1884), and *Droughts and Floods in the Province of Buenos Aires* (1884).

Argentina has a wide climatic range, from subtropical humid in the northeast to arid in the Andean northwest, humid temperate in the fertile central Pampas, and sub-Antarctic to arid in Patagonia. The Andean region has some of the highest elevations on Earth, including Aconcagua Mountain at 6,960 meters. Also, around 30 percent of the Rio de la Plata river basin, the second largest in the continent, is located in Argentina, providing about 80 percent of the country's freshwater. The country has a 5,000-kilometer-long coastline on the Atlantic Ocean to the east-southeast. Its population is largely concentrated in urban centers, with the Buenos Aires metropolitan area containing about one-third of the total. The estimated population annual growth rate is 1.1 percent, and Argentina has an average life expectancy of 71.9 years.

The country shares the environmental problems affecting the subcontinent, especially deforestation, soil degradation, desertification, air and water pollution, and the consequent decline in biological diversity. According to recent reports by the United Nations Environment Programme, about 35 percent of pasture land has been lost because of overgrazing in the Pampas, and more than 50 percent of Argentinean mammals and birds are threatened with extinction. Extreme climatic events such as droughts and floods in recent decades have affected large areas of the country, especially the Rio de la Plata basin and the Pampas. Of more concern, environmental degradation is intertwined with the vicious cycle of increased poverty levels, social breakdown, and political instability that has affected the country since the late 1990s.

José Esteban Castro

Further Reading

Bethell, L. (Ed.). (1993). *The Cambridge history of Latin America: Argentina since independence.* Cambridge, UK: Cambridge University Press.

Instituto Nacional de Estadísticas y Censos. (2002). *Argentina.* Retrieved December 19, 2002, from http://www.indec.mecon.gov.ar

United Nations Environment Programme. (2000). *GEO Latin America and the Caribbean: Environment outlook 2000.* San José, Costa Rica: United Nations Environment Programme.

United Nations Environment Programme. (2001). *GEO environmental data and statistics for Latin America and the Caribbean.* San José, Costa Rica: United Nations Environment Programme-World Bank.

Aristotle

(384–322 BCE)
Greek philosopher

Among ancient Greek philosophers, Aristotle came closest to the scientific point of view, and some of his ideas foreshadowed ecology. Born in Stagira in northern Greece, he went to Athens at eighteen to study in Plato's school, the Academy. After Plato's death, Aristotle became the tutor of Alexander the Great, then founded his own school, the Lyceum, which had a library, a garden, and an arboretum. Specimens of animals and plants were sent there by scholars who accompanied Alexander to Egypt, Persia, and India. Charged with impiety, like Socrates seventy-six years earlier, Aristotle retreated to the city of Khalkis, where he died.

Aristotle believed the world to be an organic whole, of which creatures are parts. This meant that ecological thought, including questions of the relationships of living creatures to one another and the environment, is possible.

Aristotle noted what modern ecologists would call various species' "trophic niches" (what they prefer to eat) and the competition "between animals that dwell in the same localities and subsist on the same food" (Aristotle, trans. 1965, vol. 3, 232). For example, the lion and the civet will compete for meat, and the kite will steal food from the raven.

He recorded an inadvertent experiment in population ecology. A pregnant female mouse "was shut up . . . in a vessel containing millet, and after the lid was removed, upwards of 120 mice were found inside" (Aristotle, trans. 1965, vol. 2, 346–348). He connected that to a plague of mice he had observed. Foxes, ferrets, and pigs gorged themselves on the rodents but failed to thin their numbers until the mice disappeared after a rainstorm.

Other ecological relationships described by Aristotle include territoriality, competition and dominance within species, migration, and hibernation. He discussed symbiosis, including parasitism and commensalism (a relationship between two kinds of organisms in which one receives benefit from the other without harming or benefiting it), through examples including the pinna (mussel) and a crab, the "pinna-guard." "If the pinna be deprived of this pinna-guard, it soon dies" (Aristotle, trans. 1965, vol. 3, 168).

However, much of Aristotle's thought is uncongenial to ecology. His belief in immutable species prevented him from conceiving evolution. His scheme was hierarchical, unlike the image of the web found in modern ecological thought. Aristotle subordinated the animal, vegetable, and mineral kingdoms to humankind, finding the purpose of the lower orders in the service of the rational species, just as inferior people are natural slaves of the superior. He did not justify misuse of animals, but others derived from his teach-

Aristotle, Parts of Animals, Book I, Chapter 5

Having already treated of the celestial world, as far as our conjectures could reach, we proceed to treat of animals, without omitting, to the best of our ability, any member of the kingdom, however ignoble. For if some have no graces to charm the senses, yet even these, by disclosing to perception the artistry which designed them, give immense pleasure to all who can trace links of causation, and are inclined to philosophy. Indeed, it would be strange if representations of them were attractive, because they disclose the skill of the painter or sculptor, and the originals themselves were not more interesting, to all at any rate who have eyes to discern the reasons that determine their formation . . . we should venture on the study of every kind of animal without distaste; for each will reveal to us something natural and something beautiful. Absence of chance and conduciveness to an end are to be found in Nature's works in the highest degree, and the end of her generations and combinations is a form of the beautiful.

ing the corollary that animals have no intrinsic value and can be exploited.

Aristotle believed that the ideal city should be self-sufficient but that practical considerations make trade necessary. Population must be limited; a state should have no more citizens than can see and hear each other; of course, no public address systems then existed. All the territory belonging to the city should be visible from the height of its acropolis. The site should be healthful and have sufficient water. Temples should be on high places where their sacred groves help with the water supply. Inspectors would safeguard resources of the landscape. Conservation was thus part of Aristotle's idea of the good city, and his practical suggestions supported his environmental theory.

J. Donald Hughes

Further Reading

Aristotle. (trans. 1965). *History of Animals* (Vols. 1–3) (A. L. Peck, Trans.). Cambridge, MA: Harvard University Press.

French, R. (1994). *Ancient natural history*. London: Routledge.

Hughes, J. D. (2001). Athens: Mind and practice. In *An environmental history of the world: Humankind's changing role in the community of life* (pp. 59–66). London: Routledge.

Lloyd, G. E. R. (1991). *Methods and problems in Greek science*. Cambridge, UK: Cambridge University Press.

Matthen, M. (1997). The organic unity of Aristotle's world. In L. Westra & T. M. Robinson (Eds.). *The Greeks and the environment* (pp. 133–148). Lanham, MD: Rowan and Littlefield.

McKeon, R. (1941). *The basic works of Aristotle*. New York: Random House.

Preus, A. (1975). *Science and philosophy in Aristotle's biological works*. Hildesheim, Germany: Georg Olms.

Sarton, G. (1952). *A history of science: Ancient science through the golden age of Greece*. Cambridge, MA: Harvard University Press.

Army Corps of Engineers

North America's oldest and largest construction agency, the Army Corps of Engineers has evolved over two hundred years from a fort agency—a corps of engineers who planned and built fortification for the army—to a champion of river improvement to a guardian of wetlands with broad responsibilities for environmental protection. Founded by Congress in 1802, the Army Corps of Engineers planned coastal defenses, mapped the Cumberland Road into the Ohio Valley, and transformed the U.S. Military Academy into the nation's first engineering science school. The General Survey Act of 1824 and subsequent legislation made the corps and its topographical bureau into the construction arm of Congress with broad responsibilities for surveying canals and improving rivers and harbors. During the Civil War, corpsmen such as Robert E. Lee, George G. Meade, George B. McClellan, and Pierre G. Beauregard commanded clashing armies. Roughly between 1865 and 1900, as a free-spending Congress turned to rebuilding war-torn rivers and harbors, the corps pioneered iron framing, reinforced concrete, suction dredging, underwater explosives, funnel-like river jetties, and motorized ship locks that made rivers work like canals. One corps project dear to the heartland was an ambitious plan to open a deep-draft shipping canal through the mouth of the Mississippi River. In 1885 the Corps completed a remarkable gated dam at Davis Island below Pittsburgh—the first of the Ohio River system's forty-six locks and dams. Water quality became an army concern when Section 13 of the 1899 River and Harbors Act made the corps responsible for policing refuse dumping and pollution in navigable waters. Navigation work also led the corps into hydropower development at Wilson Dam and Powerhouse on the Tennessee River, completed in 1925.

Increasingly a civilian agency with a military command, the twentieth-century corps won fame for hydraulic projects known for their size. In 1914 corpsmen finished the Panama Canal after the French had abandoned the project. In 1928, after the nation's worst flood disaster, Congress approved Chief Engineer Edgar Jadwin's plan to rein in the Mississippi with a seven-state network of levees and drains. More than three thousand laborers joined the corps's tent city on the Columbia River for the construction of Bonneville Dam and Powerhouse, opened in 1937. Monumental construction elsewhere inspired corps work on the World War II Manhattan Project facilities, the NASA launch center at Cape Canaveral, the enormous U.S.-Canadian St. Lawrence Seaway, the 698-kilometer McClellan-Kerr Waterway along the Arkansas River, and the 1,183-kilometer Pick-Sloan barge channel that remade the Missouri River into a staircase of locks and dams.

Mississippi Showcase

Herculean attempts to harness the great Mississippi River showcase the corps's approach. Above St. Louis, the corps's twenty-nine locks and dams maintain a 2.7-meter depth for slack-water (water having no horizontal motion) navigation. Below the confluence of the Ohio River, where the swollen river curves through one of the world's most dangerous floodplains, the Mississippi River and Tributaries Project funnels high water through a human-made phalanx of floodways with storage reservoirs and more than 3,220 kilometers of levees. The corps's Bonnet Carre Spillway—credited with saving New Orleans eight times since 1936—diverts torrents via Lake Pontchartrain into the Gulf of Mexico. Another remarkable feature is Old River Control above Baton Rouge. Opened in 1962 and rebuilt after a barge nearly knocked out the centerpiece struc-

ture in 1973, the five-project dam-and-powerhouse complex keeps the Mississippi from jumping west through the cypress-tupelo swamps of Louisiana's Atchafalaya River.

Nationwide the corps has spent more than $100 billion on approximately 13,700 kilometers of levees, 600 locks and dams, 300 deep-draft ports, 75 hydropower projects, and 4,400 boat landings and recreation areas along 17,700 kilometers of navigable waterways. But the corps has always faced opposition. Critics have repeatedly damned the corps for pork-barrel proposals that overstate the benefits of river construction and understate the construction cost. One controversy centers on the Red River's aquatic staircase—a five-dam shipping project that has lured little traffic beyond the barges used for construction. Another embarrassment is the 322-kilometer Tenn-Tom waterway completed in 1984. A shortcut for Appalachian coal shipments, the project, according to critics, has generated barely one-tenth of the shipping that the corps predicted when applying to Congress for funds. The Taxpayers for Common Sense and the National Wildlife Federation—two lobbies usually at opposite ends of America's political spectrum—have recently allied to denounce twenty-five boondoggle projects. Topping the list is the corps's billion-dollar irrigation development plan for Arkansas's White River. Second is a deepwater tanker channel through Delaware Bay.

Corps Consequences

While tax conservatives hammer at the expense of river construction, greens fear pollution and habitat loss. Dikes and dams alter the seasonal floods that once replenished the wetlands. Dredging kills mussels and bottom-feeders. Lock pools fill with soil and cloud the reedy places that fish need for spawning grounds. In the century since engineers began clearing the Missouri River for steamboats, the braided channel has lost almost 60 percent of its presettlement water surface area and 120,000 hectares of sandbars and river woodlands. The Ohio River, meanwhile, has trapped enough nitrate-rich farm runoff to endanger Cincinnati's water supply. Ecologists blame the corps, in part, for $15 billion in damage when rivers in the Midwest breached levees during the summer of 1993, flooding out hundreds of towns. High water devastated Davenport, Iowa, and nearly topped over the 15-meter floodwall that precariously sheltered St. Louis. Corps streambank stabilization projects may have contributed to the disaster by compressing river corridors and destroying river grasslands that once absorbed seasonal floods.

Today the crisis of vanishing wetlands moves engineering beyond the dam-it, ditch-it tradition: In Wisconsin, for example, corps ecologists use dredged material to rebuild bird habitat; in Missouri engineers notch navigation dikes to flush silted backwater; in the Yazoo River basin, levee construction pits have been redesigned for fishing and recreation; in the sink below New Orleans, freshwater diversions may restore a buffer of marsh. Biologists and wildlife experts have been a rising voice in the corps since the 1977 Clean Water Act made the engineers defenders of wetlands. The corps's newest plan for saving the Florida Everglades calls for dismantling corps-built locks and levees. Likewise in Idaho and the Pacific Northwest, where hydro projects kill off the salmon migration, a corps study calls for the breeching of four of the agency's tallest dams. A beast and a benefactor, the corps plays Jekyll and Hyde in a nation suspended between the promise of industrialization and the yearning for greener places lost to the industrial age.

Todd Shallat

Further Reading

Morgan, A. (1971). *Dams and other disasters: A century of the Army Corps of Engineers in civil works.* Boston: P. Sargent.

National Research Council. (1999). *New directions in water resources planning for the U.S. Army Corps of Engineers.* Washington, DC: National Academy Press.

Reuss, M. (1988). *Designing the bayous: The control of water in the Atchafalaya Basin: 1800–1995.* Washington, DC: U.S. Government Printing Office.

Shallat, T. (1994). *Structures in the stream: Water, science, and the rise of the U.S. Army Corps of Engineers.* Austin: University of Texas Press.

Art *See* Environmental Narratives; Hudson River School; Landscape Architecture; Landscape Art, American; Landscape Art, Chinese; Landscape Art, European; Landscape Art, Japanese; Nature Photography; Nature Writing

Asbestos

Although most people think of asbestos as being either a rock or a mineral, this is incorrect. Asbestos is an industrial term of convenience used for several different minerals of metamorphic origin that share the property of occurring in fibrous form.

Asbestos has been used at least since the time of the ancient Romans. They valued it for the properties that have made it useful in modern societies: its resistance to fire and its fibrous nature, which allowed it to be spun or woven into cloth. Common uses in the ancient world included lamp wicks and wrapping for the dead during cremation so that the ashes might be easily recovered.

There are six different minerals that have been produced and sold as asbestos at one time or another: chrysotile ("white asbestos"), $Mg_3Si_2O_5(OH)_4$; crocidolite ("blue asbestos"), "$Na_2Fe_5[(OH)Si_4O_{11}]_2$; amosite ("brown asbestos", $MgFe_6[(OH)Si_4O_{11}]$; anthophyllite, $(MgFe)_7[(OH)Si_4O_{11}]_2$; tremolite, $Ca_2Mg_5Si_8O_{22}(OH)_2$; and actinolite $Ca_2(Mg, Fe)_5Si_8O_{22}(OH)_2$. All of these minerals except chrysotile are members of the amphibole family of minerals, as can be noted by the similarity of their formulas. Chrysotile is the fibrous form of serpentine, a rather common mineral, and is considerably softer than the amphibole varieties of asbestos. On the Mohs scale of mineral hardness, chrysotile averages about 4, softer than glass, while the amphibole varieties are harder than glass.

About the only properties that chrysotile and the other minerals share is that they are resistant to heat and they occur to varying degrees in a fibrous form. They differ in their fiber length, fiber strength, and fiber thickness, with the longer fibers being more in demand commercially. Chrysotile fibers tend to be longer than those of any of the amphibole varieties, and chrysotile production has accounted for about 95 percent of the world production of asbestos.

Geology of Asbestos

Deposits of these six minerals are mostly products of metamorphic alteration of mafic and ultramafic igneous rocks (rocks rich or very rich in iron and magnesium) during regional metamorphism. The most common host rock is peridotite, but some deposits occur in dunite. The fibrous minerals occur in two different ways, either as *cross fiber* or *slip fiber* veins. Cross fiber means that the mineral fibers grow across the veins, that is, perpendicular to the long dimension of the veins. In contrast, slip fibers are orientated parallel to the length of the veins. Slip fiber is preferred by industry because it can be used to produce a greater variety of products and therefore brings a higher price. An indefinite mixture of cross and slip fiber is known as mass, or mixed, fiber.

There are four specific geologic processes than have formed deposits of asbestos. Listed in order of decreasing commercial importance, they are: hydrothermal alteration of ultramafic rocks, ultramafic intrusions into older rocks, hydrothermal alteration of dolomitic limestones, and thermal metamorphism of banded ironstone.

Perhaps the world's best-known and historically most important deposit of chrysotile is located in southeastern Canada near Thetford, Quebec. Commercial quantities of chrysotile have been produced from several different mines located along an almost 160-kilometer-long belt extending from Quebec southward into the United States along the Appalachian Mountains. The modern era of asbestos production started with the discovery of chrysotile at Thetford in 1878. Asbestos has been continually produced from this district since then, and this area still accounts for the bulk of Canada's asbestos production. The district is noted both for the large quantity of chrysotile that occurs and for its high-quality slip fiber. The mineralization occurs in a suite of ultramafic rocks and sediments thought to have formed at a mid-ocean ridge but now found on land (ophiolite complex): peridotite, dunite, and pyroxenite. The host rocks have all undergone varying degrees of a hydrothermal alteration process called serpentinization. (Complete serpentinization is less desirable than partial serpentinization because it tends to produce lower-quality cross fiber.) Intrusions of granite and shearing are also common throughout the length of the belt.

The Bazhenovo district in the southern Ural Mountains of Russia is probably the second-best-known asbestos-producing area in the world. As at Thetford, chrysotile mineralization is developed in ultramafic rocks that have undergone partial serpentinization.

Major Uses and Producers

Asbestos has been used in a large variety of products. Worldwide, but not in the United States, its most important use is in the manufacture of molded asbestos-cement products in several forms including pipes, boards, and flat sheets. In the United States, 62 percent of the asbestos used in 2001 was in roofing materials, 22 percent in various types of gaskets, and 12 percent in various friction products such as brake pads and clutch facings.

Production of asbestos has been declining rapidly since the late 1970s, particularly in the United States. Total world production in 2001, consisting almost totally of chrysotile, was approximately 1.9 million metric tons, which is 50 percent less than world production just ten years earlier. The two biggest producers are Russia (approximately 40 percent of world production in 2001) and Canada (approximately 18 percent). The bulk of the production from these countries comes from the previously described Bazhenovo and Thetford districts. Other important asbestos producers include China (13 percent of world production), Kazakhstan (12 percent), and Brazil (11 percent). The only mine still operating in the United States is located in San Benito County, California, and it produced only 5,000 metric tons in 2001, all of it chrysotile.

Asbestos Controversy

In only a little more than a decade, the public's view of asbestos completely turned around from considering it to be a mineral with marvelous and useful qualities to fear and even hysteria at the possibility of exposure. It became, and to a considerable extent remains, the most feared contaminant, a fact that is directly responsible for the decline in asbestos production described in the previous section. Each year, billions of dollars are spent in the United States on asbestos remediation, probably more than is spent on any other single contaminant. It is classified as a carcinogenic material by the U.S. Department of Health and Human Services, and its use is regulated by both the Environmental Protection Agency (EPA) and the Occupational Safety and Health Administration (OSHA). Many people who are familiar with the asbestos controversy think that much of what happened was an overreaction.

Concern about the health effects of factory air heavily laden with asbestos began in the late nineteenth century, but no governmental action occurred until 1931, when Great Britain enacted the first workplace regulations of asbestos. By the 1960s, several diseases related to asbestos exposure were recognized, including asbestosis (a scarring of lung tissues) and several forms of cancer.

Asbestos regulation began in the United States in 1971 when the newly formed EPA listed it as a hazardous air pollutant. Additional regulations were added in following years. This was in response to contemporary medical studies of workers exposed over many years to very high concentrations of asbestos-laden dust, which showed that the workers had a high incidence of asbestos-related diseases. The mass media sensationalized such studies but usually did not mention that extrapolating results from severe occupational exposure to the general population might not be justified. The publicity caused a near panic among the general public. People began to demand that asbestos be removed from schools, and attorneys began to win large damage awards based on the argument that since scientists had been unable to determine a safe level of exposure, there was no safe level. The phrase "one fiber can kill" was widely repeated by the media and became engraved on the public's consciousness. Eventually, the EPA moved to completely ban all forms of asbestos. A Federal appeals court partially overturned this ban in 1991, and currently the use of asbestos is illegal only in certain paper products, flooring felt, and rollboard. Based on the results of studies showing that the air in a building containing undisturbed and undamaged asbestos is similar to outdoor air, the EPA currently advises owners that the material is often not dangerous and removal may be unnecessary.

Most laws regulating asbestos enacted in other industrialized nations treat chrysotile differently from the amphibole forms because of scientific evidence indicating that chrysotile may not be dangerous at all, or at least less dangerous than the amphibole forms. The difference is due to the different physical properties of chrysotile, compared to amphibole, and the body's response. Amphibole fibers are not soluble in the body, and so large amounts can accumulate over time, but chrysotile tends to dissolve and therefore can be excreted. The immune system also seems to be better able to eliminate chrysotile from the body compared to amphibole.

Just how concerned should people be about asbestos? In assessing this, there are three important factors to consider: the concentration of asbestos in the air, the length of exposure, and the type of asbestos. It is important to realize that a latency period exists, so effects from a severe exposure may not show up for twenty to thirty years. Remember that asbestos is a natural substance that is present in unpolluted air. The generally accepted estimate is that a person breathing normal outdoor air will inhale approximately four thousand asbestos fibers each day, or about 100 million fibers over the course of a lifetime. Exposure to chrysotile does seem to be less worrisome than exposure to amphibole forms, which is good news because it accounted for 95 percent of past use and is the only form of asbestos currently being produced.

The debate is not yet resolved over whether chrysotile should be treated differently from other forms of asbestos and just what criteria define safe levels of exposure. It can be stated with confidence that there is no scientific basis for concluding that any exposure, no matter what the level, is dangerous. Perhaps most encouraging are studies such as the one by the independent Health Effect Institute, which calculated that the risk of dying from nonexceptional exposure to chrysotile is about five deaths per 100,000 people. This is in the same range as the risk of being killed by a lightning strike (estimated three deaths per 100,000).

Gene D. Robinson

Further Reading

Alleman, J. E., & Mossman, B. T. (1997). Asbestos revisited. *Scientific American, 277*(1), 70–75.

Craig, J. R., Vaughan, D. J., & Skinner, B. J. (2001). *Resources of the earth: Origin, use, and environmental impact.* Upper Saddle River, NJ: Pearson Education, Prentice Hall.

Harben, P. W., & Bates, R. L. (1990). *Industrial minerals: Geology and world deposits.* London: Industrial Minerals Division, Metal Bulletin.

Health Effect Institute. (1991). *Asbestos in public and commercial buildings: A literature review and synthesis of current knowledge.* Cambridge, MA: Health Effects Institute.

Ross, H. C. W., Ross, M, & Frondel, C. (1988). *Asbestos and other fibrous minerals.* New York: Oxford University Press.

Ross, H. C. W., & Ross, M. (1994). Minerals and cancer. *Geotimes, 39*(1), 13–15

Asia, Central

Central Asia consists of the republics of Turkmenistan, Kazakhstan, Uzbekistan, Kyrgyzstan, and Tajikistan, all formerly a part of the USSR and, before that, of the Russian empire. Some experts include Afghanistan, Mongolia, Tibet, and Sinkiang (Chinese Turkestan) as part of central Asia. The total area of the five republics is 2,483,998 square kilometers, about half that of the continental United States, divided as follows: Kazakhstan, 1,687,825 square kilometers; Turkmenistan, 303,414 square kilometers; Uzbekistan, 280,413 square kilometers; Kyrgyzstan, 123,392 square kilometers; and Tajikistan, 88,954 square kilometers.

Since the Neolithic period, central Asia has been home to concentrated areas of urbanites and agriculturalists in a land of pastoralists. Agriculture and cities clustered around oases and the floodplains of rivers (the Amu Dar'ya, Syr Dar'ya, Murghab, Tejen, and Zaravshan). Irrigated orchards formed the basis for wealthy sedentary empires such as that of Khorezm (Khwarizm), centered in the cities of Urgench, Bukhara, and Samarqand during the ninth to thirteenth centuries. Despite the destruction of the urban, agricultural, and political infrastructure by the Mongols in the thirteenth century, the local economy slowly recovered, and by the fifteenth century the Turkic conqueror Timur (Tamerlane), who claimed descent from the Mongol conqueror Genghis Khan, made Samarqand the capital of his empire. With the breakup of Timur's empire, the region fragmented into smaller khanates and emirates.

Russian military conquest of the region began in the 1860s, spurred by the notion of converting central Asia into a center for cotton growing. Because supplies of cotton from the southern states of the United States were not reaching Europe because of the Civil War, the czarist regime saw an opportunity not only to meet its own needs for cotton but also to become a competitive exporter.

By 1889 the conquest was complete. However, the extensive network of canals and small-scale agriculture was not affected. Farmers practiced water-conserving practices, including crop rotation, and were attentive to proper drainage of their irrigated fields. Village leaders oversaw the decisions of the *mirab*, or water master, who held responsibility for maintenance of the canal and for the equitable distribution of water.

Beginning in the 1930s, however, Russian leader Joseph Stalin's collectivization and industrialization campaigns transformed the face of the region. Small-scale traditional systems of irrigation were completely destroyed as independent farms were dissolved and merged into gigantic collective and state farms (*kolkhozy* and *sovkhozy*). With construction of the Great Fergana Canal in 1939 and the irrigation of the Hungry Steppe of Uzbekistan (between Tashkent and Samarqand), Chechens, Crimean Tatars, and ethnic Korean rice and orchard farmers, deported from the Caucasus and the Soviet Far East, were resettled in those areas.

On the steppes and semidesert pasturages that had dominated northern and central Kazakhstan, herders were ordered to pool their flocks into new livestock collective farms. Brutal implementation and resistance led to the deaths of about 1.5 million Kazakhs, 25 percent of the population. Nomadic herding as a cultural and economic form of livelihood was brought to an end.

Migration to the Steppe

On the newly emptied portions of the northern Kazakh steppe, ethnic Germans were deported during World War II to create an agricultural base, joining an appreciable number of Great Russians (members of the dominant Slavic-speaking ethnic group of Russia) and Ukrainians who had migrated to the region since its conquest. In 1954 Nikita Khrushchev, Soviet Communist Party first secretary, announced a "Virgin Lands Campaign" to turn the steppe into a grain factory. Despite initial successes, however, inappropriate tilling practices and the absence of crop rotation led to enormous soil erosion and serious duststorms (in 1963, 1965, 1968, and 1974).

In the eastern, hillier region of Kazakhstan, Stalin's revolution was industrial, with the creation of gigantic mining, refining, and manufacturing centers at Ust-Kamenogorsk, Ekibastuz, and Semipalatinsk (Semei). Air pollution, although having decreased since 1991 because of the general economic decline in the region, is still serious, as is water pollution. In 1994 an estimated 4.55 million metric tons of pollutants were discharged into the atmosphere over Kazakhstan alone. The Irtysh River, which flows north from eastern Kazakhstan, is heavily polluted by industrial effluents.

One of the grimmest environmental legacies is that of the extensive nuclear testing that was conducted in Kazakhstan from 1949 to 1989. Testing was ended partly in response to the emergence of a powerful grassroots antinuclear movement in Kazakhstan led by author Olzhas Suleimenov. An alliance, Nevada-Semipalatinsk, was formed with those exposed to nuclear tests in the U.S. West during the 1940s and 1950s. Because most of the victims in Kazakhstan were rural ethnic Kazakhs, and the tests were ordered from Moscow, the movement acquired an anticolonial tenor. Over 450 explosions, including 119 above ground, left expanses in western Kazakhstan (Kapustin Yar) and eastern Kazakhstan (near Semipalatinsk) disaster areas. Hundreds of thousands of people were exposed to dangerous levels of radiation in those areas, and the incidence of birth defects and cancers is many times higher than the average for the rest of the country or the former Soviet Union. Due to the tests, 19 million hectares of land have become unusable as well. Extensive areas in southern and central Kyrgyzstan, where uranium was mined, are also heavily polluted by mining residue.

By 1900 the oilfields in the southern Caspian Sea near Baku, Azerbaijan, made the Russian empire among the world's leaders in oil production. In recent decades, the discovery of oil and natural gas in the shallow, northern, Kazakh portion of the Caspian Sea and its coastal region (especially the Tengiz fields) has led to intensive exploitation by multinational corporations (such as Chevron). The water level in the Caspian Sea has risen notably since 1970, and protective dikes have failed to prevent breaching of well caps and other facilities. As a consequence, petroleum products in the northeastern Caspian Sea are thirty times permissible levels, and the soil cover of the coastal region has been polluted. The sturgeon catch, which amounted to 27,000 metric tons in 1985, was a mere 1,890 metric tons in 1994, although part of this decline is also a consequence of the hydropower dams on the Volga River and its tributaries and the resultant inability of sturgeon to reach their spawning streams.

Caspian Sea Mining

Another attempt to mine the Caspian Sea also led to environmental problems. In 1980 the Kara-Bogaz Gol, a shallow gulf of the Caspian, was dammed off to allow its water to evaporate. This was to allow the mining of mineral salts on the floor of the gulf. However, windstorms deposited great quantities of the salts on irrigated fields in Turkmenistan, and in 1984 authorities ordered the dam to be blown up and the gulf reflooded.

Arguably the most important environmental issue in central Asia is the availability of water. On the eve of World War II, in 1939, plans for a vast expansion of cotton growing were accelerated. Russian czarist authorities had eyed the region for this purpose in the 1860s, and the goal of cotton self-sufficiency for the USSR was posed early on by Russian Communist leader Vladimir Lenin in 1918. However, it was under Stalin that the regime undertook to harness the Amu Dar'ya and Syr Dar'ya Rivers to irrigate the cotton fields. In 1950 planning commenced for the Karakum Canal in Turkmenistan. By the 1970s central Asia could no longer feed itself because cotton replaced food crops against the backdrop of rapid population increase (the population of the central Asian republics more than doubled between 1959 and 1987). Moreover, the combination of decades of huge withdrawals of water from the river systems of the region for cotton irrigation, overwatering, indiscriminate application of fertilizers and pesticides, and poor drainage management has resulted in one of the most ruinous regional environmental catastrophes of modern history.

East of the Caspian Sea lies the Aral Sea, which only half a century ago was the fourth-largest lake in the world, with an area of 66,000 square kilometers, a volume of 1,061 cubic kilometers, and a salinity level of 10 parts per 1,000. But the Aral Sea is rapidly drying up, like Lobnor (China) and Lake Chad (Africa). By 1994 the area of the lake, now divided into a "Large Sea" and a "Small Sea," was only 31,938 square kilometers, and in 1998 it was only 28,687 square kilometers with a volume of 181 cubic kilometers, less than one-fifth of its former size. During that period salinity in the lake has quadrupled, from 10 grams per liter to 45, and the fish catch, which once amounted to 43,430 metric tons (1960), is now zero. Because the central Asian republics have been unable to shift their agricultural economies away from cotton and rice to more traditional orchard crops, the Aral Sea is certain to disappear within the next two decades.

Before cotton agribusiness, the combined inflow of the Amu and Syr Dar'ya Rivers into the Aral Sea was 52 cubic kilometers annually, with precipitation adding another 6 cubic kilometers. By 1980 inflow had effectively dwindled to nothing, whereas the evaporation rate was 57.7 cubic kilometers annually. The Karakum Canal in Turkmenistan proved particularly wasteful. Although water withdrawn from the Amu Dar'ya River to the canal increased by 93 percent from 1960 to 1968, the amount of irrigated land increased by only 10 percent. Seepage losses in the unlined canal averaged 5 cubic kilometers annually, fully one-half of the water withdrawn from the river.

Other geographical changes included the vast expansion of the human-made Lake Sarykamysh, which is a 4,830-square-kilometer drainage basin for the discharge of drainage water from the cotton fields, and the disappearance of the *tugai* (dense floodplain) habitat along the rivers and in their deltas. The *tugai*, with its reedy tall grasses, tamarisks, poplars, willows, and oleasters, once formed a rich habitat for a large variety of fishes, birds, and mammals. Only 38 of 170 indigenous species of mammals are still present. Like the Amu Dar'ya tiger, they, too, face extinction as halophytic (growing in salty soil) vegetation takes over and then itself disappears, yielding to the cracked, crusty *takyr* desert. *Takyer* deserts are desert areas of low relief, often composed of thick clay deposits that serve as catchment areas for precipitation.

Consequences of Desiccation

The most serious consequences of the desiccation of the Aral Sea have been those connected with human health. Because 41,000 square kilometers of seabed are now exposed, an estimated 35 to 135 million metric tons of sands laden with salts, pesticides, fertilizers, and other chemicals are blown across fields and human settlements each year. This has been exacerbated by an increasing frequency of days with duststorms, thought to be related to a regional climate change caused by the shrinking of the lake. The surrounding Karakalpak Autonomous Republic (in Uzbekistan), whose livelihood was once dependent on Aral Sea fishing, has been most severely affected. Infant mortality rates in the most exposed districts, such as Bogataus, are shockingly high; 111 per 1,000 die before their first birthday. According to the Asian Development Bank, deficient water quality is responsible for the widespread poor health in the region. Eighty percent of women and children suffer from anemia, and the incidence of viral hepatitis, tuberculosis, cancer, and typhoid fever is increasing.

Another epidemiological problem concerns the stocks of biological weapons that Soviet authorities tested and stored on Vozrozhdenie Island, once in the middle of the Aral Sea. These weapons were created to spread highly dangerous diseases such as Ebola virus, plague, anthrax, smallpox, and Marburg fever. If the Aral Sea continues to dry up at its current rate, the 3 kilometers of water still separating the island from the mainland will be converted into a land bridge within ten years. There will then be a danger of wildlife transporting and disseminating the pathogens to the mainland, which could in an extreme case launch a worldwide pandemic.

Cotton for Export

Although self-sufficiency in cotton was a goal of Soviet leaders, they also believed that cotton would be an enduring source of export income. However, cotton prices on the world market fell from $2.27 per kilogram to $1.38 between 1960 and 1985. Ironically, despite the expansion in irrigation, cotton production, although doubling in central Asia from 1960 to 1980, began to decrease thereafter as more and more irrigated land was damaged by salinization. Exports declined from 272 million linear meters in 1965 to 163 million meters in 1985, whereas cotton imports actually rose from 95 million meters to 419 million meters during that same period.

During the 1970s increasing recognition of the water crisis led central Asian Communist Party leaders to call for a transfer of water from northward-flowing Siberian rivers such as the Irtysh and Ob' to their region. The "Sibaral" canal, dubbed "the project of the century," was first discussed by the Aral-Caspian Expedition of the USSR Academy of Sciences in 1950. It would have stretched 2,200 kilometers across the Turgai uplands, terminating north of the Aral Sea. This project had entered the planning stage along with a parallel project to divert northward-flowing European rivers and waters southward to irrigate Ukraine, Kalmykia, and the northern Caucasus and to halt a feared further drop in the level of the Caspian Sea. But the projects elicited a crescendo of opposition from scientists, writers, nature protection advocates, and Russian nationalists who objected to exporting "Russian" water to central Asia. In 1986 all work on the diversion projects was cancelled, Russian leader Mikhail Gorbachev's first major signal to the educated public that he sought to be viewed as a reformer.

Protected Land

While central Asia was a part of the Soviet Union, environmental protection chiefly took the form of *zapovedniki*, nature reserves set aside for the protection of unique, significant, or endangered ecological communities. Chief among the people who conducted important ecological field investigations and promoted nature protection were Abram L'vovich Brodskii, Daniil Nikolaevich Kashkarov, and Nina Trofimovna Nechaeva.

The nature reserves, by republic, are:

Kazakhstan: 8 *zapovedniki* (Aksu-dzhabagly, Almaty, Barsa-Kelmes, Borovoe, Kurgaldzhin, Markakol', Naurzum, and Ust-Iurt) with 860,000 hectares, plus 60 *zakazniki* (a protected territory established for a limited time) with 5,200,000 hectares, 1 national park with 50,500 hectares, 30 breeding sanctuaries with 40,000 hectares, and 24 natural monuments with 6,000 hectares.

Kyrgyzstan: 5 *zapovedniki* (Besh Aral, Issyk Kul, Sary Chelek, Naryn, and Karakol Janyryk) with 241,150 hectares, plus 14 *zakazniki* with 264,600 hectares and 2 national parks with 13,900 hectares.

Tajikistan: 3 *zapovedniki* (Dashti-jum, Romit, and Tigro-vaia Balka) with 86,000 hectares, plus 14 *zakazniki* with 830,000 hectares and 2 national parks with 1.5 million hectares.

Turkmenistan: 8 *zapovedniki* (Amu-Dar'ya, Badkhyz, Gasan-Kuli, Kaplankyr, Kopetdagskii, Krasnovod-skii, Repetek, and Siunt-Khasardagskii) with 819,000 hectares, plus 13 *zakazniki* with 815,000 hectares and 2 natural monuments with 2,100 hectares.

Uzbekistan: 8 *zapovedniki* (Badai-Tugai, Chatkal, Gissar, Kitab, Kyzlkum, Nuratin, Surkhand—including the former Aral-Paigambar, Zaamin, and Zaraf-shan) with 178,000 hectares, plus 2 national parks with 598,750 hectares, 2 natural monuments with 3,400 hectares, and 1 breeding reserve with 5,145 hectares.

Enforcement in all of the republics, however, is not effective because of inadequate funding. Additionally, Turkmenistan has a government policy of selling licenses to hunt rare animals in reserves, and in Tajikistan an ongoing civil war has taken a heavy toll on wildlife. Over the past century, despite the establishment of *zapovedniki* and *zakazniki*, species loss in central Asia has been significant, including the Amur tiger and the leopard. Currently, of large mammals, the cheetah and the urial, mouflon, Marco Polo, and other mountain sheep and goats are endangered. Finally, reacclimatization of native animals into the wild from zoos, breeding farms, and *zapovedniki*, as well as acclimatization of exotic species were pursued during the Stalin and subsequent regimes. European bison *(Bison bonasus b.)* were implanted in the Sary Chelek *zapovednik* in Kyrgyzstan; chinchilla *(Chinchilla lanigera Mol.)* in the Pamirs of Tajikistan; nutria *(Myocastor coypus Mol.)* and muskrat *(Ondatra ondatra)* along the Ili, Amu Dar'ya, and Syr Dar'ya Rivers; American mink *(Mustela vison Brisson)* along the Naryn River valley in Kyrgyzstan; marten *(Martes martes L.)* in the Kyrgyz Tien Shan range, and a host of other species. Reacclimatized fauna include the *saiga (Saiga tatarica L.)* (large Eurasian steppe antelope), released near Almaty; *dzheiran (Gasella subgutturosa Gueld.)* (central Asian desert gazelle) on Barsa Kelmes Island *zapovednik* in the Aral Sea; *arkhar* sheep *(Ovis ammon Blith.)* in northern Kazakhstan; and the *kulan*, or Asiatic wild ass (onager) *(Equus hemionus Pall.)*, removed from the Barsa Kelmes *zapovednik* beginning in 1981 to other parts of central Asia because of the increased salinity of the Aral Sea and the degradation of the habitat on the island.

Central Asia continues to be rich in species diversity. Of the 489 species of birds, 179 of mammals, 104 of fish, 49 of reptiles, 12 of amphibians, and 3 of cyclostomata (a group of primitive fish with circular mouths adapted for sucking, including lamprey and the hagfish) that live in Kazakhstan, 113 species of birds and 48 species of mammals are hunted, whereas 129 species and subspecies of vertebrates are considered endangered. In less-developed Kyrgyzstan, 13 of 84 mammalian species, 3 of 25 reptile species, 33 of 296 bird species, 2 of 65 fish species, and 28 of 4,500 plant species are endangered.

Douglas R. Weiner

See also Aral Sea, Camels, Deserts, Pastoralism

Further Reading

Bissell, T. (2002, April). Eternal winter: Lessons of the Aral Sea disaster. *Harper's Magazine*, 41–56.

Chesnokov, N. I. (1989). *Dikie zhivotnye meniaiut adresa* [Wild Animals Change Their Addresses]. Moscow: Mysl.

Daly, J. C. K. (2000, November 8). Global implications of Aral Sea desiccation. *Central Asia—Caucasus Analyst.*

EcoStan News, Retrieved May 28, 2003, from http://www.ecostan.org

Feshbach, M., & Friendly, A., Jr. (1992). *Ecocide in the USSR: Health and nature under siege.* New York: Basic Books.

Glantz, M. H. (Ed.). (1999). *Creeping environmental problems and sustainable development in the Aral Sea basin.* Cambridge, UK: Cambridge University Press.

Grote, U. (Ed.). (1997). *Central Asian environments in transition.* Manila, Philippines: Asian Development Bank.

Micklin, P. P. (Ed.). (1992). The Aral crisis. *Post-Soviet Geography, 5.*

Pryde, P. R. (1991). *Environmental management in the Soviet Union.* Cambridge, UK: Cambridge University Press.

Weinthal, E. (2002). *State making and environmental cooperation: Linking domestic and international politics in central Asia.* Cambridge, MA: MIT Press.

Asia, Central—Ancient

Central Asia is part of the belt of arid lands reaching from northwest Africa, in the far west of the Eurasian landmass, to Manchuria in the far east. The aridity of this entire region forced the communities that lived there to construct distinctive lifeways, of which the most important involved irrigation agriculture and various forms of pastoralism. Historians use the term, "central Asia," in various ways. In this article, "central Asia" refers to the lands at the heart of the Eurasian landmass. These include the former Soviet republics of Turkmenistan, Uzbekistan, Kyrgyzstan, Tajikistan, and Kazakhstan, as well as the eastern parts of Chinese Xinjiang, and parts of northern Afghanistan (ancient Bactria) and northern Iran (ancient Khorasan). For some purposes, it also makes sense to include some of the steppe lands of southeast Russia and southern Siberia.

Modern historiography has largely neglected these lands, but the collapse of the former Soviet Union and the increasing strategic significance of the region, have broadened scholarly interest in central Asia and its past. It has become apparent that the history of Eurasia cannot be fully understood without understanding the distinctive societies that flourished at the center of the continent.

Geography and History

Most of central Asia falls within the huge zone of flatlands that dominates the northern half of Eurasia. Nevertheless, at the southern and southeastern fringes of central Asia there is a rim of mountains. These were squeezed up over many millions of years by the collision of the Indian tectonic plate with the Siberian and Chinese plates. The chain of mountains extends from the Kopet Dag, along the borders between northeast Iran and Turkmenistan, along the borders between Afghanistan and Uzbekistan, and into the Pamirs. Then it splits, the Tian Shan mountains running north and the Kunlun mountains running south of the Tarim basin in Xinjiang. Just north of the mountain ranges, much of central Asia is arid. Indeed, central Asia includes some of the world's harshest deserts, from the Kyzyl Kum and Kara-Kum in Turkmenistan and Uzbekistan to the Taklimakan desert in the Tarim basin. These are an extension of the chain of drylands that reaches from the Atlantic shores of the western Sahara to the Pacific region of Manchuria. Aridity explains why central Asia has never been a region of dense populations. But the feature that had the greatest influence on the region's history has been the combination of mountains and desert, for, flowing down from the mountains, and renewed each year by mountain snowmelt, are many rivers. These water the arid plains, cre-

ating small, but fertile oases. The major rivers of central Asia include the Amu Dar'ya and Syr Dar'ya (the ancient Oxus and Jaxartes), and the Tarim River in Xinjiang.

As a result of these features, central Asian societies combined two distinct elements: pastoralists who lived in the more arid regions, and oasis dwellers who lived near the region's major rivers. Much of the history of central Asia is shaped by relations between these two very different, but intertwined worlds. The mobility of pastoralists has complemented the wealth and commercial sophistication of cities throughout central Asian history. This is why long-distance commerce, funded by wealthy urban merchants, and protected by pastoralists, was to become a dominant feature of the region's history.

Another factor that explains the historical importance of central Asia is its centrality within Eurasia. This centrality, and the importance of commerce to the region's populations, help explain why central Asia had contacts with much of the rest of Eurasia, from Siberia to the Baltic, the Mediterranean, Mesopotamia, the Indian subcontinent, and China, over several thousand years. These myriad contacts explain why the cultures of central Asia have been so diverse, and so open to influences from other parts of Eurasia.

The First Human Settlements

The first human-like inhabitants of central Asia may have been Neanderthals. It is known that during the last Ice Age, Neanderthals sometimes lived along the southern fringes of central Asia. At Teshik-Tash, on the upper Amu Dar'ya River, Soviet archaeologists found the remains of a Neanderthal encampment, which contained what is probably the tomb of a young boy. It is decorated with the skull of a mountain goat. However, Neanderthals did not penetrate much further north, which is hardly surprising because during the ice ages, the steppelands to the north were extremely cold, plant foods were scarce, and to survive you needed to be a superb hunter, exploiting the vast herds of deer, bison, and mammoth that grazed the ice age steppes. Not until modern humans appeared in the region, from about 40,000 years ago, was it possible to settle the ice-age steppes of northern Eurasia in larger numbers. To survive, the earliest migrants needed sophisticated hunting technologies, control of fire, and warm clothes.

The first agricultural settlements appeared in central Asia about 8,000 years ago (6000 BCE). This was within two thousand years of the earliest appearance of agriculture in Mesopotamia. Indeed, it may be that agriculture was brought to central Asia by migrants from Mesopotamia, for some of the archaeological features of these settlements, including wall paintings and small figurines, are reminiscent of finds in Mesopotamia. The earliest villages in central Asia set the pattern for the agrarian history of the entire region, for they lay along rivers leading from the mountains to the south into the arid flatlands to the north. The communities of the so-called Jeitun culture lie between the foothills of the Kopet Dag mountains and the Kara-Kum desert, in southern Turkmenistan. Its farmers used simple forms of irrigation. The thawing of winter ice up in the mountains provided water for simple irrigation ditches just when the water was most needed. Similar settlements also appeared within the Tarim basin in Xinjiang, at the edge of the Taklimakan desert. Over several thousand years, farming communities multiplied in southern central Asia. Some appeared higher up in the mountains, where irrigation was less important; some appeared further out into the flatlands, where irrigation was more important. However, the aridity of regions far from the major rivers limited the number of farming communities and the size of farming populations.

In the arid regions, away from the villages, lived populations of hunters and foragers. Foragers and farmers probably exchanged goods, in a pattern that was to become typical of much of central Asia. Then, from perhaps 4000 BCE, lifeways also began to change in the non-agricultural regions. The British archaeologist Andrew Sherratt has pointed out the momentous significance of a series of technological innovations that occurred in different parts of Eurasia, between 5000 and 3000 BCE. They included horse-riding, the use of animal fibers for textiles, and the use of animal milk and blood as foodstuffs. Sherratt has described these innovations as the "Secondary Products Revolution." The Secondary Products Revolution allowed communities with domesticated animals to exploit their livestock more efficiently, until eventually, there emerged the distinctive lifeway known as pastoralism, which is based almost entirely on the exploitation of domesticated livestock. Keeping large herds of animals can be done most efficiently if they can graze over large areas, so early pastoralists were usually more nomadic than farmers. From about 4000 BCE, we begin to get evidence of communities of pastoralists living nomadic lives in the western steppes of Eurasia, north of the Black Sea and the Caspian Sea. Their remains show up mainly in burials, rather than in settlements, which is typical of nomadic communities. Livestock provided much of their food, their clothing, their tents, and their textile fibers; horses lugged their carts and belongings through the steppe and carried their soldiers into battle. For pastoralists of the Eurasian steppes, horses were particularly important, though camels and sheep were also valued.

By 3000 BCE, pastoralist communities were also living in the arid flatlands of central Asia, particularly near the major rivers. They probably spoke early forms of Indo-European languages. Some may have migrated through the steppes for much of the year, while others migrated to summer pastures in the mountains and descended to the plains in winter. The number of pastoralists was never large, but they were extremely mobile, and probably exchanged goods, genes, languages, and technologies (including that of pastoralism) over large areas.

Central Asia Emerges as the Hub of Eurasia-Wide Exchange Networks

From about 2000 BCE, central Asia emergds as the hub of the largest land-based network of exchanges ever to exist in the premodern world. Directly or indirectly, this network linked all parts of Eurasia. It included three main elements. First, there were regions of agrarian civilization—areas of dense settlement, with irrigation agriculture, cities, and states. Agrarian civilizations had already appeared in Mesopotamia and Egypt, in the far north of the Indian subcontinent, and in northern China. Second, in central Asia itself, there had also appeared a number of cities. Archaeologists describe this early cluster of central Asian cities as the Oxus civilization. Finally, pastoralist communities existed throughout the Eurasian steppelands, and their mobility, combined with their interest in trade goods from nearby cities, ensured that they would exchange goods over large areas.

These three elements—regions of dense settlement in Outer Eurasia, a region of urban settlement at the center of the continent, and pastoralist networks exchanging goods over large areas—help explain why central Asia began to play so strategic a role in Eurasian history. By 2000 BCE, visitors to the cities of the Oxus civilization could have found goods from all major regions of Eurasia: from Mesopotamia, from India, from

China, from the steppes, and even from the forested lands of Siberia.

For some time, though, these links were tenuous and easily broken. In the second millennium BCE, pastoralist communities in central Asia became more sedentary and less mobile. Many lived in villages, though livestock rearing remained the basis of their economy, and they continued to trade with the nearby cities of central Asia. Warmer, wetter climates may have caused this shift away from mobile pastoralism. Some of central Asia's pastoralist peoples also embarked on large migrations, which took them into Mesopotamia, Persia, and north India. They brought with them the religious and cultural traditions of central Asia as well as its Indo-European languages, so their migrations permanently transformed the ethnic, religious, and linguistic maps of these regions.

In the first millennium BCE, pastoralists became more mobile again, perhaps because climates became cooler and drier, and less suitable for farming. Pastoralists also began to use improved types of horse harness, as well as the small compound bows that were to make them such effective cavalry soldiers. The beautiful and animated animal art that we associate with the Scythians also belongs to this era. In the steppes, there appeared powerful regional rulers, judging by the splendor of some steppe tombs, such as the eighth-century tomb of Arzhan, in Tuva, at the border between Mongolia, Kazakhstan, and Russia. The classic descriptions of pastoralist lifeways late in the first millennium BCE come from the Greek writer, Herodotus (who wrote about the Scythians living north of the Black Sea), and from the Chinese historian, Sima Qian, who wrote about the Xiongnu, who lived in what is today Mongolia.

In central Asia, there was a new phase of urbanization, as cities spread deeper in the steppes, along the Amu Dar'ya and Syr Dar'ya Rivers, and in the region of Khorezm, near the Aral Sea. For the first time, too, neighboring agrarian empires began to take an interest in central Asia. In the middle of the sixth century BCE, Cyrus II, the founder of the Achaemenid dynasty (ruled 559–520), invaded central Asia. He faced formidable armies of pastoralists, and eventually he met his death there. His successors reestablished a loose Achaemenid hegemony over much of southern central Asia. In the fourth century, between 329 and 327 BCE, Alexander of Macedon invaded central Asia. He left behind several Greek colonies, some of which eventually established powerful states in the lands between central Asia and northern India. In the second century

BCE, a people called the Xiongnu created the first great pastoralist empire, in Mongolia. As Achaemenid and Greek power weakened, the Xiongnu began to exact tributes from the cities of central Asia. Late in the second century, the great Chinese emperor Han Wudi (147–87 BCE) sent an army to central Asia in a bid to outflank his enemies, the Xiongnu. This was the first of several Chinese bids for control of central Asia.

Increasing outside interest in the region stimulated trade through central Asia and helped create the multiple trade routes that are now called the Silk Roads. Passing through central Asia, silks traveled to Persia and on to the Mediterranean, while Roman glassware and ceramics traveled in the opposite direction. Religions also traveled the Silk Roads. Early in the first millennium, Buddhism traveled with merchant caravans to central Asia and eventually to China. Later in the millennium, Manichaeism spread from Persia through central Asia to China; and Nestorian Christianity spread along the same route. From the seventh century, Islam began to travel the Silk Roads. From the eighth century CE, it would become the dominant religion of central Asia, and a major shaping force of modern central Asian cultures.

The wealth of these flourishing trade routes made it possible to establish the first central Asian empires. The Kusana empire, created by a dynasty of pastoralist origin, the Yueji, flourished from the second to the fourth centuries CE. It was followed by the Hephthalite empire (fifth and sixth centuries). Like the leaders of later states in the region, the rulers of these dynasties were usually based in the region's cities, though their armies and sometimes their leaders often came from nearby pastoralist communities. Their wealth and power came partly from the commercial wealth that flowed through the region, while the immense variety of their commercial contacts explains why their cultural and religious life was so varied. Under the Kusana, for example, coins depicted rulers as pastoralists, but gave them titles derived from Indian or Greek traditions; Kusana coins also mentioned gods whose names would have been as familiar in the Mediterranean as in north India, and some that would also have been familiar in China. The earliest Kusana writing used the Greek alphabet, while Kusana artworks include Greek statuary, Chinese lacquers, Indian carved ivory, and Egyptian glassware. By the time Islam entered central Asia, the region was already the focus point for exchanges that linked all of Eurasia into a single huge network of exchanges, the largest and most variegated in the entire world.

David Christian

Further Reading

Barfield, T. J. (1993). *The nomadic alternative*. Englewood Cliffs, NJ: Prentice Hall.

Barthold, W. (1977). *Turkestan down to the Mongol invasion* (4th ed., trans. T. Minorsky). London: E.J.W. Gibb Memorial Trust.

Christian, D. (1998). *A history of Russia, Central Asia and Mongolia from prehistory to the present: Vol. I. Inner Eurasia from prehistory to the Mongol Empire*. Oxford, UK: Blackwell.

Christian, D. (2000). Silk roads or steppe roads? The silk roads in world history. *Journal of World History 11*(1), 1–26.

Christian, D. (2000). The rise of pastoralism in Eurasia: c. 4,000 BC to c. 1,000 BC. *Microsoft Encarta*. Redmond, WA: Microsoft Corporation.

Dani, A.H., & Masson, V. (Eds.). (1992). *History of the civilizations of Central Asia: Vol. 1. The dawn of civilization: Earliest times to 700 BC*. Paris: UNESCO.

Frye, R. N. (1996). *The heritage of Central Asia: From antiquity to the Turkish expansion*. Princeton, NJ: Markus Wiener Publishers.

Golden, P. (1998). *Nomads and sedentary societies in medieval Eurasia*. Washington, DC: The American Historical Association.

Hiebert, F. T. (1994). *Origins of the Bronze Age oasis civilization in Central Asia*. Cambridge, MA: Peabody Museum.

Harmatta, J. (Ed.). (1994). *History of the civilizations of Central Asia: Vol. 2. The development of sedentary and nomadic civilizations: 700 BC to AD 250*. Paris: UNESCO.

Khazanov, A. M. (1994). *Nomads and the outside world*. Madison: University of Wisconsin Press.

Soucek, S. (2000). *A history of inner Asia*. Cambridge, UK: Cambridge University Press.

Asia, Southeast—Ancient

The present countries of Myanmar, Thailand, Malaysia, Indonesia, East Timor, Singapore, Laos, Vietnam, Cambodia, and Philippines form Southeast Asia. Geographically, Southeast Asia stretches from the eastern Himalayas to the archipelago that exists southeast of continental Asia. The region lies between 28° N and 10° S of the equator. Part of the region is on mainland Asia while the rest comprises islands that are usually small, but include larger ones such as Sumatra, Borneo, and New Guinea. Mainland Southeast Asia has a tropical climate with seasonal monsoons during the rainy season. Insular Southeast Asia mostly lies in the equatorial climate zone that is hot, humid, and wet; though there are no monsoons per se in this region, there are distinct rainy and dry seasons.

The region is interspersed with river valleys, lakes, mountains, islands, and seacoasts, and such a varied environment has given rise a distinctive way of life. As the region is hot and humid, it is ideal for wet rice cultivation. This has resulted in high population concentrations in the plains and river valleys where the rice is cultivated. This population concentration, together with the organization required to cultivate rice and build irrigation systems, led to the emergence of social stratification. The easily navigated seas of the region promoted contacts with the external world, leading to extensive trade and the introduction of cultures and religions from outside. Spice production in the area was important for trade. The cumulative result of trade was creation of wealth that led to the emergence of large kingdoms.

People

The early population belonged to numerous tribes with diverse cultures and languages. The spiritual beliefs were mostly animistic and incorporated totemism. The most important occupations were related to agriculture, fishing, hunting, animal husbandry, and collection of forest products for the market. Forest products were an important aspect of the economy because of the presence of rich rainforests in the region.

The earliest known human habitation in what is now Malaysia has been found at the Niah caves of Sarawak (on the island of Borneo) that date back to 35,000 BCE. By 2500 BCE, the Proto-Malays migrated from China to this area. Later another ethnic group emerged, the Deutero-Malays, who had mastered iron-working technology. In northern Thailand, the earliest known settlement is the Ban-Chiang that dates back to 3,000 BCE. In Burma, the earliest known people were the Mons who came from central Asia and settled along the Thanlwin and Sittoung rivers during the pre-Christian era. Later, the Pyu came from Tibet, and then the Bamars who settled along the Irrawaddy.

Polity

The Indo-Chinese peninsula was known as the Suvarna-bhumi and Suvarna-dvipa, and was a place known for spice, gold, and mineral production. The main kingdom in Annam (present-day Vietnam) was called Champa, the ruins of which are found at Trakieu. The people were accordingly called Cham. In what is now Indonesia, the influence of Hinduism led to the formation of empires like the Sri-Wijaya, Melayu, Mataram, and Majapahit. Sumatra was the center of the Sri-Wijaya kingdom (in what is modern-day Palembang), founded in the fourth century CE. An inscription from Ligor in the Malay Peninsula dating from 775 CE refers to the power of Sri-Wijaya extending all the way to the Bay of Bandon. Burma saw the emergence of the Pyu kingdoms (100 BCE–840 CE) and the Bagan kingdom (849–1287 CE). The political origins of the Thai people can be traced back to China to about 650 BCE. Later its southern area formed part of Cambodia. Its main development was the formation of Sukhothai kingdom during 1238 CE in central Thailand. It was later eclipsed by the kingdom of Ayutthaya.

Religion and Monuments

The art and architecture of Southeast Asia were greatly affected by Hindu and Buddhist influences from India. In Myanmar (Burma), excavations at Prome, Pegu, and Pagan have revealed significant ancient artifacts. Prome is the site of old stupas and temples, and inscriptions there appear in both Sanskrit and the ancient Pyu language. During the early Christian era, Mahayana Buddhism was introduced in Burma. (Later on, the influence of Hinayana Buddhism gained ground. Today, it is the Hinayana form that is prevalent in Burma [Myanmar]). Ancient Burmese temples and pagodas were influenced by the sculpture, terracotta, and architecture of the Bengal region and the alluvial plains of northern India. The finest example of Burmese architecture is the Ananda temple, a Buddhist temple built by the king Kyanzittha.

In Java, these temples go by the name *candi*, and most of them are built according to a uniform pattern. Near Borobudur, there is a Shiva temple named Candi Banon. The Lara-Jongrang is group of Brahman temples. Of the Buddhist temples of Java, the most magnificent is the temple of Borobudur, constructed 750–850 CE under the patronage of Sailendra rulers.

Cambodia is home to the famous Vishnu temple of Angkor Wat. There are also many temple complexes at Angkor Thom, the capital city built by Jaya Varman VII. There is an important group of temples at Champa, namely Dong Duong, Po-nagar, and Myson, the last two being Shivite.

Conclusions

Ancient Southeast Asian civilizations were influenced by physical and environmental factors. Settlement concentrated on river plains and in delta regions, as these were advantageous for wet-rice cultivation and trade. Myanmar had the Irrawady River; in Thailand the Chao Phraya River was a focus of settlement; and the Mekong River fed the Indo-China region. At the same time, mountainous areas formed places of habitation for local indigenous tribes. There was a symbiotic relationship between patterns of settlement, subsistence, material culture, trade, religion, and environmental factors.

Anup Mukherjee

Further Reading

Higham, C. (2001). *The civilization of Angkor*. Berkeley: University of California Press.

Majumdar, R.C. (Ed.). (1989). *The history and culture of Indian people* (Vol. 3–5). Bombay, India: Bhartiya Vidya Bhavan.

Tarling, N. (Ed.). (1999). *The Cambridge history of Southeast Asia: Volume 1, from early times to c.1500*. Cambridge, UK: Cambridge University Press.

Weightman, B. A. (2002). *Dragons and tigers: A geography of south, east and Southeast Asia*. New York: John Wiley.

Asia, Southeast—Insular

Insular Southeast Asia includes over 20,000 islands, encompassing the Indonesian and Philippine archipelagoes, Malaysia, Brunei, and Singapore. Characterized by incredible cultural and biological diversity, the region contains numerous coral reefs and rainforests. Particularly noteworthy are the marine and terrestrial environments found within the Togean–Banggai Corridor and the Sulawesi Moist Forests in Indonesia, Palawan Province in the Philippines, Milne Bay Province in Papua New Guinea, and Sundaland—an ecological "hot spot" encompassing 17,000 islands in Indonesia, Malaysia, Singapore, Brunei, and southern Thailand. There are many endemic plants and animals within this transboundary area, 60 percent of which are found nowhere else. Deforestation is the most serious environmental problem in the region, and the populations of several large mammals—including the orangutan in Sumatra and the two rhinoceros species found in Sundaland—have been reduced to critical levels by habitat destruction and poaching.

Indonesia

Containing some of the world's richest ecosystems and 17 percent of all known species, Indonesia is the world's largest and most expansive archipelagic state. Although its land area is less than 2 percent of the Earth's total, its 13,500 islands include major parts of Sundaland, the entire Wallacea "hot spot," and almost half the New Guinea Tropical Wilderness Area. However, the country has been plagued by persistent ethnic and religious violence, indiscriminate killings committed by the military and allied militias, and in October 2002, the bombing and murder of almost 200 tourists and local residents in Bali. The violence has exacerbated the ecological crisis, and the collapse of tourism and trade is expected to worsen the situation.

Positive steps have been taken, however, to counter the continued loss of Indonesia's ecological diversity. On the island of Sulawesi, the World Wildlife Fund is working to conserve a multitude of native mammals, birds, and plants in Dumoga National Park and in the Central Sulawesi Lakes ecoregion (an important fishing area for local people and a stopover for migratory birds). Unlike much of Indonesia, in Sulawesi the rainforests remain relatively intact. Over half the island is still covered with lowland and montane rainforests that provide habitats for the moor and black-crested macaques—two rare types of monkeys—as well as the Celebes Rousette and the Sulawesi barebacked fruit bats, the Sulawesi hornbill, and hundreds of butterfly species.

Another environmental organization, Conservation International (CI), is helping local authorities identify threatened marine and terrestrial environments in the New Guinea Tropical Wilderness Area and Mamberamo Lake Basin Region, and in the archipelagos of the Togean-Banggai Corridor in central Sulawesi. Employing "rapid assessment" surveys of forty–five sites covering approximately 6,000 square kilometers in the Raja Ampat Islands in West Papua province, in 2001 and 2002 CI and The Nature Conservancy identified four new species of fish, 450 hard corals (over half the world total), 600 mollusks, and over 1,100 species of reef fish, including the most fish (283) seen in a single dive. As a result, the final report of the Center for Applied Biodiversity Science described the islands as "the world's richest in terms of its amazing diversity of marine habitats [and] biodiversity" (Center for Applied Biodiversity Science 2002, 2).

Community-based education has been initiated in Gunung Gede National Park, in cooperation with the national park authority and local non-governmental organizations (NGOs), to provide hands-on training and employment for indigenous communities, and to raise awareness of natural resource management issues in Indonesia. CI is also seeking to establish protected areas that extend beyond national borders, and to facilitate information sharing and decision making among the various management agencies in the region. Other tasks include co-management of the Leuser ecosystem under the sponsorship of the European Union, promotion of intraregional ecotourism attractions to fund conservation projects, and the creation of long-term management practices and standards to limit further damage to wilderness areas.

Philippines

The 7,000 islands of the Republic of the Philippines comprise the world's second-largest archipelago and northernmost extension of insular Southeast Asia. The expected doubling of the population within 28 years has increased concern about the impact of mining in ecologically sensitive areas, land clearing for plantations, agriculture, fuel, and hydroelectric dams, and increased urbanization. The Philippines is one of the five most biologically diverse countries on Earth, having nearly 6,000 endemic plant, 555 terrestrial vertebrate, and over 70 percent of known coral species. However, less than 7 percent of the original cloud and rainforests remain as 2,700 square kilometers are logged each year (a rate equal to almost one percent of the 31 million hectares annually deforested worldwide) to satisfy the demands of 70 million people. As a result, 123 species of animals and plants are now critically endangered, including the Philippine eagle and freshwater crocodile, giant clam, green sea turtle, and golden-crowned flying fox. The coral reefs of the Philippines are the most threatened on Earth, due to urban pollution, overfishing, and climate change.

To prevent further degradation, CI is working with local governments and communities in the Sierra Madre and Palawan Biodiversity Corridors to undertake socioeconomic and biological research that encourages community awareness and participation in resource management. In the Palawan corridor, CI works with local communities and NGOs to strengthen environmental management, and to promote tourism development that will benefit indigenous people and help protect coral reefs and coastal ecosystems. CI also recently convened a conservation priority setting workshop with the Philippine Department of Environ-

Iban Swidden Horticulture

Like many indigenous peoples of Southeast Asia, the Iban of Sarawak practiced swidden, or slash-and-burn horticulture. The following ethnographic account by Derek Freeman details the advantage of exploiting virgin land for gardens.

Despite the fact that Iban have been living in the valley of the Sut for something like fifty years, virgin jungle (kampong) was still being felled at Rumah Nyala in 1949–50, and I was fortunate in being able to witness many different types of land usage. Before beginning our survey there are several preliminary points which should be made. Iban methods of land usage are complex.

There is however, one general feature of especial significance: a marked tendency (particularly when working virgin forest) to farm land for two years in succession, before letting it revert to secondary jungle. [...]

Every land usage cycle begins with the felling of virgin jungle. During the past hundred years, many thousands of acres of primeval forest in the Rejang basin have been felled by Iban axes, and in the Baleh (and other similar pioneer areas) this onslaught is still going on. From the historical survey (presented in Part II of this report) of the Iban occupation of the Batang Rejang and its tributary rivers and streams, it emerges clearly that the Iban are a virile and resourceful people with an insatiable appetite for virgin land. The motives which prompt this appetite are many. Foremost is the knowledge that, given good weather, two and more crops of exceptional abundance may be harvested from an umai kampong. In their prayers (sampi) at the time of pemanggol, the Iban ask for:

"Land that is fat, fat in deep layers,

Luxuriant land, land that is fruitful,

Soil soft and fecund, land richly fertile;"

and they know that this is most likely to be found in tracts of kampong, on untouched slopes and terraces, where the humus of centuries lies thickly. The labour expended on an umai kampong is heavy, but it holds high promise of a surplus—a surplus that leads to property and prestige and all the other things most desired by Iban hearts.

Author: Freeman, Derek. (1955). *Iban Agriculture: A Report on the Shifting Cultivation of Hill Rice by the Iban of Sarawak.* London: Her Majesty's Stationery Office, pp. 114–115.

---

ment and Natural Resources to mobilize government agencies and scientists to help conserve lands surrounding the Northern Sierra Madre Natural Park, the largest protected area in the Philippines. Totaling 359,000 hectares, this park includes almost 10 percent of the country's remaining primary rainforest.

Singapore

Situated at the tip of the Malay Peninsula, the city-state of Singapore consists of the main island and 60 smaller ones, with a total land area of approximately 646 square kilometers. Bordered by peninsular Malaysia to the north, Sabah and Sarawak to the east, and Indonesia to the south, Singapore was originally covered by tropical rainforests. Today, fewer than 300 hectares remain in designated nature reserves. Managed by the National Parks Department, the reserves enclose remnants of both mangrove and dipterocarp forests. Mammals include the flying lemur, squirrels (slender and plantain), and the long-tailed macaque, while the only large mammal remaining in the wild is the wild pig. There are 300 species of migratory birds. Reptiles include the reticulated python (the world's longest snake), the Malayan water monitor, and a variety of lizards and turtles. Some native fish are still found in reservoirs and streams, and the island is home to over 350 species of butterflies and other insects.

In addition to wildlife and forest conservation, perhaps the biggest challenge confronting Singapore today is large-scale land reclamation. Because of Singapore's small size, authorities have resorted to reclamation since the 1960s to satisfy the need to construct new housing for a growing urban population. However, the environmental consequences of such activities have led the government more recently to evaluate alternative approaches to urban planning and sustainable community development.

Malaysia

In neighboring Malaysia, which includes northwest Borneo and the southern section of the Malay Peninsula, the biggest ecological concern is also deforestation. Though 75 percent of the country is forested and Malaysians remain primarily rural dwellers, there are increasing pressures to accommodate industrial development and urbanization. A number of environmental groups are now assisting the national government to design more appropriate policies. Among the more active are the Australian-based Mineral Policy Institute and the Nautilus Institute for Security and Sustainability.

Greg Ringer

Further Reading

Barker, R., & Herdt, R. (1985). *The rice economy of Asia.* Washington, DC: Resources for the Future.

Bautista, G. M. (1994). *Natural resources, economic development, and the state: The Philippine experience.* Singapore: Institute of Southeast Asian Studies.

Center for Applied Biodiversity Science (2002). *Marine RAP survey of the Raja Ampat islands, Papua Province, Indonesia.* Washington, DC: Conservation International.

Dauvergne, P. (1999, July 15). Environmental crisis. *Far Eastern Economic Review, 162*(24), 27.

Hirsch, P., & Warren, C. (1998). *The politics of environment in Southeast Asia: Resources and environment.* London & New York: Routledge.

Leinbach, T. R., & Ulack, R. (Eds.). (2000). *Southeast Asia: Diversity and development.* Upper Saddle River, NJ: Prentice Hall.

Mineral Policy Institute, http://www.hydra.org.au/mpi

Mrazek, R. (2000). *The memory of trade: Modernity's entanglements on an eastern Indonesian island.* Durham, NC: Duke University Press.

Nautilus Institute for Security and Sustainability, www.nautilus.org

Osborne, M. (1990). *Southeast Asia: An illustrated introductory history.* Canberra, Australia: Allen & Unwin.

SarDesai, D. R. (1997). *Southeast Asia, past and present.* 4th ed. Boulder, CO: Westview Press.

Southeast Asia START Regional Centre, Chulanlongkorn University, Thailand, www.start.or.th

Van Meijl, T., & von Benda-Beckmann, F. (Eds.). (1999). *Property rights and economic development: Land and natural resources in Southeast Asia and Oceania.* London & New York: K. Paul International.

Asia, Southeast—Mainland

Mainland Southeast Asia, composed of Cambodia, Malaysia, Myanmar (Burma), Thailand, Vietnam, Laos, and southern China, is one of the most culturally dynamic regions in the world. It is also among the more physiographically and biologically diverse regions of the world, with a number of major mountain ranges and rivers—including the Chao Phraya in Thailand, the Irrawaddy in Myanmar, the Red River in Vietnam, and the Mekong River, which connects the six countries of the Greater Mekong Subregion (Myanmar, Thailand, Laos, Cambodia, Vietnam, and Yunnan Province in southwest China).

The countries of mainland Southeast Asia share a history of colonialism and armed conflict, as well as rapid economic growth and urban development in the 1980s. However, the subsequent global economic crisis, which first appeared in Thailand in 1997, has triggered both challenges and opportunities as earnings decline throughout the region. Although the phenomenal growth experienced by Southeast Asia in the 1990s played a formative role in reuniting and empowering countries long fragmented by genocide and war and encouraged greater political stability and openness, it also stimulated more migration to the cities and a preference for large-scale development projects financed by international donors. Increased logging and the cutting of trees for fuel, overgrazing of livestock, and illegal hunting and the trade in endangered wildlife for medicine are now significant environmental threats, and national governments now struggle to balance the benefits of economic development with conservation of their marine and terrestrial environments.

In a region where financial resources are finite and political conditions remain uncertain, Asia now contains more than a dozen of the most polluted cities in the world, and half of the population of mainland Southeast Asia lacks adequate sanitation facilities or access to clean water. Although many countries have begun to enact greater environmental regulations, their efforts are hindered by the decline in foreign earnings and the value of their own currencies. The growing urbanization of Southeast Asia has also accelerated the loss of forests and the habitats they provide for wildlife, particularly in the Greater Mekong Subregion, as countries clear more land for agriculture and industrial development, and more tropical timber is exported to western Europe and North America.

Among the threatened wildlife most at risk in mainland Southeast Asia from poaching, logging, and agricultural expansion are the giant panda, Indochinese tiger, Asian elephant, Asiatic wild dog, Siamese crocodile, golden monkey, snow leopard, and gaur (Indian bison), which are used throughout the region for work animals and for meat but are now endangered by habitat destruction and human disturbance, as well as by exposure to diseases introduced by domestic cattle. Other species include the banteng (wild ox), once found throughout mainland and insular Southeast Asia but now absent because of habitat loss and war; the kouprey (gray ox), one of the rarest mammals in the world and found only in northeastern Cambodia, southern Laos, eastern Thailand, and western Vietnam; the Vu Quang ox, only recently identified and named in 1993; and the sun bear, formerly found throughout the region but now extinct in China and surviving only in protected areas of Thailand, Malaysia, and Indonesia.

China

In October 2000 Conservation International (CI), a nonprofit conservation group launched its first program in Sichuan and Yunnan Provinces in southwest China. The organization's efforts to encourage sustainable conservation and community development in the region reflect the extraordinary levels of biodiversity (biological diversity as indicated by numbers of species of animals and plants) found in both provinces, with the Hengduan Mountains in Sichuan Province considered "one of the world's most biologically rich temperate regions and a priority area for conservation" (Conservation International 2002, 4). The area is home to more than eight thousand species of plants and three hundred species of mammals, almost one-third of which are native; conservationists have recorded 686 bird species (equal to those of the United States), including 27 species of pheasants (14 percent of the world total) and 230 species of rhododendrons alone on the mountains' slopes. Meanwhile, local medical authorities have documented the healing properties of more than five thousand species of the area's plants and animals for fighting cancer and other major illnesses.

Because of this biological richness, the provincial governments recently enacted a ban on logging in the area, and local officials and Conservation International are now collaborating with indigenous communities and resource managers to stop illegal hunting and logging in forests along the country's borders, where both are a major cause of habitat loss. CI has also facilitated the government's increasing commitment to environmental conservation by donating funds and technical assistance to provincial and district authorities, so that

The beach on the island of Koi Phi Phi in the Andaman Sea just off the coast of mainland Thailand. Despite water pollution, the wide beaches and blue water have led to much tourism along the coasts of mainland Southeast Asia. COURTESY MARY CORINNE LOWENSTEIN.

they may better manage protected areas in southwest China.

Greater Mekong Subregion

In the Greater Mekong Subregion (GMS) the continuing consequences of fifty years of war have proven difficult to overcome. Although the national government of Thailand has now banned timber exports, Thai companies continue to log forests in neighboring Laos and Cambodia, and coastal mangrove forests are cleared for commercial shrimp farms along the Gulf of Thailand. Mining companies are also active in western Cambodia, where only recently guerrilla soldiers of the Khmer Rouge (insurgent Cambodian communists) fought, while large sections of central Laos, Vietnam, and southern China have been cleared for the construction of hydroelectric dams and roads. More recently, the growing trade in forest products and animal parts for medicine and food has contributed to illegal hunting and deforestation throughout the GMS. As a result, many environmentalists and economists consider the loss of marine and forest resources to be the most significant challenge to the long-term success of the region's recovery.

In response, Conservation International and the World Wildlife Fund (WWF) have joined local organizations and government agencies to restore the ecological diversity of a bioregion long decimated by war and internal conflict. In Cambodia the national government set aside 18 percent of the country as protected areas in 1993. Included in this new system were several national parks—among them, Preah Sihanouk (Ream), the smallest in the system, and Preah Suramarit Kossomak (Kirirom) in the Elephant Mountains, where King Norodom Sihanouk once had his summer palace—along with nine wildlife sanctuaries and three multiple-use zones.

To support this effort, CI recently completed the first wildlife survey of the central Cardamon Mountains in south-central Cambodia, and WWF assisted the Cambodia Environmental Management Program in banning gem mining and logging in the mountains and in designating the area as a protected forest in March 2002. Although the Cardamon Mountains cover less than 10 percent of Cambodia, their relative isolation under the Khmer Rouge government enabled many animals to survive relatively unscathed. As a result, almost half of Cambodia's native wildlife—including the majority of its known mammals—can be found in the mountainous forests today.

WWF is also working with the government of Vietnam to create eco-tourism attractions on the island of Con Dao, the country's second-largest marine park. Con Dao is also the site of a massive prison complex originally constructed by the French in the 1800s and later expanded by the U.S.-backed Saigon government in the 1960s and 1970s to include the infamous "tiger cages" that once held many of the current political leaders of Vietnam. WWF is also helping the national Forest Institute and local villages to implement the Five Million Hectare Forest Reforestation Program in the central highlands, habitat for the endangered saola, a small deer discovered just a decade ago and now in danger of extinction.

South of Ho Chi Minh City, in the mangrove forests of Ca Mau, one of the world's largest and richest in terms of species, the Institut de Recherche pour le Développement du dela du Mékong (Research Institute for the Development of the Mekong, IRDDM) instituted a program in 1990 to study the long-term impacts of shrimp farming. Using data obtained through remote sensing, IRDDM seeks to create an integrated "environmental management" geographic information system (GIS) for use by resource managers and planners. Elsewhere in the lower Mekong Basin, researchers from Lund University in Sweden are examining traditional natural resource use and wetland conservation activities in the transboundary region between Thailand, Laos, and Vietnam, with the goal of encouraging less pollution and water waste.

In collaboration with CI and WWF, the institute and the university will join together in advising educational institutions and district governments throughout the subregion on the challenges and opportunities of planning for small-scale tourism and other development projects. The goal is to encourage activities that are culturally and ecologically sustainable in an area where 60 percent of the population is under age eighteen and where mangrove forests and coral reefs are threatened by coastal development, agriculture, and aquaculture, as well as by episodic outbreaks of crown-of-thorns starfish and global climate change.

Thailand, which lost nearly half of its 435,000 square kilometers of primary forest cover between 1961 and 1985, now bans logging in its national parks and forests. However, the country continues to log almost 6,000 square kilometers of forest each year (8.4 percent of its remaining cover) from unprotected areas. Air pollution is also a major problem in the capital city of Bangkok, despite recent efforts to construct a mass transit system and to limit private automobile use in the city center. Also, a lack of sanitation and sewage treatment facilities remains a major challenge.

Laos, a landlocked country, is also taking steps in collaboration with WWF and the United Nations Development Programme to conserve its environment and to reduce the annual rate of logging (estimated at almost 1,000 square kilometers each year, or 1.5 percent of its existing primary forest cover). Although the country remains among the least developed in the region, with less than 20 percent of its population living in urban areas, its relative poorness and proximity to Vietnam, Thailand, and southern China make it the most vulnerable country in the Greater Mekong Subregion.

The Future

Although the prognosis remains uncertain, efforts to conserve the natural environments of mainland Southeast Asia continue to lag behind the social and economic pressures for development. While many of the countries in the region are signatories to international conventions that regulate resource use, including the U.N. Conference on the Law of the Seas (1982) and the Convention on Biological Diversity (1993), there is little uniformity or agreement on appropriate practices. Indeed, the Association of Southeastern Asia Nations has resisted any efforts to implement a regional protocol for preventing marine pollution in territorial waters, although it has have provided financial support in monitoring and capacity building among member nations.

In addition, a repressive military government in Myanmar and continued guerrilla warfare along the Thai border impede efforts to encourage progress in human rights and environmental conservation, while major investments in manufacturing and industrial development in Malaysia since the 1980s have led to more urbanization and the cultivation of land for rice in ecologically sensitive areas. Furthermore, as communities have shifted from nomadic lifestyles and grown in population, and as governments have begun to exercise greater control over the natural environment for energy, irrigation, and food production, their methods have significantly altered traditional practices and accelerated the degree of degradation. Rural landscapes that were once primarily agricultural have been industrialized and urbanized, and coastal waters once abundant with fish, coral reefs, and mangroves forests are now contaminated by sewage discharges and marine pollution and heavily exploited for aquaculture, tour-

ism, and oil and gas exploration. As a consequence, land-use conflicts are more frequent, and incentives to protect the region's wetlands and natural areas are less apparent. Yet, the conservation and rehabilitation of Southeast Asia's natural environments are critically important both socially—for the food and health benefits they provide—and economically, as a source of pharmaceutical drugs and attractions for eco-tourism.

The challenges of balancing development with environmental conservation—and the possibilities offered by tourism in reconnecting an area long defined by its history of conflict through expanded networks of travel and communication—remain a topic of uncertainty. However, the practices already underway in mainland Southeast Asia may yet help establish a framework for community and government leaders who truly wish to successfully market and maintain protected areas as destinations for both foreign and domestic visitors; create long-term funding support for environmental conservation and education projects that unite both parks and communities; generate economically and socially sustainable employment opportunities; and develop meaningful, collaborative partnerships between local people and government officials. Absent a willingness to consider these multiple perspectives, the prospects for the long-term survival of endangered wildlife in mainland Southeast Asia are doubtful.

Greg Ringer

Further Reading

Boothroyd, P., & Wiesman, B. (Eds.). (1993). *Development, environment and society in Vietnam.* Vancouver, Canada: Institute of Asian Research.

Conservation International. (2002). *Conservation regions, Asia-Pacific: Papua New Guinea.* Retrieved January 7, 2003, from http://www.conservation.org/xp/CIWEB/regions/ asia_pacific/png/png.xml

Easter, K. W., Dixon, J. A., & Hufschmidt, M. M. (Eds.). (1991). *Watershed resources management: Studies from Asia and the Pacific.* Honolulu, HI: Environment and Policy Institute, East-West Center.

Heyzer, N., Riker, J. V., & Quizon, A. B. (Eds.). (1995). *Government-NGO relations in Asia: Prospects and challenges for people-centered development.* Kuala Lumpur, Malaysia: Asian and Pacific Development Centre.

Hirsch, P., & Warren, C. (1998). *The politics of environment in southeast Asia: Resources and environment.* New York: Routledge.

Hudson, C. (Ed.). (1997). *The China handbook.* Chicago: Fitzroy Dearborn Publishers.

Japan Environmental Council. (Ed.). (2000). *The state of the environment in Asia 1999/2000.* Singapore: Institute of Southeast Asian Studies.

Leinbach, T. R., & Ulack, R. (Eds.). (2000). *Southeast Asia: Diversity and development.* Upper Saddle River, NJ: Prentice Hall.

Rice, E. B. (1997). *Paddy irrigation and water management in southeast Asia.* Washington, DC: World Bank.

Seda, M. (Ed.). (1993). *Environmental management in ASEAN: Perspectives on critical regional issues.* Singapore: Institute of Southeast Asian Studies.

Tai-Chee, W., & Singh, M. (Eds.). (1999). *Development and challenge: Southeast Asia in the new millennium.* Singapore: Times Academic Press.

United Nations Economic and Social Commission for Asia and the Pacific. (1998). *A demographic perspective on women in development in Cambodia, Lao People's Democratic Republic, Myanmar, and Vietnam.* New York: United Nations Economic and Social Commission for Asia and the Pacific.

Association of African Earthkeeping Churches

While studying religious influences on Zimbabwe's liberation struggle, Professor M. L. Daneel became aware of a grassroots need in the province of Masvingo for involvement in preserving the environment. Discussions with rural traditionalists and Christians led to a new liberation struggle, on behalf of God's creation. A "war of the trees" was declared targeting three concerns: tree planting, wildlife conservation, and water resources.

Two organizations joined in this effort: the Association of Zimbabwean Traditionalist Ecologists (AZTREC), and the Association of African Earthkeeping Churches (AAEC). AZTREC comprises traditionalist chiefs, elders, and spirit mediums involved in environmental conservation. AAEC comprises 150 to 180 African Initiated Churches (AICs), mainly of the prophetic or pentecostal type, representing some two million adherents throughout Zimbabwe.

AAEC and AZTREC both belong to the Zimbabwean Institute of Religious Research and Ecological Conservation (ZIRRCON), an expansion of Professor Daneel's research unit. This body today represents Zimbabwe's largest grassroots environmental organization. Some 8 million trees have been planted in several thousand woodlots since the inception of the movement (1986 to 1988). Twelve nurseries in Masvingo each produce between 50,000 and 100,000 seedlings annually. AAEC and AZTREC have mobilized peasant communities to establish their own woodlots near stable water points. Satellite nurseries are also being developed by women's and youth groups, and at AIC theological schools.

AAEC's main ceremony in its quest for a liberated creation is a "eucharist of tree planting" (Daneel 2001), referred to by AIC members as the *maporesanyika*, or "earth-healing" ceremony. A thoroughly contextualized sacrament, this ceremony represents a compelling challenge to African and world churches as regards Christian·stewardship of creation.

How then does this "green mission" affect the life and shape of an earthkeeping church? There is a noticeable shift in the healing focus at AIC headquarters. The concept *hospitara* now includes the connotation of "environmental hospital" to care for the wounded earth: the "patient" is the denuded land, while the "dispensary" is the nursery with its assortment of seedlings. The AAEC's reforestation programs have also stimulated a need for new ethical codes. Leading earthkeepers insist that the church, with its legislative and disciplinary powers, is an effective institution for opposing the forces that mindlessly exploit our limited resources.

The AAEC's message and struggle is holistic. By embracing trees at the communion table, earthkeeping communicants replace exploitation of nature with an attitude of humble stewardship. Earth care has empowered the poor and marginalized to contribute significantly and has even attracted government recognition. It has liberated people from hopeless poverty, as budding woodlots and small-scale income-generating projects revive some hope for a better future.

M. L. Daneel

Further Reading

Carmody, J. (1983). *Ecology and religion: Toward a new Christian theology of nature.* New York: Paulist Press.

Daneel, M. L. (1987). *Quest for belonging: Introduction to a study of African independent churches.* Gweru, Zimbabwe: Mambo Press.

Daneel, M. L. (2000). African initiated churches in southern Africa: Protest movements or mission churches?

Discussion Papers in the African Humanities, AH33. Boston: Boston University African Studies Center.

Daneel, M. L. (2001). *African earthkeepers: Wholistic interfaith mission*. New York: Orbis Books.

Gumbo, M. (1995). *Guerrilla snuff*. Harare, Zimbabwe: Baobab Books.

Messer D. E. (1992). *A conspiracy of goodness: Contemporary images of Christian mission*. Nashville, TN: Abingdon Press.

Sundkler, B. G. M. (1961). *Bantu prophets in South Africa*. London: Oxford University Press.

Audubon Society

The Audubon Society began as the first grassroots nationwide American conservation organization, and continues to be one of the most powerful. It was founded in 1896 when two prominent Boston women, Mrs. Augustus Hemenway and Minna Hall, formed the Massachusetts Audubon Society to halt the decimation of bird populations. The group campaigned especially against the popular fashion of using birds and feathers to decorate women's hats. It took its name from a similar, short-lived society that the New York sportsman George Grinnell had run in the late 1880s. The bird hats sparked unprecedented public outrage for a conservation issue, and the "Audubon clubs" spread swiftly state by state. In 1905, the state clubs joined to create the National Association of Audubon Societies—shortened in 1940 to the National Audubon Society.

Women founded, ran, and dominated the membership of most of the early state societies, while men, who comprised about half the leadership, tended to focus on lobbying, field research, and lectures. The Audubon women shared members, tactics, and a focus on education with the broad network of late-nineteenth-century women's clubs that worked for reform causes—as well as a firm, Victorian-era middle-class belief in women's obligation to safeguard society's morals. The societies ran children's clubs. They published the magazine *Bird-Lore* (later *Audubon*) and funded wardens for the first national wildlife refuges. Their efforts led to passage of landmark federal wildlife protection legislation, notably the 1900 Lacey Act and the 1918 Migratory Bird Treaty Act. They helped establish the legal foundations as well as the popular support and moral tone for twentieth-century conservation.

In the 1920s, the Society began to build its own network of refuges. In the 1930s and 40s, it started children's camps, and spearheaded the research and protection efforts to save the whooping crane, roseate spoonbill, and other endangered bird species. As the post-World-War-II environmental movement flowered, the National Audubon Society, a prominent player, branched out to campaign for wilderness preservation, pesticide bans, and population control. In the 1960s and 70s, it participated in the powerful lobbies to pass the critical Clean Air, Clean Water, and Endangered Species Acts. It established nature centers, and launched the *World of Audubon* television specials in 1984, while *Audubon*, a premier environmental magazine, matched glossy photographs and literary essays with advocacy and reporting.

In the 1980s, Audubon, like the Sierra Club and other powerful environmental groups, drew criticism for its corporate sponsorships, lack of racial and ethnic diversity, and emphasis on lobbying versus grassroots political action. Into the 1990s, as the Society addressed issues from the Everglades to the Arctic, some of its leaders decried the Audubon image as old-fashioned while others feared the loss of a distinctive mission and a sense of history. In 2000, Audubon's new strategic plan resolved the debate by trumpeting the Society's history and reclaiming both its focus on bird protection and its roots in grassroots action. Audubon pledged to resume its leadership in bird conservation, and to expand its education programs and devote resources to its local chapters to pursue its central goal. As of 2002, the Society had 9 regional and 27 state offices and over 500 local chapters.

Jennifer Price

Further Reading

Audubon (formerly *Bird-Lore*) (1899–).

Audubon Society website: http://www.audubon.org.

Buchheister, C., & Graham, F. (1993). From the swamps and back: A concise and candid history of the early Audubon movement. *Audubon*, 75, 7–45.

Doughty, R. W. (1975). *Feather fashions and bird protection: A study in nature protection*. Berkeley: University of California Press.

Graham, F., Jr. (1990). *The Audubon ark: A history of the National Audubon Society*. New York: Alfred A. Knopf.

Price, J. (1999). *Flight maps: Adventures with nature in modern America*. New York: Basic Books.

Audubon, John James

(1785–1851)
French artist and naturalist

Artist and naturalist John James Audubon created stunning, remarkably detailed color portraits of North American birds and mammals. Nearly two centuries after they were first produced, these widely distributed portraits continue to inspire viewers to appreciate the beauty, majesty, and mystery of the natural world.

Audubon was born in Les Cayes, Santo Domingo, the son of a French sea captain, planter, and slave dealer, Jean Audubon, and one of his mistresses, Jeanne Rabin(e?). At age six John Audubon was sent to France, where he was cared for by his father's legal spouse, Anne Moynet Audubon. He lived a relatively carefree life in Nantes, France, with a minimum of formal schooling; he also began developing an interest in nature and drawing. With the Napoleonic Wars raging in Europe, in 1803 Audubon fled to the United States to avoid military conscription. There he helped manage Mill Grove (his father's farm outside Philadelphia, Pennsylvania), began early experiments in bird banding, and met his wife, Lucy Bakewell, a neighbor's daughter. The two were married in 1808 and eventually had two sons and two daughters.

Between 1807 and 1820 he was involved in several failed business ventures, including an ill-fated general store in Kentucky that landed him in debtors' prison. At age thirty-five Audubon then began actively pursuing his dream to produce a collection of portraits that included every species of North American bird. For the next five years he held a variety of posts, including a brief stint as a taxidermist at the Western Museum of Science in Cincinnati, Ohio, while his wife raised their children and taught school. As he traveled, he collected bird specimens, recorded notes about his experiences, and filled his folio with magnificent watercolor drawings of birds. Most were produced from freshly killed specimens propped up with wire.

By 1824 Audubon began searching for a publisher for his work, first in the United States and then in England, where his watercolors enjoyed critical acclaim. There he discovered the London engraver Robert Havell Jr., with whom he collaborated for more than a decade to produce the elegant four-volume elephant folio edition of his *Birds of America* (1827–1838). This collection of 435 life-sized color engravings of birds in their natural habitat remains one of the most striking and famous natural history publications of all time. Although critics charged that Audubon tended to present his birds in unnatural poses, to overly romanticize them, and to endow them with humanlike features, the public clearly identified with his images, which were widely reproduced on prints, plates, calendars, trading cards, and more affordable editions of *Birds of America*. Audubon also joined with his two sons and the Charleston, South Carolina, naturalist John Bachman to produce a companion publication on mammals, the three-volume *Viviparous Quadrupeds of North America* (1845–1854).

In 1886, when the American naturalist George Bird Grinnell was contemplating what to call the new bird protection society he was launching, Audubon's name seemed a natural choice. Although Audubon had sacrificed the lives of many birds to create his vibrant illustrations, he had also fostered public awareness about the value of native wildlife and lamented the decline of many species. Although Grinnell's Audubon Society proved short-lived, the Audubon name was subsequently immortalized in a series of state societies that began forming in 1896 and in the National Association of Audubon Societies, established in 1905. Rechristened the National Audubon Society in 1940, this organization has continued to promote the legacy of its namesake—the appreciation of wildlife—for nearly a century.

Mark V. Barrow Jr.

Further Reading

Ford, A. (1988). *John James Audubon: A biography*. New York: Abbeville Press.

Fries, W. H. (1973). *The Double Elephant Folio: The story of Audubon's Birds of America.* Chicago: American Library Association.

Graham, F., Jr. (1990). *The Audubon ark: A history of the National Audubon Society*. New York: Alfred A. Knopf.

Herrick, F. H. (1938). *Audubon the naturalist: A history of his life and time* (2nd ed.). New York: D. Appleton-Century.

Sterling, K. B. (1999). John James Audubon. In J. A. Garraty & M. C. Carnes (Eds.), *American national biography* (pp. 745–748). New York: Oxford University Press.

Streshinsky, S. (1993). *Audubon: Life and art in the American wilderness*. New York: Villard Books.

Australia

(2002 est. pop. 19.7 million)

Australia is a country of nearly 7.7 million square kilometers. The population is mostly of European origin (but with many Asian immigrants since the 1960s); 27 percent are foreign born; the official language is English; religions are Protestant and Catholic but also Buddhist and Islamic; the capital is Canberra, and the main cities are Sydney, Melbourne, and Brisbane. Although Australia is mostly an urban society, industries include wheat, cotton, cattle and sheep ranching, gold and coal mining, and tourism as well as the urban-based service sector and manufacturing industries. The political system is based on the Westminster tradition (where the Prime Minister and his or her government is chosen on the basis of a majority Parliamentary vote, after democratic elections, and answerable to Parliament) but has a federal constitution, with a national and six state governments.

Natural and Pre-European Features

Australia is the driest continent, with the poorest soils, the least water (except Antarctica), and the lowest mountain ranges. Its forest cover is about 10 percent of the total landmass. The largest river system is the Murray-Darling, which carries less water than the Sacramento-San Joaquin river system of California. Much of the continent, apart from the fertile east coast, the southeastern crescent, and southwestern Western Australia, is covered by scrub, native grasses, and deserts. The continent is profoundly affected by the El Niño-La Niña climatological cycle and subject to debilitating droughts. Nevertheless, the climate is generally mild by European standards, merging to tropical in the north. Its unique flora and fauna, principally its marsupials and eucalyptus trees, have attracted much attention.

Europeans were not the first to change the Australian land. Australian aborigines had settled from Southeast Asia and subsisted on the continent for sixty thousand years. Aborigines burned forest undergrowth to promote better grass cover to encourage game. Some forests, such as the Pilliga of western New South Wales, have become more extensive and changed composition since the removal of aboriginal people.

Aboriginal Australians also changed their environment by introducing the dingo (a native dog) and, through their hunting practices, may have been responsible for eliminating large marsupials such as the *Diprotodron* and, on the mainland, the *Thylacine* (Tasmanian tiger). Decimation of the aboriginal populations in eastern Australia in the nineteenth century by disease and white violence led to plagues of possums and kangaroos in some areas.

European Perceptions

The foreignness of the flora and fauna profoundly influenced European attitudes and practices after the first white settlement in 1788. Although Europeans had some appreciation of indigenous species and of the grandeur of those landscapes that resembled the parks of large English estates, nature was mostly viewed as a resource. The Australian landscape was seen as deficient because it did not conform to European standards of beauty. The dearth of deciduous trees, the dull appearance of the eucalyptus forests, and the lack of distinct seasons disturbed or repelled many settlers. Although late nineteenth-century European painters displayed a greater appreciation of Australia's natural environment, the landscape depicted was pastoral and essentially a celebration of settlement's triumph over nature. Not until the 1930s were the harsher tones of the "red center"—the arid and often desert-like outback in the center of Australia—and arid lands prominently assimilated into art.

Land Settlement

The colonial governments intervened on a large scale to develop land, bringing considerable environmental change. Sales of Crown lands replaced land grants to encourage settlement from 1831, but until the 1860s most land was occupied by large landholders called "squatters" who grazed large herds of sheep (and cattle) that eroded native vegetation. From the 1860s to the 1920s colonial governments tried largely unsuccessfully to encourage small-scale development, first through land legislation for "free selection" (1860s) and then in the 1880s and after 1900 through irrigation policies.

In 1885 Alfred Deakin, minister of water supply in the state of Victoria and a future prime minister, trav-

Eucalyptus in the Australian outback. COURTESY MARK SPALDING.

laws. Further developments along these lines were implemented by the Australian-American Elwood Mead, who was chairman of the Victorian State Rivers and Water Supply Commission (1907–1915).

But irrigation led to a plethora of problems: overuse of water, especially contentious after the development of cotton farming in the 1970s in northwestern New South Wales; dams in the Murray-Darling River basin after the 1920s and on the Ord River in Western Australia after the 1960s interfering with natural river systems; and soil and water salinity problems. Irrigation was, however, only part of agriculture's negative impact on the environment.

The demand for land and for agricultural production was such that sometimes land use clashed with the limits that nature provided. An example was the marginal land of South Australia north of the so-called Goyder's line, where wheat farming was initially successful in the 1870s only to be defeated by severe droughts in the 1880s.

Agriculture produced more environmental damage than did pastoral activity, which was compatible with the survival of some native vegetation and extensive tree cover. Extensive clearing of trees through ringbarking (girdling) occurred after the 1850s to aid closer settlement. Removal of trees has caused great salinity problems. Although apparent by the 1940s, these effects were largely ignored, and by the late twentieth century much of Western Australia's wheat belt and the Murray-Darling River basin were severely affected by salinity due to excessive removal of native trees.

Furthermore, overgrazing led to removal of native grasses and vegetation, robbed the soil of nutrients, and spread introduced European and South African weeds as hoofed animals carried the seeds. Extinction of animal species, notably the *Thylacine* in Tasmania, also occurred as farmers sought to protect their flocks and crops from predators.

An extreme result of imprudent agricultural methods was the prevalence of dust storms. Francis Ratcliffe's book *Flying Fox and Drifting Sand* (1938) alerted the public to the impact of soil erosion that was exacerbated by drought, rabbits, and the combination of overgrazing and wheat farming. Farmers and governments were hampered in their responses by the absence of a national policy comparable to the New Deal in the United States. Not until the 1940s did Australia follow the U.S. lead and begin to establish soil conservation services in the states and a more coordinated approach.

eled overseas, including to California, to study irrigation policies and practices. His comprehensive report recommended government assistance to make the arid regions bloom; it was Deakin who encouraged two Canadians, George and William B. Chaffey, to come to Australia to work on the Mildura and Renmark schemes (planned towns based on company land development) situated on the Murray Riverin Victoria and South Australia, where colonial governments gave them 300,000 hectares of land grants. Although the Chaffey brothers got into financial difficulties in the 1890s, their settlements and Deakin's legislation became the foundation of Australian irrigation-based farming, which continued to grow in importance.

Irrigation systems were established to promote closer settlement on the assumption that a sound and prosperous society with a stable social structure required sturdy yeoman farmers; increasingly it was accepted that the state would be required to support these ideals with advice, cheap finances, and suitable

Australia was subjected to a vast range of invasive animals and plants, which were linked mainly to European agricultural and pastoral occupation. Exotic birds and trees were introduced by homesick English people to provide hunting for the gentry under the acclimatization movement (a movement which exchanged exotic plants and animals for economic, scientific and aesthetic "improvement" of the land), which flourished in all colonies in the mid-nineteenth century. Most damaging of the invasive species was the European wild rabbit, introduced in 1859 for hunting, and the prickly pear cactus from Central America, first cultivated in 1839 as an ornamental; the cactus covered million of hectares of land in Queensland and New South Wales by 1900; rabbits spread across all areas except the far tropics after their introduction. Both the prickly pear cactus and rabbit invasions were facilitated by low human-to-land ratios under pastoral occupation, and they threatened the viability of that pastoral economy, but also the prospects for broad-acre agriculture and small-scale farming. By the 1920s demands for biological control were growing. In 1924 introduction of the *Cactoblastis* moth proved successful against the prickly pear cactus. U.S. writer Rachel Carson in her book *Silent Spring* (1962) lauded this introduction as an outstanding example of how biological alternatives to pesticides could be found. However, use of biological controls in Australia was outweighed by the vastly greater exploitation of the new synthesized insecticides such as DDT after 1945.

Although the rabbit gravely damaged the flora of Australia, no objection was made to the comparable damage done by sheep—it was the competition for pasture by the 1880s that led to the search for controls; eventually the myxomatosis virus, introduced from South America, decimated the rabbit population after its release in 1949–1950, but subsequently rabbits gained partial immunity, and myxomatosis had to be supplemented in the 1990s with calici virus, allowing large areas of the inland to be revegetated.

Conservation and Restoration

While Australia's European population has always been predominantly urban-based, there has been relatively little historical writing on urban environmental problems, and little evidence of organized urban environmental movements until the 1970s. For one thing, the image that Australians had of themselves—until the 1960s—was one of an important connection with the "bush" (rural Australia). Moreover, Australia was urbanized, but not heavily industrialized, and even the (few) big cities were, apart from certain inner city areas, relatively free of the congestion-induced environmental problems which occurred in Britain. Since Australia (apart from the New South Wales regional towns of Newcastle and Port Kembla, as well as Botany in Sydney, and some parts of Victoria) was not industrialized until the 1940s, problems of pollution in urban areas tended to be those of small industry; domestic and some power station smoke pollution, and occasional poverty and congestion-related health problems such as the notorious outbreak of plague in the Rocks area in central Sydney in the first few years of the twentieth century. Rather, in the nineteenth century and after, Australian impacts upon the land wrought by farming and mining were the most noticeable, though these impacts included, to be sure, the demands for timber and other raw materials that urban growth required.

In the mid-nineteenth century people began to recognize the damage being done to the land by European agricultural methods. Conservation sentiment emerged after the Australian gold rushes revealed the negative impacts of removing trees to aid the mining industry and to provide fuel for the growing towns in Victoria. Ideas about nature's changing human impacts were also stimulated by U.S. writer George Perkins Marsh's book *Man and Nature* (1864). Important authorities such as Ferdinand Mueller, director of the Victorian Botanic Gardens, and John Ednie Brown, South Australian conservator of forests, emphasized the value of tree cover as a means of conserving moisture. These men favored extensive reforestation and afforestation, including planting imported Monterey pines from California. Brown elevated trees from a mere influence to an almost complete control over climate.

At the same time the first Australian national parks were established, but not as wilderness preserves; rather they were established as areas for recreation, especially for the cities of Sydney and Melbourne. Audley, south of Sydney, was in 1878 the second officially designated "national park" in the world and was stocked with European deer for the benefit of hunters, bushwalkers (hikers/wilderness campers), and picnickers.

Conservation policies were stymied by the administration of forestry services within the colonial lands or mines departments—and by fragmentation of authority through the colonial sovereignty of Crown lands. With federation (union under a federal constitution of the six colonies), this fragmentation of authority continued after 1901 as water policies and Crown lands were under control of the state governments, in contrast with U.S. public lands under control of the federal government. Thus water regulation between states for the Murray-Darling River basin—the river system that covered four of the six states—was ineffective despite interstate agreements.

After the 1880s, conservation-minded foresters such as George Perrin advocated state forests for the colonies and experimented with exotic trees in plantations; he and his supporters were influenced by European and Indian forestry service practices. Royal commissions (a formal government appointed judicial inquiry with legal powers to subpoena witnesses and recommend criminal contempt charges for false testimony) on forestry in Victoria (1897–1901) and New South Wales (1908–1909) led to acts to regulate the cutting of timber and to promote state forestry services, both—government agencies administering them for conservation, logging, and carrying out those operations—the services were established, always based on acts of parliament, in each colony, and the regulations to control cutting under them and to plant trees as well spread to other states when they all adopted their own acts followed ultimately in other states.

Conservation movements with popular support had roots in ornithology through the Gould League of Bird Lovers, founded by Jessie McMichael in Victoria in 1909. Named after nineteenth-century ornithologist John Gould, this organization enrolled hundreds of thousands of young children, encouraged the study of Australian birds, and had the prestige of Prime Minister Alfred Deakin as first president.

Conservation sentiment was in part a product of federation and nationalism; the Australian Forest League raised pride in Australian trees and their wood products; bushwalker clubs were established by the 1910s and 1920s. Led by such early conservationists as Myles Dunphy in New South Wales, these clubs promoted creation of more national parks and greater appreciation of nature.

During the years between the world wars, conservation meant efficient use of resources, especially of timber through the Imperial Forestry Conferences, development of a Commonwealth Forestry School in 1926, and water conservation measures. The most ambitious plans to harness the country's natural resources involved the push for watering the deserts by turning inland the coastal streams; although the outlandish Bradfield scheme (a scheme to turn the coastal river waters of northeastern Australia back through huge tunnels under the Great Dividing Range inland to water the dry interior of the continent) (1938–1942) and

the writing of journalist Ion Idriess were advocated without success, they were partially attained with inception of the Snowy Mountains scheme. Following the example of the Tennessee Valley Authority in the United States, the Snowy Mountains Authority was created by the Labor federal government, and the scheme was implemented in the 1950s; it diverted water from the coast, producing hydroelectric power, flood control, and recreational lakes in the Snowy Mountains and water for irrigation in the Murray-Darling River basin. Australians objected little to these vast changes to the landscape because economic benefits and efficiency came first as Australians sought to put the depression of the 1930s and wartime austerity behind them.

Modern Environmentalism

The new ecological consciousness of the 1960s and later would make Australians more aware of the environmental consequences of great national development proposals. Dam projects were subject to bitter controversy. When the Tasmanian government decided to push ahead in the 1960s with more dams for its power grid, it met resistance. The decision of Tasmania's Hydroelectric Commission to build a dam in the middle of the Lake Pedder National Park in 1967 led to the founding of the Tasmania Wilderness Society and greater emphasis on wilderness preservation. Although Lake Pedder was flooded in 1972 despite widespread protests, the Tasmania Wilderness Society led the successful effort to save the Franklin River from a similar fate in 1983, an achievement that catapulted Green Party leaders such as Bob Brown into national prominence and gave Greens political representation in the federal and state parliaments from the late 1980s onward.

In the 1960s the rebirth of the conservation movement in the United States stimulated a similar rebirth in Australia, stimulated also by mining projects and dam building. Plans to drill for oil near the Great Barrier Reef and to mine the sand dunes of Fraser Island on the Queensland coast produced pioneering modern environmental movements in the 1960s and 1970s. Active in the leadership of the Great Barrier Reef struggle was the Australian Conservation Foundation (1965). Mining on the Fraser Island sand dunes was outlawed in most parts in 1975 and a world heritage area eventually established (1992). At the same time (1975), the federal National Parks and Wildlife Conservation Act and the Great Barrier Reef Marine Park were enacted.

Conservation was aided by the election of Prime Minister (1972–75) Gough Whitlam's Labor federal government in 1972 and by the rise of a new, more socially and environmentally conscious urban middle class that was university trained and committed to environmental values. But these were strongly backed by elements within the left-wing section of the trade union movement and the Labor Party. Labor and trade unionists took the lead on urban environmental issues. The growth of Australia's cities was marked after 1950, and controlling air pollution and conserving the built environment became major campaigns by the 1970s. Trade unions established "green bans" to prevent destruction of important buildings and streetscapes, and some freeway construction was halted. Smoke from factories and exhaust fumes from the steadily building traffic in Sydney and Melbourne had produced a decline in air quality in the 1960s and 1970s, and led to the establishment of government environmental protection agencies in the states. Power stations were moved out of the cities, transferring pollution to regional communities such as the Hunter River Valley in New South Wales, and Latrobe Valley in eastern Victoria. Major environmental battles continued to rage in the 1980s and 1990s over the destruction of old-growth forests for wood chips for paper pulp—an industry established in the 1960s, principally in New South Wales and Tasmania, and over uranium mining in the Outback. Australia remained without nuclear power, except for one small research reactor, although Australia exported uranium from a few mines.

The conservative (Liberal Party) government that assumed power in 1996 moved away from the more environmentally conscious policies pursued (erratically and partially) by the Labor Party governments from 1983 to 1996. The Howard Liberal Party government refused in 2001 to endorse the Kyoto protocols on greenhouse gases as damaging to Australia's coal industry and capped fuel levies on petroleum. Fuel levies are oil produced in Australia at a (usually) lower than world price. For some two decades the price was levied so that the price of sale within Australia would be the equivalent of imported petroleum; this made petrol for cars and diesel for trucks more expensive, and the levy was a huge boost to federal government revenues. The introduction of a federal goods and services tax also advantaged private transport over public and thereby encouraged congested roads. Atmospheric pollution continues to be a threat to human health, although the decline of heavy industry and prevalent climatic conditions make skies clearer and cleaner than those in many countries. Though air pollution in the cities improved in the 1980s, impending environmental disasters await Australia with the massive growth of Sydney, as well as the swelling size of Melbourne and Brisbane. Pollution problems associated with this growth, especially in western Sydney, are now apparent, as industry and housing moved into that area in a Los Angeles like spread to the Blue Mountains some 80 kilometers to the west.

Notwithstanding urban environmental concerns, the most significant issues remain those of water, salinity, tree clearing, and other land-use practices. These issues continue to be raised by the impact of a European (and increasingly U.S.-influenced) culture and economy on a natural world that has always posed sharp physical constraints.

Ian Tyrrell

See also Biological Exchanges; Colonialism and Imperialism; Endangered Species; Extinction; Indigenous Peoples; Insects; Rabbit; Sheep

Further Reading

Bolton, G. (1981). *Spoils and spoilers: Australians make their environment, 1788–1980.* Sydney, Australia: Allen and Unwin.

Bonyhady, T. (2001). *The colonial Earth.* Melbourne, Australia: Miegunyah Press.

Dargavel, J. (1995). *Fashioning Australia's forests.* Melbourne, Australia: Oxford University Press.

Flannery, T. (1994). *The future eaters.* Sydney, Australia: Reed Books.

Griffiths, T. (2002). *Forests of ash: An environmental history.* Melbourne, Australia: Cambridge University Press.

Hutton, D., & Connors, L. (1999). *A history of the Australian environmental movement.* Sydney, Australia: Cambridge University Press.

Powell, J. (1976). *Environmental management in Australia 1788–1914.* Melbourne, Australia: Oxford University Press.

Pyne, S. (1991). *The burning bush, a fire history of Australia.* New York: Henry Holt.

Ratcliffe, F. (1938). *Flying fox and drifting sand: The adventure of a biologist in Australia.* London: Chatto and Windus.

Rolls, E. (1969). *They all ran wild.* Sydney, Australia: Angus and Robertson.

Rolls, E. (1981). *A million wild acres.* Melbourne, Australia: Thomas Nelson.

Tyrrell, I. (1999). *True gardens of the gods: Californian-Australian environmental reform, 1860–1930.* Berkeley and Los Angeles: University of California Press.

Australia, Aboriginal

Aboriginal Australia has been viewed traditionally as a classic example of hunter-gatherer, that is, pre-agricultural, society—a continent of people in equilibrium with the natural environment. More recent perspectives, however, by anthropologists, archaeologists, ethnohistorians, and indigenous people themselves have helped dispel this stereotype. Today it is recognized that a wider range of sociocultural variation existed across the continent and through time than had previously been thought, overlapping in many ways with horticultural and agricultural societies like those of nearby Papua New Guinea. Aboriginal peoples had considerable control over the natural environment and its resources and managed these in ingenious ways.

Society, Religion, Demography

Although over two hundred Australian languages and many dialects were spoken across the continent, Aboriginal society shared many similarities. Society was kinship based; clans (descent groups) inherited land that was overseen by totemic ancestors shaped in the primeval Dreamtime (in Aboriginal belief, the time of creation). Complex patterns of kinship and social networks bound together large sectors of the continent. Trade, exchange, and ritual provided a further binding force. In some cases, trade and exchange networks extended from one corner of the continent to the other. Basically egalitarian, Aboriginal society also had powerful and influential elders—men and women initiated into the hierarchies of the religious system and its cults. A conservative estimate of some 300,000 for the Australian Aboriginal population at the time of European settlement has been suggested, but more recent studies, which allow for the decimating effects of introduced diseases and conflict (byproducts of colonialism), have increased this three- or fourfold. More fertile sectors of the continent, such as the southeast and the eastern and northern coastlines, were densely populated in comparison with other parts of the world inhabited by hunter-gatherers.

Resource Management

Land and resource management practices were central to Aboriginal economies. These involved use of fire, processing techniques, and storage. For example, more intensive and costly strategies, in terms of energy expenditure, were aimed at stockpiling stores for lengthy, populous, intergroup ceremonial occasions that ran for weeks and months of each year. In arid and semi-arid Australia, which comprises two-thirds of the continent, grass seeds and other seeds were managed, stored in quantity and made into bread on a daily basis. In these harsh regions, extensive loose, open social networks cemented relations between far-flung peoples, operating as elaborate safety harnesses that could be called upon in times of need. In richer, humid regions, like the tropical north and temperate southeast, social networks were bounded territorially, reflecting denser, more competitive populations. Here, a sedentary way of life also was more common. In Victoria and the Murray River Valley, for instance, villages were constructed, often atop large earth mounds. Intensive fishing was undertaken day and night, and extensive drainage systems were dug to control eel runs and their productivity. Along the tropical coast and its offshore islands, specialized fishing societies flourished that focused on hunting dugongs (aquatic mammals similar to sea manatees) from seagoing canoes. Plants were managed in a form of domiculture (symbiotic relationship between humans and undomesticated plants) centered on more sedentary base camps.

Tasmania

The Tasmanians were isolated from mainland Australia for some 12,000 years, but were linked biologically, linguistically, and culturally to southeastern Australians. There were also some differences reflecting, no doubt, their cultural isolation and history. For example, apart from along the humid west coast, settlement appears to have been more mobile than in environmentally comparable areas of southeastern Australia. Population densities were also lower than in the latter areas. Fishing no longer was practiced and equipment was generally less extensive, as befits more-mobile economies. Archaeological investigations suggest that during the last 4,000 years rain forests were more extensively utilized, coastal strategies rearranged, and populations may have expanded on the west coast.

Aboriginal Arrival in Australia

Aboriginal colonization of Australia some time before 40,000 years ago is supported by plentiful well-dated ar-

The Worlds of the Arunta

This early account of the life of the Arunta aboriginal people of Australia shows how the human, natural, and spiritual worlds were seen as one, rather than as distinct from one another.

Starting southwards, they travelled first of all underground, and came out at a place called Arapera. Here they spent their time eating Unjiamba. Then, leaving here, they took their sacred pole or Nurtunja to pieces and travelled further on until they came to Ooraminna, in the Macdonnell Ranges, where there is a special water-hole, close beside which they camped, two great stones arising to mark the spot. Then they went south to a place called Neri-iwa, where they died . . . .

In addition to these traditions of the wanderings of various companies of men and women belonging to different totems, we meet with others which refer to the origin of special individuals, or groups of individuals, who did not wander about, but lived and died where they arose. Thus, for example, an Inarlinga or "porcupine" (Echidna) man is supposed to have arisen near to Stuart's Water–hole on the Hugh River, while at the Emily Gap, near to Alice Springs, tradition says that certain witchetty grubs became transformed into witchetty men, who formed a strong group here, and who were afterwards joined by others of the same totem, who marched over the country to the Gap.

Each of these Alchera ancestors is represented as carrying about with him, or her, one or more of the sacred stones, which are called by the Arunta natives Churinga, and each of these Churinga is intimately associated with the Kuruna or spirit part of some individual. Either where they originated and stayed, as in the case of certain of the witchetty grub people, or else where, during their wanderings, they camped for a time, there were formed what the natives call Knanikilla, each one of which is in reality a local totem centre. At each of these spots—and they are all well known to the old men, who pass the knowledge on from generation to generation—a certain number of the Alchera ancestors went into the ground, each leaving his Churinga behind. His body died, but some natural feature, such as a rock or tree, arose to mark the spot, while his spirit part remained in the Churinga. These Churinga, as well as others that the wandering parties left behind them, were stored in Pertalchera, or sacred storehouses, that usually had the form of small caves and fissures in the rocks, or even a hollow tree of a carefully concealed hole in a sand-bank. The result is that, as we follow their wanderings, we find the whole country is dotted over with Knanikilla, or local totem centres, at each of which are deposited a number of Churinga, with Kuruna, or spirit individuals, associated with them. Each Knanikilla is, of course, connected with one totem. In one part we have a definite locality, with its group of wild cat spirit individuals; in another, a group of emu; in another, a group of frog, and so on through the various totems; and it is this idea of spirit individuals associated with Churinga and resident in certain definite spots that lies at the root of the present totemic system of the Arunta tribe.

Source: Spencer, Walter Baldwin & Gillen, Francis James. (1927). *The Arunta: A Study of a Stone Age People*. London: Macmillan and Company, p. 75.

chaeological sites dating to around 40,000–30,000 years ago, when both Papua New Guinea and Tasmania were connected to Australia (Greater Australia). Earlier dates, however, are continually being entertained and heatedly debated. For example, recent redating of a Lake Mungo (New South Wales) skeleton, which was originally dated to around 30,000 years, has arrived at dates of twice that age and more. All skeletal data can be linked to the present indigenous population.

Linguistically, Australian languages share much in common and have little close association with languages outside Australia apart from some in Papua New Guinea. Archaeological data indicate that by 35,000 years ago occupation stretched from the tropics to around the temperate Tasmanian glaciers. By 30,000 years ago, most major environments of the continent were peopled, with the arid core being populated shortly after. The human population appears to have had little dramatic effect either upon major vegetation patterns, vulnerable to Aboriginal burning practices, or fauna. People and now extinct Pleistocene fauna (including megafauna) appear to have coexisted for tens of thousands of years. After the glacial maximum 18,000 years ago, the numbers and use of archaeological sites increaseed in many environments of Greater Australia. This general trend may be a reflection of climatic amelioration and continues throughout the more humid period after 10,000 years ago, becoming most marked in the last 4,000 years, even though climate at that time became drier and more stressful. In general this trend suggests increasing Aboriginal population sizes and densities even in the face of climatic reversal. Archaeological evidence of related cultural changes begins after 18,000 year ago but is most marked in the last 4,000 years. For example, from 4,000 years ago cemeteries in southeastern Australia, which begin around 13,000 years ago, are larger and more complex, and painted rock art styles in northeastern Australia become highly regionalized. At this time also, in arid and semiarid regions use of grass seeds is intensified and many environment are more intensively occupied, including the harshest deserts, some offshore tropical islands, tropical rain forests, and southeastern wetlands and highlands. This suggests increases in population sizes and densities and more intensive, more territorial socioeconomic patterns.

On reexamination, therefore, Aboriginal Australia, although culturally unique, also begins to demonstrate in many subtle ways some of the same patterns and trends found among hunter-gatherer peoples on other continents. Prior notions of a timeless people in a timeless land have given way to more dynamic portrayals.

Harry Lourandos

Further Reading

Altman, J. C. (1987). *Hunter-gatherers today: An Aboriginal economy in north Australia*. Canberra, Australia: Australian Institute of Aboriginal Studies.

Bell, D. (1983). *Daughters of the Dreaming*. Melbourne, Australia: McPhee Gribble.

Butlin, N. G. (1993). *Economics and the Dreamtime: A hypothetical history*. Cambridge, UK: Cambridge University Press.

David, B., & Lourandos, H. (1998). Rock art and sociodemography in northeastern Australian prehistory. *World Archaeology 30*(2), 193–219.

David, B., & Lourandos, H. (1999). Landscape as mind: Land use, cultural space and change in north Queensland prehistory. *Quaternary International*, 59, 107–123.

Dixon, R. M. W. (1980). *The languages of Australia*. Cambridge, UK: Cambridge University Press.

Flood, J. (1995). *Archaeology of the Dreamtime* (New ed.). Sydney, Australia: Angus and Robertson.

Hynes, R. A., & Chase, A. K. (1982). Plants, sites and domiculture: Aboriginal influence upon plant communities in Cape York Peninsula. *Archaeology in Oceania*, 17(1), 38–50.

Lourandos, H. (1980). Change or stability?: Hydraulics, hunter-gatherers and population in temperate Australia. *World Archaeology*, 11(3), 245–266.

Lourandos, H. (1997). *Continent of hunter-gatherers: New perspectives in Australian prehistory*. Cambridge, UK: Cambridge University Press.

Mulvaney, J., & Kamminga, J. (1999). *Prehistory of Australia*. Sydney, Australia: Allen and Unwin.

O'Connell, J. F., & Allen, J. (1995). Human reactions to the Pleistocene-Holocene transition in Greater Australia: A summary. *Antiquity*, 69(265), 855–862.

Pardoe, C. (1995). Riverine, biological and cultural evolution in southeastern Australia. *Antiquity*, 69(265), 696–713.

Peterson, N. (Ed.) (1976). *Tribes and boundaries in Australia*. Canberra, Australia: Australian Institute of Aboriginal Studies.

Smith, M. (1986). The antiquity of seed grinding in central Australia. *Archaeology in Oceania*, 21, 29–39.

Thorne, A. G. (2000). Age of the Lake Mungo 3 skeleton: Reply to Bowler and Magee and to Gillespie and Roberts. *Journal of Human Evolution*, 38(5), 733–741.

Thorne, A., Grun, R., Mortimer, G., Spooner, N. A., Simpson, J. J., McCulloch, M., et al. (1999). Australia's oldest human remains: age of the Lake Mungo 3 skeleton. *Journal of Human Evolution*, 36, 591–612.

Williams, N. W., & Hunn, E. S. (Eds.). (1982). *Resource managers: North American and Australian hunter-gatherers*. Boulder, CO: Westview Press.

Australian Conservation Foundation

The Australian Conservation Foundation (ACF) was founded in 1964. Although issue-based or local conservation groups had operated in Australia during the nineteenth century, the founding of the ACF was the first attempt to establish a truly national organization for environmental advocacy and campaigning. It still plays an important role but is no longer the only national conservation group, having been joined by such groups as the Wilderness Society and the Worldwide Fund for Nature. It is governed by a council with equal representation of individuals from each of the Australian states.

The ACF began as a politically conservative organization. Its founder was environmental scientist Francis Ratcliffe; its first president was High Court Chief Justice Sir Garfield Barwick; and many other conservative luminaries were on its council, including top business leaders. Prince Philip, the duke of Edinburgh, also played an important role in the ACF during its first decade, as did Australian poet Judith Wright (although she was no conservative). The ACF tended to emphasize research that would back up its lobbying efforts through "old boy networks."

However, in an era of increasing radicalization and involvement of young activists, this older group of leaders was removed in 1973, replaced by younger, more militant leaders. They were especially critical of the ACF council's failure to argue more effectively for preventing the damming of Lake Pedder in Tasmania. The new, more militant leaders included conservationists whose names would become household words— Milo Dunphy, Geoff Mosley, Jack Mundey, and John Sinclair. Dunphy was the leading conservationist in New South Wales until his death in the late 1990s; Mosley was the ACF director from 1973 to 1986 and is still active. Jack Mundey was the leader of the famous Sydney Green Bans movement, and John Sinclair was leader of the campaign to protect Fraser Island.

The ACF played an important national role, along with the Tasmanian Wilderness Society, in the massive campaign to stop the flooding of southwest Tasmania's Franklin River for hydroelectricity. This campaign, begun during the mid-1970s, ended with the 1983 river blockade, the victory of the antidam Hawke Labor Party in 1983, and the Franklin Dam High Court case that recognized a more important role for the federal government in environmental matters.

During the late 1980s the ACF enjoyed a strong relationship with the federal Labor government, and its leadership was evident in many campaigns, often resulting in significant government policy changes. These included Australian support for an end to whaling, opposition to uranium mining, opposition to the woodchipping of many old-growth forests, opposition to sand mining on Fraser Island, support for World Heritage listing of the wet tropics of far north Queensland and Kakadu in the Northern Territory, and opposition to mining in Antarctica.

The last decade has brought difficult times for many environmental advocacy groups such as the ACF as they have struggled with such problems as decreasing budgets, unsympathetic governments, and more aggressive and smarter industry groups. However, the ACF continues to provide research, lobbying, high-profile advocacy, occasional mass mobilizations, and widespread community education. Its current president is rock star Peter Garrett, and its executive director is conservationist Don Henry.

Drew Hutton

Further Reading

Broadbent, B. (1999). *Inside the greening: 25 years of the Australian Conservation Foundation.* Elwood, Australia: Insite Press.

Green, R. (Ed.). (1981). *Battle for the Franklin.* Melbourne, Australia: Fontana and ACF.

Australian Conservation Foundation. (n.d.). *Habitat.* Available at http://www.acfonline.org.au/docs/publications/habitat.asp

Hutton, D., & Connors, L. (1999). *A history of the Australian environment movement.* Cambridge, UK: Cambridge University Press.

Sinclair, J., & Corris, P. (1994). *Fighting for Fraser Island.* Alexandria, Australia: Kerr.

Wright, J. (1977). *The coral battleground.* West Melbourne, Australia: Nelson.

Austria

(2000 est. pop. 8 million)

With 83,850 square kilometers, the landlocked, alpine country of Austria is one of the smaller states of the European Union, which it joined in 1995, having a close economic integration with other member nations, mainly Germany. Its population is about 8 million, with an annual growth rate of .3 percent, an important portion of which is caused by migration. Austria is among the richest nations on earth, ranking eighth on the per-capita gross domestic product list of the Organization for Economic Cooperation and Development (OECD).

Since the Iron Age, mining has been an important source of wealth and agent of environmental change. The Roman Empire's Noricum Province, which covered part of the current territory, was important for its iron. Later, the archbishopric of Salzburg from the fifteenth century onward effectively promoted the large-scale introduction of spruce in its forests as firewood for the salt mines of Hallein. To pursue this development, extensive forest laws were created, among the first and most detailed in Europe. The Habsburg dynasty also relied on salt for part of its income (*Kammer*), hence the former salt mining district still bears the name *Salzkammergut* and shares the legacy of forest development with spruce for salt mining with the alpine valleys of the former archbishopric.

Iron, found especially in the province of Styria, proved almost equally destructive for local old-growth forests, of which only one small area still exists.

Two Events 600 Years Apart

Two Austrian events of special relevance to environmental history occurred more than six hundred years apart: The first event, a serious earthquake, occurred on 25 January 1348 in Carinthia, close to Villach. The southern part of the Dobratsch, a limestone mountain more than 2,000 meters high, slid into the valley. Several villages were buried; estimates of the number of people killed range from five thousand to ten thousand. The renowned medievalist Arno Borst has argued that the resulting earthquake and in particular the side effects such as floods and fires—together with the plague that ravaged Europe at the same time—can help to explain the change in European mentality from the medieval belief in God's creation and his ultimate wisdom to a Renaissance world view in which humans were seen as masters of creation that happened in the fourteenth century. Borst argues that the development of the Bourgeoisie is connected to these events, as is the beginning of secularization and the demise of the princely rulers for far-ranging consequences, which were probably not caused, but triggered by the catastrophe and its reverberations in distant monasteries all over Europe.

The second event was a referendum held on 5 November 1978, which might prove to be of similar long-term relevance. Austria does not operate its only nuclear power plant, which was mothballed after the referendum against it. The plant was never in operation, but was completed and ready to be started. The referendum changed the future of nuclear energy in the country with a narrow majority of 50.5 percent. Nowadays Austrians feel seriously threatened by surrounding nuclear reactors that are operated on much lower security standards than the standards that the Austrian reactor would have had, and the country's antinuclear policy is still quite firm. This policy is affordable due to Austria's terrain: The Alps offer unique possibilities for water power, and both the main river—the Danube—and many alpine valleys are dammed for hydroelectric power production. The Kaprun power plant was built in the post-World War II years with considerable monetary help from the United States.

Because Austria has more than 40 percent forest cover, forest degradation caused by long-range air and soil pollution is among the current environmental issues. The environmental legacy of high-performance agriculture is seen in widespread nitrate pollution of groundwater. Austrian farms, like those of other western European mountainous countries, are small and fragmented. Their products are relatively expensive. A successful niche strategy is organic farming. With almost 10 percent, Austria has the third-highest proportion of organic farmers in Europe, with only the petite principality of Liechtenstein showing a considerably greater number. But this is not enough to effectively halt pollution. Truck transit, especially on north-south routes through the alpine area, is a major concern, as well.

During the late twentieth century former mining areas changed into tourist areas—one of many instances of the move into the tertiary economic sector so prevalent in modern Austria. Tourism, important for its positive effect on the international trade balance, has environmental impacts on fragile mountain ecosystems. Avalanches injure and kill several people each year. The fragile mountain ecosystems will face considerable additional stress due to global environmental change. Thus, reduction of greenhouse gases is on the agenda of both nongovernmental organizations (NGOs) and the government. Several environmental NGOs are active in the country. Independent research institutes such as the Austrian Institute for Applied Ecology, founded in 1985, and branches of international organizations such as the Worldwide Fund for Nature (branch founded 1963) and Greenpeace (branch founded in 1982) are main public voices.

Protest Brings Conservation

In December 1984 part of the Danube Valley downstream of Vienna, a site designated for a dam and power plant, became the site of a cooperative protest of environmentalists of all kinds. Concern over one of the last stretches of undisturbed floodplain (close to the village of Hainburg) on a heavily utilized river found mass media support in an unprecedented way, resulting in the conservation of the area. Environmentalists in the country count the antinuclear referendum and the protest in Hainburg as their main victories.

National parks, small and seldom fully protected, are more controversial. The first, Hohe Tauern, was created in 1992, protecting a part of the central ridge of the Alps. Only part of it is internationally acknowledged. Among the fully acknowledged ones, Neusiedler See-Seewinkel (1993) is notable because it is a joint operation with Hungary, protecting one of the few saline steppe lakes in Europe. In 1996 the contested floodplain became Donau-Auen park. Austria's seven parks comprise 2,200 square kilometers, approximately 3 percent of the nation.

The country has developed a national plan for sustainable development, but governmental efforts are not considered sufficient by NGOs.

Austria's landscapes are characterized by their high diversity on a small scale. Conflicts about land use and necessary measures to ensure sustainable regional development led to a new, transdisciplinary research initiative, called "Sustainable Development of Austrian Cultural Landscapes." This initiative, started in 1995, was the first national environmental program ever to include a considerable amount of environmental history research. The field as such is not institutionalized in the country, nor does any comprehensive literature exist.

Verena Winiwarter

Further Reading

Borst, A. (1990). Das Erdbeben von 1348: Ein historischer Beitrag zur Katastrophenforschung [The earthquake of 1348: A historical contribution to catastroph research.] In *Ketzer und Artisten: Welten des Mittelalters.* Munich, Germany: Piper.

Projektgruppe Umweltgeschichte. (1999). *Landschaft hat Geschichte: Historische Entwicklung von Umwelt und Gesellschaft in Theyern* [CD-ROM]. Vienna: WUV-Verlag.

Sonnlechner, C., & Winiwarter, V. (1999). Recht und Verwaltung in grundherrschaftlichen Waldordnungen Niederösterreichs und Salzburgs (16. bis 18. Jahrhundert). In E. V. Heyen (Ed.), *Naturnutzung und Naturschutz in der europäischen Rechts- und Verwaltungsgeschichte* (pp. 57–85). (Jahrbuch für Europäische Verwaltungsgeschichte Band 11). Baden-Baden, Germany: Nomos.

Automobile

Most people think of the automobile as the invention that ushered out the nineteenth century and welcomed in the twentieth with a blast of exhaust smoke. It was in 1894, for instance, that Frank and Charles Duryea of Springfield, Massachusetts, took their first orders for a gasoline buggy, giving tentative birth to a new industry that would come to influence everything from urban planning to social life. But the very earliest cars, a strange and wonderful mélange of the practical and the eccentric, were built hundreds of years before the Duryea brothers took their first test drives down Springfield's Maple Street, and they ran on steam. Leonardo da Vinci thought about carriages that could move under their own power in the fifteenth century and left drawings showing rudimentary steering and transmission systems. In 1510, the German Renaissance painter Albrecht Durer sketched a complex and undoubtedly very heavy royal carriage, propelled by muscle power through geared cranks. The two yeoman pictured in Durer's drawing would have had to be stout hearted indeed to get the richly adorned vehicle moving.

The Age of Steam

At least until the first practical internal-combustion engine was developed in 1860, constructing a workable steam car for the road was the personal obsession of any number of scientific geniuses and eccentrics, very few of whom received anything but ribald laughter and scorn for their trouble. Automotive historians can only imagine the scene in Paris in 1769 when the Frenchman Nicholas Cugnot (1725–1824), a distinguished military engineer in the service of the Empress Maria Theresa of Austria, retired from active duty and began working, under royal commission, on his idea for a steam-powered military truck. The finished motor carriage may have been capable of only 11 kilometers per hour, but it moved. This, the world's first automotive test drive, sufficiently loosened royal purse strings to fund a second and larger model. Cugnot's second steam carriage had front-wheel drive, with the boiler hanging off the nose, a design that resulted in such an unbalanced weight distribution that the vehicle was barely steerable.

Pioneers after Cugnot

After Cugnot, the scene shifted to England, where the significance of the technical breakthroughs was matched only by the public's apathy toward them. Who could imagine that these outlandish contraptions, easily outrun by even the lamest horse, would ever become practical?

The Scottish pioneer James Watt (1736–1819), whose technical innovations made the Age of Steam possible, applied for and was granted a patent for a steam carriage in 1786, but did not actually build it. Watt was so afraid of explosions from high-pressure boilers that he had a covenant written into the lease for any potential tenants of his home, Heathfield Hall, stipulating that no steam carriage should ever be allowed to approach the house.

Richard Trevithick (1771–1833), a pioneer of the high-pressure steam engine, developed and patented a locomotivelike carriage with a boiler and smokestack that attained a heady 14 kilometers per hour on Christmas Eve, 1802. Trevithick's huge car, which had eight-foot rear wheels, made several relatively trouble-free trips, though during one the vehicle went awry and tore out some garden railing. Another intrepid British inventor, Goldsworthy Gurney (1793–1875) of the Sur-

A uniformed gas station attendant in Seoul, Korea in August 2002. COURTESY KAREN CHRISTENSEN.

rey Institute, built a long-distance steam car that in 1825 made an 136-kilometer round-trip journey without incident in ten hours. His coach was later damaged by antimachinery Luddites, who, according to a contemporary account, "considered all machinery directly injurious to their interests . . . [and] set upon the carriage and its occupants, seriously injuring Mr. Gurney and his assistant engineer, who had to be taken to Bath in an unconscious condition" (Stein 1961, 20).

Steam pioneers in the United States faced ridicule and censure, too. Oliver Evans (1755–1819) is not well-remembered today, but this unassuming and notably unsuccessful early-nineteenth-century engineer built the first self-propelled vehicle in the United States— and it also *swam*. This unsung mechanical genius also constructed the first high-pressure boiler in the United States and created an automation system for a grain mill that prefigured Henry Ford's assembly-line system by 150 years.

Evans, a Philadelphian, built his 18-metric-ton Orukter Amphibolos in 1805 as a dredger to excavate the city's waterfront. To get it to the Schuykill River, less than a kilometer from his workshop, he drove it up Market Street at between 6 and 7 kilometers per hour, attracting crowds. The 25 cents he charged onlookers was the only money Evans ever made from steam vehicles. The Amphibolos was notably unsuccessful as a dredger. It was sold for scrap, and Evans' later plan to build a fleet of produce-carrying trucks was rejected by the Lancaster Turnpike Company, which concluded that the trucks would probably shake to pieces on the terrible roads. They were undoubtedly right, and besides, the United States, like England, was developing a fast and efficient rail system. By 1850, there were 14,400 kilometers of railroads in the United States and nothing but muddy horse tracks for other traffic between most major towns and cities. Given that fact, it is remarkable that an unbowed Evans predicted in 1812 that "the time will come when people will travel in stages moved by steam engines, from one city to another, almost as fast as birds fly. . . . A carriage will set out from Washington in the morning, the passengers will breakfast in Baltimore, dine in Philadelphia and sup in New York the same day" (Georgana 1992, 11).

Obstacles to Steam-Powered Road Vehicles

The inventors struggled to make their fire-belching vehicles practical, and an English entrepreneur named Walter Hancock was the first to offer regular passenger

Cars and Pedestrian Streets

In one respect, however, people on the pedestrian streets of Boston, of Disneyland, or of shopping centers do behave differently from people on ordinary city streets heavily used by vehicles. The exception is significant. People cross over from one side to the other freely, and in using this freedom they do not seem to be inhibited by the curbs. These observations, coupled with the way people are forever sneaking across streets at forbidden places if they can get away with it—even at risk to their own lives—and coupled with the palpable impatience people so often exhibit at crossings, lead me to believe that the main virtue of pedestrian streets is not that they completely lack cars, but rather that they are not overwhelmed and dominated by floods of cars, and that they are easy to cross.

Even for children the point may be less to segregate the cars than to reduce the domination by cars and combat the erosion of sidewalk play space by cars. It would, of course, be ideal to dispose of cars entirely on city streets where children play; but worse troubles still are harvested if this means disposing of the other utilitarian purposes of sidewalks, and along with them, supervision. Sometimes such schemes, too, are automatically self-canceling. A housing project in Cincinnati affords an illustration. The houses in this project front on pedestrian precincts of lawns and sidewalks, and they back up on service alleys for cars and deliveries. All the casual coming and going occurs between the houses and the alleys and therefore, functionally, the backs of the houses have become the fronts and vice versa. Of course the alleys are where the children all are too.

Life attracts life. Where pedestrian separation is undertaken as some sort of abstract nicety and too many forms of life and activity go unaccommodated or are suppressed to make the nicety work, the arrangement goes unappreciated.

Source: Jacobs, Jane. (1961). *The Death and Life of Great American Cities.* New York: Vintage Books, p. 348.

---

routes of the type Evans imagined. For five months at some point in the years between 1824 and 1836, Hancock had nine steam coaches taking on paying customers. But Hancock's revolutionary bus service didn't attract enough brave souls; hence its financial collapse. It probably would be going too far to say a conspiracy killed the steam coaches, but certainly the powerful and established railroad interests threw some spikes in the road. As Ken Purdy reports in his classic book *Kings of the Road,*

> The railroads of the day took a very dim view indeed of the kind of competition steam coaches obviously could offer, and arrangements to make things difficult for the upstarts were not hard to contrive. A four-shilling toll-gate charge for horse-drawn coaches, for example, could easily be raised to two pounds and eight shillings for a steam coach. ... The steam coaches had received, in 1831, a clear bill of health from the House of Commons, but even Parliament could not prevail against the will of "the interests"—

not the first time it has turned out so. (Purdy 1949, 196)

Even more crippling than high road taxes was the infamous "Red Flag Act," passed in Britain in 1865, which restricted self-propelled vehicles to 2 miles an hour (3.2 kilometers an hour) in town and 4 (6.4 kilometers an hour) in the country. In addition, a person carrying a red flag had to walk in front of anything moving under its own power.

In the next half-century, steam carriages would make their mark, particularly in the United States. One particularly innovative model, shaped like a railroad locomotive, was commissioned by the government Indian agent Joseph Renshaw Brown to carry food and supplies to isolated bands of Sioux Indians before the Civil War, though the bad roads in the hinterlands of Minnesota made it impractical for the purpose. More successful were the brightly painted fire engines that appeared in several cities after the war was over. Steam cars survived the onslaught of internal combustion in the first decade of the twentieth century, and marques such as Stanley, Locomobile, and White had many admirers, who loved the cars' silent operation, range, and absence of a crank handle (a necessary accessory for cars powered by an internal-combustion engine in the days before electric starting). This latter advantage, shared by electric cars, was a prime consideration in an era when misapplied cranking could break your arm.

But Stanleys and Whites could take up to half an hour to work up a head of steam, consumed great amounts of water and wood fuel, and scared people who read accounts of boiler explosions. When rapid technological advancements radically improved the gasoline engine after 1905, the market for steam cars dried up. By 1911, White and Locomobile abandoned steamers and switched to gasoline power.

The Electric Car Plugs In

Electrics lasted longer, though they too eventually lost the race to the wider-ranging gasoline car. The dignified electric at least put up a pretty good fight before succumbing.

As the British authors of the book *Automania* suggest, the horrendous roads that had done much to stifle development of the early steam car actually worked to the advantage of the first electrics: "Until American roads were improved, almost all cars [were] kept within the city limits where the short range of the electric car was no great drawback" (Pettifer and Turner 1984, 55).

How bad were the roads? The United States had 43,200 kilometers of them as early as the 1830s, but most were dirt tracks. In 1903 only 10 percent of U.S. roads were paved, which helps explain why the first automobiles were inevitably "high wheelers." In addition to the seas of mud that formed whenever it rained, horse traffic turned streets into cesspools. In cities such as London and New York, armies of street sweepers were employed to clean up an average of 18 kilograms of dung per horse per day.

It is hardly surprising, then, that the quiet, clean electric car found favor. Electric vehicles grew out of early experiments with electric trains and trolleys and became possible only with the invention of the practical storage battery in 1859. The first true electric car may well have been a three-wheeled carriage made by Magnus Volk of Brighton, England, in 1888.

Electric cars first made a discernible impact in the United States through their use as taxis, particularly in New York City. By 1898, the Electric Carriage and Wagon Company had a fleet of twelve sturdy and stylish electric cabs—with well-appointed interiors able to accommodate gentlemen in top hats—plying the city streets. As in contemporary horse carriages, the driver sat outside on a raised platform.

Through small-scale, successful businesses like this, the electric car gradually won acceptance. By 1900, Americans could choose their motive power, and at the first-ever National Automobile Show, held that November in New York City, polled patrons overwhelmingly chose electric as their first choice, followed closely by steam. Gasoline ran a distant third, getting only 5 percent of the vote. There were 1,681 steam, 1,575 electric, and only 936 gasoline cars made that year.

Unlike the steam car tinkerers, who were sometimes lucky to escape with their lives after demonstrating their inventions, many of the early gasoline car pioneers became industrialists whose names are well remembered today. Gottlieb Daimler (1834–1900), Henry Ford (1863–1947), Ransom Olds (1864–1950), Carl Benz (1844–1929), William Durant (1861–1947; founder of a little company called General Motors), James Packard (1863–1928), and Clement Studebaker (1831–1901) are a few of the men who survived the vicious competition of the early years of motoring.

Many of the men who made their careers selling internal combustion had a lifelong fascination with electric cars. The German Ferdinand Porsche, for instance, built his first car, the Lohner Electric Chaise, in 1898 at the age of twenty-three. The Lohner-Porsche was absolutely groundbreaking in that it was the world's first front-wheel-drive car (excluding, perhaps, Nicholas Cugnot's carriage) and also introduced such revolutionary concepts as four-wheel brakes and an automatic transmission. Its use of electric motors in the four wheel hubs was revived for the 1971 moon lander and has been brought out again in some of today's hybrid cars.

Henry Ford was also fascinated by all things electrical, and he received early encouragement from the inventor Thomas Edison (1847–1931), who became a close friend. The two met at a Brooklyn dinner party in 1896, where Edison allegedly told Ford this about his gas buggies: "Young man (Ford was thirty-three), that's the thing, you have it. Keep at it. Electric cars must keep near to power stations. The storage battery is too heavy. Steam cars won't do, either, for they have to carry a boiler and fire. Your car is self-contained—

it carries its own power plant—no fire, no boiler, no smoke, no steam" (Crabb 1969, 168–169).

Nevertheless, neither Ford nor Edison gave up on electric cars, and in 1914 Ford Motor Company announced it would introduce a rechargeable vehicle of its own, powered by Edison's batteries. But by then it was clear that the electric car was on the road to nowhere, and the project never went beyond a few prototypes and some inflated press releases.

The End of an Era

The device that largely killed the electric car as a viable product—the self-starter for internal-combustion cars—was, like the electric car itself, first marketed to women. "Any Woman Can Start Your Car" read a 1911 ad from the Star Starter Company that featured a bonneted woman at the wheel of a crankless gas buggy. By "cranking from the seat, and not from the street," she was eliminating one of the last major advantages the early electric car had.

Use of the starter quickly spread throughout the industry, and sales of electrics plummeted, down to 6,000 vehicles, or 1 percent of the industry, by 1913. That same year, the Ford Model T alone sold 182,809. Electric carmakers closed or consolidated. Of the twenty companies that were selling electrics at the height of the market in 1910, less than ten survived until the end of World War I. A few specialized firms, such as industry leader Detroit Electric, limped into the 1920s, catering mainly to a diehard coterie of wealthy women.

Ironically, the electric car died out just as some of the major objections to it, such as high price, slow speed, and short range, were finally being addressed. The last Detroit Electrics could reach 56 kilometers per hour, which was competitive in the early 1920s. And the cheap, cheerful, and light Dey runabout of 1917 was offered to a largely indifferent public at just $985. No doubt electric-car technology would have continued to evolve, but with no industry to support it, research and development went as flat as one of Edison's batteries after an 80-kilometer run. Electrics, steamers, and, eventually, hydrogen cars became the province of backyard tinkerers and post-office-box entrepreneurs, who sold conversion kits in the back pages of *Popular Mechanics.*

Ironically, around this same time internal-combustion engines got a whole lot more dangerous, because tetraethyl lead—pioneered as a gasoline additive by chemist Thomas Midgley (1889–1944)—was intro-duced to prevent "knocking" and allow higher-compression engines. Although some public health officials raised an outcry about lead's potential to cause nervous-system and brain disorders when it built up in the human body, they were not heeded. Millions of metric tons of lead were pumped into the atmosphere from vehicular exhaust until it began being banned as an additive in the 1970s. Today, approximately 80 percent of worldwide gasoline sales are unleaded, and much of the remaining 20 percent have reduced lead content.

Stirrings of a Revival in Electrics

Electrics have made sporadic reappearances on the world stage, mostly in response to fuel crises such as the Arab oil embargo of 1973. Unfortunately, most have been underdeveloped conversions, such as the utility-endorsed Henney Kilowatt of 1959 to 1961, which started life as a French Renault Dauphine. Some 120 Henneys were built, which is a good run for a postwar electrical vehicle (EV).

In the early 1960s consumers around the world demonstrated their interest in small, economical cars by buying Volkswagen Beetles in the hundreds of thousands. In the United States, the three largest auto manufacturers responded to the foreign invasion with "compacts" such as the Ford Falcon and Dodge Dart, cars that seem laughably large and thirsty now. In Europe, tiny, highly fuel-efficient "microcars" such as the BMW Isetta enjoyed a brief vogue. Some independent optimists thought the time might be right for a modern electric. "Are Electric Cars Coming Back?" asked *The Saturday Evening Post* in 1960.

But many of the "new" EVs that appeared over the next two decades appeared predestined for failure, with bizarre pop-riveted bodies, tacky parts-bin interiors, and below-the-radar marketing. Consider, for example, the Urba Sports Trimuter of 1981, a "space-age" three-wheeler with a head-frying pop-up canopy, a needle nose, and a top speed of 96 kilometers per hour that the enterprising owner was supposed to build himself from $15 plans. Other half-baked monstrosities included the Free-Way Electric, which looked like a bug and was probably as easily squashed; the three-wheeled Kesling Yare, with styling straight out of *A Clockwork Orange*; and the B & Z Electric, which in photos appears to have been made of ill-fitting scrap wood.

Sebring-Vanguard actually managed to sell 2,200 two-seat, plastic-bodied CitiCars in the wake of the

1973 Arab oil embargo, but these basic phone booths on wheels, powered by golf-cart batteries with a top speed of only 48 kilometers per hour (and a range of 64 miles "in warm weather"), weren't likely to build a loyal customer base. Viable commuter EVs had to wait until the first reliable conversions appeared in the late 1980s.

Meanwhile, other would-be auto moguls were trying to revive the steam car. Robert Paxton McCulloch (1911–1977), a chainsaw millionaire, lost a sizable part of his fortune on a steam prototype, the Paxton Phoenix, between 1951 and 1954. And a colorful character named William Lear (1902–1978), who invented not only the eight-track stereo but the first aircraft automatic pilot (as well as the business jets that bear his name), spent $15 million in 1969 dollars on a turbine bus and a 250-horsepower turbine steam car concept. Both manufacturers succeeded in producing quiet, efficient, and modern steam engines with minimal pollution, but neither was fully developed. Even though his bus suffered from reliability problems and poor gas mileage, Lear was so confident that he tried (without success) to enter a steam car into the 1969 Indianapolis 500. British sports car maker Austin-Healey was also working on a steam car, one with four-wheel drive no less, in 1969.

Nevertheless, even relatively wealthy entrepreneurs like McCulloch and Lear soon discovered that they lacked the resources to successfully market a competitive car, no matter how brilliant the science behind its propulsion system. Gary Levine wrote in his 1974 book *The Car Solution*, that "the cry 'bring back the steam car' is now uttered with increasing frequency by those familiar with the nation's health, energy, and transportation problems" (123–124), but that cry proved easy to ignore.

The Modern Era: Gasoline Power and Pollution

Since 1969, the U.S. vehicle population has grown six times faster than the human population and double the rate of new drivers. Despite being only 5 percent of the world's population, Americans own 34 percent of the planet's cars. New car registrations in the United States grow at a rate of 2 percent a year. By 2100, the current 600 million cars registered worldwide (a third of them in the U.S.) could grow to 4.5 billion. China is leading the ominous Third World rush to "modernize" through the use of private cars. Although almost 80

percent of its travel is now either on foot or by bicycle, the world's most populous and rapidly industrializing country could have 100 million cars by 2015.

The global mania for private automobiles, together with the means to acquire them, translates into a huge projected increase in the world car population in the next fifty to one hundred years. Since cars account for a third of smog-related emissions and a quarter of global warming, such an increase would obviously have disastrous, deadly consequences for planetary health. The ill effects of all these automobiles are myriad. In half the world's cities, the biggest source of air pollution is exhaust emissions. The World Bank estimates that in Asia thousands of people die prematurely every year from filthy air. The problem is most acute in China, which relies heavily on coal, but the situation is bad elsewhere, as well. In Athens, Greece, the death rate climbs 500 percent on bad air days. In Sao Paulo, Brazil, dirty air and clogged streets have forced officials to set up a rotation system for drivers that keeps one-fifth of the city's cars off the road at any given time. Cars are also a huge problem in Tel Aviv, Israel, where smog is predicted to reach Mexico City levels (the worst in the world, with ozone levels three times safe limits) by 2010; already, it has led to outbreaks of asthma and bronchitis in the city and in nearby Jerusalem. In Prague, Czech Republic, smog occasionally forces police to set up roadblocks and keep all but essential traffic out of the city center. In Singapore, drivers pay a premium for licenses that allow them unlimited access to the highways.

But even as we are realizing what our continuing reliance on the private automobile is costing us, we are adding another 50 million of them to the planet's burden every year. Car making is now the largest manufacturing activity on earth.

The Growing Market in China

The U.S. auto industry sees rich opportunities in China. In 1997 General Motors joined with Shanghai Automotive Industry Corporation to build Buick Regals and Centuries in China. Wayne Booker, of Ford's international operations staff, says that the Chinese market is "vitally important to the long-term success of Ford" (Smith 1997). Chrysler recently unveiled a two-cylinder China Car, made of lightweight plastics.

China's own auto industry sold 2.4 million vehicles in 2002, according to the People's Bank of China. The country's auto industry is growing at the fastest rate in the world, and it increased by more than 30 percent between 1990 and 1998, according to the website www.just-auto.com. The industry grew by 20 percent in 2001 alone, reports the BBC, which adds that the number of passenger cars in the country is expected to double between 2002 and 2006. Other Asian countries rapidly adding cars to their roads are Vietnam, India, and Indonesia.

Whether in China or the United States, cars are pollution factories. In one year, the average gas-powered car produces five tons of carbon dioxide, which as it slowly builds up in the atmosphere causes global warming. Auto plants are also a significant source of emissions, particularly from their paint shops, though some manufacturers have switched to cleaner water-based paints. According to 1996 data from the U.S. Environmental Protection Agency, a single Mitsubishi plant in Normal, Illinois, produced 8.6 kilograms of toxic chemicals per vehicle.

There is some hope that a new generation of internal-combustion engines can eliminate the worst effects of tailpipe emissions. In 1997, Honda announced its Zero-Level Emission Vehicle, or ZLEV, whose 2.3-liter four-cylinder engine, it said, produced emissions that were actually cleaner than the ambient air. But Roland Hwang, then transportation program director of the Union of Concerned Scientists, said that Honda's claims did not take into account all the ancillary emissions associated with gasoline-powered automobiles, such as those produced by refineries and fuel transportation. A ZLEV, he said, "could be responsible for about seventy times more hydrocarbons and five times more nitrogen oxides than reported by Honda" (Job 1998).

The University of California, Riverside, announced in 2002 that preliminary results of its low-emission vehicle study show that internal-combustion engines can be as clean as gas-electric hybrids and meet strict emissions standards. Researcher Jim Lentz told the *Los Angeles Times* that since the 1970s emissions have gone from measurements like 10 grams per mile to hundredths or even thousandths of a gram per mile.

The Impact of Sports Utility Vehicles

But advances in clean engine technology have been obliterated by the rapid growth of the gas-guzzling sport utility vehicle (SUV), especially in the United States. In 1985, SUVs accounted for only 2 percent of new vehicles sold in the United States; in 2003 they were the most popular form of vehicle, accounting for more than 25 percent of sales. No other country has taken to the SUV with quite such alacrity, but they are an increasingly familiar sight on world roads.

In the United States, SUVs are considered light trucks and are allowed to pollute more than cars. A Volkswagen New Beetle (a small car) will emit close to 49 metric tons of carbon dioxide in its lifetime, according to Friends of the Earth, while a Lincoln Navigator (an SUV) will emit 90 metric tons. The National Academy of Sciences reports that light trucks (including SUVs, minivans, and pickup trucks) could reach 13 kilometers per liter (30 miles per gallon) with an expenditure of $1,200 to $1,300 per vehicle, but they are required only to meet the federal light-truck standard of 20.7 miles per gallon (approximately 9 kilometers per liter).

Automakers Ford and General Motors announced efforts in 2000 to improve fuel economy for SUVs, but the vehicles still lag behind. The Cadillac Escalade, Dodge Durango, GMC Yukon and other heavy SUVs average 5 kilometers per liter (12 miles per gallon) in city driving. The Environmental Protection Agency estimates that a 1.2 kilometer-per-liter (3 mile-per-gallon) increase in average fuel economy would save $25 billion a year in fuel costs and eliminate 140 metric tons of carbon dioxide emissions annually.

Associated Environmental Problems

Beyond the tailpipe, there is the simple fact that a third of the average U.S. city's land is devoted to serving the car, including roads, service stations and parking lots. According to anticar activist Jan Lundberg, founder of the Alliance for a Paving Moratorium, asphalt now covers 96,000 square kilometers of the United States, obliterating 16 million hectares of farmland. Two percent of the nation's surface area and 10 percent of the arable land are covered over, he says.

As cities sprawl farther into distant suburbs, daily commutes are also spiraling upward. An hour a day in the car has become the U.S. national norm. The average U.S. family takes ten car trips a day, mostly for shopping, socializing, or recreation. For every 16 kilometers traveled, approximately 14 are taken in a car. Despite the fact that the U.S. interstate highway system is completely built out, $200 million is spent every day constructing, fixing, and improving roads in the United States. Traffic management and parking enforcement on those roads costs $48 billion annually, and $20 billion is spent on routine maintenance. And yet, the National Transportation Board predicts that delays caused by congestion will increase by 5.6 billion hours in the period between 1995 and 2015, wasting an unnecessary 28 billion liters of fuel. The General Accounting Office, a federal agency, puts the loss of national productivity resulting from traffic congestion at $100 billion a year. More than half (70 percent) of all daily peak-hour travel on interstates now occurs under stop-and-go conditions.

A 2000 study prepared for the Green Party in England and Wales looked at annual costs attributable to road transport, and concluded that the basic £6 billion cost was augmented by a £19 billion cost for congestion, a £11.1 health cost, a £2.9 billion accident cost, and a £2.6 billion noise cost.

A Revolution in Technology

Given these challenges, it is perhaps fortunate for the human race that alternative fuel technology has continued to develop and that replacements for the internal-combustion engine may at last be practical. Fuel cell technology, first demonstrated in principle in 1839, can be compared to car battery technology in that both fuel cells and traditional car batteries produce electricity. But batteries store both their fuel and their oxidizer internally, which means that periodically they have to be recharged. By contrast the fuel cell, like a car engine, can run continuously because its fuel and oxygen are not sealed up inside it.

Although there are several different kinds of fuel cell, only one type, the proton-exchange membrane (PEM) cell is seriously being considered for cars. Although the modern work on fuel cells is all fairly recent, the technical problems of the cells themselves have been mostly worked out, and the main hurdles concern the building of a worldwide infrastructure for hydrogen production and distribution. Many carmakers, including Ford, DaimlerChrysler, Honda, and Toyota, expect to have fuel-cell cars on the road—at least in prototype form—by the end of 2003, but analysts don't expect hydrogen vehicles to make a serious impact on internal combustion until 2015 or 2020. When they arrive, they promise a new era of sustainable, zero-emission cars and trucks.

Meanwhile, battery-powered EVs have largely fallen by the wayside because of their limited range. When equipped with modern lead-acid batteries, the otherwise ultra-sophisticated EV1, introduced by General Motors with much fanfare in 1996, can go no farther than 112 kilometers in city driving before needing a recharge. The battery car therefore has severe handicaps in the race to become the world's mainstream automobile. In 2002 only a handful were being built around the world, and Ford announced it was disman-

tling its Th!nk division, which produced battery vehicles such as the Norwegian-sourced City car.

The batteries are the problem. Range-limited lead-acid packs—the most affordable option—were until recently the standard for most EVs, though the more exotic nickel metal hydride (NiMH) packs have rapidly taken their place. The technology graveyards are littered with dead battery technologies, including sodium-sulfur, a fiasco in early Ford EVs, and zinc-air. Other battery types are more promising, including lithium-ion, which is showing up in a wide variety of consumer products. But will lithium batteries, which could offer high energy density, long cycle life, and the ability to work in many different temperatures, ever be practical in cars? Unfortunately, like the sodium-sulfur batteries in the Ford Ecostar, lithium-ion presents a fire hazard because lithium itself is highly reactive.

One possible solution to the limitations posed by battery technology is to use the hybrid gas-electric car as a cleaner and greener interim step, plugging a gap of several years as fuel cell cars continue development. Like the fuel cell, the hybrid idea is not new, since engineers have long recognized that electric motors are great for accelerating and that gas engines work best at a steady speed.

One of the first hybrids was the Woods Interurban of 1905, which for most uses was a battery-powered electric. Long-distance drivers had the option, however, of swapping the electric power unit (supposedly a fifteen-minute job) for a two-cylinder gasoline engine and drivetrain. The Interurban didn't find many customers. Of more recent vintage was the experimental GM 512 of 1969, a very lightweight two-passenger hybrid car whose entire front was hinged, eliminating the need for a door. Like many modern hybrid designs, the 512 automatically switched from electric power to two-cylinder gas power. Other hybrid concept cars included Lincoln-Mercury's Antser, developed in the 1980s, and Ford's Synergy 2010.

The first production hybrid, when it finally arrived in 1997, came in the guise of the modest Toyota Prius, not a futuristic show car. The Prius, which has been steadily improved since its debut, achieves approximately 21 kilometers per liter (50 miles per gallon). Introduced at around the same time, the Honda Insight two-seater hybrid achieves an incredible 29 kilometers per liter (70 miles per gallon) on the highway. In 2002 Honda made a third hybrid, a 21-kilometer-per-liter version of its Civic sedan, available. By late 2002, several hundred thousand hybrids had been sold worldwide, making them the most successful EVs ever sold. But most analysts think it will be the fuel-cell car that finally replaces internal-combustion and ends the hundred-year reign of fossil fuels for the world's transportation.

Jim Motavalli

Further Reading

Angelucci, E., & Bellucci, A. (1974). *The automobile from steam to gasoline.* New York: McGraw-Hill.

Bradsher, K. (2002). *High and mighty: SUVs—the world's most dangerous vehicles and how they got that way.* New York: Public Affairs.

Crabb, A. R. (1969). *Birth of a giant: The men and incidents that gave America the motorcar.* Philadelphia: Chilton Book Co.

DeCicco, J. K, Martin, J., & Martin, T. (2000). *ACEEE's green book: The environmental guide to cars and trucks.* Washington, DC: The American Council for an Energy-Efficient Economy.

Flink, J. J. (1970). *America adopts the automobile, 1895–1910.* Cambridge, MA: MIT Press.

Furnas, J. C. (1960, March 12). Are electric cars coming back? *Saturday Evening Post.*

Georgana, N. (1992). *The American automobile: A centenary.* New York: Smithmark Publishers.

Jack, D. (2000). *Taken For a ride: Detroit's big three and the politics of pollution.* New York: Four Walls Eight Windows.

Job, A. M. (1998). Honda's truly comparable total ZLEV pollutants. *Mercury News.* Retrieved March 4, 2003, from http://www.parc.xerox.com/solutions/enhancedthumbnails/demo-enh/Demo-Hybrid/120/solstice.crest.org/efficiency/ev-list-archive/9803/msg00549.html

Kay, J. H. (1997). *Asphalt nation.* New York: Crown Publishers.

Levine, G. (1974). *The car solution: The steam engine comes of age.* New York: Horizon Press.

Montagu of Beaulieu, Edward John Barrington Douglas-Scott-Montagu, Baron, & Bird, A. (1971). *Steam Cars: 1770 to 1970.* New York: St. Martin's Press.

Nadis, S., & MacKenzie, J. J. (1993). *Car trouble: A world resources guide.* Boston: Beacon Press.

Pettifer, J., & Turner, N. (1984). *Automania.* Boston: Little, Brown and Company.

Purdy, K. (1949). *Kings of the road.* Boston: Atlantic Monthly Press.

Schiffer, B.M. (1994). *Taking charge: The electric automobile in America.* Washington, DC: Smithsonian Institute Press.

Sears, S. W. (1977). *The automobile in America.* New York: American Heritage Publishing Company.

Shnayerson, M. (1996). *The car that could: The inside story of GM's revolutionary electric vehicle.* New York: Random House.

Smith, G. (1997, Spring). Buick does Beijing. *Earth Island Journal.* Retrieved March 4, 2003, from http://www.earthisland.org/eijournal/new_articles.cfm?articl eID=320&journalID=50

Sperling, D. (1995). *Future drive: Electric vehicles and sustainable transportation.* Washington, DC: Island Press.

Stein, R. (1961). *The treasury of the automobile.* New York: Golden Press.

Whitener, B. (1981). *The electric car book.* Louisville, KY: Love Street Books.

Zuckerman, W. (1991). *End of the road: From world car crisis to sustainable transportation.* White River Junction, VT: Chelsea Green.

Avalanches

Avalanches are masses of snow—often mixed with ice, water, soil, or rock—that slide down a mountain slope. Approximately 1 million avalanches occur worldwide every year, although only a small portion threaten people. Avalanches generally occur on slopes between 30 and 60 degrees, where the incline is steep enough to produce momentum but not too steep for snow accumulation. Although avalanches vary in size, snow slides of less than 45 meters across the slope and 23 meters vertically are generally considered "sloughs," not avalanches. Two categories of avalanches exist: (1) loose snow avalanches, which start at a single point on the slope, spread out as they descend, and involve primarily surface snow and (2) slab avalanches, which consist of a rectangular-shaped block of snow that separates entirely from the slope and then descends. Even though loose snow avalanches attain the highest speeds (the fastest reach 240–320 kilometers per hour), slab avalanches are more dangerous because escape is difficult. The word *avalanche* comes from the Old French word *avalanste*, which derives from *avaler*, meaning "to descend or come down"; English usage of *avalanche* dates to the eighteenth century.

People and Avalanches

Although avalanches do not threaten most of the world's population, they occur in all mountainous areas, which cover 20 percent of the Earth's land surface. Through history, people have increasingly traveled through, lived near, worked on, and fought over the world's mountains, thus escalating exposure to avalanches. Travelers have a long history with avalanches. In 218 BCE avalanches killed thousands of soldiers—as well as several elephants—in Cartha-

ginian general Hannibal's army as it traveled across the Alps. Since the Middle Ages scores of European religious pilgrims crossing the Alps to (and from) Rome perished in avalanches or, at least, traveled in fear. Avalanches have also engulfed more modern travelers: The most deadly avalanche in United States history, for example, occurred in 1910, when ninety-

The world's most deadly avalanche in history: 31 May 1970, Cordillera Blanca, Peru. COURTESY GEORGE PLAFKER/U.S. GEOLOGICAL SURVEY.

six passengers and workers on the Great Northern Railroad in Washington State died after a single avalanche buried their entire train.

Settlers and workers have also faced avalanches. Written records from Iceland mention avalanches overtaking houses and villages since 1118 CE. Swiss inhabitants have reported destruction of churches, homes, and other buildings since the fifteenth century. Additionally, avalanches have plagued those drawn to mountains for work, such as pasturing animals, mining for precious metals, or cutting timber. In western North America, for example, the Gold Rush era from roughly 1850 to 1910 drew more people into mountains than ever before, and hundreds died in avalanches in mining centers like Alta, Utah, and Silverton, Colorado. These workers and settlers often exacerbated avalanche hazards by cutting trees, which, once cut, no longer anchored the snow.

Finally, military conflicts have exposed troops to the perils of avalanches. During World War I avalanches in the Alps killed as many as eighty thousand troops; many of the avalanches were set off by enemy troops. By World War II Frank Harper's *Military Ski Manual* (1943) taught U.S. soldiers how to prevent avalanche accidents when traveling in mountainous terrain and, additionally, how to trigger avalanches that would destroy the enemy.

Recreation and Avalanches

During the last two centuries avalanches have increasingly caused deaths as mountaineers and skiers have ventured into mountains. Mountain climbing began as a sport in the late eighteenth century and became popular by the twentieth century; skiing boomed after the 1950s. Avalanche fatalities worldwide correlate with trends in snow recreation. Between 1895 and 1989, 322 members of Himalayan mountaineering expeditions died from avalanches—the second-leading cause of death among mountaineers after falling. And the most deadly avalanche in recent European history occurred at a ski resort (Val d'Isère, France, 1970). Snow sports expose others to avalanches, too: Guides direct tourists and climbers; porters carry gear and cook food; service employees operate ski lifts, clean chalets, sell food, drive buses, and so forth; and snow patrols control avalanches and, importantly, rescue avalanche victims. All of these people can become victims themselves.

Avalanche Control

Three principal strategies have existed for preventing avalanches. First, avoidance is obviously the most effective strategy. Many Native Americans in North America avoided avalanches by descending from the Rocky Mountains onto the Great Plains during winter. Native people in the Himalayas also migrated out of avalanche-prone valleys during winter, a practice that tourism increasingly disrupts.

Second, defense against avalanches can also prove effective. As early as the ninth century Swiss inhabitants of the Valais region settled beneath heavily forested slopes that offered protection. Mountain residents in Switzerland constructed the first known walls and fences to defend against avalanches in 1518. Not until the nineteenth century, however, were defense structures widespread in the Alps.

Third, the most vigorous campaigns to control avalanches have occurred since the 1950s to protect recreationists. Although miners had experimented with dynamite, Europeans began systematic detonation of explosives during the 1930s to release avalanches when people were not present. By the 1960s avalanche control relied on a host of weapons, including 105-millimeter howitzers, recoilless rifles, and cannon-like weapons called "avalaunchers," in what became a virtual war against mountains. At the 1960 Olympic Games in Squaw Valley, California, the avalanche prevention team dropped bombs from lifts, cut cornices with torpedoes, and used delayed-fuse projectiles to release slab avalanches. Since the 1960s highways and ski resorts have been the focus for avalanche control. In the United States alone, snow patrols currently use roughly 100,000 bombs annually to control avalanches. Although the weapons are quite effective, occasional accidents occur when they malfunction or when hikers and skiers stumble on unexploded shells.

Deadliest Avalanches

Whereas the deadliest avalanches in North America, Europe, and Asia have killed hundreds, major avalanches in Peru have killed thousands. In 1725 an avalanche destroyed the town of Ancash, killing three thousand inhabitants. A 1962 avalanche inundated the town of Ranrahirca and claimed another four thousand lives. The deadliest avalanche in recorded history also occurred in Peru: An earthquake on 31 May 1970 triggered an avalanche that buried towns and killed an estimated fifteen thousand people, leaving only a few hundred survivors.

Mark Carey

Further Reading

Armstrong, B. R., & Williams, K. (1992). *The avalanche book* (Rev. ed.). Golden, CO: Fulcrum Publishing.

Atwater, M. (1968). *The avalanche hunters*. Philadelphia: Macrae Smith.

Bernbaum, E. (1990). *Sacred mountains of the world*. San Francisco: Sierra Club Books.

Fraser, C. (1978). *Avalanches and snow safety*. New York: Scribner.

Gallagher, D. (Ed.). (1967). *The snowy torrents: Avalanche accidents in the United States, 1910–1966*. Alta, UT: Alta Avalanche Study Center, United States Department of Agriculture, Forest Service.

Jenkins, M. (2000). *The white death: Tragedy and heroism in an avalanche zone*. New York: Random House.

McClung, D., & Schaerer, P. (1993). *The avalanche handbook*. Seattle, WA: The Mountaineers.

McDowell, B., & Fletcher, J. E. (1962). Avalanche! 3,500 Peruvians perish in seven minutes. *National Geographic, 121*(6), 855–880.

Oliver-Smith, A. (1986). *The martyred city: Death and rebirth in the Andes*. Albuquerque: University of New Mexico Press.

B

Bahro, Rudolf
(1935–1997)
German philosopher and economist

Rudolf Bahro wrote books critical of modern civilization, in which he predicted the early destruction of industrial societies and demanded an ecological-communitarian "Third Way" as an alternative to that destruction. He was famous as a dissident and critic of the East German political and economic systems and was among the founders of the Green Party in West Germany.

Bahro was born in Bad Flinsberg, Silesia, Germany (now Poland). He studied philosophy at Humboldt University in East Berlin, German Democratic Republic (1954–1959) and worked as an editor and ideologist for several journals between 1959 and 1967. He was an ardent Communist but came into conflict with the party line when he published an article by writer Volker Braun in *Forum*, a newspaper aimed at students. The article was unwelcome to the SED (the East German Socialist Party), and Bahro had to leave the newspaper and take work at a rubber factory in Berlin (1967–1977). According to Bahro, he ultimately realized that socialism served as only a pretense for power politics when troops from the Warsaw Pact countries invaded Czechoslovakia in 1968, and he decided then to call the system to account. In 1977 *Die Alternative*, an extensive assessment of the political and economic systems of East Germany from a Communist perspective, was published in West Germany. For this Bahro was arrested by state security and sentenced to eight years in prison in June 1978 for divulging official se-

crets. Because of international pressure, he was released in October 1979 and was expatriated to West Germany. There Bahro continued his criticism of industrial society and was among the founders of the Green Party (1980), which he left in 1985, disappointed by its increasing conformity. In 1987 Bahro's magnum opus *Logik der Rettung* (published in English as *Avoiding Social and Ecological Disaster: The Politics of World Transformation: An Inquiry into the Foundations of Spiritual and Ecological Politics*) was published. It was an apocalyptic vision of the self-destruction of humanity in industrial society. He developed the concept of a "Third Way" as an alternative to that self-destruction. Bahro saw, analogous to the New Age movement, the first step to salvation in a change of awareness and a spiritualization of each individual, leading to massive abandoning of modern society with its fixation on progress, technology, science, and individual freedom. Instead, he called for the creation of small, self-sustaining communities in harmony with nature. Bahro rejected parliamentary democracy and called for a "Government of Rescue," monitored by an ecological council, to implement the necessary restrictions on society in order to prevent ecological catastrophe. Because he considered a charismatic leader as necessary for this salvation, Bahro occasionally has been accused by the left as being eco-fascist. After reunification of the two Germanys, Bahro was appointed associate professor of social ecology at Humboldt University in Berlin in 1990. Bahro died of leukemia in Berlin.

Most of Bahro's calls for individuals to abandon industrial society in favor of small autonomous communities linked with each other remained a theory, and only a few attempts were made to put his ideas into practice. But in 1993 the model community LebensGut (a play of words rendering a double meaning: "live good" and "life estate") Pommritz was founded in Saxony, Germany, a project that is still under way. It has been aiming to combine subsistence economy, ecological agriculture, traditional handicrafts, modern technology, and cultural activities.

Ute Hasenöhrl

Further Reading

Bahro, R. (1978). *The alternative in Eastern Europe*. London: NLB.

Bahro, R. (1984). *From red to green: Interviews with New Left Review*. London: Verso.

Bahro, R. (1986). *Building the Green movement*. London: GMP.

Bahro, R. (1994). *Avoiding social and ecological disaster: The politics of world transformation: An inquiry into the foundations of spiritual and ecological politics*. Bath, UK: Gateway.

Hart, J., & Melle, U. (1999). On Rudolf Bahro. *Democracy and Nature: Irrationalism, Religion, Ecology and Democracy, 4*(11/12), 204–218.

Bailey, Florence Merriam
(1863–1948)
U.S. writer and ornithologist

The ornithologist and author Florence Augusta Merriam Bailey was one of several important American women who were nature writers and conservation advocates in the late nineteenth and early twentieth centuries. Her popular writing on birds and their habits introduced generations of children and adults to birdwatching, while her involvement in the Audubon Society in its early years aided its advocacy against the depredation of bird populations and habitats by the millinery trade. She is best known for her *Handbook of Birds of the Western United States* (first published in 1902, eleven editions by 1935), the earliest comprehensive guide to western birds. Bailey was the first female member (1885) and fellow (1929) of the American Ornithologists' Union (AOU).

Born in Locust Grove, New York, to Caroline Hart Merriam and U. S. Congressman Clinton Levi Merriam, Florence was formally educated in New York City where the family wintered. Influential in her intellectual development, however, was the wilderness surrounding the family's farm upstate where Florence walked, observed, and recorded the natural world around her. Her older brother Clinton Hart Merriam (known as Hart) shared her interest in nature. (Hart Merriam was an original founder of the American Ornithologists' Union, and would later become the first chief of the U.S. Biological Survey and co-founder of the National Geographic Society.) At Smith College as a special student during 1882–1886 (B.A. awarded belatedly in 1921), Florence Merriam formalized her study of nature and became an environmental activist, founding a college chapter of the Audubon Society to advocate against using birds and bird feathers in hat design in order to preserve rookeries and nesting sites. She initiated birdwatching expeditions, invited the naturalist John Burroughs to campus, and began publishing articles on bird behavior in the Audubon Society magazine. *Birds Through an Opera-Glass* (1889) collected her early journalism. *My Summer in a Mormon Village* (1894) described rural Utah where she was a tuberculosis convalescent. She spent 1893 at Stanford University, where she was influenced by her cousin, the evolutionary theorist David Starr Jordan, and developed a lifelong friendship with the botanist Alice Eastwood. After passing time in northern Arizona and near San Diego, she wrote an account of western birdwatching, *A-Birding on a Bronco* (1896). Upon relocating to Washington, D.C., Merriam became an active member of Women's National Science Club, and continued her environmental advocacy, working with Olive Thorne Miller on an AOU committee for the Protection of North American Birds. Merriam renewed her active support of the Audubon Society and continued to contribute articles to publications including the specialized bird publications *Bird-Lore, The Auk, The Condor*, as well as the children's magazine *St. Nicholas. Birds Of Village and Field* (1898) sought to introduce birdwatching—and by extension, bird preservation—to a widespread nonspecialist audience.

In December 1899, Florence Merriam married a mammal expert with the U.S. Biological Survey, Vernon Bailey. Together they documented western wildlife, with Merriam Bailey contributing to many of her husband's publications in addition to completing her best-known work, the encyclopedic *Handbook of Birds of the Western United States*. A sojourn in New Mexico in 1903 convinced the Baileys of the importance of preserving New Mexico's wilderness for the Taos Indians and other Native Americans, and led to Merriam Bailey's *Birds of New Mexico* (1928), which won the AOU's Brewster Medal in 1931. Other accolades Merriam Bailey earned included having a variety of California chickadee named after her (*Parus gambeli baileyae*), and earning an honorary LL.D. degree from the University of New Mexico (awarded in 1933, the same year Mary Austin earned one). *Among the Birds in the Grand Canyon National Park*, her final work, was published by the National Park Service in 1939. Bailey died 22 September 1948 in Washington, D.C.

Jen Hill

Further Reading

Bailey, F. M. (1890). *Birds through an opera glass.* Boston: Houghton Mifflin.

Bailey, F. M. (1896). *A-birding on a bronco.* Boston: Houghton Mifflin.

Bailey, F. M. (1902). *Handbook of birds of the western United States.* Boston: Houghton Mifflin.

Brooks, P. (1980, September). Birds and women. *Audubon,* 88–97.

Doughty, R. W. (1975). *Feather fashions and bird preservation.* Berkeley: University of California Press.

Edwards, T. S., & De Wolfe, E. A. (Eds.). (2001). *Such news of the land: U.S. women nature writers.* Hanover, NH: University Press of New England.

Kofalk, H. (1989). *No woman tenderfoot: Florence Merriam Bailey, pioneer naturalist.* College Station: Texas A & M University Press.

Norwood, V. (1993). *Made from this earth: American women and nature.* Chapel Hill: University of North Carolina Press.

Rossiter, M. W. (1982). *Women scientists in America.* Baltimore: Johns Hopkins University Press.

Strom, D. (Ed.). (1986). *Birdwatching with American women.* New York: W. W. Norton.

American Association of University Women. (1989). *Women of courage: Ten north country pioneers in profile.* Saint Lawrence County, NY: St. Lawrence County, New York Branch of the American Association of University Women.

Balkans

The term *Balkans* refers generally to that region comprised of either the mountain range that is found largely in Bulgaria and on the Balkan Peninsula of southeastern Europe or the peninsula itself—or both. The mountains themselves are often considered to be part of a larger system that includes the Carpathian Mountains and the Transylvanian Alps to the north. In addition, other closer ranges are often included as subsystems or as further extensions of the Balkan Mountains in this larger system (e.g., the Dinaric Alps, the North Albanian Mountains, the Rhodope Mountains, and the Stara Planina). The range itself is almost 550 kilometers in length and runs approximately along the 43rd parallel north from the Belogradchik Pass in the west to the Black Sea in the east. Mount Botev is the highest peak in the Balkans at 2,376 meters above sea level, and the range's average height is just under 725 meters above sea level. From a geological perspective, the Balkans are structurally mixed and there has been some incidence of significant earthquakes in the region.

The Balkan Peninsula is one of three large peninsulas that mark out the southern geography of the European continent, and it is defined largely as that land mass that is situated with the Mediterranean Sea to its south, the Aegean and Black Seas to its east, the Adriatic and Ionian Seas to its west, and the Danube River and its plains establishing its northern limit. Throughout the peninsula, rivers and associated valleys historically constituted the main conduits for communications, trade, and transport.

The Balkans are home to a variety of peoples that are distinguished mostly by language, divergent definitions of ethnicity and trajectories of national development, and religious affiliations, including Albanians, Bosnians, Bulgarians, Croats, Greeks, Macedonians, Muslims, Pomaks, Roma or Gypsies, Romanians, Serbs, Slovenes, and Turks. (Fewer than 50,000 Jews continue to live in the Balkans today, although there were approximately 1,200,000 prior to the late 1930s and 1940s.)

Contemporary descriptions of the Balkans as a region rarely conform to each other with respect to common physical borders as they instead imply a variety of cultural, historical, and/or political phenomena as seen from a plurality of perspectives. As a consequence, the region often refers to a core area comprised essentially of the former socialist state of Yugoslavia (i.e., today's states of Montenegro and Serbia, the Macedonian state FYROM, Bosnia and Herzegovina, Croatia, and Slovenia) and variously includes—due to cultural connections and/or physical proximity—Albania, northern parts of Greece, significant portions or all of Bulgaria, and sometimes even portions of Romania and/or of Hungary.

With respect to the ecologies of the region, there have been long-standing traditions of both settled agriculture and various forms of animal husbandry. Traditionally, the vast majority of agricultural endeavors throughout the region's histories have been undertaken on small scales by peasant farmers. Reflecting the agrarian traditions of small landholders that prevail in the region into the twenty-first century, most settlements besides the larger cities are towns and villages of relatively small size throughout much of the Balkans.

Agriculture, Nature Resources, and Industry

Animal husbandry in the lands took various forms and reflected variations both in herd/flock compositions and sizes, scales of production, and settlement preferences. Animals common in many parts of the region included sheep, goats, cattle, and pigs. Some regional traditions of livestock production have historically been depicted as causing both overgrazing and deforestation. In addition to settled traditions of husbandry, pastoral (semi-)nomadism and transhumance were common in some periods.

Concerning the extractive economies of the past and present, there have been longstanding practices of acquiring forest resources in the Balkans, with deforestation a common problem in some areas both historically and today. Also, anthracite and other varieties of coal have been mined in the region, as have copper and ferrous ores. Water resources are significant both in their own right and as sources of power generation.

Although the Ottoman empire controlled many parts of the region for almost five centuries, it has been the experiences of socialism and of postsocialist conflicts in the latter half of the twentieth century that have made the greatest impact on both the natural environments and the cultural landscapes of the region. Most processes of large-scale industrialization in the region took place during the socialist era. As in other parts of the Soviet and socialist realm, there were inadequate oversights in place to regulate both the development and appropriation of natural resources and the magnitude and nature of environmental impacts.

Environmental Issues in the Socialist and Post-Socialist Periods

The many types of environmental problems that can be seen as having their roots in the socialist period include situations associated with urban and industrial contamination and overconsumption of water resources and associated environments (e.g., wetlands). Severe problems in the Danube River and its delta are among the most apparent to international observers, but many similar situations exist in the region's other rivers, lakes, and wetlands. Also harmful and widespread in the region are situations caused by the following environmental issues: contamination of land resources from improper disposal of solid wastes, unsafe air emissions, pollution of land and water resources associated with mining activities, deforestation, contamination of land and water resources by agricultural practices, erosion of soil resources, and associated losses in biodiversity. These problems have continued into the post-socialist era due to inadequate resources to devote to necessary reforms. These environmentally and socioeconomically deleterious situations have also been further exacerbated by the conflicts following the collapse of socialism in Eastern Europe and the former Soviet Union.

Significant problems that have been created in the current environmental histories of the Balkan region can be seen to have their roots in the violent conflicts that have raged in the lands of much of the former Federal Republic of Yugoslavia and at its peripheries. In addition to the loss of human life and the destruction of significant places in the built landscapes of the region, battles and violent episodes of ethnic cleansing have produced many problems associated with the large numbers of displaced persons throughout the region. The fact that many refugees lacked the bare necessities of life (e.g., fuel, food, homes) also led to further environmental problems associated with deforestation, erosion, and despoliation of land and water resources. In addition, the environmental ramifications of civil war can be seen in other ways: areas littered with landmines and fears about the exposure of peoples to, and the contamination of lands and water sources by, dangerous types of munitions (especially the depleted uranium munitions employed by NATO peacekeeping forces) and facilities (e.g., factories, petrochemical plants) that were bombed.

In attempting to bring peace and long-term stability to the region, the United Nations is attempting to address fundamental questions of environmental security. The creation of the Joint United Nations Environment Programme (UNEP)/United Nations Centre for Human Settlements (Habitat) Balkans Task Force (BTF) has been the first of such initiatives specifically concerned with natural and human environments in the area. While the Balkans region still faces many challenges emanating from its historic and contemporary contexts, it is hoped that this initiative will resolve many of these problems and serve as a model for other regions of conflict (e.g. Afghanistan, central Africa) in dealing with environmental challenges.

Kyle Evered

Further Reading

Carter, F.W. (Ed.). (1977). *An historical geography of the Balkans*. London: Academic Press.

Todorova, M.N. (1997). *Imagining the Balkans*. New York: Oxford University Press.

United Nations Environment Programme (UNEP)/ United Nations Centre for Human Settlements (Habitat) Balkans Task Force (BTF) Retrieved March 11, 2003, from http://www.grid.unep.ch/btf/

Baltic Region

The Baltic Region is most commonly defined by the drainage basin of the Baltic Sea. From a political and administrative point of view, all nine countries bordering the Baltic Sea, namely Germany, Poland, Russia, Lithuania, Latvia, Estonia, and the Scandinavian states (Finland, Sweden, and Denmark) can be regarded as the Baltic Region. The former Soviet Russian provinces Lithuania, Latvia, and Estonia are historically known as the Baltic States.

The Baltic Sea drainage basin has a size of 1,745,100 square kilometers and is about four times larger than the Baltic Sea. About 85 million people live in the Baltic drainage area and nearly 15 million live within 10 kilometers of the coast. The population, as well as industry, is concentrated in the southern Baltic Region. Forty-five percent of the total population lives in Poland. Largest cities in the Baltic Region are St. Petersburg (5 million), Stockholm (1.6 million), and Copenhagen (1.35 million) along the Baltic Sea coast and Warsaw (1.65 million) at the Vistula River.

Landscape and Climate

Geologically, the northern Baltic Region (Sweden, Finland) is part of the Precambrian shield. The hill-studded plain landscape is characterized by magmatic and metamorphic rock partly covered by a thin layer of moraine material. During the last ice age the entire Baltic Region was covered with ice. After a fast melting (18,000–6000 BCE), the southern and eastern Baltic areas were covered with a mighty moraine layer, leaving an irregular plane landscape behind. The isostatic uplift in the northern Baltic Region still occurs, up to 8 millimeters per year. Fjords and the archipelago coast are typical for the rocky coasts of Scandinavia. Parts of the southern Baltic coast are submerging and undergo coastal erosion. Cliffs, sandy beaches, and shallow lagoons are typical features of the smooth coastline of the southern Baltic.

Due to the warm Gulf Stream, the climate in the southern Baltic Region is maritime and becomes more continental toward east and north. In northern Finland and Sweden, near the Arctic Circle, a polar-continental climate prevails. The average monthly temperature in July is around 16–18° C in the entire Baltic Region. Average January temperatures are between −12° C in the north and 0° C in the southwest. All areas receive sufficient amounts of rain and supply many rivers. Forests dominate the land cover (48 percent) followed by arable land (20 percent) and nonproductive open lands (17 percent). Only 8 percent in the Scandinavian and Russian drainage areas and 46 percent in the southern Baltic Region are arable land and pastures.

History and Economy

The large rivers and the Baltic Sea always played an important role for transport and exchange in the Baltic Region. In the ninth and tenth century the Scandinavian Vikings founded settlements and trading places along the entire Baltic coast. Their fast boats followed the large rivers and penetrated deep inland. Large areas and many cities, especially of the Russian territory, were affected. In the fourteenth century, the Hanse (a guilt of merchants) dominated trade and culture in the Baltic Region, and many Hanseatic cities were founded along the Baltic coasts. The importance of the region increased with increasing population and development especially of the eastern and northern Baltic areas. After World War II the Baltic region was divided into the western and northern countries with market economies as well as the socialistic states of Russia, Poland, and the German Democratic Republic (GDR). After the fall of the Iron Curtain in the early 1990s the Baltic Sea became a European sea of central importance again. Trade and travel intensified and the historical unity of the region is being restored. At the end of the twentieth century about $100 billion, or 6 percent of world trade, was generated in the Baltic Region. Sea transport is important in this respect. About 7 percent of the world sea trade takes place in Baltic Region (500 million tons in 1998), about 2,000 larger ships are on the Baltic Sea at every time, and seventy-six significant sea harbors are available. The Kattegat and the Kiel Canal link the Baltic Sea with the North Sea and the Atlantic Ocean. The 100-kilometer Kiel Canal is the artificial channel with the highest number of ship passages worldwide (37,600 ships in 1998).

Steep gradients in economic and social development still exist in the Baltic Region. The income per capita is 5–10 times higher in the northwestern countries (Finland, Sweden, Denmark, and Germany) compared to the east.

Environmental Situation

The gradients between east and west are visible in the state of water, land, and air pollution, especially from point sources. In 1992 the Helsinki Commission defined 132 hot spots of environmental pollution in the Baltic Region; 101 of them, as well as all priority hot spots, are located in the former eastern socialist countries. Major polluters are municipalities and industries. In the eastern and northern forested areas emissions from pulp and paper industries are significant. In the northwestern countries, measures to fight environmental pollution clearly have improved the state of the environment during the last decade. The emission and concentrations of hazardous substances in the environment, as well as the eutrophication of surface waters due to excessive nitrogen and phosphorus emission, declined significantly. In Poland and the Baltic States, progress is obvious, too, but environmental problems tend to remain in Russia. Insufficient sewage treatment, large-scale oil pollution from defective pipelines, as well as radioactive contamination from nuclear waste, nuclear-powered ships, and nuclear power stations are serious problems in Russia. Eight of the twenty-nine nuclear power stations in the Baltic Region are located in Russia and two of them in Lithuania. These power stations do not comply with international safety standards and are regarded as a serious danger for the entire region.

The emission of exhaust fumes is concentrated in the southern Baltic Region, where industries, traffic, and population density is highest. The acid atmospheric deposition resulting from these gases is regarded as one major reason for the intense forest dieback, especially in the hilly southern Baltic Region. Despite the reduction of the nitrogen and sulfur gas emissions during the last decade, forest dieback remains a serious problem. Long-distance transport of these gases and their deposition is responsible for the strong acidification of surface waters in Scandinavia, as well.

All countries bordering on the Baltic have signed the Helsinki Convention. The goal of the convention is to protect the marine environment of the Baltic Sea from all sources of pollution, and to restore and safeguard its ecological balance. Up to now, the governing body, the Helsinki Commission (HELCOM), has agreed on 134 recommendations and has positively influenced joint international environmental protection in the region. More important for the significant improvements of the environmental quality during the last two decades were the well developed, implemented, and monitored national and international environmental laws in the member states of the European Community. With the extension of the European Community by Poland and the Baltic States, a fast growth of economy and prosperity in the Baltic Region is expected. With the exception of Russia, the EC environmental laws then become valid in the entire Baltic Region and ongoing improvements of environmental quality and reductions of air, water, and soil pollution are expected, too.

In 1992 the Council of the Baltic States was founded to promote the joint political development of this region. The council consists of Norway, Iceland, and the nine states bordering the Baltic Sea.

Gerald Schernewski

See also Baltic Sea

Further Reading

Sweitzer, J., Langaas, S. & Folke, C. (1996). Land cover and population density in the Baltic Sea drainage basin: A GIS database. *AMBIO*, 25, 1991–1998.

Lozan, J. L., Lampe, R., Matthäus, W., Rachor, E., Rumohr, H., & Westerhagen, H. v. (Eds.). (1996). *Warnsignale aus der Ostsee*. Berlin, Germany: Parey.

Kononen, K. Bonsdorff, E., & Kessler, E. (Eds.). (2001). Man and the Baltic Sea. *AMBIO*, 30(4–5).

Baltic Sea

The Baltic Sea is an enclosed sea in central and northern Europe, bordered by Germany, Poland, Russia, Lithuania, Latvia, Estonia, Finland, Sweden, and Denmark. The Skagerrak and Kattegat, two arms of the Atlantic Ocean falling on the western and eastern sides of Denmark, respectively, connect the Baltic Sea to the North Sea and the Atlantic Ocean. The Baltic Sea covers an area of 412,000 square kilometers and has a volume of 21,700 cubic kilometers, an average depth of 52 meters, and a maximum depth of 459 meters, at Landsort deep. It has a maximum west-east stretch of about 1,200 kilometers and a south-north stretch of about 1,300 kilometers. The sea is divided by several sills (submerged ridges) into the Gulf of Bothnia in the north; the Gulf of Finland and the Gulf of Riga in the east; the Gotland and Bornholm Sea in the center, as well as the Arkona and Belt Sea; and Kattegat and Skagerrak in the west.

Evolution of the Baltic Sea

During the last ice age the entire Baltic Sea region was covered with ice. After the glaciers retreated, the Baltic Sea evolved during several stages. During the first stage, the Baltic Sea was what is known as the enclosed Baltic Ice Lake (11500 BCE). Due to sea level rise it became connected to the North Sea; at that point it was known as the Yoldia Sea (8300 BCE). After a land rise of up to 9 millimeters per year, it became the brackish lake-like Ancylus Sea (7500 BCE), which changed after a sea-level rise into the Littorina Sea (6000 BCE). In the following stages, when the Littorina Sea evolved into the Limnea and Mya Seas (since 600 BCE), only smaller alterations took place.

Characteristics of the Baltic Sea Today

The tidal range in the Baltic Sea is below 0.2 meters. With the exception of the northern part, water temperatures in most coastal waters reach 20 °C in summer and allow intensive seaside summer tourism. During winter, on average 150,000 square kilometers of the northern Baltic Sea are covered with ice for several months. Nowadays, ice cover in the southern and western Baltic Sea is rare. In the central Baltic Sea a vertical temperature stratification (thermocline) is established in a depth of about 20 meters and separates surface water from deeper water masses.

The Baltic Sea is the largest brackish water body in the world. About 440 cubic kilometers of freshwater per year enter the Baltic Sea from rivers. The annual precipitation of about 225 cubic kilometers per year exceeds the evaporation (185 cubic kilometers per year) and adds another 40 cubic kilometers per year to the freshwater budget. The water exchange time in the Baltic Sea is about 25 years. At the interface with the North Sea, about 470 cubic kilometers of water per year with a high salinity of 3 percent enter the Baltic Sea annually. Due to the higher density of the North Sea water, this inflow takes place near the sea bottom and is compensated by a near surface outflow of altogether 950 cubic kilometers per year. Spatial salinity gradients in the Baltic Sea are the result. In the Baltic Sea, the inflowing saline North Sea water forms a thick layer at the bottom, which is divided from overlaying water with lower salinity. This permanent salinity stratification (halocline) is most intensive in the western part of the Baltic Sea and decreases towards east. In the eastern and northern parts, salinity is below 5 parts per thousand; this increases toward the west to 20–25 parts per thousand. The inflow of saline and oxygen-rich North Sea water is driven by weather conditions. Until the 1970s these events took place nearly regularly. Between 1983 and 1992 and since 1995, no strong salt water intrusions have been observed. During these periods of stagnation, large areas of the depths of the Baltic Sea and its sediments have become oxygen free, and the consequent hydrogen sulfide formation has caused serious problems for the Baltic Sea ecosystem. Due to its brackish character, the Baltic Sea ecosystem has less diversity of fauna and flora than comparable freshwater or marine ecosystems, and many species live at the edge of their physiological ability.

The Impact of Humans on the Baltic Sea

The Baltic Sea suffers from ongoing human impact. Increasing industrial and urban development and intensified agriculture have increased the load of nitrogen in rivers that pour into the Baltic Sea to four times what it was at the beginning of the twentieth century, and have increased the phosphorus load in those rivers to eight times the levels at the beginning of the twentieth century. About 70 percent of that nitrogen load and 81 percent of the phosphorus load enter the Baltic Sea. In 1995 the Baltic Sea received 761,000 metric tons of nitrogen and 38,000 metric tons phosphorus from the drainage basin. The result is eutrophication (lack of oxygen caused by an efflorescence of plant life feeding on the nitrogen and phosphorous) of the sea, especially of the estuaries and coastal areas. The frequency and spatial coverage of excessive algal growth (algal blooms), with discoloration of the water and foam formation, as well as oxygen depletion in deeper water bodies, has increased. A reduction of water transparency has taken place and caused a decrease of depth and distribution of perennial macrophytes (large plant life). Shifts in fish and benthic (deep-water) fauna, as well as changes in the food-web, have been observed. In several cases, harmful algal blooms caused a poisoning of wild fish, fish in aquaculture farms, bottom fauna, and sea birds in coastal waters and lagoons. Since the late 1980s, the river loads of nitrogen, phosphorus, heavy metals, and pollutants have been decreasing. In some coastal areas eutrophication has already decreased in response, indicating a recovery.

Fisheries benefited from eutrophication. Between 1930 and 1980 Baltic fish catches increased from 100,000 metric tons to 1,000,000 metric tons as a result of eutrophication and intensified fishing. Cod, herring, and sprat constituted more than 80 percent of the catch and the fish biomass during that period. Changes in the ecosystem, biological interactions, and overfishing caused dramatic changes in the fish stock between 1980 and the late 1990s. An 80 percent decline in the cod stock to about 200,000 metric tons and a decline in the herring stock to 1,300,000 metric tons took place. In the same period, the commercially less valuable sprat stock tripled from approximately 667,000 metric tons to 2,000,000 metric tons. The total allowable catches in the Baltic Sea in 2001 were 105,000 metric tons for cod, 372,000 metric tons for herring, and 355,000 metric tons for sprat. To maintain minimum levels of spawning fish stocks, the total allowable catches were reduced by 30–46 percent between 1998 and 2001. This necessary reduction has serious economic consequences for the fish industry in the Baltic Sea.

Gerald Schernewski

Further Reading

Shepard, C. (Ed.). (2000). *Seas at the millennium: An environmental evaluation* (Vol. 1). Amsterdam: Pergamon.

European Enviroment Agency. (2001). *Eutrophication in Europe's coastal waters* (Topic Report July 2001). Copenhagen, Denmark: EEA.

Kononen, K. Bonsdorff, E., & Kessler, E. (Eds.). (2001). Man and the Baltic Sea. [Special Issue]. *Ambio*, 30 (4–5).

Lozan, J. L., Lampe, R., Matthäus, W., Rachor, E., Rumohr, H., & Westerhagen, H. v. (Eds.). (1996). *Warnsignale aus der Ostsee*. Berlin, Germany: Parey.

Bamboo

For centuries bamboo has played an indispensable part in the daily life of millions of people in tropical coun-

tries. Recently it has gained an increasing importance worldwide as a substitute for timber.

Bamboo is a unique group of tall grasses with woody jointed stems. Bamboo belongs to the subfamily Bambusoideae of the grass family Poaceae (or Gramineae). There are about seventy-five genera with about thirteen hundred species and varieties covering about 25 million hectares worldwide. Bamboo plants grow either single stemmed apart from each other (leptomorph type) in cooler and temperate regions (eastern Asia) or in dense clumps (pachymorph type) in warm, tropical regions (western Asia, Southeast Asia, South America). The woody culm (stem) is mostly hollow and characterized by walled septa (nodes), with internodes between. The nodes give the plant its strength.

Bamboo is the fastest-growing and most versatile plant on Earth. The culms arise from buds at the underground shoot-root system, the rhizome. Shoots emerge with the rainy season and expand within a few months to their final length of 10–30 centimeters and a diameter of 5–30 centimeters. During the growth of the culms, bamboo produces the highest amount of biomass (living matter) in the plant realm. Depending on type, location, and climate, the annual growth rate is about 10–25 metric tons, that is, 5–12 metric tons of air-dried biomass. After three to four years the culms are selectively harvested. Bamboo is a self-regenerating raw material; its production continues after individual culms have been cut due to the new shoots, which appear each year. Depending on the species, the culms of one population flower after forty to eighty years, mostly with a subsequent dying of the whole population across countries. This simultaneous flowering can have serious economic implications by depriving people of their basic natural resource.

There are over one thousand uses for the more than 10 million metric tons of bamboo produced annually. The shoots provide food and are utilized in large quantities. The culms have excellent technological properties for construction, scaffolding, handicraft products, furniture, fuel, and as material for secondary products, such as bamboo mats and boards as well as parquet. Over 1 billion people live in bamboo houses, from simple dwellings to four-story city houses and modern engineered structures. Bamboo processing is often done at craft level and needs relatively low capital investment. The fibers provide a valuable material for pulp and paper as substitute for wood. Bamboo crops are also used to provide wind protection in farming and to stabilize river banks and forest hillsides by the interlocked rhizome system. Due to the overexploitation of natural forests and the increasing demand for woody material, the increased plantation and better utilization of bamboo are strongly promoted. However, problems with stand management, harvest, storage, and biological hazards and the need for preservation against overexploitation of bamboo forests by an expanding bamboo industry have to be considered. Nevertheless, in a time of declining natural resources bamboo has a future.

Walter Liese

Further Reading

Cusack, V. (1999). *Bamboo world.* Kenthurst, Australia: Kangaroo Press.

Judziewicz, E. J., Clark, L. G., Londono, X., & Stern, M. J. (1999). *American bamboo.* Washington, DC and London: Smithsonian Institution Press.

Liese, W. (1998). *The anatomy of bamboo culms.* (INBAR Technical Report No. 18). Beijing, China: INBAR.

Meredith, T. J. (2001). *Bamboos for the gardens.* Portland, OR: Timber Press.

Bear

For hundreds of thousands of years humans and bears have had similar environments and lifestyles. For at least the last ten thousand years of that shared history, bears have also played important economic, spiritual, and symbolic roles in human cultures across the Americas, Asia, and Europe.

Why have humans found bears so fascinating for so long? Perhaps it is because humans eat many of the same foods, from fish to berries and roots and other plant parts. Bears also sometimes stand and walk erect on their hind legs, like humans, and often sit or sleep in very human-like postures. A skinned bear also looks uncannily similar to a human corpse; even today, hunters often mistake bear skeletons for human skeletons when they come across them in the deep woods.

The bear family, Ursidae, evolved from dog-like carnivores more than 20 million years ago. Omnivorous and highly adaptable, the eight species of living bears inhabit diverse environments in more than sixty countries, from Arctic tundra to dense forests, prairie grasslands, and desert steppes. Four species currently share the genus *Ursus*—polar bears *(U. maritimus)*, brown bears (also known as "grizzly bears," *U. arctos*), American black bears *(U. americanus)*, and Asiatic black bears *(U. thibetanus)*. Each of the other four species of living bears has its own genus and species—the spectacled bear of South America *(Tremarctos ornatus)*, the sun bear *(Helarctos malayanus)* and sloth bear *(Melursus ursinus)* of Asia, and the giant panda of China *(Ailuropoda melanoleuca)*. Bears vary greatly in size, from impressive 2.4-meter, 771-kilogram adult male polar bears to relatively diminutive 1.5-meter, 65-kilogram sun bears.

Whereas polar bears feed mainly on seals and other sea mammals, and giant pandas eat almost nothing but bamboo, most bears consume a wide variety of plant foods and supplement them with whatever animals they can catch or scavenge. Perhaps the best-known behavior of bears that live in cold climates is hibernation; hibernating bears may not eat, drink, or excrete for up to five months, surviving the worst of the winter by sleeping through it, snug in their dens.

Economic, Spiritual, and Symbolic Roles

Hibernating bears have served as an important source of food, fat, and furs for human hunters of the northern forests for thousands of years. These hunters often honor the spirits of the bears they have killed with elaborate ceremonies such as the Bear Festival of the Ainu people of Japan or the Bear Party of the Koyukon of Alaska, as well as with strict rules on proper ways to hunt, kill, and eat bears and on how the unusable remains, especially skulls and other skeletal parts, should be disposed of. Hunting peoples believe that only if the spirits of slain bears are properly honored will living bears allow themselves to be caught in the future.

In addition to hunting bears for food and clothing, people have tried to ritually draw on the bear's strength and ferocity. According to legend, Scandinavian warriors of the Middle Ages donned specially treated shirts made from bear skins to take on the fearlessness, strength, and stamina of enraged bears in battle. They were known as "berserkers," literally "bear sarkers" (those who wore bear shirts), and were said to be able to bite through the enemy's shields or walk through fire without injury while in their battle frenzy.

Bears have also been important for medical purposes in many cultures. Nearly all Native American tribes of the Great Plains have considered shamans with bear spirits as their allies to be the strongest healers. Many parts of bears have been used for millennia in traditional Chinese medicine as well; bear bile, for

A hunter in the Kodiak National Wildlife refuge in Alaska. COURTESY WILLIAM A. TROYER/U.S. FISH AND WILDLIFE SERVICE.

instance, is a crucial ingredient in cures for liver diseases and has been prescribed since at least the seventh century CE. The growing demand for bear bile and other medicines derived from bears has resulted in severe overhunting of many populations of Asian bears.

Evolving Attitudes

Attitudes toward bears in Western culture have changed dramatically since the Middle Ages. Many

medieval Europeans enjoyed attending bear-baiting events, in which a bear was chained to a tree, blinded, and "baited" into a frenzy by barking dogs, then forced to defend itself against human adversaries. Most contemporary Westerners prefer instead to observe bears in the wild, read about them (e.g., A. A. Milne's Winnie-the-Pooh), watch them on television (e.g., the cartoon characters Yogi Bear and Boo Boo), or cuddle them (e.g., toy "teddy bears," named after U.S. President Theodore "Teddy" Roosevelt, who reportedly refused to shoot a cub while on a bear hunt in 1902).

Like wolves, bears have become symbols of wilderness for many people today. This has led to conflicts over bear conservation. Bear species around the world face severe threats from habitat loss (polar bears face the added threat of global warming, which is literally causing much of their habitat to melt away). Whereas some people, such as environmentalists and wildlife biologists, favor protecting bear habitat from development and reintroducing bears into suitable habitat from which they had previously been removed, other people, such as farmers and ranchers, oppose these efforts, fearing that their crops or livestock would be endangered by bears.

Dave Aftandilian

Further Reading

Beecham, J. J., & Rohlman, J. (1994). *A shadow in the forest: Idaho's black bear.* Moscow: University of Idaho Press.

Coulbourne, G., & Pollard, P. (1997). *Myths.* Retrieved November 27, 2002, from www.bears.org

Coulbourne, G., & Pollard, P. (1997). *Species.* Retrieved November 27, 2002, from www.bears.org

Hallowell, A. I. (1926). Bear ceremonialism in the Northern Hemisphere. *American Anthropologist, 28*(1), 1–175.

National Wildlife Federation. (2002). *Bears of the world.* Retrieved on November 27, 2002, from http://www.nwf.org/keepthewildalive/bearsoftheworld.cfm

Nelson, R. K. (1983). *Make prayers to the raven: A Koyukon view of the northern forest.* Chicago: University of Chicago Press.

Newman, A., & Suk, J. (Eds.). (1978). *Bear crossings: An anthology of North American poets.* Los Angeles: New South Company.

Peacock, D. (1990). *Grizzly years: In search of the American wilderness.* New York: Henry Holt.

Rockwell, D. (1991). *Giving voice to bear: North American Indian myths, rituals, and images of the bear.* Niwot, CO: Roberts Rinehart.

Servheen, C., Herrero, S., & Peyton, B. (Eds.). (1999). *Bears: Status survey and conservation action plan.* Cambridge, UK: International Union for Conservation of Nature and Natural Resources (IUCN).

Shepard, P., & Sanders, B. (1985). *The sacred paw: The bear in nature, myth, and literature.* New York: Viking Penguin.

Stirling, I. (1988). *Polar bears.* Ann Arbor: University of Michigan Press.

Beaver

Once hunted and trapped to virtual extinction in both the Old and New Worlds, the beaver at first glance might seem to have had a negligible impact on environmental history. However, no other mammal besides humans has had greater impact. Left unmolested, the beaver has shaped the land, especially in North America, cutting down trees, constructing dams and canals, creating ponds and wetlands, ultimately converting, when dams break and are left in disrepair, forest into meadow. Yet the beaver was assaulted—in a centuries-long fur trade—and the changing relationship between man and this rodent was one key to historical patterns of ecological change in wide portions of North America.

Evolution and Characteristics

Living beavers are members of the genus *Castor* in the family *Castoridae*, rodents that evolved in North America and Europe during the Oligocene. Now-extinct fossil members of the family included spiral-burrowing beavers and, in North America, a giant semiaquatic beaver the size of a black bear. The genus *Castor* appeared during the late Miocene but reductions in species diversity during the Pleistocene left just two modern species, *C. canadensis* in North America and *C. fiber* in Europe and northern and western Asia.

C. canadensis and *C. fiber* are similar in size and weight (13–27 kilograms) and many other respects, but the former, with its orange, chisel-like incisors, has perfected the rodent's ability to burrow and gnaw. An excellent swimmer, it can travel up to 800 meters (one-half mile) under water at speeds of up to five miles per hour and remain submerged for fifteen minutes at a time. In pursuit of its vegetarian diet, especially tree cambium, lily roots, and shrubs, the beaver floods many acres of land by building dams of mud, grass, sticks, logs as long as six feet, and rocks. The ability to dredge canals and deepen the level of lodge entrances allows the beaver to live comfortably under the ice in shallow ponds and in safety from its major nonhuman predators—wolves and wolverines. *C. canadensis* is a social animal, living in family groups in lodges or burrows in the banks of ponds and rivers. A colony usually includes a monogamous pair of adults, one or two juveniles from the previous year's litter, and from 1 to 8 kits (usually 2 to 4) usually born in the late spring. While colonies can be distributed densely in a watershed, with neighboring colonies respecting each other's territory and with mating among family members, beavers do have a little understood pattern of population dispersal. A monogamous pair of beavers will rarely survive together more than ten years, but when unmolested, beaver colonies can thrive in an area for many more years, even adjusting to changes in riparian vegetation caused by their incessant harvesting.

Since remnant populations of *C. fiber* were found primarily in the banks of large rivers, it was long thought that it manipulated the environment far less than *C. canadensis*. However, recent experiences with rebounding *C. fiber* populations have shown that it is the near equal of its North American relative.

Environmental Impact

The habitat-transforming abilities of *C. canadensis* are nothing short of remarkable. Colonies often build a series of dams, creating a chain of terraced ponds. Beavers can build dams over 12 feet high, if necessary, and in a year or two extend dams several hundred feet to impound water. Beavers usually harvest trees within 100 yards of a pond but extend the range of their foraging with canals up to 700 feet in length.

C. canadensis alters its habitat profoundly. Its dams diminish the force of floods, raise the local water table, and hold back silt and soil nutrients. The ponds provide habitat for fish, amphibians, reptiles, aquatic insects, and crustaceans; other mammals like river otters, minks, muskrats, and raccoons; and a variety of water birds and passerines. The meadows that remain after a dam has been abandoned are fertile and especially conducive to the growth to willows and aspens—favorite beaver foods—thus inviting their return. Unlike human farmers, when beavers move on they leave the land more fertile than they found it. Indigenous people and European newcomers recognized the importance of beavers in landscape, and today the traces of beavers can be read in the countless watercourses, meadows, valleys and towns bearing their name.

Beaver as a Commodity

Humans desired beavers not just for their meat and pelts, but for castoreum, the secretions of the scent gland lauded since Herodotus's time as a medicine for all manner of ailments, and while no longer used, analysis has shown that it does contain compounds of medicinal value such as salicylic acid, a major ingredient in aspirin. Thus commodified, *C. fiber* came under constant pressure and was eradicated in different parts of Europe from the first century on. By the fifteenth century beavers were scarce throughout Europe, and by the nineteenth century only small, isolated populations were left.

In North America, Indians used beaver widely for the very practical reasons of food and clothing, and they placed great import on treating this animal with respect. Many Indians believed that this sentient, intelligent, powerful, reincarnating species—associated by some with work and provisioning, even with domestic faithfulness—would reciprocate their actions and come willingly to be used. Europeans who arrived in North America commodified the beaver everywhere (it was so important that an average-size beaver pelt—known as the Made Beaver—became the standard of exchange for the Hudson Bay Company). They valued the pelts because of the interlocking barbs of the under hairs (reflected in the HBC motto, *pro pelle cutem* [the skin for the fur or wool]), which made them without parallel as the primary raw material in felt hat production from the sixteenth through mid-nineteenth centuries, when silk made significant inroads. The beaver trade in North America was intensely competitive over several hundred years, as different companies vied for business supremacy. Beaver populations plunged from an estimated 50 million animals on the cusp of European arrival to rarity in New England and scarcity in the greater Northeast by the end of the seventeenth century. Inland, the pattern repeated itself. Everywhere, after the mid-eighteenth century, steel traps made the assault more lethal. Indians, nonindigenous independent trappers, and people of mixed Indian-European ancestry-all took part, in different places and times. By the late-nineteenth century beavers were locally extinct or scarce throughout North America.

Conservation

Concern for the decline in beaver emerged slowly in North America. Efforts in the nineteenth century by the Hudson Bay Company to leave some animals behind to replenish colonies failed for multiple reasons, including intense competition. The rise of the conservation movement in the late-nineteenth and early-twentieth centuries embraced the plight of the beaver. With only an estimated 100,000 left in North America, they became protected animals, and efforts were made to relocate beavers from areas where they remained in small numbers, like the Adirondack Mountains in New York, to areas from which they had been extirpated. By the mid-twentieth century, beaver numbers re-

A U.S. Forest Service game warden points to a bullet hole in a beaver blanket. COURTESY DAN H. RAISTON/U.S. FISH AND WILDLIFE SERVICE.

bounded enough that state governments again allowed beaver trapping.

Today: Nuisance or Savior?

Today beavers are reestablished in many former ranges and are no longer a rarity in Europe or North America. In Europe, efforts have been undertaken to restore *C. fiber* from Scotland to the Danube watershed, and in the 1990s it flourished, especially in Scandinavia, Poland, and Russia, and had attained a total population of approximately 250,000. In North America, *C. canadensis* has rebounded everywhere, especially near or in reforested areas, including the regions from which it had been extirpated, and now numbers again in the millions—at least 6–12 million and growing. The major predators of beavers have all declined: wolves, wolverines and human trappers.

In North America today, the beaver again flourishes, becoming the keystone species in many wetland areas and expanding anywhere there is water and trees. This presents contradictions for many Americans and Canadians who live increasingly in suburban areas or who farm their land for trees. On one hand, people marvel at the beaver's architectural and engineering skills and remark positively on its character and mentality, enshrining it in a cloak of cleanliness, monogamous family values and—as "eager beavers"—industriousness. On the other hand, even as some regard beavers as a key to restoring wetlands, habitat diversity, and a generally healthy environment, others increasingly denigrate beavers as a nuisance. The increase in beaver numbers has not increased their popularity. Most landowners and highway departments do not appreciate felled trees and flooded valleys. Humans prefer shaded shorelines. Beavers prefer to bring the shade—leaves are another food they relish—into the bottom of their ponds, leaving large trunks and branches helter-skelter along the shore. It was once thought that beavers confine their foraging to softwoods like aspen and birch. However, now that populations have grown, it is evident that beavers will fell and strip hardwoods, including red and white oaks, maple, ironwood, and shagbark hickory.

Although the introduction of beaver to suitable habitat guarantees an increase in biodiversity and environmental quality, in many cases its destruction of trees and flooding of land deter its introduction. Where animal rights activists have successfully lobbied against leg-hold traps, conservation managers are scrambling to find methods to control this small mammal, which has its own sense of how the environment should be managed.

Bob Arnebeck and Shepard Krech III

Further Reading

Banfield, A. W. F. (1974). Family Castoridae/Beavers. In *The mammals of Canada* (pp. 157–162). Toronto, Canada: University of Toronto Press.

Ives, R. (1942). The beaver-meadow complex. *Journal of geomorphology, 5,* 191–203.

Krech, S., III. (1999). Beaver. In *The ecological Indian: Myth and history* (pp. 173–209). New York: W. W. Norton.

Kwon, H. Y. (2000). The return of the beaver. In Schueler, T.R., & Holland, H.K. (Eds.). *The practice of watershed protection* (pp. 405–410). Ellicott City, MD: Center for Watershed Protection.

Martin, H. (1892). *Castorologia.* Montreal, Canada: Drysdale.

Mills, E. A. (1990). *In beaver world.* Lincoln: University of Nebraska Press. (Original work published 1913)

Morgan, L. H. (1986). *The American beaver.* Mineola, NY: Dover Books. (Original work published 1868)

Novak, M. (1987). Beaver. In M. Novak, et al. (Eds.). *Wild fur-bearer management and conservation in North America* (pp. 282–312). Toronto, Canada: Ontario Ministry of Natural Resources.

Outwater, A. (1996). *Water: A natural history.* New York: Basic Books

Rue, L. L., III, (2002). *Beavers.* Stillwater, MN: Voyager Press.

Ryden, H. (1989). *Lily pond: Four years with a family of beavers.* New York: HarperCollins.

Seton, E. T. (1929). *Lives of game animals.* New York: Doubleday, Doran and Co.

Bhopal Disaster

The well-known Bhopal chemical disaster, which destroyed many thousands of lives, still stands as a lesson about the long-lasting consequences of corporate mismanagement and thoughtless global development. In the early morning of 3 December 1984, a toxic cloud of methyl isocyanate (MIC) and other chemicals leaked from the Union Carbide India, Ltd. (UCIL), pesticide plant, and drifted over the sleeping inhabitants of Bhopal, India. Most heavily affected were poor people living in the crowded shanties adjacent to the plant. Choking on the deadly gas, which smelled like burning chilies, many victims suffocated within minutes, either in their homes or on the streets as they fled. Because of bureaucratic difficulties in collecting information about the victims, no death toll has ever been firmly reached, with estimates ranging from 3,000 to 7,500 immediate deaths and 150,000 to 500,000 injured. Long-term health effects include blindness, lung disease, neurological disorder, and genetic damage. The environmental effects also persist. In 1999, a study by the environmental organization Greenpeace found that the long-abandoned plant was leaking toxins into the groundwater, the only water source for the many people still living nearby.

The cause of the Bhopal accident was a runaway chemical reaction caused by leaking valves, improper storage of MIC in much larger quantities than was recommended, and lack of backup systems to prevent accidental mixing of chemicals. Safety procedures at the plant had been disregarded, and many safety systems had been shut down or were in disrepair. Furthermore, the warning siren failed to go off.

UCIL's parent company in the United States, the Union Carbide Corporation, refused responsibility for the accident. Although it owned 50.9 percent of UCIL's shares, Union Carbide claimed that the Indian owners and managers and the Indian government were responsible. It also maintained that the accident was the result of sabotage by an angry employee, though no one was ever charged with a crime. Critics of Union Carbide argued that it was responsible for the plant's technical design and safety operations, location near human habitation, and continued maintenance. Still, the settlement reached by the Indian government and Union Carbide came to only $470 million, between $370 and $533 per person, an amount that many survivors felt was inadequate and unjust.

The disaster initiated an organized protest movement in Bhopal and provoked a lasting response among environmentalists worldwide. In Bhopal, the survivors, mostly women, led frequent demonstrations, including marches to the abandoned factory site and an e-mail campaign, calling attention to their hardships and demanding that Union Carbide take responsibility and deliver adequate compensation. In 1999, they filed a new class action suit in New York, charging Union Carbide and its CEO at the time of the accident, Warren Anderson, with violations of human rights and international law and "a reckless and depraved indifference to human life" (Hedges 2000, 4). In the United States, the Bhopal disaster sparked an environmental movement in West Virginia, where similar chemical plants are located. This activism led to the passage of national environmental legislation, SARA Title III: The Emergency Planning and Community Right-To-Know Act (1986) that forced chemical companies to publicize their emissions and develop worst-case scenarios for possible accidents.

Ann Larabee

Further Reading

Bhargava, A. (1986) The Bhopal incident and Union Carbide: Ramifications of an industrial accident. *Bulletin of concerned Asian scholars* 18(4), 2–19.

Basu, A. (1994) Interview with Jabbar Khan. *Bulletin of concerned Asian scholars* 26(1–2), 14–17.

Cassels, J. (1993). *The uncertain promise of law: Lessons from Bhopal*. Toronto, Canada: University of Toronto Press.

Chouhan, T. R. (1994). *Bhopal: The inside story*. New York: Other India Press.

Fortun, K. (2001). *Advocacy after Bhopal: Environmentalism, disaster, new global orders*. Chicago: University of Chicago Press.

Hedges, C. (2000, March 5). A key figure proves elusive in a U.S. suit over Bhopal. *New York Times*, p. 4.

Ingalls, L. (1994). Toxic vapor leak: Bhopal, India (1984). In N. Schlager (Ed.), *When technology fails: Significant technological disasters, disasters, accidents, and failures of the twentieth century*. (pp. 401–416). Detroit, MI: Gale Research.

Labunska, I., Stephenson, A., Brigden, K., Stringer, R., Santillo, D., & Johnston, P. A. (1999). *The Bhopal legacy: Toxic contaminants at the former union carbide factory site, Bhopal, India: 15 years after the Bhopal accident*. Exeter, UK: Greenpeace Research Laboratories.

Biodiversity

The word *biodiversity* is a contraction of the phrase *biological diversity* and was coined in 1985 by the biologist Walter Rosen of the United States National Research Council as a title word in a seminar he was organizing to discuss biological diversity. Biologists' definitions of biodiversity differ, but as a survey of prominent scientists' opinions done by United States author David Takacs (1996) clearly illustrated, biodiversity transcends diversity as indicated by numbers of species existing on the planet. Rather, most agree it includes biological information across all levels of organization, including genes, populations, species, communities, and ecosystems, as well as the way they fit together.

Because biodiversity cuts across different levels of organization, it is often useful to focus on a particular type of biological diversity. Genetic diversity measures the amount of inherited genetic variability within a population. Even when species are not extinct, their survival can be severely compromised if genes that confer specific survival traits such as disease resistance or environmental tolerance are lost when populations become isolated or decrease.

Ecosystem diversity measures the variety of communities or habitats. Ecosystem diversity is much harder to measure because the boundaries of many communities or habitats are not fixed like that of a pond, but rather gradually change from one type to another over a transition zone.

How Many Species Are There?

Estimates of the total number of plant and animal species vary from 3 million to 30 million, but most estimates put the range between 5 and 10 million. These numbers have changed as new techniques have been developed to more accurately estimate species numbers and as new species have been identified. Each year about thirteen thousand species are discovered and added to the 1.4 million species that have been catalogued so far. The majority of new species are invertebrates, plants, and bacteria, but even large vertebrates are still being discovered. In 1990 a new species of monkey was discovered in South America. It has been estimated from catches examined in Amazon fish markets that as much as 40 percent of South American freshwater fishes are still not identified.

Measuring Biodiversity

Mathematically the two components of biodiversity are richness and evenness. Richness is a measure of how many organisms exist in a given area. Evenness is a measure of whether each species in a community is represented by about the same number of individuals or whether a few species have large populations and other species have small populations. Two communities could be equally diverse in terms of richness but differ greatly in terms of evenness. A variety of mathematical techniques have been developed to measure species diversity, but it is often most convenient for a scientist to use an index to calculate a single number that can represent both richness and evenness. The most widely used of these indices are the Shannon and the Simpson's index. Both of these indices were developed in the 1940s but gained in popularity when their use was promoted by Spanish ecologist Ramon Margalef and United States ecologist Robert MacArthur in the 1950s.

Importance of Biodiversity

A species can be considered to have either instrumental or inherent value. A species would have instrumental value if it is useful to humans, for example, if it can be used to create life-saving medicines, or if it is aesthetically beautiful. A species would have inherent value if it has some worth apart from its usefulness, for example, simply because it exists on the planet. It is extremely difficult to attach a monetary amount to inherent value.

Historically, examples of the value of biodiversity are anthropocentric (human centered), focusing on the instrumental values of species. According to most of the world's great religions, species were created to be useful to humans. In early Christianity nature and species existed to be transformed and controlled, but the tenets of piety and austerity demanded a certain respect for God's world. Only a few religions, such as Jainism and the animist religions, rate the inherent value of species over instrumental value.

Inevitably, the debate surrounding the preservation of biodiversity hinges not on science but on ethics. The decisions about how much land should be preserved in order to preserve biodiversity are typically based on value rather than function or on ethics. Clearly, not all decisions are based on pure economic value. Biodiversity has great social, ethical, and cultural values to humans. Examples of this fact are preserved in religion, art, and literature. For example, U.S. naturalist John Muir's great success in garnering public

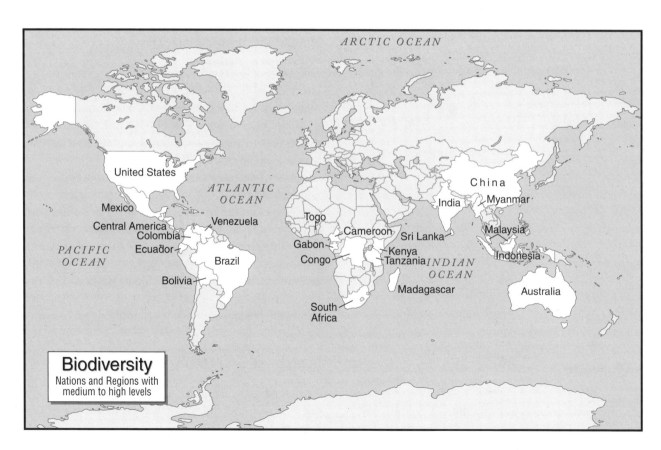

Biodiversity
Nations and Regions with medium to high levels

support to preserve large tracts of the U.S. West was due mostly to the aesthetic appreciation that humans have of nature. This appreciation is still apparent through the public's support of parks and zoos and nature and conservation organizations.

Taxonomy and the Species Concept

Scientists have always been interested in biodiversity. Humans have been formally collecting and naming biological species for at least four thousand years. Initially collections focused on the large, accessible, beautiful, and useful. Because of this people know 98 percent of the world's birds and nearly 95 percent of the world's mammals, but people know only a fraction of the world's beetles. In 1980 a sample from a Panamanian forest produced over nine hundred beetle species that were previously unknown to science.

Although much of the important work in preserving biodiversity lies in the realm of ecology and conservation biology, the conceptual basis of biological diversity is the science of taxonomy. Butterflies, bacteria, and grasses, for example, are all recognizable biological groups or taxa. Taxonomy is the science of categorizing and organizing species into groups that reflect their evolutionary relationships.

Before English naturalist Charles Darwin and the concept of evolution, early taxonomists focused on morphological (relating to the form and structure of animals and plants) similarities and differences that could be used to identify unique species. The Greek philosopher Aristotle was one of the first persons to categorize organisms based on reproductive morphology and habitat preferences. As the numbers of newly discovered species increased rapidly with exploration during the Renaissance, a new system was needed. Early taxonomists, including sixteenth-century Italian botanist Andrea Cesalpino and seventeenth-century scientists, including Italian zoologist Marcello Malpighi and the English botanist John Ray and his student zoologist Francis Willughby, developed the first hierarchical taxonomic systems. They based their systems on general morphological features to create sets of nested hierarchical categories based on natural relationships.

Perhaps the most famous taxonomist was the Swedish naturalist Carolus Linnaeus. In the mid-1700s Linnaeus, borrowing heavily from Ray and Willughby, standardized the nomenclature and hierarchical taxonomic system that is still used today. His hierarchical system grouped organisms based on structural similar-

ities. Although parts of his system have been changed, the major taxonomic groups "kingdom," "phylum," "order," "family," "class," "genus," and "species" are still used today. The universally accepted naming system he standardized is a binomial (two-term) naming system using the genus and species names from the taxonomic hierarchy to identify species. For example, *Homo sapiens* is the scientific name for humans.

Species

The basis of biodiversity is the recognition of unique species. Early taxonomists focused on the morphological definition of *species:* Some groups of individuals (species) are distinct from others because of some distinct morphological characteristics. In 1686 Ray introduced the beginnings of the biological species definition: Species are composed of individuals that can reproduce and produce viable offspring. Both of these definitions, although not perfect, are still used today.

Although Linnaeus placed chimpanzees and humans in the genus *Homo*, his decision to do so was based solely on morphology. The ideas of what a species is and how species originate have changed significantly since Linnaeus introduced his system of classification. It is clear from his writings that Linnaeus was aware that species are capable of hybridizing but that he had no understanding of the process of evolution.

Only after Darwin's publication of *The Origin of Species* in 1859 did taxonomists begin to piece together the evolutionary relationships between taxa (taxonomic groups). Because morphological similarities were used and were often representative of evolutionary relationships, many species could be easily placed into evolutionary trees that traced the history and relationships of species through the higher taxa. Sometimes morphological features did not indicate common descent, resulting in some groups that defied classification. Recently, the development of sophisticated genetic technology, such as mitochondrial DNA markers, has allowed modern taxonomists to unravel the evolutionary lineages of many groups of species.

Conservationists: Origins of Modern Biodiversity

Botanist Frederic Clements and zoologist Victor Shelford were ecologists in the United States who were pioneers in the study of community ecology. Separately they published books on community ecology, and together they published the book *Bio-Ecology* in

1936 that clearly established the importance of plant-animal interactions. English ecologist Charles Elton developed the food chain concept in the 1920s. Later, in 1957, he wrote the important and still classic work on invasive species, *The Ecology of Invasions of Plants and Animals,* in which he calls for the "conservation of variety". In the 1930s and 1940s aquatic ecologists G. Evelyn Hutchinson from the U.S. and Ramon Margalef in Spain focused their research on understanding how aquatic planktonic systems supported high levels of diversity. At the same time, U.S. ecologist Raymond Lindeman pioneered research that would become the foundation of ecosystem ecology. In the 1950s, E. P. Odum further developed ecosystem research and wrote the first ecology textbook. In 1959 G.E. Hutchinson addressed the American Society of Naturalists. In his speech titled *Homage to Santa Rosalia or Why Are There So Many Animals?* he anticipated the field of biodiversity with his consideration of how the previous fifty years of research described how so many or so few species could co exist in a given area.

U.S. forester Aldo Leopold may have been one of the first scientists to directly consider the importance of biodiversity in his writings. He spoke indirectly of biodiversity in *A Sand County Almanac,* published in 1946, discussing the diversity of wild plants that feeds the eye, and he lamented that as woodlots were grazed and fields built over, the "visual diet" became bland as more species disappeared from the landscape.

The influence of the U.S. Transcendentalist writers Ralph Waldo Emerson and Henry David Thoreau and the U.S. preservationist John Muir was also present in Leopold's ethical considerations of the value of biodiversity as he considered species' value as potential resources, from food to furniture, and as objects of aesthetic appreciation. Leopold also considered the ethics of human-mediated species extinction.

In the 1960s environmental writers, beginning with U.S. biologist Rachel Carson, were influential in presenting ideas about ecology and biological diversity to a general audience. Many authors were writing about the issues of pollution, consumption, and human population growth, but it was U.S. conservation biologist David Ehrenfeld's book *Conserving Life on Earth,* published in 1972, that presented the biological, social, and ethical issues surrounding species and habitat decline to the general public. Ehrenfeld argued for the preservation of biological diversity for scientific as well as moral and emotional reasons.

In 1981 U.S. ecologists Paul and Anne Ehrlich published the book *Extinction*, which further argued for the recognition of the importance of the increase in species extinctions. In the preface they developed an analogy that would later become an important theory in conservation biology. The Ehrlichs argue that Earth is a spacecraft and that it contains many species that are the rivets that hold together the ecosystems of the planet. Their argument is that humans are the "rivet poppers" causing the extinctions of individual species. The extinction of one or two species may be imperceptible at the global or even the ecosystem level, but each species extinction weakens the system, eventually leading to the collapse of the ecosystem. Many studies have supported the idea that extinctions can systematically weaken ecosystems.

The first book entitled *Biodiversity* was based on the National Forum of BioDiversity held in 1986. This series of essays by eminent scientists in ecology and conservation biology is still widely read and quoted by the scientific community.

Of the eminent scientists who have made biodiversity their life's work, U.S. scientist E. O. Wilson is probably the most recognized by the general public. He popularized the word *biodiversity* in his scientific and popular writings after 1986. Before that, Wilson recognized the implications of species and habitat loss. Wilson's research placed him right in the center of the biodiversity discipline. His specialty is ants, an ecologically dominant group, and he has spent his career studying the relationship between taxonomy, evolutionary biology, behavior, and ecology.

United States ecologists David Ehrenfeld, Michael Soulé, Paul Ehrlich and Jared Diamond have written extensively about biodiversity and conservation issues for the general public as well as for the scientific audience. Together they founded the field and the society of conservation biology. Ehrenfeld's research has focused on conservation of sea turtles. Soulé developed methods to determine critical population sizes for species conservation. Ehrlich is a population ecologist who studies endangered species and optimum design of nature preserves. Diamond developed theories that correlated species extinction rates to habitat size and were important in developing policy for large nature reserves.

Because so much biological diversity is concentrated in the tropics, many of the best-known scientists have focused on those regions. Thomas Lovejoy, a United States biologist who works mainly in Brazil, is best known for publicizing the issue of tropical deforestation in the late 1970s and for making the first projections of global extinction rates for the *Global 2000*

Report to the President of the United States in 1980. Peter Raven, also from the United States, is a plant taxonomist specializing in tropical flora, and has long warned about the decline of biodiversity and advocated conservation. British ecologist Norman Myers demonstrated significant declines associated with cattle grazing in the 1980s. He originated the "biodiversity hotspots" (areas where there are high levels of species richness, endemic species [species that are native only to that area], and rapid habitat loss) concept. Daniel Janzen, a U.S. ecologist who works much of the time in Costa Rica, has greatly influenced conservation efforts in the tropics. United States entomologist (a biologist who studies insects) Terry Erwin has used intensive sampling in the rainforest to determine estimates of the Earth's species biodiversity.

Current Mass Extinction

Speciation is the process of biological species formation. New species are formed, but those same species go extinct eventually. By examining the fossil record, paleobiologists are able to estimate what the normal or background (prehuman) rate of extinctions should be. It is estimated that background extinction rates are about one species per million species per year. Prominent scientists, including Wilson, Raven, and Soulé, place the rate of extinctions at hundreds to thousands of species per year.

The Earth is undergoing a mass extinction during which huge numbers of species are becoming extinct in a short time. Mass extinctions are nothing new; at least five mass extinctions have already occurred. Glaciation during the Ordovician period, 500 million years ago, caused the extinction of 50 percent of all the animal species on Earth; climate changes 250 million years ago during the Permian caused the extinction of 75 percent of all terrestrial vertebrate species and 95 percent of all marine species. Wilson suggests that it is possible that within one hundred years 50 percent of all existing plant and animal species will be extinct. However, unlike during any previous mass extinction, humans are the major agent of species loss during this sixth mass extinction through habitat fragmentation and destruction, as well as through species introduction and exploitation.

Biodiversity can recover from mass extinctions if the extinction mechanism is stopped, but the recovery process requires millions of years, which is too long to be meaningful to human society. In an effort to curb the extinction rate, the World Wildlife Fund, the World Conservation Union (IUCN), and other organizations have suggested that every country should set aside 10 percent of its total area for biodiversity protection. But Soulé, Wilson, and others argue that although this would be a great achievement in terms of public policy, it would do little to slow species loss.

In the late 1980s British tropical ecologist Norman Myers suggested that in an effort to maximize biodiversity preservation, conservation efforts should be focused in areas where there are high levels of species richness, endemic species (species that are native only to that area), and rapid habitat loss. Myers called these areas "biodiversity hotspots." He has suggested that at least one-third of all species exist in just twenty-five hotspots on less than 2 percent of the Earth's land surface. Myers has argued that if just these few locations were preserved, the effects of the current mass extinction would be greatly reduced.

Human Impacts on Biodiversity

The main mechanisms that cause biodiversity loss are habitat destruction and fragmentation, the colonization of new areas by introduced (invasive or exotic) species, exploitation of resources by harvesting for food and industry, and pollution. Classic examples of human impacts on species extinction include massive extinctions on Easter Island and Hawaii after human colonization and the numerous extinctions in Australia after the arrival of western Europeans who introduced numerous European vertebrates.

Habitat loss and fragmentation are the greatest causes of biodiversity loss and contribute to 88 percent of all recent extinctions. Habitat loss occurs when land is cleared for farming, grazing, or housing. It can also occur when land is made uninhabitable by pollution, desertification, or erosion. Habitat fragmentation can be more significant than habitat loss in some areas. As areas are divided into farms, houses, roads, urban areas, and small tracts of original habitat they take on a jigsaw appearance. Small fragments cannot support large populations, and remaining populations are more isolated and are more at risk of extinction and invasive species.

Invasive species are the second-greatest mechanism, contributing to 46 percent of losses in biodiversity, as estimated by Wilcove and colleagues. Invasive or introduced species are species that have been moved from their native habitat, either intentionally or unintentionally, by humans to a new location where they are free to reproduce without their natural predators, competitors, or diseases. Between 1840 and 1880 more than sixty species of vertebrates, including rabbits, cats, and foxes, were released in Australia, resulting in the extinctions of many endemic mammals. More than one thousand species have become extinct in Hawaii since the arrival of humans.

Conservation Biology

Conservation biology is the study of the preservation of biological diversity. It emerged simultaneously with biodiversity as a concept and has become an independent and dominant discipline within the field of biology. It applies the fields of evolutionary biology and ecology directly to answering questions concerning species extinctions. As the Society for Conservation Biology mission statement suggests, conservation biology exists not only to study biodiversity but also to develop the tools "to protect, maintain, and restore life on this planet" (Society for Conservation Biology 1996, 6). Since its conception the discipline has become important in identifying areas of special concern, preserving genetic variability of species at risk, and advising policy in the creation of preserves and parks throughout the world.

Research, Policy, and Legislation

Two ecological funding programs were instrumental in increasing scientists' understanding of biodiversity and ecosystem changes by providing some of the first integrated long-term research studies. From 1968 to 1974 $27 million was spent on large-scale ecosystem-level ecological research projects in the International Biological Program (IBP). It significantly increased the number of trained ecologists and the amount of ecological research that was being produced just as the public was becoming aware of growing environmental problems.

In 1980 the National Science Foundation established the first Long Term Ecological Research Site (LTER) in the United States. Since then the network has grown to twenty-four U.S. and international sites, involving over one thousand scientists in projects that focus on, among other things, ecosystem function, long-term monitoring of species loss, and climate change.

The first important national laws addressing endangered species were passed in the United States. In 1966 the Endangered Species Preservation Act provided land acquisition and the listing and limited protection of native animal species. The Endangered Species Conservation Act of 1969 was passed to protect species in danger of "worldwide extinction." It prevented the importation or sale of listed species within the United States and called for an international ministerial meeting to adopt a convention on the conservation of endangered species. In 1973 the Endangered Species Act was passed, combining and considerably strengthening the 1966 and 1969 acts.

The 1973 act has been influential as a model for legislation around the world, but it has its faults. It has often been criticized as a law that rescues species only when they are in imminent danger of extinction. However, it is important because it is one of the first laws that addressed human-caused extinction and species decline, and it recognized that species preservation requires habitat conservation.

From 1971 through 1973 a number of important international environmental conventions were held and led to protection and research in biological diversity. In 1971 the Ramsar Convention on Wetlands of International Importance focused on wetlands conservation to save waterfowl and wetlands. That same year the United Nations Educational, Scientific and Cultural Organization (UNESCO) Man and Biosphere (MAB) Program convention was held to develop a global network of unique nature preserves to integrate conservation, development, and scientific research.

In 1972 the UNESCO Convention for the Protection of the World Cultural and Natural Heritage established a set of protected World Heritage Sites that contain "outstanding physical, biological, and geological features; habitats of threatened plants or animal species and areas of value on scientific or aesthetic grounds or from the point of view of conservation" (UNESCO 1972). As of May 2000, 160 countries had signed the convention, and there were 630 sites worldwide.

The first U.N. Conference of the Human Environment was held in 1972 in Stockholm, Sweden, and formally declared humans as part of, and responsible for, protection of the environment. It resulted in a plan that focused on environmental assessment and management. Subsequent conferences (Earth Summits) have been held every ten years since to discuss issues of the environment, including biodiversity.

The Convention on International Trade in Endangered Species of Wild Fauna and Flora (CITES) was held in 1973 and eventually signed by 152 countries. It restricted international commerce in plant and animal species believed to be actually or potentially harmed by trade.

It wasn't until 1980 that another important suite of conferences resulted in the final Convention on Biological Diversity of 1992. The goal of this convention was to inspire countries to implement national conservation strategies.

The National Forum on BioDiversity was held in Washington, DC, in 1986—the year the Society for Conservation Biology was established. This forum of internationally recognized researchers brought together the biological and social issues surrounding diversity, extinction, and habitat loss under a single title: "biodiversity." It also brought issues surrounding biological diversity to the attention of the U.S. Congress and to the public.

Partly in response to the National Forum on BioDiversity, the Ad Hoc Working Group of Experts on Biological Diversity was organized by the U.N. in 1988 to explore the need for an international convention on biological diversity. This group decided that a separate global convention on biodiversity issues was necessary. The group's recommendations resulted in an agreement called the "Convention on Biological Diversity" presented at the 1992 United Nations Conference on Environment and Development (UNCED) in Rio de Janeiro, Brazil (the 1992 Earth Summit). The convention is a legally binding international agreement dedicated to developing a plan to preserve biodiversity, provide sustainable use of its components, and establish fair and equitable sharing of the benefits of genetic resources. As of 2003 over 174 countries and the European Union had ratified or acceded to the agreement. Although the United States signed the agreement in 1993, the U.S. Senate had yet to ratify it.

Biodiversity in the Future

The knowledge gained by studying biodiversity is being incorporated into decision-making processes about park and preserve management and species protection. Universities, museums, zoos, and other organizations are modernizing programs to more directly focus on biodiversity issues. The public is better educated about the issues of biodiversity and species loss because of increasing environmental activism, much from within the scientific community. However, the conditions in which that community operates are, as E. O. Wilson suggests, of "unprecedented urgency" because of the rampant destruction of species and be-

cause of the rapid development of research and technologies that may lead to preservation of biodiversity.

Vicki Medland

Further Reading

Ehrenfeld, D. (1972). *Conserving life on Earth*. New York: Oxford University Press.

Ehrlich, P. R., & Ehrlich, A. H. (1981). *Extinction: The causes and consequences of the disappearance of species*. New York: Random House.

Erwin, T. L., & Scott, J. C. (1980). Seasonal size patterns, trophic structure, and richness of Coleoptera in the tropical arboreal ecosystem: The fauna of the tree *Luehea seemannii Triana* and *Planch* in the Canal Zone of Panama. *Coleopterists Bulletin, 34*, 305–322.

Leopold, A. (1966). *A Sand County almanac*. Oxford, UK: Oxford University Press.

Myers, N., Mittermeier, R. A., Mittermeier, C. G., da Fonseca, G. A. B., & Kent, J. (2000). Biodiversity hotspots for conservation priorities. *Nature, 403*(6772), 853–858.

Takacs, D. (1996). *The idea of biodiversity: Philosophies of paradise*. Baltimore: Johns Hopkins University Press.

Wilcove, D. S., Rothstein, D., Dubow, J., Phillips, A., & Losos, E. (1998). Quantifying threats to imperiled species in the United States. *BioScience, 48*(8), 607–615.

Wilson, E. O. (Ed.). (1988). *Biodiversity*. Washington, DC: National Academy Press.

Wilson, E. O. (Ed.). (1999). *The diversity of life*. New York: W. W. Norton.

Wilson, E. O. (2002). *The future of life*. New York: Alfred A. Knopf.

Biological Corridors

Biological corridors are strips of land which differ from their immediately surrounding environment and connect two or more separate pieces of that surrounding environment. They serve as links between habitats, acting as conduits for the spread of plants and the movement of animals. Corridors may also function as habitats in their own right, providing resources and shelter to many species.

Corridor Types, Structure, and Function

Corridor types include natural as well as human built or influenced features. Streams and streambank vegetation make up the predominant natural corridors in most landscapes. Many linear constructed features, and the strips of vegetation alongside them, act as corridors for people and wildlife. These include powerline and pipeline rights-of-way, roads, railways, fences, ditches, and even the edges of buildings, where vegetation provides food, shelter, and rest areas for many species. Plantings such as hedgerows, shelterbelts, and windbreaks usually have a utilitarian or aesthetic function for people in agricultural or suburban areas. They are also important corridors since they often connect cultivated fields or other key habitats and are the primary conduits for safe travel for many small animals within these areas.

Corridor structure depends on several factors, the most important being width. Narrow corridors, such as most roads, paths, trails, hedgerows, and drainage features are classified as *line corridors* because they consist solely of edge environments with edge species, i.e., the type of environment and species found at a habitat edge, where one habitat meets another. Thus, line corridors contain the same plant and animal species throughout their width. *Strip corridors* are wider, and besides edge environments on either side, also contain interior environments, typically those found in the interior of a habitat, away from the perimeter. Consequently, strip corridors contain different species within their interiors than at their edges. Examples of strip corridors include very wide roads such as interstate highways, wide powerline rights-of-way, and broad strips of forest.

Corridors mainly function as conduits for the movement and dispersal of wildlife. In this capacity, corridors enable individual animals from different areas to spread to new habitats, enhancing gene flow among populations. How well corridors function for wildlife mobility depends on their structure and the species involved. Line corridors often facilitate movement across themselves but may inhibit movement along their length, especially if they contain many breaks in continuity. Conversely, strip corridors frequently offer several species the opportunity to travel lengthwise, but due to the varied habitats across their width, may restrict crosswise movement. While small streams are generally not barriers to transverse movement, large rivers may well stop many species from crossing.

Corridors may also be habitats in their own right, providing food, water, shelter, breeding opportunities, and other resources.

Environmental Effects and Biological Reserves

Corridors have a number of effects on their environment. A corridor may simultaneously connect diverse patches of habitat while also fragmenting the landscape. Vegetated corridors, such as hedgerows, often have a greater variety of vegetation than nearby habitats and may help to recolonize the environment after a disturbance such as a fire. However, some corridors may actually create disturbance by harboring disease organisms that spread to connected areas. Stream corridors provide shade and nutrients to watercourses while filtering water flowing over land before it enters the stream. Thus, they help to control runoff and reduce flooding and soil loss.

Corridors connecting biological reserves (national parks, national forests, wilderness zones, and related areas) play a crucial role in maintaining the reserves by preserving or restoring some of the natural landscape connections found in undisturbed areas. Many researchers emphasize the need for multiple links between reserves to protect against the loss of connectivity should fire or disease damage any one corridor. These corridors should be large enough to encompass not only animal movement, but also enough species diversity to enable natural communities to be maintained throughout the landscape. Ideally, a network of such corridors would link an entire continental region of reserves. This linkage would be crucial during periods of climate change, when some species need to shift locale to avoid inhospitable conditions.

Human Uses

Corridors are built to serve many human purposes. Roads, highways, railroads, and canals are used primarily for transportation by both people and wildlife. Trails through forests and parks, or paths alongside streams, also provide recreation, and frequently have aesthetic and educational value. Other corridors may supply fuel or food for local people. Some corridors are created to maintain particular environments or species, such as the roadside reserves created in Australia to preserve native wildflowers. In the United States a system of multi-use corridors was suggested by a presidential commission in 1987. The commission recommended extending and linking existing corridors, such as streams, hiking trails, biking paths, and abandoned rail lines, to create a corridor network throughout the country. This network would link urban and rural areas for the dual purposes of recreation and conservation.

Controversies

Not all researchers agree on the need for, or desirability of, biological corridors. They point to the known disadvantages, including landscape fragmentation, spread of non-native species, facilitation of poaching, and the potential spread of fire, disease, and pests. Cost is also a factor, and while natural corridors generally require little management, artificial ones often need considerable maintenance. However, the consensus is that the benefits of corridors generally outweigh the drawbacks. Consequently, in many urban and suburban areas greenways, trails, paths, and stream corridors are being constructed and interconnected. Many regional and urban planners are integrating biological corridors into new developments, and corridors are playing an increasingly larger role in public policy issues such as wetland protection, conservation of rare and endangered species, biodiversity, flood control, water quality, and recreation.

Biological corridors connect the increasingly isolated patches of natural habitats in our landscapes. Their development and maintenance are viewed as crucial to the health of our environment, and future planners will need to incorporate a variety of corridors into rural and urban developments. The importance of corridors will thus grow, and future researchers will need to learn more about corridor structure, functions, and effects on landscapes.

Salvatore DiMaria

Further Reading

Adams, L. W., & Dove, L. E. (1989). *Wildlife reserves and corridors in the urban environment: A guide to ecological landscape planning and resource conservation.* Columbia, MD: National Institute for Urban Wildlife.

Budd, W. W., Cohen, P. L., Saunders, P. R., & Steiner, F. R. (1987). Stream corridor management in the Pacific Northwest: I. Determination of stream-corridor widths. *Environmental Management, 11* 587–597.

Forman, R. T. T. (1983). Corridors in a landscape: their ecological structure and function. *Ekologia, 2* 375–387.

Forman, R. T. T., & Godron, M. (1986). *Landscape ecology.* New York: John Wiley & Sons.

Hudson, W. E. (Ed.). (1991). *Landscape linkages and biodiversity.* Washington, DC: Island Press.

Naveh, Z., & Lieberman, A. S. (1984). *Landscape ecology: theory and application.* New York: Springer-Verlag.

Saunders, D. A., & Hobbs, R. J. (1991). *Nature conservation 2: The role of corridors.* Chipping Norton, Australia: Beatty and Sons.

Shafer, C. L. (1990). *Nature reserves: Island theory and conservation practice.* Washington, DC: Smithsonian Institution Press.

Simberloff, D., & Cox, J. (1987). Consequences and costs of conservation corridors. *Conservation Biology, 1* 63–71.

Suchantke, A. (2001). *Eco-geography: What we see when we look at landscapes.* Great Barrington, MA: Lindisfarne Books.

Vink, A. P. A. (1983). *Landscape ecology and land use.* New York: Longman, Inc.

Biological Exchanges

For millions of years, most terrestrial species stayed home. Geographic barriers, such as oceans and mountain chains, inhibited migrations and divided the earth. Only birds, bats, flying insects, and good swimmers consistently bucked the trend. A few other species did so occasionally, thanks to sea-level changes and land bridges, or to chance voyages on driftwood. Natural evolution took place, for most species, in separate biogeographical provinces.

Intracontinental Biological Exchange

This long phase in the history of life ended when human beings began their long-distance migrations. Deep in prehistory, people—or hominids at any rate—walked throughout Africa and Eurasia, occasionally bringing a plant, seed, insect, rodent, or microbe to a place it would not have reached on its own. With plant and animal domestication some 10,000–12,000 years ago, people began to do this on purpose and more frequently. Most of the plants and animals susceptible to domestication were found in Eurasia, and the east-west axis of that continent eased the spread of those plants and animals sensitive to climate conditions or to day length (several flowering plants take their cues to bloom from day length). The suites of domesticated plants and animals on which agriculture and herding rest spread almost instantaneously by the standards of the past, although in fact it took a few millennia. This process no doubt proved highly disruptive biologically, as local biogeographic provinces were invaded by alien creatures that humanity spread. It also proved highly disruptive historically, obliterating peoples who did not adapt to the changing biogeography, the

Cassava in Africa

Cassava (manioc, tapioca) is a root crop native to South America that was exported to sub-Saharan Africa by European colonists. It thrived in Africa and became a major food source, in part because it is drought resistant and can be grown easily. The following account by British anthropologist Audrey Richards describes how the Bisa and Bemba peoples of Zambia use religion to protect their crops.

To protect their distant gardens from theft the Bemba resort to supernatural means only. Protective magic is used, but only to a small extent. It is interesting to find that the Bisa, whose staple crop is cassava, which is readily stolen as it remains in the ground all the year round, regularly place in their gardens charms designed to afflict a possible thief with different types of illness. This Custom, known as *ukuamba*, seemed to be universally practised on Cilubi Island. A man leaving home for a period would plant in a prominent place a stake with magic attached to it, and so strong was the belief in its powers that the owner himself was afraid to dig up the cassava on his return without first removing the charm. Among the Bemba, where the staple crop is less frequently stolen, such forms of protective magic seem to be, comparatively speaking, rare. Charms to be burned in a field to produce various diseases such as elephantiasis in garden thieves were described to me, but I never heard frequently of their use. In such cases I was told the culprit could only hope to recover if he confessed his guilt. A far more common practice is the use of a special form of curse, *ukulapishya*, uttered after a theft has been committed, not before. This is done when gourds or pumpkins are disappearing from a garden and the thief is unknown. I have heard such curses uttered constantly during the hunger months, when the pilfering of vegetables is quite frequent, and a woman has no means of guarding them. The usual procedure followed was to announce in a loud shout in the quiet of an evening some such statement as, "All you people, listen! One of my pumpkins went yesterday and another the day before. Now I am angry. I am really going to curse. Tomorrow I am going to curse. Really and truly I am."

Source: Richards, Audrey I. (1935). *Land, Labour, and Diet in Northern Rhodesia: An Economic Study of the Bemba Tribe.* Oxford, UK: Oxford University Press.

---

changing disease regimes (patterns of disease and health in a given population), and the changed political situations brought on by the spread of farmers, herders, and eventually of states. Out of this turmoil of Afro-Eurasian biological exchange emerged the great ancient civilizations from China to the Mediterranean. They all based their societies on intersecting but not identical sets of plants and animals.

Biological homogenization within Afro-Eurasia had its limits. The links between North Africa, say, and east Asia before 500 BCE were slender. Varying topography and climate also checked the spread of species. The process presumably accelerated when interregional contacts flourished—when large states created favorable conditions for the movement of goods and people. The era of the Han and Roman empires, for example, when the trans-Asian Silk Road was a well-beaten path, unleashed a small flood of biological exchanges. The Mediterranean acquired cherries at this time, and possibly smallpox and measles too; sorghum made its way from East Africa to India to China, while grapes, camels, and donkeys also arrived in China from southwest Asia and North Africa.

Within Eurasian history there were two other moments of heightened biological exchange. The first of these came during the early Tang dynasty (in China), in the seventh and eighth centuries. The Tang rulers came from various ethnic and cultural traditions, and for a century and a half showed keen interest in things foreign: trade, technology, culture (e.g., Buddhism)—and plants and animals. The court imported exotica: curious creatures, aromatic plants, and ornamental flowers. Much of this was inconsequential in social and economic terms, but some of it, such as the cultivation of cotton (imported from India), was not. The Tang were culturally receptive to strange plants and animals, but there was more to it than that. Their political power on the western frontier, and the geopolitical situation generally before 750 CE, promoted the trade, travel, and transport that make biological exchange likely. For roughly a century and half (600–750) the numerous polities of central Asia were frequently consolidated into only a few, simplifying travel by lowering protection costs. A handful of large empires held sway throughout central Asia, making the connections between China, India, Persia, and southwest Asia safer than usual. This geopolitical arrangement fell apart after 751, when Muslims defeated Tang armies, and after 755 when rebellion shook the Tang to its foundations. Thereafter both the stability of the geopolitical situation and the receptivity of the Tang to things foreign changed, waned more often than waxed, and the opportunities for biological exchange grew scarcer.

The third moment of heightened biological exchange within Eurasia came with the *Pax Mongolica* of the thirteenth and fourteenth centuries. By this time most of the feasible exchanges of plants and animals had already taken place. But the heightened transport across the desert-steppe corridor of central Asia may have brought carrots and a species of lemon to China, and a form of millet to Persia. Quite possibly, it also allowed the quick diffusion from central Asia of the bacillus that causes bubonic plague, provoking the famous Black Death, the worst bout of epidemics in the recorded history of western Eurasia and North Africa. Plague may also have afflicted China in these centuries, although the evidence is ambiguous.

While this process of Eurasian (and North African) biological exchange never truly came to an end, it slowed whenever political conditions weakened interregional contacts. It also slowed in general after around 200 CE, with the erosion of the *Pax Romana* and *Pax Sinica*, which had so encouraged long-distance travel and trade within Eurasia. By that time, sugar cane had taken root in India, spreading from its New Guinea home. Wheat had spread widely throughout most of its potential range, as had cattle, pigs, horses, sheep, and goats. Less and less was left to do even when conditions encouraged biological exchange.

Meanwhile, on other continents, similar if smaller-scale processes of biological exchange and homogenization were in train. In the Americas, maize spread from its Mesoamerican home both north and south, slowed, it seems, by difficulties in adapting to different day lengths at different latitudes. In Africa, the Bantu migrations of some 2,000 years ago probably diffused several crops throughout eastern and southern Africa, and possibly brought infectious diseases that ravaged the indigenous, previously isolated, populations of southern Africa. These events in Africa and the Americas, too, must have been biologically and politically tumultuous, although the evidence is very sparse.

In biological terms, the process of human-promoted biological exchange selected for certain kinds of species, those that coexisted easily with human activity: domesticates, commensals (such as rats), and plants that thrive on disturbed ground, most of which we usually call weeds. These species prospered under the new regimes of expanded human migration and interaction. From their point of view, history had taken a very favorable turn. Indeed, humanity was in a sense working for them, spreading their genetic footprints far and wide within the continents, and into the future.

Intercontinental Biological Exchange and Biological Invasion before 1400 CE

Intercontinental biological exchange also has a long pedigree. The first people to migrate to Australia may have accidentally brought some species with them some 40,000 years ago. About 3,500 years ago, later migrants to Australia purposely brought the dingo (a large dog), the first domesticate in Australian history. The dingo quickly spread to all Aboriginal groups outside of isolated Tasmania, and also formed feral packs. It proved an effective hunting dog and led to the extinction of some indigenous mammals. The dog (not the dingo) was also the first domesticated animal in the Americas, brought across the Siberian-Alaskan land bridge with some of the first settlers during the last Ice Age. Here dogs probably played a significant role in reducing the populations of large mammals, many of which became extinct at around the time humans arrived in North and South America. Initial human settlement of unpopulated islands also wrought major ecological changes throughout the southwest Pacific and Polynesia, including numerous extinctions, from about 4,000 years ago until the colonization of New Zealand roughly a millennium ago. All these instances were cases of invasions of "naive" lands, continents, and islands that had no prior exposure to humanity and its fellow travelers, or to the intensified fire regime that human presence normally brought. This helps to explain the dramatic effects, particularly the rash of extinctions, that followed upon human settlement of Australia, New Zealand, and the Americas.

Eventually, people began to transport animals, plants, and pathogens from one human community to another across the seas. In many cases, the only evidence for such transfers is the existence of the imported species. The sweet potato, a native of South America, somehow arrived in central Polynesia by 1000 CE and subsequently spread widely throughout Oceania. It is a delicate crop and could not survive a driftwood voyage: no one doubts that people transported it, although no one knows just when, how, or even who. It eventually became a staple food in the western Pacific, highland New Guinea, and to a lesser extent the east Asian archipelagoes and mainland.

A second mysterious transoceanic crop transfer took place across the Indian Ocean some time before 500 CE. Somebody brought bananas, Asian yams, and taro to East Africa. These crops had much to recommend them, as they do well in moist conditions, whereas the millets and sorghum that Bantu expansion brought into central and southeastern Africa were adapted to dry conditions. Plantains, of which bananas are one variety, had existed in the wild from India to New Guinea. Linguistic and genetic evidence suggests they arrived on the East African coast as early as 3,000 years ago, and reached the forest zone to the west of the great lakes around 2,000 years ago, just about the time of the Bantu migrations. Quite possibly the success—in terms of population growth and the extent of settlement—of Bantu speakers, often attributed to their use of iron, owed something to their successful adoption of these exotic crops. As relative newcomers to East and southern Africa, they had less invested in prevailing ecological patterns and fewer disincentives to experiment. Bananas, taro, and yams were probably introduced to East Africa more than once, and almost surely were brought again in the Austronesian settlement of Madagascar that took place just before 500 CE. These Asian crops assisted crucially in the epic (but unrecorded) colonization of central Africa's moist tropical forests by farmers, as well as in the settlement of Madagascar.

Several other significant intercontinental biological transfers took place before 1400, mainly between Africa and Asia, a route that posed minimal obstacles to sailors. Africa's pearl millet, derived from a West African savanna grass, is the world's sixth most important cereal today. It was introduced into India some 3,000 years ago, and today accounts for about 10 percent of India's cereal acreage. East African sorghum entered India at about the same time, and eventually became India's second most important grain after rice. Sorghum stalks were also useful as fodder for India's cattle. Finger millet, also from Africa, made it to India only around 1,000 years ago. It became the staple in

Himalayan foothill communities and in India's far south. The main effect of the transfer of African crops to south Asia was to provide India with drought-resistant dryland crops, opening new areas to settlement and providing a more reliable harvest where water supplies were uncertain. These examples suggest a very lively world of crop exchange—and probably weeds, diseases, and animals too—around the Indian Ocean Rim from around 3,000 to 1,000 years ago. The regular monsoon winds of the Indian Ocean helped make this region of the world precocious in its maritime development and hence biological exchange.

While south Asia received new crops from Africa, it sent others to the Middle East and the Mediterranean. Between the tenth and thirteenth centuries, Arab trading networks, facilitated by the relative peace supervised by the Abbasid caliphate (750–1258), brought sugar, cotton, rice, and citrus fruits from India to Egypt and the Mediterranean. These plants, and the cultivation techniques that came with them, worked a small revolution on the hot and often malarial coastlands of North Africa, Anatolia, and southern Europe. They caused many coastal plains to be brought under cultivation on a regular basis, often for the first time since the Roman Empire. Sugar and cotton could flourish with unskilled and unmotivated slave labor; their introduction may have quickened the slave-raiding that kept Mediterranean and Black Sea populations anxious for centuries. Keeping an army of laborers at work on malarial coasts—in the Levant, Egypt, Cyprus, Crete, Sicily, Tunisia, and Andalusia to mention a few centers of sugar production—required constant resupply from poorly defended peasantries. Sometimes this quest took slave raiders to the Black Sea coasts, but it also took slave merchants across the Sahara and along Atlantic coasts. Saadian Morocco, a state originally based on plantations in the Sous and Draa river valleys, brought sugar and African slaves together in a profitable mix that would soon be transplanted to Atlantic Islands such as the Canaries and Madeira, and then to the Americas.

A second avenue of exchange involving the Mediterranean basin linked it to West Africa. While this was not genuinely an intercontinental exchange, the Sahara for several millennia functioned somewhat like a sea, as the use of the Arabic term for shore (Sahel) for the West African desert edge implies. A thousand years before Columbus crossed the Atlantic, some unknown soul crossed the Sahara, reuniting the Mediterranean and the Sahel, which the increasingly arid Sahara had divided since about 3000 BCE. Trans-Saharan trade developed in salt, slaves, and gold. But no doubt this reunification included a biological dimension. Large horses seem to have made their debut in West Africa via trans-Saharan trade. Linguistic evidence suggests they came from the Maghreb to the north. These animals eventually became a decisive element in a military revolution in the Sahel, creating a mounted aristocracy that by the fourteenth century built imperial states. The Jolof, Mali, and Songhai empires of West Africa depended on horse cavalry, which undergirded their military power and, via slave-raiding, their economies. When ecological conditions permitted, these empires bred their own war horses, and when they did not, they had to import them, usually from Morocco. In any case, the social, economic, and political history of West Africa took a new direction with the arrival of big horses.

These instances show that long before the great age of oceanic navigation, the links of trade and colonization in the Pacific, in the Indian Ocean, and across the Sahara brought biological exchanges that powerfully influenced the course of history. The further exchanges attendant upon the voyages of Columbus, Magellan, Cook, and others extended this process, wrenchingly, to lands formerly quite separate in biological (as in other) terms.

Biological Globalization after 1400

After 1400, mariners linked almost every nook and cranny of the humanly habitable earth into a biologically interactive unit. The world's seas and deserts no longer served to isolate biogeographical provinces. It became a world without biological borders, as plants, animals, and diseases migrated wherever ecological conditions permitted their spread, although how soon and how thoroughly they did so often depended on patterns of trade, production, and politics.

Columbus inaugurated regular exchanges across the Atlantic, whereby the Americas acquired a large suite of new plants and animals, as well as devastating diseases that severely depopulated the American hemisphere between 1500 and 1650. Simultaneously, Africa and Eurasia acquired some very useful crops from the Americas, most notably potatoes, maize, and cassava (or manioc). Ecosystems and societies in the Americas were remade, with new biologies and new cultures. But the same was true, if less catastrophically, in Africa and Eurasia. The new food crops fueled population growth in Europe and China, and possibly in Africa too (there is no firm evidence). Maize and pota-

toes changed agriculture in Europe, and maize and sweet potatoes did similar things in China, allowing more intensive production, and allowing new lands not suited to wheat, barley, rye, or rice to come into production. In Africa, maize, cassava, and peanuts became important crops. Some 200 million Africans today rely on cassava as their staple food. Many of the rest, mainly in the south and east, rely on maize.

These modern exchanges had political meanings and contexts. European imperialism, in the Americas, Australia, and New Zealand, simultaneously promoted, and was promoted by, the spread of European (or more usually Eurasian) animals, plants, and diseases. Europeans brought a biota that unconsciously worked together as a team to favor the spread of European settlers, European power, and Eurasian species, and thereby to create what Alfred Crosby, the foremost historian of these processes, called neo-Europes—including Australia, New Zealand, most of North America, southern Brazil, Uruguay, and Argentina.

Beyond the neo-Europes, there emerged in the Americas something of a neo-Africa. More than ten million Africans arrived in the Americas in slave ships. In those same ships came yellow fever and malaria, which profoundly influenced settlement patterns in the Americas. They also brought West African rice, which became the foundation of the coastal economy in South Carolina and Georgia in the eighteenth century, and important in Surinam as well. Other African crops came too: okra, sesame, and (although not in slave ships) coffee. African biological impact on the Americas did not cease with the end of slave trade. Much later African honeybees imported into Brazil crossbred to create an "Africanized" bee that since the 1950s has colonized much of the Americas.

The age of sail brought the continents together as never before. But sailing ships did not prove hospitable carriers to every form of life. They filtered out a few, those that could not for one reason or another survive a long journey, or required conditions that sailing vessels could not provide. The age of steam, and then of air travel broke down yet further barriers to biological exchange, adding new creatures to the roster of alien intruders, and accelerating the dispersal of old and new migratory species alike. The advent of iron ships toward the end of the nineteenth century, for example, opened a new era in biological exchange involving species of the world's harbors and estuaries. After the 1880s iron ships began to carry water as ballast. Soon special water ballast tanks became standard, and so, for example, a ship from Yokohama bound for Vancouver would scoop up a tankful of water and a few marine species from Japanese shores, carry it across the wide Pacific, then release it in Puget Sound before taking on cargo.

In the 1930s, Japanese clams hitched such a ride and upon arrival began to colonize the seabeds of Puget Sound, creating a multimillion-dollar clam fishery in British Columbia and Washington State. A jellyfish that devastated Black Sea fisheries arrived from the East Coast of the United States in about 1980. The zebra mussel, a Black and Caspian Sea native, colonized the North American Great Lakes and river system from a beachhead established near Detroit in 1985 or 1986. It has cost the United States and Canada billions of dollars by blocking water intakes on city water systems, factories, and nuclear power plants. A more recent invader of the North American Great lakes is a crustacean called the fishhook flea, also a native of Caspian and Black Sea waters. It first appeared in Lake Ontario in 1998 and is now in the all the Great Lakes and New York's Finger Lakes, menacing sport and commercial fisheries, and disrupting the Lakes' food web. The failures of Soviet agriculture, and the expanded grain trade from North America in the 1970s and 1980s, created a new pattern of ship traffic that eventually brought disruptive biological exchanges. Nowadays, some thirty-five thousand ocean-going ships and three thousand marine species are in transit at any given time, linking the world's harbor and estuarine ecosystems as never before. The exchanges via ballast water are but a single variety of the swirl of biological exchange going on in modern times. Transport, travel, and trade take place on such a scale now and with such rapidity that a vast homogenization of the planet's flora and fauna is underway.

Outlook

From the Olympian height that allows a view of all life on Earth over its entire history, the last ten thousand years appear as an instantaneous homogenization of ecosystems, a new era in Earth history. Humankind has connected formerly distinct spheres of life, through trade and travel, reprising in the blink of an eye what formerly happened through continental drift. Some 300 to 250 million years ago, the world's continents fused to form a single supercontinent, called Pangaea. Creatures formerly kept apart from one another now rubbed shoulders, and large numbers of them went extinct by about 220 million years ago. Reptiles inherited the earth, spreading throughout the globe. In the last few millennia, our species has once again fused

thejycontinents, and to some extent the seas, and is probably provoking (through this and other means) the sixth great extinction spasm in the history of earth.

From less Olympian heights, other vistas present themselves. The process of biological exchange is much influenced by the technology of transportation. The invention of ships, of ballast tanks, of railroads and airplanes, all led to changes and surges in the pattern of biological exchange. This provides one rhythm. Another is political.

Some states and societies showed great eagerness to import exotic species. Monarchs of ancient Egypt and Mesopotamia buttressed their prestige by maintaining gardens and zoos filled with exotic plants and animals. The Tang, as noted, showed a similar enthusiasm. Thomas Jefferson tried his best to establish rice and silkworms in Virginia. Later, the U.S. government employed an army of plant prospectors, who scoured the globe for potentially useful species, and brought tens of thousands to the United States. In the nineteenth century, Australia and New Zealand featured "acclimatization societies" which made it their business to import species that met with their approval (usually from Britain). Nowadays the United States, Australia, New Zealand, and many other countries spend vast sums trying to prevent the importation of unwanted species, hoping to forestall biological invasions rather than foment them. Altogether, biological invasions now cost the United States more than all other natural hazards—floods, hurricanes, tornadoes, earthquakes—combined.

Beyond the disposition any society might have toward exotic species, the changing nature of geopolitics also affected biological exchange. Trade and travel—and presumably biological exchange—flourished in peacetime and contracted in times of war, brigandage, and piracy. Probably eras of imperial power provided the best political environment for biological exchange, when a single power enforced a general peace. Anarchic systems of competing states probably checked biological exchange by slowing trade and travel, notwithstanding the effects of mobile armies and navies. Furthermore, imperialism also seems to have inspired, as well as eased, the process of collection: botanical gardens and the like. Kew Gardens outside of London proved a crucial link in transferring rubber seeds from Brazil to Malaya at the end of the nineteenth century, which started a new plantation economy in Southeast Asia. The swings between moments of consolidated imperialism and anarchic struggle established another rhythm governing the history of biological exchange.

This, of course, was influenced in turn by biological exchanges, as in the case of horses on the African savanna.

One can only postulate such patterns in the history of biological exchange. Demonstrating their validity would require quantitative evidence beyond what one can reasonably hope to find. Yet one may be sure that time and again in the past ten millennia biological exchange has altered history. The next ten millennia will be quite different: fewer exchanges of existing species will take place, because so many already have. But newly engineered species will occasionally depart from their programmed scripts, fashioning unpredictable biological dramas. Some of these will help shape the future.

J.R. McNeill

See also Central Asia, Ancient; Cereals; China, Ancient; Cotton; Ecological Imperialism; Exotic Species; Exploration; Manioc; Mediterranean Basin; Potato; Sugar; Taro; Yam

Further Reading

Burney, D. (1996). Historical Perspectives on Human-Assisted Biological Invasions. *Evolutionary Anthropology, 4*, 216–221.

Carlton, J. H. (1996). Marine bioinvasions: The alteration of marine ecosystems by nonindigenous species. *Oceanography, 9*, 36–43.

Carney, J. (2001).*Black rice: The African origins of rice cultivation in the Americas.* Cambridge, MA: Harvard University Press.

Cox, G. W. (1999). *Alien species in North America and Hawaii.* Washington, DC: Island Press.

Crosby, A. (2003). *The Columbian exchange: Biological and cultural consequences of 1492.* Wesport, CT: Greenwood Press.

Crosby, A. (1986). *Ecological imperialism: The biological expansion of Europe, 900–1900.* New York: Cambridge University Press.

Curtin, P. (1993). Disease exchange across the tropical Atlantic. *History and Philosophy of the Life Sciences, 15,* 169–196.

Dodson, J. (Ed.). (1992). *The naïve lands: Prehistory and environmental change in Australia and the Southwest Pacific.* Melbourne, Australia: Longman Cheshire.

Groves, R. H., & Burdon, J. J. (1986). *Ecology of biological invasions.* Cambridge, UK: Cambridge University Press.

McNeill, W. H. (1976). *Plagues and peoples.* Garden City, NJ: Anchor Press.

Mooney, H. A., & Hobbs, R. J. (Eds.). (2000). *Invasive species in a changing world.* Washington, DC: Island Press.

Watson, A. (1983). *Agricultural innovation in the early Islamic world: The diffusion of crops and farming techniques.* Cambridge, UK: Cambridge University Press.

Biological Weapons

Biological weapons are living microorganisms and nonliving natural poisons (toxins) used to attack humans, livestock, and crops. Examples of microbial agents include the bacteria that cause anthrax, Q fever, tularemia, and plague; the viruses that cause smallpox, Venezuelan equine encephalitis, and foot-and-mouth disease; and the fungal molds that cause crop diseases. Toxin warfare agents include botulinum toxin, ricin, and saxitoxin. Some agents (such as anthrax) are highly lethal if left untreated; others (such as Q fever) are merely incapacitating. The ability of pathogenic microbes to multiply in the host means that even small quantities can be militarily significant.

Although offensive biological warfare (BW) programs are shrouded in secrecy, roughly a dozen countries are suspected of possessing or pursuing development of these weapons. In addition to Russia, proliferators are concentrated in two regions: the Middle East and North Africa (Egypt, Iraq, Iran, Israel, Libya, Sudan, and Syria) and east and Southeast Asia (Myanmar, China, Taiwan, and North Korea).

Delivery Systems and Effects

BW agents can be delivered with specialized bombs, warheads, or spray tanks that disperse the agent as an invisible, odorless aerosol of microscopic particles that remain suspended in the air for long periods and infect the targeted population through the lungs. Anthrax bacteria are well suited for aerosol delivery because they can be induced to form rugged spores that remain viable and infectious even after traveling over a hundred kilometers downwind. In contrast, tularemia and plague bacteria do not form spores and are rapidly killed by sunlight, heat, and drying.

The effects of biological weapons are delayed. Although toxins generally act within several hours, the incubation period of anthrax and bubonic plague is one to six days, and that of smallpox about twelve to fourteen days. Most BW agents can infect people who

The Biological and Toxin Weapons Convention

Below is a selection from *the Convention on the Prohibition of the Development, Production and Stockpiling of Bacteriological (Biological) and Toxin Weapons and on Their Destruction* (entered into force on 26 March 1975).

The States Parties to this Convention,

Determined to act with a view to achieving effective progress towards general and complete disarmament, including the prohibition and elimination of all types of weapons of mass destruction, and convinced that the prohibition of the development, production and stockpiling of chemical and bacteriological (biological) weapons and their elimination, through effective measures, will facilitate the achievement of general and complete disarmament under strict and effective international control,

Recognizing the important significance of the Protocol for the Prohibition of the Use in War of Asphyxiating, Poisonous or Other Gases, and of Bacteriological Methods of Warfare, signed at Geneva on June 17, 1925, and conscious also of the contribution which the said Protocol has already made, and continues to make, to mitigating the horrors of war,

Reaffirming their adherence to the principles and objectives of that Protocol and calling upon all States to comply strictly with them,

Recalling that the General Assembly of the United Nations has repeatedly condemned all actions contrary to the principles and objectives of the Geneva Protocol of June 17, 1925,

Desiring to contribute to the strengthening of confidence between peoples and the general improvement of the international atmosphere,

Desiring also to contribute to the realization of the purposes and principles of the United Nations, Convinced of the importance and urgency of eliminating from the arsenals of States, through effective measures, such dangerous weapons of mass destruction as those using chemical or bacteriological (biological) agents,

Recognizing that an agreement on the prohibition of bacteriological (biological) and toxin weapons represents a first possible step towards the achievement of agreement on effective measures also for the prohibition of the development, production and stockpiling of chemical weapons, and determined to continue negotiations to that end,

Determined for the sake of all mankind, to exclude completely the possibility of bacteriological (biological) agents and toxins being used as weapons,

Convinced that such use would be repugnant to the conscience of mankind and that no effort should be spared to minimize this risk,

Continues

Continued

Have agreed as follows:

Article I

Each State Party to this Convention undertakes never in any circumstances to develop, produce, stockpile or otherwise acquire or retain:

(1) Microbial or other biological agents, or toxins whatever their origin or method of production, of types and in quantities that have no justification for prophylactic, protective or other peaceful purposes;

(2) Weapons, equipment or means of delivery designed to use such agents or toxins for hostile purposes or in armed conflict.

Article II

Each State Party to this Convention undertakes to destroy, or to divert to peaceful purposes, as soon as possible but not later than nine months after entry into force of the Convention, all agents, toxins, weapons, equipment and means of delivery specified in article I of the Convention, which are in its possession or under its jurisdiction or control. In implementing the provisions of this article all necessary safety precautions shall be observed to protect populations and the environment.

Article III

Each State Party to this Convention undertakes not to transfer to any recipient whatsoever, directly or indirectly, and not in any way to assist, encourage, or induce any State, group of States or international organizations to manufacture or otherwise acquire any of the agents, toxins, weapons, equipment or means of delivery specified in article I of this Convention.

Article IV

Each State Party to this Convention shall, in accordance with its constitutional processes, take any necessary measures to prohibit and prevent the development, production, stockpiling, acquisition, or retention of the agents, toxins, weapons, equipment and means of delivery specified in article I of the Convention, within the territory of such State, under its jurisdiction or under its control anywhere.

Source: The Biological and Toxin Weapons Convention. Retrieved January 14, 2003, from http://projects.sipri.se/cbw/docs/bw-btwc-mainpage.html

are directly exposed but will not spread from person to person. The Soviet Union, however, developed two contagious BW agents (smallpox and plague) for long-range strategic attacks against U.S. and Chinese cities.

Historical Background

Biological weapons have been employed sporadically throughout human history. In antiquity, Greek, Persian, and Roman armies poisoned enemy wells with cadavers. In 1346, Tartar forces besieging a Genoese fort in the Crimean town of Kaffa catapulted some of their own plague victims over the ramparts. The Genoese defenders contracted plague and retreated to Italy; the disease then spread across Europe in a devastating pandemic known as the Black Death. In 1763, in the aftermath of the French and Indian Wars, British forces gave smallpox-contaminated blankets to Indian tribes besieging Fort Pitt (present-day Pittsburgh).

In World War I, German saboteurs covertly used anthrax and glanders bacteria to sicken enemy horses, which then played a key role in military logistics. During World War II, the United States, Britain, Canada, Russia, Germany, and France all did research on biological weapons, but Japan was the only country to use them. Between 1932 and 1945, the Japanese army ran a secret BW facility in occupied Manchuria (China) called Unit 731, where scientists grew pathogenic bacteria and tested them on prisoners of war. In 1940, Japanese military aircraft dropped ceramic bombs containing plague-infected fleas on 11 Chinese cities, triggering deadly epidemics.

The Biological and Toxin Weapons Convention

During the 1950s and 1960s, the U.S. and Soviet offensive BW programs made major technical advances in the large-scale production of pathogens, their stabilization and storage in liquid and dry formulations, and their dissemination as infectious aerosols. On November 25, 1969, however, President Richard M. Nixon ordered the U.S. offensive BW program halted and all agent stockpiles destroyed. In February 1970, the ban was extended to cover toxin agents, although work on BW defenses continued. U.S. renunciation of its offensive program opened the way for the negotiation of the 1972 Biological and Toxin Weapons Convention (BWC), a total ban on development, production, and stockpiling, which entered into force in 1975.

Even after ratifying the BWC, the Soviet Union secretly maintained an offensive BW program in four military laboratories and an ostensibly civilian pharmaceutical complex known as Biopreparat. In 1979, an epidemic of human anthrax in the Soviet city of Sverdlovsk claimed at least sixty-eight lives. Moscow attributed the outbreak to contaminated meat, but Washington alleged it had resulted from an accidental release of anthrax spores from a military microbiological facility. In 1992, Russian president Boris Yeltsin admitted that the Sverdlovsk anthrax outbreak had resulted from Soviet military activities and that Soviet/Russian implementation of the BWC had been "delayed" for two decades. He issued an edict ending the offensive BW program, but a residual capability may still exist.

As of mid-2002, 145 states had signed and ratified the BWC. However, some countries suspected of having clandestine BW programs have neither signed nor ratified the treaty (Israel and Sudan); other states have signed but not ratified, putting them in legal limbo (Egypt and Syria); and still others are full-fledged members of the BWC but appear to be pursuing illicit BW programs in violation of their treaty obligations (China, Iraq, Iran, Libya, North Korea, Russia, and possibly India and Pakistan).

The lack of formal measures in the BWC to check and enforce compliance has seriously weakened the treaty's effectiveness. In July 2001, a seven-year effort to strengthen the BWC by negotiating a legally binding system of on-site inspections of BW-capable facilities collapsed when the United States withdrew from the talks. The rationales given for the U.S. withdrawal included doubts about the effectiveness of the regime and concerns over the risk of compromising sensitive biodefense and industrial secrets.

The Late Twentieth Century

During the 1991 Persian Gulf War, the United States assessed that Iraq had a BW capability, but it was not until postwar investigations by the United Nations Special Commission (UNSCOM) that its full scale and scope were understood. In August 1995, a senior Iraqi defector revealed that before the Gulf War, Iraq had mass-produced three BW agents (anthrax bacteria, botulinum toxin, and aflatoxin), which were loaded into aerial bombs and Scud missile warheads but were not used.

In 1996, hearings before the South African Truth and Reconciliation Commission revealed that in the mid-1980s, the apartheid regime had launched a secret chemical and biological weapons program known as

Project Coast. Members of the South African Defense Force allegedly used BW agents against black-liberation groups in neighboring countries, the African National Congress, and anti-apartheid leaders. In 1993, then-President Frederik W. de Klerk halted the program and ordered all stocks destroyed, although production records were reportedly retained.

A few terrorist groups have also sought biological weapons. In 1984, an Oregon cult grew salmonella bacteria and used them to contaminate salad bars in a nearby town in a scheme to disrupt a local election; 750 people fell sick with food poisoning and 45 were hospitalized. The Japanese Aum Shinrikyo cult tried on nine occasions in 1990 and 1993 to release anthrax bacteria or botulinum toxin in downtown Tokyo, but failed for technical reasons.

Threats in the Twenty-First Century

In September and October 2001, a series of letters containing a powdered form of anthrax spores were sent through the U.S. mail, killing five people, infecting several more, and causing significant social disruption and economic damage The ripple effects of the anthrax-laden letters, which shut down U.S. post offices and Federal buildings for months, forced the irradiation of government mail, and terrorized millions of Americans, demonstrated the massive disruption that could result from even the limited release of a weaponized biological agent. This lesson may well have inspired other terrorists to replicate or even surpass the autumn 2001 attacks. Thus, a more extensive incident of bioterrorism remains a frightening possibility. Al-Qaeda mastermind Osama bin Laden has declared that it is his "religious duty" to acquire weapons of mass destruction, including biological weapons. Moreover, in March 2002, U.S. troops found an abandoned laboratory under construction near Kandahar, Afghanistan, where al-Qaeda apparently planned to develop BW agents.

In view of the emerging threat of bioterrorism, the United States and other countries are improving their intelligence-gathering capabilities in an attempt to prevent further attacks. Given the possibility that prevention could fail, efforts are also under way to strengthen the ability of medical and public health practitioners at the federal, state, and local levels to detect, treat, and contain deliberate outbreaks of infectious disease. These measures include stockpiling vaccines and antibiotics, and implementing improved systems for rapid

detection of and response to unusual disease outbreaks.

Jonathan B. Tucker

Further Reading

Alibek, K. with Handelman, S. (1999). *Biohazard: The chilling true story of the largest covert biological weapons program in the world, told from inside by the man who ran it.* New York: Random House.

British Medical Association (1999). *Biotechnology, weapons and humanity.* London: Harwood Academic Publishers.

Cole, L. A. (1997). *The eleventh plague: The politics of biological and chemical warfare.* New York: W. H. Freeman.

Drell, S. D., Sofaer, A. D., & Wilson, G. D. (1999). *The new terror: Facing the threat of biological and chemical weapons.* Stanford, CA: Hoover Institution Press.

Guillemin, J. (1999). *Anthrax: The investigation of a deadly outbreak.* Berkeley and Los Angeles: University of California Press.

Harris, S. H. (1994). *Factories of death: Japanese biological warfare 1932–45 and the American cover-up.* London: Routledge.

Institute of Medicine (1999). *Chemical and biological terrorism: Research and development to improve civilian medical response.* Washington, DC: National Academy Press.

Lavoy, P. R., Sagan, S. D., & Wirtz, J. J. (Eds.). (2000). *Planning the unthinkable: How new powers will use nuclear, biological, and chemical weapons.* Ithaca, NY: Cornell University Press.

Lederberg, J. (Ed.). (1999). *Biological weapons: Limiting the threat.* Cambridge, MA: MIT Press.

Miller, J., Engelberg, S., & Broad, W. (2001). *Germs: Biological weapons and America's secret war.* New York: Simon & Schuster.

Regis, E. (1999). *The biology of doom: The history of America's secret germ warfare project.* New York: Henry Holt & Co.

Tucker, J. B. (Ed.). (2000). *Toxic terror: Assessing terrorist use of chemical and biological weapons.* Cambridge, MA: MIT Press.

Tucker, J. B. (2001). *Scourge: The once and future threat of smallpox.* New York: Atlantic Monthly Press.

Zilinskas, R. A. (2000). *Biological warfare: Modern offense and defense.* Boulder, CO: Lynne Rienner Publishers.

Biophilia

A relatively new term in the environmental field, *biophilia* is now widely used to denote an innately emotional affinity of human beings to other life forms. It was brought into popular usage by Harvard University sociobiologist Edward O. Wilson with the publication of his book *Biophilia: The Human Bond with Other Species*, in 1984.

The term had been used in another context by the psychologist Erich Fromm, but Wilson gave biophilia a meaning that quickly acquired currency among scholars ranging from evolutionary biologists to deep ecologists. He observed that much of what we now experience as "human nature" appears to have been shaped by this affinity. He suggested that such inclinations as the desire to live near lakes or oceans, enjoyment of lawns, and affection for other mammals all have their roots in humanity's evolution through a million years or more of close involvement with other species. This involvement ranged from the excitement and reward of hunting other animals for food or fur to the fear of being attacked or killed by larger predators, and from satisfaction or delight in the consumption of some fruits or vegetables to fear of being poisoned by others. It ranged from the feelings of well-being associated with certain environments to feelings of isolation or foreboding associated with others. Thus, in its broadest sense, biophilia refers not only to positive attraction (as with flowers, pandas, sunsets, or birds) but also to fear or repulsion (as with spiders, snakes, and maggots). The latter responses are sometimes denoted by the separate term *biophobia*.

Wilson's interest in this phenomenon was not just one of dispassionate science, but of ethical concern about the impact of the human enterprise on other species. His own studies, along with others, indicated that the Earth is experiencing a mass extinction that could ultimately endanger the stability of ecosystems, agricultural systems, and human health worldwide. This "sixth extinction" is believed to be, in large part, a result of the rapidly growing human dominance of the planet—and seeming disregard for the plight of other species. At a conference convened at Williams College in 1990, titled "Arousing Biophilia," Wilson joined a group of other scholars to discuss the possibility that if biophilia is indeed a hard-wired human trait, it might be somehow used to help stem the planet's mounting loss of biodiversity.

In *The Biophilia Hypothesis* (1993), edited by Wilson and Yale University conservation biologist Stephen R. Kellert, a range of scholars explore the implications of biophilia for the human future. Kellert and Wilson propose that biophilia is actually not a single instinct, but a complex of "learning rules" that guide a person's

responses to nature, with those responses falling along a variety of emotional spectra: "from attraction to aversion, from awe to indifference, from peacefulness to fear-driven anxiety." They note that for 99 percent of human evolution, people lived in hunter-gatherer bands that were intimately involved with other species. The hypothesis is that as language and culture developed, it was animals and plants that provided the symbols, metaphors, and myths that mediated learned behavior and feeling—"the brain evolved in a biocentric world, not a machine-regulated world" (Kellert and Wilson, 32). Anthropologist Richard Nelson, citing a recording by ethnographer Karl Luckert, notes that young Navajo hunters were traditionally taught, "Animals are our food. They are our thoughts" (Kellert and Wilson, 204).

A central theme of Kellert, Wilson, and others is that in the relatively brief period since the rise of industrialization, humans have become increasingly separated from direct contact with nature. A key implication of the hypothesis is that if people can better understand the evolutionary adaptations that enabled them to thrive long before industrialization, they may reconsider many of the practices that could otherwise destroy not only the stability of the Earth's climate, fresh water supply, food production, and resistance to disease, but also many of the cultural and spiritual satisfactions that seem to make life most worthwhile. Other scholars, such as biologist Lynn Margulis and science writer Dorion Sagan, take a less sanguine view. In their essay "God, Gaia, and Biophilia," they write, "it is difficult to speak monolithically of biophilia, a simple love of life" (Kellert and Wilson, 345–364). They suggest that it may be more useful to speak of "prototaxis—the generalized tendency of cells and organisms to react to each other in distinct ways." Surveying the broad history of Earth, they observe that even as species develop intimate relationships with the environment, they repeatedly alter it—and what was desirable in the past may be unattainable now. "At this late juncture," they write, "we have come to see that there is no way we can expand indefinitely without imposing indefinite unpleasant changes on the environment."

Such views suggest that the hope expressed by Kellert and Wilson—to harness biophilia to stem the erosion of life at large—poses a difficult challenge. Living in environments that are now sharply altered from those we evolved in, humans may not always consciously recognize or understand the affinities that have shaped learning patterns. A possible danger is that, because the connection between people and nature is hard-wired, it cannot simply be shrugged off when it is no longer satisfying; instead, it becomes virulently antipathetic. Environmental scientist David Orr suggests that the artificial environments of industrialized or urban life in some cases may cause the human emotional response to nature to be transmuted into a deep-seated biophobia. He notes that industrialization has entailed an increasing proclivity by humans not just to live in interdependence with nature but to control it, and that this urge to control has led to a world in which it becomes ever easier to become biophobic: "Undefiled nature is being replaced by a defiled nature of landfills, junkyards, strip mines, clear cuts, blighted cities" (Kellert and Wilson, 416). He further lists ozone depletion, toxic pollution, and global warming as phenomena that trigger such antipathetic responses. "My hypothesis about the biophilia hypothesis," Orr concludes, "is that whatever is in our genes, the affinity for life is now a *choice* we must make."

Ed Ayres

Further Reading

Arousing Biophilia: A Conversation with E. O. Wilson (1990). Retrieved November 6, 2002, from http://arts.envirolink.org/interviews_and_conversations/EOWilson.html

Ayres, E. (2002, November/December). The biophilia paradox. *World Watch 3*.

Kellert, S. R., & Wilson, E. O. (1993). *The biophilia hypothesis*. Washington, DC: Island Press.

Kellert, S. R. (1997). *Kinship to mastery: Biophilia in human evolution and development*. Washington, DC: Island Press.

Levett-Olson, L. (2001). *Erich Fromm's biophilia: Socialist humanism as creative advance*. AAPT Melbourne Conference. Retrieved November 6, 2002 from http://www.alfred.north.whitehead.com/AAPT/discussion_papers/2001_LLeeLO.pdf

Wilson, E. O. (1984). *Biophilia: The human bond with other species*. Cambridge, MA: Harvard University Press.

Wolf, E. C. (1989, Summer). Arousing biophilia. *Orion*.

Bioregionalism

Bioregionalism is a philosophy and way of life based on the belief that people can fight the catastrophic negative effects of human activities on Earth's biosphere by recognizing and living in tune with the bioregions into which Earth's various areas can be classified. Bioregionalism means more than conservation of resources and environmentalism; it entails a transformation of fundamental aspects of human consciousness.

Defining Bioregions

A bioregion is defined as an area in which a unique overall pattern of natural characteristics can be found. The main features are generally distributed throughout a continuous geographic terrain and include a particular climate, local aspects of seasons, landforms, water-sheds, soils, and native plants and animals. People are also counted as an integral aspect of a place's life, as can be seen in the ecologically adaptive cultures of early inhabitants, and in the activities of present-day *reinhabitants*—people who attempt to harmonize in a sustainable way with the place in which they live. In describing a bioregion, information may be drawn not only from the natural sciences but from many other sources as well. It is a geographic terrain and a terrain of consciousness. Anthropological studies, historical accounts, social developments, customs, traditions, and arts can all play a part.

The Goals of Bioregionalism

Bioregionalism has three main goals. It aims to restore and maintain local natural systems; to satisfy basic human needs for food, water, energy, housing, and resources in sustainable ways; and to support the work of reinhabitation. The latter is accomplished through proactive projects, employment and education, and by engaging in protests against the destruction of natural elements in a bioregion.

Bioregional goals play out in a spectrum of different ways for different places. Reinhabitants of the Kansas Area Watershed Bioregion of North America, for example, are engaged in restoring native prairie grasses in order to rebuild the ecosystem, whereas bringing back salmon runs has a high priority for Shasta Bioregion in northern California. Using biomass as a renewable energy source fits Cascadia Bioregion in the rainy Pacific northwest. Less cloudy skies in the sparsely vegetated southwestern Sonoran Desert Bioregion make direct solar energy a viable alternative there. Education about local natural characteristics and conditions varies substantially from place to place, as does the degree of social and political action on bioregional issues.

Bioregionalism Begins at Home

The following statement was adopted by the first North American Bioregional Congress in 1984:

A growing number of people are recognizing that in order to secure the clean air, water and food that we need to healthfully survive, we have to become guardians of the places where we live. People sense the loss in not knowing our neighbors and natural surroundings, and are discovering that the best way to take care of our selves, and to get to know our neighbors, is to protect and restore our region.

Bioregionalism recognizes, nurtures, sustains and celebrates our local connections with:

Land

Plants and Animals

Springs, Rivers, Lakes, Groundwater and Oceans

Air

Families, Friends, Neighbors

Community

Native Traditions

Indigenous Systems of Production and Trade

It is taking the time to learn the possibilities of place. It is a mindfulness of local environment, history, and community aspirations that leads to a sustainable future. It relies on safe and renewable sources of food and energy. It ensures employment by supplying a rich diversity of services within the community, by recycling our resources, and by exchanging prudent surpluses with other regions. Bioregionalism is working to satisfy basic needs locally, such as education, health care and self-government.

The bioregional perspective recreates a widely-shared sense of regional identity founded upon a renewed critical awareness of and respect for the integrity of our ecological communities.

People are joining with neighbors to discuss ways we can work together to:

1. Learn what our special local resources are;

2. Plan how to best protect and use those natural and cultural resources;

3. Exchange our time and energy to best meet our daily and long-term needs;

4. Enrich our children's local and planetary knowledge.

Security begins by acting responsibly at home. Welcome Home!

Source: *Heartland Bioregion Communicator.* Retrieved December 30, 2002, from: http://www.tcgreens.org/gl/articles/ 20010701071729894.html

Bioregional thinking appeals to people in many fields that relate to ecological sustainability. Restoration ecology practitioners readily grasp the importance of an appreciative local culture for their efforts to revive native plants and animals. Urban ecology advocates use bioregions for "nesting" their redesigned cities in a broad natural context. Permaculturalists (supporters of sustainable, ecologically sound agriculture) and most organic farmers employ techniques that are appropriate to their particular locales and insist on maintaining soils, water sources, and native species. Poets, painters, theater groups, and other artists have embraced bioregional themes in their works, and bioregionalism encourages the support of local arts and art forms, such as distinctive regional music. Elementary school teachers introduce bioregional concepts, and graduate schools recognize theses and dissertations based on them. Followers of deep ecology claim bioregionalism is a social manifestation of their biocentric philosophy. Even traditional conservation and environmental groups, such as the Sierra Club, have adopted a system of "ecoregions" to address members' problems in home areas.

History of the Bioregionalism Movement

In the early 1970s, natural scientists, social and environmental activists, artists, writers, community leaders, and back-to-the-landers began to define the contemporary vision of bioregionalism. They wanted to do more than "just save what's left" in regard to nature, wildness, and the biosphere. Planet Drum Foundation (an ecological education and action organization that promotes sustainable living founded on an understanding of bioregions) in San Francisco became a voice for this sentiment, publishing information on applying place-based ideas to environmental practices, society, cultural expressions, philosophy, politics, and other subjects. By the late 1970s, bioregional organizations such as the Frisco Bay Mussel Group in northern California and the Ozark Area Community Congress on the Kansas-Missouri border were founded to articulate local economic, social, political, and cultural agendas. The Mussel Group eventually played a pivotal role in 1981 persuading the public to vote down a bioregionally lethal canal proposal that would have diverted fresh water away from San Francisco Bay. The Ozarks group has held continuous annual gatherings to promote and support place-based activities. At present there are hundreds of similar groups (and publications) in North and South America, Europe, Japan, and Australia.

Acting Locally, Regionally, and More Broadly

Bioregionalists are primarily concerned with their own local areas. There are a surprisingly large number of opportunities to bring the issue of sustainability into work on everyday living conditions, whether the project is resident-based reforestation in rural areas or community gardens in cities. Watershed-based organizations with bioregional priorities for basins as small as a creek or as large as the Great Lakes are a steadily growing phenomenon. Their recommendations to boards, councils, and other agencies are not limited to creek restoration, water conservation, and other obvious issues, but may also include redrawing political borders to fit watershed lines and adopting ecological urban plans.

On a broader level, representatives of the bioregional movement from around the world have held gatherings and congresses in Canada, Italy, Mexico, and the United States that have resulted in the formulation of general principles and statements of intent, including the often-reprinted proclamation "Welcome Home," first adopted by the North American Bioregional Congress in 1984. Defending bioregions from persistent globalist intrusions requires especially creative responses. When multinational land developers threatened the town of Tepoztlan in Mexico with loss of traditional water rights and political autonomy, bioregionalists from throughout North America assisted in mounting a resistance that eventually stopped the developers. Most recently, Guard Fox Watch, a monitoring group made up of bioregional activists from Japan and the United States, investigated and successfully exposed the destructive ecological impact and official "greenwashing" of the 2002 Winter Olympics in Salt Lake Bioregion. More bioregional alliances to defend particularly threatened places can be expected in the future.

Peter Berg

Further Reading

Aberley, D. (Ed.). (1993). *Boundaries of home: Mapping for local empowerment.* Philadelphia: New Society Publishers.

Andrus, V., Plant, C., Plant, J., Wright, E (Eds.). (1990). *Home! A bioregional reader.* Philadelphia, PA, Santa Cruz, CA, and Gabriola, Canada: New Society Publishers.

Berg, P. (Ed.). (1978). *Reinhabiting a separate country: A bioregional anthology of northern California.* San Francisco: Planet Drum Books.

Berg, P. (1995). *Discovering your life-place: A first bioregional workbook.* San Francisco: Planet Drum Books.

Dodge, J. (1981). Living by life: Some bioregional theory and practice. *CoEvolution Quarterly,* (32), 6–12.

House, F. (1999).*Totem salmon: Life lessons from another species.* Boston: Beacon Press.

Mills, S. (1996). *In the service of the wild.* Boston: Beacon Press.

Sale, K. (1985). *Dwellers in the land: The bioregional vision.* San Francisco: Sierra Club Books.

Synder, G. (1990). *The practice of the wild: Essays.* San Francisco: North Point Press.

Traina, F., & Darley-Hill, S. (Eds.). (1995). *Perspectives in bioregional education.* Troy, OH: North American Association for Environmental Education.

Bird, Isabella

(1831–1904)
British travel writer

Although Isabella Lucy Bird (later Bishop) began her traveling career late in life, in her forties, she established a reputation both as a popular travel writer and as a respected geographer. She was one of a group of women first admitted as full members of the Royal Geographical Society in 1892. Bird's commitment to travel began with an intense desire for solitude, a solitude that she found in mountainous regions. A skilled and experienced horsewoman, Bird sought out areas of the world inaccessible except by horseback and wrote lyrical, yet accurate, descriptions of her surroundings. Traveling in Hawaii, the Malay Archipelago, the Colorado Rocky Mountains, Tibet, and China, she felt most alive when venturing into difficult terrain. She traveled without a European male escort, and attempted to avoid other Europeans in her travels.

Bird was born in Yorkshire and grew up in Cheshire. Bird's family had an imposing religious background; her father was a minister in the Church of England and her mother was the daughter of a minister. Her aunts had worked with Christian missions in India and Persia, so the idea of women traveling was acceptable so long as a religious mission was involved. Bird and her sister, Henrietta, were home-schooled by their parents and given an excellent education in languages and natural history. Bird continued to teach herself botany, photography, and cartography, along with basic medical and veterinary care.

While growing up, Bird suffered from a range of mysterious illnesses and eventually had a tumor removed from her spine. Her doctors suggested travel to recover, and at age twenty-two, she traveled to the United States, writing of her experiences in *The English Woman in America* (1856). Another visit soon followed as she pursued her father's religious interests, and she wrote *The Aspects of Religion in the United States of America* (1859). Both books were published anonymously. Bird continued writing, producing a wide range of articles on natural history for women's magazines, but was always in ill health. It is likely that she was suffering from the intellectual frustration caused by the constricted life women faced in Victorian England.

At age forty-one, remembering how much better she felt while traveling, Bird traveled to Australia, then continued to Hawaii, where she discovered the freedom of riding astride, without sidesaddles. She wrote her sister, Henrietta, of her experiences, letters that she worked into her book *The Hawaiian Archipelago*. She continued riding in the Rocky Mountains of Colorado, describing her joy with her newly found health and freedom, themes she explores in *A Lady's Life in the Rocky Mountains* (1879), her best-known and most beloved book. Finding that she could support herself through her writing, Bird continued traveling and helped establish several medical missions. She amazed her readers with her courage as she traveled off the beaten path, finding health while facing physical hardship. Marriage to John Bishop interrupted her travels, but she continued after his death, riding through Tibet, Persia, and Kurdistan, then into China and Tibet. For each trip, she described the geography of the region and her adventures with individual horses and native guides. When she died at age seventy, she was still planning her next trips.

Lila Marz Harper

Further Reading

Barr, P. (1970). *A curious life for a lady: The story of Isabella Bird.* London: Macmillan.

Bird [Bishop], I. (1987). *A lady's life in the Rocky Mountains.* Sausalito, CA: Comstock. (Original work published 1897)

Bird [Bishop], I. (1974). *Six months among the palm groves, coral reefs and volcanoes of the Sandwich Islands.* Rutland, VT: Tuttle. (Original work published 1890)

Frawley, M. (1994). *A wider range: Travel writing by women in Victorian England.* Madison, NJ: Fairleigh Dickinson University Press.

Gergits, J. M. (1996). Isabella Lucy Bird. In *British Travel Writers, 1837–1875: Victorian Period. Dictionary of Literary Biography. Vol. 166*, pp. 29–49. Detroit, MI: Gale.

Harper, L. M. (2001). *Solitary travelers: Nineteenth-century women's travel narratives and the scientific vocation.* Rutherford, NJ: Fairleigh Dickinson University Press.

Birds

Together with insects, birds are the Earth's winged marvels. These feathered vertebrates are champions of the globe's atmosphere, and appeared in the fossil record about 150 million years ago, evolving according to many experts, from dinosaurs. In resent years avian taxonomists have revised upward the number of living birds to as many as 9,703 species in 23 orders, 142 families, and 2,057 genera.

Flying gives birds a superb advantage. They can move swiftly and easily over land and water, and adjust to shifts in weather and climate by making long-distance flights in search of food and suitable habitat in which to nest. We give the term "migration" to the cyclical nature of these movements, marveling at how far waterfowl and shorebirds travel, and how they navigate to precise destinations.

Adaptability

Flight enables birds to occupy a wide range of habitats, including forests, deserts, and grasslands, where they subsist on a variety of animal and plant foods. It has also enabled them to colonize remote islands, where isolation has resulted in some birds becoming flightless, such as penguins in the Southern Ocean. Another flightless bird, the ostrich from Africa, is the largest bird, standing 2.7 meters (9 feet), and weighing 160 kilograms (353 lbs).

Some families, such as gulls and albatrosses (the longest-winged birds), pass much of their lives over seas and oceans feeding on marine organisms, and then fly to nest on tiny atolls or remote islands.

Others families are entirely terrestrial, and like hummingbirds (the smallest bird, the bee hummingbird is 5.7 centimeters [2.2 inches] long, weighs 1.6 grams [0.056 oz.]), select a range of plant associations at different elevations in order to feed on nectar and insects. The rufous hummingbird, one of nineteen hummers in the U. S., may lower its energy consumption by growing torporous at night and during bad weather. Mountain-dwelling hummers, which have the highest metabolic rates of any animal, do likewise.

Human Relationships: Predation and Domestication

Humans relate to birds in basically two ways. First, we hunt wild birds, such as waterfowl, for their meat, eggs, skins, and feathers; or, we regard hawks and eagles as threats to livestock, or blackbirds, starlings, ands other perching birds as pests among crops, and extirpate them. As major predators, we have extinguished 33 species and subspecies over the past 200 years in North America (together with Hawaii and Puerto Rico), including remarkably abundant species, such as the passenger pigeon, Carolina parakeet, and heath hen (an eastern subspecies of the greater prairie chicken).

Some farmers regarded the Carolina parakeet, for example, as troublesome around crops and killed these gregarious birds. Others cleared old-growth forests and felled large dead trees preferred by the ivory-billed woodpecker, and extirpated ducks, shorebirds, and cranes by draining their wetland homes. Today, 92 species are threatened and endangered in the United States.

Secondly, humans relate to birds by breeding them for the house and yard, selecting pheasants for their colors and taste, turkeys for size, doves for docility and appearance in order to meet our needs. Captive domestic fowl, or chickens, reportedly the commonest bird in the world, are derived from Asia's red jungle

American egret, cattle egret, and black-necked stilts at the Salton Sea, a major bird sanctuary, in southern California.
COURTESY MILTON FRIEND.

There is nothing in which the birds differ more from man than the way in which they can build and yet leave a landscape as it was before.

—Robert Lynd, *The Blue Lion and Other*, London: Methuen, 1923.

---

fowl. As captives, these birds can be traced to India more than 5,000 years ago, and today's sixty or so breeds of chicken, plus domesticated ducks and geese, supply eggs as well as meat. In addition, we select birds as companions and pets, ornamenting our homes with their beautiful shapes and songs. Scores of species, including parrots and finches, are valuable for the pet trade.

Other Relationships

There are additional ways in which human beings relate to birds. We seek nest and roost sites in order to collect droppings, or guano, as a fertilizer; gather down from colonies of eider ducks in Iceland, for example, for sleeping bags and cold weather clothing, and tie colorful feathers of domestic fowl, pheasants (and at one time the North American wood duck), into fish lures.

Some of these practices established sustainable relationships with birds. This occurred in Peru, where cormorants, boobies, and pelicans supplied valuable guano for European and North American farmers for thirty years after 1850. Government controls and bird colony management helped restore seabird populations until quite recently, and guano continues to be used on a regional basis. In southwest Africa, similar guano mining does not destroy the birds that supply it.

Conservation

By tallying the numbers of crop and livestock insects birds consume, conservationists have stressed their benefits to horticulturists and farmers. This argument surfaced a century ago when the Audubon Society recruited members within the U.S. Then, as now, preservationists urged lawmakers to establish enforceable laws to protect useful species. Rather than kill birds, they encouraged the public to observe the life histories of common species.

This anthropocentric viewpoint expanded in ecological directions as scientists regarded birds as part of a "balance" in nature, factoring into food chains and flows of energy that characterize and sustain plant and animal communities. The direct and indirect benefits from birds encompass recreational, aesthetic, and inspirational values, typified in art, literature, and song. Ancient stories heralded birds as gods, or spirits, who carried messages to humans. This iconography continues in our love for barn swallows and purple martins, which nest around habitations. In spring, we celebrate the arrival of these feathered migrants, marveling at their powers of flight, movements, and how they are "at home" in sites and habitats thousands of miles apart.

In this sense current concern for migratory species, particularly non-game birds, reflects a broadening interest in animals for their own sakes, rather than for how they sustain us materially. The satisfaction we derive from noting birds within metropolitan areas, where most of us live, expresses an introspective, humbler concern about our activities in the landscape, and the sense of companionship among the living things, including human beings, that give distinction to this planet.

Robin Doughty

Further Reading

Ehrlich, P. R., Dobkin, D. S., & Wheye, D. (1992). *Birds in jeopardy*. Stanford, CA: Stanford University Press.

Salathe, T. (Ed.). (1991). *Conserving migratory birds*. Cambridge, UK: International Council for Bird Preservation.

Terborgh, J. (1989). *Where have all the birds gone?* Princeton, NJ: Princeton University Press.

Welty, J. C. (1982). *The life of birds*. Philadelphia: Saunders.

Bison

The bison, the largest land mammal to survive the Ice Age in North America, has long been an icon of natural abundance. Indeed, the bison is the symbol of the U.S. Department of the Interior, which manages American public lands. The association of the bison with the idea of natural abundance springs from exaggerated estimates of the bison population that flourished in the nineteenth century. Some nineteenth-century observers estimated that between 75 and 100 million bison inhabited the Great Plains (grasslands of 3 million square kilometers between Canada and west Texas). Based on drier-eyed figures of range-carrying capacity, however, recent estimates have indicated that a maximum of 30 million bison inhabited the grasslands. This population was in all likelihood constantly in flux, owing to the intermittent effects of drought, grassfire, blizzards, competing grazers, and wolf predation. Archeological evidence indicates that during the last millennium, long droughts reduced the bison population considerably.

Hunting by American Indians

Since the eighteenth century, this fluctuating bison population had to contend with invasions of people, technologies, and exotic plants, microbes, and animals into the Great Plains. By the end of the nineteenth century such invasions had nearly caused the extinction of the bison. The first of these invaders was the horse, which European colonists brought to North America in the sixteenth century. In the first half of the eighteenth century, Pueblo Indian traders in New Mexico introduced the horse to the grasslands. The arrival of the horse prompted several American Indian groups such as the Atsina, Asiniboine, Blackfeet, Comanche, Kiowa, Cheyenne, and Sioux, who had made seasonal migrations into the plains from surrounding regions to hunt bison on foot, to become year-round residents of the plains as mounted bison hunters. Such a decision meant abandoning their reliance on a broader diversity of resources; the former strategy had ensured against famine in case of the failure of certain resources.

Historians and anthropologists once assumed that nomadic American Indian bison hunters lived in harmony with their primary resource, restraining their demands through the exercise of an ethic that discouraged overhunting. Recent scholarship, however, has questioned the sustainability of the nomads' novel resource strategy, suggesting that the pressures of mounted hunters and the grazing of millions of American Indians' horses, when combined with the existing ecological pressures on the bison population, may have slowly depleted the bison's numbers.

Near-Extinction in the Nineteenth Century

Whether depletive or not, the pressures of American Indian hunters on the bison were slight compared to the effects of a series of ecological and economic invasions in the mid-nineteenth century. The arrival of steamboats on the upper Missouri River in 1831 initiated an American Indian–Euro-American trade in bison robes that consumed over 100,000 northern plains bison annually until the 1860s. The 300,000 immigrants to Oregon, Utah, and California who traversed the central plains between 1840 and 1860 drove half a million cattle through the grasslands. These animals grazed and trampled grasses, spoiling much of the bison's winter habitat in the central plains river valleys. Additionally, the cattle may have introduced bovine diseases to the bison. In the late 1860s and early 1870s railroads reached the central and southern plains, bringing thousands of Euro-Americans armed with accurate, powerful rifles that had been developed during the American Civil War. Between 1870 and the early 1880s, these Euro-American hide hunters killed perhaps 2 million bison annually and disturbed the foraging and reproduction patterns of millions more. Finally, millions of cattle were driven into the plains in the 1870s, both northward from Texas and westward from the Midwest, occupying the bison's former range and thereby effectively preventing any recovery of the bison population. By the end of the nineteenth century the bison had been reduced to a population of fewer than one thousand.

The rapid collapse of the bison population in the mid-nineteenth century spurred calls for the preservation of the species. Nascent animal protection groups and advocates of humanitarian policies toward American Indians briefly allied to protest the eradication of the bison by hide hunters. Their effort to ban the hunting of bison by non-American Indians in the western territories was obstructed by officials in the Army and Interior Departments. These officials, and their allies in Congress, anticipated that, because the nomads depended so centrally on the bison, the elimination of the species would force them to submit to the reservation system.

Preservation in the Twentieth Century

In the early twentieth century, Americans and Canadians struggled to preserve the bison from extinction. Historians once regarded those efforts as a laudable hallmark of preservationism. In more recent years,

The American Bison on the Great Plains. COURTESY STEVE MALINOWSKI/U. S. FISH AND WILDLIFE SERVICE.

they have pointed to the ironies and contradictions of those efforts. In the United States, the interests of tourism and sport hunting dictated the course of the bison's salvation from extinction. The preservationists sought not only to save the bison from extinction but to rescue them from the clutches of entrepreneurs who exhibited bison in wild west shows. Between 1902 and 1914, the federal government, under pressure from elites in the East who were nostalgic for the nineteenth-century western frontier, installed a handful of bison in small preserves from Oklahoma to Montana. By the 1920s, content that the bison was preserved for tourists, preservationists' interest in the further protection of the bison waned, and preservationists acquiesced to the destruction of large private bison herds by sport hunters. Moreover, the crowded conditions on many of the preserves reduced the bison to semidomesticates. In Canada the achievement of creating Wood Buffalo National Park on the Alberta-Northwest Territories bor-

der in 1922 was shortly thereafter compromised by the introduction of bison from the grasslands. The new arrivals introduced bovine tuberculosis to the existing bison and, by interbreeding with the bison already in the park, may have eliminated the separate subspecies of Canadian wood bison.

The management of bison preserves shifted toward less-intrusive policies by 1968, when in both Wood Buffalo National Park in Canada and Yellowstone National Park in the United States, wildlife officials ended the practice of culling bison populations. As a result, in Yellowstone, within a few years the bison population had increased significantly, and bison began transgressing park boundaries each winter in search of forage. Nearby ranchers, fearing that the bison carried bovine diseases, insisted on the enforcement of laws that mandated the killing of bison that left the park; hundreds of bison were killed during the particularly cold winters of 1988–1989 and 1996–1997. Advocates of the bison including Indians of the plains further alarmed ranchers in the 1980s and 1990s by calling for the establishment of a "Buffalo Commons" in depopulated and economically depressed areas of the plains. The remaining Euro-American inhabitants of these areas vigorously resisted this suggestion. Great Plains ranchers were receptive to the idea of raising bison themselves, however. By 2000 there were nearly 250,000 bison in North America. Over 90 percent were owned by private ranchers.

Ultimately, rather than a symbol of natural abundance, the bison's history suggests that it is a symbol of adaptation and survival. The species has endured drought, predators (human and otherwise), and domestication to survive.

Andrew C. Isenberg

Further Reading

Barsness, L. (1974). *Heads, hides, and horns: The complete buffalo book*. Fort Worth: Texas Christian University Press.

Branch, E.D. (1997). *The hunting of the buffalo*. Lincoln: University of Nebraska Press.

Dary, D. (1974). *The buffalo book*. Chicago: Swallow Press.

Flores, D. (1991). Bison ecology and bison diplomacy: The southern plains from 1800 to 1850. *Journal of American History, 78*, 465–85.

Haines, F. (1970). *The buffalo*. New York: Crowell.

Hornaday, W.T. (1887). *The extermination of the American buffalo, with a sketch of its discovery and life history*. Washington, DC: Government Princeton Office.

Isenberg, A. C. (2000). *The destruction of the bison: An environmental history, 1750–1920.* New York: Cambridge University Press.

McHugh, T. (1972). *The time of the buffalo.* Lincoln: University of Nebraska Press.

Meagher, M. (1973). *The bison of Yellowstone National Park.* Washington, D.C. : Government Printing Office.

Roe, F.G. (1951). *The North American buffalo: A critical study of the species in its wild state.* Toronto, Canada: University of Toronto Press.

Black Elk

(1866–1950)
Holy man of the Oglala

Black Elk was an Oglala (Sioux) holy man best known for what he reported in the book *Black Elk Speaks*, published in 1932. Said to be a life story, the book offered a vision of better times that were far removed from the painful realities of twentieth-century reservation existence. A "bible" of the hippie movement, *Black Elk Speaks* was required reading for the increasingly popular environmental, antiwar, New Age, back-to-nature, and Native American cultural resurgence movements of the 1960s and 1970s.

Concurrent with the interest in *Black Elk Speaks* was a "Keep America Beautiful" campaign that bolstered the holy man's association with ecology. In ubiquitous television commercials, billboard ads, and posters, the campaign featured a tearful Indian dressed in nineteenth-century Plains-culture buckskins. The image projected was that of a Native American elder who cherished the memory of a once-pristine American landscape. Now he wept upon seeing how polluted it had become. Because the most memorable passage in *Black Elk Speaks* depicted the holy man with tears on his cheek, the two images became interchangeable.

During this period, attacks against Vietnamese villages by American troops were reminiscent of forays against Native American camps described by Black Elk. Similarly, the ruin of rain forests by Agent Orange was equated with the desecration of what the holy man referred to as "mother earth." His was a voice that called people to lay down their arms and learn anew how the "Great Spirit" intended people to live. Emerging as a "wisdom keeper" for social activists in the last decades of the twentieth century, Black Elk came to be regarded as Native America's premier religious thinker.

The book *The Sacred Pipe* reinforced Black Elk's image, but it, too, contained no details about sixty years of the man's life that went unreported in *Black Elk Speaks*. Despite this void, he came to symbolize Native American experience as a whole. A victim of colonial conquest, Black Elk was resigned to live out his years and "dream of yesterday." His image was significantly altered, however, when the book *The Sixth Grandfather* provided commentary for the transcripts upon which *Black Elk Speaks* was based and when the book *Black Elk: Holy Man of the Oglala* illuminated that part of his life that had so long remained in the dark. Readers learned that Black Elk was an ardent Catholic for almost fifty years (and was not the unbending traditionalist that became his stereotype). Best known among his people for being a devout layman, he held the office of catechist and was remembered for preaching the message in the Book of Genesis that calls humans to be sensitive stewards of creation. Testimonials from those who best knew him insisted that he admirably taught and lived the Christian way. As a result, teachings that once were thought to be quintessentially "Indian" emanated, in reality, from a Christian faith that Black Elk built upon his Native American tradition.

A provocative topic, Black Elk has, over time, borne the mantle of wilderness ascetic, dejected elder, Native American ecologist, and Christian role model. As the new millennium began, some even hoped that Black Elk would be a candidate for sainthood within the Catholic church.

Michael F. Steltenkamp

Further Reading

Brown, J. E. (1953). *The sacred pipe.* Norman: University of Oklahoma Press.

DeMallie, R. J. (1984). *The sixth grandfather.* Norman: University of Oklahoma Press.

Neihardt, J. G. (1961). *Black Elk speaks.* Lincoln: University of Nebraska Press.

Steltenkamp, M. F. (1993). *Black Elk: Holy man of the Oglala.* Norman: University of Oklahoma Press.

Blackfly

Blackflies (sometimes also called "buffalo gnats") are small (body length 1.2–6.0 millimeters), dark, hump-backed flies of the family Simulidae. About 1,500 species are described from all parts of the globe except Antarctica. The eggs are mostly laid in flowing fresh water (rivers and streams) and the larvae are aquatic, filter-feeding on diatoms and microscopic particles of vegetable debris. Adult female flies suck the blood of birds and mammals (including humans) and are implicated in the spread of various debilitating diseases.

The most important disease carried by blackflies is human onchocerciasis or "river blindness," caused by the filarial nematode *Onchocera volvulus*. River blindness is widespread in tropical Africa and in Latin America from southern Mexico to Ecuador and northern Brazil. It is thought to have originated in Africa and been brought to the New World by infected African slaves.

Infection comes with a bite from a blackfly carrying larval worms in its body. When the fly bites it injects saliva into the wound. The saliva contains anticoagulants preventing clotting and ensuring a free flow of blood, and it is also contaminated with larval worms which then invade the body. About twenty-five species of blackfly, all in the genus Simulium, are implicated as disease vectors.

Worms take about eighteen months to reach sexual maturity, and although they begin life living loosely in the body tissues, they later become encapsulated in tough fibrous nodules which are the body's defense mechanism to this type of invasion. Adult female worms are 35–70 centimeters long, white, covered with close-set, ridge-like rings. Adult males are only 2.5–3.0 centimeters long and occur in the nodules with the females.

Mated female worms are viviparous, releasing many thousands of tiny embryo worms (microfilariae) about 0.275–0.3 millimeters long. The microfilariae have curved pointed tails and wriggle very actively. They migrate from the nodules into the dermis of the skin where they are likely to be sucked up with blood into another blackfly and the cycle continues.

Only a minute fraction of the microfilariae are picked up by other blackflies. Huge numbers are released during the approximately twelve-year life span of the female and the vast majority remain in the skin of the victim, leading to relentless and intolerable itching, skin thickening, and lesions. Invasion of the eyes leads to deterioration in vision, particularly as the microfilariae die and the body reacts to their increasing presence, eventually leading to the blindness of the disease's name. Although not a major killer of humans, onchoceriasis is debilitating and distressing, and a

major cause of morbidity in the mainly poor rural communities that it affects. It has been estimated that 1 million people in Africa are blind as a result of the disease and a further 17 million in 34 countries are infected.

The other major disease carried by blackflies is leucoctozoonosis, an often-fatal disease of stock birds (chickens, turkeys, ducks, and geese) caused by protozoan blood parasites of the genus Leucocytozoon. The North American turkey industry is particularly affected, with losses sometimes reaching 5 percent.

Apart from the direct spread of diseases, the unwanted attentions of blackflies can have a significant effect on the lumber, construction, mining, farming, tourism, and recreation industries, because large numbers of biting flies can make any activity out of doors unpleasant. For example, the blackfly "biting season," typically in May and June in North America, delays the tourist season in some areas until July instead of beginning in May, with the loss of six weeks potential income.

Richard Jones

Further Reading

Crosskey, R. W. (1990). *The natural history of blackflies.* New York: John Wiley & Sons.

Davies, J. B., & Crosskey, R. W. (1991). *Simulium—vectors of onchocerciasis: Advanced level training and information guide.* Geneva, Switzerland: World Health Organization.

Kim, K. C., & Merritt, R. W. (Eds.). (1987). *Black flies: Ecology, population management and annotated world list.* State College: Pennsylvania State University.

Black Sea

The Black Sea is a large (420,300 square kilometers) inland sea situated between Anatolia (Turkey) and southeastern Europe. Its maximum depth is 2,210 meters. It receives the waters of several major rivers, notably the Danube, Dnepr, and Don. Its water is brackish, only half as salty as the oceans. In recent decades it has suffered considerable biological disruption due to industrial pollution, especially in its shallow northwestern shelf.

The Black Sea was formed from an ancient lake during a great flood. With the retreat of the last ice age about twelve thousand years ago, sea levels everywhere rose, eventually overtopping the Bosporus ledge (the saddle rock that connects Europe and Anatolia, which underlies the Bosporous strait) about seventy-five hundred years ago and splashing into what then became the Black Sea. People and animals had to move to higher ground. This great flood, which may have been the basis for Sumerian and biblical flood stories, raised the ancient lake's water level 150 meters and expanded its area by thousands of square kilometers. The Black Sea is thus very young as seas go, and its plants and animals have only just begun adapting to their range of conditions.

The Black Sea is distinctive because its depths are anoxic (there is no dissolved oxygen) and hostile to all life except specially adapted bacteria. Below 150–300 meters, the water is permeated by hydrogen sulfide. The unusually weak mixing between the sea's layers, a result of the small temperature gradient, allows this "dead zone," the largest one in the world's hydrosphere (the aqueous envelope of the Earth), to persist and makes the Black Sea highly vulnerable to eutrophication (the process by which a body of water becomes enriched with nutrients).

Since ancient times Black Sea fisheries helped sustain coastal communities. Tuna, anchovy, and mullet were among the most sought-after species. But after 1970 these fisheries declined sharply in one of the world's most notable ecosystem collapses. The collapse had two main dimensions: pollution and biological invasion. With the industrialization of the river basins of the Black Sea and the chemicalization of agriculture, especially in Russia and Ukraine, the pollution entering the Black Sea grew markedly after 1960. Population growth (to about 160 million in the Black Sea basin) added to the sewage effluent. Elevated levels of nitrogen and phosphorus brought on eutrophication, especially on the shallow northwestern shelf. Oil pollution (about 90,000 metric tons annually in the 1990s) and radioactive wastes flowing in from the Don added to the stresses upon Black Sea species. Then, in the 1980s the Black Sea was invaded by an alien species, the comb jelly (*Mnemiopsis leidyi*), a native of the eastern coast of North America. It probably arrived in the ballast water of ships. Its diet includes fish larvae and the tiny creatures that fish eat. Nothing in the Black Sea would eat the comb jelly, so its population exploded, attaining a mass of 810 million metric tons (ten times the world's annual fish harvest), to the detriment of all other Black Sea species; fish landings declined 70–95 percent from 1989 to 1999. In the 1990s Black Sea

countries began to work together to address the environmental condition of the Black Sea but found cooperation difficult and funds scarce.

J. R. McNeill

Further Reading

Ascherson, N. (1995). *Black Sea*. New York: Hill and Wang.

Ryan, W., & Pitman, W. (1998). *Noah's flood: The new scientific discoveries about the event that changed history*. New York: Simon & Schuster.

Travis, J. (1993). Invader threatens the Black, Azov Seas. *Science, 262*, 1366–1367.

U.N. Environment Programme (UNEP). (2001). *A joint commitment to saving the Black Sea*. Retrieved April 15, 2001, from http://www.grid.unep/ch/bsein/tda/files

Bolivia

(2000 est. pop. 8.1 million)

Bolivia is a landlocked country in the center of South America. It has an area of 1,098,000 square kilometers and is bounded by Peru, Brazil, Paraguay, Argentina, and Chile. The capital is La Paz (1.1 million), and Sucre (190,000) is the seat of Bolivia's Supreme Court. Although Bolivia is the fifth-largest country in South America, it has one of its lowest population densities. Bolivia is one of the most indigenous areas of Latin America; 50–60 percent of the population claims to be indigenous. Recent censuses have used language, rather than ethnicity, to classify Bolivians. According to the 1992 census, 87.4 percent of Bolivians speak Spanish as their primary language. Of the entire Bolivian population, including those whose primary language is Spanish and those who do not speak Spanish, 34.3 percent speak Quechua, 23.5 percent speak Aymara, 1 percent speak Guaraní, and 6 percent speak other indigenous languages. Many Bolivians are bilingual in Spanish and a native language or in Aymara and Quechua.

Bolivia has abundant natural resources but is one of the less-developed countries in Latin America. For example, in 1992 it had an infant mortality rate of seventy-five per thousand. Bolivia also is one of the least-industrialized countries in Latin America; it has traditionally been an exporter of unprocessed ore (silver, tin, and gold) and has only recently become an exporter of oil, natural gas, timber, and agricultural products. The rural population is plagued by under-employment, malnutrition, and a lack of basic services. Most Bolivians are nominally Roman Catholic (85 percent), but there is widespread religious syncretism (the combination of different forms of belief or practice), especially among Andeans. There has also been a gradual increase of evangelical sects during the last few decades.

Ecological Regions

The rich cultural diversity of Bolivia reflects its varied geography. Although most people consider Bolivia to be an Andean country, more than 60 percent of its territory is lowlands. Despite this, most of the population (90 percent) is clustered in the Andean highlands and valleys. The Andes Mountains run through western Bolivia as two massive mountain chains (the Cordillera Occidental and the Cordillera Real) with many peaks above 6,000 meters. These two chains enclose the Altiplano, an arid high plateau of an average altitude of 3,500 to 4,000 meters that contains Lake Titicaca and other smaller lakes. The southern part of the Altiplano contains two of the world's largest salt flats, Uyuni and Comaipasa. The eastern slopes of the Cordillera Real form the humid, semitropical valleys of the Yungas, which gradually join the Amazonian lowlands. Farther south the departments of Cochabamba, Chuquisaca, and Tarija are located in drier and more temperate valleys. Between the Yungas and the northeastern Amazonian area there are extensive floodplains and drier plains around Santa Cruz. The southeastern part of the country is occupied by the arid and sparsely populated scrubland of the Gran Chaco.

History

Archeological evidence and carbon tests have demonstrated that the highlands of Bolivia have been occupied by humans for five millennia. Andean civilizations thrived in a seemingly harsh environment by using a variety of strategies. Most researchers agree that both South American tubers and camelids (llamas and alpacas) were domesticated around Lake Titicaca. Potatoes are indigenous to the Andes, and a wide variety of species are still adapted to different ecological conditions. Andeans have also cultivated other tubers that are scarcely known to the rest of the world, such as *ocas* (bitter potatoes) and *ullucus*, which can grow at altitudes of 4,200 meters. Tubers were complemented with highly nutritious Andean cereals such as quinoa (a pigweed grown for its edible seeds), amaranth, and *kañawa* and with leguminous plants that are more apt to valleys, such as *tarwi* or peanuts. In the valleys these native crops were complemented by maize, which was imported from Mesoamerica at an unknown date.

Andeans not only adapted food that was suited to their climate, but also processed it so that it could be easily stored and would ensure a food supply during harsh times. Potatoes were and still are frozen and sun dried to become *chuño* (dark freeze-dried potato) and *tunta* (white freeze-dried potato); maize was also dried, and llama flesh was sun dried and converted into *charqui* (sun-dried meat; origin of English word *jerky*).

The Tiwanaku civilization was centered in the Bolivian Altiplano and flourished from 1500 to 1200 BCE. It centered around the metropolis of Tiwanaku and reached into the Peruvian coast and northern Chile. Like all Andean civilizations, Tiwanaku had the ideal of a vertical control of resources—that is, control of access to resources from different elevations—and established colonies in warmer valleys and the Pacific coast to obtain maize, coca, and other products. It also constructed extensive water management systems to produce an intensive agriculture in the middle of the Altiplano. These systems included flooded-raised fields (*sukakollos*), terraces on the slopes of hills, artificial ponds (*qochas*), which took advantage of the high water table, and surface and underground irrigation channels. According to most researchers, Tiwanaku collapsed as a result of ecological changes that rendered the Altiplano increasingly arid.

After the collapse of Tiwanaku the Bolivian highlands were ruled by Aymara-speaking chiefdoms that were often at war. The Incas conquered the area around Lake Titicaca at around 1450 and converted it into the province of Qollasuyu. Although they subdued the Aymaras and brought Quechua-speaking colonizers to the warmer valleys, they were never able to assimilate the Aymaras. The Tiwanaku *sukacollos* were not discovered until the twentieth century, but the Incas continued to construct massive terraces and irrigation channels.

Although popular perceptions of the lowlands have equated them with barren deserts peopled by savages, recent research in the Llanos de Moxos (Amazonian flood plains of Moxos) has found ample evidence of pre-Hispanic landscape management. The floodplains of Moxos are crisscrossed with artificial ponds, channels, mounds, and causeways that date back to prehistoric

Floating reed islands constructed on Lake Titicaca, located between Bolivia and Peru. COURTESY NICOLE LALIBERTE.

times. They were used not only to regulate water levels and produce an intensive agriculture, but also to breed fish. These civilizations also disappeared without a trace until their works were discovered in the twentieth century. Whether they were Arawak immigrants or local Tacana groups is a matter of speculation.

The Spanish invasion was catastrophic for Bolivian native cultures. The demographic collapse of the conquest translated into an abandonment of labor-intensive agriculture. Because the Spaniards privileged mining, agriculture reverted to subsistence level. The Spaniards also brought new animals, plants, and agricultural techniques. The lack of population and the lack of interest that Spaniards had in traditional agriculture led to the collapse of most irrigation systems. European plows and animals, such as cows, sheep, and goats, and the practice of monoculture increased soil erosion throughout Bolivia. The mining industry also required huge amounts of timber as fuel for its smelters and to support underground shafts. The construction of Spanish towns also required more timber than traditional

Andean constructions. Deforestation compounded with soil erosion to render large areas unsuitable for cultivation. Europeans also favored their own products and dismissed local products that were much more adapted to the local ecological conditions. European domestic animals, for example, needed more pasture and were more destructive than Andean camelids, which fed on lichens and tough grasses.

After its independence from Spain in 1825, Bolivia continued to rely on mining as its main source of revenue; therefore, the deforestation and erosion of its western and southern areas continued. At the end of the nineteenth century Bolivia developed an interest in its Chaco and Amazonian territories. The colonization of these territories, by men and cattle, led to further problems with erosion and deforestation. The failure to Westernize Bolivia and its status as one of the most underdeveloped countries in Latin America have recently led to a recognition of its indigenous past and to an attempt to recover its traditional crops, agricultural techniques, and culture, which have been suitable to its environment for millennia. Therefore, products such as quinoa are no longer regarded as backward "Indian" products; they are gradually becoming a valuable export and a valuable sort of protein that thrives with little care in the barren slopes of the Andes.

The impact of globalization since the 1980s has had disastrous effects on the Bolivian environment. Deforestation has increased dramatically, particularly in the Amazonian basin. The highlands and the valleys have faced acute water problems and alarming levels of soil erosion. This has been compounded by a disastrous series of floods and droughts. The illicit cocaine production and gold mining operations have dumped harmful chemicals into Bolivian rivers. Like many other Latin American countries, Bolivia's main challenge in the twenty-first century is finding a way to reconcile its economic development needs with the need to preserve its environment for future generations.

Frederic Vallvé

Further Reading

Bakewell, P. (1984). *Miners of the red mountain: Indian labor in Potosí, 1545–1650.* Albuquerque: University of New Mexico Press.

Block, D. (1994). *Mission culture on the upper Amazon: Native tradition, Jesuit enterprise, and secular policy in Moxos, 1660–1880.* Lincoln: University of Nebraska Press.

Bouysse-Cassagne, T. (1987). *La Identidad Aymara. Una aproximación histórica* [The identity of the Aymaras: A historic approximation]. La Paz, Bolivia: Hisbol/IFEA.

Cole, J. (1985). *The Potosí Mita, 1573–1700: Compulsory Indian labor in the Andes.* Stanford, CA: University of Stanford Press.

Council, N. R. (1989). *Lost crops of the Incas: Little-known plants of the Andes with promise for worldwide cultivation.* Washington, DC: National Academy Press.

Denevan, W. M. (1966). *The aboriginal cultural geography of the Llanos de Moxos of Bolivia.* Berkeley and Los Angeles: University of California Press.

Erickson, C. (2000). An artificial landscape-scale fishery in the Bolivian Amazon. *Nature, 408,* (Nov. 9), 190–193.

Fifer, V. J. (1972). *Bolivia: Land, location and politics since 1825.* Cambridge, UK: Cambridge University Press.

Finot, E. (1978). *Historia de la Conquista del Oriente boliviano* [History of the conquest of the Bolivian east]. La Paz, Bolivia: Juventud.

Gade, D. W. (1999). *Nature and culture in the Andes.* Madison: University of Wisconsin Press.

Godoy, R. A. (1990). *Mining and agriculture in highland Bolivia ecology: History and commerce among the Jukumanis.* Tucson: University of Arizona Press.

Harris, O. (1982). Labour and produce in an ethnic economy, northern Potosí, Bolivia. In D. Lehmann (Ed.), *Ecology and exchange in the Andes* (pp. 70–96). Cambridge, UK: Cambridge University Press.

Healy, K. (2001). *Llamas, weavings, and organic chocolate: Multicultural grassroots development in the Andes and Amazon of Bolivia.* Notre Dame, IN: University of Notre Dame.

Klein, H. S. (1982). *Bolivia: The evolution of a multi-ethnic society.* Oxford, UK: Oxford University Press.

Kolata, A. L. (Ed.). (1996). *Tiwanaku and its hinterland: Archaeology and paleoecology of an Andean civilization.* Washington, DC: Smithsonian Institution Press.

Langer, E. D. (1987). *Rural society and the mining economy in southern Bolivia: Agrarian resistance in Chuquisaca, 1880–1930.* Stanford, CA: Stanford University Press.

Larson, B. (1988). *Colonialism and agrarian transformation in Bolivia: Cochabamba, 1550–1900.* Princeton, NJ: Princeton University Press.

Mazuda, S., Shimada, I., & Morris, C. (Eds.). (1985). *Andean ecology and civilization.* Tokyo: University of Tokyo Press.

Montes de Oca, I. (1997). *Geografía y recursos naturales de Bolivia* [Geography and natural resources of Bolivia] (3rd ed.). La Paz, Bolivia: EDOBOL.

Platt, T. (1982). *Estado Boliviano y Ayllu Andino. Tierra y tributo en el Norte de Potosí* (The Bolivian state and the Andean Ayllu: Land and tribute in the north of Potosí). Lima, Peru: Instituto de Estudios Peruanos.

Boone and Crockett Club

Founded in 1887 and named after two famous hunter-heroes, Daniel Boone (1734–1820) and Davy Crockett (1786–1836), the Boone and Crockett Club was the first private organization in American history to deal effectively with conservation issues of national scope. Its genesis lay in the adoption by nineteenth-century "gentlemen" hunters and anglers of the "code of the sportsman," an ethical system that defined the correct methods for pursuing wildlife considered to be game in order to give it a "sporting" chance and that demanded that sportsmen take responsibility for the perpetuation of game and its habitat.

"The Hunter's Cabin" at the World's Columbian Exposition, held at Chicago in 1893. The cabin is the headquarters of the Boone and Crockett Club. Out front is Elwood Hofer, hunter, guide, and packer from Yellowstone Park. COURTESY JOHN F. REIGER.

By the mid-1880s George Bird Grinnell (1849–1938), editor of *Forest and Stream Weekly*, the leading outdoor journal of the period, had long been exhorting his readers to create sportsman-conservationist organizations that could put this code into practice. One who found

Grinnell's message appealing was a young Theodore Roosevelt (1858–1919), who became friends with Grinnell in 1885. In 1887 Roosevelt invited Grinnell and a number of other sportsmen friends to a dinner party in New York City, at which Roosevelt proposed, and they accepted, the creation of a national hunting-conservation association.

The Boone and Crockett Club—with politically influential members, with Grinnell's *Forest and Stream* as its "natural mouthpiece," and with the knowledge that in order for people to preserve wildlife, they must also save its habitat—would have a tremendous impact on the early conservation movement. In 1891 members of the club persuaded Secretary of the Interior John W. Noble (1831–1912) to ask President Benjamin Harrison (1833–1901) to take the revolutionary step of setting aside the first national forest, the beginning of a system of forests and grasslands that now totals 77.7 million hectares. And in 1894 the club, led by Grinnell and his *Forest and Stream*, succeeded in creating enough of a public outcry over the poaching of endangered bison in the inadequately protected Yellowstone National Park to obtain passage of legislation that established the definition of a national park as an inviolate wildlife and wilderness sanctuary.

In addition to playing a major role in the passage of key environmental laws, the club during its early years provided the milieu in which the future president, Theodore Roosevelt, formulated his conservation philosophy, which is the foundation of the modern conservation program in the United States. Grinnell and a later club member, Gifford Pinchot (1865–1946), were the two strongest influences in molding that philosophy. Pinchot was chief of the U.S. Forest Service.

The departure of Roosevelt from the White House in 1909 did not lessen the club's efforts in behalf of wildlife and habitat. Environmental successes for which its members could take a large measure of credit were establishment of Glacier National Park in Montana (1910), Mount McKinley (later Denali) National Park in Alaska (1917), the Migratory Bird Treaty Act (1918), and Great Smoky Mountains National Park in Tennessee and North Carolina (1930).

With the founding in later years of organizations such as the National Wildlife Federation (1935) and the National Audubon Society (1940), the Boone and Crockett Club no longer occupies the same preeminent position in the field of wildlife conservation. But the club continues to be an advocate, especially in its financial support of wildlife research.

John F. Reiger

Further Reading

Cutright, P. R. (1985). *Theodore Roosevelt: The making of a conservationist*. Urbana: University of Illinois Press.

Grinnell, G. B., & Sheldon, C. (Eds.). (1925). *Hunting and conservation: The book of the Boone and Crockett Club*. New Haven, CT: Yale University Press.

Reiger, J. F. (2001). *American sportsmen and the origins of conservation* (3rd ed.). Corvallis: Oregon State University Press.

Trefethen, J. B. (1961). *Crusade for wildlife: Highlights in conservation progress*. Harrisburg, PA: Stackpole.

Trefethen, J. B. (1975). *An American crusade for wildlife*. New York: Winchester Press.

Boserup, Ester
(1910–1999)
Danish social theorist

Ester Boserup spent most of her professional life as a civil servant, yet few have had greater impact on academic social theory. Her analysis of population growth as a principle impetus to technological change has had a profound effect on theories of human and social evolution, while her effective reversal of previous beliefs about the relative productivity of agriculture and industry have had an at least equal effect on practical development planning.

Boserup was born in 1910 in Frederiksberg, Denmark, the daughter of the director of a textile company. In 1931, she married Mogens Boserup, a professor at the University of Copenhagen and writer in the tradition of democratic socialism. She was a civil servant for the Danish government from 1935 to 1947, a researcher for the United Nations in Geneva from 1947 to 1957, and a member of the United Nations Committee of Development Planning from 1972 and the Danish Council of Research Planning from 1973. From 1957 she was also a free-lance writer, with projects involving extended stays in India and Senegal.

Boserup's central focus was on two questions: the relationship between agriculture and industry in development and the relation between invention and population growth in social evolution. Previous evolutionary theories had generally dissociated agriculture from industry by attributing them to various key "inventions" that occurred in various evolutionary stages. Boserup argued that invention is not an explanation but something to explain. There is abundant evidence that that in any given area at any give time many more innovations are known than are actually adopted. We must explain why some are adopted and others are not. She saw the explanation in increasing population pressure creating demands for efficient ways to increase agricultural intensification, not just at one stage but along the entire course of evolutionary development.

No less important than Boserup's substantive claims were the simple but innovative ways she marshalled evidence, especially her measures of agricultural intensification and efficiency. Her measure of intensification is the ratio of the area cultivated to the total area occupied, which for agriculture she connected to the length of the fallow period. That is, in a system of shifting agriculture, if farmers return to a field every thirty years and farm it for one year, then the ratio is 1:29. In a system of settled agriculture in which each farm has three fields of the same size and one is left fallow each year, the ratio is 2:1. The measure of efficiency was equally direct. In place of monetary budgets she used energy budgets: calories gained for calories expended. Such ratios can be established quite readily for crops that can be examined in the field and inferred with at least reasonable precision from historical and archaeological records.

Although Boserup's analyses have been subject to much criticism in detail, particularly in relation to modern industrial countries, they have led to greatly increased precision in understanding and comparing various agricultural and related technologies and the organizational arrangements through which they are deployed, both over the long run of historical time and across the enormous variety of contemporary cultural adjustments.

Murray J. Leaf

Further Reading

Bayless-Smith, T. P. (1982). *The ecology of agricultural systems.* Cambridge, UK: Cambridge University Press.

Boserup, E. (1965). *The conditions for agricultural growth.* London: Allen and Unwin.

Boserup, E. (1970). *Women's role in economic development.* New York: St. Martins.

Boserup, E. (1981). *Population and technological change: A study of long-term trends.* Chicago: University of Chicago Press.

Turner, B. L., & Brush, S. B. (1987). *Comparative farming systems.* New York and London: Guilford Press.

Brazil

(2000 est. pop. 169 million)

Brazil is the largest country in South America, occupying about 47.7 percent of the landmass of the South America and 20 percent of the landmass of North and South America put together. With an area of 8.5 million square kilometers, it is the world's fifth-largest country (behind the Russian Federation, Canada, China, and the United States) and the largest country in the Southern Hemisphere. Because about 92 percent of the country is located in the intertropical zone, it is also the largest tropical country in the world.

The Brazilian population of 169 million makes it the fifth largest in the world (behind China, India, the United States, and Indonesia). Eighty-two percent of Brazilians are considered urban dwellers, although a fair number of them live in very small towns in predominantly rural or unsettled areas. In the 1950s and 1960s, Brazil's population, which was mostly rural, grew and became urbanized faster than that of almost all other countries, but the growth rate fell sharply after the 1980s. Today the growth rate is moderate and tends to continue declining. Brazilians are distributed quite unevenly, with a large majority of the people and almost all large cities located along (or close to) its Atlantic coastline. Vast central and western areas have low population densities.

Brazil is a fully industrialized country, although it is not considered developed because of its strongly skewed wealth distribution and deep social inequalities. In 1999, its gross domestic product, at US $751.5 billion, was the eighth largest in the world, following that of the United States, Japan, Germany, United Kingdom, France, Italy, and China. Brazil was also the tenth-largest consumer of energy in the world during 2001. Almost every type of modern industry can be found in Brazil. It is a world-class producer of steel and metallurgical products, motor vehicles and parts, airplanes, machinery, electronics, paper and cardboard, clothes, and shoes. It also has a vast—although uneven—agricultural and animal husbandry sector. Soybeans, corn, rice, sugarcane, coffee, oranges, and cotton are some of its major agricultural products. Brazil has the world's second-largest number of cattle and third-largest poultry and hog industries. Its service sector is also diversified and dynamic.

The economic system is a mix of private enterprise (including foreign and multinational companies) and

The Sugar Plantation in Brazil

The following overview of the annual farming cycle focuses on the community of Vila Reconcavo in the sugar-producing region of the state of Bahia in northeastern Brazil in the early 1950s.

The agricultural cycle and the work on a plantation may be divided into two broad epochs, summer and winter. Summer is the busiest season, for it is harvest time and all hands are occupied, including the migrant workers. The cutters with their machetes cut an average of three to four tons a day apiece, which must be quickly loaded and carried to the factory and milled, for the longer the lapse of time between the two operations, the greater the loss of sugar content. After a field has been cut, one of two things occurs. If it is to be turned into pasture, it is fenced, and the draft animals are turned loose in it. Otherwise the leaves which were cut from the top of the plant and left lying on the ground are burned, and within a short time the roots start sending up new shoots. This old planting (soca) each year gives a decreased yield. As a rule a field is cut and burned three to four years before being turned into pasture. In the days of the old plantations, when the soil was more vigorous, cane of twelve years was considered "new cane." Now, however, the yield is so decreased by the increasing poverty of the soil that three to four years is the best, depending upon the amount of rain. During the summer, if land is prepared and there are prospects of heavy showers, "summer plantings" may be made. They are never as good as those done in the winter, for the sun frequently kills the new shoots. Toward the end of summer, the pastures or garden plots which are to be made into new plantations (rego novo) are prepared, for such work is usually done in accordance with conditions of the land rather than only at the time of planting. New plantings yield an average of thirty to forty tons per acre. Cutting, transporting, burning, and planting are done by the resident workers, while the weeding and general cultivating are carried out by the migrant laborers.

Work in the winter period can usually be handled by the resident workers alone. The planting of cane goes on throughout the year, but the most favorable time is during July and August, when the rains begin to diminish in constancy and the sun shines longer. Cane planted at this time gives the greatest yield. The seed used is the top part of the cane itself, the "eye" which appears just below the leaves. As a rule each plantation furnishes most of its own seed. That for the summer planting comes from the cane which is cut to go to the factory, and that for the winter from small plantings made previously for the purpose. The state government also maintains an agricultural station in the area, from which the planters can get seed. During the winter all repairs are made on houses, fences, and equipment, and of course the necessary drainage ditches must be built or repaired and seasonal cultivation and clearing work must be done.

Source: Hutchinson, Harry William. (1957). *Village and Plantation Life in Northeastern Brazil.* Seattle: University of Washington Press, pp. 67–68.

strong state investments and companies. Over the last decade, however, private companies have taken over or advanced strongly into many economic sectors previously dominated by the state (such as telecommunications, steel production, railroads, and electric, gas, and phone utilities). Brazil's economy is dynamic, attains high growth rates, and was built mostly on the voracious—and often wasteful—extraction and transformation of natural resources.

Brazil has been an independent country since 1822. Until 1889 it was a monarchy, and it is now a federated republic, with twenty-six states and a federal district that includes the national capital, Brasília. Portugal colonized Brazil, and thus the national language is Portuguese. Brazilian culture is a blend of European (specifically Iberian), African, and native influences. However, European and African contributions were diversified in their respective origins and formed many blends with each other and with native cultures. Ethnically, Brazilian society is a rich blend of these interactions, including extensive miscegenation. Therefore, racial tensions and conflicts range from moderate to weak. Brazil has the largest number of Catholics in the world, although several Protestant and evangelical denominations gained many followers over the last few decades. Afro-American religions are also more widely practiced than previously. Brazilians have a tolerant attitude about religion, however, and many people have more than one orientation, lessening religious conflict.

Brazil's Relevance to Environmental History

Brazil is relevant to the world's environmental history and future for at least seven reasons: (1) Brazilian territory is large, spanning about 37 degrees of latitude and about 38 degrees of longitude, which corresponds to four time zones. This expanse allows sharp variations in ecological processes, ecosystems, and landscapes. (2) Most of Brazil is tropical. Biodiversity (biological diversity in an environment) is richer in the warmer and moister areas of the planet. Indeed, Brazil, being so large, so tropical, and mostly moist, is frequently cited as being endowed with a "megabiodiversity," along with Mexico, Peru, and Indonesia, among others. (3) The distribution of biomes (major biological community types) enhances this biodiversity. The biologically rich tropical rain forests (in their Amazon and Atlantic formations) cover or covered most (approximately 55 percent) of the Brazilian territory, interfacing with the extensive and also biologically rich savannas (cerrados, 25 percent). Then there are the more confined and less diverse desert scrub formations (caatinga, 13 percent) and tropical and temperate grasslands (2.5 percent). The Pantanal (freshwater wetlands) biome is relatively small (1.0 percent) but biologically rich. This terrestrial biodiversity is capped by extensive coastal mangroves and shoreline scrub formations (about 3.5 percent) along the almost 8,000 kilometers of Atlantic seashore and complemented by the Atlantic Ocean's own marine lifeforms. (4) The Americas in general, and Brazil in particular, were among the last areas of the globe to be reached and occupied by populations of *Homo sapiens*. The oldest undisputed records of human presence in Brazil date back to a maximum of only eight thousand years, quite recent in relative terms. This means that in Brazil, as in the rest of the Americas, Australia, and Oceania (islands of the Pacific Ocean), in contrast to the "Old World" (the mainlands of Af-

rica, Asia, and Europe), human-made changes in natural processes and landscapes have had much less time to happen and accumulate. Brazil's rich tropical ecology was disturbed by humans much later and to lesser degrees than were Old World ecosystems and is therefore considered to be, in the broad sense of the word, "wilder." (5) The bulk of human experience in the Americas occurred under the regimes of small groups of nomadic hunter-gatherers or small, semipermanent villages of tropical gardeners, and not under complex civilizations based on intensive agriculture, specialized social classes, centralized states, permanent towns and cities, and organized religions. This holds true even if Mexican, Mayan, and Inca civilizations are taken into account together with other more complex societies who prevailed for some time in other parts of the Americas, including the Brazilian Amazon. Many of the remaining peoples of the world who are still influenced by or actually experiencing such "traditional," low-impact lifestyles of hunting-gathering-tropical gardening live in Brazil. Over the last few centuries there has been opportunity to record their forms of interaction with the natural environment. (6) The European colonization of Brazil (and the rest of the New World countries) left relatively abundant records about the interactions between many types of colonizers and colonized peoples in many ecological settings and under many socioeconomic and cultural circumstances. The sharp cultural distinctions between natives and colonizers (including African slaves transferred by force to Brazil) are in themselves full of recorded lessons in environmental history—exchanges in domesticated and semidomesticated plants and animals, deliberate and accidental introductions of other plants and animals, spread of contagious diseases, the uses of fire, extraction of floral resources, hunting and fishing, gardening, agricultural expansion, values and perceptions, technology, and so forth. (7) Brazil has vast amounts of many of the natural resources most useful to humanity. It is rich in fresh water (the Amazon River basin alone is said to hold 20 percent of the world's fresh water) and in the associated hydroelectric potential of many long rivers. It also has extensive deposits of the world's most useful ores and minerals (iron, aluminum, manganese, tin, copper, kaolin, quartz), besides gold, silver, and precious stones. Its tropical forests, the most extensive in the world, yield wood and dozens of other products. It also has a vast stock of agricultural soils, in addition to its fauna and flora and their respective genetic endowments.

Nature and Society Shaping Each Other

Brazilian prehistory and history encompass many episodes in the unfolding of environmental history in the form of eloquent relationships between natural landscapes, processes and features, and human societies.

What's in a Name?

Brazil is reportedly the only modern nation named after a tree. The brazilwood tree—*pau-brasil* in Portuguese and *Cesalpinia echinata* in scientific nomenclature—was the first commodity that the Brazilian natural treasure chest sent to the rest of the world in modern times. The dense hardwood of this tree, endemic to the coastal formations of the Atlantic Forest, with its striking red color, prompted the Portuguese to baptize it with a name derived from the word *brasa* (red coal). Eventually, the name *brazil* went beyond the tree and the commodity and became the name of the colony and the country.

Of course, this naming is related to the economic importance of the tree and not to any preservationist sensitivity of the pragmatic Portuguese colonizers. The wood yielded a valued deep-red dye used in garments, carpets, and drapes. It was also used for cabinet making and crafts. The brazilwood trade started immediately after the arrival of the Portuguese in 1500 and continued until the 1870s, when dye was replaced by synthetic dyes created in European laboratories. Selected for its commercial value from among literally hundreds of trees of the tropical Atlantic Forest, the brazilwood tree became the country's national tree. Today, although it is hard to find mature individual trees in the wild, the species is protected and reproduced in botanical gardens and used for landscaping and plantations. Only a residual trade in brazilwood remains, mainly for cello and violin bows.

Recent Arrivals and Recent Extinctions

The very fact that the human occupation of Brazil is so recent relates to many matters of environmental history. As humans expanded into the Americas they found a vast and diverse territory in which biological processes had been evolving without human intervention. Life had not been static. Plants, animals, ecosystems, and landscapes had gone through many changes over time—migration, expanding or shrinking ranges, speciation (formation of new species), adaptation, extinction, erosion, climate shifts, and so forth—but until twelve thousand years ago no humans were present in the Americas to influence (or even witness) them. Several species of large land animals (megafauna)—such as mastodons, giant sloths, armadillos, felines, and a camel-like species—became extinct just as the first humans were spreading around the continent. There is evidence of this scenario because these animals had evolved in isolation from human hunters, thus being easy prey to their keen hunting skills. Combined with other factors, such as climate and ecosystem change and the slow rates of reproduction of these large animals, human hunting may thus have contributed decisively to the impoverishment of the continental fauna in relatively recent times. Brazil is among the areas in which the fossilized remains of these species are found.

Putting New Plants and Animals to Work

A distinct aspect of the timing of the original human migration into the Americas was the independent domestication of plants and animals. If the dates of early migrations into the Americas and of the domestication of plants and animals in the Old World are correct, it can safely be said that the original migrants entered the Americas without the "safeguard" or cache of domesticated plants and animals.

Thus, whereas several Old World populations, starting around eleven thousand years ago, began to master the more famous and lasting of the domesticated plants (such as wheat and rice) and animals (such as cattle, goats, pigs, horses, and sheep), populations in the Americas, arriving there without these resources, had to start from scratch, in an entirely different natural setting, with a different set of plants and animals. Nonetheless, archeologists have identified at least three major centers of plant and animal domestication in the Americas—two in the high plateaus of present-day Mexico and Peru-Bolivia and one in the present-day eastern United States. In those centers were domesticated, among others, corn (*Zea mays*), beans (*Phaseolus* sp.), potatoes (*Solanum tuberosum*), sweet potatoes (*Ipomoea batatus*), squash (*Cucurbita pepo*), peanuts (*Arachis hygogaea*), tomatoes (*Lycopersicum esculentum*), cotton (*Gossypium hirsutum* or *G. barbadensi*), the llama (*Lama glama*)(the only large animal native to the New World to be domesticated before contact with Europeans), and the turkey (*Gallipavo meleagris*).

In contrast, the vast lowlands of South America, in which Brazil is located, contributed much less to the stock of regionally or globally significant domesticates.

Manioc *(Manihot esculenta)* and sweet potatoes seem to be the only food plants from the lowlands (although not necessarily from Brazilian territory) to have been domesticated before European contact and to have gained wider importance as sources of food, spreading to Africa, Asia, and Oceania. Besides manioc, several other native or transplanted Meso-American or South American species of food plants (yams [*Dioscorea* sp], squash, and beans) were already found by Europeans in or around the modest gardens of the tribal natives of Brazilian lowlands, but they gained only local importance. Other useful plants (cotton tobacco [*Nicotiana tabacum*] and gourds [*Crescentia cujete*]) were also cultivated or protected by Brazilian natives, and some of them became world-class commodities. However, not a single domesticated animal taken from the lowland fauna was recorded, although some native groups confined modest flocks of muscovy ducks *(Cairina moschata)* and several species of fresh-water turtles (such as *Podocnemis unifilis and Podocnemis expansa).*

Bounty of the Wild

One lens through which to examine the relations between humans and nature in Brazil is the contrast between its relatively meager contribution to the portfolio of humanity's cultivated plants and animals and its rich biodiversity. Indeed, Brazil's biodiversity has yielded many useful plant and animal products that were or are mostly extracted, as opposed to domesticated. Among the more famous of these are rubber and the Brazil nut, products of huge trees *(Hevea brasiliensis* and *Bertholletia excelsia)* endemic to mature Amazonian forests. But many other extractive goods, such as ornamental and medicinal plants, fibers, the hides of caimans (reptiles similar to alligators; *Melanosushus niger* was one of the targeted species), the pelts of several wild animals—such as peccary *(Tayassu tajacu, Tayassu pecari),* jaguar *(Pantera onca),* and otter *(Pteronura brasiliensis)*—bird feathers, fish, and whale oils, have been important products of Brazil, especially for export. There still is a dynamic global trade in live animals—most of it illegal—in which Brazil participates prominently as a supplier, selling tropical fish, birds (*Psitacidae* parakeets, parrots, macaws, *Ramphustidae* toucans, many songbirds, etc.), tamarin monkeys and other primates, felines, reptiles (such as iguanas), scorpions, tarantulas, and butterflies.

Brazil is also the source of accidental exports of "unwanted" species. This is eloquently illustrated by the infamous "fire ant" *(Solenopsis invicta).* Probably hidden in the crevices of tropical tree trunks imported through the port of Mobile, Alabama, in the 1930s, this aggressive species native to Brazil, Argentina, and Paraguay spread throughout the South of the United States and became a major problem for farmers and wildlife managers. The so-called African bee (*Apis mellifera adansonii*), another notorious insect invader of the United States and other countries of the Americas, although not native to Brazil, started a forty-year spree from São Paulo. A set of these highly aggressive bees, under study in a Brazilian lab, accidentally escaped in 1956 and spread over tropical and parts of temperate America, either blending with or extinguishing *Apis mellifera* bee populations introduced earlier from Europe, creating havoc in bee-keeping industries and killing hundreds of people and livestock. Thus many natural elements found in Brazil—including reproductive and genetic materials—are still regularly taken from their natural settings and integrated into social and economic networks, bypassing local domestication and sometimes even local knowledge.

Domestication in the Making

Brazil's rich fauna and flora also provide the opportunity for contemporary and fairly well-documented episodes of attempted domestication. The world's most important acts of domestication were prehistoric and thus left meager traces, inferred from archeological sites, myths, and genetic information. The exact details of the domestication of, for example, wheat, corn, and rice (humanity's three most important and widely cultivated foods today), or cattle, chickens, and sheep may never be known. However, latter-day episodes of domestication reveal much about the demands that societies place on nature.

Brazil provides several opportunities for examining such episodes. For example, the floral dye *urucum,* made from seeds of the native bush *Bixa orellana,* was once an entirely extractive product. The plant was domesticated and planted in Brazil and elsewhere in the early twentieth century. Starting in the 1940s, however, synthetic dyes devalued *urucum* plantations, but after the 1980s *urucum* made a strong agricultural and commercial comeback as a natural dye because its synthetic substitutes were proven to be carcinogenic.

Domestication of the Brazilian rubber tree (*Hevea brasiliensis)* was not achieved in Brazil, nor by Brazilians, but rather by scientists and technicians in Europe and by colonial administrators and farmers in South and Southeast Asia. For many decades the rubber tree had been exploited in Brazil exclusively as an extractive good, based on wild populations spread throughout large sections of Amazonia. Domestication, mastered in England and executed in Asia, virtually extinguished the commercial importance of extractive production in Brazil. The huge economic importance of natural rubber made the tree's domestication in the late 1800s one of the most documented episodes in the human quest for mastering plants, especially because the global scope of production and consumption of rubber created equally global connections and rivalries.

Three other examples of domestication with remarkable commercial success are the cashew *(Anacardium occidentale)*, guaraná *(Paulinia cupana)*, and cocoa *(Theobroma cacao)* trees, also native to Brazil and also once exploited as entirely extractive. These trees were domesticated at different times and planted in extensive plantations (in Brazil and, in the case of cocoa, in other countries as well) that sold fruit, pulp, seeds, and nuts around the world. The *jaborandi* tree *(Pilocarpus microphyllus)* is an even more recent example. This native tree yields bark and leaves with important medicinal uses, including in the treatment of glaucoma. Over the last two decades its production, once entirely extractive, shifted toward cultivation. The Amazonian palm tree *açaí (Euterpe oleracea)* is increasingly managed in its wild stands, and soon plantations may prevail over wild populations. Two other Amazonian fruit trees that are going through processes of domestication are *cupuaçu (Theobroma grandiflorium)* and *graviola (Anona muricata)*.

Also, Brazilian research and environmental agencies, in association with farmers, are trying to domesticate (or at least establish captive breeding) a variety of wild native animals, such as the capybara *(Hidrochaeris hydrochaeris,* the world's largest rodent), several species of freshwater fish and turtles, and caimans.

Historical Introductions

After European contact, Brazil's soils were systematically and extensively used for the cultivation of many nonnative plants brought by the colonizers. The plantations and mills for sugarcane *(Saccharum sp.,* domesticated in southeastern Asia or New Guinea) of the Brazilian northeast, for example, were the first permanent, large-scale, and commercially successful economic activity developed by Europeans anywhere in the Americas. Begun in the 1550s, they later spread to other parts of Brazil, which has been a world-class producer of sugar for almost five centuries. The coffee plant *(Coffea arabica* and *Coffea robusta),* a native of Africa and possibly domesticated in Arabia, also began a successful career in plantations in Brazil's mid-south in the 1770s and has now spread into the midwest and even into southern Amazonia. For about 160 years (1790–1950), Brazil was the largest coffee producer and exporter in the world, and coffee cultivation is expanding again in the country.

A more recent introduction was the Asian fiber plant jute *(Corchulos capsularis).* Introduced in the Amazonian floodplains in the 1930s, it grew well and expanded for about forty years but was swiftly defeated in the 1970s by the development of plastic fibers.

This string of successful introductions continues to this day. Soybeans *(Glycine hispida),* introduced on a large scale only in the 1970s, have prospered, as have Brazil's herds of cattle, chickens, and hogs. Brazil is also a world-class producer of introduced citrus fruits, namely oranges *(Citrus aurantium),* lemons *(Citrus limonum),* and tangerines *(Citrus reticulata).* Tropical fruit species introduced from other areas of the world—such as mangoes *(Mangifera indica)* and jackfruit *(Artocarpus integra)*—also grow well in Brazil. And recently, Brazil has also started to produce larger yields of temperate fruits such as grapes, apples, and melons.

Rushing for Gold and Precious Stones

The mining of gold and precious stones in Brazil had a profound impact on the country's environmental history. These mineral riches were found in the 1690s by Portuguese explorers after almost two hundred years of frantic searches all over Brazil. Gold and precious stones were spread throughout a vast and unsettled area deservedly named "Minas Gerais" ("general mines"), which has remained the name of a Brazilian state.

This vast frontier of gold and precious stones produced well for about one hundred years, with different locations reaching peaks at different times. Most of the digging and sifting was done in rivers and along their banks and floodplains, uprooting native vegetation, silting the rivers and changing their courses, churning soils, and creating scarred landscapes. Each location successively attracted, was settled by, and then pushed away tens of thousands of Portuguese, Brazilian Creoles, and African slaves involved in mining, transportation, government, supervision, farming, and support activities. Besides inundating Portugal and the rest of Europe with tons of gold and precious stones and accelerating commercial and industrial changes there, this gold rush caused thousands of square kilometers of the Brazilian backlands to be surveyed and mined, with massive environmental transformations of the topography and the vegetation—forests, savannas, and desert scrub. Such transformations, many of them almost invisible today to the untrained eye, remain to be studied and compared to smaller, contemporary gold and precious stone frontiers in other areas of the country, such as Amazonia.

Frontiers into the Twenty-First Century

Brazil is one of the few countries of the world in which extensive frontiers remain to be settled by the core of the national society. A vast portion of Brazil's immense Amazon region still displays frontier features such as low population density, difficulty of access, unassigned and abundant natural resources, and loose governmental controls. These features attract big government and private initiatives, besides massive migrations of small-scale settlers and adventurers.

The social and environmental dimensions of this process have been strong enough to earn Brazil a bad reputation among many contemporary environmentalists, particularly concerning recent policies and moves toward the occupation of the Amazonian frontier. The economy of Brazil's settled areas—and of other countries—sends out strong and multiple demands for ores, water, timber, and energy (in the forms of firewood, charcoal, hydroelectric dams, agricultural soils, land for agrarian reform and colonization, roads, and railroads) to these frontiers, and they respond to these demands. These demands obviously create local social and environmental impacts such as deforestation, encroachment on native peoples' homelands, migrations, displacements, conflicts over land, and new and often antagonistic social arrangements. These impacts have been harshly criticized by an international public opinion. Although population increase and resource use are still limited for the Amazon frontier as a whole, local cases are indeed ridden with personal drama, social conflict, and environmental wastefulness.

One Tropical Forest Down, One to Go?

Brazil can be singled out as the country that removed the world's largest continuous stretch of tropical rain forest—the Atlantic Forest. Despite the fact that a relatively long time was spent in eliminating more than 90 percent of this forest and despite the fact that Brazilian society is richest and most developed inside its former borders, the Atlantic Forest is mostly gone. During the five hundred years of Brazil's national history, this forest, which was found in seventeen of Brazil's twenty-

six states (with an original and mostly continuous range of 1.1 million square kilometers), took most of the brunt of the new and expanding human demands created by European colonization and lifestyles. There are many lessons to be learned from this forest, its resilience, its recovery, its reclamation, its conservation—lessons to be learned by Brazilians and by the peoples of other countries who have eliminated or are pressing their own tropical or temperate forests.

Until 1970 only 1 percent of Brazil's still vast Amazon rain forests had been deforested. By 2000 the deforestation had climbed to 13 percent. Will its deforestation proceed or will the lessons of the Atlantic Forest sink in? This is a major topic to be investigated by environmental historians.

Exploration of Biodiversity

The organisms of Brazil's little-studied biodiversity offer many subjects of research for environmental historians. Brazil's capacity for studying and researching this part of its natural endowment is still limited, and international cooperation will be needed, creating or expanding multinational networks of scientists, companies, universities, and government agencies.

Prospecting, researching, and manipulating genetic resources, in particular, may have significant consequences for humanity. Although the future is usually not the domain of historians, they should not close their eyes to the possibilities of new cultivated plants (or new variants of already cultivated plants), new principles to be used in medication and treatments, transplantable genes, and other promises of genetic engineering. Brazil's biodiversity is one source of the required biological and genetic materials.

A branch of biodiversity research is the study of so-called emerging diseases. Brazilian public health institutions are researching at least a dozen contagious, fatal, or potentially fatal diseases that are suspected to have infected human beings only quite recently. These diseases are linked to the opening of new frontiers or to the settlement of denser populations in recently opened frontiers, because they were recorded mostly among individuals who lived along roads or in mining camps, particularly in Amazonia. Personnel in isolated military outposts and missionaries also seem to be major targets. Much like the Ebola virus, they probably have non-identified wild animals as hosts and transmitters. These native diseases, coming from frontier areas, seem to be a counterpoint to the Old World infectious diseases that ravaged Native American populations everywhere, including Brazil. Thus, for all its bright promises, Brazilian biodiversity also carries threats to humans.

Urban Environmental Issues

As an urban and industrialized country, Brazil displays almost every known urban-industrial environmental problem. Large and medium-sized cities, especially in the southeast and along the Atlantic coast, suffer from polluting industries, hazardous materials, toxic wastes, poor sanitation and related waterborne diseases, poorly managed garbage collection and disposal, dirty air and water, noise, and intensive traffic. Several measures to control or overcome these problems deserve attention. For example, the city of São Paulo, in Brazil's industrial heartland, conducts the world's largest and most aggressive program for limiting the use of private automobiles to limit air pollution. When the program is in effect, 20 percent of private cars are banned on any given day from a large central area of the city. The more modernized agricultural areas of Brazil are also afflicted by modern problems, such as the excessive use of chemicals, outbreaks of pests, erosion, and silted rivers.

Environmental Laws and Management

Brazil is going through a "third generation" of environmental laws, agencies, and policies. Since the 1930s Brazil has gone from loose regulations on specific resources to today's encompassing laws concerning water, ores, genetic materials, flora, and fauna, and from multiple federal agencies in charge of regulation and management to a single federal executive agency under the Secretariat for the Environment (created in the 1990s). Every state has a similar secretariat and an environmental control agency. Since the late 1980s hundreds of environmental-impact statements have been drafted as part of the requirements for licensing many kinds of productive and infrastructural activities. An encompassing management system allows the cooperation of federal and state agencies, workers, scientists, businesses, and nongovernmental organizations through the National Environmental Council and equivalent councils in each state. Forty-six national parks and hundreds of other federal and state conservation units have been managed since 1937. At least two large and lasting animal conservation programs in Brazil have achieved success—one focused on the golden-lion tamarin (*Leontopithecus rosalia rosalia)* and another focused on several species of marine turtles (such as *Dermochelys coriacea* and *Chelonia mydas*).

United Nations Conference on Environment and Development, known as the Rio–92 environmental summit, spurred Brazilians to become concerned with environmental issues, resulting in the creation of hundreds of citizen groups who have legal standing to use the judicial system in the defense of the environment. Many other international meetings of scientists, managers, and activists have kept this concern alive. Brazil is also host to the largest multilateral environmental program in the world, the Pilot Program to Conserve the Brazilian Rain Forests, supported by the G7 countries (world's seven richest countries—United States, Japan, Canada, United Kingdom, France, Italy and Germany). The program deals with community-based demonstration projects, scientific institutions, state environmental agencies, indigenous homelands, logging and fishing companies, and so forth.

For all this, Brazil should continue to be a focal point for the study of past and current events and processes that make the fabric of environmental history.

José Drummond

See also Amazon River; Coffee; Forests, Tropical; Gold; Mendes, Chico; Orinoco River; Sugar and Sugarcane

Further Reading

Becker, B. & Egler, C. (1992) *Brazil: A new regional power in the world economy.* Cambridge, UK: Cambridge University Press.

Dean, W. (1987). *Brazil and the struggle for rubber: A study in environmental history.* Cambridge, UK: Cambridge University Press.

Dean, W. (1995). *With Broadax and Firebrand: The destruction of the Brazilian Atlantic Forest.* Berkeley: University of California Press.

de Onis, J. (1992). *The green cathedral.* New York: Oxford University Press.

Diamond, J. (1998). *Guns, germs and steel—the fate of human societies.* New York: Norton.

Dillehay, T. (2000). *The settlement of the Americas: A new prehistory.* New York: Basic Books.

Goulding, M, Smith, N., & D. Mahar. (1996). *Floods of fortune: Ecology & economy along the Amazon.* New York: Columbia University Press.

Guimaraes, R. (1992). *Politics and the environment in Brazil.* Boulder, CO: Tynne Rienner.

Hall, A. (1989). *Developing Amazonia: Deforestation and social conflict in Brazil's Carajás Program.* Manchester, UK: Manchester University Press.

Miller, S. (2000). *Fruitless trees—Portuguese conservation and Brazil's colonial yimber.* Stanford, CA: Stanford University Press.

British Empire

By the late nineteenth century, the British Empire administered roughly one-fourth of the world's land. Given their wide geographic range, the nations of the former Empire are not easily characterized. Each former colony has a complex local, regional, and national environmental history, shaped by a variety of geological, climatic, economic, cultural, and political factors. However, these widespread territories all share the experience of administrative and economic control by England (after 1707, Great Britain), control that left an ecological imprint.

The British Environmental Regime

The question as to when the British Empire began has occasioned persistent debate. Did the Empire begin with the "internal colonialism" that brought Wales, Scotland, and Ireland under English control? Did it begin when England established colonies in North America, or when Britain assumed control of India and Australia in the eighteenth century? The English words "colony" and "plantation" first appear in the sixteenth century, and an environmental perspective on the origins of the Empire argues for a similarly early date. Beginning in the Tudor era (1485–1603) there are already indications of a British "environmental regime," a set of developmental attitudes and practices that shaped the Empire.

As Patricia Seed (1995) demonstrates, English colonizers established land "ownership" in North America by erecting fences or hedges, and beginning to graze animals and farm. This practice was also prevalent in the sixteenth- and seventeenth-century plantations of Ireland, the late eighteenth-century settlement of Australia, and the late nineteenth-century acquisition of modern-day Zimbabwe. Some claim that the British marked India even more dramatically by erecting a "great hedge" thousands of kilometers long, but evidence for this is inconclusive.

The English also surveyed and mapped the land: "no other European country employed surveyors so extensively; no other European colonists considered establishing either private property or boundaries in the New World as central to legitimate possession" (Seed 1995, 24). Rationalizing a colony by mapping it was often preliminary to reshaping it in characteristic ways, including by forest clearance, biological exchange, and extension of trade infrastructure.

British colonizers cleared woodland for various purposes: to supply naval timber, as was the case with white pines from North America; to provide fuel for local development, as in India; to create export commodities, such as New Zealand's kauri and kahikatea woods; to create farmland and pasture, as in northern Australia; and to enhance security, as was the case with the military roads cut through County Wicklow, Ireland and northwest India.

Biota exchange in the Empire was a complex interplay of accident and intent. British crop seed inevitably contained weeds (most notoriously the dandelion), and British colonists carried diseases unknown to indigenous peoples. Some animals were intentionally introduced—for example, pigs into New Zealand and sheep into Australia—with profound ecological effects. The naturalist interests of British colonizers also led them to collect colonial flora and fauna, a form of scientific acquisition apotheosized in the Royal Botanical Gardens at Kew (developed after 1772) and the London Zoo (founded 1828, opened to the public 1847).

The British developed harbors and port facilities in their colonies, notably in India, Australia, and New Zealand, to promote their nineteenth-century industrial economy. While *coastal* development was common in European colonization, the British also extended trade infrastructure, such as steamboat facilities, roads, bridges, and railways, far inland. In the 1860s the British laid 8,000 kilometers of railway track in India; by the end of the nineteenth century, there was a total of 38,000 kilometers.

Environmental Legacy of British Empire

British practices transformed colonial environments. Monocultural farming and grazing in Australia, New Zealand, and southern Africa required the clearing of indigenous trees and shrubs, and this contributed to soil salination. In western Australia, "shallow-rooted annual crops, growing mainly in the warmer months, used far less water than the deep-rooted native perennials. Within a period of between five and 20 years after clearing, seepage salting began" (Young 1996, 60). Extending agriculture and trade infrastructure often meant draining swamps and damming rivers. Factories, railways, and steamships needed fuel—initially wood and coal, later petroleum—and all produced smoke and soot. In fact, by 1863 air pollution in Calcutta had become so bad that it "became one of the first cities in the world to adopt smoke nuisance legislation . . . only ten years after London, and well before many European and North American cities" (Anderson, in Arnold and Guha 1995, 294). Mineral extraction could also exact a high environmental cost, as in South Africa's Rand region: "in other gold-bearing regions most of the recoverable metal was found in nuggets or at least in flakes that could be separated from the soil simply by washing it, but on the Rand the work of separating little flecks of gold from the soil soon became an industrial undertaking" (Lloyd 1984, 214).

In addition to such immediate environmental impact, British colonial policies shaped future internal developments that continue to affect the landscape and culture of the former colonies. Some areas (in Burma, for instance) which had practiced small-scale mixed farming and agroforestry well-suited to their ecosystems were transformed into commodity exporters, with long-lasting residual effects on labor and food supply. Massive population relocation, such as sending British and Irish prisoners to Australia and importing slave labor from West Africa to the West Indies, left an environmental and human legacy that permanently altered these societies.

Imperial historiography is now paying more attention to the impact of the Empire on the "metropole," or the colonizing power itself. The most obvious of these effects on Great Britain was the promotion of industrialization. Ports such as Liverpool and industrial centers such as Manchester partly owed their nineteenth-century growth to Indian cotton, Australian wool, and Irish laborers. This explosive urban growth facilitated by supplies of raw materials, food, and labor from the Empire produced the challenges characteristic of modern British environmental history.

While British imperial dominion undeniably shaped world environmental history, the impact was not apocalyptic. There was no pre-colonial "golden age" when the environment was not altered; precolonial cultures, for example, used fire to clear woodland, and hunted some species to extinction. Moreover, Richard Grove (1995) has demonstrated that the colonial encounter with "tropical island Edens" was an important inspiration for modern environmentalism. Beyond fostering environmentalist principles, administering these lands also produced practical innova-

tion. For example, the interrelated challenges of population, intensive cultivation, and waste led to Albert Howard's composting experiments in India in the 1920s and 1930s, which became a source of modern agroecology. The naturalist and hunting interests of British colonizers also led to the preservation and then conservation of endangered species in Africa.

Michael R. Hutcheson

See also Colonialism and Imperialism; Exploration; United Kingdom

Further Reading

Arnold, D., & Guha, R. (Eds.). (1995). *Nature, culture, imperialism: Essays on the environmental history of south Asia.* Delhi, India: Oxford University Press.

Canny, N. (1988). *Kingdom and colony: Ireland in the Atlantic world, 1560–1800.* Baltimore: Johns Hopkins University Press.

Crosby, A. W. (1986). *Ecological imperialism: The biological expansion of Europe, 900–1900.* Cambridge, UK: Cambridge University Press.

Gadgil, M., & Guha, R. (1992). *This fissured land: An ecological history of India.* Berkeley: University of California Press.

Griffiths, T., & Robin, L. (Eds.). (1997). *Ecology and empire: Environmental history of settler societies.* Seattle: University of Washington Press.

Grove, R. H. (1995). *Green imperialism: Colonial expansion, tropical island edens and the origins of environmentalism, 1600–1860.* Cambridge, UK: Cambridge University Press.

Lloyd, T. O. (1984). *The British Empire 1558–1983.* Oxford, UK: Oxford University Press.

Louis, W. R. (1998–1999). *The Oxford history of the British Empire* (5 vols.). Oxford, UK: Oxford University Press.

MacKenzie, J. M. (1988). *The empire of nature: Hunting, conservation and British imperialism.* Manchester, UK: Manchester University Press.

Meinig, D. W. (1988). *The shaping of America: A geographical perspective on 500 years of history; Atlantic America, 1492–1800.* New Haven, CT: Yale University Press.

Seed, P. (1995). *Ceremonies of possession in Europe's conquest of the New World, 1492–1640.* Cambridge, UK: Cambridge University Press.

Young, A. R. M. (1996). *Environmental change in Australia since 1788.* Melbourne, Australia: Oxford University Press.

Brower, David
(1912–2000)
U.S. environmentalist

Environmental historians credit David R. Brower, the first executive director of the Sierra Club and founder of the Earth Island Institute and Friends of the Earth, with helping transform the conservation movement in America into modern-day environmentalism. Brower worked for the creation of so-called wilderness areas in America and fought to create national parks and seashores in Kings Canyon, California; North Cascades, Washington; Redwood, California; Point Reyes, California; and Great Basin, Nevada. As an early environmental advocate, Brower helped to define the political landscape of postwar environmental issues— dams, wilderness designation, and population growth.

Born in Berkeley, California, Brower joined the Sierra Club in 1933. Brower used the *Sierra Club Bulletin* to publicize and promote the out-of-doors spaces frequented by the club's members and became a director of the organization in 1941. During World War II he served as an instructor and intelligence officer for the U.S. Army 10th Mountain Division in the Italian Alps. When Brower returned to the United States he went back to the Sierra Club and in 1952 became its first executive director.

In 1950 Brower helped move the Sierra Club into environmental politics. When the U.S. Bureau of Reclamation proposed to build dams that threatened to flood Echo Park in Dinosaur National Monument in Utah and Colorado, Brower and the Sierra Club joined with Howard Zahniser of the Wilderness Society to oppose legislation authorizing eleven dams, including two in Echo Park. They won removal of the Echo Park dams from the legislation by agreeing not to oppose the other dams. The compromise bill, passed in 1956, included a measure to dam the Colorado River at Glen Canyon, Arizona, which Brower had never seen. Brower visited Glen Canyon before it was flooded and, from then on, considered the compromise his biggest failure. Just before workers and engineers finished construction in 1963, Brower published a eulogy for the canyon, *Glen Canyon: The Place No One Knew*.

After Glen Canyon, Brower focused his energies on building up the Sierra Club as an activist organization focused on defining the boundaries of "wilderness." During Brower's tenure, the club's membership rose from five thousand to seventy thousand. With Zah-

niser, he lobbied for the 1964 Wilderness Act, which set aside 3.6 million hectares of "wild lands" (now over 40 million hectares). He used the Sierra Club to combat federal dam proposals that threatened Grand Canyon National Park in Arizona, financing full-page ads in the *New York Times* that included slogans such as "Should we also flood the Sistine Chapel, so tourists can get nearer the ceiling?" However, Brower's activist politics upset colleagues at the Sierra Club, and his penchant for using the Sierra Club press to advertise threats to wilderness (by the end of his life he had published 115 books on wild spaces) led to a large organizational debt. In 1969 he was forced to resign his position as executive director.

Discontent with organizational bureaucracy characterized Brower's later career. In 1969 he started another environmental action group, Friends of the Earth, but problems with its board of directors forced a split in the mid-1980s. In 1982 he founded the Earth Island Institute in hopes of avoiding bureaucracies. Earth Island was a project-based organization focused on coordinating different organizations. In 1983 Brower was reelected to the Sierra Club board of directors but resigned just before his death in 2000, claiming that its bureaucracy got in the way of action.

Ryan J. Carey

Further Reading

Brower, D. (1990). *For Earth's sake: The life and times of David Brower.* Salt Lake City, UT: Peregrine Smith Books.
Devall, B. (1981). David Brower. *Environmental Review, 9*(3), 238–253.
McPhee, J. (1971). *Encounters with the archdruid.* New York: Farrar, Straus and Giroux.
Miller, C., & Rothman, H. K. (1997). *Out of the woods: Essays in environmental history.* Pittsburgh, PA: University of Pittsburgh Press.
Rothman, H. K. (2000). *Saving the planet: The American response to the environment in the twentieth-century.* Chicago: Ivan R. Dee.

Brown-Headed Cowbird

The brown-headed cowbird (*Molothrus ater*) is one of five species of cowbirds, a genus of the New World family Icteridae, which includes blackbirds, orioles, caciques, oropendolas and meadowlarks. Male plumage is black with a brown head; females are entirely grayish. Cowbirds often forage in association with large ungulates to feed on insects disturbed by the grazing mammals, bison in the past and now cattle. The original distribution of brown-headed cowbirds was centered in the Great Plains in habitats comprising mixtures of grasslands and woodlands. European settlement of North America altered the original vegetation of the continent in a manner that favored cowbirds: the clearing of eastern forests and conversion of land to agriculture allowed cowbirds to spread east. In the fall and winter, cowbirds flock with other blackbird species (red-winged blackbirds, common grackles) and European starlings.

All cowbird species are brood parasitic. Brood parasites lay their eggs in the nests of other species (called hosts), which then incubate the interloper's eggs and care for their young, often at the expense of the host's own offspring. Female cowbirds search for host nests in the morning; having chosen one, they lay an egg before sunrise during a 30-second visit. They often remove one host egg from the nest that they parasitize. Brown-headed cowbirds are very general in their host selection. Over 200 species have been parasitized, and almost 150 of these are known to have reared cowbird young. Most cowbird hosts are smaller than cowbirds (for example, yellow warblers and chipping sparrows), and nests of these species produce none of their own species if a cowbird egg hatches. Larger host species (such as the song sparrow and the red-winged blackbird) are more tolerant of intranest competition.

Because of the abundance of cowbirds, there are sometimes conservation concerns for host species. For threatened and endangered species (such as Kirtland's warbler and the black-capped vireo), nesting failure due to cowbird parasitism is one form of loss that can be controlled; management plans often call for cowbird removal from breeding areas of the endangered populations.

Interactions between host and parasite provide good examples of coevolution. It is of obvious and strong selective advantage for hosts to recognize and respond to cowbird parasitism. Some species do so by ejecting cowbird eggs, deserting nests, or even burying cowbird eggs in the lining of their nests. Cowbirds, just as obviously, need to select hosts that will accept their eggs.

Brood parasitism as manner of reproduction offers two general themes for study and research on cowbirds: what criteria do cowbirds use in selecting host species? and How do cowbirds come to know their own species identity? Radio tracking and DNA sampling have been used to identify specific host nests chosen by individual female cowbirds in an attempt to answer the first question, and young cowbirds have been raised in laboratories to allow study of development of song and innate behavior in an attempt to answer the second. With regard to host species, researchers have examined if host species identify cowbirds as a threat, if hosts can recognize their own eggs, and whether they respond to a foreign egg in the nest.

Peter E. Lowther

Further Reading

King, A. P., & West, M. J. (1977). Species identification in the North American cowbird: appropriate responses to abnormal song. *Science, 195*(4282), 1002–1004.

Ortega, C. (1998). *Cowbirds and other brood parasites.* Tucson: Arizona University Press.

Rothstein, S. I., & Robinson, S. K. (Eds.). (1998). *Parasitic birds and their hosts: Studies in coevolution.* Oxford, U.K.: Oxford University Press.

Brundtland Commission

The World Commission on Environment and Development (WCED) was popularly known as the "Brundtland Commission" after its chairperson, the former Norwegian prime minister Gro Harlem Brundtland. It was established in 1983 by the United Nations to formulate a global action plan to reconcile social and economic development with resource conservation.

The WCED's subsequent work was summed up in its influential study, *Our Common Future*, or the "Brundtland Report" (1987). The WCED proposed a strategy of "sustainable development," defined as "development that meets the needs of the present without compromising the ability of future generations to meet their own needs."

The thinking behind the Brundtland Report was actually far from new; its roots go back to the early twentieth century. Then, there had been increasing alarm in the United States at the wanton destruction of forests and other natural resources. The United States Forest Service under the leadership of its chief forester

Gifford Pinchot argued for a new policy of "sustained yield."

This view was echoed by the WCED, whose main focus was the inefficiency of current resource use. The WCED endorsed further conventional economic growth, something the Commission's critics regard as possible only at the expense of the environment.

It also supported greater world trade, which many anti-globalization campaigners regard as a major cause of global environmental problems, not a cure. Nuclear power, which most environmentalists see as incompatible with long-term environmental security, also received WCED support.

Some disputed the notion of a "common future," saying it was inapplicable to a society characterized by deep social divisions. Others attacked its definition of sustainability, arguing that it was impossible to predict what future generations might need. Some criticisms went further, questioning whether any sort of *global* strategy could really succeed: only local initiatives coming from people in their own communities, they felt, could do the job. Others attacked the Brundtland Commission for its failure to consider the future needs of non-human life-forms. Such critics believed that humans must learn to treat the rest of nature as something with intrinsic value, worthy of respect and protection for its own sake.

The WCED tried to shift the thinking of politicians and other decision-makers. Given the threats made by many post-WCED governments to sacrifice wildlife reserves and lift other forms of environmental protection, perhaps the debate has not shifted very far.

Sandy Irvine

Further Reading

Daly, H. E. (1997). *Beyond growth: The economics of sustainable development*. Boston: Beacon Press.

Devall, B., & Sessions, G. (1984). The development of natural resources and the conservation of nature. *Environmental ethics, 6*, 293–322.

Hays, S. (1959). *Conservation and the gospel of efficiency*. Cambridge, MA: Harvard University Press.

Hueting, R. (1990). The Brundtland Report: a matter of conflicting goals. *Ecological economics, 2*, 109–117.

Jacobs, M. (1996). *The politics of the real world*. London: Earthscan.

Kovel, J. (2002). *The enemy of nature: The end of capitalism or the end of the world?* London: Zed.

Lohmann, L. (1990). Whose common future? *The Ecologist, 20*(3), 82–84.

MacDonald, M. (1998). *Agendas for sustainability : Environment and development into the twenty-first century*. London: Routledge.

McLaughlin, A. (1993). *Regarding nature: Industrialism and deep ecology*. Albany: State University of New York Press.

Naess, A. (1988). Sustainable development and the deep ecology movement. *The trumpeter, 4*, 138–142.

Rees, W. (1988). Sustainable development: Economic myths & ecological realities. *The trumpeter, 5*(4), 133–138.

Sachs, W. (1991). Environment & development: The story of a dangerous liaison. *The ecologist, 21*(6), 252–257.

Sarkar, S. (1990). Accommodating industrialism. *The Ecologist, 20*(4), 147–152.

Buddhism

Buddhism is a religion that was founded by a sage who lived in northern India in the fifth and sixth centuries BCE and who was given the title Buddha, which means "the one who is enlightened." This enlightenment experience and the way in which the Buddha explained it to other people is at the heart of Buddhism. The essence of the Buddha's teaching is that human experience is characterized by suffering in various forms, and yet it is possible to live life in such a way that suffering is at least minimized and possibly eliminated. The Buddha advocated a way of life that would help to achieve this goal.

The Life of the Buddha

The boy who was to become known as the Buddha was born in what is now southern Nepal in 563 BCE. His name was Siddhartha Gautama, and he was the son of the king of the Sakya people. Siddhartha's life was extremely affluent and comfortable; he lived in his father's palace, and it appears that the king was reluctant to allow his son to leave their secure and luxurious surroundings. Nevertheless, it seems likely that Siddhartha had by his mid- to late twenties begun to question the ethics of this materialistic lifestyle.

One day he apparently set off to ride outside the palace walls, where he presumably encountered the poverty of ordinary people. It is recorded that he witnessed an elderly person, a person with a serious illness, and a dead body. These were sights that were

Buddhism—Ideal and Real

As with all religions, there are significant differences in Buddhism between how the religion is understood and experienced by the educated elite and how it is understood and experienced by the common person. In addition, in money nations in Asia, people who are Buddhists also combine elements from other religions such as Daoism and Confucianism with Buddhism. The text below describes these multiple expression of Buddhism in Central Thailand.

The farmers, as well as the educated classes call themselves Buddhists. It should be recognised, however, that the two types of Buddhism are quite distinct. The elite often appear to be aware of the philosophical message of the teachings of Siddhartha Gautama and its implications for those who wish to follow his path to salvation. The farmers, on the other hand, have little or no idea of the philosophy of Buddhism. Instead, the practices and beliefs which are derived from Buddhism have been re-interpreted in the farmers' religion to fit their particular worldview. . . .

The religion of the farmer is basically animistic, whilst the elite may be regarded as having organized an intellectual appreciation of their religion. It is because of the incorporation of Buddhism in the animistic worldview that the villagers 'do not feel that they are members of several different religious systems at the same time'. On the other hand, the sophisticated Buddhist may well feel that there exists a discrepancy between the Great Tradition and the manifold accretions.

Though the farmer uses the same Buddhist institutions, concepts and ideas with which the elite are familiar, he gives them a different meaning. In the course of this book it will be seen that in rural areas the role of the monk is intimately connected with the idea of creating a certain type of magical power. Similarly, whilst the educated Buddhist may accept the five precepts as an ethical guide, in the countryside they are often used in a cleansing ritual. And the acquisition of merit is important for both types of Buddhists, but in the eyes of the farmer the concept of merit is closely connected with beneficial magical power and good luck.

Source: Terweil, Jan Barend. (1975). *Monks and Magic: An Analysis of Religious Ceremonies in Central Thailand.* London: Curzon Press, pp. 3–5.

not normally seen within the palace walls, and must have had a profound impact on Siddhartha. In addition, he also saw a wandering sage, who appeared to have relinquished the material things of life and to have gained something of a sense of equanimity about life.

Siddhartha was greatly disturbed by these sights, and determined that he could not sustain his present lifestyle. He decided to leave the palace and his family secretly, and to assume the life of a wandering mendicant or sadhu. Siddhartha fasted and adopted other ascetic practices, with the purpose of gaining spiritual insight. He was accompanied at this time by five other ascetics. Eventually Siddhartha decided that extreme asceticism was unlikely to lead to enlightenment, and he decided to lead a more moderate life. His five companions left him, as they felt that he was no longer adhering to his spiritual ideals.

Then, in a celebrated event in Buddhist history, Siddhartha sat in meditation under a tree, and determined that he would continue in meditation until he gained insights into the nature of life. Eventually, he became enlightened and was henceforth known as the Buddha. He felt that he had comprehended the nature of human suffering, and that he now knew how human beings might eliminate suffering from their lives. Initially, he was uncertain whether his analysis would be too complex for people to appreciate, and he wondered whether he should attempt to teach his spiritual discoveries. He walked to the deer park at Sarnath, near the city of Varanasi (Benares) on the river Ganges, and there met his previous five companions. The Buddha then delivered to them his first sermon, which is now known as "The Setting in Motion of the Wheel of the Law." The five ascetics were impressed by the teaching and became his disciples. They were ordained as the first Buddhist monks, and became the first members of the *sangha* or community of committed Buddhists.

The Buddha subsequently devoted the remainder of his life to teaching his practical philosophy of living. He led the life of an itinerant preacher, accompanied by his disciples. He would explain his teaching wherever there were groups of people who were willing to listen. In about 486 BCE, after a life of traveling and teaching in northern India, the Buddha fell ill, perhaps as a result of eating food that caused an infection. He died near the town of Kusinara, with the monk Ananda (the Buddha's "beloved disciple") at his side.

The Buddha's Teaching

The heart of the Buddha's teaching is contained in four propositions known as the Four Noble Truths. The first of these is the observation that suffering exists in the world. This is not intended to signify simply the kind of suffering that accompanies a bad headache or a grazed knee. Rather, it is intended to be an observation on the entire nature of the world and of human existence: separation from loved ones, death, disappointments and failure in one's undertakings, and the inequities of life.

The second Noble Truth is the proposition that the cause of the suffering and pain that people feel under such circumstances is not brought about by the circumstances themselves, but by our perceptions of those events. Suppose that we apply for a new job that seems very attractive, and we go for an interview full of great hopes, but then fail to get the job. It is likely that we would be very disappointed. Buddhism argues however, that it is not the failure to get the job that causes suffering, but the way in which we respond psychologically to that. If we could manage to keep it in perspective, then we would not suffer as much.

This leads us to the third Noble Truth. The Buddha argued that it was possible to end suffering, partly by adopting a different mental attitude. Suppose that we suffer a sports injury and can no longer play our favorite sport. This could lead to our feeling very demoralized and depressed. Buddhism argues, however, that if we can manage to stop wishing things were different, and put our energies into something else, then our suffering might be at least reduced. Finally, in the Fourth Noble Truth, the Buddha proposed a clear sequence of steps by which an individual can learn to change the attitudes that lead to suffering, and hence eliminate suffering itself. This strategy is known as the Noble Eightfold Path.

The first step on the Eightfold Path is that the aspirant should hold Right Views. One of the central aspects of this is that people should try to appreciate that there is no real self. We tend to the assumption that within each person is a tangible self. The Buddha argued however, that this was not so, and that if we recognize that fact, we will also understand that there is no self to experience suffering. He also stressed that people should contemplate the impermanence of all life. He argued that an understanding of impermanence helps to maintain what we might call nowadays a sense of proportion about things.

The second step is that of Right Resolve. Among other things, the Buddhist determines to show compassion and kindness to other living things. It is perhaps here, through an appreciation of impermanence, and also through the exercise of compassion towards other life forms, that we begin to recognize the basis of the Buddhist sensitivity to the environment.

The next two steps involve the exercise of Right Speech and Right Conduct. The former asks the Buddhist to be thoughtful and careful in all the things that she or he says, in order to be sensitive to the feelings of others. Right Conduct involves being careful not to take the life of other living things, not to steal, and generally to try to be moderate in terms of lifestyle. The fifth step involves adopting an occupation that is in keeping with the philosophy of Buddhism. Such occupations as butcher or hunter are regarded as unsuitable for a Buddhist.

The sixth step, usually known as Right Effort, involves an individual trying to maintain an appropriate psychological approach to the world. Detachment from objects or feelings in the world is very important here. For example, we all tend to have our favorite foods and to enjoy certain meals. The Buddhist however, tries to refrain from developing an attachment to one kind of food and not to another. Food is treated simply as nourishment for the body rather than as something that generates either pleasure or distaste.

The penultimate step on the Noble Eightfold Path is Right Attention. This emphasizes the importance of being mindful at all times. Mindfulness is a mental state of full awareness of one's surroundings and also of one's mental states. True mindfulness prevents inappropriate thoughts from distracting us from the Buddhist practice. In addition, mindfulness helps to calm the mind and make it less receptive to becoming attached to worldly things.

The final stage of the Eightfold Path is Right Meditation. The ultimate purpose of this discipline is to acquire an insight into the nature of reality, and hence to fully appreciate the nature of suffering and the way to its elimination. Both Buddhist clergy (monks and nuns) and laypeople practice meditation regularly. Some meditation techniques are designed to help create a calmness in the mind that makes the mind more receptive to the *vipassana*, or insight meditation, which reveals the way in which the mind and mental processes reflect the world. The Buddhist observes the manner in which thoughts come and go in the mind, and analyzes those thoughts according to the principles and concepts of the Noble Eightfold Path. The Buddhist who follows the Path may attain enlightenment and exist in a state of supreme peace sometimes known as nirvana.

Buddhism and the Environment

The basic precepts and philosophy of Buddhism tend to encourage a sensitive approach to the environment. The whole approach of Buddhism is designed to eliminate suffering, and hence Buddhism discourages any action that might harm living things. Buddhists tend to be mindful of their actions in the natural world, and so would not thoughtlessly saw down a tree or pull up plants without very careful consideration. They would be equally thoughtful with regard to animals, and would tend not to use resources from the natural world without careful thought. Indeed, Buddhists would normally only wish to use resources to the extent required to sustain life. The excessive use of resources, particularly to make money, would be regarded as a form of greed and desire. The Buddhist attitude would preclude excessive mining for minerals, the destruction of forests for building purposes, or the pollution of rivers with industrial waste.

Much of the Buddhist approach to the living world derives from an appreciation of the impermanence of all things. This sense of a shared impermanence tends to result in the development of compassion towards all living creatures. This attitude toward the environment is evident in Buddhist aesthetics in painting and garden design, especially in China and Japan.

In the sixth century, the Indian monk Bodhidharma traveled to China, bringing with him a school of Buddhism that emphasized meditation. This school became known as Chan in China and Zen in Japan. Chinese and Japanese paintings often depict the solitary sage or philosopher, alone in a vast landscape of mountains and pine forests with which he seems in harmony. In particular, the paintings are often characterized by large areas of empty space, with the trees and mountains located on one side. This may be taken as a metaphor for the process of meditation, whereby the individual seeks to become unattached from the material world and to empty the mind of worldly concerns.

The emphasis upon empty space may also be seen in the simplicity of formal Zen gardens such the one at Ryoanji in Kyoto, Japan. This consists of a rectangular-shaped area covered with white sand, which has been carefully raked smooth. Several rocks and stones of various sizes are placed in apparently random positions in the sand, although the main impression is one of unadorned white sand. This minimalist design may be seen as an aesthetic in its own right, or as a metaphor for the creative emptiness to be cultivated during meditation. In addition to garden design, the succinct Japanese poetic form known as haiku often takes as its subject natural objects such as pine trees, cherry blossom, and birds. Haiku often seem to capture in a few lines the essence of a natural event.

Buddhism represents a philosophy which is intended to help people overcome suffering, while at the same time living in harmony with their surroundings. Zen Buddhism uses paradoxical statements as one technique for breaking through the barriers of conventional thinking to a realization of the true nature of reality. Whatever the approach, Buddhism is a religion that encourages people to have a balanced view of the world and to promote mindful care of the environment and all living things.

Paul Oliver

Further Reading

Bancroft, A. (1974). *Religions of the East.* London: Heinemann.

Batchelor, M., & Brown, K. (Eds.) (1992). *Buddhism and ecology.* London: Cassell.

Conze, E. (1993). *Buddhism: A short history.* Oxford, UK: One World.

Pye, M. (1979). *The Buddha.* London: Duckworth.

Saddhatissa, H. (1971). *The Buddha's way.* London: Allen and Unwin.

Bush Meat

The term *bush meat* refers to meat obtained in the wild. *Bush* itself, referring to wild areas outside of town, is probably of colonial origin, derived from the Dutch *bosch*. But indigenous words also exist to describe landscapes inhabited by wild animals and spirits and modified by human activities such as farming, hunting, and livestock raising. The processes of hunting, skinning, and ultimately consuming bush meat have cultural meanings inscribed in art, rituals, food taboos, and territorial organization that vary over time, place, and by ethnic group.

Hunting, one of the oldest human economic activities, continues to be a major source of protein and income despite being banned in many tropical countries. Conflicts are common between local hunters, who view hunting as a moral right to subsistence, and national governments and international conservation organizations that seek to control hunting for ecotourism, safari hunting, and conservation of biodiversity. Nevertheless, the bush meat sector forms an important part of many national economies. A million metric tons of bush meat, the equivalent of 4 million cattle, is consumed annually in the Congo Basin of central Africa. Game marketing accounted for 1.4 percent of the Ivory Coast's gross national product in 1996. In that year,

hunters sold 120,000 metric tons of bush meat worth an estimated US $150 million. The income earned from hunting often surpasses revenues earned from cash crop cultivation. This dynamic but generally illicit commerce links rural hunters, urban-based merchants, and restaurant owners who serve game dishes to urban elites for whom bush meat is both a status food and a way to maintain ties with rural areas. Expanding urban populations and increased demand for bush meat in Latin America and Africa have driven prices beyond the means of most rural consumers.

Hunters will shoot almost anything to cash in on the booming trade in bush meat. In the tropical forest regions of Southeast Asia, South America, and Africa, they typically follow logging roads that open up formerly inaccessible areas. More effective hunting techniques and weapons (shotguns, wire snares) have further heightened pressure on wild animals. The species most commonly appearing in African bush meat markets are antelope (duikers, bushbucks) and primates, especially monkeys. Farmers view monkeys as agricultural pests and ask hunters to eliminate then before they cause too much crop damage. Bush meat mer-

Senufo hunter skinning bushbuck (*Tragelaphus scriptus*) in the Korhogo region of northern Côte d'Ivoire. COURTESY T. BASSETT, 1981.

chants pay top prices for monkey, cane rat, porcupine, and hare for which there is high consumer demand. Another factor in wildlife decline is the transformation of animal habitats due to deforestation and the expansion of agriculture and livestock raising. Since wild animals play important roles as pollinators and dispersers of seeds, their decline inevitably alters savanna and forest ecologies.

Innovative wildlife conservation policies are urgently needed that combine sustainable use of nonprotected species with better protection of endangered species. A number of comanagement programs in which local communities collaborate with government and nongovernmental organizations in wildlife conservation are currently being pursued with uneven results.

Thomas J. Bassett

Further Reading

Bennett, E. L., & Robinson, J. G. (2000). *Hunting for sustainability in tropical forests.* New York: Columbia University Press.

Gibson, C. C. (1999). *Politicians and poachers: The political economy of wildlife policy in Africa.* Cambridge, UK: Cambridge University Press.

Neumann, R. (1999). *Imposing wilderness: Struggles over livelihood and nature preservation in Africa.* Berkeley & Los Angeles: University of California Press.

Newmark, W.D., & Hough, J. L. (2000). Conserving wildlife in Africa: Integrated conservation and development projects and beyond. *Bioscience, 50*(7), 585–592.

Oates, J. F. (1999). *Myth and reality in the rain forest: How conservation strategies are failing in West Africa.* Berkeley & Los Angeles: University of California Press.

Cacao

Cacao is a tree native to the neotropics (the tropics of the New World) whose place of origin was most likely the Amazon basin of South America. Each tree produces pods that sprout directly from the trunk. The pods are filled with a white, sweet pulp and about a dozen dark, bitter beans. The pre-Columbian indigenous peoples of Amazonia harvested the tree, probably for the pulp at first. The tree was diffused, probably by humans, from its place of origin along the Orinoco River to the Caribbean and then to Mesoamerica. Cacao was first cultivated on a large scale in Mesoamerica, where the civilizations developed a taste for the dried, fermented beans. They ground these beans into a powder and mixed them with water, chilis, and spices and consumed them as a drink. In the indigenous Nahuatl language, this drink was known as *xocolatl*, from which the word *chocolate* derives. The Spanish conquerors developed a taste for this drink after the conquest of the New World in the sixteenth century. Growing demand from both the New World and Spain fueled a series of cacao booms in the Spanish empire—in El Salvador during the sixteenth century and in Venezuela during the eighteenth century. Ecuador emerged as the world's largest producer after 1820, when Venezuela's cacao haciendas were destroyed during the wars of independence. Global demand for chocolate declined for several decades in the early nineteenth century. The invention of milk chocolate and the chocolate bar in Europe during the 1870s, however, greatly increased the global demand for cacao. Global consumption of chocolate grew 800 percent between 1880 and 1900 alone.

This rapid growth in global demand also spurred rapid globalization of production during the late nineteenth and early twentieth centuries. New areas of production emerged far from cacao's historical native and cultural range: in southern Brazil and, above all, in the British and French colonies of West Africa. The environmental history of cacao since the early twentieth century has been one of cycles of booms and busts. Growers found that cacao could be produced most economically on the rich soils of newly cleared forest. In order to maximize production—and therefore profits—they cultivated cacao as a monoculture. For most of the twentieth century, then, the expansion of the cacao frontier caused extensive deforestation throughout the tropics. Such plantations remained productive for several decades but then gradually fell into decline as the soil fertility was exhausted. Planting cacao in such monocultures also created the ideal conditions for the outbreak of epidemic crop diseases, which plagued cacao plantations worldwide for most of the twentieth century. Recently scientists have begun working with cacao planters throughout the tropics on new ways of cultivating cacao. Instead of the classic open monocultures of the twentieth century, they are practicing agroforestry, in which cacao is planted among the rain forest's native plants. This practice—although not yet widespread—helps preserve rain forests and their biological diversity. Preliminary results suggest it is also more ecologically sustainable than monoculture because the other plants help sustain soil fertility and discourage the diffusion of crop epidemics.

Stuart McCook

179

The Magic of Cacao

The following extract of ethnographic text describes the use of cacao in healing rituals of the Kuna people of Panama.

Some diseases are the work of evil spirits and it is necessary to oppose and defeat the purpose of these in order to effect a cure. When it is believed that spirit demons have the soul of a patient and carried it to their abode in one of the several lower strata of the earth, a ceremonial treatment is indicated. In a high fever accompanied by delirium it is evident that the rational soul of the sufferer has left his body. It is then the duty of the siaigartulet to restore this captive of the spirit demons by invoking the aid of good spirits. Wooden images or miniatures may be used for this. Smoke is of great assistance. A brazier is placed near the hammock of the patient and cacao beans are burned in it. The wooden images are held in the smoke. The siaigartulet chants instructions for the actions that are to the place and the details of the journey of the good spirits in pursuit of the demons. This may take several hours or even days, for there are many impediments to be overcome. A close watch of the patient is maintained for evidence of the return of his soul.

Source: McKim, Fred. (1947). "San Blas: An Account of the Cuna Indians of Panama, 1936. *Etnologiska Studier 15*, 61.

Further Reading

Clarence-Smith, W. G. (Ed.). (1996). *Cocoa pioneer fronts since 1800: The role of smallholders, planters, and merchants.* New York: St. Martin's Press.

Clarence-Smith, W. G. (2000). *Cocoa and chocolate, 1765–1914.* New York: Routledge.

Coe, S. D., & Coe, M. D. (1996). *The true history of chocolate.* London: Thames and Hudson.

Knapp, A. W. (1920). *Cocoa and chocolate: Their history from plantation to consumer.* London: Chapman and Hall.

Ruf, F. (1995). *Booms et crises du cacao: les vertiges de l'or brun* [Cacao booms and busts: the vacillations of "brown gold"]. Paris: Ministre de la coopération.

Young, A. M. (1994). *The chocolate tree: A natural history of cacao.* Washington, DC: Smithsonian Institution Press.

California Condor

The California condor (*Gymnogyps californianus*) is a spectacular and highly endangered bird, and is the largest of the three North-American vultures. Similar in size and weight to the Andean condor of South America, California condor males average 8.8 kilogram in weight, while females average only 8.1 kilogram; their wingspan is about 2.8 meters and the body is about 1.2 to 1.3 meter long. A scavenger, the condor feeds on dead animal flesh. With its powerful gliding flight it can cover hundreds of kilometers in a day's foraging.

California condors are social birds, gathering at feeding, roosting, and bathing sites. Pairs nest solitarily in cliff-side caves, laying a single-egg clutch on the sand or gravel substrate. Incubation lasts about fifty-seven days. The chick takes it first flight at about six months, and depends on its parents for food for another six months.

The California condor's range in the nineteenth and early twentieth centuries extended from the Canadian border to Mexico in the western United States, and probably east into Colorado, Wyoming, and Arizona. By the mid 1900s its range was reduced dramatically, when an estimated 150 condors survived only in the mountains surrounding California's Central Valley. The causes of the decline were thought to include DDT, shooting, power-line collision and electrocution, habitat loss, ritual sacrifice by Native Americans, and poisoning incidental to predator control.

In 1980 the U.S. Fish and Wildlife Service began an intensive research and conservation program to identify limiting factors and start a captive-breeding program. Researchers used radio telemetry and intensive necropsies to identify lead poisoning, caused by ingesting hunter's ammunition, as the primary cause of catastrophic recent, and probably historic, wild condor mortality.

By double- and triple-clutching of the remaining wild nesting pairs and by ultimately trapping all remaining wild condors, biologists built up a captive population at the San Diego and Los Angeles zoos and quickly produced enough birds to start releases to the wild. In 1988 Andean condors were released experimentally in California in order to develop a protocol for California condor releases in the same area, which followed in 1992. Condors were first released in California in the historic range, and later in the Grand Canyon area of Arizona where a nesting population existed in the late Pleistocene. By late 2002, total captive condors numbered 198 with 70 being released birds living in the wild.

Two problems have plagued the release efforts. Husbandry techniques using puppets to rear baby condors, as opposed to allowing parent condors to rear their own young, have rendered the young release candidates too tame and approachable for survival. Parent rearing must become the norm for releases.

In addition, the primary limiting factor has not been corrected to date. Released California condors have unfortunately fallen victim to the same lead-poisoning problem that caused the near-extinction of the species in the 1980s. Alternatives to lead ammunition exist but until their use becomes widespread, high mortality will continue to prevent re-establishment of the California condor.

Helen A. Snyder

Further Reading

Koford, C. B. (1953). *The California condor. National Audubon Society Research Report, 4,* 1–154.

Snyder, N., & Snyder, H. A. (2000). *The California condor: A saga of natural history and conservation.* London: Academic Press.

Snyder, N. F. R., & Schmitt, N. J. (2002). California condor (*Gymnogyps californianus*). In A. Poole & F. Gill (Eds.), *The birds of North America, No. 610.* Philadelphia: Birds of North America, Inc.

Camels

The camel has played an important role in the environmental history of Africa and Eurasia since its domesti-

cation. Superbly adapted to arid environments, the camel has allowed human beings to negotiate the deserts and mountains of northern Africa and central Asia, and in this sense the camel has been instrumental both in connecting the African societies and ecologies immediately to the south of the Sahara with the intercommunicating zone around the Mediterranean and in linking societies and ecologies across the southern axis of Eurasia itself, from the Mediterranean to China. Along with the horse, cow, donkey, and yak, it is one of the few domesticated animals that is large enough to carry an adult human.

There are two species of camels, the dromedary, or Arabian camel *(Camelus dromedaries)*, which has a single hump, and the Bactrian camel *(Camelus bactrianus)*, which has two. The domestication of the dromedary in Arabia sometime around 1200 BCE allowed it to replace the ass in desert transport, strengthened the hand of desert-edge communities around the Arabian peninsula, and launched the career of bedouin culture. It likely strengthened the states of the desert fringe and may possibly have played a role in the decline of the riverine civilizations of Egypt and Mesopotamia. In North Africa during the course of the fourth, fifth, and sixth centuries CE, the use of the dromedary as a draft animal largely replaced a system of haulage in horse- or ox-drawn carts. The economics of camel transport encouraged Muslim societies in both North Africa and the Middle East to reduce and finally abandon their commitment to carted vehicles and to roads.

The Bactrian camel, which has been less intensively researched than the dromedary, was domesticated in southwest Asia before 2500 BCE and spread to Iraq, India, central Asia and into China. Like the drome-

Domesticated camel in Kenya. COURTESY D. BRUCE DICKSON.

Boys and Camels among the Somali of Northeast Africa

When they have reached the age of seven or eight years, and sometimes earlier, boys are sent out with their brothers and cousins to look after the camels. Their life, as has been said, is a hard one, particularly in the dry seasons. Indeed the camel camps are in effect the initiation schools for the nomadic life.

In a camel-camp the eldest herdsman is its natural leader (except in the case of a hired servant), but there is no formal differentiation of roles or offices. The young lads sent out to the camps are trained to go without water and to live on milk alone. They learn the art of camel-husbandry, the care of the stock, and their water and pasture requirements. They are taught which are the best grasses, and which pasture is noxious and to be avoided. Thus they learn to adapt themselves to living with the herds, to seek the best grazing, to deal with sickness and to count, water and milk the camels. To illustrate, the care and affection which the camel-boys lavish on their stock I mention an incident which occurred while I was in one camel encampment. In extreme drought and heat few camels were in milk and the camel-boys were living just at subsistence level with no water to alleviate their thirst. One morning a young camel-herd came to my tent to beg water, not, as he emphasized, for himself, but for two young camels which were sorely in need. My companions amused by the boy's solicitude for his stock, did not lose the opportunity of pointing out how this incident typified the pastoralist's regard for the camels.

Source: Lewis, Ioan M. (1961). *A Pastoral Democracy; a Study of Pastoralism and Politics among the Northern Somali of the Horn of Africa.* London: Oxford University Press.

---

dary, the Bactrian camel could be used as draft animal as well as a pack animal and a military mount. The Bactrian camel, however, was not as large or fast as the dromedary, and over time its range diminished. In central Asia during the second half of the second century BCE, a hybrid camel produced from the interbreeding of the dromedary and the Bactrian took over the role once held by the Bactrian. The pure Bactrians were retained as stud animals.

The economic advantages of the camel over other beasts of burden in arid lands are several. It can consume vegetation that other mammals avoid, thanks to its rapid and frequent digestive cycle that efficiently breaks down dry matter and fiber, cellulose, and crude protein. The camel can go without water for longer than any other working animal and is able to survive extreme desiccation, up to the loss of forty percent of body weight in a lean animal. The amount of time that a camel can continue without water is a function of many variables, including temperature, age of the camel, and weight of the freight burden, among others. On occasion, fully loaded camels have been able to push through desert terrain for more than ten days without water.

Today, camels are principally found in a broad band that stretches east through the North Africa, the Sahara, and the African grasslands just below the Sahara through Turkey and the Middle East to the western half of India. Within this zone, camels are considered to be extremely important to the nomadic livestock economies of Somalia, Mauritania, and the western Sahara and to be of major importance in Tunisia, Jordan, Saudi Arabia, Yemen, Sudan, Niger, and Chad. Camels have adapted themselves to a variety of different environments, and specialists today distinguish between the physical characteristics of lowland, mountain, riverine, and desert camels.

James L. A. Webb Jr.

Further Reading

Beebe, H. K. (1990). *The dromedary revolution* (Occasional Papers No. 18). Claremont, CA: Claremont Graduate School, Institute for Antiquity and Christianity.

Bulliet, R. W. (1975). *The camel and the wheel.* Cambridge, MA: Harvard University Press.

Gauthier-Pilters, H., & Dagg, A. I. (1981). *The camel: Its evolution, ecology, behavior, and relationship to Man.* Chicago: University of Chicago Press.

Wilson, R.T. (1984). *The camel.* London: Longman Publishing Co.

Canada

(2001 est. pop. 31 million)

Canada encompasses North America, between the United States and the Arctic islands, and from the Atlantic to the Pacific Ocean. Intense cold, aridity, and thin soils pose significant challenges to agriculture and settlement. Covering 9,203,054 square kilometers, this area was sparsely inhabited by indigenous peoples (except on the Pacific coast, which accounted for 200,000 of the estimated precontact population of 500,000), and only slowly brought within the realm of European settlement. Fewer than 3 million people of European descent occupied this area in the 1850s. By 1901 the total Canadian population was 5.3 million, and in 1951, 14 million. Canada is a plural society, with two official languages (English and French), a complex regional and immigrant background, and diverse forms of religious observance.

Colonialism, Settlement, and Resource Development

As in all settler societies, the occupation and development of the land was a significant part of the colonization process. Early interactions between Europeans and aboriginal peoples led to significant demographic shifts. Epidemic diseases reduced populations on both the Atlantic and Pacific coasts and in the St. Lawrence Valley before the development of extensive trade networks or settler colonialism. As European trade connections extended into the interior and north, patterns of demographic collapse and rapid cultural change followed.

From the banks of the St. Lawrence in the seventeenth century to the western plains in the twentieth, immigrants and their descendants cleared forests and turned prairie sod to establish farms and families. The cumulative impact was enormous. By 1911, forest covered less than 10 percent of once heavily treed southern Ontario. Many wetlands and swamps were drained. A grid of roads and farms lay over much of southern Canada. Fields of wheat replaced grasslands, and cattle roamed the short-grass prairie. New plant and animal species were introduced and indigenous flora and fauna were displaced. Some of the introductions became pests; some native species were driven to extinction (the passenger pigeon), others were dramatically reduced in numbers (the bison).

As early Canada was brought within the expanding orbit of Atlantic and world commerce, its environment also came to be seen as a storehouse of valuable resources open to exploitation. Supplying external markets, and yielding valuable returns to developing colonial and Canadian economies, these resources were described by the historian Harold Innis as "staple products," and he and other Canadian scholars developed a theory of economic development in new-settled lands from studies of their exploitation. Cod, beaver, timber, and minerals were the most notable of the Canadian staples, but wheat and other agricultural products can be counted among them.

In the sixteenth and seventeenth centuries explorers believed the codfish stocks of the western Atlantic to be "a kind of inexhaustible manna." As a rising European population and an ever greater number of religious fast days pushed up the demand for fish, the banks of Newfoundland and the waters of the Gulf of St. Lawrence attracted hundreds of fishing voyages from Portugal, France, and England each year. As the "wet" fishery (in which the catch was preserved in brine on board the fishing vessels) gave way to the "dry" fishery (in which cod were salted and air-dried on large wooden flakes on shore) settlement in Newfoundland quickened. By the early eighteenth century, much of the catch came from small settlements (outports), whose families fished the in-shore. Some local stocks showed signs of depletion and communities sought to control exploitation through a loose form of moral economy. But changing economic, social, and demographic circumstances eventually undermined most such efforts to limit exploitation. With the introduction of new technologies through the twentieth century, the diffuse, loosely structured and difficult-to-control fishery began overfishing cod stocks. Despite efforts to regulate the catch by extending jurisdiction over international waters to 200 miles, the Newfoundland fishery fell into crisis. In 1993 the Canadian government closed the Atlantic cod fishery.

In contrast to the fishery, which looked outward from widely scattered coves and harbors to migratory offshore resources and thus had a broadly radial structure, the fur trade was linear in its organization, and much more easily controlled. Heavily, but not exclusively focused on the beaver, it ran into the northern heart of the continent through two portals, the St. Lawrence-Great Lakes, and Hudson Bay. In Montreal the Northwest Company established the command center of a trade carried inland along the waterways of the Canadian Shield and beyond across the prairies by voyagers whose canoes carried supplies and trade goods into the interior and returned laden with furs. From posts on the shores of the northern entry to the continent, the Hudson's Bay Company (HBC) also engaged aboriginal people in this trade. With new markets for beaver and other pelts, and new goods (from copper kettles to blankets, axes, and beads) to be acquired in exchange, aboriginal exploitation of fur-bearing animals increased markedly. Pressure on the resource only increased as trade expanded and HBC and Montreal traders competed with each other for native suppliers. In 1821, the competing factions amalgamated, but the onslaught continued. By 1840, parts of northern Ontario, once rich in beaver, were virtually hunted out. Only a few years later, and well aware of the need for conservation, the HBC encouraged the devastation of beaver stocks in an area beyond the Rocky Mountains in an effort to reduce its value and attractiveness to American rivals.

Devastation of another sort followed the fur trade. Commercial networks brought new diseases among aboriginal peoples. Between the last decades of the eighteenth century and the middle years of the nineteenth, the common cold, measles, whooping cough, smallpox, and other ills killed tens of thousands of aboriginal peoples who lacked previous exposure to and immunity from these virulent invaders.

The gold and silver brought to Europe from Spanish America inspired hopes that the north would also yield mineral wealth, but mining was slow to develop in British North America. Gold rushes occurred in several places in the mid-nineteenth century, but most were small and ephemeral. The most significant was in British Columbia, where discoveries along the Fraser River in 1858 brought some 30,000 placer miners. Demographic, economic, social, and environmental transformations occurred in short order. On sand and gravel bars along the Fraser, surface material was washed through sluice boxes and into the Fraser River. Rockfields were left behind, and at the mouth of the river the increased sediment load advanced the delta front at a rapid rate. Some forty years later, the basic patterns of extraction and environmental transformation were repeated during the Klondike rush to the Yukon.

Coal fueled the Canadian industrial revolution in the late nineteenth century, but there were significant reserves only in the eastern provinces and in the then-remote far west. In parts of Nova Scotia, mine towns, hills of refuse shale, and later land subsidence mark the environmental legacies of the industry. Less evident but nonetheless important were the pollutants spread across the land and into human lungs by the industries that burned local coal. Late in the nineteenth and through the twentieth century, deep, expensive new mines in the hard rock of the Canadian Shield and western cordillera yielded fortunes in gold, silver, and other metals such as lead, zinc, copper, nickel, and eventually uranium. In Alberta, after 1945, oil and natural gas development expanded massively; today the tar sands of northern Alberta hold one of the richest unrealized oil sources in North America. Again, environmental impacts have been largely local, but toxic materials released or utilized in the processing of ore and petroleum products sometimes destroyed downwind vegetation and/or poisoned streams and lakes.

The forest has been one of Canada's richest and most enduring resources. Its exploitation underpinned much nineteenth-century development as the pine forests of eastern and central Canada were heavily used to meet British and American demand for lumber. In the twentieth century pulp mills depended on hitherto underutilized species such as spruce, and the logging frontier expanded west and north. British Columbia, and in time the boreal forests, became major producers. Conservation and silvicultural initiatives and the natural resilience of the forest have sustained the resource into the twenty-first century. Today, Canada has more land in forest (over 45 percent of the national land area) than in 1900, and in the 1990s forest products accounted for approximately 14 percent of Canadian manufacturing. Since 1980 the industry has changed dramatically. Rapidly altering economic conditions, changing societal expectations, and strong opposition to prevalent logging practices, particularly the extensive clear-cutting practiced in coastal British Columbia, have forced the introduction of new regulations and greater levels of public participation in decision making to achieve more sustainable forest practices.

Water became an especially important resource in the twentieth century. Hydroelectric dams provided energy for resource development in remote regions and for urban industrial and consumer demand. Cheap electricity underwrote growth in mineral and pulp and paper industries that required large amounts of energy. In Quebec and British Columbia, for example, aluminum processors located in non-metropolitan areas, distant from bauxite sources in the Caribbean, to benefit from cheap water power on the Saguenay and Nechako Rivers, respectively. Although some advocated hydroelectricity as a green fuel, critics pointed to the deleterious consequences of reservoir flooding and damming on wildlife, fisheries, and human settlements. Water development has also been an important driver of agricultural intensification. By extending irrigation systems, semiarid portions of the prairie provinces and of British Columbia were incorporated into range and cattle operations and developed for crops as diverse as stone fruits and sugar beets. Irrigated agriculture accounts for a significant portion of total water consumption in the prairie provinces and faces increasing criticism as population and urban growth pushes domestic consumption levels upwards.

Staple resource development occurred within an evolving trade and communications pattern and exerted different influences across the country. An industrial heartland emerged in central Canada around the St. Lawrence and Great Lakes. Canada's two largest cities, Montreal and Toronto, created commercial linkages across the continent and commanded transportation corridors, particularly after the advent of the transcontinental railroad in the 1880s. In outlying areas, smaller cities shaped regional hinterlands; beyond, dispersed settlements pressed into marginal environments and extracted commodities for export. By the late nineteenth century, the power of metropolitan centers in Canada, steam-powered technologies, and new transportation connections facilitated the rise of a national economy based upon industrial resource extraction. By 1940, most Canadians lived in cities on the southern fringe of the country. Canada's vast land increasingly came under the power of an industrial extractive economy, supporting local development and feeding international markets for raw and semiprocessed natural resources.

Environmental Policy

Environmental policy in Canada has been shaped by the problems of jurisdiction in a federal state. Since Canadian Confederation, jurisdiction over natural resources has been split between the federal government and the provinces. Sections 92 and 102 of Canada's foundational constitutional legislation, the British North America Act (1867), assign broad powers over land and resources to the provinces. The Act also gives the federal government jurisdiction over ocean-based and anadromous fisheries, and navigable and international rivers, and grants significant powers related to

natural resources under section 91 (particularly in trade and commerce, taxation policy, and most broadly "Peace, Order and good Government"). Before constitutional changes in 1982, the basic outlines of Canada's provincial-federal division of powers gave rise to an environmental policy regime marked by "provincially led intergovernmental collaboration" (Hessing and Howlett 1999). Policy analysts argue that the division of powers under the constitution has hindered environmental management at the national level. However, a national parks program was initiated with the creation of Rocky Mountain Park (later Banff National Park) in 1885, and by the 1930s a national system of parks extended across the country. In the early twentieth century, a federally led commission of conservation organized inventories of forests, rivers, fur-bearing animals, and other resources, but its effects on policy were limited. Federal jurisdiction over fisheries was one of the strongest national levers in environmental policy and had important implications for conservation and habitat planning. Beyond these examples, there are instances of interprovincial cooperation in areas such as water planning. Primarily, however, resources are managed and regulated at the provincial level; a diverse body of legislation and policy shapes environmental issues and resource development across the country.

Canada and the United States

Canada's relationship with the United States has also shaped the evolution of environmental issues and policy in the twentieth century. Canada and the United States share a boundary across North America that interrupts north-south aligned ecological zones, and crosses major rivers and lakes. Most Canadians live within one hundred miles of this boundary and much Canadian economic activity revolves around cross-border trade.

Managing nature and shared resources across the Canada-U.S. boundary has produced a number of innovative policies and institutions. To protect nature that does not respect national boundaries, policies have sought to coordinate wildlife management. Many of these attempts died in negotiation, but the Migratory Birds Treaty (1916), which seeks to protect migratory birds over a wide continental space, represents an early and enduring achievement. Other institutions have sought to coordinate transboundary development. The International Joint Commission (IJC), established in 1909, has overseen a cooperative approach to water development. It supplies national governments with expert recommendations on shared water resource and air pollution disputes. The IJC has been particularly important in shaping major transnational development projects, such as that embodied in the Columbia River Treaty (1964), and in addressing water and air pollution problems in the Great Lakes region. Like other transboundary institutions, however, the IJC has limited jurisdiction and authority. It has operated, primarily, as a diplomatic instrument to provide arms-length recommendations. The more recently created Environmental Commission of the North American Free Trade Agreement (NAFTA) bears the same promise and limitations.

Other resource sectors have produced seemingly as much conflict as cooperation. The Pacific salmon fishery of British Columbia, the U.S. Pacific Northwest, and Alaska has been torn by disputes over appropriate catch levels between national fisheries. Early twentieth-century attempts to coordinate fisheries regulations and set national limits failed. Only in 1937, after years of diplomatic effort and signs of resource decline, did the Pacific Salmon Convention establish a bi-national commission to study the resource and recommend catch levels. Despite fifty years of constructive activity, the institution was dissolved in the mid-1980s under intense political pressure. Since that time, a new Treaty and Pacific Salmon Commission has sought to address national and regional demands within the context of a continuously declining fishery. Conflict and high-level diplomacy remains a constant.

Canada's economy and natural resource trade has become progressively integrated with the United States. During World War II and after, the two national economies were increasingly intertwined, as a result of military cooperation and cold war strategic considerations. Exports of strategic minerals spiked and all natural resources were more intensively developed and traded. Despite several bouts of protectionism in the 1930s and 1970s, continental integration advanced during the twentieth century. In 1989, Canada and the United States signed a Free Trade Agreement (FTA) to remove tariff barriers to trade and to establish agreements about specific sectors, such as energy. In 1992, NAFTA extended the FTA to include Mexico. A side agreement established the Environmental Commission.

There have been several implications of closer integration for environmental issues: first, the trade in natural resources has soared over the last hundred years, hindering, to some extent, the development of secondary manufacturing in Canada, while driving expansionist development policies, particularly in less-settled interior regions and the middle north. Since the 1970s, for example, Quebec Hydro has expanded its hydroelectric energy supply in northern Quebec, flooding Cree hunting territories, to profit from energy markets in the United States and particularly New York State. Second, Canada has been pressured to harmonize environmental and trade policies with the United States, in order to level the playing field in competitive resource sectors (such as forestry products), and to insure resource security for the United States in fields such as energy and strategic minerals. The Canadian export trade in softwood lumber has been particularly contentious. Before and after the NAFTA, U.S. competitors and legislators charged that the pattern of resource tenure rights in Canada constituted unfair trading practices. Canadian exporters and governments have, in turn, fought these charges and decried U.S. protectionism.

Matthew Evenden and Graeme Wynn

Further Reading

Harris, C. (1997). *The resettlement of British Columbia: Essays on colonialism and geographical change*. Vancouver, Canada: University of British Columbia Press.

Hessing, M., & Howlett, M. (1999). *Canadian natural resource and environmental policy: Political economy and public policy*. Vancouver, Canada: University of British Columbia Press.

Innis, H. A. (1978 [1940]). *The cod fisheries: The history of an international economy*. Toronto, Canada: University of Toronto Press.

Kiy, R., & Wirth, J. (Eds.). (1998). *Environmental management on North America's borders*. College Station: Texas A & M University Press.

MacEachern, A. (2001). *Natural selections: National Parks in Atlantic Canada*. Montreal & Kingston, Canada: McGill-Queen's University Press.

Mitchell, B. (1995). *Resource and environmental management in Canada: Addressing conflict and uncertainty*. Toronto, Canada: Oxford University Press.

Nelles, H. V. (1974). *The politics of development: Forests, mines & hydro-electric power in Ontario, 1849–1941*. Toronto: Macmillan of Canada.

Rajala, R. A. (1998). *Clearcutting the Pacific rainforest: Production, science and regulation*. Vancouver, Canada: University of British Columbia Press.

Ray, A. J. (1974). *Indians in the fur trade*. Toronto, Canada: University of Toronto Press.

Wood, J. D. (2000). *Making Ontario: Agricultural coloniza-tion and landscape re-creation before the railway.* Toronto, Canada: University of Toronto Press.

Wynn, G. (1981). *Timber colony: A historical geography of early nineteenth century New Brunswick.* Toronto, Canada: University of Toronto Press.

Capitalism

Definitions of capitalism tend to reveal the ideology of the person or institution making the definition. The commonsense, neoclassical understanding of capital-ism is as an economic system defined by private own-ership of productive goods and services. Here the re-quired inputs (including labor power) and produced outputs are secured through the operation of a compet-itive market in which prices for such are set. In the neoclassical view, numerous consumers and sellers freely enter a frictionless market space, invest with per-fect rationality and knowledge, and respond to price signals so that each secures a fair price.

While one might quibble with the prescription of-fered, Karl Marx (1818–1883) and Friedrich Engels (1820–1895) provide a prognosis of the limits of capital-ism and moreover in a form that provides insight into the historically specific relationship between capital-ism and the environment. In their broad interpretation, capitalism is much more than an economic system for exchange; rather, it defines the dominant social system of our age, one that shapes the cultural, economic, and political institutions of our lives as well as our under-standing of them and our commitment to change within them.

Capitalism as a Mode of Production

To understand both the neoclassical and Marxist inter-pretations of capitalism as it impacts the environment, we have to go back and explain the basis for the capital-ist commitment to material growth, for it is this growth that has been recognized as incompatible with environ-mental sustainability. To begin, all living organisms transform nature, taken here as matter and energy, into other forms of matter and energy in order to survive. So-called higher organisms, including humans, do this not only as individuals, but also as members of social groupings; together they—and we—secure shelter, procure food, and obtain the other essentials for sur-

vival. The *mode of production* refers to the social rela-tions we enter into in order to transform nature into the products necessary for our survival, while the *means of production* are the tools we use to effect that transforma-tion. In addition to digging sticks, hunting implements, machines, factories, and other tools, the latter also in-clude our own labor power. The Marxist commitment to the laborer (or proletarian) is based on the fact that labor power is used to fashion and employ all the other means of production. Neoclassical economists also rec-ognize and value the contribution of entrepreneurs (or capitalists), who own and mobilize the other means of production.

While there are many ways to distinguish different modes of production, basic characteristics include the social structure of the production system as deter-mined by who owns the means of production, and how the goods that are captured, grown, and produced are distributed. An understanding of the social structure of ownership and of the distribution system can, in turn, predict the relationship of a particular mode of production with the environment. To illustrate, under the hunting and gathering mode of production, the bows, arrows, slings, and other means of production were widely held, while the products procured were distributed according to kinship and tribal obligations. In the absence of a market system whereby surplus goods could be exchanged for other products, and given direct access to the means of production, partici-pants tended toward subsistence living, in which sur-plus accumulation was dysfunctional and even dis-couraged. Under feudalism, landlords owned and rented out the land to peasants, tenant farmers, or serfs, with the latter, in turn, owning most of the other means of production, such as oxen and plows. The peasants paid out a portion of their harvest as rent to the land-lord or served in his fields or army for a designated period. Here there was a weak town-based market sys-tem whereby goods and services produced beyond subsistence needs were bartered for or exchanged through the emerging medium of money. As yet, there was no well-defined mechanism whereby the subsis-tence farmers could be induced to produce much more than they consumed or had to pay out in tribute to the landlords.

As described by Marx in *Capital* (1867), capitalism in its classic form is a mode of production in which the means of production are owned and controlled by a social class known as the capitalist class, or bourgeoi-sie. The majority of the population belongs to the labor, or proletariat, class; within the production process, they only own their labor power. This they sell to capitalists for a wage. Capitalism acquires its forceful quality (some would say its "genius") through the presence of a well-articulated competitive market. Here the goods that are produced through labor power are exchanged by many private market participants (buyers and sellers) for other goods, with money the medium for exchange.

The dynamic of capitalism arises through the process of commodity exchange in a competitive marketplace in which the private capitalist entrepreneur is forced to reinvest a portion of the surplus value left after paying for maintenance of the means of production (wages, rent, interest, and so on). That surplus must be plowed back into new research, development, and other means for market expansion; the capitalist cannot squander it as might a feudal landlord in the absence of competitive pressure. Reinvestment is a requirement of the competitive market, for without reinvestment one runs the risk of losing one's competitive edge and, in the end, one's business. In short, the competitive market forces the capitalist to either keep moving forward or sink, as even the entrepreneur with a patented (protected) product risks being undone by innovative competitors. Furthermore, insofar as capitalism is defined by the presence of a wage-earning labor class and a competitive market, it actually depends on a certain level of perceived scarcity in order both to motivate worker participation in production and to secure necessary market expansion through consumer demand. Common consequences of this need for scarcity include the presence of unemployed workers (Marx's "industrial reserve army") ready to take jobs and undercut worker wage demands, as well as the constant creation of new consumer wants and desires regardless of the environmental consequences generated.

The Rise of Capitalism

Currently the dominant mode of production worldwide, capitalism emerged first in the city-states of Renaissance Italy during the fifteenth century before taking hold most firmly in northern Europe, principally in England and the Netherlands during the sixteenth century. Here a new class of bourgeoisie entrepreneurs, raising money through an emerging banking system, first commodified and then greatly expanded agriculture, mining, textiles, shipbuilding and other industries for market production. In the process they undercut the power of feudal landlords and displaced

self-sufficient subsistence farmers, medieval artisans, and others involved in a more sustainable relationship with nature. They also contributed to the rise of strong nation-states necessary for colonial expansion in search of new resources and markets, greatly increasing the pressure on the environment in the process. The displaced peasants and workers, in turn, became available labor for the capitalist enterprises that were concentrated in emerging urban centers toward which the rural population was forced to migrate.

To summarize, capitalism as a unique mode of production is defined by the presence of a competitive market for commodity exchange in which capitalists control the means of production (except for labor itself) and the majority of the population sells its labor power for a wage. In response to the requirements of the competitive market, the capitalist entrepreneur constantly seeks to lower the cost of production, including labor and other resource inputs, while expanding market control and, ultimately, profits. As a result, capitalism became very aggressive toward labor (the primary Marxist concern) as well as toward the environment as it spread out from its birthplace in Europe in search of cheaper sources of labor and natural resources as well as new markets for its products.

As defined by Marx and Engels, communism, the fourth major mode of production (after hunting and gathering, feudalism, and capitalism) is characterized by public (state) ownership of the means of production in the name of the workers. Here the state itself allocates resources in the absence of a competitive market. Communism is not as materially aggressive as capitalism toward the environment because there is no structural necessity for market expansion. Nonetheless, as has been demonstrated at the nation-state level, it has failed to achieve any semblance of environmental sustainability due to other structural defects, such as an inability to properly price natural resources in the absence of a market test for value.

The Contradiction for Capitalism

Both conventional economists and Marxists agree that under capitalism there is a constant drive to expand. This continuous drive is not exclusive to capitalism, and indeed Communism may also be growth-oriented. Nevertheless, for capitalism accumulation is a basic structural requirement. To understand the environmental manifestation of this requirement we have to consider the concept of *contradiction*. A contradiction is an unavoidable structural defect in a mode of production, the permanent solution to which requires a change in the basic social structure defining that mode of production. For communism, the basic contradiction is found in the defining dictum used for planning and distribution: "From each according to his ability, to each according to his needs" (Marx [1875]1974, 347). The contradiction emerges as the individual incentive to produce, and even to work, particularly at larger (nation-state) levels, falls aside when one's needs are secured and there is no material reward for superior effort. Thus early on in their revolutions both the Soviet Union and China found it necessary to move beyond reliance on altruism and peer pressure and to introduce material incentive systems to spur production, particularly when they were forced to compete with the capitalist West.

Turning back to capitalism, according to Marx, the basic contradiction for capitalism is between the social nature of production and its private appropriation. That is, while different classes and different factions within classes work together to produce products, the surplus value is distributed to individuals in varying sizes. This leads to class struggle over the size and distribution of surplus value, pitting labor against capitalists and, within classes, different factions (for example, finance versus industrial capital) against one another. In addition, when individual capitalists, each acting in their own self interest, appropriate surplus value, they produce aggregate results adverse to their collective class interests, such as the wasteful use of common resources, including air and water, and underinvestment in common needs such as education and infrastructure. As a result, capitalism requires state intervention to assure the conditions necessary for continued accumulation, even if popular capitalist ideology favors minimum state intervention in market allocation.

Growth as a Response to Contradiction

In a system of class conflict, a growing economy temporarily supports social harmony, as each segment hopes to share in the larger surplus generated. While perhaps more fancy than fact, this "trickle-down" expectation is nevertheless deeply ingrained as a popular notion and, moreover, is promoted by the state to ensure both social harmony and legitimation of the state. In this manner, continued economic expansion is a necessary condition for capitalism despite attending environmental consequences. Insofar as capitalism has been able to "deliver the goods," it has succeeded in securing most of the population's allegiance, at least in prosperous regions such as Europe and North America.

The Social and Environmental Manifestations of Contradiction

Capitalism's constant drive for accumulation, while temporarily contributing to social harmony, generates new manifestations of contradiction and crisis as the search for cheaper resource inputs and new markets leads to uneven development, volatile pockets of unemployed and displaced labor, contamination of the environment, and damage to workers' health. Basically there are three interrelated manifestations of the primary contradiction (between the social nature of production and its private appropriation). Economically there is a declining rate of profit per dollar invested as capitalists squander the world's resources, using up the cheapest sources first while also substituting capital investment for labor (automation) in an attempt to reduce labor's power over the production process. This declining organic composition of capital, as Marx calls it, in turn leads to the social manifestation of contradiction through unemployment and increasing violence on labor, which necessitates state intervention both through police control and socialist welfare reforms (the latter most forcibly in modern western Europe). Finally, the environmental manifestation of contradiction is clear, not only through the way capitalists treat common resources, again necessitating state intervention, but even through the despoilment of privately held resources in the quest for profit. In short, capitalism must commodify nature itself as an input into the production process. In order for this to happen, nature must be appropriated as dead and available for human benefit. This is an idea supported by mechanistic cosmology. It gained prominence, at least among the emerging bourgeoisie of northern Europe, during the sixteenth century and at the expense of the now dysfunctional organic cosmology that considered nature to be alive and capable of retribution if misused.

Capitalism Today

To be sure, capitalism as a dynamic social system has evolved since the tooth and claw labor struggles Marx and Engels described. Over time class consciousness was blurred in advanced capitalist states by worker participation in ownership, if not actual control, of production resources through pension plans and other stock-holding options. Moreover, popular allegiance was secured through major expansion of home ownership and other consumption amenities, with homes, as well as nature, portrayed as a locus for social reproduction of the labor force and ideologically as a refuge from the alienating forces of production, such as commodification of the fruits of one's labor as well as damage to workers' health and safety. Critics such as Max Weber (1864–1920) and Thorstein Veblen (1857–1929) rejected Marxist class analysis as materially too deterministic and as overlooking other properties arising from shared consumption characteristics (for example, lower-, middle-, and upper-class consumption) as well as from religious and cultural practices that both pre- and postdate capitalism. The Marxist analysis of capitalism and class consciousness, however, and its understanding of the relation between capitalism and the environment, goes to the heart of the necessary relationship between those constructs and capitalism itself, whereas the contingent categories postulated by Weber, Veblen, and neo-classical analysts are merely descriptive and bear no necessary relation to the defining structure of capitalism.

Michael K. Heiman

See also Club of Rome; Commodification; Ford, Henry

Further Reading

Engels, F. (1940). *Dialectics of nature* (C. Dutt, Trans.). New York: International Publishers. (Original work published 1878)

Heiman, M. (1988). *The quiet evolution: Power, planning, and profits in New York State.* New York: Praeger.

Merchant, C. (1980). *The death of nature.* San Francisco: Harper & Row.

Marx, K. (1974). Critique of the Gotha programme. In D. Fernback (Ed.), *Karl Marx: The First International and after* (pp. 339–359). New York: Vintage Books. (Original article published 1875)

Marx, K. (1977–1981). *Capital: A critique of political economy* (D. Fernbach, Trans.). New York: Vintage. (Original work published 1867–1894)

Marx, K. (1973). *Grunrisse: Foundations of the critique of political economy.* London: Harmondsworth/Penguin. (Original work published 1858)

Smith, A. (1976). *An inquiry into the nature and causes of the wealth of nations.* (R. H. Campbell & A. S. Skinner, Eds.). Oxford, U.K.: Clarendon Press. (Original work published 1776)

Veblen, T. (1899). *The theory of the leisure class: An economic study of institutions.* New York: Charles Scribner's Sons.

Weber, M. (1968). *Economy and society.* (E. Fischoff et al., Trans.) New York: Bedminster Press. (Original work published 1922)

Caribbean

The Caribbean region extends 4,000 kilometers along an arc from northwestern Cuba to the southern tip of Trinidad. This arc forms the northern and eastern boundaries of the Caribbean Sea, a basin of 2.7 million square kilometers. To the west, the sea is bounded by the Yucatán Peninsula of Mexico, Belize, Guatemala, Honduras, Nicaragua, and Costa Rica and to the south by Panama, Colombia, and Venezuela. The hundreds of islands that make up the Caribbean region are highly diverse in size, landforms, geology, and climate. Cuba, for example, occupies an area of more than 110,000 square kilometers, whereas the smallest of the region's independent island nations, such as St. Kitts and Nevis, occupy an area of scarcely 258 square kilometers. Geographers conventionally divide the region into the Greater Antilles (the large islands of Cuba, Hispaniola, Jamaica, and Puerto Rico) and the much smaller but more numerous Lesser Antilles to the east, which run in a north-south axis separating the Caribbean Sea from the Atlantic Ocean.

The Caribbean is a polyglot (using several languages) region whose history includes centuries of imperial conflict over the land, resources, and people of the region. Most of the population is descended from nonnative peoples brought to the region between the sixteenth and twentieth centuries as slaves or indentured laborers. Little remains of the region's indigenous peoples, other than some Carib native communities on St. Vincent and Dominica. Despite the common circumstances of coerced migration that populated the Caribbean following European conquest and the collapse of native societies, the now-independent nations of the Caribbean reflect the linguistic, cultural, and political characteristics of their colonizing powers, whether Spain, France, Britain, or Holland. In many instances, islands repeatedly changed hands between rival imperial powers during the colonial era, giving rise to contemporary societies such as St. Lucia and

Columbus' Impression of the Caribbean Islands

I understand sufficiently from other Indians, whom I had already taken, that continually this land was an island, and so I followed its coast eastward 107 leagues up to where it ended. And from that cape I saw toward the east another island, distant 18 leagues from the former, to which I at once gave the name *La Spanola*. And I went there and followed its northern part, as I had in the case of Juana, to the eastward for 178 great leagues in a straight line. As Juana, so all the others are very fertile to an excessive degree, and this one especially. In it there are many harbors on the sea coast, beyond comparison with others which I know in Christendom, and numerous rivers, good and large, which is marvelous. Its lands are lofty and in it there are many sierras and very high mountains, to which the island *Centrefrei* is not comparable. All are most beautiful, of a thousand shapes, and all accessible, and filled with trees of a thousand kinds and tall, and they seem to touch the sky; and I am told that they never lose their foliage, which I can believe, for I saw them as green and beautiful as they are in Spain in May, and some of them were flowering, some with fruit, and some in another condition, according to their quality. And there were singing the nightingale and other little birds of a thousand kinds in the month of November, there where I went. There are palm trees of six or eight kinds, which are a wonder to behold because of their beautiful variety, and so are the other trees and fruits and plants; therein are marvelous pine groves, and extensive meadow country; and there is honey, and there are many kinds of birds and a great variety of fruits. Upcountry thee are many mines of metals, and the population is innumerable. *La Spanola* is marvelous, the sierras and the mountains and the plains and the meadows and the lands are so beautiful and rich for planting and sowing, and for livestock of every sort and for building towns and villages. The harbors of the sea here are such as you could not believe it without seeing them; and so the rivers, many and great, and good streams, the most of which bear gold. And the trees and fruits and plants have great differences from those of La Juana; in this [island] there are many spices and great mines of gold and of other metals.

Source: *Journals and Other Documents on the Life and Voyages of Christopher Columbus* (1963), edited by Samuel Eliot Morison. New York: Heritage Press, pp. 182–183.

Dominica whose official language is English but whose spoken vernacular is a French patois.

Landforms throughout the Caribbean tend to be mountainous and plunge into deep oceanic trenches. With the exception of the Bahamas, Barbados, Antigua, and Trinidad, flat, low landscapes are uncommon in most of the region. The interiors of the Greater Antilles islands are geological extensions of the highlands of southern Mexico and reach elevations of more than 2,700 meters in the Dominican Republic on Hispaniola. Most of the Lesser Antilles lie along the intersection of two tectonic plates that yield both mountainous uplifting and geological instability. Earthquakes occur with some frequency on these islands, and dramatic and occasionally devastating volcanic eruptions have occurred on some. The 1902 eruption of Mount Pelée on Martinique killed nearly all of the thirty thousand inhabitants of St. Pierre, the island's largest town. A 1997 volcanic eruption on Montserrat forced the evacuation of most of that island's eleven thousand residents.

Natural vegetation patterns on the islands are likewise diverse, ranging from tropical rain forest, tropical seasonal forest, and mountain forest to savanna, dry scrub, and even desert. Maximum rainfall usually occurs from June through November, yielding to a comparatively dry season in the first half of the year. Rainfall generally increases from north to south throughout the Caribbean, but island topography is at least as critical as latitude in determining climate and associated vegetation. The high peaks on many islands trigger rainfall from easterly winds, whereas low-lying islands receive less rainfall and may experience frequent drought. Because of the mountainous terrain throughout the Lesser Antilles, entirely distinct climatic patterns are often found in close proximity even on small islands. In general, wetter, more heavily forested zones face the Caribbean (leeward) sides of the Lesser Antilles islands, and drier zones occupy the windward sides facing the Atlantic. As important as latitude and topography are in determining climate and vegetation, the biogeography (geographical distribution of plants and animals) of each island has been massively affected by ecological changes wrought by five hundred years of European colonialism and settlement.

Pre-Columbian Human Environments

Prior to human settlement, forest cover throughout the Caribbean region was extensive, although it was periodically diminished by natural environmental disturbances. Forces such as hurricanes and volcanic eruptions precluded the development of climax forests (stable plant communities achieved through long-term ecological adaptation) and associated fauna and in some instances led to complete recolonization by floral and faunal species of adjacent islands. Before the arrival of humans, the only mammal species north of Trinidad consisted of bats and rodents. Earliest human settlement in the Caribbean was by a variety of preceramic (nomadic, pre-agricultural) foraging and fishing peoples who sailed or drifted to the Greater Antilles from Central America as early as 5000 BCE. Much later, around the time of Christ, Native Americans from Venezuela and Guyana migrated northward through the Lesser Antilles in pursuit of the region's aquatic resources (primarily fish, turtles, and sea mammals). These peoples, collectively known as Taino (formerly Arawaks), brought about the first significant human modification of Caribbean island environments. The Taino introduced South American cultigens (cultivated varieties or species for which a wild ancestor is unknown) such as cassava, sweet potato, yams, peanuts, beans, and maize, all of which were grown on plots (conucos) under tropical forest shifting cultivation. Caribbean peoples also made extensive use of inshore mammal and fish species, as well as birds and lizards. After 1200 CE the Taino were steadily supplanted by more militaristic island Caribs, who swept northward through the Lesser Antilles by incorporating existing populations through conquest and intermarriage. At the time of European conquest, indigenous populations of the Caribbean were estimated at 2–4 million. In some areas of high population density, soil erosion apparently resulted from native cultivation techniques. Yet, most indigenous peoples in the Caribbean appear to have lived in relative harmony with their environments, if not always with each other.

Ecological Effects of Conquest

Hispanic colonization of the Caribbean commenced in 1493, but entailed small numbers of actual settlers: the entire Spanish population of the region never exceeded ten thousand during the fifteenth and sixteenth centuries. Similarly, neither Britain, France, nor Holland sought to extensively populate the Caribbean with their citizens, however much they fought each other over the region's resources. Yet, the ecological consequences of European conquest were immediate and irreversible and were felt through a massive depopulation of the region. Horrified colonial-era chroniclers such as Fray Bartolome de las Casas graphically documented the mistreatment of Caribbean natives forced to mine gold for the Spanish. It is likely, however, that Old World diseases such as plague, smallpox, measles, and malaria, to which indigenous populations lacked any acquired immunity, exacted a far greater toll than did European slavery and other abuses. By 1524 all of the native populations of the Greater Antilles and the Bahamas, as well as most of those of the Lesser Antilles, had been extinguished.

As native populations died out, their agricultural lands were abandoned and quickly reverted to forest cover, a process that occurred in other former aboriginal areas of the Americas as well. In the Caribbean, this process was extraordinarily rapid, and most traces of native agriculture and even settlements were quickly swallowed by encroaching forest. Barbados, for example, had been one of the most heavily populated of the Lesser Antilles during the pre-Columbian period. Yet, when the first English settlers arrived one hundred years after the demise of the native population they encountered nothing but dense forests growing down to the shoreline. Although the Spanish introduced many nonnative plant species into the region, most were initially unable to establish themselves in the new environment, primarily because of direct competition with species from the encroaching forest or because of the lack of available space within it. Nonnative plants did not gain a foothold until the later removal of island forests to make way for sugarcane. Introduced faunal species, however, multiplied rapidly in habitats that lacked natural predators and had known no previous hoofed animals. The Spanish left pigs on virtually every island as a potential food source for colonists, and these animals adapted readily to Caribbean forests. By 1514 more than thirty thousand pigs, most of them wild, were reported on Cuba. Pigs, in particular, competed with the declining native human population and may have hastened its demise by rooting up conucos and destroying native crops. Spanish cattle also thrived on Caribbean islands, further compounding long-term environmental problems. The hooves of both cattle and pigs compacted the soil along their trackways, resulting in severe gully erosion in the form of *barrancas* (ravines or gorges) on Cuba and Hispaniola by the late sixteenth century.

As readily accessible sources of gold were depleted, together with the native population compelled to mine it, colonists sought other sources of wealth during the sixteenth century. Throughout the Caribbean, European settlers and Crown authorities turned to an array of agricultural commodities. Tobacco, cotton, indigo, and ginger were introduced with varying levels of success, typically among the few thousand European yeoman farmers who settled in the region. Yet, none of these crops transformed human-environmental relations in the Caribbean as much as sugarcane did. Originally domesticated in Asia from a wild grass species, sugarcane was introduced by the British to Barbados and by the French to St. Kitts in the 1640s. The crop grows well throughout all but the driest parts of the Caribbean, but its demands posed sweeping environmental consequences for the islands of the region. Intolerant of competition for sunlight, water, and nutrients, sugarcane could be successfully cultivated only after the clear-cutting of native forest, followed by continuous weeding. Lowland seasonal forest soils provided the best soil and nutrient combinations for cane cultivation, and consequently these areas were most extensively cleared to make way for the crop. Soon the only areas remaining under forest cover were the highland zones of mountainous islands; low-lying islands were rapidly stripped of all forest cover. Yet, even higher elevations were rarely spared the effects of sugar cultivation because the boilers used to refine sugar were usually fueled by firewood cut from upland forests. In Barbados virtually all of the island's seasonal forests had been cut and replanted with cane by 1665, just twenty years after English settlement. St. Kitts, Nevis, and Montserrat followed suit by the 1680s, Antigua, Guadeloupe, Martinique, and lowland Jamaica by the 1750s, and the Spanish territories of Santo Domingo, Cuba, Puerto Rico, and Trinidad by 1800.

Human and Ecological Consequences of Sugar Production

The ecological consequences of sugarcane cultivation in the Caribbean would be difficult to overstate. It is estimated that hundreds, or even thousands, of plant and animal species were driven to extinction in this process. On Barbados writers of the 1650s commented on the marked absence of songbirds compared to other islands. Indeed, by that time all forest-based birds, other than several hummingbird species, had already disappeared, together with their forest habitats. The region's shift to a monocrop plantation economy also accentuated ecological problems as varying metropolitan demands for sugar dictated cultivation practices and intensity. When European markets became glutted with sugar or prices fell, Caribbean planters typically fallowed some of their land, opening a niche for other plant species on their farms. After the native forest cover had been decimated, more often than not these niches were filled by weed species introduced (usually unwittingly) from abroad. The legacy of this pattern is an extraordinarily high level of nonnative plant species found on most of the islands of the Caribbean. On Barbados, 88.7 percent of the wild plant species recorded in the 1960s originated from outside the island, one of the highest levels of nonnative vegetation of any country in the world.

The clearing of native forest and cultivation and harvest of sugarcane required vast quantities of human labor, a vexing problem for colonists witnessing the virtual extinction of native populations. The demand for agricultural labor was resolved in the sixteenth century by the onset of the Atlantic slave trade, during which an estimated 1.7 million Africans were transported to Britain's Caribbean holdings alone. The presence of African slaves and demand for plantation land quickly swallowed the small-scale tobacco and subsistence farms earlier established by European yeoman farmers. On the sugar-growing islands, African populations soon vastly outnumbered European settlers. Because of the sheer size of the workforce required for cane production (on St. Kitts, for example, the slave population by the late 1700s reached a density of 360 per 2.6 square kilometers) and the devotion of virtually all arable land to sugarcane, the Caribbean came to rely heavily on imported food. In some instances, however, plantation owners allotted gardens to their slaves to defray some of the costs of their subsistence.

Throughout the Caribbean, the era of slavery was marked by a continual hemorrhage of labor through defection and flight as slaves sought refuge in maroon (fugitive slave) communities created in remote upland areas. With the formal end of slavery, plantation owners sought other mechanisms to bind workers to their farms, but many freed slaves were reluctant to resume work on sugar plantations. Because the end of slavery was not accompanied by a redistribution of land, however, former slaves who wished to cultivate farms of their own were forced to do so in areas of marginal productivity, such as swamps and hillsides. Such farming was all but impossible on islands such as Montserrat and Barbados, where there simply was no land apart from that owned by the planter class. Elsewhere, however, subsistence farming on hillsides produced erosion and topsoil loss within a few decades of the end of slavery. Planters' efforts to recruit replacement laborers through indentured servitude (primarily of natives of the East Indies) in the late nineteenth century further aggravated the already high person-to-land ratios, food deficits, and environmental problems associated with farming in marginal zones. For many residents of the Caribbean, environmental pressures and the absence of occupational opportunities apart from estate labor stimulated a rising tide of emigration. By the early twentieth century numerous Afro-Caribbean communities had been formed along the coast of Central America by migrants seeking work on the Panama Canal or the region's banana plantations. High levels of emigration continue today. Most families in the English-speaking Caribbean can identify numerous close relatives living in the United States, Britain, or Canada, and many are heavily dependent on the money sent home by migrants living abroad.

Contemporary Environmental Issues

Although few nations in the Caribbean, other than Cuba, the Dominican Republic, and Haiti, rely heavily on sugar any longer as their primary export, the legacies of sugar production continue to plague the region. A highly inequitable pattern of land ownership (much of it now under absentee control) and extremely high population density continue to cause destructive hillside farming, the loss of topsoil, and outmigration. Since the early 1950s several islands in the eastern Caribbean, among them St. Lucia, St. Vincent, Dominica, and Grenada, have developed export-oriented banana industries based exclusively on peasant production. Eastern Caribbean farmers produce high-quality, commercial-grade fruit using less of the toxic chemicals associated with banana production elsewhere in the Americas. It is no coincidence that these islands have experienced lower rates of outmigration than have islands that have failed to develop viable alternatives to a moribund plantation sugar economy. Following a recent World Trade Organization ruling against the tariff protection that Caribbean banana growers receive from Europe, however, the future of banana production in the region appears less than promising.

For much of the Caribbean, local livelihoods and government revenues since the 1960s have been tied ever more closely to tourism. The region's famed expanses of white beaches and turquoise water have created a proliferation of hotels, all-inclusive resorts, port facilities for ocean liners, and casinos. Within the Caribbean, the heavy reliance on foreign tourists as a primary source of hard currency remains an issue of much debate, given that the changing tastes of the tourist industry often preclude long-term national economic planning. Others assert that the transformation of Afro-Caribbean residents into maids, cooks, and sex workers who cater to the needs of affluent whites creates an unwanted parallel with the era of slavery. There seems little doubt that tourism has caused already high land prices to skyrocket, further excluding many local residents from access to farming. Apart from such questions, the development of Caribbean coastlines to accommodate millions of visitors each year poses formidable environmental problems of its own. The filling of estuaries and mangrove swamps to create resorts and golf courses contributes to siltation of the once-crystalline waters eagerly sought by tourists and has dire consequences for coral reefs and local fisheries. Nor do most islands possess adequate sewage and solid-waste disposal infrastructure to maintain large-scale tourist facilities on a environmentally sustainable basis. Perhaps the most ironic illustration of this process was the decision of the government of Barbados to construct a new landfill during the late 1990s, mostly to accommodate waste from tourist hotels and ocean liners. The site chosen for the new landfill was a national park once promoted by the tourist industry as one of the island's most scenic natural environments.

Mark Moberg

See also Colonialism and Imperialism; Migration; South America; Sugar

Further Reading

Collinson, H. (Ed.). (1996). *Green guerrillas: Environmental conflicts and initiatives in Latin America and the Caribbean: A reader.* London: Latin American Bureau.

Grossman, L. S. (1998). *The political ecology of bananas: Contract farming, peasants and agrarian change in the eastern Caribbean.* Chapel Hill: University of North Carolina Press.

Lentz, D. L. (2000). *An imperfect balance: Landscape transformations in the Precolumbian Americas.* New York: Columbia University Press.

Mintz, S. (1985). *Sweetness and power: The place of sugar in modern history.* New York: Viking.

Richardson, B. (1983). *Caribbean migrants: Environment and human survival on St. Kitts and Nevis.* Knoxville: University of Tennessee Press.

Watts, D. (1990). *The West Indies: Patterns of development, culture, and environmental change since 1492.* Cambridge, UK: Cambridge University Press.

Watts, D. (1995). Ecological responses to ecosystem shock in the island Caribbean: The aftermath of Columbus, 1492–1992. In R. A. Butlin & N. Roberts (Eds.), *Ecological relations in historic times* (pp. 267–279). Oxford, UK: Blackwell.

Caribbean Coastlands

The Caribbean coastlands are a region defined by geography, topography, climate, and history. The region includes the terrains of the Caribbean Sea basin lying between sea level and 1,000 meters in altitude. The annual average temperature in these coastlands is 20–30° C, with no cool season. The region is geographically fragmented and dispersed over a large area. It includes the coastal plains and forests of the Greater Antilles—Cuba, Jamaica, Hispaniola (shared by Haiti and the Dominican Republic), and Puerto Rico. The eastern part of the region is enclosed by an arc of small islands, the Lesser Antilles. The southern and eastern boundaries of the region include the costal regions of South and Central America. Although the region is geographically fragmented, its similar landscapes and patterns of economic development have given it a common environmental history.

During the pre-Columbian period there were two main centers of population in the region. One main center of population was in the Greater Antilles, home to the Taino (Arawak). They practiced *conuco* agriculture—the shifting cultivation of root crops in small plots. The soil was then often heaped into small mounds and planted with a variety of staple crops, especially cassava (a tropical plant with an edible rootstock) and sweet potato. *Conuco* agriculture made effective use of soil nutrients. Individual plots could produce for fifteen to twenty years before the soil was exhausted. The tremendous productivity of *conuco* agriculture, supplemented with hunting and fishing, allowed the Taino to sustain large populations. For example, scholars estimate that Hispaniola's pre-contact population was likely between 300,000 and 750,000. (Colonial authorities authorized the importation of slaves from Africa to make up for the labor shortages.) The Lesser Antilles were home to the Caribs. While they also practiced *conuco* agriculture, their main base of subsistence was fishing. The second main center of population in the pre-Columbian Caribbean was in northern Colombia. The Tairona and Cenu peoples had developed elaborate techniques for fishing the region's rivers, and the Tairona made extensive use of irrigation and terracing in the foothills of the Sierra Santa Marta. Smaller, less technologically developed societies inhabited the Lesser Antilles and Central America. The Caribbean coastlands societies had developed extensive networks of communication and exchange both within the region and beyond. These networks allowed for the introduction of new plants. Cacao and cassava, for example, were probably introduced to the Caribbean coastlands from the Amazon River basin.

New Environments

The European conquest of the New World destroyed the pre-Columbian environments, in the process creating distinctly new colonized environments. Europeans introduced new plants, animals, and diseases. The conquest also caused the catastrophic collapse of the indigenous populations. This complex phenomenon was caused by many factors. Old World epidemic diseases such as smallpox, cholera, and influenza decimated the indigenous populations. Old World livestock, such as pigs, cattle, and goats, trampled indigenous farms and ate their crops. Warfare, famine, slave raids, and declining birthrates also contributed to the long-term decline in the indigenous populations. By 1600 the indigenous populations of the Bahamas and Hispaniola had disappeared entirely. Elsewhere in the coastlands, only fragmented indigenous populations survived.

From the sixteenth to the twentieth century, the colonized environments were defined by the production of export crops. Some of these crops, such as indigo and the banana, were introduced from other parts of the tropical world. But Europeans also developed a taste for plants native to the region, such as tobacco and cacao, and began cultivating them on a large scale. The crop that defined the Caribbean coastlands was sugarcane. The Spanish introduced sugarcane to the Caribbean, bringing it to Hispaniola early in the 1500s. It was the British, however, who inaugurated the Caribbean sugar boom early in the seventeenth century. For a few decades in the seventeenth century, the sugar boom made Barbados the richest colony in the world. The sugar boom generated untold wealth, but it also produced widespread deforestation and environmental decline. Late in the seventeenth century other British and French colonies in the Caribbean began developing their own sugar industries, inaugurating a period known as "the great clearing." Smaller islands, such as Barbados and St. Croix, were entirely deforested in one or two decades. The industrialization of sugar agriculture in the nineteenth century, with the introduction of railroads and mechanized sugar refineries, accelerated the pace of forest clearance. Cuba's vast forests were almost completely destroyed during the nineteenth-century expansion of its sugar industry. Similar environmental transformations accompanied the spread of other tropical coastlands crops, such as tobacco in Cuba, cacao in Venezuela, and bananas in Central America.

Population Changes

The export boom also transformed the region's human populations. After the collapse of indigenous populations, colonial authorities began importing African slaves to work on the plantations. Within a few generations the majority of the region's population was of African descent, with the exceptions of Cuba and Puerto Rico. All the inhabitants of the Caribbean coastlands were plagued by tropical diseases, particularly malaria and yellow fever, until the late nineteenth century, limiting population growth. As a result of the growing commercial and military presence of the United States in the Caribbean, the U.S government and U.S. foundations took an interest in tropical diseases. The U.S.-based Rockefeller Foundation, for example, led a largely successful campaign to eradicate yellow fever. Government-sponsored sanitation campaigns also greatly reduced the incidence of malaria.

In the mid-nineteenth century the environmental order of the Caribbean coastlands began to slowly change. The gradual decline of the region's plantation economies has led to the pursuit of other forms of economic development. After the abolition of slavery, former slaves and their descendants shifted from producing export crops to producing staple crops. These peasant producers have often been forced to cultivate their crops on marginal lands, either because of population pressure or because plantations continued to control the best farmlands. Cultivation on marginal lands has produced catastrophic soil erosion, particularly in Haiti.

Some countries began exploiting their mineral wealth. Venezuela, Trinidad, and Colombia have become major oil exporters, whereas Jamaica exports significant quantities of bauxite. Tourism, the Caribbean's other main path of development since World War II, has allowed many countries to profit from their tropical landscapes. But tourism has also placed additional strains on already scarce supplies of freshwater and food in a region where the local population alone already exceeds the viable carrying capacity (the population that an area will support without undergoing deterioration).

Stuart McCook

Further Reading

Crosby, A. C. (1986). *Ecological imperialism: The biological expansion of Europe, 900–1900*. Cambridge, UK: Cambridge University Press.

Galloway, J. H. (1989). *The sugar cane industry: An historical geography from its origins to 1914*. Cambridge, UK: Cambridge University Press.

Grossman, L. S. (1998). *The political ecology of bananas: Contract farming, peasants, and agrarian change in the eastern Caribbean*. Chapel Hill: University of North Carolina Press.

Patullo, P. (1996). *Last resorts: The cost of tourism in the Caribbean*. London: Cassell.

Richardson, B. C. (1992). *The Caribbean in the wider world, 1492–1992*. Cambridge, UK: Cambridge University Press.

Richardson, B. C. (1997). *Economy and environment in the Caribbean: Barbados and the windwards in the late 1800s*. Gainesville: University Press of Florida.

Sauer, C. (1966). *The early Spanish main*. Berkeley and Los Angeles: University of California Press.

Watts, D. (1987). *The West Indies: Patterns of development, culture, and environmental change since 1492*. Cambridge, UK: Cambridge University Press.

Caribou

Caribou is the North American term for the wild reindeer (*Rangifer tarandus*), which inhabits and migrates over vast areas of the circumpolar North. This same species, called simply "wild reindeer" on the Eurasian continent or "reindeer" in its domesticated variety, plays a key role for northern environments. It forms

Caribou bulls in velvet near the Bering Sea in Alaska. COURTESY JOHN SARVIS/U. S. FISH AND WILDLIFE SERVICE.

the dominant large mammal and herd species of the north, constituting a basic food resource to the wolf, lynx, and wolverine, at times even eagle and bear. Its own grazing and trampling of the tundra and taiga has enormous impact upon the northern flora. While herd increase can be explosive, so can population crashes be equally drastic, depending not necessarily on grazing depletion, but commonly on the "locking" of available grazing under heavy snow crusting. The species also holds a significant position with respect to the maintenance of human populations. Seven subspecies of *Rangifer tarandus* are recognized, but taken as a whole, the worldwide species population is estimated to be about 5 million. Their wide-spreading toed "feet" enable them to traverse deep snows, wet marshlands, and even to swim most effectively. They are also very buoyant in water, thanks to their air-filled tube-formed hairs, which also make their fur an excellent insulator against cold. During the bare-ground period they can eat a wide variety of green plants, and during the period of snow cover, they eat lichen, which they can smell through the snow and dig deep craters to reach. Both males and females grow antlers. Caribou are known to follow seasonally shifting migration routes over hundreds of miles in herds in the tens of thousands.

Rangifer tarandus (hereafter "reindeer") has served human purposes in a remarkable variety of ways. Reindeer have been trained as decoy animals to lure reindeer for the kill; they have been milked for the production of cheese; they have been used as pack animals for bare-ground transport and harnessed to sleds for winter use; they are also mounted and ridden. Not only do reindeer provide food, clothing, transport, and marketable commodities such as meat and antlers for medicinal purposes, they also have formed an essential basis on which many distinct hunting and pastoral cultures have developed.

Today special rights to hunt or herd reindeer compose fundamental aspects of indigenous resource use ranging from that of the Saami in the northwestern corner of Europe, eastward to the twenty–six so-called small peoples of the Russian north (as well as the larger ethnic groups of Komi and Yakut), and on across the Bering Sea to Alaska, where domestic reindeer stock and management skills were imported toward the close of the 1800s to save the native Inuit from conjectured starvation as a result of the crash of the caribou herds. Herding of domestic reindeer has spread to places in both Canada and Greenland as well, but the predominant economic benefit of the species for mankind in the New World has been and still is as an object of the hunt. In Eurasia on the other hand, the occasional swelling of wild reindeer herds poses a real threat to the continuity of herding practices, as the wild reindeer not infrequently sweep into the rangelands of domestic stock, mix, and carry away the reindeer herd. In Alaska, where reindeer herding never approached caribou hunting in either economic or cultural importance for the great majority of native people, the same phenomenon of range conflict between domesticated and wild herds does not attain the same critical proportions as in Eurasia. For hunters, the "comeback" of wild herds is regarded as a blessing. Moreover, reindeer hunting and herding are by no means necessarily separated in either time or place for the same people. The dynamics of wild and domestic herd fluctuations in combination with variable codifications of indigenous rights to reindeer in different nation states, along with the weight of cultural herding and/or hunting heritage, generate a wide array of impacts and survival strategies.

Hugh Beach

Further Reading

Banfield, A. (1961). *A revision of the reindeer and caribou genus rangifer*. National Museum of Canada. Bulletin No. 177.

Beach, H. (1990). Comparative systems of reindeer herding. In J. Galaty & D. Johnson, D. (Eds.), *The world of pastoralism: Herding systems in comparative perspective* (pp. 255–298). New York: Guilford Publications.

Ingold, T. (1980). *Hunters, pastoralists and ranchers*. Cambridge, UK: Cambridge University Press.

Carson, Rachel

(1907–1964)
Biologist and writer

Rachel Louise Carson was a biologist and writer whose work championed the ecological view that human beings are part of the natural world and that any abuse done to nature is reflected in harm to human life. She was born in Springdale, Pennsylvania, near Pittsburgh. Her family was poor, but her well-educated mother was a proponent of the nature study movement and nurtured in her youngest child a deep respect for the natural world and a love of literature. Carson read and contributed to *St. Nicholas Magazine* and won the first of several literary prizes at the age of ten.

She entered Pennsylvania College for Women, now Chatham College, in Pittsburgh, on a scholarship, determined to become a writer. But a required course in zoology and its brilliant professor, Mary Scott Skinker, inspired Carson to change her major to biology, a field in which there were few professional opportunities for women. She received her B.A. degree in 1929 and won a place at the Woods Hole Marine Biological Laboratory in Massachusetts, where she saw the sea for the first time and began a lifelong interest in its ecology. She entered Johns Hopkins University on a scholarship to study marine biology. While there she taught zoology at the college and at the Dental School of the University of Maryland, but she also worked in the genetics laboratory of Raymond Pearl, who influenced her scientific perspective. In 1932, Carson received her M.A., but the Great Depression and the death of her father and older sister in 1935 and 1937 necessitated the end of her graduate studies. She became financially responsible for her mother and her sister's two small children.

Biology Career Begins

Carson found part-time work as an aide at the U.S. Commerce Department's Bureau of Fisheries field office in Baltimore. There she wrote radio scripts for a series on marine life. At night she wrote natural history features for the *Baltimore Sunday Sun*. In 1936, Carson entered federal service as a junior aquatic biologist, one of two professional women at the Bureau of Fisheries, which became part of the U.S. Fish and Wildlife Service in 1939.

She gained literary notice with the publication of *Under the Sea-Wind* in 1941 and moved up the ranks of the service as an editor and information officer rather than a field scientist. By 1949, she was editor-in-chief of all U.S. Fish and Wildlife publications.

Her work at the U.S. Fish and Wildlife Service required her to have a broad knowledge of biology and natural science. She created a series of publications called "Conservation in Action" to highlight a new refuge system. The series was distinguished by its sensitivity to the interrelationships of wildlife and habitat and by its scientific accuracy. As editor, Carson was exposed to a broad range of research and reviewed the latest field trials. Her career in government provided a valuable perspective on the problems of managing the environment and enriched her personal connections with nature.

The increasing responsibilities of her job dramatically slowed the pace of her own writing. It took her ten years to synthesize the latest research on oceanography

> The "control of nature" is a phrase conceived in arrogance, born of the Neanderthal age of biology and philosophy, when it was supposed that nature exists for the convenience of man.
>
> —Rachel Carson, *Silent Spring*, p. 297

and to write her most popular book, *The Sea around Us* (1951), which garnered international acclaim. First serialized in the *New Yorker*, it remained on the *New York Times* best-seller list for a record eighty-six weeks. Through Carson's clear analysis of waves, tides, islands, and the deepest regions of the sea, readers were made aware of the fragile interdependence of life. *The Sea around Us* won the John Burroughs Medal and the National Book Award for 1952 and vaulted Carson to a preeminent position as a science writer. Carson followed in 1955 with *The Edge of the Sea*, which examined the ecology of sea and shore and was also a best-seller.

With her financial life secure, Carson left government service in 1952. As early as 1945, she had been skeptical of the benefits of the newly developed synthetic hydrocarbon pesticides, particularly DDT, (dichloro-diphenyl-trichloro-ethane), which were widely used in domestic agriculture in the United States. By 1957, she believed that the long-term effects of such chemical pesticides were potentially harmful to the whole biota (flora and fauna of a region). Her investigation of the subject took nearly four years and included the impact of pesticides on wildlife, especially birds, soil, water, and air. She found compelling evidence that certain cancers in humans were related to pesticide exposure.

Silent Spring Stirs Controversy

Silent Spring first appeared in 1962 in the *New Yorker*, where it caused a sensation. The chemical industry and the agricultural lobby rushed to judge Carson as an alarmist and a poor scientist. Industry attempts to prevent publication of the book failed, but Carson was maligned as a woman who had overstepped her bounds, and she was subjected to personal attack by industry and by some in government.

Silent Spring caught the attention of President John F. Kennedy, who called for an investigation of her claims. Carson testified before congressional committees urging federal and state regulation of pesticide control programs and the elimination of DDT use in domestic agriculture.

Acclaimed by the public, she received numerous scientific and literary awards, including the National Audubon Society medal and election to the American Academy of Arts and Sciences. Writing *Silent Spring* required moral and physical courage because during that time Carson battled breast cancer. She died in Silver Spring, Maryland, at age fifty-six, just eighteen months after publication of her most important book.

Rachel Carson inspired younger activists to demand greater environmental protection by government. Her work expanded the definition of the environment to include the interrelationships between humans and the rest of the living world. She is credited with beginning the contemporary environmental movement by democratizing science and calling for greater governmental vigilance. Her *The Sense of Wonder* was published posthumously in 1965. In it Carson urged adults to expose children to the wonders of nature as a source of lifelong enrichment. Carson was also awarded the Presidential Medal of Freedom posthumously by President Jimmy Carter in 1980.

Linda Lear

Further Reading

Carson, R. (1998). *The discovered writing of Rachel Carson* (L. Lear, Ed.). Boston: Beacon Press.

Carson, R. (2002). *Silent spring*. Boston: Houghton Mifflin.

Gottlieb, R. (1993). *Forcing the spring*. Washington, DC: Island Press.

Lear, L. (1997). *Rachel Carson: Witness for nature*. New York: Henry Holt.

Carver, George Washington

(c. 1863–1943)

U.S. agronomist

George Washington Carver was born a slave at Diamond Grove, Missouri. Orphaned as a baby, he was raised by his mother's owners. On their farm, Carver grew to have a keen interest in, and a gift for, understanding the workings of nature. As an African-American, he struggled to get an education, finally earning a master's degree in agriculture from Iowa State University in 1896. His professors, who included two future secretaries of agriculture, recognized that his genius in mycology (the study of fungi) came from a rare insight into habitats and symbiotic relationships. In Iowa he could have continued his research in hybridization as well as mycology, but he instead accepted a job as director of agriculture at Tuskegee Institute in rural Alabama. Founded by Booker T. Washington (1856–1915), the school was a leader in the education of black farmers and teachers.

When Carver arrived in Alabama, he soon realized that much of contemporary scientific agriculture could not possibly be duplicated by poor tenant farmers. Most black farmers worked other people's land for a share of the crops. Sharecroppers often had to borrow money to purchase food and supplies until the crops were harvested. Debtor laws trapped them in virtual peonage, making them stay with a landowner until they had paid all their debts. Such farmers could not afford cutting-edge technology. Carver therefore pioneered what would later be called appropriate technology and sustainability during his forty-seven years at the school.

Operating the only agricultural experiment station run entirely by African-Americans, Carver sought to keep all experiments within reach of "the poor tenant farmer with one-horse equipment" (McMurry 1981, 81). His teachings included green fertilization (the growing of ground cover that either enriches the soil as it grows, as with nitrogen-fixing crops, or does so when it is plowed under), crop rotation, composting, and use of readily available natural resources. Although he later became famous as a chemist who pioneered numerous peanut products, Carver initially sought to provide through "cookstove chemistry" alternatives to purchased goods to help break the cycle of debt. He taught sharecroppers to use easily grown crops for food, native clays for paints, and wild plants for landscaping, so that the sharecroppers could become as self-sufficient as possible. Peanuts were a good source of protein, so Carver provided recipes in experiment station bulletins to turn this soil-enriching plant into such commodities as a milk substitute, ink, coffee, and "chicken loaf." He provided similar recipes for other plants and taught how to preserve foods so they would last the winter.

A deeply religious man, Carver believed in the interconnection of all life and taught a reverence for the works of the "Great Creator." People, he taught, could harness but not defy the forces of nature. Speaking of conservation, he noted, "It is fundamental that nature will drive away those who commit sins against it" (Ferrell 1995, 30). His ideas caught the attention of Henry Ford, who made the professor his guest of honor at a conference in Dearborn, Michigan in 1937 of supporters of chemurgy, a movement which sought to find industrial uses for farm products. Carver became a hero of that movement. Business promoters tried to manufacture some of Carver's products, but most were readily created by consumers themselves and thus not commercially feasible. By the time he died on 5 January 1943, Carver had returned to his original vision, dedicating his waning years to establish the Carver Museum and Carver Foundation to preserve and continue his attempts to work with renewable and abundant resources to improve the lives of poor farmers.

Linda O. McMurry Edwards

Further Reading

Carver, G. W. (1905). *How to build up worn out soils* (Bulletin 6). [Pamphlet]. Tuskegee, AL: Tuskegee Institute Experiment Station.

Ferrell, J. S. (1995). *Fruits of creation: A look at global sustainability as seen through the eyes of George Washington Carver*. Shakopee, MN: Macalester Park Publishing Company.

Kremer, G. R. (Ed.). (1987). *George Washington Carver in his own words*. Columbia: University of Missouri Press.

McMurry, L. O. (1981). *George Washington Carver: Scientist and symbol*. New York: Oxford University Press.

Catholicism

Christians generally profess belief in a holy catholic church, with the term "catholic" meaning "universal," signifying the hope that people everywhere will become followers of Jesus. Christians believe Jesus to be the savior of humanity, the Christ (the Messiah, or "anointed one"), the Son of God, and indeed the incarnation or embodiment of God. All Christians profess to be catholic in the sense that they believe their faith is open to everyone. Today, however, the term Catholicism (with a capital C), more properly Roman Catholicism, refers to the Church of Rome led by the bishop of Rome, the pope. Catholics consider the pope to be the successor to St. Peter, one of the original twelve disciples of Jesus and the first leader of the early Christian church.

Christian and Catholic Beliefs

Roman Catholics makes up more than half the Christians in the world today, and estimates are that Catholics now comprise about 17 percent of all people on earth. Geographically, Catholics have been concentrated especially in Europe, and more recently in Latin America. In the United States, although the combined members of all the various Protestant Christian denominations still outnumber Catholics, the latter are that country's largest single religious denomination.

The Roman Catholic Church shares with other Christians the fundamental beliefs recited in the Nicene Creed: that there is only one God, that this one God is known to believers in a Trinitarian manner as Father, Son, and Holy Spirit; that God is the creator of all things seen and unseen; that the world and humans are in some way estranged from God, but that the love of God, expressed especially in the crucifixion and death of Jesus, has conquered that estrangement; that Jesus has been raised from the dead; that the Spirit of God has now been poured out so as to renew all creation; that sins have been forgiven, and that human beings will be raised up bodily by God after death so as to be finally united with the risen Christ.

Within the framework of their adherence to the central teachings of Christian tradition, Roman Catholics also emphasize the importance of seven sacraments. These are baptism, confirmation, reconciliation, Eucharist, marriage, holy orders and final anointing. The Eucharist ("thanksgiving"), is especially important: Catholics believe that bread and wine are transformed into the body and blood of Christ. The transformed bread and wine are then shared by the congregation in reenactment of the last meal that Jesus shared with his disciples. This sacrament is often called Communion, as Catholics believe that those who share in the body and blood of Christ share a most intimate communion with one another and with God.

What has distinguished Catholic Christianity from most of the Protestant sects, for whom the word of God is central, is Catholicism's emphasis on sacraments. Generally speaking, a sacrament is anything (water, bread, wine, oil, sunlight, rain, soil, life, etc.) through which a sacred or divine presence is made visible. It was especially through the wonders of nature that early in the history of religion all religious people first gained a sense of how a sacred reality influences the world. For example, the way in which the sun lights up the daytime world may be taken as a symbol of how divinity illuminates human existence. Historically, many religions have been heavily sacramental, and Catholicism has inherited this motif from its religious predecessors, often embracing and transforming their religious symbols and practices.

Sacramentality and Ecology

By the beginning of the twenty-first century a sacramental emphasis had become especially important among Catholic scholars, including especially feminist theologians, as a religious foundation for ecological responsibility. Thomas Berry, the world's best-known Catholic ecological visionary, has often emphasized that a rich sense of God depends upon the integrity of nature. If we lose nature, he argues, the religious sense of God will wither and die along with it. Berry, a Catholic priest and religious scholar, is the most prominent proponent of the sacramental approach. He even goes so far as to say that the universe is the "primary" revelation of God. His theology is quite in tune with the sacramental emphasis in Catholic tradition, but it gives a much more subordinate role to the Bible than do other approaches. The sacramental theme is also exemplified in the creation-centered theology associated with Matthew Fox—a Dominican priest turned Episcopalian—and in the ecological visions of feminist theologians who have observed a close connection between the death of nature and the social oppression of women.

If nature can be interpreted as a sacramental disclosure of God, then this implies that God is, for this stream of Catholicism, much more embodied and related to nature than is the case in other religions and other versions of Christianity. Advocates of the sacramental approach urge people today to listen attentively to native peoples, who have always experienced the sacred in nature. And they encourage ecologists also to look again at cultures of the Neolithic period, when the power and presence of the sacred apparently came into people's awareness through maternal representations and goddess figures. Since sacramental ecologists consider the roots of the ecological crisis to be intertwined with patriarchal (male-dominated) cultures, they often claim that people must learn to think once again of God in terms of feminine as well as masculine imagery. Because of its sacramental orientation, therefore, Catholic Christianity is said to be essentially, and not just incidentally, concerned with the well-being of the natural world.

Since the 1970s a considerable body of reflection on the relevance of religion to ecological concern has emerged in Catholic circles under the designation of ecological theology. One of the responsibilities of the discipline of theology is to scan religious traditions to determine whether and how they may illuminate and respond to contemporary concerns. In the case of ecological issues the task has not always been easy, since the integrity of the natural world was not a major preoccupation during the emergence of Christianity as a dominant world religion. In fact, at times Catholic Christianity has shown little concern for the well-being of the nonhuman natural world. However, by the end of the twentieth century it was beginning to undergo a "green revolution."

Catholic theologians have discovered a wealth of ecologically relevant material in the religious classics of their own tradition. They have gone far beyond simply repeating the familiar biblical exhortation to responsible stewardship of the natural world. A growing body of Catholic ecological theology now hopes to make a difference in the shaping of environmental policy.

This theology begins with the assumption that what ecological responsibility needs first and foremost is a recognition that the nonhuman natural world is valuable in itself. This means that nature must be seen as more than mere "stuff" to be shaped into human projects. Insofar as nature is sacramental—transparent to the sacred—it is worth saving even apart from its utility for humans.

Church Statements on Faith and the Environment

In a message delivered on 1 January 1990, Pope John Paul II spoke of the world's ecological crisis as a moral issue. He condemned the reckless exploitation of natural resources and asserted that a refusal to respect nature is a threat to world peace. He then exhorted his followers to undertake a change of lifestyle and engage in environmental education.

In 1991, the U.S. National Conference of Catholic Bishops issued a pastoral letter entitled *Renewing the Earth* with the purpose of awakening a spirituality and religious ethic sensitive to environmental issues. Emphasizing that environmental matters are religious and

moral in nature, the letter states that the ecological crisis requires nothing less than a complete change of heart in order to save the planet. Similar exhortations have appeared in Catholic conferences in other countries. In June of 2001, the American Catholic bishops also issued a statement on the dangers of global climate change: "Global Climate Change: A Plea for Dialogue, Prudence and the Common Good." The document argued that the United States, the world's heaviest producer of greenhouse gases, must play a special role in addressing the planetary problem.

Most significantly, official Catholic statements have emphasized that the relief of ecological damage is inseparable from issues of social and economic justice, locally and globally. Catholic ecological teaching consistently maintains that unless and until economic justice reigns over the entire earth, ecological problems will not disappear. It also implies that Catholics must now connect questions concerning the life and dignity of the human person to the wider fabric of terrestrial life as a whole. The American bishops noted that there is a single web of life and that the mistreatment of nature diminishes human life along with other kinds.

Catholic ecological theologians have applauded this linking of ecology to concerns for justice (eco-justice), but many of them contend that neither the pope nor the world's bishops have realistically faced the fact that ecological problems are exacerbated by the sheer pressure of human numbers.

Renewing the Earth also declared explicitly that the fundamental ecological virtue is *hope*. Hope is essential because the bleakness that shows up on the ecological horizon is sometimes overwhelming. It can easily tempt religious believers to a world-despising escapism. Quoting the famous Jesuit poet Gerard Manley Hopkins, *Renewing the Earth* invited American Catholics always to look for "the dearest freshness deep down things." There is never a good reason to stop hoping, even when, to quote from "God's Grandeur," a poem by Hopkins, "all is seared with trade; bleared, smeared with toil." Theologically interpreted, this has been taken to mean that a realistic hope neither denies the harsh realities of the present nor gives itself over to premature flight from the world. Instead, hope inspires an ethic that prepares the world for an indefinite and incalculable future.

Catholic teaching and theology also emphasize the ecological significance of the doctrine of the incarnation, whereby God is believed to have become fully embodied in the life of Christ. Since the "body of Christ" is composed of the same atomic and molecular stuff that make up the rest of the universe, there is an inseparable connection between God and matter. Thus the doctrine of the incarnation allows humans to give thanks that they are a part of nature. A dualistic, world-escaping piety that separates matter from spirit has influenced much of Christianity, but the incarnational and sacramental emphasis in Catholic teaching and theology implicitly affirms the union of God and nature. In this regard, Pope John Paul II's official acknowledgment of the evidence for biological evolution is not without ecological implications. It is a fundamental axiom of ecological ethics that humans must learn to feel deeply that they belong to nature. Religion, however, at times seems to have detached humans from earth, locating them essentially in a spiritual world beyond nature. In the world of science, on the other hand, probably no idea makes humans more aware of their belonging to nature than that of evolution. Evolutionary biology, genetics, and cosmology have drawn the connection of human existence to the rest of life and the whole universe much more tightly than previous ages were able to do.

Catholic thought has become increasingly comfortable with evolutionary science, though not without considerable resistance at times. In the twentieth century the adventurous religious thought of the Jesuit geologist Teilhard de Chardin (1881–1955) in particular made it possible for many Catholics to embrace evolution with great enthusiasm. Although ecological considerations did not enter formally into Teilhard's voluminous reflections, his ideas have had a major impact on the "greening" of Catholic as well as much Protestant theology. What Teilhard emphasized to his fellow Christians was that they could love the earth deeply without being anxious that they are thereby turning their backs on God. He justified this exhortation by way of a creative synthesis of evolutionary ideas and incarnational theology.

For centuries Catholics and other Christians had often (though not always) assumed that the natural world was a stage for the human drama, or a "soul school" in which people are supposed to prepare for the journey to heaven. Nature, it is true, was also viewed by such luminaries as St. Francis of Assisi, Thomas Aquinas, and Hildegaard of Bingen as a sacramental manifestation of the creator, and therefore as something to be revered. But in some of the more mystical strains of Christian piety the earth was more a point of departure for the spiritual journey to the next world than something that humans should take special pains to preserve here and now.

Especially since the time of the Second Vatican Council (1962–1965), however, Catholic thought has emphasized that there can be no salvation of humans apart from the renewal of the entire universe. And because of its firm belief in the intimate presence of God's Spirit in creation, Christian faith allows itself to be animated by a hope for the new creation of *this* world. In contemporary Catholic teaching, religious hope does not look for an eventual substitution of another world for this one. So the hope for resurrection implies not only that the human body must be respected here and now, but that the entire natural context in which living bodies abide deserves a religious reverence.

John Haught

Further Reading

Berry, T. (1988). *The dream of the earth.* San Francisco: Sierra Club Books.

Edwards, D. (1995). *Jesus the wisdom of God: An ecological theology.* Maryknoll, NY: Orbis Books.

Haught, J. F. (1993). *The promise of nature.* New York: Paulist Press.

McDonagh, S. (1990). *The greening of the church.* New York: Orbis Books.

Ruether, R. R. (Ed.). (2000). *Christianity and ecology: Seeking the well-being of Earth and humans.* Cambridge, MA: Harvard University Press.

Smith, P. (1997).*What are they saying about environmental ethics?* Mahwah, NJ: Paulist Press.

Catlin, George

(1796–1872)
U.S. painter

Born in Wilkes-Barre, Pennsylvania, George Catlin abandoned an early law career for art, through which he explored a lifelong passion for the natural world and its inhabitants. Apparently—his myth-making left his biography a challenge—Catlin had ambitions as a history painter but his earliest portraits were lackluster and so he decided to exploit the uncompetitive niche as a painter of Indians. Determined to capture Indians first-hand on canvas, Catlin went west in the 1830s, where he encountered many.

Catlin's output, generated by his habit of sketching in the field and filling in details later, was prodigious:

one wag supposedly remarked that he was the fastest brush in the West. His strength was people's faces, but he was lackadaisical about bodily proportions, poses, and features. His landscapes, including early scenes like a bird's-eye panorama of Niagara Falls, were notable. His western spaces range from green prairie grasses and rolling hills to striking representations of Missouri River shoreline, are animated with buffaloes and other animals (as well as Indians), and reflect his transcendental emotions concerning nature.

In 1837, Catlin opened an Indian gallery in New York, charging admission to see nearly 500 paintings and Indian artifacts, and to hear his lectures. He took his show on the road but interest flagged, and he hoped to no avail that Congress would purchase his collection. In 1839 he moved to Europe where the boom-and-bust pattern repeated itself. Imprisoned for unpaid debts, Catlin was rescued by a wealthy American who purchased the collection of paintings held by his creditors. Later, Catlin produced 300 copies or adaptations of the originals from cartoons, or pencil and ink drawings, as the core of a new 600-painting collection. He returned to the United States in 1870 but died two years later. In 1879, his benefactor's heirs gave the original paintings to the Smithsonian Institution and much of the cartoon collection ultimately followed.

Catlin was a romantic and primitivist. In his day, most Americans of European descent regarded Indians as an impediment to manifest destiny, their traditional lives to be in inevitable decline, and their future to lie in "civilized" agrarian pursuits. Catlin agreed that American Indians were vanishing, but he also insisted that their natural state was noble and worthy. His thoughts about civilization's corrupting influence were acerbic. Not surprisingly, others criticized Catlin for being blind to the fullness of Indian lives and characters.

Catlin secured a place in the annals of environmental history not simply because of his paintings, but for his "melancholy contemplation" in the 1830s on the demise of buffaloes and Indians: "And what a splendid contemplation too, when one . . . imagines them as they *might* in future be seen, . . . preserved in their pristine beauty and wildness, in a *magnificent park*, where the world could see for ages to come, the native Indian in his classic attire, galloping his wild horse . . . amid the fleeting herds of elks and buffaloes. . . . A *nation's Park*, containing man and beast, in all the wild and freshness of their nature's beauty!" (Catlin 1973, 261–262).

As romantic, paternalistic, ethnocentric, and appropriative as these ideas may seem today, Catlin was both a creature of and decades ahead of his time. Many scoffed at his romantic vision, and his words about a national park fell on deaf ears, but sentiments like his grew and eventually led to the policy which established Yellowstone as the first national park in 1872. Catlin hoped that his epitaph would commemorate him as the founder of a national park; but today he is known mainly as a painter of Indian portraits and as the person who gave his name to the red steatite (catlinite) quarried by the Sioux to be used as pipestone.

Shepard Krech III

Further Reading

Catlin, G. (1973). *Letters and notes on the manners, customs, and conditions of North American Indians* (2 vols.). New York: Dover.

Dippie, B. W. (1990). *Catlin and his contemporaries: The politics of patronage.* Lincoln: University of Nebraska Press.

Mitchell, L. C. (1981). *Witnesses to a vanishing America: The nineteenth-century response.* Princeton, NJ: Princeton University Press.

Truettner, W. (1979). *The natural man observed.* Washington, DC: Smithsonian Institution Press.

Central America

History and environment go hand in hand in Central America, which consists of Belize, Guatemala, El Salvador, Honduras, Nicaragua, Costa Rica, and Panama. These seven small countries form an isthmus—an area roughly the size of Italy—that connects South America with North America. The isthmus is one of the most distinctive places in the world because it is a bridge between two continents and two oceans (the Atlantic and the Pacific). It was formed during the Pliocene epoch (3–4 million years ago) when an uplift united a small archipelago into a narrow landmass. Dominating this bridge is a range of volcanic mountains that has been a barrier to transportation and communication. The volcanoes are as high as 4,267 meters, and some remain active. On their slopes exist different life zones (regions characterized by specific plants and animals), ranging from dry deciduous forests to wet tropical forests and, in the higher elevations, cloud forests. A lack of major navigable rivers has also hindered travel and communication throughout the region.

Central America's two coasts have different climates and ecosystems. The Atlantic side has tropical lowland plains with high rainfall, dense forests, and banana plantations. The Pacific side is dryer and historically was covered with deciduous forest, although today most of that has been cleared for farmland and pastures. The variety of elevations and tropical life zones, combined with the region's being both intercontinental and interoceanic, created a high degree of biodiversity (biological diversity as indicated by numbers of species of animals and plants). There are hundreds of species of birds, mammals, fishes, reptiles, and amphibians, thousands of species of plants, and literally hundreds of thousands of species of insects. Many of these life forms are endemic to the region (found there and nowhere else).

Between the mountains exist many valleys and plateaus, where most of the region's cities are found. The coastal regions have few good ports or deep harbors, and the heat, humidity, insects, and tropical storms retarded urban development there. But even in the valleys residents were exposed to a variety of natural disasters such as earthquakes and volcanic eruptions. As one Costa Rican historian has written, "living with earthquakes and volcanoes has been an inescapable part of Central American life for centuries" (Pérez-Brignoli 1989, 2).

Indigenous Mesoamerica (Middle America)

In this diverse environmental setting lived a variety of peoples who learned to survive and create vibrant cultures. Although some anthropologists claim that Asian people migrated to the region thirty to forty thousand years ago, many native peoples believe that they originated from a specific place within the region—that they have always been there. Either way, the region became densely populated in Belize, Guatemala, and Honduras by people under the hegemony of Mayan culture and less densely populated in El Salvador and Nicaragua by Pipil and Nicarao natives who trace their roots to the Nahua (Aztecs) from Mexico. Along the Caribbean coast of Honduras and Nicaragua live the Miskito native peoples, and in Costa Rica and Panama a variety of native peoples (such as the Guaymí and Cabécar) were related to tribes from South America and formed more nomadic societies than the sedentary, technologically advanced Maya.

The Maya, who today still speak over fifty dialects, formed an advanced civilization based on city-states that were only loosely unified. Individual cities such as Tikal (in Guatemala) or Copán (in Honduras), which were also ceremonial centers with great temples and pyramids, retained their own self-rule. Sustaining such large population centers meant developing an agricultural system that provided enough food for the residents and surplus for lean times. Corn (maize), which became the vital staple of this system, was grown under a slash-and-burn cultivation system. Also called "swidden agriculture," the system required the clearing and burning of forests for cornfields (milpas). Between cornrows, the natives planted nitrogen-fixing beans whose vines could climb the corn stalks, and squashes whose leaves provided shade cover for the beans and acted as a natural pest control. This efficient intercropping system was used throughout the Americas and helped native peoples survive for thousands of years. Native peoples also supplemented their diet with a variety of fruits, vegetables, fish, mammals (especially deer), and chocolate from cacao.

Nature figured prominently in Mayan cosmology (a branch of metaphysics that deals with the nature of the universe). The ceiba tree was thought to hold up the four corners of the world and was also the tree under which people's souls went after they died. Thus, many Mayan people planted the trees in their homes and plazas and would not cut them down in the forests—a practice continued today. Likewise, animals such as the jaguar were considered deities.

But all native groups in Central America left their mark on the environment. Although many pre-Columbian native peoples maintained a sustainable population suitable to their environments, clearing great sections of the forests for milpas and cities could have been part of the reason for the eventual decline of the Maya. Scholars are not in complete agreement on this point, but some research shows how the Maya exceeded their carrying capacity (the population that an area will support without deterioration), which helped cause the collapse of their cities prior to the arrival of Europeans. But overall for the region it is a question of scale and lifestyle. Most indigenous groups were small enough to avoid exceeding their resources, but if in areas they did, they simply moved to other areas to allow natural replenishment to occur.

Arrival of Europeans and the Colonial Period

European explorers with different perspectives on the environment entered this world in the early sixteenth century. Columbus, on his fourth trip to the New World in 1502, explored Central America's Atlantic coast and named part of it "Costa Rica" (rich coast) for the wealth he was hoping to find. That mentality of extracting riches underscored the European attitudes about nature. Columbus also left a legacy of naming places in Spanish, and he collected a great deal of geographical data for the Crown. Meanwhile, Vasco Núñez de Balboa and his men crossed the isthmus of Panama in 1513 and "discovered" the Pacific Ocean. That set in motion Spain's need to secure the isthmus as a strategic crossing point in its trade of gold from Peru to Europe.

The Spaniards established cities in the region as early as 1519 to service the needs of incoming settlers and to serve as garrisons for Spanish control of the land. The cities were built in great part by local native peoples whom the Spaniards had brutally enslaved. But with such ventures came what caused perhaps the most enduring biological change to the region: diseases. What has been called "the Columbian exchange" (Crosby 1972, 2) includes the microbial invasion from Europe that caused epidemics of diseases such as smallpox, typhus, dysentery, pneumonia, and the plague to decimate native populations who had built up no immunities to the diseases.

Unlike mineral-rich Mexico and Peru, Central America was seen as a kind of backwater by Europeans during the colonial period (1500–1800). Thus, the region did not attract as many immigrants as other parts of the Spanish empire. But those who did move there discovered that Central America had other commodities to export. Indigo and cochineal dyes were in high demand in Europe and became Central America's first colonial exports. Later sugar, cotton, and tobacco became important crops. But these monocrops altered the environmental and social landscapes. They required huge conversion of native vegetation and were dependent on a slave labor system that the Spaniards introduced. Known as the *encomienda*, Spanish planters were "entrusted" with native peoples to work the fields and tend the cattle. The idea of private land ownership was in complete contrast to the native communal farming system.

But certainly not all of Central America was changed in this way. The Spanish preferred to settle in climates and terrains that reminded them of home, such as the central valley of Costa Rica and the highlands of Guatemala. In those places, referred to as "neo-Europes" (Crosby 1986, 134), Spaniards could create wheat and barley fields, olives and fruit orchards, vineyards, and cattle pastures to provide them with the commodities they were used to in Europe.

The coastal lowlands and montane (relating to the biogeographic zone of moist, cool upland slopes below the timberline dominated by large coniferous trees) forests were no good for this kind of agriculture and were thus avoided.

Independence and the Nineteenth Century

Independence came to Central America in 1821. After a two-year period of incorporation by Mexico (when Chiapas elected to remain with that country), leaders in the region formed the United Provinces of Central America with Guatemala City as the capital. Unity, however, was fleeting—Guatemalan predominance, territorial jealousies, and the environment itself thwarted its success. The mountainous terrain and slow communications prevented political cohesion, so that by 1838 Nicaragua and Costa Rica had withdrawn from the union, and the other three provinces followed their lead soon after. Thus five small nations emerged on the isthmus, with Guatemala having the greatest population (660,000) and Costa Rica the smallest (70,000).

The new nations and the majority of the people in them were poor. Because the region lacked large quantities of natural resources, most Central Americans maintained a subsistence economy. That changed in the 1850s when Europeans saw that the volcanic soil of the highlands and plateaus was perfect for the production of coffee beans. The coffee industry thrived, setting Central America on an even more export-dependent pathway and converting a great many hillsides in Guatemala, El Salvador, and Costa Rica into coffee plantations. The pattern was accelerated with the introduction of bananas in the late nineteenth century. To meet a growing demand for the fruit, U.S. investors converted millions of acres of coastal lowlands into banana plantations, developed railroads around the region to bring the fruit to ports, and established a multinational export network. Leading this effort was the United Fruit Company, which by 1910 came to control 75 percent of the international banana trade and made Costa Rica the world's largest banana producer. Honduras and Guatemala became close competitors. But sigatoka (a leaf blight) and Panama disease (a root fungus), which thrive in plantation settings, destroyed many thousands of acres, causing the banana producers to move on and convert other lowland areas into plantations.

Much of this late nineteenth- and early twentieth-century development was spawned by a belief in positivism. Positivism, advanced by economists in Europe, holds private property, scientific education, technological advancement, and modernization in high regard, which meant for Central America a large degree of foreign investment to pay for such changes. The foreign investment set in motion a tradition of becoming dependent on outside areas for local development projects, which, as in the case with bananas, often brought severe environmental change.

The Twentieth Century

Construction of the Panama Canal in the early twentieth century created one of the biggest environmental changes in Central America. Opened in 1914, the canal was an engineering masterpiece and was viewed by Americans as an important commercial and military advantage. But no one seemed to worry about the environmental impact of digging the ditch and creating locks, dams, and diversion weirs in this tropical and biologically sensitive area.

The canal not only transformed the isthmus but also set the stage for an even larger U.S. presence in the region. That presence was manifested in policies that supported Central American leaders (often dictators) friendly to U.S. business. Like their positivism-oriented predecessors, these leaders were eager to continue modernization and development schemes that hastened economic growth but that did not benefit the majority of the people of their countries. Such were the cases especially in Nicaragua, El Salvador, and Guatemala in the early and middle parts of the century. In Guatemala, United Fruit's empire was threatened when Jacobo Arbenz, an avowed socialist with plans to nationalize foreign holdings via land reform, was elected president in 1950. His land reform efforts were cut short, however, when the United States acted on behalf of United Fruit and on the fear that Arbenz represented a "communist" threat to the region. The Central Intelligence Agency engineered a coup that ousted Arbenz and propped up a government friendlier to U.S. interests. The result was the beginning of a thirty-year civil war that left hundreds of thousands of Guatemalans dead and the land scorched from constant warfare.

Other wars and revolutions in the region in the 1970s and 1980s had similar causes and effects. As one scholar has explained, the root of these upheavals "can be summed up in one word: land" (Weinberg 1991, 5). The inequitable uses and ownership of land and resources prompted revolts for political and economic reforms in Nicaragua and El Salvador in those years. And while the revolts raged, prolonged in Nicaragua by U.S. support of the Contras (counterrevolutionaries opposed to Sandinista government that came to power in 1979 by ousting the Somoza dictatorship), great damage was done to the tropical forests and agricultural fields.

Thus there has been a move to conserve tropical resources and environments. Costa Rica has been a regional leader in this move, with over 25 percent of its land dedicated to preservation through national parks and biological reserves. There are many pressures (i.e., logging, mineral exploration, cattle grazing) on this "model," but it at least represents a framework for future environmental protection. Costa Ricans have also been at the forefront of inventorying their biodiversity with the understanding that to protect nature means first understanding what biological resources they have. But to make the parks "pay their way," ecotourism is now a flourishing industry but also puts other pressures on the environment in some, although perhaps gentler, ways. Belize, Guatemala, Panama, and Nicaragua are also marketing their tropical beauty and archeological riches to foreign tourists.

Outlook for the Twenty-First Century

Tourism, now the leading industry in Costa Rica and growing in other nations, will need to be monitored closely for its environmental side effects. Central Americans are also concerned about energy production and consumption, improved tropical conservation, effects of export agriculture (including chemical pesticide dependence), and mining. Each nation has a department of *medio ambiente* (environment) or natural resources with many of these issues to monitor. They are all strapped for economic resources, however, and thus there has been much international attention from nongovernmental organizations to assist in the environmental protection of such an ecologically diverse and rich region.

Likewise, urban issues such as congestion, sprawl, pollution, expanding greenbelts and parks, improving mass transit, and dealing with waste and recycling are all urgent issues facing Central American cities, especially as they continue to grow rapidly. Millions of *campesinos* (rural farm workers) migrate to Guatemala City, San Salvador, Tegucigalpa, San Pedro Sula, Managua, San Jose, and Panama City each year looking for work and a better life. They often do not find these, however, as they are forced to live in marginalized housing or slums without access to public services.

Thus municipal and national leaders have many responsible planning challenges ahead.

Sterling Evans

See also Biological Exchanges; Caribbean; Mexico

Further Reading

Adams, R. E. W. (1991). *Prehistoric Mesoamerica*. Norman: University of Oklahoma Press.

Barry, T. (1987). *Roots of rebellion: Land and hunger in Central America*. Boston: South End Press.

Barry, T., & Preusch, D. (1986). *The Central America fact book*. New York: Grove Press.

Barzetti, V., & Rovinski, R. (Eds.). (1992). *Toward a green Central America: Integrating conservation and development*. West Hartford, CT: Kumarian Press.

Brockett, C. D. (1998). *Land, power, and poverty: Agrarian transformation and political conflict in Central America*. Boulder, CO: Westview Press.

Carrasco, D. (1990). *Religions of Mesoamerica*. San Francisco: Harper-San Francisco.

Castro Herrera, G. (1996). *Naturaleza y sociedad en la historia de latinoamérica* [Nature and society in Latin American history]. Panama City, Panama: CELA.

Coatsworth, J. H. (1994). *Central America and the United States: The clients and the colossus*. New York: Twayne Publishers.

Collins, J. (1986). *Nicaragua: What difference could a revolution make (food and farming in the new Nicaragua)*. New York: Grove Press.

Collinson, H. (Ed.). (1997). *Green guerrillas: Environmental conflicts and initiatives in Latin America and the Caribbean*. Montreal, Canada: Black Rose Books.

Crosby, A. W. (1972). *The Columbian exchange: Biological and cultural consequences of 1492*. Westport, CT: Greenwood Press.

Crosby, A. W. (1986). *Ecological imperialism: The biological expansion of Europe, 900–1900*. Cambridge, UK: Cambridge University Press.

Evans, S. (1999). *The green republic: A conservation history of Costa Rica*. Austin: University of Texas Press.

Franke, J. (1993). *Costa Rica's national parks and preserves: A visitor's guide*. Seattle, WA: Mountaineers.

Karnes, T. L. (1961). *The failure of union: Central America, 1824–1960*. Chapel Hill: University of North Carolina Press.

LaFeber, W. (1993). *Inevitable revolutions: The United States in Central America*. New York: W. W. Norton.

McCollough, D. (1977). *The path between the seas: The creation of the Panama Canal, 1870–1914*. New York: Simon and Schuster.

Meza Ocampo, T. A. (1999). *Costa Rica: Naturaleza y sociedad*. [Costa Rica: Nature and society]. Cartago, Costa Rica: Editorial Tecnológica de Costa Rica.

Pérez-Brignoli, H. (1989). *A brief history of Central America*. Berkeley & Los Angeles: University of California Press.

Schlesinger, S., & Kinzer, S. (1999). *Bitter fruit: The story of the American coup in Guatemala*. Cambridge, MA: Harvard University Press.

Wallace, D. R. (1992). *The quetzal and the macaw: The story of Costa Rica's national parks*. San Francisco: Sierra Club Books.

Weinberg, B. (1991). *War on the land: Ecology and politics in Central America*. London: Zed Books.

Woodward, R. L. (1985). *Central America: A nation divided*. New York: Oxford University Press.

Chang River

The Chang (Yangtze) River is the longest river in China and one of the country's most important waterways. From its headwaters in the Tibetan Plateau, the Chang stretches eastward more than 6,276 kilometers before emptying into the Pacific Ocean near the industrial port city of Shanghai. It is fed by over three thousand smaller tributaries and covers a watershed of almost 1.8 million square kilometers. In its upper reaches the river flows through mountainous terrain marked by numerous rapids and gorges. After crossing through the Chang Gorges region (also known as the Three Gorges region), about 1000 kilometers inland from the coast, the Chang becomes much wider and gentler for the remainder of its length.

Over 350 million people, around one-third of China's total population, live within the boundaries of the Chang River valley, and the river runs through many of China's largest cities, including Chongqing, Wuhan, and Nanjing. The Chang has been an important trade route for thousands of years, and it is navigable by ocean-going vessels up to the Three Gorges region. It also flows through many of China's most fertile and highly developed agricultural areas and provides irrigation for thousands of square kilometers of farmland. The floodplains in Jiangsu Province at the mouth of the Chang are an especially important center of rice production.

The Chang River valley has been prone to extensive flooding throughout China's recorded history, with major floods occurring once every ten years on average. During the twentieth century the region was hit by particularly devastating floods in 1931 and 1954, both of which killed tens of thousands of people. China's recent economic development has compounded the problem. Not only has deforestation in the hinterland created significantly higher erosion levels, but also many of China's new industrial centers have sprung up within the flood zone along the river's lower reaches. Despite government flood control efforts, the river flooded again in 1991 and 1998, causing significant property damage. In an effort to solve the problem and promote industrial development in the region, the Chinese government has launched a mammoth hydroelectric dam project at the Three Gorges site. When completed, the controversial project will be the world's largest dam and create a 650-kilometer-long reservoir that will require the relocation of more than 1 million people.

With increased industrial development along its banks, the Chang has also experienced significantly rising pollution levels in recent years. The river currently receives almost half of China's industrial sewage, much of which is untreated. Although the government announced a series of new environmental protection measures in the 1980s and 1990s, more than 21 billion metric tons of industrial waste and sewage were discharged into the Chang in 2000. In addition to causing serious health problems for the region's inhabitants, the increased pollution levels also threaten several of the river's indigenous species, including the Baiji dolphin and the Chinese river sturgeon.

James H. Lide

Further Reading

Cannon, T., & Jenkins, A. (Eds.). (1990). *The geography of contemporary China: The impact of Deng Xioping's decade.* New York: Routledge.

Chao, S. (1994). *Geography of China: Environment, resources, population, and development.* New York: John Wiley.

Edmonds, R. L. (1994). *Patterns of China's lost harmony: A survey of the country's environmental degradation and protection.* New York: Routledge.

Geping, Q., & Jinchang, L. (1994). *Population and the environment in China.* Boulder, CO: Lynne Rienner.

Leeming, F. (1993). *The changing geography of China.* Cambridge, MA: Blackwell.

Chávez, César
(1927–1993)
U.S. labor leader

"César Chávez was the most important Latino leader this country has ever seen," wrote filmmakers Rick Tejada-Flores and Ray Telles. In part, "his greatness was that his vision reached out to touch millions of Americans—not just Mexican Americans, but ordinary people of all sorts." As founder and leader of the United Farm Workers union and an uncompromising promoter of social justice and environmental protection, he forged a connection "between the haves and the have-nots [that] created a remarkable moment in American history—an era in which people who would not normally meet connected and worked together to correct terrible injustices" (Ferriss & Sandoval 1997, ix–x). Born near Yuma, Arizona, Chávez grew up in a family who lost its small farm and business during the Great Depression and became migrant farmworkers in California. There he experienced hard work, terrible living conditions, poor pay, the uncertainty and lack of opportunity faced by all migrants, and, as a Mexican American, the racism and segregation endured by all minorities in pre-civil rights America. Forced to drop out of school after the eighth grade, he was profoundly influenced by these experiences and by his mother's teachings of social justice and nonviolence.

After a brief (1944–1946) stint in the U.S. Navy, Chávez returned to Delano, California, married Helen Fabela in 1948, and eventually fathered eight children. The Community Service Organization (CSO), an important vehicle to empower the powerless, hired Chávez and enabled him to develop his organizing skills. While fighting for the rights of local farmworkers, accompanied by social activists Dolores Huerta and Gilbert Padilla, Chávez learned the importance of boycotts, marches, political lobbying, and the use of religious symbols to win adherents and achieve justice for workers. He left the CSO in 1962, however, when its policy board refused to allow him to organize agricultural workers. Working with Huerta and others, Chávez formed the Farm Workers Association (FWA) that year.

Delano Grape Strike

In the famous Delano grape strike (1965–1970), the FWA joined with the AFL-CIO–affiliated Agricultural Workers Organizing Committee (AWOC) to demand recognition and contracts from the powerful California grape producers. Presenting the strike as part of a national movement for greater social justice and workers' civil rights, Chávez employed tactics of nonviolence, civil disobedience, coalition building, massive protest marches, and nationwide boycotts to win national support and recognition.

The decade of the 1970s proved difficult for Chávez and the United Farm Workers (UFW), as the union was called after 1973. Confronting challenges from the growers-backed Teamsters union, charges of mismanagement and incompetence, and the companies' refusal to renew contracts, the union called more strikes, some punctuated with violence as corporate agriculture stiffened its resistance. Despite sympathetic support from Governor Jerry Brown and Chávez's efforts to establish the state Agricultural Labor Relations Board (ALRB), which brought about government supervision of elections and collective bargaining, strife in the fields continued. Dissension emerged within the union over Chávez's management style, resulting in the disruption of long-term friendships and the defection of key leaders. UFW membership began to decline. With Ronald Reagan's election to the presidency, the 1980s proved especially difficult for unions in general and for the UFW in particular.

Pesticide Threats

Chávez was well aware of the dangers posed by exposure to pesticides used in the fields. In the late 1960s he had encouraged young farmworkers and activists to study medicine and return as doctors and nurses to help their fellow farmworkers protect themselves from the health threats posed by working around such chemicals. The union's pressure in the mid-1980s led Monterey County, California, to enact some of the toughest laws in the nation regulating pesticide use, and raised "the consciousness of everyone, including the farmers" (Ferriss & Sandoval 1997, 234). His controversial documentary film *The Wrath of Grapes* and his thirty-six-day fast in 1988 focused the nation's attention on the use of pesticides in food production.

The Significance of Chávez and His Work

In 1990 the president of Mexico awarded César Chávez that country's highest award given to a foreigner. While in San Luis, Arizona, not far from his birthplace, Chávez died in his sleep on 23 April 1993. In 1994 President William Clinton posthumously awarded him America's highest civilian honor, the Medal of Freedom.

Chávez's importance goes beyond organizing farmworkers and giving them some control over their lives. His goal was greater than that. "We have to build more clinics and coops, [and] . . . to participate in the governing of towns and school boards. We have to make our influence felt everywhere and anywhere" (Levy 1975, 537). Besides helping to inspire the Chicano civil rights movement of the 1960s, he got people from other ethnic groups and other classes involved in working for social justice and increasing awareness of the dangers posed by pesticides used in food production.

Errol D. Jones

Further Reading

Ferriss, S., & Sandoval, R. (1997). *The fight in the fields: Cesar Chavez and the farmworkers movement.* New York: Harcourt Brace.

Griswold del Castillo, R., & Garcia, R. (1995). *César Chávez: A triumph of spirit.* Norman: University of Oklahoma Press.

Hammerback, J. C., & Jensen. R. J. (1998). *The rhetorical career of César Chávez.* College Station: Texas A&M University Press.

Levy, J. (1975). *Cesar Chavez: Autobiography of La Causa.* New York: W. W. Norton.

Matthiessen, P. (1969). *Sal Si Puedes: Cesar Chavez and the new American Revolution.* New York: Random House.

Tejada-Flores, R., & Telles, R. (Producers). (1997). *The fight in the fields: Cesar Chavez and the farmworkers struggle* [Motion picture]. United States: Paradigm Productions.

Chesapeake Bay

Chesapeake Bay is America's largest estuary and, as such, has played an important role in the nation's economic, political, and environmental history. Bounded by Virginia and Maryland, the bay is 297 kilometers long but only 56 kilometers at its greatest width. Draining a watershed of over 155,000 square kilometers, which covers portions of six states, the bay flows to the Atlantic Ocean through a 27-kilometer-wide opening just north of Cape Henry, Virginia, at the bay's southern extreme. Although the bay is large, with several thousand kilometers of shoreline, it is not deep. The average depth is just over 6 meters, with its deepest point only 53 meters. With many marshes and wetlands, the bay is home to approximately thirty-five hundred species of plants and animals, including over three hundred species of fish. Its waters are vital to seasonal bird migrations along the Atlantic seaboard.

Chesapeake Bay's name was derived from a Native American term meaning "Great Shellfish Bay," and the bay has always played a prominent role in American history. Along its wide tributaries the English established their earliest settlements in the seventeenth century, the bay's abundant resources first noted by the famed Jamestown colonist John Smith. The emergent colonies developed extensive fishing industries, and the area's reputation was solidified not only by tobacco but also by extensive crab and oyster populations. Protected from coastal storms, port cities such as Norfolk, Virginia, and Baltimore, Maryland, prospered and remain terminals of trade with Europe and the rest of the world. Today a growing population of over 15 million people live in the bay's watershed, their economy still largely dependent upon the bay. Approximately 90 million metric tons of imports and exports pass through its major ports annually. Recreation and tourism are critical to the local economies, and the shipbuilding industry in the Hampton Roads area is one of the largest in the world. Norfolk is home to one of the world's largest naval bases.

Centuries of growth, however, have threatened the fragile ecosystem of the bay. Today the federal Environmental Protection Agency includes the bay on its list of impaired waterways, its most damaged tributaries including the Patapsco, Anacostia, and Elizabeth Rivers. With environmental regulations over the last thirty years constraining direct industrial discharge, the greatest threat to the bay today comes from nonpoint (diffuse) pollution. Constituting this are contaminants or toxins washed into the bay's tributaries by a variety of human activities, including agriculture and construction. Excess nutrients have led to eutrophication (excess algal growth that blocks sunlight from the underwater grasses critical to the bay's ecosystem). Over the last two decades the condition of the bay has prompted public and private efforts at conservation. In 1983 local governments created the Chesapeake Bay Program to coordinate restoration efforts, with private initiatives such as the Chesapeake Bay Foundation assisting. Thanks to such efforts, the bay today has begun to show improvements.

Brooks Flippen

Further Reading

Curtin, P. D., Brush, G. S., & Fisher, G. W. (2001). *Discovering the Chesapeake: The history of an ecosystem*. Baltimore: Johns Hopkins University Press.

Dorbin, Ann E. (2001). *Saving the bay: People working for the future of Chesapeake*. Baltimore: Johns Hopkins University Press.

Lippson, A. J., & Lippson, R. J. (1984). *Life in the Chesapeake Bay*. Baltimore: Johns Hopkins University Press.

Shubel, J. R. (1981). *The living Chesapeake*. Baltimore: Johns Hopkins University Press.

Wennersten, J. R. (2001). *The Chesapeake: An environmental biography*. Baltimore: Maryland Historical Society.

Chile

Chile is heralded throughout Latin America as a model of democracy and free-market economic reform. However, ecological crises and their accompanying social problems threaten its macroeconomic stability and the political peace that underwrote its transition from dictatorship to democracy in the 1990s.

Geography and Pre-Colombian History

Chile acquired its current borders in the late nineteenth century, when it wrested control of the nitrate-rich northern Atacama Desert from Peru and Bolivia in the War of the Pacific (1879–1883). In the 1880s Chile defeated independent indigenous Araucanian groups that had controlled the territories south of the Biobío River. At this time Chile pushed its northern border to the city of Arica, incorporating the Atacama Desert, and through the plains of Patagonia, Tierra del Fuego, and past the Strait of Magellan in the south. It also took control of Easter Island, 2,700 kilometers off its coast.

Chile extends 4350 kilometers north to south and an average of 200 kilometers from the Andes in the east to the Pacific Ocean on the west coast. At their highest, the Andes reach 6,900 meters, becoming smaller south of the Biobío River. The extraordinary natural diversity of this unusual geography was reflected in the varied socioeconomic characteristics of indigenous groups before the Spanish conquest.

Compared to the major imperial states like the differentiated social structures, and large sedentary peasant populations of Peru and Mexico, Chile's pre-conquestindigenous societies were less dense, organized in small units, and mostly semi-sedentary and nomadic.

Chile's *norte grande*, or "great north," is dominated by the Atacama Desert, the driest in the world, which stretches from the northern border with Peru to the Copiapó River. Below the Atacama lies the *norte chico*, or "small north," where transverse rivers run from the mountains to the ocean.

Further south lies Chile's central valley, which enjoys a temperate Mediterranean climate and fertile soils. South of the Biobío River, the valley is dominated by one of the world's largest temperate rainforests, containing rare species including the Chilean pine. At the time of conquest, Araucanian Indians lived in small semi-sedentary units engaging in agriculture and in hunting and gathering in the central valleys and foothills of the cordillera, and in fishing in coastal areas. The mountain-dwelling Pehuenche were largely nomadic and engaged in hunting and gathering.

Colonial Chile

Spanish colonization extended into Chile from Peru between 1541 and 1553; however, the Araucanians maintained their resistance in the region south of the Biobío River for centuries. In addition to continual warfare with the militarily effective Araucanians (today referred to as Mapuche), ecological constraints eroded Spanish interest in Chile. Arid northern deserts, dense southern rain forests, and scarce mineral riches made Chile a marginal region of the Spanish empire

Chilean colonial society was centered in the fertile central valley. The Spanish enslaved Mapuche captured in battle, and employed the *encomienda* system of Crown grants to demand tribute and labor from indigenous communities. Most Mapuche worked on Spanish estates (*haciendas*) in the central valley or in small placer gold mines. Spanish ranchers pastured livestock year-round in various ecological niches. Landowners accumulated extensive tracts of land because each animal required several hectares of the sparse grasses, bushes, and trees.

The Spanish colonial economy introduced a number of major environmental changes. Spaniards cultivated European crops on their estates, while indigenous laborers produced native foods for their own subsistence. In addition, landowners raised cattle and sheep in the central valley and the *norte chico*. Stepped up mining in the *norte chico* in the eighteenth and nineteenth centuries and livestock pasturing contributed to progressive deforestation. Similarly, forests of the hills and mountain slopes of the central valleys were destroyed as *haciendas* expanded. Finally, the Spanish introduced new biological agents, including smallpox and measles, that with chronic warfare and forced labor, took a toll on Chile's indigenous population. During the colonial era a large *mestizo* population arose, but not until the mid-nineteenth century did the population of Chile approach pre-conquest levels.

Modern Chile

Following the independence wars (1808–1817) and a series of civil conflicts (1817–1830) Chile acquired a degree of stability and prosperity. Rapid economic growth was fueled by exports of Chilean wheat, copper, and, following the War of the Pacific, nitrates. By the 1860s, Chile produced the world's largest supply of copper in mines in the *norte chico*. The territory south of the Atacama Desert had dense forests of *algarrobo* and *chañar* trees whose fruit was central to the pre-Colombian diet. These forests were mostly destroyed by the expansion of copper production and timber production for construction. The largely foreign-owned nitrate industry, the motor of Chile's economic growth between the 1880s and 1930, rapidly destroyed 90 percent of the native forests of the north.

Export-driven growth in the 1880s led to the final conquest of the independent Araucanian/Mapuche and the colonization of the regions south of the Biobío River. The Mapuche were settled on reservations, and huge tracts of forested land were auctioned off or granted to colonists who earned titles from the state by clearing forest and cultivating crops. Despite efforts to bolster small landholders, large estates producing grains and livestock came to dominate the south.

After 1930, Chile experienced a major crisis in its export-based economy and initiated a process of import substitution industrialization. Protective tariffs and government subsidies spurred new economic growth based on manufacturing. Industrial growth and the stagnation of the export sector caused a population shift to large cities, particularly Santiago. As of 2003 Santiago has about forty percent of Chile's population of 15 million, and shares the social and environmental problems of similar Latin American megalopolises: sprawling slums lacking basic infrastructure, deficient public transportation, and dangerous air pollution caused by dust from unpaved streets on the city's periphery, industry, and an unregulated fleet of thousands of diesel-powered buses. Emissions from buses make Santiago's air pollution among the world's worst, reaching levels four times those deemed unsafe by the United States Environmental Protection Agency. Air pollution from smelters has also been a problem in mining regions. As recently as 1999, five of seven smelters in large copper mines did not meet Chile's air quality requirements.

During this period the Chilean state began to develop commercial forestry. Deforested lands in the southern region and central valleys were replaced by plantations of North American Monterey pine, intended to address soil erosion and degradation, and supply new mills and cellulose industries. From 1930 to 1973 the state promoted commercial forestry and subsidized the planting of pine. This culminated during the 1970–1973 socialist government of Salvador Allende, which attempted to balance forestry with the preservation of Chile's remaining native forests. Allende's government linked environmental degradation to unregulated resource exploitation by North-American mining companies and large private estates. It nationalized the copper industry, whose mines supplied over 80 percent of Chile's foreign earnings, and intensified the agrarian reform initiated by Allende's predecessor.

Post–1973, Free-Market Reform

Experiments in land reform and state-directed forest management were short-lived. In 1973, Allende's government fell to a military coup supported by the United States. The dictatorship of Augusto Pinochet, which lasted from 1973 to 1990, brought dramatic economic and ecological change to Chile. Economic policies included the reversal of the agrarian reform, privatization, and deregulation of trade and investment. The result was deindustrialization, increased foreign investment, and the emergence of an economy driven by the export of primary commodities.

The transition to democracy after 1990 did not significantly alter this course, and during the late 1980s and 1990s Chile achieved rapid economic growth. The governments of the Coalition of Parties for Democracy (1990–present) have basically maintained Pinochet's economic policies, while implementing gradual reforms to democratize the state, combat poverty, and address looming ecological disasters that threaten the sustainability of Chile's resource-based development. In 1990, the democratic government of Patricio Aylwin created a National Commission on the Environment to formulate environmental policy, but implementation

laws drafted in 1994 were not passed until 1997. The new regulations have been assailed by trade organizations and by environmentalist groups alike.

Contemporary Environmental Problems

In the fruit sector, the reversal of agrarian reform has led to the creation of new large commercial estates that employ a migratory labor force. The massive use of pesticides has created serious health problems, including skin diseases, sterility, miscarriages, and birth defects. Monoculture, soil depletion, and new disease-resistant crops have created a cycle of dependency on ever-larger quantities of chemical inputs.

Deregulation opened Chile's coast to factory trawlers from Japan, Korea, and Spain. This was followed by the development of hundreds of factories producing fish meal and other processed fish products. Chile has also experienced an explosion of shellfish and fish farming, primarily of salmon. The waste produced by fish farming has polluted Chile's southern lakes and coast, and wild fish stocks have been depleted to produce fish meal for feed in salmon farms. Wild species also risk catching exotic diseases carried by farmed salmon that escape their pens.

In the forestry sector, privatization and state subsidies after 1974 stimulated the massive replacement of temperate rainforest with plantations of Monterey pine, which in Chilean soil grows at five times its North-American rate. National and transnational forestry companies have purchased cellulose and pulp companies and large tracts of land throughout Chile's southern provinces. Environmental groups in Chile have denounced the destruction of native forests and the ecological impact of pine plantations.

The growth of commercial forestry has led to massive protests against new forestry projects in southern Chile. Forestry development has led to the expulsion of thousands of peasants and Mapuche communities who have lost land to pine plantations or whose subsistence base has been undermined by the ecological impact of commercial forestry. Mapuche organizations have organized militant protests against forestry companies and projects to build new hydroelectric plants in Mapuche-dominated regions. Today their demands for ethnic autonomy and the return of lands lost since the nineteenth century challenge the neoliberal model of economic development and political stability during the ongoing transition to democracy.

Thomas Miller Klubock

See also Andes

Further Reading

Bauer, A. J. (1975). *Chilean rural society from the Spanish conquest to 1930*. Cambridge, UK: Cambridge University Press.

Camus, P., & Hajek, E.R. (1998). *Historia ambiental de Chile* [Environmental history of Chile]. Santiago, Chile: Andros Impresores.

Collins, J., & Lear, J. (1995). *Chile's free-market miracle: A second look*. Oakland, CA: Food First.

Crosby, A. W. (1972). *The Columbian exchange: Biological and cultural consequences of 1492*. Westport, CT: Greenwood Press.

Defensores del Bosque Chileno. (1998). *La tragedia del bosque chileno* [The tragedy of Chile's forests]. Santiago, Chile: Ocho Libros.

Klubock, T. M. (Forthcoming 2003). Land, labor, and ecological change in Chile, 1973–1998. In P. Winn, (Ed.), *Victims of the miracle? Chilean workers and the neoliberal model, 1973–1998*. Durham, NC: Duke University Press.

Loveman, B. (2001). *Chile: The legacy of Hispanic capitalism*. New York: Oxford University Press.

Quiroga, R. (1994). *El tigre sin selva: consecuencias ambientales de la transfromación económica de Chile, 1974–1993* [The tiger without a jungle: The environmental consequences of Chile's economic transformation]. (1994). Santiago, Chile: Instituto de Ecología Política.

Steward, J.H. (Ed.). (1946). *Handbook of South American Indians*. Washington, DC: Smithsonian Institution Bureau of American Ethnology.

Chimurenga

In the aftermath of *chimurenga*, Zimbabwe's liberation struggle that culminated in political independence in 1980, peasant society became increasingly aware of the paradox that the "lost lands" (farmlands taken from black Zimbabweans and occupied by white farmers during the colonial era), having been recaptured politically, were still being lost ecologically at an alarming rate. A green force was mobilized to engage in a new *chimurenga* by waging a "war of the trees." Aimed at the "liberation of creation" (restoration of the environment from destruction and exploitation through responsible Earth-care), the struggle was based on the religious ten-ets and holistic African worldviews of the earlier struggle for political independence; hence the development of two distinct components within the "army" of "Earthkeepers": African traditional and Christian.

As Professor M. L. Daneel, who was then at the University South Africa, and his team of field workers over a three-year period did the groundwork for the new struggle throughout Masvingo Province, his research unit evolved as a financially empowering agency under the name of ZIRRCON (Zimbabwean Institute of Religious Research and Ecological Conservation). This unit took responsibility for founding and developing two sister organizations: AZTREC (Association of Zimbabwean Traditionalist Ecologists), formed in 1988 and currently comprising a powerful green force of African chiefs, headmen, spirit mediums, and former guerrilla fighters; and its Christian counterpart, the AAEC (Association of African Earthkeeping Churches), founded a couple of years later and currently comprising 150 to 180 African Independent Churches (AICs), with a total estimated membership of 2 million adherents throughout Zimbabwe.

AZTREC and AAEC together control fourteen main tree nurseries in Masvingo Province, each of which cultivates between 50,000 and 100,000 seedlings annually. Women and youth add additional seedlings from their satellite nurseries as they strive to push the annual production rate to 1 million seedlings. Over the years peasant communities that have been mobilized in the "war of the trees" have planted 8 million trees in several thousand woodlots, mainly fruit trees, exotics, and a wide variety of indigenous trees. ZIRRCON and its sister organizations currently cultivate more indigenous tree seedlings than any other institution in Zimbabwe.

Women have played pivotal roles in the green movement from its inception. Two of the key figures in AZTREC's first executive were spirit mediums VaZarira Marambatemwa and Lydia Chabata. Both were known for their prominent roles in the liberation war. VaZarira, who at one stage was AZTREC's president, chose the name "Marambatemwa" (literally "refusal to have the trees felled," the traditional name used for ancestral holy groves) to underscore her dedication to the "war of the trees." Together the traditionalist and Christian women have formed eighty women's clubs in Masvingo Province, each of which engages in a combination of ecological activities—nursery development and tree planting—and income-generating projects, such as bakeries, soap production, clothes manufacturing, vegetable and fruit sales, sunflower oil production, and so forth.

Religious Inspiration

The success and persistence of AZTREC's contribution in the "war of the trees" derive from religious inspiration. In the rural areas all tree-planting ceremonies are ritual events, modeled largely on traditional *mukwerere* rain rituals. Like the *mukwerere*, AZTREC's *mafukidzanyika* ("Earth clothing") ceremonies focus on the barren environment and the need for rain—in this instance to enable newly planted seedlings to survive and grow. Due to the attendance of numerous AZTREC chiefs and elders from various chiefdoms, a broader spectrum of tribal authority is present at tree-planting ceremonies than was normally the case with local traditional rain rituals. Thus the *mafukidzanyika* ritual unit implies the interaction of a whole range of spirit hierarchies in a kind of multi-tribal ecumenism. This is reminiscent of the *chimurenga* war council, comprising the top ancestors of the entire country under the jurisdiction of the African creator-god, in which regional concerns were dealt with in the spirit world from the perspective of provincial and national ones.

At the start of each *mafukidzanyika* ceremony there is a presentation of beer and snuff, together with a ritual address of the land's guardian ancestors. On 2 December 1990, at an AZTREC tree-planting event in Chief Nhema's area in Zaka District, a tribal elder addressed the regional ancestors as follows:

> We have gathered here in your honor, our ancestor, father Nhema. Your children want to clothe the Earth, for it is naked . . . We ask for rain because your children are being scorched by the heat of the sun. Give us the coolness of rain . . . This land is barren because we have been chopping down all the trees. You *mhondoro* ["lion spirits," i.e., tribal spirits] have no wilderness left in which to dwell. We want to restore the forests to cover the naked land. [Beer libation and snuff offered at this point.] Pass our plea to Musikavanhu [the creator of people] so that the trees we plant will be watered sufficiently to survive.

In such ritual address the reaffirmation of mystical union between the living, the living dead, and the Creator features as a premise of the ecological struggle. True to the worldview of Shona, Zimbabwe's largest tribe, major environmental endeavors cannot be attempted without the guidance and approval of the mystical forces regulating land issues. Implicit in this union is the rejection of exploitive individualism as offensive and destructive. It is the ancestors who provoke confessions of guilt about environmental destruction, as it is their privileges that are curtailed by wanton destruction of "their" forests. Thus the ancestors represent the ethical dimension in the "war of the trees." In a sense they are the ecological conscience of their living descendants.

Appeals to Divinity

Appeals to the traditional African creator-god during *mafukidzanyika* ceremonies underscore dependence of the traditionalist "Earthkeepers" on this divinity. At the conclusion of the tree-planting season in Masvingo Province, an AZTREC delegation is sent to the distant Matopo hills to report on the latest environmental achievements and to consult with Mwari, the creator-god, who addresses his/her people as an oracle from granite cave-shrines. Mwari invariably responds positively to tree-planting reports, urges greater ecological effort, and promises guidance for the future. But the oracle does not prescribe detailed green battle strategies. The details of the actual struggle out in the country are taken care of by the ancestral war council, in this instance the senior guardian ancestors of the various districts. Nevertheless, Mwari emerges in the tree war as liberator from environmental catastrophe, in similar fashion as he/she provided supernatural affirmation in the quest for political liberation during the 1896 rebellions and the second *chimurenga* (1966–1980), prior to independence. Significantly, oracular inspiration has caused AZTREC chiefs to develop strict control measures to prevent riverbank cultivation and wanton tree felling in their chiefdoms and has caused their spirit mediums to enforce customary laws, such as the protection of wildlife, fruit trees, rivulets, and pools in the neglected holy groves (*marambatemwa*) under their jurisdiction.

AZTREC's contribution to the "war of the trees" clearly illustrates the ability of African elders, once motivated and empowered, to appropriate, reinterpret, and revitalize Africa's age-old religious beliefs in modern programs of environmental reform.

Inus Daneel

Further Reading

Daneel, M. L. (1971). *Old and new in southern Shona independent churches.* The Hague, Netherlands: Mouton.

Daneel, M. L. (1995). Mwari the liberator—Oracular intervention and Zimbabwe's quest for the lost lands. *Missionalia, 23*(2), 216–244.

Daneel, M. L. (2001). *African Earthkeepers—Holistic interfaith mission.* New York: Orbis Books.

China

(2000 est. pop. 1.2 billion)

Under the rule of the Manchu dynasty (1644–1912) the Chinese empire more than doubled its territory. Its size and geographical and cultural diversity were unlike those of any other country. In the northern and western regions camels passed through the inner Asian desert oases in Xinjiang, yaks filled the stables of Buddhist monasteries on the plateau of Tibet, sheep grazed the pastures of Mongolia, and horses and deer roamed the plains and forests of Manchuria. In the southwestern and southern regions indigenous peoples had fought losing battles against the invasions of Han-Chinese colonists, miners, traders, and soldiers who came to exploit the riches of the tropical rain forests, timber, copper, iron, tin, and eventually their farming soils. In the fertile river valleys and plains in the eastern half of China the Han-Chinese population had grown from about 150 million in 1700 to maybe 350 million in 1800 and to 450 million in 1900, creating an enormous demand for metals, timber, cotton, wool, fuel, pork, and many other products. Spurred on by the new American crops such as maize, potatoes and tobacco and growing demand for tea, many farmers went to exploit the hills and mountains of central and south China, and millions even went overseas. Economic growth was uneven, and so were its environmental effects on different regions, but population pressure on natural resources increased wherever people could move.

Landscape Made by Human Hand

After the eighteenth century forests were felled with increasing speed and the land reclaimed for growing maize or tubers. Farmers and other settlers ruthlessly exploited the shrinking natural vegetation and other resources of the hills and upstream areas. Many mountain soils could not sustain a long period of farming, rapidly eroded, and became too thin and stony. Most land was never officially registered, which makes it difficult to estimate the speed of the agricultural reclamation process. On gentler slopes and along river valleys terraces were built to conserve water, soil, and nutritional elements. Lakes and low-lying land in river floodplains were reclaimed for irrigated agriculture. The resulting anthropogenic (human-created) soils became stable and gave high yields of rice. Thus much of China's landscape was created by human hand.

However, land and people became vulnerable to floods and droughts as riverbeds were raised and natural vegetation and flood retention capacities reduced. Along the coast the silt-laden rivers deposited much sediment, and land was reclaimed from the sea on a large scale, not only at the mouth of the Yellow River, but also near those of the Yangtze and other rivers.

Dry and Irrigated Farming in North and South

Water is in short supply in northern China but ample in southern China. The monsoon climate brings an uneven distribution of rainfall, with spring droughts and summer floods. Traditionally, some land along the rivers of northern China and near mountains was irrigated by surface water, but most farming was dry. Shallow wells supplied water for vegetables and drinking. Wheat, millet, sorghum, and maize were dominant crops. Diets were poor and particularly lacking in animal protein. Constrained by poverty and difficult transport, only some farmers could afford to grow cotton, tobacco, peanuts, and other cash crops or to keep pigs for manure and pork. Most people lived in walled rectangular villages spread evenly across the North China Plain. In contrast, in the Yangtze River basin in central and southern China, water was abundant and where necessary was caught in tanks and reservoirs in the hills and subsequently stored in paddy fields. Rice yields were high, transport was convenient, and income was supplemented by sericulture (silk production), tea growing, weaving, and other industries. Population was dense, crowding the cities, market towns, and villages that stretched along rivers, roads, and canals.

New Factors of Change

During the final years of the Manchu dynasty four new elements began to change China's traditional environment.

First was modern transport. Concessions were given to build railroads, and Chinese and foreign railway companies began to develop land and to exploit mines and forests, and new cities sprang up. Because of improved railway transport, millions of colonists moved into Manchuria and other outlying regions. Famines were much reduced. Great droughts in northern China during 1876–1878 and in northwestern China during 1899–1900 and 1929–1930 had cost millions of lives, but in 1922 the North China Plain was saved by its railroads. During the 1930s China had over

Rice Paddy Construction

The following account of building a rice paddy in rural Taiwan makes clear the level of knowledge and skill required to farm wet rice successfully in China.

In San-lin village, rice paddies were still being constructed during my research period. The farm land near the Ta-an River was occasionally washed away by the strong torrents in the rainy seasons and had to be rebuilt. Construction is tedious and slow. First, the topsoil must be skimmed off and put aside for later use. The stony subsurface must be culled and the rocks broken into smaller pieces with hand chisels, if they are too large, or removed from a higher terrace to a lower one. Villagers call this process "digging out soil, and inserting the stones" (tsup-to dzip-dze).

After the stony layer is levelled, the topsoil is evenly redistributed. Since the original topsoil usually is not sufficiently deep for crop growth, more earth must be purchased or found and hauled to the area. All the while the workers continually consult their water level to ensure that the land is level. [. . .]

Even after additional earth has been added, the land is not suitable for rice growing. Since the topsoil is still thin and its capillary structure unformed, any irrigation water would soon filter away, carrying off any organic nutrients. According to the villagers, the best utilization of this kind of land is to grow sugar cane, which requires far less water and fertilizer than rice, for the first three or four years. During this period, large amounts of rice straw and sugar cane leaves are plowed into the field to improve organic composition and provide tissue elements. Another common practice is to channel irrigation water into the new field during the rainy season, when the heavy precipitation upstream leaches deeply into the earth and carries off soil components. When this stagnant muddy water is left on the field it releases its heavier elements. The water then is drained off, and the field is flooded with fresh water. After another such treatment the soil layer has been thickened, the earth structure changed, and the organic nutrients increased. Then the land can be used for rice growing.

Source: Huang, Shu-min. (1978). *Agricultural Degradation: Changing Community Systems in Rural Taiwan.* Ann Arbor, MI: University Microfilms pp. 62–64.

20,000 kilometers of railways. Modern tar roads and rubber-tired carts and trucks greatly reduced short-distance transport cost. Old city walls were torn down to make way for new development. Nevertheless, political strife between warlords continued to tear China apart. Modern development other than mining remained concentrated in the coastal areas, particularly in Japan-controlled Manchuria and Taiwan, and a few cities.

Second, after 1870 modern mining and other industries developed, such as the Pingyuan coal mines near Beijing, the Hanye iron works in Hubei, the Shuikoushan lead mines in Hunan, and the Dongchuan copper mines in Yunnan. Traditionally, mines and kilns for porcelain and bricks had used up much wood fuel in their immediate surroundings, but the new large-scale mines needed much more and soon were served by railways. After 1895 foreign industries were introduced in the western treaty ports. Under foreign protection Shanghai, Tianjin, Canton, and other cities rapidly developed into industrial and commercial centers. The 1933 industrial survey reported thirty-eight hundred mostly-urban, modern factories. New large-scale technologies were adopted in textiles, coal mining, iron smelting, oil pressing, and flour milling. New products were introduced, and cigarettes, matches, electricity, and machinery changed people's lives. The urban population expanded rapidly, leading to crowded housing, crime (Shanghai became associated with kidnapping and vice), and unsanitary conditions.

A barge makes its way on the Huangpu tributary of the Change (Yangtze) River in Shanghai.

Even so, city life was more secure than life in the countryside. The crisis of the 1930s, World War II, and subsequent civil war retarded China's modern industrial development, and in 1949 only some coastal cities and Manchuria had modern industry.

Third, new crops, animal breeds, and cultivation techniques were brought into China by Chinese entrepreneurs living overseas, Western missionaries, and (mainly) U.S. agricultural scientists. U.S. cotton, Italian wheat, British pigs, Swiss goats, and Russian and Dutch dairy cattle gave higher returns than most local varieties. Eventually, many local varieties disappeared, although some qualities were maintained in cross-breeds. Chinese cotton growers and soybean growers began to produce for the Japanese market and native factories. Through increasing commercialization, the rural standard of living improved slightly in most regions.

Fourth, China's government became more economically exploitative and socially invasive. Traditional property regimes (regular patterns of occurrence or action) were replaced by legal arrangements allowing fuller exploitation of land and other natural resources. For instance, traditional Mongolian land rights were revoked and sold to Japanese, Russian, and Chinese chartered companies. Improved communications, modern arms, and new bureaucracies strengthened the reach of the state. Nationalism and other ideologies demanded that China should be strong and its people be lifted from poverty. Rising expectations led to revolutionary movements and civil wars, in which warring parties mobilized available natural and human resources on an unprecedented scale.

Rural Misery

In spite of such modernization efforts, the image of China as a country plagued by bandits, soldiers, opium, and natural disasters remained a valid one. The 1931 and 1935 floods of the Yangtze River and the deliberate dike breaks in Shandong to force the Yellow River into a southern course in 1938 destroyed millions of people, cattle, and homes. The Japanese invasion and atrocities, such as the mass-murders in Nanking, made millions flee to the interior, from where the government of Free China continued its struggle. Less dramatic but ever present were stark poverty, high infant and child mortality, and many epidemic diseases. About 1 million Chinese, mostly urban young adults working indoors, died of tuberculosis every year; cholera and malaria were common. Most farmers, working barefoot in the paddy fields, spreading night soil (human excrement) over their vegetables, living with their pigs, and drinking unsanitary water, were infested with parasites and affected by viruses and died before the age of sixty. Families split up early, and few managed to attain Chinese philosopher Confucius's ideal of three generations living under one roof.

Loss of Forests and Vegetation Cover

By 1800 most of China's original forest had already been felled, with some stands remaining in the northeast and southwest. China's forest cover decreased more rapidly because railroads made commercial exploitation feasible and also because land was reclaimed for agricultural use. Official data (91 million hectares of forest in 1934 and 84 million hectares with 6 billion cubic meters of timber in 1947) are highly questionable. By 1940 Manchuria's forest cover and timber stocks had been halved, and by 1985 halved again. In the Yangtze River upper basin, forest cover shrank from 50 percent to less than 20 percent and in Sichuan from 34 percent to 12 percent by 1962. In particular the Great Leap Forward of 1958–1961 (an unsuccessful attempt to decentralize the economy by establishing a nationwide system of people's communes) has been blamed for large-scale wanton felling of forests to acquire building material and fuel for new rural industries. Commercial logging, agricultural land reclamation, household fuel use, and desiccation all had great impact. The consequent changes in river regimes caused greater vulnerability to floods and droughts.

Under communism and the communes established in 1958, afforestation campaigns were organized on a massive scale. Villages were obliged to plant a hundred trees per inhabitant, mostly along roads but also on waste hills to provide fuel and to combat erosion. Often done without sustained followup, tree planting had more failures than successes. For instance, along the northern deserts where pastures had been reclaimed to create farmland, a giant shelterbelt was created to reduce wind velocity and protect the new farmland against desertification—an almost hopeless effort. Planting tea or fruit trees on wasteland did not always

help against erosion. The forest area grew to 125 million hectares in 1988 and to 160 million hectares today, but most forests are young and low in quality. In 1988 the government raised the price of timber, severely restricted its use for building purposes and railway sleepers, and began importing pulp and paper. Reserving land for forest growth (by now 1 million square kilometers) and selling long-term land leases of local forests, pastures, and wasteland to individual farmers have been adopted as solutions for collective squandering of resources and failing common property regimes, but with mixed success. China's timber stock seems to be rising again, and some erosion-prone farmland in the hills has been taken out of cultivation. However, global warming has intensified droughts in the north and floods in the south.

Population and Birth Control Measures

China's population increased from 583 million in 1953 (the first census) to 1 billion in 1982 and more slowly to 1.2 billion in 2000. Natural growth is down to .9 percent per year now. Remarkably, as the Chinese people became more affluent and resource constraints eased, birth control policies became stricter. In 1958 new household registration rules were adopted, requiring rural migrants to urban areas to have urban work or school permits or settlement permits from urban authorities. This started the formal separation of rural and urban households. Strict urban rationing of food, cloth, and housing and strict controls on population movement succeeded in cutting off the rural-urban flow. Consequently, urbanization rates remained low, and the rural population increase had to be accommodated within each village, regardless of its land and other economic resources. The communist regime made great efforts in health care and education. Vaccination programs put an end to most childhood diseases, and primary school enrollment increased from 50 percent in 1952 to 85 percent in 1965 and became almost universal after 1975. Life expectancy at birth increased dramatically after the early 1960s, also because of improved diets, and during the 1990s it has continued to rise more slowly by another two years to 69.1 for men and 73.5 for women, which is already close to levels in the advanced world.

Many factors contributed to China's fertility decline during the 1950–1990 period. Total Fertility Rates dropped from 5.8 in the late 1960s to less than 3 by 1980 and below replacement value in the 1990s (TFR is always measured per woman over her entire life time). Women's liberation, education, full female employment in rural collectives and cities, cramped urban housing, decreases in child mortality, and greater availability and knowledge of contraceptive methods all played a role. However, specific to China were its severe state measures, with heavy penalties and collective pressure and different policies for urban and rural areas. Politicians were and still are driven by Malthusian (relating to the theories of English economist Thomas Malthus) concerns about limited natural resources and food supply. During the 1980s scientists calculated an "optimal" population of 700–800 million people. Chinese governments at all levels feared the social burden of more children. State family-planning policies started in 1971 with the slogan "late, sparse, and few," meaning late marriages and only two children per couple. The rule of "only one child" was instituted for the urban population and state employees in 1978 and later spread to suburban and affluent rural areas. A "one-child certificate," a contract that rewarded complying mothers but carried severe penalties for offenders, backed up the rule.

In many rural areas a second child is allowed only if the first is a girl. After ultrasound scans became widely available, sex-selective abortion escalated. The birth ratio of boys to girls for second children rose from 1.2 in 1990 to over 1.5 in 2000. Popular acceptance of the one-child policy has increased in urban areas but less so in rural areas. The 2001 family-planning law severely restricts citizens' reproductive rights while extending legal protection and quality health services to mothers and infants who abide by the law. Its prohibition against using coercion to enforce birth control is mainly cosmetic because the law gives unlimited powers to local governments to impose severe sanctions on offending couples.

China's population policies supposedly have reduced its population growth by 300 million people. Based on a total fertility rate of 1.8 and adjusted for the slanted sex ratio, China's population may be forecast to peak at 1.45 billion in 2033 and to decline thereafter. Thus within a century its share of world population will have dropped from one-fourth to one-sixth.

The Effects of Socialist Planning in Agriculture and Industry

Central socialist planning is known for its great successes and even greater failures. Communist leader Mao Tse-tung's megalomaniac Great Leap Forward was different in that it combined central targets and directives with local autarchy (absolute sovereignty) and mass campaigns. Results were disastrous. In 1958 large people's communes organized farming along military lines and started a mass campaign to produce iron in 600,000 small furnaces. Urban population jumped from 90 million in 1957 to 130 million in 1960. The cities could not sustain this influx, and food shortage followed. The idea to open up new land, terrace hills, and build reservoirs everywhere proved counterproductive and environmentally destructive. Distribution networks broke down, grain output dropped, and during 1960–1961 the resulting famine cost 25 million lives. There were long-lasting effects on natural resources; for instance, the decimated fish population of China's largest lake, Qinghai, has not recovered since. It also created an obsession with local self-reliance in food grain.

The large fields created under collective farming, although more efficient in the use of oxen, machinery, irrigation, fertilizers, and pesticides, were more vulnerable to erosion and salinization. Since 1958 about 35 million hectares (one-third of China's farm acreage) have been lost or diverted to other uses. Twice as much was reclaimed for agriculture, mostly poor soils, remote areas, or steep hill slopes. Chinese colonists were settled in border regions, from the Sanjiang marshes in the extreme north to the tropical forests of Hainan and the deserts of Xinjang. Their irrigated agriculture destroyed the pastures and livelihood of native people. By the 1970s land reclamation, overgrazing, and reduced precipitation—another consequence of deforestation—had turned a half-million square kilometers of northern prairies into deserts and reduced grass by one-third to one-half on remaining prairies. One-sixth of China suffered from serious soil erosion. One-quarter of China's reservoir capacity had silted up, and natural lakes such as the Dongtinghu had lost most of their flood-retention capacity. During the 1990s, on average, 5–15 million hectares were seriously stricken by flood every year, and 5–20 million hectares by drought. Nevertheless, continuous increases in grain yield were achieved with improved varieties and expanded irrigation since the late 1960s with everincreasing application of chemical fertilizers and electric pumps. Recently China has promoted bioengineering, and now half of its cotton and much of its soybeans and maize have been genetically modified to increase pest resistance.

Fearing foreign invasion, after 1965 China set up many heavy industries in remote mountain areas. In socialism, big was beautiful, but all provinces and cities tried to, or had to, become self-reliant. Socialist planning invited local governments and factories to maximize output and distribute according to plan, regardless of efficiency or cost. Resources such as land, water, and ores had no value in their own right, rather only from invested labor. This led to wasteful use of energy, hoarding of resources of raw materials, and blind production. Moreover, China was isolated, and without access to foreign technology, most industries continued to copy or adapt the Soviet technology of the 1950s. When China finally woke up to the demands of the market in the 1980s, it found that large parts of its industrial apparatus were mislocated and that almost all were outdated. Thus traditional industries could not compete with the new industries established with foreign technology (and, increasingly, with foreign capital) in the coastal regions.

As direct state involvement in the economy declined, the central government concentrated on planning and implementing large projects. In spite of government efforts to restrict urban inflow, increasing differentials in development and income made tens of millions of poor farmers migrate to nearby cities or to the east. Average rural income in poor provinces was only one-tenth or less of that in Shanghai and Guangzhou. Government subsidization of village antipoverty programs proved effective in providing a minimal sustenance of life, primary education, and health care. The rural population still depended on the collective provisions of its own villages and was not entitled to any urban employment or social security. However, as agriculture became less and less rewarding, more was needed. At the end of the 1990s the government tried to direct the rural outflow toward rural towns and to create employment there. Urbanization is now accepted as inevitable and even positive for socioeconomic development. Political priorities are urban housing, drinking water, sanitation, and improved indoor air quality by changeover to use of gas from coal.

A grand scheme to "develop the west" aims at developing the physical and social infrastructure of twelve western provinces and integrating them into China's economy. New railroads, highways, mines, and factories will lead to fuller exploitation of the resources of the west. Coal-fired power plants will send their electricity to the east, pipelines will transport gas and oil from Xinjiang to Shanghai, and a railway from Lhasa to Qinghai will finally connect Tibet with China. Reducing the negative environmental effects of forced rapid development will be a great challenge to local governments. The giant Sanxia hydropower station on

the Yangtze River is nearing completion, and over 1 million people must be resettled from its reservoir. Original plans for resettlement of farmers in upland areas have been modified after the 1998 Yangtze River flood disaster alerted authorities to the dangers of water and soil erosion because of farming the hills. Another grand scheme transfers water from the Yangtze River basin to the dry north. It is a long-cherished dream but poses enormous problems. So far the water pumped north through the Grand Canal has been polluted by industries and rather costly. In 2000 engineering work started on a middle route to transport water from the Hanshui River at Danjiangkou to Henan and across the Yellow River.

Industrial Pollution and Remedial Measures

In 1972 pollution accidents affected the fish supply to Beijing from the Guanting reservoir and the shellfish of Dalian Bay. The government disclosed that mercury and other heavy metals dumped into the Sungari and Nenni Rivers were poisoning fish and people. Such disclosure reflected a beginning awareness of the need to check pollution and prepared China for participation in the Stockholm conference on the environment and adoption of its first environmental regulations. A 1977 survey of sea pollution found high industrial discharges of heavy metals and serious oil spills; 15,000 square kilometers of oil covered the Bo Hai (an arm of the Yellow Sea), a traditional provider of shrimp and fish to the banquets of China's politicians and administrators.

Early remedial policies focused on management of river systems, waste-release standards for new or expanding large industries, cleanup of major cities, reduction in pesticide use, food safety inspection, and research and monitoring. After 1979 industrial expansion plans were screened for their discharge standards. Regulators first focused on the metallurgy, oil, textile, paper, food, building materials, and machinery industries. However, compliance was uneven, depending on the development level and financial resources of the responsible local governments.

A trial environmental law was passed in 1979. It focused on prevention and the principle of "the polluter pays." Surface water-quality standards were introduced in 1983 and 1986, and local governments were made responsible for monitoring water quality and preventing further degradation. Three standards of ambient air quality were set for different types of areas. Polluting enterprises were charged for above-standard emissions. Laws for conservation of forests, grasslands, fisheries, and wild animals were passed during the mid–1980s. By 2000 over twelve hundred nature reserves occupied 10 percent of China's territory, one-half of which were in Tibet and Xinjiang. Environmental laws were introduced for the marine environment (1982), water pollution (1984), air pollution (1987), solid waste (1995), and noise (1996). Environmental-impact assessments were required for a growing number of construction projects. In 2000 a total emission-control permit system was introduced for certain areas, whereby emission quotas are distributed or traded.

The 1980s were a period of rapid, visible, and cost-effective early advances in pollution prevention and treatment efforts. Between 1982 and 1984 the State Council ruled that 6 or 7 percent of investments in capital construction and renovation projects should go to pollution prevention and treatment. An important financial source for local government was created with the tax on urban construction. Environmental protection became a standard part of the government's five-year plans. By 1987, .8 percent of the gross domestic product (GDP) was spent on environmental protection, and its proponents demanded that this should rise to 1.5 to 2 percent eventually. However, subsequently this percentage fell, and only at the end of the 1990s did it increase to a level of around 1 percent.

Weak Enforcement of Rules

Why was followup of early advances so difficult? In practice, sanctions against polluting by enterprises were weak. Pollution charges being lower than treatment costs, it paid to pollute. State-owned enterprises saw pollution charges (which totaled 6 billion yuan in 2001) as just one more state tax. Management was lax, inspections were few and sloppy, and treatment installations might have been turned off to save costs. As in other socialist countries, in China local governments were owner of the enterprise, monitor of its environmental performance, and judge at the same time. They feared that investments in the environment might come at the expense of employment and profits. Local environmental protection bureaus had their staffs increased to 130,000, but their hands were tied. Decisions were made by bureaucracies rather than imposed by law or public opinion. The diversity in technological levels and scale within many industrial branches in China further complicated an imposition of uniform standards. China set ambitious targets for reduction of

emissions by its industries, but monitoring has been uneven, and small industries and farmers are hardly covered.

Industrial pollution has been spreading. By the mid-1990s one-half of China's industrial production came from township and village enterprises, largely outside of the control of local environmental protection bureaus. It took time, considerable political effort, and concentrated action to close down the worst-polluting industries in the most affected eastern areas of China. Prompted by unacceptable levels of water pollution and drinking water disasters, cleanup programs were started for major cities, Taihu Lake, and medium-size river basins. Eighty-two percent of industrial wastewater discharged by urban industries is up to standard now, compared with 50 percent in 1990. Polluting industries were driven to interior provinces and rural areas.

Problems are greatest in the dry north, where industries and households make great demands on shrinking water sources. Economically, the most rational solution is to raise water prices and reduce the allocation of irrigation water to farmers, but this solution has met with political and practical objections. Since the 1990s the lower reaches of the Yellow River run dry for several months a year and have become a sandy sewer. All main lakes and one-half of the sections of the Huai River, the Hai River, the Liao River, and other rivers in the east are worse than the lowest quality standard grade V. The north and west of China also burn much coal. In spite of greater energy efficiency and coal washing, rapid industrial growth of around 10 percent a year pushed China's total sulfur dioxide and soot emissions to 18 and 9.9 billion metric tons, respectively, in 2000. Highest levels are found in the interior coal-burning cities in Shaanxi, Hebei, Chongqing, Guizhou, and Sichuan Provinces.

Eventually, rather than legislation or punitive sanctions, China's fast economic growth, improvements in education, foreign investment, and increased environmental awareness (leading to greater political pressure on municipal leaders to clean up their cities) were the more important contributors to technological innovation, improved efficiency, and cleaner production of China's industries. Shortages in energy (in particular electricity and oil) and water during the past two decades led to more economic resource use and a shift to more efficient technology. China has become an importer of raw materials such as cotton, pulp, steel, and oil and an exporter of finished industrial products.

Natural Disasters

In recent decades the worst natural disaster in China was the Tangshan earthquake, which killed 242,000 people (mostly miners), injured another 164,000, and destroyed 10 million homes in 1976. The annual death toll of earthquakes and landslides is about one thousand. Severe droughts affect 10 million hectares of farmland every year, and serious floods about 5 million hectares, with one to three thousand lives lost and 3 million homes destroyed. Although their death toll pales in comparison to the traffic death toll (almost 100,000 per year), their economic costs are enormous because of damage to homes, other buildings, infrastructure, crops, and domestic animals. Official estimates note that annual direct economic damages have increased: 50 billion yuan in the 1950s, 60 billion yuan in the 1970s, over 100 billion yuan in the 1990s. However, if one includes indirect losses because of deforestation, desiccation, pollution, and natural resource degradation, annual economic losses quadrupled to almost 20 percent of China's GDP in the 1990s.

The vulnerability to flood disaster will be reduced as people move out of low-lying areas along major rivers and as stricter building limits are imposed. China's eighty-four thousand reservoirs have helped to reduce floods and store water for irrigation, but many reservoirs have become old, silted up, and outright dangerous. Dikes along main rivers have offered greater protection, but riverbeds have been raised by sediments and constricted by bridges and other buildings (and dikes). Antiflood standards are low: twenty to thirty years for most cities and only three to five years for rural areas. Increased afforestation programs and decreased grain cultivation in erosion-prone areas will help reduce both flood and drought damages.

International Cooperation

China's environmental efforts have received considerable support—both institutional support, such as in legislation and training programs, and support for investment projects—from foreign countries and international organizations such as the World Bank. For instance, other countries mainly financed the phasing out of chlorofluorocarbon (CFC) coolants in China's refrigerator industry.

China's principles in global environmental issues were laid down in 1990: Environment should remain linked to the need for economic development; developed countries are mainly responsible for present pollution; the interests of developing countries should not be hurt by "green" demands; the world economic order should promote participation of developing countries in solving global problems; and by reducing its own environmental problems China as a large country will contribute to the global situation. China has subscribed to most international treaties, and its World Trade Organization accession has brought it closer to international product standards. Its international stand is a clever combination of global concerns and self-interest in continued economic growth, which invites Western countries and companies to contribute to and participate in environmental improvements in China.

Eduard B. Vermeer

See also Desertification; Endangered Species

Further Reading

China Environment Yearbook Society. (1990–2000). *Zhongguo Huanjing Nianjian* (China environment yearbooks). Beijing, China: China Environment Yearbook Publisher.

Dodgen, R. A. (2001). *Controlling the dragon: Confucian engineers and the Yellow River in the late imperial China.* Honolulu: University of Hawaii Press.

Edmonds, R. (Ed.). (1998). *Managing the Chinese environment.* Oxford, UK: Oxford University Press.

Elvin. M., & Liu T. J. (1998). *Sediments of time: Environment and society in Chinese history.* Cambridge, UK: Cambridge University Press,

Fairbank, J. & Feuerwerker, A. (Eds.). (1983–1987). *The Cambridge history of China* (Vols. 12–15). New York: Cambridge University Press.

Lee, J., & Wang, F. (Eds.). (1999). *One quarter of humanity: Malthusian mythology and Chinese realities. 1700–2000.* Cambridge, MA: Harvard University Press.

Ma, X. Y., & Ortolano, L. (2000). *Environmental regulation in China: Institutions, enforcement and compliance.* Boulder, CO: Rowman and Littlefield.

Mallory, W. H. (1922). *China: Land of famine.* New York: American Geographical Society.

Marks, R. (1997). *Tigers, rice, silk, and silt: Environment and economy in late imperial south China.* Cambridge, UK: Cambridge University Press.

McEllroy, M. B., Nielsen, C. P., & Lydon, P. (Eds.). (1998). *Energizing China: Reconciling environmental protection and economic growth.* Cambridge, MA: Harvard University Press.

Myers, R. H. (1970). *The Chinese peasant economy: Agricultural development in Hopei and Shantung, 1890–1949.* Cambridge, MA: Harvard University Press.

Shapiro, J. (2001). *Mao's war against nature: Politics and the environment in revolutionary China*. Cambridge, UK: Cambridge University Press.

Smil, V. (1984). *The bad Earth: Environmental degradation in China*. New York: M. E. Sharpe.

Smil, V. (1993). *China's environmental crisis: An inquiry into the limits of national development*. New York: M. E. Sharpe.

State Environmental Protection Administration. (2002). *Report on the state of the environment in China 2001*. Retrieved February 4, 2003, from http://www.zhb.gov.cn/english/SOE/soechina2001/index.htm

State Environmental Protection Bureau (1994). *Zhongguo Huanjing Baohu Xingzheng Ershi-nian* (Twenty years of environmental protection administration). Beijing, China: China Environmental Sciences Press.

Vermeer, E. B. (1988). *Economic development in provincial China: The central Shaanxi since 1930*. New York: Cambridge University Press.

Vermeer, E. B. (1998, December). Industrial pollution in China and remedial policies. *The China Quarterly, 156*, 952–985.

Wang, H. C. (1992). *Deforestation and desiccation in China: A preliminary study*. Retrieved February 4, 2003, from http://www.library.utoronto.ca/pcs/state/chinaeco/forest.htm

World Bank. (1997). *Clear water, blue skies, China's environment in the new century*. Washington, DC: author.

Xia, G. (1998). *An estimate of the economic consequences of environmental pollution in China*. Retrieved February 4, 2003, from http://www.library.utoronto.ca/pcs/state/chinaeco/pollut.htm

Xiong, D. T. (1989). *Zhongguo jindai linyeshi* (A history of forestry in modern China). Beijing, China: Zhongguo linye chubanshe.

China, Ancient

China, as described in this entry, is generally considered "China Proper," that is, the drainages of the Huang (Yellow) River, the Chang (Yangtze) River, and the Pearl and Huai Rivers, as well as the coastal areas of the south. The time period is a span roughly from the seventh century BCE to the seventh century CE.

China is a vast land with a great variety of terrain as well as weather, making it difficult to speak of a single ecology or environment in this region. Never-

theless, there are four environmentally relevant issues that a majority of ancient Chinese had to contend with, regardless of their location. These relate to water, deforestation, farming, and regional interdependence.

Water Issues

The climate in North China is arid and subject to the influence of cold-air blocks from Mongolia and Siberia. The preservation of water for domestic use and irrigation was one of the most precarious tasks that individuals and communities had to undertake. Torrential rains could come in summer, and huge flows of melted snow and ice from high mountains in the spring could create nearly instantaneous floods, sometimes lasting for very long periods of time. Fields and houses would be washed away, topsoil carried off, and thick deposits of silt left after the waters receded. All of these created adverse conditions that no simple water control project could handle. It is not surprising, then, that the legend of Emperor Yu, the founder of China's mythical first dynasty, held that he had channeled the overflowing waters of the Huang back into their proper course. Yu's father, according to the same legend, had previously attempted a dike-building project that failed, resulting in renewed flooding—and Yu's father's punishment by execution. This legend may well reflect a collective memory of great inundations that (unlike the flood in the story of Noah) did not occur only once.

In South China (below the Chang River Valley and the high mountain barriers north of Guangdong Province) monsoon rains regularly bring in huge amounts of water. Torrential rains can generate raging torrents in moments. For these reasons, Chinese farmers worried constantly about water conditions that could bring disaster to their daily lives. Lack of rain in the south could be just as dangerous as a flood. Rice paddies require large amounts of water, and a few days of severe drought could wipe out an entire season's crop. Thus, water issues were just as problematic in the south as they were in the north.

The most common way of handling the problem of managing water for irrigation and daily use was to sink wells and to use small ponds to preserve surplus rainfall. Every Chinese village in ancient days had a public well, and larger households might have their own in the backyard or kitchen. Ancient Chinese hydraulic engineers created marvels of technology such as the Du Jiang dam in Sichuan (in western China), which split an entire river into two basins to irrigate the Chengdu basin. A water gate built from basic mate-

Mencius on Resource Management

If close-meshed nets are not allowed in the pools and ponds, there will be more fish and turtles than can be eaten. And if axes are allowed in the mountains and forests only in the appropriate seasons, there will be more timbers than can be used

Source: *Sources of Chinese Tradition* (Vol. 1), compiled and translated by Wm Theodore De Bary and Irene Bloom. (1999). New York: Columbia University Press, p. 118.

rials—bamboo, pebbles, and timber—could be opened and closed to adjust an enormous water flow that irrigated several tens of thousands of hectares of land. Amazingly, it still works today, with only minor adjustments, 2,200 years after it was built.

Chinese hydraulic engineers also built many canals to link lakes and rivers of different systems into wider networks. One canal system in Liangqu (in the present-day Guangxi Zhuang Autonomous Region, in the far south of China) linked two river systems at their origins high in the mountains. This mini-prototype of the Panama canal had its own dam and reservoirs, and an intricate system of locks to raise and lower the water level so that ships could literally move up and down mountains. As with the dam in Sichuan, this project is still in operation two thousand years later.

Deforestation

The Chinese used wood as a building material as early as the Neolithic Age (7000–2000 BCE) to construct houses, especially in the south. The frames were wood, with mud brick and stamped earth used to complete the walls. Wooden materials do not last as long as stone, which why very little ancient architecture survives in China. Eventually a house would need to be repaired, or replaced completely, and more timber was thus consumed. Chinese originally cooked with firewood over open fires, a practice that evolved into the use of stoves. Wood-burning kilns for the production of pottery and ceramics, and foundries for bronze and iron also consumed enormous amounts of wood.

In North China, arid and cold weather meant that new trees grew only slowly on formerly forested land; this new growth had no chance of keeping up with the speed with which trees were cut down for construction and fuel. Barren hills and fields therefore became commonplace in the northern countryside. As early as the fourth century BCE, the great philosopher Mencius

commented that cities all seemed to be surrounded by barren hills like bald heads freshly washed. Northern soil was a fine yellow powder that simply could not be preserved without vegetation, and the phenomenon of rapid desertification had been noticed in China since very early days. Loose sand carried away by river systems eventually came to rest as heavy silt deposits that raised riverbeds higher and higher, until the dikes and banks bordering them literally lifted some of China's northern rivers into the air. The waters of these so-called hanging rivers flowed at a higher level than the surrounding lands. The Huang is the most notorious of these.

In the south, warm and humid weather allowed cutover vegetation to grow back more quickly than in the north, but the speed with which trees were cut down was faster still. Southern hills were normally covered with dwarf trees and bushes whose shallow root systems were completely inadequate to hold the soil in place during torrential rains. Firewood became so expensive that eventually Chinese had to find creative ways of conserving fuel. They invented a fuel-efficient stove as early as the second century BCE in which a small amount of straw, haystalks or the stalks of crops could be burned and generate a short but intense heat. The Chinese method of stir-fry cooking was extremely fuel-efficient, as the ingredients were chopped and prepared ahead of time, and needed only a minimal time on the fire to be cooked thoroughly. The stove was structured in such a way that the remnant heat in the stove and ash after cooking two or three stir-fry dishes could be used to boil water or cook rice. Indeed, the art of Chinese gourmet cooking is the direct result of a conservation-minded lifestyle.

In North China, where animal husbandry was more common, people used dried animal dung (either in cakes or powder form) and husks of grains as basic fuels for cooking food and heating the home on winter days. Such fuels burned at a lower temperature than wood, but they produced a sustained heat that made the houses comfortable. While there is no literary record nor archeological evidence that indicate precise dates, heat channels under the floors and bed that conduct heat from the stove throughout the home are believed to have been invented no later than the second century BCE and became commonplace in north China no later than the ninth century BCE. The northern Chinese cuisine relies heavily on steamed breads, fried pancakes, and boiled noodle soups, all of which can be produced economically by using just a small portion of such long-lasting heat.

Farming

Chinese agriculture emerged in North China as early as 6,000 to 7,000 BCE, when millet was domesticated. The main crop in the south was rice, which was domesticated at about the same time. Early on, Chinese farmers practiced slash-and-burn agriculture to open new fields; they also knew to leave some fields fallow to preserve the richness of already opened land. By the third or fourth century BCE, population pressures in the highly crowded central plain (around the middle reaches of the Chang River) led to an extremely high population density that put a great burden on what little agricultural land was available. Farmers had to use relatively small patches of land to produce enough food to feed a large population, and as noted above, environmental conditions were hardly favorable. Under such challenging conditions, Chinese farmers developed practices that were highly labor-intensive. Chinese farming tied down an enormous amount of human labor for producing food, and had to draw upon extra labor during the busy harvest seasons. Farmers had to develop labor-consuming field management in order to utilize the soil, and the population, to their maximum capacities. The soil needed more workers, and the working population thus needed an increasing supply of food. It was a vicious circle.

To maximize the use of limited resources, Chinese farmers would carefully calculate timing in order to catch all available moisture when the winter snows melted, and they would cover the snow with mats in order to prevent it—and the water it would provide in the spring—from being blown away. They found various methods of shortening the growing seasons, such as interpolating crops. Planting different crops alternately on a plot of land meant that nutrients that had been removed from the soil by one crop could be replenished by the one planted subsequently, thereby conserving the soil's fertility. Rice farmers used concentrated fields as nurseries, growing densely-planted sprouts in a very small area while another crop reached maturity in the larger fields. After the mature crop was harvested, the partially grown sprouts could be painstakingly transplanted into the larger field. For fertilizers, they used burned ash, silt dredged from the bottoms of ponds, crumbled earthen walls, and the excrement of animals and humans. From about the second century CE on, the size of China's population meant that the country could no longer afford to leave more than a very few fields fallow. Most were in constant use for food production, and their soils came to depend entirely on fertilizers, as the original topsoil was completely exhausted. Skills for making the most effective use of intensely crowded land area eventually spread throughout China, even finding their way into neighboring countries.

The necessity for intensive cultivation also meant that there was little or no pasture in which domestic animals could graze. The Chinese countryside was dotted with pigs and chickens, but these animals did not run wild. Rather, they were carefully kept in yards or cages, and their waste was collected for use as fertilizer. Fish grew in hatcheries surrounded by fruit trees and other plants. Ducks were kept in ponds. The silt that collected at the bottom could be dredged up periodically and used to fertilize the fields. A small, nearly independent ecosystem thus could thus grow up around a pond next to a village.

Regional Interdependence

These local farming ecosystems were not completely independent of each other; rather, they were part of a much larger system that integrated regional labor, land, and crops into a network of exchange that constantly sought the most economic and efficient way to draw upon local conditions and resources to produce needed products. Such products might include staple goods, preserved or cooked foods, clothing, furniture, utensils, or tools. These products were not made for subsistence (that is, for personal use), but rather for trade. They were gathered by itinerant merchants to be sold in other regions. A network of hierarchically arranged market centers based in towns and cities spread all over China and siphoned local products from rural areas, redistributing them elsewhere. Even when China suffered the throes of internal division and civil war, the interregional economy was so tightly integrated that political divisions could not stop the exchange of goods and wealth.

The sixth century BCE in China witnessed a sustained and ongoing process of debate in which several schools of philosophy (Confucianism and Taoism chief among them) eventually shaped the Chinese way of thinking. In the emergent Chinese worldview, the cosmic order, the natural world, human society, and human individuals are all integrated into a comprehensive system in which energy and resources constantly circulate. The parts are indivisible from the whole. Consider for example the term *mai*, which means the veins and arteries of the human body. The very same term is also used to denote mountain ranges, a river's course, a network of human relationships, a family's lines of descent, or even a system of highways. The constant and unimpeded flow and circulation of energy, or *qi* through such systems—in the sky as atmosphere, in a person as spirit—is the very definition to vitality. Without a proper circulation of *qi*, there is death. Chinese acupuncturists have a term *xue* that denotes an important point of juncture in which the human body's circulating *qi* gathers and disseminates. The same term *xue* is also applied in feng shui (Chinese geomancy) to describe an auspicious site on which to construct a city, a house, or a grave.

The Chinese mentality, as reflected in the Confucian and Taoist philosophies, strives to achieve and maintain a balance between the order of the cosmos and nature on the one hand, and the order of human society on the other. Human effort should not be used for the conquest or exploitation of nature. Rather, it should accord as much as possible with the movements of natural forces. Therefore, the ancient Chinese formed in their minds a network of interaction between and among the cosmos, nature, human society and the human individual. These various levels are understood to be interlocked and constantly interacting with one another in a carefully maintained dynamic equilibrium. To upset any part of the balance is to invite adverse repercussions throughout the entire system. Hence, the Chinese believe that human abuse of nature will return in the form of nature's retaliation. In the same mode, the Confucian motto of forbearance states: "Do not do unto others what you do not wish them to do to you." The system of interrelations and balances includes the small ecosystem around a pond, the larger farmstead and its natural surroundings, and the enormous marketing network for the exchange of resources. Feng shui, literally translated, means "wind and water." The terminology is quite telling, in that it reveals the fundamental belief that human life is heavily influenced by the blowing winds and the flow of the waters.

Cho-yun Hsu

See also Biological Exchanges; Confucianism; Taoism

Further Reading

Elvin, M., & Liu, T. J. (Eds.). (1998). *Sediments of time: Environment and society in Chinese history*. New York: Cambridge University Press.

Hsu, C. 1980. *Han agriculture*. Seattle: University of Washington Press.

Tucker, M. E., & Berthrong, J. (Eds.). (1998). *Confucianism and ecology: The interrelation of heaven, earth and humans*. Cambridge, MA: Harvard University Press.

Chipko

The effectiveness of any religion in protecting the environment depends upon how much faith its believers have in its precepts. Its value depends upon how those precepts are transmitted and adapted in everyday social interactions. In the case of the Hindu religion, some of its precepts have become ingrained in daily life and social institutions. An example is the Chipko movement.

The movement began in March 1973 when villagers in the Himalayan town of Gopeshwar in Uttaranchal Province, India, formed a human chain and encircled trees to keep them from being cut down to supply a factory producing sports equipment. The movement leader, Chandi Prasad Bhatt, declared: "Let them know we will not allow the felling of a single tree. When their men raise their axes, we will embrace the trees to protect them" (Shephard 1987, 69). The same scenario occurred later in another village when logging contractors wanted to cut trees under license from the provincial government's Department of Forests.

The Chipko movement acquired a special significance in 1974. Lured by the provincial government to receive a long-disputed war compensation payment (from the 1962 China-India conflict), men of Gopeshwar had gone to Chamoli (a district headquarter), leaving only women, children, and older people behind. In the absence of the men, when lumber company employees arrived to begin logging in the Reni forest, near Joshimath (an ancient town and place of pilgrimage for Hindus), thirty women marched into the forest to resist by hugging the trees. One of the women, Gaura Devi, said that the forest was like her mother and that loggers would have to shoot her to cut a single tree. After a heated confrontation, loggers turned back without felling a single tree. Those thirty women used the satyagraha (passive resistance) philosophy of Indian nationalist and spiritual leader Mohandas Gandhi (1869–1948) to fight against an ecological abuse. Since then the Chipko *andolan* (movement) has grown from a grassroots eco-development movement to a worldwide phenomenon.

After an understanding of the Chipko movement and its relevance to environmental protection in the context of spirituality is accepted, then a common strategy for environmental stewardship can be developed. Such a strategy will depend upon how people (1) perceive a common future for humanity, (2) insist upon respect and compassion for all creatures as well as for nature itself, (3) consider integrating human values with a land ethic in the sense that any erosion of land results in turn in the erosion of human values, (4) interweave the spirituality of ahimsa (Hindu doctrine of refraining from harming any living being) into the economic, political, social, and technological domains of the secular world, and (5) believe in the crusade for the preservation and sustenance of *Vasudhaiv-kutumbkam* (the family of Mother Earth).

O. P. Dwivedi

Further Reading

Dwivedi, O. P. (2000). Dharmic ecology. In C. K. Chapple & M. E. Tucker (Eds.), *Hinduism and ecology: The intersection of Earth, sky, and water* (pp. 3–22). Cambridge, MA: Harvard University Press.

James, G. A. (2000). Ethical and religious dimensions of Chipko resistance. In C. K. Chapple & M. E. Tucker (Eds.), *Hinduism and ecology: The intersection of Earth, sky, and water* (pp. 499–530). Cambridge, MA: Harvard University Press.

Shephard, M. (1987). *Gandhi today: The story of Mahatma Gandhi's successors.* Cabin John, MD: Seven Locks Press.

Christianity *See* Catholicism; Ecology, Christian; Ecology, Spirtual; Protestantism

Circumpolar Regions

The circumpolar regions include high-latitude lands, oceans, and icecaps of the Northern and Southern Hemispheres – traditionally the Arctic, Sub-arctic, and Antarctic regions. Hard to define politically—especially in the Northern Hemisphere, where eight countries share borders—the circumpolar regions are best delineated by the distinctive plants, animals, and traditional human ways of life that have evolved in response to a harsh, cold climate.

Terrestrial Ecological Regions

The circumpolar regions occur within the Polar Domain, a large ecological region that spans Arctic, subarctic, and Antarctic environments. The Polar Domain covers 38 million square kilometers—26 percent of the Earth's surface. In the Northern Hemisphere the Polar Domain is comprised of three terrestrial divisions: icecap, tundra, and taiga (a moist subarctic forest dominated by conifers that begins where the tundra ends). Only icecap and tundra divisions occur in the Southern Hemisphere. Low temperatures and precipitation and harsh, long winters define the climate of the circumpolar regions.

Icecaps—permanent ice sheets characteristic of Greenland and Antarctica—comprise about 37 percent of the Polar Domain's area. The world's largest icecap—covering 98 percent of Antarctica—has an average depth of 1,916 meters and a maximum depth of 4,776 meters. Icecaps have the lowest mean annual temperatures of circumpolar ecological regions; no month is above freezing. Mean temperatures in the interior icecap of Antarctica—the most extreme in the Polar Domain —range from −40° C in summer to −68° C in winter. A global record low temperature, −89.2° C, was recorded in July 1983 at Vostok Station. Mean annual temperatures for the Greenland icecap—the Arctic's largest—range from −20° C to −30° C; a record low of −70° C was logged at Northice Station in 1953. Because icecaps occur at the highest latitudes, day length can range from zero hours in winter to twenty-four hours in summer. Precipitation is low, mainly fall-

The Harsh Realities of Life in the Arctic

Except among the Kanhiryuarmiut the winter from October to April is generally a hand to mouth struggle. Starvation may, and does, occur at any time, but generally the sunless days are most feared. There is seldom a winter that among one or another of the Copper tribes dogs do not die of hunger; dried sinew and clothing are eaten and the houses are without light or fuel. Specific instances of deaths from hunger are detailed in another place.

Source: Stefansson, Vilhjalmur. *The Stefansson-Anderson Arctic Expedition of the American Museum: Preliminary Ethnological Report.* (1914). Anthropological Papers of the American Museum of Natural History, Vol. XIV, Part 1. New York, p. 53.

ing as snow; it readily accumulates because of constant cold.

Tundra and taiga are defining ecological elements of the northern circumpolar region. Primarily restricted to the Arctic, tundra comprises about 15 percent of the Polar Domain's area. Short-stature grasses, sedges, dwarf shrubs, and mosses are characteristic Arctic tundra plants. In Antarctica tundra is restricted to ice-free areas of the Antarctic Peninsula and some nearby islands. Low-stature mosses, lichens, and two vascular plants, the grass *Deschampsia antarctica* and the cushion plant *Colobanthus quitensis*, occur in Antarctic tundra. Taiga—typically considered Sub-arctic—occurs entirely in the northern circumpolar region and comprises about 48 percent of the Polar Domain's area. A forested biome (a major ecological region), taiga is dominated by conifers, particularly spruce *(Picea)* and fir *(Abies)*. Taiga merges with tundra at northern latitudes and deciduous (leaf-dropping) forest at southern latitudes.

Oceans

The Polar Domain's oceans—the Arctic Ocean and the Southern Ocean—are generally low in temperature and salt content and rich in plankton (microscopic plants and animals that form the base of the food web). Ice is a characteristic feature of polar oceans; duration of ice cover during the year is the basis for classifying polar oceans into two ecological zones: the predominantly coastal inner polar division, where ice cover persists year around; and the largely marine outer polar division, where ice is probable during winter and spring. Due to drift, wind, and currents, ice is in constant motion around the poles.

The Arctic inner polar ocean division includes the Arctic Ocean and northern passages of the Canadian Archipelago. The Antarctic inner polar division is confined to a narrow perimeter around the ice shelf—large areas of ice anchored to the continent. The Arctic Ocean is contained by landmasses; thus pack ice covers the basin year around. In the Antarctic, open ocean bounds pack ice, and ice may drift north into warmer latitudes. As a result, Antarctic pack ice does not extend past 60°S in the winter. In the Arctic and Antarctica the outer polar ocean division is regularly covered by pack ice in winter, carried there by currents from the inner polar division. Oceanic currents largely shape the external boundaries of the outer polar division. In the Arctic the cold East Greenland and Labrador currents carry pack ice as far south as 46°N—the Grand Banks; the warm Gulf Stream keeps the eastern Norwegian Sea and southern Barent's Sea ice-free year around.

The circumpolar oceans are productive and support a unique array of life. In Antarctica, spring phytoplankton (planktonic plant life) blooms feed the shrimp-like krill *(Euphasia superba)* that forms the base of a Southern Ocean food web that includes ten species of whale, six species of seal, seven species of penguin—the signature species of the Antarctic—and two hundred species of fish. The Southern Ocean's productivity is made possible by a marine upwelling that surrounds the Antarctica—a zone where deep, nutrient-rich water rises upward when warmer surface waters are pushed southward by wind and deflected by the Coriolis force (an apparent force that, as a result of the Earth's rotation, deflects moving objects to the right in the Northern Hemisphere and to the left in the Southern Hemisphere). The pack ice that covers the Arctic Ocean during much of the year restricts mixing and limits light penetration; thus most productivity occurs in ice-free areas near land or in nearby subarctic regions. The Arctic marine food web is distinctive, including icons such as polar bear *(Ursus maritimus)*, walrus *(Odobenus rosmarus)*, narwhal *(Monodon monoceros)*, and beluga *(Delphinapterus leucas).*

Human Influences

Humans have inhabited the northern circumpolar region for millennia; Antarctica's isolation and extreme conditions have prevented settlement. Today, under the Antarctic Treaty of 1959, signatory nations maintain scientific research bases in the world's largest protected area.

The marine environment has been a key resource for many Arctic peoples, whose cultures were sustained by fishing and by hunting marine mammals and seabirds. Harvests by subsistence hunting and fishing were dwarfed by large-scale commercial harvest, which rose dramatically in the late 1800s to the mid-1900s. Whaling was an important early industry, especially in the Arctic: baleen (a horny substance in two rows of plates along the upper jaws of baleen whales), oil, and meat were the products. Whaling did not begin on a large scale in Antarctica until 1904; four baleen whale species, including blue whale *(Balaeoptera musculus)*, were driven to near extinction shortly thereafter, causing shifts in the food web. Over-fishing is a concern, especially in the Antarctic, where Patagonian toothfish *(Dissostichus eleginoides)* and Antarctic cod *(Notothenia coriiceps)* stocks have plummeted, and harvest of krill may threaten food web integrity.

Pollution from the developed world is a major concern for the circumpolar regions. Heavy metals, radioactive cesium, and persistent organic pollutants such as polychlorinated biphenyls, dumped or borne by winds, have entered Arctic food webs. In the Antarctic, ozone depletion—caused in part by chlorofluorocarbons—threatens phytoplankton sensitive to excess ultraviolet radiation. Global warming threatens the circumpolar region—and the world—by melting icecaps and diminishing sea ice, causing sea levels to rise, and by melting tundra and taiga permafrost, which may release greenhouse gases, including carbon dioxide and methane. Melting Arctic ice may also disrupt the global ocean circulation system—the ocean conveyor—that transports heat worldwide. The plunge of cold, dense, salty water in the North Atlantic sets the conveyor in motion by drawing warm, tropical waters

northward to replace the cold sinking waters. Freshwater from melting ice could either dilute the North Atlantic's salinity, stopping the sinking of water or insulating the surface of the ocean, limiting transfer of heat to the atmosphere. The net result would either be a cooling of the North Atlantic that could occur abruptly—in decades—and cause great ecological and economic disruption or a slow cooling over a century that may offset the effects of global warming in the region.

Charles E. Williams

Further Reading

Armstrong, T., Rogers, G., & Rowley, G. (1978). *The circumpolar north: A political and economic geography of the Arctic and Sub-arctic*. London: Routledge.

Gagosian, R. (2003). *Abrupt climate change: Should we be worried?* Woods Hole, MA: Woods Hole Oceanographic Institution.

Kerr, R. (1999). Will the Arctic Ocean lose all its ice? *Science, 286*, 1828.

Lopez, B. (1986). *Arctic dreams: Imagination and desire in a northern landscape*. New York: Scribner.

McGonigal, D., Woodworth, L., & Hillary, E. (2001). *Antarctica and the Arctic: The complete encyclopedia*. Westport, CT: Firefly Books.

Montaigne, F. (2002). Boreal: The great northern forest. *National Geographic, 201*(6), 42–65.

Mulvaney, K. (2001). *At the ends of the Earth: A history of the polar regions*. Washington, DC: Island Press.

Smith. R. (2001). Frozen under. *National Geographic, 200*(6), 2–35.

Stone, G. S. (2001). Exploring Antarctica's islands of ice. *National Geographic, 200*(6), 36–51.

Vaughan, R. (1999). *The Arctic: A history*. Phoenix Mill, UK: Sutton Publishing.

Civilian Conservation Corps (CCC)

The Civilian Conservation Corps (CCC) was a major conservation initiative of President Franklin D. Roosevelt's first administration. The CCC reflected Roosevelt's strong interest in conservation, which dated back to his days in the New York State Senate. Created by the Unemployment Relief Act of March 1933, the CCC, first known as "Emergency Conservation Work," was designed to help alleviate unemployment during the Great Depression. Its name was changed to "Civilian Conservation Corps" by the Conservation Corps Act of June 1937.

During the CCC's nine-year existence, more than 3 million men, of whom 225,000 were World War I veterans and 15,000 were Native Americans, undertook a wide range of conservation projects. A modest number of African Americans were also employed, but their ranks were limited because of the requirement that the majority of them be housed in segregated units. The CCC men were involved in soil conservation projects that included building 6 million dams to control erosion, reforesting, fire fighting, constructing and upgrading roads in national forests, managing wildlife, restoring and protecting historic sites, and repairing reservoirs. The CCC men, aged eighteen to twenty-five, all of whom volunteered, were paid $30 a month, $25 of which went to their hard-pressed families. They were provided meals, uniforms, and housing in units of two hundred men placed in twenty-five hundred CCC camps around the country. The unemployed men who participated in the program were selected by the Department of Labor, and the War Department had responsibility for transporting the men to the camps, which were administered by U.S. Army officers. In 1935, its peak year, the CCC employed about five hundred thousand men. Southern-born Robert Fechner (1876–1939), the agency's first director and a former vice president of the American Federation of Labor, instituted the segregation policy. His successor, James J. McEntee (1884–1957), another labor union man who had been Fechner's assistant, took over for the remaining three years that the CCC was in operation.

With the coming of World War II, national unemployment pressures eased, and many of the CCC men were needed in the armed forces. Despite the agency's popularity—it was probably the New Deal's best-liked initiative—and in spite of vigorous objections from President Roosevelt, Congress closed the agency in July 1942. The CCC is perhaps best remembered for the planting of trees. Three-quarters of all trees planted in the United States from 1776 to 1942 were planted by CCC men. Citizens generally were grateful for the fact that CCC enrollees were in safe hands under U.S. Army management. In addition, residents in communities located near CCC camps appreciated the money spent by the CCC men in those communities during their off-duty hours, which did much to shore up local economies.

Keir B. Sterling

Further Reading

Lacy, L. A. (1976). *The soil soldiers: The Civilian Conservation Corps in the Great Depression.* Radnor, PA: Chilton.

Pinkett, H. T. (Comp.). (1948). *Preliminary inventory of the records of the Civilian Conservation Corps* (Preliminary Inventories No. 11). Washington, DC: National Archives.

Rawick, G. P. (1957). *The New Deal and youth: The Civilian Conservation Corps, the National Youth Administration, and the American Youth Congress.* Unpublished doctoral dissertation, University of Wisconsin-Madison.

Salmond, J. A. (1967). *The Civilian Conservation Corps, 1933–1942: A New Deal case study.* Durham, NC: Duke University Press.

Clamshell Alliance

The Clamshell Alliance was a citizen action group formed in 1976 to oppose the construction of a nuclear power station in Seabrook, New Hampshire. The alliance consisted of loosely knit antinuclear groups in New England. A central office coordinated activities and disseminated information between groups, which included environmentalists, members of the fishing community, and concerned citizens. The Clamshell Alliance adopted nonviolent tactics as part of its Declaration of Nuclear Resistance to protest Seabrook Station.

Seabrook Station is located 21 kilometers south of Portsmouth, New Hampshire, on the Atlantic coast, near a salt marsh estuary. It is one of the most controversial and litigated reactors in the United States. Opposition to Seabrook Station began mobilizing in 1972 through state proceedings against the dangers of nuclear power and related environmental issues. Legal battles that challenged the federal licensing and regulatory proceedings began in 1975 and lasted twenty-five years.

When construction of twin 1,150-megawatt power plants began in 1976, the Clamshell Alliance staged a series of nonviolent site occupations and demonstrations. Within a year, the alliance had attracted thousands of antinuclear activists. On 30 April 1977 Clamshell Alliance affinity groups and supporters camped out at the construction site to halt progress. When they marched together on the site, singing and chanting, 1,414 activists were arrested. Noncooperation was one of the tactics recommended by the Clamshell Alliance, so state police arresting noncooperating demonstrators had to drag them to buses. The police buses were filled quickly; the National Guard was called in to assist with arrests. It took twelve hours to remove all the demonstrators. Reporters and photographers were arrested as well.

This Clamshell Alliance demonstration was the first major mass occupation of a nuclear plant site in the United States. The alliance actions were based on consensus decision making. When planning the occupation at Seabrook, hundreds of participants discussed and agreed to the scenario. As the police began arresting the perceived leaders of the group, the occupation was not abandoned. Protestors were charged with a misdemeanor. New Hampshire Governor Meldrim Thomson ordered that protestors be held in county jails and National Guard armories for up to two weeks.

The Clamshell Alliance received unprecedented media attention and sparked opposition to proposed nuclear power stations across the country. With the national visibility that it generated, the Seabrook protest was considered a great success. Prior to the protest, the federal Nuclear Regulatory Commission had never denied a plant permit or halted construction on a project. Due to efforts by the alliance, the growth of nuclear power in the United States was stalled for more than two decades, and many plant projects were cancelled. Although the alliance eventually disbanded, citizen groups continued to protest the Seabrook construction. Despite this opposition, the Seabrook Station opened for commercial operation in 1990.

Two concepts—nonviolent direct action and consensus decision making—governed the Clamshell Alliance. The alliance stimulated other peaceful antinuclear activities in New England through the late 1980s. Protests were waged against proposed nuclear reactors in Montague and Plymouth, Massachusetts, and in Millbrook, Connecticut; the alliance also took action toward dismantling an existing facility in Vernon, Vermont. Regional organizations modeled after the Clamshell Alliance and its civil disobedience tactics initiated antinuclear campaigns across the United States.

In 1990 Clamshell Alliance cofounder Guy Chichester ran for governor of New Hampshire on the platform of "no nukes." During his campaign as a Green Party candidate, Chichester was under indictment for cutting down one of the test sirens that the government-utility owner of the Seabrook reactor had installed. Chichester won 1.3 percent of votes as a write-in gubernatorial candidate and was acquitted

by a jury of his peers, who, like most New Hampshire residents, were also opposed to the Seabrook Station.

Owned and operated by the North Atlantic Energy Service Corporation, the Seabrook reactor continues to be a controversial site and is the focus of a public radiological monitoring program called Citizens Within the Ten Mile Radius.

Robin O'Sullivan

Further Reading

Asinof, R. (1977). No-nukers demonstrate their strength at Seabrook. *The Valley Advocate*.

Bedford, H. F. (1992). *Seabrook Station, citizen politics and nuclear power*. Amherst: University of Massachusetts Press.

Belisle, M., & Fitz, D. (1997). A green campaign for governor of New Hampshire. *Synthesis/Regeneration, 12*. Retrieved January 2, 2003, from http://web.greens.org/s-r/12/12–10.html

Mowrey, M. (1993). *Not in our backyard: The people and events that shaped America's modern environmental movement*. New York: W. Morrow.

Steven, D. W. (1980). *Seabrook & the Nuclear Regulatory Commission: The licensing of a nuclear power plant*. Hanover, NH: University Press of New England.

Wasserman, H. (1996). Slaying the nuclear dragon. *Mother Jones*. Retrieved January 2, 2003, from http://www.motherjones.com/mother_jones/MJ96/wasserman.htm l

Clements, Frederic

(1874–1945)
U.S. ecologist

Frederic E. Clements was a key proponent of "the prairie school" of American ecology. His "dynamic ecology" constructed an image of vegetation growth, primarily under the environmental influence of climate, passing through "successions" from the primitive to the complex toward stable, enduring climax plant communities that were in themselves virtual organisms. As the leader of the Nebraska wing of the "prairie school," Clements's views clashed with the less doctrinaire Chicago school. The University of Chicago professor Henry C. Cowles studied the dunes of Lake Michigan where he detected a less predictable, capricious nature that ran contrary to the exactness of the Clementsian paradigm.

The "succession model" appealed to federal land managers in the new resource agencies who adopted the terminology and methodology of Clements in an effort to ground their policy decisions in science. By mid-twentieth century Clements's ideas passed out of vogue, but agencies and range technicians still employed "succession and climax" terms to describe and analyze vegetation.

Clements also infused American botanical science with ideas of evolutionary progress prevailing in other disciplines—biology and even history with Frederick Jackson Turner's thesis that settlement of the American frontier evolved from simple pioneer colonies to complex communities through successive stages of development.

Clements's career began in the summer of 1893 with an investigation of the effect of recurring droughts upon the vegetation of his native Nebraska. In Clements's studies at the University of Nebraska, the innovative botanist Charles Bessey made Clements aware of European botanical studies of plant communities and the implications for practical application in serving the purposes of a land grant university. Clements received his Bachelors degree in 1894, his masters in 1896, and doctorate in 1898.

Clements's dissertation was in collaboration with the future legal scholar, Roscoe Pound, entitled "The Phytogeography of Nebraska." This "reconnaissance" of the vegetation mantle of Nebraska foreshowed more ambitious studies emphasizing dynamic processes in vegetation growth. His 1905 *Research Methods in Ecology* outlined an approach to vegetation studies emphasizing measurement and experimentation to understand the composition of vegetation—not just the individual plant but the community. His emphasis upon counting the number of plants in marked plots ("the quadrat method") appears as a methodological forerunner of modern population ecology.

In 1916, Clements's *Plant Succession: An Analysis of the Development of Vegetation* emphasized "dynamic ecology" or change, process, and direction. This work, plus his *Plant Indicators: The Relation of Plant Communities to Process and Practice* (1920) brought his studies to the tasks of the practical world—to understand natural processes for concrete utilitarian reasons, e.g. range science, livestock forage production, and erosion control. Clements's career took him from the University of Nebraska to the University of Minnesota and finally to the Carnegie Foundation in 1919 as a research scientist

where he remained until his retirement in 1941. During these years he traveled widely by automobile, with his wife and colleague Edith Schwartz Clements behind the wheel, driving more than 300,000 miles to every part of the American West for their investigations. He and Edith maintained an alpine laboratory on the slopes of Pikes Peak west of Colorado Springs where university graduate students supported by his research grants conducted experiments for their graduate degrees, disseminating his ideas over the course their own careers. His succession and climax theories became popular primarily among ecologists in North America, Australia, and South Africa.

William D. Rowley

Further Reading

Hagen, J. B. (1992). *An entangled bank: The origins of ecosystem ecology*. New Brunswick, NJ: Rutgers University Press.

Overfield, R. (1993). *Science with practice: Charles E. Bessey and the maturing of American botany*. Ames: Iowa State University Press.

Steen, H. K. (Ed.). (1999). *Forest and wildlife science in America: A history*. Durham, NC: Forest History Society.

Tobey, R. C. (1981). *Saving the prairies: The life cycle of the founding school of American plant ecology, 1895–1955*. Berkeley: University of California Press.

Climate

Climate is the average condition of the weather at a place over a period of years. The issue of whether changes in climate have had a significant impact on history is controversial. It should not be overlooked that both *climate* and *history* are blanket terms located on such a high level of abstraction that relationships between them cannot be investigated according to the rules of scientific methodology. To be more meaningful, the issue needs to be broken down to lower scales of analysis, for example, by focusing on specific human activities and/or needs in relation to a given set of climatic variables. Regarding preindustrial societies this concerns primarily the availability of biomass (the amount of living matter, e.g., food, fodder) and energy (e.g., wind, water power, draft animals), secondly population dynamics (e.g., patterns of disease, fertility of humans and livestock), and thirdly communications as well as military and naval operations. Undoubtedly, beneficial climatic effects tend to enlarge the scope of human action, whereas climatic shocks restrict it or even lead to emergency situations. Seasonal patterns of temperature and rainfall mattered for energy availability and population dynamics depended on the environmental, cultural, and historical context.

Regular instrumental observations of temperature and precipitation were taken within national networks from the 1860s. For the previous period the study of climate draws on proxy (indirect) data from natural and human archives. Data from natural archives (e.g., corals, varves [pairs of layers of alternately finer and coarser silt or clay believed to comprise an annual cycle of deposition in a body of water], fossil pollen, tree rings, ocean and lake sediments, ice cores) are essential for those times and places for which documentary evidence is sparse or nonexistent, such as precolonial United States or the high latitudes.

Documentary evidence (human archives) allows reconstructing seasonal or monthly conditions and disentangling temperature and precipitation. Therefore, documentary evidence is better suited for investigating the human dimension of climatic change. Documentary evidence is well researched in Europe and eastern Asia. In Latin America promising research has begun. For the major oceanic areas a worldwide database of daily weather information is gathered from naval logbooks. For Africa documentary evidence is still spotty. In the Islamic world the possibly abundant documentary evidence remains to be explored.

Documentary evidence is investigated by the historical climatology branch of science, which is situated at the interface between climatology and environmental history. Historical climatology focuses on interpreting current natural disasters within a historical context, investigates the vulnerability of past economies and societies, and explores past discourses on, and social representations of, climate. Documentary evidence is classified according to several criteria. (See table 1.)

Direct observations include chroniclers' narratives of weather patterns memorable to a particular region. A special focus is on rare but socioeconomically significant extreme events. In China records have been kept for more than two thousand years, in Europe for nearly one thousand years. Daily weather observations were promoted in Europe beginning in the late fifteenth century by the rise of planetary astronomy. Narrative and/or early instrumental observations were discontinuous.

In order to more objectively portray the character of extreme climatic events, chroniclers often referred to physical and biological proxy indicators, such as the duration of snow cover, the freezing and altitude of water bodies, or the development of crops. Some kinds of indirect data were the product of routine administrative processes; that is, they were recorded in an institutional framework for socioeconomic reasons. In this case they were often continuous. For example, for centuries the beginning of wine and grain harvests was regulated by many communities in order to prevent tax evasion. For another example, wages paid on Saturdays for community work (e.g., cutting ice at the mills, harvesting) in the town of Louny (northwestern Bohemia) were record regularly. These were scrupulously recorded in a book of accounts from 1450 to 1632 and can be used as proxies for temperature reconstruction. In Spain the Catholic Church organized *rogativas* (rogations), which were standardized liturgical actions meant to end climatic stress situations connected with long dry (*pro pluvia* [for rain] rogations) or wet spells (*pro serenitate* [for sun] rogations) that jeopardized crops.

Reconstructing climate from documentary evidence involves the construction of temperature and precipitation intensity indices ranging from −3 (very cold or dry) to +3 (very warm or wet). Series of intensity indices are included in statistical models to reconstruct monthly gridded mean air pressure at sea level and temperature for the eastern North Atlantic-European region. These spatial reconstructions of climate in terms of colored charts are made on a monthly level dating back to 1659 and on a seasonal level dating back to 1500.

Climate before 1000 CE

Climate during the last 2 million years is characterized by alternating warm and cool periods. These variations are initiated by changes in the Earth's orbital parameters. During the last ice age temperatures were generally lower and were characterized by large and irregular fluctuations. A global warming trend, starting eighteen thousand years ago, put a provisional end to full glacial climate conditions. Five thousand years later temperatures plummeted again about 3 to 4° C within a few decades. This last ice age relapse, called the "Younger Dryas," lasted about a thousand years and put an end to the last ice age. The climate of the subsequent and current postglacial period, the Holocene, has so far remained fairly stable. In Europe it is

TABLE 1.
CLASSIFICATION OF DOCUMENTARY EVIDENCE

Perception of Weather and Climate	Kind of Evidence	
Direct	*Observed*	*Measured*
	Weather anomalies	Barometric pressure
	Natural hazards	Temperature
	Weather spells	Precipitation
	Daily weather	Water-gauge, etc.
Indirect (Proxy Data)	*Organic*	*Inorganic*
	Phenology	Water levels
	Crop yields	Duration of snow, frost, and ice
	Time of crop harvests	
	Cultural	*Epigraphical*
	Rogation ceremonies	Archeological remains

Source: Pfister, Brázdil, & Glaser (1999).

divided into century-long cold periods that alternate with warm periods. The longest and most pronounced warm period took place nine thousand to fifty-five hundred years ago. Since then a more rapid irregular alternation of warm and cold periods has been observed.

The Last Millennium

The best known of these periods are the Medieval Warm Epoch (the more appropriate term *Medieval Climatic Anomaly* is suggested because it removes the emphasis on temperature as its defining characteristic) from about 900 to 1300 and a subsequent cool period lasting to the late nineteenth century that is called the "Little Ice Age" because glaciers in most regions of the globe were expanding during that time. In the Northern Hemisphere the average annual temperature during the twentieth century was the highest of the last millennium, the 1990s being the warmest decade of the millennium, partly as a consequence of the increased greenhouse effect (warming of the surface and lower atmosphere of the Earth caused by conversion of solar radiation into heat). The primary sources of interannual variability in global surface temperature patterns during past centuries are the El Niño Southern Oscillation (ENSO) in the Pacific and the North Atlantic Oscillation (NAO).

However, such generalizations mask a broad array of regional and local trends. In order to investigate human vulnerability to climatic impacts, the perspective of "ages" needs to be broken down to monthly or seasonal temperature and precipitation patterns on the regional level. So far this time resolution is available only for Europe and China.

Central Europe

After a cold relapse in the twelfth century winters were mild from 1180 to 1300. Subsequently the winter half-year was colder than today until the end of the nineteenth century. This is connected to a more frequent and sustained advection (horizontal transfer) of cold-dry continental air masses from the northeast. Icy winters were frequent during the periods of 1306–1328, 1430–1490, 1565–1615, 1655–1710, 1755–1860, and 1880–1895. From 1365 to 1400, 1520 to 1560, and 1610 to 1650 winters were somewhat warmer. Springs were particularly chilly in the 1690s and in the 1740s. Temperature and precipitation in winter increased over most of the twentieth century.

Summers do not show distinct long-term characteristics. Those during the thirteenth century were warm and dry. During the fourteenth century clusters of cool and wet summers occurred repeatedly (e.g., in the 1310s and 1340s). From 1380 to 1430 and again from 1530 to 1565 the summer half-year was as warm as during the twentieth century. During the last one-third of the sixteenth century cold spells and long rains in midsummer expanded at the expense of warm anticyclonic (relating to a system of winds that rotates about a center of high atmospheric pressure clockwise in the Northern Hemisphere and counterclockwise in the Southern Hemisphere) weather. This trend culminated in the 1590s. Summers in the early and late seventeenth century were rather cool; temperatures from 1630 to 1687 were close to the twentieth-century average. During the 1700s several warm decades (1720s, 1730s, and 1780s) stand out in England and in central Europe, whereas the first half of the nineteenth century, particularly the 1810s, was markedly cooler.

Russia

Winters became severe during the final decades of the sixteenth century, particularly from 1620 to 1680, and during the first half of the nineteenth century. Summer droughts were frequent between 1201 and 1230, between 1351 and 1380, and between 1411 and 1440. Conditions were rather warm in all seasons in the first half of the sixteenth century. Subsequently, pronounced cold spells stand out from 1590 to 1620 and from 1690 to 1740. Summer droughts were frequent from 1640 to 1659 and from 1680 to 1699. The period from 1770 to 1830 was warm, and numerous droughts were reported from 1801 to 1860. Summers from 1890 to 1920 were by far the chilliest of the last five hundred years; this period also included an unusually large number of extreme dry and wet seasons.

China

In southern China the thirteenth century was the warmest of the last millennium. The Little Ice Age, the long cooling trend from the high Middle Ages until the late nineteenth century, was well documented in Europe and also evident in China. Three cold periods—1470–1520, 1620–1740, and 1840–1890—are identified, the 1650s being by far the coldest decade. After 1310 the temperature plummeted at a rate of .1° C per century. Temperatures during four cold periods were .6–.9° C lower than the modern mean: 1321–1350 (−.6° C), 1441–1470 (−.7° C), −1680 (−1.1° C), and 1861–1890 (−.9° C). The 1650s were 1.1° C below the modern mean. Subsequently the winter half-year grew warmer. Climate variability increased markedly throughout the nineteenth century to a maximum in the early twentieth century. In northern China two cold periods—1500 to 1690 and 1800 to 1860—stand out over the last six centuries. Considering all seasons, the period from 1650 to 1670 was the coldest, but the summer half-year was almost equally cold from 1580 to 1600.

Mediterranean

After a cold twelfth century the period from 1200 to 1400 was warm in the southwestern part of the Medi-

terranean basin. Annual precipitation in Morocco was generally lower from the sixteenth to nineteenth centuries. In Catalonia (northeastern Spain) dry spells during the winter half-year were frequent in the mid-sixteenth century but almost absent from 1580 to 1620. Numerous autumnal floods were reported from 1580 to 1630, from 1770 to 1800, and again from 1840 to 1870.

Africa

In Africa the critical issue in most regions is the precipitation in the monsoon season. Annual rainfall levels mark the boundaries of vegetation zones, for example, between the Sahelian (semidesert fringe of the southern Sahara Desert) cattle zone and the savanna where rain-fed crops are grown. During wetter periods isohyets (lines on a map connecting areas of equal rainfall) advanced northward, during drier periods, they advanced southward. In western Africa a wet period stands out from 700 to 1300. It was followed by a drier period from 1300 to 1500. Between 1500 and 1700 rainfall was so plentiful that the savanna zone extended to Timbuktu (16° N latitude). Beginning in the eighteenth century the monsoon receded again. By 1850 the savanna had moved 200 to 300 kilometers southward. Arab camel nomads advanced in the wake of this shift, and black cattle raisers retreated. In the 1820s and 1830s rainfall was below average in large parts of the continent. From 1870 to 1900 rainfall increased. Lake levels and the discharge of major streams exceeded the twentieth-century average.

Latin America

In Latin America there seemed to have been a trend toward greater aridity in the 1700s compared to the previous century. Dendroclimatic evidence (obtained by analyzing the rings in the cross-section of a tree trunk) for central Chile indicates higher-than-average rainfall from 1450 to 1600, whereas several severe droughts were reported over the subsequent centuries (e.g., 1637–1640, 1770–1773, 1790s, and 1810s). In the Buenos Aires region (Argentina) the 1700s were drier than the 1600s. Severe droughts occurred in the 1690s, the 1710s, the 1750s, and 1771–1774.

ENSO and the Pacific

The El Niño Southern Oscillation (ENSO) is the result of a cyclic warming and cooling of the surface of the central and eastern Pacific Ocean that strongly affects rainfall in the areas around the Pacific and the Indian Ocean. It was defined in 1891, in northern Peru, as a combination of anomalously warm sea temperature, stronger-than-usual southward coastal current, and high rainfall in the Sechura Desert. Archival data suggest that the effects of the ENSO episodes from 1600 to 1900 were more intense and more global than those of the twentieth century. For example, the worst droughts in the colonial history of India (mid–1590s, 1629–1633, 1685–1688, 1788–1793, and 1877–1878) were caused by ENSO-related failures of the monsoon. The last two events in particular had global effects. Beyond ENSO, global weather anomalies are also induced by large volcanic eruptions (e.g., the 1815 explosion of Tambora, Indonesia).

Historical Significance of Climatic Change

Models of climatic effects on society are often framed as a chain of causation. Climatic patterns have a first-order, or biophysical, impact on agricultural production or on the outbreak of diseases or epizootics. These may have second-order impacts (caused by the first-order impacts) on prices of food or raw materials, which may then ramify into the wider economy and society (third-order impacts). The farther people move away from first-order impacts, the greater the complexity of the factors masking the climatic effects. It is easier to investigate the effects of short-term (annual and perennial) effects. In dealing with the effects of multi-decadal climate variations, researchers must account for modifications in the economic, institutional, and environmental settings so great as to flaw any attempt at strict comparison or measurement. Societies tend to adapt to climate changes.

Christian Pfister

See also Droughts; Earthquakes; Floods; Weather Events, Extreme

Further Reading

Alverson, K. D., Bradley, R. S., & Pedersen, T. (2003). *Paleoclimate, global change and the future.* Heidelberg, Germany: Springer.

Bradley, R. S., & Jones, P. D. (Eds.). (1996). *Climate since A.D. 1500* (2nd ed.). London: Routledge.

Brázdil, R., & Kotyza, O. (2000). *History of weather and climate in the Czech lands: Vol. 4. Utilisation of economic sources for the study of climate fluctuation at Louny and surroundings in the fifteenth–seventeenth centuries.* Brno, Czech Republic: Masaryk University.

Claxton, R. H. (1993). The record of drought and its impact in colonial Spanish America. In R. Herr (Ed.), *Themes in rural history of the Western world* (pp. 194–226). Ames: Iowa State University Press.

Grove, R. H., & Chappell, J. (Eds.). (2000). *El Niño: History and crisis.* Isle of Harris, Scotland: White Horse Press.

Luterbacher, J., Xoplaki, E., Dietrich, D., Jones, P. D., Davies, T. D., Portis, D., Gonzales-Rouco, J. F., von Storch, H., Gyalistras, D., Casty, C., & Wanner, H. (2002). Extending North Atlantic oscillation reconstructions back to 1500. *Atmospheric Science Letters, 3*(2), 114–124.

Luterbacher, J., Xoplaki, E., Dietrich, D., Rickli, R., Jacobeit, J., Beck, C., Gyalistras, D., Schmutz, C., & Wanner, H. (2002). Reconstruction of sea level pressure fields over the eastern North Atlantic and Europe back to 1500. *Climate Dynamics, 18,* 545–561.

Mann, M. E., Bradley, R. S., & Hughes, M. K. (1999). Northern Hemisphere temperatures during the past millennium: Inferences, uncertainties, and limitations. *Geophysical Research Letters, 26,* 759–762.

Martin Vide, J., & Barriendos, M. (1995). The use of rogation ceremony records in climatic reconstruction: A case study from Catalonia (Spain). *Climatic Change, 30,* 201–221.

McCann, J. (1999). Climate and causation in African history. *The International Journal of African Historical Studies, 32*(2–3), 261–279.

Metcalfe, S. E., del Rosario Prieto, M., Endfield, G. H., Davies, S. J., & O'Hara, S. L. (2002). The potential of archival sources for reconstructing climate and climate-related processes in Latin America. *PAGES News, 10*(3), 11–14.

Ortlieb, L., Gabriel Vargas, G., & Hocquenghem, A. M. (2002). ENSO reconstruction based on documentary data from Ecuador, Peru and Chile. *PAGES News, 10*(3), 14–17.

Pfister, C., Brázdil, R., & Barriendos, M. (2002). Reconstructing past climate and natural disasters in Europe using documentary evidence. *PAGES News, 10*(3), 6–8.

Pfister, C., Brázdil, R., & Glaser, R. (1999). *Climatic variability in sixteenth century Europe and its social dimension.* Dordrecht, Netherlands: Kluwer.

Trenberth, K. E. (2001). Climate: El Niño-Southern Oscillation (ENSO). In J. Steele, S. Thorpe, & K. Turekian (Eds.), *Encyclopedia of ocean sciences* (pp. 815–827). San Diego, CA: Academic Press.

Wang, S. W. (1991). Reconstruction of temperature series of North China from 1380s to 1980s. *Science in China, Series B, 34*(6), 751–759.

Watson, R. T. (Ed.). (2002). *Climate change 2001: Synthesis report: Third assessment report of the Intergovernmental Panel on Climate Change (IPCC)*. Cambridge, UK: Cambridge University Press.

Climate Change *See* Global Warming

Club of Rome

Founded in 1968 in the Italian capital, the Club of Rome is a private think tank that brings together a diverse mix of former politicians, civil servants, and scientists. One of its reports—*Limits to Growth*—provoked widespread public debate when it was published in 1972.

This Report argued that not only was infinite growth impossible on a finite planet, but also that environmental constraints upon human activity would begin to bite in the not-too-distant future. Furthermore, the consequences of ignoring those limits could only be disastrous.

The arguments contained in *Limits* were not new in themselves. Obviously, there are limits to the Earth's resources, just as there are limits to the amount of pollution it can absorb. The most distinctive aspect of *Limits* was its use of computer-generated mathematical models to illustrate what was happening to the world.

Critics argued that the Club's dismal view of the future was based on an unwarranted extrapolation of selected trends, many of which could change. The report was particularly attacked for underestimating human creativity and the potential of technology to solve problems. Yet, given the signs of disastrous climatic change and other serious environmental dysfunction, perhaps the Club of Rome was closer to the truth after all; the Club's stance on the limits to technology-based solutions also seems vindicated. The most serious defect of the Club's report was its focus on individual resources such as minerals. Though many resource prices have not followed the predicted upward spiral, prices often do not reflect *total* costs, especially environmental ones. More importantly, the problem is not that resources are going to "run out," but rather that the Earth cannot sustain the side-effects of general environmental degradation that unavoidably result from current levels of resource use. The real question is not how much fossil fuel remains to be tapped, but rather what will happen if we continue to burn it at current rates.

A distinctive part in the Club's work is identifying future scenarios. To deal with these, the Club stresses countries' interdependence and the need for a cooperative approach. Also emphasized is the need to think holistically and see connections between the political, social, economic, technological, environmental, psychological, and cultural dimensions. The Club views the challenge not in terms of individual crises but rather as a constellation of crises.

Sandy Irvine

Further Reading

Hardin, G. (1980). Limited world, limited rights. *Society, 17*(4), 5–8.

Hodson, H. V. (1977). *The diseconomies of growth*. London: Earth Island.

Kassiola, J. (1990). *The death of industrial civilization*. Albany, NY: State University of New York Press.

Ophuls, W. (1993). *Ecology and the politics of scarcity*. San Francisco: Freeman.

Sears, P. (1958). The inexorable problem of space. *Science, 127*, 9–16.

Meadows, D., et al (1992). *Beyond the limits: Global collapse or sustainable future*. London: Earthscan.

Tinbergen, J. (Ed.). (1976). *Rio report: Reshaping the international order*. New York: Dutton.

Dieren, W. Van, (Ed.). (1995). *Taking nature into account: Towards a sustainable national income*. New York: Springer.

Borgese, E. M. (1998). *The oceanic circle: Governing the seas as a global resource*. Tokyo: United Nations University Press.

Cook, E. (1982). The consumer as creator: A criticism of faith in limitless ingenuity. *Energy exploration & exploitation, 1*(3), 189–201.

Daly, H. (1990). Boundless bull. *Cannett centre journal, 4*(3), 113–118.

Ehrlich, P. (1989). The limits to substitution. *Ecological economics, 1*(1), 9–16.

Georgescu-Roegen, N. (1971). *The entropy law and the economic process*. Cambridge, MA: Harvard University Press.

Meadows, D., et al. (1972). *The limits to growth*. New York: Universe Books.

Coal

The combustion of coal for fuel energized the transition from traditional to modern economies, and coal continues to supply about one-quarter of the world's primary energy, which includes fossil and biomass fuels and hydro and nuclear electricity. People have known about coal since prehistory (outcropping of seams is common), but its documented use as a fuel in antiquity was limited (the most important application was in ironmaking during the Han dynasty in China, from about 200 BCE to 9 CE). European extraction of coal began in Belgium in the early twelfth century, and regional wood shortages—caused not only by rising demand for fuelwood and charcoal but also by rising demands for construction and shipbuilding timber—were the main reason for the gradual transition to coal in parts of early modern Europe. This transition took place first in England, where most of the coalfields that operated during the twentieth century were already exploited between 1540 and 1640, and then in other deforested or industrializing regions (the Dutch "Golden Age" of the seventeenth century was a notable exception because it was fueled by large-scale extraction of peat).

In spite of its low productivity and high risk, traditional coal mining, which relied solely on human labor for extraction and loading, expanded roughly one hundredfold during the nineteenth century, from about 10 million metric tons in the early 1800s to 1 billion metric ton a century later. By that time U.S. production was dominant, but the United States was, in turn, surpassed after 1950 by the Soviet Union and during the 1980s by China. Gradual mechanization of coal cutting and loading eventually doubled and even tripled productivity in underground mining, but the greatest advances came from a radical shift from underground to surface mining. Surface mines now produce about 60 percent of U.S. output, and China remains the only major coal producer with marginal surface extraction. In addition to increasing productivity (commonly ten to fifteen times higher than underground mining, with peak output surpassing 30 metric tons per worker a day), surface mining has drastically reduced accidents and exposure to coal dust.Underground mining, which is also much safer in the United States now, continues to be deadly in the Ukraine and China; chronic dust inhalation causing black lung disease continues to be a major problem even in U.S. and European underground mines.

Coal Uses

Households and small manufacturers (ranging from brick makers to soap makers) were the earliest users of coal for fuel. Coke (a residue of coal) became the dominant fuel in British blast furnaces after 1750, but in the United States charcoal, which was abundant, was the leading metallurgical fuel until the 1880s. James Watt's improved steam engine (patented in 1769) and its even more efficient successors became the largest coal consumers for the next 130 years. The rise of coal-fired electricity generation shifted most of the demand for coal to larger boilers producing pressurized steam for turbogenerators. After World War II steam engines also disappeared from rail and water transportation. With household coal combustion almost completely displaced by fuel oil and more recently by natural gas and with chemical syntheses relying almost exclusively on hydrocarbons, the Western coal market now has just two components: high-quality fuel to produce coke for blast furnace smelting iron and medium- to low-quality bituminous coals and lignites to produce steam for electricity generation.

During the early 1970s, with cheap crude oil and a rapid rise of nuclear electricity generation, coal was widely predicted to become a marginal fuel by the year 2000. But global coal output kept on increasing, and by 1988, when it peaked with about 3.6 billion metric tons of bituminous coal and 1.3 billion metric tons of lignites, it was about 30 percent above the 1975 level. Even with the abrupt decline in production by countries of the former Soviet Union during the early 1990s and with an equally abrupt decline in China's coal extraction before the decade's end, coal output was about 18 percent higher in 2000 than in 1975. Coal's share of the world's total primary energy supply—25 percent—is virtually identical to that of natural gas. Coal was the energy foundation of Western industrialization, and it continues to be a critical primary energy source in affluent North America and Europe as well as in rapidly modernizing Asia—but a significant environmental price has been paid.

Impacts on the Atmosphere

Even high-quality coal contains 1–2 percent sulfur and about 10 percent ash, and low-quality steam coal can contain as much as 3–5 percent and 25–40 percent, respectively. Uncontrolled coal combustion is thus a large source of particulate matter (soot and fly ash) and sulfur dioxide. The combination of these air pollutants created smog whose semipermanent presence caused chronic lung diseases and whose episodic peaks caused deaths in all highly polluted areas from the late nineteenth century until the 1950s. This pollution decreased radically after 1955 with the widespread installation of electrostatic precipitators that can remove more than 99 percent of fly ash. During the 1970s, as evidence showed that sulfur dioxide from coal combustion is the single largest contributor to acid rain, many power plants began installing flue gas desulfurization. Together with a switch to natural gas and low-sulfur coal, these controls reversed the trend of rising sulfurous emissions in Europe and North America. In contrast, coal combustion—be it in simple household stoves, in boilers producing steam for residential heating or industrial enterprises, and in electricity-generating plants of all sizes—continues to be the single largest source of often-severe air pollution in China as well as in parts of India.

Coal resources are sufficient to maintain, or even to increase, coal's share of global energy use. Coal resources, estimated at 6.2–11.4 trillion metric tons, are so immense that there is no possibility of shortages not only during the twenty-first but also during the twenty-second century. At about 230 years in the year 2000, coal's global reserves to production ratio is more than three times that of natural gas and more than four times that of crude oil. Environmental concerns will determine coal's eventual fate. Although even the difficult challenge of removing nitrogen oxide generated during high-temperature combustion of coal now appears to have an effective technical solution, there are no practical, large-scale means of eliminating or sequestering carbon dioxide generated during coal combustion. Coal is the most carbonaceous fossil fuel (typically with a carbon to hydrogen ratio of 1, compared to 0.5 for crude oil and 0.25 for natural gas), and the only viable partial solution to coal's greenhouse gas burden is to make its conversion more efficient and hence less carbon dioxide intensive. In any case, coal's fate will depend on the rate and the magnitude of future global climate change.

Vaclav Smil

See also Air Pollution; Climate Change; Energy; Industrialization

Further Reading

British Petroleum. (2002). *Review of world energy*. London: British Petroleum.

Flinn, M. W., et al. (1984–1993). *History of the British coal industry*. Oxford, UK: Oxford University Press.

Nef, U. (1932). *The rise of the British coal industry*. London: George Routledge & Sons.

Odell, P. R. (1999). *Fossil fuel resources in the 21st century*. London: Financial Times Energy.

Rogner, H.-H. (2000). Energy resources. In J. Goldemberg (Ed.), *World energy assessment* (pp. 135–171). New York: United Nations Development Programme.

Rose, A., Torries, T., & Labys, W. (1991). Clean coal technologies and future prospects for coal. *Annual Review of Energy and the Environment, 16*, 59–90.

Sieferle, R. P. (2001). *The subterranean forest*. Cambridge, UK: White Horse Press.

Smil, V. (1994). *Energy in world history*. Boulder, CO: Westview.

Smil, V. (2003). *Energy at the crossroads*. Cambridge, MA: MIT Press.

von Tunzelmann, G. N. (1978). *Steam power and British industrialization to 1860*. Oxford, UK: Clarendon Press.

Cod

Cod are one of the most commercially important fish, being a source of food and cod-liver oil. Cod have long been an integral part of human history, especially in the areas around the North Atlantic, where the Atlantic cod (*Gadus morhua*) is widely distributed in the moderate zones of the continental shelf, forming several separated stocks.

Cod gather in large numbers during the winter to spawn, forming the basis for intensive seasonal cod fisheries. Female cod lay 4–7 million eggs; hatchlings drift with ocean currents about ten weeks. Adult cod live near the bottom of the ocean at depths up to 300–600 meters and often occur in dense aggregations, particularly in areas with a good food supply. The usual weight of cod is 3–4 kilograms (up to 90 kilograms). They are voracious predators, eating mostly shoal fish such as capelin and herring but also mollusks, crabs, starfish, worms, squids, and their own young. They undertake long migrations to the productive shallow areas, such as ocean banks and bays. These migratory populations could be fished as well, for example in the Barents Sea. Climate changes influence the abundance and distribution of cod stocks.

The cod fisheries caused the establishing of settlements and further economic development of many remote territories such as Iceland, Newfoundland, New England and the northern coasts of Norway and Russia.

Cod have been an important food source since ancient times but began to develop as an international commodity only in the thirteenth century. Cod meat is rich in protein without being fatty. Cured by salting or air drying, it provides a valuable and easily transportable product. During preindustrial times fishers used mostly baited hooks on lines to fish for cod. By the fifteenth-sixteenth centuries the quest for cod increased due to population growth and climatic changes in northern Europe and fierce competition for cod occurred between fleets of the Hanseatic League (mercantile union of medieval German towns) and the Dano-Norwegian state on one side and England on the other. At that time the crucial factors that affected cod fisheries and cod trade were the availability of salt, which was expensive until the late seventeenth century, and a cool and dry climate, which was important

A Yupik Inuit woman in Alaska fishing for cod through a hole in the ice. COURTESY U. S. FISH AND WILDLIFE SERVICE.

for cod drying. English ships sailed in the spring to Portugal for salt, then to Iceland for fish, then back to Portugal, where the fish were sold, and then back to England with wine, oil, and salt. After the fifteenth century English, French, Spanish, and Portuguese fishers established even more extensive fisheries along the North American coast. Cod became an important part of international trade.

After the second half of the nineteenth century catches of cod increased considerably due to the introduction of trawling technology. The maximum catch of Atlantic cod—as much as 4 million metric tons—took place during the late 1960s. Overexploitation of many regions in the North Atlantic encouraged fish-producing nations to nationalize cod resources, generating interstate conflicts known as "cod wars." Especially large catches of cod were taken from the ocean banks off Newfoundland and Labrador, where during the 1950s through the 1970s multinational cod fisheries developed using huge factory trawlers. To protect fish resources and to avoid conflicts, in 1977 the 200-mile (320-kilometer) national zone, within which no other country may fish, was established. However, cod stocks dramatically dropped during the early 1990s, causing a cod-fishing moratorium to be declared on the Grand Banks and surroundings off the coast of Newfoundland. The collapse of the cod fisheries in that area had significant social consequences and became known as the "Newfoundland crisis." Restrictions in the cod catch did not lead to recovery of stocks until recently. The fish that gave Cape Cod its name is severely overfished in New England waters as well. In total, due to overfishing, mistakes in fishery regulation, and climate changes, cod catches in the North Atlantic dropped three- to fourfold during the 1990s. Cod hatcheries were developed at the end of the nineteenth century, but their positive effect is doubtful. At present the development of cultivation of cod in artificial conditions (aquaculture) represents a potential way to increase its production.

Julia Lajus and Dmitry Lajus

Further Reading

Candow, J. E., & Corbin, C. (1996). *How deep is the ocean? Historical essays on Canada's Atlantic fishery.* Sydney, Canada: University College of Cape Breton Press.

Jakobsson, J. et al. (Eds.). (1994). *Cod and climate* (ICES Marine Science Symposium Vol. 198). Copenhagen, Denmark: International Council for the Exploration of the Sea.

Harris, M. (1998). *Lament for an ocean: The collapse of the Atlantic cod fishery: A true crime story.* Toronto, Canada: McClelland & Stewart.

Innis, H. A. (1978). *The cod fisheries: The history of an international economy.* Buffalo, NY: University of Toronto Press.

Kurlansky, M. (1997). *Cod: A biography of the fish that changed the world.* New York: Walker.

Starkey, D. J., Reid, C., & Ashcroft, N. (Eds.). (2000). *England's sea fisheries: The commercial sea fisheries of England and Wales since 1300.* London: Chatham Publishing.

Thor, J. T. (1995). *British trawlers and Iceland, 1919–1976.* Esbjerg, Denmark: Fiskeri-og Sofartsmuseets Studieserie.

Thor, J. T. (2000). The quest for cod: Some causes of fishing conflicts in the North Atlantic. *Acta Borealia, 1,* 41–50.

Coffee

Coffee is a woody shrub of the genus *Coffea* in the family Rubiaceae native to the understory of tropical African forests. The two main species of international commerce are *Coffea arabica*, known as arabica, and *Coffea canephora* var robusta, know as robusta. Arabica is native to the highland forests of Ethiopia and has been a major item of international trade for a millennium, while robusta is native to the lowland forests of central Africa and was developed as a significant export industry only in the second half of the twentieth century for use in lower quality products such as instant coffee.

Coffee can be cultivated in regions that share the geoclimatic characteristics of its native habitats. For robusta this means tropical lowlands both within its native range in Africa and in such countries as Vietnam, Indonesia, and Brazil. Arabica is grown commercially in tropical highlands in such areas as Brazil, Colombia, Mexico and Central America, East Africa, and Southeast Asia. A total of eighty countries grow coffee for export.

A Brief History of Coffee

Coffee was originally cultivated for mass consumption in the fifteenth century in the southern part of the Arabian Peninsula, mostly in the modern nation of Yemen, for export throughout the region. Its arrival and spread coincided with the spread of Islam, particularly since coffee—a beverage that engenders convivial social interaction—was viewed as preferable to alcohol, which is proscribed by Islam.

Coffee consumption spread to Europe in the seventeenth century, where it was greeted enthusiastically by the growing middle classes. It was seen as a more socially beneficial alternative to alcohol and coffeehouses spread throughout the continent. Coming at a time of social change in Europe, these coffeehouses provided a new social space to convene, socialize, and do business. Indeed, many modern institutions, including Lloyd's of London and the New York Stock Exchange, began as coffeehouses. Ruling elites, both in Europe and the Muslim world, viewed these "penny universities" with suspicion. They considered the free exchange of ideas and intellectual foment of the coffeehouses to be politically dangerous. Furthermore, in the European case, coffee imports contributed to large trade deficits with the Arab world, which added an economic element to the drive to suppress coffee. Nowhere was this undertaken more vigorously than in the German states, where coffee was systematically prohibited in terms very similar to the modern prohibitions on various other psychoactive drugs. The European elite's antipathy to coffee changed with the development of European colonies in the tropics beginning in the seventeenth century. Coffee was the perfect crop for the European mercantile powers. It was readily and enthusiastically consumed in their home countries, it traveled well, and grew easily with two elements the colonies had in abundance: land and labor.

The result was a global increase in forced labor and environmental degradation. Large tracts of native forest were cleared, often by slaves, in the Dutch colonies of Ceylon and Indonesia, in the French Caribbean and African colonies, in the Portuguese colony of Angola, and in the English colonies of the Indian Subcontinent and East Africa. This pattern was also followed in the former Spanish colonies of South and Central America and in the former Portuguese colony of Brazil.

Regions that became major coffee producers suffered a near to total removal of the natural forest, with the largest example being that of Brazil's state of Sao Paulo, which today is completely free of its original forest cover.

The ecosystems in which coffee thrives also tend to be ecologically fragile habitats. Montane tropical forest in particular, where arabica is grown, is a notably rich and relatively scarce habitat. Colombia's highland coffee growing areas are estimated to contain 10 percent of the world's biodiversity. The economic and political forces that encourage coffee cultivation thus frequently result in concomitant degradation or disappearance of

Perfect Coffee

Beeton's has long been a source of advice on etiquette and family life in England. The following excerpt from the 1890 edition of the advice manual tells readers how to make good coffee.

To have good coffee, the berries must be not only of the first quality, but fresh ground. Very much also depends upon the roasting. To have coffee in perfection the berries should be roasted fresh every morning. In most families, however, this is impossible; the consumption would never warrant it. The plan recommended, therefore, is to buy fresh-roasted coffee, and to grind at home as much as is required for the day's consumption. A supply for a week or a fortnight of fresh-roasted coffee-berries will keep quite well, if put into a tin canister and covered down closely. Never buy ground coffee for the purpose of keeping it, as it soon loses its flavour. The mill used for coffee should be one that grinds very coarsely. It is a great mistake to grind coffee to a fine powder, for the liquid never clears so well, and much of the flavour is destroyed. In many countries where coffee is grown and its use well understood, the berries are never ground, but merely bruised in a mortar. All the virtue is thus soon extracted by boiling, and none lost in the prolonged process of grinding. Coffee requires to be kept in a very dry place and apart from other things which give off an aroma, for it very readily absorbs the flavour of anything that is placed near to it. It is therefore best kept in an air-tight canister. Properly made, it requires no other ingredients to clear it, no isinglass or egg-shells, which can only interfere with the delicate flavour of really good coffee. The pot in which it is made should be of metal, kept clean and dry, and the proportion of coffee required is half an ounce of ground coffee to every half-pint of water. First scald out the pot, put in the quantity of coffee required, and pour the water boiling hot upon it. Set the pot on the fire, and let it boil till the bubbles are clear, removing the pot whenever it seems inclined to boil over; then pour out a cupful and put it back again. This will clear the spout of the pot, as well as help to clear the coffee. Let it stand for ten minutes or a quarter of an hour near the fire, to be kept hot, but not to simmer, and it will be fit for use. According to Francatelli, "the simplest, the easiest, and most effectual means whereby to produce well-made coffee, is to procure one of Adam's coffee percolators, No. 57, Haymarket, London; put the coffee in the well, place the perforated presser upon it, then pour in the boiling water gently and gradually, until the quantity required is completed; put the lid on the percolator, and set it by the fire to run through. By strict attention to the foregoing instructions excellent coffee will be produced in a few minutes; the proportion of coffee and water being 1 oz. of coffee to a large breakfast cup of water."

Source: *Beeton's All About Everything: Being a Dictionary of Practical Recipes and Every-Day Information.* (1890). London: Ward, Lock and Co., p. 69.

---

these unique habitats. This has been the case ever since coffee was first established as a major export crop in the Arabian Peninsula, has been repeated during the period of European colonial expansion in Ceylon, Haiti, Brazil, and Kenya, and continues today in ascendant coffee growing countries such as Vietnam, Indonesia, and Papua New Guinea.

Coffee as the Link between Rich and Poor Nations

One of the major recurring patterns of the international coffee trade is that, while coffee is grown in tropical areas and developing countries, it is consumed mostly in developed temperate countries. This arrangement has three important ramifications. First, coffee is the most direct economic connection between the average consumer in the developed world and some of the poorest, most marginalized people on earth. The flow of money from developed countries to developing regions represented by the coffee trade exceeds that of every other commodity (today coffee is the second most valuable item of legal international trade, after petroleum). This trade dwarfs the flow of aid money to the developing nations. Second, the structure of the trade concentrates environmental externalities—

chiefly habitat destruction, pesticide contamination, and water pollution due to processing—in poor areas on behalf of rich consumers. Finally, the relationship of coffee-producing economies with consuming economies is often a continuation of the lopsided economic patterns established under colonialism.

With the end of colonialism in the nineteenth and twentieth centuries, elites in coffee-producing countries continued the pattern of environmental and social exploitation. In most countries the majority of coffee is produced by rural smallholders who remain trapped in cycles of debt and dependence on traders and exporters. This relationship is repeated to some extent on the international scale, with coffee trading companies and consuming countries wielding extraordinary power over producers, particularly those nations that earn a substantial part of their foreign exchange through coffee (well over half for many African and Central American countries).

In the second half of the twentieth century, worldwide coffee production surged as coffee-consuming nations grew wealthy and coffee became a staple drink. By the end of the century, a land area approximately equal to the size of Portugal (11 million hectares)—all former tropical forest and savanna—was being used for coffee production. Coffee production increased during this period in two ways. In newly producing countries, more land was cleared and put into coffee production. This trend continues in the twenty-first century in emergent coffee producers like Vietnam (which, in the 1990s, leapt from being a negligible exporter to the world's second largest) and Papua New Guinea.

Technification

In long-established producing countries, output was increased through a process known as *technification*. As an extension of Green Revolution technologies to coffee, this process entailed the use of new varieties of coffee, intensive fertilizer and pesticide use, and the conversion of traditionally diverse agroforestry systems into coffee monocultures. This process was promoted by international lending and development agencies like the World Bank and the U.S. Agency for International Development and was undertaken most vigorously in Colombia.

Technification has had a number of deleterious effects on the environments of coffee producing regions. Pesticide and fertilizer pollution has impacted people and ecosystems dramatically. The removal of agro-

forestry and shade systems (farming techniques in which coffee grows under a canopy of larger trees) destroyed a critical element of diversity from these already compromised ecosystems.

The result of the expansion and technification of coffee production has led to a decline in suitable habitat for migratory songbirds, which spend the winter in tropical regions such as Central America and central Africa and the summer in North America and Europe. This has resulted in a dramatic decline in songbird numbers. The decline constituted direct feedback between coffee drinkers in developed countries and the environmental impacts of their consumption and prompted, in the 1990s, the emergence of a consumer movement to favor shade-grown (or "bird friendly") coffee in an effort to restore bird habitat.

Organic coffee (grown without synthetic pesticides or fertilizers) and Fair Trade coffee (traded in a manner that does not exploit farmers) emerged as growing sectors of the industry as a result of increased awareness of the environmental and social impacts of coffee production. Because coffee is such a direct linkage between the people of developing and developed countries, it has come to the forefront of a more general consciousness of the consequences of consumerism.

Gregory Dicum and Nina Luttinger

Further Reading

Clarke, R. J., & Macrae, R. (Eds.). (1985). *Coffee.* London: Elsevier Applied Science.

Dicum, G, & Luttinger, N. (1999). *The Coffee Book: Anatomy of an industry from crop to the last drop.* New York: The New Press.

Rice, P, & MacLean, J. (1999). *Sustainable Coffee at the Crossroads.* Washington, DC: Consumers Choice Council.

Ukers, W. H. (1935). *All about coffee* (2nd ed.). New York: The Tea & Coffee Trade Journal Company.

Colombia

(2002 est. pop. 40 million)

Colombia lies at the northwestern corner of continental South America. Its complex geography has given it one of the most ecologically diverse environments in South America, and contributed to the country's enduring social fragmentation. Most of Colombia's population has lived in the western third of the country. Western Colombia consists of three major geographical regions: extensive tropical lowlands along both the Caribbean and Pacific coasts, and the Andean highlands. Most of Colombia's major cities, including Bogotá and Medellin, are found in the highland valleys between the three major chains of the Andes—the *cordillera occidental*, the *cordillera central*, and the *cordillera oriental*. The eastern two-thirds of the country consists of the sparsely inhabited lowlands of the Orinoco River and Amazon River basins.

Colombia's pre-Columbian Indian societies, particularly the Tairona, the Cenu, and the Muisca (or Chibcha), had developed settled, extensive agriculture. Their diets were based on a combination of corn, potatoes, and quinoa, which they cultivated in terraced hillsides and large planting beds. All three groups supplemented their diets with hunting and fishing. This tremendous productivity gave Colombia the highest population density outside the Aztec and Inca empires. The Muisca alone had a population of some 600,000. These groups also exploited nature for political and economic power. Each group's power depended heavily on its control over the production and trade of critical natural resources, such as salt, emeralds, seashells, and cotton, which they exchanged over extensive regional trading networks.

The Spanish conquest and colonization of Colombia (c. 1530–1819) produced a new environmental order. The most dramatic environmental consequence of the conquest was the demographic collapse of the Indian population. The main cause of this complex phenomenon was the introduction of Old World epidemic diseases such as smallpox, measles, and influenza. Mortality rates from these epidemics were high. In 1539, for example, a single epidemic in the southern province of Popayán killed some 100,000 Indians. Records from the cities of Tunja and Pamplona suggest that by the mid-1600s, Colombia's Indian population was only one-fifth of what it had been at the moment of conquest. This demographic collapse led to labor shortages, particularly in the gold mining regions of western Colombia. To make up for these shortages, the Spanish began importing African slaves. Colombia's European population also grew rapidly, both through immigration and natural increase. By late 1700s, Colombia's total population had almost recovered to the pre-Conquest levels. Only a quarter of the population was fully Indian, while the rest was white, black, or mestizo (a mix of Indian and white).

Spanish colonial policy and practice also transformed Colombia's landscapes. The major force for environmental change was the Spanish requirement that their Indian subjects pay tribute in specific crops, livestock, and other necessities. The tribute requirement caused the simplification of the Indian communities' complex agricultural systems. It also served as a vehicle for the introduction of Old World crops and animals. Tribute obligations forced Indians to cultivate Old World crops such as wheat, which they were reluctant to cultivate on their own. Old World livestock, particularly cattle, pigs, and sheep, also flourished in Colombia's environments.

Colombia's independence from Spain in 1819 marked the beginning of a century-long era of expanding agricultural frontiers. This generated a wave of internal migration, rapid population growth, and new environmental problems. After independence, many Colombian farmers began cultivating cash crops for overseas markets, to meet growing overseas demand for tropical commodities such as tobacco, rubber, cotton, chinchona bark, and indigo. These crops could best be cultivated in the lowlands or on the medium-altitude mountainsides, and waves of settlers began to migrate to these regions from the overpopulated highlands. They saw agriculture primarily as an extractive, transient activity. They cleared a patch of forest, cultivated it until the nutrients were exhausted, and then moved on to clear new forest. In the space of two generations, they converted thousands of acres of diverse primary forest into desolate pastures. The settlers also harvested wild crops—such as rubber and chinchona—so aggressively that they killed them. This extractive frontier agriculture was neither economically nor environmentally sustainable. The growth of the coffee industry in Colombia, beginning in the last two decades of the nineteenth century, marked the beginning of a more sustainable approach to agriculture. By 1930, Colombia was the world's second largest exporter of coffee. Colombia's population grew rapidly during these years, as illustrated by the province of Antioquia's population, which grew from 158,000 in 1828 to more than 2.2 million in 1938.

Since 1930, Colombia has been struggling with environmental problems associated with sustaining a rapidly growing, increasingly urban population, pursuing economic development, and managing rampant civil strife and a powerful drug industry. Colombia's population stood at 4 million in 1900; by 2002, it was calculated at 40 million. The percentage of Colombians living in urban areas leapt from a third in 1938 to more than three quarters in 1994. This rapid, uncontrolled urbanization has produced air pollution, poor sanitation, and other problems. For example, almost a quarter of Colombia's population has no access to clean drinking water. In the rural areas deforestation is a growing problem, caused by legal activities such as cattle ranching, and by illegal activities such as coca farming. In 1986, some 25,000 hectares of forest were cleared for the cultivation of coca; by 1999 that figure had reached 123,000. Colombia's national government has started taking steps to manage these environmental crises, establishing a Ministry of Environment in 1993. Most environmental activism in Colombia, however, is still to be found at the grassroots level. One symbol of this is the community of Gaviotas, founded as a model sustainable community by an eclectic mix of Colombian environmental activists in the 1970s. Since the late 1990s, Colombian environmental and social activists have worked to halt the government's plans to use glyphosate herbicide sprays to control coca production in the Andes and Amazonian regions, fearing that this program would cause widespread health and environmental problems.

Stuart McCook

Further Reading

Area handbook for Colombia (4th ed.).(1990). Washington, DC: Government Printing Office.

Bushnell, D. (1993). *The making of modern Colombia: A nation in spite of itself*. Berkeley: University of California Press.

Cook, N. D. (1993). *Born to die: Disease and the New World conquest, 1492–1650*. Cambridge, UK: Cambridge University Press.

Helms, M. W. (1984). The Indians of the Caribbean and Circum-Caribbean at the end of the fifteenth century. In L. Bethell (Ed.), *Cambridge history of Latin America*, (Vol. 1; pp. 37–57). Cambridge, UK: Cambridge University Press.

James, P. E. (1968). *Antioqueño colonization in western Colombia*. Berkeley: University of California Press.

James, P. E. (1969). Colombia [Monograph]. *Latin America* (4th ed., pp. 384–427). New York: Odyssey Press.

Peterson, S. (2002). People and ecosystems in Colombia. *Independent Review* 6, 427–441.

Sánchez-Albornóz, N. (1974). *The population of Latin America: A history*. Berkeley: University of California Press.

Weisman, A. (1998). *Gaviotas: A village to reinvent the world*. White River Junction, VT: Chelsea Green.

Colonialism and Imperialism

At the heart of any consideration of imperial and colonial relations is the issue of territory and its control. Simply defined, imperialism entails one country imposing its rule over another; colonization, if distinguished from imperialism, usually refers to the occupation of a conquered land by those establishing foreign governance. Not only have these dynamics involved intense social upheavals, they have also invariably reconfigured natural environments. By establishing borders, delimiting frontiers, and taking inventories of the natural world, imperial authorities have attempted to exert their power not only over peoples, but also places. Such exertions, however, have often belied the tenuous nature of colonial control and exposed the uncertainties of territorial and overseas expansion.

Geopolitical and Juridical Foundations

The impetus for Spanish and Portuguese explorations in the fifteenth century was neither conquest nor colonization but, at least initially, trade and Christian proselytizing. Yet as voyagers traveled around the coast of Africa and across the Atlantic to the Americas, they rapidly amended their ambitions to include the possibility of future settlement. Islands along trade routes were often the first and most easily settled, but soon these travelers laid claim, on behalf of their government sponsors, to vast stretches of land along coasts and inland water routes. Explorers often justified this with the rhetoric of "discovery," asserting that the land was *"terra nullius"*—land belonging to nobody—effectively erasing indigenous peoples' presence and their pre-existing land rights. If territory were not taken by these means, it was either seized through conquest or ceded through treaties with the ostensible consent of local chiefs and princes. It is no coincidence that colonial activities often coincided with a rapacious extraction of natural resources such as gold, silver, coffee, sugar, tea, cocoa, furs, and wood.

By the time countries such as England, France, and Netherlands joined the imperial fray in the sixteenth and seventeenth centuries, inter-state conflicts over legal and trading rights within territories in the New World, the East Indies, and Africa, had become heated. Cartography played a part in these imperial disputes since maps could be used as a state tool to capture geographical spaces for political and economic ends. *The Map of Africa by Treaty* (1896), a four-volume study produced following the late-nineteenth-century European "Scramble for Africa," provides a graphic example of this.

Disease and Empire

Imperial endeavors involved more than territorial dispossession. European colonizers carried with them a complex "portmanteau biota" of pathogens, plants, and animals (Crosby, 1986, 89). Although there remains some dispute over the disease environments of the Americas and Pacific islands prior to colonial conquest, scholars are certain that vast numbers of indigenous peoples died from the introduction of new diseases including smallpox, measles, influenza, and typhus. While the Europeans' superior military technologies and Amerindians' internal conflicts were important in the triumph of Europeans, the unintentional spread of lethal diseases among populations lacking resistance or immunity was undoubtedly a central factor.

Yet disease was a double-edged sword for colonizers. The west coast of Africa was designated "the white man's grave" in the eighteenth and nineteenth centuries, in view of the high mortality rates Europeans experienced there. Tropical environments generally came to be characterized by many European explorers as undeniably dangerous for those "acclimatized" to the temperate zones of Europe or North America. Attempts to explain these differences in terms of disease susceptibility laid the foundations for both racial and climatic theories that continued to underpin "tropical medicine" well into the twentieth century.

Science, Empire and the Natural World

Imperialism also affected the realm of ideas. Coinciding with a concerted push to develop such fields as natural philosophy, natural history, and medicine, European expansion grew in tandem with a range of what are today known as scientific disciplines. Whether in terms of the physician Garcia d'Orta in Goa (on the west coast of India), the botanist Joseph Banks accompanying James Cook in the Pacific, or even Alfred Russel Wallace and Charles Darwin in South America and the Pacific, many scientists drew inspiration from their experiences outside their home environments. An enduring question is the extent to which local populations—acting as translators, guides, informants, and in some cases as "scientific professionals" in their own right—influenced these innovations.

Scientific endeavors in colonial contexts did more than generate ideas; they also influenced the kinds of interventions colonists pursued. As forestry, agriculture, geology, botany, medicine, and even anthropology became the domain of experts, not only were local forms of environmental management pushed aside, but so too were whole populations. Debates over who would have access to and control over natural resources spawned numerous conflicts both within different departments of colonial regimes and between colonists and indigenous populations. Perhaps one of the greatest ironies of these experiences, documented by Richard Grove in *Green Imperialism*, is that colonial territories served as a significant venue in which ideas about humans as destroyers rather than improvers of their environments first emerged.

Future Research

As environmental history becomes more comparative and global in scope, perhaps these historical narratives will be expanded to include empires from antiquity to the Renaissance as well as non-European imperialism in Asia and the Middle East. In such contexts, the differences between imperialism and colonialism, and between formal and informal spheres of influence will likely be extremely important. How were the environmental experiences of overseas empires such as those of Britain, France, Netherlands, and Japan different from empires derived from extensive territorial expansion, as was the case with the Ottoman, Mughal, Safavid, Russian, and Chinese empires? Finally, an important theme deserving closer scrutiny is the role of technology in imperial environmental histories.

Helen Tilley

Further Reading

Arnold, D. (Ed.). (1996). *Warm climates and western medicine: The emergence of tropical medicine, 1500–1900*. Amsterdam: Rodopi.

Arnold, D., & Guha, R. (Eds.). (1995). *Nature, culture, imperialism: Essays on the environmental history of South Asia*. New Delhi, India: Oxford University Press.

Chamberlain, M. E. (2000). *Formation of the European empires, 1488–1920*. Harlow, UK: Pearson Education.

Crosby, A. W. (1986). *Ecological imperialism: The biological expansion of Europe, 900–1900*. Cambridge, UK: Cambridge University Press.

Griffiths, T., & Robin, L. (Eds.). (1997). *Ecology and empire: Environmental history of settler societies*. Edinburgh, UK: Keele University Press.

Grove, R. H. (1996). *Green imperialism: Colonial expansion, tropical island edens and the origins of environmentalism, 1600–1860*. Cambridge, UK: Cambridge University Press.

Grove, R. H., Damodaran, V., & Sangwan, S. (Eds.). (1998). *Nature and the Orient: The environmental history of South and Southeast Asia*. New Delhi, India: Oxford University Press.

Headrick, D. (1988). *The tentacles of progress: Technology transfer in the age of imperialism, 1850–1940*. New York: Oxford University Press.

MacKenzie, J. (Ed.). (1990). *Imperialism and the natural world*. Manchester, UK: Manchester University Press.

MacLeod, R, & Lewis, M. (Eds.). (1988). *Disease, medicine, and empire: Perspectives on western medicine and the experience of European expansion*. New York: Routledge.

Sluyter, A. (2002). *Colonialism and landscape: Postcolonial theory and applications*. New York: Rowman & Littlefield Publishers.

Tignor, R., Adelman, J., Aron, S., Kotkin, S., Marchand, S., Prakash, G., et al. (2002). *Worlds together, world apart: A history of the modern world from the Mongol Empire to the present*. New York: Norton and Company.

Verzijl, J. H. W. (1970). *International law in historical perspective*. Utrecht, Netherlands: A. W. Sijthoff-Leyden.

Colorado River

The Colorado River is the eighth-longest river in North America and ranks among the fifty longest rivers in the world. From its headwaters in the Rocky Mountains of northern Colorado, it flows generally southwest for 2,330 kilometers through a portion of five western states—Colorado, Utah, Arizona, Nevada, and California—and Mexico to its delta at the Gulf of California. Major historic tributaries include the Green, San Juan, Little Colorado, and Gila Rivers. The Colorado's watershed encompasses 626,780 square kilometers in the United States, which is nearly one-twelfth of the land area of the continental United States, and 5,180 square kilometers in Mexico. The greater portion of the Colorado's watershed is arid or semiarid land and contributes very little runoff to the river. The Colorado's average annual flow of about 17 cubic kilometers is roughly one-fourteenth of the volume of the comparably sized Columbia River.

The Colorado is one of the most geologically remarkable rivers in the world. Over millions of years, the Colorado cut its way through layers of sandstone, shale, limestone and gneiss, creating spectacular canyons. The largest is the Grand Canyon, one of the natural wonders of the world; it reaches depths of 1.6 kilometers, varies in width from 8 to 29 kilometers from rim to rim, and is 446 kilometers long. The canyon's multihued rock walls reveal, and helped geologists better comprehend, almost 2 billion years of Earth history. The Colorado is also notable for the large amount of sediment it carries. Before its main-stem (along the river's main course) dams were erected, the Colorado deposited an estimated 127–152 million metric tons of sediment annually into its rich delta country below Yuma, Arizona—a sediment load approximating those of the much larger Mississippi and Nile Rivers.

The Colorado is the lifeblood of the American Southwest. Its watershed was inhabited by Anasazi, Hohokam, Hopi, and other Native American peoples for thousands of years prior to European settlement. The first person of European descent to explore the Colorado was John Wesley Powell (1834–1902), who descended the river in 1869. Since then, the Colorado has been transformed into one of the most fully utilized and fought-over rivers in the world. The first major development on the Colorado was completed in 1936, when Boulder (now Hoover) Dam was finished and 175-kilometer-long Lake Mead began filling behind it. Subsequent major developments have included the construction of seven other main-stem dams: Imperial (1938), Parker (1938), Headgate Rock (1941), Davis (1953), Palo Verde (1957), Glen Canyon (1964), and, just below the United States-Mexico border, Morelos (1950). Most of these dams were designed as multipurpose water-storage projects, providing hydroelectric power, flood control, irrigation, recreation, and domestic water. Together, they have turned the Colorado into a liquid staircase, holding back about five years of the river's annual flow. The dams generate an enormous amount of hydroelectricity, approximately 11–12 billion kilowatt-hours annually. Diversion projects—such as the All-American Canal, California Aqueduct, Central Arizona Project, and Colorado-Big Thompson Project—provide water to distant cities such as Phoenix and Los Angeles and irrigate millions of hectares of ranch and farmland across the Southwest.

This development has come at great cost to the natural environment. The dams have radically altered the river's biology and endangered many native fish, reptile, and amphibian species. Since about 1960, the Colorado has been virtually wrung dry along its course and seldom reaches the Gulf of California. Current issues include perennial allocation disputes, sediment accumulation, rising salinity levels, and the environmentalists' fight to remove Glen Canyon Dam.

George Vrtis

Further Reading

Fleck, R. F. (Ed.). (2000). *A Colorado River reader.* Salt Lake City: University of Utah Press.

Fradkin, P. L. (1996). *A river no more: The Colorado River and the West.* Berkeley: University of California Press.

Hundley, N., Jr. (1975). *Water and the West: The Colorado River Compact and the politics of water in the American West.* Berkeley: University of California Press.

Powell, J. W. (2002). *The exploration of the Colorado River and its canyons.* Washington, DC: National Geographic Society. (Original work published 1895)

Reisner, M. (1993). *Cadillac desert: The American West and its disappearing water.* New York: Penguin Books.

Columbia River

The Columbia River is 1,953 kilometers long and is the second-largest U.S. river by volume. Along with its largest tributary, the Snake River, the Columbia drains 668,220 square kilometers of the Pacific Northwest and western Canada, an area roughly equal to France. Its major tributaries include the Bitterroot, Blackfoot, Bruneau, Canoe, Clarks Fork, Clearwater, Cowlitz, Deschutes, Flathead, Grande Ronde, John Day, Kootenai, Malheur, Okanogan, Owyhee, Pend d'Oreille, Salmon, Spokane, Umatilla, Wenatchee, Willamette, and Yakima Rivers. The river's power is exemplified at the Columbia Gorge, the only place where water breaches the great mountain barriers of the western United States. The river's historically important lifeforms include six species of salmon, several species of western trout, two species of sturgeon, the sardine-like eulachon, and beaver. In the last century many additional species have been introduced, including warmwater fishes such as pike and bass, and anadromous species (species that swim upstream from the sea to breed) from the Atlantic coast, such as striped bass and shad. At one time the Columbia also provided important wetlands for birds on the western North American flyway, but it now has an extensive system of dams for navigation, hydroelectricity, irrigation, and flood protection, and the socially and culturally divergent human communities that live along it can no longer agree on how to manage the basin's waters to serve all these diverse interests.

The Columbia Basin is arguably the most ecologically and socially diverse watershed in North America. The basin extends from tundra-like areas of the Canadian Rockies across the world's largest basaltic plateau to the Great Basin of Utah and Nevada, and from the continental divide in Yellowstone to rain-drenched forests at Astoria, Oregon. The region's peoples are equally diverse. Aboriginal groups have included densely settled salmon specialists along the lower Columbia, small, migratory bands at the edge of the Great Basin, and buffalo-hunting horse tribes in the Rockies. Contact with Euro-Americans wrought tremendous social and environmental change in the basin. Indian populations declined and were forced to shift their economic focus away from precontact activities, but some have managed to maintain close ties to salmon despite mounting social and ecological obstacles. Present-day non-Indian settlements include resource-extractive communities such as Libby, Montana, and Mica, British Columbia, agricultural areas such as Yakima, Washington, and Twin Falls, Idaho, urban centers such as Portland, Oregon, and Spokane, Washington, and tourist meccas such as Jackson, Wyoming, and Bend, Oregon. The Columbia's course takes it past both the largest wilderness area in the continental United States and the most polluted sites in North America. Governing the Columbia is equally complex, as it traverses one province, two nations, seven states, and many tribes, and managing its salmon runs involves two additional states and four Asian nations.

The basin's complexity is a central factor in environmental issues. Industrial, military, and agricultural development, especially the river's famed dam system, has bolstered economies in western Canada and the United States, but development also altered habitat and released pollutants that threaten humans and nature alike. Nuclear wastes at Hanford, Washington, and Arco, Idaho, and chemical and heavy-metal deposits from mining near Coeur d'Alene, Idaho, and Butte, Montana, have made those sites eligible for Superfund dollars for cleanup of hazardous wastes; the cleanup is calculated to cost several billion dollars. Development and fishing extinguished many salmon runs, and many more are listed as threatened or endangered under the U.S. Environmental Protection Act. Resolving such problems poses daunting challenges because the region's economy is intrinsically dependent on activities that cause environmental degradation, and the basin's social and cultural diversity stymies consensus on how to resolve problems.

Joseph E. Taylor III

Further Reading

Lang, W. L., & Carriker, R. C. (Eds.). (1999). *Great river of the West: Essays on the Columbia River.* Seattle: University of Washington Press.

Meinig, D. W. (1968). *The great Columbia Plateau: A historical geography, 1805–1910.* Seattle: University of Washington Press.

White, R. (1995). *The organic machine: The remaking of the Columbia River.* New York: Hill and Wang.

Comanagement

Comanagement is the process of sharing responsibility for the management of natural resources between a government agency (or other formal institution) and local stakeholders, such as rural communities, indigenous peoples, and nongovernmental organizations. Also referred to as *community-based conservation, collaborative resource management, joint management,* or *conservation partnerships,* comanagement has been applied to marine and freshwater fisheries, wildlife populations, and other natural resources, as well as to national parks, forest reserves, and many other conservation settings worldwide. Although not without its challenges, comanagement represents one of the most important innovations in natural resource conservation to emerge during the last three decades.

Rise of State-Centered Conservation

Although comanagement is often touted as a novel approach to conservation, the concept actually is not entirely new. Cases in which governments have passed responsibility for managing natural resources to local communities go back to at least the nineteenth century, such as at Lofoten, Norway, where a major cod fishery has been managed with oversight by participating fishers for over a century.

When the modern conservation movement took shape in the late 1800s, however, most conservationists in North America and western Europe argued that the protection and management of natural resources were the responsibility of the state, employing the knowledge and wisdom of professional managers and scientists trained in forestry, biology, engineering, and other emerging scientific disciplines. As societies industrialized and transportation and economic links improved, the exploitation of forests, wildlife, and water sources advanced on an unprecedented scale, involving powerful national and international economic interests. Conservationists argued persuasively that a strong and progressive central government was the best way to counterbalance the juggernaut of exploitation and achieve conservation goals, be they the preservation of wild lands or the wise management of natural resources. The role of the state was duly codified in legislation authorizing government action to protect wildlife and endangered species, establish forest reserves and national parks, manage fisheries, and control environmental contamination.

Although the scale at which federal and colonial governments established parks and reserves during the late nineteenth and early twentieth centuries was impressive, these accomplishments came with a price. Many units were superimposed over territory that had been farmed, fished, hunted upon, gathered over, grazed, and otherwise called home by indigenous cultures and traditional communities. For instance, the territory that in 1872 became Yellowstone National Park (Wyoming, Montana, and Idaho) was used seasonally by Shoshone Native American bands. Likewise, Yosemite National Park in California, designated in 1890, was inhabited by Miwok peoples who gathered a wide variety of plant and animal resources from the Yosemite environment.

As conservationists strove to preserve nature, they often failed to recognize that many landscapes they perceived as pristine actually resulted from traditional habitat modification activities such as regular burning, seasonal grazing, or shifting cultivation. Local residents who relied on plants and animals as subsistence resources often were forced to abandon or greatly modify their traditional harvests. Indeed, in many cases they were physically evicted from parks and reserves. In some instances, to protest such treatment, communities purposefully exploited or overharvested animal and plant resources they previously had managed with care. All too often, the centralized model of conservation that took shape in the nations of the Americas and in European colonial empires produced highly polarized relations between local residents and natural resource professionals, each with different perspectives on their interaction with the natural world.

Changing Assumptions, Changing Policies

The first major instance in which modern conservation began to chart an alternative course occurred in western Europe when nations such as Great Britain began to establish modern protected area networks in the years after World War II. Working in rural landscapes that had been settled and managed by agrarian populations for centuries, conservation planners realized from the onset that a U.S.-style national parks system would not be feasible. The agencies that they ultimately established to design and manage national parks and reserves, such as Britain's National Parks Commission (later renamed the Countryside Commission), did not acquire large extensions of land for protection. Rather, from the start they functioned more as regional advisory committees, working closely with local planning authorities inside designated park boundaries and attempting to provide incentives for land uses that would be compatible with landscape conservation goals.

By the 1960s and 1970s a broader consensus had begun to emerge that governments needed to give greater consideration to local people's concerns when managing natural resources. The more progressive social climate of the time made it possible for disenfranchised indigenous communities, native peoples, and minority cultures to consolidate their fundamental human rights. In legal and political arenas, as well as in the court of public opinion, indigenous peoples began to press conservation and resource management agencies to give them a greater role in managing natural resources of traditional importance, including forest estates, fish stocks, wildlife populations, and public lands with religious, subsistence, or culturally relevant historical value. In the United States, for instance, federal court rulings such as *U.S. v. Washington* (1974) reaffirmed the right of Native American tribes to manage, in conjunction with state agencies, fisheries resources originally granted to the tribes in treaties signed with the U.S. government.

At about the same time, concern over the economic, social, and environmental costs of centralized, statesponsored development models began to spur a shift to more democratic grassroots development approaches. This provided an opportunity for rural communities to claim a greater role in managing natural resources upon which they depended and would prove particularly important in developing countries. By the early 1980s conservation and development in Africa, Asia, and Latin America were being discussed as potentially complementary rather than opposing concepts, further emphasizing the importance of addressing local people's concerns in formal conservation and management.

The claims of local communities also were buoyed indirectly through advancements in academic arenas, where a growing body of research in ecological anthropology, ethnobiology, and human geography fueled appreciation of the complexity and sophistication of local and indigenous resource management traditions. Rather than mere opportunists and exploiters of natural resources, local people were revealed in many studies to be careful and effective stewards of land, fish, forests, and fauna. As early as the 1960s and 1970s, farsighted scientists were drawing on these new views of local capacities to argue for the adoption of comanagement approaches, as biologists Raymond Dasmann, from the United States, and David Western, from Kenya, did while studying wildlife populations and nature preserves in eastern and southern Africa.

By the end of the 1970s it was clear that a major shift in natural resource policy was taking hold at both national and international levels. In the case of protected areas, a systematic attempt to promote comanagement began in 1979 with the establishment of the Man and the Biosphere Program within the United Nations Educational, Scientific, and Cultural Organization (UNESCO). The term *biosphere reserve* describes a conservation area where a core protected zone (such as a national park) is surrounded by buffer zones and transition areas allowing traditional land use and economic activities, such as eco-tourism, that are compatible with conservation goals. The program has promoted the designation of biosphere reserves by national governments worldwide, with more than 360 designations in eighty-five nations to date.

By the 1980s even the venerable U.S. National Park Service (NPS) was embracing more collaborative approaches to park management, through designations of new national parks, national heritage areas, and national trail and river corridors in which the federal government owned little land and management was shared with state and private partners. At longestablished parks, the NPS increasingly began to collaborate with volunteer groups and neighboring communities in order to address management issues, such as development pressures on adjacent lands, that could not be dealt with adequately through more traditional administrative channels alone.

Putting Comanagement into Practice

Amid the lofty rhetoric of collaboration, natural resource professionals have faced an ongoing challenge of translating the ideals of comanagement into a new kind of conservation on the ground. In practice comanagement can encompass a range of approaches that is likely to vary in how well it achieves meaningful collaboration. At one end of the scale, under what is termed "passive collaboration," natural resource managers may simply inform local resource users about management decisions or seek their input and opinions prior to implementing management prescriptions. At the other end of the scale, self-determinant collaboration may mean that local residents themselves make and implement management decisions, with government professionals serving in an advisory role to help analyze problems and resolve conflicts.

Initially, comanagement efforts tended to proceed in a piecemeal, experimental fashion, often beginning at the initiative of dynamic individuals—perceptive local leaders as well as innovative resource management professionals—who advocated collaborative management of natural resources particularly important for local residents. Comanagement of state-owned forestlands in parts of India, for instance, was spurred initially by concerned villagers and later expanded with the support of professional foresters.

Nongovernmental organizations (NGOs) have also played a prominent role in sparking the implementation of comanagement, particularly in developing countries. In 1985 a leading conservation NGO, the World Wildlife Fund, launched a program called "Wildlands and Human Needs," which sponsored model comanagement projects in Latin America, Asia, and Africa. Another major conservation NGO, the Nature Conservancy, shifted its emphasis in the early 1990s from establishing strict nature preserves to one of protecting larger "bioreserves," where the organization helps brings together government actors and local residents and private landowners to protect the biological wealth of native ecological landscapes.

Natural resource agencies in the United States, Australia, Brazil, Canada, India, and other nations have had mandates to implement comanagement since the 1970s and 1980s. Initially, however, most were reluctant to share decision-making authority that previously had been theirs alone and often resorted to court appeals and bureaucratic foot dragging in an attempt to delay implementation. Over time more progressive administrators began to recognize that comanagement offers the possibility of stretching limited agency budgets further and of helping satisfy public demands for reforms and change. By the 1990s natural resource agencies were moving much more rapidly on implementing comanagement agreements for fisheries, forest products, wildlife populations, and public lands.

Yet, even with clear incentives, many government agencies have had difficulty accepting local communities as equal partners in natural resource management, particularly when indigenous communities or minority cultures are involved. In New Zealand, Parliament passed the Conservation Act in 1987, authorizing the government to pursue collaborative arrangements with native Maori communities for managing wildlife populations and protected areas, but implementation has been slow. Cultural differences play a role. For instance, certain Maori concepts of resource stewardship are not easily translated into the scientific language of ecology that natural resource professionals are accustomed to using. A lack of prior models for collaboration has also slowed the transition to comanagement, along with inadequate funding of new institutions on the part of the government and objections by more preservation-oriented conservation activists.

Even for the countries and institutions that have gone the furthest in embracing comanagement approaches for natural resources, positive results have not been automatic. The integration of traditional management practices for flora and fauna populations is no guarantee that every group or community will be effective stewards in all situations, particularly when cultural belief systems and subsistence patterns are undergoing rapid flux. Inequities or corruption in governance systems can overwhelm even the best intentions at collaborative management, as can social or ethnic divisions within local communities.

In the case of the Dzanga-Shanga forest region of Central African Republic, over ten years of work by conservation groups have yet to foster workable comanagement regimes. The region is populated by a variety of ethnic groups, many of whom have emigrated from other parts of the country, and communal management traditions for forest resources are not well developed. It has been difficult for conservationists to offer to local residents incentives for conservation that are equivalent to the lure of easy profits promised by organized wildlife poaching and logging companies active in the region.

Future Prospects

The role of local communities in resource conservation and their capacity to enhance sustainable management approaches are now unquestioned, but examples of successful comanagement arrangements still remain elusive in many settings. Perhaps the single most important factor in continuing to refine and improve comanagement regimes is the commitment of federal and state governments to continue supporting partnerships and collaboration with funding and resources. Comanagement is not a panacea by itself, but it remains the most viable approach available to governments, communities, and organizations alike for meeting twenty-first-century conservation challenges.

John Tuxill

Further Reading

Batisse, M. (1982). The biosphere reserve: A tool for environmental conservation and management. *Environmental Conservation, 9*(2), 101–111.

Berkes, F. (1989). *Common property resources: Ecology and community-based sustainable development*. London: Bellhaven Press.

Bernard, T., & Young, J. (1997). *The ecology of hope: Communities collaborate for sustainability*. Gabriola Island, Canada: New Society Publishers.

Brown, J., & Kothari, A. (Eds.). (2002). Local communities and protected areas. *Parks, 12*(2), 1–96.

Jentoft, S., & Kristoffersen, T. (1989). Fishermen's co-management: The case of the Lofoten fishery. *Human Organization, 48*(4), 355–365.

Kruse, J., Klein, D., Braund, S., Moorehead, L., & Simeone, B. (1998). Co-management of natural resources: A comparison of two caribou management systems. *Human Organization, 57*(4), 447–458.

Pinkerton, E. W. (1992). Translating legal rights into management practice: Overcoming barriers to the exercise of co-management. *Human Organization, 51*(4), 330–341.

Taiepa, T., Lyver, P., Horsley, P., Davis, J., Bragg, M., & Moller, M. (1997). Co-management of New Zealand's conservation estate by Maori and Pakeha: A review. *Environmental Conservation, 24*(3), 236–250.

Tuxill, J. L. (2000). *The landscape of conservation stewardship*. Woodstock, VT: Conservation Study Institute.

Wells, M. P., & Brandon, K. E. (1993). The principles and practice of buffer zones and local participation in biodiversity conservation. *Ambio, 22*(2–3), 157–162.

West, P. C., & Brechin, S. R. (Eds.). (1991). *Resident peoples and national parks: Social dilemmas and strategies in international conservation*. Tucson: University of Arizona Press.

Western, D., Wright, R. M., & Strum, S. C. (Eds.). (1994). *Natural connections: Perspectives in community-based conservation*. Washington, DC: Island Press.

Wollendeck, J. M., & Yaffee, S. L. (2000). *Making collaboration work: Lessons from innovation in natural resource management*. Washington, DC: Island Press.

Commission for Environmental Cooperation

One of the most prominent trade agreements signed in North America was the North American Free Trade Agreement (NAFTA). This agreement between Canada, Mexico, and the United States came into effect in 1994 and created one of the world's largest trading blocks. While most people are aware of this agreement, very few know that two parallel agreements were signed following NAFTA. One of them is the North American Agreement for Environmental Cooperation (NAAEC). NAAEC was formed to reduce the concerns that some environmentalists had about potential degradation of the environment caused by increased trade and industrial activities on some parts of the continent. The main role of NAAEC was to "address regional environmental concerns, help prevent potential trade and environmental conflicts and to promote the effective enforcement of environmental law" (CEC 1998, ii). This environmental agreement came into effect on 1 January 1994, and along with it, the Commission for Environmental Cooperation (CEC) was created.

The Mission of the CEC

In the context of NAFTA and increased trade and economy, the mission of the CEC is to encourage cooperation and public participation of all North American communities in the protection and sustainable use of the environment for present and future generations. During the development of the NAAEC, the three countries (often cited as parties) established the following objectives for the CEC: "(1) to protect the environment through cooperation, (2) to promote sustainable development based on mutually supportive environmental and economic policies, (3) to support the environmental goals of NAFTA and avoid creating trade distortions or new trade barriers, (4) to strengthen cooperation in the development of environmental laws and enhance their enforcement, and (5) to promote transparency and public participation" (CEC 1998, 3).

The Three Components of the CEC

The CEC accomplishes its tasks through the combined efforts of its three principal components: the Council, the Secretariat, and the Joint Public Advisory Committee (JPAC). The Council is the governing body of the CEC and is composed of the highest-level environmental authorities from each country. In 2002, Canada's David Anderson (head of Environment Canada, Canada's ministry of the environment), Mexico's Secretary of the Environment and Natural Resources Victor Lichtenger, and the United State's Christine Todd Whitman (head of the U.S. Environmental Protection Agency) made up the Council. The Council is responsible for the global activities of the CEC. Depending on NAAEC's need for information or action, the Council can assign committees, working groups, or expert groups to which it can turn for advice and for help in decision making. The Council also oversees the activities of the Secretariat. Under the obligations of NAAEC, the Council cooperates with the NAFTA Free Trade Commission to ensure that environmental goals are respected.

The Secretariat is located in Montreal, Canada. An executive director heads the Secretariat. The executive director is selected by the Council and has a mandate of three years (renewable for three more years). The Secretariat's staff is composed of professionals and experts from the three countries who are hired and supervised by the executive director. The Secretariat implements the annual work program and provides administrative, technical, and operational support to the Council. It is an independent administrative body. Under Article 13 of NAAEC, the Secretariat has the potential "to prepare a report for the Council on any matter within the scope of the annual program" (CEC 1998, 19). For example, under this article, the Secretariat prepared a report on the bird migratory habitat in San Pedro watershed (CEC 1999), a transboundary ecosystem between the United States and Mexico, and analyzed the electricity market in North America (CEC 2001). The most controversial articles that the Secretar-

iat has to deal with are articles 14 and 15. These articles are unique as they allow "submission from any NGO [nongovernmental organization] or person asserting that a Party is failing to effectively enforce its environmental law" (CEC 1998, 20). If the submission was considered valid, the Council could request the Secretariat to develop a factual record. A factual record is a report from any technical, scientific, or other relevant sources that can help make clear what happened in the case under submission. In the first seven years of the CEC only two factual records were developed, but in 2002 seven more were added.

The Secretariat's activities are diverse, and in addition to specific obligations, it can initiate activities connected to the mission of NAAEC. The Secretariat's activities are developed in a three-year work plan. The 2002–2004 work plan of the Secretariat includes four programs: environment, economy, and trade; conservation of biodiversity; pollutants and health; and law and policy. The CEC also supports the North American Fund for Environmental Cooperation, a granting program that promotes public participation in community-based environmental cooperation in North America.

The Joint Public Advisory Committee (JPAC) is composed of fifteen citizens, five from each of the three countries, and advises the Council on any matter within the scope of the agreement. Through regular meetings with the public of North America or the creation of working groups, JPAC has the capacity to provide scientific or technical information to the Council. The information can be used for the development of factual records or to prepare advice to the Council on relevant matters (for example, Advice to Council 02–01 on Children's Health and the Environment in North America). It is a unique vehicle to promote transparency and public participation.

Each party can also create two additional advisory committees within their country for further advice and elaboration of NAAEC. These are a National Advisory Committee (NAC) and a Governmental Advisory Committee (GAC). Membership in the NAC is drawn from the public and can include NGOs and experts. The GAC includes representatives from the federal, state, or provincial governments. Both committees help in decision making and give advice in relation to NAAEC.

The CEC is unique, as no other international free trade agreement has included such a prominent body to oversee the issues related to trade and the environment. CEC works in the three official languages,

French, English and Spanish. Its uniqueness lies in its capacity to deal with environmental concerns in a transparent manner, and to promote public participation. For many citizens and NGOs of North America, CEC offers a very effective forum to promote environmental stewardship at the continental scale.

Liette Vasseur

Further Reading

Commission for Environmental Cooperation. (1998). *North American environmental law and policy*. Québec, Canada: Editions Yvon Blais Inc.

Commission for Environmental Cooperation. (1999). *Ribbon of life: An agenda for preserving transboundary migratory bird habitat on the Upper San Pedro River*. Montreal, Canada: CEC Secretariat.

Commission for Environmental Cooperation. (2001). *Electricity and the environment: An article 13 initiative of the North American Commission for Environmental Cooperation*. Montreal, Canada: CEC Secretariat.

Commission for Environmental Cooperation. (2001). *North American agenda for action: 2002–004. A three-year program plan for Commission for Environmental Cooperation of North America*. Montreal, Canada: CEC Secretariat.

Markell, D. L. (2000). The Commission for Environmental Cooperation's citizen submission process. *The Georgetown International Environmental Law Review, 7*, 545–574.

Commodification

Commodification refers to the process through which relations between human beings and the natural environment become increasingly transformed into market transactions and the elements of nature converted into tradable commodities. It is important to differentiate between (1) the application of market institutions and mechanisms as instruments to enhance human capacities in dealing with the natural environment and (2) the transformation of elements of nature into marketable commodities for private profit. Although these processes are closely intertwined, the notion of commodification refers primarily to the latter.

Commodification of Nature

The concept of commodification derives from the theory of capitalist society of German political philosopher Karl Marx (1818–1883), whereby the exchange of privately owned commensurable commodities becomes the centerpiece of the social system. Drawing on the value theory elaborated by classical political economists such as Scotsman Adam Smith (1723–1790) and Englishman David Ricardo (1772–1823), Marx argued that commodities have a doubled-edged characteristic. On the one hand, commodities have "use value" because they can satisfy human needs, and this characteristic makes individual commodities qualitatively different and incommensurable with each other. On the other hand, commodities have also exchange "value" because they can be exchanged for other commodities on the basis of their comparative quantitative value. The exchange value of different commodities is eventually expressed in the form of a general equivalent such as money, which is itself a particular type of commodity.

For Marx the key commodity in capitalist society is labor, which is abstracted from the material activity of individual workers and transformed into a commodity that can be treated as commensurate with other commodities that intervene in the production process. He argued that this commodity-centered system of production has a fundamental contradiction: although the labor incorporated in the commodities acquires a social character in the exchange process, this social character is not apparent for the individual producers. In the marketplace the transactions assume an impersonal nature whereby the underlying social relations of production are perceived by the actors as relations between things, the commodities. He called this reduction of an essentially social relation into relations between things "commodity fetishism": in the market the products of human labor appear as independent entities controlled by a self-organizing mechanism completely alien to the wills and beyond the control of the human beings involved.

In Marx's analysis, the development of capitalist social relations entails an increasing expansion of the commodification process that tends to involve all elements of nature in the circuit of commerce. For instance, writing in the mid-nineteenth century he theorized about the commodification of soil that was taking place through the intensification of capitalist agriculture, whereby the natural wealth contained in the soil nutrients had become the object of private appropriation, unchecked exploitation, and depletion. In this connection he argued that one of the preconditions of the future communist social order that he envisaged

> **Modern man seems to believe he can get everything he needs from the supermarket and corner drugstore. He doesn't understand that everything has a source in the land or sea.**
>
> —Thor Heyerdahl, 1954

as the superior form of social organization that would replace capitalist society will be transcending the contradictions of the commodity-centered social organization, which among other issues will imply the abolition of the private property of natural resources. In the new order human beings would be temporary beneficiaries and not private owners of nature. Common possession and the free association of producers would be the main principles for achieving a rational government of the relationship between human beings and the natural environment.

Although the marketization of natural resources has always been constitutive of the capitalist production process, the use of the concept of commodification in relation to the environment has acquired renewed saliency since the 1980s. Policies adopted worldwide to tackle the global environmental crisis caused by extensive degradation of ecosystems have increasingly resorted to applying market mechanisms in order to bring under control environmental problems such as depletion of pastures, forests, and fisheries, desertification, or water and air pollution. One of the central tenets of these policies has been that environmental management should be organized around market principles because this would allow the achievment of a more efficient allocation of available resources and the provision of incentives for the conservation of natural resources. However, the actual enforcement of these policies requires the creation of private property rights over natural resources that are often in the public domain or are owned in common by local communities. Also, this process of reform has led to the reconceptualization of the status granted previously to goods and services such as water supply and sanitation that were historically considered to be public goods but that have been increasingly transformed into commodities as a result of these policies. This development has led to bitter and ongoing controversies.

From "Market Failures" to Market-Based Environmental Policy

Historically the process of commodification of the natural environment has faced enormous obstacles, some of which were traditionally conceptualized by economic theorists as "market failures." For instance, the environmental costs and benefits of economic activities have seldom been incorporated into the calculations involved in market transactions. Welfare economists (welfare economics is a field of economics developed since the 1870s as a critique of classical liberal economic thinking; its main tenet is the need for state intervention to preserve the conditions of the market economy) suggested that the problem originated in one particular type of market failure: the hidden costs and benefits, that is, the "negative and positive externalities" arising from a given activity affecting the environment. These externalities arise from market transactions that have costs and benefits for third parties that are not captured in the market price of the goods or services involved. For instance, the provision of water supply has positive externalities because it produces benefits not only for those agents directly involved in water transactions but also for the public in general, given that, among other issues, it enhances public health and cleanliness. Contrariwise, the disposal of untreated industrial and urban effluents has negative externalities because the damage caused to natural resources not only affects those agents directly involved in the activity but also has a negative impact on society and the environment at large. The conventional argument has been that externalities produce allocative inefficiency (in standard economic theory, when a given economy deviates from the optimal equilibrium characterized by the provision of the right amounts and types of goods and services preferred by the economic agents), given that part or all of the costs arising from them are socialized and not paid by the individual economic agents involved in the exchange. English economist Arthur Cecil Pigou (1877–1959) famously argued in favor of taxing negative externalities, such as the discharge of polluting effluents, through the implementation of the "polluter pays" principle. He also suggested that positive externalities could be induced through subsidization.

Another type of market failure theorized by welfare economists is the existence of public goods, that is, goods characterized by their low or nondivisibility and excludability (the feasibility to exclude non-payers from access to a given good or service). As public goods or services are consumed collectively it is difficult—if possible at all—to charge individual users for their actual consumption and to exclude non-payers, as in the case of, for instance, flood control or prevention of water-related diseases, which are normally provided by the public sector and funded through general taxation.

However, theories of market failure have been severely criticized, in particular by scholars working in the traditions of the New Institutional Economics, Public Choice Theory, and Property Rights Theory. In this connection, there is one argument that has become particularly influential in the elaboration of environmental policy since the 1980s: The concept of market failure would be a fallacy because all that exist are transaction costs. According to these critics, the failure to organize markets for particular goods or services arises because often the transaction costs are too high, but not because environmental costs are intrinsically intractable externalities (e.g., the cost of air or water pollution) or because certain goods or services merit a differential treatment (e.g., as public goods). Thus, the argument continues, if transaction costs can be lowered to affordable levels, then all goods and services could be managed through the market. The key to lower transaction costs is to assign private property rights over goods or services that are in the public domain or that are owned in common because these (anachronistic) forms of property would be the main cause of high transaction costs and therefore the main obstacle for the full marketization of these goods and services.

These arguments have become highly influential since the 1980s and have fostered a radical transformation in the policies of environmental management. The principle behind these new policies is that the environment is best served if natural resources are treated as economic goods because this would allow the otherwise-intractable problem of making both environmental values and risks commensurate with mar-

ketable goods and services. A complementary principle is that natural resources must become private property because commodity markets require a system of private property rights as the precondition to make the transactions possible. A classical example of this position was popularized in the late 1960s through U.S. biologist Garrett Hardin's well-known argument of the "tragedy of the commons" with reference to the over-exploitation of common-property resources. However, whereas in the 1960s there was a strong belief that private property systems should be strictly enforced and controlled by the state, since the 1980s there has been a shift, and the prevailing policies have been predicated on the principle that, once created, markets for environmental goods should be coordinated through the self-regulated operation of market mechanisms. The resulting policies have been often conceptualized by the critics as a commodification of nature, which implies an extension of capitalist forms of production and consumption to areas that had remained relatively outside the circuit of capitalist socioeconomic organization.

One particular example of this process is the creation of water markets to induce a more efficient allocation of water resources across competing uses of water. Tradable water rights are created with the assumption that water can be transformed into (1) an economic good that can be made commensurable with others and therefore can be priced in the marketplace and (2) private property that can be owned and traded by economic agents in a free market. The principle at work is that in a free market for water rights, prices will be determined by the balance between supply and demand and that this would provide a solution for the growing conflicts characterizing the management of water resources in the face of increasing demand for competing uses. This approach to water management became well established in the Fourth Principle of the Dublin Declaration adopted at the 1992 United Nations Conference on Water and the Environment, which stated that "water has an economic value in all its competing uses and should be recognized as an economic good" (United Nations, 1992).

Another example is the creation of markets to trade in air pollution permits within a restricted volume of total allowable pollution emissions. Similar models have been implemented for the management of water pollution, where a market for commodified pollution effluents is created. Under this system, polluters can buy time-limited pollution allowances where the only restriction is the total annual pollution allowance for each individual market. Unused permits can be freely traded, even for use in future periods. In a similar way to the previous case, the principle at work here is that in a free market for pollution permits, prices will be determined by the balance between supply and demand and that this would provide a solution for the otherwise-intractable problem of internalizing environmental costs in production processes.

Discernible Trends and Controversies

Market-based environmental policies have been widely adopted since the 1980s and form part of the main policy tools recommended by multilateral organizations such as the World Bank or aid agencies working in developing countries. However, the model has been strongly criticized both on theoretical and empirical grounds, and the controversy is set to continue. One of the main criticisms, put forward by authors working in the fields of ecological economics and political ecology, concerns the fact that the treatment of elements of the natural environment as tradable commodities is based on the false assumption that the values that human beings attach to nature are commensurable and, therefore, reducible to finding the right transaction cost for them. Contrary to this assumption, these critics argue, most ecological distribution conflicts, such as those derived from competing demand for water resources or from the impact of air and water pollution, constitute a clash of incommensurable values that are not reducible to a monetary expression. For instance, local communities may value their water resources not just because of their potential exchange value in the market but also—and often mainly—on the basis of traditional, religious, cultural, or other valuation frameworks that may not be reconcilable with the commodity-centered valuation system of capitalism. Therefore, these critics argue that resolving environmental problems such as depletion of water resources and forests often requires a pluralist approach that can accommodate alternative and even irreconcilable value systems rather than reducing the problem to the particular standards of valuation prevailing in capitalist markets. Furthermore, imposing the particular valuation framework underlying the policies of environmental commodification would imply an undemocratic exercise of power that rules out alternative value frameworks in the name of simplifying the increasing complexity of contemporary society.

As mentioned, it is necessary to distinguish between the deployment of market mechanisms to achieve public policy objectives and the commodification of environmental goods and services for private profit. It is mainly the latter that has been and will likely continue to be the object of fierce controversy and political conflict.

José Esteban Castro

Further Reading

Bromley, D. W. (1991). *Environment and economy: Property rights and public policy.* Oxford, UK: Blackwell.

Connelly, J., & Smith, G. (1999). *Politics and the environment: From theory to practice.* London: Routledge.

Dasgupta, P., & Heal, G. (1985). *Economic theory and exhaustible resources.* Cambridge, UK: Cambridge University Press.

Dryzek, J. (1997). *The politics of the Earth.* Oxford, UK: Oxford University Press.

Eckersley, R. (Ed.). (1995). *Markets, the state and the environment: Towards integration.* London: Macmillan.

Gordon, S. (1954). The economic theory of a common-property resource: The fishery. *The Journal of Political Economy, 62*(2), 124–142.

Grundmann, R. (1991). *Marxism and ecology.* Oxford, UK: Oxford University Press.

Hardin, G. (1968). The tragedy of the commons. *Science, 162*, 1243–1248.

Harvey, D. (1996). *Justice, nature, and the geography of difference.* Cambridge, MA: Blackwell.

Martínez-Allier, J. (1987). *Ecological economics.* Oxford, UK: Basil Blackwell.

Marx, K. (1976). *Capital.* New York: Vintage. (Original work published 1867)

Marx, K., & Engels, F. (1967). *The communist manifesto.* Harmondsworth, UK: Penguin. (Original work published 1848)

O'Connor, M., & Spash, C. (Eds.). (1999). *Valuation and the environment: Theory, methods and practice.* Cheltenham, UK: Edward Elgar.

Ostrom, E. (1990). *Governing the commons: The evolution of institutions for collective action.* New York: Cambridge University Press.

Parsons, H. (Ed.). (1977). *Marx and Engels on ecology.* Westport, CT: Greenwood.

Pigou, A. C. (1962). *The economics of welfare* (4th ed.). New York: St. Martin's Press. (Original work published 1920)

Redclift, M., & Benton, T. (Eds.). (1994). *Social theory and the global environment.* London: Routledge.

Rubin, I. I. (1972). *Essays on Marx's theory of value*. Montreal, Canada: Our Generation Press. (Original work published 1928)

Schmidt, A. (1971). *The concept of nature in Marx*. London: New Left.

United Nations. (1992). *The Dublin statement on water and sustainable development*. Retrieved January 22, 2003, from http: //www.gdrc.org /uem /water /dublin-statement.html

Communal Areas Management Programme for Indigenous Resources (CAMPFIRE)

CAMPFIRE, an acronym for Communal Areas Management Programme for Indigenous Resources, is an innovative community conservation project launched in Zimbabwe in 1986. Settler governments in South Africa and Zimbabwe, as well as British colonial authorities elsewhere, had responded to diminishing wildlife stocks from the early twentieth century by establishing protected game reserves or national parks where hunting was not allowed and access largely restricted to scientists and tourists. But game reserves could only cover a very limited area, and wildlife destruction continued elsewhere on privately and communally held land. Moreover, the game reserves excluded most African communities, who drew little benefit from them, and they precluded the economic utilization of wildlife, except for tourism.

As in the sphere of forestry, advocates of community-based management criticized this approach in the 1980s. Some argued that wildlife would be more ecologically sustainable than livestock in fragile and hard-pressed African lands, especially in drier zones. Wild species, it was suggested, were adapted to the local environment and could make best use of the range of vegetation. Community management of such natural resources could become a key development tool, and smallholders could benefit economically. The Department of National Parks in the new Zimbabwean government, which came to power in 1980, acting with the World Wildlife Fund (WWF) and researchers at the University of Zimbabwe, developed the CAMPFIRE policy around these aims. By 1988, the scheme was working in two rural district councils, Nyaminyami and Guruve. By 1995, twenty-five districts had joined and considera-

ble revenue was being generated from hunting, tourism, and sale of venison.

The scheme attracted a great deal of publicity and large amounts of donor funding, especially from USAID (US Agency for International Development). In this sense it brought the added benefit of foreign aid to the economy as a whole. It was coterminous with important developments in international organizations, such as United Nations agencies, which laid greater stress on indigenous rights and the link between biodiversity and local knowledge. CAMPFIRE served as a model for similar projects throughout the region of southern Africa; East Africa has also developed community management schemes, although they rest partly on earlier experiments in Kenya.

A considerable academic literature has examined CAMPFIRE's difficulties as well as its successes. Communities that generate income do not always benefit as much as they might wish, because the councils controlling the appropriation of resources may reallocate income. The scheme is run through local council bodies whose interests are not always the same as those of the producing groups. Direct individual income is usually irregular or absent, and some of the most profitable commodities, such as ivory, have been subject to unpredictable international regulation. While venison is one product, tourism and hunting provide larger returns; in 2000–2002, this source of revenue has declined sharply as a result of national politics and internal conflict. If local families, often poor, are partly to sacrifice their individually owned cattle and agricultural system in favor of wildlife, they require a more immediate economic incentive. In the northwestern Nkayi and Lupane districts, which on paper looked like a good site for the scheme because of their marginality and low population densities, CAMPFIRE became viewed with great suspicion for the above reasons, and also because some saw increasing wildlife numbers as a cultural step backwards and a threat to modernity and development. Many believed that earlier wildlife eradication programs to control the tsetse fly had, overall, been beneficial. Here and elsewhere, local political conflict often intensified around wildlife projects.

CAMPFIRE has been enormously influential in debates about wildlife conservation, management of natural resources, and formation of development policies. It has stimulated debate both internationally and within local communities. It has not been an unqualified success: conservationists have become concerned that community management may not always be a reliable method of protecting rare species and biodiversity; communities have questioned whether wildlife can produce a regular income and social progress. Because of external funding and the participation of non-governmental organizations, it is difficult to say whether CAMPFIRE has been financially viable as a development strategy. Some also see it as another route by which the central state can control rural communities and commodify their resources. Yet the program has helped to create a new baseline for theory and practice. Fresh ideas and directions, such as local shares in the revenue from reserved areas and national parks, are being developed. The success of private game farms in some African countries suggests that further innovation along these lines is feasible.

William Beinart

Further Reading

Alexander, J. & McGregor, J. (2000). Wildlife and politics: CAMPFIRE in Zimbabwe. *Development and Change, 31*(3), 605–628.

Child, B. (1996). The practice and principles of community-based wildlife management in Zimbabwe: The CAMPFIRE programme. *Biodiversity and Conservation, 5*(3), 369–382.

Hulme, D., & Murphree, M. (Eds.). (2001). *African wildlife and livelihoods: The promise and performance of community conservation*. Oxford, UK: James Currey.

Murombedzi, J. C. (1991). *Decentralising common property resources management: A case study of the Nyaminyami District Council in Zimbabwe's wildlife management programme* (Issues paper no. 30). London: International Institute for Environment and Development, Dryland Network Programme.

Condor *See* California Condor

Confucianism

Confucianism is the system of ethical behavior founded by the Chinese sage Confucius (551–479 BCE). It is a combination of an ethical system, a political philosophy, and a set of prescriptions for the way in which people should conduct their social lives. It also has some of the characteristics of a religion. "Confucius"

is the Westernized version of the Chinese name K'ung Ch'iu, which may be translated as "Master Kung." Confucius was born in the province of Lu, which is located in what is now Shandong Province. Confucius's father died when he was young, although it appears that his mother managed to ensure that he received an adequate education. As a young man he obtained a post as a civil servant but in middle age embarked on an extensive period of travel that included studying and teaching. He finally returned to Lu, where he devoted his remaining years to teaching.

Confucian teachings are contained in a number of texts. The so-called Five Classics may well have been written during the lifetime of Confucius, but they almost certainly used substantial source material from previous writings. They consist of *The Book of Odes, The Book of Documents, The Book of Ceremonial Rites, The Book of Changes,* and *The Book of Spring and Autumn Annals.* Besides these, there are the Four Books, which consist of writings collected by the followers of Confucius, perhaps a hundred years after his death. These are *The Doctrine of the Mean, The Analects, The Great Learning,* and *The Book of Mencius.* The Four Books gradually became regarded as more significant than the Five Classics, with *The Analects* in particular regarded as representative of the teachings of Confucius. By about 200 BCE, Confucianism had begun to spread fairly widely in China and gradually became accepted as the religion of the state. This continued for almost two thousand years—until 1912. Confucianism also spread beyond the borders of China: to Korea during the Yi dynasty (1392–1910) and to Japan in 405 CE in conjunction with an understanding of the Chinese script. Neo-Confucianism evolved during the Sung dynasty (960–1279 CE) and was in some ways a reaction to the increasing popularity of Buddhism and Taoism.

The essence of the teaching of Confucius was that human beings should act in a moral way toward each other, trying to show such characteristics as compassion, sensitivity, humanity, and consideration. He asserted that individuals should treat others as they would prefer to be treated themselves. Confucius suggested that if individuals would act according to these principles, then a more peaceful, harmonious, and integrated society would result. He placed great emphasis upon the stability of the family and upon the need for people to show respect to their elders and to parents. Confucius encouraged political rulers to demonstrate the same kind of ethical principles in their administration of the state. He argued that the political ideal is for rulers to show compassion and humanity toward their subjects, whereas subjects should show respect and loyalty toward their rulers. It is also perhaps significant that Confucius taught people of all social backgrounds, whereas in the China of the time, education tended to be restricted to the higher social classes.

The development of Confucianism proceeded in parallel with that of Taoism, and there was to some extent continual interchange between the two sets of teachings. Both developed in China but tended to appeal to different groups of people. Confucianism was more concerned with prescribing a set of ethical principles for those in administrative authority, whereas Taoism appealed to those with more mystical leanings and emphasized the importance of being in harmony with nature.

Confucianism emphasizes the creation of a moral harmony between people and their environment. One may compare this with the tradition of *feng shui* (wind and water). Adherents of *feng shui* believe that there is an all-pervading energy named *ch'i*, which varies depending upon the distribution of hills, valleys, and rivers. *Feng shui* diviners provide advice on the location of new buildings or temples in order to determine the most beneficial distribution of *ch'i*. The ultimate aim is a sense of harmony between people and the natural world.

Paul Oliver

Further Reading

Dawson, R. (1981). *Confucius.* Oxford, UK: Oxford University Press.

Lau, D. C. (Ed.). (1979). *Confucius: The Analects.* Harmondsworth, UK: Penguin.

Legge, J. (1971). *Confucius: Confucian Analects, The Great Learning, and The Doctrine of the Mean.* New York: Dover.

Smith, H. D. (1973). *Confucius.* New York: Scribner.

Congo (Zaire) River

With a length of over 4,377 kilometers, the Congo River (also called the Zaire River) is the fifth-longest river in the world and the second longest in Africa (after the Nile). It is also the second-most powerful river in the world, discharging 33,980 cubic meters of water per second. So powerful is the Congo River that its brown waters surge nearly 144 kilometers out into the Atlantic Ocean. The city nearest its mouth is the town of Banana in the Democratic Republic of the Congo. Its width ranges from .8 kilometers to 16 kilometers, and it contains more than four thousand islands.

The Congo River crosses the equator twice while cutting an arc through the basin-like depression in the equatorial African rain forest known as the *cuvette* (basin). The river's drainage basin covers almost all of the Democratic Republic of the Congo (formerly Zaire), the Republic of the Congo, the Central African Republic, and parts of Zambia, Angola, Cameroon, and Tanzania. Because it receives water from tributaries both north and south of the equator, the river maintains a strong flow all year.

The Congo River can be divided into three sections. From its source in the savannas of the Democratic Republic of the Congo's Shaba Province, it is called the "Lualaba," and it flows northward for over 1,600 kilometers to Wagenia Falls, in the heart of the equatorial rain forest near Kisangani. There it takes the name "Congo" and flows in a lazy arc through the rain forest. The banks are not always clearly delineated, and during periods of high water the river spills over into floodplains that stretch as far as 19 kilometers inland. The third section begins at Malebo Pool, where the two national capitals of Kinshasa (Democratic Republic of the Congo) and Brazzaville (Republic of the Congo) face each other. Between the pool and the Atlantic Ocean, the river plunges nearly 304 meters, creating the largest reserve of waterpower in the world.

Cataracts along the lower Congo served as a barrier to European penetration during the era of the slave trade, although there was a lively river trade along the upper Congo that was dominated by networks of indigenous traders such as the Bobangi, the Boloki, and the Ngombe. Control of the Congo River was seen as crucial to the French and the Belgians, who were trying to establish colonies in equatorial Africa beginning in the late nineteenth century. They transported steamboats piece by piece from the Congo estuary to Malebo Pool for use on the upper Congo, and they used conscripted African labor to build railroads that bypassed the cataracts. With riverboat transportation in place, the Congo River became major transportation artery in equatorial Africa.

Since independence from Belgium in 1960 the government of the Democratic Republic of the Congo has attempted to harness some of the water power of the lower Congo's rapids by building two dams, Inga I and Inga II, which provide more electricity than the country is able to consume at the present. Because the

Democratic Republic of the Congo and the Republic of the Congo have not developed industrial centers along the banks of the Congo, it remains one of the world's least polluted rivers, according to a recent survey by the World Commission on Water for the 21st Century, a Paris-based group supported by the World Bank and the United Nations.

Robert Harms

Further Reading

Caputo, R. (1991). Lifeline for a nation: Zaire River. *National Geographic, 180*(5), 35.

Devroey, E. (1941). *Le bassin hydrographique congolais* [The hydrographic basin of Congo]. Brussels, Belgium: [G. Van Campenhout.

Fay, R. (n.d.). *Congo River*. Retrieved November 8, 2002, from http://www.africana.com/Articles/tt_236.htm

Forbath, P. (1977). *The river Congo*. New York: Harper & Row.

Harms, Robert (1981). *River of wealth, river of sorrow: The central Zaire Basin in the era of the slave and ivory trade*. New Haven, CT: Yale University Press.

Johnson, D. (n.d.). *Congo River called one of world's cleanest*. Retrieved November 8, 2002 from http://www.africana.com/DailyArticles/index_19991203.htm

Thinkquest Team 16645. (n.d.). *Congo River*. Retrieved November 8, 2002, from http://library.thinkquest.org/16645/the_land/congo_river.shtml

Conservation

Although it could be argued that every human society endeavors to mediate its members' relations with the natural world, the term *conservation* refers to a specific set of policies that arose in the late nineteenth century, particularly (although not uniquely) in the United States. Born in an age marked by industrialization, urbanization, nationalism, and imperialism, conservation bore the imprint of all these developments. Above all, however, it represented an effort to make science and government the arbiters of natural resource policy. As such, many of its most fundamental features continue to influence environmental policymaking into the twenty-first century.

Origins

For a movement that has long been standard to environmental history and the history of the Progressive Era, conservation's chronological limits remain curiously indistinct. While the word *conservation* itself is an old term, apparently having first been used in English in the 1700s to refer to the "conservancy" of London's Thames River, it was not employed during the first attempts to reform natural resource policy in the latter half of the nineteenth century. As a result, historians have reached differing conclusions as to the conservation movement's precise starting point. Although the term *conservation* never appears in its 300-plus pages, many scholars would point to the publication of George Perkins Marsh's *Man and Nature; Or, Physical Geography as Modified by Human Action* in 1864 as the clearest beginning of the movement. A Vermonter who served in Europe for many years as a diplomat for the Lincoln administration, Marsh was also arguably the first environmental historian. In *Man and Nature*, he asserted that overcutting of forests led to erosion, loss of soil fertility, and, if unchecked, the destruction of civilizations. Such a scenario, according to Marsh, explained the collapse of ancient Greece and Rome; it would repeat itself in the Americas unless the government took steps to protect the remaining forests.

Recently, scholars focusing on other areas of the globe have advanced findings that diminish Marsh's uniqueness as the originator of the conservation movement. In particular, historians of European expansion have noted that Marsh's theories derived in large part from earlier findings about deforestation, especially in the tropical areas subjected to European colonization from the fifteenth century onward. Thus, even before *Man and Nature*'s publication, colonial administrations adopted what would today be termed conservation measures. In 1859, for example, the Government of the Cape Colony of Southern Africa passed a Forest and Herbiage Protection Act. Three years later, the French began to establish forest reserves in their colonies in Cochin China (present-day Vietnam). Marsh himself conducted an extensive correspondence with Dietrich Brandis, the German forester who in 1864 (the same year as *Man and Nature*'s publication) founded the Indian Forest Department, the agency charged with managing the forest reserves in Great Britain's colonies in India. While none of these findings undermines the acuity of Marsh's insights, they do suggest that his thought, rather than being ahead of its time, emerged instead out of an ongoing, transnational conversation about the environmental risks of human behavior—and, moreover, that there may be no single, simple starting point for a movement as broad and varied as conservation.

Opie, you haven't finished your milk. We can't put it back in the cow, you know.

—Aunt Bee Taylor, *The Andy Griffith Show*

Although conservationists such as Marsh typically spoke in terms of protecting nature, their policies had dramatic social consequences. In Europe, where scientific forestry first emerged, the solution that Marsh and others advanced—government ownership and management of forests and other environmentally sensitive areas—often prompted bitter struggles with peasant populations who had long depended on nearby forests for game, firewood, forage, building supplies, and the like. As European powers exported their forestry practices to their colonies in the nineteenth and twentieth centuries, these confrontations became if anything more heated, for, as colonial subjects, the indigenous inhabitants of Africa, Asia, and elsewhere typically enjoyed even less official recognition of their customary rights to woodlands than did their European peasant counterparts. In India, for example, Brandis's Forest Department, in an effort to protect economically valuable species of trees for use by the British, enacted rules limiting rural communities' ability to hunt, graze livestock, farm, lumber, or set fires in the forests, despite the longtime dependence of Indian peasants and tribal peoples upon local woodlands. The native population responded not only with widespread avoidance of the new rules but also with arson, the defacement of government boundary markers, and even attacks upon agents of the Forest Department.

Such conflicts with indigenous peoples were not entirely absent from the United States. In much of the American West, the creation of conservation areas in the late nineteenth century meant removing locations from the control of American Indians. This process of dispossession was facilitated not only by the rise of the reservation system, but also by new hunting and fishing codes, which governed how, when, and how much fish and game American Indians could catch, and by the creation of new conservation areas, which limited Native American access to much of their previous territory. In 1880, for instance, Philetus Norris, an early superintendent of Yellowstone National Park (created in 1872 to protect the spectacular scenery in the mountains of northwestern Wyoming), extracted a

"solemn promise" from the nearby Crow, Shoshone, and Bannock Indian peoples "not [to] enter the Park," where they had long hunted elk, mountain sheep, and other game. The authorities at the forest reserves created after 1891 often placed similar limits on Indian mobility. Although such efforts typically met with only partial success, as Native Americans, like their counterparts in British India, were seldom willing to surrender their access to the material and cultural resources conservation areas contained, they were effective enough to disrupt American Indians' subsistence patterns and to trigger prolonged conflicts between Native Americans and conservation authorities.

Conservation also reshaped Euro-American environmental practices. The notion at the heart of conservation—government ownership and stewardship of the natural world—represented a radical deviation from the widely shared Euro-American belief that the public domain ought to be transformed into privately owned farm land as expeditiously as possible (an ideal that reached its most complete statement in the United States with the Homestead Act of 1862). As a result, even though *Man and Nature* was a bestseller by the standards of the 1860s, its suggestions were not implemented into American natural resource policy for almost two decades. This sustained pause in the United States between Marsh's warnings and governmental action—between the movement's intellectual precursors and its shaping of actual policy—in turn explains much of the scholarly confusion about conservation's precise starting date.

The first to adopt Marsh's proposed solution of government ownership and management of the forests was New York State. In 1883, the state created a forest preserve in the Adirondack Mountains in its far northern counties, primarily out of concerns that deforestation in this region would threaten the water flow necessary for its mills and canals. In 1891, the federal government, similarly concerned about water supplies, passed the Forest Reserve Act, which authorized the president to withdraw from settlement any plot of public land "wholly or in part covered with timber

Your State Forester and the
National Association of State Foresters

NASF-FP-1

The "Conservation Pledge" used by the National Association of State Foresters as an educational tool with school children.

or undergrowth" as a permanent forest reservation. Within ten years, there would be fifty-four forest reserves (later renamed national forests) containing some sixty million acres throughout the United States. The majority clustered west of the Mississippi River, where the ongoing federal ownership of the public domain facilitated the carving out of large reserves, but by the early twentieth century forest reserves could also be found in New Hampshire, Florida, North Carolina, and Puerto Rico.

The inhabitants of the American countryside developed a deeply ambivalent relationship to the forest reserves and other conservation sites emerging in their midst in the late nineteenth century. While some welcomed conservation's efforts to protect the forests and game so essential to country life, others resented the movement's imposition of new laws criminalizing such rural practices as hunting or fishing for food, cutting trees for building supplies or firewood, or grazing livestock on open land. In the face of frequent local hostility to conservation, government officials soon realized that establishing a functioning conservation policy necessitated not only passing new laws but creating enforcement mechanisms as well. New York State, for example, early on created a force of foresters to patrol its preserve in the Adirondacks. In 1886, the federal government, lacking an efficient administrative agency for its nascent conservation efforts, turned the management of the national parks over to the United States Army. This ostensibly temporary measure remained in effect for thirty-two years, ending only after Congress created the National Park Service in 1916.

Americans were not alone in finding enforcement essential to their conservation plans or even in assigning the military to this task. A similar linkage between conservation and the military took place in Asia and Africa during both the colonial and post-colonial eras. Officers in the British Army were early proponents of conservation in colonial India, while after 1945 several of the newly independent nations in Africa turned to the military to prevent poaching on the conservation lands that they inherited from colonial regimes.

The Progressive Era

Even as the conservation movement achieved prominence in the United States in the late nineteenth century, it continued to be influenced by people and ideas from overseas. The federal government's Division of Forestry, established in 1881 with an advisory rather than administrative function, was directed from 1886 to 1898 by Bernhard E. Fernow, a graduate of one of the famed forest academies of his native Prussia. In 1898, another German immigrant, Carl Schenk, founded the first school of forestry in the United States on the grounds of the Vanderbilt family's sprawling Biltmore estate in North Carolina. Even the American at the forefront of establishing a national conservation policy in the United States, Gifford Pinchot, acquired his early training abroad, first at the French forestry school at Nancy and later through travels to Germany and Switzerland. Thus, like Marsh before him, at the same time that Pinchot was involved in a nationalist project—protecting the United States's natural resources—he was also a participant in a transnational circuit of ideas about human interactions with the environment, one that linked North America with Europe and its colonies in Africa, Asia, Australia, and the Caribbean.

Although Pinchot shared with his European counterparts an abiding belief in scientific expertise, the differing forest ecologies, labor supplies, and legal and political contexts between the Old and New Worlds led him to develop distinct management policies. Above all, Pinchot believed that in the United States the national government needed to take a central role in conservation policy. When an assassin's bullet elevated Theodore Roosevelt to the presidency in 1901, Pinchot developed an uncommonly fruitful alliance with the new chief executive. Cementing their ties through their shared enthusiasm for "strenuous manhood" (on one of their first meetings, Roosevelt and Pinchot wrestled and then boxed before discussing natural resource policy), Pinchot persuaded the new president to use the powers of the executive office to expand dramatically the federal government's conservation program.

The result was an unprecedented flurry of conservation measures over the next few years. In 1902, Roosevelt signed into law the National Reclamation Act, which authorized the Secretary of the Interior to construct reservoirs in the arid regions of the West and to sell the resulting irrigated cropland to settlers. In 1905, Pinchot persuaded Roosevelt to create the Forest Service. This new agency, with Pinchot as its first chief forester, combined the supervisory and enforcement responsibilities for the forest reserves that had previously been scattered through several offices into a single bureaucracy. (In recognition of the government's growing need for scientifically trained foresters, Pinchot had already helped establish the Yale Forestry School in 1900; many of its graduates soon ended up employed by their school's founder at his new Forest Service). The 1906 American Antiquities Act authorized the president "to declare . . . objects of historic or scientific interest . . . situated upon the lands owned or controlled by the Government of the United States to be national monuments." Acting upon his new powers, Roosevelt created Devil's Tower National Monument in Wyoming and the Petrified Forest National Monument in Arizona shortly after signing the act into law. In 1907, Roosevelt and Pinchot inaugurated the Inland Waterways Commission, a task force dedicated to improving inland navigation in the United States. The following year, Roosevelt and Pinchot convened a national conservation congress at the White House, a measure that led to the creation of the National Conservation Commission in 1908.

Pinchot's role during this era extended beyond shaping federal policy to popularizing the conservation movement. In 1910, after being forced from office because of his disagreements with Roosevelt's more laissez-faire successor, William Taft, the former chief forester published *The Fight for Conservation*, which contained what has become the single best-known definition of conservation: "Conservation means the greatest good to the greatest number for the longest time." This definition, an updated version of utilitarianism's goal of achieving the "greatest good to the greatest number," reverberated through American culture in the early twentieth century, elevating the term conservation from forestry circles to popular discourse. In the process, it also complicated further questions about conservation's starting point, since Pinchot's book gave the misleading impression that conservation was a new movement, when in fact the term described a process that was already well underway. Within a brief period of time, one could witness conservation being applied to a variety of new issues, some seemingly quite distant from natural resource policy. Reformers in the 1910s spoke of conserving the United States' "racial stock" and "the energies of its citizens," and of embracing "efficiency" in all aspects of American life. This wide embrace of conservation's central tenets—scientific expertise, governmental oversight, and efficiency—rendered the movement arguably the archetype of the Progressive Era and its efforts to reform an ever-more industrial, urban America.

Despite such remarkable achievements, tensions existed within and without the conservation movement during this time. Representatives from the American West, where most initial conservation measures had been focused because of the region's greater aridity and higher concentration of public lands, early on expressed concern that the expanding federal conservation program was limiting private ownership and impinging on each state's ability to guide its own development as it saw best. In 1907, several representatives added an amendment to an agricultural appropriation bill transferring the power to create forest reserves in the western states of Colorado, Idaho, Montana, Oregon, Washington, and Wyoming from the president to Congress. Pinchot and Roosevelt responded by setting aside sixteen million acres in new reserves (dubbed "midnight forests" by their detractors) the night before the law was to go into effect. This act only solidified the suspicion in the minds of some Westerners that the federal government was undertaking a conservation program without respecting Western wishes, thus setting in motion a series of federal-local conflicts over conservation that remains prominent in the American West to this day.

Hetch Hetchy

If the events of 1907 illuminate some of the resistance that conservation encountered from those outside the movement, another incident from the early twentieth century revealed the fault lines within the movement. In 1901, the city of San Francisco, searching for a more reliable source of water, applied for a permit to build a reservoir in Hetch Hetchy, a valley located in Yosemite National Park, some 150 miles outside the city limits. This act eventually precipitated a sharp break between Pinchot and his one-time friend John Muir, the founder and first president of the Sierra Club. Muir, like Pinchot, had been an early proponent of forest reserves in California's Sierra Nevada Mountains—indeed, Muir and Pinchot had worked together on the National Forest Commission in 1896, during which they spent a memorable evening camping out together at the Grand Canyon. But while Muir objected to San Francisco's plans to dam Hetch Hetchy, which he thought would destroy a site of unsurpassed natural beauty, Pinchot supported the project in the belief that it was a more rational and efficient to use the valley as a reservoir than as mere scenery. Roosevelt, who shared both Muir's "preservationist" viewpoint as well as Pinchot's "utilitarian" perspective, wavered but eventually backed San Francisco's plans. Following a bitter, twelve-year campaign, the dam was finally built after President Woodrow Wilson signed the Raker Bill in 1913. Although Muir and his allies lost this particular battle, their campaign revitalized the Sierra Club and resulted in the creation of the National Park Service in 1916, thus ensuring a greater federal commitment to protecting the national parks.

The confrontation between Muir and Pinchot at Hetch Hetchy has often overshadowed much of the rest of the history of early conservation. For many scholars, the incident stands as an exemplar of the still-unresolved divisions between "preservationist" conservationists, who want nature protected from any human impact, and "utilitarian" conservationists, who believe that nature can be managed to meet human needs. While there is much to this interpretation, it has had the unfortunate effect of making the disagreement between Muir and Pinchot into the defining feature of the conservation movement. Such a conclusion not only obscures how much "preservationists" and "utilitarians" shared—such as a common belief in government ownership and expert supervision of environmentally sensitive areas—it also seems a poor fit with conservation's history outside of the United States. In much of Asia, Latin America, or Africa, after all, the central conflicts have tended not to be between conservationists but instead between conservationists and a rural population seeking control of the conservation areas in their midst.

The events that unfolded in Africa at almost the same time as the Hetch Hetchy controversy began provide an illuminating point of comparison. In 1900, the British Foreign Office called the world's first international environmental conference, which sought to preserve Africa's wild animals. The continent's colonial powers—France, Germany, Belgium, Italy, Spain, Portugal, and Great Britain—all attended, at which they established a number of agreements about protected and "vermin" species (the latter, which at the time included lions, hyenas, and leopards because of the threat they posed to humans and livestock alike, were assigned bounties so as to encourage their destruction) and laid the groundwork for a network of game reserves and parks across Africa. Notably absent from the conference were sharp divisions between "preservationists" and "utilitarians" as well as any representatives from indigenous Africa. Indeed, native Africans found themselves, rather than white hunters, depicted as the cause of the recent wildlife decline in the continent and, as such, the targets of many of the measures that emerged from the 1900 conference. New game laws, for example, restricted African hunting, while many of the new national parks involved the relocation of native African populations that had previously in-

habited the park territory, creating a bitter legacy between conservationists and local populations.

In North America, conservation policy did not undergo a dramatic expansion until the 1930s, when Theodore Roosevelt's distant cousin, Franklin Roosevelt, made conservation a cornerstone of his recovery plans during the Great Depression. Some of these measures built upon precedents established by the elder Roosevelt. The reclamation policies enacted during Theodore Roosevelt's administration, for example, bore their greatest fruit in the 1930s with such enormous water management projects as Hoover Dam and the Tennessee Valley Authority. Other measures represented more novel solutions to environmental problems. During the 1930s, for instance, the newly formed Civilian Conservation Corps sent thousands of young men into the countryside to battle forest fires and soil erosion, while the ecological damage manifested by the dust storms that swirled above the Great Plains during the "dirty thirties" prompted Congress to pass the Taylor Grazing Act in 1934. Attributing the Dust Bowl to the expansion of farming onto marginal lands, the Taylor Grazing Act withdrew all remaining federal lands from public entry—in essence ending, in the name of conservation, the policy of creating new agricultural homesteads that had guided the federal government for most of its existence.

Conservation and Environmentalism

If conservation's starting points remain indistinct, so too do its end points. In the United States, historians have typically presented the conservation movement as superseded by the environmental movement sometime in the 1960s and 1970s, the precise turning point being either the release of Rachel Carson's groundbreaking expose of DDT, *Silent Spring*, in 1962 or the first Earth Day of April 22, 1970. In either scenario, scholars distinguish environmentalism from conservation by a number of features: its mass popular appeal, its concern with threats to the human body, and its consumerist rather than producerist orientation towards nature. While recent research has muddied this taxonomy somewhat (concerns about the health effects of industrial processes, for example, now appear to predate *Silent Spring* by decades), it does seem, as measured by the membership in advocacy groups such as the Sierra Club, that the public concern for environmental issues underwent a remarkable explosion during the 1960s and 1970s. Still, it may be a mistake to regard this as constituting a sharp break with the conservation movement, as many of the institutions that became so important to Americans during this time—the National Park Service, the Forest Service, the Bureau of Land Management, or, for that matter, the Sierra Club—can trace their origins to conservation's emergence at the turn of the century.

Positing a clear end to conservation becomes even more complicated if one looks outside the United States to the developing world. In many cases, the newly independent nations of Africa and Asia continued the environmental policies of their colonial predecessors, maintaining the parks, forest reserves, and game preserves that had been established during the imperial era, while in Central and Latin America and elsewhere, countries imported the national forest and park models developed in the United States. Perhaps as a result, although struggles over natural resource policy remain prominent in much of the developing world, there is little evidence of a definable transition from conservation to environmentalism. Instead, much of the debate in these countries has focused on how to make the present conservation framework more accommodating to the needs of rural inhabitants. Some areas of Africa and south Asia, for example, have witnessed the rise of "community conservation," a policy of enlisting local communities in the decision-making processes for conservation areas. Such efforts at creating a new, more inclusive conservation, however, have not supplanted more ambitious and interventionist conservation policies. Especially controversial have been enormous dam and irrigation projects in India, China, and elsewhere, some of which dwarf even the United States's undertakings of the 1930s. Although the debates over such programs are sometimes cast in terms of "sustainable development" rather than conservation per se, the core assumption of sustainable development—that nature, when appropriately managed, can meet human needs over an extended period of time—shares much in common with conservation's principles of efficiency, expert management, and sustained yield, demonstrating the movement's enduring legacy for the global environment.

Karl Jacoby

See also Civilian Conservation Corps; Marsh, George Perkins; Nature; Nature Conservancy; Pinchot, Gifford; Roosevelt, Franklin Delano; Roosevelt, Theodore; Women and Conservation

Further Reading

Beinart, W., & Coates, P. (1995). *Environment and history: The taming of nature in the USA and South Africa.* New York: Routledge.

Grove, R. (1995). *Green imperialism: Colonial expansion, tropical island edens and the origins of environmentalism, 1600–1860.* New York: Cambridge University Press.

Guha, R. (2000). *Environmentalism: A global history.* New York: Longman.

Hays, S. (1959). *Conservation and the gospel of efficiency: The progressive conservation movement, 1890–1920.* Cambridge, MA: Harvard University Press.

Jacoby, K. (2001). *Crimes against nature: Squatters, poachers, thieves, and the hidden history of American conservation.* Berkeley: University of California Press.

Spence, M. (1999). *Dispossessing the wilderness: Indian removal and the making of the national parks.* New York: Oxford University Press.

Consumer Movement

The consumer movement, a movement to give consumers both more information about the many products in their daily lives and more power to pressure manufactures to make products meet certain standards, began in the 1960s in reaction to public concerns about product safety and the completeness and reliability of information provided to purchasers. It was a natural reaction to modern consumerism, which dates back to the period after World War I. At that time, starting in the United States, manufacturers and retailers began to realize that their businesses would boom if the mass of ordinary working people could become consumers for the flood of goods that increasingly productive technology could now release into the market.

Items such as the domestic washing machine, the radio and later the television, and, of course, the family car, symbolized this transformation from an economy in which consumer goods had been confined to a comparatively small section of society. Before, affluence had been confined to the circles immortalized in novels such as *The Great Gatsby*, in which the rich lived lives of conspicuous consumption. For the majority, however, consumption patterns were rather more austere. Indeed, when many people went to the luxurious new cinemas known as picture palaces being opened in the

1920s, it was the first time that they walked on proper carpets.

Selling Dreams

The fast-expanding advertising industry played its part by persuading people that the route to happiness lay in spending their monies on the fast-growing array of goods and services now on offer. Modern ideas about marketing developed hand in hand with the growth of mass production. Marketing people study human psychology to identify feelings that can be converted to desires, which could, the marketers claimed, be fulfilled by the purchase of goods and services. Feature movies (and later television) also encouraged such desires, since the medium of film enabled ordinary people to see how the rich apparently lived. A revolution of rising expectations was under way and today has reached every corner of the world.

However, many of those goods and services fell far short of what consumers had expected. Be it in terms of fair pricing, performance, durability, or other unwarranted claims made by sellers, consumers sometimes got short measure. The problem was not new. In the nineteenth century, for example, food adulteration was a common problem, and action had been taken to prevent it in many countries. After World War II, a number of critics, perhaps most notably writer and social critic Vance Packard, denounced practices such as planned obsolescence (the making of goods with deliberately and unnecessarily short lifespans). Ralph Nader's *Unsafe At Any Speed* (1965), an exposé of dangerous car designs, also reflected concern for consumers.

Growth of the Consumer Movement

The activities of critics and crusaders such as Vance Packard and Ralph Nader heralded the birth of the consumer movement, and the notion of *consumer sovereignty* became integrated into mainstream economic theory. Consumer sovereignty recognized that a market economy might be far from perfect, but, it was argued, any imperfections could, in part, be corrected by consumers themselves if they became more discriminating in their purchases—as the name of the magazine of the British Consumer Association, *Which?*, suggests. Organizations such as the British Consumer Association strive to help people make wiser choices. They have made many constructive suggestions for improving legislation concerning the description and sale of goods.

The consumer movement has organized itself internationally as well as within individual countries. The Consumers International, for example, was founded in 1960 as the International Organization of Consumer Unions (IOCU) by a group of national consumer organizations that recognized that they would become stronger by working across national borders. The organization campaigns on issues such as product and food standards, health and patients' rights, the environment and sustainable consumption, and the regulation of international trade and of public utilities.

Unlike the green-lifestyle movement, the various consumer pressure groups do not question consumerism per se; they content themselves with attempting to protect consumers against unfair trading practices and generally help shoppers select the best-value goods and services. Sometimes, this leads to startling contradictions. Thus in *Which?*, it is common to see an article on environmental protection sitting next to ones on the best buy in disposable cameras and high-speed sports cars—both quite environmentally irresponsible products. Electric salad shakers are, in the consumer test laboratory, as worthy a use of natural resources and human creativity as anything else. Most traditional consumer organizations seldom ask whether such items are necessary, or whose interests and priorities those items serve.

Consumerism

Though individual leaders such as Ralph Nader have become involved in more radical politics, the consumer movement as a whole remains wedded to the values and lifestyles dominant in contemporary society. In particular, the movement reflects the concept of the individual as self-interested consumer, rather than as cooperating citizen. In other words, it reflects the very individualism that some critics hold to be a major root of both societal breakdown and unsustainable demands upon environmental systems. The equation of consumption with personal happiness is seldom questioned, nor is it fully recognized that the trappings of affluence can in fact turn into traps, whether in the form of crushing personal debt or perpetual dissatisfaction with what one owns (since it seems, there is always something better about to be released). Instead, it is assumed that human needs can be met with the purchase of commodities: happiness, it seems, is there for the buying.

Consumer Choice?

The reality is different. Given the volume and rapidly changing range of products on the market, many with specifications comprehensible only to the expert, an individual's judgment is bound to be inadequate. Even experts do not know the potential consequences of many of the complex chemical substances in some of today's manufactured goods. Even with all the relevant information, making wise choices can be a time-consuming process, and when the right product is identified, the price may be beyond the consumer's means. Many have recommended a collective rather than a private approach. In the former, society would set appropriate standards for the quantity and quality of goods and services available. Durability, shared consumption (for example, renting instead of personally owning equipment needed only on an infrequent basis), satisfaction from less or, most significantly, satisfaction from nonmaterial pleasures are all hallmarks of a truly green pattern of consumption.

Sandy Irvine

Further Reading

Carley, M., & Spapens, P. (1998). *Sharing the world: Sustainable living and global equity in the 21st century*. London: Earthscan.

Durning, A. (1992). *How much is enough? The consumer society and the future of the earth*. Washington, DC: Worldwatch Institute.

Easterlin, R. (1973). Does money buy happiness? *Public Interest, 30*, 3–10.

Easterlin, R., & Crimmins, E. (1991). Private materialism, personal fulfilment, family life and public interest. *Public Opinion Quarterly, 55*, 499–533.

Ehrlich, P., & Ehrlich, A. (1989). Too many rich folks. *Populi, 16*(3), 3–29.

Fox, R., & Jackson, T. (Eds.). (1983). *The culture of consumption: Critical essays in American history, 1880–1980*. New York: Pantheon.

Goodwin, N. R., Ackerman, F., & Kiron, D. (Eds.). (1997). *The consumer society*. Covelo, CA: Island Press.

Hirsh, F. (1976). *Social limits to growth*. Cambridge, MA: Harvard University Press.

Irvine, S. (1989). *The limits of green consumerism*. London: Friends of the Earth.

Lansley, S. (1994). *After the gold rush: The trouble with affluence*. Henley, UK: Henley Centre/Century Books.

Leach, W. (1993). *Land of desire: Merchants, power and the rise of a new America*. New York: Pantheon Books.

Lury, C. (1996). *Consumer culture*. Cambridge, UK: Polity Press.

Mander, J. (1980). Four arguments for the elimination of advertising. In K. Rotzoll (Ed.), *Advertising and the public*. Champaign: University of Illinois Press.

Mander, K. & Boston, A. (1995). Wal-Mart worldwide: The making of a global retailer. *The Ecologist, 25*(6), 232–237.

Packard, V. (1960). *The wastemakers*. New York: McKay.

Rees, W., & Wackernagel, M. (1995). *Our ecological footprint*. Philadelphia: New Society.

Samuelson, R. J. (1997). *The good life and its discontents: The American dream in the age of entitlement*. New York: Vintage Books.

Seabrook J. (1988). *The race for riches: The human cost of wealth*. Dartington, UK: Green Print.

Trainer, F. E. (1985). *Abandon affluence*. Atlantic Highlands, NJ: Zed Books.

Wachtel, P. (1983). *The poverty of affluence*. New York: The Free Press.

Copper

Ten thousand years ago, in the first known use of metal, people in southwest Asia collected native copper they found associated with copper ores and hammered it into artifacts that are speculated to be awls, hooks, and beads. Later they learned how to smelt the ore, to alloy copper with arsenic to obtain a stronger metal, and to make bronze by alloying copper with tin. People chose bronze for personal display, ritual objects, and grave goods. The use of copper and bronze spread, or developed independently, throughout the world except in Australia and Oceania. The Chinese bronze ritual vessels from 750 BCE in museum collections are among the best known ancient artifacts. Brass, an alloy of copper and zinc, found favor in India and the Mediterranean around 300 BCE. The native peoples of North America exploited the abundant resources of native copper in present-day upper Michigan to make widely traded items, but never smelted it or made bronze. In Peru and Ecuador sophisticated artisans made decorative objects and tools from copper and bronze in pre-Columbian times.

Copper in the Industrial Age

The corrosion resistance and ease of fabrication of copper and its alloys made them attractive metals for industrial uses. The beginning of large-scale industrialization in the eighteenth century brought increased demand for copper, first for sheathing the wooden hulls of ships trading in tropical waters and later for locomotive boilers and for brass piping and fittings for machinery. Another large increase in demand followed the adoption of electrical power in the 1880s. Since copper is an excellent conductor of electricity and can be easily drawn into wire, it was the ideal material for carrying power from central generating stations to consumers. Electrical wiring soon became, and remains today, the largest single use for copper.

Copper is a scarce element constituting only 0.0058 percent of the Earth's crust. (Iron stands at 5.6 percent in the abundance rankings.) It can be obtained only where natural processes have concentrated it into ore. Some places—Chile, Arizona, and Zambia—have large deposits of copper ores while many parts of the world have none. People have traded copper since earliest times, and today most industrial nations depend on international trade for their copper.

From Ore to Refined Copper

The deposits of ore containing 25 percent or more copper that people found in the past have been mined out since the ancient times until the recent past. Even the best ores today contain only 0.5 percent copper. Despite this decrease in the grade, increased efficiency achieved at copper mines and smelters has kept the price of copper (corrected for inflation) nearly constant for the last seventy years. Nevertheless, two important consequences arise from the use of lower-grade ore: Modern copper mines are among the largest man-made holes in the ground and, since so much of the ore is unusable material, huge quantities of waste result from copper production, which can be divided into milling and smelting. Milling is the process of separating the copper mineral from the rest of the constituents in the ore first by grinding the ore and then by suspending the ground material in water. The various constituents used to be separated out by density differences and since the early twentieth century the copper can be extracted by wetting properties of minerals in appropriate frothing reagents. The waste, called tailings, is deposited in large ponds.

The concentrate from the mill is then shipped to a smelter, which may be far removed from the mine and mill site. Smelters make impure blister copper that retains not just copper, but other metals (some of them precious) from the ore. Since these impurities spoil the

electrical conductivity of the metal, blister copper is refined by electrolysis. Electric current passing through a solution of dilute acid (the electrolyte) transfers the copper to plates (called cathodes) while the impurities are left behind. Gold, silver, and other metals are important by-products of the copper refinery.

The Effect of Copper Mining on the Environment

Nearly all copper ores are made up of sulfide minerals such as chalcopyrite, a copper-iron-sulfide, and contain small amounts of arsenic, silver, gold, and other metals. Copper smelting techniques used into the twentieth century dispersed the sulfur in the ore into the atmosphere. The "copper smoke" emitted by smelters consisted of dilute sulfuric acid laced with arsenic and other constituents of the ore. Damage to farm crops and animals from copper smoke led to lawsuits and trials, first in South Wales, and later in the United States, where the issue reached the Supreme Court in 1907. Smelter operators responded by building tall stacks, allowing the smoke to traveler farther afield, which made it more diluted and less hazardous when it came back down. They also installed sulfuric acid by-product plants and used electrostatic precipitators to trap the arsenic fumes. The cost of meeting increasingly stringent environmental regulations has been a factor in the transfer of copper smelting operations from industrialized countries such as the United States to less-developed countries that are more tolerant of pollution.

The fate of the abandoned copper mines and smelters found in industrialized countries is a serious environmental concern. Ground water flowing through abandoned underground workings becomes acidified from contact with the remaining copper and other sulfide minerals, and emerges as acid mine drainage. The huge Berkeley pit in Butte, Montana, an abandoned copper mine, is being filled with water flowing into it from the mine workings that honeycomb the surrounding land. The resulting lake is so acidic that birds landing on its surface promptly die. Eventually the pit will fill; where the acidic water will go then no one knows.

The Future of Copper Use

The high value of copper assures that most copper products are recycled. This recycled metal makes up about a third of the world's current supply of copper.

Nevertheless, increased demand for new metal means that copper made from ore of ever-decreasing copper content continues to increase. The worked-out mines now on the landscape of copper-producing regions suggests that extraction of copper in the future will be increasingly costly, both initially and in terms of environmental consequences. Fortunately, there are few uses for copper for which other metals cannot be substituted. Aluminum, for example, is an excellent conductor of electricity and heat, and is already substituting for the copper formerly used for electric transmission lines and automobile radiators. Fiber-optic cables have replaced much of the copper formerly used in telecommunication systems, and plastic increasingly supplants copper plumbing. Thus, it is unlikely that any future shortage of copper will be a serious problem for society.

Robert B. Gordon

Further Reading

Gordon, R. B., et al. (1987). *Toward a new iron age? Quantitative modeling of resource exhaustion.* Cambridge, MA: Harvard University Press.

Hyde, C. K. (1998). *Copper for America: The United States copper industry from colonial times to the 1900s.* Tucson: University of Arizona Press.

Joralemon, I. B. (1973). *Copper, the encompassing story of mankind's first metal.* Berkeley, CA: Howell-North.

Joseph, G. (1999). *Copper: Its trade, manufacture, use, and environmental status.* Materials Park, OH: ASM International.

Molloy, P. (1986). *History of metal mining and metallurgy: An annotated bibliography.* New York: Garland.

Rees, R. (2000). *King Copper, South Wales and the copper trade 1854–1895,* Cardiff, UK: University of Wales Press.

Coral and Coral Reefs

Living coral reefs occur throughout the tropical latitudes of the world's oceans. Formed by associations of individual coral organisms and colonies, but hosting extensive biodiversity, coral reefs are highly productive. They usually grow where conditions for marine life would otherwise be unconducive. Fossil corals and coral reefs, found in sedimentary rock strata around the world, attest to the varied climates and paleoecological conditions of the past 600 million years. Coral reefs worldwide are currently threatened by local human-induced disturbances and rising global ocean temperatures.

In their adult form, corals are sedentary, multicelled organisms that form an endoskeleton of calcium carbonate. It is this endoskeletal structure that provides the geological structure of coral reefs, is found as fossils in rock strata, and is valued for ornamental purposes.

Members of the Phylum Cnidaria, corals comprise about 800 living species. Modern corals process nutrients in symbiosis with zooxanthellae, photosynthetic algae that live within the coral organism. This relationship creates the conditions for the robust productivity of entire reef ecosystems, but the requirements of photosynthesis—sunlight, and therefore shallow ocean depths—constrain the distribution of coral reefs throughout the world's oceans.

Reefs and Reef Environments

Marine organisms have been constructing landmasses at and just below sea level for about three-quarters of the Earth's geological history. The dominant reef-building organisms for much of that time were stromatolites. Corals are more recent, having appeared with other multicellular organisms in the Cambrian, about 600 million years ago.

Living reefs and their underlying structures of dead coral are youthful by geological standards, because the ocean floors on which they form are relatively young. Living species of coral are even younger, many having evolved over the past 65 million years. Paleontological studies of fossil corals and reefs suggest that surviving coral taxa recover slowly from mass extinction events.

Living coral reefs are of three primary kinds: *fringing reefs* form in shallow water close to island and continental landmasses; *barrier reefs* occur in deeper water farther from shorelines; and ring-shaped coral *atolls* occur separate from landmasses. More recently, two additional kinds of reef have been recognized: submerged reefs and reef communities, the latter so named due to the absence of reef structure.

The role of photosynthesis in coral physiology restricts the distribution of corals and coral reefs to shallower depths and tropical waters. Coral reefs are nevertheless abundant in the Indian and Pacific Oceans and are also distributed throughout the tropical portions of the Atlantic Ocean and in the Caribbean Sea.

As ecosystems, coral reefs are home to significant biodiversity. Reefs host related species, such as sea anemones, and a wide variety of other invertebrates, such as sponges, bryozoans, sea urchins, sea stars, worms, crustaceans, and mollusks. Among the vertebrates, fishes abound in healthy reef ecosystems. Taken together, the associations of organisms inhabiting coral reefs place them among the most productive of the Earth's ecosystems per unit area, on par with rainforests.

Coral Reefs in Human Prehistory and History

Because of how they alter their marine environments, coral reefs provide favorable conditions for migratory and sedentary human populations, and for human enterprise. Barrier and fringing reefs protect the shorelines of landmasses from destructive waves and storms, while the biomass associated with reefs helps sustain human life. Coral atolls have similar characteristics, with the addition of a large central lagoon. These advantages permitted the spread of Asian peoples throughout a vast region of the eastern Indian Ocean and the Pacific Ocean.

European exploration and colonization also benefited from coral reefs. In many cases, reefs provided safe anchorage for ships, provisions for continued voyaging, and resources for exploitation. European contact substantially altered the human ecologies of Caribbean reefs, displacing Native American populations with European colonists and African slaves. Pacific and Indian Ocean populations, though effected by colonial enterprises, remained largely intact until the twentieth century, but modern commerce and warfare had a profound effect on island and reef cultures.

The introduction of industrial technologies and economies of scale have severely affected reefs throughout the world. Reef fisheries are currently threatened by over fishing and loss of reef biomass. Pollution and tourism-related exploitation of reef resources contribute to the decline of reefs, as they inhibit the ability of reef organisms to recover from natural damage. The use of Pacific coral atolls as test grounds for nuclear weapons is a highly visible cause of reef destruction.

Marine biologists also credit global warming for "bleaching," a destructive process by which rising water temperatures cause corals to expel zooxanthellae, leading to loss of photosynthetic activity. Bleaching seriously threatens entire reef ecosystems. Global warming may also increase the severity of ocean storms, further threatening reef structures.

A variety of environmental organizations and governmental agencies have called attention to threatened reef ecosystems. In the United States, the National Oceanic and Atmospheric Administration promotes research into the causes of reef degradation and invites initiatives to monitor and mitigate adverse effects. These, however, only affect reefs in the territorial waters of the United States.

Mark L. Hineline

Further Reading

Bryant, D., Burke, L., McManus, J., & Spalding. M. (1998). *Reefs at risk: A map-based indicator of threats to the world's coral reefs.* Washington, DC: World Resources Institute.

Davis, W. M. (1928). *The coral reef problem.* New York: American Geographical Society.

Hodgson, G. (1999). A global assessment of human effects on coral reefs. *Marine pollution bulletin, 38*(5), 345–355.

Reaka-Kudla, M. L. (1997). The global biodiversity of coral reefs: a comparison with rain forests. In M. L. Reaka-Kudla, D. E. Wilson, & E. O. Wilson (Eds.), *Biodiversity II* (83–108). Washington, DC: Joseph Henry Press.

Schopf, T.J.M. (1979). The role of biogeographic provinces in regulating marine faunal diversity through geologic time. In J. Gray & A. J. Boucot (Eds.), *Historical biogeography, plate tectonics, and the changing environment* (449–457). Corvalis: Oregon State University Press.

Stoddart, D. R. (1969). Ecology and morphology of recent coral reefs. *Biological Reviews, 44,* 435–499.

U.S. Coral Reef Task Force. (2000). *The national action plan to conserve coral reefs.* Washington, DC: The Task Force.

Cosmology

Cosmology is the study of the universe as a whole: its structure, composition, history, and probable future. Because human records only extend over a tiny fraction of the lifetime of the universe and human exploration has been restricted to a very small region, cosmologists are forced to rely on extrapolations and speculation beyond what would be acceptable in the other sciences. While much of cosmological theory has no immediate relevance to understanding the environment of living organisms on earth, cosmology sheds light on the time scale of biological evolution and the possibility of new resources being discovered. Cosmology touches at several points on issues also of concern to religion and has for many thinkers required a revision of their estimate of the place of humans in nature.

The Geocentric Universe and Astrology

As ancient man watched the daily transit of the sky by sun and moon and the stars, it was only natural to assume that the Earth was the center about which they moved. On closer observation it became apparent that a few star-like objects moved a bit differently, seeming to wander against the background of stars that traveled together across the sky as if attached to a transparent sphere. The movements of the wanderers, called planets, was thought to influence human affairs and a group of professional astrologers began to predict the future for individual clients by casting horoscopes, based on the position of the planets at the time of their births. Tables of planetary positions were worked out, assuming the planets moved in circular orbits about the earth. The most famous of these, the Almagest of Ptolemy (90–168 CE) is the basis for astrological tables used today.

A Heliocentric Universe

The Ptolemaic model held sway until the Polish clergyman Nicolas Copernicus (1473–1543) published his book, *On the Revolutions of the Celestial Orbs* in 1512. Realizing that his views would meet with disapproval by church authorities, he postponed publication of his book until his dying year. The Copernican model was popularized by the Italian mathematician Galileo Galilei (1564–1642) who did incur censure for his views. In actuality, though, both the Ptolemaic and Copernican systems were defective in assuming on philosophical grounds that planetary motion must be circular. Based on the careful observations of the Danish nobleman Tycho Brahe (1546–1601), the German scholar Johannes Kepler (1571–1630) demonstrated that the planets moved about the sun in elliptical orbits. It remained for the great English mathematician Sir Isaac Newton (1642–1727) to discover the laws of motion and of universal gravitation that explained the elliptical orbits and confirmed the heliocentric model.

A Very Large and Old Universe

By the beginning of the twentieth century, astronomers were in general agreement that the sun was just one of many stars and that the visible stars in the sky were clustered together in a large structure, the Milky Way galaxy. A group of indistinct fuzzy objects called nebulae had yet to be explained. In 1918, the American astronomer Harlow Shapley (1875–1972) was able to demonstrate that the sun was quite far removed from the center of the Milky Way. In 1923 the American astronomer Edwin Hubble measured the distance to the Andromeda nebula, showing that it and the other nebulae were actually galaxies in their own right. The universe was understood then to consist of many galaxies like our own and thus to be very much larger than anyone had previously expected.

A theoretical result known as Olber's paradox implies that the universe, or at least the stars in it, could not be of infinite age, since, if it were, the sky would be as bright at night as during the day. In 1929 Edwin Hubble, working with the world's then largest telescope on Mount Palomar in California, was able to demonstrate that galaxies far from the Earth were moving away from it with a velocity that increased with distance. This fact, along with other evidence, leads to the conclusion that the universe we know was, at its beginning some ten to twenty billion years ago, confined to a very small region of space and began to separate as the result of a giant explosion: the "big bang."

The Life Cycles of the Stars and Origin of the Chemical Elements

Until the twentieth century the energy source of the sun was a mystery. In the 1930s it was discovered that the fusion of small nuclei to form a large nuclei would result in the transformation of a small fraction of the smaller nuclei's mass into heat energy according to Einstein's famous formula, $E = mc^2$. It is now known that the power source of the sun is the fusion of hydrogen nuclei to form helium nuclei. Computer modeling now shows that after the sun, which is now about five billion years old, has transformed most of its hydrogen into helium, its inner regions will contract and become hotter until the combining of helium nuclei to form carbon and oxygen nuclei becomes feasible. After that, further contractions will occur until atoms as heavy as iron will occur. The formation of nuclei heavier than iron requires an additional input of energy and only occurs when massive stars explode as supernovas.

Our current understanding of the distribution of chemical elements is as follows: Hydrogen and a certain amount of helium were formed during the big bang, some ten to twenty billion years ago. The basic elements of life and those found in large quantities on earth had to be formed in stars that had passed the hydrogen burning stage and ultimately returned their substance to the interstellar medium where it could condense as a new star, the sun, and planets formed. Elements with atomic numbers higher than iron are formed in supernova explosions, and therefore are destined to remain rare regardless of how thoroughly the mineral resources of Earth are explored.

Cosmology Today

Modern cosmologists apply the principles of relativity theory and the discoveries arising from experiments in particle physics to try to understand the origin and the ultimate fate of the universe as we know it. In contrast to the assumption that the Earth held a privileged position in the universe, most cosmologists today make assumptions of isotropy and homogeneity, that is, that the universe looks pretty much the same from any point in it and in any direction in space. Perhaps the biggest question in cosmology is whether the current expansion of the universe, begun at the big bang, will continue indefinitely, or will at some point in time be reversed, resulting ultimately in a "big crunch" after which the universe might begin to expand again. The answer, which depends, according to current theory, on the total amount of mass in the universe, is being actively debated as the twenty-first century begins.

Donald R. Franceschetti

Further Reading

Chaisson, E. J. (2001). *Cosmic evolution.* Cambridge, MA: Harvard University Press.

Hartquist, T. W., & Williams, D. A. (1995). *The chemically controlled cosmos.* New York: Cambridge University Press.

Kaufmann, W. J., III & Comins, N. F. (1996). *Discovering the universe* (4th ed.). New York: W. H. Freeman.

Kippenhahn, R. *100 Billion Suns.* (1983). New York: Basic Books.

Seeds, M. A. (1994). *Foundations of Astronomy.* Belmont, CA: Wadsworth.

Cotton

Cotton has been one of the world's leading agricultural crops for several millennia. Its role in the development of several countries and cultures makes it one of the most important agricultural crops in human history.

Cotton is the seed-hair fiber of a variety of plants of the genus *Gossypium*, which belongs to the Malvaceae family and is native to most subtropical countries. It is most successfully cultivated in temperate climates with well-distributed rainfall and typically ranges from 1 to 2 meters in height when under cultivation in that climate. It produces creamy-white flowers that soon turn deep pink and fall off, leaving the small green seedpods, known as "cotton bolls," which contain the seeds. Seed hairs, or fibers, growing from the outer skin of the seeds become tightly packed within the boll, which bursts open upon maturity, revealing masses of the fibers. These are white to yellowish white in color, ranging from 2 to 4 centimeters in length. Cotton is harvested when the bolls open.

Cotton fibers may be classified in three large groups, based on staple length (average length of the fibers making up a sample or bale of cotton) and appearance. The first group, long-staple cottons, includes the fine, lustrous fibers with staple length ranging from 2.5 to 6.5 centimeters and includes types of the highest quality, such as Sea Island, Egyptian, and pima cottons. Long-staple cottons are costly because they are the least plentiful and most difficult to grow. They are used mainly for fine fabrics, yarns, and hosiery. The second group contains the standard medium-staple cotton, such as American Upland, with staple length from 1.3 to 3.3 centimeters. The third group includes the short-staple, coarse cottons, ranging from 1 to 2.5 centimeters in length, used to make carpets and blankets, coarse and inexpensive fabrics, and blends with other fibers.

Because cotton is plentiful and economically produced, cotton products are relatively inexpensive. The fibers can be made into a wide variety of fabrics suitable for a great variety of wearing apparel, home furnishings, and industrial uses.

Cotton in History

Cotton has been spun, woven, and dyed since prehistoric times. It was widely used in ancient Egypt, China, and especially India. Hundreds of years before the Christian era, India's craftsmen excelled at weaving cotton textiles, and the use of such textiles spread to the Mediterranean countries. Native Americans skillfully spun and wove cotton into fine garments and dyed tapestries. Cotton fabrics found in Peruvian tombs are believed to belong to a pre-Inca culture. In color and

The Boll Weevil

The chief problem facing cotton growers in the United States is the boll weevil, a beetle that punctures cotton buds and places its larvae that hatch and damage or destroy cotton bolls. Since the pest invaded U.S. cotton farms from Mexico in the late 1800s, it has cost America's cotton producers more than $15 billion in yield losses and costs to control the insect pest. As of 2003, the weevil has been eradicated in the southeastern states of Virginia, North Carolina, South Carolina, Georgia, Florida and Alabama and the Western states of Arizona and California.

Researchers have been looking for a natural predator for the boll weevil for 100 years with no success. Combating the weevil has created many problems. The USDA implemented its Boll Weevil Eradication Program in May 1995 in South Texas. The initial results of the eradication program were ruinous. Lower Rio Grande Valley cotton growers lost an estimated 365,000 acres of cotton, valued at $140 million. The region produced about 54,000 bales of cotton, compared to almost 308,000 bales the previous year. Cotton farmers in the San Angelo area who participated in the program lost more than half their crop, with losses valued at about $60 million.

The USDA research office in the Lower Rio Grande Valley discovered that the eradication program directly caused the crop destruction. The boll weevil was eliminated but the malathion spraying killed beneficial insects, such as spiders and wasps, which usually control other pests. In this case, the predators of beet army worms were eradicated, causing the cotton-eating worms to take over the cotton fields. The study found the density of beet army worms in Valley cotton fields to be 164 times the density of the worms in Mexican cotton fields 15 miles away. Less than one percent of the cotton leaves in Mexico were damaged by the worm, while 71.4 percent of the leaves on valley plants were worm-eaten.

—James G. Lewis

Further Reading

Daniel, Pete. (1985). *Breaking the Land: The Transformation of Cotton, Tobacco, and Rice Cultures since 1880*. Urbana and Chicago: University of Illinois Press.

The Boll Weevil War. Texas Environmental Profiles. Retrieved March 6, 2003 from http://www.texasep.org/html/pes/ pes_2tex_riog.html

---

texture the ancient Peruvian textiles resemble those found in Egyptian tombs.

As important as cotton was to ancient civilizations, its greatest impact came much later, when, with Britain at the fore, cotton revolutionized Western civilization. Britain imported little cotton cloth before the fifteenth century. By the beginning of the seventeenth century, the British trading company, the East India Company, was importing rare fabrics from India. At the end of the eighteenth century, Britain found itself at the center of the cotton trade. The development of the cotton industry took a dramatic turn in the eighteenth century when Britain acquired colonies in North America suitable for the growing of cotton and struck deals in India for cotton. Cotton was the catalyst for the Industrial Revolution in Britain. Mechanized cotton spinning and mechanized weaving expanded the volume of cloth that could be produced and increased the need for raw cotton. Cotton soon superseded flax and wool textiles and became central to Britain's economy.

Although the factory system began in Britain in 1785, not until the invention of the cotton gin (short for *engine*) could cotton growers meet demand for their product. The cotton gin was a machine that separated seeds from fiber; it was invented in the United States in 1793. Britain's textile manufacturers had already become dependent on cheap sources of cotton and cheap labor to run its mills by the time the cotton gin was invented. The cotton gin deepened this dependence. Britain's need for imported cotton fiber encouraged

Cotton in Central Africa in the Nineteenth Century

The following extract from the travel account of British explorer Richard F. Burton of his travels in central Africa in the mid-nineteenth century points to the importance of cotton as a trade good.

The principal of the minor items are colored cloths, called by the people "cloths with names:" of these, many kinds are imported by every caravan. In some regions, Ugogo for instance, the people will not sell their goats and more valuable provisions for plain piece-goods; their gross and gaudy tastes lead them to despise sober and uniform colors. The sultans invariably demand for themselves and their wives showy goods, and complete their honga or black-mail with domestics and indigo-dyed cottons, which they divide among their followers. Often, too, a bit of scarlet broadcloth, thrown in at the end of a lengthened haggle, opens a road and renders impossibilities possible.

The colored cloths may be divided into three kinds—woolens, cottons, and silks mixed with cotton. Of the former, the principal varieties now imported are joho or broadcloth; of the second, beginning with the cheapest, are barsati, dabwani, jamdani, bandira, shi't (chintz), khuzarangi, ukaya, sohari, shali, taujiri, msutu, kikoi, and shazar or mukunguru; the mixed and most expensive varieties are the subai, dewli, sabuni, khesi, and masnafu. Traveling Arabs usually take a piece of baftah or white calico as kafan or shrouds for themselves or their companions in case of accidents. At Zanzibar the value of a piece of 24 yds. is 1 dollar 25 cents. Blankets were at first imported by the Arabs, but being unsuited to the climate and to the habits of the people, they soon became a drug in the market.

Joho (a corruption of the Arabic Johh) is a coarse article, either blue or scarlet. As a rule, even Asiatics ignore the value of broadcloth, estimating it, as they do guns and watches, by the shine of the exterior; the African looks only at the length of the pile and the depth of the tint. The Zanzibar valuation of the cheap English article is usually 50 cents (2s. 1d.) per year; in the interior, rising rapidly through double and treble to four times that price, it becomes a present for a prince. At Ujiji and other great ivory-marts there is a demand for this article, blue as well as red; it is worn, like the shukkah merkani, round the loins by men and round the bosom by women, who therefore, require a tobe or double length. At Unyanyembe there are generally pauper Arabs or Wasawahili artisans who can fashion the merchants' supplies into the kizboa or waistcoats affected by the African chiefs in imitation of their more civilized visitors.

Of the second division the cheapest is barsati, called by the Africans kitambi; it is a blue cotton cloth, with a broad red stripe extending along one quarter of the depth, the other three quarters being dark blue; [the red it either or European or Cutch dye.] The former is preferred upon the coast for the purchase of copal. Of this Indian stuff there are three kinds, varying in size, color, and quality; the cheapest is worth at Zanzibar (where, however, like dabwani, it is usually sold by the gorah of two uzar or loin-cloths) from 5 to 7 dollars per score; the second 10 dollars 50 cents; and the best 14 to 15 dollars. The barsati in the interior represents the doti or tobe or merkani. On the coast it is a favorite article of wear with the poorer freemen, slaves, and women. Beyond the maritime region the chiefs will often refuse a barsati, if of small dimensions and flimsy texture. Formerly, the barsati was made of silk, and cost 7 dollars per loin-cloth. Of late years the Wanyamwezi have taken into favor the barsati or kitambi banyani; it is a thin white long cloth, called in Bombay kora (Corah, or cotton piece-goods), with a narrow reddish border of madder or other dye stamped in India or at Zanzibar. The piece of 39 yards, which is divided into 20 shukkah, costs at Bombay 4.50 Co.'s rs.; at Zanzibar 2 dollar 50 cents; and the price of printing the edge is 1 dollar 75 cents.

Source: Burton, Richard F. (1995). *The Lake Regions of Central Africa.* New York: Dover Publications, Inc., pp. 531–532. (Originally published 1860)

Britain's consent to the Monroe Doctrine (a foreign-policy statement by U.S. President James Monroe declaring that any attempt by a European power to control any nation in the Western Hemisphere would be viewed as a hostile act against the United States) in part because it protected it's burgeoning trade with Latin America. Britain's need for access to vast African and Indian markets for its cotton manufactures influenced its role as an imperial sea power and led to colonizing efforts in those two areas.

The Deep South

In the early seventeenth century Britain's colonies in North America began growing cotton for domestic use and export to Britain on a limited basis. The cotton gin changed that. The cotton gin revitalized slavery, which had been dying out. By the early nineteenth century the southern U.S. states became the biggest supplier of cotton to Britain while also supplying the textile mills established in the northern United States. Cotton cultivation became the basis of the one-crop, slave-labor economy of the Deep South and a principal economic cause of the Civil War. Slavery formally ended in 1865, only to be replaced by share cropping and tenant farming, a form of economic slavery that dominated the southern economy well into the twentieth century.

Soil exhaustion in the eastern United States pushed the "Cotton Belt" westward from the Carolinas eventually to eastern Texas. Soil erosion became a problem in the Cotton Belt. Soil easily wore out and eroded from years of growing the same crop on the same land. Despite these and other problems, such as boll weevil infestation, by the end of the 1920s the United States was growing more than half the world's cotton. Since then many other countries have increased their production, with manufacturing being carried out chiefly in Europe and Asia.

From the early 1800s until recent years the United States was the world's leading cotton producer and second only to Britain in the manufacture of cotton goods. In the 1990s China became the leading cotton-producing country, followed by the United States and the republics of the former Soviet Union. Other important cotton producers are Pakistan, India, Brazil, and Egypt. China and India are the leading cotton manufacturers, followed by the United States.

James G. Lewis

Further Reading

Brown, H. B. (1938). *Cotton: History, species, varieties, morphology, breeding, culture, diseases, marketing, and uses* (2nd ed.). New York: McGraw-Hill.

Burton, A. (1984). *The rise and fall of king cotton.* London: British Broadcasting Corporation.

Daniel, P. (1985). *Breaking the land: The transformation of cotton, tobacco, and rice cultures since 1880.* Chicago: University of Illinois Press.

Munro, J. M. (1987). *Cotton* (2nd ed.). New York: Wiley.

Smith, C. W., & Cothren, J. T. (Eds.). (1999). *Cotton: Origin, history, technology, and production.* New York: Wiley.

Council on Environmental Quality

The U.S. Council on Environmental Quality (CEQ) is the highest legal advisory body to the president on environmental affairs. During the late 1960s, as problems with environmental quality became more apparent and environmentalism grew, Washington State's Democratic Senator Henry Jackson introduced legislation to formalize a coherent national environmental policy. The result was the National Environmental Policy Act (NEPA), which President Richard Nixon signed into law on 1 January 1970. NEPA not only established environmental protection as a national priority, but also established CEQ to assist the president on environmental issues and to issue annual public reports. Whereas the Environmental Protection Agency, also established in 1970, focused on pollution and served as the mainline agency for policy implementation, CEQ's mandate was broader and in more of an advisory capacity. Three experts, appointed by the president and confirmed by the Senate, composed CEQ, which relied on a support staff in the Executive Office of the President. One of the most important functions of CEQ was to review environmental-impact statements (EIS), which NEPA required of every substantive federal or federally funded project. In the years that followed, CEQ formalized the guidelines and regulations by which the EIS process operated. It therefore played an important role as federal administrators for the first time completed careful assessments of the consequences of their proposals and, in turn, subjected them to public review.

The importance and power of CEQ are completely dependent upon the president, and over the years its influence has varied according to changes in public opinion and the interests of the successive administrations. Although Nixon initially did not stress CEQ, he staffed it with strong environmental advocates, including its first chairman, Russell Train, former head of the Conservation Foundation. Train and his colleagues took the initiative and shaped much of Nixon's early agenda, a period of remarkable legislative success. Throughout the 1970s CEQ's professional staff grew to almost fifty, including members with expertise in ecology and environmental science as well as economics, policy, and law. CEQ regularly issued studies of emerging problems, most notably its 1980 "Global 2000" report on international environmental trends. Many of these studies provoked controversy but were still influential in framing the issues for political discourse.

In recent years CEQ has suffered declining budgets and influence. President Ronald Reagan first proposed abolishing the council but withdrew his proposal when prominent Republicans objected. In the end, he reduced CEQ's staff to fewer than ten and transferred real authority to the cabinet Council on Natural Resources, headed by James Watt, an advocate of development. President George H. W. Bush appointed an experienced professional to head CEQ but did not completely restore its budget or staff. President Bill Clinton also proposed eliminating the council in favor of elevating the EPA to cabinet level, a reorganization that ultimately failed. Today critics argue that the CEQ's studies and reports are nothing more than political cover, hardly the unbiased and scientific advice intended by NEPA.

Brooks Flippen

Further Reading

Council on Environmental Quality. (1997). *The National Environmental Policy Act: A study of its effectiveness after twenty-five years*. Washington, DC: U.S. Government Printing Office.

Flippen, J. B. (2000). *Nixon and the environment*. Albuquerque: University of New Mexico Press.

Hays, S. P. (1987). *Beauty, health, and permanence: Environmental politics in the United States, 1955–1985*. New York: Cambridge University Press.

Shaw, B. (1979). *Council on Environmental Quality*. Austin, TX: Bureau of Business Research.

Soden, D. L. (Ed.). (1999). *The environmental presidency*. Albany: State University of New York Press.

Czechia
(2001 pop. 10.2 million)

Czechia (Czech Republic)—located in central Europe between Germany, Poland, Slovakia, and Austria—has an area of 78,866 square kilometers. The capital city is Praha (Prague), with a population of 1.2 million. Czechia is highly industrialized, with coal mining, construction, transportation, metallurgy, and production of machinery, chemicals, textiles, electronics, glass and china, and foodstuffs. It also has intensive agriculture. Tourism is based on its natural beauty, historic cities and sites, and hundreds of castles and chateaus.

The Czech Republic was created in 1993 by a peaceful division of Czechoslovakia. Czechoslovakia was a founding member of the United Nations in 1945, and Czechia is a member of the North Atlantic Treaty Organization, Organisation for Economic Co-Operation and Development. In 2002, the Czech Republic was invited into the European Union.

The Czech state was created in the tenth and eleventh centuries by uniting Bohemia and Moravia and, in the fourteenth century, Silesia. From 1526 until 1918 the Czech state was the most industrialized part of the Habsburg monarchy. The Czech Republic arose from the breakup of Austria-Hungary in 1918 late in World War I, when two regions with different cultural heritages and economic levels, Czechia and Slovakia (with Ruthenia, which in 1945 was ceded to the Soviet Union), joined as one state—Czechoslovakia. In 1969 Czechoslovakia became a federation of the Czech and Slovak Republics until they were separated in 1992.

Czechia's highest peak is 1,602 meters above sea level; its lowest point is 115 meters above sea level. Because of thousands of years of settlement, many types of cultural landscape exist, and hardly any truly natural landscape remains. One thousand years ago forests covered about 70 percent of the landscape; today forests—largely secondary and coniferous—cover only 33 percent of the landscape. Human impact on the environment has been heavy: arable land accounts for 40 percent, permanent cultures (e.g. gardens, orchards, vineyards, etc.) for 3 percent, permanent grasslands for 12 percent, and other areas (e.g., roads, built-up sections) for 12 percent.

The transformation of the mostly forested landscape of Czechia lasted thousands of years. Slavonic settlement and agriculture spread from fertile and less forested inland lowlands toward mountainous border regions with a broad belt of frontier forest. The largest deforestation took place in the twelfth through the fourteenth centuries, during the time of so called great colonization. Its peak occurred during the thirteenth century when the border regions were colonized mostly by people from German and Austrian regions, who were invited by Czech kings and nobility. Within this period the Czech landscape was transformed into rural countryside subsequently threatened by erosion. In the nineteenth and twentieth centuries, industrialization, a fast growth of population, and urbanization, created urban landscapes. The quality of the environment was consequently rapidly declining. In the period of Communism the diversity of agricultural landscapes decreased dramatically due to intensive collective farming.

Intensive mining of coal for use in power plants and the development of heavy industries, including chemicals, grew, especially under the Communist regime from 1948 to 1989, and bear the greatest responsibility for environmental deterioration. During the 1980s, air, water, and soil pollution—as well as environmental damage to forests—were at their worst. By 1989 the government characterized the environmental situation as catastrophic. A radical improvement began after the "Velvet Revolution" (the fall of Communism in November 1989), especially because of an active environmental state policy and industry restructuring. Since 1990 Czechia has changed from a centrally driven and planned economy to a market-oriented economy. Environment improvements followed. Between 1990 and 1999 air pollution decreased by 50 percent. Water quality markedly improved, and now no major watercourses are listed in the "worst" category. In 2000 16.2 percent of Czechia's land was protected. Four national parks cover 1.3 percent, 24 protected landscape areas cover 13.2 percent, and 1,921 small-scale protected natural sites cover 1.3 percent. Czechia has six United Nations Educational, Scientific and Cultural Organization biosphere reserves.

Landscape conservation has a tradition dating back to 1838, when the first landscape area was privately conserved. The Ministry of Environment (formerly part of the Ministry of Interior) was established in 1990. The State Environmental Policy Program was approved in 1999; the implementation plan for the European Union Environmental Acquis was approved in 2000. Hundreds of environmental nongovernmental organizations exist; major ones are the Czech Union of Nature Conservation (established in 1979), Brontosaurus Movement (1974), and Society for Sustainable Living (1992). Other environmental organizations include Duha (Rainbow) and Deti Zeme (Children of the Earth). Greenpeace and the politically weak Green Party are also active.

Leoš Jeleěk

Further Reading

Institute of Geography of the CSAS and Federal Committee for the Environment. (1992). *Atlas zivotniho prostredi a zdravi CSFR* [Atlas of the environment and health of population of the CSFR]. Brno-Prague, Czech Republic: Institute of Geography of the CSAS and Federal Committee for the Environment.

Holecek, M., et al. (1995). *Czech Republic in brief: Prague.* Prague, Czech Republic: Publishing House of the Czech Geographical Society.

Jelecek, L., & Bohac, Z. (1989). Mountains, forests, rivers: Medieval Bohemia in the context of central Europe. In J. F. Bergier (Ed.), *Montagnes, fleuves, forêts dans l'histoire: Barrières ou lignes de convergence?* [Mountains, rivers, forests in history: Barriers or lines of convergence?] (pp. 147–166). St. Katharinen, Germany: Scripta Mercaturae Verlag.

Ministry of the Environment of the Czech Republic. *State of environmental policy 2001.* Retrieved January 13, 2003, from: http://www.env.cz/env.nsf/homeie?OpenFrameSet

Moldan, B., & Hak, T. (2000). *Czech Republic 2000: Ten years on: Environment and quality of life after ten years of transition.* Prague, Czech Republic: Charles University.

State of the environment in Czechoslovakia. (2000). Prague, Czech Republic: Czech Committee for the Environment and Vesmir.

D

Dams, Reservoirs, and Artificial Lakes

The construction of large dams and their reservoirs has been an integral part of human efforts to harness nature for subsistence and economic needs. Dams and reservoirs have been used for irrigation, flood control, storage of drinking water, navigation, warfare, and power production. From early irrigation efforts in the Zagros Mountains of Iran roughly 8,000 years ago to irrigation canals along the Tigris and Euphrates rivers 6,500 years ago, humans used dams to collect and distribute water for increased agricultural production.

Dams have been used for other reasons than irrigation and flood control. Some societies used dams and water manipulation for warfare. In 514–515 BCE a large dam was built on the Huai River in central China measuring about 32 meters high and 4,000 meters long. The goal of this dam was to flood an enemy position upstream. When this dam breached four months later, the waters released killed over 10,000 people.

An irrigation dam built in southeastern Spain demonstrated some of the dangers inherent in large dams. The original dam foundation was built in 1647–1648 and washed away the following summer. A later dam was built on the same site in 1802, with an intended height of 50 meters. Unfortunately it was built on deposited gravel rather than bedrock and when the reservoir was almost full a washout of the dam resulted in a flood that killed 608 people in the town of Lorca and 328 in the surrounding countryside.

The dangers to human life presented by dams did nothing to slow down the pace of their construction throughout the world, and the emergence of industrial capitalism led a continuing boom of dam construction for the production of first mechanical and later electrical power. In Great Britain dams were integral to the early industrial revolution. In the nineteenth century, British industrialists built almost 200 dams of over 15 meters in height to provide industrial power. In the Northeastern region of the United States, dams were built on rivers running from the Appalachian Mountains to the Atlantic Ocean to provide power for textile mills and sawmills. Protest arose over many of these dams because they flooded fields used for pasture and agriculture and destroyed fish runs that provided important economic and subsistence resources for farmers and fishermen. In the early nineteenth century American courts found in favor of these protests, but as the industrial economy became a centerpiece of the American economy, the interests of development won out over ecological concerns.

Not all large dams were built for industrial development and irrigation. A hunting and fishing club in Pennsylvania bought an old dam and rebuilt it in order to create a resort and fishing for local elites. When 6 to 10 inches of rain fell in a twenty-four-hour period the dam gave way and initiated one of the worst disasters in United States history. The washout of that dam in 1889 led to the Johnstown flood, which resulted in the deaths of over 2,200 people.

Dams built in the Pacific Northwest region of the United States during the Great Depression in the 1930s played important roles in not only controlling floods and providing water for irrigation in vast, fertile desert regions but also provided the electrical power necessary for the United States and its allies to emerge victorious at the end of World War II. A river of electricity from Columbia River dams to shipyards and aircraft manufacturing companies in Oregon and Washington drove the industrial production that was key to the Allies' success.

The Impacts of Large Dams and Reservoirs

In the twentieth century, the fever of dam construction exploded in such a way as to leave almost no river in the world untouched, radically altering the watersheds and ecosystems of thousands of rivers around the world. More than 40,000 large dams block rivers and approximately 35,000 of these were built after 1950. While dams have been built to serve human needs, their legacy is a mixed one; for dams are much more than tools, they are also symbols. President Nehru of India declared more than fifty years ago that dams are temples. More than almost any other manmade object, they signify humanity's control and domination over nature and more accurately, reflect the desire for continual progress and development. However, symbols can signify negative meanings as well and the construction and use of large dams carries negative ramifications.

Historian Donald Worster has written on the dangers of dams to society and argues that the construction of large-scale dam and irrigation projects leads to the rise of a technical elite and a consolidation of control over irrigated lands by elite landowners. His theory has been validated in several cases. The construction of dams and irrigation systems in the Imperial Valley of Southern California was predicted to create a utopia of independent small-scale farmers. Historian Norris Hundley, Jr. described what actually happened instead.

> The financiers and speculators snapped up small plots, transforming them into large-scale factory farms under managers who naturally sought to secure maximum returns on their investments. Most of the few farmers who did not sell out to handsome offers used their agricultural profits and expanded bank credit to enlarge their own holdings, hire managers, and retire to the cooler temperatures and comforts of the coastal cities. That left the valley populated by a handful of owners and operators at the top of the social pyramid and a large underclass of laborers, most of Mexican origin, who toiled for agribusiness by keeping the irrigation ditches open and bringing in the bountiful crops. (Hundley 1992, 220–221)

The vast Columbia River Irrigation District created by damming the Columbia River with the Grand Cou-

lee dam also brought thousands of acres into agricultural production and like the Imperial Valley led to the consolidation of the land into fewer landowners and agribusinesses.

The physical danger inherent in large dams and reservoirs may be best exemplified by an unmitigated disaster on the Yangtze River in China in 1975. In August of that year, "indestructible" dams collapsed following heavy rains in the monsoon season. The surge of water collapsed first two dams and then another. Roughly sixty dams fell like dominoes leading to the deaths of approximately 200,000 people in Henan Province. These dams were built as part of the massive transformation of the landscape that accompanied the Great Leap Forward, an attempt in communist China to rapidly move from an agrarian to an industrial economy. Famines and other ecological disasters resulted from this effort and a series of large dams were built that the Chinese government says displaced approximately 10 million residents from their homes and villages, but which more likely displaced 40 to 60 million.

There are other dangers that arise from large dams and reservoirs besides flooding. Disease is commonly associated with dam projects. Malaria, dysentery, hepatitis, and sleeping sickness are only a few of the devastating diseases that increase in incidence with the creation of large reservoirs, sitting bodies of water that facilitate the growth of bacteria and parasites. One of the more prevalent diseases associated with reservoirs and standing water is schistosomiasis. This disease is caused by the blood fluke parasite, which is carried by snails in water (often irrigation ditches) and then finishes its lifecycle in human bodies. There is no doubt that the expansion of this disease and many others results from the growth of large dams and reservoirs.

At least as important as health dangers to people are the social and ecological changes that result from large dams and reservoirs. Many recent large-scale projects displaced numerous people. The Three Gorge Dam in China is expected to force approximately 2 million Chinese from traditional homes, land, and communities that have been inhabited for multiple generations. Many of those displaced from their land by these projects receive little or no compensation; in fact, most of the Chinese have yet to receive their promised compensation. The compensation received, in many cases, is often less than the value of the land, and land offered in compensation is often of poorer quality than the fertile river bottoms covered by reservoirs. Many are forced to move to already overcrowded urban centers in pursuit of employment.

The ecological consequences of dams and irrigation systems are numerous. Constant irrigation of farm soils contributes salt to the soil to the degree that the land often becomes unproductive. Water tables also rise from lost water and this turns productive farmland into waterlogged land that is no longer usable and contributes to the spread of parasites and malaria. Finally, the efficiency of large-scale irrigation projects must be questioned because so much of the water is wasted, particularly through evaporation losses.

The control of rivers through dams has contributed to the destruction of once-rich ecosystems. Historically, humans have avoided living in flood plains due to the perennial potential danger. Now, with governments promising to control floods and also due to human population pressures, flood plains are opened for settlement and while important riparian ecosystems are lost, humans are increasingly vulnerable to floods. Another important negative result of large dams is the blocking of silt from traveling downstream and being deposited in rivers and in floodplains. These silts traditionally serve a number of functions. They create habitat for fish and fish reproduction on river bottoms. Deposition of riverborne sediments has traditionally enriched farm soil, something farmers along the Nile River understood for thousands of years. Finally, the loss of silt behind large dams is causing many deltas to diminish and reducing the nutrients flowing into large lakes and oceans. Also, without the deposition of riverborne sediments in oceans, beaches are more likely to be washed away and not replenished. Many communities are forced to haul in rocks and sand to fill in beaches that were at one time replenished by rivers that no longer function completely.

Sometimes violence erupts as landowners try to protect their land. Indians protesting the loss of their land for construction of the Chixoy Dam in Guatemala were slaughtered by government forces. In another incident in the African nation of Mauritania in 1979, interethnic conflict emerged over control of land to be irrigated by a dam project in the Senegal Valley. Over 200 people died in the fighting and the government placed some Mauritanians under protection and about 180,000 more were airlifted away from the site of the conflict.

Resistance to Large Dams and Reservoirs

What Marc Reisner called the "go-go era" in dam building in the American West began to close in the 1950s. In that decade the Sierra Club and Wilderness Society cooperatively opposed the construction of a dam in Dinosaur National Monument on the Green and Yampa rivers in beautiful desert terrain. This was an important turning point in the American environmental movement and led to continued efforts to create a wilderness plan and block other dam projects throughout the country so that by the 1970s it became virtually impossible to build a major dam in the United States.

Austrians opposed the construction of a dam on the Danube River in 1984. The dam to be built at Hainburg would have destroyed an important forest ecosystem and organized protest led the Austrian government to abandon the project. Protestors of the Three Gorges Dam in China have suffered from government oppression. Dia Qing, an active opponent of the project, was imprisoned for ten months for editing the book *Yangtze! Yangtze!*, which criticized the dam project. The book was also banned in China and remaining copies were collected and burned. According to Human Rights Watch, opponents of the dam have been jailed.

One of the strongest conflicts has been over the Narmada River Project in India, a plan that has engendered massive national and worldwide protest as well as opposition by leaders in Indian society. The plan to build 3,200 dams on one river is one of the most ambitious engineering projects in human history and has triggered protest and created several negative consequences. Tens of millions of Indians, many of them dependent on the river for their livelihood, are being forced into city slums and wage labor jobs. Those who have refused to leave their land have been threatened with drowning, had their water pipes filled with cement, and their crops bulldozed into the ground.

While projects in China, India, and Turkey move forward, there have been calls to remove large dams in the United States. Environmentalists, Indians, and other fish advocates have demanded that large dams on the Snake River and even on the Columbia be removed due to the damage they have inflicted on salmon and steelhead species of fish. The dams on the Snake and Columbia Rivers have reduced a one-time salmon and steelhead run of 18 million fish a year to about 2 million a year currently and have caused many fish to go extinct. Though the Department of Interior made the decision to maintain the four dams on the Lower Snake River in Washington State, if the fish continue to decline there will be further consideration of dam removal in the future.

In the final analysis it is important to note that while large dams and reservoirs provide benefits to irrigation, power production, flood control, and drinking water, those benefits come with human and ecological costs. Too often those benefits accrue to the state and the wealthiest members of a particular society while the lower rungs are forced from their homes and traditional ways of life into cities or onto inferior farmland. Furthermore, large dams and reservoirs result in radical changes to ecosystems and farmlands that destroy native habitat and those lands that are under productive human use. While there are protests against various dam projects throughout the world, there is increased understanding of their impacts and the possibility that the era of large dams may be slowly coming to a close.

Jeffrey Crane

See also Colorado River; Columbia River; Irrigation; Narmada Dam; Nile Valley; Salinization; Water Energy

Further Reading

Adams, W. M. (1992). *Wasting the rain: Rivers, people and planning in Africa.* Minneapolis: University of Minnesota Press.

Goldsmith, E., & Hildyard, N. (1984). *The social and environmental effects of large dams.* San Francisco: Sierra Club Books.

Hundley, N., Jr. (1992). *The great thirst: Californians and water, 1770s–1990s.* Berkeley: University of California Press.

McCully, P. (1996). *Silenced rivers: The ecology and politics of large dams.* London: Zed Books.

Mikesell, R. F., & Williams, L. (1992). *International banks and the environment: From growth to sustainability, an unfinished agenda.* San Francisco: Sierra Club Books.

Qing, D. (1998). *The river dragon has come! The Three Gorges Dam and the fate of China's Yangtze River and its people.* Armonk, NY: M. E. Sharpe.

Reisner, M. (1993). *Cadillac desert: The American West and its disappearing water.* New York: Penguin Books.

Roy, A. (1999). *The cost of living.* New York: The Modern Library.

Schnitter, N. J. (1994). *A history of dams: The useful pyramids.* Rotterdam, Netherlands: A. A. Balkema.

Worster, D. (1985). *Rivers of empire: Water, aridity, and the growth of the American West.* New York: Oxford University Press.

Danube River

Originating in Germany's Black Forest at the confluence of the Brig and Brigach streams at Donauschingen, the Danube River flows southeast through central and southeastern Europe into the Black Sea. At 2,850 kilometers, the Danube is the second-longest river in Europe (after the Volga). The Danube is the world's most international river, passing through eight countries—Germany, Austria, Slovakia, Hungary, Yugoslavia, Bulgaria, Romania, and Ukraine. These countries, along with parts of Switzerland, Slovenia, Croatia, Bosnia and Herzegovina, and Moldova, form the 816,000-square-kilometer catchment area of the Danube basin, inhabited by 76 million people. Major tributaries include the Inn, Morava, Tisza, Drava, Sava, and Prut Rivers.

The Danube basin has three subregions. The Upper Danube reaches southwest from the river's source in southern Germany, through Austria's Wachau Valley to Vienna, ending at the point where the Morava enters the Danube at Devin, Slovakia. After Devin, the Middle Danube passes east through Bratislava and the large inland deltas of the Szigetkoz (Hungary) and Zitny-Ostrav (Slovakia) before taking a sharp turn south at Visegrad. From there the Middle Danube passes through Budapest and Belgrade to the Iron Gates, a gorge on the Yugoslav-Romanian border that is now the site of a large hydroelectric dam. The Lower Danube moves east, forming the border between Romania and Bulgaria. As it nears the Black Sea, the river turns north and splits into three branches at the Danube Delta: the Chilia, the Sulina, and the Saint George. The 6,000-square-kilometer Danube Delta spans the Black Sea coast of Romania and Ukraine. Approximately two-thirds of the delta is submerged seasonally.

The alluvial floodplains and wetlands of the Danube remain important areas for European biodiversity. Important wildlife include the pygmy cormorant (*Phalacrocorax pygmeus*), the red-breasted goose (*Branta ruficollis*), and the European otter (*Lutra lutra*). Several rare karst hyrogeological ecosystems exist along the Danube; these areas are especially vulnerable to ecological degradation.

Social History of the River

Humans have inhabited the Danube Basin for at least 7,000 years. The Neolithic Danubian culture lived along the river between 5,000 and 4,000 BCE. The ancient Greeks called the river the *Istros*, a name the Romans later used to distinguish the lower reaches of the Danube, the *Ister*, from the upper section, the *Danubius*. The Danube was an important trade artery in the Middle Ages and Renaissance, carrying grain, people, and goods between central and southeastern Europe.

Floods occur regularly on the Danube in the early spring and early summer of each year. The 1501 flood remains one of the worst flood events on the Danube ever recorded. Composer Franz Liszt gave a concert to benefit the Hungarian victims of the catastrophic Danube flood of 1838. Serious floods occurred again in 1876, 1884, 1954, 1965, 1999, and 2000.

Human regulation of the river for flood control and navigation began as early as 1426, when Hungarian villages on the riverbanks instituted a small-scale irrigation system. Prior to large-scale river regulation, the river shifted its course often and divided into several smaller channels in many stretches. Hungarian Count István Szechényi initiated several major engineering projects on the Danube in the mid-nineteenth century. The 1856 Danube Convention, signed after the Crimean War (1853–1856), guaranteed free international navigation and laid the groundwork for twentieth-century international institutions such as the Danube Commission and the International Commission for the Protection of the Danube River (ICPDR). Armed conflicts and embargoes disrupted river transit during the first and second world wars and again during the Yugoslavian civil war of the 1990s.

Contemporary River Protection Issues and Institutions

The eight industrialized countries through which the Danube flows before entering the Black Sea have harnessed the river for generating hydroelectricity, cooling nuclear power plants, irrigating agricultural land, and providing a sink for effluents from chemical plants, paper mills, and oil refineries. Nitrogen and phosphorus pollution from agriculture and industries along the Danube causes eutrophication (lack of oxygen due to an efflorescence of plant life feeding on the nitrogen and phosphorus) and other environmental problems in the Black Sea.

A tide of environmental awareness set in motion waves of citizens' actions along the Danube. In 1984, when Austria's government proposed a hydroelectric dam at Hainburg, a large wetland east of Vienna, thousands of activists lodged a successful protest. In Ruse, an industrial city on the Danube, Bulgarian citizens protested chemical plant emissions in 1987.

A dam planned at Gabíkovo-Nagymaros, on the border of Hungary and Czechoslovakia, provoked a mass movement in Hungary during the 1980s. At the peak of the Danube movement in 1988, forty thousand protesters demonstrated against the dam in Budapest. Following the collapse of state socialism in 1989, the Hungarian government abandoned construction, and the newly formed Slovak government diverted 80 percent of the river's flow to make its part of the dam system operable. The Danube movement became a symbol of Hungary's transformation from state socialism, while building the dam symbolized national development in Slovakia. In 1993, Hungary and Slovakia entered into a decade-long lawsuit in the European Court, and the two countries continue negotiations over sharing use of the river.

In 2000, the Danube was affected by a major cyanide spill on the Tisza, its largest tributary. The spill originated at a gold mining operation in Romania and passed through Hungary, Yugoslavia, and Bulgaria. Cyanide from the accident reached as far as the Danube Delta.

In response to this history of transboundary environmental problems, policy makers in the Danube region instituted several new international nature preserves along the river, including the Danube-Ipel between Slovakia and Hungary and the Danube-Drava between Hungary and Croatia. The Danube Delta is protected by the international Ramsar Convention on Wetlands, and UNESCO (United Nations Educational, Scientific, and Cultural Organization) created the Danube Delta Biosphere Reserve in Romania in 1979. Ongoing citizens' actions, state-level environmental protection, and international environmental coordination efforts will all protect the Danube's ecosystems for future generations.

Krista Harper

Further Reading

Carter, F. W., & Turnock, D. (1993). *Environmental problems in eastern Europe.* New York: Routledge.

Commission of the European Communities. (2001). *Environmental cooperation in the Danube-Black Sea region.* Brussels, Belgium: Commission of the European Communities.

Cousteau Society. (1993). *The Danube: For whom and for what?* Paris: Cousteau Foundation.

Fitzmaurice, J. (1996). *Damming the Danube.* Boulder, CO: Westview.

Held, J. (Ed.). (1994). *Dictionary of East European history since 1945*. Westport, CT: Greenwood.

Darwin, Charles

(1809–1882)
English naturalist

Charles Robert Darwin was born in Shrewsbury (pronounced "Shrowsbury"), England, the son of physician Robert Darwin and Susannah Wedgwood Darwin of the wealthy Wedgwood pottery dynasty. After education at Shrewsbury School, Charles started a medical degree at Edinburgh University, but, repelled by the sight of surgery performed without anesthetics, he did not finish his studies. He went later to Cambridge University in preparation for becoming a clergyman in the Church of England.

He showed an early interest in natural history and in 1831 took the unpaid position of naturalist aboard the *H.M.S. Beagle* on its surveying voyage to South America and the Pacific and Indian Oceans under the command of Captain Robert Fitzroy (1805–1865). On his return he published an account of the journey as the third volume of Fitzroy's *Narrative of the Surveying Voyages of the Adventure and Beagle* (1839). Over the next four years he oversaw the publication of reports by experts of the day on the mammal, bird, fish, and reptile specimens he had collected. He also wrote an important book entitled *The Structure and Distribution of Coral Reefs* (1842) and several monographs on fossil and living barnacles (1851–1854). He was by then firmly established as a worldly and knowledgeable naturalist; when his travelogue was reissued in an enlarged edition as *Journal of Researches into the Natural History and Geology of the Countries Visited during the Voyage of H.M.S. Beagle round the World* (1845), he received more widespread and popular acclaim.

Throughout his years of patient observation Darwin had pondered the variety of life. He was greatly influenced by the work of geologist Charles Lyell (1797–1875), who had outlined the idea that geological changes to the Earth had happened slowly over millions of years, rather than over the thousands of years deduced from the biblical account of Genesis and the great flood. The economist Thomas Malthus (1766–1834) had also written an influential book entitled *An Essay on the Principle of Population* (1798), in which he argued that the burgeoning population of the Earth could not expand forever and that at some point starvation, disease, pestilence, war, and other "natural" causes would prevent further increase.

Theory of Evolution

During Darwin's travels, including famously those through the Galapagos Islands, he had regularly come across unusual groups of closely related species, for example, the Galapagos finches; he likened them to variations on a theme. And through his gentlemanly pursuits he had come across bird, dog, and horse breeders who, having an eye for a minor variation in shape, color, strength, or temperament, had created new breeds as different from one another as one wild species might be from another. These ideas were at the forefront of Darwin's mind as he constructed his famous theory of evolution by natural selection.

As Darwin wrote in his introduction to *On the Origin of Species* ([1859] 1999):

> As many more individuals of each species are born than can possibly survive; and as consequently, there is a frequently recurring struggle for existence, it follows that any being, if it vary however slightly in any manner profitable to itself, under the complex and sometimes varying conditions of life, will have a better chance of surviving and thus be naturally selected. From the strong principle of inheritance, any selected variety will tend to propagate its new and modified form.

Darwin had been working slowly on a manuscript of his evolutionary thoughts for many years when, in June 1858, he received from a fellow world traveler and naturalist, Alfred Russell Wallace (1823–1913), an essay entitled "On the Tendencies of Varieties to Depart Indefinitely from the Original Type." Wallace had independently arrived at exactly the same conclusion: that the huge reproductive ability of living organisms, subtle variation within species, and the struggle for survival would result in the selection of any slight advantage and the inheritance of that advantage in offspring.

Darwin was a famous and authoritative naturalist, whereas Wallace was younger and less known, but Darwin knew that he would have to publish soon or lose the originality of his ideas. Through the support of his close colleagues, Charles Lyell and botanist Joseph Hooker (1817–1911), Darwin was persuaded to act. The following month Darwin and Wallace gave a joint paper (lecture) to the Linnean Society of London, and a year later, in 1859, Darwin's most famous book, *On the Origin of Species*, was published.

The book soon generated a storm of controversy. At the beginning of the nineteenth century, the study of natural science was intricately intertwined with an appreciation of the wonders of God's creation—many of the most important naturalists of the day were clergymen. It was assumed that species are fixed, created by a divine hand and therefore immutable. However, as Darwin pondered, several authors had already suggested that species are not fixed. The French naturalist Jean-Baptiste de Monet de Lamarck (1744–1829) had been suggesting that environmental effects on a creature might be passed on to its offspring. Thus the ancestors of giraffes could have acquired longer and longer necks by the act of continually stretching upward to higher and higher branches. Unfortunately there was no direct evidence that this had occurred, and, for example, no matter how often animals' tails are docked, the offspring are always born with fully functional tails.

With Darwin and Wallace came, for the first time, an obvious explanation of how species might change— an explanation that was coherent, plausible, and readily acceptable to the scientific community. It was not, however, acceptable to the clergy. They took Darwin's book to suggest that the world had not, after all, been created in a week and not in 4004 BCE, as had been calculated from the Bible, and that humans had not been created in God's image but rather had begun as something more primitive. To them, Darwin's book reduced the story of Creation, and of Adam and Eve, to a myth.

Darwinism Debated

In June 1860 at Oxford a debate was held at a meeting of the British Association. Darwin was unwell and did not attend, but his friend and supporter Thomas Henry Huxley (1825–1895) spoke "for" Darwinism. The levelheaded scientific content of the debate over three days is somewhat overshadowed by a famous confrontation between Huxley and Samuel Wilberforce, bishop of Oxford—a vociferous opponent of the theory. Addressing Huxley from the floor of the meeting, Wilberforce demanded to know whether it was through his grandmother or his grandfather that he was descended from apes. Huxley's reply was that he would rather be descended from an ape than from a cultivated

man who prostituted the gifts of culture and eloquence to the service of prejudice and falsehood.

Darwin died comfortable and content but without any formal recognition from the state. Today, however, Darwin is recognized as one of the most important figures in the history of science and, with Wallace, is credited with producing the theory that underlies all of biological science. Every aspect of the study of living things, from form and function to ecology and genetics, is underpinned by the two men's concept of evolution by natural selection.

Richard A. Jones

Further Reading

Bettany, G. T. (1887). *Life of Charles Darwin*. London: Walter Scott.

Burkhardt, F. et al. (1985–2001). *The correspondence of Charles Darwin* (12 vols.). Cambridge, UK: Cambridge University Press.

Darwin, C. (1999). *On the origin of species by means of natural selection, or the preservation of favoured races in the struggle for life*. New York: Bantam. (Original work published 1859)

Darwin, C. (1868). *The variation of animals and plants under domestication*. London: John Murray.

Darwin, C. (1871). *The descent of man and selection in relation to sex*. London: John Murray.

Desmond, A., & Moore, J. R. (1992). *Darwin*. London: Penguin.

Wallace, A. R. (1889). *Darwinism*. London: Macmillan.

Deer *See* White-tailed Deer

Defenders of Wildlife

Defenders of Wildlife is a nonprofit conservation organization that focuses on progressive advocacy for wildlife and its habitat. Defenders of Wildlife is dedicated to the protection of all native wild animals and plants in their natural communities. The organization focuses on species conservation, habitat conservation, and policy leadership. The protection of ecosystems, biological diversity, and interconnected habitats are priorities.

Defenders of Wildlife uses education, litigation, research, legislation, media campaigns, and advocacy to defend wildlife and its habitat. Scientists, attorneys, wildlife specialists, and educators work together to promote solutions to wildlife problems. Defenders of Wildlife advocates new approaches to wildlife conservation that will help prevent species from becoming endangered.

Defenders of Wildlife endorsed the passage of, and aided in the enforcement of, the Endangered Species Act (ESA) of 1973. The organization also helped draft the Convention on International Trade in Endangered Species of wild fauna and flora (CITES). Defenders of Wildlife is the main organization promoting gap analysis, a habitat inventory designed to preserve biodiversity. It also initiated the Habitat for Bears campaign, an effort to save Florida's dwindling population of black bears. The organization helped win enactment of laws to protect dolphins from death in tuna nets, requiring "dolphin-safe" labels on cans of tuna. Defenders of Wildlife assisted in drafting the Wild Bird Conservation Act, passed in 1992, and helped strengthen the 1994 Marine Mammal Protection Act. In 2001 Defenders of Wildlife was instrumental in passage of the Historic Lands Legacy Conservation Initiative, providing $12 billion in funding for comprehensive wildlife and biodiversity conservation. Defenders of Wildlife opposes legislation that would open the Arctic National Wildlife Refuge to oil exploration and development.

Defenders of Wildlife has been a champion of wolves and other predators since its inception. The organization led a controversial fight to restore the gray wolf to its former habitat in Yellowstone National Park and central Idaho. Ranchers in nearby states protested the effort because wolves outside the park often prey on livestock. Defenders of Wildlife attempted to reduce opposition by creating the $100,000 Wolf Compensation Trust to reimburse ranchers at fair market value for losses of livestock to wolves. The wolf reintroduction program has been successful in recent years, although critics remain vocal. In 2001 Defenders organized the first Carnivore Conservation Conference. The organization is also working to restore wolves to the southwestern and northeastern United States.

Another volatile issue is the management of bison that wander from Yellowstone National Park. The Montana Stockgrowers Association insists that bison, as potential carriers of the disease brucellosis, pose a threat to cattle and a potential disaster for the state's livestock industry. Defenders of Wildlife protested that the Montana Livestock Department's policy of killing bison that leave Yellowstone's boundaries is unnecessarily brutal because the risk of bison passing the disease is small. Defenders of Wildlife supports the federal government's position that more low-risk bison should be released. The state of Montana refused to relax its policy in 2002 but continues to work with the National Park Service on bison management, under pressure from both sides.

Founded in 1947, Defenders of Wildlife has 430,000 members and publishes *Defenders*, a bimonthly magazine on environmental issues. The organization is currently involved in many conservation efforts, such as restoring grizzly bears to the Bitterroot ecosystem in Idaho and Montana; protecting polar bear habitat in Alaska; and promoting recovery of the vaquita porpoise and other imperiled marine mammals.

Robin O'Sullivan

Further Reading

Burton, J. (1992). *Close to extinction*. Chicago: Franklin Watts.

Defenders of Wildlife. Retrieved May 13, 2002, from http://www.defenders.org

DiSilvestro, R. L. (1991). *The endangered kingdom: The struggle to save America's wildlife*. New York: John Wiley & Sons.

Ehrlich, P. R., & Ehrlich, A. H. (1981). *Extinction: The causes and consequences of the disappearance of species*. New York: Random House.

Hudson, W. E. (1991). *Landscape linkages and biodiversity: Defenders of wildlife*. Washington, DC: Island Press.

Defoliation

Defoliation occurs when a plant loses its leaves. It is a common natural occurrence when plants suffer stress from drought, unavailability of nutrients, disease, or insect or other damage. In the broadest sense of the term, autumn leaf fall by deciduous (leaf-dropping) plants is also defoliation. Plants prepare themselves for dormancy and the challenges of cold weather by shedding their leaves. The term is used, however, to designate untimely leaf fall. Excessive and unseasonable defoliation can signal a larger environmental problem and lead to significant environmental change. Deliberate human-caused defoliation is also a management technique in some kinds of industrial agriculture, such as cotton or soybean production, where the leaves impede mechanized harvesting. Defoliation was also a major constituent of the environmental warfare waged by U.S. forces in southeastern Asia during the Vietnam War.

Insect-Caused Defoliation

Defoliation because of insect damage is the "natural" defoliation that seems to bother scientists most—because insect damage can signal larger environmental problems, but it can often be moderated or controlled. Infestations of forest tent caterpillars, for example, can cause large-scale defoliation that affects growth rates of trees but also the aesthetic qualities of the forest. When population explosions of tent caterpillars occur, the larvae will move on in search of additional food after they have stripped the leaves of the trees they infest. While migrating, they defoliate deciduous trees and shrubs in their path. Forest tent caterpillar epidemics last in most cases from three to five years and therefore cause not only extensive defoliation, but also repeated defoliation. Plants that are defoliated by caterpillars, gypsy moths (major defoliators in North America, especially in eastern forests), or other insects suffer, first of all, growth loss. If they also suffer from drought, disease, or other stresses, defoliation can also cause widespread plant mortality. Defoliation can also reduce seed production for several years after it occurs, and plants that are affected can also be weakened and made more vulnerable to future environmental challenges. Extensive defoliation also allows more light to penetrate to the forest floor and affects water and nitrogen cycling.

In other words, defoliation in general can cause extensive forest ecosystem change and is usually regarded as ecologically and aesthetically undesirable. Many forest managers regard insect infestations as amenable to management by pesticides and other management tools and therefore find defoliation caused by insects an especially undesirable occurrence.

Human-Caused Defoliation

Insect infestations often occur in forests or in individual trees that are weakened by other stresses, some of them human-made. Humans much more directly cause defoliation in other ways. Anthropogenic (human-caused) defoliation is usually more extensive and comprehensive than defoliation from natural causes and is also considered a desirable goal. Crop managers in the United States have for a half-century used herbicides to defoliate plants in cotton and soybean fields to open the fields up to mechanical harvesting. Defoliated fields dry out faster, allowing more picking hours per day and sooner after rain. Defoliation removes the food supply for most insects, thereby eliminating late-season pest problems. In certain conditions, defoliation reduces boll rot by creating fields that dry out faster and that then generally—in the absence of precipitation—stay dry.

Defoliation is a controversial procedure among cotton and soybean farmers, not so much because of reluctance to use herbicides on crop plants, but because the timing of the application of herbicides is tricky. When plants are stripped of their leaves, fiber and seed development ceases. If too many soybeans or cotton bolls are still immature when defoliating herbicides are applied, the overall yield is reduced. If the crop plants are suffering some stress from insects, diseases, or drought, they will not respond in predictable ways to defoliating chemicals. Weather conditions at the time of application, as well as several days after, can affect the success of the process. The application of defoliants must also be done carefully. An application that is too heavy can cause the leaves to die but "stick" to the plant; an application that is too light can cause only a few leaves to fall. Defoliation as a crop management tool, in other words, works only within a specific range of conditions and requires a level of predictability that cannot always be attained.

When the U.S. forces used herbicides to defoliate thousands of hectares of forests and croplands during the Vietnam War, they either did not care if the treated plants lived or died, or they deliberately sought to destroy both plants and harvests. Under the auspices of Operation Ranch Hand, about 10 percent of the total land area of Vietnam was sprayed with about 41 million liters of the defoliant Agent Orange between 1965 and 1970. The herbicides that made up Agent Orange worked by defoliation, and when they were sprayed from the air on upland forests and coastal mangrove forests, they encouraged the trees in these forests to drop their leaves during the two to eight weeks following application. When they were sprayed on rice and other crop fields, they stunted or killed the plants. The main goal of defoliation was to remove cover for the movement of opposing forces. When defoliants were sprayed on crops, they were meant not to facilitate harvests, but to destroy them. Operation Ranch Hand's applications of defoliating herbicides, in other words, did not need to take into account tricky variables that compromised their use in industrial agriculture and were relatively wanton.

Humans have also caused defoliation, although unintentionally, of forest trees in another quarter because of the long-range effects of acid rain. Rain that has absorbed high levels of acidic pollutants—most notably, sulfur dioxide and nitrogen oxide—causes a variety of reactions in the vegetation and soils on which it falls. The chemical and physical properties of affected soils, the biological properties of affected vegetation, and the patterns of precipitation and other climate variables shape the impact of acid rain. In those soils and forests where acid rain has an impact, defoliation is caused in two ways. Acid rain damages the foliage surface of the plant, thereby diminishing the ability of leaves to function properly. Eventually, the plant affected in this way begins to lose its leaves. Acid rain also changes the chemistry of the soil, compromising the plant's ability to take up nutrients or doing damage to the plant's root system. Defoliation in this case is more indirect. Damage to the plant's ability to take up nutrients eventually forces leaf-drop in deciduous trees or "crown dieback" in conifers.

Again, other factors contribute to defoliation and forest death: drought, insect damage, disease, and the removal of acid-neutralizing vegetation by logging. But acid rain has been one of the major causes of tree death in several deciduous and conifer forests in North America and Europe. Some estimates of what the Germans call "Waldsterben" (forest death) blame acid rain for causing damage to over half of German forests by the mid–1980s. Defoliation is only one consequence of acid rain, and not always the first one. But extensive defoliation is an important indication of larger problems; And in many forests in Europe and North America in which it has occurred, acid rain is one of these problems.

Defoliation as Environmental Signal

Whatever the cause, the unseasonable loss of leaves by plants signals something amiss in the functioning of individual plants as well as in populations of plants in a forest. Defoliation is an especially good indication of relative tree and forest health. Scientists concerned about forest health in Europe, for example, acknowledged the value of defoliation rate as an overall measure of forest health in a program established in 1985 to study the effects of pollutants on European forests. A special program, the International Cooperative Programme on the Assessment and Monitoring of Air Pollution Effects on Forests, established under the United Nations Economic Commission for Europe, initiated a large-scale forest condition survey in European countries and began to survey permanent sample forest plots to measure tree health. By 2002 the survey included six thousand permanent general assessment plots and 860 intensive monitoring plots in thirty-nine participating countries. In this survey, surveyors look at the crown condition of "idealized trees" of constituent species of a forest or trees with full foliage in the same locales as the survey plots to set baselines for forest "health." They then carefully survey the crowns of trees in the assessment plot to determine their health relative to the baseline trees. The results of these surveys, along with a general large-scale annual survey of soil and foliage conditions of sample plots and a much more thorough and intensive monitoring of a smaller set of plots, have produced data that clearly point to an overall reduction in crown density, which, along with other data, point to acid rain as a cause. In all cases in this study, the condition of the foliage has been used to measure tree and forest health.

It is not always easy for scientists to distinguish between defoliation caused by "natural" causes and human-caused defoliation because insects and disease often invade, and drought or other "natural" factors sometimes kill trees and forests that have been weakened by pollution or poor management, and vice versa. A sick forest usually suffers from a variety of ailments that express a complicated exchange between human-made and other causes. But the dramatic increase in defoliation in temperate zone forests during the last quarter of the twentieth century indicates that human activity is a major contributing factor to defoliation. Percentages and rates of defoliation are at the same time especially good indications of relative tree and forest health.

Mart A. Stewart

Further Reading

Cecil, P. F. (1986). *Herbicidal warfare: The Ranch Hand project in Vietnam*. New York: Praeger.

European Union Scheme on the Protection of Forests against Atmospheric Pollution, United Nations European Commission for Europe, & European Commission. (2002). *The condition of forests in Europe: 2002 executive report*. Geneva, Switzerland: United Nations European Commission for Europe & European Commission.

Lovett, G. M., Christenson, L. M., Groffman, P. M., Jones, C. J., Hart, J. E., & Mitchell, M. J. (2002). Insect defoliation and nitrogen cycling in forests. *Bioscience, 52*(4), 335–342.

Deforestation

Deforestation is commonly thought of as a modern phenomenon that has gained momentum only since about 1950 in the tropical regions of the world. But deforestation is as old as the human occupation of the Earth, deliberate and controlled burning to clear trees and to drive game probably beginning with the emergence of *Homo erectus* a half-million years ago. All that has changed since 1950 is that an old process has been greatly accelerated and that environments more biologically sensitive and irreversibly damaged have been affected. It is possible that as much as nine-tenths of *all* deforestation occurred *before* 1950.

Forested environments have attracted human attention because of their diverse products. Trees provide wood for construction, shelter, and implements. Wood provides the fuel to keep warm, to cook food and make it palatable, and to smelt metals. The fruits and nuts of trees are useful for human foods, medicines, and dyes, and the roots, nuts, young shoots and branches, and particularly the flush of young grass after burning provide forage for wild and domesticated animals. Initially, at least, cleared forest provides naturally friable (easily crumbled) and nutrient-rich soils for growing crops. Clearing requires no sophisticated technology. Humans with stone axes need only boundless energy to fell trees; in contrast, fire and browsing animals can wreak havoc with little effort. The substitution of metal for stone axes about thirty-five hundred years ago, and then for saws in the medieval period, merely eased the back-breaking task of clearing and thus accelerated the rate of destruction and land-use transformation. Power saws during the last fifty years have had a catastrophic impact. One person can clear in a few days what took between ten and twenty days before.

If there is uncertainty about the current pace and locale of deforestation, then how much more confused must it have been in the past when few records were kept and when clearing was regarded as the first and "natural" stage in improvement and agricultural expansion, and hence rarely commented on. Addition-ally, the multiple meanings given to three definitions are crucial to the shaky knowledge about the history of deforestation. What is "a forest," what were the extent and density of trees at any past given time, and what constitutes "deforestation"? Pragmatically, a forest is a closed-canopy tree cover, and more open tree cover is woodland, all of which affects density. "Deforestation" is any process that modifies the original tree cover, from clear felling to thinning to occasional fire. However, it is not a one-way process; forests are dynamic entities, and whenever population pressures on forests are relaxed they can regrow with amazing vigor, for example, after the Mayan population collapse in Central America about 800 CE, after the Great Plague in Europe in the mid-fourteenth century, after the initial European encounter with the Americas and the decimation of the native population by disease, and after agricultural land abandonment in post–1910 eastern United States and post–1980 Europe.

So how much forest was cleared? If "human history" is taken to mean "after the last ice age ten thousand years ago," then not until about eight thousand years ago did climatic fluctuations and ice sheet movements abate and global forests stop responding dynamically to environmental changes and assume something like their present distribution. Then agriculture began in earnest. Climatic modelers have tried to recreate past vegetation because of the role it plays in the radiation balance of the Earth (the balance between incoming radiation from the sun and back radiation to clouds and the atmosphere which is affected by different sorts of vegetation) and in bio-geochemical cycles (e.g., global atmospheric carbon, nitrogen, water moisture, and temperature movements, with forest vegetation absorbing more carbon than, say, grass) related to climatic change. According to the climatic modler, Elaine Matthews the preagricultural closed forest probably once covered 46.28 million square kilometers and more open woodland 15.23 million square kilometers, and these have been reduced by 7.01 million square kilometres and 2.13 million square kilometers, respectively. Historical reconstructions of known clearing episodes and potential rates of clearing based on population numbers in the past support the general magnitude of change as being between 8.05 million square kilometers and 7.44 million square kilometers. Thus the total area of global forest has possibly decreased by 15.15 percent and the woodlands by 13.8 percent, a massive amount to be sure, but not, perhaps the worldwide devastation that is commonly supposed. Further refinement of these figures is unlikely because of the lack of reliable records. Modern clearing must be increasing that amount.

Prehistoric Clearing

Preliterate societies everywhere had a far more severe impact on the forests than is commonly supposed. The increase and spread of people, cultivation, and animal domestication took place in largely forested environments. In Europe, Mesolithic cultures (c. 9000–5000 BCE) cleared the forest edges for cultivation and used fire for game hunting. On the fringes of the upland areas of northern and southwestern England, successive clearings were accompanied by pollens of light-demanding plants, such as sorrel and ribwort plantain, which can flourish only as a result of reduced tree cover. Contrary to conventional archeological wisdom that the subsequent twenty-five hundred years of Neolithic agriculture (c. 4500–2000 BCE) were characterized by sporadic swidden agriculture (rotational burning and clearing for cropping), recent evidence suggests a more sedentary society and greater impacts. The recent excavation of the large, timbered longhouses across Europe shows that many were occupied for centuries, which suggests permanence of settlement. The Neolithic peoples were discerning farmer/pastoralists who sought out floodplain edges and selected the loessic (relating to an unstratified loamy deposit) soils because of their fertility and not because of their supposed treelessness. Stone axes made short shrift of the forest. The floodplains supported intensive garden cultivation and meadows. The cleared soils sustained yields of cereal crops for surprisingly long periods, and shortfalls in diet were supplemented by a hitherto-unsuspected reliance on stock, particularly cattle, which supplied meat, blood, milk, and cheese. A typical six-household, thirty-person settlement would have needed to plant about 13 hectares of wheat and run a thirty-to-fifty-head herd of cattle (the number needed to make it economically feasible to extract milk and meat produce) with forty sheep/goats and innumerable pigs. If the area used for crops, housing, garden plots, a woodlot, construction timber, pasture land, meadows, and rotational forest browse is totaled, then each settlement needed over 6 square kilometers of woodland to survive, or a staggering 20 hectares per person. If the forest was not cleared with axes, it was thinned or destroyed by burning and animal grazing Throughout the subsequent late Neolithic to early Bronze ages (c. 3000–1000 BCE) the process continued unabated. Charcoal layers, decreases in forest pollens, increases in cereal and weed pollens, and farming and clearing implements, laying between changing pollen layers or beds, all point to intensive farming and forest clearing.

Recent archeological and botanical evidence in the Americas tells a similar story of impacts and disturbance, so that any romantic idea of the presence of untouched, virgin forests before European contact is a myth. Burning, swiddens (plots produced by cutting back and burning off vegetation), and manipulation of useful trees in the rain forest of the equatorial upland areas may date from as early as the first retreat of the ice (c. 12,000 BCE), and most soils there and in the Amazon River basin are studded with charcoal. Ethnobotanists (people who study the plant lore of a race or people) think that much of the Amazonian forest is a cultural artifact created by successive native resource management strategies to cope with fluctuations in population. The Maya lowlands and other parts of tropical Central America have a similar history. In temperate North America the travel accounts of Americans William Bartram, Benjamin Hawkins, and others in what would become the southeastern states in the eighteenth and nineteenth centuries have detailed descriptions of indigenous clearing and agriculture, which are substantiated by recent archeological and paleobotanical evidence. From at least 10,000 BCE the aboriginal population occupied the rich bottom lands of the continental river systems. Progressive clearing on the floodplains and lower terraces and the intensification of cropping gradually converted the landscape into a mosaic of permanent settlements and cultivated fields, with early successional deciduous (leaf-dropping) forests invading abandoned Native American fields, the original forest remaining only in the uplands. By 1000 CE the Native Americans were colonizing the fire-prone eastern woodlands. Knowledge about deforestation in Africa is sparse, and with the exception of settlement in the savanna-woodland and adjacent belts in western Africa, deforestation may not have been extensive.

In every continent fire and the ax, together with dibble-and-hoe cultivation and later the light plow (often significantly integrated with considerable pastoral activity in Old World situations), resulted in the creation of nonforested patches. Forest structure was changed by the selective utilization of useful plants (e.g., olive, walnut, pistachio, bamboo, palm) by humans and animals, which altered the distribution of tree species and left distinctive "gardens" in the forest. In sum, the impact of early humans on the forest was greater than suspected; it may well be one of the major deforestation episodes.

The Classical World

From about 1000 BCE to the end of the Dark Ages, increasing population, burgeoning urbanization, and trade by different cultures, mainly on the northern rim of the Mediterranean basin, caused widespread coastal and some inland deforestation. The contemporary literature of the classical age of Greece and Rome—for example, the works of Greek geographer Strabo, Greek scientist Theophrastus, Roman orator Cicero, Roman writers Varro and Columella—supplements archeological and paleoecological evidence. For the first time people recorded what they saw, did to, and thought of their external world and were conscious of their power to control and even "create" nature. The primary cause of clearing was either to grow food or to facilitate grazing, followed in impact by procuring domestic fuel, building ships, and smelting metal. The detail of each process comes in roughly reverse order to its importance. Thus, as always, clearing to grow food was the most important change but gets little mention because it is subsumed into the larger everyday, taken-for-granted practice of agriculture. Yet, the industrious farmer who, Roman poet Virgil said, "subdues his woodland with flames and plough" and who "carted off the timber he has felled" (Virgil, 2:177) was the prime cause of change. Once-extensive forests are known to have become either greatly diminished or eliminated. On the other hand, metal smelting and its subsequent woodland needs loom disproportionately large because of their intense localized impact, as at the mines of Rio Tinto (southwestern Spain), Populonia (Italy, opposite the isle of Elba), Lauarion (southeast of Athens), or Cyprus, although it is doubtful that they were nearly as devastating as they are commonly made out to have been. Abundant evidence of clearing relates also to fuelwood procurement for domestic use and baths, to the general timber trade to imperial Rome and other cities, and to an outcome of warfare, particularly through ship building by Venetian and Arab traders during the seventh to eleventh centuries CE.

The marked seasonality of the climate and the prevalence of fire and overgrazing by stock, particularly goats, resulted in the succession of an inferior woodland—garigue (low, open scrublands) or marquis (thick, scrubby underbrush)—which in turn could be degraded to poor pasture. Ultimately, massive erosion, with associated deposition in shallow coastal locations, led to the widespread onset of malaria by the fourth century BCE. Centuries of overgrazing and clearing during the medieval period continued the process. Nevertheless, forest degradation and erosion should not be overstated, and they did not contribute to economic decline. Although a picture emerges of considerable change, with a few exceptions the forests furnished the timber needs of the time and during the later part of the early Renaissance period, as evidenced by the great fleets launched by Venice, Genoa, and Catalonia. It is likely that the final woodland denudation of the Mediterranean world was the product of population pressure as late as the nineteenth and early twentieth centuries.

The Middle Ages

Western and central Europe and northern China during the Middle Ages were energetic and inventive societies. Both witnessed a surge of economic activity in which the forest and its multiple riches played a central part. The historian of European medieval technology, Lynn White, talked of the "cultural climate" of invention, innovation, and religious belief that characterized the Middle Ages in the continent, and it is a useful concept when thinking about clearing. People had an intense religious belief in creating a divine, designed Earth, coupled with a need to understand and use nature for practical ends. Lay and ecclesiastical owners cleared vast areas both for the glory of God and for personal territorial gain; piety was accompanied by a zeal to improve. The underlying driving force was a sixfold increase of population between 650 and 1350, and more food was needed to avert famine. Underutilized and marginal lands were colonized in the western European heartland, and a massive expansion was made into the forests of central and eastern Europe. Three technical innovations helped raise production. First, the dominant system of two fields with one fallow was replaced by a three-field system, thus shortening the fallow period. This was possible because new crops such as oats and legumes helped to fertilize the soil and supplemented animal and human nutrition. Second, the development of the wheeled plow with coulter (a cutting tool attached to the beam of a plow) and moldboard (a curved iron plate attached above a plowshare to lift and turn the soil) allowed cultivation to move from the light soils onto the heavy, moist soils that were usually forested. Third, plowing efficiency was improved by the invention of the rigid horse collar and nailed horseshoes, which favored the horse over the ox by increasing speed and pulling power.

Whereas the society of the traditional manorial system was hierarchical, custom bound, and socially immobile, the new clearing and expansion produced a more fluid society. Aggrandizing landlords everywhere encouraged new settlers onto their lands and offered generous terms of ownership and personal freedom in return for clearing and cultivation. In a general way clearing contributed to the emancipation of the common people by giving them property, freedom, and status. Organized colonization by Germanic settlers on the forest frontier of central and eastern Europe changed the ethnic and settlement map of that part of the continent. The high point of clearing was between 1100 and 1350, the detail of this spectacular expansion being the subject of a vast literature. Place names indicate clearing and new settlements in once-forested areas, and rent rolls, charters, and leases show how expansion occurred. Cultivation rose from about 5 percent of land use in the sixth century CE to 30–40 percent by the late Middle Ages, and the vast tracts of forest were fragmented, thinned, or eliminated.

Experts estimate that the forests of France were reduced from 30 million hectares to 13 million hectares between about 800 and 1300—but still one-quarter of the country was forest covered. Farther east in Germany and central Europe, perhaps 70 percent of the land was forest covered in 900 CE, but only about one-quarter remained by 1900.

As the forest became less extensive, so it became more valued. The new upwardly mobile and increasingly powerful nobility now claimed the remaining forest as their personal hunting grounds by the end of twelfth century. The peasants, who gathered fuel, grazed stock, and made good use of the forest products, opposed this. Subsequently, a vast body of customs and rights emerged to govern forest use, which was a measure of increasing woodland scarcity.

The "agricultural revolution of the Middle Ages," (White, 1962: 77–8) as Lynn White called it, had a significance wider than local forest clearing alone, great as it was. The dominance of humans over nature was asserted, and the focus of Europe shifted from south to north—from the restricted lowlands around the Mediterranean to the great forested plains drained by the Loire, Seine, Rhine, Elbe, Danube, and Thames Rivers. There the distinctive features of the medieval world blossomed—a buildup of technological competence, self-confidence, and accelerated change—and after 1500 enabled Europe to invade and colonize the rest of the world. In that long process of global expansion the forest and the wealth released from it played a central part.

In contrast, little is known about clearing in China, where massive deforestation must have happened also. As usual, the detail of agricultural clearing is murky, but the demands of industry are clearer. A flourishing iron and steel industry in the Shantung region in northeastern China during the Northern Sung Dynasty (910–1126 CE) and the early substitution of coal for charcoal suggest not only precocious technological development but also widespread devastation and shortages of fuel. Just after the *Domesday Book* of England was completed in 1086, iron production in China was about 113,000 to 136,000 metric tons, only a little less than total European production at the beginning of the eighteenth century. Production then declined by half, whether through exhaustion of fuel, the Mongol invasions, or some other factor is not known.

Details of peasant life and livelihood are sparse, but peasants must have waged an unrelenting struggle to create the new agricultural land, which quadrupled between 400 and 1770 CE to feed a population that rose from 65–80 million to 270 million. River valleys were irrigated, and large swathes of forested uplands in the central and tropical southern provinces were cleared for potatoes, maize, and other imported crops in order to cope with the enormous migration of peoples from the north.

Early Modern Times

During the 450 years from 1492 to about 1950 Europe burst out of the confines of its continent, with far-reaching consequences for the global forests. Energetic and innovative capitalistic economies created wealth out of their new-found land, trees, animals, plants, and people overseas. Nature was expropriated and commodified. Enormous strains were put on domestic and overseas forest resources by a steadily increasing population (just over 400 million in 1500 to nearly 2.5 billion in 1950) and by rising demands for fuel, raw materials, and food with urbanization, industrialization, and generally rising affluence, first in Europe and, after the mid-nineteenth century, in the United States.

Expansion was broadly of two kinds. In the mainly temperate neo-European areas—a shorthand term for territories newly settled by Europeans from the seventeenth century onwards (e.g., North America, Australia, New Zealand, parts of southern Africa and Latin America), settler societies were planted and created. Permanent settlement began in earnest by the mid-seventeenth century after the near-elimination of the indigenous peoples by virulent Old World pathogens (agents of disease) such as smallpox, measles, and flu. The imported Old World crops and stock flourished wonderfully. The dominant ethos of freehold (a tenure of real property by which an estate of inheritance in fee simple or fee tail or an estate for life is held) tenure, dispersed settlement, "improvement," and personal and political freedom led to a rapid and successful expansion of settlement, although much environmentally destructive exploitation also occurred. Tree growth was considered a good indicator of soil fertility in all pioneer societies, and the bigger the trees, the quicker they were felled to make way for farms. The United States was the classic example of this neo-European agricultural clearing. The pioneer farmer, through "sweat, skill, and strength," was seen as the heroic subduer of a sullen and untamed wilderness. Clearing was widespread, universal, and an integral part of rural life; about 460,300 square kilometers of dense forest were felled in the eastern and southern states by about 1850 and a further 770,900 square kilometers by 1910. It was one of the biggest deforestation episodes ever. A similar process of pioneers hacking out a life for themselves and their family in the forest occurred in Canada, New Zealand, South Africa, and Australia. In Australia, for example, nearly 400,000 square kilometers of the southeastern forests and sparse woodland were cleared by the early twentieth century.

In the European colonized areas of the subtropical and tropical forests, exploitation was somewhat different. Harvesting of indigenous tree crops (e.g., rubber, nuts, hardwoods) gave way in time to the systematic replacement of the original forest by "plantation" crops grown for maximum returns in relation to the capital and labor (usually slave or indentured) inputs. Classic examples of this were the highly profitable crops of sugar in the Caribbean, coffee and sugar in the subtropical coastal forests of Brazil, cotton and tobacco in the southern United States, tea in Sri Lanka and India, and later rubber in Malaysia and Indonesia.

In eastern Brazil over half of the original 780,000 square kilometers of the huge subtropical "Atlantic" forest that ran down the eastern portions of the country had disappeared by 1950 through agricultural exploitation and mining. In Sao Paulo State alone the original 204,500 square kilometers of forest were reduced to 45,500 square kilometers by 1952.

Indigenous peasant proprietors were not immune to the pressures of the global commercial market. Outstanding was the expansion of peasant cultivation in the Irrawaddy River delta of lower Burma (Myanmar) (encouraged by British administrators) between 1850 and 1950, which resulted in the destruction of about 35,000 square kilometers of imposing equatorial (kanazo) rain forests and their replacement by rice; the same occurred in other delta areas in southeastern Asia. Throughout the Indian subcontinent the early network of railways meant an expansion of all types of crops by small-scale farmers, often for cash, which led to forest clearing everywhere.

Societies not yet affected by European penetration did not exploit their forests any less vigorously or in any more egalitarian or caring a manner than did their ultimate colonial, commercial European overlords. There is plenty of evidence from, for example, southwestern India and Hunan Province in south-central China from the sixteenth century onward to show that the commercialization of the forest was well established. In the former, permanent indigenous agricultural settlement existed side by side with shifting cultivation, and village councils regulated forest exploitation by agriculturalists. The forest was not regarded as a community resource; larger landowners dominated forest use in their local areas. Scarce commodities such as sandalwood, ebony, cinnamon, and pepper were under state and/or royal control. In Hunan Province a highly centralized administration encouraged land clearance in order to enhance local state revenues so as to increase the tax base and support a bigger bureaucracy and militia. State encouragement was also given later to migrations into the forested hill country of southern China. Simply put, forests everywhere were being exploited and were diminishing in size as a response to increasing population numbers and increasing complexity of society. In the subtropical world change was just slower—but no less severe—than that unleashed by the Europeans with their new aims, technologies, and intercontinental trade links. Measures of destruction are hard to come by, but in south and southeastern Asia between 1860 and 1950, 216,000 square kilometers of forest and 62,000 square kilometers of interrupted or open forest were destroyed for cropland.

During these centuries clearing was also nibbling away at the edges of all forests in Europe itself. Outstanding was the elimination of over 67,000 square kilometers in the mixed-forest zone of central European Russia between the end of the seventeenth century and the beginning of the twentieth century.

The insatiable demand in all societies for new land to grow crops and settle has been matched by a rising demand for the products of the forest themselves. For example, the European quest for strategic naval stores (masts, pitch, tar, turpentine) and ship timbers made major inroads into the forests of the Baltic Sea coastal region from the fourteenth century onward and those of the southern United States after about 1700. Alternative construction timbers such as teak and mahogany were discovered in the tropical hardwood forests after about 1800, with dire effects on those forests.

The Twentieth Century

The pace of land transformation increased during the first half of the twentieth century. In the Western world demands for timber accelerated. New uses (pulp, paper, packaging, plywood, chipboard) and relatively little substitution of other materials boosted use, while traditional uses in energy production, construction, and industry continued to loom large. The indispensable and crucial nature of timber in many Western economies gave it a strategic value akin to that of petroleum in economies today. In the tropical world the massive expansion of population by more than a half-billion on a base of 1.1 billion resulted in extensive clearing for subsistence, accompanied by an expansion of commercial plantation agriculture. In all, perhaps 2.3 million square kilometers of tropical forest were lost between 1920 and 1949. The only encouraging feature in the global picture during these years was the reversion of farmland to forest. This had begun in the eastern United States with the abandonment of "difficult" and hard-to-farm lands in New England in favor of easier-to-farm open grasslands and continued with the abandonment of the cotton- and tobacco-growing lands in the southern states. A similar story unfolded in northern Europe with "marginal" farms.

The most publicized deforestation—the deforestation that everyone thinks of when the word is mentioned—occurred after 1950. While temperate coniferous softwood forests have about kept up with the demands of industrial societies for supplies of timber and pulp, the focus of deforestation has shifted firmly to the tropical world. There better health and nutrition have resulted in a population explosion. These often-landless people have moved deeper into the remaining forests and further up steep forested slopes. They have no stake in the land and therefore little commitment to sustainable management. Since 1950 about 5.5 million square kilometers of tropical forests have disappeared, Central and Latin America being classic examples. In addition, the tropical hardwood forests are being logged out for construction timber at an alarming rate, while wood is cut for domestic fuel in prodigious quantities in Africa, India, and Latin America. Globally fuelwood cutting now roughly equals saw timber extraction—about 1.8 billion cubic meters compared to 1.9 billion cubic meters. It is forecast to rise rapidly in line with world population increase.

The history of deforestation is long and complex and is a sizable portion of the history of the world. It is one of the main causes of terrestrial transformation whereby humankind has modified the world's surface, a process that is now reaching critical proportions. One thing is certain: With an ever-increasing world population many people will want to exploit resources, and the process of deforestation will not abate. Other people will want to restrict the use of forests and preserve them. The tensions between exploitation and preservation will continue.

Michael Williams

See also Agroecology and Agroforestry; Forestry

Further Reading

Bechmann, R. (1990). *Trees and man: The forest in the Middle Ages* (K. Dunham, trans.). New York: Paragon House.

Bogucki, P. I. (1988). *Forest farmers and stockholders: Early agriculture and its consequences in north-central Europe.* Cambridge, UK: Cambridge University Press.

Darby, H. C. (1956). The clearing of the woodland in Europe. In W. L. Thomas (Ed.), *Man's role in changing the face of the Earth* (pp. 183–216). Chicago: University of Chicago Press.

Dean, W. (1995). *With broadax and firebrand: The destruction of the Brazilian Atlantic forest.* Berkeley and Los Angeles: University of California Press.

Meiggs, R. (1982). *Trees and timber in the ancient Mediterranean world.* Oxford, UK: Clarendon Press.

Virgil. (1984). *The Georgics* (L.P. Wilkinson, Trans.). Harmondsworth, UK: Penguin Books.

White, L. (1962). *Medieval Technology and Social Change.* Oxford, UK: Clarendon Press.

Williams, M. (1989). *The Americans and their forests.* New York: Cambridge University Press.

Williams, M. (1991). Forests. In B. L. Turner, W. C. Clark, R. W. Kates, J. Mathews, W. B. Meyer, & J. F. Richards (Eds.), *The Earth as transformed by human action: Global and regional changes in the biosphere over the past 300 years* (pp. 179–201). Cambridge, UK: Cambridge University Press.

Williams, M. (2003). *Deforesting the Earth: From prehistory to global crisis.* Chicago: University of Chicago Press.

Desertification

The term *desertification*, taken literally, means the process of creating a desert. It is, however, a controversial term that has evoked images of marching sands overrunning villages and deserts spreading at the hands of man. Much literature has been devoted to giving a meaning to this term, which is now understood by most scientists to refer primarily to various processes of land degradation.

The term desertification came into common use in the mid–1970s, when there was worldwide concern that human activities may be changing the earth's surface in such profound ways that serious climatic consequences resulted. This concern probably arose from a combination of factors that occurred at roughly the same time. One was the publication of the SMIC Report, a technical report detailing the findings of a panel of atmospheric scientists concerning the impact of land surface changes on climate. This report represented the first serious and comprehensive look at this issue. Another was the onset, around 1968, of what seemed to be an unprecedented and devastating drought in the Sahel of West Africa. A third was the availability of satellite images of large sections of the earth's surface. These showed the extent of human-induced changes of the land surface. A link was made between these changes and the drought in a much-publicized study by eminent meteorologist Jule Charney of the Massachusetts Institute of Technology.

The world's attention was focused on the desertification problem when the United Nations convened an international meeting in Nairobi, Kenya, in the summer of 1977. Unfortunately, the event was more a political one than a scientific one and much misinformation resulted. Humans were blamed for a worldwide disaster. At a later meeting in Rio de Janeiro in 1992 the U.N. took a more moderate view, one that recognized the role played by natural processes. Nonetheless, much of the misinformation is still widespread; but fortunately, numerous attempts have been made to present a more balanced view. It is now recognized that land degradation is a serious concern and that it probably has some impact on meteorological processes. It is also recognized that the extent and degree of the changes and their impact has been greatly exaggerated.

Definition and History of the Concept

Concern about landscape change and its possible impact on climate goes back at least to the fifteenth century, when Columbus speculated that deforestation had reduced rainfall in the Canary Islands. At the beginning of the beginning of the twentieth century there was considerable speculation that the Kalahari and surrounding semiarid regions of Southern Africa were further drying up. A much touted solution was to flood the Kalahari in order to bring back the good rains. Not long afterward several authors, most notably Bovill and Stebbing, hypothesized that deforestation was producing drought in Africa.

This idea was revived when drought struck the region again in 1968. The United Nations commissioned several studies prior to the Nairobi conference. National science organizations and individual scientists provided additional literature, little of which was peer reviewed.

At the Nairobi conference desertification was defined as "the diminution or destruction of the biological potential of land [which] can lead to desert-like conditions." This is closely akin to the concept of a living environment becoming sterile and barren. The process was further defined as human-induced, with the role of climate being essentially one of producing susceptibility. However, the United Nations Environment Programme (UNEP) produced a map of desertification status in Africa (See map on p. 26) that looked remarkably

Grazing animals around a well in Morocco; desertification often begins as a result of the grazing pressure around such isolated wells. COURTESY OF SHARON NICHOLSON.

like a map of rainfall. Other definitions abound, with the emphasis ranging from human impacts on the land to economic impacts, landforms and vegetation, and even phenomena on geologic time scales. Most, however, emphasize the concept of diminished land productivity and they restrict it to cases wherein the cause is human and not climatic.

Thus, the published definitions of desertification tend to encapsule the idea that desertification is "the expansion of desert-like conditions and landscapes to areas where they should not occur climatically" (Graetz 1991, 60). Unfortunately, most of the evidence of desertification derives from locations and time periods that were simultaneously affected by either drought or long-term declines in rainfall. Consequently, there is disagreement concerning the causes and processes of degradation, the extent to which the observed changes are natural or man-made, the amount of land affected or at risk, and the reversibility of desertification.

Mainguet (1991, 4) proposed a more encompassing definition: "Desertification, revealed by drought, is caused by human activities in which the carrying capacity of land is exceeded; it proceeds by exacerbated natural or man-induced mechanisms, and is made manifest by intricate steps of vegetation and soil deterioration which result, in human terms, in an irreversible decrease or destruction of the biological potential of the land and its ability to support population." Finally recognizing the climatic controls on the process, the United Nations changed its definition to read "land degradation in arid, semiarid and dry sub-humid areas resulting from various factors, including climate variations and human activities" (Puigdefabregas 1995, 311 & Warren 1996, 348).

Forms, Processes, and Physical Manifestations of Desertification

The concept of desertification that emerged from the 1977 Nairobi conference was one in which land degradation began in core areas around intensively utilized sites, such as villages, wells, and water holes. These degraded areas would grow, causing the desert to encroach into formerly productive regions of arid and semiarid land. The changes that took place were viewed as more or less irreversible.

The processes of desertification that were enumerated include removal of vegetation, erosion and compaction of soils, excessive water consumption, irriga-

tion, inappropriate use of agricultural technology and other examples of poor land management practices. Natural vegetation is cleared for agriculture; savanna lands, fields, and pastures are burned at the end of the dry season; wood is gathered for firewood, charcoal, and building supplies; animals overgraze grasslands. This generally leaves the surface more barren and more susceptible to wind and water erosion. The erosion removes the organic topsoil, fine materials, and sometimes tracts of the surface. In many arid regions, use of tractors and other technologies further enhance the erodibility. Animals trample the soil surface, compacting and aggregating materials in ways that hinder drainage and infiltration. When irrigated land is improperly drained, salt and other chemical residues are left behind.

Many general causes of desertification have been identified. There is a belief that its roots lie in societal changes such as increasing population, sedentarization of the indigenous nomadic peoples, breakdown of traditional market and livelihood systems in developing countries, implementation of new and inappropriate technology in these regions, and bad strategies of land management. Associated with these changes are growing livestock numbers, cultivation in marginal areas, intensive irrigation, and deforestation.

In West Africa, where desertification is considered to be intense, much of the problem has been attributed to government policies and their effects on the pastoral societies of the Sahel. Incentives were given for growing cash crops, at the expense of subsistence agriculture, and cultivation expanded into the southern Sahelian fringes traditionally left for dry-season pastures. The result was over use or "over-cultivation" of the land. Also, the sedentarization of nomads was encouraged for a variety of reasons, such as centralized government control of education and health, and their traditional migration routes became blocked by national borders. Their impact became more localized, instead of spread out over the vast region as they migrated. Their animals clustered around the few available wells, overgrazing the surrounding land; this had dramatic effects in the face of the drought that prevailed in the 1960s and 1970s. These policies were exacerbated by an increase in population of both pastoralists and cattle by about 3 percent per year, a result of access to medical and veterinary services.

Desertification is manifested as changes of the vegetation cover, soil, and surface topography. Soil structure and texture are altered, materials are leached, and nutrients and organic materials are lost. Soil fertility is thereby reduced and impervious horizons, such as lateritic crusts, may form. Vast amounts of topsoil are removed by water and wind, producing huge gullies and badlands. Poor irrigation and management practices lead to salinization, alkalinization, and waterlogging of the soil, processes that further reduce soil fertility. Water supplies become enriched with salt. Bare ground is exposed. Sand dunes build up or are mobilized, often encroaching upon vegetation. The amount of vegetation or primary productivity may be reduced, or vegetation composition may change, with diverse and nutrient-rich species of grasses, forbs, and herbs replaced by less palatable shrubs. The spatial distribution of vegetation and water supply is unfavorably altered, the landscape becoming more heterogeneous and resources contracted. The carrying capacity of the land is dramatically reduced.

Desertification can be viewed as resulting from disturbance in an ecosystem that is otherwise stabilized by a series of feedbacks, many of them negative, between society, man, herbivores, vegetation, soil, and climate. When a vegetated surface is degraded, such as by uncontrolled grazing, the result is an alteration of soil water and nutrient flow in the vicinity of plants. The removal of organic litter also alters the partitioning of rainwater on the surface. The removal of litter and exposure of soil has two positive feedbacks: the bare soil is more susceptible to crusting by rainfall impact and to wind and water erosion. A second feedback is the altering of the microclimate over the disturbed land: the extremes of temperature and evaporation are amplified when plants are removed, thus making regrowth more difficult. In undisturbed arid and semi-arid environments that are in equilibrium, the feedback loops tend to be negative, hence preserving the status quo. The disturbances associated with desertification turn some of the feedback loops from negative to positive. This allows the environmental disturbance to be amplified, in other words, the desertification becomes self-accelerating. Drought similarly destabilizes the equilibrium and is thus associated with many of the instances in which desertification has been identified as a serious problem.

Magnitude and Extent of the Problem

During the 1977 conference the United Nations released figures indicating that desertification had affected some 35 million square kilometers of land glob-ally and that overall 35 percent of the Earth's land surface was at risk of becoming desertified. This estimate was gleaned from maps produced by U.N.-sponsored studies showing desertification risk and desertification severity. Unfortunately, there was little rigor in the studies upon which the maps were based. Moreover, desertification processes had been intensely studied in only a few isolated areas, generally those where desertification is indicated as "very severe" on the map in Fig. 1. The broad brush strokes on the map are clearly evident over the Sahara desert. The extent of desertification, defined as human-induced, is indicated as "slight" in areas of extreme desert where only a handful of humans, if any, crossed during the course of the last century and moderate in areas nearly devoid of inhabitants.

Another case in point is the common estimate that the desert is advancing over West Africa into the Sahelian region to the south at a rate of 7.5 kilometers per year. The source of this figure is not quite clear but it appears to be based on only two measurements made by Hugh Lamprey in the Sudan in 1958 and 1975. He determined the geographical limits of *Acacia* growth around Khartoum and concluded from this that the desert had advanced southward in the western Sudan by 90 to 100 kilometers.

Thus, the extent of desertification worldwide has never been adequately assessed. However, two studies have made steps in the right direction. One is the desertification atlas of Nick Middleton and David Thomas (1992). The atlas contains maps of individual processes and effects of desertification: soil degradation, water erosion, wind erosion, and chemical and physical deterioration. Unfortunately, these are also based on little actual data and the methodology of the assessment is not well defined. However, select, well-defined, quantitative case studies are also included in the atlas. The second is the work of Stephen Prince and colleagues (1998), which examined land degradation in West Africa on a nearly continental scale. This study keyed in on the definition of desertification as a decline in land productivity, which they assessed using the concept of "rain-use efficiency" (RUE, the ratio of net primary production to rainfall). The satellite-derived Normalized Difference Vegetation Index (NDVI) was used to quantify vegetation growth. During the nine years of analysis, 1982 to 1990, when steady desertification was supposedly occurring, RUE actually increased. Overall the study showed that there was no widespread, sub-continental scale desertification over west Africa, although pockets of heavily degraded land were detected.

The Controversy Surrounding Desertification

From the onset of interest in desertification in the 1970s, the issue has caused considerable controversy. A major point of contention is the relative roles of climate and people in the process. There are also uncertainties concerning the amount of land that has been affected or is at risk, and concerning the reversibility of desertification. The nature and impacts of desertification were also disputed.

Much of the controversy resulted from the lack of scientific rigor in the studies of the 1970s and the information disseminated by the United Nations. An abundance of reports were produced, documenting case studies from around the world, but in them was a virtual absence of ecological detail. Attention was paid to such parameters as numbers of livestock and harvest quality but not to the manifestations of desertification on soils and vegetation. Sweeping conclusions were drawn from miscellaneous observations, with no measurements or systematic assessments of the actual changes. Desertification estimates for Africa, in particular, were problematic for two reasons (Nicholson et al. 1998). For one, the information was largely anecdotal. Secondly, the few actual assessments extended over periods of drought or rainfall decline. The UNEP map supposedly depicting desertification severity, was largely extrapolated from risk factors in the environment; de facto, it was a map of vegetation and climate and contained virtually no information on desertification status. Consequentially, the extent and severity of desertification were largely exaggerated.

At the heart of the problem was the intentional elimination of climate as a possible cause of desertification. This was unfortunate because nearly all of the few actual assessments extended over periods of drought or rainfall decline. Thus, while desertification itself was defined as anthropogenic, the evidence used to assess it could equally have been a product of climatic variability. A good example is the pivotal work of Hugh Lamprey. During the period that Lamprey took measurements, rainfall in the Sahel declined by nearly 50 percent, with a somewhat lesser reduction in the area surveyed by Lamprey. Thus, while desertification itself was defined as anthropogenic, the evidence used to assess it could equally have been a product of climatic variability.

This is true of many other instances of supposed widespread desertification in areas of the United States, Australia, and elsewhere. At the beginning of the twentieth century there was a common belief that the Kalahari of Southern Africa had been progressively drying up. Various authors noted the desiccation of the Senegal River and nearby the degradation of the forests in the Sahel about this same time. Landscape degradation also affected huge regions of Australia at the end of the twentieth century and livestock numbers plummeted. At the time these phenomena were all attributed to human activities, but all were roughly contemporaneous with a climatic desiccation that affected nearly the entire global tropics. The desiccation was particularly apparent in Australia and Africa. Thus, in these examples, landscape degradation accompanied climatic perturbations. Likewise, farmland was ruined and soil was eroded during the Dust Bowl days of the 1930s in the Great Plains of the U.S. during the worst drought conditions on record in the region. These examples illustrate the inseparability of climate and desertification. This tandem of events occurred again with the Sahel drought of the late 1960s and early 1970s. The increased aridity affected nearly all of Africa by the 1980s and 1990s. Thus, it is virtually impossible to separate the impact of drought from that of desertification.

Equally problematic is the perception that has developed of the process of desertification. The term evokes an image of the "advancing desert," a living environment becoming irreversibly sterile and barren. This paradigm is used in climatic studies of desertification, but it has long been recognized that the process has a much different character. Studies in the Sudan by Ulf Hellden and his students at the University of Lund showed through a combination of field work and analysis of satellite photos that there was neither a systematic advance of the desert or other vegetation zones, nor a reduction in vegetation cover, although degradation and replacement of forage with woody species was apparent. There was no evidence of a systematic spread of desertified land around villages and waterholes or of reduced crop yield due to cultivation of marginal or vulnerable areas.

On the other hand, these studies clearly demonstrated that changes took place in response to drought, with full recovery of the land productivity at the end of the drought. Compton J. Tucker, of NASA, and Sharon Nicholson, of Florida State University, published several studies that demonstrated that the same is true for the Sahel as a whole. The "advances" of the desert during recent years closely mimic the fluctuations of rainfall in the Sahelian region. Stephen Prince and colleagues at the University of Maryland likewise showed that net primary productivity (NPP) varies in step with rainfall.

None of above facts belies the idea that "desertification" is a problem. It is a process of land degradation with many biophysical components. The topsoil is eroded, adding to the atmospheric dust loading, and tracts of land are washed away, producing huge gullies. The soil's texture, organic matter, and nutrient content are changed in ways that reduce its fertility. Poor irrigation and management practices lead to salinization and waterlogging of the soil. Although land may become more barren, it is more commonly the case that diverse and nutrient-rich species are replaced by vegetation of poorer quality.

Meteorological Consequences

The complexity of desertification causes and consequences is recognized in new assessments. Unfortunately, this complexity is all too often ignored in descriptions of the process. This is particularly true of the studies that have attempted to evaluate the possible climatic effects of desertification. For that reason, the meteorological consequences have never been firmly established and many studies have exaggerated the importance of desertification for climatic variability in areas such as West Africa.

The Impact of Desertification on Climate: Charney and the "Albedo Effect"

One of the first concerns about the meteorological consequences of desertification is that raised by Charney: that it may have caused drought in the Sahelian region of West Africa. Although this idea has been proven wrong by numerous studies, it still occasionally appears in the literature.

Charney's mechanism was based on the exposure of highly reflective soil as a result of overgrazing. The percent of solar radiation reflected back towards space, termed albedo, would increase, thus reducing the amount of surface heating. Theoretically, to maintain a heat balance and prevent the surface from constantly cooling, the heat loss from the increased albedo would have to be offset by another source of heat. In this case the source would be sinking of the air over the desertified region, a process that heats the air via compression as it encounters increasingly high pressure. The sink-

ing of the air mass would suppress rainfall. Charney's hypothesis, supported by mathematical models, was interpreted as a way that drought could be created by human activity or a positive feedback mechanism by which natural droughts could be self-accelerating. The drought would reduce vegetation cover, exposing more soil, increasing the surface albedo, and further reducing rainfall.

There were numerous flaws in this thinking. For one, Charney tested his idea using a highly unrealistic desertification scenario: increasing albedo from 14 percent to 35 percent over a vast region of West Africa. Isolated studies of relatively small, highly grazed areas which indicate some change: the albedo of soil in the overgrazed Sinai was 46 percent, compared to 25 percent in unperturbed areas and in Tunisia the albedo of protected grazing sites was 4 percent to 10 percent lower than that of unprotected, desertified areas. However, studies of the Sahel as a whole have suggested that albedo there has been relatively stable over time, despite droughts and human pressure on the environment. Moreover, the grassland albedo in West Africa is determined much less by vegetation than by soil moisture, which is strongly dependent on rainfall. Thus any positive feedback related to surface albedo is more likely to be a result of a drought than of human-induced desertification.

More importantly, Charney's idea has been inappropriately applied to areas beyond the Sahel. There it appeared to be reasonable as a result of the region being one where radiative effects actually create a net heat loss. This is an unusual situation found only in the desert areas of West Africa and the Arabian peninsula. The mechanism also requires that the underlying soil have a very high albedo, something that is generally not true of the soils in more humid regions. Perhaps more importantly, in the woodlands south of the Sahel, removal of the vegetation actually decreases rather than increases surface albedo. This happens because the number of reflecting surfaces (the leaves of the trees) is reduced when the region is deforested.

Other Climate Issues Related to Desertification

Although the albedo effect probably plays at most a small role, Charney's hypothesis led the way to many other ideas concerning feedback between the land surface and climate. Some of the proposed mechanisms involve soil moisture, temperature, surface roughness, and aerosol generation. The two most important are probably soil moisture and aerosols.

The ability to hold moisture is determined to a first approximation by the texture and structure of the soil. A fine-textured soil, with a high clay content, tends to hold moisture and promote plant growth more than a coarse-textured sandy soil. Thus, over Southern Africa the areas with clay-rich vertisols support a much denser vegetation cover than the Kalahari sands, despite similar amounts of rainfall. Soil texture, in particular removal of the finer particles, is one of the important physical effects of the various processes of desertification. Vegetation also promotes the retention of soil moisture by way of surface shading, retardation of runoff, and the impact of the roots on the soil. Thus, the reduced vegetation cover and the structural and textural changes of a degraded soil reduce the soil's ability to retain moisture. This has two effects: it further reduces plant growth and it modifies the partitioning of rainfall into runoff and evaporation, altering both the amount of evaporation and its timing. In general, the result will be reduced evaporation and, consequently, reduced heating of the atmosphere via latent heat release.

Numerical modelling studies have shown the effects of soil moisture, surface evaporation, and latent heat on hydrology and climate. For example, models have shown that there is greater daily precipitation variability with shorter time scales of soil moisture retention. Also, evaporation responds more slowly to the input of precipitation when hydrologic processes in the soil are included in the model.

The implications of these theoretical results are that modification of the land surface characteristics can probably alter weather patterns. Much research in the Great Plains and in Florida has shown that this is unequivocally true on small scales. Elsewhere observational evidence of land-atmosphere feedback processes has been more difficult to establish. In this context, the Hydrological-Atmospheric Pilot Experiment (HAPEX) Sahel field experiment that took place in Sahelian Africa in 1992 has produced some interesting results.

Chris Taylor and Thierry Lebel (1998) used HAPEX-Sahel results to show evidence of a link between surface fluxes and persistent rainfall patterns at convective length scales. During individual rainfall events the probability of rainfall at a given location was strongly correlated with that location having received antecedent rainfall from a previous event; thus, rainfall is correlated with evaporation anomalies. The approach to demonstrating this is based on comparison of pairs of rain gauges within the area. After one gauge randomly receives much more rainfall, a large gradient builds up as that gauge continues to receive a higher amount of rainfall during nearly all subsequent rainfall events. This phenomenon was observed at numerous pairs of gauges. In many cases, the gradient during the season was several times larger and in the opposite direction as the climatological rainfall gradient. This feedback thus enhances the patchy nature of the rainfall and creates pockets of very wet and very dry conditions within the overall rainfall field. It has not been shown, however, that a net change in the total amount of rainfall results.

Dust

Fortunately, atmospheric visibility is related to dust concentration and visibility data has been useful for examining the spatial and temporal distribution of dust in the region over multi-year periods. From visibility analyses it is apparent that there has been a steady increase in the frequency of occurrence of dust conditions over West Africa since the early 1970s and that it has paralleled a downward trend in rainfall. This steady build up of dust over West Africa since the early 1970s has been confirmed by a consistent upward trend in African dust measured at sites downstream.

West Africa is the source of nearly half of the mineral aerosols residing in the atmosphere. Commonly termed "Saharan dust" or "desert dust," it was long assumed to originate in the Sahara. Recent evidence suggests instead that most of it originates in the semi-arid Sahel/Soudan region and throughout North Africa the build-up of dust is better correlated with Sahelian rainfall than with local conditions.

The impact of the dust build-up on meteorological processes over West Africa is not adequately known, but several recent studies suggest that its effect could be quite significant. Modelling studies of the general atmospheric circulation have shown that regional climate cannot be realistically simulated without including the effects of dust in the model. The models in fact suggested that "disturbed" sources resulting from climate variability, cultivation, deforestation and wind erosion contribute some 30 to 50 percent of the total atmospheric dust loading. Models of convection have shown that the dust has an impact on synoptic conditions and, therefore, presumably on rainfall as well. Over West Africa the dust layer is important for the maintenance and possible growth of some wave disturbances and therefore it affects the mid-level African Easterly Jet, which in turn affects the development of weather systems in the region. The effect of the dust relates to its modification of atmospheric heating. The effect is quite complex because the dust modifies both the shortwave solar radiation transmitted through to the surface and the longwave infrared radiation emitted to space. Dust also modifies the physical properties of clouds, reducing their ability to produce rainfall.

Outlook

Desertification is a decline in the productivity of the land surface. The term itself is somewhat of a misnomer, evoking images of the "advancing desert." This concept has resurged from time to time since the beginning of the twentieth century. With the claims of some scientists that the 1970s Sahel drought was a *result* of desertification and the U.N. proclamation that some 35 million kilometers of land had already been lost, desertification became the focus of much scientific, political and institutional attention. Recent work has shown that such claims of the worldwide extent of desertification and their influence on climate have been greatly exaggerated. However, we do not have any true understanding of the process nor any accurate assessment of the extent and degree of desertification globally.

Desertification is often assumed to be a result of human activities, but in reality the productivity of the land can be reduced from either human mismanagement or adverse climatic conditions. Generally, a combination of these factors is the cause. Unfortunately, most of the evidence of desertification is from locations and time periods which were simultaneously affected by drought or long-term declines in rainfall. Consequently, there is disagreement concerning the causes and processes of degradation, the extent to which the changes are natural or man-made, the amount of land affected or at risk, and the reversibility of desertification.

Although it is unlikely that desertification has produced major climatic changes, such as drought in the African Sahel, it is clear that changes in the surface conditions of the land can alter meteorological processes on local and regional scales. Further work is needed into the mechanisms of this influence. Of particular concern is the global increase in mineral aerosols eminating from the West African Sahel, an increase that might be influencing the region's climate.

Sharon Nicholson

See also China; Sahara; Sahel; United States—Southwest

Further Reading

Biswas, M. K., & Biswas, A. K. (Eds.). (1980). *Desertification*. Oxford, UK: Pergamon Press.

Charney, J. G. (1975). The dynamics of deserts and droughts. *Quarterly Journal of the Royal Meteorological Society, 101*, 193–202.

Eckholm, E. P. (1975). Desertification: A world problem. *Ambio, 4*, 137–145.

Graetz, R. D. (1991). Desertification: A tale of two feedbacks. In H. A. Mooney, et al. (Eds.), *Ecosystem experiments* (pp. 59–87). Chichester, UK: John Wiley and Sons.

Hellden, U. (1991). Desertification—Time for an assessment? *Ambio, 20*, 372–383.

Inadventent climate modification: Report of the study of man's impact on climate (SMIC). (1971). Cambridge, MA: MIT Press.

Mainguet, M. (1991). *Desertification, natural background and human mismanagement*. Berlin, Germany: Springer Verlag.

Middleton, N. J., & Thomas, D. S. G. (1992). *World atlas of desertification*. London: Edward Arnold.

Nicholson, S. E. (2000). Land surface processes and Sahel climate. *Reviews of Geophysics, 38*, 117–139.

Nicholson, S. E. (2002). What are the key components of climate as a driver of desertification? In J. R. Reynolds, & D. M. Stafford Smith (Eds.), *Global desertification: Do humans cause deserts?* Berlin, Germany: Dahlem University Press.

Nicholson, S. E., Tucker, C. J., & Ba, M. B. (1998). Desertification, drought and surface vegetation: An example from the West African Sahel. *Bulletin of the American Meteorological Society, 79*, 815–829.

Puigdefabregas, J. (1995). Desertification: Stress beyond resilience, exploring a unifying process structure. *Ambio, 24*, 311–313.

Taylor, C. M., & Lebel, T. (1998). Observational evidence of persistent convective scale rainfall patterns. *Monthly Weather Review, 126*, 1597–1607.

Thomas, D. S. G., & Middleton, N. J. (1994). *Desertification: Exploding the myth*. Chichester, UK: John Wiley and Sons.

Tucker, C. J., & Nicholson, S. E. (1998). Variations in the size of the Sahara 1980 to 1997. *Ambio, 28*, 587–591.

Warren, A. (1996). Desertification. In W. M. Adams, A. S. Goudie, & A. R. Orme (Eds.), *The physical geography of Africa* (pp. 342–355). New York: Oxford University Press.

Deserts

Deserts cover approximately 30 percent of Earth's surface. A rudimentary classification divides them into two broad types: hot deserts (tropical and subtropical deserts) and temperate or mid-latitude deserts. Hot deserts, in which temperatures remain high or very high all year round, are found in both hemispheres around the tropics between latitudes 20° and 30° north and south. In temperate deserts temperatures differ widely between winter and summer (in winter there is often at least one month in which the mean temperature falls below 5° C and snow may accumulate for several days). Such deserts are found mainly in the interior of Eurasia and in the southwest of North America. Besides these two broad classes there are other types that in part coincide with tropical deserts, but whose formation is affected by different factors such as cold coastal currents.

Despite their great diversity, the earth's arid zones share some common characteristics, principally their aridity, which is the result of high temperatures and low, irregular rainfall. The irregularity of rainfall ex-

plains another typical characteristic of dry ecosystems: large fluctuations of biomass above and below very low mean values.

Apart from deep subterranean resources, which in most cases remained unexploited until the twentieth century, deserts provide two important kinds of natural resources: scarce but relatively long-lasting water and food resources; and episodic but abundant resources (such as a sudden deluge of rain after which a pasture may develop). In any event, it must be emphasized that it is the interaction, by way of technology and social relations, between a given society and an arid environment that causes certain aspects of a desert to be perceived as limitations or as resources.

Hunter-Gatherer Societies

Some hunter-gatherer societies of semiarid zones survived into the nineteenth century in America and into the twentieth century in Australia and southwest Africa. In general these societies had little ability to modify their environment (although they sometimes did so with fire) and they depended on the spontaneous reproduction of spatially dispersed natural resources. They all displayed an astonishing knowledge of their ecosystems and were able to exploit a large variety of ecological niches, which constituted their productive base. They lived in small groups around temporary sources of water. When the water dried up or the resources situated at a short distance from the pool ran out, they were obliged to move away and find another source of water, which means they were constantly on the move. Lack of water was for them an almost absolute constraint (if food was located too far from the water, they could not exploit it and therefore it did not constitute a resource). Different local groups maintained close kinship relations or alliances with neighboring groups in the same or nearby territories. When there was extreme drought or shortage of food, these social relations allowed them to move into territories occupied by their relatives and allies. It has been suggested that the enormous complexity in the kinship systems of some Australian Aborigines, which created strong ties of obligation among different groups, may have been a way of adapting to the uncertain nature of arid environments.

Travelers cross the Sahara Desert in Egypt on camels. COURTESY OF NICOLE LALIBERTE.

Nomadic Pastoralists

For thousands of years the typical way of life in the deserts of Eurasia and Africa (though not in those of

Camels in the Libyan Desert

The following text makes clear why the camel is so important to the desert-dwelling bedouin of Libya in North Africa.

The nomadic movements of the two small herd species, sheep and goats, are predicated upon the ability of these animals to extract all the water they need from their food whenever fresh, green graze is abundant. Like the small herd animals, camels can go without drinking in times of good winter and spring pastures, but camels carry the tendency toward mobility one step further.

In summer the small herd animals must be watered about twice a week, and their movements accordingly are limited to the area they can reach in a day's travel to and from their water supply. Camels can water as infrequently as twice a month, which in theory allows them to graze areas up to 150 kilometers from the watering point. One hundred fifty kilometers represents the outside limits of the camel's endurance, and while this figure does not represent the normal situation, it does indicate the vast resources at the disposal of the species in dealing with drought in exceptionally bad years. More commonly, camels water every seventh to ninth day and the distances grazed are correspondingly reduced.

Still, the camel's speed, plus the infrequency with which it needs water, means that camels retain a high degree of mobility year-round. Unlike the other species, camels are not dependent upon the fortuitous occurrence of both water and summer graze in one place.

Source: Behnke, Roy H., Jr. (1980) *The Herders of Cyrenaica: Ecology, Economy and Kinship among the Bedouin of Eastern Libya*. Urbana: University of Illinois Press, 28–29.

America or Australia) has been that of nomadic pastoralism, a complex, sophisticated mode of subsistence that has played a major role in the history of the Old World. Most researchers believe that nomadic pastoralism arose at the edges of cultivable zones after the neolithic advent of agriculture and domestication of animals, in regions that were too dry for the development of settled agriculture and cattle-raising.

Nomadism specialized in exploiting an ecological niche that the mixed economies (sedentary agriculture and stockbreeding) could not take advantage of. It seems that almost all nomad societies originated directly or indirectly in the Near East. This region, which suffers acute summer droughts or has clearly arid climates, was inhabited by wild animals (goats, sheep, dromedaries) that, owing to their specific characteristics, fullfilled two conditions: They were easily domesticated and were more or less naturally adapted (or could become so, with the help of man) to the arid or semiarid environmental conditions. The other early agricultural and cattle-raising centers of the world, in

Asia and America, were not populated with these kinds of animals. Some argue that pastoral nomadism arose independently in the Sahara, but that theory continues to be controversial.

A secondary center of nomadic pastoralism may have had its origin in the steppes of southern Russia, where it would have emerged between the third and second millennia BCE in mixed-economy societies of eastern Europe. In the south of Russia the horse, domesticated around 3000 BCE, gave herders of sheep and goats (which had originated in the Near East) great mobility. The theory is that the domestication of the Bactrian camel (between the third and second millennia BCE), which is similar to the dromedary but better adapted to cold winters, allowed nomads to penetrate the deserts of central Asia. The discovery of Caucasian mummies, some of them from the second millennium BCE, and of texts written in Indo-European languages in the desert of Taklimakan (in the northwestern Chinese region of Xinjiang) may testify to the extent of this movement.

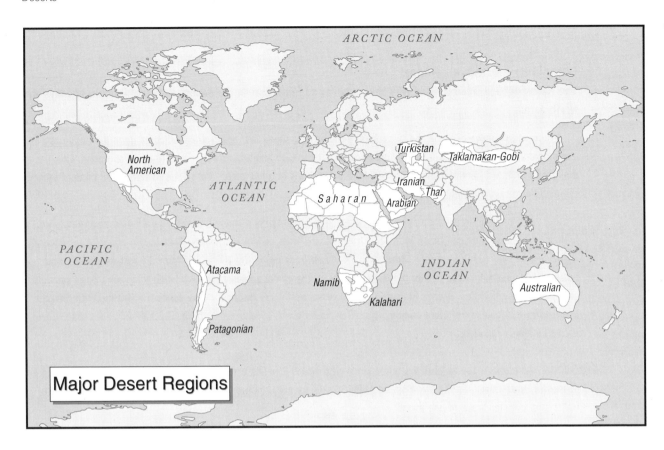

Major Desert Regions

Analyzing the way nomadic societies interact with the environment helps us to understand the great influence that arid and semiarid regions have exercised on the development of Eurasian and African civilizations. Nomadic pastoralism, as a mode of subsistence, is essentially unstable and expansionist. Herds undergo great fluctuations in size and composition in arid environments. Both ethnographic studies and computer techniques demonstrate the potentially explosive growth of a simple flock of sheep or goats. Nomadic societies exploit this potential in order to accumulate a lot of animals. From the standpoint of basic units of production, it is an intelligent and adaptive response to environmental fluctuations, but on a regional scale it prepares the way for social and ecological disaster. Assertions that nomads, although they do not consciously attempt to modify their environment, create their own steppes and deserts may contain a certain element of truth. The combination of sudden fluctuations and expansive tendencies gives rise to another of the most well-known aspects of nomadic societies: quick and radical shifts along migratory tracks, which sometimes historically appear as invasions or attacks on settled civilizations. It should be borne in mind that

mobility and the lack of fixed settlements has always given great military advantages to desert peoples.

Nomads exploit their resources in small units of production (households or encampments), but, as with hunter-gatherers, these basic units are linked to each other, generally by means of kinship relations. It is these links that form the basis of larger units when organizing migratory tracks, when regulating rights of access to grazing land, and when facing environmental changes. It is membership in these higher-ranking units that in fact grants rights to territory and its resources. As in many hunter-gatherer societies, among nomads kinship relations have great importance because they operate like economic institutions. The manner in which hunter-gatherers and pastoral nomads relate to nature is very different, however. Whilst the hunter-gatherers exploit a great variety of ecological niches in different places and seasons, the nomads always exploit the same basic resource: pasture (either in different environmental zones or in the same one). Whereas the hunter-gatherer's territorial system is based on moving himself towards the resources, that of the nomad involves moving an entire infrastructure of production, with little regard to the regional availability of microresources (such as small mammals and birds, and wild nuts and fruit, all of which are important to hunter-gatherers). For the hunter-gatherer the great waterless spaces of the desert represent a constraint that prevents him from exploiting resources that are too remote from pools and streams. For the nomad, those spaces only represent a relative limitation, since he can travel long distances transporting water on his animals.

Trading Routes and Oases

From the Atlantic to western China, deserts form a gigantic arid belt that for centuries separated the principal civilizations of the Old World. The nomads, on their constant journeys in search of new pastures, discovered the routes that would allow Chinese silk to travel to Europe across the deserts of central Asia and that would move gold, ivory, and slaves from tropical Africa to the Mediterranean across the Sahara. They became intermediaries operating between ecologically and culturally different regions, which allowed them to divert surpluses from the agrarian societies of Africa, Europe, and Asia to the arid lands. Thus there emerged, in the oases and at the edges of deserts, fabulously wealthy cities, such as Palmyra, Petra, Samarqand, Tombouctou (Timbuktu), and Almería, in extremely poor environments. The wealth of medieval Islam, which culturally unified the deserts of Asia and Africa, is very much connected with the control of trade between remote civilizations and with the irrigation systems in arid countries.

The oases, like islands in the sea, played a crucial role along the trading routes. But life in these land-locked islands would have been impossible without agriculture, and the main limiting factor for the growth of plants in deserts is water. What characterizes the agriculture of oases is the use of ingenious techniques and complex irrigation systems that permit the extraction and exploitation of water from surface aquifers. The expansion of the Arabs in the Middle Ages helped to spread hydraulic technologies and crops from different regions. The result was the appearance of agricultural ecosystems that were largely freed from the environmental constraints of arid climates, in which man was able to introduce species from different regions. Before the discovery of America the greatest relocation of vegetable species in history occurred precisely across the deserts and oases of Asia and Africa in the medieval Islamic world.

Juan García Latorre

See also China; Sahara; Sahel; United States—Southwest

Further Reading

Amin, S. (1972). *Sullo sviluppo desiguale delle formazioni sociali.* Milan: Terzo Mondo.

Barich, B. E. (1998). *People, water and grain: The beginnings of domestication in the Sahara and the Nile Valley.* (Studia Archaeologica No. 98.) Rome: "L'"Erma" di Bretschneider.

Clouldsley-Thowson, J. L. (Ed.). (1984). *Sahara Desert.* Oxford, U.K.: Pergamon Press.

Cremaschi, M., & Lernia, S. (Eds.). (1998). *Wadi Teshuinat: Palaeoenviroment and Prehistory in south-western Fezzan (Lybian Sahara).* Florence, Italy: C.I.R.S.A.

Cribb, R. (1993). *Nomads in archaeology.* New York: Cambridge University Press.

Evenari, M., Schulze, E.-D., Lange, O. L., & Kappen, L. (1976). Plant production in arid and semi-arid areas. In: O. L. Lange, L. Kappe, and E.-D. Schulze (Eds.), *Water and plant life* (pp. 439–451). Berlin, Germany: Springer-Verlag.

Godelier, M. (1984). *L' idéel et le matériel.* Paris: Librairie Arthème Fayard.

Gumilev, L. N. (1988). *Searches for an imaginary kingdom: The legend of the kingdom of Prester John.* Cambridge, UK: Cambridge University Press.

Harris, D. R. (Ed.). (1996). *The origins and spread of agriculture and pastoralism in Eurasia.* Washington, DC: Smithsonian Institution Press.

Howell, N. (1979). *Demography of the Dobe Arca Kung.* New York: Academic Press.

Hunter-Anderson, R. L. (1986). *Prehistoric adaptation in the American South-West.* Cambridge, UK: Cambridge University Press.

Jabbur, J. S. (1995). *The Bedouins and the desert.* New York: State University of New York Press.

Khazanov, A. M. (1984). *Nomads and the outside world.* Cambridge, UK: Cambridge University Press.

Lee, R. B. (1979). *The Kung San: Men, women and work in a foraging society.* Cambridge, UK: Cambridge University Press.

Mc Neill, J. (2001). *Something new under the sun. An environmental history of the twentieth century.* London: Penguin History.

Renfrew, C. (1987). *Archaeology and language. The puzzle of Indo-European origins.* London: Jonathan Cape.

Schultz, J. (1995). *The ecozones of the world: The ecological divisions of the geosphere.* Berlin, Germany: Springer-Verlag.

Shmida, A., Evenari, M., & Noy-Meir, I. (1986). Hot deserts ecosystems: An integrated view. In M. Evenari, I. Noy-Meir, & D. W. Goodall (Eds.), *Hot deserts and arid shrublands* (Vol. B., pp. 379–387). Amsterdam: Elsevier.

Webb, J. L. (1995). *Desert frontier: Ecological and economic change along the western sahel, 1600–1850.* Madison: University of Wisconsin Press.

West, N. E. (Ed.). (1983). *Temperate deserts and semi-deserts.* Amsterdam: Elsevier.

Development Narratives

In their simplest form, development narratives are the rules of thumb, arguments, crisis narratives, "war stories," and other scenarios about how development has, can, and should proceed. Development narratives enable decision makers to take action, whether the decision makers be farmers, bureaucrats, policy makers, agency managers, outside experts, or others. More formally, development narratives are scenarios (stories and arguments) that articulate the assumptions that guide decision making about development in situations of high complexity, uncertainty, and conflict—which is to say, most situations. Each narrative has a beginning, middle, and end (or premises and conclusions, if cast as an argument) and revolves around a sequence of events or positions in which something is said to happen or from which something is said to follow.

The most extreme of these development narratives are well-known and often environmental. If resource extraction is going up, it must be because of globalization. If trees are being cut, it must be deforestation, however many trees are being planted elsewhere. If the Sahel (the arid semidesert region bordering the Sahara) advances a measurable amount, it must be because of desertification or global climate change. But it gets worse: Development narratives can be connected together. Pity the poor nation in a continent called "Except-Africa" (as in "development works everywhere . . . except Africa") facing its doomsday scenario of rising populations, devastating disease, human-induced droughts and land degradation, mass exodus of poor people from the countryside, rising urban unemployment, political unrest, riots in the streets, another coup . . . another basket case!

Many development narratives may be much less invidious, but people just do not know if this is so. For the point about development narratives is that they persist precisely because rural and urban development is so difficult. Development is a genuinely difficult activity, and one of the principal ways practitioners, bureaucrats, policy makers, and other decision makers (including citizens) articulate and make sense of its complexity, uncertainty, conflict, and unfinished business is to tell scenarios and formulate arguments that fix and steady that reality enough to make decisions about it. People undertaking development want to do something now—often urgently so—without waiting for the world to become more certain, simple, agreeable, and complete. Indeed, the pressure to generate narratives about development is directly related to the difficulty decision makers experience over that development.

There are many ways to change development narratives. One is to critique a narrative's arguments and story line, which may reveal that its points are empirically unfounded or implausible. Unfortunately, critique on its own does little to make the process of arriving at a decision easier or clearer, since critiques do not replace the debunked narrative with anything useful to the decision makers. Thus, there is often pressure to generate counternarrative—scenarios or arguments that people find more convincing than the development narrative critiqued. Indeed, many would argue that there can be no true rural or urban development, especially in the environmental arena, without these alternative counternarratives. The literature on development narratives gives other examples of how to displace discredited narratives.

Emery Roe

Further Reading

Escobar, A. (1996). *Encountering development: The making and unmaking of the Third World.* Princeton: Princeton University Press.

Gasper, D., & Apthorpe, R. (1996). Introduction: Discourse analysis and policy discourse. *The European Journal of Development Research, 8*(1), 1–15.

Hoben, A. (1995). Paradigms and politics: The cultural construction of environmental policy in Ethiopia. In: *World Development, 23*(6), 1007–1022.

Leach, M., & Mearns, R. (1996). *The lie of the land.* Oxford, UK and Portsmouth, NH: International African Institute in association with James Currey and Heinemann.

Rocheleau, D. E., Steinberg, P., & Benjamin, P. (1995). Environment, development, crisis and crusade: Ukambani, Kenya 1890–1990. *World Development, 23*(6), 1037–1051.

Roe, E. (1999). *Except-Africa: Remaking development, rethinking power*. New Brunswick, NJ: Transaction Publishers.

Dewey, John
(1859–1952)
U.S. philosopher

U.S. philosopher John Dewey was the leading proponent of pragmatism, an early twentieth-century philosophical movement that rejected belief in universal truth for the proposition that knowledge and experience are ever-evolving modes of an organism adapting to its environment. Dewey and his fellow pragmatists abandoned the search for philosophical methods that best discover reality in favor of applied intelligence that successfully engages reality. Dewey's unique achievement was to reinterpret the traditional concerns of continental philosophy (such as metaphysics, logic, ethics, and aesthetics) in light of pragmatist convictions. He also championed a strong conception of democracy as the core of pragmatism. Throughout his career Dewey remained politically active and conceived his philosophy as a form of social criticism.

Dewey's activism and insistence on judging ideas by their application in social situations resulted in part from the tumultuous upheavals that characterized American history during his life. Born in Vermont, Dewey spent his youth in Burlington, which was a growing city bustling with Irish and French-Canadian workers who were often at odds with the local Yankee business owners. The social conflicts visible in Burlington typified the dramatic transformations that were rapidly changing American society. The Industrial Revolution transformed America from a loosely organized, largely rural society into an urban, technical, industrial, and multinational capitalist world power. Dewey called for and theorized the reform of the liberal democratic tradition so that it could effectively grapple with urbanization and industrialization. To that end he sought to extend the experimental methods of the natural sciences to the social and cultural spheres; suggestively, he preferred to call his philosophy "experimentalism" rather than "pragmatism." He argued that the concrete achievements of the natural sciences serve as an example of democratic social intelligence.

Although Dewey wrote on many topics of public concern, his greatest fame came from his championing of progressive education. As a professor at the University of Chicago he worked with the renowned Cook County Normal School and soon opened his own institution, the Laboratory School (widely known as the "Dewey School") in 1896. Dewey advocated a flexible curriculum that recognized the autonomy of each student yet provided each student with relevant and intelligent guidance. Furthermore, Dewey conceived of education as preparation for democratic citizenship, helping students learn the social intelligence and problem-solving skills upon which democratic societies depend.

Dewey's legacy to environmental thought is his insistence on using an ecological organism/environment model to understand human behavior. All elements of Dewey's philosophy theorized humans as inexorably intertwined with nature. Occasionally he commented on conservation: "Without abundant store of natural resources, equal liberty for all is out of the question," argued Dewey in a 1937 essay "Freedom" (251). "Conservation of not only the public domain but restoration of worn-out land to fertility, the combating of floods and erosion which have reduced vast portions of our national heritage to something like desert, are the penalties we have to pay for past indulgence in an orgy of so-called economic liberty."

Kevin C. Armitage

Further Reading

Dewey, J. (1987). "Freedom." In J. A. Boyston (Ed.), *The later works, 1935–1937*. Carbondale: Southern Illinois Press, pp. 247–255.

Fott, D. (1998). *John Dewey: America's philosopher of democracy*. Lanham, MD: Rowman & Littlefield.

Hickman, L. A. (1990). *John Dewey's pragmatic technology*. Bloomington: Indiana University Press.

Menand, L. (2001). *The metaphysical club*. New York: Farrar, Straus and Giroux.

Ryan, A. (1995). *John Dewey and the high tide of American liberalism*. New York: W.W. Norton.

Rockefeller, S. (1991). *John Dewey, religious faith and democratic humanism*. New York: Columbia University Press.

West, C. (1989). *The American evasion of philosophy*. Madison: University of Wisconsin Press.

Westbrook, R. B. (1991). *John Dewey and American democracy*. Ithaca, NY: Cornell University Press.

Diamonds

The word *diamond* comes from two Greek words: *diaphanes* and *adamas*. The former means "transparent" and the latter, "invincible," two characteristics of diamonds that are evident in their clarity, brightness, and hardness. Diamonds have been valued for their hardness since antiquity, because they cannot be damaged by any other stone or destroyed by fire.

Diamonds have been prized as jewelry for millennia because of the beauty of their brightness. The quality of a diamond is measured by the combination of the number of carats, color, transparence, and lapidary (the art of cutting gems). Diamonds are found in every color, red being the rarest. Brightness is achieved by cutting a diamond at perfect and proportional angles.

Origins

Diamonds were formed 150 to 200 kilometers below the Earth's surface over the course of millions of years. They were brought closer to the Earth's surface by volcanic eruptions and other natural cataclysms that occurred around 100 million years ago.

Several methods are used to find diamonds, such as the use of open mines, river mines, subterranean mines, and, more rarely, sea mines. The rarity of diamonds increases their value; from 226 metric tons of rock and sand comes only one carat of diamond, which corresponds to one-fifth of a gram of weight. World production is estimated at 100 million carats a year, but only 20 percent of diamonds are used in jewelry.

Like the graphite used in lead pencils, diamonds are made of carbon, but the atomic structures of graphite and diamonds are different. The carbon atoms in diamonds are strongly attached and remain very closed in contrast to the carbon atoms in graphite, which are distant and weakly connected. This is because diamonds were produced under very great pressure deep in the Earth, enclosing the carbon atoms in a compact and dense cubic structure.

Mining and Production

Exploration for diamonds began in India between 800 and 600 BCE. For two thousand years India monopolized world production. In Europe diamonds were used during Greek times, and their use spread during Roman times, but for a long time diamonds were the privilege of kings and religious authorities. During the Middle Ages people believed diamonds could ward off poisons, fears, and magic spells. But diamonds were prized most for the beauty of their brightness. In the fifteenth century people began to associate diamonds with love, engagement, and marriage. For example, in 1477 Archduke Maximiliano Austria gave his fiancée, Mary Burgundy, a diamond as the symbol of their engagement.

During the eighteenth century Brazil became an important source of diamonds. The main area of diamond exploration is in northeastern Minas Gerais State near Diamantina City. Diamonds were found there in the 1720s, and several laws were passed in order to organize and control their production. Diamonds were found in rivers, and thus the use of water was important for diamond exploitation. At first exploration was open to anyone who paid a tax had slaves to work a piece of land. But in 1739 the Portuguese crown, which controlled Brazil, granted a monopoly to contractors, who bought the right to mine diamonds. By 1753, with diamond contractors retaining the right of exploitation, the Portuguese crown held a monopoly on the trade. Finally, in 1771, under the administration of the marquis of Pombal, the Portuguese crown also monopolized the exploitation of diamonds and created a state company, the Diamond Royal Extraction.

The mother rock, in which diamonds are found, is called "kimberlite" because it was first found in Kimberley, South Africa, which became important in diamond production after the nineteenth century. Kimberlite wasn't found in Brazil until the 1990s, and it was not found in Diamantina, as had been expected, but rather in another area of Minas Gerais State called Triângulo Mineiro and also in Mato Grosso do Sul State. Today the most important sources of diamonds are Australia and Zaire for industrial use and South Africa, Australia, and Namibia for use in jewelry.

Environmental Implications

The exploration for diamonds causes a great deal of ecological damage, especially when diamonds are located in rivers. The surrounding forests are devastated to provide space and materials for the exploration and subsequent mining—a fact that was observed by the Brazilian naturalist José Vieira Couto in the eighteenth

Renowned Diamonds

Since the Middle Ages people have given names to the most remarkable diamonds. The largest and most beautiful diamonds have intriguing histories, and today they usually belong to museums and private collections. A slave in Minas Gerais in Brazil used the South Star diamond in 1853 to buy her freedom. After being polished it weighed 128 carats and was clear white. The Hope diamond, also known as "the cursed diamond," was found in India in 1642. It is blue and weighs 112 carats. It was taken to Europe, where it was bought by French King Louis XIV, who named it the "Crown Blue diamond." It was stolen during the French Revolution and reappeared in 1830 in London when Henry Thomas Hope, a banker, bought it. His son died just after inheriting it, starting the dark history that surrounds the diamond. In 1908 the sultan of Turkey Abdul Harmid got sick just after he bought the diamond, and in 1911 Evelyn MacLean, a North American millionaire, lost her son and her fortune and killed herself just after she bought it. Today the Hope diamond can be seen in the Smithsonian Museum in Washington, DC. The Koh-I-Noor diamond, also known as the "Light Mountain," belonged to an Indian rajah and a Persian shah. An Englishman stole it from a Hindu temple and gave it to Queen Victoria. It weighs 108.92 carats and remains in the Tower of London as part of a crown that belonged to Queen Mary. The story of the Florentine diamond—yellow and 137.27 carats—began in 1657 when the Medici family of Italy bought it. It also belonged to the Habsburg dynasty. It disappeared just after World War I.

—Junia Furtado

century. There are also alterations in the course of the rivers and erosion of the riverbanks, and chemicals used in the exploration and mining process may poison both the fish and those who derive their livelihoods from fishing. In addition, exploration and mining without control or precautions cause changes in climate, the extinction of certain species of animal and plant life, and deterioration of the soil.

Junia Furtado

Further Reading

Diamants, exposition au museum national d'histoire naturelle [Diamonds, exposition at the National Museum of Natural History]. (2001). Paris: Société Française de Promotion Artistique.

Erlich, E., & Hausel, W. D. (2002). *Diamond deposits: Origin, exploration, and history of discovery.* Littleton, CO: Society for Mining, Metallurgy, and Exploration.

Furtado, J. F. (1996). *O Livro da Capa Verde: a vida no Distrito Diamantino no período Real Extração* [The book of the green cover: life in the diamond district]. São Paulo, Brazil: Anna Blume.

Dioxins

Dioxins are chlorinated organic compounds that are classified, along with polychlorinated biphenyls (PCBs) and similar chemicals, as persistent organic pollutants. Described as "the archetype of toxic chemicals" (Webster and Commoner 1994, 1), dioxins have generated scientific and political controversies over their production, distribution, and health and environmental effects. Since the late 1960s several high-profile incidents have fueled public fears about dioxin exposure and led to attempts to reduce production of dioxins.

Environmental Fate and Behavior

The term *dioxins* refers generically to 210 polychlorinated dibenzo-p-dioxins (PCDDs) and polychlorinated dibenzofurans (PCDFs or furans), distinguished by their chemical structure, which determines their environmental behavior and health effects. This structure consists of two benzene (hydrocarbon) rings connected by a bridge of one oxygen atom (PCDFs) or two oxygen atoms (PCDDs) and up to eight chlorine atoms attached to the benzene rings. Of these 210 compounds, only 7 PCDDs and 10 PCDFs are considered toxic. The most extensively studied and most toxic of this group is 2,3,7,8-tetrachlorodibenzo-p-dioxin (TCDD), often called simply "dioxin."

Unlike PCBs, dioxins have never been intentionally produced; rather they are byproducts of combustion and industrial processes. The leading source appears to be chemical, hospital, sewage, and municipal waste incineration; other important sources include the synthesis of pesticides and herbicides (including 2,4,5-T and 2,4-D), leaded gasoline combustion, pulp and paper bleaching, polyvinyl chloride (PVC) plastic production, aluminum smelting, coal-fired utilities, and production of magnesium, nickel, iron, and steel. In the environment, dioxins and other persistent organic pollutants are characterized by the potential for long-range atmospheric transport, toxicity, resistance to degradation, and bioaccumulation and concentration in the food chain. Their global distribution, far from production sources, makes these chemicals a concern worldwide.

Despite extensive study and testing, considerable debate remains over the precise human health effects of dioxins and the levels of exposure that produce them. Most observers agree that acute exposure produces the severe skin condition chloracne. Dioxins produce cancer, genetic mutations, birth defects, reproductive abnormalities, immunotoxic effects, and endocrine disruption in laboratory tests, but translating these results to human effects, especially at low doses, is controversial. Epidemiological studies of human occupational, accidental, or environmental exposures are likewise sources of scientific and public dispute.

Because they are fat soluble, dioxins concentrate in animal and human fatty tissues, and most human exposure is via the food chain. Samples from around the world reveal background concentrations in human tissues in the parts per trillion. Although this "body burden" has reportedly declined since the 1980s due to the control or elimination of many sources, the persistence of dioxins in environmental "reservoirs" and animal tissues means they may still pose a significant risk. Regulatory agencies worldwide have set safe human tissue levels for dioxins in the low parts per trillion, reflecting the concern and uncertainty surrounding their toxicity.

Origins and History of Human Exposure

Soil samples show a rapid increase in dioxin levels coinciding with the development of the industrial chlorine chemistry in the twentieth century. Scientists identified dioxins in the 1950s when chemical workers developed chloracne after spills or other releases. Animal testing in the 1970s revealed dioxins, especially TCDD, to be potent carcinogens. However, studies of pesticide and waste-disposal workers in Sweden, Germany, and the United States failed to definitively connect human dioxin exposure to cancer, although a wide range of noncancerous effects were documented.

Dioxin exploded into public consciousness through two episodes of acute public exposure. In 1968 almost two thousand Japanese were poisoned by PCB- and PCDF-contaminated rice oil in the Yusho, or "oil disease," incident. Confirmed health effects included severe chloracne and skin pigmentation, developmental problems in breast-feeding infants and children exposed in utero, and some liver function disruption. Cancer deaths have not been conclusively linked to the Yusho incident. Similar health effects resulted from the exposure of residents of Seveso, Italy, in 1976 after an industrial accident at a pesticide plant released a chemical cloud containing a large amount of TCDD. Affected neighborhoods were not evacuated for three weeks, even though many domestic animals died within days. Some Seveso studies have suggested links between TCDD exposure and elevated cancer risk.

Uncertainty also surrounds the exposure of American soldiers during Operation Ranch Hand, the U.S. Army's use of the defoliant Agent Orange (which was laced with dioxins) during the Vietnam War. In the late 1970s and early 1980s some veterans reported health problems including cancers, birth defects in their children, and neurological and hormonal conditions. Veterans' lawsuits and battles with government scientists instigated U.S. congressional hearings in 1989 and led to the eventual compensation of "Ranch Hands" for a limited number of medical conditions. Other major dioxin controversies in the United States included the discovery of soil and groundwater contamination at Love Canal, New York, in 1978 and at Times Beach, Missouri, in 1983.

Toward Dioxin Regulation

Heightened public anxiety has meant that attempts to regulate dioxins and determine acceptable health risks have been deeply politicized. Prominent scientists such as Barry Commoner have confronted government and industry scientists with evidence of the cellular mechanism by which dioxins enter and disrupt human systems. Other scientists have cast doubt on the purported carcinogenic effects of dioxins at the low levels encountered by the general public. Environmental groups have accused the U.S. Environmental Protection Agency (EPA) of stalling or covering up assessments linking dioxins with health and environmental problems and of colluding with industry to conceal dioxin pollution from pulp and paper mill effluent. An EPA reassessment of dioxins begun in 1991 attempted to characterize dioxin health risks, sparking a flurry of criticism from scientists and the chlorine industry; delays and scientific reviews meant that in 2002 the reassessment remained in draft form.

Improved scientific understanding of dioxins has spurred global efforts to reduce emissions. In the 1980s the United Nations Environment Programme initiated studies and conventions for the control of persistent organic pollutants, and the International Agency for Research into Cancer has since classified TCDD as a "known human carcinogen." More recently, the Stockholm Convention on Persistent Organic Pollutants was signed by 151 countries in 2001–2002, paving the way for a global program to identify and reduce dioxins in the environment.

Arn Keeling

Further Reading

Bartlett, R. A. (1991). *Troubled waters: Champion International and the Pigeon River controversy*. Knoxville: University of Tennessee Press.

De Vito, M. J., & Gallo, M. A. (2000). Dioxins and dioxin-like chemicals. In M. Lippman (Ed.), *Environmental toxicants: Human exposures and their health effects* (pp.243–266). New York: John Wiley & Sons.

Gibbs, L. M. (1995). *Dying from dioxin: A citizen's guide to reclaiming our health and rebuilding our democracy*. Boston: South End Press.

Gough, M. (1986). *Dioxin, Agent Orange: The facts*. New York: Plenum Press.

Harrad, S. (2001). The environmental behaviour of persistent organic pollutants. In R. Harrison (Ed.), *Pollution: Causes, effects and control* (4th ed., pp. 445–473). Cambridge, UK: Royal Society of Chemistry.

Schecter, A. (Ed.). (1994). *Dioxins and health*. New York: Plenum Press.

Thornton, J. (2000). *Pandora's poison: Chlorine, health, and a new environmental strategy*. Cambridge, MA: MIT Press.

U.S. Environmental Protection Agency, National Center for Environmental Assessment. *Dioxin and related compounds*. Retrieved January 24, 2003, from http://cfpub.epa.gov/ncea/cfm/dioxin.cfm

Van Strum, C., & Merrell, P. (1987). *No margin of safety: A preliminary report on dioxin pollution and the need for emergency action in the pulp and paper industry*. Seattle, WA: Greenpeace USA.

Webster, T., & Commoner, B. (1994). Overview: The dioxin debate. In A. Schecter (Ed.), *Dioxins and health* (pp. 1–50). New York: Plenum Press.

World Health Organization. *Dioxins and their effects on human health*. Retrieved January 25, 2003, http://www.who.int/fsf/Chemicalcontaminants/

Diseases, Animal

Almost all of the contagious diseases that have caused major health problems for humans have originated in nonhuman animals and have "jumped the species barrier." Thus animal diseases and human diseases cannot clearly be separated when discussing the impact of animal diseases on human environments. Noncontagious animal diseases rarely cause environmental problems of any significance. It is also important to emphasize that humans are mammals, so diseases found in other nonhuman animals, especially mammals, can often cross readily into humans.

Prominent examples include smallpox, cholera, tuberculosis, bubonic plague, influenza, and AIDS. In recent years there have been panics over other animal diseases such as brucellosis and hoof-and-mouth disease, Hanta virus, and so-called mad cow disease, which may not be a disease in the usual sense at all. The impact of the latter diseases are trivial compared to the impact of the former, yet they have received more publicity, perhaps because of media-inspired fear and ignorance.

Most animal diseases that jump to humans are caused by bacteria and viruses whose small size and evolutionary history make them highly volatile, hence more likely to be transmitted from one individual to another, which is the basis of contagion. A few diseases, such as malaria and sleeping sickness, are caused by single-celled organisms, but their larger size means they cannot be transmitted as aerosols and are transmitted primarily by injection, for example, through insect bites.

What makes most of these diseases so virulent in human populations is that they have coevolved in interactions with other species, which have also co-evolved an immune response to them so that they are not serious illnesses in their original host species. When first exposed, humans have no evolved immune response to these pathogens (agents of disease); for example, smallpox is related to bovine pox, which causes minor problems in cattle but is often fatal in its mutated form in humans. Similarly, the AIDS virus is closely related to a viral infection that occurs in African primates, where it causes only mild influenza-like symptoms. Other examples include measles, which is closely related to the ungulate disease rinderpest; tuberculosis, which is closely related to a similar disease in cattle; and influenza, which is actually a complex of viral diseases derived repeatedly from similar pathogens occurring both in pigs (swine flu) and birds such as ducks and chickens.

Contagious diseases that managed to cross the species barrier from nonhumans into humans have been a major environmental factor in shaping the history of Europe and Asia. The development of agricultural practices, in particular domestication of ungulates, set up a scenario whereby humans were continually exposed to a wide range of epidemic diseases that already afflicted the ungulate populations and thrived within the high densities at which human societies kept cattle and pigs. Farmers are sedentary, living among both their own sewage and that of the domestic animals with whom they live in an intimate and symbiotic fashion. In many agrarian societies farmers take cattle and pigs into their homes at night, both for warmth and to protect their livestock from predators. These conditions prolong exposure to bacterial and viral pathogens.

Agriculture sustains much higher human densities than the hunting-gathering lifestyle that agriculture replaced. The large concentrations of humans resulting from increased urbanization provided fertile ground for the rapid spread of infectious diseases that originated in other species. Only within the last century did European cities achieve self-sustaining populations because so many city dwellers died from disease that constant immigration from rural areas was required to sustain urban areas. For example, bubonic plague is spread by fleas that pick up the plague bacillus from the fur-bearing mammals that are their normal hosts. Plague first appeared in Europe in the mid-sixth century CE and had a devastating impact in the fourteenth century in continental Europe (the "Black Death"), where it killed as many as 25 million people. In the British Isles in the seventeenth century plague killed

25–30 percent of the total population. One of the major vectors (agents of transmission) for plague appears to have been furs brought from areas of low population density in central Asia with the opening of trade routes to China in the mid-fourteenth century.

Old and New Worlds

The importance of animal diseases in shaping both human history and cultural attitudes toward the environment can be illustrated by comparing the Old World (Eurasia and north Africa) with the New World (the Americas). Many cultures in the Americas developed agriculture, but it was based almost exclusively around agronomy (a branch of agriculture dealing with field-crop production and soil management), for example, corn, potatoes, squash, and beans, rather than on pastoralism. The only animals domesticated in the Americas were dogs, guinea pigs, guanacos (llama and alpaca), and turkeys. Unlike the domesticated ungulates of the Old World, these New World domesticates were never maintained at high densities, humans did not drink their milk, nor were any of these animals except dogs kept in close proximity to humans, as livestock were in the Old World.

Many New World cultures existed at densities comparable to those in Europe. The Aztec capital of Tenochtitlan in Mexico may have been one of the largest cities in the world during its heyday. Similarly, many other New World communities such as cities of the Mayans, Incas, and the Mound Builder cultures along the Mississippi and Ohio River valleys lived at densities comparable to those in European and Asian cultures. Epidemic diseases appear to have been virtually nonexistent in these indigenous New World cultures, which is almost certainly attributable to the absence of domestic ungulates, which have been the source of epidemic diseases in Europe, Asia, and northern Africa.

The absence of nonhuman-derived contagious diseases and associated immune responses in New World humans was certainly a major factor in the successful invasion of the New World by Europeans. The most devastating environmental consequence of the introduction of animal diseases into susceptible human populations was what has been referred to as the first, or microbial, phase of the European conquest of the Americas. Contrary to popular mythology this did not begin with the "discovery of the Americas" by Columbus in 1492 but rather was initiated earlier by Basque whalers, Viking settlers, and English fishermen who began landing along the Atlantic coast of the Americas well before Columbus arrived in the Caribbean and other Spanish explorers (conquistadors) arrived in the New World.

Despite the success of conquistadors such as Hernan Cortes and Francisco Pizarro, it was actually smallpox that led to the collapse of the Aztec and Inca empires. Cortes's initial 1519 foray into the Aztec civilization was much less successful than his subsequent 1520 foray after smallpox arrived in Tenochtitlan. By the early seventeenth century the indigenous population of Mexico had fallen from an estimated 20 million to less than 2 million. Similarly, smallpox arrived in Inca territory in 1526, setting up the opportunity for Pizarro's successful "invasion" in 1531. There are well-documented cases of 90 percent or more of indigenous populations being wiped out by these new contagious diseases that arrived with both Europeans and their symbiotic nonhumans. The Mandans, one of the most elaborate of the Great Plains cultures, suffered mortality of more than 95 percent of their population after arrival of smallpox on a Missouri riverboat in 1837.

Not only humans suffered as a result of the introduction of these diseases. Many natural populations of animals, including deer, caribou, moose, bison, and beaver, also experienced massive die-offs from west of Hudson's Bay to the Rocky Mountains during the latter part of the eighteenth century. These deaths probably resulted from disease introduced by Europeans through their domestic animals. It is worth noting that these die-offs were almost exclusively among ungulate populations, which would have been most susceptible to the ungulate-derived contagious diseases characteristic of Europe and Asia. Carnivores appeared relatively unaffected by these illnesses but suffered as a result of loss of their ungulate food supplies.

One ironic consequence of this introduction of nonhuman-derived diseases was the destruction of cultural traditions based on respect for nonhumans. Most, if not all, of the indigenous cultures of North America had philosophical traditions in which nonhumans were regarded as creator spirits, and the concept of relatedness was based upon ecological relationships. It has been argued that the devastating impact of introduced disease on these cultures caused them to turn on their nonhuman relatives, leading some tribes to be willing to wipe out local populations of beaver, deer, bison, and wolves in order to trade furs for European trade goods and metal.

Different Perspectives

The invading European tradition, derived primarily from English and Scottish cultures, had a different relationship with the natural world. Western European cultural tradition consistently works to separate itself from any association with the natural world, except as a source of resources for exploitation. Protestant Christian sects developed philosophical traditions that offered no encouragement for investigation into the ways of God's creatures. God had given humans "dominion" over the creatures, and that was sufficient justification for any action regarding the natural world.

Europeans regarded mountainous country as unpleasant and dangerous, and forests were considered to be even worse. That these places were wild, hence untamed, was sufficient to trigger terror and hostility in western Europeans. The "wild" (natural world) was so unreasonably fearsome that encroachment of wild creatures into the human domain was highly alarming. A bee flying into a cottage or a bird rapping at the window was enough to frighten people. The English House of Commons rejected a bill in 1604 because a jackdaw (a bird related to the crow) flew through the chamber during the speech of its sponsor.

This difference in response to the nonhuman (natural) world continues to manifest itself in contemporary responses to animal-borne diseases that are often extreme in comparison to the actual threat posed. The most egregious response in recent years has been the slaughter of hundreds of thousands of farm animals, particularly in the British Isles and their cultural descendant, the United States, in response to minor outbreaks of hoof-and-mouth disease and the sporadic and highly unusual occurrence of so-called mad cow disease.

In the case of hoof-and-mouth disease the threat is almost exclusively economic. There is little evidence that hoof-and-mouth disease represents any serious threat to human health. Still, the economic threat is deemed sufficient to destroy hundreds of thousands of animals, mostly because the possibility exists that they may have been exposed to the disease. Similarly, wild bison that stray beyond the borders of Yellowstone National Park in the United States are summarily slaughtered by agents of the state of Montana on the grounds that these animals might act as reservoirs for the cattle disease brucellosis. The irony in this case is that brucellosis is a disease that evolved in Old World bovids and was introduced into the United States along with cattle. No bison has ever been demonstrated to show the symptoms of brucellosis, yet the fact that a low percentage of bison test positive for exposure to the pathogen is deemed sufficient reason to kill them.

Mad Cow Disease

The response to so-called mad cow disease, more properly called "bovine spongiform encephalopathy" (BSE), is even more absurd. BSE appears to be one of a group of related pathological conditions that may be caused by "prions," which appear to be protein molecules capable of self-replication. Other diseases in this group are scrapie in sheep and kuru and Creutzfeldt-Jakob syndrome in humans. Such pathological conditions impact the central nervous system and gradually destroy the brain. The damage to the central nervous system is what produces the symptoms that have led to this condition being designated as "mad cow disease." A more accurate term would be "acutely distressed cow disease," but this does not scan as well in headlines or roll off the tongues of newscasters as readily. These apparently prion-based conditions are not directly communicable and can be passed only through consumption of central nervous system tissue, including brain and spinal cord. The only reason these conditions appeared to spread in the United States and England is because slaughterhouses in those countries use "wastes" remaining after butchering to be ground up and added to cattle feed as a protein supplement.

In humans it is obvious that only by consuming central nervous system material can humans become infected. Outbreaks of kuru in New Guinea are clearly related to the cultural tradition of consuming the brains of other humans as part of a cannibalistic tradition. In England BSE-type syndromes have shown up in humans who consumed low-grade commercial hamburgers. It seems obvious that banning use of the waste products of slaughterhouses in both hamburger for human consumption and in cattle feed could stop any possible outbreak, yet commercial pressures have slowed or prevented such moves. Still, the total number of BSE human victims numbers less than twenty, and there is little likelihood of an outbreak or of a human contracting BSE by eating regular beef in the form of roasts or steaks.

Hanta virus is a rodent-borne viral pathogen. There is actually an entire class of Hanta-like viruses in a variety of murid (the family of mice and rats) rodents. The one described as "Hanta virus" appears to have only one species, deer mice (*Peromyscus maniculatus*),

as its primary host, where it does not appear to cause significant health problems. In humans, however, this virus causes pneumonia-like symptoms that result in death about 50 percent of the time. This disease is well known to indigenous peoples of the U.S. Southwest and may be one of the reasons why traditional Navajo people destroy a hogan after a person has died in it. In recent years this disease has caused a minor panic in the United States because deer mice are a common rodent. Hanta virus does not appear to be transmissible among humans, so it is unlikely to ever become a true epidemic. The number of recorded cases in the United States is less than two hundred since the Centers for Disease Control have been keeping records.

To summarize, the major environmental and health problems in humans result primarily from close association with domestic animals. This association has allowed several diseases to jump from their ungulate or avian hosts and cross the species barrier into humans. Almost all of these problems result from a lack of proper respect for nonhumans, which is a legacy of the western European philosophical and economic traditions.

Raymond Pierotti

Further Reading

Cockburn, A. (1967) *Infectious diseases: Their evolution and eradication.* Springfield, IL: Thomas Press.

Diamond, J. (1997). *Guns, germs, and steel: The fates of human societies.* New York: W. W. Norton.

Dobyns, H. (1983). *Their numbers become thinned.* Knoxville: University of Tennessee Press.

Ewald, P. (1994). *Evolution of infectious disease.* Oxford, UK: Oxford University Press.

Martin, C. L. (1978). *Keepers of the game: Indian animal relationships and the fur trade.* Berkeley and Los Angeles: University of California Press.

May, J. M. (1958). *The ecology of human disease.* New York: MD Publications.

May, J. M. (1961). *Studies in disease ecology.* New York: Hapner Publishing.

Diseases, Human

The environments of human diseases have geographical/climatic, cultural, and biological factors. Prior to the development of urbanism, agriculture, increased sedentism (settlement), and large population centers, humans throughout the world lived in smaller, more mobile communities that were not disease free but did not suffer the epidemic diseases and crowd-type diseases that came later. Early populations suffered from trauma (mostly accidental as opposed to interpersonal), parasites, and various forms of infection, including those that involved bone disease, dental disease, and arthritic conditions. The infectious diseases that contributed to great human morbidity and mortality later are believed to have originated mostly in southeastern Asia and Africa. In the Old World several environmental factors combined to change the pattern of disease. The development of agriculture involved larger human communities, which were more stationery and had less dietary variety. Although agriculture offered control over the food supply, it also made it more vulnerable in some environments to the destructive nature of weather-related events. The resulting famine and malnutrition were problems themselves and lowered human resistance to pathogens (agents of disease). Irrigation techniques created breeding grounds for disease organisms, and associated plowing techniques may have increased the risk of fungal diseases. The semipermanent settlements that frequently were associated with agriculture increased the likelihood of contaminated water supply and pathogen exposure due to human contact with compromised environments.

Urbanism brought even larger crowd-type disease problems. The associated social stratification may have limited food access and variety. Migration and merchant travel increased contact among communities and allowed mobility of human-associated pathogens as well. With population growth, urbanism, travel, and many other cultural/environmental factors, Europeans witnessed leprosy as a major health problem in the Middle Ages, followed by tuberculosis and the Black Death. Bubonic plague reached Europe by 547 CE, likely from the Himalayan area. It returned in the middle of the fourteenth century, likely from China, and periodically ravaged European populations until the early eighteenth century. Obviously, the climate and location were suitable for the organism, *Yersinia pestis*, but also present were host rodents and perhaps cultural factors that contributed to the impact of the disease, such as thatch-roof houses that provided rodent habitat and stimulated contact between infected fleas and human occupants. In various times and places, measles, smallpox, typhus, cholera, dysentery, tuberculosis, influenza, schistosomiasis, and other diseases

in addition to bubonic plague have caused much loss of human life and affected survivors as well. Factors influencing the rise and impact of these diseases are complex but are deeply rooted in culture and population dynamics. In general, the mortality impact has been greatest when reaching a population with no or minimal previous exposure. Cultural factors such as trade, exploration, and warfare have created such long-range contacts stimulating epidemics.

Tuberculosis is a disease caused by the bacillus *Mycobacterium tuberculosis*. The disease is easily spread through aerial transmission, but complex factors influence the disease expression (the impact of a disease on any particular person), such as biological attributes of the person affected and such cultural associations as nutrition and working and general living conditions.

Typhus is a disease caused by the organism *Rickettsia prowazekii*, transmitted by body lice. Obviously it requires a conducive human environment and is influenced by personal hygiene.

Transmission by Mosquito

Yellow fever, malaria, and dengue fever depend on the mosquito for human transmission and thus are confined to environments—climatic and cultural—in which mosquitoes are present. Yellow fever is caused by a group B virus and normally is a disease of nonhuman primates. When affecting humans it is usually transmitted by the mosquito *Aedes aegypti*, commonly associated with human occupation. Yellow fever can produce fever, hemorrhage into the digestive tract, jaundice, and headache. During historic epidemics, mortality was relatively high. During the seventeenth century severe epidemics occurred among people living in the Caribbean. Epidemics also occurred during this time and later in other areas of the world, especially port cities with Caribbean contacts. In 1900 the role of the mosquito in disease transmission was recognized, and plans were implemented to eradicate *Aedes aegypti* in troubled areas. Reduction of mosquito populations and the successful development of a vaccine greatly reduced the impact of this disease on human populations.

Malaria is a disease caused by the plasmodium—a protozoan—transmitted by the bite of a female Anopheles mosquito. Classic symptoms include chills, fever, sweating, drowsiness, and nausea. Although this disease appears to be of Old World origin, it spread throughout the Americas after European contact in areas harboring the mosquitoes. By the nineteenth cen-

The Epidemic Ghost

The following ethnographic account tells the tale of a ghost who was thought to be responsible for epidemics in Thailand.

Until the Twentieth Century, Thailand was visited by terrifying epidemics of cholera, smallpox, and other devastating diseases. The physiological and psychological consequences of these sudden epidemics were shattering, and it is not at all surprising that the culture has evolved a specialized ghost which is considered peculiarly responsible for these visitations. Since buffaloes and other farm animals are also of vital importance in the livelihood of the Bang Chan farmer, this same ghost is considered responsible for epidemics of rinderpest and other economically disastrous animal diseases.

One frequently hears the word *haa* (epidemic) in everyday speech, usually of a rough sort. *Taaj* haa means to die of an epidemic disease. *Aaj haa* is an insulting term implying that the person spoken about derives from, or is associated with, the hated and feared *haa* ghosts.

The sole effect of Epidemic Ghost is to inflict sickness in the form of epidemic diseases. Conversely, diseases of epidemic proportions are caused only by Epidemic Ghost, among all the S-s [subjects] found in the culture. If a person is stricken by a disease which, at the time, is endemic rather than epidemic or nearly so, then the diagnosis will invariably be rendered in terms of some S other than Epidemic Ghost.

Although there are no standardized notions as to the derivation of Epidemic Ghost, it is not surprising that idiosyncratic notions tend to define this S as deriving from an out-group. Thus, Monk Doctor Marvin told me that Epidemic Ghost derives from a dead Muslim or Lao—explaining that those ethnic groups like to eat fresh raw meat. The Laos do in fact like raw meat prepared in certain ways. Nai Sin, on the other hand, believes that this S derives from a Muslim who, before death, specialized in slaughtering buffaloes and chickens, and who now, as a ghost, continued to indulge in killing those animals. Muslims around Bang Chan do in fact engage disproportionately in slaughtering, a service which they render commercially to their Buddhist neighbors, whose Merit-Moral System includes a firm prohibition against the taking of animal life.

Source: Textor, Robert B. (1973). *Roster of the Gods; An Ethnography of the Supernatural in a Thai Village.* New Haven, CT: Human Relations Area Files, pp. 391–392.

tury malaria had become endemic in tropical and subtropical areas of the Americas. In the Old World malaria may have contributed to the decline of the Roman Empire and was a European health problem in the seventeenth and eighteenth centuries. As with yellow fever, control of the disease began with recognition of the mosquito as the vector and campaigns to reduce mosquito populations.

Dengue fever results from infection with an arbovirus (transmitted by infected arthropods such as mosquitoes and other insects). Symptoms include chills, headache, backache, exhaustion, high fever, slow heart rate, low blood pressure, lymph node enlargement, and skin rash. Dengue can be fatal, especially if quality treatment is not available. The disease remains a problem worldwide in areas with mosquito concentrations.

Culture is an important factor in the ecology of human disease. Mosquito-transmitted diseases require proximity of human victims to mosquito breeding grounds. Urban crowding in the tropics with lax measures to control mosquito populations contributes to the spread of these diseases.

Disease impact can be worsened by social factors. Starvation and malnutrition can weaken the human host, perhaps leading to failure of the immune system. In some cultures, poverty places humans in proximity to nonhuman animals and their potential disease vectors. Agriculture-related irrigation can provide breeding grounds for mosquitoes.

Disease impact was especially lethal in New Zealand and Hawaii because the newly introduced pathogens were associated with economic disruption and land displacement. Such social factors limit health care and contribute to the spread of disease.

The measles epidemic of 1875 in the Fiji Islands is thought to have produced exceptionally high mortality because of associated social and psychological factors. Public panic limited proper care of those affected and increased the severity of the disease.

Immunity as a Factor

The extent of immunity created by previous exposure represents a major variable in the ecology of human disease. In the history of world epidemics, those with greatest morbidity and mortality frequently have involved the introductions of new pathogens into populations with little or no recent previous exposure. Warfare, trade, and exploration create new contact among previously separated populations and thus have been factors in major epidemics.

It has been estimated that European exploration and colonization introduced diseases into previously isolated populations and killed 56 million people worldwide. Early European arrival in the Fiji Islands, Hawaii, and Tahiti brought measles, whooping cough, influenza, smallpox, tuberculosis, and venereal diseases that decimated populations.

Epidemic disease has played an important role in military campaigns. Typhus is credited with defeating Napoleon in Russia and has been a major factor in numerous other military actions. Typhoid and dysentery frequently have been associated with military operations. Disease also is cited as having slowed European expansion into Africa.

Populations arrived in the New World relatively late, mostly from Asia through the Bering Strait. The ancient geographical isolation of the Americas from the Old World impeded the spread of Old World diseases. Diseases present in pre-Columbian America were largely those supported by the environment and those that were present in the parent populations in Asia and that could survive the migration.

Research on human skeletal remains recovered from well-dated archeological contexts in the New World suggests that many diseases were present prior to European arrival. The most common health problems documented in the skeletal remains were dental disease (tooth decay, alveolar abscesses, tooth loss, periodontitis, excessive occlusal wear [wear on the biting surfaces of the teeth]), nonspecific stress indicators (lines of increased density in long bones, enamel hypoplasia [an area of the dental enamel that is underdevel-

oped], abnormal periosteal [bone deposits on the external surfaces] bone formation), fractures, arthritic conditions, and various congenital disorders. Diseases included tuberculosis, treponemal disease, leishmaniasis, and such parasites as tapeworm, pinworm, roundworm, and hookworm. Many skeletal samples also document high infant mortality.

The skeletal studies document not only that significant morbidity and mortality were present in the pre-Columbian Americas, but also that in many areas they were increasing through time. Much of this temporal increase in health problems has been linked to the development of agriculture. The shift from hunting, fishing, and gathering to domesticated food production produced not only a more restricted diet in some areas, but also a change in settlement pattern toward greater sedentism and greater population size and density. In some environments population density was sufficient to promote such diseases as tuberculosis.

Environmental Factors

The impact of disease on early American populations was influenced by not only cultural but also geographical/environmental factors. For example, studies in Ecuador have suggested a general, widespread temporal increase in mortality and morbidity during prehistory. These patterns also show regional differences, reflecting the highly varied environment of Ecuador. In a comparison of coastal and highland groups, the highland groups fared better with fewer nutritional problems and less evidence of infection. Within the coastal samples, those from the higher rainfall North showed greater stature but more evidence of infectious disease than did their counterparts from the more arid south coast.

The possible impact of hookworm in ancient Ecuador is an example of how both cultural and geographical aspects of the environment contribute to disease expression. Although hookworm is generally thought of as a disease introduced from Africa, studies of mummified human remains from ancient Peru have documented the pre-Columbian presence of hookworm. Severe hookworm infections can lead to anemia, which can provoke skeletal alterations in the form of increased bone porosity and expansion of the areas of blood-forming tissue. Such skeletal alterations are included in the condition porotic hyperostosis. In ancient Ecuador this condition occurred primarily on the coast and during times when agriculture was practiced. This condition was not common in highland areas of similar times. The likely explanation is that hookworm became a problem on the coast when, with agriculture, the settlement pattern shifted toward larger communities with increased sedentism. This development allowed the hookworm to complete its life cycle, which involves humans excreting feces containing eggs that hatch to produce larvae, which then must enter a human walking barefoot. Among more nomadic groups the population traveled on before the larvae appeared. But with agricultural groups living in the same area for extended periods, the opportunities for hookworm increased. In the highlands, an agricultural settlement pattern was present, but the environment was too cool for the hookworm larvae.

Europeans entering the New World beginning the late fifteenth century brought with them many diseases that apparently were previously unknown in the New World. Smallpox, measles, mumps, influenza, bubonic plague, typhus, diphtheria, scarlet fever, cholera, malaria, and whooping cough, among others, arrived in the Americas for the first time. The impact of these diseases was devastating, and the size of the aboriginal population was reduced to a fraction of its former number. Still, the timing and nature of the impact were shaped by cultural and geographical environmental factors. The earliest declines came from the Caribbean and North America, where initial European contact occurred. The diseases and population reductions then worked their way westward in North America, largely following movements of European settlers. Among Plains groups, the sedentary farmers living along the rivers were affected first, whereas the more nomadic groups were initially spared.

Discussion of the role of environment in the development of human disease must consider both cultural and geographical factors. Climatic factors such as humidity, rainfall, and temperature can affect the nature and impact of human disease. Geographical factors also can influence human settlements, population movements, warfare, trade, and many other aspects of culture that play key roles in human disease. Culture itself—in particular, the dynamics of food procurement, settlement pattern, sanitation practices, trade, status roles, and warfare—dramatically influences the occurrence and impact of human disease. All of these factors are linked in complex and dynamic ways with great variety of expression. Human disease must be viewed in its environmental perspective. Because it is *human* disease, human culture plays a dominant role.

Douglas H. Ubelaker

Further Reading

Crawford, M. H. (1998). *The origins of Native Americans: Evidence from anthropological genetics.* Cambridge, UK: Cambridge University Press.

Fischer, E. P., & Klose, S. (1996). *The diagnostic challenge: Knowledge for health.* Munich, Germany: R. Piper.

Greenblatt, C. L. (1998). *Digging for pathogens.* Philadelphia: Balaban.

Haines, M. R., & Steckel, R. H. (2000). *A population history of North America.* Cambridge, UK: Cambridge University Press.

Kiple, K. F. (1993). *The Cambridge world history of human disease.* Cambridge, UK: Cambridge University Press.

Larsen, C. S., & Milner, G. R. (1994). *In the wake of contact: Biological responses to conquest.* New York: Wiley-Liss.

Ubelaker, D. H. (1992, June). Patterns of demographic change in the Americas. *Human Biology, 64*(3), 361–379.

Verano, J. W., & Ubelaker, D. H. (1992). *Disease and demography in the Americas.* Washington, DC: Smithsonian Institution Press.

Viola, H. J., & Margolis, C. (1991). *Seeds of change: Five hundred years since Columbus.* Washington, DC: Smithsonian Institution Press.

Diseases, Plant

Plant diseases result from infection by certain viruses, viroids (simple virus-like particles that lack a protein coat), mollicutes (mycoplasma-like organisms), bacteria, protozoa, fungi, parasitic angiosperms (higher plants), and nematodes. (See table 1.)

When such an organism infects a plant (the host) and lives in association with it, the association is said to be symbiotic (Greek *syn* = "together with" + *bios* = "life"). The relationship may be mutualistic (reciprocal) if both organisms benefit (as with mycorrhizas and nitrogen-fixing bacteria) or parasitic (Greek *parasitos* = "one who dines at another's table") if the infecting organism benefits at the expense of the host. The infecting organism (the parasite) is said to be a pathogen if it causes disease (damage, debilitation, necrosis, or death) in the host. The study of plant diseases is plant pathology, and those who conduct such study are plant pathologists. Plant diseases cause massive economic losses in cultivated plants worldwide (e.g., 20 percent of the world cereal crop is lost annually) and

TABLE 1.
MAIN TAXONOMIC GROUPS THAT INCLUDE PLANT PATHOGENS

Group	Description	Examples
Superkingdom: Prokaryotae Kingdom: Monera (bacteria and mollicutes)	Bacteria exist largely as single cells, without a true nucleus, that may grow in or between host cells. Cells may secrete cytolytic enzymes, pathotoxins, plant growth regulators other pathogenicity factors, often encoded by plasmids. Reproduce by fission and/or by spores. Dispersed as spores or whole cells by wind, water, and sometimes vectors. Exhibit a wide range of ecophysiological and nutritional strategies. (See tables 2, 3, and 4). Mollicutes (phytoplasmas and spiroplasmas) lack a rigid cell wall, live within the cells of the host, and nutritionally are holobiotrophic. Transmitted by vectors, notably arthropods, and by mechanical means such as injury or grafting	*Agrobacterium* (crown gall); *Erwinia* (fire blight, soft rots and wilt); pytoplasmas (yellows, witches'-brooms)
Superkingdom: Eukaryotae Kingdom: Fungi (true fungi)	Normally composed of microscopic tubelike structures (hyphae) with chitin-rich walls with haploid nuclei, which may grow between and through plant cells. Hyphae may secrete extracellular cytolytic enzymes, pathotoxins, growth regulators, and other pathogenicity factors. Reproduce asexually and sexually by means of nonmotile spores, which may be dispersed by wind or water or occasionally by vectors such as insects. Sexually produced spores often have a thick wall and considerable powers of survival. Exhibit wide range of ecophysiological and nutritional strategies (See tables 2, 3, 4, and 6.)	uredinales (rusts); ustilaginales (smuts); erysiphales (powdery mildews); *Septoria* (eye-spot); *Colletotrichum* (anthracnose); *Verticillium* and *Fusarium* (vascular wilts); penicillium (blue mold); peronosporales and sclerosporales (downy mildews); *Phytophthora* (late blight); *Pythium* (rots and damping-off)
Kingdom: Chromista (referred to colloquially as "fungi" and until recently included in the kingdom fungi)	Normally composed of microscopic, tubelike structures (hyphae), with cellulosic cell walls and diploid nuclei; usually produce motile spores; otherwise as for fungi	Peronosporales and Sclerosporales (downy mildews); *Phytophthora* spp. (late blight and other blights); *Pythium* spp. (rots and damping-off)
Kingdom: Protozoa	Multicellular plasmodia without a cell wall that are obligate, intracellular parasites that reproduce by motile spores and sexual, resting spores.	*Plasmodiophora* (club root) (until recently classified in the kingdom fungi)
	Or flagellate, unicellular organisms belonging to Euglenophyta that inhabit the phloem of infected hosts. Spread by vectors and mechanical means such as injury or grafting	*Phytomonas* (phloem necrosis, heartrot, sudden wilt, and empty root) holoparasites: *Viscum* (true mistletoe); *Orobanche* (broomrape); *Rafflesia*; *Striga* (witchweed)
Kingdom: Plantae (flowering plants)	About 1 percent (300,000 species) of flowering plants are parasitic on other plants. Reproduce by seeds that germinate to produce seedlings that develop a close association with the vascular system of a living host for the exchange of nutrients via a multicellular structure called a "haustorium." Some are obligate parasites (Holoparasites), and of these some are also photosynthetic (e.g., *Striga*) and others not (e.g., *Rafflesia*). Others are facultative parasites (hemiparasites) that have photosynthetic leaves and can live part of their life cycle away from a host. Most hemiparasites are components of natural grasslands.	hemiparasites: *Euphrasia* (eyebright); *Rhinanthus* (yellow rattle)
Kingdom: Animalia (nematodes or eelworms)	Simple, small, usually microscopic wormlike organisms 300 micrometers – 4 millimeters by 15–35 micrometers). Reproduce by means of eggs that hatch, usually in the soil. Usually facultative parasites that spread by swimming or are dispersed in water or soil as eggs or individuals. Penetrate host roots, occasionally leaves, by means of "stylet" causing symptoms that include galls, root lesions, root proliferation, debilitation, and stunting	*Meloidogyne* (root knot nematodes); *Heterodera* (cyst nematodes); *Pratylenchus* (lesion nematodes); *Ditylenchus* (stem and bulb nematodes); *Aphelenchoides* (leaf nematodes)
Kingdom: Viruses	Viruses are submicroscopic obligate, intracellular parasites capable of growth and replication only in association with another, more complex organism (animal, plant, or fungus). Lack any cellular structure, consisting only of nucleic acid (RNA or DNA, double or single stranded) with a protein coat, usually either rod shaped or isometric. Spread by vectors (usually arthropods) or by mechanical means such as wounding or grafting. Symptoms include dwarfing, stunting, mosaic, necrosis, and yellowing.	RNA viruses: rod shaped: tobamovirus (tobacco mosaic); hordeivirus (barley stripe mosaic); potyvirus (potato virus Y) isometric particles: tombusvirus (tomato bushy stunt); comovirus (cowpea mosaic); cucumovirus (cucumber mosaic) DNA viruses: caulimovirus (cauliflower mosaic;
	Viroids are simple viruses that lack a protein coat.	coconut cadang viroid; potato spindle tuber viroid

are significant components of most natural and semi-natural ecosystems.

Plant pathogens may also be grouped according to their ecophysiological and nutritional strategies. (See tables 2 and 3.) The latter have a direct bearing on the range of symptoms produced. (See table 4.)

Landmarks in Research

Fungi are organisms belonging to the kingdoms Fungi and Chromista. These are the most important and widely studied groups of plant pathogens. The fossil record shows that fungi and fungus-like organisms infected the tissues of fossilized plants as far back as the Devonian period (306–408 million years ago). Some of these were probably mutualistic; others bear a close resemblance to rot-forming fungi of the present day and may have been the cause of disease. Further evidence of fungal diseases may be found in pollen deposits of the more recent geological periods. For example, the significant decline in elm (*Ulmus* spp.) pollen during the Atlantic period (c. 5000–3000 BCE) has been attributed in part to epidemics of the Dutch elm disease caused by *Ceratocystis* spp. There is also evidence of

the spores of pathogenic fungi in archeological remains, for example, in the windings of Egyptian mummies.

In the historical record, fungal diseases of plants have been known from the earliest times. A common explanation was that they were sent as a punishment from God, as when the Hebrew prophet Amos wrote, "I have smitten you with blasting and mildew" (Amos 4:9). During the seventh century BCE the Romans, under Numa Pompilius, established an annual festival, the Rubigalia. On 25 April each year a procession left Rome by the Flavian Gate and marched to the fifth milestone on the Claudian Way. There a red dog was sacrificed in the hope of persuading the corn god Rubigus to control the rust disease (caused by the fungus *Puccinia graminis*), which causes reddish lesions on infected leaves, by chaining up the dog star Sirius, thought to be the cause of the disease. Theophrastus, the Greek philosopher, was the first to study plant diseases and in about 300 BCE wrote about diseases of trees, cereals, and beans, observing, for example, that rust diseases were more prevalent in valleys than on hillsides.

In the seventeenth century, having noted that rust disease of wheat flourished where barberry *(Berberis*

TABLE 2.
THE DIVERSITY OF ECOPHYSIOLOGICAL STRATEGIES OF PLANT PATHOGENIC ORGANISMS

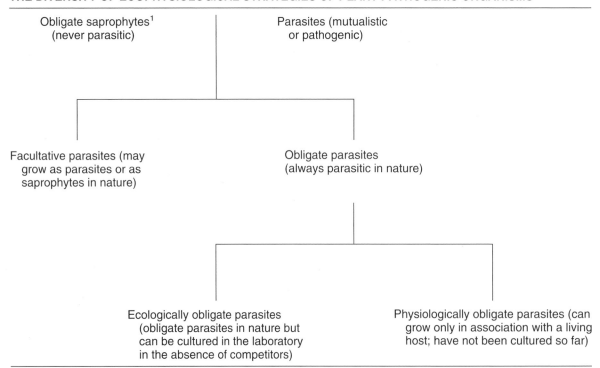

1. Many species currently placed in this group may be capable of parasitism but have not yet been studied in sufficient detail to confirm this.
    Source: Brian (1967).

TABLE 3.
RANGE OF NUTRITIONAL STRATEGIES EXHIBITED BY PLANT PATHOGENIC FUNGI

Nutritional Strategy[1]	Definition	Examples
Holobiotrophs[2]	Pathogens that in nature grow only in association with a living host plant	Uredinales (rusts); stilaginales (smuts); Erysiphales (powdery mildews)
Hemibiotrophs[3]	Pathogens that grow for part of their cycle in the living tissues of a host plant and part in tissues they have killed with cytolytic enzymes and/or pathotoxins	mainly biotropic: *Guignardia* (black rot); *Septoria* (eye spot) mainly necrotrophic: *Colletotrichum* (anthracnose)
Necrotrophs (or perthotrophs)	Parasites that in nature grow in dead host tissues they have killed with cytolytic enzymes and/or pathotoxins	*Penicillium* (blue mold); *Sclerotinia* (soft rots); *Sclerotium* (damping-off, cankers and rots)
Saprotrophs[4]	Nonparasites that in nature grow only on dead substrates	Up to 92 percent of all fungi

1. These categories may also be used to classify plant pathogenic chromista and bacteria, which include examples of all strategies, and to a lesser extent plant pathogenic nematodes. All plant pathogenic mollicutes, protozoa, flowering plants, viruses, and viroids are holobiotrophs.
2. The pathogen may be entirely intercellular, intercellular and intracellular, or intercellular with specialized intracellular feeding branches (haustoria).
3. Most plant pathogens currently thought to be necrotrophs may, in fact, be hemibiotrophs with an extended necrotrophic phase, but research is required to confirm this.
4. Many fungi currently thought to be saprotrophs may, in fact, have an unnoticed holobiotrophic, endophytic phase in their life cycles, as in the cases of *Acremonium*.
Source: Parbery (1996).

vulgaris) was found, farmers concluded that this plant exerted a magical and malign influence on the wheat and therefore grubbed it out from the hedgerows. This practice was most astute because scientists now know that *Puccinia graminis*, the cause of rust disease of wheat, has a complicated life cycle, with some stages occurring on wheat and others on barberry. Indeed, the removal of barberry as a method of control of rust disease has been widely and successfully practiced in the United States for more than two hundred years.

Other causes of plant disease were held to be the stars—but not the sun, according to Theophrastus— meteors, witchcraft, animals, and various environmental factors. In the biblical account Pharaoh, for example, retelling one of his dreams to Moses, said that he had seen "Seven ears, withered thin and blasted with the east wind" (Gen. 41:23). Even as late as the first half of the nineteenth century, at the time of the Irish potato famine (1845, 1846), it was widely held that the potato late blight disease (then called "potato murrain") was the result of the saturation of plants by heavy rain: a plant equivalent of human dropsy. Even people, such as botany professor Lindley at the University of London, who saw mold growing on plants afflicted by disease held that the mold was a consequence of disease,

as when mold grows on stale bread, rather than the cause of it.

By this time, however, more enlightened minds were getting closer to the truth. The scientific study of plant disease began in the seventeenth century with J. S. Elsholz (1684), and by 1705 French botanist J. P. de Tournefort had distinguished two groups of diseases, caused by internal and external forces, respectively. By 1723 C. S. Eysfarth was grouping plant diseases according to the stage of development of the plant on which they occurred. In 1751 Swedish botanist Carl von Linné (Linnaeus) distinguished plant diseases as mildew, rust, smut, ergot, and various kinds of insect damage. During the late eighteenth and early nineteenth centuries descriptions of plant diseases were much influenced by medical terminology. For example, Danish biologist Johann Fabricus, in his seminal work of 1774 on the diseases of plants, recognized six classes of disease: rendering unproductive, wasting, decaying, discharging, rendering misshapen, and being extraneous (i.e., due to injury). He was also aware that plant diseases might be caused by microorganisms, as when he referred to the "small worms" that Linnaeus believed were the cause of smut, concluding that the symptoms of smut could be best ex-

TABLE 4.
EXAMPLES OF THE DIVERSITY OF SYMPTOMS CAUSED BY PLANT PATHOGENIC FUNGI AND BACTERIA

Symptom	Description
Rusts	Usually limited lesions in which spores of the holobiotropic[1] Uredinales (Fungi) break through the cuticle of living, infected hosts. "Green islands" of chlorophyll may remain around lesions as infected leaves age. Intercellular hyphae usually form haustoria (specialized feeding branches). Some are systemic, and spores may then be produced over large areas of the hosts, which may also grow abnormally.
Smuts	Usually limited lesions in which black ustilospores of the holobiotrophic Ustilaginales (Fungi) break through the cuticle or burst from reproductive structures of living hosts. Hyphae may be intercellular or intracellular in living cells. Many are systemic.
Powdery Mildew	White to gray hyphae and conidia of the holobiotropic Erysiphales (Fungi) grow on surfaces of living hosts, connected to epidermal cells by haustoria. Green islands of chlorophyll may remain around lesions as infected leaves age.
Downy Mildews	Masses of white to gray sporangia of the holobiotrophic Peronosporales and Sclerosporales (Chromista) grow through the cuticle or stomata of living hosts. Hyphae are usually intercellular and form haustoria. Some are systemic.
Galls, Leaf Curls, and Witches'-Brooms	Overgrowth, distortion, or proliferation of host tissues induced by hormonal imbalance caused by wide diversity of holobiotrophic or hemibiotrophic pathogens. Symptoms may be caused by some members of all main groups of bacteria and fungi.
Scabs	Limited dry surface lesions with scabby host deposits of corky, lignified, and pigmented cells induced by infection by certain hemibiotrophic or necrotrophic bacteria (*Streptomyces* spp.) and Fungi (mainly Ascomycota).
Necrotic Spots	Limited necrotic lesions formed on leaves, stems, or flowers of hosts by wide range of necrotrophic or hemibiotrophic bacteria and fungi. Pathotoxins and cytolytic enzymes may contribute to symptoms. Character of lesion also affected by host responses to infection, including deposition of phenolics.
Cankers, Die-Backs, and Stem and Twig Blights	Stem lesions and twig and shoot death caused by some necrotrophic bacteria and fungi (mainly ascomycota) that infect and destroy stem and twig tissues of woody hosts.
Vascular Wilts	Wilt of foliage and stems followed by death of infected plant, caused by invasion of vascular system and release of pathotoxins and cytolytic enzymes by certain necrotrophic fungi and sometimes bacteria.
Blights	Killing of host leaves and shoots by pathotoxins and/or cytolytic enzymes produced by wide diversity of necrotrophic or hemibiotrophic bacteria and fungi.
Rots	Destruction of host tissues by cytolytic enzymes of wide diversity of necrotrophic and hemibiotrophic bacterial and fungal pathogens. Enzymes involved may include cellulases, hemicellulases, pectic enzymes, and lignases.
Hypersensitive Flecks	Rapid death, lignification, and pigmentation of one or small group of cells of resistant host following challenge by spores of avirulent strain of bacterium or fungus. Usually associated with gene-for-gene resistance of holobiotrophs and hemibiotrophs and with nonhost resistance.

1. For definitions of *necrotrophic, holobiotroph,* and *hemibiotroph* see table 3.
Source: Ingram and Robertson (1999).

plained by assuming that something organized was the cause. In fact, research on smut diseases of cereals, including loose smut *(Ustilago nuda)* and stinking smut or bunt *(Tillelia caries),* was to play a crucial part in establishing that microorganisms are, in fact, the cause of most plant diseases. Bunt had been known to the early herbalists such as German botanist Jerome Bock (1552) and in 1733 was attributed by English agriculturalist Jethro Tull in *The Horse-Hoing Husbandry* to cold, wet summers. Subsequently Mathieu Tillet (1755) studied smut diseases in detail and recognized the spores as being critical to the development of the diseases but was unable to identify these as being produced by fungi. The breakthrough came more than fifty years later when Bénédict Prévost (1807) published for the first time experimental proof that bunt is caused by a microorganism, later named *Tilletia caries* by French botanists C. and E. L. R. Tulasne in 1847.

Studies of another major group of plant pathogenic fungi, the rusts, were also of critical importance in the history of plant disease research. It is now known that most rust fungi have complex life cycles involving two or more spore types. In some species these all occur on a single host species (autecious rusts), but in others such as *Puccinia graminis*, the cause of black stem rust of wheat, two hosts (heteroecious rusts) are involved—wheat and barberry. Black stem rust was known to the ancients, but not until the latter half of the eighteenth century, with the work of the Italians Giovanni Targioni-Tozzetti and Felice Fontana, were the spore stages recognized and described. These scientists, with English naturalist Sir Joseph Banks in the early nineteenth century, believed that the cause of the disease was a small parasitic plant. That the spore stages of rusts are related was not proven until 1854 with the publication by Tulasne of a study of rose rust (*Phragmidium*).

The nature of heteroecism (the quality of passing through stages in the life cycle on alternate and often unrelated hosts) took longer to establish. For a long time farmers had been aware of the link between barberry bushes and the appearance of wheat rust, and by 1755 the Barberry Law of Massachusetts had been enacted to "prevent danger to English grain arising from Barberry bushes." Similar laws followed in Connecticut, Rhode Island, and France. In 1805 Banks, following observations of rust in Norfolk, United Kingdom, proposed that "the parasitic fungus of the barberry and that of the wheat are one and the same species," and in 1806 L. G. Windt, working in Germany, came to a similar conclusion for rust on rye.

Thomas Andrew Knight tried, but failed, to establish the connection by experiment in 1805. However, Niels Pederson Scholar, in Denmark, in 1816 experimentally infected rye with rust from barberry. Proof ultimately came from the work of German botanist Anton de Bary who, in 1865 and 1866, described experiments in which he infected barberry with sporidia from teliospores produced on wheat and rye with aeciospores from barberry.

Studies of the potato blight disease in the mid-nineteenth century were also seminal in establishing that plant diseases are a consequence of infection by microorganisms. One of the experts brought in to advise on the cause of the epidemic was an English country parson, the Reverend Miles Berkeley. In a seminal paper published in 1846 he stated unequivocally that "The decay (of potatoes) is the consequence of the presence of the mould, and not the mould of decay." A similar view had been reached by others in the United States,

Belgium, and France, notably J. F. L. Montagne, a former surgeon of Napoleon's army, as Berkeley was careful to note. Indeed, it was Berkeley who in 1845 first named the causal fungus of the disease as *Botytis infestans* (now renamed *Phytophthora infestans*). The dispute continued into the second half of the century and did not end until publication of the definitive memoirs on plant disease by de Bary in 1861 and 1863.

During the rest of the nineteenth century through to the mid-twentieth century the science of plant pathology was dominated by detailed studies of the life cycles of fungi that cause plant diseases. Such studies led to few major conceptual advances but were, nevertheless, important in laying the foundations for subsequent research on the control epidemiology and ecology of plant diseases and on the basic mechanisms involved in plant-pathogen interaction.

Plant pathologists had been concerned from the earliest times with the practical business of controlling or preventing infections of crop plants by pathogens, especially fungi. One strategy is a form of "cultural control," meaning adopting horticultural or agricultural practices such as avoiding sources of infection, removing the alternate host, reducing humidity, and changing the pH of soils that might encourage disease. Few of these approaches are completely effective, and plant pathologists therefore sought chemicals with which to combat disease.

The earliest use of chemicals for disease control came in the late seventeenth century when sodium chloride (common salt) was applied to wheat seed to prevent infection by bunt (*Tulletia*) following the observations that seed salvaged from a wrecked ship remained free of disease when planted. Later, copper sulfate was substituted for salt, and in the late nineteenth century this chemical mixed with lime ("Bordeaux mixture") was used to prevent infection of vines with vine downy mildew (*Plasmopara*) following the observation in 1882 by French botanist P. M. A. Millardet that vines in the Bordeaux region of France sprayed with this mixture to deter thieves remained free of disease. Bordeaux mixture has been used ever since as a "protective" fungicide to control a wide diversity of fungal diseases, notably blight of potatoes. Major disadvantages are that the mixture is easily washed off of leaves by rain and so must be reapplied at regular intervals and that copper itself is toxic to plants and humans. Other toxic compounds used subsequently as protective fungicides include compounds containing sulfur and compounds containing heavy metals such as tin, zinc, and mercury. Finally, in the 1960s organic "systemic fungicides" were discovered. These are taken up by the cells of the treated plant and kill or debilitate pathogens by limiting postinfection growth. They persist in the plant for greater periods of time, and therefore fewer applications are required, although these fungicides suffer from the disadvantages of being expensive to develop and produce and being easily overcome by mutations to insensitivity in the pathogens they are designed to control (fungi are genetically very plastic).

Another approach to the control of plant diseases pioneered by research on fungi is that in which a non-pathogenic organism is used instead of a chemical to prevent infection. The pioneering ecological research of British pathologist S. D. Garrett laid the foundation for such an approach. The first such "biological control"—and still one of the most effective—is the use of the saprophytic (obtaining food by absorbing dissolved organic material) fungus *Peniophora* to prevent infection of pine stumps by the butt rot fungus *Heterobiasidion*. There are now many other effective biological control procedures, but few have been adopted for widespread use.

Perhaps the most effective approach to control is through the development of disease resistance. Most plants possess characteristics such as a waxy surface that might promote the run-off of water carrying pathogen spores or a thick cuticle that slows down the infection process. Such preformed factors may be enhanced by breeding or selection, but none is completely effective. During the first half of the twentieth century it became apparent that most plants possess "active" mechanisms that may prevent infection. In such cases attempted invasion by a potential pathogen usually leads to death of the initially invaded cell, the "hypersensitive response," and the accumulation at the infection site of toxic chemicals such as superoxides and secondary metabolites (substances essential to the metabolism of an organism). Together these processes restrict the growth of the invading pathogen. During the second half of the twentieth century research in plant pathology was dominated by studies of the physiological and biochemical control of such active defense.

Meanwhile, during the early years of the twentieth century, Roland Biffen, in Cambridge, United Kingdom, was laying the foundations to explain the genetic mechanisms involved in active defense through his studies of the inheritance of resistance to rust disease in wheat. By the middle of the century H. H. Flor was working in the United States on the inheritance of resis-

tance to rust (*Melampsora*) in flax. The result was the exposition of the "gene-for-gene hypothesis" (see table 5) that now underpins not only the breeding of disease-resistant plants, but also studies of the basic mechanisms of plant-pathogen interaction. The hypothesis states, in essence, that single, dominant genes in the host and pathogen control resistance (*R*-genes) and avirulence (*Av*-genes; nonpathogenic), respectively, and that resistant phenotypes (the visible properties of an organism that are produced by the interaction of the genotype and the environment) result from the interaction between the products of one *R*-gene in the host and the products of a single, specific avirulence gene in the pathogen. Conversely, a susceptible reaction results if the *R*-gene is absent or recessive in the host or if the *Av*-gene is absent or recessive in the pathogen. (See table 6.) There may be several *R*-genes in any one host and several avirulence genes in the pathogen. The work of Biffen, Flor, and others made it possible during most of the twentieth and twenty-first centuries to breed a wide range of disease-resistant cultivars (organisms originating and persisting under cultivation) of plants, and these were widely deployed as a means of controlling plant diseases. As with systemic fungicides, however, a major problem was the genetic plasticity of pathogenic fungi leading to the evolution of new races capable of overcoming the resistance genes, even where several resistance genes were combined in one host cultivar, with the accompanying need to breed further resistant cultivars and so on—an expensive proposition.

In recent years the approach to disease control has been to deploy a range of disease-control measures in combination, so-called integrated control, to reduce disease to acceptable levels while minimizing inputs, especially of toxic chemicals.

Toward the middle of the twentieth century, in parallel with research on resistance, the field of plant disease epidemiology began to develop, most notably as

TABLE 5.
THE GENE-FOR-GENE RELATIONSHIP

		Host Genotype	
		R1 R1	*r1 r1*
Pathogen	*AV1*	−	+
Genotype	*av1*	+	+

− = Resistant interaction
+ = Susceptible interaction
Source: Flor (1971).

TABLE 6.
DIVERSITY OF EFFECTS OF PATHOGENIC FUNGI AND BACTERIA ON THE ECOLOGICAL FITNESS OF HOST PLANTS

Group	Description	Examples
Destroyers	Kill whole plant	damping-off (e.g., *Pythium* spp.); and jarrah die-back (*Phytophthora* spp.); vascular wilts (e.g., *Fusarium* spp. and Dutch elm disease *[Ceratocystis]*); many plant pathogenic bacteria
Debili tators	Cause discrete lesions or systemic infections, with variable effects on host growth rate and fitness; do not normally kill host	many ruts (Uredinales); powdery mildews (Erysiphales); downy mildews (Peronosporales and Sclerosporales); club root *(Plasmodiophora)*; leaf spotting diseases (many members of the ascomycota); many plant pathogenic bacteria
Sexual Inhibitors	Reduce fecundity with little effect on growth	some smuts (ustilaginales) and rusts (uredinales); ergot *(Claviceps); Erwinia*; phytoplasmas

Source: Burdon (1993).

a means of understanding better how epidemics of fungal pathogens develop in crops with a view to forecasting such epidemics more accurately and therefore deploying control strategies more effectively. In their simplest form plant disease epidemics follow an S-shaped (sigmoidal) pattern, with an initial slow buildup of infection followed by a rapid rise as more spores are produced and then a plateau as all infection sites are occupied or a rapid decline as the host is destroyed. This basic pattern varies greatly according to the host and pathogen in question and the prevailing environmental conditions. The South African plant pathologist Van de Plank in 1963 first put studies of disease epidemics on a firm experimental and theoretical footing, ultimately leading to effective computer simulation of epidemics and accurate forecasting of disease.

From the mid-twentieth century onward there was also a fever of theoretical research on the physiology and biochemistry of pathogen-host interaction, notably with fungi but also with bacteria, pioneered by R. K. S. Wood in the United Kingdom and Arthur Kelman in the United States. The toxins, enzymes, and hormones involved in infection, pathogen nutrition, and the reorientation of host metabolism following infection were all described, as were the metabolic changes in the host following infection and in resistance responses. By the late twentieth century molecular biological techniques made possible the cloning of *R*-genes, avirulence genes, and pathogenicity genes and the explanation of the molecular mechanisms by which hosts and pathogens recognize or fail to recognize one another, leading either to resistance or disease, respectively. Now genetic modification (GM) technology is being used to develop disease-resistant crops as a result of such research.

Viruses and Viroids

The effects of virus infections on plants were first recognized, although not understood, in the sixteenth century when the "breaking" of flower color in tulips became a popular study for flower painters, particularly in the Netherlands. Various potato diseases now known to be of viral origin were described in the eighteenth century, and at the time of the potato blight epidemic, the curl disease, caused by potato leaf roll virus and other mosaic viruses, was causing significant crop losses. By 1869 the variegation of *Abutilon striatum*, a decorative plant widely used in conservatories, was found to be infectious when variegated scions (a detached living portion of a plant joined to a stock in grafting) were grafted on to green stocks.

Earlier in the century French scientist Louis Pasteur had noted that no microscopically visible organisms could be found in infectious fluid causing rabies in dogs and speculated that pathogens too small to be seen might be responsible for the disease. In 1886 K. Mayer used sap from tobacco plants infected with mosaic disease to infect healthy plants. In 1892 Ivanowski showed that the sap from infected plants remained infective after passage through a bacterium-proof filter, and in 1898 Beijernick confirmed this result and called the infective material *contagium vivum fluidum* (infectious living fluid).

By the start of the twentieth century virus diseases were being described, the mechanisms for their transmission from plant to plant by vectors (organisms that transmit a pathogen) such as sucking and biting insects, nematodes, fungi, and mechanical injury were being explained, and the procedures for the experimental infection of plants were being developed. However, the identity of the infective agents remained a mystery. In 1935 W. M. Stanley in the United States isolated and purified a "protein" from plants infected with tobacco mosaic virus. This protein remained infective after serial dilution and even after successive recrystalizations. In 1937 Bawden and Pirie in England showed that this "protein" from infected tobacco was, in fact, a nucleo-protein that appeared as liquid crystals of 5 percent protein and an associated ribonucleic acid (RNA).

After the chemical nature of viruses was established, scientists could study these organisms using a range of physical and chemical techniques. It was found that some were rodlike in form (e.g., tobacco mosaic virus), consisting of a coiled core of RNA enclosed within a protein coat of regularly positioned molecules. This coat was characteristic for each virus but was not necessary for infection. In other cases, such as turnip yellows virus, for example, the particles were roughly spherical, with the protein subunits forming an icosahedral lattice and the RNA closely associated in a regular pattern with the inner surface of this shell. Some viroids may also cause plant diseases. Virus structure was studied by U.S. geneticist James Watson and English biophysicist Francis Crick in the 1950s, and there is little doubt that this was a significant precursor of their work on the helical structure of DNA.

During the early part of the twentieth century the quantitative study of viruses infecting plants was based on the ability of infecting virus particles to induce a local necrotic lesion response on certain hosts, it being possible to establish a relationship between the concentration of virus particles in a given sample and the number of local lesions induced on a leaf of the test plant. Explanation of the chemical structures of viruses made possible the development of more sophisticated techniques based on their antigenic (relating to a protein or carbohydrate substance capable of stimulating an immune response) properties, notably the enzyme-linked immunosorbent assay (ELISA) and, more recently, a variety of molecular biological techniques. (ELISA is a process in which an enzyme-labeled antibody binding to a specific virus sample precipitates and digests a chemical dye, leading to a color change; the intensity of the color change gives a measure of the virus in the sample.) Nevertheless, the study of plant viruses was dominated during the first three-quarters of the twentieth century by descriptions of symptoms, identification of the vast range of causal viruses and vectors, and descriptions of the particles and host cell responses derived from electron-microscopic studies. Not until introduction of molecular biological techniques in the last decades of the twentieth century were scientists able to explain details of the mechanisms of interaction between host and viral genomes (haploid sets of chromosomes with the genes they contain) and the mechanisms whereby plant hosts recognize and then resist infection by potentially pathogenic viruses.

Mollicutes and Bacteria

One group of plant diseases thought to have been caused by viruses resulted in yellowing and reddening of the infected tissues and/or proliferation of the shoot apex to form a mass of shoots called a witches'-broom (an abnormal tufted growth of small branches on a tree or shrub caused by fungi or viruses). Despite extensive research over more than seventy years, however, no viral pathogen could be detected in infected tissues. In 1976 Doi and collaborators in Japan identified the cause as wallless, mycoplasma-like organisms (mollicutes), subsequently named "phytoplasmas" and "spiroplasmas." These organisms do not appear to be of major importance in causing plant disease and, as yet, have not been the subject of any extensive research in the way that fungi, viruses, and bacteria have.

Bacteria were shown to be the cause of disease in animals through the studies of anthrax in France by Pasteur and Robert Koch in 1876, and by 1878 Burrill, in the United States, had shown that fire blight of apple and pear was also caused by bacterial infections. Thereafter, the pioneering work of Erwin Smith in the United States showed that a significant number of plant diseases were bacterial in origin, although this view was disputed by some eminent botanists until the end of the nineteenth century.

Studies of bacterial diseases continued through the first part of the twentieth century but were largely descriptive in nature and concerned with the control of the diseases in crops. A significant exception was the study of crown gall disease, caused by *Agrobacterium tumefaciens*, notably by Armin C. Braun in the United States. The bacterium gains entry to a variety of hosts through wounds and then cases tumorous grown. Braun showed that this tumorization is irreversible, the hosts cells having been "transformed." This discovery laid the foundations for later research that revealed that transformation is caused by transfer of the plasmid DNA (having an extrachromosomal ring of DNA) coding for tumorous growth from the bacterial cells to the hosts cells, where it is permanently incorporated into the genome, a discovery that ultimately led to the development of GM technology in plants. During the latter half of the twentieth century studies of bacteria, as with fungi, contributed to knowledge of plant diseases in a variety of other ways, notably because of their facility as experimental tools for studies of the molecular biology of host-pathogen interaction. Thus in 1984 Brian Staskawicz and colleagues in the United States cloned for the first time a pathogenicity gene using the bacterial soybean pathogen *Pseudomonas syringae* pv. *glycinea*. Bacterial pathogens such as *Pseudomonas, Xanthomonas*, and *Ralstonia* species are now playing a central role in molecular plant pathology, notably in the explanation of the mechanism whereby bacteria deliver pathogenicity factors into host cells and are recognized and excluded by resistant hosts.

Nematodes

Nematodes were first associated with a plant disease by Needham in England in 1743 when he observed these minute "worms" in small, abnormally rounded wheat grains (wheat galls). A second nematode disease, root knot of cucumber, was noted in 1855, and by the end of the century two more had been identified: bulb nematode disease and sugar beet cyst nematode disease. Others were identified by Cobb in the early part of the twentieth century. Nematode diseases are significant but not of major importance, and most studies have been descriptive or concerned with control.

Plant Disease in Natural Ecosystems and Conservation

Studies of the occurrence and control of plant diseases in crop plants have dominated the science of plant pathology until recently. It has always been known that a great diversity of plant diseases occurs in natural ecosystems. (See table 6.) Sometimes such diseases cause major damage on a national or international scale, as in the case of jarrah die-back of native species in Australia and New Zealand as a result of infection by *Phytophthora cinnamomi* and the widespread destruction of elms in the United States and Europe as a result of infection by *Ceratocystis novo-ulmae*, the cause of Dutch elm disease. For the most part, however, it is

not yet known whether plant pathogen diversity plays an important role in ecosystem dynamics and productivity or is simply another level of biological complexity of no structural significance. Research on this important topic is now being pursued around the world and, with the development of appropriate molecular markers, is set to make rapid strides in the future.

Conservation of plant pathogen diversity in natural ecosystems is counterintuitive because of the great economic threat that pathogens pose to crops and wild plant species in natural ecosystems.

However, the threats to pathogen diversity are significant, being related to the threats to host plant diversity, intensified by the agricultural tradition of destroying plant pathogens wherever they occur. Both *ex situ* (out of the natural place) and *in situ* (in the natural place) approaches to conservation are of potential value but pose the threat of escape, with potentially devastating consequences for adjacent crops and natural hosts. *Ex situ* conservation strategies (in gene banks) pose fewer risks than *in situ* strategies but are less effective for conserving a broad spectrum of diversity and suffer from the serious disadvantage of not allowing continuing host-pathogen co-evolution. Research on plant pathogen conservation is still in its infancy.

David S. Ingram

Further Reading

Agrios, G. N. (1998). *Plant pathology* (4th ed.). San Diego, CA: Academic Press.

Berkeley, M. J. (1846). Observations botanical and physiological on the potato murrain. *Journal of the Horticultural Society of London, 1*, 9–35.

Brian, P. W. (1967). Obligate parasitism in fungi. *Proceedings of the Royal Society Series B 168*, 101–118.

Burdon, J. J. (1993). The structure of pathogen populations in natural plant communities. *Annual Review of Phytopatholgy 31*, 305–323.

Flor, H. H. (1971). Current status of the gene-for-gene concept. *Annual Review of Phytopathology 9*, 275–296.

Holliday, P. (1998). *A dictionary of plant pathology* (2nd ed.). Cambridge, UK: Cambridge University Press.

Ingram, D., & Robertson, N. (1999). *Plant disease: A natural history*. London: HarperCollins.

Large, E. C. (1940). *The advance of the fungi*. London: Jonathan Cape.

Parbery, D. G. (1996). Trophism and the ecology of fungi associated with plants. *Biological Reviews 71*, 473–527.

Sivasithamparam, K., Dixon, K. W., & Barrett, R. L. (Eds.). (2002). *Microorganisms in plant conservation and biodiversity*. Boston: Kluwer Academic Publishers.

Webster, R. K., Shaner, G., & Van Alfen, N. K. (Eds.). (1963–2003). *Annual review of phytopathology* (Vols. 1– 41). Palo Alto, CA: Annual Reviews.

Dodo

Ninety-nine percent of all species that ever lived are extinct. Countless numbers were birds, many of which in recent times were hastened to their end by the gustatory, commodifying, and habitat-transforming activities of humans: moas in New Zealand and innumerable other species throughout the Pacific, the Carolina parakeet and Labrador duck in North America, the great auk and Eskimo curlew, and so on. Heading the list are several poster birds for extinction: the (surely extinct) ivory-billed woodpecker; a passenger pigeon named Martha, which expired in the Cincinnati Zoo in 1914 as the last of a species that, just a short time before, had been staggeringly abundant; and the dodo, which disappeared before the end of the seventeenth century, by which time it had entered the realm of popular culture, that is to say, of misconception.

One major fallacy about the dodo (*Raphus cucullatus*) comes from its common name, whose origin is a Dutch word meaning "sluggard or round-heavy ass" or a Portuguese word meaning "simpleton or fool." The dodo has always been considered in negative terms as simple, plodding, uncomprehending, and lazy. (Swedish botanist Carl von Linne [Linnaeus] later assigned it the species name *ineptus*, but *cucullatus* had preference in nomenclature.) For at least a century, "dumb as a dodo" has been applied to persons considered stupid—and a dodo was also an inactive or unenlightened person—despite English writer Lewis Henry Carroll (Charles L. Dodgson), who invested the dodo in *Alice's Adventures in Wonderland* with the simple wisdom to figure out that all one had to do to dry off after being immersed in Alice's sea of tears was run in a circle for a while.

John Tenniel's engravings in *Alice's Adventures in Wonderland* depict the dodo as a rotund character (with human hands beneath his wings!) clearly derivative of the famously round, blankly droll dodos painted by Roelandt Savery, a Dutch artist of Flemish origin, in 1626–1628. Savery's dodos have had remarkable staying power through the ages, dominating representations of the dodo in stamps, children's books, cartoons, and kitsch.

A Few Facts

But was the dodo either stupid or shaped like a beach ball? What is known about it is that it lived only on the island of Mauritius, east of Madagascar, and that according to a recent analysis of mitochondrial DNA, it was a member of the family Columbidae in the order Columbiformes (pigeons and doves), and related to the extinct solitaire of Rodriguez Island and the Nicobar pigeon of the Nicobar Islands and southeastern Asia. Millions of years ago ancestors of these birds probably island-hopped from southeastern Asia across the Indian Ocean—flying or flightless is not known—and in time evolved to the dodo and solitaires.

Furthermore, dodos, especially males, were indeed large (12–18 kilograms) and, with stubby wings and a breastbone too small to support the pectoral muscles required to lift them into flight, confined to the ground. Their plumage was gray and rather uniform but for several plumes curling up from the rump. Their heavy bills (especially in males) and large stones in the crop were used to tear, crush, and digest thick-hulled fruits, nuts, and seeds. Ground-nesters and territorial, females laid only a single egg in each clutch. Their physical remains—a rich trove of bones from Mauritian bogs and other remains in some two dozen museums (no stuffed specimens exist)—as well as a range of less-known engravings, other images, and texts suggest that although massive in skeletal structure, dodos were sleeker, more upright, and substantially more active than depicted by Savery.

The Beginning of the End

Moreover, for millennia the dodo evolved on an island free of large predators—until humans with their biota (the flora and fauna of a region) arrived. The first record of human presence is of Portuguese who came to Mauritius in the early sixteenth century; the prior arrival of Arab seafarers, although reasonable, is speculative absent documentation. The Portuguese were largely transient, and their influence on the dodo is poorly understood. Next came the Dutch, who arrived in 1598 with domesticated animals, sugarcane, and colonial designs. By 1681, some eight decades after the Dutch and approximately 175 years after the Portuguese arrived, the dodo had disappeared.

Why did the dodo become extinct? Some reasons can surely be traced to its low reproductive rate, slowness to mature, ground-dwelling habits, inability to fly, lack of experience with predators, and circumscribed island habitat. In this light, the Portuguese and Dutch who arrived on Mauritius considered a large, unwary (rather than stupid), flightless bird an easy mark, despite its formidable bill. Some Dutch called dodos "disgusting birds" because their flesh was tough except for the breast and preferred other animals as food; yet, they caught dodos by the dozens, cooking and eating them on the spot or, for those sailing away, salting them down for future consumption.

Of as profound a consequence for the dodo was the exotic biota introduced principally by the Dutch: rats and other stowaways, as well as crab-eating macaques, pigs, goats, dogs, and cats, most intentionally imported as part of a larger agenda to deforest and transform lands for agricultural production, to introduce (and let loose) animals that were a ready source of protein and other products, and to construct culturally familiar surroundings. The new omnivorous fauna and environmental transformations, all at the behest of humans, together with humans' gustatory interest, had a cumulative fatal impact on the dodo. One can only imagine the effect of macaques, pigs, dogs, and cats on eggs and fledgling dodos, as well as on slow-reproducing Earth-bound adult birds. In the end, the story of the dodo is the familiar one of island extirpation (since 1600 almost all birds that have disappeared lived on islands), but this extinction registered in a way that earlier ones had not because the dodo gave its name to the expression that stands for the end of life: "as dead as a dodo."

Shepard Krech III

Further Reading

Fuller, E. (2001). *Extinct birds* (Rev. ed.). Ithaca, NY: Comstock Publishing Associates/Cornell University Press.

Fuller, E. (2002). *Dodo: From extinction to icon*. London: Collins.

Gould, S. J. (1996). The dodo and the caucus race. *Natural History, 105*(11), 22–33.

Kitchener, A. (1993). Justice at last for the dodo. *New Scientist, 139*(1888), 24.

Quammen, D. (1996). *The song of the dodo: Island biogeography in an age of extinctions*. New York: Scribner.

Shapiro, B., et al. (2002). Flight of the dodo. *Science, 295*, 1683.

Strickland, H. E., & Melville, A. G. (1848). *The dodo and its kindred*. London: Reeve, Benham, and Reeve.

Dogs

Though by no means universally beloved, dogs live in a greater intimacy with human beings than any other animal. They traditionally share human homes, and they eat scraps and leftovers from human meals. Perhaps still more significantly, dogs appear to show a considerable range of emotions that, superficially at least, resemble those of human beings, including guilt and love. Furthermore, dogs have an enormous genetic variability, unparalleled among other animals, which resembles cultural variation among humans. Thus, a Pekinese and a Labrador dog seem at first to have little resemblance, yet they can reproduce together and are considered members of a single species. In mythology, legend, and literature, dogs often appear as mediators between human beings and nature as well as between the living and the dead.

Dogs were domesticated from wolves throughout much of Eurasia at least 1,400 years ago. Ethnologists believe this relationship grew out of a symbiosis, which may have begun long before, but about which little is known. Wolves probably followed human beings, eating remains left at campfires and sometimes leading hunters to game. Eventually, people began to adopt and raise wolf pups, and these eventually became the domestic dog. The period in which the dog was domesticated corresponds roughly to transition from societies of nomadic hunter-gatherers to a partially settled existence as herders and agriculturalists. Dogs must have helped to control flocks and to guard homes.

The most glamorous use of dogs has been in hunting, an activity that came to be surrounded by increasingly elaborate rituals. Kings of ancient Egypt and Mesopotamia were depicted in all their splendor pursuing game with their dogs. The ability of dogs to locate game by scent appeared clairvoyant. People have often credited dogs with the ability to see spirits, an idea that persists in folklore today. In consequence, dogs have often been regarded as guides for the deceased to the next world. In Egypt, Anubis, who leads the spirits of the departed to the place of judgment, is traditionally depicted with the body of a man but the head of a dog or jackal. In diverse traditions from the Greeks to the Aztecs, dogs guard the entrance to the underworld.

Attitudes towards dogs have varied widely. The ancient Greek historian Herdotus reported that in Egypt the entire family would go into mourning when the household dog died. Dogs were also highly regarded among the Babylonians, Greeks, and Romans, where they were closely associated with healing. A rare moment of tenderness in Homer's *Odyssey* is when the hero returns home and is recognized only by his dog Argus. Among the Hebrews, however, dogs were considered unclean and repugnant, an attitude that carried over into Christianity and Islam.

Even when the dominant view of dogs has been negative, however, they were sometimes praised for their loyalty. Both Christians and Muslims honor Kasmir, a dog that according to legend guarded the seven sleepers of Ephesus for two hundred years after these young men took refuge in a cave to escape persecution for their beliefs by the Roman Emperor Decius (249–251 CE). According to one medieval legend, the dog Guinefort on an estate near Lyon in France saved a baby from a snake but was then killed in anger by its master, who saw blood and failed to realize what had happened. Peasants in the surrounding area considered the dog a saint, and pilgrims soon began to come from distant towns to venerate the site of its martyrdom.

Dogs have often symbolized absolute loyalty, a virtue that was especially important in feudal societies. The Japanese tell of a romantic rebel named Yorozo, who single-handedly fought off the imperial guard but was finally wounded and committed ritual suicide. His dog took the corpse of Yorozo from the enemy, dragged it to a burial ground, and kept vigil there until it died of hunger. The most famous faithful dog in Japan is probably Hachiko (c. 1923–1925), who has a bronze statue commemorating his faithfulness at Shibuya station. Every day he met his master at the station; after his master died he continued to wait at the station and eventually died there himself. Few people could reciprocate that sort of devotion, but Yudhisthira, a hero in the Hindu epic *Mahabarabta*, refused to enter heaven if his dog could not accompany him. By about the twelfth century it became common for lords and ladies in Europe to have themselves depicted on their tombs with beloved dogs at their feet. In the latter eighteenth and early nineteenth centuries, there was a great expansion in pet keeping, and the dog became a central part of family life. Among aristocrats, dogs were used to show the presumed virtues of careful breeding, and elaborate records were kept of their pedigrees.

In Germany after World War I, dogs were for the first time systematically trained to serve as guides for the handicapped. Technology, however, would soon make most of the traditional functions of the dog in guarding and herding largely obsolete. By the middle of the twentieth century dogs in industrialized countries were largely depicted as nostalgic reminders of a rural past, as, for example, in the television show *Lassie* (1954–1971). The latter twentieth century saw a minor revival of interest in dog ownership throughout Europe and North America, as social scientists began to document the psychological and even physiological benefits of keeping a pet. Dogs, like human beings, have, however, become increasingly removed from the natural world, as they shared the benefits, follies, and frustrations of contemporary life. There are now designer clothes, hairdressers, spas, psychologists, and gourmet restaurants for dogs, and the first commercial use of cloning is likely to be for dogs and other pets.

Boria Sax

Further Reading

Budiansky, S. (1992). *The covenant of the wild: Why animals chose domestication.* New York: William Morrow.

Leach, M. (1961). *God had a dog: Folklore of the dog.* New Brunswick, NJ: Rutgers University Press.

Schwarz, M. (1997). *A history of dogs in the early Americas.* New Haven, CT: Yale University Press.

Serpell, J. (Ed.). (1995). *The domestic dog: Its evolution, behavior and interactions with people.* New York: Cambridge University Press.

Thurston, M. L. (1996). *The lost history of the canine race: Our 15,000-Year affair with dogs.* Kansas City, MO: Andrew and McMeel.

Domestication, Plant and Animal

Domestication of plants and animals is the most fundamental subsistence change in human history. For 100,000 years or more, humans subsisted only by foraging and hunting. Then, near the end of the Pleistocene epoch (1.9 million–10,000 BCE), people in a few regions of the Earth independently began to control and breed the species they had hitherto only collected. Between 12,000 and 5000 BCE food producing began to replace food collecting. In the process humanity gained unprecedented control of the natural world, and human populations grew geometrically. However, adaptive success was purchased at the price of ecological disruption, new infectious diseases, and accelerated environmental destruction.

Hopi Blue Corn Meal

Corn was domesticated in Middle America and later became the staple food of the indigenous peoples of the U. S. Southwest and East. The following text describes the importance of corn to the Hopi of Arizona and provides a recipe for making blue corn meal.

Corn, whether growing in lush green fields or hanging in colorful dried clusters from the roof rafters, is more than food to the Hopi people, it is life. At the naming ceremony of the newborn, a special ear of corn is selected as the "mother corn" and is held sacred by the family, until it is used much later as food. Some families also put a taste of blue cornmeal into the baby's mouth, saying, "This corn is your life's strength. Eat this and grow strong and have a long, happy life."

Making Blue Corn Flour

1. Shell dried blue corn.
2. Wash corn until the water runs clear.
3. Coarsely grind corn in a hand-powered corn mill.
4. Put ground corn in a shallow pan and bake at 350°F until the corn puffs and smells like popcorn—about twenty minutes.
5. Remove corn from pan and cool.
6. Grind puffed corn on grinding stones or in a food mill until it is as fine as flour.
7. Store cornmeal in a covered container in a cool place.

Blue corn flour is available commercially as harinella, but this product is a mixture of blue and white cornmeals so it doesn't have as strong a flavor and color as pure blue cornmeal.

Source: Kavena, Juanita Tiger. (1980). *Hopi Cookery*. Tucson: University of Arizona Press, pp. 13, 16.

The theory that domestication took place in a single limited area and then spread by diffusion throughout the rest of the world has been discredited. It now appears that plant and animal domestication occurred independently and repeatedly within six or more primary "hearths" in southwestern Asia, sub-Saharan Africa, peninsular southeastern Asia, Eastern Asia, Mesoamerica, and Andean South America. Later, more limited domestication took place in secondary "hearths" such as southeastern North America and southern Asia.

Locating these hearths is easier than determining why such profound adaptive changes occurred within them. The ethnographic (relating to the study of human cultures) record indicates that, as a rule, foraging peoples do not farm unless new circumstances make foraging difficult or impossible. Therefore, the transformations of food-collecting systems into food-producing ones at the end of the Pleistocene epoch may have been caused by worldwide (1) climate changes, (2) mammalian extinctions, (3) sea-level rise, and (4) apparent human population increases that also occurred around that time. Archeologist Mark Cohen (1977) argues that, although prehistoric foraging populations grew throughout the Pleistocene epoch, the pressure of population on food resources became critical only when climatic and environmental changes at the epoch's close undercut existing foraging economies. As environments became increasingly less productive, population pressure forced foragers to intensify and expand their subsistence activities. According to economic historian Frederic Pryor (1983), such intensification might have included taming animals and tending plants in order to (1) reduce the risks arising from overreliance on increasingly unreliable wild foodstuffs, (2) supplement wild foodstuffs available primarily in one season with cultivated foodstuffs available in another, (3) utilize the labor of marginal members of societies who were unable to participate fully in the primary food-collection activities, or (4) simply add variety to the diet.

Where taming and tending were practiced over the long term on suitably malleable species, it likely resulted in domestication. However, not all scholars accept the "food crisis theory" and instead favor other causes, including human population growth, differentiation and specialization within human adaptive systems, or creative human manipulation of the environment.

Plant Domestication

Whatever their reasons for doing it, after people began to systematically replant the seeds they gathered, they interposed *human* selection between the organisms and the *natural* selective forces of the environment.

> A common procedure at harvest time is for the cultivator to go through his field and carefully select

Two llamas in Huaraz, Peru. COURTESY NICOLE LALIBERTE.

heads to be saved as stock seed for the next planting. The rest of the field is harvested for consumption. In this situation, selection is total. The components of the population that contribute to the next generation are those chosen by the cultivator. The rest are eliminated from the gene pool. (Harlan, De Wet, & Stemler 1976, 8)

As a result, some genetic mutations that would ordinarily be eliminated in the wild come to be favored in the cultivator's field. In cereal grasses such as wild wheat, barley, oats, or rye, seed-dispersal mechanisms are the first to change under cultivation. Wild grains have excellent means of scattering their ripe seeds because natural selection allows only the genes of plants with efficient dispersal mechanisms to be transmitted to succeeding generations. Although genetic mutations retarding seed dispersal occur in each generation in wild populations, they are fatal to the progeny of the plants that carry them. Yet, the seeds of wild plants with retarded seed-dispersal mechanisms are easier for humans to collect. It is their seeds that are unconsciously selected by collectors. When collectors began to *reseed* their fields, such mutations began to survive. Reseeding may have first been done by collectors seeking to introduce wild cereals into habitats outside their natural range. Whatever the reason, when collectors began saving and planting some of the seeds they harvested, greater and greater numbers of the dispersal-retarding mutations were concentrated in the grain populations. Generations of unconscious human selection genetically altered the grain and increased its harvestability and, therefore, the productivity per unit of labor invested in its collection.

Harvesters also unconsciously favored uniform rates of seed maturation. Wild cereal seeds do not ger-

A Bedouin man with a donkey, a beast of burden, in Egypt in 2002. COURTESY NICOLE LALIBERTE.

minate at the same time but rather tend to sprout throughout the growing season. Some even remain dormant for years. Cultivated cereals are harvested all at once. Individual plants that produce the most seeds at harvest time thus make the greatest contribution to the next generation. In this way, harvesting narrows seed germination ranges and reduces prolonged seed dormancy.

A trend toward larger seeds is also common, although not entirely universal, in cereals under cultivation. The increased size of domesticated seeds is partly due to conscious human selection of the largest seeds for replanting, but larger seeds also result from seedling competition. Seed size is closely related to seedling vigor, and the seedlings that sprout first and grow fastest in the seed bed are the ones most likely to contribute genes to the next generation.

In addition to these unconscious selective behaviors, a variety of others are imposed by the cultivators' conscious preferences in taste, color, ease of processing, and storage. As a general rule, the part of the plant most used by humans is the part most modified by human selection. Consequently, little resemblance exists between the ears in maize, the tubers in yams, or the pods in peas and the comparable organs in the wild ancestors of these plants. Domesticated plants have been sculpted by human selection. As the process continues through time, plants lose, to a greater or lesser degree, their capacity to survive without direct human intervention in their life cycles.

Domestic wheat, a cereal grass of the genus *Triticum*, has proven to be the most significant cultivated plant in human history. Yet, such minor genetic differences separate wild and domestic wheats that they might readily be included in the same species. This genetic proximity suggests that the domestication of wheat was both simple and rapid. Recent experiments in the measurement of domestication rates done by archeologist Gordon Hillman and plant scientist Stuart Davies (1990) indicate that wild einkorn and emmer wheats could have become completely domesticated in twenty to two hundred years. By contrast, the domestication of maize or corn appears to have taken upward of two thousand years.

Maize *(Zea mays spp.)* evolved from the wild grasslike perennial *teosinte* in Mesoamerica and northern South America. The earliest evidence of what is probably maize comes from a pollen profile dating to 5100 BCE. The earliest definite archeological maize remains were recovered at Guilá Naquitz, a dry rockshelter in Oaxaca, Mexico. These tiny cobs date to about 4200 BCE

and came from plants in an early stage of domestication. Maize does not appear to have been fully domesticated until about 3000 BCE. From that time forward, it was widely cultivated in North and South America. The slow pace of maize domestication is striking considering that squash *(Cucurbita spp.)*, another New World cultigen (an organism of a variety or species for which a wild ancestor is unknown), was first cultivated between 8000 and 6000 BCE.

Although maize produces more foodstuffs per unit of cultivated land than any of the other Native American crops, it has nutritional disadvantages. Most notably, certain of its amino acids are difficult for humans to process. Native Americans learned to enhance the nutritional quality of maize by boiling dried kernels in a lime solution before grinding them into flour. Beans *(Phaseolus spp.)* supply many of the nutrients missing in maize, and Native Americans also learned to grow and consume the two crops together.

Although a vast array of vegetables is grown in Eastern Asia, dry and wet rice *(Oryza spp.)* are the focus of cultivation there. In the world at large, only wheat exceeds rice in dietary importance. Although it has been suggested that rice domestication began about 15,000 BCE, the earliest archeological evidence of domesticated rice, recovered at sites from northern Thailand and the well-watered, tropical regions of southern China, is no earlier than about 5500 BCE. Rice cultivation spread to—or emerged independently in—northern China shortly after this time.

Millet is the common name for a number of drought-resistant cereal grasses widely used as human food, animal forage, and hay. Most species tilled today were apparently domesticated in northern China. As one moves from south to north in China, rainfall levels and mean annual temperatures decline. Not surprisingly, the plants domesticated in northern China contrast markedly with those in southern China. Foxtail *(Setaria italica)*, pearl millet *(Pennisetum americanum)*, broomcorn millet *(Panicum miliaceum)*, and other species were probably domesticated on the upper and middle reaches of the Yellow River. After millet's domestication, various millet races spread throughout semiarid mainland Asia and arrived in Taiwan between 4000 and 2500 BCE.

In tropical and subtropical regions of the world, cultivation traditionally centered on asexually or vegetatively reproduced root crops such as arrowroot *(Maranta spp.)*, yams *(Dioscorea spp.)*, potatoes *(Solanum tuberosum)*, taro *(Colocasia spp.)*, cassava or manioc *(Manihot spp.)*, and fruit trees such as bananas *(Musa* spp.). Seeds are not necessary for their reproduction. These plants all have the capacity to regenerate tissues and structural parts either naturally or through human cutting or grafting. By reproducing plants asexually, farmers are able to preserve desired characteristics from generation to generation. Intensive human vegetative husbandry has caused some species to lose their capacity for sexual reproduction altogether. The ease of this manner of horticulture suggests that root crop domestication by vegetative reproduction may have preceded the domestication of cereal grains and other seed crops. Domesticated root crops were present in Panama by 5000 BCE.

Animal Domestication

It is generally assumed that, confronted by humans, wild animals instinctively either fight or flee. However, zooarcheologist Charles Reed (1986) contends that most, in fact, are easily tamed. In his view, the major impediment to their domestication was human hunting. Subsistence systems that minimized hunting were the most likely to have initiated the domestication process; those that specialized in hunting were the least likely to have done so. Recognizing the signs of domestication in skeletal remains from archeological sites is not often easy. Fortunately, in recent years the analysis of DNA has proved a helpful supplement to archeology.

The skeletons of dogs (Canis familiaris) dated to about 12,000 BCE recovered from hunting camps in Palestine constitute the earliest definite archeological evidence of animal domestication of any kind. One can see why dogs were the first to enter the human orbit. Canines are willing scavengers; their wolf ancestors must have skulked around the edges of human camps since time immemorial. Eventually such skulkers would have become semidomesticated. Full domestication—and human recognition of the utility of dogs in the hunt—no doubt came later. But how much later? A recent comparison of wolf and dog DNA sequences suggests the two species diverged more than 100,000 years ago. Few prehistorians are prepared to accept such an early date for the onset of domestication. Genetic analysis of a large sample of contemporary dogs worldwide suggests that the domestic dog is most likely to have originated in Eastern Asia fifteen thousand years ago and to have spread from there. Related DNA analysis suggests that New World dogs originated in the Old World and then, in company with peoples crossing the Bering Strait land bridge, entered North America near the end of the Pleistocene epoch.

Ovicaprines—sheep (Ovis spp.) and goats (Capra spp.)—were the next animal species to enter the human orbit. Archeological evidence suggests that their domestication probably occurred as early as 9000 BCE in the mountainous regions of eastern Turkey and western Iran. Wild ovicaprines were "preadapted" for life with humans; easy to tame when young, they can digest a wide range of plants that humans find inedible. More importantly, their alpha (dominant) males neither defend individual territories nor assemble exclusive harems. Ovicaprines thus can be kept in sociable, mixed-sex herds. Between about 7000 and 6000 BCE domestic goats and sheep became the principal source of meat and hides for the earliest farmers of southwestern Asia. Their dispersal throughout Eurasia and Africa after that time appears to have been rapid.

Domestic pigs are descended from the wild boar (Sus scrofa), a species originally found throughout broad-leafed, deciduous (leaf-dropping) forests from Eurasia to northern Africa. Although adult boars are dangerous, wild piglets are easily tamed. Archeological evidence suggests that pig domestication began slightly later than ovicaprines, independently in southwestern and eastern Asia.

The placid domestic cow of modern times, Bos taurus, is a descendant of Bos primigenius, the Old World wild cow or auroch (plural aurochsen). Aurochsen became extinct in the seventeenth century. However, their behavior can be inferred from accounts of Spanish longhorn cattle that reverted to the wild in frontier Texas and California. Longhorns were fierce, quick, willing to attack without provocation, and hard to kill. If aurochsen, which often reached 2 meters at the withers, behaved like longhorns, they must have been among the most formidable creatures encountered by prehistoric people. This leaves researchers wondering what possessed human forebears to domesticate them. Perhaps only religious motivation would have induced people to do so. Aurochsen might have been driven into natural enclosures from which individual animals were extracted for sacrifice. Eventually herds thus impounded might have been kept and bred. Whatever the motive for it, cattle domestication began about 7000 BCE in Anatolia, Greece, and parts of southwestern Asia. Significantly, archeological evidence of bull worship at around 6000 BCE has come to light at early sites such as Çatal Hüyük in Turkey and elsewhere in the eastern Mediterranean. Once domesticated, cattle spread quickly. Bos taurus bones dating to about 4500

BCE have been recovered in northern Africa at Capeletti. Cattle herders expanded south into the Sahara Desert during a moist period there between about 5500 and 2500 BCE. Rock paintings at Tassili in the central Sahara depict long-horned, humpless cattle of apparent *Bos taurus* stock. The desiccating Sahara pushed herders farther south. Domesticated cattle, presumably taurines, were present in eastern Africa by about 3000 BCE. The expansion of herders throughout sub-Saharan Africa was well underway after that date. However, recent DNA evidence suggests the possibility that native African cattle were already domesticated in sub-Saharan Africa prior to the arrival of taurine stock.

Southern Asia was a third center of independent cattle domestication. It was a primary hearth for the domestication of the water buffalo *(Bubalus bubalis)* and humped Zebu cattle *(Bos indicus)*. Zebu cattle from the Indian subcontinent appeared in eastern Africa sometime after about 1000 BCE. Infusion of such stock must have improved African herds. Zebu cattle generally need less water and forage than taurines and gain back weight more quickly after droughts. Crossing Zebu with local breeds may also have produced more disease-resistant cattle capable of greater milk yields.

Cattle were the earliest pack transport and traction animals but, following their domestication, horses *(Equus caballus)*, donkeys *(Equus asinus)*, and camels *(Camelus spp.)* performed both tasks more efficiently. Although all three were likely domesticated for their meat, hides, and milk, the subsequent mastery of riding of these species revolutionized human trade, transportation, and warfare. The donkey, apparently the first of the horse family *(Equidae)* to be domesticated, appears in the archeological record of Mesopotamia about 4000 BCE. DNA analyses of modern horses suggest that their domestication occurred in many centers in Eurasia. Archeological remains indicate that horses were certainly being raised on the steppes north of the Black Sea by 3000 BCE. Archeological evidence of domesticated camels is poor, but these animals were probably present in southwestern Asia by 3000 BCE.

The late Pleistocene extinctions that swept through the New World eliminated wild species, such as horses and giant camels, that might otherwise have been domesticated. The key grazing animal species to survive—pronghorn antelope *(Antilocapra americana)* and American buffalo *(Bison bison)*—make poor domesticants. Although social like ovicaprines, pronghorns differ from them in the amount of body contact they will tolerate. They are not "contact animals" but rather maintain distance between each other. Adult male pronghorns have a well-developed sense of territory. They strive mightily to keep females inside their territory and other males outside of it. These traits render domesticating pronghorns difficult and herding them nearly impossible. Bison also exhibit behavioral traits that make handling difficult even for contemporary herders. Not surprisingly, both species remained wild into modern times. Thus, the number of potentially domesticable animals in the Americas was limited. Compared to the extraordinary array of New World domesticated plants, the array of domesticated animals was paltry indeed. It included only dogs, Muscovy ducks *(Cairina moschata)*, turkeys *(Mele agris gallopavo)*, Guinea pigs *(Cavia porcellus)*, and various forms of New World camelids *(Lama spp.)* such as the llama, vicuña, guanaco, and alpaca. This dearth of domesticated animals had fatal consequences for New World peoples—a fact dramatically illustrated in Mexico and Peru by the rapid military triumphs of mounted sixteenth-century Spanish conquistadores. However, the low number of pre-Columbian domesticated animals had a positive side: It reduced Native American exposure to deadly diseases passed from animals to humans.

Silent Domestication

Domestication of plants and animals in the visible world was accompanied by domestication of organisms in the invisible microbial world. Many of these microbes were benign or useful. Yeast, for example, makes fermentation possible. Systematic fermentation is impractical, even impossible, in the absence of sealable pottery jars. Yeast domestication must therefore have been an unintended consequence of ceramic manufacture. Fermentation processes dependent upon yeast include pickling, cheese making, bread making, culturing, and producing vinegars, sauces (especially fish sauces), and lactic acid fermentations of various vegetables such as sauerkraut. Fermentation can preserve food, remove toxic components, utilize food wastes, and supply essential secondary food constituents. Fermented sauces and relishes improve flavor or disguise its defects.

The fermentation of wine and beer must not be forgotten. Early wine was made from honey, palm sap, dates, figs, raisins, apples, pomegranates, and numerous other fruits. Beer, fermented chiefly from wheat and barley, made an important contribution to the nutrition of the grain farmers who consumed it. Cereal porridge lacks vitamins of the B-complex. Happily, most beers are rich in B-complex vitamins. But human adaptation proceeds on the mental plane as well as the material. Beer and wine help here, too; English poet A. E. Houseman wrote, "And malt does more than Milton can / To justify God's ways to man" (1988).

The achievement of early farmers in harnessing the microbes of fermentation is impressive indeed. Their practical understanding of the ferments is especially remarkable because it was gained by trial and error in a prescientific context. In addition to yeasts and bacteria, early farmers domesticated numerous lower plants such as mushrooms, fungi, and algae. Cultivation of yeasts, bacteria, and lower plants offers three advantages: short production cycles, modest space needs, and low water requirements. Further, the relative simplicity of their husbandry requirements allows the character of the final product to be precisely controlled.

Unfortunately, silent domestication had a more sinister aspect. By living intimately with their domestic animals, humans altered the transmission patterns of existing animal pathogens (agents of disease) and stimulated the evolution of new ones. Humans came to share the diseases of the creatures they exploited. Old World examples include measles, tuberculosis, and smallpox (derived from cattle) and influenza and pertussis (from pigs and perhaps ducks and dogs). There are many others, some of which spill back from domestic animals to wildlife that come in contact with them.

By making life more sedentary, early farming brought people into sustained contact with fecal wastes, both human and animal. Absent a clear recognition of the relationship between feces and disease, farmers were not overly careful about the disposal of human and animal waste and seemed to have made little systematic effort at preventing their food and water from becoming contaminated by sewage. Such contamination provides ideal environments for the transmission of diseases such as diarrhea (particularly dangerous for small children), typhoid, and cholera. Intestinal parasites such as worms and protozoa also spread readily in this environment.

This brings the discussion once more to beer. To a certain extent, these diseases can be avoided by not drinking the water and making do with beer and wine instead. Alcoholic ferments were thus an important cultural adaptation to the new conditions of disease and health created by the silent domestication processes active in early farming life.

Weeds

Microbes were not the only set of unintended domesticants. Another set, weeds, was found on the margins of the cultivators' fields. *Weed* is a folk, not a scientific, term. It refers to plants that rapidly colonize soils disturbed and stripped of vegetation by fires, landslides, windstorms, floods, and so forth. Before the advent of agriculture, there were relatively few of these plants. However, land clearance for agriculture dramatically expanded the habitat of such pioneers and, eventually, turned them into unintended cultivars (organisms originating and persisting under cultivation) dependent upon human environmental disturbance and subject to human manipulation. In this way, new varieties of weeds were produced as the by-products of cultivation. These new varieties emerged as hybrids when wild and domesticated races of cereals and other plants were grown together in the same fields. Some weed species were ultimately domesticated. Both rye and oats were European weeds that entered the repertoire of Old World domesticates when farmer-colonists began farming the interior of that continent. But most weeds remain semidomesticated pests and bedevil cultivators to this day.

The spread of farming carried these weedy pests into new territories. The best evidence for the arrival of agricultural peoples in northern Europe is the appearance of such characteristic Mediterranean weeds as ribwort plantain (*Plantago lanceolata*), stinging nettle (*Urtica dioica*), and various kinds of sorrels (*Rumex spp.*). The later spread of European agriculture into the New World, Australia, and the islands of the Pacific introduced these Old World weeds with devastating effect.

Human-Caused Environmental Destruction

By late prehistoric times few of the Earth's terrestrial ecosystems had not felt the impacts of humankind. Not all impacts were of the same magnitude, however. Hunting-and-gathering peoples had a comparatively modest effect, whereas farmers radically changed natural conditions wherever they went. By clearing, burning, and killing wild predators, and later by plowing and irrigating, they overrode local constraints and created new, relatively homogeneous environments. Agriculture represents an ecological simplification of human subsistence. It narrows human dependence to a limited range of plant and animal species largely controlled by the farmers themselves. When tended by humans, this array of domesticated species can adapt to a wide range of environments. The adaptability of their animals and plants, combined with their efforts at transforming the environment, meant that agriculturalists were less obliged to learn the ins and outs of their new ecologies and cared little for preserving wild food resources. By altering their environment and increasing the size of the human population supported by it, farmers made it difficult for hunting-and-gathering peoples to subsist. Along with agricultural peoples and their animals came deadly zoonoses (diseases communicable from animals to humans). As prehistory drew to a close, continued population growth generated by agriculture stimulated ever-more-intensive forms of cultivation and husbandry such as dairying, wool raising, irrigation agriculture, and its twin, fully nomadic pastoralism. Inexorably, growth and intensification led to the rise of cities, states, and civilization. From then on, there was no going back.

D. Bruce Dickson

See also Agriculture; Cereals; Horse; Patoralism; Rice

Further Reading

Clutton-Brock, J. (1999). *A history of domesticated mammals.* London: Cambridge University Press.

Cohen, M. (1977). *The food crisis in prehistory.* New Haven, CT: Yale University Press.

Crawford, G. W., & Shen, C. (1998). The origins of rice agriculture: Recent progress in east Asia. *Antiquity, 72*(278), 856–866.

Crosby, A. W. (1986). *Ecological imperialism: The biological expansion of Europe.* New York: Cambridge University Press.

Daszak, P., Cunningham, A. A., & Hyatt, A. D. (2000). Emerging infectious diseases of wildlife—Threats to biodiversity and human health. *Science, 287*(5452), 443–449.

Dickson, D. B. (1988). Anthropological utopias and geographical epidemics: Competing models of social change and the problem of the origins of agriculture. In P. Hugill & D. B. Dickson (Eds.), *The Transfer and Transformation of Ideas and Material Culture* (pp. 45–72). College Station: Texas A&M University Press.

Flannery, K. V. (1969). Origins and ecological effects of early domestication in Iran and the Near East. In P. J. Ucko & G. W. Dimbleby (Eds.), *The domestication and exploitation of plants and animals* (pp. 73–100). Chicago: Aldine.

Giuffra, E., Kijas, J. M. H., Amarger, V., Carlborg, Ö., Jeon, J.-T., & Anderson, L. (2000). The origin of the domestic pig: Independent domestication and subsequent introgression. *Genetics 154*(4), 1785–1791.

Haeun, M., Schäfer-Pregi, R., Klawan, D., Castagna, R., Accerbi, M., Borghi, B., & Salamini, F.(1997). Site of einkorn wheat domestication identified by DNA fingerprinting. *Science, 278*(5341), 1312–1314.

Harlan, J. R., De Wet, J. M. J., & Stemler, A. (1976). Plant domestication and indigenous African agriculture. In J. R. Harlan, J. M. De Wet, & A. Stemler (Eds.), *Origins of African plant domestication* (pp. 3–19). The Hague, Netherlands: Mouton.

Hillman, G. C., & Davies, M. S. (1990). Measured domestication rates in wild wheats and barley under primitive cultivation, and their archaeological implications. *Journal of World Prehistory,* (2), 157–222.

Housman, A. E. (1988). A Shropshire lad (verse LXII). In *Collected poems and selected prose.* New York: Penguin.

MacHugh, D. E., & Bradley, D. G. (2001). Livestock genetic origins: Goats buck the trend. *Proceedings of the National Academy of Sciences, 98*(10), 5382–5384.

Pennisi, E. (2002). Shaggy dog history. *Science, 298*(5598), 1540–1542.

Piperno, D. R., & Flannery, K. V. (2001). The earliest archaeological maize (*Zea mays* L.) from highland Mexico: New accelerator mass spectrometry dates and their implications. *Proceedings of the National Academy of Sciences, 98*(4), 2101–2103.

Piperno, D. R., Ranere, A. J., Holst, I., & Hansell, P. (2000). Starch grains reveal early root crop horticulture in the Panamanian tropical forest. *Nature, 407*(6806), 894–897.

Pryor, F. L. (1983). Causal theories about the origins of agriculture. *Research in Economic History, 8*, 93–124.

Reed, C. (1986). Wild animals ain't so wild, domesticating them not so difficult. *Expedition, 28*(2), 8–15.

Savolainen, P., Zhang, Y.-P., Luo, J., Lundeberg, J., & Leitner, T. (2002). Genetic evidence for an east Asian origin of domestic dogs. *Science, 298*(5598), 1610–1613.

Smith, B. D. (1997). The initial domestication of *Cucurbita pepo* in the Americas 10,000 years ago. *Science, 276*(5314), 932–934.

Stanton, W. R. (1969). Some domesticated lower plants in south east Asian food technology. In P. J. Ucko & G. W. Dimbleby (Eds.), *The domestication and exploitation of plants and animals* (pp. 463–469). Chicago: Aldine.

Troy, C. S., MacHugh, D. E., Bailley, J. F., Magee, D. A., Loftus, R. T., Cunningham, P., Chamberlain, A. T., Sykes, B. C., & Bradley, D. G. (2001). Genetic evidence for Near-Eastern origins of European cattle. *Nature, 410*(6832),1088–1091.

Vilà, C., Leonard, J. A., Götherström, A., Marklund, S., Sandberg, K., Lindén, K., Wayne, R. K., & Ellegren, H. (2001). Widespread origins of domestic horse lineages. *Science, 291*(5503), 474–477.

Vilà, C., Savolainen, P., Maldonado, J. E., Amorim, I. R., Rice, J. E., Honeycutt, R. L., Cranndall, K. A., Lundeberg, J., & Wayne, R. K. (1997). Multiple and ancient origins of the domestic dog. *Science, 276*(5319), 1687–1689.

Zhao, Z. (1998). The middle Yangtze region in China is one place where rice was domesticated: Phytolith evidence from the Diaotonghuan cave, northern Jiangxi. *Antiquity, 72*(278), 885–897.

Zohary, D., & Hopf, M. (2000). Domestication of Plants in the Old World (3rd ed.). Oxford, UK: Oxford University Press.

Douglas, Marjorie Stoneman
(1890–1998)

U.S. conservationist

Marjorie Stoneman Douglas was born in Minneapolis, Minnesota, the only child of Florence Lillian Trefethen and Frank B. Stoneman. When she was a young child, her father left, eventually settling in Florida, and she moved with her mother to her mother's family in Taunton, Massachusetts, her home until she finished college. In 1912 she graduated from Wellesley College, where she majored in English but also studied geology and geography.

In 1915, after a short career training salesgirls in department stores and a brief childless marriage to Kenneth Douglas, a journalist with the *Newark* (New Jersey) *Evening News*, she joined her father in Miami and successfully filed for divorce. Because her father had become editor of the *Miami Herald*, Douglas was soon able to begin her career as a writer.

Except for a year of service with the American Red Cross in Europe during World War I, Douglas devoted the rest of her life to presenting the characteristics and needs of South Florida to the public. For three years she wrote a daily column for the *Herald* that included nature studies and social comment. She served on the first committee organized to establish an Everglades National Park, authorized by Congress in 1934 and established in 1947. Her book, *The Everglades: River of Grass* (1947), was the first work to publicize the concept that water moved like a river almost imperceptibly through the saw grass of the Everglades to the sea. In 1970, when nearby Big Cypress Swamp was threatened by a proposed jetport, she organized the Friends of the Everglades. From then on, she spoke out publicly and wrote articles in support of efforts to restore the flow of water from the Kissimee River through Lake Okeechobee into the Everglades.

Earlier, Douglas wrote short stories for general-interest magazines that helped define South Florida as a region and often included plots about threats to the environment. She published full-length fiction with similar themes, including *Road to the Sun* (1951), *Freedom River Florida 1845* (1953), and *Alligator Crossing* (1959). Her other full-length nonfiction works were *Hurricane* (1958) and *Florida, the Long Frontier* (1967).

Douglas spent the last years of her long life as an ardent proponent of projects to restore the Everglades, using her voice and her pen. She presented to the public the concept that the whole of South Florida was one ecosystem blocked from functioning by canals and channels and polluted by agricultural interests, particularly sugarcane growers. Although she died before Congress passed the Comprehensive Everglades Restoration Plan in 2000, Douglas and her Friends of the Everglades had served as the powerful lobby that had kept the issues before the public.

Douglas died at the age of 108 in her beloved home in Coconut Grove. The National Park Service scattered her ashes in the park's Marjory Stoneman Douglas Wilderness Area, established in 1978 with approximately 518,600 hectares (1.3 million acres).

Polly Welts Kaufman

Further Reading

Douglas, M. S., & Davis, J. E. (2002). *The wide brim: Early poems and ponderings of Marjory Stoneman Douglas.* Gainesville: University Press of Florida.

Douglas, M. S., & Rothchild, J. (1987). *Marjorie Stoneman Douglas: Voice of the river.* Sarasota, FL: Pineapple Press.

McCarthy, K. M., (Ed.). (1990). *Nine Florida stories by Marjory Stoneman Douglas.* Jacksonville: University of North Florida

McCarthy, K. M. (Ed.). (1998). *"A river in flood" and other Florida stories by Marjorie Stoneman Douglas.* Gainesville: University Press of Florida.

Leposky, R. E. (1997). Marjorie Stoneman Douglas: Bibliography. *The Marjorie Kinnan Rawlings Journal of Florida Literature, 8,* 55–73.

Douglas, William O.
(1898–1980)
U.S. Supreme Court Justice, author, environmentalist

William O. Douglas used his stature as a U.S. Supreme Court Justice to popularize environmental issues. Douglas's public activism, his environmental writings, and various legal opinions assured Douglas an important place in the American environmental movement from the 1950s to the 1970s.

Born in Minnesota in 1898, Douglas spent most of his early years living in Yakima, Washington. To strengthen himself from weakness caused by infantile paralysis, he hiked in the hills and mountains of central Washington. The hiking increased Douglas's strength and made him a lifelong believer in the healing power of nature.

Douglas graduated from Whitman College in 1920 and from Columbia Law School in 1925. Following teaching stints at Columbia and Yale law schools, Douglas served on the Securities and Exchange Commission until appointed to the Supreme Court in 1939. He quickly associated with the liberal justices of the Court and by the early 1950s was an established national figure.

Using that prominence, Douglas first began his public environmental activism in 1954. The National Park Service proposed a scenic highway along the Chesapeake and Ohio Canal in the suburbs of Washington, D.C., and the *Washington Post* published an editorial supporting the road. The towpath along the canal was a favorite refuge for Douglas, and he wrote to the *Post* on 15 January 1954, calling the canal a "Sanctuary" and urging the editorialist to join him for a hike, upon which Douglas believed he would change his mind supporting the road. Douglas's public challenge worked, and two *Post* editors and several well-known American wilderness advocates joined Douglas for a

189-mile protest hike. Eventually, due to this public exposure and continued activism, the road proposal was defeated, and the C & O Canal became designated a National Historical Park in 1971. The National Park Service dedicated the park to Douglas in 1977.

Douglas took public stands at several other places during the ensuing two decades. In 1958, Douglas led another protest against a road, this time in the Olympic National Park. Like the C & O Canal hike, this successful protest hike included leading environmentalists and drew significant media exposure. He also lent his name, time, and energy to environmental causes for forests and mountains, rivers and lakes, and fish and wildlife throughout the nation. Douglas wrote about much of his environmental activism and philosophy in a series of popular books published in the 1960s, including *My Wilderness: The Pacific West* (1960), *My Wilderness: East to Katahdin* (1961), *A Wilderness Bill of Rights* (1965), and *Farewell to Texas: A Vanishing Wilderness* (1967).

Furthermore, as a Supreme Court Justice, Douglas heard some cases concerning environmental issues. In *Udall v. Federal Power Commission* (1967), for example, Douglas wrote a majority opinion that considered the interests of fish and recreation in river management and refused to endorse a dam proposal for the Snake River. In several dissents, including *Scenic River Preservation Conference v. Federal Power Commission* (1972) and *Aberdeen & Rockfish R. Co. v. Students Challenging Regulatory Agency Procedures* (1975), the justice worried about the weakening of the National Environmental Policy Act (1969) and advocated stronger application of the law. His most important environmental legal opinion came in *Sierra Club v. Morton* (1972) in which Douglas argued that natural entities, such as valleys, rivers, or forests, ought to have the standing to sue in court. It was a radical legal idea that a majority on the Court was unable to support.

I realized that Eastern thought had somewhat more compassion for all living things. Man was a form of life that in another reincarnation might possibly be a horsefly or a bird of paradise or a deer. So a man of such a faith, looking at animals, might be looking at old friends or ancestors. In the East the wilderness has no evil connotation; it is thought of as an expression of the unity and harmony of the universe.

William O. Douglas. (1974). *Go East, Young Man*. New York: Random House.

Douglas lent his reputation to environmental causes at a momentous time in American environmental history, and his work made a difference.

Adam M. Sowards

Further Reading

Douglas, W. O. (1965). *A wilderness bill of rights.* Boston: Little, Brown and Company.

Douglas, W. O. (1972). *The three hundred year war: A chronicle of ecological disaster.* New York: Random House.

O'Fallon, J. M. (Ed.). (2000). *Nature's justice: Writings of William O. Douglas.* Corvallis: Oregon State University Press.

Sowards, A. M. (2002). William O. Douglas: The environmental justice. In B. Tong & R. A. Lutz (Eds.), *The human tradition in the American west* (pp. 155–170). Wilmington, DE: Scholarly Resources.

Wasby, S. L. (Ed.). (1990). *"He shall not pass this way again": The legacy of justice William O. Douglas.* Pittsburgh, PA: University of Pittsburgh Press, for the William O. Douglas Institute.

Droughts

Droughts are a deficit of precipitation over a period of time. Droughts are normal, recurrent, and menacing events that are part of the climate of a place. They occur in almost all climatic zones of the world, and their characteristics vary from one place to another. Droughts can be short or long. They can be local or widespread. Throughout human history, droughts have posed a threat to the survival of civilizations by creating a lack of water for agriculture and the natural environment. Some societies have been decimated by droughts as people were forced to migrate and disperse. Droughts have caused famines and wars and have altered the course of history.

Droughts are especially common in arid regions (deserts that receive less than 25 centimeters of precipitation a year) and semiarid regions (steppes that receive between 25 and 50 centimeters of precipitation per year). Generally, drier regions have a greater variability of precipitation and a greater vulnerability to drought. Droughts are a concern in wetter regions because they can have an impact on agriculture and other economic activities as well as pose a fire hazard. About half the people who live in the most populated areas of the world are vulnerable to droughts. The United Nations Development Programme, which is working to halve world poverty by 2015, is providing advisory services and institutional strengthening to people in the drylands of the world, empowering the poor so that they can reduce their vulnerability to climatic shocks such as droughts and improve their adaptation to climatic change.

Definitions

Scientists classify droughts by conceptual and operational definitions. Conceptual definitions are generic and help people understand the concept of drought. An example of an operational definition is "an extended period of dry weather," which refers to deficient precipitation for a period of time that can be as long as a season, a year, or several years.

Operational definitions identify the inception, persistence, conclusion, and severity of a drought. Operational definitions vary according to different discipline perspectives. The inception of a drought can be defined by how much the amount of precipitation has deviated from the average. In the field of agriculture, the definition of a drought could compare the amount of precipitation received to the amount of evapotranspiration (evaporation plus transpiration [moisture given off by vegetation]) in order to determine how much soil moisture is lost and the impact it will have on plant growth.

A meteorological drought is defined by how dry it is in comparison to the average amount of precipitation that is received in a given area, as well as by how long the drought has lasted. A meteorological drought ends when precipitation returns. The length of time that a place takes to recover from a meteorological drought is dependent on the drought's intensity, duration, and the amount of precipitation after the drought ends.

A hydrological drought is defined by the effects that the lack of precipitation has on both surface and subsurface water supplies. The lack of water supplies affects streamflow, lake levels, and aquifers. This affects such economic activities as agriculture, recreation, navigation, and the production of hydroelectricity. Lack of water supplies also affects the natural habitat of plants and animals, land use (i.e., deforestation), and land degradation (i.e., desertification). It can also have political implications. For example, a country could build dams to create catchment basins or reservoirs to trap as much water as possible along a river that flows into another country.

War and Drought, Peace and Milk

For peoples whose lives and ways of life are dependent on the food they grow and the animals they raise, drought is a threat to their very existence. The Somali of northeast Africa equate drought with everything bad and rain with everything good.

At this point, let me add a word on the meaning of "evil" and "good." What are the evils and the virtues we talk about in connection with the days and the year? By "evil" I mean drought, for drought is said to be the source of all evil. The source of all virtue, then, is rain. From this pastoral base, the metaphors can be expanded. Drought, *ABAAR*, is said to be accompanied by war, *COL*; rain is accompanied by peace, *NABAD*. Hence one hears the saying, *COL IYO ABAAR, NABAD IYO CAANO*: "war and drought, peace and milk," milk here being synonymous with rain, a further extension of the metaphor. Inter-clan strife may easily result from different families, *REER*s, arriving at a well at the same time during a drought. If immediate action is not taken, war may result. The opposite is true during a year of plenty. A further extension of the metaphor is, with drought and war, disease, *CUDUR*; with rain and peace, health, *CAAFIMAD*. Also accompanying rain are enjoyment, *RAHHO*, marriage, worshipping, education, etc. Thus the metaphor of drought and rain is extended to all aspects of the nomadic way of life.

Source: Galaal, Muusa-Haaji-Ismaa'iil. (1968). *The Terminology and Practice of Somali Weather Lore, Astronomy, and Astrology*. Mogadishu, Somalia: Published by the author, 11.

Some scientists suggest that the two processes that should be included in a definition of a drought are the time and space processes of supply and demand. Therefore, a socioeconomic drought links the supply and demand of goods to agricultural, hydrological, and meterological droughts. In other words, a drought could be defined as occurring when the demand for a good exceeds supply due to a weather-related deficit in water supply. For example, the supply of corn, beef, water, and many other economic goods is dependent on the weather.

Causes of Drought

High air temperatures and winds and a lack of moisture in the air can affect the severity of droughts. One of the factors that controls air temperature is ground radiation. Radiation of heat from the Earth warms the air over a dry surface more than over a moist surface. This is because when a surface is dry, the absorbed solar radiation is reradiated into the atmosphere as terrestrial radiation and is primarily used to heat the atmosphere by conduction and convection of heat from the surface into the overlying air. When a surface is moist, much of the terrestrial radiation is used to vaporize water. This is why high air temperatures often accompany a drought. Therefore, the lack of moisture

in the air and the higher air temperature cause soils to dry, crops to die, and bodies of water to shrink.

Droughts also can be caused when wide undulations in the westerly wind system create huge cutoff masses of air that rotate in a cyclonic direction (a low-pressure, counterclockwise wind circulation in the Northern Hemisphere) or an anticyclonic direction (a high-pressure, clockwise wind circulation in the Northern Hemisphere). These cutoff lows and highs, referred to as "blocking systems," prevent the usual west-to-east circulation of weather systems. These blocking systems can persist for several weeks.

The weather phenomenon known as *El Niño* also produces droughts. Named by Peruvian fishermen about two hundred years ago, El Niño refers to the Christ Child because it is around Christmas (every three to seven years) that the cold coastal waters become warm. Scientists later learned that this was caused by changes in the surface temperature of the sea and shifts in the Earth's atmospheric and oceanic circulations. The changes that occur in the atmosphere and ocean circulation are in turn caused by temperature and pressure changes in the atmosphere between the eastern and western tropical parts of the southern Pacific Ocean. Warm winds and the Equatorial South Pacific Current begin to blow eastward toward South America causing precipitation, while drying out the southwestern Pacific, which is usually wet. This causes droughts in India, Indonesia, eastern Australia, Hawaii, and other islands.

Some scientists have linked the variations in precipitation to sunspot activity. A study of tree rings in the western United States has found that the drought that occurs approximately every twenty-two years coincides with the twenty-two-year cycle of magnetic polarity reversals of sunspot clusters, which reverse every eleven years after the eleven-year cycle of sunspot activity. However, many scientists have stated that there is no link between solar variation and weather.

High-pressure systems, which are areas of dry air common in deserts, can increase in size and prevent the small amount of moisture present in deserts from penetrating the region, thus increasing the probability of drought. This can also occur in other climatic regions if a high-pressure system becomes stagnant over an area. The clear skies of high-pressure systems allow the sun to warm the Earth more than normal, and in return the atmosphere is heated more by ground radiation. Therefore, deserts can experience drought, as did the Sahara late in the twentieth century.

Global warming has also been implicated as a cause of more serious and prolonged drought. The greenhouse effect—caused by the emission of carbon dioxide and other gases—increases the retention of infrared heat radiated by the Earth. However, climatologists state that droughts are completely natural and do not need an unusual event, such greenhouse warming, for their development.

History of Droughts

Desertification is the natural process of an area becoming a desert due to climatic change, but it can be accelerated by human activities. The planting of crops can add moisture to the air, but the opposite effect can occur when people remove vegetation from the land, contributing to the development of droughts and causing the climate to become drier, as has occurred in Africa. From 1968 to 1974 a severe drought occurred in the Sahel, the area along the southern margin of the Sahara Desert. Due to the drought, desertification occurred. The amount of grazing land decreased, millions of herding animals died, and over one hundred thousand people died of starvation. The Sahel suffered severe droughts in the late 1600s and mid–1700s, but the drought of 1968–1974 was devastating because a larger population lived in the region. The drought ended with above-normal rains for the area.

Pollution in the form of sulfate aerosols from factories and power plants in the industrialized Northern Hemisphere affected the Sahel thousands of miles away. The pollution may have reduced rainfall by as much as 50 percent. Scientists in Australia and Nova Scotia performed computer simulations using climatic models to test this hypothesis. They found that simulations that did not take into consideration pollutant emissions showed no drought in the Sahel. But when they factored in pollutant emissions from Europe and North America, the tropical rains of Africa shifted southward and produced less rain in northern Africa.

Droughts have also had a great socioeconomic impact on the Great Plains of the United States. When European settlers settled the Great Plains in the 1860s and 1870s, the region was experiencing an unusually wet period. To promote settlement in the region, the railroads used the slogan "Rain follows the plow," a respected scientific opinion in the mid-nineteenth century. However, a drought from 1887 to 1896 disrupted the agriculture of the region and caused many people to leave.

From 1934 to 1941 a drought affected most of the United States but especially the Midwest. The years 1934 and 1936 were the driest on record in the United States. In the Midwest, where people had broken the sod and denuded the land of its natural grassland vegetation to plant crops, dust blew into the eastern part of the region and this area became known as the "Dust Bowl." John Steinbeck wrote in his 1939 novel *The Grapes of Wrath* that thousands of homeless and hungry people fled from Arkansas, Kansas, Oklahoma, New Mexico, Nevada, and Texas looking for any kind of work. The Midwest suffered more droughts in the 1950s and from 1987 to 1989. In places, it was more severe than the 1934–1941 drought.

Extended droughts have led to permanent climatic changes in some areas. Dendrochronology (the study of tree rings) has provided a history of droughts and climatic changes. In the late thirteenth century the Anasazi people of Mesa Verde in the Colorado Plateau of southwestern Colorado fled the area due to a great drought. Dendrochronology has also revealed severe droughts that lasted several decades in the Sierra Nevada from about 900 to 1400 CE. A drought caused the demise of the ancient city of Mycenae in Greece around 1200 BCE when residents of the thriving city dispersed from the area. The drought affected Mycenae but not Athens only 96 kilometers away because moisture brought in by winds crossing the Mediterranean shifted direction, and a mountain range blocked the winds from reaching Mycenae. In eastern Pakistan and western India, agricultural activities of people of the Indus Valley, coupled with an extended drought when the summer monsoon winds failed to bring in moisture from the Arabian Sea because expansion of westerly winds to the north kept the monsoon winds from penetrating the region, created the Rajputana Desert within the span of a millennium, starting from around 2500 BCE.

Many areas of the world—such as Australia, India, Mexico, the United States, China, Africa, the Middle East, New Zealand, Canada, Russia, and northeastern Brazil, which is known as the "Drought Polygon"—are experiencing drought. These areas are part of the Earth's drylands, which cover 40 percent of the land surface. Drylands are part of semiarid or subhumid climates. They also are grasslands, which are important grain producers, serving as the breadbaskets of the world and supporting millions of people. Although drought can occur in just about any climatic region, drylands are vulnerable to desertification and are especially susceptible to experiencing a drought with permanent consequences.

Planning for Drought

Drought historically has not been given the scientific and political attention that other natural disasters, such as earthquakes, hurricanes, and floods, have been given. But recently attention has been given to the question of how the impact of a drought can be minimized. This new attention has been the result of concern over the global increase in drought and famine, desertification, deforestation, and the effect that these factors can have on climatic change, which can affect the frequency and harshness of drought.

Internationally, many countries have drought plans. In the United States drought management has been practiced by individual states. Most states now have drought plans. California and Florida delegate drought planning to local authorities. The 2000 National Drought Policy Commission report to Congress and the president, *Preparing for Drought in the 21st Century*, emphasized that drought planning needs to occur at the local, state, tribal, and federal levels. Drought planning involves taking action before a drought occurs in order to minimize its long-term damage.

In 1995 the National Drought Mitigation Center was established at the University of Nebraska-Lincoln. It assists institutions in developing and implementing measures that will reduce American society's suscepti-

bility to drought. It stresses preparedness and risk management, not crisis management. The center maintains an information clearinghouse and provides drought monitoring, planning, and mitigation. It conducts research and provides services to state, regional, tribal, and federal agencies as well as to international governments and organizations.

Each drought has its own characteristics, which are dependent on its temporal extent, severity, geographical extent, and social conditions. A drought has two components: the natural event itself, known as "the hazard," and the social factor, which is the susceptibility of a society to the hazard. Susceptibility to the hazard involves the capacity of a society to anticipate, cope, and recover. Monitoring, predicting, providing early warning, mitigation, and preparedness are components of the risk management process that helps a society deal with a drought. Scientists have to consider society's susceptibility to drought by taking into consideration such factors as population growth and shifts, technology, and environmental awareness, among others.

Indicators of Drought

The atmospheric parameters that scientists use to predict drought are precipitation and temperature, and the analysis of precipitation, streamflow, and snowpack data is used as drought indicators. However, predicting droughts is difficult. One reason is that depending on the area and the types of activities that are carried out in the area, different indicators need to be considered. For example, to gauge the possible impact of a drought, soil moisture and rates of evapotranspiration would be important factors to consider in agricultural areas, whereas a whole different set of factors need to be considered in metropolitan areas. Another problem is the lack of universal drought criteria that could allow for comparison of droughts on different continents, which would allow effective sharing of data and knowledge.

Drought indices (numerical standards that indicate the severity of a drought) rely on gathering atmospheric information (precipitation), hydrologic information (streamflow and snowpack), and soil and vegetation information (the health of plants determined by measuring reflectivity of leaf surfaces, which gives an indication of water stress).

The U.S. Department of Agriculture uses the Palmer Drought Severity Index, which takes into consideration monthly temperature and precipitation data, to determine when to grant drought assistance. The index is a soil-moisture algorithm that is used in an area of similar terrain. Another index is the Surface Water Supply Index, which is used in mountainous areas where snowpack is important to the water supply. This index is calculated by drainage basin and is based on precipitation, snowpack, streamflow, and reservoir storage.

The National Drought Mitigation Center uses the Standardized Precipitation Index, which takes into account the probability of a precipitation deficit for any time period, such as three, six, twelve, twenty-four, or forty-eight months. This index can provide an early warning of drought and helps in assessing drought severity.

Information collected from weather stations is used for drought monitoring and impact assessment. The scarcity of weather stations in some parts of the world, such as Africa, makes it difficult to monitor an impending drought. And in some areas weather information is collected only at certain locations.

Satellites are another means of global drought detection and assessment. The U.S. National Oceanic and Atmospheric Administration (NOAA) uses measurements made by the Advanced Very High Resolution Radiometer (AVHRR) on polar-orbiting satellites to improve early drought detection and to monitor a drought's impact on agriculture. AVHRR collects reflectance information in the visible, near infrared, and thermal bands of the solar spectrum. This information is combined to create a Vegetation Condition Index (VCI) and a Temperature Condition Index (TCI).

This technology works on the principle that vegetation has low reflectance in the visible and near infrared bands of the solar spectrum. Because plants absorb visible energy for the purpose of photosynthesis, the reflectance is low when plants have a normal chlorophyll content but increases when chlorophyll content decreases. Water content prevents plants from absorbing high amounts of solar energy in the near infrared band. This helps keep plants cooler. When the amount of water decreases in plants, the near infrared reflectance drops. This, in turn, leads to an increase in the vegetation surface temperature and ultimately to vegetation stress. Because AVHRR-based indices are excellent indicators of drought, they can be used to estimate agricultural losses. This method of drought measurement has been used in Africa and other parts of the world.

Famine and Drought

The primary cause of famine is political strife or a civil war, rather than drought, as had once been thought.

However, a drought can disrupt food production and can be a natural trigger for famine. The lack of water leads to crop failures, which cause food scarcity and lead to demand for food in the international market, which, in turn, harms stocks and food prices and leads to malnutrition and famines. Drought also affects forest yield: It causes an increase in fire risk; it increases livestock and wildlife death rates; it affects wildlife habitats; and it causes the destruction of crop and range land. Drought affects the economy of a society as a whole: It can cause an increase in crime; it can harm the health of a society; and it can cause a reduction on the quality of life in general. Unemployment increases, and tax revenue for government decreases. Indirect impacts of a drought include a reduction in agribusiness, which affects farmers' income and the price of food.

Drought also may cause people to migrate from the impacted area. After the drought has ended, people may not return to their homes. The area that they migrated to will experience an increase in population, which will place an increased burden on the area's infrastructure and environment. This situation has occurred in the Sahel, where people, many of whom had lived in rural areas, can no longer sustain themselves by living with nature. The coastal desert city of Nouakchott, Mauritania, on the western edge of the Sahel, in 1958 was built as the capital with a population of fifteen thousand. It now has a population of six hundred thousand due to the recurring droughts of the Sahara and Sahel. Another example is the drought-plagued area of northeastern Brazil, where human and animal pressures on the land have depleted the vegetation and overall environmental quality of the land, causing aridity to increase. Millions of people have migrated from this area. The area abandoned by a migrating population will also suffer because its economic infrastructure will decline.

Natural and Complex

The absence of an exact and widely accepted definition of drought has added to the confusion of whether drought even exists. Droughts are, in part, natural phenomena that are components of a broader physical process entailing the interaction of solar energy and upper wind and oceanic circulations. Scientists have concluded that drought is a normal and recurring feature of virtually all climatic regions, whether they experience high or low amounts of precipitation. Drought, therefore, is a temporary deviation from the norm.

Droughts, considered the most complex natural hazard, are affected by population growth, shifting population patterns, urbanization, technology, water usage, governmental policies, social behavior, and environmental awareness. Thus a society's exposure to drought is affected by its own actions. Increasing population and increasing urbanization in developing countries are increasing pressure on water, land, and other resources. Therefore, planning for a drought helps reduce its impact through mitigation and risk management.

Roberto Garza

See also Deserts; Irrigation; Water

Further Reading

Allan, T., & Warren A. (Eds.). (1993). *Deserts: The encroaching wilderness: A world conservation atlas.* New York: Oxford University Press.

Boerma, A. H. (Ed.). (1975). *Drought in the Sahel: International relief operations 1973–75* Rome: Eliograf.

Bryson, R. A., & Murray, T. J. (1977). *Climates of hunger: Mankind and the world's changing weather.* Madison: University of Wisconsin Press.

Dando, W. A. (1980). *The geography of famine.* New York: Halsted Press.

Dolan, E. F. (1990). *Drought: The past, present, and future enemy.* New York: F. Watts.

Gabler, R. E., Sager, R. J., Wise, D. L., & Petersen, J. F. (1999). *Essentials of physical geography* (6th ed.). Philadelphia: Saunders College Publishing.

Garcia, R. V. (1981). *Drought and man: Vol. 1. Nature pleads not guilty.* Oxford, UK: Pergamon Press.

Garcia, R. V. (1986). *Drought and man: Vol. 3. The roots of catastrophe.* Oxford, UK: Pergamon Press.

Garcia, R. V., & Escudero, J. C. (1982). *Drought and man: Vol. 2. The constant catastrophe: Malnutrition, famines and drought.* Oxford, UK: Pergamon Press.

Gill, R. B. (2000). *The great Maya droughts: Water, live, and death.* Albuquerque: University of New Mexico Press.

Glantz, M. H. (Ed.). (1976). *The politics of natural disaster: The case of the Sahel drought.* New York: Praeger.

Glantz, M. H. (1994). *Drought follows the plow.* Cambridge, UK: Cambridge University Press.

Gribben, J. (1976). *Forecasts, famines and freezes.* New York: Walker Publishing.

Grove, R. H., & Chappell, J. (2000). *El Nino—history and crisis: Studies from the Asia-Pacific region.* Cambridge, UK: White Horse Press.

Hall, A. L. (1978). *Drought and irrigation in north-east Brazil.* Cambridge, UK: Cambridge University Press.

Lutgens, F. K., & Tarbuck, E. J. (2001). *The atmosphere: An introduction to meteorology.* Upper Saddle River, NJ: Prentice Hall.

Marsh, W. M., & Grossa, J. M. (1996). *Environmental geography: Science, land use, and Earth systems.* New York: John Wiley & Sons.

Moran, J. M., & Morgan, M. D. (1997). *Meteorology: The atmosphere and the science of weather* (5th ed.). Upper Saddle River, NJ: Prentice Hall.

Mortimore, M. (1989). *Adapting to drought: Farmers, famines and desertification in west Africa.* Cambridge, UK: Cambridge University Press.

National Geographic Society. (1978). *Powers of nature.* Washington, DC: National Geographic Society.

Newman, J. L. (Ed.). (1975). *Drought, famine and population movements in Africa.* Syracuse, NY: Maxwell School of Citizenship and Public Affairs, Syracuse University.

Organisation for Economic Co-Operation and Development. (1988). *The Sahel facing the future: Increasing dependence or structural transformation.* Paris: Organisation for Economic Co-Operation and Development.

Saarinen, T. F. (1966). *Perception of the drought hazard on the Great Plains.* Chicago: University of Chicago.

Somerville, C. M. (1986). *Drought and aid in the Sahel.* Boulder, CO: Westview Press.

Subrahmanyam, V. P. (1967). *Incidence and spread of continental drought.* Geneva, Switzerland: Secretariat of the World Meteorological Organization.

Tannehill, I. R. (1947). *Drought: Its causes and effects.* Princeton, NJ: Princeton University Press.

U.S. Department of Agriculture, National Drought Policy Commission. (2000). *Preparing for drought in the 21st century.* Washington, DC: U.S. Department of Agriculture.

Wilhite, D. A. (Ed.). (2000). *Drought: A global assessment.* New York: Routledge.

Wilhite, D. A., Easterling, W. E., & Wood, D. A. (Eds.). (1987). *Planning for drought: Toward a reduction of societal vulnerability.* Boulder, CO: Westview Press.

Williams, J. (1992). *USA Today: The weather book.* New York: Vintage Books.

World Meteorological Organization. (1975). *Drought: Lectures presented at the twenty-sixth session of the WMO executive committee.* Geneva, Switzerland: Secretariat of the World Meteorological Organization.

Drug Production and Trade

The first drugs—psychoactive substances that alter states of consciousness or increase metabolic performance—were found in the plant world, and since that time plants from which drugs are derived have interacted with humans in countless relationships between plants and society, between nature and culture.

For ages the use of such psychoactive drugs, at first mainly through consumption of parts of certain plants—has been widespread. From so-called primitive people to modern societies, on each continent and in every religion, all kinds of people have resorted to drug-produced stimulations—from the mild ones created by tea and coffee to the more potent ones created by other natural drugs such as cannabis (marijuana), coca, kola, khat (a shrub whose leaves contain a stimulant), opium, and so on and to chemical or even medicinal drugs such as cocaine, heroin, crack, LSD, ecstasy, Prozac, Valium, and so on.

As Jean-Marie Pelt, a French pharmacognosist (descriptive pharmacologist dealing with crude drugs and simples), writes, "drug sticks to Man like skin to his flesh" (Pelt 1983, 14). Botanist Richard E. Schultes and pharmacochemist Albert Hofmann have shown the great diversity of drug plants and their worldwide use, the tropical regions being by far the richest in natural psychoactive substances. Only the Inuit of Arctic latitudes were known for their ignorance of mind-altering substances, until the introduction of alcohol.

However, since their early use by primitive societies as entheogens (generating inner divinity), drugs have been perceived as harmful to both individuals and societies. Thus they have been classified—according to their potency and harmfulness—as legal or illegal, often without scientific evidence of their toxicity or addictiveness. Hence the term *drug* is now almost uniquely used to mean an illegal mind-altering substance, even though alcohol and nicotine are as addictive as heroin—and kill many more people.

The one hundred-year global prohibition on many plants and plant-based drugs has had unintended consequences on their production, trade, and consumption. Criminalization of the drug industry and of drug consumers has had dire socioeconomic, political, and even ecological effects both in the developing world, where most illicit plant-based production occurs, and in the developed world, where the consumption of cannabis, cocaine, and heroin is concentrated. However, the long-accepted dichotomy between a drug-producing South and a drug-consuming North is no longer valid. Indeed, recent trends have shown a fast-growing consumption of heroin and amphetamine-style stimulants in major producing countries but even more so in key transit countries (Afghanistan, Pakistan, Iran,

Turkey, Myanmar [Burma], Thailand, Laos, Central Asia, Russia, China). The North still represents a huge market for the consumption of illegal drugs, but it is also engaged in illegal production of among other drugs, cannabis and amphetamine-style stimulants being produced in Canada, the United States, and Europe.

Agricultural Techniques

With most plant-based drug-producing countries being located in the South, most environmental issues are related to traditional slash-and-burn agricultural techniques. Indeed, swiddening, or shifting cultivation, is a common practice among opium producers in the forests of southeastern Asia and among coca growers in the Andes. Living on poor tropical soils, these farmers burn the vegetation to clear fields and to ensure that their crops thrive on the nutrients contained in the ash. Such fields are commonly cultivated for three to four years before being left to regenerate for seven to ten years; other fields are then cleared. For small productions and in low human densities, this agricultural technique is ecologically benign. However, with greater population densities and greater opium and coca production, tropical rain forests have been under greater pressure, especially when increasing commercial logging also occurs (for example, the harvesting of teak in Myanmar [Burma] and Thailand).

The coca plant and the opium poppy are mainly grown on the sides of mountains or hills, which are vulnerable to water erosion. In the tropical areas of the world, the combination of excessive swiddening and heavy rainfall leads to severe soil depletion.

To increase production in such contexts, most illegal farmers have resorted to modern agricultural technologies without the counseling to which legal farmers have access. Thus excessive use of fertilizers, herbicides, and pesticides is harmful to the environment, polluting the soils of areas that are already ecologically threatened and contaminating lower lands where food crops are grown.

Soil contamination also occurs when chemicals used in drug-processing laboratories are dumped into streams. Cocaine production, for example, leads to huge amounts of ammonia, sulfuric acid, and kerosene being dumped into Amazonian streams. In Asia, heroin refining and production involve acetic anhydride, hydrochloric acid, ammonium chloride, and sodium carbonate, residues of which are dumped into local river systems. Thus the illicit drug industry causes soil exhaustion and soil pollution and is detrimental to the environment.

Drug plants, however, have long been cultivated and harvested in traditional ways that are respectful of the environment. The opium poppy, for example, a plant with an ancient record of symbiosis with human societies, has spread around the world through the earliest human migrations and settlements. However, today the opium poppy is targeted for eradication, sometimes with the help of other "natural" agents.

The Opium Poppy

The opium poppy, *Papaver somniferum Lewin*, is one of the earliest known medical plants and has provided modern medicine with a major pain reliever—morphine. Among the Papaveraceae family, the genus *Papaver* comprises about 110 species of both annual and perennial herbs whose fruit is a capsule containing numerous seeds and latex tissue. The family is rich in alkaloids such as the opium alkaloids. However, *Papaver somniferum* and *Papaver setigerum* are the only two species known to contain morphine, whose content defines the potency of opium. Only morphine is retained to process heroin, while other alkaloids—such as thebaine and doeine, which, with some forty other alkaloids, provide much of the medical value of opium—are removed during drug refining. Thus *Papaver somniferum* is cultivated as the main source of commercial opium and heroin.

History Archeological evidence suggests that the opium poppy first grew between the western Mediterranean and Asia Minor. Where and when people began to cultivate the poppy and harvest its opium and how the plant spread to the Far East are not known. Only cultivated and semi-wild populations—no truly wild populations—have been accounted for. Thus the opium poppy is a cultivar (an organism originating and persistent under cultivation), and all varieties are closely linked to their relationship with humans. Indeed, they are "known only from pioneer habitat created and maintained by humans either consciously, in the form of cultivated fields, or unconsciously, in the form of 'waste areas' or disturbed environments adjacent to or in the near vicinity of these fields" (Merlin 1984, 54).

The opium poppy has provided humans with numerous resources since early times (food, animal fodder, oil, medicinal as well as ritualistic and recreational drugs) and has most likely spread with human societies along early migrational and trading routes, from western to eastern Eurasia, from one pioneer habitat to another. Originally, the relationship between the plant and human societies seems to have been beneficial, although for the last two centuries it has been perceived as clearly detrimental, enough at least to cause people to prohibit opium and advocate eradication of the plant.

Consequences of Prohibition

The global prohibition of certain drugs has been progressively enforced since the early twentieth century when, at the instigation of President Theodore Roosevelt, the International Opium Commission was convened in Shanghai in 1909 and the International Opium Convention, confining the use of opiates and cocaine to medicinal purposes, was signed at the Hague Conference on 23 January 1912. This prohibition has created the world's most lucrative illicit market for some psychoactive substances and encouraged their production and trafficking. As a result, the global war on drugs, devised by the administration of President Richard Nixon in 1969 and perpetuated by subsequent U.S. administrations, has escalated.

In broad environmental terms, the production, trafficking, and consumption of illicit psychoactive substances have had harmful ecological, social, economic, and political consequences. As Richard Davenport-Hines puts it, "It is not the supply of a drug that turns a user into a criminal but the illicitness of that supply" and "Criminal sanctions against drug-trafficking may be well intentioned, and may enjoy temporary or localized success; but overall the primary role of these laws is a business incentive" (Davenport-Hines 2001, xiv). Only 10 to 15 percent of illicit heroin is intercepted worldwide as drug traffickers keep gross profit margins of up to 300 percent; illicit opium production tripled between 1985 and 1996, with Afghanistan and Myanmar (Burma) being by far the main producers.

Thus a failed war has been waged globally for decades in Asia against the opium poppy and all its illicit derivatives and even in Latin America against coca plants. Criminalization of the drug economy and militarization of its repression are two effects of prohibition in producing countries as well as in transit countries—such as Myanmar (Burma), Laos, Thailand, China, Afghanistan, Iran, Pakistan, and the former Soviet republics of Central Asia. Armed violence is frequent and has dire consequences on life conditions, worsening the ecological impact of opium poppy cultivation and heroin refining.

Eradication Agenda

Some eradication techniques—for example, aerial spraying of herbicides—directly harm the environment, notably legal crops grown close to illegal crops. Moreover, in the war against drugs, techniques are being developed to eradicate the plants themselves through "natural" ways. For example, in Uzbekistan, in a facility known for germ warfare research where horticultural pathogens such as wheat rust and cereal blight were produced, scientists have developed the deadly strain of a benign fungus well known to opium poppy growers. *Pleospora papaveracea* could, if used, become a seedborne mycoherbicide (a fungus-based herbicide) specifically aimed at eradicating the opium poppy, spreading naturally on the wind and causing poppies to whither and die. Such a fungus could wipe out opium poppy crops in a few seasons if it is ever tried on a large scale, which nobody seems ready to do because of the environmental risks.

If the poppy-killer fungus is used, it would not be the first time that a natural agent was spread as a biological weapon, either to protect legal crops or to eradicate illegal ones. Indeed, the Pleospora program was part of a broader program named "Strategy for Coca and Opium Poppy Elimination" (SCOPE) devised by the United Nations International Drug Control Programme. SCOPE is a worldwide eradication program that targets coca plants as well as opium poppies. It was started to study the potential impact of another fungus, *Fusarium oxysporum*, which was accidentally discovered in the 1970s when it destroyed an experimental commercial coca plantation owned by the Coca-Cola company in Hawaii. Scientists concluded that mutation risks were too high to use the fungus to eradicate cannabis plants in the United States.

Psychoactive plants and substances derived from them have always been deeply rooted in most human societies. People have used such plants and their derivatives for many purposes, integrating them into numerous cultures, thus shaping unique and complex relationships between nature and culture. Recently attitudes toward these plants and their derivatives have changed—not because the plants themselves have changed but rather because people's relationships with them have changed. With the global prohibition that the increasingly global society has placed upon certain drugs that have played significant roles in societies, some of these plants are targeted for eradication, sometimes putting the ecological and cultural environment at risk in a struggle between nature and culture.

Pierre-Arnaud Chouvy

Further Reading

Booth, M. (1998). *Opium: A history*. New York: St. Martin's Press.

Chouvy, P. A. (2002). *Les territoires de l'opium. Conflits et trafics du Triangle d'Or et du Croissant d'Or* [The territories of opium. Conflicts and trafficking in the Golden Triangle and the Golden Crescent]. Geneva, Switzerland: Olizane.

Davenport-Hines, R. (2001). *The pursuit of oblivion: A social history of drugs*. London: Phoenix.

Escohotado, A. (1999). *A brief history of drugs: From the Stone Age to the stoned age*. Rochester, NY: Park Street Press.

Merlin, M. D. (1984). *On the trail of the ancient opium poppy*. Rutherford, NJ: Fairleigh Dickinson University Press.

Pelt, J. M. (1983). *Drogues et plantes magiques* [Drugs and magic plants]. Paris: Fayard.

Rudgley, R. (1993). *Essential substances: A cultural history of intoxicants in society*. New York: Kodansha.

Schultes, R. E., Hofmann, A., & Ratsch, C. (2002). *Plants of the gods*. Rochester, NY: Healing Arts Press.

Tullis, L. (1995). *Unintended consequences: Illegal drugs and drug policies in nine countries*. Boulder, CO: Lynne Rienner.

Dubos, René
(1901–1982)
French microbiologist and environmentalist

Soil microbiologist, environmentalist, humanist, and philosopher, René Dubos promoted the adoption of a more holistic environmental science and was among the vanguard of a group of post–World War II scientists who researched questions pertaining to the environmental relationship between science and ethics.

René Jules Dubos was born in Saint-Brice in the rural region of Ile-de-France just north of Paris. As a youth, Dubos took long walks in the countryside, cultivating a deep-seated appreciation for the pastoral landscape. Later in life Dubos would promote the beauty of pastoral landscapes as a desirable and sustainable combination of the finer qualities of wilderness and civilization. After World War I Dubos entered the National Institute of Agronomy, where he earned his B.S. degree in 1921. He then moved to Rome, where he worked as an associate editor for an agricultural journal. In Rome, Dubos read a paper by the Russian

Man will survive as a species for one reason: He can adapt to the destructive effects of our power-intoxicated technology and of our ungoverned population growth, to the dirt, pollution and noise of a New York or Tokyo. And that is the tragedy. It is not man the ecological crisis threatens to destroy but the quality of human life.

René Dubos, quoted in *Life*, July 28, 1970.

soil bacteriologist Sergei Winogradsky that argued that soil microbes should not be studied in isolation but instead should be studied in their own environment so as to appreciate their interactions with other soil bacteria. The paper encouraged Dubos to return to microbiology, and he moved to the United States, where he studied at Rutgers, receiving his Ph.D. in soil microbiology in 1927. Dubos then spent most of the rest of his career at the Rockefeller Institute for Medical Research, where in 1947 he opened a new department dedicated to tuberculosis research; this department was inspired by the death of his wife, Marie Louise Bonnet, who succumbed to tuberculosis in 1942. Dubos's research indicated that nutrition and environment have long-term influences on human health. Turning toward social ethics, Dubos came to believe that social reforms would improve environmental conditions and that social progress is a moral necessity for ensuring improved health for subsequent generations.

Dubos dedicated much of his professional career to the study of microbial diseases. Indeed, he discovered the enzymes in soil microbes that were used as the first antibiotic drugs. In his research Dubos learned that environmental conditions affect soil microbes to the extent that they can alter many of the microbes' characteristics and capabilities. Dubos then applied that observation to the larger world and realized that all organisms are similarly affected by their environment. The increased reckless environmental destruction after World War II prompted Dubos to move his political interests toward the still-developing modern environmental movement.

These more holistic social and environmental patterns became the cornerstone for Dubos's books for popular audiences. In *So Human an Animal* (1968), for which he was awarded the Pulitzer Prize, and *A God Within* (1972) Dubos articulated a new social and environmental ethic. He saw science as rendering itself irrelevant as it lurched toward reductionism, the practice of sacrificing breadth in favor of scientific depth. The disadvantage of this endeavor was that discoveries

failed to appreciate the significance of the relationship between organisms and their environment. This shortcoming led Dubos to champion for the greater acceptance of the new science of ecology. In addition to asking probing intellectual questions regarding environmental protection, Dubos was an active participant in local environmental struggles. He was particularly involved in the efforts to save Jamaica Bay in New York. Dubos and others thwarted an attempt to convert a landfill into additional runways for John F. Kennedy airport. The peninsula into Jamaica Bay is now named Dubos Point Wetland Park. The restoration of the land and the establishment of the park there constitute a valuable case study for grassroots environmental activism as well as for philosophical questions regarding "nature."

On 20 February 1982, his eighty-first birthday, René Dubos died in New York City.

Michael Egan

Further Reading

Benison, S. (1976). Rene Dubos and the capsular polysaccharide of pneumococcus. *Bulletin of the History of Medicine, 50*(4), 459–477.

Dubos, R. (1968). *So human an animal.* New York: Scribner.

Dubos, R. (1972). *A god within.* New York: Scribner.

Moberg, C. L. (1996). Rene Dubos: A harbinger of microbial resistance to antibiotics. *Microbial Drug Resistance, 2*(3), 287–297.

Piel, G., & Segerberg, O., Jr. (Eds.). (1990). *The world of Rene Dubos: A collection from his writings.* New York: H. Holt.

Dung

Dung is a common English term meaning "semisolid animal excrement." Dung has had three principal uses throughout history. By far the most important use has been its application to crop fields, gardens, and pastures to return the essential macronutrients (nitrogen, phosphorus, and potassium), to replenish organic matter, and to improve the water-holding capacity of cultivated soils. Also, dried dung was once a necessity for fuel in arid, treeless areas of Asia, Africa, and the Americas. And in some arid regions dung, together with chopped straw or sand, was added to clay to make sun-dried mud bricks.

Animal dung is a relatively poor source of recycled nutrients. Freshly voided wastes of large domesticated animals are mostly water, and even on a dry-weight basis, manure of poorly fed Indian cattle may have less than 1 percent nitrogen. Only poultry wastes are relatively rich in nitrogen and phosphorus. All traditional Old World agricultures returned most of their barnyard manures to fields, and collection, fermentation, transport, and application of these manures added up to one of the most labor-intensive tasks in preindustrial farming. Today's recycling rates range from only about 30 percent in the United States, where only about 40 percent of all animal wastes are voided in confinement, to more than 90 percent in several small European countries. Leaching (loss by percolation), volatilization (loss by vaporization), and denitrification reduce the nitrogen content of applied manures to a fraction of the original nutrient content.

Regions where dung was commonly used for cooking and, to a lesser extent, for indoor heating included the arid interior of Asia, the entire Indian subcontinent, virtually all of the Middle East, the Saharan and some Sahelian parts of Africa, and arid and high-altitude regions of both Americas. In India, where dung is still widely used for cooking by millions of poor peasants, both cow and water buffalo droppings are gathered daily, mostly by children and women, both for their own household use and for sale. Dry chips are ready for use, whereas fresh dung is often mixed with straw or chaff, then hand molded into patties and sun dried before burning. Dung of cattle and wild buffalo made an indispensable contribution to America's westward expansion as it provided the fuel needed for the pioneering continental crossings and for the subsequent colonization of the Great Plains during the nineteenth century. Westward-bound travelers on the Oregon and Mormon Trails collected "buffalo wood," and the early settlers stacked winter supplies of "cow wood" in igloo shapes or against house walls.

Cattle dung and camel dung continue to be used in the Sahelian fringe of the Sahara Desert of Africa, as well as in many Egyptian villages. The yak has been the dominant supplier of dung for fuel on the high Tibetan Plateau, and in South America llama dung was the principal fuel on the Altiplano of the Andes, the core of the Inca empire in today's southern Peru, eastern Bolivia, and northern Chile and Argentina. Only sheep dung has been generally avoided because its burning produces an acrid smoke. Although many nineteenth-century American reports noted that buffalo dung burned very cleanly (albeit too fast, necessitating constant stoking), unvented indoor cooking with most kinds of dry dung generates more smoke than does the burning of seasoned wood. In terms of gross energy content, air-dried dung (10–20 percent moisture, energy content up to 14 million Joules per kilogram) is at least 20 percent below dry straw, and it has only half of charcoal's high heat content.

Vaclav Smil

Further Reading

Pathwardan, S. (1973). *Change among India's harijans.* New Delhi, India: Orient Longman.

Smil, V. (1985). *Biomass energies.* New York: Plenum Press.

Smil, V. (1994). *Energy in world history.* Boulder, CO: Westview.

Smil, V. (2003). *Energy at the crossroads.* Cambridge, MA: MIT Press.

Welsch, R. L. (1980). No fuel like an old fuel. *Natural History, 89*(11), 76–81.

Dust Bowl

Today the term *dust bowl* is applied to any area that is badly affected by wind erosion. Originally, in the 1930s (the so-called dirty thirties), the term *Dust Bowl* referred to an area on the Great Plains of North America that experienced huge clouds of blowing dirt, leading to severe economic and social dislocation. A reporter invented the term, but exactly what he meant has never been clear. Perhaps he was thinking of the vast interior of the continent, with the Rocky Mountains as the rim, as a vessel that had been producing cereal grains but then was producing only dust. The U.S. Soil Conservation Service adopted the term officially, designating the western third of Kansas, southeastern Colorado, the Oklahoma Panhandle, the northern two-thirds of the Texas Panhandle, and northeastern New Mexico. But during the 1930s there was a fluctuating but enormous fringe area that covered almost 40 million hectares, so that at times dust bowl conditions extended northward into the Dakotas and Canada.

These conditions of severe wind erosion first appeared in the spring of 1934, when a massive dust storm swept eastward out of Montana and Wyoming. As it blew along, it picked up more and more dirt, until 315 million metric tons of it were blowing eastward. On May 9th that storm reached Chicago, then moved on to New York, Boston, and Washington, D.C. Ships in the Atlantic, some of them 483 kilometers off the coast, found dust on their decks during the next day or two. Later dust storms were mostly confined to the Southern Plains. Some of them were dramatic "black blizzards" that came with rolling turbulence, rising like a long wall 2,100–2,400 meters high. The Soil Conservation Service compiled a frequency chart of dust storms of regional extent, when visibility was cut to less than a mile. There were 22 in 1934, 40 in 1935, 68 in 1936, 72 in 1937, 61 in 1938, 30 in 1939, 17 in 1940, and finally only 17 in 1941, the last year of the storms. A single storm might rage for only an hour or for days.

Income and Health Suffer

This catastrophic erosion led to a devastating loss of farm income as crops failed and livestock (along with wildlife) died from ingesting dust. Many people suffered from lung damage, or "dust pneumonia," as well as from the psychological trauma of the storms, the destruction of their homes and property, and huge financial losses. Recurring years of such conditions turned many people into environmental refugees seeking homes elsewhere—in Arizona, California, or the Pacific Northwest. In the worst-hit counties, one-third to one-half of the population left during the decade. For those who stayed, bankruptcies were common among both farmers and the townspeople who depended on them.

The causes of this environmental disaster, the worst in American history, remain a matter of controversy. Some historians, along with many surviving residents of the area, tend to see humans as innocent victims of a natural disaster; without drought, they say, there would have been good crops and no wind erosion. Certainly, the drought experienced in the 1930s was unprecedented for severity and duration in the previous half-century of white settlement of the Great Plains. But other historians and scientists have argued that the Dust Bowl owed much to human actions as well as to natural cycles. Agriculture, they say, was largely to blame for its own misfortunes—particularly

an agriculture that was more attentive to short-term economic gain and distant urban market prices than to long-term ecological patterns and local environmental realities.

During World War I and the 1920s, wheat farming expanded at a phenomenal rate into the windy, drought-prone plains, driven by the same speculative fever that gripped the whole American economy. The farming that came to the area was commercial, market driven, and characterized by rapid mechanization (gasoline tractors, wheat combines), by a high degree of monoculture specialization, and by heavy borrowing and intense capitalization. Although the typical plains farm was family owned and operated, many operators were tenants moving from place to place, whereas others were "suitcase farmers"— speculators from town who invested in wheat cropping as others invested in the stock market. Just as Wall Street collapsed in 1929, setting off the Great Depression, so historians have argued, the wheat boom collapsed about the same time. Overproduction led to declining prices, which in turn led to more plowing of fragile grasslands and more risk taking with the weather. The Dust Bowl, by this interpretation, was a disaster created by modern farming methods and motives, an extreme example of the ecological damage caused by commercial agriculture planetwide.

Federal Aid Provided

The federal government quickly launched a massive rescue effort in the 1930s, sending over $1 billion into western counties in an attempt to keep people on the land and in the region. Whether wisely or not, that aid provided a cushion for failure. Federal disaster assistance, soil-saving techniques, and crop subsidies became a permanent way of life. In 1941 the rainfall returned, leading to a long, wet period of recovery and a return to production expansion. Besides government help, farmers came to depend on the new technology of deep-well irrigation—pumping up groundwater from the Ogallala aquifer to supplement the moisture supply. Severe but short-lived droughts continued to occur over the next fifty years, but none had the environmental or economic consequences of the Dust Bowl years, leading many optimists to believe that human ingenuity and improved technology had made another disaster impossible. More realistically, a constant flow of federal dollars, peaking in drought years, along with the mining of groundwater, is why farmers and ranchers have managed to stave off another general catastrophe. Neither panacea is dependable, however, and an agricultural system driven by market opportunism in a highly volatile climate must always face an uncertain future. Meanwhile, in other arid and semiarid parts of the world, similar patterns of desertification and dust bowls have proliferated, raising questions about how agriculture in marginal environments can ever be made safe and reliable.

Donald Worster

Further Reading

Bonnifield, P. (1979). *The Dust Bowl: Men, dirt, and depression.* Albuquerque: University of New Mexico Press.

Riney-Kehrberg, P. (1994). *Rooted in dust: Surviving drought and depression in southwestern Kansas.* Lawrence: University Press of Kansas.

Tobey, R. C. (1981). *Saving the prairies: The life cycle of the founding school of American plant ecology, 1895–1955.* Berkeley and Los Angeles: University of California Press.

Worster, D. (1979). *Dust Bowl: The Southern Plains in the 1930s.* New York: Oxford University Press.

Dutch Elm Disease

Shortly after World War I, a previously unknown disease affecting elm trees (*Ulmus*) was reported in the Netherlands. The disease, known as Dutch elm disease because of the seminal work between 1919 and 1934 by several notable Dutch women researchers, is a wilt disease caused by the fungus *Ophiostoma ulmi*. It is transmitted from tree to tree by elm bark beetles (scolytid) or through interlocked root systems of neighboring trees.

It is thought that the disease originally came from Central Asia and was transported to Europe and North America on imported logs. After 1920, it spread rapidly over the European continent and beyond, arriving in Britain in 1927, the United States in 1930, and Canada in 1945. Initially, the disease caused widespread destruction of elm trees, but after 1937 it became less virulent and came to be regarded as an endemic problem of less importance. However, in the 1960s a new, more virulent strain of the fungus emerged in Canada and arrived several years later in Europe, causing devastation on a larger scale than before. Millions of elm trees died since the mid–1960s leaving entire landscapes denuded of

one of the more important trees of natural and cultural landscapes of the northern temperate zone.

Elm has been used and cultivated since Neolithic times because of its resistance to rotting and splitting. This made the wood suitable for the construction of coffins, water pipes, drains, and furniture. During the seventeenth and eighteenth centuries landowners widely planted elm trees in hedgerows between their fields. This was also the time that landscape architects recognized its ornamental characteristics and starting plantings in landscape parks, especially in England. This tradition continued during the nineteenth and twentieth centuries when millions of elms were planted in parks, along roads, and in gardens throughout North America and Europe. Around 1930, just before Dutch elm disease arrived, it is estimated that there were 77 million elm trees in cities and towns across North America. By 1976, municipalities in the northeastern United States had lost over 50 percent of their original elm population. Similar losses also occurred in other countries. Britain, for example, lost 95 percent of its pre-epidemic elm population between 1927 and 1995.

Since the 1920s, attempts to breed elm hybrids resistant to *Ophiostoma ulmi* have been carried out in the Netherlands, Great Britain, and North America, with only moderately successfully results. Attempts to control the disease have been concentrated on the reduction of beetle populations, the injection of fungicides, breeding of resistant elm hybrids, and the use of parasites feeding on the fungus. Recent advances in molecular biology and genetic engineering have provided new, powerful tools to study the disease and assist in the resistant breeding programs.

K. Jan Oosthoek

Further Reading

Campana, R. J., & Sinclair, W. A. (1978). *Dutch elm disease, perspectives after 60 years.* Ithaca, NY: Cornell University Agricultural Experiment Station.

Holmes, F. W., & Heybroek, H. M. (Eds.). (1990). *Dutch elm disease—The early papers. Selected works of seven Dutch women phytopathologists.* St. Paul, MN: APS Press.

Rackham, O. (2001). *The history of the countryside: The classic history of Britain's landscape, flora and fauna.* London: Phoenix Press.

Richens, R. H. (1983). *Elm.* Cambridge, UK: Cambridge University Press.

Welwig, A. (1993). The battle against Dutch elm disease: Still fighting the fatal fungus. *Geographical, 65*(11), 27–30.

E

Earth Day

Earth Day is a special day devoted to educating people about the environmental crises and opportunities facing the world. It has been celebrated each year on 22 April since 1970.

By the end of the 1960s, air pollution had been linked to lung disease, and smog was becoming endemic in America's largest cities. Huge fish kills were reported in the Great Lakes. Cleveland's Cuyahoga River, inundated with oil and petrochemicals, had ignited in a spectacular fire. Grassroots organizations were emerging to fight freeways and power plants that threatened their neighborhoods. Industrial forestry was invading the national forests. In 1969, a giant oil spill in Santa Barbara, California, filled the evening news with pictures of dying wildlife. Rachel Carson's *Silent Spring* (1962) and Paul Ehrlich's *The Population Bomb* (1968) found huge audiences.

In 1969, those various events were still largely viewed as discrete, unrelated phenomena. None by itself was important enough to carry much political clout. Then in September 1969, Wisconsin's Senator Gaylord Nelson, a Democrat, gave a speech at the University of Washington that described the oil spill in Santa Barbara as emblematic of the deterioration of the quality of American life. He called for a nationwide college teach-in, modeled on antiwar teach-ins, to start a public debate about environmental problems.

After receiving an enthusiastic response, Nelson asked Republican congressman Paul N. "Pete" McCloskey to cochair a national nonprofit organization to promote the teach-in. They recruited Denis Hayes, a political activist who had graduated that spring from Stanford University, to hire a staff and serve as national coordinator. Within a few weeks, the young staff had christened the teach-in "Earth Day," and launched a campaign to create a new social movement.

Earth Day was conceived in the activism and idealism of the 1960s. It grew out of the same ferment that produced the civil-rights movement and the antiwar movement. But whereas by 1970, in the wake of several assassinations, many of the more visible leaders in those movements were becoming frustrated, violent, and exclusionary, Earth Day explicitly sought to develop a broad constituency for its message. The *New York Times* (23 April 1970) described the resulting campaign: "Conservatives were for it. Liberals were for it. Democrats, Republicans, and Independents were for it. So were the ins, the outs, the Executive and Legislative branches of government." Earth Day forged links between traditional conservation groups, who were concerned with wildlife and habitat, and newer groups worried about industrial pollution, agricultural pesticides, and urban blight.

Earth Day was a spectacular success. An estimated 20 million Americans took part in that first campaign in 1970. The traffic was shut off on Fifth Avenue in New York City, and it was turned into a giant pedestrian mall filled with educational displays, recruiting tables for environmental groups, street vendors, and so on. Hundreds of thousands of people gathered in Central Park for a free concert and to demonstrate against air pollution. Huge rallies were held across the country, with special television coverage focused on Washington D.C., Chicago, Philadelphia, and San Francisco. Congress adjourned for the day so that all

There are no passengers on Spaceship Earth. We are all crew.

—Marshall McLuhan, 1964

members could return to their districts to take part in events that were held in virtually every city, town, and village in the United States.

Earth Day changed the American political landscape. It led directly to the creation of the Environmental Protection Agency and made inevitable the swift passage of landmark legislation to protect the air, the water, and endangered species.

Approaching 1990, with Hayes serving as chair, the Earth Day Network began recruiting organizers around the world for its twentieth anniversary. One hundred forty one countries held Earth Day events that year. Typical Earth Day events have included a gathering of more than 100,000 red-robed Buddhist monks in Thailand to celebrate life; rallies across Tanzania to protest the climate change that is melting Mount Kilimajaro's snowcaps; and car-free days in Canada, the Czech Republic, India, Taiwan, and South Korea. By 2000, hundreds of millions of people in 183 nations were participating. Earth Day is now well established as the world's first secular, theme-driven, global holiday.

Denis Hayes

Further Reading

Earth Day: The beginning. (1970, April 23). *New York Times*. Lead editorial.

Hayes, D. (2000). *The official Earth Day guide to planet repair*. Washington, DC: Island Press.

National Staff of Environmental Action. (1970). *Earth Day: The beginning: A guide for survival*. New York: Bantam Books.

Shabecoff, P. (2000). *Earth rising: American environmentalism in the 21st century*. Washington, DC: Island Press.

Earth First!

A U.S. organization created by mainstream environmentalists and fringe political activists, Earth First!'s

intention from its establishment in 1980 was to radically change the complexion of U.S. environmentalism.

In the early 1980s, support for the Endangered Species Act appeared to be waning after Congress allowed an exemption to the Act that killed the only known population of snail darters, a tiny fish. Ronald Reagan, elected president in 1980, ran on a platform that explicitly placed economic growth before environmental protection. The U.S. Forest Service's close ties to the timber and mining industries led it to largely abandon its multiple, or "wise" use policies. Worst of all, according to environmental activists, in an era of high inflation and high unemployment, the public appeared supportive of all of these actions.

Against this backdrop, Earth First!'s founders, including former Wilderness Society lobbyist Dave Foreman and Yippie Mike Roselle, felt compelled to "say what needs to be said" (Scarce 1990, 58), namely that the sacrifice of America's wilderness areas was an intolerable ecological and social blow. They envisioned a group that would be so extreme in its rhetoric and its tactics that mainstream environmental organizations such as the Wilderness Society and Sierra Club would seem reasonable by contrast and could win the day in political struggles. Earth First! would oppose wilderness destroyers at corporate headquarters and in the wilderness itself.

Organizationally, it patterned itself after Native American tribes that had no leader but, instead, operated anarchically, with all tribal members having an equal say in what should be done. Earth First! developed without a hierarchical structure. It has no headquarters, nor is there an elected or appointed leader to direct the group; the closest thing it has to a central clearinghouse of any sort is whatever building houses the group's newspaper, the *Earth First! Journal*.

Earth First! established no requirements to become a "member," nor are there any dues. Membership is a set of beliefs that one accepts and a set of behaviors that one enacts, especially the belief that wilderness protection is the foremost environmental concern facing the planet and that direct action needs to be taken to preserve wilderness. Locally, Earth First! chapters control their own destinies. Members enjoy so much freedom that anyone may act in the name of Earth First! without sanction from the organization. From its earliest days this freedom caused dissension within the group and disdain from outsiders.

New Environmentalism

Unique as Earth First! was in its organizational form, its rhetoric and its tactics would prove to be the most controversial thing about the "tribe," as many members call it. Earth First! took as its motto "No Compromise in Defense of Mother Earth," and it meant it. If, for example, the U.S. Forest Service identified 10 million acres in a given state as undeclared but de facto wilderness, Earth First! insisted that all 10 million acres be set aside as wilderness. In contrast, "mainstream" environmental organizations were willing to accept far less from the governmental agencies, ranchers, motorized recreationists, and "extractive" industries like timber and mining with which they negotiated.

The group's tactics infuriated suit-and-tie environmentalists. The tribe redefined "action." No longer was it enough to write a check and feel good about one's contribution to saving the planet. Earth First!ers were expected to take *direct* action, going to the source of the problem and confronting it directly—ideally with news cameras present to spread the word and raise awareness. Their campaigns included blocking roads used by logging trucks and conducting tree-sits, during which activists live high in trees for days—or, in the case of Julia Hill—years at a time.

However, what most angered the mainstream was the practice by some Earth First!ers, and the acceptance by many others, of "ecotage:" ecological sabotage. In the pages of the *Journal* and in *Ecodefense: A Field Guide to Monkeywrenching*, activists described the rationale behind—and provided step-by-step instructions for—wrecking the machinery used to destroy wilderness. Perhaps the most controversial of the ecotage tactics was "tree spiking," which involves driving long nails into trees to ruin their commercial value. The trees are not harmed, but milling spiked trees can be extremely dangerous to those operating the saws.

Few, if any, persons have been injured by wilderness activists. In contrast, Earth First!ers have paid dearly for their behavior. Some have received jail terms for acts of ecotage, but more often tribal members have been the victims of harassment and worse while they have conducted peaceful, nondestructive activities. Law enforcement agents in California were filmed dabbing pepper spray into activists' eyes as

they sat chained to a table in a Congressman's office, and at least one activist was killed when loggers felled a tree on him. In the most notorious case of all, the Federal Bureau of Investigation and the Oakland, California Police Department attempted to frame activists Judi Bari and Darryl Cherney after a bomb blew up in their car; in response to their lawsuit, Bari's estate (she died of cancer before the trial began) and Cherney were awarded $4.4 million by a federal jury in 2002.

Earth First! Conflict and Culture

As controversial as direct action has proven to be, many Earth First!ers sought respectability in an Earth-centered philosophy, "deep ecology," and early on, the tribe adopted the new but respected science of conservation biology as its own. Activists also contribute scientific treatises to the *Earth First! Journal* on a host of issues. At the outer edge of Earth First! rhetoric, some activists have given voice to misanthropy, arguing that *Homo sapiens* is a plague on the planet.

As is common in grassroots social movements, Earth First! activists feel a need to create their own communal identity to reaffirm their cause and their individual commitment to it. Many activists live simply, often in group homes or cooperatives. They ride bicycles when they can and make their automobiles last as long as they are able. They work at food cooperatives, ecology centers, and operate or are employed by businesses that they see as minimally harmful to the planet. Men and women alike wear their hair long and dress in well-worn but serviceable clothing. Music and art also have emerged from the Earth First! community.

Impact

Earth First!'s import is easiest seen at the local level, in keeping with the tribe's emphasis on grassroots activism. In controversies across the United States, and increasingly around the world, Earth First! activists have confronted powerful political and corporate interests. Those confrontations themselves have been victories of sorts, for without Earth First! activists, a host of environmental disputes—including the continued cutting of redwood trees, the importation of beef raised on former rainforest land, and the plight of dozens of plants, animals, places, and peoples—would not have received the attention that they have. Earth First! made it acceptable to carry a picket sign for the environment and to hold a sit-in for an endangered species. Compelled by its no-compromise ethic, the tribe is, above all else, the environmental movement's conscience.

Rik Scarce

Further Reading

Bari, J. (1994). *Timber wars*. Monroe, ME: Common Courage.

Devall, B., & Sessions, G. (1985). *Deep ecology: Living as if nature mattered*. Layton, UT: Peregrine Smith.

Earth First! Journal. Various issues.

Foreman, D. (1993). *Confessions of an eco-warrior*. New York: Crown.

Foreman, D., & Haywood, B. (1993). *Ecodefense: A field guide to monkeywrenching*. Chico, CA: Abbzug Press.

Hill, J. (2001). *The legacy of Luna: The story of a tree, a woman and the struggle to save the redwoods*. San Francisco: Harper.

Scarce, R. (1990). *Eco-warriors: Understanding the radical environmental movement*. Chicago: The Noble Press.

Earth Keepers *See* Association of African Earthkeeping Churches; Chimurenga

Earthquakes

Earthquakes are vibrations of the Earth caused by waves radiating from some source of elastic energy. Earthquakes have disastrous effects on densely populated areas as well as on nuclear power plants, dumping grounds for hazardous wastes, nuclear waste depositories, and large-scale technical constructions.

Early Explanations

People have come a long way in their understanding of the causes of earthquakes. At first myths, legends, and apocalyptic imaginations were used to explain processes in the Earth's interior. Prior to the knowledge that the Earth is a sphere, the Earth was thought to be a disk carried by something. Hindu mythology taught that the god Vishnu, preserver of the world, is lying on the "world snake"(a snake that provides a resting place for Vishnu) and that under the world is a turtle. On the turtle stand four elephants that carry the Earth. Movement of the elephants causes earthquakes. Japanese people believed that a huge catfish

causes the trembling of the Earth by his vehement movements. Sometimes gods also were held responsible for earthquakes, for example, Poseidon by the ancient Greeks and Neptune by the ancient Romans.

Classical Antiquity

The theory that air (vapors) in the cavities of the Earth are the cause of earthquakes was upheld, with slight variations, from the time of Greek philosopher Anaxagoras (500–428 BCE) to the time of German Canon and Councillor Konrad von Megenberg (1309–1374) in the late Middle Ages. Only Tales of Milet (c. 625–547 BCE), the founder of Ionian natural philosophy, attributed earthquakes to the rocking of the Earth on water. Greek philosopher Anaxamines of Milet (585–526 BCE) thought that periods of dryness and wetness were responsible for earthquakes. Greek philosopher Democritus (460–371 BCE) considered water to be the cause.

The Greek philosopher Aristotle (384–322 BCE) described earthquakes as the consequence of compressed air captured in caves. Aristotle's ideas were used to explain meteorological phenomena and earthquakes until the Middle Ages.

The Roman poet Lucretius (98–55 BCE) gave a vivid description of the reason for earthquakes in his philosophical poem "De Rerum Natura." Lucretius thought that the knowledge of correlations according to the laws of nature would eliminate the erroneous notion of "punishment and reward"—the lives of people being determined by gods. Roman statesman and philosopher Seneca (4 BCE–65 CE) was much influenced by the devastating earthquake at Pompeii and Herculaneum on 5 February 62 (or 63). He supported the views of Aristotle and also adopted his classification. Plinius (23–79), the Roman historian and author of *Historia Naturalis*, considered earthquakes to be merely underground thunderstorms.

Middle Ages

When classical antiquity was rediscovered by the Christian Occident (the term used to describe what is now Europe during the Middle Ages) around the year 1200, significant parts of Greek ideology were merged with Christian ideas. Albertus Magnus (1193–1280), the German scientist and philosopher, supported the spreading of the still-forbidden writings of Aristotle and Arabic and Jewish commentators. His own works, in which he also opposed mystical conceptions, were an outstanding contribution to the development of the sciences. His concept of earthquakes was founded on

Aristotle on Earthquakes

The famous Greek philosopher Aristotle (384–322 BCE) described earthquake as consequences of compressed air, captured in caves.

. . . Many times compressed air (pneuma) generated in the interior, which had reached the required mixture and was then pushed into cave ducts, shakes many parts (of the earth surface) because it is separated from where it was generated. Often a mass of such pneuma from outside gets caught in the earth cavities, becomes separated and shakes the earth in trying to force its way out; in doing so, it causes the phenomenon called earthquake . . .

Earthquakes which act in a transverse direction under an acute angle we call inclining earthquakes; those which move vertically up and down are called shakers, and collapse earthquakes are those which cause a sagging into interior cavities; if they open up crevices and rupture the earth, they are called bursters. Some topple with a thrust, they are called thrust quakes. Earthquakes causing a recoil are called swingers, i.e. they keep the affected object permanently in its position by lateral inclination and a backswing; their effect is a type of trembling. There are also "Howlers" among the earthquakes, which cause the earth to shudder with a roaring like thunder . . .

Source: Aristotle. (1970). *Meteorologie*. Berlin: n.p., pp. 63, 73, 248.

Aristotle's theory and repeated Anaxagora's concept of clogged pores of the Earth but made distinctions. His disciple, the Italian scholastic Thomas of Aquino (1225–1274), continued the Aristotelian bent of his teacher. Due to Thomas's belief in a synthesis between God and nature, he believed that earthquakes were caused by God and may, merely secondarily, also have had natural causes, such as vapors and winds; otherwise his theory was based on Aristotle's ideas.

Italian poet Petrarch (1304–1374) and Konrad von Megenberg, on the other hand, passed on the theories of antiquity. Petrarch often mentioned earthquakes in his letters, quoting ancient authors such as the Roman poets Horace and Virgil. *The Book of Nature*, written in 1349 by von Megenberg, the first so-called natural history written in German, counts earthquakes among the natural phenomena and largely leaves out mysticism.

Some later philosophers, as well as the German humanist, physician, and mineralogist Georgius Agricola (1494–1555), believed that earthquakes were the consequence of an subterranean fire that was ignited by the sun itself. The long-lasting hypothesis of a central subterranean fire, which was presumed by Greek philosopher Pythagoras (570–500 BCE), was revived in the book *Mundus Subterraneus* by German scholar Athanasius Kircher (1601–1680). But the hypothesis of a central fire as the cause for all earthquakes and volcanoes was not sufficient to Kircher. So he considered additional focal points of fire that were connected to the central fire.

The Enlightenment

During the eighteenth century scientists became more and more convinced that no natural phenomenon is unexplainable; thus an explanation for earthquakes became a challenge for scientists during the Enlightenment. English physician William Stukeley (1687–1765) wrote in his book *Philosophy of Earthquakes* that earthquakes are caused by electrostatic discharge between sky and Earth, like lightning. This new idea was motivated by the general discussion of electricity by scientists at that time.

The biggest catastrophe of the eighteenth century occurred in 1755 when an earthquake struck Lisbon, Portugal, and initiated an enormous debate about the cause of earthquakes. About sixty thousand people were killed by the Lisbon earthquake, and suddenly the optimists' way of thinking in that century was debatable. François Marie Arouet Voltaire (1694–1778), French writer and philosopher, discussed the Lisbon earthquake in his novel *Candide* (1759). The German philosopher Immanuel Kant (1724–1804) was deeply impressed by the earthquake, too. Kant published in 1756 the paper "Von den Ursachen der Erschütterungen bei Gelegenheit des Unglücks, welches die Länder von Europa gegen das Ende des vorigen Jahres betroffen hat" ("About the causes of shocks during the disaster, which affected the countries of Europe at the end of the last year"), in which he found chemical causes for earthquakes. He negated all mystical and

TABLE 1.
EUROPEAN MACROSEISMIC SCALE (EMS-98)

Intensity	Definition	Description
I	Not felt	Not felt
II	Scarcely felt	Felt only by a few people at rest in houses
III	Weak	Felt indoors by a few people. People at rest feel a swaying or light trembling.
IV	Largely observed	Felt indoors by many people, outdoors by few. A few people are awakened. Windows, doors and dishes rattle.
V	Strong	Felt indoors by most, outdoors by few. Many sleeping people are awakened. A few are frightened. Buildings tremble throughout. Hanging objects swing considerably. Small objects are shifted. Doors and windows swing open or shut.
VI	Slightly damaging	Many people are frightened and run outdoors. Some objects fall. Many houses suffer slight nonstructural damage like hair-line cracks and fall of small pieces of plaster.
VII	Damaging	Most people are frightened and run outdoors. Furniture is shifted, and objects fall from shelves in large numbers. Many well-built buildings suffer moderate damage: small cracks in walls, fall of plaster, fall of parts of chimneys; older buildings may show large cracks in walls and failure of fill-in walls.
VIII	Heavily damaging	Many people find it difficult to stand. Many houses have large cracks in walls. A few well-built buildings show serious failure of walls; weak older structures may collapse.
IX	Destructive	General panic. Many weak structures collapse. Even well-built buildings show heavy damage: serious failure of walls and partial structural failure.
X	Very destructive	Many well-built buildings collapse.
XI	Devastating	Most well-built buildings collapse; even some with good earthquake – resistant design are destroyed.
XII	Completely devastating	Almost all buildings are destroyed.

Source: G. Grünthal (Ed.). (1998). *European Macroseismic Scale 1998 (EMS-98).* Luxembourg-City, Luxembourg: Centre Européen de Géodynamique et de Séismologie.

religious explanations and held that ". . . we have the cause below our feet" (Kant, 1968, 469).

The so-called optimists such as Kant and French philosopher Jean-Jacques Rousseau (1712–1778) sought to find also positive consequences of earthquakes, such as the detection of hot springs. Rousseau took the view that people should return to nature and live in the open air.

Earthquakes Are Waves – an Important Discovery

Englishmen John Winthrop (1606–1676) and John Michell (1724–1793), also impressed by the Lisbon earthquake, began to reflect on not only the causes but also the effects of an earthquake. Winthrop, a mathematician and natural philosopher, made the important discovery that earthquakes are waves; this discovery would be revived a hundred years later. Michell, lecturer at Cambridge University, in 1760 published a study in which he recognized wavelike motions of the ground. With that study he anticipated the perception that would lead to an understanding of the cause of earthquakes.

A big step forward in the development of seismology (the study of earthquakes) was taken by the Irish engineer Robert Mallet (1810–1881) when he began collecting worldwide earthquake occurrences. He compiled a catalog of six thousand earthquakes, from which he was able to draw the most complete earthquake map of the world in 1857. The cause of earthquakes was still unknown, but Mallet's research, which led to the understanding of the origin of mountains and continents, was the basic approach to answering the question. In 1912 the German meteorologist and geophysicist Alfred Wegener (1880–1930) presented his theory of continental drift, which states that parts of the Earth's crust slowly drift atop a liquid core. Weg-

TABLE 2.
DISASTROUS EARTHQUAKES

Date	Country	Epicenter	Casualties	Recomputed Magnitude	Comment
28 Dec. 1908	Messina, Italy	38° N, 15.5° E	70,000 to 100,000	7.5	Deaths from earthquake and tsunami (tidal wave)
22 May 1927	near Xining, China	36.8° N, 102.8° E	200,000	8.3	Large fractures
30 May 1935	Quetta, Pakistan	29.6° N, 66.5° E	30,000 to 60,000	7.5	Quetta almost completely destroyed
25 Jan. 1939	Chillan, Chile	36.2° S, 72.2° W	28,000	8.3	
5 Oct. 1948	Ashgabat, Turkmenistan, USSR	38° N, 58.3° E	110,000	7.3	
29 Feb. 1960	Agadir, Morocco	30° N, 9° W	10,000 to 15,000	5.9	Occurred at shallow depth just under city
31 May 1970	Peru	9.2° S, 78.8° W	66,000	7.8	$530,000 damage, great rock slide, floods
20 June 1990	Western Iran	37° N, 49.4° E	40,000 to 50,000	7.7	Landslides
29 Sept. 1993	Southern India	18.1° N, 76.5° E	9,748	6.3	
17 Aug. 1999	Turkey	40.7° N, 30° E	17,118	7.4	At least 50,000 injured, thousands homeless. Damage estimated at $3–6.5 billion.
26 Jan. 2001	India	23.3° N, 70.3° E	19,988	7.7	166,812 injured, 600,000 homeless.
25 March 2002	Hindu Kush Region, Afghanistan	35.9° N, 69.2° E	800–1,000	6.1	At least 1,000 killed, several hundred injured, and several thousand homeless in Baghlan Province. At least 1,500 houses destroyed or damaged at Nahrin and several hundred more in other areas of Baghlan Province. Landslides blocked many roads in the epicentral area. Felt strongly in much of northern Afghanistan. Also felt in the Islamabad-Peshawar area, Pakistan, and at Dushanbe, Tajikistan.

Source: U.S. Geological Survey. (2003). Earthquake hazards program. Retrieved Jan 24, 2003, from http://neic.usgs.gov/neis/eqlists/eqsmajr.html

ener hypothesized that there was a gigantic continent (Pangaea) 200 million years ago.

Causes

Earthquakes are classified as natural and induced. Natural earthquakes are further classified as tectonic (the most common, more than 90 percent; resulting from sudden release of energy stored by major deformation of the Earth), volcanic (in conjunction with volcanic activity), and collapse (e.g., in the regions of caverns). Induced earthquakes are vibrations of the ground caused by human activities such as construction of dams, mining, and nuclear explosions. For example, a reservoir filling in Koyna, India, induced a catastrophic earthquake that caused 177 deaths.

The majority of earthquakes are caused by the movement of tectonic plates, as explained first by the continental drift theory of Wegener. Tectonic plates are large segments of the Earth's lithosphere (the outer, rigid shell of the Earth that contains the crust, continents, and plates). The Earth's surface consists of nine major plates: six continental plates (the North American, South American, Eurasian, African, Indo-Australian, and Antarctic plates) and three oceanic plates (the Pacific, Nazca, and Cocos plates). Tectonic plates move in relation to other tectonic plates and along faults over the deeper interior. Faults are fractures or zones of fractures in rock along which the two sides have been displaced relative to each other parallel to the fractures, for example, the well-known San Andreas fault in California, which separates the Pacific plate (with San Francisco and Los Angeles on it) from the North American plate.

When lava is upwelling at the midoceanic (mid-Pacific, mid-Atlantic) ridges, rock moves slowly away from either side of the ridges across the surface of the Earth, creating new sea floor. As new plates are constantly being created, plates must also be absorbed. This happens in the so-called subduction-zones, where dipping ocean plates descend into the Earth by way of an ocean trench. These subduction-zones are where most deep-focus earthquakes (below 300km depth) occur. Earthquakes, volcanoes, mountain building, and subduction zones are therefore generally explained as consequences of steady, large, horizontal surface motions. Most tectonic plates contain both continents and ocean floor. At present, those plates containing Africa, Antarctica, and North and South America are growing, whereas the Pacific plate is getting smaller. When plates collide—for example, the African and the Eurasian or the Indo-Australian and the Eurasian—big mountain chains, such as the Alps and the Himalayas, arise, accompanied by persistent earthquake activity.

Seismographs and Seismograms

Earthquakes are recorded by sensitive instruments called "seismographs." Today's digital seismographs record ground shaking over a large band of frequencies and seismic amplitudes. A seismogram (the record created by a seismograph) shows the motions of the Earth's surface caused by seismic waves as a function of time. Earthquakes generate different kinds of seismic waves. P (primary) waves move in a compressional motion, meaning that they alternately compress and dilate the rock, whereas S (secondary) waves move in a shear motion, perpendicular to the direction the wave is traveling. From a seismogram the distance and energy of an earthquake can be determined. At least three seismograms are needed to locate where an earthquake occurred. The place at which rupture commences is called the "focus" or "hypocenter," whereas the point on the Earth's surface directly above the focus of an earthquake is called the "epicenter." The distance between the focus and the epicenter is called the "focal depth" of an earthquake.

Scales—magnitude

The magnitude of an earthquake is a measure of the amount of energy released. One common type of magnitude measurement is the Richter scale, named after the U.S. seismologist Charles Francis Richter (1900–1985). The Richter scale is logarithmic. For example, the seismic energy of a magnitude 7 earthquake is one thousand times greater than that of a magnitude 5 earthquake.

Scales—intensity

Another scale measures the seismic intensity of an earthquake at different sites. Seismological services (services in charge of maintaining the national seismic network, evaluating recent earthquakes, updating the earthquake catalog, and determining earthquake hazards) mail questionnaires to local inhabitants and authorities after an earthquake to ask them to estimate its effects. Commonly used are the European Macroseismic Scale 1998 (EMS–98, see table 1) in Europe and the Modified Mercalli Intensity Scale in the United States, both with intensity ratings between I and XII. Japan uses the Omori Scale, with intensity ratings between 0 and VII. The damage distribution of an earthquake is visualized on maps on which lines of equal intensity (isoseismals) on the Earth's surface are drawn.

Seismological Services

Most countries have national seismological services, for example, the Swiss Seismological Service, the British Geological Survey, and the U.S. Geological Survey. Seismic data collected by the seismological services are submitted to, for example, the World Data Center in Colorado in the United States and the International Seismological Centre in Edinburgh, Scotland.

Recent Earthquake Catastrophes

The most destructive earthquakes have occurred along the subduction zones between the Indo-Australian and the Pacific plates. (See table 2.) Three earthquakes with the most casualties in 2002 occurred in Turkey on 3 February, in Afghanistan on 25 March, and in western Iran on 22 June.

The 3 February earthquake in Turkey, with a magnitude of 6.5, caused at least 44 deaths, 318 injuries, and damage to 622 buildings in Afyon Province. It was felt in much of west-central Turkey and in the Dodecanese Islands of Greece.

The 25 March earthquake in Afghanistan was localized in the highly seismic Hindu Kush region with a magnitude of 6.1. It killed at least one thousand and injured several hundred. At least fifteen hundred houses were destroyed or damaged at Nahrin and several hundred more in other areas of Baghlan Province. This shallow earthquake at a depth of 8 kilometers occurred near the boundary of the Eurasian and Indian tectonic plates, which are converging to generate complex stresses in the region, resulting on the one hand from subduction and on the other hand from rotation of continental blocks.

The 22 June earthquake in western Iran, with a magnitude of 6.5, occurred in a highly seismic region on the boundary between the Arabian and Eurasian plates. It killed at least 261, injured 1,300, and damaged thousands of buildings. Damage was estimated at $91 million. The earthquake was felt strongly in much of western Iran. The Arabian plate is a small plate split from the African plate, and as it collides with the Eurasian plate it causes uplift of the Zagros Mountains and damaging earthquakes. Several severe earthquakes have occurred nearby, for example, the 20 June 1990 earthquake (40,000–50,000 casualties) about 150 kilometers north of the 22 June 2002 earthquake.

Strategies Against Earthquakes

The increasing density of population increases the potential effects of earthquakes, especially in urban areas with high seismic activity, for example, San Francisco, which was struck by an earthquake on 18 April 1906. For this reason, antiseismic building codes are important. Proper planning and regulation of new buildings and seismic upgrading of existing buildings can now safeguard most types of buildings against earthquake shocks. One obstacle to adhering to antiseismic building codes is the high cost; this is true particularly in cities of the Third World and of newly industrializing countries. The 19 September 1985 Mexico City earthquake occurred 200 kilometers from Mexico City, but the shaking of loose sediments in the city was much stronger than at the epicenter. Nearly ten thousand people died, and the city was heavily damaged as poorly constructed buildings collapsed. The earthquake destroyed as many as 100,000 housing units and countless public buildings. Even with all the tools of modern technology, the time, location, and magnitude of earthquakes cannot be predicted precisely. However, damage and casualties can be lessened if builders adhere to building codes based on the seismic hazards of their area.

Christa Hammerl

Further Reading

Agricola, G. (1558). *De ortu et causis subterreaneorum* [About the origin and the causes of subterranean] (Vol. II). Basel, Switzerland: Frobenius.

Aristotle. (1970). *Meteorologie* [Meteorology]. Darmstadt, Germany: Wissenschaftliche Buchgesellschaft.

Bolt, B. A. (1976). *Nuclear explosions and earthquakes: The parted veil.* San Francisco: Freeman.

Bolt, B. A. (1982). *Inside the earth: Evidence from earthquakes.* San Francisco: Freeman.

Bolt, B. A. (1993). *Earthquakes.* San Francisco: Freeman.

Grünthal, G. (Ed.). (1998). *European Macroseismic Scale 1998 (EMS–98).* Luxembourg-City, Luxembourg: Conseil de l'Europe, Cahiers du Centre Européen de Géodynamique et de Séismologie.

Gubbins, D. (1990). *Seismology and plate tectonics.* Cambridge, UK: Cambridge University Press.

Gutdeutsch, R., Grünthal, G., & Musson, R. (Eds.). (1992). *Historical earthquakes in central Europe.* Vienna: Abhandlungen der Geologischen Bundesanstalt.

Hammerl, C., & Lenhardt, W. (1997). *Erdbeben in Österreich* [Earthquakes in Austria]. Graz, Austria: Leykam.

Kant, I. (1968). *Von den Ursachen der Erderschütterungen bei der Gelegenheit des Unglücks, welches die westlichen Länder von Europa gegen das Ende des vorigen Jahres getroffen hat, 1776* [About the causes of earthquakes on the occasion of the disaster, which struck countries in western Europe at the end of the last year, 1776]. Berlin, Germany: Akademie-Textausgabe.

Kashara, K. (1981). *Earthquake mechanics.* Cambridge, UK: Cambridge University Press.

Kircher, A. (1678). *Mundus subterraneus* [The subterranean world] (3rd ed.). Amsterdam: Joannes Janssonius.

Kostrov, B., & Das, S. (1988). *Principles of earthquake source mechanics.* Cambridge, UK: Cambridge University Press.

Lay, T., & Wallace, T. C. (1995). *Modern global seismology.* San Diego, CA: Academic Press.

Mallet, R. (1851). *First report on the facts of earthquake phenomena.* London: British Association.

Michell, J. (1760). *The nature and origin of earthquakes.* London: Philosophical Transactions.

Giese, P. (1985). *Ozeane und Kontinente: Spektrum der Wissenschaft* [Oceans and continents: spectrum of the science]. Heidelberg, Germany: Akademie Verlag.

Pfeiffer, F. (Ed.). (1877). *Konrad von Megenberg: Das Buch der Natur* [Konrad von Megenberg: The Book of Nature]. Stuttgart, Germany.

Richter, C. F. (1958). *Elementary seismology.* San Francisco: Freeman.

Titus Lucretius Carus. (1986). *De rerum natura* [About nature]. Leipzig, Germany: Reclam.

U.S. Geological Survey, Earthquake Hazards Program. (n.d.). *National Earthquake Information Center, World Data Center for Seismology.* Retrieved November 28, 2002, from http://neic.usgs.gov/neis/bulletin/

Voltaire, F. M. A. (2000). *Candide oder Der Optimismus* [Candide or optimism]. Frankfurt, Germany: Insel Taschenbücher. (Originally published, 1759.)

Walker, B. (1982). *Erdbeben: Der Planet Erde* [Earthquakes: Planet Earth]. Amsterdam: Time-Life Bücher.

Wegener, A. (1915). *Die Entstehung der Kontinente und Ozeane* [The origin of continents and oceans]. Braunschweig, Germany: Friedrich Vieweg and Sohn.

Eastman, Charles

(1858–1939)
Native American writer

Charles Eastman, a Native American physician, writer, and activist, left a significant record of the Santee or Eastern Sioux relationship with nature and helped fuel the American wilderness movement during the first decades of the twentieth century.

Eastman, who was first given the name Hakadah and later renamed Ohiyesa ("Winner"), came into the world during a turbulent period for the Santee Sioux. After the failed uprising of 1862, Ohiyesa fled Minnesota with his grandmother (Ohiyesa's mother died in childbirth, and the U.S. government imprisoned his father), eventually ending up in southern Manitoba, Canada. After ten years of exile, Ohiyesa was finally reunited with his father, who convinced his son to accept Christianity and to enroll in the Santee Normal Training School in Nebraska. There Ohiyesa took the name Charles Eastman. Eastman excelled as a student and went on to study at Beloit, Knox, and Dartmouth Colleges and Boston University, where, in 1889, he graduated with an M.D. After his schooling, Eastman served as Bureau of Indian Affairs's physician at the Pine Ridge reservation, where he introduced many suspicious Sioux to the value of Euro-American medicine, treated survivors of the 1890 Wounded Knee massacre, and met his future wife, the educator and reformer Elaine Goodale. After repeated disagreements with Bureau of Indian Affairs officials, Eastman resigned and started an unsuccessful private practice in St. Paul, Minnesota. He later served as physician on the Crow Creek Agency and at the Carlisle Indian School, took an appointment as a U.S. Indian inspector, and lobbied in Washington on behalf of the Santee Sioux. Eastman also established Y.M.C.A. chapters on reservations, ran a youth camp in New Hampshire with his wife, and worked with the Boy Scouts and Camp Fire Girls. Eastman ultimately became one of the most prominent early twentieth-century Native American voices calling for reform of the federal government's treatment of Native Americans.

But it is for his writing that Eastman is best remembered. In collaboration with his wife, he wrote dozens of articles and ten books, many of which told the story of his early life prior to prolonged contact with Euro-American culture. Eastman's writings were well received by middle-class Anglo Americans who, in the early twentieth century, had discovered wilderness and traditional Native American life as a source of regeneration from the stress of urban life. In fact, much of the Native American lore appropriated by the Boy Scouts and the Camp Fire Girls came from Eastman's writings. As several historians have pointed out, by feeding nostalgia for "authentic" Native American life in the wilderness, Eastman dismantled more pernicious Native American stereotypes and generated sympathy for Native American political causes.

Many have criticized Eastman for his romanticized views of Sioux life, his tendency to universalize Native American cultures, his use of the evolutionary language of savagery and civilization, and his portrayals of Native Americans as living in perfect balance with the American wilderness. Still, for the careful reader, Eastman's writings provide an indispensable account of the place of nature in Santee Sioux life.

Colin Fisher

Further Reading

Deloria, P. J. (1998). *Playing Indian.* New Haven, CT: Yale University Press.

Stensland, A. L. (1977). Charles Alexander Eastman: Sioux storyteller and historian. *American Indian Quarterly*, 3(4), 199–207.

Wilson, R. (1983). *Ohiyesa: Charles Eastman, Santee Sioux*. Urbana: University of Illinois Press.

Ecofeminism

Ecofeminism (the term is short for *ecological feminism*) is a combination of ecological and feminist analyses and movements. *Ecofeminism* has become an umbrella term for historical associations between women and nature, for studies of and resistance to domination as a mode of interhuman and human-Earth relations, for in-depth understanding of patriarchal social structures and worldviews, and for social movements that see the oppression of women and the domination of the natural world as connected. Ecofeminist theorists reflect differently on the relationships between women and the natural world and between misogyny (hatred of women) and the ecological crisis. Foundational assumptions differ, as do the goals and means to achieve them. This has led to a divergence wherein the feminist analysis could be liberal (equality between women and men), Marxist or socialist (economic disparities are central), cultural (maintain divisions between feminine and masculine ideas, but promote the feminine), radical (autonomy for women), postmodernist, postcolonialist, or ecowomanist. The environmental analysis ranges from an anthropocentric (human-centred) viewpoint, as seen in mainstream environmental resource management, to looking at the centrality of economic structures that cause environmental ruin, such as social ecology. Others do not accept anthropocentrism at all, as seen within the deep ecology or cosmology frameworks. Much of ecofeminism has emerged in North America, but a variety of regional, ethnic, and cultural ecofeminisms exists. There are ecofeminist reflections from Latin and South America, Asia, India, and Africa. For some, religion is a central element, and there are Buddhist, Native American, Goddess, Hindu, Muslim, Christian, and Jewish ecofeminists. From the beginning, those who agreed that ecology is a feminist issue and that solutions to ecological problems must include feminist analyses disagreed as to the nature of these connections. As ecofeminist philosopher Karen Warren writes:

> The varieties of ecofeminism reflect not only the differences in the analysis of the woman/nature connection, but also differences on such fundamental matters as the nature of and the solutions to women's oppression, the theory of human nature, and the conceptions of freedom, equality, epistemology on which various feminist theories depend. (Warren 1987, 4)

Origins

Ecofeminism appeared in the 1970s, predominantly in North America, although the term was introduced by French feminist Françoise d'Eaubonne. In her 1974 book *Le Féminisme ou la Mort* (Feminism or Death), she called upon women to lead an ecological revolution to save the planet. In 1975 theologian Rosemary Radford Ruether wrote:

> Women must see that there can be no liberation for them and no solution to the ecological crisis within a society whose fundamental model of relationships continues to be one of domination. They must unite the demands of the women's movement with those of the ecological movement to envision a radical reshaping of the basic socioeconomic relations and the underlying values of this society. (Ruether 1975, 204)

Ecofeminism became a useful lens through which to assess connections and layers of associations between women's oppression and ecological crisis. Critical links were being made between race, class, gender, militarism, and environmental destruction. Ecofeminism in North America has roots in activism and analyses of the antinuclear, antiwar, environmental, and lesbian-feminist movements. Conferences and popular ecofeminist publications in the 1980s were forerunners of academic ecofeminist writings, particularly in philosophy, sociology, and religious studies. The development of a coherent body of ecofeminist theory, or an understanding of ecofeminism as a specific subject, began in the mid-1980s in North America. In general, ecofeminism developed with two distinct approaches: theoretical and material associations.

Theoretical Associations

The inquiry into the Western woman-nature construct has been a prolific area of ecofeminist theory, coming predominantly from philosophy and religion. The basic realization of ecofeminism is that the oppression of women and the natural world is built into the very mode of perceiving both. Central to ecofeminist theory is that dualisms are embedded in the Western worldview, values, and actions. These hierarchical dualisms are concepts about the world, human relations, and the place of humans within the scheme of things. Dualistic conceptual structures are those such as women-men, feminine-masculine, Earth-heaven, nature-culture, reproduction-production, body-mind, emotion-reason, intuition-thought, private-public, passive-active, natural-supernatural, and slave-master. The first half of each dualism is subordinate to the second. These dualisms are ideologically grouped together such that women are connected to feminine, Earth, nature, reproduction, body, emotion, intuition, private, and slave, and the same grouping of the second halves applies to men. These ideas are taken as truth and are structured within the social and economic order. They point to a logic of domination embedded in Western worldviews. Ecofeminists show how this worldview sanctions an understanding that men have innate power over both women and nature and that the twin dominations of women and nature are justified and appear as "natural." Religion, philosophy, science, and most cultural symbols have reinforced this worldview.

Ecofeminists have discussed the origin of domination and oppression, identifying roots in the development of hierarchy, misogyny, agricultural mastery, slavery, anthropocentrism (human centeredness), androcentrism (male centeredness), and the conquest of reason over nature. Both patriarchy and domination have long and complex histories within human communities, and little is certain. However, ecofeminists contend that the history of the intertwined oppression of women and nature can help to resist the daily oppression of women and escalating ecological crisis.

Material Associations

During the 1970s there was much debate about development theory and practice—development meaning the idea that all societies around the world had to "develop" the same way, and move from an agricultural to an industrial economy. The results of such "development" led some countries to plunge into extreme poverty. There began a debate about what the development agenda was in fact doing, and whether it was contributing to sustainable societies. Within this debate there was a focus on gender and development, asking questions about how development affects women and what role women play in economic and social concerns. The United Nations Decade for Women (1975–1985) ended with evidence that the situation of women was worsening everywhere in the world. It was evident that, with few exceptions, women's access to economic resources, income, and employment had worsened, work was increasing, and health, nutritional, and educational status was declining. Many antipoverty activists began to see the development model as destructive of existing agricultural, social, cultural, and ecological systems.

As the Earth's primary life support systems of air, water, and land become unstable, people are forced into new and more burdensome relations with the environment. In some areas of Africa and India women must travel for days to collect fuel or find water for basic survival. Often entire communities of people are forced to become environmental refugees, moving to overcrowded urban settings. Currently the United Nations estimates that there are over 25 million refugees throughout the world and that more than half are environmental refugees, meaning persons whose motivation for moving is environmental. Between 75 and 90 percent of all refugees are women and children.

Ecofeminists claim that in most parts of the world environmental problems disproportionately affect women and that poor women are the first victims. Problems of unsustainable food sources, soil erosion, undrinkable water, deforestation, toxic waste, lack of access to fuel, and reduction of common land often directly affect women. Yet, the increased burdens that women face result not from just environmental deterioration. A gender-based division of labor found in most societies considers family sustenance to be women's work. As the primary care-givers, women are responsible for the food and health of family members. Studies show that virtually everywhere women not only work longer hours than men, but also perform physically heavier work. Women have title to just 1 percent of owned land, yet they produce the bulk of the world's food.

The ecofeminist material approach examines sociopolitical and economic structures that restrict many women's lives to poverty, ecological deprivation, and economic powerlessness. This approach also reveals how gender and environmental issues are lived in different cultures. In North America ecofeminists have addressed issues such as environmental racism, toxic waste sites, agrobusinesses, corporate control, militarism, children's health and the environment, and access to drinkable water.

Ecofeminism has never been a homogeneous, unified theory or movement. Some proponents celebrate the diversity, whereas others find the diversity troublesome. Two issues debated within eco-feminism are the issue of theory, data, and action and the issue of cross-cultural concerns.

Theory, Data, and Action

Ecofeminist theory has predominantly come from academics in North America. While increasingly sophisticated ecofeminist analyses evolved, environmental issues affecting many of the world's women accelerated. The ecofeminism of northern nations was criticized for being blind to these material issues and for not realizing that consumerist cultures are a significant cause of the environmental and economic deprivation of southern nations. It has taken time for ecofeminism to find clarity in the relationship between theory and action and between privilege and poverty. In addition, each ecofeminist writer or activist is often dedicated to a specific concern, such as Western philosophy, religion, militarism, vegetarianism, animal rights, lesbian communities, poverty, North-South and global voices, solidarity, political action, citizens movements, ethics, economics, ethnicity, ritual, or art. Within each of these the emphases are varied, and there is little agreement as to what exactly ecofeminism is and how it should be used. The result can be a disconnect. For example, ecofeminists can be astute about the historical processes of the feminizing of nature, the naturalizing of women, and their mutual domination, but be oblivious to the corporate takeover of water rights in their own neighborhood. Ecofeminist activists can proclaim that women are "natural" leaders and healers in environmental movements without thinking through the political consequences of such ideas.

Other controversies within ecofeminism involve the use of spirituality. Some ecofeminists claim that spirituality is central, whereas others denounce spirituality as apolitical and irrelevant. Some use spirituality in romantic ways and for individual comfort, and others see spirituality as the base of political, social, and ecological transformation. Some ecofeminists say that research shows that prior to patriarchy there was a matriarchal or goddess period of ecological and social health. Others say that such research is faulty and that even if partially accurate, it is not relevant today.

Ecofeminism is a convergence of ecology and feminism into a new social theory and political movement. For many, ecofeminism represents a third wave of feminist critique and action. Ecofeminism is now a lens through which many issues are voiced, academic analyses sharpened, and actions taken. There is a loosely connected theoretical base, but it contains inner tensions, contradictions, and differing emphases. No single viewpoint embraces it all, and no single person is representative of ecofeminism. The division between the path of ecofeminist theory and an orientation to analysis for praxis (practice) and political transformation has lessened over the years, although the division serves as a reminder that larger horizons are relevant and that thought disconnected from action is void of political potential.

Cross-Cultural Concerns

Eco-feminism is emerging in many countries, and the women-nature association does not look the same everywhere. Context, culture, and religion play a significant role in understanding the history of the women-nature connection and if and how it can be used to resist the oppression of women and ecological ruin. Although hierarchical dualisms are endemic (native) to Western societies, this is not true elsewhere. Whereas most ecofeminists want to deconstruct the hierarchical dualisms, others want to reclaim and rejoice in the connections among women, femininity, emotion, body, intuition, and nature while rejecting the slave-master relationship. Contexts and strategies differ. Also, in some cultures and for some ecofeminists, the essence of women is understood to be closer to nature than that of men, or what is called "essentialism." Essentialism is a viewpoint that considers all women to have the same attributes, such as being naturally caring, peaceful, maternal, and sensitive to suffering and thus more apt to be ecologically responsible. Some add that women are connected to a Goddess, or a form of a Mother Earth wisdom spirituality. Most North American ecofeminist theorists reject essentialism but may accept that it is viable in particular cultures or contexts or even strategically useful.

Cross-cultural ecofeminism also reveals that ecological and feminist concerns are not equal everywhere. In some regions women are the custodians of the land but have no social rights and experience much violence. In other regions ecological deterioration is severe, and survival is at stake. For some, ecofeminism needs to become more aware of the role of economics and the systemic forces causing material and ecological deprivation around the world. The challenge is for ecofeminism to continue expanding to appreciate the cross-cultural issues, the range of suffering, and the potential solutions.

Contributions

Eco-feminism has developed into an interdisciplinary project, a social theory, and a third wave of feminism. Since the 1990s ecofeminism has addressed an endless variety of topics, researching and collecting statistics on the relations between ecological stress and human health, gender and ecological critiques of militarism, analyses of globalization, implications of the World Trade Organization, and exposition of the players in particular ecological disasters (the *Exxon Valdez* oil spill; the Union Carbide gas peak at Bhopal, India; the nuclear plant accident at Chernobyl, Russia; the Persian Gulf War; megadams; and rain forest destruction). Ecofeminists are engaging in agricultural issues, including the use of pesticides, organic farming, genetically modified foods, and cancer-causing chlorides. Clean air, clean water, reproductive rights, and environmentally safe schools for children are among issues being addressed within ecofeminist frameworks.

National organizations with an ecofeminist orientation have emerged, such as the Women's Environment and Development Organization (WEDO) in New York and Women, Environment, Education and Development (WEED) in Toronto. In conjunction with the United Nations Earth Summit in 1992, the theme of "Women for a Healthy Planet" became the impetus for the creation of local activist and education groups in North America and throughout the world. Hundreds of local, national, and international groups throughout the world connect women and ecological issues.

Academics continue to navigate through the many elements that have gathered under the umbrella of ecofeminism, and not everyone is comfortable with the range of expressions and issues. Still, ecofeminism is being studied at most universities in North America in several disciplines—women's studies, philosophy, theology, religious studies, environmental programs, and political science—as women and men, inspired by ecofeminism, become involved in projects to improve their part of the world.

Heather Eaton

Further Reading

Adams, C. (Ed.). (1993). *Ecofeminism and the sacred*. New York: Continuum.

Cuomo, C. J. (1998). *Feminism and ecological communities: An ethic of flourishing*. New York: Routledge.

d'Eaubonne, F. (1974). *Le féminisme ou la mort* [Feminism or death]. Paris: Pierre Horay.

Eaton, H., & Lorentzen, L. A. (Eds.). (2003). *Ecofeminism and globalization: Exploring religion, culture and context*. Lanham, MD: Rowman & Littlefield.

Griffin, S. (1978). *Woman and nature: The roaring inside her*. London: Woman's Press.

Mellor, M. (1995). *Earthcare: Women and the environment*. New York: Routledge.

Mellor, M. (1997). *Feminism and ecology*. Cambridge, UK: Polity Press.

Mies, M., & Shiva, V. (1993). *Ecofeminism*. London: Zed Books.

Ruether, R. R. (Ed.). (1975). *New woman/new earth: Sexist ideologies and human liberation*. New York: Seabury Press.

Ruether, R. R. (Ed.). (1996). *Women healing Earth: Third World women on ecology, feminism, and religion*. Maryknoll, NY: Orbis Books.

Warren, K. J. (1987). Feminism and ecology: Making connections. *Environmental Ethics, 9*, 3–19.

Warren, K. J. (2000). *Ecofeminist philosophy: A Western perspective on what it is and why it matters*. Lanham, MD: Rowman & Littlefield.

Ecological Imperialism

Imperialism is usually considered to be a political and sometimes an economic or religious phenomenon. But it also has an ecological side: Imperialists have intentionally, more often unintentionally, and always inevitably carried with them plants, animals, and microlife from their lands of origin to their new lands. Where imperialists have been successful not simply in conquest but also in settlement, they have done so with the indispensable assistance of the life forms they brought with them. The most successful imperialists have been those who have, as much by chance as intention, changed the flora and fauna, macro and micro, of their new environments to be much like their old environments.

Immigrant life forms often have done poorly in their new homes: for instance, attempts to permanently establish the European nightingale in North America have never succeeded. But some of these immigrants, moving into environments where organisms were not preadapted to prey on or effectively resist them, have often done well indeed.

The Days of the Smallpox Epidemics among the Chippewa of The Great Lakes

Several very old informants spoke of the days of smallpox epidemics. The disease being unknown to the Indians, they had no cure for it; remedies that it was hoped might help were applied without success.

"We had no cure for white men's sickness like smallpox. I remember an event of the smallpox time [said a Red Lake informant]. Some Canadian Indians who happened to come down our way found all the Indians in one place dead—all but two children. One of these children was Ghost Head. This woman grew up and lived in Red lake a long time; I knew her well. The Canadians found Ghost Head suckling her mother who had been dead of smallpox 3 to 4 days. Big flies were on her body, but still the child nursed on the woman. They put the children into their canoe, took them home, and cared for them."

Source: Hilger, M. Inez. (1951). *Chippewa Child Life and Its Cultural Background*. Bureau of American Ethnology, Bulletin 146. Washington, DC: Smithsonian Institution, p. 93.

Examples of Ecological Imperialism

Ecological imperialism is as old as human migration. For example, the ancestors of the Australian aborigines arrived in Australia from the Malay Archipelago fifty or so thousand years ago and some millennia afterward imported their dog, the dingo, the continent's first domesticated animal, which figured importantly in their success there.

The best examples pertain to European expansion because the Europeans were the first to habitually cross oceans, that is to say, to travel between continents with sharply contrasting biotas (flora and fauna). The human invaders' attendant organisms spearheaded alterations in local ecosystems essential for the biological and economic success of the humans. This can be considered under three headings: crops, animals, and diseases.

Crops

Europeans learned to eat the foods of America and Oceania (lands of the Pacific Ocean) but generally preferred their own food, planting wheat, barley, rice, turnips, peas, bananas, and so forth in their colonies wherever they would grow and as soon as was practical after arrival. These crops were often particularly important in enabling the imperialists to live in numbers in areas where indigenous crops did not grow well. A good example of a successful European crop is wheat, which prospers where Native American cereals do not and provided the nutritional and economic foundation for large populations in the temperate zone grasslands of North and South America and Australia.

Animals

European imperialists were most successful where there were few domesticated animals prior to their arrival. In America imported pigs fed on a great variety of locally available substances propagated wildly, and pigs generously provided proteins and fats for the imperialists. Imported cattle turned what humans cannot eat—grasses and forbs (nongrass herbs)—into what they can eat—meat and milk—and were running in vast feral herds in northern Mexico and Argentina within a century or so of their arrival. Old World sheep also thrived in many of the colonies, and their numbers exploded in Australia and New Zealand. Where these and like quadrupeds, goats, for instance, did well, so did the Europeans.

Horses were slower than most imported quadrupeds to have population explosions, but they did so in time. They made supermen of the invaders in battle with native foot soldiers, most of whom had never seen such large animals before and none of whom had ever seen an animal carry a human and obey human will.

The biological revolutions underlying these successes were much more complicated than simply bringing crops and animals ashore. Whole ecosystems or at least several of their components had to be imported, too. For example, in the thirteen colonies and then the early states of the United States one of the problems of establishing large herds of domesticated animals from Europe was the fact that native grasses and forbs, products of millennia free from the tread and teeth of domesticated herds, did not tolerate heavy grazing pressure well. The importation and then often-rapid expansion of European forage plants—for instance, white clover and what Americans inaccurately call Kentucky bluegrass—unrolled a carpet of food for immigrant quadrupeds. Much the same thing happened in the humid zones of Argentina, Australia, and Argentina.

Diseases

In the first stage of European imperialism in the Americas and Oceania, the triumph of the invaders over the natives seemed unlikely. The newcomers were always outnumbered. They were isolated by whole oceans from their home bases and were inexperienced in even how to survive in the new and alien environments. They were in need of powerful allies, such as the animals cited earlier and the germs they and their animals brought in their blood and breath. The Old World invaders' advantage was that their microorganic evolution and human history were different than those of the natives of the New World.

Heavy populations dependent on agriculture appeared earlier in the Old World than elsewhere, most significantly in crowded and filthy cities, providing the pathogens with food, habitat, and opportunity for transmission. Heavy populations of domesticated animals first appeared there likewise, providing more habitats for pathogens and opportunities for jumping from one species to another, including humans. The possibilities for epidemiological disasters were multiplied by the penchant of Old World peoples for long-range commerce.

When European imperialists crossed the oceans they brought with them infections unknown to American and Oceanic peoples, whose general density of population was low or relatively new, as were their cities. Large herds of domesticated animals were rare or nonexistent, and the tempo of long-range commerce was relatively low. Thus native peoples were unfamiliar with such infections as smallpox, measles, typhus, influenza, yellow fever, and malaria.

The most important or at least most spectacular of these infections in ecological imperialism was smallpox. It first arrived in the West Indies at the end of 1518, spread rapidly through the Greater Antilles and then on to Mexico, where Hernán Cortes and his conquistadors had just been driven out of the Aztec capital. All or nearly all of the Spaniards had already had the disease on the other side of the Atlantic and were immune. The peoples of Mexico were universally susceptible and died in droves.

Similar sequences of events occurred elsewhere in the Americas and Oceania. For example, the way was cleared for the Pilgrims who arrived in Plymouth, Massachusetts, in 1620 by some sort of devastating epidemic in 1616. For another example, smallpox raced through the aborigines of New South Wales in 1789 soon after the arrival of the Botany Bay colonists.

Where Ecological Imperialism Failed

Where the Europeans' attendant organisms, macro and micro, triumphed, as in temperate zone regions of America and the southwest Pacific, the Europeans took over demographically. Where the triumph was mixed, as in tropical America and South Africa, the Europeans conquered militarily but not demographically. Where the attendant organisms had only minor effect, as in tropical Africa and Asia, the Europeans failed to found colonies of settlement and were ejected in the twentieth century.

Alfred W. Crosby

See also Biological Exchanges; British Empire; Diseases, Human; Exploration

Further Reading

Cook, N. D. (1998). *Born to die: Disease and New World conquest, 1493–1650*. Cambridge, UK: Cambridge University Press.

Campbell, J. (2002). *Invisible invaders: Smallpox and other diseases in aboriginal Australia, 1780–1880*. Victoria, Australia: Melbourne University Press.

Cronon, W. (1994). *Changes in the land: Indians, colonists, and the ecology of New England*. New York: Hill and Wang.

Crosby, A. W. (1972). *The Columbian exchange: Biological and cultural consequences of 1492*. Westport, CT: Greenwood Press.

Crosby, A. W. (1986). *Ecological imperialism: The biological expansion of Europe, 900–1900*. Cambridge, UK: Cambridge University Press.

Diamond, J. (1996). *Guns, germs, and steel*. New York: W. W. Norton and Co.

Melville, E. G. K. (1994). *A plague of sheep: Environmental consequences of the conquest of Mexico*. Cambridge, UK: Cambridge University Press.

Merchant, C. (1989). *Ecological revolutions: Nature, gender, and science in New England*. Chapel Hill: University of North Carolina Press.

Thornton, R. (1987). *American Indian holocaust and survival: A population history since 1492*. Norman: University of Oklahoma Press.

Todd, K. (2001). *Tinkering with Eden: A natural history of exotics in America*. New York: W. W. Norton and Co.

Ecological Restoration

To restore a thing means to return it to a previous condition, and ecological—or environmental—restoration returns a landscape or ecological system such as a forest, grassland, or lake to a previous condition. Examples of ecological restoration include replanting vegetation on land disturbed by surface mining to control soil erosion or return the land to productive use, replanting prairie species on farmland originally occupied by prairie, or even reestablishing historic vegetation at a historic site such as a battlefield to re-create historic conditions.

As these examples illustrate, environmentalists and environmental managers give the term *restoration* quite different meanings, depending on exactly how the "original"—or model—ecosystem or landscape is defined and what attributes are selected as goals of restoration.

Thus the term *restoration* may be used broadly to refer to attempts to restore selected attributes of a landscape, such as its productivity, its beauty, its historic value, or its value as habitat for certain species of plants or animals. Used in this way, *restoration* includes various forms of restorative land management, which may be referred to more generally as "rehabilitation" (restoration of selected features), "reclamation" (rehabilitation carried out on severely degraded sites such as surface mines), "reforestation," "revegetation," or even "healing" (restoration of the health of an ecosystem). In all of these cases, restoration projects may be motivated by human interests such as a desire for clean water or timber production or opportunities for hunting, fishing, backpacking, or other recreational activities.

Alternatively, *restoration* may be used in a narrower and more demanding sense to refer not to restoration of selected attributes of the historic, or "model" ecosystem, but rather to restoration of the entire system, including elements such as dangerous or unattractive animals or events such as wildfires or flooding, whether these are regarded as useful or desirable or not. In such cases it may be difficult to justify restoration in purely economic or even aesthetic terms, and restoration takes on a different value, becoming less an attempt to return land to productivity or ecological health than a gesture of respect for the natural landscape apart from its immediate value for humans and, not incidentally, a way of ensuring its survival by compensating in an ecologically effective way for novel influences—usually the result of human activities—coming from "outside" the ecosystem.

Although efforts of this kind are often necessary to ensure the survival and well-being of an historic landscape and although restoration in this narrower sense has been practiced since the early decades of the twentieth century, environmentalists and environmental managers ignored restoration for many decades, in part because they feared that the promise of restoration might be used to undermine arguments for the preservation of natural areas. Since the mid-1980s, however, restoration, in both the broader and narrower senses, has rapidly gained in importance as a strategy for the conservation of natural areas.

Broadly understood, ecological restoration dates to the earliest times of which people have any record of practices such as shifting agriculture, crop rotation, fallowing of land, soil replenishment, game management, and reforestation. Even more fundamentally, it may be rooted in human anxiety regarding nature itself as the source of all life, including human life, and in the ceremonies and rituals of world renewal, the maintenance of populations of plants and animals, and the regeneration of souls or spirits that are characteristic of many traditional societies.

Basic Assumptions

Precisely because both the idea and the practice of restoration have so long a history, this history is best understood not simply as the development of these forms of restorative management, but rather as the change of attitudes toward environmental damage and repair. Because restoration in its broadest sense is the process of returning land to a former condition, usually regarded as in some way preferable to the present "degraded" condition, restoration efforts always reflect basic assumptions about what is desirable in an ecosystem and what is regarded as "degraded" land.

These assumptions vary widely from culture to culture and have often changed dramatically over time. Today, for example, most environmentalists blame humans for damaging the Earth, but as recently as two

Though historically related to land-management practices such as reforestation, reclamation, and rehabilitation, ecological restoration is distinct from these practices in its commitment to guiding an ecosystem or landscape back to a previous condition in ecological history. Reproduced here is a rare photo of an early ecological restoration project initiated by botany professor Edith Roberts at Vassar College in Poughkeepsie, New York in the 1920s. The project illustrates the emergence of this relatively new form of management out of a marriage of wildflower gardening and ecology. This attempt to create in miniature a collection of the plant associations native to Dutchess County anticipated similar projects that would take place in other parts of the United States in subsequent decades. PHOTO FROM ECOLOGY, APRIL 1933; COURTESY OF LOIS KOMAI WHO DISCOVERED THE RARE PHOTO AND WILLIAM JORDAN III WHO PROVIDED IT FOR USE HERE.

centuries ago most people in the West had a different view. Regarding natural landscapes as "fallen" and unredeemed by human effort, they took it for granted that humans improved on "raw" nature through activities such as gardening, farming, and building, and that damage to land, rivers, and seas was due to the unrestrained and undirected influences of nonhuman, natural forces such as fires, floods, catastrophic storms, or even ecological processes such as predation or natural changes in vegetation. This is what the eighteenth-century French naturalist Compte de Buffon had in mind when he claimed that "wild nature is hideous and dying; it is I, I alone who can make it agreeable and living" (Glacken 1967, 495). Like Buffon, those who wrote about "restoring" forests or productivity in the seventeenth and earlier centuries saw damage as largely the result of human neglect rather than of human activities involving exploitation or abuse of the land. For them, restoration was a way of maintaining

human improvements—or gardens—that had been created from wild nature and that required more or less continual maintenance to prevent their return to chaos.

This view of nature was not peculiar to the West. Europeans rejuvenating hayfields by adding cow manure viewed nature in this way. So did Asians rebuilding rice paddies by consolidating terraces and Native Americans maintaining wildlife populations by burning forests or grasslands or creating elaborate rituals designed to ensure the periodic renewal or "fixing" of the world.

All of these activities might be called "restorative improvement," and work of this kind and the ideas about nature it reflects underlie conservation projects aimed at "reclaiming" land from nature or maintaining it for human use. Other examples include the irrigation of desert land to create conditions suitable for agriculture, as was done extensively in parts of the western

United States early in the twentieth century, the creation of arable land by filling of wetlands, and even the management of forests to ensure sustained yields of timber.

Different as these activities are, they all reflect the idea that nature is always in a sense running down, deteriorating or *degenerating*, and that it requires human effort to maintain it or put it back in working condition. A different idea took shape in the United States during the nineteenth century as a result of the work of a handful of thinkers and land managers who essentially turned the old idea of degradation upside down. A leading figure was George Perkins Marsh (1801–1882), a scholar, diplomat, and author of the classic *Man and Nature* (1864). In this revolutionary book Marsh argued that humans, not natural forces, are the primary cause of environmental damage and of calamitous events such as floods, droughts, or extinctions. Challenging the conventional idea of humans as an ordering influence in the landscape, Marsh declared that "Man is everywhere a disturbing agent" (Marsh 1965, 36). In Marsh's view, land does not naturally or spontaneously degenerate but rather is actively *degraded* as a result of human activities such as the clearing of forests, damming of rivers, or cultivating of land. Describing a network of ecological relationships and interdependencies linking forest and river, rainfall and erosion, Marsh argued that humans disturb nature's balances not only in direct and obvious ways, but also in indirect and subtle ways.

Co-Workers with Nature

Marsh's novel views about damage also made him one of his period's leading advocates of restoration. Indeed, *Man and Nature* is a long essay not just about environmental damage, but also about environmental restoration, which Marsh mentions repeatedly. Seeing humans as the cause of environmental damage, Marsh was hopeful that humans could also improve ecosystems they had damaged. Drawing on his observations of Mediterranean landscapes, especially in Italy, where he was U.S. ambassador from 1861 until his death in 1882, Marsh wrote that humans must become coworkers with nature "in the reconstruction of the damaged fabric which the negligence or the wantonness of former lodgers has rendered untenantable" (Marsh 1965, 35). All modern restorationists who see themselves returning nature to a condition that existed before humans damaged or corrupted it are working within this nineteenth-century vision of degradation.

Because this degradation is supposed to have been caused by humans disrupting or "breaking" the natural integrity of the ecosystem, this might be called "restorative repair." Soil conservation, land reclamation, fertility renewal, streambed reconstruction, environmental engineering, natural gardening and landscaping, land stewardship, and wildlife renewal can all be seen as either improvement or repair, depending on what the practitioner supposes the source of damage to be.

One result of the emerging idea of restorative repair was a growing interest in historic landscapes as models for environmental management projects. By 1900 U.S. Department of Agriculture investigators seeking information about historic landscapes in the western states were querying elderly ranchers and farmers about pre-ranching and prefarming conditions. In the 1930s geographer Carl Sauer directed a major "erosion history" project within the Soil Conservation Service to assemble and catalogue information about the pre-European landscapes of the United States. Leading plant ecologists such as Henry Cowles and Frederick Clements also were interested in describing presettlement landscapes because these were the baseline upon which their theories of ecological processes and change were built. Their interest was also stimulated by environmental catastrophes such as the Dust Bowl of the 1930s, which led Americans to reflect on their history and the social and ecological consequences of settlement. Another reason for the growth of interest may have been the disillusionment following World War I, ushering in what historians such as Michael Kammen say was a new period of U.S. sensitivity to history.

This new period of sensitivity lent support to a third form of environmental restoration, which might be called "restorative naturalizing." This form developed as land managers who saw humans as the cause of environmental damage began attempting to restore landscapes to a condition that they regarded as natural and unpeopled rather than as gardened or in some way improved. Some range managers and foresters who were interested in productivity, along with a handful of landscape architects and designers interested in the beauty of designed landscapes, began experimenting with restoration by naturalizing. In the 1910s, for example, range scientist Arthur Sampson in the western United States began experimenting with native grasses in projects undertaken to return vegetation to overgrazed mountain meadows. Around the same time landscape architects such as Frederick Law Olmsted in the East and Jens Jensen in the Midwest helped establish a style of landscape design that emphasized the use of native plants in naturalistic arrangements. Although their aims were dissimilar—Sampson working in remote mountain areas in Utah and designers such as Olmsted and Jensen working on public lands and private estates in and around major cities—both adopted landscapes that existed prior to the time of European settlement as models and sought to re-create elements of these former landscapes.

Natural Landscapes

The growing popularity of restorative naturalizing early in the twentieth century was linked to a growing concern about the preservation of natural landscapes, at least in New World settings such as Australia and North America. Throughout the nineteenth century artists—including landscape designers working in the naturalistic tradition, the romantic poets, and painters such as those of the Hudson River Valley school—reflected and gave shape to a growing interest in unsettled lands. By the end of the century this interest, together with the closing of the U.S. frontier, led to a growing movement for preservation of lands such as those set aside as natural parks. In some areas, however, little or nothing of the precontact landscape remained to be preserved, and it was in such areas, notably in the Midwest—where the vast tallgrass prairies had been virtually eliminated from the landscape since the time of European settlement—that conservationists began concentrating on restoration as a way of ensuring the survival of increasingly rare kinds of natural landscapes.

Despite their different goals and philosophies, all of these restoration "schools" had one thing in common: Their goals, whether economic, environmental, historical or aesthetic, were defined in large part by human interests. Foresters, for example, whether they worked in the U.S. Rockies or the French Alps, focused on utility when replanting forests, their primary goal being to prevent floods, halt avalanches, or build up timber supplies. Similarly, landscape architects such as Olmsted and Jensen tried to create landscapes that people would find attractive and also in many instances practical because they involved relatively little maintenance and in some cases contributed to solving environmental problems such as erosion, flooding, or loss of habitat for native species.

By the 1920s, however, a few practitioners were experimenting with an approach to restoration that was quite different in this respect. Setting aside, insofar as they could, human considerations of all kinds, these restorationists began trying to re-create entire ecosystems for their own sake, deliberately ignoring their utility or value to humans. In an early example of such a project, botany professor Edith Roberts and her students created a "collection" of plant communities native to the area on the campus of Vassar College in eastern New York in the 1920s. Although they did this in part for scientific and educational purposes, their aim—to create realistic representations of various community types regardless of their practical value or interest to humans—marked a definite shift from the aims of earlier restorationists. A decade later a group at the University of Wisconsin Arboretum in Madison undertook a similar project on a considerably larger scale. Their aim, like that of Roberts, was to re-create a microcosm of the presettlement landscape, creating, in the words of U.S. forester Aldo Leopold, who played a key role in the project during its early years, "a sample of original Wisconsin—a sample of what Dane county looked like when our ancestors arrived here during the 1840s" (Jordan 1984).

At the arboretum, as in the earlier project at Vassar College, the project was undertaken for a variety of human reasons, the project planners pointing out its scientific, historic, and aesthetic as well as its environmental value. Their aim, however, was to re-create authentic replicas of the "original" natural ecosystems of the area, regardless of their utility or appeal to humans, and to include all their attributes, even those that might seem useless, ugly, or even dangerous.

Projects such as these represented a fourth approach to ecological restoration, which might be called "literal restoration" or "holistic restoration"—that is, restoration of the whole. In its early stages of development this approach was a form of restorative naturalizing because practitioners taking this approach regarded the landscapes and ecosystems they chose as models for their projects to be natural—that is, more or less "pristine" and reflecting little or no human influence. This idea has changed some in recent years as conservationists have become more aware of the extent to which many landscapes once regarded as pristine or "natural" actually reflect long and complex histories of interaction with humans. Even more significant, however, was the way in which those practicing this form of restoration defined their objectives. Whereas "naturalizers" such as Sampson or Jensen had always taken human interests such as productivity or beauty into consideration when planning and justifying their work, the holistic restorationists explicitly ignored human interests and preferences, adopting a studied disregard for human interests in choosing models and defining goals for their projects.

A good example was fire. Historically, many New World ecosystems—notably the tallgrass prairies of the Midwest and also many of the forests of the Southeast and West—were fire-dependent ecosystems, maintained by fires that were started either naturally by lightning or by Native Americans, who, like people in many parts of the world, used fire extensively to manage their environment. Europeans, however, had little understanding of the role fire played in these landscapes. In most areas land-management agencies such as the U.S. Forest Service devoted considerable energy to the suppression of fire, and the use of fire as a tool for managing (or restoring) wildlands was highly controversial not only in the public arena but also among conservationists through much of the twentieth century. Despite this controversy, managers seeking effective ways to manage certain forests and prairies did experiment with fire, often taking their cue from their knowledge of historic practices of Native Americans. Because these experiments proved successful in many instances, these managers rapidly became proponents of prescribed burning, often in defiance of both conventional wisdom and professional practice.

"Undesirable" Elements

In the same spirit of disregard for immediate human interests and cultural tastes, holistic restorationists insist on including other "undesirable" elements such as poisonous snakes, predators such as wolves, or unpopular species of plants in their restoration projects in order to make them as authentic as possible.

No doubt partly for this reason, holistic restoration at first played a negligible role in conservation thinking, policy, and practice. Although the earliest holistic restoration projects were carried out as early as the 1920s, these projects gained little attention from the conservation community, and even the handful of people involved in such projects generally overlooked or downplayed their value as a model for environmental management and conservation. Pioneering conservationist Leopold provides a good example. Leopold was deeply involved in various kinds of restorative management projects during much of his career. He was also an effective advocate of such work and played a key role in the early holistic restoration project at the University of Wisconsin. Despite this involvement, he never placed much emphasis on this form of restora-

tion as a strategy for the conservation of natural landscapes, and in *A Sand County Almanac*, his best-known and most influential writing, his accounts of his own efforts at holistic restoration at his family's rural retreat in central Wisconsin are generally downbeat in tone.

Considering the growing importance of holistic restoration as a conservation strategy during the past decade or two, it is important to consider why conservationists and environmentalists neglected it for so long. In part this was because, in contrast with other forms of restorative land management, holistic restoration is inconsistent with the assumptions and concerns of the major schools of environmentalism. To the conservationists of the first half of the twentieth century, who generally adopted a utilitarian idea of the value of the natural landscape, the holistic restorationist's concern for elements—such as "minor" species or processes such as fire or flooding—that might actually reduce the economic value of a landscape seemed impractical and even self-indulgent. Such a concern seemed a kind of boutique conservation that had little relevance to a program of conservation designed to repair environmental damage on the continental scale represented by the Dust Bowl or extensive deforestation in the Southeast, Northeast, Northwest, and upper Midwest. As a result, virtually all of the restorative work done during this period by programs such as the Civilian Conservation Corps and by new agencies such as the Soil Conservation Service fell into the categories of restorative repair or improvement. In the context of the large-scale conservation programs that were undertaken during this period, the few projects that people would today recognize as holistic restoration projects were exceptional and, in fact, had little influence on land-management policy or practice.

A generation later the environmentalists of the 1960s and 1970s also downplayed the importance of holistic restoration as a conservation strategy but for different reasons. Whereas the conservationists of their parents' generation had regarded this highly ambitious and demanding form of restoration as impractical, the new generation regarded it as presumptuous. Environmentalists, more concerned than conservationists had been about the conservation of natural landscapes for their own sake, worried that the promise of restoration might be used to undermine arguments for the preservation of existing natural areas. Arguing that natural areas such as prairies, wetlands, and old-growth forests were not only vulnerable but also "irreplaceable," they developed a way of talking about the natural landscape that precluded serious discussion of restoration. As a result, whereas other forms of restorative management, such as restorative improvement, repair, and naturalizing, developed during this period, assuming growing importance in areas such as reclamation of lands disturbed by surface mining or draining of wetlands, holistic restoration was virtually ignored.

This situation began to change during the 1980s for several reasons. One was that, with the supply of high-quality natural areas dwindling as the best areas were either acquired for preservation or lost to development or other forms of exploitation, environmentalists and managers began looking for alternative approaches to conservation. An obvious possibility was holistic restoration, which not only provided an alternative of sorts to preservation, but also opened up the possibility of expanding and upgrading existing preserves.

Preservation Not Enough

More fundamentally, ecologists were becoming increasingly aware that preservation by itself is often not enough to ensure the conservation of a high-quality natural area over a long period of time. Because a basic principle of ecology is that everything interacts with and influences everything else, preservation in the strict sense is actually impossible because ultimately an ecosystem cannot be protected from "outside" influences. Even if these influences are subtle and indirect, they can affect the ecosystem in important ways and can even lead to its complete replacement by another kind of ecosystem. Here again, the tallgrass prairies of central North America provide a good example. Most of these prairies were destroyed by the plow during the nineteenth century. However, those areas of prairie that escaped direct destruction have in many cases been lost as they were replaced by oak forests in the absence of fire—an indirect and often unintended result of settlement and the creation of plowlands that prevented the spread of the fires on which the prairies depended.

The implications of this base system of ecology were becoming clear by the 1980s: Preservation is not a satisfactory strategy for the conservation of natural areas. In fact, in the last analysis preservation is not a conservation strategy at all but is better regarded as a goal. The best way to reach that goal is first to do what one can to reduce "outside" influences and then to identify "outside" or novel influences that still exist and to find ecologically effective ways of compensating for them. Because this process of active compensation actually is "holistic restoration," this form of restoration, understood in this way, is the key to the long-term conservation of natural areas everywhere. In the long run the "best" natural areas will not be those that have simply been "protected" from outside—or novel—influences, but rather those that have benefited from ongoing programs of holistic restoration understood in this way.

The importance of this process is now becoming clear as catastrophic fires in ponderosa pine forests of the U.S. Southwest dramatize the need for restorative management to reduce fuel loads and open up fire-prone canopies following a century of fire suppression in these fire-dependent ecosystems. Although the early development of holistic restoration took place mainly on the prairies of the Midwest, the need for restoration is actually far more urgent in these forests: while the prairies merely fade into oak forest in the absence of restorative fire, ponderosa pine forests become prone to catastrophic fires that can denude slopes, leading to erosion that destroys not only the community but also the soil on which it depends, effectively destroying the entire ecosystem, which on some sites with steep slopes may not recover for centuries.

Growing awareness of the dependence of at least some natural landscape on human activities has played an important role in the emergence of holistic restoration as a conservation strategy since the 1980s, but other considerations have also played a role. One of these has been the growing recognition of the value of the process of restoration itself, not only for the landscape or ecosystem being restored, but also for those carrying out the work. An early step in this "discovery" of restoration as a way of interacting with natural landscapes in a positive way was the realization that restoration is a valuable way to learn about the ecosystems being restored by raising questions and testing ideas about those ecosystems. Obviously, one way to learn about a complex system such as a radio, for example, is to try to repair it when it is broken, and this is true of ecosystems as well. The discovery of the role of fire in some kinds of ecosystems noted earlier is an example. However, restoration efforts have also led to important insights into ecological processes as diverse as the cycling of nutrients in lakes, interactions between plants and complexes of fungi that inhabit their roots and genetic (or "evolutionary") changes in plants in response to altered conditions. They have also led to better understanding of the habitat requirements of species—the relationships between ecosystems, soil, and climates, interactions between predator and prey species, and even the composition of historic ecosystems, such as the oak savannas of the Midwest, that no longer exist in their historic form. Reflecting on the value of restoration as a way of gaining ecological insight, British ecologist Anthony Bradshaw has suggested that restoration should be regarded as the "acid test" of ecological understanding.

Today ecologists often undertake restoration projects specifically in order to test ideas about the ecosystems being restored, and environmental educators have extended the idea of learning in this way into outdoor classrooms, developing restoration projects in schoolyards and neighborhoods as a way of introducing students to the natural history, ecology, and environmental history of the area in which they live.

More generally, practitioners have discovered that participating in restoration projects in urban, suburban, or even wilderness areas can be rewarding for participants—a way of interacting with the natural landscape that is both active and positive in its effect on the landscape. In addition, restoration provides a context for confronting the negative as well as the positive aspects of people's relationship with the rest of nature. Restoration forces the practitioner to acknowledge the damage that led to the need for restoration and his or her complicity in it. It also requires the participant to take responsibility for the life processes such as killing and discriminating among species that restoration efforts always entail, and to confront and acknowledge the uncertainty of the restoration process itself. Like preservation, restoration is, after all, impossible in the strict sense. For one thing, the idea that people can copy nature accurately is open to serious question. Because the way people think about the landscape is conditioned by their culture, once people affect a landscape, knowingly or not, they cannot help but recreate it at least partly in their own image. In addition, although some kinds of change are reversible, others are not. Also, as critics have pointed out, however perfectly restored a landscape may be in an ecological sense, it will never have the same kind of value that the original did because it has a different history.

These negative aspects of ecological restoration may, however, prove to be one of the most important things about it because they offer environmentalism a way to escape from a naive and ecologically destructive innocence and to achieve the knowledge of history and the recognition of the mutual dependence of humans and the landscapes they inhabit that is prerequisite for ecological adulthood and true membership in the land community.

Although practitioners are only beginning to explore the benefits of participation in ecological restoration efforts, they have made considerable progress in recent years. Today the value—and appeal—of this constructive and troubling way of "using" the natural landscape and negotiating people's relationship with it is evident in the growing number of community-based projects. These are often planned and carried out largely by volunteers and often involve the addition of restoration projects to more-traditional forms of outdoor recreation such as backpacking and birding, often incorporating or complementing these activities as part of ecotourism experiences. These activities, some have suggested, provide a model for the human "use" of natural landscapes such as parks, preserves, and even wilderness areas.

Efforts such as these are also forcing practitioners to think more clearly about restoration, what it means, and the relationship between humans and the landscape it implies. Practitioners in New World settings such as North America and Australia, for example, have often been inspired by the idea that the landscapes they choose as models for their restoration projects are "natural." This idea, however, fails to take into account the influence of indigenous peoples on the landscapes they inhabit and makes little sense in Old World settings, where human influences on the landscape are well documented over hundreds and even thousands of years. In fact, New World or Old, most ecosystems reflect at least some human influence. A tallgrass prairie in Iowa, for example, may not really be any more "natural" than a meadow in England or a forest in Japan that has been managed intensively since medieval times. If the meadow and forest developed under the influence of frequent mowing or cutting by humans, and the prairie developed under the influence of frequent burning, also by humans, then all three may have the complex structures, self-supporting dynamics, and rich species composition often regarded as distinctive characteristics of "natural" systems.

Thus, although it may be useful to use the word *natural* when people want to distinguish between humans and the rest of nature, in most cases it may be better to use the more neutral—and usually more accurate—word *historic* or *classic* when referring to the landscapes most often selected as models for ecological restoration projects.

Since the 1980s ecological restoration has grown rapidly in importance as a conservation strategy, a discipline, and a context for negotiating the relationship between humans and the landscapes they inhabit. Milestones in this growth have included the creation of an international professional society, the Society for Ecological Restoration (SER), in 1987, and the creation of two journals, *Ecological Restoration* in 1981 and *Restoration Ecology* in 1993. Whereas SER is concerned with what has been called "holistic restoration," other organizations, such as the American Society for Surface Mine Reclamation and the Canadian Land Reclamation Association, support other forms of restorative management such as reclamation, rehabilitation, and restorative repair.

William R. Jordan III and Marcus Hall

See also Reforestation

Further Reading

Glacken, C. (1967). *Traces on the Rhodian Shore: Nature and culture in western thought from ancient times to the end of the eighteenth centure.* Berkeley: University of California Press.

Hall, M. H. (1999). *American nature, Italian culture: Restoring the land in two continents.* Unpublished doctoral dissertation, University of Wisconsin, Madison.

Hall, M. (2001). Repairing mountains: Restoration, ecology, and wilderness in twentieth-century Utah. *Environmental History, 6*(4), 574–601.

House, F. (1999). *Totem salmon: Life lessons from another species.* Boston: Beacon.

Jordan, W. R., III.(2003). *The sunflower forest: Ecological restoration and the new communion with nature.* Berkeley and Los Angeles: University of California Press.

Marsh, G. P.(1965). *Man and nature; or, physical geography as modified by human action.* Cambridge, MA: Belknap. (Original work published 1864)

Mills, S. (1995). *In service of the wild: Restoring and reinhabiting damaged land.* Boston: Beacon.

Roberts, E. A., & Rehmann, E. (1996). *American plants for American gardens.* Athens: University of Georgia Press. (Original work published 1929)

Ecological Simplicity

Persons practicing ecological simplicity make as few demands on their environment as possible. In the developed world this usually involves decreasing consumption and making environmentally responsible consumer choices. Ecological simplicity is not a new concept: Buddhism, Taoism, and Christianity all include references to the virtues of an ecologically simple life. It does not imply living in a state of deprivation or technological simplicity. Simplicity movements, including ecological simplicity, are generally a voluntary rejection of the complexity of the dominant lifestyle and are usually driven by moral philosophy.

Early History and the Transcendentalists

Numerous simplicity movements have occurred throughout history. Interest in ecological simplicity often depends on the current economic, social, and ethical climates. Initially people were attracted to ecological simplicity for religious reasons, but to most of these people ecological simplicity meant rural agrarian living. Many groups, most notably the Quakers, had a respect for nature and a desire to "neither hurt nor destroy" the environment. Not until the Transcendentalist movement was limiting the deterioration of the natural environment directly expressed.

Transcendentalism required one to go beyond the empirical and use intuition to gain the true knowledge of things. One could best find inspiration and eventually the answer to any question through contemplation of the symbolism present in nature because nature is the embodiment of the divine and follows its own order. American writers Ralph Waldo Emerson and Henry David Thoreau espoused the "deliberate life" to best understand the order of nature and rise above mundane existence. Deliberate or simple living required one to exert oneself intellectually and physically and to maintain material self-control in order to develop virtue and character. Living in the present and in nature was a way to reach the goal of happiness in life.

Progressive Simplicity

After the American Civil War, science, technology, and capitalism seized the collective mind of the industrialized world, and the Transcendentalist view of nature went out of fashion. But industrialism and the rapidly growing human population were leading to pollution, poverty, and increasing social strife. Many of the new middle-class professionals were joining the wealthy in a quest for satisfaction that had not come with increased wealth and consumption. They returned to the Progressive social reforms that Transcendentalists had promoted decades earlier. In addition to addressing

Thoreau on Simplifying One's Life

I left the woods for as good a reason as I went there. Perhaps it seemed to me that I had several more lives to live, and could not spare any more time for that one. It is remarkable how easily and insensibly we fall into a particular route, and make a beaten track for ourselves. I had not lived there a week before my feet wore a path from my door to the pond-side; and though it is five or six years since I trod it, it is still quite distinct. It is true, I fear, that others may have fallen into it, and so helped to keep it open. The surface of the earth is soft and impressible by the feet of men; and so with the paths which the mind travels. How worn and dusty, then, must be the highways of the world, how deep the ruts of tradition and conformity! I did not wish to take a cabin passage, but rather to go before the mast and on the deck of the world, for there I could best see the moonlight amid the mountains. I do not wish to go below now.

I learned this, at least, by my experiment: that if one advances confidently in the direction of his dreams, and endeavors to live the life which he has imagined, he will meet with a success unexpected in common hours. He will put some things behind, will pass an invisible boundary; new, universal, and more liberal laws will begin to establish themselves around and within him; or the old laws be expanded, and interpreted in his favor in a more liberal sense, and he will live with the license of a higher order of beings. In proportion as he simplifies his life, the laws of the universe will appear less complex, and solitude will not be solitude, nor poverty poverty, nor weakness weakness. If you have built castles in the air, your work need not be lost; that is where they should be. Now put the foundations under them.

Source: Thoreau, Henry David. (1854). *Walden*. Chapter 18.

---

poverty, child labor, and women's suffrage, Progressives tackled issues related to overconsumption, urban blight, and land degradation.

Contact with nature was considered imperative to survival in the stressful "modern world," and nature as recreation became popular. Landscape design, including the design of Central Park in New York City, incorporated native species in natural displays rather than horticultural exotics in formal gardens. As American historian David Shi points out in his book, *In Search of the Simple Life*, the "arts and crafts" simplicity movement boomed as the wealthy sought out comfortable houses with exceptional views. *The Ladies Home Journal* magazine, which reached a large middle class, presented simplicity and the nature aesthetic as a desirable lifestyle, and more people moved to the country to build the small houses pictured in the magazine.

American naturalist John Muir had already published numerous articles in popular periodicals about the natural areas of the West in the late 1800s, and people sought out those areas. Camping, hiking, and bird watching became popular pastimes for the middle classes. Muir started the Sierra Club in 1892, and it was an immediate success in helping Muir to gain popular

backing and to lobby U.S. President Theodore Roosevelt for the creation of several national parks, including Yosemite in California and Grand Canyon in Arizona. Muir was heavily influenced by Transcendentalism and believed strongly in the spirituality of nature. However, the majority of people in the United States at that time, although they read Muir, camped, and bird watched, were still consumers enamored with technological progress.

Modern Environmental Simplicity

The fascination with nature continued into the 1920s, as did increasing prosperity that made even higher demands on the environment. In 1926 regional plans that included greenbelts and integrated open areas of green space in urban areas were created. However, the economic depression of the 1930s ended green development before it ever got started. The Great Depression and two world wars established a sort of forced simplicity for a while. After World War II, led by creative corporate marketing and planned obsolescence, people embraced consumerism with vigor. Development, technological production, overconsumption, and the new "throw away" mentality brought an abandonment of the ideals of simplicity and led to increased waste, pollution, and environmental degradation.

Not until the 1960s did concern over increasingly visible environmental damage lead large numbers of people to reevaluate the effects of their lifestyles on themselves and their surroundings. Ecology was coming into its own as a scientific discipline. The emergence of environmental ethics and the growing body of scientific literature about human impacts on the environment inspired people who were already active in the peace and civil rights movements to act for change. The new environmental reformists were educated and developed strong antipollution grassroots organizations. For the first time environmental activism was driven by a real sense of urgency. There was great concern that civilization was destroying itself through overconsumption of resources and overproduction of toxic wastes.

Several important events during the 1970s resulted in mass interest in ecological simplicity. The first Earth Day was held to educate and motivate people to reduce their impacts on the environment and to bring politicians and activists together. The controversial bestsellers *The Greening of America* by Charles Reich and *Ecotopia* by Ernest Callenbach, as well as other books that touted the virtues of a simpler ecological lifestyle, were published. There was growing concern over the upper limits of carrying capacity (the population that an area will support without deterioration) as world population reached 4 billion. An embargo by oil-producing nations resulted in shortages and high prices worldwide. Ecological "footprint" analyses that measured the amount of ecological space each person used were introduced. Late in the decade the Green Party emerged in Europe, promoting a political platform based on social justice, peace, and environmental protection, and quickly gained membership throughout the world. People began discussing "sustainable development" in which production and consumption are balanced by environmental protection. People bought smaller cars and houses, turned down thermostats, and invested in emerging sustainable technologies.

Even though consumption and waste increased with economic growth in the 1980s, ecological simplicity, as a concept, was firmly established in world society. In 1983, 1992, and 2002 Earth Summits were convened by U.N. member countries to discuss strategies for sustainable development, population control, environmental protection, and pollution reduction. Today the number of people embracing ecological simplicity as a lifestyle is slowly growing in the developing world. Participation in ecological simplicity is still mostly limited to the wealthy and middle classes because environmental choices like purchasing sustainable products are more expensive. At least two U.S. magazines—*Real Simple* (published by Time Inc.) and *Organic Style* (published by Rodale)—are targeted specifically toward helping affluent women embrace ecological simplicity in their everyday lives.

Future strategies for ecological simplicity will require sophisticated approaches to sustainable development that reduce human impacts on the environment. More important, they will require all persons to make difficult personal choices that lessen their own environmental impact.

Vicki Medland

Further Reading

Callenbach, E. (1975). *Ecotopia*. Berkeley, CA: Banyan Tree Books.

Diamond, J. (1995, August). Easters End. *Discover, 16*(8), 63–69.

Elgin, D. (1981). *Voluntary simplicity: An ecological lifestyle that promotes personal and social renewal*. New York: Bantam.

Rees, W., & Wackernagel, M. (1996). *Our ecological footprint—Measuring human impact on the Earth*. Gabriola Island, Canada: New Society Publishers.

Reich, C. (1970). *The greening of America*. New York: Random House.

Shi, D. E. (1986). *In search of the simple life*. Layton, UT: Gibbs and Smith.

Thoreau, H. D. (1995). *Walden: An annotated edition*. Boston: Houghton Mifflin.

Ecology, Christian

The Christian churches, not unlike other institutions, paid little attention to ecological issues until late into the twentieth century. By the beginning of the new millennium, however, there had appeared a rather large body of official ecclesiastical documents and theological works in Catholic, Protestant and Orthodox settings emphasizing the importance of ecological concern as both a moral and religious issue.

Behind this new emphasis lies the conviction that ecological ethics needs to be grounded in a vision of reality that will offer ethically inspiring reasons for taking care of the nonhuman natural world across many generations. By the beginning of the twenty-first century a growing body of Christian thought maintained that a sense of God's creative blessing of creation and delight in living diversity may help believers to nurture and sustain ecological concern.

Such a claim has been issued in response to the charge by some environmental thinkers that a pure secularism or naturalism (the belief that nature is all there is) provides a more coherent basis for ecological responsibility than does Christianity. Philosopher John Passmore, for example, argued that Christianity, because of its otherworldly preoccupations, is inherently hostile to ecological responsibility. Obsession with the supernatural and life beyond death, he asserted, leads the faithful to concentrate so exclusively on the next world that they pay little attention to this one. Ecological critics of Christianity have also often cited the controversial thesis of historian Lynn White, Jr., that the book of Genesis, by granting humans dominion over life on earth (Gen 1: 26), has sanctioned much of the Christian West's aggressive domination of the natural world.

Ecologically informed Christian thinkers agree that their tradition has been at best ambiguous in its attitude toward nature. Nevertheless, they contend that there are rich resources in the scriptures and Christian doctrine for an effective ecological spirituality and morality. Of course, the survival of nature has not been a religious priority until recently, and Christian thinkers do not pretend that biblical and other classic sources contain prepackaged remedies for contemporary ecological problems. Still, they consider central teachings of their faith to be powerfully relevant to ecological ethics.

The Tradition-Centered Approach to Christian Ecology

There are two main ways in which Christian thought has dealt with the question of its ecological relevance. The first is a tradition-centered approach, which insists that the classic Christian writings and teachings offer an adequate foundation for a robust ecological ethic. Not only the summons to stewardship of creation, but also the Christian tradition's call to live a virtuous life, should help alleviate the stress that humans have been putting on the natural world. Serious practice of the virtues of moderation, humility, justice, gratitude, and compassion is a necessary response to the greed, arrogance, inequity, and apathy that have led to the ruination of nature in many places. The tradition-centered approach proposes that immoderate consumption, ingratitude, and economic injustice have done much to bring about the poisoning and depletion of Earth's resources and life systems. Without a massive popular return to the pursuit of time-tested virtues, humans will have great difficulty restoring the planet to health.

Environmental abuse, this argument continues, follows from disobedience to Christianity's moral precepts, not from any weaknesses inherent in Christianity itself. Accordingly, the current threat of global catastrophe does not arise from Christianity, but instead from a failure to accept its message. Moreover, Lynn White, Jr.'s, thesis that the Bible's giving humans dominion over the earth is the main historical cause of the ecological is based on mistaken biblical exegesis. Even though Christians may often have interpreted dominion to mean domination, biblical scholarship has shown that dominion really means that humans should have a nourishing and protective attitude toward nature. The supporters of the tradition-centered approach to Christian ecology are not arguing that we translate the Hebrew with a different word; rather, they are trying to identify more accurately what aspect of dominion they think the text means in this case. Furthermore, the real causes of ecological problems are entirely too complex to make any single religious tradition the prime culprit.

The Sacramental Approach to Christian Ecology

However, a second group of Christians is less tradition-centered. Its response to ecological abuse is more focused on nature itself and less on classic religious texts. Although it embraces the traditional teachings and classic literary sources associated with Christianity, it also reminds Christians that nature itself is revelatory of God. This second option seeks to recapture the lost sense that nature is sacramental—that nature participates in and discloses the sacred reality that Christians call God. It observes that humans have by and large forgotten that the entire universe is revelatory of its creator. Nature's sacramental transparency to God gives it an intrinsic value that should spark in Christians a strong impulse to protect it from human abuse.

Genesis 1:26 (King James Version)

26. And God said, Let us make man in our image, after our likeness: and let them have dominion over the fish of the sea, and over the fowl of the air, and over the cattle, and over all the earth, and over every creeping thing that creepeth upon the earth.

The text-based, tradition-centered ecological theology is more typical of traditional Protestant Christianity, which historically emphasized the word of God, as revealed in scripture, more than sacraments as the place of human encounter with God. The nature-focused theological posture, on the other hand, is more characteristically Catholic and Orthodox, although an increasing number of Protestants now endorse it also. Advocates of the sacramental position doubt that stewardship, the practice of virtue, and the adherence to traditional church doctrine, necessary though these may be, provide Christians with a sufficiently energizing basis for ecological responsibility. What is needed, they think, is a radical shift in Christianity's understanding of both nature and God.

On the basis of the sacramental approach, ecological theology makes the case that Christian faith is essentially, and not just accidentally, bound to the preservation of nature. The loss of nature leads directly to a diminishment of the sense of God. It is useful to ask what religions would look like if humans lived on a lunar landscape. From the beginning of religious history on Earth the mystery of the sacred has been revealed through such natural phenomena as clean water, fresh air, fertile soil, clear skies, bright light, thunder and rain, living trees, plants and animals, and life's fertility. Nature, viewed in sacramental perspective, is not primarily raw material to serve human purposes, but essentially the showing forth of a divine goodness and generosity. As such, according to many Christian ecologists, it commands a care and concern that a purely secularist view cannot provide.

John Haught

Further Reading

Berry, T. (1988). *The dream of the Earth.* San Francisco: Sierra Club Books.

Hessel, D. T. (Ed.). (1996). *Theology for Earth community: A field guide.* Maryknoll, NY: Orbis Books.

Moltmann, J. (1985). *God in creation.* (M. Kohl, Trans.). San Francisco: Harper & Row.

Nash, J. (1991). *Loving nature.* Nashville, TN: Abingdon Press.

Oelschlaeger, M. (1996). *Caring for creation: An ecumenical approach to the environmental crisis.* New Haven, CT: Yale University Press.

Passmore, J. (1974). *Man's responsibility for nature: Ecological problems and Western traditions.* New York: Charles Scribner's Sons.

Santmire, P. (1985). *The travail of nature.* Philadelphia: Fortress Press.

White, L., Jr. The historical roots of our ecological crisis. *Science, 155,* 1203–1207.

Ecology, Cultural

Cultural ecology has become one of the most widely recognized terms used in the social and biophysical sciences when people look at culture, society, and environmental interactions. The broad scope of the term *cultural ecology* defies a single definition, but in general it represents a field of study aiming to understand the interactions among socio–cultural, economic, and environmental systems. Cultural ecologists pay attention to the process of human adaptation to the environment and linkages among forms of socio-political organization, technological development, and strategies of resource management. The term can be traced to U.S. anthropologist Julian Steward's 1938 work *Basin Plateau Arboriginal Sociopolitical Groups* and his 1955 seminal book *The Theory of Culture Change: The Methodology of Multilinear Evolution.* Since then the term "cultural ecology" has provided a heuristic (an aid to learning) device for understanding the interactions between environment and culture, not only in anthropology, but also in geography. During the fifty years since Steward's book, cultural ecology has evolved as a dynamic field, incorporating an increasing number of concepts and methods while broadening the scope of investigation from small and isolated societies to include emerging contemporary socio-cultural changes and problems around the world. Cultural ecology was the basis for what became ecological anthropology, which later developed into the environmental anthropology of the present. At the same time, however, the term *cultural ecology* has also been used by many interchangeably with the older and more general term *human ecology*. Today, although most anthropologists use the term (and field) *environmental anthropology*, the term *cultural ecology* is still widely used, for instance, among geographers (the Association of American Geographers named its annual prize in cultural ecology after anthropologist Robert McNetting, whose work exemplified the interdisciplinary, collaborative nature of the field). Although in its earlier stages cultural ecology was largely recognized as a U.S. "specialty" in anthropology, it has since expanded across both academic and geographic borders.

In this context cultural ecology has necessarily passed through a long interdisciplinary history marked by shifting frameworks within disciplines. One can understand this history in three broad stages. First, it emerged as a product of turn-of-the-century debates involving the frameworks of environmental determinism, cultural evolutionism, and the so-called U.S. historical possibilism (i.e., stress the unique conditions in which different cultures emerge), all of which marked the emergence of anthropology as a discipline. Second, cultural ecology evolved as a product of the interactions among cognitive and behavioral anthropology, ecology (and the ecosystem concept), geography, and economics, which were all seeking complementary explanations and methods in order to understand culture and nature relationships. Third, cultural ecology developed as a result of a changing world, particularly after World War II, as small "isolated" societies became affected by growing international economic and political systems and as environmental problems arose as an issue of social and political concern.

Emerging as a discipline, the anthropology that nurtured cultural ecology was characterized by theoretical arguments such as those among proponents of the mostly European "cultural evolutionism" and the U.S. historical possibilism of Franz Boas and later A. Kroeber. Explanations for variations in cultural complexity and change were marked by somewhat deterministic approaches that emphasized either the role of the biophysical environment (or culture itself) or linear models of Eurocentric social evolution; in both cases, however, the physical environment and culture were seen as static—and to some extent "superorganic" (i.e., emphasizing the overall importance of culture over internal variability)—entities lacking dynamics and internal diversity.

Early Works

Earlier works of Boas and Kroeber—including the analysis of "cultural elements and traits" and the delineation of "cultural areas" as organizing "cultural-environmental units"—became the basis from which cultural ecology developed. Initially the environment was considered as a limiting rather than determining factor in culture. During this period the linear social evolutionary perspective (i.e., progressive stages towards "civilization") that developed during the nineteenth century and that was used as a tool to explain forms of cultural evolution and development was largely dismissed. As a student of Kroeber, Steward advanced the cultural area approach (for instance, as reflected in Steward's important *Handbook of South American Indians*) into a comparative tool to understand cultural complexity, economic systems, and material culture and added to it an emphasis on adaptive "processes." Also important, although in parallel, to the development of cultural ecology was the work of Leslie White regarding the relationship between social complexity, production systems, and the accumulation of "energy" in the manipulation of environmental resources.

Steward's cultural ecology, although embedded in a "multilinear evolutionary" perspective (i.e., social groups organize and change following different forms and pathways, such as in prevailing modes of production), put emphasis on what he called the "culture core," that is, the set of social institutions most closely related to the environment, or more precisely, to production systems and economy. This brought attention to variables related to social, political, and religious patterns empirically perceived as connected with economic activities, and thus environmental resources and conditions. The central idea in Steward's model is the relationship between forms of social organization and institutions and environmental resources (availability, fluctuations, and distribution thereof) as mediated by technology (material culture and forms of resource management). Methodologically, Steward's cultural ecology placed value on the ethnographic (relating to the study of human cultures) method, qualitative and quantitative empirical data, and comparative analysis.

Although emphasizing the interaction between social organization and environmental resources, to some extent culture was seen as an expression of patterns of subsistence (modes of production). In other words, society reveals culture by means of adaptation to its environment, thus hypothetically cultural ecology also advanced the idea that similar biophysical environments could give rise to cross-cultural similarities. In this context the concept of culture started to encompass more than norms, values, and taboos and began to focus strongly on forms of sociopolitical organization, economy and food production systems, and material culture (e.g., foragers, horticulturalists). An important outcome of this trend has been the increase in ethnographies of production systems, thus revealing a wealth of knowledge (and misconceptions) about agricultural and resource management technologies among indigenous and peasant populations.

Equally important to cultural ecology was the parallel development of the so-called ethnosciences, particularly ethnoecology and ethnobiology, during the 1950s. Focusing on a cognitive perspective (the way we perceive and understand the environment) and management of environmental resources, these fields emerged as a combination of approaches from linguistics, biology and systematics (i.e., organization and classification of organisms), and ethnographic methods and built upon the already established field of ethnobotany (decades old by that time). Ethnoecological interest in understanding human-environmental relationships and production systems converged closely to the cultural ecology focus. For instance, Harold Conklin's studies on the ethnoecology of shifting cultivators provide much of the basis for cultural ecologists working on agricultural production systems. During the following decades ethnoecology evolved toward an increasing fusion with cultural ecology.

Ecosystem Approach

During the 1960s cultural ecology emerged as an important field in anthropology and gave way to an ever-increasing incorporation of ecological, political, and economic factors into the analysis of culture and environment. The integration of different perspectives, such as Steward and White's cultural ecology, with ecosystem ecology provided a basic theoretical structure, and methods borrowed from systems analysis, ethnoecology, and vegetation and animal ecology characterized the scenario that marked the emergence of the so-called ecological anthropology. Examples that highlight the diversity of this period can be seen in the works of R. A. Rappaport, A. P. Vayda and Rappaport,

C. Geertz, J. Bennett, and R. Netting. Perhaps the first attempt to use the ecosystem approach in anthropology was made by Geertz in his work *Agricultural Involution: The Process of Ecological Change in Indonesia*. The ecosystem approach provided an organizing structure to analyze the role of historical and political factors in explaining forms of agricultural change in parts of Indonesia. Directly and indirectly, the ecosystem approach in anthropology may also be noted in other important works of the 1960s. Bennett's *Northern Plainsmen* drew the attention of cultural ecologists to the importance of regional studies and placed more emphasis on socio-political and institutional adaptation. In the same period Netting's work among the Kofyars in Africa *(The Hill Farmers of Nigeria)* gave emphasis to the processes of agricultural intensification and the organization of labor in rural communities.

However, it was Rappaport's *Pigs for the Ancestors* that marked definitively (and somewhat controversially) the assimilation of the ecosystem approach into mainstream anthropology and the emergence of ecological anthropology. He studied the relationship between cultural and noncultural variables among the Tsembaga people in highland New Guinea using the ecosystemic analogy as a basic structure. In his analysis he showed the relationship between rituals and other aspects of social and ecological life, such as animal husbandry, gardening, hunting, warfare, and food distribution. He defined the ecosystem in terms of trophic (energy and matter) and nontrophic (human and social interaction) exchanges and proposed the use of "population" as a unit of analysis, in a way comparable to ecological theory. This position was revised and reinforced by Vayda and Rappaport. The adoption of the ecosystem concept increased the emphasis on a biological approach to cultural ecology, characterizing an important period of transition to ecological anthropology. This process reinforced the emphasis on the relationship between social institutions and organization and production systems, continuing Steward's tradition on new ground. No less important, one may argue, has been the parallel so-called formalist-substantivist debate in economic anthropology, discussing views on the nature of the individual and social behaviors regarding economic maximization and cultural norms; despite its particularities, this is a relevant debate for cultural ecologists engaging in research, particularly among peasant/rural communities, and dealing with the spread of markets and infrastructure into "isolated" communities.

During this period few scholars influenced cultural ecology more than did Ester Boserup and her book *The Conditions of Agricultural Growth*. Boserup's seminal work used an alternative view to define the relationship between population growth and food production, questioning the traditional classical economic approach to agriculture based on the Malthusian (relating to the theories of British economist Thomas Malthus) model. Whereas Malthusian advocates had placed population growth as a dependent variable on food production, Boserup did the opposite. Her model defined population growth as the independent variable that induces intensification and increases food production. To some extent, it provided a "missing" conceptual framework to understand the formation of social complexities in different conditions of environmental resources and limitations. Arguably, Boserup's work and theoretical framework are the most cited reference in cultural ecology to date.

Despite the frequent labeling of this period as "functionalist" (i.e., every aspect of culture and behavior serves to fulfill a role) and "materialist" (i.e., emphasis on human basic needs such as food and resources) when considered as a whole the sum of these approaches is characterized by a multifactorial explanation that includes historical, political, demographic, and institutional elements in the explanation of sociocultural systems. To some extent the ecological approach of the 1960s was an attempt to address the affinities between the Steward and White models and biological theory. On the one hand, this approach challenged the scope of culture in anthropology to encompass processual interactions (i.e., connected actions or events that lead to continuing changes) between social groups and their environment. On the other hand, the concept of culture was narrowed to an ordinary set of adaptive pathways and technologies by which a society sustains itself within its habitat. Such an ecological view tends to fit culture within the adaptation model, which stresses the role of environmental constraints in social development.

Criticism

Criticism of ecological anthropology abounded in the 1970s and early 1980s. The use of the ecosystem approach was epistemologically (relating to the study of knowledge) bound to problematic concepts such as stability and equilibrium—concepts that contradict the dynamic nature of culture and society. In summary, despite the work of scholars such as Netting and Bennett showing the importance of history and sociopolitical structure to explaining cultural change, there was a tendency to criticize the field of "ecologically oriented anthropology" as functionalist and homeostatic (in equilibrium).

Numerous works were done during the 1970s within the interfaces of cultural ecology and ecological anthropology perspectives combining social, ecological, and political variables. During this period the stress on individual-oriented models, as well as on more policy-oriented models, also increased. Netting's book *Cultural Ecology* illustrates the diversity of the field during this time, such as by his statement that "there is only one way to explain what cultural ecology is: to show what it is doing" (Netting 1977, 7). In this book Netting then departs to an interesting ethnological analysis of production systems, including foraging, horticulture, pastoralism, and fisheries, as well as a chapter on using field methods, conducting comparative work, and testing ecological explanations used in cultural ecology.

The 1980s were characterized by epistemological revisions in cultural ecology and related fields. Cultural ecology and ecological anthropology in general have benefited from the revision of the ecosystem concept during this time, which allowed it to maintain a dialogue with other disciplines. Of particular importance has been the emergence of a political ecology approach, combining to some extent approaches from political economy, world system theory (i.e., political inter-societal system and dependency among nation states and other social structures emphasizing levels of appropriation of capital, raw material, and modes of production, for instance, between developed and developing nations), and cultural ecology. The concern with a problem-oriented approach has increased the role of cultural ecologists in development issues and policy while maintaining their theoretical concerns with human behavior.

Although the use of the ecosystem concept has provided cultural ecologists with a powerful tool in the study of human behavior, numerous problems have appeared. The emphasis on equilibrium models, the focus on energy, and the subjectivity of boundaries and units of analysis have placed human populations in an ambiguous condition in relation to ecological systems. The biological legacy that ecological anthropology inherited along with ecosystem theory in the 1960s placed humans outside ecological "equilibrium." On the other hand, several works were expressing concern about the dismissal of the ecosystem concept in anthropology (but largely in ecological anthropology), such as E. F. Moran's *Human Adaptability* and Roy Ellen's *Environment, Subsistence and System*. Scholars from both fields reflected a consensus that the concept had more to offer than problems. Interestingly, similar considerations were taking place in biology and ecology. They proposed separating ecosystem analysis from homeostatic models and criticized the focus on energy flow models and the lack of history on ecological analysis. Examples of these criticisms and revisions of the concept in anthropology can be tracked in Moran's *The Ecosystem Approach in Anthropology* (containing contributions from a diverse group of anthropologists).

Adapting to Change

Maintaining a tradition of a constantly evolving and changing field, cultural ecology continued to adapt to a changing world and new disciplinary boundaries during the 1980s and 1990s. Attention to conservation issues increased with the growing concern over related topics such as tropical deforestation, indigenous land rights, traditional ecological knowledge, globalization, and market expansion. Knowledge about indigenous production systems, agroforestry (land management for the simultaneous production of food, crops, and trees), and other management technologies was brought to light as an alternative to rural development and also as a venue of cultural survival. New generations of cultural ecologists, whether in geography or anthropology, expanded the methodological repertoire to include tools for spatial-temporal analysis such as remote sensing and geographic information systems. Actually, cultural ecologists paved the way for the application of these tools in the social sciences in general. For example, a special issue of the journal *Human Ecology* was dedicated to the topic of "recent advances in the regional analysis of indigenous land use and tropical deforestation." The issue brings together recognized cultural ecologists presenting their work using a combination of theoretical approaches, putting emphasis on teamwork, and including the integration of ethnographic, remote sensing, and geoprocessing techniques (i.e., analysis and integration of data containing spatial attributes). Similarly, cultural ecologists entered the 1990s as the "cultural brokers" of the social sciences on the emerging research agenda of "human dimensions of global environmental change." The growing concern over (and international geo-political recognition of) global climate change as well as other macro-scale changes in cultural and bio-

logical diversity brought an opportunity for social scientists in general—and the community of cultural ecology in particular—to bring their knowledge and approaches toward macro-scale analysis and policy. In this context, however, cultural ecology's local-scale approach (whether in anthropology or geography) tends to be overwritten by large-scale analysis offered, for instance, by sociologists and demographers looking at population-environment linkages. As it has been from time to time, the challenge of finding appropriate levels of analysis and conceptual frameworks to understand culture, society, and environment continues. Another important area benefiting from the intellectual history of cultural ecology is the growing interdisciplinary community working on the so-called common property resources. The wealth of knowledge about management systems and social institutions developed by half a century of cultural ecology has provided a fundamental basis for a research community truly ranging from the analysis of local resources (e.g., forests, irrigation) to the biosphere (the part of the world in which life can exist, e.g., atmosphere, oceans).

Cultural ecology continues to thrive because of its constructive, flexible, and always-improving approach to human and environment linkages. Debate and criticism are cultural ecology's main asset. While moving away from "monolithic theories" to explain environment and culture, it has become relevant and respectful of its own diversity. Working in emerging fields such as historical ecology and political ecology, new and old generations of cultural ecologists continue to evolve to work in new domains of culture, society, and environment, bringing attention to political issues, historical trends, transnational realities, and the implications of globalization. As A. Biersack and C. Kottak put it, the field has evolved (and matured) while including interests such as symbolic, historic, political, and economic concerns and bringing together interests in environmental values and religion, cultural construction of the environment (space and place), globalization and consumerism, gender and ethnicity, human rights, and the human dimensions of global environmental change.

Cultural ecology has offered a variety of approaches that allow people to understand their social complexities and differences—a legacy embedded today (but not always recognized) in the majority of fields dealing with socio-environmental problems, a legacy essential to the understanding of contemporary human problems at all scales of analysis.

Eduardo S. Brondizio

Further Reading

Arzipe, L. (Ed). (1996). *The cultural dimensions of global change: An anthropological approach.* Paris: United Nations Educational, Scientific and Cultural Organization.

Balée, W. (Ed.). (1998). *Advances in historical ecology.* New York: Columbia University Press.

Behrens, C. A. (Ed.). (1994). Recent advances in the regional analysis of indigenous land use and tropical deforestation. *Human Ecology, 22*(3), 243–247.

Bennett, J. (1969). *Northern plainsmen: Adaptive strategies and agrarian life.* Chicago: Aldine.

Bennett, J. (1976). Anticipation, adaptation and the concept of culture in anthropology. *Science, 192,* 847–853.

Biersack, A., & Kottak, C. (1999). Introduction: From the "new ecology" to the "new ecologies." *American Anthropologist, 101*(1), 5–18.

Boaz, F. (1911). *The mind of primitive man.* New York: Macmillan.

Boserup, E. (1965). *The conditions of agricultural growth: The economics of agrarian change under population pressure.* Chicago: Aldine.

Conklin, H. (1954). An ethnoecological approach to shifting agriculture. *Transactions of the New York Academy of Sciences, 17*(2), 133–142.

Conklin, H. (1957). *Hanunóo agriculture.* Rome: United Nations Food and Agricultural Organization.

Conklin, H. (1961). The study of shifting cultivation. *Current Anthropology, 2,* 27–61.

Crumley, C. (Ed.). (1994). *Historical ecology: Cultural knowledge and changing landscapes.* Santa Fe, NM: School of American Research Press.

Crumley. C. (2001). *New directions in anthropology and environment: Intersections.* Walnut Creek, CA: Altamira Press.

Geertz, C. (1963). *Agricultural involution: The process of ecological change in Indonesia.* Berkeley and Los Angeles: University of California Press.

Kottak, C. (1999). The new ecological anthropology. *American Anthropologist, 101*(1), 19–28.

Kroeber, A. (1939). *Cultural and natural areas of native North America.* Berkeley and Los Angeles: University of California Press.

Malthus, T. (1992). *An essay on the principle of population.* Cambridge, UK: Cambridge University Press,.

Moran, E. F. (1979). *Human adaptability.* Boulder, CO: Westview Press.

Moran, E. F. (Ed.). (1990). *The ecosystem approach in anthropology: From practice to concept.* Ann Arbor: University of Michigan Press.

Netting, R. (1968). *Hill farmers of Nigeria: Cultural ecology of the Kofyar of the Jos Plateau.* Seattle: University of Washington Press.

Netting, R. (1977). *Cultural ecology.* Prospect Heights, IL: Waveland Press.

Nietschmann, B. (1973). *Between land and water: The subsistence ecology of the Miskito Indians, eastern Nicaragua.* New York: Seminar Press.

Orlove, B. (1980). Ecological anthropology. *Annual Review of Anthropology, (9),* 235–273.

Rappaport, R. A. (1984). *Pigs for the ancestors: Ritual in the ecology of a New Guinea people.* New Haven, CT: Yale University Press.

Rappaport, R. A. (1990). Ecosystems, populations, and people. In E. F. Moran (Ed.), *The ecosystem approach in anthropology: From concept to practice* (pp. 41–72). Ann Arbor: University of Michigan Press.

Sheridan, T. (1988). *Where the dove calls: The political ecology of a peasant corporate community in northwestern Mexico.* Tucson: University of Arizona Press.

Steward, J. (Ed.). (1939–1946). *Handbook of South American Indians.* Washington, DC: Smithsonian Institution.

Steward, J. (1955). *Theory of cultural change.* Urbana: University of Illinois Press.

Vayda, A. P., & MacCay, B. (1975). New directions in ecology, cultural and ecological anthropology. *Annual Review of Anthropology, 4,* 293–306.

Vayda, A. P., & Rappaport, R. (1968). Ecology, cultural and noncultural. In J. A. Clinton (Ed.), *Introduction to cultural anthropology* (pp. 476–497). Boston: Houghton Mifflin.

White, L. (1943). Energy and the evolution of culture. *American Anthropologist, 45,* 335–356.

White, L. (1949). *The science of culture.* New York: Free Books.

Ecology, Deep

The term *deep ecology* was coined in 1973 by the Norwegian philospher Arne Naess (b. 1912) in a brief article entitled "The Shallow and the Deep, Long-Range Ecology Movements: A Summary," in which Naess contrasted two starkly different approaches to solving the emerging ecological crisis. Shallow, or reform, ecology suggests that the world's ecological crisis can be solved by reforming mainstream industrial society without questioning or challenging consumerism and economic growth. Shallow ecology is human-centered (anthropocentric), regarding nature merely as a resource to be used for the benefit of humans. Deep ecology encourages us to develop an ecocentric (nature-centered) outlook in which nature is seen as part of one's self, and as intrinsically valuable. In asking deep questions about why and how industrial society has produced the ecological crisis, deep ecology points to the need for radical changes in mainstream values, policies, and lifestyles in order to bring about lasting ecological harmony.

The philosophers Bill Devall and George Sessions championed Naess's approach, and have explored how Naess and the deep ecology movement in general have been inspired by the writings of individuals who lived ecocentric lives. Saint Francis of Assisi, Spinoza, Henry David Thoreau, John Muir, Aldo Leopold, Rachel Carson, and David Brower are examples of such figures in the West. Ecocentric perspectives can also be found in many non-Western societies.

Arne Naess and the Concept of Ecosophy

From a young age, Naess had deep love of nature and a particularly profound relationship with a mountain known as Halingskarvet in south central Norway. After thirty years as a professor of philosophy at the University of Oslo, Naess took early retirement in 1969 so that he could turn his energies to the resolution of the ecological crisis. His major work on deep ecology is *Ecology, Community and Lifestyle.* In this book, and indeed in many of his prolific writings in this area, he indicates that one of the aims of deep ecology is to enable individuals to articulate and act upon their own ecological wisdom, or *ecosophy*, (from the Greek, *oikos*, meaning household , and *sophia*, meaning wisdom).

An ecosophy (which Naess also refers to as a "total view") can be said to comprise three interdependent senses of depth: deep experience, deep questioning, and deep commitment. Perhaps the most important of these is the aspect of deep experience that Naess calls "wide identification": direct, intuitive perception of our utter embeddedness in and radical communion with all levels of the Earth community, from other organisms, to rivers and ecosystems, and eventually to Gaia, the self-regulating Earth. Wide identification puts human beings in the realm of their ecological selves joyfully recognizing that all entities in nature have intrinsic value irrespective of their usefulness to

humans. These deep realizations are often spontaneous, and involve gestalt perception, in which one's "normal" sense of isolated objects is replaced by a sensitivity to the contexts and relationships in which every object is utterly embedded.

Deep experience gives people the energy and inspiration to deeply question assumptions and values with respect to our relationship with nature, and also to question the assumptions of the wider culture. In deep questioning we adopt a skeptical attitude towards our culture in order to try to understand why it is so destructive of nature. We also ask ourselves how we might develop lifestyles that would be in harmony with our deep experiences of wide identification.

Deep questioning in turn leads to deep commitment when engaging in actions aimed at bringing about ecological harmony through peaceful and democratic means. Thus deep ecology is more than a philosophy. Its end point is action, and as such it is a movement, inspired by our ecological relationships with the world. The emphasis on action distinguishes deep ecology from ecophilosophy, which mainly concerns itself with thinking about human-nature relationships.

The Deep-Ecology Approach

Naess has developed a process for helping each individual to articulate his or her own ecosophy and for applying it in daily life. Harold Glasser has called this process the *deep-ecology approach* to distinguish it from other interpretations of deep ecology. For Glasser, the deep-ecology approach "represents a logical culmination and fusing of Naess's earlier philosophical work with his political activism and his love of nature"(Glasser 1999, 360). The deep-ecology approach encourages individuals and policy makers to explore and, with luck, resolve conflicts between fundamental beliefs and actions in order to bring about ecological harmony.

The deep-ecology approach comprises four levels. Level one is the philosophical or religious realm, where our fundamental intuitions about the nature of the world reside. This is the domain of our deep experience. Naess stresses the importance of tolerance and radical pluralism at this level. To take a religious example, Buddhists and Christians would differ with respect to the existence of a transcendent God, but both would agree about the importance and sacredness of life. Naess asks us to articulate our first-level intuitions in the form of an ultimate norm—a principle for right action based on our most fundamental understanding

The Deep Ecology Platform

1. The well-being and flourishing of human and nonhuman life on Earth have value in themselves (synonyms: inherent worth; intrinsic value; inherent value). These values are independent of the usefulness of the nonhuman world for human purposes.

2. Richness and diversity of life forms contribute to the realization of these values and are also values in themselves.

3. Humans have no right to reduce this richness and diversity except to satisfy vital needs.

4. Present human interference with the nonhuman world is excessive, and the situation is rapidly worsening.

5. The flourishing of human life and cultures is compatible with a substantial decrease of the human population. The flourishing of nonhuman life requires such a decrease.

6. Policies must therefore be changed. The changes in policies affect basic economic, technological structures. The resulting state of affairs will be deeply different from the present.

7. The ideological change is mainly that of appreciating *life quality* (dwelling in situations of inherent worth) rather than adhering to an increasingly higher standard of living. There will be a profound awareness of the difference between big and great.

8. Those who subscribe to the forgoing points have an obligation directly or indirectly to participate in the attempt to implement the necessary changes.

Source: Naess, Arne, & Sessions, George. (1984). *Deep Ecology Platform*. Retrieved November 26, 2002, from http://www.deepecology.org/deepplatform.html

and insight. "Obey God!" and "Richness of life for all!" are examples of ultimate norms. Ultimate norms are necessarily vague statements that cannot be logically derived or defended, since they stem from deep intuition and experience.

The remainder of Naess's process is concerned with achieving consistency between ultimate norms, lifestyles, and policies. Level two constitutes the *deep-ecology platform*, which Naess wrote with fellow philosopher George Sessions in 1984. The platform consists of eight points intended to outline a worldview shared by supporters of the deep-ecology movement and to stimulate discussion and debate. The platform is not intended as set of unmodifiable dogmatic statements or as a strict definition of the movement.

The platform begins by stating that all life is intrinsically valuable irrespective of its usefulness to human beings. Points two and three recognize that richness and diversity are valuable in themselves, and state that we should utilize nature only to satisfy vital needs, which must be decided upon according to local con-

texts and circumstances. Exceeding our vital needs leads to unsustainable impacts on nature. Points four and five state that most unsustainable impact arises in the West, as Western or Westernized consumers utilize 80 percent of the world's resources while constituting only 20 percent of the world's population. Point six suggests that there must be radical changes at the level of policy to correct these impacts and imbalances, and point seven urges us to focus on life quality rather than on high levels of consumption. Naess uses the slogan "simple in means, rich in ends," suggesting that voluntary simplicity can give rise to deep experiences of connectedness at all levels of human existence. The platform's final point is that if people broadly agree with the platform statements, they are obliged to help to bring about change.

At level three of the deep-ecology approach, we consider options for action that derive from level two's platform. Level four is the realm of concrete consequences, where we implement specific actions and decisions. Because many options are derivable from the

www.greenribbonpledge.org

THE Green Ribbon PLEDGE

Please join us as part of the Green Ribbon Pledge to conserve energy for a secure future. Together, we can make a difference.

Wear or display this ribbon as a sign of your commitment to conserving energy and take the pledge online at www.greenribbonpledge.org

Conserving Energy for a Secure Future

The Green Ribbon Pledge, endorsed by many environmental organizations in the United States: The pledge advocates basic lifestyle changes to facilitate energy conservation.

platform, the principle of radical pluralism reappears here. Naess stresses that there are many ways in which deep-ecology supporters can act according to their eco-sophies, and that tolerance of different perspectives is very important in order to avoid conflicts within the movement.

Ecosophy "T"

Naess's own ecosophy, called ecosophy T, is a good example of how the deep-ecology approach can be used to outline an ecosophy. Inspired partly by his contemplation and study of Gandhi, Spinoza, Maha-yana Buddhism, and Indian philosophy, the ultimate norm in Naess's ecosophy is "Self-realization!" The ex-clamation mark, which is common to all normative statements in Naess's process, shows that an active principle is intended—a restatement might be, "Let there be as much self-realization as possible." Naess's ultimate norm reflects the insight that every being has the right to realize its innate potential, and that humans must interfere as little as possible other beings' need to live and blossom.

It would be a mistake to regard self-realization as the activity of the human ego. In this respect, Naess acknowledges the influence of Gandhi, who believed in the essential unity of all that lives. For Gandhi, the self-realization of any being enhances the self-realization of all, since all beings are connected inti-mately through the wider Self, or *atman*. The fact that every being is connected in this nondual Self leads seamlessly and naturally to nonviolence, since violence of any kind is directed against what Gandhi referred to as the "great oneness" of all life.

Further Articulation of an Ecosophy

The next step in the detailed exploration and elabora-tion of an ecosophy is to derive lower-level norms and actions using a process that Naess calls *loose derivation* because a loose, tentative logic is involved. The best way to understand it is to look again at ecosophy T. A hypothesis derivable from Naess's ultimate norm is "Diversity of life increases self-realization potentials." The hypothesis makes an assumption about what the preceding norm might mean in the real world. One then proceeds to derive more specific, derived norms that flow from the hypothesis. In ecosophy T, one such derived norm is "Diversity of life!" As with all norms, this is a prescription for right action, but now the required action is more focused: We are urged to promote as much diversity in life as we can. A whole suite of lower-level hypotheses can be derived from this norm, one of which is "Exploitation reduces the diversity of life." Naess then seeks to articulate norms that stem from this new hypothesis, an obvious one being "No exploitation!" From this a further chain of norms and hypotheses can be derived, until we finally reach a concrete action. Naess has taken several concrete actions stemming from this particular derivational sequence in ecosophy T. One has been to support organizations dedicated to stopping and preventing abuses of political prisoners. Another has been to become involved in demonstrations and other modes of political activism to protect threatened Norwegian nature. Naess points out that ecosophy T is just one of many possible ecosophies, and that it must not thought of as definitive in any way.

Critiques of Deep Ecology

A major criticism of deep ecology has been that it is antihuman. One such critic has been Murray Bookchin, the cofounder of the Institute for Social Ecology. In the late 1980's Bookchin reacted against statements made in the *Earth First!* journal by authors purporting to be deep-ecology supporters. Those authors asserted that Ethiopa's famines and the AIDS virus were to be encouraged because they reduced the human population. Genuine deep-ecology supporters responded by pointing out that the key insight of deep ecology, that all life has intrinsic value, also applies to humans, who are therefore to be as deeply cared for as the rest of the natural world. Bookchin has also criticized deep ecology for not seeing that inequality and injustice in the human social domain are the roots of our domination of nature. Deep-ecology supporters point out that even completely egalitarian, classless societies remain in principle perfectly capable of devastating nature.

Eco-feminist thinkers have criticized deep ecology for not recognizing that it is androcentrism (male-centeredness), and not anthropocentrism (human-centeredness) that leads to the destruction of nature. Deep-ecology supporters such as Warwick Fox have countered by saying that it is too simplistic to place the blame for the destruction of nature solely on male domination of women, since many factors, not just an-

drocentrism, are involved. Fox points out that concern with problems among humans, such as gender issues and social inequality, important as they are, divert attention from the fundamental problem of the human domination of nature.

Recent Developments in Deep Ecology

Joanna Macy, an accomplished Buddhist scholar, and John Seed, an energetic forest campaigner, have developed experiential deep-ecology workshops such as the Council of all Beings, in which the emphasis is on experiencing the destruction of the Earth's ecological integrity as if one were a member of the more-than-human world. Participants in these workshops are helped to move through intense feelings of despair and hopelessness to a deep sense of personal empowerment from which they can act to bring about positive change in the world. Together, Macy and Seed have empowered activists all over the world with this approach to deep ecology.

Warwick Fox has written of the need to develop what he calls a "transpersonal ecology," based on Naess's approach to self-realization. Others, such as Andrew McLaughlin and Richard Sylvan, have worked out a "left biocentrism," in which issues of social justice are explored from an ecocentric perspective. Michael Zimmerman has examined the overlaps between the deep-ecology movement and other modern movements such as eco-feminism, transpersonal psychology, and postmodernism. Patsy Hallen explores the links between eco-feminism and deep ecology, and takes her students on extended ecophilosophical expeditions into the Australian outback. Alan Drengson has looked into how the deep-ecology platform can be used to examine the relationships between technology practices and design and the ecological crisis. Harold Glasser is investigating the implications of the deep-ecology approach for policy making, and Per Ingvar Haukeland uses the deep-ecology approach to help people develop their own ecosophies through nature experience, storytelling, and artistic expression. The eminent writer and poet, Gary Snyder, is exploring how deep ecology can be applied in the development of a bioregionalism movement in North America.

Stephan Harding

See also Naess, Arne

Further Reading

Devall, B., & Sessions, G. (1985). *Deep ecology*, Layton, UT: Peregrin Smith Books.

Drengson, A., & Inoue, Y. (1995). *The deep ecology movement: An introductory anthology.* Berkeley, CA: North Atlantic Books.

Fox, W. (1995). *Towards a transpersonal ecology.* Dartington, UK: Green Books.

Glasser, H. (1999). Naess's deep ecology approach and environmental policy. In N. Witoszek & A. Brennan (Eds.), *Philosophical dialogues: Arne Naess and the progress of ecophilosophy.* (pp. 360–390). Lanham, MD: Rowan and Littlefield.

Harding, S. (1997). What is deep ecology? *Resurgence.* 185, 14–17.

Naess, A. (1989). *Ecology, community and lifestyle.* Cambridge, UK: Cambridge University Press.

McLaughlin, Andrew, (1993) *Regarding nature.* Albany: State University of New York Press.

Seed, J., Macy, J., Fleming, P. & Naess, A. (1988). *Thinking like a mountain.* Philadelphia: New Society Publishers.

Sessions, G. (Ed.). (1995). *Deep Ecology for the 21st Century.* Boston and London: Shambhala.

Witoszek, N., & Brennan, A. (Eds.). (1999). *Philosophical dialogues: Arne Naess and the progress of ecophilosophy.* Lanham, MD: Rowan and Littlefield.

Zimmerman, M. (1994). *Contesting earth's future: Radical ecology and postmodernity.* Berkeley: University of California Press.

Ecology, Historical

Historical ecology is a viewpoint on relations between human beings and the biosphere (the part of the world in which life can exist) of Earth. Historical ecology proceeds from the axiom that humanity in its historic paths across Earth has interfered in material and measurable ways in a biotic (relating to flora and fauna) world that evolved previously by natural selection and other evolutionary forces and that the changes thus imposed on nature have, in turn, been reflected in human cultures, societies, and languages through time. In effect, historical ecology holds that wherever humans have trodden, the natural environment is somehow different, sometimes in barely perceptible ways, sometimes in dramatic ways. Proponents of historical ecology today have been trained in various disciplines, including anthropology (especially the subdisciplines of archeology and sociocultural anthropology), geography, history, integrative biology, and general ecology, and they tend to recognize the interdependence of their fields in attempting to comprehend the effects and countereffects of human behavior in the physical environment. Some biological scientists have also been employing the "new" ecology, which seeks to overturn notions of equilibrium in nature and instead to focus on dynamic forces, including human history and the seeming chaos that attends it, which prevent predetermined balance and order among species and their environments—the new ecology is fundamentally similar to historical ecology in this respect.

Historical ecology is an interdisciplinary approach. It focuses on the landscape, a multidimensional physical entity (having both spatial and temporal characteristics) that has been modified by human activity such that human intentions and actions can be inferred, if not read, from it. The landscape is like a text but not one that is readily accessible to the methods of historians and epigraphers (those who study inscriptions) because it is not written in decipherable scripts but rather is inscribed in a subtle, physical sense by learned behavior and action, sometimes remote enough from the present time to be considered part of prehistory. Landscapes in historical ecology are always related to human-environmental relations through time. As such, landscape ecology, which has been practiced almost exclusively by population ecologists and biologists, is not the same as historical ecology because landscape ecology has distinguished between landscapes without human influence and landscapes with (usually degrading, simplifying) human influence. Natural environments, once modified, may never regenerate themselves as such; rather, the product of the collision between nature and culture, wherever it has occurred, is a landscape, the central object of analysis in historical ecology. American archeologist and historical ecologist Carole Crumley points out that "Historical ecology traces the ongoing dialectical relations between human acts and acts of nature, made manifest in the *landscape.* Practices are maintained or modified, decisions are made, and ideas are given shape; a landscape retains the physical evidence of these mental activities" (Crumley 1994, 9). The notion of a dialectic in historical ecology means that human acts modify nature and that the landscape that results from those acts alters culture in an ongoing, energetic, and material dialogue between people and the environment. The landscape is where people and the environment can be seen as a totality, that is, as a diachronic (relating to time) and holistic (relating to complete systems) unit of study and analysis.

"Two Cultures"

Other fields and approaches have contributed to historical ecology. These fields and approaches historically have been limited to one or another major arena of intellectual and scholarly endeavor, either in the social sciences or the natural sciences. Historical ecology, in contrast, seems to represent a bridge between these two arenas of academic life, which are artificial constructs of higher education that have been received from the German nineteenth-century idea of a university and the ways that idea has flourished and developed (for the most part) in the United States, particularly after World War II, with the great surge in higher education afforded mostly by the G.I. Bill. These two arenas have been seen as with the "two cultures" of the academy by English physicist and novelist C. P. Snow (Crumley 1998, x) and as the historic contrast in ideologies and objectives between the West and the rest of the world; bridging the void between the two cultures for the purpose of furthering and unifying knowledge has not tended to be part of the scholarly mission in practice, let alone its central tenet. But it seems likely that the critical problems of the global environment that are facing people of the twenty-first century require such furthering and unification of knowledge. The two-cultures concept refers to the fact that for most of the twentieth century, the social sciences together with the humanities, on the one hand, and the natural sciences, on the other hand, basically represented a divide across which few specialists ventured communication of research problems, and fewer still dared submerge their careers because promotion and tenure systems together with research funding priorities reflected that basic division of the academy. Scholars and scientists learned about that divide and their place on either side of it, hence the notion of two "cultures." Historical ecology proposes to bridge those cultures under the assumption that the essential research questions concerning relationships through time between the human species and the biosphere cannot be addressed adequately and holistically without drawing liberally on the expertise of multiple fields that have otherwise developed in a certain isolation if not alienation from each other.

In the natural sciences, general ecology had championed the notion of an ecosystem wherein communities of organisms live out functional existences in commensalism (a relation between two kinds of organisms in which one obtains food or other benefits from the other without damaging or benefiting it) and associa-

tion as species that experience exchanges of energy across their borders in predictable, repetitive fashion; the ecosystem is, therefore, a synchronic (concerned with events existing in a limited time period) concept that disallows fundamental transformation of its character. It is analogous to, and to some extent derived from, the concept of static equilibrium in the physical sciences. This notion means that equivalent objects in a state of motion in opposition to each other return to a steady, stationary state at predictable and invariable rates. The ecosystem represents a model of the environment that does not permit fluidity at its margins nor fundamental change in its basic operative mechanisms (rates of energy flow, competitive exclusion of one species by another, feedback mechanisms that return the system to a steady state, and the like). Landscapes in the historical-ecological sense, in contrast, are always changing, and their unfolding development has been sometimes conditioned by humanity, which in traditional, general ecology (or ecosystem ecology) has been normally taken to be an alien factor in the analysis of ecosystems. The social sciences for their part have tended to envision humanity and cultural behavior as the result of evolutionary forces that operate in environments constrained by limits on one or another material condition or element, particularly in the approach known as "cultural ecology." To the extent that humanity perturbs nature, it must live with the result, which for its part is also transforming itself in a diachronic process that accompanies histories, lives, and specific activities. This point of view is not intuitively obvious, and it is not part of common sense and received wisdom. If historical ecology were based on only one dialectical axiom, it would lack a niche either in the natural sciences or in the social sciences. But historical ecology is inextricably immersed and fluid within the seeming void of the two cultures.

Program, Not a Paradigm

Historical ecology is probably not a paradigm (an overarching body of theories in a given subject field built upon widely agreed upon axioms and assumptions) in the sense of American historian and philosopher of science Thomas Kuhn, who doubted that such paradigms occur at all in the social sciences; paradigms require overwhelming consensus in the scientific community, and all essential problems in the field (in this case, research problems concerning humans and the environment) need to have their own models of explication and deduction—that is, highly particularistic, predictive theories of given phenomena within the field—generated from the paradigm in order to have validity; such consensus does not yet exist in regard to historical ecology, nor has historical ecology yet developed a wide range of models—historical ecology is still relatively new to science. Historical ecology has tended to reject the assumptions of earlier approaches, such as cultural ecology and ecosystem ecology, in proposing its own. Perhaps a better philosophical guideline is to consider historical ecology as a research program. The natural sciences have mechanisms for comprehending change in the environment, such as the laws of thermodynamics, relativity, and natural selection. Natural selection explains the evolution of species, whereas the social sciences have tended only to approximate such a mechanism by focusing on historical events, their chronology, and (to use present information to explain a past event, predict) the motivating forces of history. What historical ecology proposes is that the human species is itself a mechanism of change in the natural world, qualitatively as significant as natural selection, and that the human species is not just a product of natural selection because it, too, makes histories and specific landscapes that bear its inscriptions. The cumulative effects of these undertakings influence the diachronic development of the exact cultural qualities of contemporary landscapes and are manifested in them.

That is, there are two kinds of selection: One is historical, and the other is properly evolutionary—and one is not simply a variety of the other. The forms of manipulation of nature by human beings are multiple and to some degree chaotic. One can identify domestication of plants and animals and the introduction of these in exotic habitats; the construction of terraces for the cultivation of food and other crops in rocks and mountains; the digging and extending of irrigation systems and navigable channels in deserts; the destruction and burning of tropical forests and the replacement of these by ranches harboring domesticated animals that have predetermined value on financial markets; the monumental construction in large urban centers, both modern and prehistoric; the industrial pollution of waters, atmospheres, and lands; extinctions and extirpations (local exterminations of species, but not necessarily extinctions of their entire gene pools) above the background rate of plants and animals (the rate that occurs whether humans have any effect on it or not—the "natural" rate of extinction of species); the cloning of body parts and entire living beings; and so on. But these forms of manipulation of the biotic and abiotic environment are still not well defined merely by listing the effects that humanity has in nature because such effects have originated not only in complex societies, both historic and prehistoric, that have had centralized authority, that is, the state, but also in countless societies that historically have been considered to be egalitarian (bands and autonomous villages) or, at their most complex, ranked (chiefdoms), that is, "simple" societies. Yet, these societies also show evidence of their paths through today's nature that sometimes seem difficult to see and comprehend unless one is open to the idea that where human beings have made pathways through the physical environment of Earth, they have also left measurable material vestiges in the living landscape, regardless of whether they lived in complex society.

Neutral Stance

Historical ecology is neutral, in principle, as to the custodial or destructive influence that human societies have exerted on landscapes. If, in some instances, nonhuman species have become extinct because of predatory hunting and expansion of settlements or have been eliminated locally by similar practices, in other instances local biodiversity (biological diversity as indicated by numbers of species of animals and plants) has increased thanks to human modifications of the landscape. Likewise, soils have become organically and chemically impoverished under certain agricultural regimes, whereas under others, soils have actually become enhanced in terms of their nutrient content and physico-chemical properties: topsoils have been eroded in Iowa due to industrial agriculture, whereas the organic black and brown earths of upland Amazonia, typically the result of prehistoric slash-and-burn agriculture and settlement, are actually much more fertile than surrounding soils not so utilized and subject to management. *Homo sapien*, as an agent of landscape modification and artificial selection, is synonymous neither with the ecologically noble savage (*Homo ecologicus*, i.e., the idealized human species that is inherently custodial and nurturing of nonhuman nature), nor with the ecologically ignoble savage (*Homo devastans*, i.e., the idealized human species that is biologically programmed to destroy nonhuman nature). Rather, sociopolitical systems in specific environments have led historically to landscapes that are either impoverished or enriched in species diversity, soil quality, and other palpable features that are the object of modern conservationist efforts. Historical ecology studies and compares the similarities and differences among these sociopolitical systems in relationship to local landscapes and to the larger biosphere of which these are but one part. Each landscape has a history of human activities, the effects of which in principle can be evaluated on their merits and not a priori (relating to or derived by reasoning from self-evident propositions) presumed to be conservationist or anticonservationist in character. Historical ecology examines the long-term effects of human behavior in the environment (what is sometimes called *la longue durée*, the genuinely long haul of historical time), and as a consequence, it proposes solutions to understanding and managing environmental problems that are equally long term.

Beneficial Human Impacts

Regardless of its neutrality on the human capacity for landscape degradation, historical ecology demonstrates nevertheless numerous cases of low-intensity human impacts that by conservation standards actually have benefited biological and environmental diversity. Forests are typically more species rich than adjacent savannas and grasslands per unit area. Forest islands in the savannas of Guinea (western Africa) are now understood not to be relics of Pleistocene epoch (beginning 1.6 million years ago) events, but rather direct and inescapable outgrowths of generations of human settlement and resource management. Forest islands in the upland savannas of central Brazil have been likewise seen as anthropogenic (human caused), thanks to activities of the Kayapó peoples, although some controversy has hinged on this point. Forest islands on the wet savanna of the Beni, eastern Bolivian Amazon, are now understood to be the result of mound building by ancient inhabitants; the upland island forests of the region today, which account for one-third of the total area of the Beni, can be comprehended only as effects of human management of the landscape in the past. In these cases of forest expansion directed by humans—that is, cultural forests—local biodiversity itself cannot be fully accounted for by using only a model of natural selection but rather should be seen as artificially established by cultural conventions acting in tandem with given genotypes (all or part of the genetic constitution of an individual or group) with regard to landscapes of the past. The human activity

that built earthworks and constructed forests where there was none was not selected for by evolutionary forces, such as natural selection, alone, but is rather the product of history, which is sometimes chaotic, and a given, biologically determined, human substrate; the various species present on the forest islands, which are richer in diversity than the surrounding savannas, are likewise products both of natural and artificial selection acting in tandem, not isolation. The formation of forest islands by human activity is one of the most dramatic examples of landscape research in historical ecology; many other less dramatic but equally intriguing examples of the dialogue between humans and nature can be noted. Large portions of tropical forests not surrounded by savannas, which harbor among the richest concentrations of (the flora and fauna of a region) in the world, in South America and Africa are probably anthropogenic, and the distribution of semidomesticated and sometimes feral domesticated species in these forests is evidence of their manipulation in the past. Biological and ecological diversity cannot be understood without taking into account the historical, human factor. Historical ecology focuses on this factor in deciphering the chronology of events that occurred in the landscape.

Specific mechanisms used by humans in modifying the landscape, sometimes for its enrichment and sometimes not, include anthropogenic fire, epidemic diseases, soil mounding and earthwork construction, introduction and nurturing of semidomesticated and domesticated biota in new environments, and various techniques for encouraging and discouraging the growth of weeds and other pests that in other contexts may become useful species. These specific mechanisms of human influence on the landscape, and the subsequent influences that emanate onto human societies from the landscape altered in the past, suggest that a coherent, interdisciplinary approach to the relationship between humans and the environment is sorely needed for the human and environmental sciences of the twenty-first century. The Portuguese philosopher of science Boaventura de Sousa Santos indicated that in the contemporary academic world, "The distinction between natural and social science is beginning to seem meaningless" (1992, 12). To the extent that his statement is true, historical ecology represents a promising research program for a more unified science that takes account equally in principle of both human and natural factors in understanding the long-term construction and deconstruction of landscapes and the biosphere in which human progeny will seek to live.

William Balée

See also Ethnobotany; Pristine Myth

Further Reading

Balée, W. (1989). The culture of Amazonian forests. In D. A. Posey & W. Balée (Eds.), *Resource management in Amazonia: Vol. 7. Indigenous and folk strategies: Advances in economic botany* (pp. 1–21). New York: New York Botanical Garden.

Balée, W. (Ed.). (1998). *Advances in historical ecology*. New York: Columbia University Press.

Biersack, A. (1999). Introduction: From the "new ecology" the new ecologies. *American Anthropologist, 101*(1), 5–18.

Botkin, D. (1990). *Discordant harmonies: A new ecology for the twenty-first century*. Oxford, UK: Oxford University Press.

Crosby, A. W. (1986). *Ecological imperialism: The ecological expansion of Europe, 900–1900*. Cambridge, UK: Cambridge University Press.

Crumley, C.L. (Ed.). (1994). *Historical ecology: Cultural knowledge and changing landscapes*. Santa Fe, NM: School of American Research Press.

Crumley, C. L. (Ed.). (1998). Foreword. In W. Balée (Ed.), *Advances in historical ecology* (pp. ix–xiv). New York: Columbia University Press.

Crumley, C. L. (Ed.). (2001). *New directions in anthropology and environment: Intersections*. Walnut Creek, CA: Altamira Press.

Denevan, W. M. (2001). *Cultivated landscapes of native Amazonia and the Andes: Triumph over soil*. New York: Oxford University Press.

Fairhead, J., & Leach, M. (1996). *Misreading the African landscape: Society and ecology in the forest-savanna mosaic*. Cambridge, UK: Cambridge University Press.

Kirch, P. V., & Hunt, T. L. (Eds.). (1997). *Historical ecology in the Pacific islands: Prehistoric environmental and landscape change*. New Haven, CT: Yale University Press.

Kuhn, T. (1970). *The structure of scientific revolutions* (2nd ed.). Chicago: University of Chicago Press.

Lakatos, I. (1980). *The methodology of scientific research programmes* (Philosophical Papers, Vol. 1). Cambridge, UK: Cambridge University Press.

Mann, C. (2002). 1491. *The Atlantic Monthly, 289*(3), 41–53.

Parker, E. (1992). Forest islands and Kayapó resource management in Amazonia: A reappraisal of the *apêtê*. *American Anthropologist, 94*, 406–428.

Posey, D. A. (1992). Reply to Parker. *American Anthropologist, 94*(2), 441–443.

Posey, D. A. (2002). *Kayapó ethnoecology and culture*. New York: Oxford University Press.

Santos, B. (1992). A discourse on the sciences. *Review Fernand Braudel, 15*, 9–47.

Sponsel, L., Headland, T., & Bailey, R. C. (Eds.). (1996). *Tropical deforestation*. New York: Columbia University Press.

Ecology, Social

Social ecology is a field of research that views societies and their environments as biophysically linked systems. Societies ultimately sustain themselves on environmental systems and reproduce not only their population, but also their physical artifacts and their animal livestock on them. In doing so, they intentionally alter—or colonize—natural systems to better suit socioeconomic reproduction. In contrast to animal populations—which, of course, also sustain themselves by means of metabolic exchanges within their habitats and in some cases may also be considered to colonize their environments (such as termites building large structures to create "artificial" environments of stable temperature for their offspring)—human populations' relations with their environments are historically highly variable and thereby generate colonized environments of great historical variability. Social ecology seeks to understand and to explain the specific economic and cultural features of societies and their environments from the angle of these biophysical linkages. By using the term *social* rather than *human* ecology, reference is made to the specific sociocultural and economic modes of systemic integration on the part of societies: the focus is not so much on humans as a biological species as on particular historically variable modes of subsistence of human communities on various levels of scale (local, national, regional, or, finally, global).

Although specific socioecological approaches are of recent origin, as even natural science systems ecology dates back only a few decades, attempts at explaining features of societies by looking for metabolic linkages with nature date back into the early history of social theory.

History of Social Metabolism and Some of the Controversies

Four intellectual traditions contributed to the development of the sociometabolic paradigm.

Providing for Society's Metabolism by Human Labor

Karl Marx first applied the term *metabolism* to society. The exchange of matter between humans and nature, created by human labor, "is the everlasting nature-imposed condition of human existence, and therefore independent of every social phase of that existence, or rather, is common to every such phase" (Marx 1976, 183f).

Although most later Marxist writers ignore this material exchange relation in favor of an economic focus on profits and wages on the one hand and technological progress on the other hand, the French anthropologist and historian Maurice Godelier, arguing partially from a Marxist perspective, makes the exchange relation between humans and nature *the* focal point of human history. "Human beings have a history because they transform nature. . . . Of all the forces which set them in movement and prompt them to invent new forms of society, the most profound is their ability to transform their relation with nature by transforming nature itself" (Godelier 1986, 1).

Positioning a Society in Evolution by Energetics

For Herbert Spencer in the 1860s, historical progress from "barbarian" to "civilized" states depended on society's ability to control energy and use it efficiently. This "energetic evolutionism" resounded through nineteenth- and twentieth-century social theory. While energetic theories of social change soon disappeared from the mainstream of sociology, they had a substantial impact on cultural anthropology. Societal material and energetic metabolism is a main focus of anthropologists grouped as "neofunctionalists." They "see the social organization and culture of specific populations as functional adaptations which permit the populations to exploit their environments successfully without exceeding their carrying capacity" (Orlove 1980, 240). From a more technical perspective, the intimate relation between social activities on the one hand and energy availability and utilization on the other hand was demonstrated by technology historian Vaclav Smil in 1994. Although some criticized the progressist bias and others the energetic "reductionism" in trying to explain social change, contemporary social ecological analysis cannot dismiss energetic metabolism as a core feature of any society.

The Threat of Resource Overexploitation

The overexploitation of natural resources as a consequence of society's metabolism was one of the early issues in geography. Whereas George P. Marsh in 1864 focused on the destruction of forests in the midlatitudes, Nathaniel S. Shaler in 1905 discussed the problem of dwindling mineral resources. Similar concerns, nourished by wartime rather than environmental considerations, resounded in a report in 1952 by the President's Materials Policy Commission in the United States.

From the late 1960s onward, a broad "limits to growth" debate kicked off by the so-called Club of Rome Report by Dennis and Donella Meadows and Jorgen Randers in 1972 found much resonance both in science and in the public media across the world. The model used in this report is basically a metabolic model, simulating the linkages between population growth, economic growth, resource consumption, and pollution on a worldwide and medium-term basis. According to its business-as-usual scenario, the exhaustion of resources and a health-impairing level of pollution were expected to come within a few decades. These suppositions came under heavy attack by defenders of a "cornucopian worldview" who argued that scarcity because of resource exhaustion was not a serious threat: It could easily be overcome by human ingenuity and proper functioning of markets. However, with the declining trust in nuclear energy as a feasible alternative and the unfolding of the debate on "sustainable development," the threat of exhausting resources as well as the threat of exhausting the environment's capacity to absorb wastes and emissions have remained integral elements of the debate ever since.

A Distinction between Economic and Material Growths

In *The Economics of the Coming Spaceship Earth* in 1966, Kenneth Boulding, one of the founders of ecological economics, briefly outlined an impending change from what he called a "cowboy economy" to a "spaceman economy." The present world economy, according to this view, is an open system with regard to energy, matter, and information ("econosphere"). There is a "total capital stock, that is, the set of all objects, people, organizations and so on that have inputs and outputs. Objects pass from the noneconomic to the economic set in the process of production, and objects pass out of the economic set as their value becomes zero. . . .

Thus we see the econosphere as a material process" (Boulding 1966, 5). In 1969 Robert Ayres, a physicist, and Allen Kneese, an economist, claimed "that the common failure (of economics) . . . may result from viewing the production and consumption processes in a manner that is somewhat at variance with the fundamental law of the conservation of mass" (Ayres and Kneese 1969, 283). "Almost all of standard economic theory is in reality concerned with services. Material objects are merely vehicles which carry some of these services . . . Yet we [the economists] persist in referring to the 'final consumption' of goods as though material objects . . . somehow disappeared into the void . . . Of course, residuals from both the production and consumption processes remain and they usually render disservices . . . rather than services" (Ayres and Kneese 1969, 283f). Ayres and Kneese propose to "view environmental pollution and its control as a *materials balance problem* for the entire economy" (Ayres and Kneese 1969, 284, emphasis added). By this approach it became established that economic activity and prosperity in terms of monetary units, and the material turnover of a society, in terms of tons (as measuring weight) and joules (as measuring energy), were something that had to be monitored differently. Prosperity in monetary units might grow without any harm to the environment as long as growth in materials and energy use did not follow suit. Politically, this turn allowed environmentalists to escape the confrontation to economic growth and to seek pathways toward "dematerialization" of the economy—that is, economic activity adding value but not matter.

Research on Socioeconomic Metabolism

Interpretations referring to socioeconomic metabolism are not used frequently by historians. Exceptions to this rule may be found in fields like human ecology, agroecology, and population and epidemiological history. The most important European author using a sociometabolic paradigm in environmental history is the German historian Rolf Peter Sieferle, who, by analyzing historical energy systems, seeks to provide functional explanations for the structure of different social formations across human history and their environmental consequences. He outlined his basic approach in 1982. He describes paleolithic hunter-and-gatherer societies by "passive solar energy utilization," tapping the stream of solar energy stored in plants by photosynthesis and converted by herbivores and carnivores. Many generic features of these societies are related to this sociometabolic regime. Although some of this has been described before, Sieferle constructed a very stringent systemic and evolutionary context for these arguments. In sociometabolic studies of isolated foraging societies, these views have recently been empirically confirmed. Sieferle described agrarian societies as "controlled solar energy systems." Agriculture not only taps a flow of free energy, but also controls its conditions of flow and storage by plants and animals that are selected, bred, and cultivated in such a way that a large part of their biomass (amount of living matter) can be monopolized for human purposes. From this energy regime, again several generic features of agrarian societies can be explained. The first and most important feature is dependence on territory: The upper limit of total quantity of energy available to an agrarian society can be surpassed only by spatial expansion or by the import of energy fixed in biomass. Because incoming solar energy has a very low energy density, to be utilized by humans it must first be concentrated spatially, which is always associated with a significant expenditure in transportation that must not consume more energy than the load contains. Thus, there necessarily is a high degree of decentralization, and larger agglomerations could form only where there were possibilities for employing water and wind power for transportation. Departing from this, Sieferle functionally related several other features, such as the need for (and risks involved in) planning and organizing over extended time cycles, the ability to store, and the need to protect stored goods by fortifications and armed specialists.

> "Agrarian society was caught in a sort of dynamic trap: an upper limit was set by its energy basis but it must permanently attempt to reach these limits and even to transgress them, whether as an answer to scarcity or as autonomous cultural innovation. Therefore, it was straining against the natural bonds the solar energy system had put on it, and as long as there was some leeway it was successful: the limits to growth then merely turned out to be growing limits" (Sieferle 2001b, 34).

In recent years Sieferle brought together a number of researchers to collaborate in an effort to explain "Europe's special course" from an agrarian civilization into an industrial formation. They try to clarify why it was Europe's agrarian civilization that did manage a transition to the fundamentally different "fossil-energy regime" effective at present. They are looking for not one or more causative "reasons" but rather a particular constellation of factors that may have been present also in other agrarian civilizations but in Europe may have been buffered by countervailing circumstances. Whatever other factors come into play, the ready availability of fossil fuels and iron ores figured prominently. Indepth historical studies on the metabolism of preindustrial agriculture in Europe, changes in socioeconomic biomass metabolism in the course of industrialization, and the interdependence of changes in land-use and socioeconomic metabolism during the nineteenth century pave the way to a more-detailed understanding of this transition.

Résumé

Social ecology as a new field of research draws on a tradition of sociometabolic approaches from social theory, geography, ecology, and history. Its emergence was inspired by the debate on environmental concerns. Within its framework, a set of new methods was established, such as energy and material flow analysis and related forms of land-use analysis. Its core message is that historical changes in the economy and in society are systemically linked to changes in the environment, and this in turn limits and stimulates socioeconomic change. In a broad, world-history perspective, the research done so far tells us that consecutive social formations tend to display a fourfold to fivefold increase in per-capita energy and materials consumption over their predecessors, and this provides a better measure of "environmental pressure" than do population numbers and economic activity, let alone singular hygienic or pollution risks. It may turn out that historical research of socioeconomic metabolism will provide a valuable bridge between traditional economic history on the one hand and environmental history on the other hand.

Another major strength comes from systemically linking the material aspects of culture to land use and it environmental consequences. This linkage is very close in paleolithic societies as well as in agrarian societies. Industrial societies, however, function in a "deterritorialized" way (meaning that prosperity no longer depends much on territory). Finally, because the socioecological approach is rooted both in ecological theory and economic theory, it promises to draw from history for future sustainability.

Marina Fischer-Kowalski

See also Boserup, Ester; Club of Rome; Marx, Karl

Further Reading

Ayres, R. U., & Kneese, A. V. (1969). Production, consumption and externalities. *American Economic Review, 59*(3), 282–297.

Boserup, E. (1965). *The conditions of agricultural growth.* Chicago: Aldine/Earthscan.

Boulding, K. (1966). The economics of the coming spaceship Earth. In H. Jarrett (Ed.), *Environmental quality in a growing economy: Essays from the sixth RFF forum* (pp. 3–14). Baltimore: John Hopkins Press.

Boyden, S. (1987). *Western civilization in biological perspective.* Oxford, UK: Oxford University Press.

Cohen, M. N. (1977). *The food crisis in prehistory.* New Haven, CT: Yale University Press.

Cottrell, F. (1955). *Energy and society: The relation between energy, social change, and economic development.* New York: McGraw-Hill.

Glaeser, B. (1995). *Environment, development, agriculture: Integrated policy through human ecology.* London: UCL Press.

Godelier, M. (1986). *The mental and the material: Thought economy and society.* London: Blackwell Verso.

Harris, M. (1979). *Cultural materialism: The struggle for a science of culture.* New York: Vintage.

Krausmann, F. (2001). Land use and industrial modernisation: An empirical analysis of human influence on the functioning of ecosystems in Austria 1830–1995. *Land Use Policy, 18*(1), 17–26.

Lee, R. B. (1979). *The Kung San: Men, women and work in a foraging society.* New York: Cambridge University Press.

Marsh, G. P. (1864). *Man and nature; or, physical geography as modified by human action.* New York: Scribners & Sampson Low.

Marx, K. (1976). *Capital volume I.* New York: Vintage.

Meadows, D. L., Meadows, D. H., & Randers, J. (1972). *The limits to growth.* New York: Universe Books.

Odum, E. P. (1959). *Fundamentals of ecology.* Philadelphia: Saunders.

Sahlins, M. (1972). *Stone age economics.* New York: Aldine de Gruyter.

Shaler, N. S. (1905). *Man and the Earth.* New York: Duffield.

Sieferle, R. P. (2001a). *Europe's special course: Outline of a research program.* Stuttgart, Germany: Breuninger Stiftung.

Sieferle, R. P. (2001b). *The subterranean forest: Energy systems and the Industrial Revolution.* Cambridge, UK: White Horse Press.

Simon, J., & Kahn, H. (Eds.). (1984). *The resourceful Earth: A response to global 2000.* New York: Basil Blackwell.

Singh, S. J., Grünbühel, C. M., Schandl, H., & Schulz, N. B. (2001). Social metabolism and labour in a local context: Changing environmental relations on Trinket Island. *Population and Environment*, 23(1), 71–104.

Smil, V. (1994). *Energy in world history.* Boulder, CO: Westview Press.

Spencer, H. (1862). *First principles.* London: Williams and Norgate.

Vayda, A. P., & Rappaport, R. A. (1968). Ecology, cultural and non-cultural. In J. A. Clifton (Ed.), *Introduction to cultural anthropology* (pp. 476–498). Boston: Houghton Mifflin.

Weisz, H., Fischer-Kowalski, M., Grünbühel, C. M., Haberl, H., Krausmann, F., & Winiwarter, V. (2001). Global environmental change and historical transitions. *Innovation*, 14(2), 117–142.

Young, G. L. (1983). *Origins of human ecology.* Stroudsburg, PA: Hutchinson Ross.

Ecology, Spiritual

The term *spiritual ecology* refers to two cultural phenomena, one newly emergent in the twentieth and twenty-first centuries and one more ancient. The newer phenomenon is an emergent theory and developing practice within world religious traditions and among spiritually oriented individuals. The planet's environmental crises, which are generally seen to have resulted from the extractive practices and materialist assumptions characteristic of the industrial culture of the Western world, have resulted in the need for a religious understanding of the human as embedded in the ecology and dynamic processes of nature. Spiritual ecology, as a response to environmental crises and issues, is a worldview that involves reverence and awe for the creative processes of nature and is marked by attitudes of humility, simplicity, respect, and a sense of the sacredness of planet Earth and its creatures.

Spiritual Ecology and Indigenous Peoples

The more ancient spiritual ecology involves the cultures, lifestyles, and mythologies of indigenous peoples around the world. For indigenous peoples, spiritual ecology is practice rather than a theory. Although one cannot apply all practices equally to the cultures of all indigenous peoples past and present, it is possible to distinguish certain common practices that might be considered as constituting a consistent orientation to-

ward spiritual ecology as a way of life. These practices include certain shamanic practices that draw on the primal powers of the natural world, extended notions of kinship beyond human beings, a systematic observation and knowledge of plants and animals passed from generation to generation through story and myth, the notion of Earth as Mother, ancestor worship, humans seen as one strand in a created order, sacredness of place, and ceremonial rites tied to agriculture and the hunt. Another consideration is that although the principles and beliefs involved in spiritual ecology might be considered ancient, *ecology* did not emerge as a term until the latter part of the nineteenth century. Thus ancient peoples and indigenous peoples today would not generally make use of the term *spiritual ecology* to describe their way of life or worldview, making the term a descriptive one used primarily for ethnographic purposes.

Spiritual Ecology as an Integral Philosophy

It is useful, in defining *spiritual ecology*, to clarify the use of the distinct terms *ecology* and *spirituality*. The term *ecology* first appeared in 1866 when Ernst Haeckel, a disciple of Charles Darwin, derived the term from the Greek *oikos*, referring to the household and its maintenance. *Ecology* also refers to the branch of science concerned with interrelationships. *Spirituality* refers to an experience of the numinous, or divine, order of reality. In the context of ecology, *spirituality* may further refer to a vivid awareness of the interconnectedness of the metaphysical and phenomenal orders. Spiritual ecology posits the sanctity of the planet as a "home" to be cared for and maintained with respect for the health of its integral functions. Spiritual practice then, in an ecological sense, becomes the application in everyday life of such awareness and actions that affect other living beings and the planet. Thus spiritual ecology forms the basis for an ethical code of conduct based on an awareness of the principles of ecology and Earth processes combined with an experience of the divine, sacred aspect of reality.

As an integral philosophy, spiritual ecology posits a worldview that encompasses a sense of the sacredness of planet Earth (Gaia) and of the evolution of the cosmos as a divine process headed in the direction of deeper expressions of "Spirit." Chief characteristics of spiritual ecology as an integral philosophy include a shift away from an anthropocentric worldview toward a heightened sense of the sacredness of all life; a deepening awareness of the relationship between spiritual life and the planetary ecological crisis; and the encour-

The Significance of Location

The cat has the chance to make the sunlight
Beautifully stop it and turn it immediately
Into black and motion, to take it
As shifting branch and brown feather
Into the back of the brain forever.
The cardinal has flown the sun in red
Through the oak forest to the lawn.
The finch has caught it in yellow
And taken it among the thorns. By the spider
It has been bound tightly and tied
In an eight-stringed knot.
The sun has been intercepted in its one
Basic state and changed to a million varieties
Of green stick and tassel. It has been broken
Into pieces by glass rings, by mist
Over the river. Its heat
Has been given the board fence for body,
The desert rock for fact. On winter hills
It has been laid down in white like a martyr.
This afternoon we could spread gold scarves
Clear across the field and say in truth, "Sun you are silk."
Imagine the sun totally isolated,
Its brightness shot in continuous streaks straight out
Into the black, never arrested,
Never once being made light.
Someone should take note
Of how the Earth has saved the sun from oblivion.

Source: Rogers, Pattiann. (2002, Spring). "The Significance of Location." *Earth Light*, n.p.

agement of a conscious, sustainable lifestyle characterized by living simply and with wisdom and ecological integrity.

Spiritual Ecology and the Kinship Model

A debate has emerged within religious groups and among people of faith over the place of humans within the natural order. Three primary spiritual models have been operative in human history: domination of nature for human use, the stewardship of nature primarily through technological innovation, and a kinship relationship in which humans are seen as one part of an evolving whole. Each model gives rise to distinct value systems. The dominator model holds that humans have rights to exploit the natural world solely to their own ends and benefit. No discernable environmental ethic derives from this model. The stewardship model holds that humans are part of an order created by a transcendent deity and that environmental ethics derive primarily from a religious duty to care for the planet as a gift from the Creator. The kinship model holds that humans evolved out of an evolutionary process and share a kinship and interconnectedness with an emergent community of life. In this model an environmental ethic derives from feelings of wonder, reverence, and awe at the evolutionary process and from a belief in the sanctity and inherent worth of all forms of life. Within the kinship model, religious questions of the role, origin, and destiny of humans become interwoven with a knowledge of and appreciation and respect for nature, resulting in a contemporary philosophy and practice of spiritual ecology. Thus spiritual ecology addresses basic human values and cultural worldviews at their root as a way of solving intractable environmental issues and concerns.

The Practical Application of Spiritual Ecology

Despite philosophical and religious differences, the practice of spiritual ecology involves similar actions within the stewardship and kinship models. Religion and spiritual practice, historically rooted in the simplest things in life, brings the worldview of spiritual ecology, the awareness of ecological principles and the need for reverence, into the practicalities and conditions of everyday life. Bringing this awareness into everyday life is seen as a means for living sustainably and in harmony with the planet. Energy use, design principles for houses and cities, food and agricultural systems, ecological education, the exchange of services and good (economics), and levels of resource consumption are some of the considerations that fall under a contemporary practice of spiritual ecology.

K. Lauren de Boer

See also Ecology, Deep; Gaia Theory

Further Reading

Anderson, E. N. (1996). *Ecologies of the heart: Emotion, belief, and the environment.* New York: Oxford University Press.

Barnhill, D. L., & Gottlieb, R. S. (Eds.). (2001). *Deep ecology and world religions: New essays on sacred ground.* Albany: State University of New York Press.

Edwards, J., & Palmer, M. (1997). *Holy ground: The guide to faith and ecology.* Northamptonshire, UK: Pilkington Press.

Gottlieb, R. S. (Ed.). (1996). *This sacred Earth: Religion, nature, environment.* New York: Routledge.

Grim, J. A. (Ed.). (2001). *Indigenous traditions and ecology: The interbeing of cosmology and community.* Cambridge, MA: Harvard University Press.

Hessel, D. T., & Ruether, R. R. (Eds.). (2000). *Christianity and ecology.* Cambridge, MA: Harvard University Press.

Kaza, S., & Kraft, K. (Eds.). (2000). *Dharma rain: Sources of Buddhist environmentalism.* Boston: Shambhala.

Kinsley, D. (1995). *Ecology and religion: Ecological spirituality in cross-cultural perspective.* Englewood Cliffs, NJ: Prentice Hall.

Rockefeller, S. C., & Elder, J. (1992). *Spirit and nature: Why the environment is a religious issue: An interfaith dialogue.* Boston: Beacon Press.

Tucker, M. E., & Grim, J. (Eds.). (1994). *Worldviews and ecology: Religion, philosophy, and the environment.* Maryknoll, NY: Orbis Books.

Ecopsychology

In his introduction to his book *Earth in the Balance*, former U.S. Vice President Al Gore writes, "we seem to share a restlessness of spirit that rises out of the lost connection to our world" (Gore 1992, 2). The field of ecopsychology emerged in the 1990s as an attempt to address this restlessness of spirit and to find ways of reestablishing the lost connection. Just as environmental history expands the traditional scope of history by grounding human activity in the context of the natural environment, ecopsychology expands the traditional scope of psychology to include humanity's relationship with the natural world.

Ecopsychology begins with the assumptions that humanity is facing a crisis in its relationship with the natural environment, that this crisis has significant psychological roots, and that an essential dimension of the solution to the problem of increased environmental degradation lies in the realm of the psyche. Ecopsychology arises out of a relationship between the fields of ecology and psychology, applying psychological insights in understanding the sources of current ecological imbalances and bringing an ecological perspective to bear in the quest to understand and heal the modern human soul. How has humanity come to face such devastating environmental problems as massive extinctions, deforestation, topsoil erosion, global climate change, overpopulation, and worldwide pollution of air, water, and soil? Why do people continue to act in ways that they now know to be destructive? And how can people begin to change some of their most destructive habits in order to solve the problems they have created, albeit unwittingly, through their tremendous ability to transform the world?

A psychological orientation to ecology and the environment brings an appreciation for the emotional and motivational dimensions of human behavior. It highlights the importance of helping people deal with the difficult emotions that arise in learning about and seeking to address the overwhelming challenges facing humanity at this unique stage in the evolution of humans as a species. In addition, it challenges the environmental movement to examine its modus operandi in seeking change. Recognizing that the tactics of fear, guilt, sacrifice, and coercion are ineffective and counterproductive in motivating individuals to change their behavior, ecopsychology counsels those who seek constructive change in humanity's relationship with nature to find more positive motivation—to entice humanity to seek a more joyful and loving relationship with what ecopsychologist David Abram (1996) calls the "more-than-human" world.

Origins

In 1992 Theodore Roszak, professor of history at California State University in Hayward, introduced the term *ecopsychology* into the popular lexicon in *The Voice of the Earth: An Exploration of Ecopsychology*, although much of his earlier work had addressed similar themes. Independently, a small group of psychologists (including Mary Gomes, Robert Greenway, Allan Kanner, and Elan Shapiro) had begun meeting in 1989 in Berkeley (just ten blocks from Roszak's home) to articulate a psychological framework for understanding the relationship between the individual and the environment, which they had also labeled "ecopsychology." Roszak joined the group in the early 1990s, and its members were approached by Michael Murphy, founder and director of the Esalen Institute, to organize a conference that would introduce ecopsychology as a new field of inquiry. As a center for innovative and transformative approaches in psychotherapy, the Esalen Institute had recently undertaken a project of ecological renovation, which led Murphy to explore the relationship between ecology and therapy.

Two conferences on ecopsychology were held at Esalen in 1993 and 1994. In addition to members of the Berkeley group, participants included a number of scholars whose writings would come to define the emerging field—David Abram, Anita Barrows, James Hillman, Jerry Mander, Ralph Metzner, Betty Roszak, and Laura Sewall, among others. Conference participants were asked to consider several questions that helped to shape the further evolution of the field. What is the most effective way to encourage healthy environ-

mental behavior? Is consumer culture a form of psychopathology? Is the city an enemy of nature? Can modern societies recapture the ecological insights buried in their indigenous past? What is the role of religious and legal institutions? How can the new field be introduced in universities?

With funding from the Goldman Environmental Foundation, Roszak founded the Ecopsychology Institute at Hayward in 1994 in order to facilitate a dialogue between psychologists, ecological scientists, and environmental activists. The institute published a newsletter and created the Web site Ecopsychology On-Line, which featured a quarterly journal from 1996 through 1998. Growing out of their collaborative work in launching the new field and drawing on the work of conference participants, Roszak, Gomes, and Kanner in 1995 published a wide-ranging anthology of articles entitled *Ecopsychology: Restoring the Earth, Healing the Mind*, which provides a comprehensive overview of the new field.

Although the term is new, ecopsychology as a concept has much older roots. Working with American psychologist Abraham Maslow in the graduate program in psychology at Brandeis University, Robert Greenway was influenced by such notable prophets of social transformation as Timothy Leary, B. F. Skinner, Erik Erikson, Rollo May, Carl Rogers, and Aldous Huxley in association with the Center for Psychology and Social Change at Cambridge University. With fellow graduate students, Greenway coined the term *psychoecology* in 1963 to describe what they saw as a necessary joining of the fields of psychology and ecology, extending the insights of humanistic and transpersonal psychology beyond their human-centered focus to embrace ecology and the natural world.

The central idea motivating the psychoecology group was the essential identity of mind and nature. Exploring the universal symbolic patterns, or archetypes, that psychologist Carl Jung identified in his work on the collective unconscious, and drawing on the work of Alan Watts (philosopher and Zen scholar), Paul Shepard (the environmental philosopher), and Gregory Bateson (anthropologist and systems thinker), Greenway continued to explore the origins of the separation between culture and the natural world as a professor of psychology at Sonoma State University, connecting with the Berkeley group in 1989. He has written several articles for the International Community for Ecopsychology (ICE), which began publishing an online journal, *Gatherings*, in 1999 as a public forum for exploring the human-nature relationship in order to foster more harmonious ways of living on the Earth.

Understood in its broadest terms as a quest for greater harmony between humanity and nature, ecopsychology has far more ancient roots. It can be traced to the Romantic tradition in Europe, in the work of French philosopher Jean-Jacques Rousseau, German poet Johann von Goethe, and English poet Samuel Taylor Coleridge, which might be seen as a reaction of the soul to the dawning industrial age and its potential for dehumanization and the destruction of natural beauty. Similarly, ecopsychology draws on the American tradition of transcendentalism, the prophetic voices of American writers Henry David Thoreau and Ralph Waldo Emerson, and the pioneering work of American naturalist John Muir and American forester Aldo Leopold, which paved the way for the American environmental movement. Older still are ecopsychology's roots in the Western mystical tradition, Buddhist teachings on interdependence, and the nature-based spirituality of Taoism. Because most traditional indigenous cultures embody a sense of reciprocity with the natural world, ecopsychologists often identify the origins of the field in the ancient heritage of human ancestors, which they seek to recover through experiential practices that reconnect people with their roots in the living Earth.

Defining the Concept

Echoing Roszak, "as if the soul might be saved while the biosphere crumbles," Ralph Metzner describes ecopsychology as a critique of existing schools of psychology for their failure to consider the ecological foundation of human life (Roszak 1992, 17). Greenway identifies six faces of ecopsychology: (1) a context for general discussions about nature; (2) a foundation for healing, identifying the source of psychological problems in modern culture's alienation from nature and drawing on nature for healing; (3) a primarily experiential orientation, integrating the vision quest (an initiatory rite of passage in the Native American tradition) and other forms of wilderness experience in educational and therapeutic practice; (4) a spiritual practice drawing on the identity of nature and spirit; (5) a call for a new academic discipline; and (6) an attempt to articulate a philosophically coherent and consistent language for the emerging field.

An aspect that Greenway's faces fail to highlight is Roszak's emphasis on the need to include the human psyche in people's consideration of nature. Citing Aus-

trian psychoanalyst Sigmund Freud, Roszak suggests that the psychopathology of everyday life (reflected in such phenomena as ozone depletion, toxic waste, and the greenhouse effect) reveals a parallel psychopathology of the soul. He faults ecologists and environmental activists for relying on prophecies of gloom and the psychology of shame to motivate changes in human behavior, seeing in such tactics a kind of "environmental puritanism that almost delights in castigating our sins of self-indulgence . . . as if guilt were the only way to instill virtue." In contrast, he is seeking "an alternative to scare tactics and guilt trips that will lend ecological necessity both intelligence and passion" (Roszak 1992, 36, 39).

In his efforts to establish ecopsychology as a mainstream academic discipline that would address the emotional, motivational, and psychological aspects of environmental issues, Roszak sought to articulate an environmentally based definition of mental health. In the epilogue to his first book, he identifies eight basic principles of ecopsychology: (1) The root of the madness of industrial society is the repression of the ecological unconscious, which is the core of the mind. (2) This ecological unconscious represents "the living record of cosmic evolution" (Roszack 1992, 320). (3) The goal of ecopsychology is to heal the "fundamental alienation between the person and the natural environment" (Roszak 1992, 321). (4) Focusing on childhood as the critical stage of development, ecopsychology seeks to recover the animistic perception of nature (i.e., the perception of nature as a living, conscious identity) characteristic of this stage, drawing on the healing techniques of traditional peoples, nature mysticism, wilderness experience, and deep ecology in order to nurture an "ecological ego." (5) Building on this foundation, ecopsychology seeks to nurture a sense of ethical responsibility for the planet that will become an integral factor in social and political relations. (6) Drawing on ecofeminism and feminist spirituality, ecopsychology seeks to reevaluate gender roles and character traits that underlie humanity's domination of nature. (7) Ecopsychology suggests that small-scale social forms are better than large-scale urban-industrial culture for cultivating the ecological ego. (8) There is a synergistic relationship between personal and planetary well-being.

The 1995 anthology by Roszak, Gomes, and Kanner opens with the "Environmental Foreword" by Lester Brown, editor of the World Watch Institute's annual *State of the World* reports, who notes that ecopsychology offers environmental politics an understanding of the "irrational forces that tie people to their bad environmental habits," drawing on the ecological sciences in reexamining "the human psyche as an integral part of the web of nature" (Roszak, Gomes, & Kanner 1995, xvi). The psychologist James Hillman offers the "Psychological Foreword," entitled "A Psyche the Size of the Earth," highlighting the concept of the ecological self. Identifying the roots of cultural isolation and fragmentation in specialization and professionalism, Hillman sees potential for change in fresh ideas that are "blowing in from the world, the ecological psyche, the soul of the world . . . to which the human soul is commencing to turn with fresh interest, because in this world the human soul has always had its home" (Roszak, Gomes, & Kanner 1995, xxiii).

Topics addressed in the anthology provide an overview of the concerns encompassed in the field. Paul Shepard describes the chronic madness in humanity's treatment of the world, which he traces to the emergence of agriculture. The psychologist Chellis Glendenning explores elements of addiction and denial in dysfunctional environmental relations. Kanner and Gomes discuss the relationship between consumerism and modern advertising, which they describe as the "largest single psychological project ever undertaken by the human race" (Roszak, Gomes, & Kanner 1995, 80). Joanna Macy, a Buddhist scholar and deep ecologist, emphasizes the need to help people deal with the sense of despair that learning about environmental problems can engender. Greenway discusses the role of wilderness in restoring ecological sanity, and Elan Shapiro describes the psychological healing effects of environmental restoration projects. Articulating the multicultural self as an integral aspect of the ecological self, Carl Anthony, the leader in the environmental justice movement, offers a vision of a global civil society freed from the divisiveness of racism, and Jeannette Armstrong, the leader in international indigenous people's political movement, draws on her heritage in the Okanagan community (indigenous community in British Columbia) to present a compelling analysis of contemporary society from the perspective of a traditional indigenous culture.

Related Fields

Ecopsychology is probably closest in spirit to deep ecology because both perspectives seek to cultivate a more relational and inclusive notion of the self, drawing on insights from Buddhism, cosmology (a branch of metaphysics that deals with the nature of the universe), and systems science to challenge the individualism and dualism inherent in Western culture. Ralph Metzner describes a paradigm shift from physics to ecology and evolution as the foundational sciences, noting Shepard's characterization of ecology as the subversive science, which challenges the foundations of the modern industrial worldview through a transdisciplinary inquiry into systemic interrelationships. Roszak appeals to the Gaia hypothesis (the idea that the Earth is itself a living organism) and the anthropic principle (the idea that life and mind are inherent in the universe from the beginning) as examples of an emerging cosmology that transcends the separation between matter and spirit. Although still controversial and not widely accepted in the scientific community, such perspectives offer a sense of belonging to an increasingly alienated humanity.

In contrast to the predominantly anthropocentric (human-centered) orientation of other branches of ecophilosophy and environmental ethics, deep ecology seeks to foster an expanded sense of self that embraces the natural world. Like Greenway, the deep ecologist Warrick Fox seeks to "ecologize" transpersonal psychology, challenging the Freudian model of the tripartite self, which relies on moral constraint (the superego) to hold the impulsive id in check, through the agency of the rational ego. Ethical appeals to the intrinsic value of nature, according to Fox, only reify (regard as concrete or material) the "atomistic, particle-like volitional self." He cites George Sessions, one of the founders of deep ecology, who suggests that "our problems seem to channel down ultimately to human psychology" (Fox 1990, 217, 225).

According to David Abram, the transition from oral to written language shifted the focus of perception away from direct sensual experience toward more abstract and rational cognition, thus diminishing the magical presence of the world experienced by more traditional cultures. John Seed, a deep ecologist, invites people "to hear within ourselves the sound of the earth crying" (Seed, Macy, Fleming, & Naess 1988, 5). Efforts to reclaim and honor the sensual aspect of being link ecopsychology with eco-feminism and the reemergence of Earth-based spirituality. Spiritual ecofeminists offer the goddess as a symbol of divinity that is immanent in the world, whereas social and cultural ecofeminists seek gender equity and the revaluation of women's essential (although generally invisible) role in the world's economy, grounding the economy in the household of nature. Drawing on shamanic traditions throughout the world, ecopsychology seeks to rekindle the animistic view that all of nature is alive with conscious intelligence. Honoring the wisdom of traditional people, who cultivated a far more sustainable relationship with the land, ecopsychology fosters solidarity with native peoples and their struggle for autonomy, seeking to embody similar values in the context of the postindustrial world.

Efforts to "reinhabit" the places where people live join ecopsychology with bioregionalism, a movement that seeks to ground human identity in the land, redefine the concept of home, and value the essential role of community and face-to-face interaction in the cultivation of healthier relationships, both with each other and with the Earth. Roszak writes about the madness of the cities, triggering critics who fault ecopsychology for its antagonism to urban culture. Nevertheless, ecopsychology aligns itself with social ecology and the environmental justice and urban restoration movements. Hillman suggests that people need to rediscover the gods of the city and find ways to embody organic values in urban design. Social justice is an essential foundation. Articulating the relationship between social oppression and environmental devastation is a critical task for ecopsychology if it hopes to overcome the psychological resistance to change and mobilize humanity's energies in more constructive directions.

Vision for the Future

Subject to some of the same tensions that divide the deep ecology, eco-feminism, and social ecology camps within the ecophilosophy community, ecopsychology offers another lens through which to view the dysfunctional nature of people's relations with one another and with the world around them. Whether it is rooted in anthropocentrism, patriarchy, or political, economic, and military forms of domination, the current human situation as a species on the brink of self-destruction calls upon all people to reexamine their own relationships. Ecopsychology counsels people to acknowledge their emotions and to channel emotional energy into constructive change. It invites people to examine both the belief systems and the material conditions that separate people from one another and to slowly dismantle the walls that they have constructed to keep the rest of the world out.

Environmental history examines the evolution of humanity's relationship with nature and clarifies the connections between the human-nature relationship and human social relations. Ecopsychology offers an

analysis of the psychological dimensions of humanity's evolutionary journey, suggesting that the path to further evolution lies in expanding human identity to embrace the world in which people are inextricably embedded. Unlike sociobiology, which explains human behavior in purely biological terms as the result of selfish genes competing to maximize their reproduction, ecopsychology highlights the subjective dimension of human experience, affirming the potential for the emergence of more harmonious relationships through the cultivation of a consciousness of relatedness. The course of evolution has bestowed upon humanity the gift of self-conscious reflection; the fate of life on this planet now lies in human hands, hearts, and minds. Ecopsychology focuses on humanity's understanding of itself and its place in the world as the key to reorienting the goals motivating human behavior away from notions of progress, growth, control, and domination toward more sustainable notions that honor the gift of life.

Debora Hammond

See also Ecology, Deep; Ecology, Spiritual

Further Reading

Abram, D. (1996). *The spell of the sensuous: Perception and language in a more-than-human world*. New York: Vintage Books.

Bateson, G. (1972). *Steps to an ecology of mind*. New York: Ballantine Books.

Berry, T. (1988). *The dream of the Earth*. San Francisco: Sierra Club Books.

Cohen, M. J. (1997). *Reconnecting with nature: Finding wellness through restoring your bond with the Earth*. Corvallis, OR: Ecopress.

Fisher, A., & Abram, D. (2002). *Radical ecopsychology: Psychology in the service of life*. New York: State University of New York Press.

Fox, W. (1990). *Toward a transpersonal ecology: Developing new foundations for environmentalism*. Boston: Shambhala.

Gore, A. (1992). *Earth in the balance*. New York: Houghton Mifflin.

Hayden, T. (1996). *The lost gospel: A call for renewing nature, spirit, and politics*. San Francisco: Sierra Club Books.

Heller, C. (1999). *Ecology of everyday life: Rethinking the desire for nature*. Montreal, Canada: Black Rose Books.

Hillman, J. (1992). *The thought of the heart and the soul of the world*. Dallas, TX: Spring Publications.

Mander, J. (1991). *In the absence of the sacred*. San Francisco: Sierra Club Books.

Mathews, F. (1991). *The ecological self*. Savage, MD: Barnes and Noble Books.

Merchant, C. (1992). *Radical ecology: The search for a livable world*. New York: Routledge.

Metzner, R. (1999). *Green psychology: Transforming our relationship to the Earth*. Rochester, VT: Park Street Press.

Roszak, T. (1992). *The voice of the Earth: An exploration of ecopsychology*. New York: Touchstone.

Roszak, T., Gomes, M. E., & Kanner, A. D. (1995). *Ecopsychology: Restoring the Earth, healing the mind*. San Francisco: Sierra Club Books.

Seed, J., Macy, J., Fleming, P., & Naess, A. (1988). *Thinking like a mountain: Toward a council of all beings*. Philadelphia: New Society Publishers.

Sewall, L. (1999). *Sight and sensibility: The ecopsychology of perception*. New York: J. P. Tarcher.

Shepard, P. (1982). *Nature and madness*. San Francisco: Sierra Club Books.

Suzuki, D. (1997). *The sacred balance: Rediscovering our place in nature*. Vancouver, Canada: Greystone Books.

Watts, A. W. (1958). *Nature, man and woman*. New York: Random House.

Winter, D. D. (1996). *Ecological psychology: Healing the split between planet and self*. San Francisco: HarperCollins.

Zimmerman, M. E., Callicott, J. B., Sessions, G., Warren, K. J., & Clark, J. (1993). *Environmental philosophy: From animal rights to radical ecology*. Englewood Cliffs, NJ: Prentice Hall.

Ecosystems

Ecology is the branch of biology that investigates the relationships between living things and their environments. More specifically, ecosystem ecology focuses on how organisms obtain and transform energy and materials. The concept of ecosystem builds from the notion that organisms utilize energy to transform basic elements or nutrients with resulting increases in living (organic) matter and alterations to their environments. An ecosystem, therefore, includes the organisms of a defined area and their associated resources.

The ecosystem concept originated with A. G. Tansley, an English ecologist. Prior to Tansley, most ecologists (scientists who study ecology) focused primarily on organisms and their interactions in ecological communities, commonly called associations. Tansley argued that the organisms could not be understood without considering their relationships to the "whole complex of physical factors" that constituted their environment. These factors include light, soil, minerals, water, and atmospheric gases, and effects of temperature, pH, and other variables that change over space and time.

Literally, *ecosystem* means an ecological system, implying the flow of energy and cycles of materials from the soil, water, and air through living organisms and back again. This system involves a biotic component, comprising all of the living organisms involved in the system, and an abiotic component, meaning the nonliving parts of the system. The nonliving, of course, is the energy and the minerals, gases, and other molecules that make up the soil, water, and air. While community ecology focuses primarily on biotic interactions, ecosystem ecology focuses on relationships between biotic and abiotic components.

Scale, Size, and Scope

Communities must be defined at scales involving biotic interactions, but ecosystems can be defined at nearly any scale. Community ecology is defined by interactions such as competition, predation, and mutualism. Ecosystem ecology is not necessarily limited to interactions between organisms. For example, the global carbon cycle not only involves photosynthesis and carbon uptake by plants, but it also relates to absorption of carbon dioxide by the ocean, burning of fossil fuels, and accumulation or loss of organic matter in the soil. Atmospheric carbon dioxide balance, therefore, can and, indeed, must be addressed at a global scale. Accumulation or loss of organic matter in soil, on the other hand, could be addressed at a scale of a few square meters to perhaps a few hectares, but cannot realistically be addressed at a scale larger than a plant community where this process occurs.

Ecologists define the scale of ecosystems according to the questions they are investigating. For example, if one is interested in global warming and its relationships to atmospheric carbon dioxide, the appropriate ecosystem might well be the entire Earth. On the other hand, if one is investigating the rate of carbon uptake through photosynthesis by a forest, the appropriate ecosystem might be a hectare (10,000 square meters) or less. The study of carbon conversion from fallen leaves to leaf-eating mites on the forest floor might focus on a square meter.

Temporal scales vary with spatial scales. For example, global carbon cycles are on the order of hundreds of years or longer, depending on what aspect of the cycle one is investigating. Carbon uptake by a forest relates to tree growth and turnover on a scale of a decade to a hundred years or more. Decomposition processes and turnover of invertebrate organisms, such as mites in the forest litter, is on a temporal scale of weeks to a year or two at most.

Succession and Ecosystem Development

Early in the twentieth century, during the formative years of ecology, ecologists were divided over the degree to which associations of organisms, called ecological communities, functioned as an integrated unit, much like the cells or organs of an organism. This debate stemmed from two consistent sets of observations of natural communities: (1) organisms are assembled to varying degrees into recognizable natural associations; and (2) the composition of each association, or community, reflects local environmental conditions and disturbance. Although our understanding of these observations is much clearer now, the generalizations have withstood a century of ecological study and observation.

F. E. Clements, an American ecologist, published two seminal works in which he argued that associations (natural communities) functioned like superorganisms. Contemporary ecologists, especially H. C. Cowles and W. S. Cooper, had previously established that distinct communities developed as species became established on newly exposed abiotic resources, such as sand dunes or moraines formed by retreating glaciers. Moreover, they observed that disturbance to established communities resulted in changes in the composition of species making up the association. In both cases, following disturbance, the communities proceeded in a more or less predictable pattern of species change over time, eventually, in the absence of further disturbance, leading to a stable association of species that reflected local environmental conditions. This process, which so occupied Clements's attention, was called succession. Where the community developed on virgin resources without prior alteration by previous life, it was called *primary succession.* When an existing community was disturbed, the subsequent process was called *secondary succession.* If not disturbed by subsequent disturbance, the two successional processes, in theory, will arrive at the same mature association, the composition determined by local environmental conditions. Clements equated this successional process to the aging process of an organism, and even now, mature ecosystems are commonly referred to as "old growth."

In contrast to the views of Clements, another contemporary, H. A. Gleason, argued that associations were mere chance occurrences of species that were responding to similar environmental requirements. Although Gleason acknowledged that it might be useful to classify associations for convenience, communities in his view represented only casual relationships, and identifiable patterns in species associations were merely the result of parallel adaptations to environmental conditions.

Most ecologists now accept that associations are more than mere chance occurrences of species in the same location, but communities function much differently than organisms. Individual species interact with one another at the community level in both complementary and antagonistic ways. Indeed, succession occurs in part because of these relationships. Those organisms that become established first, sometimes referred to as "pioneer species," modify the environment through their interactions. For example, annual plants become established in disturbed soil. They compete with one another for needed resources, but they also contribute organic matter to the soil, and by their presence, they provide shade favorable to different species that are not well adapted to full sunlight. Some may also produce chemicals that interfere with the establishment of other species, and may even release chemicals that prevent their own offspring from remaining on the same site. Certain herbivores may be attracted to the site because of the presence of the pioneer plants, and in turn, the herbivores may favor a different suite of species. Thus, as organisms become established, they directly or indirectly create conditions that favor a different suite of species. Over time, the association changes. As the species change, the abiotic environment changes, in part because of the change in species, and in part, the change in the abiotic environment causes a change in species.

Our modern view of succession is a more or less predictable pattern of change in the ecosystem over time leading to a mature association in which the biotic and abiotic components are stabilized. This mature community maintains itself indefinitely in the absence of disturbance or environmental change. Organisms and abiotic factors in the mature community are essentially constant within the limits of year-to-year climatic and population cycles. This is the old growth condition, which Clements called the "climax community."

Biomes and Communities

Associations, based largely on vegetation, have been classified throughout much of the world. This greatly facilitates the sharing of information and ideas about their composition and ecology. Like the classification of organisms, associations are often organized in a hierarchy. At the broadest scale, associations reflect climatic conditions, especially average temperature and precipitation. Ecologists call these *biomes*. We find, for instance, a tropical rain forest biome in climates that are very warm and humid. Deserts, on the other hand, occur in dry climates, irrespective of temperature. Grasslands and savannas occur in moderate climates that tend to be drier than those supporting forests. The species of vegetation in each of these biomes will vary from one region to another, but the form of the vegetation is consistent. For example, savannas are characterized by a ground cover of many species of grasses and broad-leaved flowering plants with scattered shrubs and trees. The species present in the Serengeti savanna of Africa are quite different from those found in the Midwest of North America, but the structure of the savannas is remarkably similar.

Within each biome, there will be many types of ecological *communities*. For example, there may be streams, lakes, riparian communities along streams, and different types of wetlands. Each community type within a biome has similar structure and may have some of the same species. At the community scale of association, certain species will consistently be associated on similar soils and topography and undergo similar successional patterns when disturbed. It is this community level of organization that Clements likened to an organism.

Food Chains and Food Webs

The animals within each association primarily reflect both the composition and structure of the vegetation. Composition of vegetation refers to the actual species present whereas structure refers to the form, that is, trees, shrubs, grasses, broad-leaved herbaceous plants, and their spatial distribution. Structure also refers to dead vegetation, especially standing dead trees, called snags, and coarse woody debris on the ground, as well as organic material over and in the soil. The relationship between plants and animals is certainly not passive. Animals coevolved with plants and interact with them in a myriad of ways. Most obviously, perhaps, plants represent food for certain animals, called herbi-

vores. The relationships, however, go far beyond herbivory. Some animals, called carnivores or predators, prey on other animals. Carnivores provide a degree of protection to plants by preventing overpopulation of herbivores. As plants evolved ways to minimize herbivory, herbivores evolved ways to overcome the plants' defenses. Some animals eat seeds while others aid in seed dissemination. Birds and other insect-eating animals, such as spiders, provide some protection to plants from herbivorous insects. The interactions are endless. Every species in the community interacts directly or indirectly with every other species in the community in either complementary or antagonistic ways. This includes the countless species of fungi and microbes, some of which are disease agents, but most of which are involved in decomposition and nutrient cycling processes. It is this coevolution among the interacting organisms in the community that results in finely tuned relationships within local ecosystems.

The importance of these interactions was first championed by Charles Elton, a British ecologist, who pointed out that ecosystems are organized, among other ways, through feeding relationships. Elton introduced the concepts of food chains and what we now call food webs. A food chain is a series of species linked through herbivory and predation. Certain plant species are eaten by various species of herbivores that, in turn, are eaten by certain species of primary carnivores that are eaten by certain species of secondary carnivores, and so on. In nearly all communities, however, most plant species are consumed by a variety of different herbivorous species, each of which is preyed upon by a variety of carnivorous species. These cross-linked food chains are called food webs.

Computer models are now commonly used to examine ecological relationships. Ecological modeling, however, originated with A. J. Lotka in 1925. Populations and communities, Lotka suggested, can be represented by a set of equations that describe the thermodynamic relationships of energy and material transformations in food webs. Lotka's ideas went largely unnoticed until they were incorporated into an important paper published in 1942 by Raymond Lindeman, an aquatic ecologist. Lindeman studied food webs in a temperate lake and realized that he could characterize the organisms representing the community by how they fit into the energy transformations that were occurring. Lindeman theorized that the second law of thermodynamics suggests some loss of energy as heat through each transformation.

Trophic Structure

Green plants utilize light through the process of photosynthesis. They are called autotrophs because they provide their own energy in contrast to animals and most microbes that are heterotrophs, meaning they must obtain their energy from other sources. Ultimately, of course, heterotrophs must get their energy directly or indirectly from autotrophs. Lindeman observed that all of the energy captured by green plants, however, could not be converted to energy in herbivores, and likewise, primary carnivores could not capture all of the energy from herbivores. Energy is not transformed completely because (1) some is needed to maintain the host species from one generation to the next, and (2) not all of the material consumed can be converted to energy. Just as the energy from gasoline used to propel a car is converted to heat, energy used to maintain the metabolism of an organism is converted to heat, which is then lost from the ecosystem.

Lindeman recognized that there is a movement of energy from sunlight, into chemical bonds in green plants, to compounds in herbivores, to compounds in primary carnivores, and so on. All of the energy entering an ecosystem is ultimately lost as heat when the chemical bond energy is released through metabolism. He called each energy level a *trophic level* (from Greek *trophe*, meaning food or nourishment). Because energy cannot be completely transformed from one trophic level to the next, Lindeman suggested that the organisms of an ecosystem could be visualized as a trophic pyramid, with the base level representing autotrophs, the second level herbivores, the third level primary carnivores, and so on. It is rare in most ecosystems for more than four or five trophic levels to be represented. There simply is not sufficient energy to support higher levels of consumers.

Although many contributed to the continued development of ecosystem concepts, it was Eugene P. Odum of the University of Georgia who arguably had the greatest influence. Building from his predecessors' ideas, Odum published a textbook in 1953 in which he provided a clear framework of how energy allocation and transformations could be used to explain the structure and function of ecosystems, including the movement of nutrients. During the following three decades, Odum revised and updated his book several times, and influenced the thinking of thousands of ecology students, many of whom have gone on to successful careers in ecology.

Nutrient Cycles

Although energy can be considered the currency of ecological systems, it is the elements making up organic molecules that are the substance of life. Beyond the physiological knowledge of how nutrients are transformed and used by cells, much of our ecological understanding of nutrients is based on large-scale ecosystem studies, primarily watersheds. A watershed is that landscape area encompassing a single drainage system. When precipitation falls on the land it either filters through the soil to groundwater, evaporates, or runs off. Water flowing off the land soon enters a stream, which may join a second-order (larger) stream, leading to a third-order stream, and so on until it reaches the ocean. First-order streams represent relatively small watersheds, and it was at this scale that hydrologists (scientists who study water movement in the landscape) and ecologists teamed up to examine how nutrients were being retained and lost from the ecosystem. Of the more intensively studied watersheds, those at Hubbard Brook in New Hampshire are noteworthy. It was here that G. E. Likens and F. H. Bormann, along with many co-workers, began experiments that revealed much of what we know about nutrient cycling in ecosystems.

As ecosystems develop through successional processes, their ability to hold and cycle nutrients generally increases. Of the approximately 96 naturally occurring elements, about 26 are used by living organisms in various amounts. The bulk of living material is carbohydrate, meaning it is made up of compounds comprised largely of carbon, hydrogen, and oxygen. These elements are obtained by green plants from the atmosphere through the process of photosynthesis, where energy of sunlight is used to break apart water molecules and recombine the electrons with carbon dioxide to form carbohydrate molecules. Some of the light energy is transformed to energy in the chemical bonds of the carbohydrate molecule. All aerobic organisms (those requiring oxygen, as opposed to anaerobic organisms that can survive without oxygen) also absorb oxygen from air or water for use in respiration, transforming it in the process to water. Molecules can be transformed within an organism, such as sugar to fat or cellulose, or transformed from molecules in one organism to those in another, as when one organism eats and digests another organism. It was this energy transformation that Lindeman first characterized and which greatly influenced our understanding of how ecosystems function through food webs and trophic structure.

In addition to carbon, hydrogen, and oxygen, some twenty-three other elements are needed in various amounts. All of the elements enter the biotic component of ecosystems through autotrophs that absorb them as dissolved nutrients. Four of the twenty-three elements are needed in fairly large amounts by living organisms. They are nitrogen, phosphorus, potassium, and sulfur. These elements are important in proteins, nucleic acids, and enzymes needed by all living cells. Other elements are needed in lesser amounts, primarily as components of enzyme systems or in specialized molecules such as chlorophyll and hemoglobin.

Nitrogen and phosphorus, in particular, are needed in relatively large amounts but generally are available in limited quantities, for quite different reasons. Nitrogen gas is abundant, composing 78 percent of Earth's atmosphere. Nitrogen gas, however, is inert and must be converted to a soluble compound before plants can absorb it, a process called nitrogen fixation. Nitrogen gas is converted to usable forms either by biological fixation by specialized microbes, or through lightning. Once absorbed by plants, nitrogen is converted to protein and nucleic acid molecules in plant cells; other organisms, including humans, must acquire their nitrogen from the plant or animal tissues they consume. When metabolic wastes are eliminated by animals, or when tissues or organisms die, nitrogen-containing compounds are quickly broken down by microbes, and are ultimately released into the soil or water as soluble nitrogen compounds that can be reabsorbed by plants.

Phosphorus must be obtained through the weathering of phosphorous minerals during the formation of soil, one of the critical processes associated with succession. Phosphorus is seldom abundant in soil-forming minerals. Moreover, phosphorus is easily rendered insoluble by chemical reactions in the soil or water. As with nitrogen, soluble phosphorus is incorporated into plant compounds, from which consumer organisms can obtain it for use in their own metabolism. Because phosphorus is often limiting, organic waste products or dead organisms are quickly attacked by microbes that absorb phosphorus for use in their metabolism. Eventually, phosphorus is released back to the soil or water where plants compete for it.

Other nutrients are relatively more abundant and are needed in lesser amounts. Like phosphorus, they are released into the soil from weathering of minerals, absorbed by plants from the soil solution, moved through food webs, and recycled following waste elimination or death of organisms. Energy flows through an ecosystem, entering as light, transformed over and over in metabolic reactions, and ultimately is lost as heat. In contrast, nutrients are recycled in ecosystems through well-established processes called nutrient or biogeochemical cycles.

As soil develops during succession, more nutrients are released by weathering of minerals. Also, the soil and the organisms living in the developing ecosystem can retain and cycle more nutrients. Consequently, the productivity of ecosystems increase as they mature, leading to more living matter (biomass), until the old growth condition is attained.

When ecosystems are disturbed, such as when forests are cut or burned, nutrients tend to "leak" from the system. By disturbing watersheds, and measuring the amount of water and dissolved or suspended material in the water, over several years, Likens and Bormann found that although some nutrients are lost more easily than others, all can be lost. The leakage of nutrients from ecosystems, however, quickly tapers off as succession occurs. Some of the leakage is associated with soil erosion, and some occurs from dissolved nutrients in runoff water. Both soil erosion and loss of dissolved nutrients causes the ecosystem to be less productive until nutrients and soil can be replenished through succession. Most nutrients are replenished by weathering from minerals, but nitrogen must be replaced from the atmosphere. Nutrient loss from a disturbed ecosystem can be very rapid, such as with a storm event, whereas replenishment may take many years. If most of the soil is lost, the ecosystem may require many centuries to regain its full potential productivity.

Eutrophication

Nutrients lost from a terrestrial ecosystem, such as a watershed, enrich the lakes or streams that receive them in a process called *eutrophication*. Under natural conditions, eutrophication is ordinarily very gradual. Human alterations to natural ecosystems, however, can greatly accelerate eutrophication. Consider, for example, when we replace natural ecosystems with intensive agriculture or cities. These highly altered ecosystems are very "leaky," with runoff or erosion vastly greater than from undisturbed ecosystems. Moreover, we frequently use fertilizer to enhance agricultural production, and our farms and sewage treatment systems are very incomplete compared to the nutrient cycling that occurs in natural ecosystems. Simplification of ecosystems leads to large amounts of nitrogen and phosphorus compounds entering the streams draining farmland and cities.

High levels of soluble nitrogen and phosphorus stimulate growth of aquatic plants, which leads to higher populations of consumers and decomposers in eutrophic streams and lakes. During the day, when photosynthesis replenishes the oxygen in water, this elevated productivity is of less concern, but at night, as respiration continues without photosynthesis, dissolved oxygen in eutrophic water commonly reaches a critically low level, often leading to the death of the more oxygen-demanding species. Eutrophic water, therefore, becomes clogged with plants and tends to support fish and other organisms tolerant of low oxygen levels. Eutrophication has become a serious environmental concern, not only in many lakes and streams, but in estuaries and associated oceanic areas.

Ecosystem Management

Our understanding of ecosystems has had a great influence on environmental protection and management of natural resources. We now understand how our use of ecosystems can compromise their ability to function, leading to environmental problems. One of the most striking developments in ecosystem management stemmed from the growing concern over the loss of biodiversity. Species are lost for a host of reasons, but one of the most important is loss of habitat. As we use natural resources, we inevitably fragment and alter habitats. Most species are sensitive to habitat characteristics, and some are even sensitive to nearby changes. Large, expansive natural ecosystems have been fragmented into smaller and smaller reserves. Altered natural disturbance patterns associated with human use have upset successional processes. Further stress has been placed on native species by widespread introduction of exotics, most of which are more tolerant of damaged ecosystems.

Historically, we have simplified ecosystems to maximize desired outputs. For example, we replace extraordinarily complex prairie or forest ecosystems with farm fields in which we grow one species. When we build suburban homes in a forest we replace most of the species with a bluegrass lawn and a few shade trees and shrubs. Our lakes have been managed for recreation and game fish, wildlife for a few game animals, and forests for a handful of the most monetarily valuable tree species. We now realize that we need healthy ecosystems if we want healthy, sustainable environments. Soil erosion, eutrophication, and loss of

biodiversity are symptoms of dysfunctional ecosystems. The underlying causes, however, are the demands a burgeoning human population is placing upon ecosystems. During the last decades of the twentieth century, ecologists, environmentalists, and natural resource managers struggled for solutions. Although our understanding of ecosystems has continued to increase and the tools ecologists now have available, such as computers and monitoring devices, are tremendously powerful, the environmental challenges are greater than ever. For example, there remains much debate about global warming, primarily because of the complexity of the global ecosystem. While there remains no doubt that much of the cause for global warming stems from increasing carbon dioxide in the atmosphere, and most of this increase can be attributed to burning of fossil fuels, it is impossible to predict how global warming will vary in different locations around the globe. Indeed, some areas are expected to get cooler even as the overall temperature increases. Within this environment of uncertainty, those with vested interests in use of fossil fuels argue that more information is needed before actions are taken that might have negative economic impacts or limit our materialistic freedoms. While our growing knowledge of ecosystems provides us great insights into how to better protect our environments, actions are limited by the political and social environments in which we live and work.

Alan Haney

See also Biodiversity; Succession

Further Reading

Clements, F. E. (1926). Nature and structure of the climax. *Ecology, 24,* 252–284.

Likens, G. E., & Bormann, F. H. (1995). *Biochemistry of a Forested Ecosystems* (2nd ed.). New York: Springer-Verlag.

Lindeman, R. (1942). The trophic-dynamic aspect of ecology. *Ecology, 23,* 399–418.

Miller, Jr., G. T. (2003). *Environmental science.* Pacific Grove, CA: Brooks/Cole.

Molles, Jr., .M. C. (2002). *Ecology.* New York: McGraw-Hill.

Odum, E. P. (1953). *Fundamentals of Ecology.* Philadelphia: Saunders.

Shimwell, D. W. (1971). *Description and classification of vegetation.* Seattle, WA: University of Washington Press.

Ecotourism

Ecotourism is traveling responsibly by causing minimal damage to the environment and helping to preserve indigenous cultures. More and more people are traveling today. The World Tourism Organization (WTO) estimates that international tourist arrivals in 2000 increased to 688 million—an increase of 7.4 percent, which was double the growth rate in 1999. Receipts from international travel, excluding airfares, increased to $476 billion. This total is predicted to increase by 6.7 percent annually in the next two decades.

With such tourism overload comes the question of its impact on local environments and local cultures. Consider these facts:

1. In Cancun, Mexico, and in Hawaii, beach erosion has been caused by construction of hotels along the beaches. This erosion has caused flooding and damaged natural wetlands. Culturally significant sites like burial grounds have been bulldozed and desecrated to build many resorts in those areas.
2. Safari activities in Kenya have doomed wildlife populations, which are retreating from their original habitats to less-suitable territories.
3. In Nepal growth of the trekking industry has contributed to pollution and caused overcrowding and trail destruction. Since 1989 the number of trekkers to the Annapurna area of Nepal increased at an annual rate of 18 percent.
4. In the Philippines and Maldives, fisheries have been depleted and local people affected by dynamiting and mining for resort building materials, which have destroyed coral reefs that took ages to form.
5. In India's most popular destination, Goa, local people are unhappy about the proliferation of five-star hotels. One five-star hotel consumes as much water as five local villages, and one five-star tourist consumes twenty times more electricity per day than does a Goan resident.
6. Three-quarters of the sand dunes on the Mediterranean coast between Spain and Sicily have now disappeared. This can be attributed to the construction of hotels and holiday apartments.

The damage wrought on mountain systems, coastlines, unique scenic and historical sites, aquatic systems, islands, and countryside is growing, and the negative fallout of tourism is drawing the attention of the world. Against this backdrop, an emerging buzzword is *ecotourism.* Ecotourism has become big business. The latest fad is for people to be adventurous, watching wildlife and enjoying pristine cultures. The market for nature holidays is expanding. In 1993 the WTO estimated that nature tourism generated 7 percent of all international travel expenditures. Now that number is around 20 percent. Nature tourism is probably the fastest-growing sector in the tourism industry, accounting for 10 percent of the market in 1989 and increasing at the rate of 30 percent.

Nature Tourism Revenues Important

Understandably, governments are investing to woo this type of tourist. Revenues from nature tourism are all too important for the economy. The tourism industry and local governments realize that income from tourism can go a long way in funding conservation projects and supporting indigenous people. For instance, in Belize, a $3.75 departure tax goes directly to the Protected Area Conservation Trust to conserve the barrier reef and rain forest. Likewise, the San people of Namibia and southern Africa have recently regained management or ownership of traditional national park land, operating ecolodges (twenty-first century facilities that offer environmentally advanced accommodation, which feature items such as natural wool carpeting and organic mattresses) and serving as guides and rangers while keeping their heritage intact. The Cofan people of the Amazon are running an ecotourism enterprise in their territory, where they sustain a thriving home-based craft industry for local visitors. Nepalese women are becoming guides for trekkers and earning a livelihood with the help of community-based tourism programs. Locals in Vietnam and Tanzania are participating in a sustainable tourist economy via locally owned hotels, tour companies, wildlife park management, and farming cooperatives that supply food to hotels and resorts. In Natal, South Africa, the park service ensures that villages have free access to parks to meet local needs and to sell their handicrafts at local lodges. In the Peruvian Amazon, an ecolodge built with the local community uses natural material and low-impact technologies. In Alice Springs, Australia, all tour fees benefit the aboriginal peoples, enabling them to continue their traditions. In Cuba's western Pinar del Rio Province, the four-star Moka Ecolodge's electricity comes from solar panels, and 40 percent of hotel revenues goes into a community development fund. In Sri Lanka the government has decided to develop ecotourism in rural areas under the Medirigiriya Community Based Ecotourism Programme, a local government-community project that integrates conservation with

---

Leave Nothing But Footprints
Take nothing but pictures.
Leave nothing but footprints.
Kill nothing but time.

Source: Motto of the Baltimore Grotto, a caving society.

---

development. In Thailand five major areas have been prioritized and five new types of management identified for coastal ecotourism development, with an emphasis on increased community participation.

Ecotourism can conserve the ecology of tourist sites and extend patronage to local people. However, because the ecotourism concept and industry are relatively new, countries are struggling to develop institutions that can meet these twin objectives. It is crucial that management institutions are put in place as ecotourism moves into the mainstream tourism sector; otherwise, the negative impact of ecotourism will be substantial. Today, in most developing countries, where tourism is increasing at the rate of 28 percent compared to 6 percent in developed countries, even if such institutions are in place, they have limited capability to run tourism at sustainable levels. In these countries, the tourism and recreation industry is at a crossroads in its development. The industry is increasingly being confronted with sustainability and compatibility with environmental protection and community development. Also, tourism is undergoing a fundamental change worldwide. In a recent poll, 65 percent of California travelers stated that a place that takes care of the environment is very important in choosing a destination outside of the state. And research indicated that 85 percent of United Kingdom holidaymakers believed that it is important not to damage the environment. Around 77 percent thought it is important that their visits include experiences of local culture and food, and 71 percent thought that tourism should benefit the people of the destination visited. The link between environment as an attraction and economic impact can be major. For example, about half of the economic impact of Montana's tourism industry can be attributed to recreation activities occurring in wildland settings.

Protests Increase

As the ecotourism wave is surging, so are the protests against faulty ecotourism development and policies.

In 1987 the Anuha Island Resort in the Solomon Islands was closed and later burned to the ground during indigenous protests. In Mexico a proposal for a golf course in Tepotztlan was abandoned after the police shot a protester. More than one hundred agitated villagers in Khao Sok National Park in Surat Thani Province in Thailand seized a bulldozer owned by the Royal Forestry Department and the trunks of trees that had been felled to build a 1,000-square-meter parking lot, an 800-meter-long road, and ten toilets. The challenge is obvious: to develop ecotourism around unique natural features and traditional cultures and simultaneously conserve resources and provide benefits to local communities. The pressure created by a high volume of tourism has to be reduced by providing alternatives to conventional tourism activities and diffusing the tourism concentration from one place. Ecotourism, which is meant to ease pressure on the ecology, can instead damage the ecology. Ecotourism does not guarantee long-term protection of the environment. In many countries proceeds from ecotourism are not being channeled to the management of natural systems or to help the local people.

Ecotourism faces many complex problems. It has no specific standards or certification system to serve as a benchmark or a yardstick and no international monitoring body for products marketed under the label of ecotourism. Even the label itself is used loosely. Paradoxically, ecotourists may visit areas of natural beauty and wildlife without realizing that local people have been evicted in order for ecotourism to be developed. More ecolodges mean more tourists flocking to them and putting even more pressure on the natural resources. Ironically, ecotourism is taking its own toll. Biopiracy is on the rise as foreign tourists, under the guise of ecotourism, smuggle indigenous herbs and other plants for the multimillion-dollar biotechnology industry.

Already the rush for ecotourism dollars is posing a threat to endangered species. No doubt hiking trails

Tourists view Mt. Kilimanjaro, a stratovolcano in Tanzania reaching 19,340 feet (5,898.7 meters). COURTESY MARY CORINNE LOWENSTEIN.

increase awareness about ecology, but they can be overextended. Between 1990 and 1994 five new hiking trails opened in Algonquin Park in Canada; if that rate continued, what might the park be like after fifty years? The Galapagos Islands are the best example of a place where ecotourism expanded too rapidly and lacked sufficient planning and controls. Phi Phi Island near Bangkok, Thailand, has also become badly polluted because of lack of facilities for coping with the tourism boom.

United Nations Designation Opposed

A coalition of nongovernmental organizations (NGOs) protested the UN decision to designate 2002 as the International Year of Ecotourism. The coalition was coordinated by the Malaysia-based Third World Network

(TWN), working with the Thailand-based Tourism Information Monitoring team. The coalition opposed the ecotourism policy promoted by the tourism working group under the Greater Mekong Subregion (GMS) development scheme, which covers a vast area of Myanmar, Thailand, Vietnam, and China. The policy focuses on the construction of highways, airports, and other tourist facilities. TWN questioned the long-term impact of promoting ecotourism in this fashion, but the UN's decision prevailed.

Around the world, conferences on ecotourism have urged that greater attention be paid to the vital role of local community in planning for ecotourism activities. Local communities are custodians of natural wealth, and they should be included in tourism planning. Specific ecotourism policies and programs are required for each nation and region. They cannot be the same everywhere. However, UN Deputy Secretary-General Louise Frechette believes it is still possible to agree on the key principles and guidelines for ecotourism development. These guidelines are the same for everyone. Each region needs appropriate standards for ecotourism facilities. Besides, labeling tourism patterns and practices can be a way to regulate ecotourism and promote ecotourism programs for tour operators. For example, the Nature and Ecotourism Accreditation Programme in Australia was developed to recognize and reward operators of genuine nature tourism and services.

Above all, as more and more people travel, tourists should follow the creed of ecotourism: Leave nothing but footprints and take nothing but photographs.

Tirtho Banerjee

Further Reading

Buettner, Dan. (2001). *Investigating ecotourism*. Retrieved January 14, 2003, from http://www.cnn.com/2001/TECH/science/10/01/amazon.quest.7/

Environment News Service (ENS). (2002). *Ecotourists urged to walk lightly on the Earth*. Retrieved January 14, 2003, from http://forests.org/articles/reader.asp?linkid=7129

Honey, M. (1998). *Where's the "eco" in "ecotourism"?* Retrieved January 14, 2003, from http://www.americas.org/events/travel/tourism_turns_green.htm

International Ecotourism Society. (2000). *Ecotourism statistical fact sheet*. Retrieved January 14, 2003, from http://www.ecotourism.org/textfiles/statsfaq.pdf

Wheat, S. (2001). Ecotourism: Hope and reality. *People & Planet*. Retrieved January 14, 2003, from http://www.peopleandplanet.net/doc.php?id=1143

Ecuador

(2001 est. pop. 12.1 million)

The Republic of Ecuador (República del Ecuador) is a nation of roughly 269,000 square kilometers, straddling the equator on the western side of South America. Although relatively small in size by South American standards, Ecuador has remarkable natural and cultural diversity and has played an important role in the development of environmental ideas and policy.

The environmental diversity is a result of the country's geographic situation, including a cross section of South America's Pacific coastal plain, the Andes mountain system, and the Amazonian lowlands. The extremely high elevation of the Andes mountains (culminating in Chimborazo, 6,310 meters) and rugged topography creates a great range of temperature, precipitation, and frost regime, from icy peaks to rain-drenched cloud forest environments to dry valleys. The coastal part of the country includes a transition from very high precipitation near the Colombian border to very low precipitation on the Santa Elena Peninsula and the border with Peru, but most regions have a pronounced dry season. The Amazonian lowlands are wet all year long with high precipitation totals. The country has many active volcanoes, which have created deep layers of relatively fertile soils in the highlands. Massive eruptions, ash falls, and erosion have resulted in fertile volcanic materials being deposited widely in the lowlands as well, especially in the numerous river floodplains. The Guayas floodplain, on the central Ecuadorian coast, is particularly rich in fertile flat soils. The diversity of plants and animals, which have taken advantage of these environmental opportunities, is staggering. They include, for example, about 1,600 species of birds, more than twice as many as are found in continental Canada and the United States combined. The country includes rain forests, high mountain *páramos* (high elevation perennial grasslands), coastal mangroves, and many types of wet and dry woodland vegetation. The country also includes the environmentally unique Galápagos Islands, with their isolated fauna.

Over 60 percent of the population now lives in cities and towns, especially Guayaquil (the largest city, with over 2 million people) and Quito (the capital). Between half a million and a million people would identify themselves as Native Americans (*indios* or *indígenas*), but many more have indigenous ancestry or practice some aspects of indigenous culture. The great majority of self-identifying indigenous people live in rural areas, where they often constitute the majority. Indeed, probably over half of Ecuador's territory could be considered to be indigenous based on the heritage of the long-term occupants. These areas include much of the central highlands and the central and southern parts of the eastern lowlands. This has led to a growing level of involvement of indigenous organizations (at local, regional, and national scales) in the politics of land and territory.

Ecuador's economy is relatively diverse, with exports divided between oil, shrimp, and agricultural products (especially bananas and cacao). Oil has provided the stimulus for recent growth, while agricultural products will likely be the long-term mainstay. Since 1979 the country has chosen its president via quite honest national elections, with numerous political parties. In actual practice, however, the country's governance has been determined by shifting coalitions between powerful interest groups, including the military, the Catholic Church, landed and entrepreneurial elites, populist coastal political machines, and (very recently) indigenous organizations. The state remains weak, and the linkage between government policy and events on the ground is often tenuous.

There is a long history of environmental change in Ecuador. Ecuador was the site of some of the earliest agricultural villages in the Americas, and much of the area was deforested by indigenous farmers beginning in the lowlands and extending into the highlands by 1500 BCE. Large areas were converted to agriculture using raised fields, irrigation, and shifting cultivation, while deliberately set fires maintained and expanded grasslands at high elevations. Massive eruptions such as that of Quilotoa in the thirteenth century devastated wide areas due to ash falls, lahar flows, and lava flows, and the threat of volcanic activity remains severe. Early Spanish observers reported that although much of the forest had been cleared, many isolated patches of woodland remained. Hunting was often controlled and regulated by chiefs. The Spanish conquest and subsequent depopulation allowed some forests to come back, but since 1800 population growth and the development of export crops created a new wave of deforestation and drainage of wetlands, with adverse impacts on avifauna and mammals.

Paintings and photographs from the nineteenth century show that the highlands had been almost completely deforested; most land was in the hands of hacienda owners for grain production and cattle and sheep grazing. Old World grasses such as kikuyu replaced native grasses. Much of the highland soils show signs of erosion, in some cases soils have eroded down to underlying hardpan (*cangagua*). Efforts at reforestation with eucalyptus and Monterey pine have helped stabilize watersheds, but these non-native species do not enhance biodiversity. On the coast, production for export of cacao and (later) banana and oil palms, coupled with the expansion of small and medium sized farms in frontier areas, led to almost complete deforestation by the end of the twentieth century. Only isolated tracts of mature forest remain on the coast, coupled with scattered areas of secondary vegetation.

Quilatoa Lagoon, a major environmental attraction, in the mountains south of Quito, Ecuador. COURTESY NICOLE LALIBERTE.

Export-oriented shrimp farming has resulted in massive destruction of mangrove ecosystems, some of it illegal. In the Amazonian lowlands, construction of roads to petroleum-producing areas in the northeast also led to colonization and deforestation. Oil spills from wells and pipelines have contaminated rivers. Since 1990, changes in environmental regulations and empowerment of local peoples have helped reduce adverse impacts.

Ecuador was the site of many early developments in geography and environmental studies. Spanish observers of the environment were remarkably sophisticated as reflected in their geographic reports of the sixteenth century. The French geodetic expedition of the 1700s produced excellent reports, and their work inspired Alexander von Humboldt to undertake his trip to the Americas, where his study of the Chimborazo volcano was particularly important for his invention of the discipline of biogeography. Later Charles Darwin's visit to the Galápagos Islands helped stimulate his thinking about evolution. Although Darwin collected widely and used some island species as evidence, he was not able to use bird diversity to prove his theory. He had not been careful enough in identifying the geographical origin of specimens. It was left to a later scientist, David Lack, using better geographical data, to show that the Galápagos finches provide evidence for natural selection. As a result, the islands became a kind of shrine of natural selection, and were declared a national park relatively early, in the 1930s. The North American painter Frederic Edwin Church used Ecuador's volcano Cotopaxi as the focus of many of his landscape paintings in the 1850s and 1860s, creating an enduring (if misleading) image of Ecuador as a wilderness of pristine volcanoes, waterfalls, and forests.

Military dictators in the 1970s declared many more areas to be national parks, as shrines to nationalism and ways to enhance international public relations, including Cotopaxi National Park. As a result of these and subsequent endeavors, Ecuador has one of the largest national park systems in the world. The parks, however, are not always well patrolled and maintained, and significant ecosystems (especially on the coast) remain poorly protected. Furthermore, the national park and wilderness ideals are probably not best suited to preserving biodiversity in areas such as Ecuador where rural people utilize much land under traditional resource management systems.

The Nature Conservancy, the World Wildlife Fund, and numerous other international organizations have promoted environmental protection. Literally hundreds of local organizations have become involved with conservation, including urban think tanks such as Ecociencia and the Natura foundation, as well as indigenous organizations at local and national scales. In some cases, organizations have lacked willingness or skill in sharing power, resulting in some organizations acting to sabotage solutions brokered by others. Critical environmental problems include water pollution from urban sewers, landfills, and oil and mineral exploitation; deforestation from ongoing agricultural development on the coast and in parts of the Amazon basin; and destruction of mangroves and other wetlands. The Galápagos Islands have experienced pressure from tourism and fishing activities, as well as oil spills. In most of these cases, the government's response has been weak, and international environmental organizations have not always acted with understanding and sympathy for the needs of local people. The country's great remaining biodiversity, cultural diversity, ecotourism, and lively grassroots politics are, however, positive factors for the future.

Gregory Knapp

Further Reading

Anhalzer, J. (1987). *Ecuador: National parks of Ecuador.* Quito, Ecuador: Imprenta Mariscal.

Ashley, J. M. (1987). *The social and environmental effects of the palm-oil industry in the Oriente of Ecuador* (Research paper series no. 19). Albuquerque: Latin American Institute, University of New Mexico.

Kimerling, J., et al. (1991). *Amazon crude.* New York: Natural Resources Defense Council.

Knapp, G. (1991). *Andean ecology: Adaptive dynamics in Ecuador.* Boulder, CO: Westview Press.

Larson, E. J. (2001). *Evolution's workshop: God and science on the Galapagos Islands.* New York: Basic Books.

Manthorne, K. (1985). *Creation & renewal: Views of Cotopaxi by Frederic Edwin Church.* Washington, DC: Published for the National Museum of American Art by the Smithsonian Institution Press.

Pearson, D. L., & Middleton, D. W. (1999). *The new key to Ecuador and the Galápagos* (3rd ed). Berkeley, CA: Ulysses Press.

Southgate, D. D., & Whitaker, M. (1994). *Economic progress and the environment: One developing country's policy crisis.* New York: Oxford University Press.

Eden

The biblical story of the Garden of Eden is a formative narrative of Western culture, influencing the colonization and settlement of the New World. The Eden story of creation, temptation, and expulsion, told in Genesis 2 and 3, derives from writers in Judah in the ninth century BCE who recorded oral traditions embodied in songs and folk stories. The writers produced a version of the Pentateuch (the first five books of the Old Testament) known as the "J source," *The Book of J*, or the Yahwist version (Yahweh is the Hebrew deity). In addition to the Eden story, these records include accounts of Abraham, Jacob, Joseph, and Moses; the escape of the Israelites from Egypt and their settlement in the promised land of Canaan.

In the Eden story told in Genesis 2, God created "the man" Adam from the dust, the word *Adam* deriving from the Hebrew word *adama*, a feminine word meaning "Earth or arable land that gives rise to plants." God then created the Garden of Eden, watered by springs out of which four rivers flowed. After he created the Trees of Life and of the Knowledge of Good and Evil he put "the man" in the garden "to dress and keep it." He formed the birds and beasts from dust, presenting them to Adam for naming. Then he created "the woman" from Adam's rib. The story of a well-watered Garden of Eden in which animals, plants, man, and woman live together in peaceful abundance is a powerful cultural image.

According to biblical scholar Theodore Hiebert in *The Yawist's Landscape* (1996), the Edenic landscape was spring fed, river based, and irrigated, typical of the river valley civilizations of Mesopotamia and Egypt in which rivers overflowed onto the land and water was channeled into ditches running to fields. The post-Edenic landscape initiated by the temptation and expulsion, on the other hand, was rain based. That landscape has been described by biblical scholar Evan Eisenberg in *The Ecology of Eden* (1998). By 1100 BCE the Israelites were farming the hills of Judea and Samaria in Canaan with ox-drawn plows and planting wheat, barley, and legumes such as peas and lentils. They pastured sheep, goats, and cattle and grew grapes in vineyards, olives on hillside groves, and figs, apricots, almonds, and pomegranates in orchards. They captured water in cisterns and terraced the land to retain the rich, but shallow, red soil for planting, using the drier areas for pasturage. The arid hill country in which ara-

Genesis 2

1 Thus the heavens and the earth were finished, and all the host of them.

2 And on the seventh day God ended his work which he had made; and he rested on the seventh day from all his work which he had made.

3 And God blessed the seventh day, and sanctified it: because that in it he had rested from all his work which God created and made.

4 These are the generations of the heavens and of the earth when they were created, in the day that the LORD God made the earth and the heavens,

5 And every plant of the field before it was in the earth, and every herb of the field before it grew: for the LORD God had not caused it to rain upon the earth, and there was not a man to till the ground.

6 But there went up a mist from the earth, and watered the whole face of the ground.

7 And the LORD God formed man of the dust of the ground, and breathed into his nostrils the breath of life; and man became a living soul.

8 And the LORD God planted a garden eastward in Eden; and there he put the man whom he had formed.

9 And out of the ground made the LORD God to grow every tree that is pleasant to the sight, and good for food; the tree of life also in the midst of the garden, and the tree of knowledge of good and evil.

10 And a river went out of Eden to water the garden; and from thence it was parted, and became into four heads.

11 The name of the first is Pison: that is it which compasseth the whole land of Havilah, where there is gold;

12 And the gold of that land is good: there is bdellium and the onyx stone.

13 And the name of the second river is Gihon: the same is it that compasseth the whole land of Ethiopia.

14 And the name of the third river is Hiddekel: that is it which goeth toward the east of Assyria. And the fourth river is Euphrates.

15 And the LORD God took the man, and put him into the garden of Eden to dress it and to keep it.

16 And the LORD God commanded the man, saying, Of every tree of the garden thou mayest freely eat:

17 But of the tree of the knowledge of good and evil, thou shalt not eat of it: for in the day that thou eatest thereof thou shalt surely die.

18 And the LORD God said, It is not good that the man should be alone; I will make him an help meet for him.

19 And out of the ground the LORD God formed every beast of the field, and every fowl of the air; and brought them unto Adam to see what he would call them: and whatsoever Adam called every living creature, that was the name thereof.

20 And Adam gave names to all cattle, and to the fowl of the air, and to every beast of the field; but for Adam there was not found an help meet for him.

Continues

Continued

21 And the LORD God caused a deep sleep to fall upon Adam and he slept: and he took one of his ribs, and closed up the flesh instead thereof;

22 And the rib, which the LORD God had taken from man, made he a woman, and brought her unto the man.

23 And Adam said, This is now bone of my bones, and flesh of my flesh: she shall be called Woman, because she was taken out of Man.

24 Therefore shall a man leave his father and his mother, and shall cleave unto his wife: and they shall be one flesh.

25 And they were both naked, the man and his wife, and were not ashamed.

ble land and pasturage lands mingled was the landscape inhabited by the descendants of Adam and Eve.

The word *Eden* is often equated with the word *paradise*, defined as "heaven, a state of bliss, or an enclosed garden." Derived from a Sumerian word, the word *paradise* meant a fertile place that had become dry and barren. The Persian word for "park" or "enclosure" evolved through Greek and Latin to take on the meaning of "garden," so that by the medieval period, Eden was depicted as an enclosed garden. Ideas of paradise as a place of peace, harmony, and material abundance are prevalent in many cultures throughout the world. In Western culture the religious path to a heavenly paradise, as envisioned throughout the early Christian and medieval periods, was based on the promise of salvation to atone for the original sin of tasting the forbidden fruit. Writers and artists portrayed the loss of Eden and the hope of human salvation in powerful imagery.

The Search for Paradise

Italian poet Dante's *Divine Comedy* (1300) illustrates the outcome of the search for paradise as a heavenly Garden of Eden. Dante and his guide, the pagan Roman philosopher Virgil, journey downward through limbo and Hell to the center of the Earth. Then they progress upward to the earthly Paradise on the mountain of Purgatory, where Virgil leaves Dante, and the Christian guide Beatrice takes over. Together Dante and Beatrice ascend through the highest levels of the celestial spheres to the Empyrean sphere of the heavenly Paradise, where Dante first focuses on the Virgin Mary,

gaining the strength to see the garden flowering in Christ. Adam, who has paid the penalty for his sin, has been redeemed and is now in Paradise. In the late fourteenth century Ludolphus of Saxony (d. 1378) wrote *Speculum humanae salvationis (The Mirror of Man's Salvation)*, popularizing the biblical narrative and making Eve responsible for the loss of Eden.

During the Renaissance, artists illustrated the Creation story, the temptation of Eve, and the loss of the Garden of Eden in woodcuts and paintings. Among the most famous is Italian artist Michelangelo's *Creation of Adam*, in which God transmits the spark of life to Adam's outstretched hand. Less known is his *Creation of Eve*, in which God draws Eve out of a sleeping Adam's rib. German painter Albrecht Dürer's *The Fall of Man* (1504) depicts Adam and Eve in a dark forest surrounded by animals as the snake offers the apple to Eve. German painter Lucas Cranach's 1526 painting shows Eve extending the apple to Adam, after having been enticed by the snake coiled around the Tree of the Knowledge of Good and Evil. In *Garden of Eden* by Flemish painter Jan Brueghel the elder (1568–1625), animals and all of nature live in harmony, depicting the possibility of a peace kingdom.

Explorers also searched the world for the Garden of Eden. On his third voyage in 1498, Christopher Columbus believed he had discovered the Garden of Eden on the mainland of South America. He associated the rivers he found there with the four rivers flowing out of Eden. Other explorers corroborated this Edenic description of the new lands of the Americas. In 1518 explorer Alonxo da Zuarza described the Caribbean island of Hispaniola as an enchanted island filled with the fruits of nature. The flowers of South America reminded Italian navigator Amerigo Vespucci of Eden, whereas explorer Simao di Vasconcelos located the earthly paradise in Brazil. Explorations into the Pacific region led to reports of the discovery of tropical island Edens and of peoples living within the peaceful abundance of nature.

Some writers and artists placed Eden in the Old World. English navigator Sir Walter Raleigh, in his 1614 *History of the World*, located Eden in Mesopotamia across the Arabian Desert. The book depicted paradise and the four rivers flowing from it—the Tigris, Euphrates, Gihon, and Pison—and included an image of the Tree of the Knowledge of Good and Evil with Adam and Eve below the tree. French scholar P.D. Huet's *De la situation du paradis terrestre* (On the location of the terrestrial paradise) (1691) set the terrestrial paradise in Mesopotamia near the Persian Gulf, and in 1719 commentator Solomon van Til illustrated Eden as a plantation of regularly planted trees located in Mesopotamia.

Modern Edens

Early modern scientists attempted to re-create the Garden of Eden in the form of botanical gardens and zoos by reassembling the parts of the garden thought to be dispersed over the entire Earth after the fall from Eden and the flood of Noah. Expanding beyond the medieval cloistered, enclosed garden, modern formal gardens were designed, planned, and superimposed on a vast landscape as Edenic spaces. The gardens at Padua, Italy (1545); Leiden, Netherlands (1587); Oxford (1621); and Paris (1626) were laid out in squares with numbered beds and central fountains, featuring plants collected from the four quarters of the globe—Asia, Africa, Europe, and America.

Colonization of the New World also drew on Edenic imagery. Many early explorers and settlers saw the New World as an Eden overflowing with bounty. Explorer Arthur Barlowe in 1584 reported that off the coast of the future state of North Carolina his expedition had encountered "so sweet and so strong a smel, as if we had bene in the midst of some delicate garden." He described the soil on Roanoke Island as "the most plentifull, sweete, fruitful and wholesome of all the world". The following year English colonist Ralph Lane wrote an account of a land that abounded in "sweete trees," "pleasant gummes," and "grapes of such greatness" as not found in all of Europe. (Barlowe and Lane quoted in Lefler and Newsome 1954, 4–5.)

To other settlers the New World had the potential to become a new paradise, but it required improvement. A land of enormous natural advantages, it would nevertheless require European refinement before it could be deemed civilized. In his 1632 *New English Canaan*, American colonist Thomas Morton described the New England environment as a paradise containing groves of trees, crystal fountains, and clear streams, filled with vast numbers of fish and fowl, awaiting European development. During the ensuing years settlers transformed the Edenic eastern landscape into farms and extracted natural resources from the land.

The goal of reclaiming the American West as an Edenic landscape differed from that goal in the eastern states, where forests could be cleared for farms and gardens. West of the one-hundredth meridian, running roughly from eastern North Dakota through the southern tip of Texas, rainfall became unreliable, in most years falling below the 51 centimeters per year it took for successful farming. On the Great Plains, the Great Basin, the Southwest, and California's Central Valley and southern deserts, rainfall had to be supplemented by irrigation.

When settlers, such as the Mormons, arrived in their promised land of Utah, they brought with them a religious mandate to make the desert bloom and to re-create the Garden of Eden on Earth. Irrigated Edens were established in Idaho and Washington, and desert transformed into Edenic gardens epitomized California's development. By the late nineteenth century water had replaced gold as California's premier resource. Access to vast resources of "white gold" water was the quintessential condition for reclaiming desert lands for the "green gold" produced by agriculture. Settlers in the San Joaquin Valley converted the desert into gardens and transformed southern California's San Fernando Valley into orchards. Irrigation demanded new technologies of damming rivers and digging canals to channel water to fields and pastures as well as new laws and regulations to distribute that water in times of drought. Throughout the West, communities tapped into streams and channeled water in ditches to gardens and fields.

The image of Eden on Earth remained powerful throughout the twentieth century as wilderness areas were set aside to preserve pristine environments, suburbs were created as idyllic communities, and shopping malls became enclosed protected spaces for fulfilling the dream of material abundance.

Carolyn Merchant

Further Reading

Eisenberg, E. (1998). *The ecology of Eden*. New York: Alfred Knopf.

Fiege, M. (1999). *Irrigated Eden: The making of an agricultural landscape in the American West*. Seattle: University of Washington Press.

Grove, R. (1995). *Green imperialism: Colonial expansion, tropical island Edens, and the origins of environmentalism, 1600–1860*. New York: Cambridge University Press.

Heinberg, R. (1995). *Memories and visions of paradise: Exploring the universal myth of a lost golden age* (Rev. ed.). Wheaton, IL: Quest Books.

Hiebert, T. (1996). *The Yahwist's landscape: Nature and religion in early Israel*. New York: Oxford University Press.

Lefler, H. T. & Newsome, A. R. (1954). *North Carolina: the history of a southern state*. Chapel Hill: University of North Carolina Press.

Merchant, C. (2003). *Reinventing Eden: The fate of nature in Western culture*. New York: Routledge.

Prest, J. (1981). *The Garden of Eden: The botanic garden and the re-creation of paradise*. New Haven, CT: Yale University Press.

Edison, Thomas Alva

(1847–1931)
U.S. inventor

Perhaps the most prolific inventor of modern times, Thomas Alva Edison left his mark on almost every aspect of life in the industrialized world. Best known as the inventor of the incandescent lightbulb, Edison was instrumental in starting the electrical power distribution system that reaches nearly every American home today. Beyond his electrical inventions and others of a chemical or mechanical nature, Edison was one of the inventors of the system of industrial research, which insures the continuing flow of new consumer products that characterizes a consumer economy. Edison's many inventions greatly increased the amount of leisure time available to American families and their consumption of energy resources in both work and leisure. His inventions, plus the appearance of motorcar, greatly increased the amount of energy demanded each year, leading to an expanded dependence on fossil fuels with the concomitant problems of air and water pollution.

Edison was born in Milan, Ohio, but moved in 1854 with his family to Port Huron, Michigan. Somewhat hard of hearing even as a child, Edison found schooling difficult and began work at the age of twelve, selling newspapers, snack items, and magazines on the Grand Trunk Railroad, which ran daily between Port Huron and Detroit. Slack periods on the train and in Detroit allowed him time for reading and access to chemical and electrical supplies. By 1863 he mastered the operation of the newly invented telegraph. In 1867 he obtained a job as telegrapher at the Western Union office in Boston, continuing his self-education there. A year later he had acquired sufficient financial backing to devote full time to inventing. Within a year, he had applied for his first patent, for a system of recording votes that he tried to market, unsuccessfully, to the United States Congress.

Edison established a laboratory in at Menlo Park, New Jersey, in 1876. There he began his efforts to produce a long-lasting electric light. Edison was but one of the inventors to develop a form of electric light, but he has generally been credited with the invention because his light proved particularly durable and because he was able to manufacture quickly, in quantity, and while implementing a compatible electrical distribution system. Following a test of the illumination and power supply system, Edison undertook the illumination of the financial district in lower Manhattan from the Pearl Street station completed in 1882.

Once it became clear that an electrical distribution network was inevitable, a decision had to be made between direct and alternating current systems. Edison was distrustful of alternating current and strongly advocated the conceptually simpler direct current system. The alternating current system, championed by George Westinghouse (1846–1914), triumphed following Westinghouse's acquisition in 1885 of patent rights to the transformer, which made it possible to transmit power at high voltages with minimum power loss. Had Edison's systems been chosen instead, a generating station would have been required within a mile or two of every customer of electrical power.

In 1887 Edison built a new and larger laboratory at West Orange, New Jersey. Edison continued inventing for the rest of his life, later turning most of the business aspects of his operations over to his grown children. Over his lifetime Edison acquired more than a thousand U.S. patents, a record for any individual. Other of Edison's inventions include the phonograph, the motion picture camera, and an alkaline storage battery with which Edison hoped initially to power electric automobiles and that later powered the starter motors in the gasoline-powered automobiles of his friend, Henry Ford. Acting at the suggestion of President Herbert Hoover, numerous American households turned off their lights for a few moments at 10:00 P.M. on the day of Edison's funeral.

Donald R. Franceschetti

Further Reading

Friedel, R., & Israel, P. (1986). *Edison's electric light: Biography of an invention.* New Brunswick, NJ: Rutgers University Press.

Josephson, M. (1959). *Edison: A biography.* New York: McGraw-Hill.

Vanderbilt, B. M. (1971). *Thomas Edison, chemist.* Washington, DC: American Chemical Society.

Education *See* Environmental Education

Egypt, Ancient

Ancient Egypt illustrates several themes important to environmental history for several reasons. It was one of the earliest major civilizations, with a unified government and written records dating from about 3200 BCE, providing information on the interaction of a complex human society with the natural environment from the beginnings of civilization. The ancient Egyptians, with few exceptions, were in charge of their lands and able to set their policies in regard to the environment for more than two thousand years. No other ancient civilization lasted so long while maintaining a relatively stable pattern in its economy, government, religion, and ecological viewpoints and techniques. Also, the environment of Egypt provided a relatively stable framework for agriculture and other means of subsistence, and within that framework the Egyptians made major ecological changes.

Environment of Egypt

Located within the dry desert belt of North Africa, Egypt is watered by and ecologically defined by the Nile River. As the Greek historian Herodotus correctly wrote, "Egypt is the gift of the Nile" (*Histories* 2.5). Flowing northward more than 6,400 kilometers from its distant sources in East Africa, the Nile is the longest river in the world, although not one of the largest in volume of flow. The Nile was a relatively dependable river, flooding its banks at the same time every year (from early August to early October), bringing moisture and new soil to the fields, and then subsiding just as regularly. The sustainability of Egyptian agriculture was supported by this annual flood and the deposition of fertile alluvial soil containing mineral material and organic debris brought down from the mountains and swamps of lands farther south. Crops could be planted only in the land moistened by the Nile, called the "Black Land" (*Kemet*) by the Egyptians. This productive land lay in long, narrow strips along each side of the river in Upper Egypt, the southern part of the country, but in the north the river became shallow, spreading out in branches to feed the fertile low-lying delta of Lower Egypt before spilling into the Mediterranean Sea. Therefore, the people could depend on adequate harvests in most years. Even though there was little rain, the climate was warm and stable without freezing or wintry storms. In the spring, however, dusty windstorms could howl out of the Sahara Desert.

The Nile was not totally predictable. Disasters occurred in years when a high flood washed away irrigation works and villages or when a low Nile failed to water the Black Land adequately. Works of art such as the causeway of the pharaoh Unas at Sakkara show people starving, with their ribs prominently visible. Rebels or invaders sometimes took advantage of weakness produced by flood and famine. As a result, Egyptian history is punctuated by difficult times such as the Intermediate Periods, when the central government headed by the pharaoh collapsed. But traditional patterns of culture, including environmental relationships, reasserted themselves after these intervals with admirable tenacity. The Nile dwindled in some years but never disappeared, and "fat years" eventually followed the "lean years."

Thus the natural ebb and flow of the Nile made a kind of environmental insurance available to the Egyptians. But the river by itself could not guarantee sustainability; for that the perceptive efforts of the Egyptian people were necessary. Many historians speak of

Selection from *Adoration of the Nile*, an Ancient Egyptian Prayer

Praise to you, O Nile, that issues from the Earth, and comes to nourish Egypt . . .

That waters the meadows, he whom Re has created to nourish all cattle. That gives drink to the desert places . . .

Beloved of Geb (the Earth-god), director of the grain-god . . .

That makes barley and creates wheat, so that he may cause the temples to keep festivals.

If his flood is low, breath fails, and all people are impoverished; the offerings to the gods are diminished, and millions of people perish.

The whole land is in terror and great and small lament . . .

When he rises, the land is in exultation and everybody is in joy.

All mouths begin to laugh and every tooth is revealed.

It is he that brings victuals and is rich in food, that creates all that is good . . .

He gives herbage for the cattle that are sacrificed to every god . . .

He fills the storehouses, and makes wide the granaries; he gives things to the poor.

He makes trees to grow . . . and people have no lack of them . . .

Your young people and your children shout for joy over you, and the people hail you as king.

Your laws are unchanging . . .

People drink your water.

You come in flood, giving water to the fields to drink and making the people strong.

Musicians play to you on the harp, and singers sing to you, keeping time with their hands . . .

When you flood, O Nile, offerings are made to you, cattle are slaughtered for you, a great oblation is made for you.

Birds are fattened for you, antelopes are hunted for you in the desert . . .

Offering is made to every god, even as is done for the Nile, with incense, oxen, cattle, and birds upon the flame . . .

He makes green the two riverbanks.

You are verdant, O Nile, you are verdant.

He makes folk live on their cattle, and their cattle on the meadow.

You are verdant, you are verdant, O Nile, you are verdant.

Source: Erman, Adolf. (1971). *Life in Ancient Egypt* (Reprint ed.). New York: Dover. Modernized and abridged by J. Donald Hughes. (Originally published 1894)

the stability of the Egyptian culture through so many centuries in a derogatory tone, as if stability were merely stagnation. But in fact the Egyptians constantly changed the landscape of their country, and the results of those changes were at times positive, at other times negative.

Changes in the Egyptian Landscape

The changing landscape of Egypt is the result of at least two causes: climatic change and the efforts of human beings. Many centuries before the rise of Egyptian civilization, the Sahara was a humid land with rivers, lakes, and forests. The gradual desiccation of North Africa may have been one reason why people moved into the Nile Valley, where forests, marshes, and grasslands persisted, beginning processes leading to intensive agriculture and civilization. By the time of the Old Kingdom (2700–2200 BCE), the Sahara had dried to conditions like those existing today. Egyptian agriculture used crops such as wheat and barley for bread and beer, flax for linen textiles, and a number of garden plants to vary the table diet.

Land was cleared in order to plant these crops. Before clearing, the Nile Valley supported an evergreen forest of fig, jujube, and acacia. The floodplains had grassland, savanna with acacia and shrubs, and wetlands of papyrus, reeds, and sedge. Pollen analyses of ancient soil deposits in the delta show that there were reeds, bulrushes, papyrus, ferns, cattail, lotus, and tam-

A pyramid at Giza, Egypt in 2002. COURTESY NICOLE LALIBERTE.

arisk. Lagoons and swamps covered the northern delta. All this changed as cultivation was extended. Tomb paintings show trees being felled. Egypt had firewood and fine woods for carving and cabinet making but had few tall, straight trees and had to import timber from Phoenicia. Egyptian ships sailed there as early as the reign of the pharaoh Snefru (2650 BCE) to obtain cedar, juniper, fir, pine, and other timber for construction. During the Middle Kingdom, as excavation of tombs in Lebanon reveals, Egyptian influence was dominant on the Phoenician coast, following the timber trade. During the New Kingdom, Egypt conquered the same area. In Egypt itself, in addition to cutting trees, the grazing of domestic animals depleted the vegetation. Nothing deforests a dry land more thoroughly than the cutting of trees followed by the grazing of goats, which often destroy the shrubs and small trees before the forest can reestablish itself. Canals helped bring the floodwaters to the land but also drained the marshes. Papyrus, a swamp-loving plant that provided the raw material for the paper on which Egyptian literature was painted, could not survive when the marshes were transformed into fields. There was still papyrus in Egypt as late as Roman times, but it later disappeared and had to be replanted in modern times with rootstock from Uganda.

Irrigation was a major form of landscape change. Art shows it as an activity of the pharaoh, but, of course, the work was really done by peasants. Irrigation increased the cropland area beyond what had been earlier flooded by the Nile. Workmen dredged channels, dug ditches, built earthen dams, constructed dikes and basins, and lifted water. The floodwaters were directed into basins, where they soaked the soil and deposited silt and organic material.

Habitats of wild land animals, birds, and fish gradually shrank and then disappeared, perhaps so slowly that few people were aware of what was happening. Eventually, large animals almost disappeared from the Nile Valley, so that when the pharaoh wished to have ritual hunts, animals had to be imported from farther up the Nile where they survived. Animals were sacred to the Egyptians, but worship did not prevent animals from being hunted. Still less did worship save animals from the destruction of their habitats. In early times, according to the evidence of petroglyphs and works of art, Egypt had a variety of species such as that now found in Kenya. But many species disappeared, including elephants, rhinoceroses, giraffes, and gazelles. Barbary sheep, lions, and leopards were reduced in numbers. The ranges of antelope species shrank.

The numbers of birds, particularly waterfowl, were astounding in Egypt as late as the New Kingdom but gradually became less abundant. As paintings show, nobles hunted birds in marshes, but there were fewer marshes as drainage proceeded. Captured birds were prepared as temple offerings. The sacred ibis is scarcely seen in Egypt today, and of the fourteen species of duck in ancient Egyptian art, only one now breeds there. A similar fate awaited fishes, which were often caught and eaten.

Environmentally, Egypt at the end of the ancient period was much changed but still productive and full of life. The Nile still brought annual floods with enough water and sediment in most years to enable the Egyptians to plant and harvest crops sufficient to meet domestic needs and to be exported as well. This success is due to the foresight of the ancient Egyptians, which was at least in part a result of their reverence for the land and its life.

J. Donald Hughes

Further Reading

Baines, J., & Malek, J. (1980). *Atlas of ancient Egypt*. New York: Facts on File Publications.

Brewer, D. J., & Friedman, R. F. (1989). *Fish and fishing in ancient Egypt*. Warminster, UK: Aris & Phillips.

Erman, A. E. (1971). *Life in ancient Egypt*. New York: Dover Publications. (Original work published 1894).

Germond, P. (2001). *An Egyptian bestiary*. London: Thames and Hudson.

Houlihan, P. F. (1996). *The animal world of the pharaohs*. London: Thames and Hudson.

Hughes, J. D. (2001). The Nile Valley: Ancient Egypt and sustainability. In *An environmental history of the world:*

Humankind's changing role in the community of life (pp. 38–42). New York: Routledge.

Kees, H. (1961). *Ancient Egypt: A cultural topography*. Chicago: University of Chicago Press.

Manniche, L. (1989). *An ancient Egyptian herbal*. Austin: University of Texas Press.

Wilkinson, A. (1998). *The garden in ancient Egypt*. London: Rubicon Press.

El Niño and La Niña

El Niño has become a household phrase around the globe. But as late as 1969 the nature of El Niño as a natural phenomenon in the equatorial Pacific was of interest only to a relatively few researchers. In that year meteorologist Jakob Bjerknes, a professor at the University of California at Los Angeles, linked atmospheric and oceanic processes in the Pacific, making El Niño a Pacific phenomenon with implications for climate anomalies around the globe. The 1972–1973 El Niño attracted the attention of oceanographic and fishery scientists because of its implications in the collapse of the anchovy fishery off the coast of Peru. The 1982–1983 El Niño caught researchers by surprise. Not only was it unforeseen by prominent researchers, but also those researchers denied that it could occur because certain expected precursors to El Niño were not yet evident as late as October 1982. That event became known as the "El Niño of the century" because of its devastating and costly impacts around the globe: droughts, floods, fires, frosts, and famines. This event sparked sharp interest in the phenomenon and its impacts on societies and economies worldwide, such as droughts and famines in Ethiopia and Papua New Guinea and crop failures in Australia, Indonesia, and the Philippines.

A few weak El Niño events occurred during the next decade or so, until the onset of the 1997–1998 event. The societal impacts of that event have been estimated in the tens of billions of dollars. It also was labeled the "El Niño of the century," displacing the 1982–1983 event from that title. This El Niño generated considerable interest by governments in El Niño forecasts. El Niño is now known to spawn climate anomalies and can be viewed as the earliest warning of potential climate-related problems that a society might have to cope with.

Non-El Niño Conditions (Conditions Perceived to be Normal)

By the early 1970s the scientific community had come to realize that changes across the sea surface temperatures (SSTs) in the tropical Pacific Ocean affect atmospheric temperatures and processes around the globe. Those temperatures vary seasonally, annually, and even on decade-long time periods. Under conditions that many observers view as normal, the winds flowing from east to west (referred to as "easterlies" by meteorologists), in combination with the rotation of the Earth, help to push water from the eastern and central Pacific toward the western part of the Pacific Ocean basin. Under normal conditions, the sea level in the western part of the Pacific basin is higher by about 60 centimeters than it is along the western coast of South America. This is a result of the strong westward-blowing winds along the equator. When the winds push the surface water away from the coast of Peru and Ecuador, cold, nutrient-rich deep water wells up to the surface to replace the displaced surface water. The physical process by which water wells up to the surface is referred to as "coastal upwelling." Such upwelling systems are fertile habitats for living marine resources and ultimately for the fishing activities of birds and fishers. As a result of this strong, productive upwelling region, Peru has become one of the world's top fishing nations.

El Niño: What It Is

Today the phrase *El Niño* is used to describe both a localized warming of the coastal ocean off Peru and Ecuador and the much larger basinwide air-sea interactions that occur across the equatorial Pacific Ocean. It is also referred to as an "El Niño-Southern Oscillation" (ENSO) warm event. ENSO is the combination of the warm changes in the SSTs combined with the changes in sea level pressure (called the "Southern Oscillation") across the tropical Pacific in general and, more specifically, between Darwin (Australia) and Tahiti. When sea level pressure is high in Tahiti, it is usually low in Darwin, and vice versa. Australians have focused on using the Southern Oscillation Index as an early warning of drought, whereas Peruvians have tended to rely on changes in sea surface temperatures in the eastern equatorial Pacific.

Every few years (four and one-half years on average), the westward winds weaken and sometimes reverse, flowing eastward. As a result, the warm water that "piles up" in the western part of the basin begins to shift eastward toward the central and eastern Pacific. The sea level drops in the west and rises in the east. When an El Niño occurs, the SSTs in the western Pacific drop by a couple of degrees Celsius, and in the east they increase by 2–3° C and higher along the Peruvian and Ecuadorian coasts. In 1997–1998 the SSTs increased by 5–6° C.

Several hundred meters below the sea's surface, the thermocline, a sharp ocean temperature gradient that separates the body of warm surface waters from the deep cold water, also changes under El Niño conditions. As the westward-flowing winds slacken and the sea level begins to drop in the western Pacific, the thermocline moves upward toward the surface in the west while it deepens in the central and eastern Pacific.

El Niño events typically last twelve to eighteen months, evolving through onset, growth, maturation, and decay. There appear to be decadal shifts in the frequency of El Niño events. For example, cold events (that is, La Niña conditions or colder-than-average SSTs in the eastern Pacific, conditions viewed by some as normal) were more frequent from 1950 to 1975. El Niño events appeared to become more frequent during the 1976–2000 period. Whereas some scientists believe that this shift from cold to warm events is a response to global warming, others contend that there is a decadal-scale shift in frequency between these two extremes of ENSO.

El Niño: What It Does

El Niño conditions bring devastatingly heavy rains to Peru's normally arid coastal areas and droughts to Bolivia and southern Peru. They have been associated with severe drought in the semiarid Brazilian *Nordeste* (northeast) and flooding in the southern part of the country. El Niño has usually, but not always, been associated with droughts in Australia, Indonesia, Philippines, Papua New Guinea, southern and eastern Africa, and the Horn of Africa. Floods occur in Argentina, Paraguay, and Uruguay.

The 1997–1998 El Niño event was linked to major forest fires in Indonesia and resultant haze in southeastern Asia. Those fires encompassed 9 million hectares, and, although they were blamed on El Niño-related drought conditions, it was discovered that unscrupulous business people (and government ministers) paid people to set the fires, knowing that a forecast of El Niño would translate into "no rain" to extinguish the fires. They could then buy the burned forest

areas. The costs attributed to the climate and weather anomalies alleged to have been spawned by (or correlated with) this El Niño event were estimated at $32–96 billion.

A study was undertaken in 1999 by the United Nations Environment Programme, in collaboration with the U.S. National Center for Atmospheric Research, the World Meteorological Organization, the United Nations University, and the International Strategy for Disaster Reduction, to examine the societal impacts of El Niño in sixteen countries. Particular attention was given to how societies reacted to the El Niño-related events, especially the existing government infrastructure, management approaches, information flow, forecasting capabilities, early warning, and disaster preparedness. The study was completed in 2000. The sixteen reports were reviewed in a search for common lessons from which the countries in the study, as well as those not included, could benefit in attempts to respond to future forecasts of El Niño (and La Niña) and to prepare strategies and tactics for coping with El Niño (or La Niña) events of varying intensities.

What People Need to Know about El Niño

El Niño does not represent unusual behavior of the global climate system. El Niño events are a part of the natural climate system and not separate from it. El Niño is known to have occurred for thousands of years. It is a quasi-periodic phenomenon that results from the constant but changing interactions between the ocean and the atmosphere above it. It can have different levels of intensity: weak, moderate, strong, and extraordinary. It appears to be a new phenomenon, but that is because it was not recognized as a phenomenon that affects regional climate around the globe.

El Niño is part of a cycle. Before the late 1960s El Niño was viewed as a local phenomenon off the west coast of South America. In the late 1960s Bjerknes linked changes in sea surface temperatures and sea level pressure, making El Niño a Pacific basinwide phenomenon. In the early 1980s researchers coined the term *ENSO* (El Niño-Southern Oscillation) to represent the constantly varying combination of changes in sea surface temperatures (El Niño) and changes in sea level pressure (the Southern Oscillation as measured at two locations across the southern Pacific—Darwin and Tahiti). Thus El Niño is now viewed as the extreme warm phase of ENSO, and *La Niña* is the label given to the extreme cold phase of ENSO.

Every weather anomaly throughout the world that occurs during an El Niño year is not caused by that El Niño. Weather anomalies and their impacts on societies occur every year, not just during the extreme phases of ENSO. In many instances local and regional geophysical and climatic factors can overshadow the potential influences on local climate of an El Niño event in the distant tropical Pacific. Great care must be taken before blaming an adverse impact on a specific El Niño.

El Niño has a positive side as well. Traditionally, researchers have for the most part focused on the adverse impacts of El Niño. Several studies have attempted to identify the cost of an El Niño on a country or a socioeconomic sector of society (crops, fisheries, sales). However, they have failed to account for the positive aspects that might be associated with, for example, more rainfall in arid areas, the availability of different fish populations in coastal waters, and the absence of forest fires, hurricanes, or cold energy-consuming winters.

There will continue to be surprises associated with future El Niño events. Researchers have been focusing on El Niño as a basinwide phenomenon that can disrupt what is perceived to be normal or average global and regional climate conditions only for the past few decades. They have not yet witnessed all of the ways that an event might develop or the various ways that its impacts might spawn climate-related hazards around the globe. It is not unreasonable to expect that each El Niño will bring surprises about how, when, and where it developed or how intense it turned out to be.

The impact of global warming on El Niño is not as yet known. Despite the considerable speculation about how the characteristics of the ENSO cycle will be affected by global warming of the Earth's atmosphere, the scientific community remains uncertain about what to expect from a warming of the atmosphere by a few degrees Celsius.

Forecasting El Niño is different from forecasting the impacts of El Niño. Until the late 1990s research attention was primarily focused on forecasting the onset of an El Niño event. Since then, however, there has been increased interest in forecasting the impacts of El Niño on different regions around the globe, on different crops, and on a wide range of climate sensitive human activities. Each El Niño spawns its own set of climate-related hazards, with considerable overlap among them. But there are also considerable differences among these sets of hazards in terms of location and intensity.

Forecasting El Niño's onset does not tell experts much about its other characteristics (e.g., intensity, frequency, duration). Forecasting its onset does not provide much usable information about its magnitude, duration, or impacts. Several examples now suggest that experts do not know enough about the behavior of the air-sea interactions during and surrounding El Niño events to state far in advance with any degree of confidence how the event will evolve.

Monitoring El Niño is different from forecasting it. Great strides in the monitoring of air-sea interactions have been taken in the tropical Pacific since the mid-1980s. People interested in ENSO can use the Internet to monitor daily, if not hourly, the changes in the sea surface conditions in this region. Monitoring El Niño instantaneously, however, is not the same as forecasting its development. Although monitoring El Niño has progressed sharply, success at forecasting its onset has been considerably slower. There are examples of attempts, showing little success to date, to forecast El Niño's development on a weekly basis based on data derived from monitoring it. In some instances El Niño conditions began to develop only to collapse a short time later.

In sum, for some countries the association of climate-related anomalies with El Niño events is strong and is, therefore, reliable enough for use in decision making. Forecasts about the potential societal impacts of El Niño are needed as urgently, if not more urgently, than forecasts about El Niño's onset. Armed with information about the possible impacts of an El Niño, a society can put in place coping mechanisms to soften, if not avoid, those expected impacts. El Niño-related forecasts should be of interest to **all** government ministries and not just those that are primarily concerned with disaster. Institutions must review their operations during the 1997–1998 El Niño event and identify strengths, weaknesses, jurisdictional constraints, and conflicts in institutional responses to the forecasts and impacts of El Niño. "Looking back to look ahead" can provide disaster and other agencies with an opportunity to review how well their contingency plans worked in 1997–1998 and, if necessary, make adjustments.

Michael H. Glantz

Further Reading

Canby, T. Y. (1984). El Nino's ill wind. *National Geographic*, *165*(2), 144–183.

Caviedes, C. N. (2001). *El Nino in history: Storming through the ages.* Gainesville, FL: University Press of Florida.

Davis, M. (2001). *Late Victorian holocausts: El Nino famines and the making of the Third World.* London: Verso Books.

Glantz, M. H. (2001). *Currents of change: Impacts of El Nino and La Nina on climate and society.* Cambridge, UK: Cambridge University Press.

Glantz, M. H. (Ed.). (2002). *La Nina and its impacts: Facts and speculation.* Tokyo: UN University Press.

Suplee, C. (1999). *El Nino/La Nina: Nature's vicious cycle.* Retrieved January 24, 2003, from http://www.nationalgeographic.com/elnino/mainpage.html

Elephants

The modern-day elephant belongs to the order Proboscidea, which once contained more than 350 species. All became extinct except for the Asian elephant *(Elephas maximus)* and the African elephant *(Loxodonta africana)*, although poachers, the international ivory trade, and loss of habitat threaten their continued existence.

Elephants are the largest land animals. Bulls (males) can reach a height of 2.7 to 3.9 meters and weigh between 2.7 and 5.4 metric tons, with cows (females) slightly smaller in size. They have many distinguishing characteristics: massive ears, which can measure almost 1.8 meters high and 1.2 meters wide; immense tusks, which are actually long upper incisors; and a trunk, which is an elongated nose used for breathing, trumpeting, smelling, drinking, eating, fighting, and communicating. Their wrinkled skin ranges from light gray to dark grayish brown. Their habitat varies from rain forests to semideserts, but most elephants live in the savanna. They are strictly vegetarian and feed on leaves, buds, branches, and other vegetation, using their trunks to dig up roots. They typically live up to seventy years and can have offspring until they are fifty. They are group oriented, living in bands of six to twenty. Elephant families are led by a matriarch, which rules over her female offspring and their young. Various "bond groups" move and feed together. Males, when they reach puberty at thirteen to fourteen years, eventually leave the family and join other bulls. There are still many unanswered questions about elephants, including the extent of their intelligence, relationship dynamics, and ecological behavior.

Most Asian elephants live in India, Cambodia, Laos, Vietnam, Thailand, and Indonesia. The African elephant, which is slightly bigger than its Asian relation, lives in the African savanna and forests, although it has completely disappeared from northern Africa and is endangered throughout the rest of the continent. Although they share many characteristics, the two elephants are genetically distinct—the Asian elephant is more closely related to the extinct mammoth than to the African elephant.

Elephants occupy a vital role in their ecosystems. Although they are often seen as "living bulldozers" that trample everything in their path, elephants return almost 80 percent of what they consume to the soil as fertile manure. They modify their habitat by converting savanna and woodlands to grasslands, and their paths act as firebreaks and rainwater channels.

As with other endangered species, management questions surround the fate of the elephant, whose numbers have dropped sharply in the last century. Poachers sell their meat, hides, and valuable ivory tusks. Similarly, their habitat is disappearing as forests are harvested for commercial purposes. Between 1979 and 1989, more than 700,000 elephants were slaughtered, reducing the worldwide population by half. Africa's savanna elephants are disappearing the fastest. Kenya alone lost 85 percent of its elephant population between 1973 and 1989.

International conservation groups are working to reverse this trend. CITES (the 1990 Convention on International Trade in Endangered Species) approved a worldwide ivory trade ban in 1989. Although the ivory market collapsed, limited "experimental" trades are still being conducted by Japan (the world's largest

A guide steers an elephant up to a loading platform in Thailand. COURTESY MARY CORINNE LOWENSTEIN.

ivory market), Zimbabwe, Namibia, and Botswana. Ecotourism in Africa and national parks in Asia have made elephants an important part of the local economies. The World Wildlife Federation, whose conservation program helps preserve biological and ecological diversity, has designated the Asian elephant as a "flagship" species over large areas.

Jessica B. Teisch

Further Reading

Alexander, S. (2000). *The astonishing elephant.* New York: Random House.

Hall, T. (2000). *To the elephant graveyard.* New York: Atlantic Monthly Press.

Harland, D. J. (1994). *Killing game: International law and the African elephant.* Westport, CT: Praeger.

Moss, C. (1988). *Elephant memories: Thirteen years in the life of an elephant family.* New York: W. Morrow.

Norton, B. (1991). *The African elephant: Last days of Eden.* Stillwater, MN: Voyager Press.

Spinage, C. A. (1994). *Elephants.* London: T & A. D. Poyser.

Sukumar, R. (1989). *The Asian elephant: Ecology and management.* New York: Cambridge University Press.

Endangered Species

Human manipulation and destruction of species and ecosystems have greatly accelerated the rate of extinction of animals and have made it necessary for people to identify and protect those species that are near extinction. A species is considered endangered scientifically and usually legally when it is in danger of extinction throughout all or most of its range. Although the term *endangered* had been used for decades, only in 1971 did the World Conservation Union (IUCN) develop a definition of *endangered* that is solely based in biology. That definition says a species is endangered when it is consistently being removed from the environment faster than it can reproduce itself.

A species labeled "threatened" is likely to become endangered in the near future. A species that is labeled "rare" naturally has restricted ranges and low population sizes. Rare species are not necessarily endangered or threatened, but because they are often restricted to one or a few locations, they are more susceptible to human perturbation and are often at risk of endangerment. The category "vulnerable" (also called "at risk"

or "of special concern") was added as people started to monitor population declines in species that appeared to be particularly sensitive to human activity. It is important to remember that organizations such as IUCN and legal documents such as the U.S. Endangered Species Act (ESA) have specific definitions and alternative categories. For example, the categories "threatened" as used by the ESA and "vulnerable" as used by the IUCN are equivalent because both mean "may become endangered."

Habitat loss and fragmentation are the most important causes of species endangerment and extinction. Habitat loss is cited as the reason for listing 85 percent of the IUCN endangered or vulnerable species. Natural ecosystems are destroyed for agriculture, industry, or human habitation. Roads further fragment remaining natural habitats and prevent movement of species. Chemical pollution from industry and agriculture enters ecosystems and eventually food webs or causes climate change that alters ecosystems on a global scale.

Introduced species (species moved into new areas by humans) reduce and fragment the populations of native species through competition and predation. Invasive species are the second-most important cause of species extinctions. In many cases introduced species are free of the diseases and predators that limit native populations, so introduced populations grow quickly, displacing or depleting native populations. For example, the introduction of two invasive predators, the Red Fox (*Vulpes vulpes*) and the Domestic Cat (*Felis sylvestris*), into Australia in the 1800s brought the mala (*Lagorchestes hirsutus*), the smallest of the wallabies, to the brink of extinction by 1950.

Species are typically placed at risk because they are of value as a resource or because they are in the way. Hunting for food and collecting wild species for pets, gardens, or museums are probably the causes of endangerment obvious to most people. Humans also commonly persecute species they perceive as threats, such as predators like wolves or eagles. This persecution is different from hunting because the species are not used as a resource but rather are killed or are purposely prevented from feeding or reproducing. The most famous example, perhaps, is the U.S. bison, which decreased from an estimated population of 60 million in 1850 to a population of only 150 in 1890 because of a combination of hunting and habitat loss to ranchers and farmers.

An increasing number of studies suggest that other types of unintentional disturbance, such as sounds from music devices, hikers, and motor vehicles, can also interfere with reproduction and cause population failures. Perhaps the best-known example of this type of unintentional disturbance is light pollution, which causes decreased nesting success and hatchling survival of endangered sea turtles. Adult and newly hatched turtles find their way to the ocean by the moonlight reflecting off the water. Artificial lights inland disorient the turtles and result in higher mortality.

Bycatch is another threat. Bycatch occurs when nontarget species happen into nets or traps meant to capture other species, and results in significant reductions in populations of certain fish and marine mammals. Sea turtles and dolphins are the most familiar victims of bycatch, but scientists are recognizing that this type of mortality can affect fish species as well. About one-quarter of the world's catch of seafood is destroyed as bycatch.

Poaching

Poaching is the theft of legally protected plants or animals. Poaching was created by a class system in which a few wealthy, often nonresident, individuals controlled vast tracts of natural areas, whereas the majority of residents were poor and had access to few sources of good-quality protein. Poaching became at once a source of nutrition and a source of income. In 1080 the Norman Forest Laws were enacted in England that made all poaching a punishable offense. Penalties were sometimes severe, but in 1217 laws that reduced the severity of poaching penalties were enacted.

In the fourteenth and fifteenth centuries a series of game laws were passed to limit local people's access to forests for hunting and grazing, but a growing gentried class was demanding the royal privilege to hunt. By the 1600s hunting licenses were granted under strict policy as political favors to certain members of the aristocracy. Not until the nineteenth century were laws such as the Game Reform Bill in England (1831) passed to allow the sale of wild game and hunting licenses to all people.

Although the locations changed from Europe in the Middle Ages to Africa and South America in the nineteenth and early twentieth centuries, the situations were somewhat similar. For example, prior to European occupation some African tribes were careful managers of wild game and limited killing of female elephants or the numbers of animals that could be taken in a particular area. After Europeans colonized Zimbabwe and other African countries, the local popula-

tions were forced off the best lands, hunting became illegal, and poaching became a more serious problem.

However, poaching continued to increase even after laws made hunting more equitable. Starting in the nineteenth century an increasing population of wealthy and middle-class people demanded exotic goods, including wild game. By the twentieth century the demand for poached goods expanded to the exotic fur and feather industry, ivory goods, alternative medicines, and the pet and early zoo and museum trade. Poaching has become a way of life in some poor countries where unemployment is high. Hunting illegal bushmeat (wild game) can earn an individual three to ten times the average income in some African countries.

Although international efforts to curb the trade in protected species, such as the Convention on International Trade in Endangered Species of Wild Fauna and Flora (CITES), have been important in slowing poaching, poaching is still a serious threat to some of the most endangered species. Demand is high for certain items, such as rhinoceros horns, which are valued for medicine and for dagger handles. Horns can be sold for between $750 and $1,500 per kilogram, depending on quality, and because only a few thousand rhinoceros are still living, prices are unlikely to decline unless changes are made in demand.

History of Endangered Species

Humans' earliest impacts on animal and plant species were probably due to hunting and collecting. Evidence from prehistoric shell middens (refuse piles) indicates that certain species of shellfish declined because of over harvesting. Experts have hypothesized that human hunters caused at least some of the many extinctions of large mammals that occurred in North America ten thousand to twelve thousand years ago at the end of the Pleistocene epoch U.S. ecologist Paul Martin and others developed the "overkill" model, which predicts that even moderately sized populations of hunters could have caused rapid declines and extinctions of many large mammals. Other scientists suggest that changes in climate may also have contributed to the decline of these species.

There is also increasing evidence that prehistoric hunter-gatherers manipulated ecosystems, especially through the use of fire. Some scientists have argued that hunter-gatherers used fire to convert and maintain large areas of forest as grassland. Beginning ten thousand years ago in west Asia and about five thousand years ago in the Americas fire was also used in the maintenance of agricultural plots.

Evidence of the large-scale effects of early humans on continental species is inconclusive, but there is extensive evidence for species declines and extinctions caused by early agriculturalists who colonized islands. For example, human colonization of Easter Island (Rapanui) about sixteen hundred years ago resulted in the extinction of all the native bird and all but two native tree species. Species declines were due to overexploitation of resources by hunting and by deforestation, which changed soil conditions and resulted in plant and animal population declines and further extinctions. The colonists also introduced nonnative plant species, chickens, and rats that contributed to the devastation of the native species on the island. Island species, as well as continental species, suffered declines as human hunters and agriculturalists colonized new habitats.

There are few records of endangered species in early history. Over twenty-five hundred years ago Persian weavers discovered that purple dye could be extracted from certain species of mollusks in the *Muricidae* (murex) family. The dye became popular among the ruling classes and later, as the Roman Empire grew, among the wealthy classes as well. By seventeen hundred years ago sumptuary laws (regulating extravagant expenditures) were passed in some areas to forbid commoners from wearing clothing dyed purple, partly to reserve the color for royalty but partly to preserve the dwindling populations of murex mollusks in the Mediterranean. The laws went unenforced, and overharvesting continued until the Roman economy collapsed around fifteen hundred years ago. The mollusks recovered but are again at risk because of pollution and collectors.

The aurochs *(Bos primigenius)* or wild ox was severely overhunted in Europe during the Middle Ages and would have been considered endangered by the 1300s. A small population remained in Poland in the 1550s and was closely monitored and protected from hunting by the Polish king, but apparently due to competition with domesticated cattle and poor management, only four individuals were known by 1600, and the species did not recover.

Between the sixteenth and nineteenth centuries great numbers of species were being discovered and described, and the collections of the world's great museums and botanical gardens were being amassed. Although people did realize that species were becoming rare and even extinct, little action was being taken to protect or even document endangered species. Museum collections were often made at great costs to natural populations because many animals were killed, lost in transport, or lost to poor preservation in order to gain a single quality specimen. Almost all species protection was occurring at the private level in the form of game ranches or preserves and was limited to certain valuable species. Zoos and botanical gardens were collecting species but were not very successful at breeding captive populations.

Toward the end of the nineteenth century public interest in conservation increased significantly worldwide and was especially strong in the United States because of naturalists and writers such as John Muir and Henry David Thoreau. In 1886 U.S. conservationist George Bird Grinnell started a local bird club that would later be the model for the National Audubon Society. The next year he and Theodore Roosevelt formed the Boone and Crockett Club to try to protect large game animals, such as bison and elk, that had declined to small populations in the United States and had been eliminated from several states.

Early in the twentieth century almost all legislation protecting species that were recognized as declining was focused on species of economic value. In 1900 concern over valuable game species resulted in the London Convention for the Protection of Wild Animals, Birds and Fish in Africa. In 1902 in Europe and in 1916 in North America, recognition of the extinction of bird species, such as the Passenger Pigeon *(Ectopistes migratorius)* in North America, that were important to agriculture or hunting led to the first international treaties limiting hunting of migratory bird species. Other treaties protecting specific species were signed during this period, but not until 1933 was the first general continent-wide convention, the London Convention on Preservation of Fauna and Flora in Their Natural State, signed. Although it mainly focused on species in Africa, it also included plants. In 1940 the Washington Convention on Nature Protection and Wild Life Preservation (in the Americas) was signed.

The U.S. writer and biologist Rachel Carson's book *Silent Spring* brought to the attention of the U.S. public the decline in many bird species caused by the spraying of chemical pesticides, especially DDT. In her book Carson said the precipitous decline of bald eagles "may well make it necessary for us to find a new national emblem" (Carson 1962). Public outcry over the endangerment of the bald eagle and other charismatic species led in 1973 to enactment of the U.S. Endangered Species Act, which became model legislation for other countries. CITES banned international trade in endangered species in 1975. Since that time considerable advancements have been made to protect species through legislation and public and private conservation efforts worldwide.

World Conservation Union (IUCN)

In 1948 the International Union for the Preservation of Nature (IUPN, later renamed the International Union for the Conservation of Nature and Natural Resources [IUCN], and often shortened to "World Conservation Union") was established, and the first international lists of endangered species and categories of endangerment were developed. The IUCN has been responsible for many important conservation efforts since its inception, including protection of species such as polar bears and areas such as the Galapagos Islands, but it is perhaps best known for the creation of its "Red Lists" of endangered and threatened species.

The IUCN was also responsible for drafting CITES in 1961. CITES was signed by eighty countries in 1973 and put into force in 1975. This international agreement between 160 countries limits the international trade of endangered and threatened wild animals and plants, whether traded as live or dead specimens, and trade goods containing parts of those species, such as ivory goods or fur coats. CITES protects over thirty thousand species.

Endangered Species Lists

IUCN and World Wildlife Fund biologist Paul Munson comprehensively summarizes the development of endangered species lists in *The Road to Extinction*. The earliest known list of rare plant species and their locations was recorded in 1634 for England by the English botanist Thomas Johnson. Other lists appeared soon after, but their creators did not assign any particular concern or risk of extinction to these species. The first list of endangered animal species, collated by Frederic Lucas for the American Museum of Natural History, was published in 1891. In 1913 the U.S. conservationist William T. Hornaday published *Our Vanishing Wildlife*, the first book that listed rare species in the United States, but more importantly, it also detailed the status of each listed population. Between 1933 and 1945 the American Committee for International Wildlife Protection funded the publication of lists of endangered and extinct mammals in Africa, the Americas, Europe, and Asia.

In 1948 the first international lists of endangered species and categories of endangerment were developed by IUPN. Originally its Service Survival Committee (renamed "Species Survival Commission" in 1981) began compiling endangered species in a card file. Not until 1966 were the first fully categorized lists of mammals and birds published.

The lists are called "Red Lists." The first included only "rare" and "endangered" species, but by 1969 they also included the categories "depleted" (similar to "threatened") and "indeterminate" (in need of further study). The first Red List of plants was not published until 1978. The first Red List of invertebrates was published in 1982. In 1996 the most complete Red List, listing 5,205 threatened animals (including one-quarter of all known mammal species), was published. The following year a list of thirty thousand threatened plants was published.

In 1971 the Audubon Society began publishing a list of North American bird species that had suffered serious population declines but that were not yet in imminent danger of extinction. This "Blue List," which was published in the journal *American Birds*, was meant to be an early warning system and does not duplicate the IUCN or U.S. endangered species lists. The list reporting methods were made more rigorous, and the name was changed to "Watch List" in 1996. Canada also maintains a Blue List of species of special concern.

In 1993 a trial for an international Blue List of a different type was begun in Switzerland by the botanists Andreas Gigon and Regula Langenauer. Species on the Swiss IUCN Red List that were found to have recovered sufficiently in a given area to no longer be considered endangered or threatened (vulnerable) were removed from the Red List and placed on the Blue List. The IUCN Blue Lists, as they become available, will be important because they will provide a tally of the successes of conservation efforts.

Which Species Are Most at Risk?

The IUCN Red Lists indicate that many of the world's taxonomic (relating to classification) groups are being greatly depleted. As of 2002, 18 percent of all vertebrates—including 24 percent of mammals (33 percent, over 20 percent of reptiles, 25 percent of amphibians, and 30 percent of fish species)—were threatened (endangered or vulnerable), 29% of invertebrates (including nearly 30 percent of mollusks and 60 percent of insects) were threatened, and almost 50 percent of all plants were threatened. At least five species of trees have four or fewer individuals remaining. The U.S. ecologist E. O. Wilson recently introduced "100 Heartbeat Club," a list that contains species that are so critically endangered that they have global populations of one hundred or fewer individuals. The Javan rhinoceros *(Rhinocerus sondaicus)* (sixty), Hawaiian crow *(Corvus Hawaiiensis)* (ten), and Chinese river dolphin *(Lipotes vexillifer)* (five) are a few of the species on the list.

How do scientists determine which species are most at risk? Scientists measure population size, genetic variability, remaining habitat quality, and likelihood for survival. Sometimes, as in the case of the black-footed ferret *(Mustela nigripes)* or the red wolf *(Canis rufus)*, individuals can be captured, bred in captivity, and then released into protected habitat when populations recover. The encouraging news is that 40 percent of the species that have been protected under the U.S. Endangered Species Act are now stable or are recovering, although only a few have been successfully removed from endangered status. The initial IUCN Blue List study conducted in northern Switzerland by Gigon and Langenauer indicates a 33 percent success rate there. Ultimately success will depend not on the protection of individually listed species, but rather on the recognition that human activities that endanger all species must be controlled. Attention must be focused on the protection of biodiversity (biological diversity as indicated by numbers of species of animals and plants) through decreased human consumption, waste, and population growth, as well as better conservation and management practices.

Vicki Medland

See also Biodiversity; Biological Corridors; Endangered Species Act; Snail Darter

Further Reading

Baillie, J., & Groombridge, B. (1996). *IUCN Red List of threatened animals.* Washington, DC: Conservation International.

Botkin, D. B. (1990). *Discordant harmonies: A new ecology for the twenty-first century.* New York: Oxford University Press.

Fitter, R., & Fitter, M. (Eds.). (1987). *The road to extinction.* Gland, Switzerland: IUCN.

Favre, D. S. (1989). *International trade in endangered species: A guide to CITES.* Norwell, MA: Kluwer Academic Publishers.

Jacoby, K. (2001). *Crimes against nature: Squatters, poachers, thieves, and the hidden history of American conservation.* Berkeley and Los Angeles: University of California Press.

Nilsson, G. (1990). *The endangered species handbook.* Washington, DC: Animal Welfare Institute.

Pyne, J. (1983). Indian fires: The fire practices of North American Indians transformed large areas from forest to grassland. *Natural History, 92*(3), 6, 8, 10–11.

Endangered Species Act

After the American Revolution the doctrine of state ownership of wildlife in the United States emerged as the powers held by the English crown and Parliament devolved to the states. By the end of the nineteenth century the federal government began to assert itself. As federal wildlife law evolved in the United States it came to encompass four basic tools: regulation of commerce in wildlife and derivative products, restrictions on taking, the acquisition and maintenance of habitat, and the requirement that particular forms of economic development consider their impact on wildlife. One consequence of these tools is that in March 2002, 515 U.S. animal species and 743 plant species were listed as either endangered or threatened. Another 33 animal species and 7 plant species were proposed for listing; another 107 animal species and 139 plant species are candidate species.

The Lacey Act (1900) established the first of these tools by prohibiting interstate commerce in "any wild animals or birds" killed in violation of state law. It permitted states to bar imports of animals legally killed in another state; they already had the right to prohibit exports. Finally, presaging both the third and fourth tools, the secretary of agriculture was instructed to adopt whatever measures proved necessary for the "preservation, distribution, introduction, and restoration of game birds and other wild birds" (Chap. 553). The second tool was introduced in the Migratory Bird Act (1913). All migratory and insectivorous (insect-eating) birds were declared "to be within the custody and protection" (Chap. 145) of the federal government. By claiming that the federal government could limit takings, the act was clearly contrary to the doctrine of state ownership. Consequently, the government entered into a 1916 treaty with Great Britain, acting on behalf of Canada, for the protection of migratory birds.

ОХРАНА ПРИРОДЫ
Орган Всероссийского Общества
охраны природы при ГЛАВНАУКЕНКП

ОХРАНА И ПРИРОДЫ!

ЗЕМЛЕДЕЛИЕ.
ОХОТА.
НАРОДНОЕ ЗДОРОВЬЕ.
КРАЕВЕДЕНИЕ.
ХУДОЖЕСТВЕННЫЕ ЦЕННОСТИ.
ДЕТИ, ЮНОШЕСТВО, ШКОЛА
КРАСНАЯ АРМИЯ.
ПУТИ СООБЩЕНИЯ.
ТУРИЗМ.

№ 4   1928

Москва-центр, Чистые Пруды, 6.

ОВЦЫ-БЫКИ.
Эти животные находятся под угрозой истребления.

This photo of the endangered musk oxen appeared on the cover of the Russian periodical *Okhrana Prirody* (Protection of Nature) in 1928. COURTESY DOUG WEINER.

Thus the constitutional right of the federal government to make treaties and to enact laws consonant with those treaties was brought to the service of wildlife.

Although the Lacey Act presumably applied to all "wild animals or birds," its application had been limited to fur-bearing mammals and game birds. The Black Bass Act (1926) extended Lacey-type protections to two fish species. Both the Lacey and Black Bass Acts were amended on several occasions. Lacey Act prohibitions were extended internationally in 1935; Black Bass Act probitions, in 1969. In 1949 the Lacey Act was again amended to prohibit the importation of animals shipped under "inhumane and unhealthful" conditions. In 1981 the two acts were merged under the Lacey Act amendments of that year.

The passage of the Tariff Act (1930) first extended these basic concepts to the international arena. If the laws of any foreign country (or one of its subdivisions) forbade the taking or exportation of any wild mammal or bird (in whole or in part), that specimen could not be imported into the United States without the U.S. consul at the export point certifying that the original taking was lawful.

Although these and other early statutes were motivated, at least in part, by what was perceived as an accelerating rate of species extinction, both the extent of wildlife protected and the nature of the protection were narrowly defined. The Endangered Species Preservation Act (1966) signaled the start of a broader-based approach that provided help on a case-by-case basis. According to environmentalist S. L. Yaffee, the motivation for the act was the "broadening knowledge about endangered species, growing public concern for protecting nongame animals, pressure from administrative experts, and congressional awareness of a symbolic issue that 'no one was against' . . ." (Yaffee 1982, 39). The "administrative experts" were largely housed in what was then the Bureau of Sports Fisheries and Wildlife in the Interior Department. The bureau appointed nine biologists to the Committee on Rare and Endangered Wildlife Species. In August 1964 they published a preliminary copy of the "Redbook," the first official federal list of endangered species. The sixty-three vertebrate species were selected solely on the basis of informal expert opinion. The copy was "preliminary" because, as the committee explicitly admitted, the criteria for listing were not clearly defined. In particular, the committee relied exclusively on biological data; it did not address criteria that might have forced a consideration of tradeoffs. Because the Red-

book listing did not signify formal federal protection, there could be no harm.

Habitat Protection

In June 1965 Interior Secretary Stewart Udall sent draft legislation to Congress that would charge his department with developing a program for "conserving, protecting, restoring and propagating selected species" (Endangered Species Preservation Act, Section 2 [a]) of mammals, birds, and fish. This ultimately passed both Houses of Congress by voice vote; the only real debate was over the further erosion of a state's right to regulate wildlife. Although the Endangered Species Preservation Act (1966) noted several reasons why species were endangered, it proposed only one solution: habitat protection. The interior secretary was authorized to use the land acquisition authority of existing laws to meet the act's goals. Congress considered the act to be little more than an enabling act for the purchase of refuges for "threatened species" (by then the third tool was a well-established function of the federal government). A threatened species was defined as one whose ". . . existence is endangered because its habitat is threatened with destruction, drastic modification, or severe curtailment, or because of overexploitation, disease, predation, or because of other factors, and that its survival requires assistance" (Endangered Species Preservation Act, Section 1[c]). The interior secretary was to make the determination "after consultation with the affected States" (Endangered Species Preservation Act, Section 1[a]) and all other interested parties. None of this was viewed as incurring any real costs, especially because the Interior Department testified that only seventy-eight species were involved (an increase of fifteen in the years since the publication of the "preliminary" copy of the Redbook).

The Endangered Species Conservation Act (1969) extended this approach internationally. The interior secretary was directed to publish a list of endangered wildlife and to ban imports of those animals and their products. The act did spell out a limited number of exceptions, such as "for zoological, education, and scientific purposes, and for . . . propagation . . . in captivity . . . for preservation purposes" (Section 3[c]). Only minor changes were made on the domestic side. The words "fish or wildlife" had been interpreted as "vertebrates;" the new act refined the definition to "any wild mammal, fish, wild bird, amphibian, reptile, mollusk, or crustacean" (Section 1[2]).

In 1969, unlike in 1966, some balancing provisions were included because of potential harm to economic interests. The motivation to add the international dimension came from conservation groups that railed against the fur industry's overexploitation of large cat species, leopards and jaguars in particular. Draft legislation appeared almost immediately after the 1966 act was signed. Little opposition was expressed during the hearings held on the bill, and the House version passed unanimously in August 1967. A Senate vote was delayed when the fur industry expressed concern; it had not recognized the potential impact of this legislation until the House vote.

The fur industry's belated concern was attributable, at least in part, to the fact that the bureau's experts did not notify economic interests of its intent to submit this legislation; the bureau considered it to be a simple technical correction of a problem associated with the 1966 act. The industry argued that unilateral action by the United States would cause inequitable economic damage to U.S. furriers. If other countries continued to permit the processing of these skins, jobs would be exported from the United States without any real gain to the affected species. The language in the draft legislation was prohibitive, but a compromise was reached where species listed as "endangered" had to be "threatened with worldwide extinction" (Section 1).

The delay in the Senate required the legislation to be reintroduced in the following session. The legislation directed the government to encourage other countries to join the effort to conserve wildlife. In particular, it was to convene an "international ministerial meeting" that would lead to "a binding international convention on the conservation of endangered species" (Section 5[b]).

CITES Agreement

That meeting led to an agreement called the "Convention on International Trade in Endangered Species of Wild Fauna and Flora" (1973), which, as the title suggests, is limited to trade; it does not provide a comprehensive blueprint for species preservation. This agreement, commonly known as "CITES," is the result of a resolution at the 1963 meeting of the World Conservation Union. Eighty countries signed the original agreement, but, as of 2002, there are 154 parties to the agreement. International trade involving selected species is subject to control. The thirty thousand species (five thousand animal and twenty-five thousand plant) currently covered by CITES are organized into three appendices that reflect the degree of required protection. Appendix I lists the species threatened with extinction and allows trade only in "exceptional circumstances." Appendix II lists species that are not necessarily "threatened" with extinction but for which trade is controlled in order to avoid circumstances that would threaten their survival. Appendix III lists species protected in at least one country, providing that country has requested assistance in controlling trade. Compliance with the CITES agreement is essentially voluntary, but the agreement is legally binding on the countries party to it. It does not replace national laws but rather provides a blueprint for domestic legislation that will implement the CITES agreement.

President Richard Nixon, in his environmental message of 8 February 1972, noted that this body of environmental law (from the Lacey Act through the CITES agreement) "simply does not provide the kind of management tool needed to act early enough to save a vanishing species." Such a concern was first addressed in the Marine Mammal Protection Act (1972); special protection was available after a species was considered "depleted" but not yet "endangered." Nixon proposed legislation that "would make the taking of endangered species a federal offense, and would permit protection measures to be undertaken before a species is so depleted that restoration is impossible" (Yaffee 1982, 49).

The Endangered Species Act (ESA) (1973) was passed to correct the weaknesses that Nixon and others identified in the existing laws. Once again the scope of federal wildlife legislation was broadened. This act applies to endangered species of both wildlife and plants and (allegedly) provides "a means whereby the ecosystems upon which [they] depend may be conserved" (Section 1531[b]). The act divides species into "endangered" and "threatened." This division was limited to animals in 1973; it was extended to plants in the 1978 amendments; the compromise with the fur industry that species be "threatened with worldwide extinction" was dropped. This division includes not only the true species, but also subspecies and distinct populations. The "threatened" category was designed to protect species before they become endangered and to continue to protect them after they are removed from the endangered list. The act includes species that might be abundant in specific locations but that are threatened in "a significant portion of their range" (Section 1532[20]). Further, it allows the listing of any species whose appearance is similar to that of a listed species, so protection for the latter requires protection for the former. The taking of an endangered species anywhere within the United States was made a federal offense, completely eliminating what had been viewed as a right of the states. Responsibility for administering federal law resides in the Fish and Wildlife Service of the Interior Department and the National Marine Fisheries Service of the Commerce Department.

Prohibitive Policy

Yaffee argues that the ESA embraced a "prohibitive policy" for three reasons. First, the issue of endangered species was symbolic, perhaps the epitome of the "quality of life" movement. No one seemed to notice that Congress, trying to minimize the contribution of humans, essentially banned a natural process—extinction. Second, the endangered species problem was defined as a technical one by scientific experts rather than as one involving a tradeoff between conflicting social goals—economic growth versus species preservation. There was no attempt to make even a rudimentary cost-benefit calculation. Third, it was not clear whose interest would be harmed before the fact; "Congress defined the law prohibitively because no one told them not to" (Yaffee 1982, 47). Congressional hearings revealed little opposition. In fact, there was no testimony from anyone who could be considered as having a direct economic interest. The bill passed the Senate 92–0 on July 24 and the House 390–12 on September 18.

One concern reflected the broad interpretation given to the word *species*. Until the 1960s scientists estimated the total number of mammal species at approximately 3 million. Advances in both taxonomy (classification) and statistics over the next two decades caused that estimate to be raised to 10 million. This explosion suggests the possibility that many more species, especially "minor" ones, were endangered than originally believed. The staff of the Fish and Wildlife Service's Office of Endangered Species had to establish some priorities in selecting species for review. Consequently, a triage mentality developed; those species that could be saved were given priority over those that could not. Higher-order species were given priority over more primitive ones, full species over subspecies, native species over foreign species. There was also an explicit "priority index" to help determine which listed endangered species would be helped. This occurred just before the listing process became political.

An important part of the listing process was the designation of "critical habitat." Unfortunately, this was not defined, nor was a procedure specified for determining such areas. "Critical" came to mean what was deemed essential for preservation. In practice, this could include all or just a portion of the existing habitat. Interest group "watchdogs" were expected to complain when they perceived that "a critical habitat" was endangered. Because economic concerns were not considered explicitly, critical habitat became the most contentious issue in the species preservation debate.

The 1978 amendments to the Endangered Species Act, passed by voice vote, reflected economic interests in two places; both were intended to provide balance. One was during the phase when critical habitat was *determined*. The other was the creation of the Endangered Species Committee (also known as "the God Committee") in which a supermajority could exempt a project (such as the building of a dam) from the act's prohibitions. To date, this committee has not authorized an exemption.

These amendments were passed the same year that Congress voted to exempt Tennessee's Tellico Dam from the Endangered Species Act. The economic concerns that led to that vote are concerns that were slowly integrated into the act as reauthorizations occurred over its first two decades; they have come to play an even larger role as reauthorizations have been stalled in the last decade.

In 1982, after months of negotiations with industry representatives, state wildlife managers, and environmentalists, a "streamlined" ESA was reauthorized for three years by voice vote in both houses. Loggers, miners, and electric utilities argued that the existing law delayed or blocked private and public projects, a legacy of the Tellico controversy. The administration of President Ronald Reagan suggested that potential economic costs be included among the criteria considered for listing a species, but the criteria remained exclusively biological. The industries whose projects required federal permits complained that the existing law did not allow them to learn in a timely fashion whether projects would imperil an endangered species or its critical habitat.

As a result of the Northern spotted owl case—in which habitat protection severely restricted foresting in the Pacific Northwest—one of the 1982 amendments allowed a regional authority, firm, or individual to receive a permit for "incidental takings" of endangered species if it has created and implemented an approved habitat conservation plan (HCP). In spite of their costly nature, by March 2002 the Fish and Wildlife Service had approved 374 HCPs, and there is no reason why the HCP alternative cannot be extended to other large landholders (e.g., ranchers). Using authority granted in the 1982 revision, the secretary of the interior exempted many small landholders in the 1990s, thereby mitigating their potential costs. In March 1997 the U.S. Supreme Court ruled that property owners had legal standing to bring suits against the federal government for "failing to consider the economic effect or scientific necessity of protecting endangered or threatened species"(*San Francisco Chronicle* 1997, A1). Economist Richard Stroup's suggestion that compensation be paid is yet another possibility for introducing balancing. The likelihood of successfully revamping the Endangered Species Act to directly include economic costs keeps dwindling. Any revamping will have to be a compromise between landowners and environmentalists, and, unfortunately, the two camps currently are entrenched in their positions regarding the act's costs to themselves and society.

Louis P. Cain

Further Reading

Bean, M. J., & Rowland, M. J. (1997). *The evolution of national wildlife law* (3rd ed.). Westport, CT: Praeger.

Endangered Species Act, PL 93–205, 87 Stat. 884. (1973).

Endangered Species Conservation Act, PL 91–135, 83 Stat. 275. (1969).

Endangered Species Preservation Act, PL 89–669, 80 Stat. 926. (1966).

Foster, J. (1978). *Working for wildlife: The beginning of preservation in Canada*. Toronto, Canada: University of Toronto Press.

Lacey Act, 31 Stat. 187. (1900).

Migratory Bird Act, 37 Stat. 828. (1913).

Public Law No. 89–669, 80 Stat. 926. (1966).

Souder, J. A. (1993, Fall). Chasing armadillos down yellow lines: Economics in the Endangered Species Act. *Natural Resources Journal, 33,* 1095–1139.

Stroup, R. L. (1997, October). The economics of compensating property owners. *Contemporary Economic Policy, 15,* 55–65.

Yaffee, S. L. (1982). *Prohibitive policy: Implementing the federal Endangered Species Act*. Cambridge, MA: MIT Press.

Energy *See* Coal; Geothermal Energy; Industrial Revolution; Natural Gas; Nuclear Power; Oil; Peat; Solar Energy; Trans-Alaska Pipeline; Water Energy; Wind Energy; Wind Energy; Wood

Environmental Defense

One of the ten largest national environmental advocacy groups in the United States, Environmental Defense (ED)—formerly the Environmental Defense Fund—employs more than two hundred attorneys, economists, scientists, and other experts to address climate change, energy, biodiversity (biological diversity as indicated by numbers of species of animals and plants), environmental health, oceans, and other issues. Supported by 300,000 members, the New York-based organization has accomplished a number of notable environmental achievements since its founding in 1967. Nonetheless, its positions and strategies sometimes raise concerns among other environmental groups, who argue that ED provides political comfort to industry. ED has traditionally embraced twin strategies to affect policy: employing economics to improve public policy and regulation and establishing agreements with leading corporations to leverage industry-wide environmentally beneficial actions. For example, ED has entered into partnerships with the McDonald's corporation to reduce container waste and with Federal Express to field fuel-efficient trucks. ED has also employed economists to advocate market-based solutions to environmental problems, whereas other more left-wing environmental organizations such as Greenpeace argue that economic considerations should never trump environmental concerns. ED was one of the prime movers in the introduction of a marketable emissions-rights plan for acid-rain pollutants, a Clean Air Act program that many believe exemplifies a successful market-based approach to environmental controls. ED staff members were involved in proposing the plan, serving on congressional committees that crafted the acid-rain bill, and implementing the trading scheme that governed the exchange of pollution rights after the legislation became law. The staff experts also sued the U.S. Environmental Protection Agency (EPA) over what they viewed as improper implementation of the program. Other advocacy work has included spurring passage of the 1987 Montreal Accord to phase out ozone-depleting gases and a 1985 push to overcome industry pressure in convincing federal regulators to phase out lead in gasoline. ED was formed during the effort to ban the pesticide DDT in 1967 and has continued major advocacy work on toxics until fairly recently. The organization's 1997 report *Toxic Ignorance* found that basic health data are not publicly available for over 80 percent of the most common chemicals in commerce. The findings sparked a partnership with EPA and the chemical industry to launch several voluntary chemical-testing initiatives after industry executives confirmed ED's findings. In 2000 ED was one of the first groups to harness the power of the Internet by launching a sophisticated Web site, www.scorecard.org, which allows users to track chemical releases by U.S. ZIP code. This database empowers citizen groups by compiling information on major sources of pollution in their communities and providing related health-risk profiles. The ease with which users can access information on the site has served to simplify EPA's complex environmental assessments of chemicals and allowed citizens to join debates on environmental risks that have increasingly been dominated by experts. ED's commitment to advocacy on toxics has slowed somewhat over the last two years as the organization shifted its focus to rain forest conservation, biodiversity, global warming, and other issues for which foundation grant funding is more readily available.

Steven Gibb

Further Reading

Environmental Defense. (2002). *2001 annual report*. New York: Author.

Gibb, S. (1997). EDF will broaden "toxic ignorance" campaign via Internet. In S. Gibb (Ed.), *Risk policy report* (p. 5). Arlington, VA: Inside Washington Publishers.

Obey. D. (2002). Environmental groups split over Senate bill for CO2 controls. In R. Urdan (Ed.), *Inside EPA* (p. 8). Arlington, VA: Inside Washington Publishers.

Pianin, E. (2002, July 31). Surge in carbon dioxide emissions cited. *The Washington Post*, p. A2.

Environmental Education

Because educators believe they have the responsibility to alert students to emerging environmental prob-

lems and the appropriate ways to resolve them, environmental education increasingly plays a critical role in abating the destruction of the world's resources and improving the urban environment. Environmental education can be traced to the onset of Western industrialization when educators, reformers, and conservationists became concerned that children were losing touch with the natural world. Its educational forerunners—nature education or nature study, conservation education, manual arts training, and outdoor education—contributed to environmental education's content and methods throughout the world. Environmental education is derived from a unique interdisciplinary social and educational movement that has vacillated between the poles of idealism and utilitarianism.

The most important forerunner, nature study, was a link between the eighteenth-century European educational reformers and twentieth-century international environmental education reformers. Nature study was the first major U.S. educational movement to attempt general education reform by combining education reform theory with study of the environment. Nature study not only answered the need to educate the young about the natural world, but also provided students with training in aesthetics, culture, and the manual arts. As an interdisciplinary movement based on science and arts, nature study was a prototype of present-day environmental education.

The pedagogical (relating to teaching) counterpart of the nature-study movement originated in educational theories emphasizing the importance of each child's full sensory participation in his or her learning, stretching beyond learning through books to learning through experience. Object teaching (drawing from the object at hand versus copying from a book), which became popular in the United States in the latter part of the nineteenth century, was the precursor to nature study.

Nature-study movement leaders recognized European education reformers such as Comenius, Pestalozzi, Rousseau, and Froebel as forerunners of the nature-study movement.

Nature-Study Leaders

John Amos Comenius (1592–1670), a seventeenth-century Moravian monk, promoted education reform in order to develop socially useful, practical skills. The goal of his educational approach was to awaken the interests of children and to produce zeal for hard work.

Comenius emphasized child activity and direct experience in the learning process. The French philosopher Jean Jacques Rousseau (1712–1778) enlarged Comenius's approach to pedagogy in *Emil* (1762), in which the goal was not only to give children knowledge, but also to teach them how to acquire it. He preached a return to nature and the necessity of a social contract that guarantees the rights of all. Laying the foundation of today's educational psychology, Rousseau believed that the principles of science should be discovered by the child, not merely learned as facts.

Johann Heinrich Pestalozzi (1746–1826), the "father of object teaching," advocated using material objects as a way of focusing the attention of the learner. In 1744 he started a school on his farm in Yverdon, Switzerland, to train fifty poor children in gardening and the three *R*'s. His methods included replacing recitation with discussion, individual teaching with group

A display of environmental books in the window of Blackwell's Bookshop in Oxford, England in 1990. COURTESY KAREN CHRISTENSEN.

instruction, and catechism with thinking. He maintained that observation is the basis of all knowledge and that the first goal in education is accuracy in observation and correct expression of what has been observed. Friedrich Froebel (1782–1852), a student of Pestalozzi, opened his own school with an emphasis on developing the inborn moral, social, and intellectual capabilities of the child through nature study, gardening, and play. Froebel focused on nature as the source of experience for child development.

Edward Sheldon (1832–1897), superintendent of schools in Oswego, New York, sought improvement of teacher training and adopted the Pestalozzian "object training" method of pedagogy. As object teaching came to be seen as dull and limited, and as interest grew in school reform, a new generation of individuals initiated the nature-study movement. In the United States, reflecting the growing emphasis on child happiness, Clement Durgan, an early proponent of the ecological viewpoint in education, established the important principle that education should be preparation for life and that childhood experience and training determine the adult's interaction with the environment.

Historically, plants have served as the pedagogical focal point for environmental education. Asa Gray (1810–1888) wrote *Gray's Manual of Botany* (1848), a classic in the field. He published *Elements of Botany* (1836) and other textbooks for young people. Learning from nature adapted well to the larger mid-1800s movement of universal education. The child-centered branch of the progressive education reform movement drew heavily on the English naturalist Charles Darwin and believed that adult functioning depends on the experience of the child. Progressive educators influenced nature-study leaders who based their programs on these child-centered pedagogical concepts, making nature an increasingly popular subject of study.

Conservation Education and Nature Study

In 1864 *Man and Nature*, the ground-breaking book by the U.S. diplomat George Perkins Marsh (1801–1882), symbolized the growing concern for the environment. Emphasizing people's responsibility for their environment, the book marked the beginning of the preservation phase of the conservation movement and reflected the growing awareness of the need to view nature as an integrated system in danger of misuse. The Swiss doctor Louis Agassiz (1807–1874), influenced by the ideas of Comenius, Rousseau, and Pestalozzi, established an enthusiastic following when he established a summer school for teachers on Penikese Island in Buzzard's Bay off the coast of Massachusetts. The summer school energized a leading group of educators who believed in the importance of natural science education.

Frank Owen Payne, a teacher and prolific author of nature-study books from Corry, Pennsylvania, first used the term *nature study* in 1884. By the late 1880s the term *nature study* was replacing such terms as *natural history, objects lessons*, and *plant work*.

Francis Wayland Parker, superintendent of schools in Quincy, Massachusetts, developed the first major school program that emphasized combining an understanding of the universe and scientific techniques as a method to solve problems. He designed an integrated, holistic approach to education about the environment. Parker in 1883 became principal of Cook County Normal School in Chicago, where he worked with Wilbur S. Jackman (1855–1907), who had developed a program that reflected an understanding of ecological principles with the natural sciences as the core of the curriculum. Jackman published *Nature Study for the Common Schools* in 1891. Some of Parker's followers founded the elite Quincy School in Poughkeepsie, New York, for the children of faculty members at Vassar College. Ultimately, the scientific methods of Agassiz, object teaching, nature study, and Parker and Jackman's progressive curriculum structure overlapped and came together. *How We Think* by the U.S. educator John Dewey (1859–1952) was an extensive treatment of this concept of the role of reason and the use of generalizations in the learning and thinking process within a modern education context. Dewey went to work for Parker at Cook County Normal School, linking Jackman and Dewey through Parker, and thus linking the nature-study movement to the progressive era.

In 1889 the Plymouth County, Massachusetts, Teachers Association, under the leadership of Arthur C. Boyden (1852–1933) and his son, Albert G. Boyden (b. 1871), set up a committee to introduce nature study into the county schools. The Bridgewater Normal School established a summer school at Cottage City, Martha's Vineyard, Massachusetts, which the elder Boyden ran until 1901. In 1890 Boyden and the Massachusetts Board of Education established a committee on nature study and promoted it around the state and nationwide. A leader in classroom pedagogy, Albert G. Boyden succeeded his father as principal at Bridgewater and shared his interest in nature study. Their promotion of nature study was embraced by teachers, writers, illustrators, and philosophical leaders who shared a love of nature and romanticized the return to an Arcadian (simple) past.

Many educators who contributed to the nature-study mystique are today only modestly known, but their influence is still felt in classrooms. The botanist Liberty Hyde Bailey (1858–1954), a teacher of teachers at Cornell University, feared that city children might lose interest in nature. His popular ideas included the belief that nature study possessed beneficial emotional, intellectual, and physical properties. Nature study in the classroom meant that not only would young people learn how to draw by focusing on nature, but also that they would grow up to learn about, understand, appreciate, and later be attracted to the healthful outdoors. In 1894 Cornell University inaugurated a nature-study program for children designed to keep them on the farm. Cornell issued pamphlets, leaflets, and periodicals and was a bustling headquarters of hundreds of nature-study clubs. In 1903 Liberty Hyde Bailey published *The Nature Study Idea*, in which he emphasized the importance of educating the city child about the natural world. Convinced that city dwellers need outdoor life, in 1901 he began editing publisher Doubleday Page's new suburban journal, *Country Life in America*, the most popular of all suburban periodicals. In 1911 Anna Botsford Comstock (1854–1930), a prominent teacher of children affiliated with the movement, wrote the *Handbook of Nature-Study*, a book she based largely on Cornell's leaflets.

Liberty Hyde Bailey's efforts to promote nature study in the schools were boosted by Henry Turner Bailey (1865–1931, no relation to Liberty Hyde Bailey), an energetic promoter of nature study in the service of manual arts training. Editor of *School Arts* magazine, published during the early twentieth century, he guided art teachers in the methods of teaching art by drawing from nature. Bailey published the book *Tree Folk*, which contained pencil sketches and informal essays and convinced readers to approach their teaching with an added appreciation for nature. Ultimately, through Bailey's efforts and influence, drawing from nature was formally introduced into Massachusetts schools.

Henry Turner Bailey's ideas about art training dovetailed well with science study programs, such as Arthur Boyden's, that were already in schools in Massachusetts in the early 1890s. Many teachers embraced this pedagogical approach in city schools, where they were required to train the coming generation of industrial workers in the manual arts. By the beginning of the twentieth century, cross-curriculum nature study was well established in classrooms throughout the nation, especially in elementary schools, where it was integrated into the natural history of the local community. Both Henry Turner Bailey's and Liberty Hyde Bailey's theories led the teacher out of the classroom and into the outdoors. The School Garden movement—which was enacted primarily through city schools and was an urban offshoot of the nature-study movement and the urban settlement movements—centered on social hygiene and nature appreciation. Importantly, women led the way as teachers of nature study and appreciation and as popularizers of science, illustrating, writing and publishing both fiction and nonfiction on natural subjects.

Many nature-study enthusiasts' devotion stemmed from a spiritual dimension. Their love of nature as a kind of neoplatonism (Platonism modified in later antiquity to accord with Aristotelian, post-Aristotelian, and oriental conceptions) was one that had been transmitted by the Puritans, purified by the Transcendentalists (adherents of a philosophy that emphasizes the a priori condition of knowledge and experience or the unknowable character of ultimate reality), and disseminated by contemporary nineteenth-century conservationists and nature writers such as John Muir (1838–1914) and John Burroughs (1837–1921) of the United States. In this way, as popularizers of nature, they spread nature appreciation to the country as a whole, their nature-study enthusiasm adding a crucial spiritual element to their insistence that children study nature.

Nature-Study Organizations and Publications

The Boston Society of Natural History, established in 1830, promoted the study of natural history in the United States by encouraging research, education, and publication of books. In 1870 the society founded the Teacher's School of Science, which offered courses, teaching guides, and lectures. The science education activist Lucretia Crocker (1829–1886) introduced nature study to Boston schools in 1876. The publication *Nature Study Review* was an important source of nature-study ideas. First published in 1905, it encompassed the principles of observational study of common material objects by children (as differentiated from science, which was considered to be for adults). The American Nature Study Society was formed in 1908 to provide direction for the movement, and it continues today to work to improve the quality of nature interpretation in schools, parks, literature, and nature organizations.

Underlying these efforts is the premise that if people become interested in their environment, they will become concerned about environmental problems and issues.

Demise of Nature Study

By the early 1930s critics claimed that nature study was anthropocentric (having human characteristics) and sentimental and focused on the lack of teacher training as a weakness of the movement. Lacking broad educational support at the local and district school levels, nature study eventually split into the conservation education movement, the outdoor education movement, and elementary science.

The conservation education movement emerged during the 1930s when focus on the ideas of "wise use" and "natural resource management" was given impetus by state and federal agencies whose goal was to cope with a particular resource problem. Citizen organizations supplemented these efforts. Legislative acts endorsing conservation education in the schools became widespread during the 1930s, 1940s, and 1950s in the United States.

Whereas conservation education was considered a substantive area of utilitarian academic study, outdoor education, with antecedents from the 1920s, was an educational approach that used resources outside the classroom for educational purposes.

Classroom elementary science focused on the beneficial social properties of scientific advancements. Science and technology, given great boosts by military needs during World War II, continued to grow at an accelerated pace following the war. The use of nuclear weapons portended the global environmental impact of technological "fixes" such as pesticides, industrial forestry, and the wholesale destruction of fragile ecosystems around the world. Women contributed important voices to environmental awareness dialogues. The U.S. biologist and writer Rachel Carson (1907–1964), educated in the nature-study tradition, wrote *Silent Spring*, which marked the beginning of widespread popular concern that technological "fixes" had a dark side. The "spaceship Earth" speech of the U.S. statesman Adlai Stevenson (1900–1965) before the United Nations in 1965 dealt with the reality of a finite planet. The speech was widely quoted and was underscored by the first photograph of Earth from the moon on 21 July 1969. The first Earth Day on 22 April 1970, also boosted popular environmental awareness.

Emergence of Environmental Education

Such responses to environmental problems alone were not enough to sustain the environmental movement and to bring about needed reforms. Many believed that environmental education is the solution to environmental problems. The term *environmental education* first appeared at the National Conference on Environmental Education held in New Jersey in May 1968. In 1970 the U.S. Congress passed the Environmental Education Act, which established environmental education not only as a term, but also signaled the importance of the new movement. Reflecting the principles of ecology, most definitions of environmental education have tended to conceptualize rather than compartmentalize content. Environmental education's most significant difference from nature study is that its emotional component is based on fear of destruction rather than love of nature; moreover, conservation stood for "economic development" under the old classification, whereas the new environmentalism reflects the ideology that less can be more.

Because issues of population and environmental impact were interwoven, population education became part of the environmental quality movement. Several groups, such as Zero Population Growth, the Council on Population and Environment, and the Population Reference Bureau, have provided leadership, materials, and direction for this movement. An array of conservation and land-trust organizations is closely allied with the conservation and environmental education movements, highlighting the lesson that an array of individual education efforts can be amplified through organization.

International Environmental Education

By the mid-1970s environmental education was an international movement. The Belgrade Charter, developed from the first world conference on environmental education in October 1975, called for an international, interdisciplinary program in environmental education, both in and out of school, encompassing all levels of education and directed toward the general public. In December 1975 an environmental education course for youth was held in Hong Kong. One hundred education specialists from sixty-four countries met for eight days to examine the aims of worldwide environmental education and the best ways of promoting it.

In 1978 the United Nations Educational, Scientific and Cultural Organization (UNESCO) defined *environ-mental education* as a learning process that increases people's knowledge and awareness about the environment, develops the necessary skills and expertise to address its challenges, and fosters attitudes, motivation, and commitment to make informed decisions and take responsible actions. On an international scale, environmental education seeks to foster awareness of, and concern about, economic, social, political, and ecological interdependence. It seeks to provide opportunities to acquire the knowledge, values, attitudes, commitment, and skills to protect and improve the environment and to create new patterns of behavior for individuals, groups, and society as a whole toward the environment.

UNESCO prepared its *International Directory of Environmental Education Institutions* in cooperation with the United Nations Environmental Programme (UNEP), and a first edition was published in 1971. Since then, new environmental education institutions have adopted training and research programs. Green Cross International enlightens and motivates people to act in accord with the guiding sense of its charter. It integrates environmental principles into traditional classroom education.

The Foundation for Environmental Education in Europe (FEEE) was established in 1981 to raise awareness of environmental issues and to effect change through education. In 2001 FEEE became the Foundation for Environmental Education (FEE) as South Africa joined as the first non-European member, the organization's first step toward worldwide expansion. Its central objectives are information and awareness of sustainability. Education is a key component of these efforts.

Environmental education has grown from an elite, local, and middle-class Western education reform movement to a global effort that embraces people of all races, classes, nations, and religions and teaches them to learn about and to protect the fragile world environment.

Cynthia Richardson

Further Reading

Able, G. A., Aldrich, J., Blackburn, A. M., & Stapp, W. B. (1977). Environmental education: A major advance. In G. A. Able (Ed.), *A report of the North American regional seminar on environmental education.* Columbus, OH: SMEAC Information Reference Center.

Bailey, H. T. (1925). *The tree folk.* Cambridge, UK: Washburn & Thomas.

Bailey, L. H. (1903). *The nature study idea.* New York: Doubleday, Page.

Bailey, L. H. (1915). *The holy Earth.* New York: Charles Scribner's & Sons.

Boyden, A. C. (1898). *Nature study by months. Pt. 1, for elementary grades.* Chicago: New England Publishing.

Comenius, J. A. (1728). *Orbis pictus* (Charles Hoole, Trans.). London: J. H. Spring. (Original work published 1658).

Comstock, A. B. (1915). Growth and influence of the nature study idea. *Nature Study Review, 11*(7).

Comstock, A. B. (1939). *Handbook of nature study.* Ithaca, New York: Comstock Publishing.

Cremin, L. A. (1961). *The transformation of the school.* New York: Vintage Books.

Froebel, F. W. (1974). *The education of man* (W. N. Hailman, Trans.). New York: D. Appleton.

Funderburk, R. S. (1948). *The history of conservation education in the United States.* Nashville, TN: McQuiddy.

Gough, A. G. (1993). *Founders in environmental education.* Geelong, Australia: Deakin University Press.

Gray, A. (1836). *Elements of botany.* New York: G. C. Carvill.

Hodge, C. H. (1902). *Nature study and life.* Boston: Ginn.

Jackman, W. (1891). *Nature study for the common schools.* New York: Henry Holt.

Martlett, R. (Ed.). (1976). *Current issues in environmental education II.* Columbus, OH: ERIC Center for Mathematics and Environmental Education.

McInnis, N., & Albrecht, D. (Eds.). (1975). *What makes education environmental?* Louisville, KY: Data Courier.

Mitchell, D. (1922, May). A history of nature study. *Nature Study Review, 19.*

Olmsted, R. (1967). *The nature-study movement in American education.* Bloomington: Indiana University Press.

Palmer, J., & Neal, P. (1994). *The handbook of environmental education.* London: Routledge.

Rogers, D. (1961). *Oswego: Fountainhead of teacher education.* New York: Appleton, Century, Crofts.

Rousseau, J. J. (1925). *Emile* (B. Foxely, Trans.). London: J. M. Dent & Sons.

Scott, C. B. (1900). *Nature study and the child.* New York: D. C. Heath.

Stapp, W. B., & Swan, J. A. (Eds.). (1975). *Environmental education.* Detroit, MI: Gale Research.

Troost, C. J., & Altman, H. (1972). *Environmental education: A sourcebook.* New York: Wiley.

Underhill, O. E. (1941). *The origins and development of elementary-school science.* Chicago: Scott, Foresman.

Environmental Ethics

Environmental ethics is a subdiscipline of philosophy originating in the early 1970s. It is principally interested in questions of the nature and value of the human and nonhuman world, and with what an appropriate human-to-nonhuman relationship might look like, or how it is that humans ought to interact with nature.

Environmental Crisis and Environmental Ethics

From the early 1960s until the present, nearly every work dealing with environmental issues begins with and assumes the truth of the premise that the world is in the throes of an unprecedented "environmental crisis." In fact, some works contain nothing but a recounting of the myriad of global and anthropogenic environmental horrors. Over this same period, environmentally concerned philosophers began to explore the philosophical issues underlying this sense of crisis in order to both understand and remedy it.

In the 1960s and 1970s the assumption of the presence of an "environmental crisis" was manifest in a growing awareness of and concern about such things as the noticeable increase in air and water pollution in large cities, rapid and irreplaceable soil erosion, and the threat of industrial and agricultural chemical poisoning (no doubt due in large part to the widespread success of Rachel Carson's landmark 1962 book *Silent Spring*). This first phase of the environmental movement was centered principally on local and regional environmental concerns. It was also characterized by the conviction that the environmental crisis was a problem of an inequitable distribution of environmental "goods" (e.g., clean water and air) and environmental "bads" (e.g., water and air pollution). This era of environmental thinking also spawned much of the "doomsday literature" that contended that we are rapidly heading toward an ecological and social (as these things are intertwined) catastrophe, and that the only thing that will avert our course is a significant alteration in our most fundamental institutions (e.g., "abandon capitalism," "reject the market economy," "stop consumerism," etc.). In short, the distinctive feature of this first wave of environmentalism was the intense concern for the survival of the human species and the view of the nonhuman environment as simply a means to secure this continued human existence. Anthropocentrism, then, underlies the era's concern about various environmental goods, their longevity, and their

Aldo Leopold Defines the "Land Ethic"

The land ethic simply enlarges the boundaries of the community to include soils, waters, plants, and animals, or collectively: the land.

This sounds simple: do we not already sing our love for and obligation to the land of the free and the home of the brave? Yes, but just what and whom do we love? Certainly not the soil, which we are sending helter-skelter downriver. Certainly not the waters, which we assume have no function except to turn turbines, float barges, and carry off sewage. Certainly not the plants, of which we exterminate whole communities without batting an eye. Certainly not the animals, of which we have already extirpated many of the largest and most beautiful species. A land ethic of course cannot prevent the alteration, management, and use of these "resources," but it does affirm their right to continued existence, and, at least in spots, their continued existence in a natural state.

Source: Leopold, Aldo: (1987). *A Sand County Almanac.* New York: Oxford University Press, p. 204.

distribution. Interestingly, some philosophers came to suggest an expanded anthropocentrism as the appropriate response to the environmental crisis at this same time.

The late 1980s to the present have witnessed the second phase of this environmental crisis. In addition to the more local, point-source issues of the 1960s and 1970s, the present focus of concern has become planetary in scope. Such things as rapid global warming due to the greenhouse effect, massive and abrupt loss of biological diversity, the poisoning of the world's lakes and rivers by acid rain, and the suspected hole in the Earth's ozone layer due to CFC (chlorofluorocarbon) emissions, have become the rallying points of more recent environmental concern. It appears that we have now attained the never before imagined (much less realized) ability to alter the condition of the planet itself. With this second phase of the environmental crisis, we are forced to grapple with the realization that our ability to increase the amount and rate of environmental damage has so greatly increased in degree that it has actually changed in kind. Primarily because global damage by its very nature precludes replenishment or regeneration from elsewhere—as more localized point-source impact does—environmental degradation on a global scale is an entirely different condition. While some philosophers view this second phase of environmental concern as perfectly compatible with anthropocentric concern and are still clearly arguing from this point of view, others find such a position lacking. For them, this second phase of environmentalism is marked by a turning away from solely anthropocentric

justifications for environmental concern and action in favor of more expanded and non-anthropocentric ethical motivations: granting value directly to the nonhuman, as well as the human world, and rejecting the narrow view of "nature as resource." Additionally, during this second era of environmentalism, a belief developed that our environmental situation is not only, or chiefly, a matter of resource distribution and human survival but equally (and maybe even more fundamentally) a cultural and value issue. A primary assertion of this current era of environmental concern is that our inherited and collective ideas, beliefs, knowledge, and values are also in part responsible for our environmental situation and are also therefore in dire need of examination.

Origin of Environmental Ethics

In the early 1970s a small cadre of philosophers began to realize that underlying our concern for and discussions about land use, biodiversity loss, and pollution were very real, interesting, and novel ethical questions. They also began to see that at the core of our disagreements about what we should do with land, how we should value other species, and which policies we should enact to mitigate pollution were very complex philosophical notions about the nature of humanity, the nature of the nonhuman world, and the nature of an appropriate relationship between the two. These philosophers quickly realized that environmental issues are inherently and intractably philosophical and ethical issues.

Those outside of philosophy have increasingly recognized how critical the work of environmental ethics and environmental ethicists is to natural-resource issues. Courses in environmental ethics were promptly required for natural-resource majors in college. Environmental ethicists were granted joint appointments in colleges of natural resources, invited to sit on natural resource advisory boards, on editorial boards of natural-resource journals, requested to participate in and join typically scientifically orientated organizations and conferences, and welcomed to contribute articles to journals and chapters to textbooks in conservation biology, forestry, environmental policy, and other natural-resource areas.

Typology of Theories

As the subdiscipline has evolved over the past three decades, environmental philosophers have separated into a number of distinct camps. Such camps distinguish themselves most profoundly by the value that they assume nature possesses and hence by the method or standard by which they believe we ought to go about addressing our environmental woes.

Anthropocentrism

First, there are those who believe that environmental policies ought to be motivated and justified by their effects upon humans. Of course these anthropocentrists often (but not always) recognize both the full range of human values and the fact that human well-being is intimately entwined with the well-being of at least certain parts of the nonhuman world. For the anthropocentrist, only humans possess intrinsic value (i.e., value beyond merely instrumental value as a means to an end), all else is only instrumentally valuable: the nonhuman is valuable only insofar as it impacts humans. Anthropocentrists, then, agree with Immanuel Kant who argues that "all duties towards animals, towards immaterial beings and towards inanimate objects are aimed indirectly at our duties towards mankind," or John Passmore who claims that "the supposition that anything but a human being has 'rights' is . . . quite untenable" (1980). Hence, for the anthropocentrist, we ought to be concerned about environmental destruction and act to mitigate it only because such destruction does or might negatively impact human beings: plant biodiversity in the rainforest is valuable, for example, because it might provide cures for certain human diseases.

Zoocentrism

Second, there are philosophers who believe that, in addition to humans, certain nonhuman animals possess intrinsic value and garner direct moral standing. These animal-centered, or zoocentric, ethicists argue that for all the reasons that we directly consider humans as intrinsically valuable, logical consistency demonstrates that we ought also to value certain nonhumans as intrinsically valuable given only that these nonhuman animals possess the same trait that makes humans morally relevant. For the zoocentrist, humans and certain nonhuman animals possess intrinsic value, all else maintains only instrumental value. Hence, the zoocentrist would be concerned about environmental destruction because of the actual and potential negative impact that it has on both humans and certain nonhuman animals: rainforest biodiversity preservation is important, for example, because it might provide cures for both human and certain nonhuman animal diseases.

Biocentrism

Third, some philosophers have argued that the only way to avoid logical moral inconsistency is to directly include all living things within the moral community. These life-centered, or biocentric, thinkers argue for the intrinsic value and direct moral standing of all individual living things, leaving only non-individual living things as possessive of merely instrumental value. Albert Schweitzer, perhaps the most popularly recognized "biocentrist," summarizes the position: "Ethics thus consists in this, that I experience the necessity of practicing the same reverence for life toward all with a will-to-live, as toward my own. Therein I have already the needed fundamental principle of morality. It is good to maintain and cherish life; it is *evil* to destroy and check life" (1923, 254).

For the biocentrist concern for, or policy regarding, environmental degradation is motivated and justified by the impact that it might have on *all* individual living things: we ought to be concerned about biodiversity loss, for example, because of the effect it has on humans, fish, and trees.

Universal Consideration

Fourth, some have even gone so far as to argue that the only sensible and logically consistent moral community would be one inclusive of all individual things, whether living or not. Those advocating this "universal consideration" suggest that we live in a morally rich world where we ought to begin with the assumption that everything is imbued with intrinsic value and possessive of direct moral standing. As Thomas Birch puts the position: "Universal consideration—giving attention to others of all sorts, with the goal of ascertaining what, if any, direct ethical obligations arise from relating with them—should be adopted as one of the central constitutive principles of practical reasonableness" (1993, 313). Hence, their reaction to or policy proposals attempting to curb environmental degradation would be motivated not only by the impact that such loss has on all living things, but also by the impact that such loss has on even nonliving things such as mountains, rivers, or rocks.

Ethical Holism

Fifth, reacting against the atomism or individualism of all of the above approaches to environmental ethics, and appealing to the science of ecology and the notion of holism, some philosophers have argued that the biosphere as a whole, as well as the systems that constitute it ought to also be directly morally considerable. Although their approaches and arguments vary, this ethical holism refocuses moral concern on the maintenance of the health of biotic communities, species, ecosystems, and even the earth as a whole—if one were to extend this idea as far as James Lovelock's Gaia Hypothesis. The most recognized version of this ethical holism is expressed by Aldo Leopold when he asserts that "A thing is right when it tends to preserve the integrity, stability, and beauty of the biotic community. It is wrong when it tends otherwise" (1949). The various forms of deep ecology are also popular representations of this position. Hence, environmental degradation, as it manifests itself in biodiversity loss for example, is a matter of concern because the health of species as well as specimens, watersheds as well as rivers, and forest ecosystems as well as individual trees are negatively impacted.

Ecofeminism and Ecojustice

The discussions within environmental ethics have also spawned a variety of interesting and exciting areas of specialty. For example, "ecofeminism," as defined by leading ecofeminist scholar Val Plumwood, "is essentially a response to a set of key problems thrown up by the two great social currents of the later part of this century—feminism and the environmental movement—and addresses a number of shared problems" (1993). Ecofeminists have developed most insightful analogies between the historical oppression of nature by humans, and that of women by men; suggesting that Western environmental problems should be—perhaps even that they can only be—understood in light of a larger historical attempt to bifurcate the world in such a way where women and nature are linked with that which is morally degraded or downgraded, and men and the nonnatural are conceptually tied to the morally relevant or superior.

Other thinkers have focused on how it is that various forms of environmental degradation, and even various proposals to remedy this degradation, play out in terms of justice between and within societies. Critiquing such notions as gross national product (GNP) as a measure of progress, capitalism and free market economics, technological fixes to environmental problems, wilderness area and park importation to third-world countries, and economic development, those interested in issues of environmental justice (or ecojustice) have dramatically illustrated the negative global result of our current environmental problems but especially how the costs of environmentally negligent behavior must be unfairly borne by some but not others. As philosopher Peter Wenz puts it, "questions about justice arise concerning those things that are, or are perceived to be, in short supply relative to the demand for them" (1988). Given that the Earth's resources are finite, and given that we are all concerned with getting our fair share of those resources, environmental issues and ethics are inherently a matter of justice.

In his classic 1949 essay "The Land Ethic," Aldo Leopold declared that conservation would remain trivial—unable to assert itself as a genuine alternative to the rampant despoliation of the land—until it could muster an ethical underpinning; unless and until, in Leopold's words, philosophy and religion had heard about it. The work begun by environmental ethics in the early 1970s and continuing today serves to fulfill Leopold's vision. Environmental ethics is proof that philosophy has indeed taken serious notice of conservation.

Michael P. Nelson

Further Reading

Attfield, R. (1991). *The ethics of environmental concern* (2nd ed.). Athens: University of Georgia Press.

Baxter, W. (1974). *People or penguins: The case for optimal pollution*. New York: Columbia University Press.

Birch, T. (1993). Moral considerability and universal consideration. *Environmental Ethics, 15*(4), 313–332.

Callicott, J. B. (1989). *In defense of the land ethic*. Albany: State University of New York Press.

Callicott, J. B. (1999). *Beyond the land ethic*. Albany: State University of New York Press.

Carson, R. (1962). *Silent spring*. New York: Penguin.

Goodpaster, K. (1978). On being morally considerable. *Journal of Philosophy, 75*, 308–325.

Guha, R. (1989). Radical American environmentalism and wilderness preservation: A third world critique. *Environmental ethics, 11*(1), 71–83.

Johnson, L. (1993). *A morally deep world*. Cambridge, UK: Cambridge University Press.

Leopold, A. (1949). *A Sand County almanac*. New York: Oxford University Press.

Naess, A. (1990). *Ecology, community, and lifestyle*. Cambridge, UK: Cambridge University Press.

Norton, B. (1988). *Why preserve natural variety?* Princeton, NJ: Princeton University Press.

Passmore, J. (1980). *Man's responsibility for nature* (2nd ed.). London: Duckworth.

Plumwood, V. (1993). *Feminism and the mastery of nature*. London: Routledge.

Regan, T. (1983). *The case for animal rights*. Berkeley: University of California Press.

Singer, P. (1990). *Animal liberation* (2d ed.). New York: Random House.

Schweitzer, A. (1923). *Civilization and ethics*. London: A. & C. Black.

Shiva, V. (1989.) *Staying alive: Women, ecology, and development*. London: Zed Books.

Taylor, P. W. (1986). *Respect for nature: A theory of environmental ethics*. Princeton, NJ: Princeton University Press.

Warren, K. (1990) The power and the promise of ecological feminism. *Environmental ethics, 12*(2), 125–146.

Wenz, P. (1988) *Environmental justice*. Albany: State University of New York Press.

Environmental Impact Statement

An environmental impact statement, sometimes called an environmental assessment, generally refers to a public document, prepared by a governmental agency, which discusses the potential environmental consequences of a proposed project, as well as alternatives and a recommended course of action. In preparing the document, the government agency generally determines (1) whether the proposed activity will have an environmental impact, (2) what the impact will be, and (3) alternatives to conducting the proposed activity that may have different or less environmental impact. Environmental impact statements as used in the United States also generally incorporate and respond to comments made by members of the public, local or state governments, or other federal governmental entities.

The document is prepared prior to the project getting under way, so that the project can be modified or even stopped if the environmental impact appears too great. In the United States, federal agencies are required to prepare environmental impact statements for "major" projects pursuant to the National Environmental Policy Act of 1969 (NEPA). Most U.S. states have similar provisions, which require state agencies to undertake similar analyses of proposed projects. Additionally, many other countries have established their own environmental impact assessment requirements.

Specific NEPA Requirements

NEPA requires each federal agency to prepare for each law or major federal action a detailed statement by the responsible official, which must include:

1. the environmental impact of the proposed action,
2. any adverse environmental effects that cannot be avoided should the proposal be implemented,
3. alternatives to the proposed action,
4. the relationship between local short-term uses of the environment and the maintenance and enhancement of long-term productivity, and
5. any irreversible and irretrievable commitments of resources that would be involved in the proposed action should it be implemented. (*NEPA*. 1969. *U.S. Code* Vol. 42, sec. 4332 C i–v.)

Additionally, NEPA requires federal agencies to consult with and obtain comments from any federal agency having special knowledge of any potential environmental impact, and to make available copies of the report to the public and all levels (local, state, and federal) of governmental agencies.

Once the responsible agency has obtained comments on its proposal, the agency prepares a "Record of Decision" document that sets out the decision the agency has decided to take, reviews the alternatives the agency considered, reviews the environmental consequences of the chosen action and the alternatives, and summarizes how the agency reached its decision based on the written record. If the agency's chosen action will have a harmful environmental impact, the agency should state how this impact will be mitigated, through monitoring or other actions. If the agency finds that a planned activity has no environmental impact, it prepares a "Finding of No Significant Impact" document.

Pursuant to court decisions interpreting NEPA, "major federal actions" have been defined as actions directly performed by a federal agency, activities that would be performed by an individual or governmental entity under a federal permit or license, or activities funded by the federal government through grants or subsidies, including grants or subsidies to private entities or individuals. Specific examples include construction of a highway or building using federal funds, designation of a wilderness area or logging area on federal lands, and development of a land use management plan.

The requirement to prepare an environmental impact statement does not mean that federal projects move forward only when an agency can guarantee an optimal environmental outcome, nor does NEPA prescribe any particular weighing of the social, economic, ecological, and technological factors that may be involved in any specific action. NEPA merely establishes a process that requires a federal agency, or in some cases other entities, to prepare a written report that can serve to inform public debate, with the goal of ensuring well-informed, open discussion prior to a decision on whether a particular federal action should take place. An agency could decide, for example, that the benefits of its action may outweigh any environmental costs.

NEPA also provides an opportunity for citizens to bring their own lawsuits ("citizen suits") to request that a federal court review an agency's decision to go forward with a project after having completed all the NEPA requirements. Under NEPA, federal courts have stated that they will review an agency's decision to ensure that the agency has adequately considered the factors that have been raised and has made a rational decision based on the written record. However, the courts are not entitled to substitute their own judgment for that of the governmental agency when it comes to such specifics as deciding the best way to build a project, design a plan, or take some other action.

Little NEPAs

Many U.S. states have passed their own versions of NEPA's requirement for environmental impact state-

ments. Sometimes these state laws are referred to as "little NEPAs." Most of these laws require agencies of the state government to prepare environmental-impact statements prior to undertaking certain projects. These state laws vary in (1) the scope of actions requiring environmental impact statements, (2) which levels of state, local, or municipal government are subject to the state's requirement, (3) the standards that apply to preparing the statement itself and the level of detail required, and (4) what standards a reviewing state court must use to decide whether a particular report is sufficient.

Environmental-Impact Statements Outside the United States

Countries outside the United States have developed their own equivalents to the environmental-impact statement required by NEPA. Such laws, like NEPA, seek to integrate broad national goals of environmental protection into the planning process of governmental entities. Variations in these laws can involve (1) which governmental agencies or branches are subject to the requirement to prepare an environmental impact statement; (2) how early in the planning process an environmental impact statement is required; (3) whether public participation is allowed, and to what extent; and (4) whether it is possible to enforce a requirement to prepare an environmental-impact statement, to address deficiencies in a statement once it is prepared, or to require a governmental agency to follow the statement's recommended course of action. Because environmental impact statements can be such useful planning tools, the United National Economic Commission for Europe, the European Commission, and the World Bank are all considering instituting them.

Barbara L. Wester

Note: The views expressed in this article are the personal views of the author and do not necessarily represent those of U.S. Environmental Protection Administration.

Further Reading

Andreen, W. L. (2000). Environmental law and international assistance: The challenge of strengthening environmental law in the developing world. *Columbia Journal of Environmental Law, 25*(1), 17–69.

Briffet, C. (1996). Monitoring the effectiveness of environmental impact assessment in Southeast Asia. *Asian Journal of Environmental Management, 4*(1), 53–66.

Caldwell, L. K. (1998). *The National Environmental Policy Act: An agenda for the future*. Bloomington: Indiana University Press.

Frey, B. C. (2001). Environmental law. In H. Kritzer (Ed.), *Legal systems of the world: A political, social, and cultural encyclopedia* (vol. 2, pp. 481–488). Santa Barbara, CA: ABC Clio.

Caldwell, L. K. (2000). Is that all? A review of the the National Environmental Policy Act, an agenda for the future. *Duke Environmental Law and Policy Forum*, 11(1), 173–191.

National Environmental Policy Act of 1969, 42 U.S.C.A. §§ 4321–4370 (West 2001).

NEPA and Agency Decision Making; 40 C.F.R. §§ 1506; Other Requirements of NEPA, 40 C.F.R. §§ 1505–1506; Agency Compliance; 40 C.F.R. §§ 1507; Terminology and Index 40 C.F.R. §§ 1508. Retrieved January 22, 2003, from http://www.uncwil.edu/evs/module/envlaw.html

Teel, J. (2001). International Environmental Impact Assessment: A Case Study in Implementation. *Environmental Law Reporter*, 31, 10291.

Environmental Justice

The environmental justice movement emerged in the 1980s at the intersection of environmentalist concerns about natural resources and social justice projects for health, equality, and civil and human rights. Environmental justice brings up questions about who pays the price for the development enjoyed by others.

Background

Activists credit the launching of this social movement to a poor, rural, mostly black community in Warren County, North Carolina, which organized against a landfill laced with polychlorinated biphenyls (PCBs). In 1987, after the Warren County protests, the United Church of Christ commissioned a study that concluded race was the most significant variable associated with the location of waste facilities. Then in 1991 the first National People of Color Environmental Leadership Summit convened in Washington, D.C. Delegates issued seventeen principles of environmental justice, calling for just public policy, clean cities, ethical uses of land and resources, universal protection from nuclear testing and the production and disposal of toxic wastes, economic self-determination for all people, the right of all workers to a safe and healthy workplace, and full compensation and reparations for victims of environmental injustice.

Movement activists argue that poor people disproportionately bear the costs of war and the underside of progress. Their communities are most likely to be the sites of dangerous experiments, toxic wastes, and unwanted facilities, such as incinerators and power plants. Often residents are forced to accept contamination of their neighborhoods as the price for the creation of jobs.

People who live in these communities thus experience threats to their resources, their livelihood, and their health. Activists have redefined the environment to include both natural and social resources, and they argue for equal access to jobs, housing, safety, sovereignty, schools, land, water, and air.

Local Focus, Worldwide Issues

Environmental justice activism is largely locally based, but activists work on environmental justice projects all around the world.

Activists have protested corporations that mine for copper in Peru, where sheep die in the Mantaro Valley because of smoke and waste from the La Oroya smelter. In Brazil, they have also protested gold mining among the Yanomami, which polluted the Orinoco River. Noisy machinery frightened away game, and Indians died in epidemics of flu and malaria. Gold and copper mining in the Star Mountains of Papua New Guinea devoured fertile croplands and pushed sediment and wastes into the Fly River system. This increased water turbidity and restricted light, thus inhibiting the formation of algae so that the fish have died, the turtles have no banks for laying their eggs, and prawns, lobsters, and birds have all abandoned the poisoned water. Even after mining ceased, contamination continues as heavy rains leach metals from the tailings pile, and the Yonggom people downstream face health risks from exposure to arsenic, cyanide, copper, lead, zinc, and cadmium.

Environmental justice activists have also protested corporations that extract teak, lay oil lines, and destroy wetlands in Burma; drill for oil in the Ecuadorian tropical forest or on the farmlands of the Ogoni people in Nigeria; flood once-fertile rice paddies with ruinous saltwater to raise commercial shrimp in Bangladesh; or destroy the mangrove trees that stabilize the shoreline habitats of bottom feeders, birds, and shellfish in Hon-

The Sacredness of Trees

Even in times of war, Hebrews received specific prohibitions about how trees could be used, as these passages from the Book of Deuteronomy indicate:

19. When thou shalt besiege a city a long time, in making war against it to take it, thou shalt not destroy the trees thereof by forcing an axe against them: for thou mayest eat of them, and thou shalt not cut them down (for the tree of the field is man's life) to employ them in the siege:

20. Only the trees which thou knowest that they be not trees for meat, thou shalt destroy and cut them down; and thou shalt build bulwarks against the city that maketh war with thee, until it be subdued.

Source: Deuteronomy 20: 19–20 (King James Version).

---

duras. Shrimp farming also poses problems along the Rufiji Delta in Tanzania, where mangrove forests stabilize the coastline, serve as windbreaks, and provide a livelihood for the people who live there.

Activists have helped seek reparations for health problems and contamination caused by nuclear testing and accidents. Nuclear testing in 1954 in the Marshall Islands brought thyroid cancer, leukemia, and reproductive problems, including miscarriages, still births, and deformed babies to future generations of residents on Rongelap and Uterik. Nuclear accidents poisoned the land and water in communities such as Chelyabinsk in the former USSR.

Environmental justice advocates also criticize international lending agencies that press for high-profile projects as conditions of their loans. These projects include cash crops, hydroelectric dams, and hotel and tourist complexes that may ignore long-term environmental consequences and result in ecological imbalance, displacement of residents, and the proliferation of communicable diseases.

In eastern Europe, activists argue that the West appropriates the world's periphery for the disposal of toxic detritus. They have also protested the damming of the Danube, the relocation of nuclear technologies, and the introduction of non-recyclable packaging and potentially harmful products such as genetically engineered foods. These activists consider the emerging culture of consumption a threat to democratic political culture, and approach access to public debates and decision-making as environmental issues.

U.S. Activism

In the United States, activists have battled plastic factories and chemical companies in Louisiana's Cancer Alley, where toxic pollution is released every day in rural communities where the streets are narrow, evacuation is difficult, and rescue efforts are hampered because the volunteers' fire trucks cannot get in and out.

Also targeted are pesticides that launch reproductive cancers among Mexican-American migrant farmworkers in California. Mango and banana plantations in Puerto Rico also rely on intensive pesticide use. In 1996, more than thirty different insecticides, fungicides, and herbicides were identified on these plantations. High-pressure sprayers apply these chemicals, causing toxic clouds to hover over the community. Health problems such as bronchial spasms and asthma, skin disorders, and partial paralysis of the extremities have plagued the residents for years.

In Augusta, Georgia, neighbors in Hyde Park have protested contamination from a nearby junkyard and chemical plant that has resulted in high death rates from rare cancers. Like many other southerners, they discovered that industrial pollution kept them from gathering fruits and planting vegetable gardens. These losses have created more poverty because residents are now forced to rely solely on wage income in a community with high unemployment.

Tucson, Arizona's southside neighborhoods, predominantly Mexican American, inhaled dangerous fumes, drank, bathed, and cooked in city well water laced with toxic chemicals, including the deadly trichloroethylene (TCE). TCE, an industrial solvent, was used by military defense contractors for their degreasing operations. It was later dumped in large volumes on the ground and in unlined industrial pits. The TCE seeped into the aquifer and created a toxic groundwater plume five miles long and two miles wide.

Neighborhoods in northern Manhattan are surrounded by three major highways, and they also house two sewage treatment facilities, a marine garbage collection transfer station, several truck routes, a diesel-fueled Amtrak line, eight diesel bus depots and the New York/New Jersey Port Authority bus station. New York City's asthma death rate is higher than that of any other city in the country. In uptown neighborhoods, diesel bus depots are located next to schools, hospitals, recreational facilities, large housing complexes, and busy shopping districts. Buses are parked on the streets surrounding the depots. During the winter months, many of them are left idling overnight. The impact of diesel bus soot is compounded by the fact that it is discharged at street level, where pedestrians are walking and breathing. People living nearby suffer from asthma, cancer, skin rashes, and kidney and liver problems.

Chicago's southside neighborhood, Altgeld Gardens, is surrounded by landfills, incinerators, smelters, steel mills, chemical companies, paint manufacturing plants, a municipal sewage treatment facility, and more than fifty abandoned toxic waste dumps. Activists and residents designate Altgeld Gardens a "toxic doughnut." In addition to living with constant noxious odors, residents face high risks of troubled pregnancies, chronic emphysemas, bronchitis, and asthma.

Northern peoples have lobbied against redirecting their rivers to provide electricity for the lower United States and building a pipeline for oil that would block the migratory routes of caribou. They have taken community action against Alaska's chronic toxic pollution problems, for Alaska is used as a dumping ground by the oil, gas, and mining industries, which endanger native villages and traditional hunting and fishing sites. More than 648 military installations pollute the land, food, groundwater, wetlands, streams, and air with fuel spills, pesticides, solvents, PCBs, dioxins, munitions, chemical weapons, and radioactive materials. Along the St. Lawrence River straddling the United States and Canada, Akwesane Mohawk activists have found environmentally persistent organic pollutants that are neurotoxic and can interfere with the endocrine system, causing infertility, cancers, hormone disorders, and growth problems.

Hopi and Dine (Navajo) peoples gathered in April 2002 for a Prayer Run to protest the loss of drinking water from beneath Black Mesa. They charged that the coal industry has contaminated their aquifers with uranium and coal, interfering with drinking, subsistence farming, and sacred religious practices. They argue that expanded mining will bring more air pollution, respiratory problems, the destruction of burial sites, ancient trails, medicinal plants, and the habitat of antelope and golden eagles in areas that are traditional cultural properties. They are concerned about the fate of Zuni Salt Lake, where people have come for centuries to collect salt and to make sacred offerings to the deity Salt Mother.

Environmental justice movements have also emerged in river cities such as Chicago, Louisville, and Washington, D.C. Today the Mississippi River is so polluted that the fish are not safe to eat. In Washington, D.C., the Anacostia River is precious to those who live along its shores. The river holds memories of days of segregation and integration, civil rights activism, and times of social change. Many people have boated and fished there with friends and relatives for most of their lives. Residents appreciate the serenity of the river, and they go there to seek solitude or to extend social and domestic space. They enjoy the wildlife of the shores, which includes salamanders, newt, deer, beavers, osprey, egrets, cranes, ducks, geese, and other migratory birds. People often gather along the shores for picnics, softball or soccer games, hiking, jogging, dog-walking, bicycling, and family reunions.

However, many people who live nearby cannot get to the river because of the highways that separate their communities from the shore. These highways, in addition to denying river access, are composed of a solid surface that cannot filter rainwater, which, soaked with gas and oil, flows into the river. In addition, the Anacostia has become the receptacle of exhaust fumes, lead, used motor oil, tires, metal parts, antifreeze, and pesticides. Overflow from the city's trash transfer station, the Metrobus maintenance yard, weapons waste from the Washington Navy Yard, and urban sewage are also discharged into the slow-circulating habitat. Biodiversity has vanished on the river bottom, where silt blocks the sunlight and the fish cannot see to catch their food.

Environmental justice activists have organized cleanup campaigns that have removed 150 tons of trash from the Anacostia River. They have protested further development along this fragile waterway and have worked to restore its endangered plants and animals and make the water safe for people to use.

Issues for the Future

These difficulties plague many river cities in the United States and highlight a larger environmental justice problem: the world is running out of water. Because of the rapid chaotic urbanization of the global south, the World Bank predicts that two-thirds of the world's population will run out of adequate water in the next twenty years.

The lack of organized local government problem-solving with regard to this chronic water shortage has created yet another concern: the privatization of common water. In the past few years, trans-national corporations have taken control of all or parts of the water systems of such cities as Atlanta, Georgia; Berlin, Germany; Buenos Aires, Argentina; Casablanca, Morocco; Chattanooga, Tennessee, and San Francisco, California; as well as in Ontario, Canada; Ghana, and Bolivia. Activists charge that this has resulted in layoffs, debris and rust in tap water, slower service, billing errors, and rate increases. Additionally, private buyers are claiming the right to extract, move, and sell massive amounts of fresh water, serving one consumer at the expense of another. For example, 65 billion gallons of water a year are piped from the Ogallala aquifer to San Antonio and Dallas, Texas. The Ogallala, which underlies the Texas Panhandle and is the water source for the whole area, already is severely depleted and cannot be replenished. A potentially bizarre scenario could occur if San Diego, California, which imports almost 100 percent of its water, approves a business proposal from a private individual to pump 65 billion gallons of fresh water a year out of two Northern California rivers, pipe it into inflatable bags bigger than three football fields, which then would be towed by tugboat to the thirsty city.

The examples illustrate the most pressing goals of the environmental justice movement: to put the survival of poor, marginalized, racially marked people in the center of environmental concerns; to document inequalities in protection against environmental hazards and to seek compensation for and elimination of such inequalities; and to respect local knowledge and cultural values when addressing various ecological problems. The movement presses global issues about the shared commons, the health of tomorrow's peoples, the unjust tradeoffs they face between job creation and industrial pollution, the environmental space over-occupied by industrial economies, the ecological debt they believe these nations must pay, and the racial discrimination that links racially marked others to pollution, defilement, impurity, and degradation.

Environmental justice is a grassroots movement, with a network of at least 7,000 local groups in the United States alone, and an unusual number of women in its leadership, perhaps because they are the primary caregivers of children and the stewards of domestic space. Their strategies include using community right-to-know laws, investigating and exposing polluters through mapping, research, and community-based environmental sampling and land use surveys, and offering training and technical assistance to individuals and groups. The movement's future organizational goals include building the base, connecting groups, and broadening its reach to deepen the impact of its work.

Brett Williams and Jon Adelson

Further Reading

Bullard, R. (2000). *Dumping in Dixie*. Boulder, CO: Westview Press.

Davis, M. (1999). *Ecology of fear*. New York: Vintage Books.

Farmer, P. (1999). *Infections and inequalities*. Berkeley: University of California Press.

Harvey, D. (1996). *Justice, nature and the geography of difference*. Cambridge, MA: Blackwell.

Johnston, B. R. (Ed.). (1997). *Life and death matters*. Walnut Creek, CA: AltaMira Press.

Environmental Narratives

Environmental narratives are accounts that describe either the physical characteristics and natural history of a place or its transformation over time. Human populations construct narratives about the places in which they live or travel for a number of reasons: to suffuse them with meaning, to heighten awareness and appreciation of them, to better understand or come to terms with environmental change, and, increasingly, to contest the assumed or official environmental account put forward by authorities.

The Meaning of Narratives

Even before it was labeled as such, "environmental history" has generally featured narratives that ascribe to environmental change—either the nobility or triumph of human actions or intentions on a landscape (for example, Frederick Jackson Turner's 1894 classic *The Significance of The Frontier In American History*) or the folly and tragedy of human experience in bringing about the degradation of place (Donald Worster's *Rivers Of*

Empire: Water, Aridity And The Growth Of The American West, published in 1985).

Often, the same sequence of biophysical events in one region has produced two or more wildly contrasting narratives. William Cronon writes in his 1992 essay "A Place for Stories: Nature, History, and Narrative," that this is because this is what historians do: impose human value and discover meaning in all the stories we tell—environmental stories included. His analysis is centered on books written by Donald Worster and Paul Bonnifield, who provide two very different tales of the same essential chronicle of environmental change in the Dust Bowl of the 1930s. Bonnifield tells a story of human determination and valor in the face of desperately grim natural forces; Worster sees human arrogance and ignorance in the same raw materials. Environmental histories are given "narrative plots," says Cronon, because all human history aspires to some kind of "moral center" with the "human struggle over values" at the core of that endeavor. Cronon's landmark essay spawned a discussion in the field and influenced the work of subsequent environmental historians, including James McCann and Alan Taylor.

Cronon's 1990 essay "Modes of Prophecy and Production: Placing Nature in History" urged environmental historians to move beyond the sweeping, global "metanarrative" of capitalism as the culprit in most of the planet's severe environmental degradation, and, generally speaking, to explore such complicating factors as class, race, gender, and shifting political systems over time that can more fully tell environmental stories.

Anthropological and Folkloric Texts

In the decades after the emergence of folklore as an academic discipline in the mid-nineteenth century, anthropologists and folklorists began exploring the complex relationships that indigenous peoples around the world had developed with their environments. In Europe and the United States folklorists collected the mythical stories of legendary figures and events, songs of prayer and supplication to the spirits of the natural world, and systems of place naming—all of which had linked people with their local environments in profound ways for centuries. These folkloric forms of expression had helped indigenous peoples throughout the nonindustrialized world better understand the life- and death-giving properties of nature and to live within the limits of their environments. Place names affixed the particular life-giving property of a locale.

Among Native American peoples, ritualized taboos warned male members of the tribe of the consequences of overhunting or not properly thanking a defeated animal for giving its life for the survival of the people.

The academic investigation of the ways in which "backward" societies understood their place in the universe and maintained their traditions occurred simultaneously with (and was in part prompted by) the rapid modernization of Europe, the United States, and Japan. As those civilizations became more urban and industrialized, and as they scrambled for control over the resources and labor supply of Africa, Asia, and Latin America, political and economic elites of these modern powers sought intellectual justification for imperialistic policies and often used anthropological texts toward those ends. In addition, during the late Victorian era came the expansion of a traveling leisure class increasingly fascinated with exotic peoples who still lived—inexplicably in the face of a presumedly superior, modernizing world—"close to nature."

Natural History, Poetic, and Ecological Narratives

The birth of the natural history narrative as a conventional literary form is often marked in the late eighteenth century with the publication of Gilbert White's *The Natural History of Selborne* (1789), which explored the landscape, wildlife, and seasonal changes of a quiet English village, and William Bartram's *Travels and Other Writings* (1791), a thoroughly multidisciplinary examination of the southeastern United States. Later American writers such as Henry David Thoreau, John Burroughs, Mary Austin, and Annie Dillard would ground their prose in similarly close explorations of place, although they often probed inward as well, seeking insights from nature on the human world and the tension between nature and civilization.

Twentieth-century natural scientists often infused their scientific writings with similarly philosophical reflections. Wildlife biologist Aldo Leopold's *Sand County Almanac* (1949) featured two personal narratives: a tale of the author's awakening on the issue of predator control and a natural history of an abandoned Wisconsin farm that Leopold worked to restore. The book called in the end for a new "land ethic" for the postmodern age. Well known for her popular narratives on oceans, Rachel Carson wrote the landmark *Silent Spring* (1962) with a combination of poetic eloquence and scientific method, although her use of personal narratives of people around the country acquainted with the horrors of indiscriminate pesticide use made her and the book vulnerable to attack by the forces most threatened by it.

Beyond the narratives of natural scientists are the works of poets, artists, and novelists that provide colored and distilled accounts of place and reflect on the dilemma of modern society and nature. William Cullen Bryant (1794–1878) and Robinson Jeffers (1887–1962) are among the luminaries whose poetic narratives honored the beauty, grandeur, and simplicity of nature and eulogized its degradation at human hands.

Expeditionary and Travel Narratives

No genre of narrative has had greater impact on the physical transformation of the land than European and American explorers' accounts of their expeditions into lands that would eventually succumb to imperial conquest. Christopher Columbus wrote glowing descriptive accounts of his four voyages to the Americas that captured the European imagination. The first, in the form of a letter to his sponsors Ferdinand and Isabella of Spain, spoke enthusiastically of the beauty and bounty of the land he had claimed, as well as of the simplicity and docility of the natives. The florid language of Columbus and of subsequent Spanish explorers to the Americas—often hyperbolic and occasionally inventive in content, particularly when it came to the presence of gold and the willingness of natives to be converted to Christianity—stimulated continued interest of European powers in hemispheric exploration and conquest.

The imperialist thrust of expeditionary writing continued. Three centuries later Alexander von Humboldt's thirty-volume *Travels to the Equinoctial Regions of the New Continent* (1805–1834), an exhaustive study of South America, contained a bounty of botanical, physiographical, climatological, and anthropological information about the continent and, because of the narrative's commandeering tone, fueled the colonialist desires of Britain, France, and Germany for its possession. In the age of exploration and conquest, expeditionary narratives opened up exotic distant worlds for readers and regaled readers with the exciting adventures of their authors. Such accounts proved enormously popular. And because they were written by learned men sent from the seat of national power, expeditionary narratives were taken as unmitigated scientific truth when, in fact, both their substance and tone were influenced by personal and national ambition

and the ethnocentric cultural assumptions of their writers.

Early accounts of the American West advanced scientific and popular understanding of the region, as well as the American romantic infatuation with the West and its conquest. The *Journal of Lewis and Clark* (1814) exemplifies this tradition. Indeed, the Lewis and Clark journal rendered the West a *national* narrative. In the 1830s artist George Catlin compiled voluminous documentation of the land and indigenous peoples of the Great Plains. Soldier, explorer, and self-promoter John C. Fremont's guidebook proved essential to thousands of pioneers on the Overland Trails who established permanent U.S. settlement of the Pacific Northwest. The romantic narrative of the Yellowstone region written by Nathaniel Pitt Langford in 1871 proved instrumental in the sequence of events that led to the establishment of the world's first national park in 1872.

Beyond those of Columbus, several other voyage narratives are worth noting for their cultural and scientific impact. The writings of William Dampier (1652–1715), a buccaneer and British navy captain, became widely influential, particularly *A New Voyage around the* World (1697). Romantic poet Samuel Coleridge drew on Dampier's vivid language and inspired imagery. William Scoresby (1789–1857), an English scientist and explorer, produced *An Account of the Arctic Regions*, which proved pivotal in the development of modern Arctic geography. Finally, serving as an unpaid naturalist aboard the *H.M.S. Beagle* on a voyage to the South Pacific, Charles Darwin returned nearly certain that all life on the planet had evolved through the process of natural selection. More than twenty years after the journey, Darwin's *The Origin of Species* (1859) outlined his theory, and *The Voyage of the Beagle* (1880) became a natural history classic.

Popular Tales

With the flowering of mass culture in the late nineteenth century, the public's growing infatuation with nature found new forms of expression. The genteel sportsmen's publication *Forest and Stream* was filled with tales of big-game adventures from around the world. Middle-class magazines featured fantastic animal narratives written by writers such as Ernest Thompson Seton, who sold nearly 3 million copies of his books, the most popular of which was *Wild Animals I Have Known* (1898). Although criticized by naturalists like John Burroughs for imposing human traits onto their animal characters, Seton and the other "nature fakers," as they were labeled, presented a "combination of folklore, fiction and tall tale humor" that proved irresistible to readers (Schmitt 1969, 46). During the Progressive Era of reform, children's outdoor fiction also proved an increasingly popular form of nature narrative that reformers believed could help instill Christian morality and traditional American virtues. Youthful members of the newly formed Boy Scouts and Camp Fire Girls absorbed such titles as *Canoe Boys and Campfires* and *The Campfire Girls at Pine Tree Camp*. Also of note was the romantic wilderness novel that caught the public fancy at the turn of the twentieth century. Exemplified by such works as Jack London's *The Call of the Wild* (1903) and Irving Bacheller's bestselling *Silas Strong* (1906), the wilderness novel appealed to urban Americans who had lost contact with the wilderness of their forebears.

Anthropomorphic (having human traits) animals and images of a vanishing, wild America found voluminous expression in film and television in the second half of the twentieth century. Walt Disney's version of Felix Salten's novel *Bambi* (1942) became the archetype of the animated nature film. The narrative's features—cute and talking animals, villainous humans, and richly animated scenery—became staples of the genre. The wilderness novel was replicated on the big screen in countless children's adventure films. Beginning in the 1950s television featured a number of nature-centered dramas geared to children and families, the most popular and enduring of which was *Lassie*. Beginning with Dr. Seuss's *The Lorax* (1971), environmental narratives became a staple of children's literature in the environmental era.

Local Narratives, Witnesses to Environmental Change

Far more obscure than Bambi or Lassie are the real-life narratives of people all over the planet who over the past several decades have increasingly informed the environmental debate. With the passage of waves of legislation in the 1960s and 1970s, environmental problems increasingly fell under the purview of scientific and governmental experts to solve. One unfortunate result of that trend, say many environmental health advocates, has been the discouragement of local and meaningful participation in discussions of the history and origins of environmental problems, the degree of their severity and threat to human health, and how best to solve them. Simultaneously, the emerging global economy advanced by transnational corpora-

tions, multinational lending institutions, and developed nations has also tended to weaken the capacity of local populations to confront environmental crises, which are increasingly transnational and global in nature. The "metanarrative" (the larger political narrative that assumes the logic, inevitability, and progressive outcome of global capitalism) formed by scientists and policymakers that has advanced the interests of global capitalization has met increasing challenge, however, from a wide array of academic disciplines and local organizations. For example, with assistance from anthropologists, folklorists, biologists, and others, residents of the coal-mining region of Appalachia in the United States have injected generations of knowledge and personal experience into the official conversation about how to reclaim the regional environment. Environmental narratives, in the end, provide people with a historical perspective of one dimension of a vast and dynamic planet.

Chris J. Magoc

Further Reading

Allen, P. G. (1986). *The sacred hoop: Recovering the feminine in American Indian traditions*. Boston: Beacon Press.

Bonnifield, P. (1979). *The dust bowl: Men, dirt, and depression*. Albuquerque: University of New Mexico Press.

Cronon, W. (1990). Modes of prophecy and production: Placing nature in history. *Journal of American History, 76*, 1087–1147.

Cronon, W. (1992). A place for stories: Nature, history, and narrative. *Journal of American History, 78*, 1347–1376.

Cronon, W. (Ed.). (1996). *Uncommon ground: Rethinking the human place in nature*. New York: W.W. Norton.

Darwin, C. (1989). *The voyage of the Beagle*. New York: Penguin Books. (Original work published 1880)

Diamond, I., & Orenstein, G. (1990). *Reweaving the world: The emergence of ecofeminism*. San Francisco: Sierra Club Books.

Eiler, L. S., & the Appalachian Forest Action Project. (1996). *Stalking the mother forest: Voices beneath the canopy*. Washington, DC: Library of Congress American Folklife Center.

Glotfelty, C., & Fromm, H. (1996). *The ecocriticism reader: Landmarks in literary ecology*. Athens: University of Georgia Press.

Halpern, D. (Ed.). (1987). *On nature: Nature, landscape, and natural history*. San Francisco: North Point Press.

Huth, H. (1990). *Nature and the American: Three centuries of changing attitudes*. Lincoln: University of Nebraska Press. (Original work published 1957)

Mackenzie, J. (1990). *Imperialism and the natural world.* Manchester, UK: Manchester University Press.

Magoc, C. J. (2002). *So glorious a landscape: Nature and the environment in American history and culture.* Wilmington, DE: Scholarly Resources.

McCann, J. C. (1997, April). The plow and the forest: Narratives of deforestation in Ethiopia, 1840–1992. *Environmental History, 2*(2), 138–159.

Merchant, C. (1989). *Ecological revolutions: Nature, gender, and science in New England.* Chapel Hill: University of North Carolina Press.

Price, J. (1999). *Flight maps: Adventures with nature in modern America.* New York: Basic Books.

Regis, P. (1992). *Describing early America: Bartram, Jefferson, Crevecoeur, and the rhetoric of natural history.* Philadelphia: University of Pennsylvania Press.

Schmitt, P. J. (1969). *Back to nature: The Arcadian myth in urban America.* Baltimore: Johns Hopkins University Press.

Taylor, A. (1998, July). "Wasty ways": Stories of American settlement. *Environmental History, 3*(3), 291–310.

Turner, F. (1989). *Spirit of place: The making of an American literary landscape.* San Francisco: Sierra Club Books.

Turner, F. J. (1894). *The significance of the frontier in American history.* Madison: State Historical Society of Wisconsin.

Weigle, M., & White, P. (1989). *The lore of New Mexico.* Albuquerque: University of New Mexico Press.

White, R. (1995). *The organic machine.* New York: Hill and Wang.

Worster, D. (1979). *Dust bowl: The southern plains in the 1930s.* New York: Oxford University Press.

Worster, D. (1985). *Rivers of empire: Water, aridity, and the growth of the American west.* New York: Pantheon.

Environmental Philosophy

It is impossible to assign a definitive beginning to environmental philosophy. A case can be made that several Asian religions—Theravadic Buddhism, say, or Taoism, or certain forms of mystical Islam—constituted the first environmentalist philosophies. Other people will argue that traditional peoples have customarily developed Earth-friendly cosmologies (branches of metaphysics that deal with the nature of the universe) that, even if not formally codified in script, merit acknowledgment as the first systems of environmental philosophy.

Within Western traditions of thought, the Greek philosopher Heraclitus, the Pythagoreans (followers of the Greek philosopher Pythagoras), and Greek biographer Plutarch have all been instanced as thinkers who provide at least a pointer in the direction that environmental thought would later take, whereas Greek philosopher Aristotle's notion of the Great Chain of Being, in which all forms of life are accorded a share of the cosmic "soul," can be seen as a first important, if qualified, expression of an ethically portentous ecological interconnectedness. One contemporary Aristotelian, John O'Neill, has based an influential environmental philosophy upon Aristotle's principle of well-being, in which "the flourishing of many other living things ought to be promoted because they are constitutive of our own flourishing" (O'Neill 1993, 24). From medieval times, the zoocentrically (animal-centered) democratic theology of Italian friar St. Francis of Assisi and the "ecological" theology of the so-called Rhineland mystics—Hildegard of Bingen, Meister Eckhart, Mechtild of Magdeburg, Julian of Norwich, Nicholas of Cusa—can also be instanced as proto-formulations of what are now categorized as environmental philosophy.

Environmental philosophy is, however, most commonly thought of as Western and modern (or, in some interpretations, constructed in reaction to the "modern")—and to seek its beginning, as distinct from its precursors, one must look to more recent times, to the post-Renaissance world. The American political theorist John Rodman, an early chronicler of environmentalism's foundational influences, advanced the credentials of French essayist Michel de Montaigne (1533–1592) who, during the late Renaissance, observed that beasts are "closer to God and virtue" (Rodman 1974, 18) than are humans; and those of the important seventeenth-century Scottish philosopher, David Hume (1711–1776), who insisted that beasts are capable of all the emotions that characterize humankind and that they also have a capacity for reason. In terms of influencing subsequent formulations of environmental philosophy, more important is Dutch philosopher Baruch Spinoza (1632–1677). In Spinoza's pantheist (worshipping all gods) cosmology, all life is an expression of an immanent God; there is, then, no ethical hierarchy among forms of life—all are on an equal footing *within* God. Spinoza's influence upon the strand of environmental philosophy known as "deep ecology" (discussed below) is particularly important.

But, as emphatic as these positions appear out of context, in each case they are comparatively minor preoccupations within the wider scheme of their respective thought. Look up the entries for Montaigne, Hume, and Spinoza in generalist encyclopedias, and the aspects of their thought that accord them a place within the oeuvre (body of work) of environmental philosophy are either not mentioned or are accorded marginal status within their larger philosophical outline. To find a primary focus on the themes that constitute the terrain of environmental philosophy it is necessary to move much closer to today—to the nineteenth century, when the ravages of the raw young phase of the Industrial Revolution brought a concern for the fate of natural processes to the forefront of many people's consciousnesses. Even then, some philosophers of the time whose work was taken up and developed by environmental philosophers in the late twentieth century—English philosophers John Stuart Mill, Jeremy Bentham, and T. H. Green, and, although controversially, German political philosopher Karl Marx—still fit the old pattern: Within the general context of their work, it is impossible to make a case for them as the founders of environmental philosophy. It is easier to make such a case for the Russian anarchist prince, Peter Kropotkin (1842–1921), or the English writers William Cobbett (1763–1835), John Ruskin (1819–1900), and William Morris (1834–1896). In the work of all of these, what would now be called "environmental" concerns were foregrounded. On the other hand, none of them was conventionally "philosophical," their work fitting more into the category of political theory than environmental philosophy.

The contested fulcrum on which environmental philosophy as it is known today pivots is the ethics of the transactions taking place between *Homo sapiens* and other forms and processes of life. This being so, environmental philosophy can most plausibly be held to begin with the Romantic movement in the nineteenth century, and the positions and people noted earlier are best accorded the status of precursor. The *central* preoccupation of contemporary environmental philosophy was also the *central* preoccupation of the Romantics. Lacking a coherent philosophical core, and manifesting differently within different national traditions, Romanticism is best understood as a reaction against the massive physical and social dislocations occasioned by the onset of industrialism. Its most important articulators, German writer Johann von Goethe (1803–1882), English poet William Wordsworth (1770–1850), English poet Samuel Taylor Coleridge (1772–1834), and the "new world" Transcendentalists, U.S. writers Ralph Waldo Emerson (1803–1882) and Henry David Tho-

reau (1817–1862), differed greatly in preoccupation, approach, and, often, in the particulars of their positions. But all sought to make a case for nature as a prior sustaining context that humans need for the nurture of their souls. Goethe, Wordsworth, and Thoreau in particular were nature focused, and opinions differ over the extent to which theirs was a developed ecological sensibility, with the negative view holding that, for the Romantics, nature was merely the medium through which one might approach the presence of God—or at least attain heights of sublime inspiration not attainable by other means. Nature, in other words, has the status of conduit for individual enlightenment. It is not seen in the first instance as a network of ecological relationships needing no human presence to acquire meaning. In terms of ethics, the injunction is to come humbly to nature, to listen, to let one's self be absorbed within it, and to hope, thereby, to attain transcendent insight.

The ecological possibilities within Romanticism were first made manifest by U.S. naturalist John Muir, a tireless campaigner on behalf of wilderness preservation in North America, from the 1880s until his death in 1914. Muir articulated a wilderness theology that joined the Scottish Calvinism of his upbringing with a Romantic's belief in the proximity of God within the "temple" of his wild creation. Wilderness, he wrote, is "full of God's thoughts" (Muir 1970, 78), and, through contact with the wild, people could not only obtain refreshment for their individual souls and bodies, but also directly apprehend the universal soul. But Muir's writings also show that he viewed nature as constituted through what would not be called "ecological relationships."

The Land Ethic

The need to find an in-principle defense of "wilderness" (*wilderness* is a term that has come to be much contested within the literature but that was largely unproblematic until the last quarter of the twentieth century) became, in the twentieth century, the evolutionary driver within environmental philosophy and explains why most foundational contributions to environmental philosophy (there are conspicuous exceptions) were generated in non-European intellectual contexts.

Muir's preservationist mantle was taken up in the 1930s by the American forester, Aldo Leopold, the first person to overtly and unambiguously base a scheme of ethics upon insights derived from ecology. For Leopold the web of relatedness in which all life is dependently bound is "the outstanding discovery of the twentieth century" (Nash 1982, 196). Drawing upon principles of ecological science familiar to himself but with little currency in the wider world, Leopold argued for an "ecological conscience"—a broad sympathy for all life that would halt the rush to species extermination that was apparent to him even in the 1930s, before incontrovertible evidence for same became widely apparent.

Leopold formulated a "land ethic": "a thing is right when it tends to preserve the integrity, stability and beauty of the biotic community. It is wrong when it tends otherwise" (Leopold 1968, 224–225). In this, the first customized formulation of an ecological ethic, he sought to extend the ethical realm beyond the human species boundary to include the community of all life. "The land ethic," he wrote, "enlarges the boundaries of the community to include soils, waters, plants and animals" (Leopold 1968, 204), and humans assume the behavioral obligations that community membership necessarily entails.

Environmental Philosophy in the 1970s: The "Classical" Phase

Although Leopold's works remained in circulation through the 1950s, that decade constitutes something of a hiatus in the development of environmental philosophy. The line of environmental thought that remains unbroken to this day begins with the publication in 1962 of Murray Bookchin's *Our Synthetic Environment* (written under the pseudonym of Lewis Herber) and, more particularly, of U.S. writer Rachel Carson's *Silent Spring*. Other factors conspired to create a potent environmental movement in the 1960s and early 1970s: the climate of dissent and critical inquiry generated by the "counterculture" generally and opposition to the Vietnam War in particular and the alarmist scientific prognostications of U.S. biologist Paul Ehrlich and the Limits to Growth team. At this time "environmentalism" was overwhelmingly a science-informed movement. Activism proceeded with little regard, or felt need, for ethical theory, and insofar as environmental philosophy did have an impact upon the wider movement and public, it was in the gaps of eco-political thought that this was to be found, whereas the environment movement's preferred politics at this time was authoritarian and antidemocratic.

But environmental philosophy would flourish in the 1980s, and the groundwork for this was laid in

the 1970s, when the "classical" pioneering works of environmental philosophy were written and the contested philosophical terrain of the 1980s was staked. The Australian author Peter Singer's *Animal Liberation* was published in 1975. Norwegian philosopher Arne Naess wrote his influential paper, "The Shallow and the Deep, Long-Range Ecology Movement: A Summary" in 1973. John Rodman published several brilliantly written papers arguing for a radical liberal ecology in the tradition of John Stuart Mill. Val and Richard Routley (each would later make major contributions under the names of Richard Sylvan and Val Plumwood), separately and together, published a series of important articles that laid the footings of axiological (value-based; seeking to arrive at objective principles of "ought" and "ought not") environmental philosophy. In different ways, so did J. Baird Callicott, who extended and developed Leopold's land ethic, Paul Taylor, Holmes Rolston III, William Godfrey-Smith, and others. Rosemary Radford Ruether published *New Woman, New Earth* in 1975. Each of these seminal works prefigured the major positions in environmental philosophy that emerged in the 1980s.

Rival Schools in the 1980s

Singer's book struck a considerable chord, and animal liberation became the first school of environmental philosophy to attain broad prominence. Employing the utilitarian calculus of Jeremy Bentham's pleasure-pain principle—that an act is wrong if the sum of pain that ensues outweighs the sum of pleasure—Singer argued that the higher animals must be moral subjects, with interests that humans are duty bound to acknowledge and respect, because they demonstrably have a capacity for experiencing pain. His formulation extended the bounds of moral subjectivity well beyond the human species boundary, with far-reaching implications for such practices as meat consumption and animal experimentation. Rival "animalist" philosophies were also developed, most prominently the case for animal "rights" that Tom Regan set against Singer's sentience-sourced case from "interests."

The ecological limitations of a scheme of thought in which the relevant ethical unit is the individual item of life were under attack by the late 1970s. Animal liberation gave no ethical status to any of the plant kingdom, or to ecological processes, nor did it provide a means to privilege the interests of a member of a threatened sentient species over a member of an abundant sentient species. By the early 1980s a much more ecologically informed holism (a theory that the universe should be seen in terms of interacting wholes that are more than the mere sum of elementary particles) had become the dominant school of environmental philosophy. This is "deep ecology," a nonaxiological philosophy wherein environmentally responsible behavior is attained through the perceiving individual self, via a process of empathetic identification, taking as his/her own a broad compass of life interests. It is a process defined by its founder, Arne Naess, as "Self-realization." One constructs an enlarged sense of "Self" (the capital *S* is used to distinguish this from the narrow, corporeal "self") in which the time-sanctioned assumption of human centeredness (anthropocentricism) is displaced by a habitual assumption of "ecocentricism" (finding meaning in ecological relationships).

By the late 1980s deep ecology and the writings of its key elaborators, Arne Naess, George Sessions, Bill Devall, and Warwick Fox, were themselves undergoing sustained criticism—from axiologists such as Richard Sylvan, from the veteran eco-anarchist, Murray Bookchin, and from eco-feminists. For Bookchin and for eco-feminism the irredeemable flaw within deep ecology is that, in positing a generalized attitude of anthropocentrism as the key to environmental pathologies, deep ecology is blind to the systemic injustices within intrahuman structures that are the prime cause of environmentally destructive activities. For Bookchin this is hierarchy; for eco-feminists it is patriarchy.

Eco-feminism posits a deeply ingrained conceptual link between the domination of nature and the patriarchal domination of women. Organized in a series of mutually reinforcing dominance-dependence dualisms (for example mind/body, abstraction/embodiment, rationality/intuition, culture/nature), these ingrained attitudinal biases powerfully militate against the interests of both women and nature. Eco-feminism thus supplies a theory of power that is seen to be absent in deep ecology. It also has a more specifically ethical dimension; here emphasis falls upon an ethic of care, an ethic characterized by fellow-feeling and respect for what is "other than I." U.S. Eco-feminist Karen Warren describes this as a "shift in attitude from 'arrogant perception' to 'loving perception' of the nonhuman world ... in such a way that perception of other as other is an expression of love for one who/which is recognised at the outset as independent, dissimilar, different" (Warren 1990, 137).

Fragmentation in the 1990s and Beyond

Although ecofeminism remains robust, since the early 1990s the conceptual coherence of environmental philosophy has been lost as rival perspectives have come into existence at a bewilderingly rapid rate. The somewhat belated interest in environmental philosophy shown by European philosophers from the 1980s is in large part responsible for this. With little intellectual sympathy for wilderness-derived eco-philosophies, most of these thinkers have found within familiar philosophical forebears and precepts all that is necessary to construct an adequate environment-regarding ethic. Environmental anthropocentrisms have again attained prominence, for example, and there has also been a pronounced shift from "pure" ethics to practical ethics. It is unlikely that the simple lines of contestation that characterize environmental philosophy up until the late 1980s will return.

Peter Hay

See also Aristotle; Dewey, John; Ecofeminism; Ecology, Deep; Environmental Ethics; Fascism; Gandhi, Mohandas; Laozi; Mencius; Muir, John; Plato; Romanticism; Steiner, Rudolf; Taoism; Theophrastus; Utopianism; Vegetarianism

Further Reading

Benton, T. (1993). *Natural relations: Ecology, animal rights and social justice.* London: Verso.

Callicott, J. B. (1980). Animal liberation: A triangular affair. *Environmental Ethics, 2*(4), 311–338.

Callicott, J. B., & Nelson, M. P. (Eds.). (1998). *The great new wilderness debate.* Athens: University of Georgia Press.

Devall, B., & Sessions, G. (1985). *Deep ecology: Living as if nature mattered.* Salt Lake City, UT: Gibbs M. Smith.

Fox, W. (1990). *Toward a transpersonal ecology: Developing new foundations for environmentalism.* Boston: Shambhala.

Fox, W. (1996). A critical overview of environmental ethics. *World Futures, 46*(1), 1–21.

Godfrey-Smith, W. (1979). The value of wilderness. *Environmental Ethics, 1*(4), 309–319.

Hay, P. (2002). *A companion to environmental thought.* Edinburgh, UK: Edinburgh University Press.

Hayward, T. (1995). *Ecological thought: An introduction.* Cambridge, UK: Polity.

King, Y. (1981). Feminism and the revolt of nature. *Heresies, 13*(4), 12–16.

Leopold, A. (1968). *A Sand County almanac, and sketches here and there.* New York: Oxford University Press.

Light, A., & Katz, E. (Eds.). (1996). *Environmental pragmatism.* New York: Routledge.

Marshall, P. (1992). *Nature's web: An exploration of ecological thinking*. London: Simon & Schuster.

Merchant, C. (1992). *Radical ecology: The search for a livable world*. New York: Routledge.

Muir, J. (1970). *Our national parks*. New York: AMS Press.

Naess, A. (1973). The shallow and the deep, long-range ecology movement: A summary. *Inquiry, 16*(1), 95–100.

Nash, R. (1982). *Wilderness and the American mind* (3rd ed.). New Haven, CT: Yale University Press.

Norton, B. G. (1991). *Toward unity among environmentalists*. New York: Oxford University Press.

Oelschlaeger, M. (1991). *The idea of wilderness: From prehistory to the age of ecology*. New Haven, CT: Yale University Press.

O'Neill, J. (1993). *Ecology, policy and politics: Human wellbeing and the natural world*. London: Routledge.

Plumwood, V. (1993). *Feminism and the mastery of nature*. London: Routledge.

Plumwood, V. (2002). *Environmental culture: The ecological crisis of reason*. London: Routledge.

Rodman, J. (1974). The dolphin papers. *North American Review, 259*(1), 12–26.

Rodman, J. (1977). The liberation of nature? *Inquiry, 20*(1), 83–145.

Rolston, H., III. (1998). *Environmental ethics: Duties and values in the natural world*. Philadelphia: Temple University Press.

Ruether, R. R. (1975). *New woman, new Earth: Sexist ideologies and human liberation*. New York: Seabury.

Salleh, A. K. (1984). Deeper than deep ecology: The ecofeminist connection. *Environmental Ethics, 6*(4), 339–345.

Singer, P. (1975). *Animal liberation: A new ethics for our treatment of animals*. New York: New York Review/Random House.

Sylvan, R., & Bennett, D. (1994). *The greening of ethics*. Cambridge, UK: White Horse Press.

Taylor, P. W. (1987). *Respect for nature: A theory of environmental ethics*. Princeton, NJ: Princeton University Press.

Warren, K. (1990). The power and the promise of ecological feminism. *Environmental Ethics, 12*(2), 121–146.

Warren, K. (2000). *Ecofeminist philosophy: A Western perspective on what it is, and why it matters*. New York: Rowman & Littlefield.

Environmental Politics

People value the environment because their livelihood and quality of life depend on it. As threats to the environment grow, so, too, do efforts to protect their interests in the environment. Environmental politics is concerned with the way people organize themselves and structure behavior to protect those interests. It considers the dynamics of social movements, institutions, and government policymaking and the way these interact. As an academic subject, environmental politics is relatively young and interdisciplinary, with significant contributions coming from history, political science, geography, sociology, anthropology, and environmental science. Although clearly influenced by traditional political studies, environmental politics is unique in a number of respects.

Ecology of Environmental Politics

The ecology of environmental problems poses unique challenges to politics. Notable among these is the transboundary nature of environmental phenomena. In short, ecological processes do not respect political boundaries: Coastal nations share the same ocean waters and mobile fish stocks; rivers traverse state boundaries; and the air and atmosphere disperse pollutants widely and distantly from their origin. Much apathy and political conflict emerge from the frequent mismatch between such transboundary environmental concerns and existing political structures and jurisdictions. The benefits of economic development typically accrue to one jurisdiction, yet the environmental costs of such development are often passed on to other jurisdictions in the form of fouled air, polluted waters, and dumped wastes, providing little incentive to regulate pollution at its source. Furthermore, governments may be less compelled to impose regulatory costs on polluting industries within their own jurisdictions when it can be shown that local pollution problems result, in part, from outside sources.

The environment is also extremely complex and continuously changing due to myriad human and natural influences. This makes it difficult to assess environmental problems and a challenge to act on them. In virtually no other political field does science play such a central role: the evolution of environmental politics has been closely linked to advances in scientific understanding about the environment and human interactions with it. Yet, the complexity of the natural environment and human societies that shape it, combined with people's inability to study most environmental changes under rigorous and controlled conditions, greatly limits what scientific research can tell people. The resulting uncertainties create considerable space for political maneuvering and often justify inaction, especially where the costs of action are potentially large.

Such complexity also has academic consequences for the study of environmental politics. Theoretical models, often borrowed from traditional social science disciplines, tend not to stand up well when applied to understanding the highly dynamic and context-laden field of environmental politics. Experience has shown that political engagement in environmental causes is unpredictable and waxes and wanes with time, and progress varies from incremental to revolutionary, depending on changing contexts and opportunities. As one seasoned political analyst astutely observed, "the whole history of international environmental action has been of arriving at destinations which looked impossibly distant at the moment of the departure" (Brenton 1994, 251). For these reasons, the study of environmental politics remains strongly anchored in the historical and comparative analysis of case studies.

The Environmental Movement

The emergence of significant political concern for the environment is often dated to the late 1800s, when governments in Europe and North America began to invest in institutions and policies aimed at conserving natural resources. This "early conservation movement" witnessed the birth of national parks systems in North America and the creation of a professional cadre of bureaucrats trained in forestry and wildlife management at the turn of the twentieth century. As well, the first environmental nongovernmental organizations (ENGOs) formed during this period, and the earliest international environmental agreements concerning the management of transboundary rivers and migratory wildlife were negotiated in North America and Europe.

This political momentum slowed during the two world wars and Great Depression years but picked up with voracity in the 1960s. Unlike the early conservation movement, the defining issues of the "modern environmental movement" were pollution and toxics. Advances in scientific research and events such as London's "killer smog" of 1954 and the publication of U.S. writer Rachel Carson's *Silent Spring* in 1962 gave the public reason for concern. And society was changing in ways that made it especially receptive to such messages. The postwar economic boom created additional environmental stresses, but the explosion in affluence also meant that material concerns were less press-

10 November 2002

Dear Friends of Hudson member:

We're about to embark on an exciting new project to raise funds for the ongoing fight to **stop SLC :**

A quilt, fashioned from individual 10" squares designed & sewn by our many talented members, to be auctioned to the highest bidder at our March party!

The FoH Quilt Project

is spearheaded by two FoH Board members: Judy Grunberg, chair of the Events Committee and a past fiber artist, and Susan Falzon, an experienced quilter and chair of the Personnel Committee who will be joined by Laura Teague, also an experienced quilter & FoH volunteer.

We know you're out there: many of you may be professional textile artists & craftsmen, many more are amateurs extremely gifted with needle and/or sewing machine.

If you think you might be interested in participating in this community effort, please fill out the coupon below and send to:

Quilt Project
% FoH
pob 326
Hudson NY 12354

YES! THE **FoHQP** SOUNDS LIKE FUN! Please send further information to

name _____

address _____

phone _____ e-mail _____

This fundraising flyer was distributed by the Friends of Hudson, a grassroots organization formed to prevent the building of a new cement plant on the Hudson River in Hudson, New York.

ing for many people. Investments in education and other quality-of-life concerns expanded, and vibrant counterculture and civil protest movements against the status quo emerged. These various factors came together in the 1960s, triggering an unprecedented rise in public concern and political activism over the environment. Government responses between 1968 and the mid-1970s were especially impressive: omnibus environmental agencies were established, and a complex array of policies was put in place in many countries to combat pollution, improve waste management, and conserve natural resources.

Concurrent with these changes were a dramatic proliferation and expansion of ENGOs such that, by the mid-1980s, their influence had become pervasive in both domestic and international environmental politics. In fact, it is to the international scene that political actors have turned much of their attention in the last twenty years. Global environmental issues such as biodiversity (biological diversity as indicated by numbers of species of animals and plants) loss, ozone depletion, and climate change have emerged and increasingly dominate environmental discourse and politics. Since the groundbreaking United Nations Conference on the Human Environment was held in Stockholm, Sweden, in 1972, national governments have met with growing frequency under the guise of international forums to consider a range of environmental problems. International agreements to regulate production of ozone-depleting chemicals, trade in hazardous waste, and ship-based marine pollution are just a few examples of multinational environmental cooperation that has, in turn, increasingly shaped policy development at the domestic level in many countries.

Policy Responses

Governments have responded in various ways to environmental problems. In the 1960s and 1970s the preferred strategy was based on strict regulatory interventions, often referred to as "command and control," whereby environmental standards are set and enforcement is backed by the threat of sanctions. Such approaches typically relied on the deployment of best available technology and practices and were often cited as inflexible and unduly costly for regulated interests. Nonetheless, they proved successful for the management of many environmental problems.

However, the competitive pressures of globalization, combined with government downsizing beginning in the 1980s, created pressure to develop regulatory strategies that were more flexible and less costly to industry. Governments have since explored a wider range of strategies, including market-based approaches that differentially tax or subsidize some practices over others; performance-based standards that enable regulated industries to achieve set targets on their own terms; and voluntary approaches that encourage progress through information sharing and recognition of industry leadership. The courts have also become an important battle ground for environmental politics during the last ten to twenty years. Frustrated over perceived back-peddling by governments on environmental commitments, ENGOs have been using the courts to pressure governments to implement existing environmental laws and more aggressively prosecute industry offenders. As well, the courts have become arbitrators of critical constitutional issues, including questions of federal-state/provincial jurisdiction, aboriginal rights, and citizen rights to a clean environment.

Regulatory influences have also migrated significantly into the marketplace. Influenced by a mixture of consumer, government, and ENGO pressures, many companies have come to realize the benefits of marketing "green" products and a green image to the public. To the extent that specific cases of such marketing reflect legitimate environmental progress or simply "green-washing" is debatable. But it is clear that environmental and related health concerns are increasingly important in consumer decision making. Eco-labeling schemes that certify quality standards for such products as recycled content and organic foods have been adopted by many governments. As well, ENGOs regularly use consumer boycotts as a strategy to change government and industry policies, and some, such as the international Forest Stewardship Council, have even developed their own consumer standards for specific products.

Inequality and the Environment

The unequal distribution of political power and its consequences in society have long been a central concern in political studies. Such perspectives entered environmental politics relatively recently (early 1980s), but they have been quick to take root, and their influence continues to grow. Environmental "justice" issues highlight the unequal distribution of environmental impacts borne by different members of society. Thus, for example, some studies have shown that polluting industries and toxic waste sites are more likely to be found adjacent to lower-income and minority residential areas. Patterns such as this are seen to reflect the relative powerlessness of certain members of society who are unable to prevent the local siting of noxious industries or relocate to cleaner areas.

Not surprisingly, this kind of Marxist-structuralist thinking, which emphasizes in its analysis wider social factors like inequality, has proven attractive to many analysts of environmental problems in the global South. That wealthier countries may be "exporting" their environmental problems to the Third World was literally confirmed by research of the toxic waste trade in the 1980s. More complex is the consequence of differences in power that countries and regions bring to international environmental negotiations.

Perhaps the greatest scrutiny has been leveled at Third World governments themselves. Domestic corruption, cronyism, and incompetence are frequently cited as causes of environmental mismanagement in these countries. They are also seen as contributing to the ongoing political and environmental marginalization of the rural poor and, especially, indigenous peoples. Often characterized as environmental stewards, indigenous and other rural peoples have become the focus of international concern and campaigns that aim to protect local rights to land while enhancing resource conservation. Although the relationship between local empowerment and conservation is often a dubious one, it has considerable political appeal and so is likely to remain central to the discourse on Third World environmental politics for some time.

Globalization and Nonstate Actors

Although claims about the demise of the nation-state are premature, it seems likely that the influence of nonstate actors will continue to grow in environmental politics. In no other field of politics has the nonprofit, nongovernment sector become so influential. Many ENGOs today control large operating budgets, are staffed by experienced and highly trained professionals, and are global in reach. ENGOs exert influence on the course of public policy from the local to international levels of governance. Whether this be in the form of providing clean drinking water to rural villages, scrutinizing the environmental practices of multinational companies, or representing the environment's interest at UN conferences, ENGOs are no longer content to assume a peripheral role in environmental politics. Instead, they demonstrate an increasing willingness to bypass state structures altogether, "picking up where government action stops—or has yet to begin" (Princen, Finger, & Manno 1995, 54).

The influence of the private, for-profit sector in environmental politics will likewise continue to grow. The world has witnessed a tenfold increase in absolute trade during the last forty years, and the economic size of larger multinational companies sometimes exceeds the gross domestic product of nations in which they invest. In this highly competitive global economy, domestic governments strive for ever more cost-effective and business-friendly regulatory strategies. Market-based and voluntary approaches for greening industry are widely embraced, even if their effectiveness is not always evident. At the same time, pressures to harmo-

nize standards and regulations internationally are likely to continue to grow. The reconciliation of trade and investment liberalization with environmental conservation has become one of the defining challenges in environmental politics.

Managing the environmental impacts of business investment and trade will be especially difficult for many lesser-developed countries (LDCs). Multinational, private-sector investments in many regions of the Third World now dwarf those of the bilateral and multilateral aid agencies. Less-affluent nations are understandably eager to entice foreign-based companies to invest in them, but weak institutions and lack of political determination decrease the likelihood that environmental regulations are followed. On the positive side, multinational companies often bring with them more advanced and cleaner production processes that gradually displace dirtier domestic industries. Either way, the pace of economic change in many LDCs is astonishing and overwhelming in its impacts. Environmental and developmental challenges facing countries such as China and India are unprecedented and of growing concern for the global community. The industrialized North can no longer assure its own environmental future without the effective participation of these and other nations of the global "South" in future environmental agreements.

Securing the Environmental Future

These and other concerns will redefine environmental protection increasingly as a security issue. Competition over scarce resources such as water, oil, and arable land will grow and, with greater affluence to spend on militarization, increase the specter of regional and possibly global conflict. The possibility of calamitous events associated with global climate change may hasten periods of great economic and political instability, as are now occurring in Indonesia. Whether the global community fractures or comes together in response to (or in anticipation of) such change may well be one of the next great tests of multilateral governing systems. Either way, environmental concerns will garner an increasing share of political efforts in years to come.

Bradley B. Walters

See also Agribusiness; Carson, Rachel; Clamshell Alliance; Club of Rome; Consumer Movement; Cross-Border Pollution; Defenders of Wildlife; Earth Day; Earth First!; Ecofeminism; Environmental Defense Fund; Environmental Justice; Environmental Protection Agency; Environmental Regulation; Fascism; Friends of the Earth; Green Parties; Johnson, Lyndon; League of Conservation Voters; Nixon, Richard; Nongovernmental Organizations; Public Interest Research Groups; Roosevelt, Franklin Delano; Roosevelt, Theodore

Further Reading

Adams, W. M. (2001). *Green development: Environment and sustainability in the Third World.* London: Routledge.

Barnes, P. M., & Barnes, I. G. (Eds.). (1999). *Environmental policy in the European Union.* Northampton, MA: Edward Elgar.

Barry, J., & Frankland, E. G. (Eds.). (2002). *International encyclopedia of environmental politics.* London: Routledge.

Brenton, T. (1994). *The greening of Machiavelli.* London: Earthscan.

Conklin, B. A., & Graham, L. R. (1995). The shifting middle ground: Amazonian Indians and eco-politics. *American Anthropologist, 97*(4), 695–710.

Dryzek, J. S., & Schlosberg, D. (Eds.). (1998). *Debating the Earth: The environmental politics reader.* Oxford, UK: Oxford University Press.

Elliot, L. (1998). *The global politics of the environment.* New York: New York University Press.

Haas, P. M., Keohane, R. O., & Levy, M. A. (Eds.). (1993). *Institutions for the Earth.* Cambridge, MA: MIT Press.

Hayes, S. P. (2000). *A history of environmental politics since 1945.* Pittsburgh, PA: University of Pittsburgh Press.

Honadle, G. (1999). *How context matters: Linking environmental policy to place and people.* West Hartford, CT: Kumarian Press.

Korten, D. C. (1990). *Getting to the 21st century: Voluntary action and the global agenda.* West Hartford, CT: Kumarian Press.

Ostrom, E. (1990). *Governing the commons.* Cambridge, MA: Cambridge University Press.

Paehlke, R. C. (1989). *Environmentalism and the future of progressive politics.* New Haven, CT: Yale University Press.

Princen, T., Finger, M., & Manno, J. (1995). Nongovernmental organizations in world environmental politics. *International Environmental Affairs, 7*(1), 42–58.

Rosenbaum, W. A. (2001). *Environmental politics and policy* (5th ed.). Washington, DC: Congressional Quarterly Press.

VanNijnatten, D. L., & Boardman, R. (Eds.). (2002). *Canadian environmental policy: Contexts and cases* (2nd ed.). New York: Oxford University Press.

Vayda, A. P., & Walters, B. B. (1999) Against political ecology. *Human Ecology, 27*(1), 167–179.

Vig, N. J., & Kraft, M. E. (Eds.). (2002). *Environmental policy: New directions in the 21st century* (5th ed.). Washington, DC: Congressional Quarterly Press.

World Commission on Environment and Development. (1987). *Our common future.* New York: Oxford University Press.

Young, O. R. (Ed.). (1997). *Global governance: Drawing insights from the environmental experience.* Cambridge, MA: MIT Press.

Young, O. R. (Ed.). (1999). *The effectiveness of international environmental regimes.* Cambridge, MA: MIT Press.

Environmental Protection Agency

The U.S. Environmental Protection Agency (EPA) is the federal executive agency responsible for protecting human health and the environment, including water, land, and air resources. EPA is headed by an administrator who is appointed by the president. EPA has a national office located in Washington, D.C., and has ten regional offices located throughout the United States. Regional offices implement EPA's programs within the states for which they are responsible. EPA also includes numerous laboratories and special project offices, which conduct research, education, and outreach and bring stakeholders together to manage regional environmental issues.

EPA implements federal laws protecting the environment by enacting regulations, enforcing requirements in federal laws and regulations, and authorizing states and federally recognized Native American tribes to carry out permitting and enforcement programs consistent with federal requirements. EPA's laboratories conduct and fund research, which can form the basis for the agency to set national environmental standards to protect human health and the environment. EPA works with stakeholder groups, including industries, citizens, and local and state government agencies, to develop management plans for shared resources, such as the Great Lakes, the Gulf of Mexico, and Chesapeake Bay. EPA also has programs that address redevelopment of formerly contaminated properties (Brownfields properties), encourage industries to develop energy-efficient products (Energy Star program), and that attempt to prevent pollution (Pollution Pre-

The Individual Versus Society

The telling comment below was made by William D. Ruckelshaus, former administrator of the Environmental Protection Agency:

You go into a community and they will vote 80 percent to 20 percent in favor of a tougher Clean Air Act, but if you ask them to devote 20 minutes a year to having their car emissions inspected, they will vote 80 to 20 against it. We are a long way in this country from taking individual responsibility for the environmental problem.

Source: *New York Times*, November 30, 1988.

vention [P2] Program, Wastewise [solid waste reduction], recycling, and refrigerant recovery).

History

Before the National Environmental Policy Act (NEPA) was enacted in 1969, the federal government was responsible mainly for preserving natural resources and providing incentives for the states to do so rather than for crafting the standards necessary to proactively protect and enhance natural resources, human health, and the environment. As impacts of industrialism on the environment and public health became more visible during the 1960s, people began to look to the federal government to offer broad protections from environmental problems that increasingly crossed local and state government boundaries. By enacting NEPA, Congress declared that the federal government would play an important role in protecting natural resources and safeguarding public health. Although the federal government had many programs related to isolated aspects of environment or public health prior to 1970, EPA was created to bring together these many programs into one central agency that could be responsible for coordinating their actions and implementing new programs that could more comprehensively address environmental problems.

In setting the mission of EPA, President Richard Nixon emphasized that the agency would carry out the following functions: (1) set and enforce national environmental standards, (2) carry out research to better understand the public health impacts of pollution and how to control it, both through technologies and policies, (3) provide assistance to other government units to abate pollution by providing grants and technical assistance, and (4) work with the Council on Environmental Quality in creating new policies for environmental protection.

To do this work, EPA brought together many smaller programs that had been carried out by other federal agencies. These agencies included, for example, the Federal Water Quality Administration, which was then located in the Department of Interior. Also included were the National Air Pollution Control Administration and the Bureaus of Solid Waste Management and Water Hygiene, all of which had been part of the Department of Health, Education, and Welfare. Also included was pesticide work being done by several offices, including the Department of Interior, Department of Health, Education, and Welfare, the Food and Drug Administration, and the Department of Agriculture. The new agency would also undertake ecological research then being done by the Council on Environmental Quality. In addition, EPA would take on some functions of the Bureau of Radiological Health, the Atomic Energy Commission, and the Federal Radiation Council.

The first administrator of EPA, William D. Ruckelshaus, took office in 1970, beginning with a staff whose members were brought together from the many offices whose responsibilities had been consolidated within EPA. Ruckelshaus organized the new agency to focus on five major environmental programs: water quality, air pollution, solid waste, pesticides, and radiation. In addition to offices for these five programs, Ruckelshaus established offices that would handle planning and management, establish standards, enforce environmental statutes and regulations, provide legal counsel, and conduct research and monitoring for pollutants.

Structure and Programs

EPA was designed to carry out its work both in its headquarters offices in Washington, D.C., and in its ten regional offices. Generally, the headquarters offices set environmental policies, which are carried out through the regional offices. Each regional office is responsible for implementing federal environmental programs in designated states. The regional offices are Region 1 (located in Boston and covering Connecticut, Maine, New Hampshire, Rhode Island, and Vermont), Region 2 (located in New York City and covering New Jersey, New York, Puerto Rico, and the Virgin Islands), Region 3 (located in Philadelphia and covering Delaware, the District of Columbia, Maryland, Pennsylvania, Virginia, and West Virginia), Region 4 (located in Atlanta and covering Alabama, Florida, Georgia, Kentucky, Mississippi, North Carolina, South Carolina, and Tennessee), Region 5 (located in Chicago and covering Illinois, Indiana, Michigan, Minnesota, Ohio, and Wisconsin), Region 6 (located in Dallas and covering Arkansas, Louisiana, New Mexico, Oklahoma, and Texas), Region 7 (located in Kansas City and covering Iowa, Kansas, Missouri, and Nebraska), Region 8 (located in Denver and covering Colorado, Montana, North Dakota, South Dakota, and Utah), Region 9 (located in San Francisco and covering Arizona, California, Hawaii, Nevada, American Samoa, and Guam), and Region 10 (located in Seattle and covering Alaska, Idaho, Oregon, and Washington).

EPA also includes many specialized program offices located within national or regional offices or in other locations throughout the states. For example, EPA's Research Triangle Park complex in North Carolina houses several national laboratories that study how pollutants impact the health of ecosystems and human populations. Other specialized program offices include those that implement management regimes for shared natural resources, such as the Great Lakes, the Gulf of Mexico, and Chesapeake Bay. Through these offices, EPA can assist stakeholders in planning and coordinating goals for managing these resources. The Great Lakes National Program Office (GLNPO), for example, which is located in EPA's Region 5 office in Chicago, in April 2002 released a strategy for restoring and managing the Great Lakes that will be implemented cooperatively through state, tribal and federal agencies. The long-range plan includes objectives for reducing toxic chemicals in fish, restoring wetlands, cleaning sediments, reducing invasive fish and plant species in the lakes, and addressing beach pollution.

EPA's enforcement of environmental regulations and statutes covers both civil and criminal matters. The agency's civil enforcement program includes both administrative enforcement actions, which EPA has the authority to prosecute through its administrative

courts, and judicial enforcement actions, which EPA initiates through the Department of Justice. Civil cases may result in payment of penalties as well as injunctive relief. The agency established a criminal enforcement program in 1982 to target the most serious violations of federal environmental laws. In 1988 Congress granted full law enforcement authority to EPA and provided additional authority through the Pollution Prosecution Act of 1990. The agency's Criminal Investigations Division coordinates closely with other federal, state, tribal, and local law enforcement agencies and has successfully prosecuted cases, including cases involving illegal dumping of hazardous materials, ocean dumping, falsification of laboratory data, oil spills, and illegal sale and disposal of pesticides and hazardous chemicals. EPA's enforcement programs can also offer help to industry to meet the requirements of federal environmental statutes and regulations and to prevent violations from occurring (compliance assistance).

Many EPA programs are carried out with other federal agencies or with states and tribes. For example, both EPA and the U.S. Army Corps of Engineers (COE) have responsibilities for issuing permits for activities under the Clean Water Act that may impact dredging and filling of water bodies, including wetlands. Although COE has the authority to issue the permits, EPA has the obligation to study the potential impact of an activity on water quality standards and decide whether the activity is consistent with those standards or whether the activity should be modified to be more protective of the receiving waters. Such standards may be set by an authorized state or tribe, in which case EPA would work with the standard-setting authority as well as COE to ensure that a permitted discharge will meet applicable water quality standards. Accordingly, the two agencies work together to share information and to consult on permit applications. Similarly, EPA may consult with the Bureau of Indian Affairs or the U.S. Forest Service when it receives a permit application or disburses grant funds for activities that may impact federal Native American lands or federal forest land. Where an EPA-authorized action may impact an endangered species, EPA works closely with the U.S. Fish and Wildlife Service, as well as state natural resource trustees, to obtain information and to assess impacts of a planned activity. Where EPA and other agencies have frequent contact regarding similar issues, the agencies may choose to enter into a memorandum of agreement to streamline the procedures they will follow in each case.

Similarly, EPA may authorize or approve states and federally recognized American Indian tribes to implement many portions of federal programs when EPA has determined that the state or tribal programs are as protective of the environment as the federal program. Many statutes, such as the Clean Water Act and Clean Air Act, allow states and tribes to implement programs that are more stringent than federal requirements. EPA also has the authority to delegate to a state or tribe portions of its own authority under some environmental statutes, such as the Clean Air Act. Where EPA and a state or tribe reach an agreement on how a federal program will be implemented, EPA and the state or tribe will often formalize this agreement through a memorandum of understanding that will describe how the parties will carry out facility inspections, notification to one another, processing of permit applications, and enforcement of permit conditions.

Through its Office of International Affairs (OIA), EPA works with other countries to address international environmental issues, including transboundary pollution, global warming, marine pollution, and persistent organic pollutants (POPs). For example, EPA and Canada have an agreement on air quality whose objectives include reducing emissions of volatile organic compounds and nitrogen oxides, which contribute to smog. EPA's OIA has also developed monitoring, analyzing, and planning tools that are available for use by other countries to assist in creating emissions inventories or in setting air quality goals. OIA also provides educational programs and technical assistance to developing countries that are seeking to address such issues as disposal of expired pesticides, lead abatement, and mobile source air pollution (air pollution caused by cars, trucks, buses, and other vehicles).

Authority

Although EPA has periodically reorganized its divisions and offices, its mission of establishing and enforcing national standards for the protection of public health and the environment has remained unchanged. One of the most important sources of EPA's authority comes from the statutes that Congress has enacted that protect public health and the environment. Many of these statutes empower EPA's administrator to conduct studies to establish specific standards or to develop regulations that can more specifically implement the protections that Congress has legislated. EPA is responsible for implementing the following major statutes: the Clean Air Act (1970), the Water Pollution and

Control Act (1972), Federal Insecticide, Fungicide, and Rodenticide Act (1972), Safe Drinking Water Act (1974), Toxic Substances Control Act (1976), Resource Conservation and Recovery Act (1976), Clean Water Act (1977), Comprehensive Environmental Response Compensation and Liability Act (the Superfund [1980]), Emergency Planning and Community Right-to-Know Act (1986), and the Brownfields Act (2002). EPA is also responsible for implementing many other laws targeting specific areas of pollution such as oil pollution, underground storage tanks, and the safe redevelopment of former hazardous waste sites (Brownfields sites). Federal environmental laws can be found in the U.S. Code. EPA's environmental regulations are found in the Code of Federal Regulations.

In addition to the direct implementation of federal environmental programs (that is, those laws and regulations that EPA enforces directly against industries, individuals, or other government entities), EPA is empowered to authorize state and tribal governments to implement certain federal environmental programs. For example, most states have been authorized by EPA, or have been granted federal authority by EPA, to implement programs addressing environmental and public health threats under the majority of statutes mentioned earlier. Implementation of the Superfund, Toxic Substances Control Act, and Emergency Planning and Community Right-to-Know Act, however, generally cannot be granted to the states or tribes. All states and most tribes have their own agencies or departments to address public health and environmental protection issues as well. Many of EPA's programs provide grants or technical assistance to these tribal, state, or other government entities to address specific public health issues or to fund research to develop a better understanding of health and environmental risks and the tools necessary to control them.

Current Issues

EPA programs span the full range of federal environmental statutes, but the agency's budget is set annually by Congress, and the agency must also set priorities that are used to allocate resources on an annual basis. Although many of EPA's employees are scientists, including experts on public health and environmental issues, EPA, like any other federal agency, does not operate in a political vacuum. EPA's administrator is a political appointee selected by the president. Many top EPA officials are also political appointees. Therefore, the agency's work is sensitive to and can be influenced by political change.

Current environmental issues in which EPA has become involved include the national debate over how to best control air emissions from utility plants, including evaluation of current regulations that apply to these plants and possible new legislation that may revise existing law (Clear Skies Initiative). The final reach of any new regulatory program will depend upon the scope of new legislation set in congressional debate, stakeholder comments, and scientific studies.

EPA has also been involved in the international debate over global warming, which is the gradual warming of the Earth's atmosphere as a result of growing emissions of carbon dioxide and other chemicals that trap heat when released into the air. The United States's position on international global warming has changed under different presidential administrations. The United States chose not to participate in the Bonn Climate Change conference in 2001, when a coalition of international governments, including the European Union, Japan, Canada, Russia, and India, agreed to modify the 1997 Kyoto protocol on global climate change (which was signed in 1997 by the United States and 177 other countries but not ratified by the U.S. Congress) to reduce emissions of six gases believed to contribute to global warming to 2 percent of 1990 emission levels by 2012. Although an EPA report issued in 2002 directly linked human activities to global warming and predicted that impacts from global warming would increase during the next decades, the administration of President George W. Bush has publicly distanced itself from the findings in that report.

EPA's less-controversial programs include its Brownfields Initiative, which is a regulatory program that provides incentives, such as grants and protections against liability, to promote the cleanup and reuse of formerly contaminated properties. Rehabilitating contaminated properties might include capping areas of contaminated waste by covering the waste with a thick soil, clay, or impermeable barrier; routing rainfall and runoff into pipes to prevent groundwater contamination as precipitation filters through land-filled wastes; removing and transporting wastes to a treatment and disposal facility; or treating wastes left onsite to render them inert. These strategies can be incorporated directly into the redevelopment of a property where contaminants are capped, or removed from a property to make way for construction of new businesses, such as shopping centers, parks, golf courses, and even new areas for wildlife habitat. In creating Brownfields redevelopment projects, EPA works directly with industry stakeholders and community groups to set cleanup and redevelopment goals. Some examples of successful Brownfields projects include the Old Works Golf Course (formerly a closed copper-smelting facility in Anaconda, Montana), the Warm Springs Pond wetlands areas (formerly a copper-mining residue dump at the headwaters of the Clark Fork River in Montana), a public housing complex (on a former lead-smelting site in West Dallas, Texas), and Chisolm Creek and Wolf Trap recreational parks (on property formerly contaminated with more than 450,000 metric tons of ash from a Virginia Power Company facility in York County, Virginia).

Barbara L. Wester

See also Ruckelshaus, William D.

Further Reading

Durant, R. F. (1985). *When government regulates itself: EPA, TVA, and pollution control in the 1970s.* Knoxville: University of Tennessee Press.

Fiorino, D. J. (1995). *Making environmental policy.* Berkeley & Los Angeles: University of California Press.

Harris, R. A., & Milkis, S. M. (1989). *The politics of regulatory change: A tale of two agencies.* New York: Oxford University Press.

Landy, M. K., Roberts, M. J., & Thomas, S. R. (1994). *The Environmental Protection Agency: Asking the wrong questions: From Nixon to Clinton.* New York: Oxford University Press.

Mintz, J. A. (1995). *Enforcement at the EPA: High stakes and hard choices.* Austin: University of Texas Press.

National Research Council. (1995). *Review of EPA's environmental monitoring and assessment program: Overall evaluation.* Washington, DC: National Academy Press.

O'Leary, R. (1993). *Environmental change: Federal courts and the EPA.* Philadelphia: Temple University Press.

Powell, M. R. (1999). *Science at EPA: Information and the regulatory process.* Washington, DC: Resources for the Future.

Quarles, J. (1976). *Cleaning up America: An insider's view of the Environmental Protection Agency.* Boston: Houghton Mifflin.

U.S. EPA. (1993). *U.S. EPA oral history interview–1, William D. Ruckelshaus.* Washington, DC: U.S. Environmental Protection Agency.

U.S. EPA. (1993). *U.S. EPA oral history interview–2, Russel E. Train.* Washington, DC: U.S. Environmental Protection Agency.

U.S. EPA. (1994). *U.S. EPA oral history interview–3, Alvin L. Alm.* Washington, DC: U.S. Environmental Protection Agency.

U.S. EPA. (1998). *Agenda for action.* Chicago: U.S. Environmental Protection Agency.

U.S. EPA. (2000). *Reusing Superfund sites, turning toxic wastelands into productive assets.* Washington, DC: U.S. Environmental Protection Agency.

U.S. EPA. (2001, November 15). Preparation of third annual U.S. climate action report. *Federal Register, 66,* 57456–57456.

U.S. EPA. (2002). *Climate action report 2002, communication under the United Nations' framework convention on climate change, final version.* Retrieved September 18, 2002, from http//www.epa.gov/globalwarming/publications/car/index.html

U.S. EPA. *Global Warming.* Retrieved September 18, 2002, from http://yosemite.epa.gov/oar/globalwarming.nsf/content/index.html

U.S. EPA, History Office. *An agency for the environment.* Retrieved September 18, 2002, from http://www.epa.gov/history/publications/origins6.htm

U.S. EPA, History Office. *An environmental revolution.* Retrieved September 18, 2002, from http://www.epa.gov/history/publications/origins5.htm

U.S. EPA, Office of International Affairs. *Role of EPA's Office of International Affairs.* Retrieved September 18, 2002, from http://www.epa.gov/oia/about/roleofoia.html

U.S. EPA, Office of International Affairs. *Office of International Affairs annual report: 2000.* http://www.epa.gov/oia/about/rpt2000.html

Williams, D. C. (1993). *The guardian, EPA's formative years, 1970–1973.* Washington, DC: U.S. Environmental Protection Agency.

Environmental Regulation

Environmental regulation combats both the pollution and misuse of natural areas and resources, but also allows certain authorized emissions of pollutants and uses of natural areas and resources. It addresses the effect of pollution and misuse not only upon human health and welfare, but also upon the integrity and quality of ecosystems. In addition, environmental regulation promotes conservation, preservation, and protection of the environment. Just as the term environment covers the broad range of interrelationships among and between air, land, water, and all living things, environmental regulations cover an increasing range of human and corporate activity. Specific environmental regulations include measures to limit emissions of pollutants into the environment; preventive measures; measures to remedy harm or the risk of harm to human health and welfare, wild animals and plants, or ecosystems; restorative measures; and measures that assign legal liability.

Internationally, environmental regulation has developed in response to a number of global environmental trends, especially the following: unsustainable use of nonrenewable resources, increasing greenhouse gas emissions, reduction in and degradation of natural areas (with a corresponding loss of biodiversity), increasing use and misuse of chemicals, escalating use of energy, unplanned urbanization, increasing waste generation, stratospheric ozone depletion, disruption of biogeochemical cycles, and human population growth. Around the world, environmental laws and regulations now cover the following subject areas: air, atmosphere, conservation (of nature, natural areas, and natural resources), environmental impact assessments, fishing, forests (conservation and management), hazardous substances and radiation, hunting (harvestable species), land use and land use planning, noise, nonrenewable-resource use and mining, protected areas, the sea, soil, wastes (for example, garbage and rubbish), water, and wild animals and plants (including species protection and management, control of pests and diseases, and vegetation cover). Since 1970, regulation of the environment has expanded explosively worldwide. Tremendous growth has occurred in both the number and breadth of international treaties, conventions, and agreements as well as national environmental laws and regulations. Alarmingly, this growth has coincided with the continuing decline and in some regions decimation of the ecological systems that nurture and sustain all life on earth.

Variations

There are multiple sources of international environmental regulation. Comprehensive international treaties and conventions, regional multilateral agreements, bilateral agreements, and the rulings and interpretations of international tribunals such as the International Court of Justice and the World Trade Organization all play a role. Examples of comprehensive international agreements include the Rio Declaration on Environment and Development (which addresses sustainable development), the Convention on Biological Diversity, the Convention on Long-Range Transboundary Pollution (which addresses air pollution), and the United Nations Convention on the Law of the Sea. Examples of regional multilateral agreements include the Convention for the Protection of the Mediterranean Sea against Pollution and the North American Agreement on Environmental Cooperation (among Canada, Mexico, and the United States). An example of a bilateral agreement is the Great Lakes Water Quality Agreement between Canada and the United States. The environmental rules issued by the European Union can be considered intermediary between international and national environmental regulation.

Regulation of the environment in individual countries generally has focused initially on abatement of nuisances, next on conservation (the protection of resources, natural areas, and esthetic values) and later on control and prevention of pollution. Domestic environmental laws are an amalgam of statutes, codes, regulations, ordinances, executive orders, case decisions, and, in many jurisdictions, constitutional provisions. These environmental laws also include the bilateral and multilateral environmental treaties, conventions, and agreements to which a particular nation is a party. Most domestic environmental law, however, is statutory, consisting of regulation of activities such as air, water and land pollution, coastline use, noise, forest and wildlife management, the use of pesticides, the disposal of hazardous and toxic substances, and the preparation of environmental impact assessments. United States examples include federal laws such as the Clean Air Act (1970); the Clean Water Act (1972); the Federal Insecticide, Fungicide and Rodenticide Act (1972); the Safe Drinking Water Act (1974); the Toxic Substances Control Act (1976); the Resource Conservation and Recovery Act, which regulates solid and hazardous wastes and underground storage tanks (1976); the Comprehensive Environmental Response, Compensation, and Liability Act (1980); the Emergency Planning and Community Right-to-Know Act (1986); and regulations for their implementation. There are also laws and ordinances at the state and local level.

Environmental regulation explores the complexity of natural systems. Environmental regulations govern many parties and interests in flux; issues are interlinked, and sometimes the regulations explore the limits of knowledge in a variety of scientific disciplines. Environmental regulations also increasingly incorporate technological considerations and dictate what technologies or range of alternatives can or must be used in implementing and enforcing environmental standards. As scientific understanding of health and environmental risks increases, nations commensurately refine their environmental standards and develop new technologies to meet the refined standards. Environmental regulations thus are always awaiting inevitable revision.

History and Development

Regulation of the environment can be traced back to Roman law concerning public use of common waterways. During the Middle Ages, private tort and trespass remedies, enforced by courts, developed in some European countries. In the sixteenth century, some European governments began to regulate coal burning. The first regulation of sewage disposal began in the nineteenth century. While some domestic conservation laws date from the late 1800s, nearly all national pollution abatement statutes worldwide were enacted beginning in 1970. Indeed, what is now recognized as environmental regulation began to be identified as such only as recently as the late 1960s. Similarly, until the late 1960s, most international agreements aimed at protecting the environment served narrowly defined utilitarian purposes and were not specifically identified as environmental agreements. Beginning with the Stockholm Declaration of the United Nations Conference on the Human Environment in 1972, however, international agreements started to reflect a desire to limit damage to the global environment. In general, these international agreements paralleled national legislation that increasingly sought to preserve, protect, and enhance the environment.

Procedural Requirements: Assessments of Environmental Impact

Since 1970, the environmental-impact assessment feature of environmental regulation has spread rapidly, not only in the United States, but also in many other nations, in international treaties, conventions and agreements, and in the activities of international aid organizations such as the World Bank and the International Monetary Fund. An environmental assessment, sometimes also referred to as an environmental impact statement, generally refers to a public document, prepared by a government agency, which discusses the potential environmental consequences of a proposed project, as well as alternatives, and recommends a course of action. With its procedural emphasis, the assessment requirement is seen as not directly impacting on the sovereign rights of nations. In most instances, the requirement operates in a relatively nonthreatening and incremental way through compromise. Environmental assessments generate primary scientific data and analyses that are otherwise unavailable. In contrast to environmental laws that regulate private conduct that has an impact on the environment, environmental-impact assessment requirements exert control at the discretion of government itself as a developer, financier, and manager of activities that affect the environment. In many countries, the impact assessments can also alert park or wildlife authorities and environmental groups about environmentally dangerous plans of military, mining, or road-building agencies.

In the United States, the National Environmental Policy Act (NEPA, 1969) requires federal agencies to prepare environmental-impact statements for major federal actions that will significantly affect the quality of the human environment. A procedural rather than a substantive requirement, the impact assessment controls *how* an agency is to go about its decision making, not *what* the agency ultimately decides to do. The assessment must identify the policy goals of the project, present alternatives for public consideration, and set forth the preferred alternative or alternatives. NEPA requires decision makers to consider a no-action alternative. NEPA also encourages scientific and, particularly, ecological analysis of environmental problems. In addition, NEPA counsels decision makers to consider natural systems holistically, to evaluate the interrelatedness of impacts and the nonlinear consequences of a project, and to understand better the unexpected consequences of an action. Moreover, by obligating an agency to solicit, record, and respond to outside comments, NEPA requires public participation. In effect, NEPA encourages federal agencies to experiment in reasonable ways.

Substantive Environmental Laws and Regulations

Regulation of the environment has been heavily influenced by several ideas. As discussed above, the procedural requirement of an environmental-impact assessment has let individuals and environmental groups participate more fully in governmental decision making. On the substantive side, concepts such as control of pollution, preservation of natural areas, the reduction of wastes, sustainable development, maintenance

of biological diversity, and concern about worldwide climate change have strongly impacted the development of environmental regulation. Examples of pollution control laws include those mentioned earlier, which address air and water quality, hazardous substances, and the use of pesticides. National, regional and local parks have preserved many natural areas, some of them unique and of great biological and ecological value. International treaties on the shipment and disposal of hazardous wastes have furthered conservation through the reduction of wastes. This theme has also been advanced by domestic laws that require or encourage industrial process changes that reduce pollutants and wastes by promoting greater efficiency in the use of raw materials, placing greater emphasis on recycling and reuse, and emphasizing the use of returnable bottles and packaging and the production of more durable goods. The concept of sustainable development has long been a feature of forest and fishery management laws. In the twenty-first century, it is increasingly important in the use and management of other natural resources, including fossil fuels, minerals, soils, and the sea; in urban planning; and in understanding the limits that "Spaceship Earth" imposes upon the activities of human populations.

Efforts to maintain biological diversity are evident in several international conventions and domestic laws that protect endangered species, parks, and wilderness areas. Diversity in a related sense has been protected as a result of laws that regulate open space, preserve historic areas and buildings, and preserve the historically and culturally significant sites of native peoples. Concerns about climate change and disruptions of biogeochemical cycles are evidenced in international agreements to reduce ozone-depleting chemicals and greenhouse gases. But certain countries, notably the United States, continue to cause controversy by their failure to ratify or agree to international conventions on climate change.

Domestic environmental regulation, especially in affluent countries, has progressed through several stages. Environmental law and policy making have typically focused first on institutional and constitutional issues, then on implementation and enforcement of command-and-control laws and measures, and more recently on market-based incentives, voluntary action, and widespread public participation. In developing countries (whose economies are mainly agriculturally based), the development of environmental regulatory programs has often been constrained by weak institutions, insufficient human and financial resources, ineffective legislation, a lack of access to information about health and environmental risks, and a lack of compliance monitoring and enforcement capabilities.

In more developed countries—those with industrialized economies—experience with environmental regulation, management, and conservation is more extensive and longstanding. Those countries have achieved adequate environmental safeguards through implementation of command-and-control environmental laws and policies. In particular, they have relied on measures such as emission standards and limits as well as on maximum permitted rates of resource use and waste disposal.

Affluent countries are increasingly relying on a mix of command-and-control measures, strategic planning, market-based incentives and some voluntary measures to achieve a cleaner environment. Recent environmental laws and policies in those countries go beyond end-of-the-pipe controls and rely to a growing extent on integrated approaches that include cradle-to-grave environmental accounting, environmental auditing, and management systems to achieve cleaner production in a number of sectors of the national economy. In some affluent jurisdictions, a growing body of domestic toxic tort, environmental insurance, and brownfields (i.e., contaminated property or property perceived to be contaminated, generally in urban areas) redevelopment law is considered a part of environmental law and regulation.

Relationships among National, Regional, and Subregional Jurisdictions

Domestic environmental regulation exists in many forms. In addition to national environmental laws that have countrywide application, many political subdivisions of nations have comprehensive environmental laws that apply within the boundaries of their jurisdiction. There are as many systems of relationships among national, regional, and subregional jurisdictions in environmental law as there are countries. In China, for example, cities exercise controlling authority over many environmental matters to a far greater extent than in many other countries. In Germany, both federal and *laender* (regional) administrative agencies in each of the sixteen regions of the country exercise jurisdiction (sometimes overlapping) over certain administrative environmental matters and disputes. For the Russian Federation the most important environmental law is the 1991 Federation Law on the Protection of the Ambient Natural Environment. In the United States, both the federal and state governments have authority to regulate activities to protect the environment. In many instances, those authorities are overlapping, but in some instances only federal or only state law applies. In addition, some cities, counties, and Native American tribes have environmental regulatory programs that in general are independent of federal environmental regulatory programs and laws.

Proliferating Regulations and Court Decisions

Domestic environmental law is increasingly embodied in regulations that implement statutory provisions. As of June 2002, ECOLEX (a web-based gateway to environmental law created as a joint project of the United Nations Environment Programme and the World Conservation Union) contained references to over 19,000 domestic environmental laws and regulations at both the national and political subdivision levels in 480 different jurisdictions. The environmental laws and the regulations that implement them in the United States are the most voluminous in the world. Particularly numerous, voluminous, and complex are the environmental quality standards, pollutant measurement standards, requirements for licenses or permits, and emission limitations that federal and state environmental agencies have promulgated to implement the environmental statutes.

Lastly, an even larger and increasing body of court and administrative decisions, particularly in developed countries, parallels the proliferation of environmental laws and regulations. As a result of litigation, environmental statutes and regulations have been interpreted and fleshed out with case law. One of the chief challenges worldwide is how to have more effective environmental laws that are consistently implemented and fairly enforced, both by administrative agencies and by the judicial system. In almost all countries, de facto environmental law equals the pollution control and limitations on resource use that are actually enforced, rather than what is stated on the books. In addition, just because an environmental limit exists does not mean that there is effective legal redress when that limit is violated. This can be the case even in countries that have strong environmental standards, relatively effective environmental enforcement programs, and fair judicial systems. To work, environmental regulations must be able both to assign legal responsibility for environmental damage and then to remedy the situation effectively.

Bertram C. Frey

The views expressed in this article are those of the author and are not necessarily those of the U.S. Environmental Protection Agency.

Further Reading

Black's law dictionary (7th ed.). (1999). St. Paul, MN: West Group.

Bonine, J. E., & McGarity, T. O. (1991). *The law of environmental protection* (2nd ed.). St. Paul, MN: West Publishing Co.

Burnett, A. (2002). *ASIL guide to electronic resources for international law.* Retrieved June 24, 2002, from American Society of International Law Web site: http://www.asil.org/resource/envl.htm

Campbell-Mohn, C, Breen, B., & Futrell, J. W. (1993). *Environmental law: From resources to recovery.* St. Paul, MN: West Publishing Co.

Center for International Environmental Law. (n.d.) *Center for International Law home page.* Retrieved June 24, 2002, from http://www.ciel.org

Dolgin, Erica L., & Guilbert, Thomas G. P., (Eds.) (1974). *Federal Environmental Law.* St. Paul, MN: West Publishing Co.

ECOLEX. (n.d.). *Gateway to environmental law.* Retrieved June 24, 2002, from http://www.ecolex.org

Environmental Law. (1984). In *The guide to American law.* (Vol. 4, pp. 321–330). St. Paul, MN: West Publishing Co.

Environmental Law. (1998). In *West's encyclopedia of American law.* (Vol. 4, pp. 265–276). St. Paul, MN: West Group.

Federal environmental laws. (2001). St. Paul, MN: West Group.

Frey, B. C. (2002). Environmental Law. In H. Kritzer (Ed.), *Legal systems of the world: A political, social and cultural encyclopedia.* (Vol. II, pp. 481–488). Denver, CO: ABC-CLIO.

Grad, F. P. (1985). *Treatise on environmental law* (3rd ed.). New York: Matthew Bender.

Gündling, L. (1995). Environment, international protection. In R. Bernhardt (general ed.), *Encyclopedia of public international law.* (Vol. 2, pp. 96–104). Amsterdam, Elsevier Science B.V.

Guruswamy, L. D., & Hendricks, B. H. (1997). *International environmental law in a nutshell.* St. Paul, MN: West Publishing Co.

Hunter, D, Salzman, J., & Zaelke, D. (1998). *International environmental law and policy.* New York: Foundation Press.

Kiss, A C., & Shelton, D. (1991). *International environmental law.* New York: Transnational Publishing.

Kiss, A. (1992). Environmental law. In M. Boes (Ed.), *International Encyclopaedia of Laws: Vol 1 Environmental Law* (pp. 1–80). Deventer, The Netherlands: Klower Law and Taxation Publishers.

Legal Information Institute. (n.d.) *Environmental law: An overview.* Retrieved June 24, 2002, from Cornell Law School's Legal Information Institute Web site: http://www.law.cornell.edu/topics/environmental.html

Novick, S. (Ed.). (1999). *Law of environmental protection.* (Includes Release 24, June 2000). St. Paul, MN: West Group.

Percival, R. V. (1995). Environmental federalism: Historical roots and contemporary models. *Maryland Law Review,* 54 (4), 1141, 1171–1178.

Rodgers, W. H., Jr. (1994). *Environmental law* (2nd ed.). St. Paul, MN: West Publishing Co.

Rodgers, W. H., Jr. (2000). The most creative moments in the history of environmental law: "The Whats." *University of Illinois Law Review,* 2000 (1), 1–33.

United Nations Environmental Programme. (n.d.) *Global environmental outlook–1.* Retrieved April 16, 2001, from http://www.unep.org/unep/eia/geo1

Environmentalism

Environmentalism signifies a changed view of the relationship between human beings and nature. This view, which became clearly recognizable as well as culturally and politically significant in the latter half of the twentieth century, drew into question the common industrialist belief that human beings have the collective right and ability to dominate nature. Environmentalism has thereby posed a challenge to industrialism's enthusiastic confidence in human progress.

With its changed understanding, environmentalism also promotes changes in human practices, particularly through a diverse social movement seeking to reform or radically transform institutions. The limits of the human ability to control nature are vividly demonstrated, according to the environmentalist view, by the various forms of environmental damage and ecological disruption created, often in unanticipated and unintended ways, by advanced technological societies. Environmentalism generally considers the wide range of environmental problems to constitute a crisis, en-

Principles Set Forth in the Earth Charter

I. RESPECT AND CARE FOR THE COMMUNITY OF LIFE

1. Respect Earth and life in all its diversity.
2. Care for the community of life with understanding, compassion, and love.
3. Build democratic societies that are just, participatory, sustainable, and peaceful.
4. Secure Earth's bounty and beauty for present and future generations.

In order to fulfill these four broad commitments, it is necessary to:

II. ECOLOGICAL INTEGRITY

5. Protect and restore the integrity of Earth's ecological systems, with special concern for biological diversity and the natural processes that sustain life.
6. Prevent harm as the best method of environmental protection and, when knowledge is limited, apply a precautionary approach.
7. Adopt patterns of production, consumption, and reproduction that safeguard Earth's regenerative capacities, human rights, and community well-being.
8. Advance the study of ecological sustainability and promote the open exchange and wide application of the knowledge acquired.

III. SOCIAL AND ECONOMIC JUSTICE

9. Eradicate poverty as an ethical, social, and environmental imperative.
10. Ensure that economic activities and institutions at all levels promote human development in an equitable and sustainable manner.
11. Affirm gender equality and equity as prerequisites to sustainable development and ensure universal access to education, health care, and economic opportunity.
12. Uphold the right of all, without discrimination, to a natural and social environment supportive of human dignity, bodily health, and spiritual well-being, with special attention to the rights of indigenous peoples and minorities.

IV. DEMOCRACY, NONVIOLENCE, AND PEACE

13. Strengthen democratic institutions at all levels, and provide transparency and accountability in governance, inclusive participation in decision making, and access to justice.
14. Integrate into formal education and life-long learning the knowledge, values, and skills needed for a sustainable way of life.
15. Treat all living beings with respect and consideration.
16. Promote a culture of tolerance, nonviolence, and peace.

Source: The Earth Charter Initiative. Retrieved January 10, 2003, from www.earthcharter.org.

---

dangering both the interests of human beings and the values of the natural world.

What can be said about environmentalism in general is limited by the fact that its identity has been and remains contested. When environmentalism first gained public prominence—during the late 1960s and early 1970s in North America—its central concept was of man, a unified humanity, standing in a problematic relationship with nature. During the subsequent development of environmentalism, this concept of a unified

humanity was thrown into question, along with the meaning of environmentalism itself.

Ecology has been central to environmentalism in complex ways. From ecological science, environmentalism has derived certain basic tenets about the complexity, diversity, interdependencies, and unpredictability of the natural world that challenge simplifying assumptions involved in technological and industrial development. In a larger cultural context, ecology has also been viewed as a source of insight into the natural

Man has been endowed with reason, with the power to create, so that he can add to what he's been given. But up to now he hasn't been a creator, only a destroyer. Forests keep disappearing, rivers dry up, wild life's become extinct, the climate's ruined and the land grows poorer and uglier every day

—Anton Chekhov, Uncle Vanya, 1897.

world and the human place in it. Ethics, aesthetics, and spirituality have thus all been linked to ecological consciousness.

Emergence of Environmentalism: The First Wave

Environmentalism emerged in two main waves of attention and action about twenty years apart—the first in the late 1960s and early 1970s, the second in the late 1980s and early 1990s. The cresting of the first wave came in the spring of 1970 with Earth Day on 22 April. Earth Day was to become an annual and widely observed event.

The first Earth Day, centered in the United States and involving the participation of more than 20 million people, occurred in the context of widespread public agreement that environmental problems require a concerted response. Environmentalism was in fashion. Despite this apparent consensus, however, Earth Day provoked tensions that were to persist in the development of environmentalism. A key question was whether Earth Day was the manifestation of a genuinely popular movement or the result of the manipulation of public opinion by elites in government, business, and the media. In fact, the event was modeled on "teach-ins" being organized during the period to protest the war in Vietnam and was the idea of Senator Gaylord Nelson. Antiwar activists complained that Earth Day served to divert energy and attention away from the struggle against the war toward the relatively safe issue of the environment. The question of co-optation by elites thus became a key issue, dividing reform and radical environmentalists and promoting an often-conflicting relationship, in particular, between business interests and environmentalists.

During the 1960s and the early 1970s a series of environmentalist books gained significant public attention and prepared the way for the kind of consensus the appeared on Earth Day. Rachel Carson's *Silent Spring* (1962) generated intense controversy and aided efforts to establish restrictions on pesticide use. Carson's book was also noteworthy because it combined an ecologically informed scientific account of a problem with a literary style evocative of a sensitive appreciation for the natural world. Later, Paul Ehrlich's *The Population Bomb* (1968) raised fears about the environmental impact of exponential increases in human population, and Barry Commoner's *The Closing Circle* (1971) argued that the prevailing mode of technological design in postwar industrialism ran counter to the lessons of ecology.

Although Earth Day signaled significant public perception of an environmental crisis, much of the environmental literature up to that time tended to focus on particular problems that were deemed especially important. This tendency changed with *The Limits to Growth* (1972), a report by Massachusetts Institute of Technology systems scientists sponsored by the Club of Rome, an international group of leaders in business, government, and science. Modelling a dynamic world system in terms of various growth factors (pollution, population, resource use, food production, and industrial output), the report projected scenarios of catastrophic collapse if substantial limits on growth were not achieved. Although environmentalists were generally sympathetic to the report's conclusions regarding growth, concerns were voiced both because of the elite composition of the Club of Rome and because the systems science orientation of the report gave it a style and focus in keeping with technocracy and industrialism. However, these aspects of *The Limits to Growth*—including its reliance on a computer at a time when the computer still had the mystique of a miraculous new technology—served to enhance the credibility and influence of the report.

The aura of crisis during the period increased the appeal of calls for an authoritarian response. The authoritarian approach especially advocated rigorous controls on population growth, but the proposed policies were often criticized, by environmentalists as well

477

as by opponents of environmentalism, as being coercive and unjust.

The main institutional response to environmental concern during the first wave involved modest reforms, taking the shape of new administrative agencies and legislation. In the United States, for example, during the period from 1970 to 1972 the Environmental Protection Agency was established, as well as legislation against air and water pollution and a provision for environmental-impact statements on projects under public purview. Similar actions were taken in Canada during those years and in western Europe and Australia by the middle of the decade. In 1972 the United Nations responded to the rise of environmental concern by holding the Conference on the Human Environment in Stockholm, followed later that year with the establishment of the UN Environment Program.

The first wave of environmentalism also brought the emergence of a range of nongovernmental organizations. For example, Greenpeace and Friends of the Earth began in North America at the end of the 1960s and spread internationally by the mid-1970s. Green parties made an initial showing in Australia and New Zealand in the early 1970s and had become significant in Europe, especially Germany, by the early 1980s.

As concern about environmental problems developed during the first wave of environmentalism, attention also turned to cases of environmental problems found throughout human history. Resource depletion and pollution were traced to earlier periods of human interaction with the natural environment in the form of such activities as hunting, agriculture, and urbanization. Earlier population concerns were found in the contention by Thomas Robert Malthus (1766–1834) that population growth would persistently outpace food production.

In connection with this attention to the past, there were suggestions that the current focus on environmental problems and claims of environmental crisis lacked historical perspective and involved misplaced emphasis. The contention was that there had always been environmental problems and that these seemed rather endemic to the relationship between humanity and nature. Environmentalists were alleged to have overstated contemporary problems, which could in fact be satisfactorily handled through human ingenuity and progress.

Environmentalism found itself challenged by a vigorous antienvironmentalism that particularly attempted to discredit as prophets of doom those who advocated limits to growth. There were, for example, both careful academic critiques of *The Limits to Growth* and disparaging reactions to the irrationality of anyone lacking the common faith in science and technology. Antienvironmentalism, especially evident by the tenth anniversary of Earth Day in efforts among U.S. business interests to promote a coalition for growth, signaled a collapse of the apparent early consensus on environmentalism and served to give clearer definition to environmentalism.

Attempts to discredit environmentalism were accompanied by efforts to fundamentally reorient it. Although environmental problems were acknowledged, their solution was supposed to reside within the framework of industrialism. Either continued economic growth was required to make environmental cleanups affordable, or a dramatic extension of privatization and the free market was needed in order to eliminate the problem of externalities—costs and benefits that fall outside the market exchange.

In broad historical terms, environmentalism represents a response to the emergence of industrialism, which began with the promotion of a technologically focused scientific revolution by early modern figures such as Francis Bacon in the sixteenth and seventeenth centuries. The idea that humanity has both the right and ability to dominate nature was clearly asserted during this period and supported the emergence of industrialism in the ensuing centuries. Although environmentalism was to challenge this idea during the late twentieth century, a critical response had already begun in the midst of the Industrial Revolution. Ernst Haeckel, for example, not only prepared the way for ecological science by coining the term *ecology* (in German, *Oekologie*) in the 1860s, but also anticipated an aspect of environmentalism in his belief that humanity should live in harmony with the natural world.

The most direct precursor of the first wave of environmentalism was the conservation movement that arose in the early twentieth century in the United States. Particularly significant were two key figures—Gifford Pinchot (1865–1946) and John Muir (1838–1914)—and a tension between them that signified different concerns in the conservation movement. Pinchot, a central figure in the development of natural resource management in the U.S. government, followed the principles of Progressivism by opposing waste and promoting efficiency in the use of resources for human benefit. Muir, founder of the Sierra Club, followed such figures as John James Audubon (1785–1851) and Henry David Thoreau (1817–1862) to focus on the preservation of wilderness as being important for the well-being of the human spirit. Aldo Leopold (1867–1948) later introduced a distinctly nonanthropocentric orientation—that is, one that does not consider humankind as the central entity of the universe—by proposing the ethical principle that conservation policy be set in accord with the interests of ecological communities.

What distinguishes the first wave of environmentalism from the conservation movement is not simply the content—for example, a sense of crisis anticipating global catastrophe—but also the context of 1960s social activism. This context included a range of social movements emerging against "the establishment" (for example, civil rights, peace, antiwar, black power, feminism), and these were sometimes portrayed as a single movement of the new left for radical social change. This context of social movement activism is reflected, for example, both in David Brower's founding of the activist Friends of the Earth in 1969 (after leaving the leadership of the Sierra Club) and in concerns at the time of the first Earth Day that the establishment might co-opt environmentalism.

From First to Second Wave: Issues and Institutions

With its first wave, environmentalism became fashionable. By the mid-1970s, however, environmentalism was going out of fashion. During this time, worries about an environmental crisis were displaced by worries about an energy crisis—in particular, the specter of an insufficient oil supply raised by the policy of decreasing exports and dramatically increasing prices initiated in 1973 by the Organization of Petroleum Exporting Countries (OPEC). In the United States, a shift in public focus from environmental crisis to energy crisis was particularly significant in the context of controversy over the proposed construction of a pipeline to transport oil from the north of Alaska to the southern port of Valdez (to then be shipped to market via tankers). This proposal, the first to come under newly legislated environmental-impact statement requirements, was opposed by environmentalists through court action. With the energy crisis atmosphere surrounding OPEC actions, however, Congress allowed construction of the pipeline by providing what was, in effect, an exemption from the legislated requirements.

Antienvironmentalism gained an advantage in the context of the energy crisis, enabled to more effectively criticize the idea of limiting growth. Concern about energy, however, also led to a change in the focus of

environmentalism. With the first wave of environmentalism, pollution emerged as the most significant environmental issue, even though potential constraints on energy and other natural resources were also then an environmentalist concern. With the energy crisis, environmentalists sharply turned their attention to confront directly the question of energy resources. A key figure in this regard was Amory Lovins, who in the mid-1970s significantly reformulated the energy problem by proposing a soft energy strategy. In this strategy, the problem is viewed principally not as one of an insufficient supply of oil and other conventional energy sources, but rather as one of inefficient energy use, coupled with a lack of development of alternative energy sources (for example, wind, solar, biomass). At the same time, Lovins pointed out that conventional energy production was both energy intensive and a source of substantial pollution. With this reformulation of the energy problem, environmentalists criticized plans for large-scale energy supply developments, especially those relying heavily on nuclear electricity.

The environmentalist shift in focus from pollution to energy began a phase that included the development in the 1980s of a wider, complex range of environmental issues that set the agenda for the second wave of environmentalism. Prominent among these issues were problems of hazardous and toxic waste, acid rain, ozone depletion, loss of biodiversity, and climate change. A series of dramatic environmental disasters also occurred, each disaster becoming a household name during the period and helping to prompt a sense of urgency about environmental matters—for example, Love Canal (1978), Three Mile Island (1979), Bhopal (1984), Chernobyl (1986), and the *Exxon Valdez* (1989). Although Earth Day had been observed each 22 April since 1970, the twentieth anniversary in 1990 was remarkable in scale, involving the participation of more than 200 million people in 141 countries.

Even though environmentalism had gone out of fashion in the mid-1970s, a relatively quiet process of institutionalization had ensued. Despite antienvironmentalist opposition, government environmental policy and administration generally remained in place and continued to develop, although there was a tendency for the earlier passion of environmental politics to be displaced by an aura of professionalism. Nongovernmental organizations, such as Friends of the Earth and Greenpeace, became more fully institutionalized and spread beyond their point of origin in North America to Europe and a more broadly international context. At the same time, environmental studies became widely established as an interdisciplinary field in academia, often including the social sciences and humanities as well as the natural sciences.

As the second wave of environmentalism emerged in the context of these developments, the World Commission on Environment and Development, established under the auspices of the UN secretary-general in 1983, became centrally important. Widely known as the Brundtland Commission for its chair, former Norwegian Prime Minister Gro Harlem Brundtland, the commission popularized the term *sustainable development* in its 1987 report, *Our Common Future.* As this term gained ascendance, the earlier environmentalist focus on limits to growth was displaced by a focus presupposing the compatibility of economic progress and environmental constraints. The report explicitly championed the cause of alleviating global poverty. At the same time, business interests, largely repelled by the earlier idea of limits to growth, now tended to engage more sympathetically in discussions of environmental problems and found it possible at times to cooperate with reform-oriented environmentalists. Radical environmentalists tended to be critical of the new term, stressing that a turn of phrase does not suffice to make development sustainable.

The focus on sustainable development was reinforced by the Rio Summit, the UN Conference on Environment and Development, held in Rio de Janeiro in 1992. As had been the case with the Stockholm conference twenty years earlier, the Rio Summit had disagreements between industrialized northern nations and poorer southern nations over the environmental agenda. Although the outcomes of the summit—such as the Rio Declaration and the Agenda 21 implementation framework—were often criticized by nongovernmental organizations as well as southern nations for following the lead of international business interests, the summit marked the culmination of the second wave of environmentalism by bringing together leaders from nearly all nations of the world to discuss environmental issues. During the summit a division emerged among industrialized nations, as the United States resisted proposals advanced by European nations. This division reappeared some ten years later when the United States, refusing to join a global agreement on climate change, effectively resumed its Rio posture.

Many Environmentalisms

The first wave of environmentalism fostered the image of a united humanity facing a common predicament.

Because there is only one Earth, as photographs from space graphically demonstrated, everyone shared an interest in the care and maintenance of spaceship Earth as the common home of humanity. The protection of the human environment was thus everyone's concern, and the environmental movement should include everyone.

The image of a common humanity and a unified movement has been significantly challenged, however, particularly during and after the second wave of environmentalism, by the emerging idea that there is not one environmentalism, but rather many environmentalisms. Environmentalisms are seen to involve not one but rather many interests and perspectives—differences over both means and ends that make a single, coherent movement impossible: there is no one movement, in this view, but rather a plurality of movements.

Differences within environmentalism were already evident in Earth Day 1970 concerns about the problem of co-optation. What emerged at this juncture was the division between a reform environmentalism fostering change within established institutions and a radical environmentalism seeking a thorough transformation of established institutions. Reform environmentalism promoted legislative changes, new administrative agencies, and the development of environmental professionalism. With an uncompromising posture, radical environmentalism found itself in confrontation not only with established institutions but, at times, also with reform environmentalism.

Radical environmentalists, who often distance themselves from the term *environmentalism* in favor of terms linked explicitly to ecology, are themselves at times divided. Already in the mid-1960s, social critic Murray Bookchin set out his basic idea of social ecology. He argued that the science of ecology offers the intellectual basis for an emancipatory revolution that would, with the development of egalitarian communities, abolish hierarchy while establishing harmony both among human beings and between humans and nature. Bookchin would later sharply differentiate not only between his radical social ecology and a reformist environmentalism, but also between social ecology and the particular radicalism of deep ecology. As conceived by Arne Naess, a Norwegian philosopher, *deep ecology* means asking deeper questions about the relations between human beings and nature than were posed by shallow ecology. Deep ecology does include basic tenets, such as the nonanthropocentric normative principle of biospheric egalitarianism, which denies ethically sanctioned privilege to any part of nature, particularly the human species. Especially as taken up by adherents in the United States, moreover, deep ecology is meant to foster a deeper connection between humans and nature, to indeed promote through ecological consciousness a transformative self-understanding by human beings of themselves as fully part of nature. Critics of deep ecology—such as social ecologists and eco-feminists—argue that its concern about the human domination of nature does not extend to concern about the domination of humans by humans. The focus of deep ecology, in this view, is implicitly authoritarian, even fascistic (uncomfortably reminiscent of the irrational blood-and-soil nature worship of Nazism).

Many environmentalisms are especially evident in connection with inequities of gender, class, race, and region. Eco-feminism, emerging during the 1980s, focused attention on gender by linking the domination of nature and the domination of women through the argument that both are features of patriarchy. Among the differences within eco-feminism, a key distinction can be drawn between a politically active social eco-feminism and an eco-feminism more concerned with problems of spirituality and consciousness. Many Marxists and socialists were suspicious of environmentalism, as it emerged during its first wave, because they saw it diverting attention from problems of class conflict and social inequality. Since the founding of the journal *Capitalism, Nature, Socialism* in 1988, however, eco-Marxism and eco-socialism have made significant developments. Under capitalism, according to this approach, human beings do not share a common interest because environmental costs are borne disproportionately by workers and the poor. From this approach, nineteenth- and early twentieth-century efforts to improve living conditions in the cities must be counted as much a part of environmental history as attempts to preserve wilderness.

The environmental justice movement, representing yet another type of environmentalism, does not dispute the importance of class inequality but maintains that attention to race points to further inequality—indeed, environmental racism. Focused initially in the 1980s on the condition of African-American communities in the U.S. South, the environmental justice movement had by the time of the First National People of Color Environmental Leadership Summit in 1991 expanded to include other U.S. areas and other racial and cultural groups, notably Native Americans and Hispanics. By the mid-1990s, the focus of the environmental justice movement had further expanded to in-clude global regional inequities, particularly as expressed in the idea of a planet divided between the rich countries of the north and the poor countries of the south. A distinctive environmentalism has been identified in the latter countries in the form of understandings and practices that, previously without the name "environmentalism," have opposed the disruption of traditional and indigenous ways of life, as well as the environmental damage associated with colonization, industrialization, and globalization.

The many environmentalisms have challenged the initial focus of environmentalism. Concerned with different inequities in human relationships, these environmentalisms reinforce the charge that a focus on a unified humanity has obscured connections between human inequity and environmental impact. The rise of these many environmentalisms indicates, nonetheless, that concerns about inequity have been significantly influenced by environmentalist challenges to the belief that human beings have the collective right and ability to dominate nature.

Douglas Torgerson

See also Earth Day; Earth First!; Sierra Club

Further Reading

Athanasiou, T. (1996). *Divided planet: The ecology of rich and poor.* Boston: Little Brown.

Carson, R. (1962). *Silent spring.* Boston: Houghton Mifflin.

Commoner, B. (1971). *The closing circle: Nature, man and technology.* New York: Alfred A. Knopf.

Connelly, J., & Smith, G. (1999). *Politics and the environment: From theory to practice.* London and New York: Routledge.

Diamond, I., & Orenstein, G. F. (Eds.). (1990). *Reweaving the world: The emergence of ecofeminism.* San Francisco: Sierra Club Books.

Dowie, M. (1995). *Losing ground: American environmentalism at the close of the twentieth century.* Cambridge, MA: MIT Press.

Dryzek, J. S. (1997). *The politics of the Earth: Environmental discourses.* Oxford, UK: Oxford University Press.

Ehrlich, P. (1968). *The population bomb.* New York: Ballantine Books.

Gottlieb, R. (1993). *Forcing the spring: The transformation of the American environmental movement.* Washington, DC: Island Press.

Guha, R., & Martinez-Alier, J. (1997). *Varieties of environmentalism: Essays north and south.* London: Earthscan.

Hays, S. P. (1975). *Conservation and the gospel of efficiency: The progressive conservation movement, 1890–1920.* New York: Atheneum.

Hays, S. P. (1989). *Beauty, health, and permanence: Environmental politics in the United States, 1955–1985.* Cambridge, UK: Cambridge University Press.

Hjelmar, U. (1996). *The political practice of environmental organizations.* Aldershot, UK: Averbury.

Leiss, W. (1972). *The domination of nature.* Boston: Beacon Press.

Lovins, A. B. (1977). *Soft energy paths.* Cambridge, MA: Ballinger Publishing.

Meadows, D. H., Meadows, D. L., Randers, J.,& Behrens III, W. W. (1972). *The limits to growth: A report for the Club of Rome's project on the predicament of mankind.* New York: Universe Books.

Merchant, C. (1983). *The death of nature: Women, ecology and the scientific revolution.* New York: Harper and Row.

Merchant, C. (1992). *Radical ecology.* London: Routledge.

Paehlke, R. (1989). *Environmentalism and the future of progressive politics.* New Haven, CT: Yale University Press.

Paehlke, R. (1992). Eco-history: Two waves in the evolution of environmentalism. *Alternatives: Perspectives on Society, Technology and Environment, 19*(1), 18–23.

Rodman, J. (1983). Four forms of ecological consciousness reconsidered. In D. Scherer & T. Attig (Eds.), *Ethics and the environment.* Englewood Cliffs, NJ: Prentice Hall.

Schlosberg, D. (1999). *Environmental justice and the new pluralism: The challenge of difference for environmentalism.* Oxford, UK: Oxford University Press.

Torgerson, D. (1999). *The promise of green politics: Environmentalism and the public sphere.* Durham, NC: Duke University Press.

Wapner, P. (1996). *Environmental activism and world civic politics.* Albany, NY: SUNY Press.

World Commission on Environment and Development. (1987). *Our common future.* Oxford, UK: Oxford University Press.

Worster, D. (1979). *Nature's economy: The roots of ecology.* Garden City, NY: Anchor Books.

Estuaries

Estuaries are water passages formed wherever freshwater streams discharge into a marine environment. Estuaries are defined by the resultant mixing of freshwater and saltwater. Such mixing can occur in deltas, bays, sounds, river mouths, marshes, sloughs, lagoons, and other geographies, many of which are classed as wetlands. Estuaries are among the most varied environments on Earth.

Estuaries are highly productive ecosystems, ranking below only rain forests and coral reefs in production of biomass (the amount of living matter) per unit area. Because of this productivity, as well as a variety of other advantages they provide to human habitations, estuaries host vast human populations worldwide. In Australia, for instance, 80 percent of the human population lives in coastal areas, many of which are estuaries.

Because estuarine habitats are sensitive to a wide range of environmental disturbances—some occurring hundreds, even thousands of miles away—they are threatened throughout the world. Threats can be as local and direct as overfishing and the reclamation of wetlands, or as distant and indirect as a dam that changes sediment transport or global climate change.

Land and Water

Estuaries form by the interaction of terrestrial drainage basins and coastal marine environments. As a result, estuaries have some of the characteristics of both environments. They also have unique features, such as the occurrence of brackish water, which is neither as fresh nor as saline as that of the marine environment. In tidal rivers, such as the Thames, the Hudson, and the Amazon, saltwater and brackish water may extend many miles upstream. In such a case, the extent of the estuarine environment depends, over time, on the volume of stream discharges, the height of tides, and the possibility of storm surges. In times of drought saltwater can extend farther upstream; at times of high stream flow, freshwater may flush the estuary.

The character of an estuary derives in large measure from the kinds and amounts of sediments transported by streams. When freshwater streams meet waters of greater salinity, sediments tend to drop out of suspension. Sediments provide estuaries with many of their characteristic landforms: islands, deltas, mudflats, sandbars, and the like. Once deposited in the estuary, sediments may be reworked by currents, waves, floods, and storm surges.

Over time estuaries may change as the sea level rises or falls. Some estuaries occur in "drowned valleys"—river valleys that subsided under the burden of ice during the Pleistocene epoch (beginning 1.6 million years ago) and that have not yet fully rebounded in the absence of that burden.

Human-induced disturbances in estuarine landscapes can be extensive. Dammed and diverted rivers, for instance, may have vastly decreased discharges and sediment loads. An extreme example of this is the former estuary in the Colorado River delta, where river flow no longer discharges into the Gulf of California. There estuarine life has all but disappeared. Increased stream discharge from urban areas or agricultural run-off can increase the extent and energy of floods, sending freshwater flows into an estuary, reworking unconsolidated sediments, and increasing the turbidity (muddiness) of estuarine and coastal waters.

Biology of Estuaries

Plants such as marsh grasses and mangrove make substantial contributions to the stability of estuaries by anchoring estuarine sediments and are the foundation for estuarine productivity. Marshes are composed of a variety of grasses that are adapted to marine waters, intertidal zones, brackish water, and freshwater. Marsh grasses provide nursery conditions and nutrients for a variety of invertebrate and vertebrate fauna. Mangroves occur primarily in intertidal zones and shorelines and make similar contributions to estuarine ecologies. On the Malaysian Peninsula, for instance, the value of mangroves and other estuarine areas for fisheries in 1985 was estimated at $277,000 per square kilometer.

Estuaries support fisheries, migratory and breeding bird populations, and other land and amphibious vertebrates. These include human populations, which have inhabited estuaries and associated littorals (coastal regions) for tens of thousands of years.

Disturbance and Mitigation

As mentioned, disturbances to an estuary caused by human development often begin far from the estuary itself in the broad watershed that provides freshwater and sediment discharge. Estuaries are subject to more localized disturbances as well. Throughout the industrialized world, for instance, estuaries have been subject to landfill, especially in or near cities. Back Bay Boston, for example, is constructed on the formally estuarine "fens" (lowlands) of the Charles River, which is no longer tidal. In the United States both the Clean Water Act and the Rivers and Harbors Act regulate developmental impacts on estuarine and other wet-

lands. Pollution, such as sewage and industrial effluent, affects estuaries; increased nutrients can increase algal blooms and cause eutrophication (the process by which a body of water becomes enriched in dissolved nutrients). Sediments may contain heightened levels of heavy metals, such as copper, lead, and mercury. Agricultural runoffs may damage estuaries through sediments from increased erosion of topsoil in watersheds as well as agricultural amendments such as fertilizers.

Restoration of estuarine environments has been attempted at a variety of sites in Australia, Europe, North and South America, and the Philippines. Such efforts usually involve the reintroduction of marsh and sea grass and mangrove. Restoration efforts are labor intensive and relatively small in scale.

Mark L. Hineline

Further Reading

Allanson, B., & Baird, D. (Eds.). (1999). *Estuaries of South Africa.* New York: Cambridge University Press.

Coats, R., & Williams, P. (1990). Hydrologic techniques for coastal wetland restoration illustrated by two case studies. In J. J. Berg (Ed.), *Environmental restoration: Science and strategies for restoring the Earth* (pp. 236–246). Washington, DC: Island Press.

Dyer, K. R. (1997). *Estuaries: A physical introduction.* New York: John Wiley & Sons.

Hobbie, J. E. (2000). *Estuarine science.* Washington, DC: Island Press.

Kennish, M. J. (1992). *Ecology of estuaries: Anthropogenic effects.* Boca Raton, FL: CRC Press.

Little, C. (2000). *The biology of soft shores and estuaries.* Oxford, UK: Oxford University Press.

Officer, C. B. (1976). *Physical oceanography of estuaries (and associated coastal waters).* New York: John Wiley & Sons.

Thorhaug, A. (1990). Restoration of mangroves and seagrasses—economic benefits for fisheries and mariculture. In J. J. Berg (Ed.), *Environmental restoration: Science and strategies for restoring the Earth* (pp. 265–281). Washington, DC: Island Press.

Ethics *See* Environmental Ethics

Ethnobotany

Ethnobotany examines the cultural and biological relationships between plants and people, usually human populations organized into communities or linguistic groups. Ethnobotanists study how people use plants, modify habitats to benefit plant species, alter entire landscapes, and create new plants through genetic selection (domestication) and unnatural places to grow them (gardens and fields).

People without metal or advanced technology have been regarded as incapable of transforming the environment from its "pristine," pre-European contact condition. Ethnobotanists have demonstrated through extensive fieldwork that indigenous people worldwide had the means and knowledge to modify the landscape and to create anthropogenic plant communities. In North America their interactions were extensive enough to make a "domesticated" plant environment where the actual presence of plants, their distribution, associations, quantity, and physical condition were determined by indigenous people's behavior, utilitarian needs, and worldview. A wilderness without people and their impact on plants has not existed in the Americas for 15,000 years!

Plant Species Management

Many techniques are used to target individual plant species to increase their productivity, ease of harvest, or spatial proximity to benefit people. Non-sedentary foragers, small-scale farmers, and agriculturists employ them. Burning clumps of a species will encourage sprouting for basketry or wooden tools. Redbud, hazel, and oak are manipulated by this means in California. Some plants are burned seasonally to encourage edible seed production or greens for humans and grazing animals.

Weeding seasonally "useless" plants to reduce competition and raise visibility, shaking propagules to increase seedlings, and creating monotypic plots encourages other plants. These are forms of selective harvesting and tending. Another form of plant life-cycle intervention is harvesting plants' subterranean roots, tubers, or bulbs with a digging stick. This technique incidentally replants root cuttings (e.g., Jerusalem artichokes and sweet flag) and bulblets (e.g., onions and camas). Through cultivation, the soil seeds are sowed, the soil is aerated, allelopaths are oxidized, and nutrients are recycled. Sedge and bulrush rhizomes for baskets grow longer from these tilling practices. Another method to assure the availability of important plants, especially rare medicines found some distance from a community, is transplanting them in a garden or protected track. A final procedure commonly used

is pruning or coppicing perennial trees or shrubs for basket canes, cordage, and firewood. Breaking fruit-laden branches of serviceberry and huckleberry reinvigorates them to stimulate vegetative growth, flowering, and fruits. The Pueblo Indians in the Southwest pruned dead limbs from piñon pines for firewood and knocked the branches to stimulate growth of more nuts from a healthier tree.

Anthropogenic Ecosystems

Humans create heterogeneous environments through their broad-scale management practices. Plant manipulation and harvest methods follow a multiyear cycle of plant management according to species and their locality. The result is an ecosystem composed of a mosaic of communities maintained by human cultural practices. Wildernesses only came to be when the indigenous managers lost their land, were killed in wars or by disease, or were replaced by foreign colonists.

Fire is a common tool throughout the world to alter plant communities. Fires set locally around acorn, hickory, and other nut trees clear brush, aid collecting or, indirectly, establish shade-intolerant seedlings. By burning grasslands and berry patches, new growth is stimulated and plant competitors are eliminated. By using fire, nutrients are recycled simultaneously, pests killed, and lower stages of plant succession maintained. The overall result is a patchwork of communities characterized by species diversity and vigorous growth.

The entire landscape is not managed the same way annually. Patches are burned in different years and harvests varied according to biological factors but aided by human practices of settlement, social dispersion, and even ritual regulation for determining which plants can be harvested at different times and places.

Special anthropogenic spaces are gardens. These are not a duplication of other plant communities but instead are associations of plants, which exist nowhere else, brought together and maintained by humans, often women. They are convenient for procuring plant products, for their high productivity, and for their great diversity of utilitarian species. Gardens may consist of native species alone, domesticated plants, or a mixture of both categories.

Wild versus Domesticated Plants

Wild or domesticated is a difficult distinction. Most plants have been selected for by many cultivation techniques. Few have avoided these human-induced, life-cycle alterations to be called truly "wild." Agricultural plants, on the other hand, have been selected for features useful to people. Their new genetic expressions are plant "artifacts" that do not exist in nature and probably would not reproduce without the assistance and habitat maintenance of people. Domesticated plants are found in all temperate and tropical continents except Australia. They include annual plant seed foods (wheat, barley, rice, millet, maize), vegetables (tomatoes, potatoes, onions, squash, spinach, cabbage), herbal spices (chilies, coriander, parsley), perennial tree fruits (apples, peaches, mangos), nuts (walnuts, coconuts), and beverages (coffee and tea). People also domesticated utilitarian plants (bottle gourds, cotton, hemp). Each requires a beneficial habitat for growth, and people determine these. In arid lands, irrigation canals and lithic mulch fields are necessary to conserve water for plants. Examples are found in Arizona, Israel, India, and China. The soil is improved with the addition of animal manure and kitchen waste. Heat and the impact of direct sunlight are mitigated by inter-cropping shade plants with tea, coffee, and fruits. Stone terracing to create more arable land surface alters topography in Peru, Mexico, and China. Women often maintain gardens for culinary variation, dietary supplements, or the aesthetics of flowers. Small fields are maintained for subsistence and are weeded according to local cultural rules of plant use. Large fields are cleared for staple crops or for surplus to sell in markets.

Ethnobotany of Environmental History

Ethnobotany tracks the actions of people, guided by their belief systems, to learn about alternative management techniques, and to understand how plant worlds are manipulated by different cultures. People use many techniques to secure a harvest of utilitarian plants. They have many management principles that regulate exploitation through scheduling their harvest activities, rotating collection areas, and limiting access by applying social and religious sanctions. These practices may benefit individual species and, simultaneously, increase habitat diversity through communities at different stages of plant succession and diverse landscapes of more productive plant associations.

The domestication of maize (Zea mays) and it methods of production present an example of the ethnobotany of environmental change. Maize is an artifact, created throughout human selection of phenotypic traits, which cannot reproduce without human assistance. To grow it humans must eliminate plant competition by clearing the land and providing the environmental qualities required for growth, mainly control over water and temperature. By clearing the land a habitat is created for ruderals, like pigweed (Amaranthus) or lamb's quarters (Chenopodium), that can be eaten as leaves and seeds by farmers or weeded according to cultural practices. After the field is abandoned, new plants volunteer that might be useful as well and create successional patches of diverse plants and animals. None would occur in nature without human manipulation of the environment for cultural purposes.

Richard I. Ford

Further Reading

Anderson, E. N. (1996). *Ecologies of the heart. Emotion, belief and the environment.* New York: Oxford University Press.

Blackburn, T. C., & Anderson, K. (Eds.). (1993). *Before the wilderness: Environmental management by native Californians.* Menlo Park, CA: Ballena Press.

Boyd, R. (1999). *Indians, fire and the land in the Pacific Northwest.* Corvallis: Oregon State University Press.

Day, G. M. (1953). The Indian as an ecological factor in the northeastern forest. *Ecology, 34(2),* 329–346.

Doolittle, W. E. (2000). *Cultivated landscapes of native North America.* Oxford, UK: Oxford University Press.

Ford, R. I. (Ed.). (1985). *Prehistoric food production in North America* (Museum of Anthropology, Anthropological Papers No. 75). Ann Arbor: University of Michigan.

Harris, D. R., & Hillman, G. C. (Eds.). (1989). *Foraging and farming: The evolution of plant exploitation.* London: Unwin, Hyman.

Minnis, P. E. (Ed.). (2000). *Ethnobotany, a reader.* Norman: University of Oklahoma Press.

Minnis, P. E., & Elisens, W. J. (Eds.). (2000). *Biodiversity & Native America.* Norman: University of Oklahoma Press.

Peacock, S. L. (1998). *Putting down roots: The emergence of wild plant food production on the Canadian Plateau.* Unpublished doctoral dissertation, University of Victoria, BC, Canada.

Soule, M. E., & Lease, G. (Eds.). (1995). *Reinventing nature: Responses to postmodern deconstruction.* Washington, DC: Island Press.

Eucalyptus

Eucalyptus is a genus of more than six hundred species of hardwood trees largely native to Australia, although a few species extend to the southern Philippines and eastern Indonesia. Known as the "gum tree" because of a distinctive resinous substance exuded by many species, the eucalyptus is identified by characteristics of its bark, leaves, flower buds, and fruits. During the nineteenth century, confusion occurred due to variability of these characteristics, the profusion of subspecies, hybridization, and the indiscriminate development of vernacular names. There was no universally accepted way of categorizing the genus. Some eucalyptus are tall (*Regnans* and *grandis*), others stunted; some grow in forests, others in open country. They tolerate many climatic variations but not extreme cold or even, in most cases, prolonged frost. Combustible material in the leaves encourages fearsome fires. However, fire regimes—the way different species of trees burn and regenerate through fire, which allows germination and created space and light for new seedlings—differ between species. Fire is important to the survival of eucalypts in opening and germinating seed and clearing space for seedlings to grow.

Controversy continues over how much impact the aboriginal people had on the shaping of eucalyptus forests, the forest's composition, the species that are dominant, and the presence of open pasture. However, it is generally conceded that aboriginal "firestick farming" (the practice of creating small fires with sticks to clear undergrowth for better game hunting) promoted more open hunting country in many places prior to European occupation in 1788.

European settlers initially regarded the eucalyptus with a mixture of dismay and contempt. Culturally, until the 1880s eucalyptus were regarded as strange and aesthetically inferior to European trees. They shed their bark instead of their leaves and have a drab, straggly appearance. As an obstacle to European expansion, large tracts of eucalyptus were cut or burned for farmland in eastern Australia from the 1850s to the 1920s.

At the same time, settlers began to exploit the hardwood's durability and strength to build wharfs, bridges, roads, and railroad ties. Some species, such as *Obliqua*, in the late nineteenth century were found to be suitable for furniture and house timbers, and medicinal uses for the oils were also explored. Experimental forestry plantations soon followed but mostly abroad.

Eucalyptus seeds have been extensively exported from Australia to many countries, mainly to replace deforested areas with quick-growing plants as wind belts and to control erosion, but also to provide fuel wood and ornamental material. In 1770 British botanist Sir Joseph Banks returned to England with seeds from British explorer James Cook's exploratory voyage to the east coast of Australia, but the genus spread most extensively from the 1850s to 1880s under the acclimatization movement—an extensive movement to exchange plants and animals to improve scientific knowledge and economic capacities of the colonies. As in Australia, eucalyptus did best in subtropical and coastal temperate climates, with *Globulus* or "blue gum" the chief variety exported. Major destinations included the Mediterranean Sea basin, especially southern Italy, where it was called the "fever tree" because of its ability to soak up malarial swamps; Brazil, where extensive plantings for railroad ties were undertaken; and California, as well as many places in Africa.

Meanwhile, greater appreciation of the tree appeared as a result of the work of painters of the Heidelberg School (1890s) and German-Australian botanist Ferdinand Mueller's tireless promotion of the aesthetic beauty of eucalyptus forests and their unique botanical qualities. Australian nationalism also favored reassessment of the tree. One species, *Regnans*, was claimed to be the world's tallest tree. (In fact it is only the tallest hardwood.)

Despite rising conservation issues and Australian national pride from Federation (political federation of the separate colonies into the Commonwealth of Australia [1901]) onward, perceptions of eucalypts remained ambivalent. The trees seemed to block economic development, and their great fires threatened human settlement, as evidenced in the famous Black Friday fire of 1939 in the Dandenong ranges near Melbourne. Since the 1960s conservation battles have raged over the survival of old-growth eucalyptus forests that are threatened by the production of wood chips for export to Japan and other places for paper making.

Abroad from Australia, the tree has come under repeated attack for its success in replacing native trees and promoting unintended environmental outcomes. Californians objected to eucalyptus forest fires, and in poorer countries monoculture plantings of eucalypts imperiled biodiversity, and local peoples fought to preserve indigenous forest uses for subsistence against foreign forestry experts who emphasized the need for "development" through growing wood in plantations of exotic trees. The trees, when transplanted, often did not live up to their economic performance in their native land but remained useful—economically and ornamentally—in many instances.

Ian Tyrrell

Further Reading

Dargavel, J. (1995). *Fashioning Australia's forests*. Melbourne, Australia: Oxford University Press.

Doughty, R. W. (2000). *The eucalyptus: A natural and commercial history of the gum tree*. Baltimore: Johns Hopkins University Press.

Griffiths, T. (2001). *Forests of ash: An environmental history*. Melbourne, Australia: Cambridge University Press.

Tyrrell, I. (1999). *True gardens of the gods: Californian-Australian environmental reform, 1860–1930*. Berkeley: University of California Press.

Europe, Ancient

Europe's geological history extends back 5 billion years to the formation of the Earth. Since then energy systems and matter transfers have altered the configuration of the continents and influenced their topographies. Climate has been significant in this, as it has reacted to such factors as atmospheric chemistry and the development of life forms that have reciprocally influenced climate.

By 3 million years ago the Earth had witnessed dramatic environmental change: it had already experienced cooling, and oscillations of global temperature were occurring. Cold periods, some sufficiently cold to promote development of greater ice cover than at present, alternated with warm periods characterized by temperatures similar to those of today. Many such cold/warm cycles have occurred. They have altered the distribution of plants and animals and the characteristics of global ecosystems: polar and montane ice caps have waxed and waned and sea levels have risen and fallen. Humans are also part of this dynamic, and it is possible that the cooling of 5 million years ago influenced the evolution of modern humans from apelike ancestors. Hominid evolution culminated in modern humans (*Homo sapiens sapiens*), whose spread and resource use was influenced by environmental change. From these geologically recent beginnings, hominids and especially modern humans have substantially altered the world's surface characteristics and climate, especially over the last 300 years.

Understanding both the stimuli and repercussions of past climate change is essential for predicting future climatic change and its impact. Insight into past environmental change has prompted the collection of "archival" material that profiles this change. Such material includes ocean, lake, and cave sediments, loess, glacial deposits, and peat deposits. In combination with relative and absolute dating, the physical, chemical, and biological evidence from such archives has facilitated the reconstruction of past environments and rates of environmental change worldwide. Such research has, however, traditionally focused on Europe, where many of the investigative techniques originated, and its surrounding oceans.

The archaeological and anthropological investigation of past human impact on the environment also originated in Europe. Archaeological finds range from stone implements deposited in river terraces to the vestiges of vast urban complexes with remnants of their citizens' material culture. With the emergence of new, increasingly scientific archaeological techniques, the evidence has permitted reconstruction of human-environment relationships. Many of these natural archives of environmental change also contain records of culturally induced environmental changes, such as deforestation and soil erosion. Such records have debunked the belief that ancient societies enjoyed harmonious and sustainable relationships with their environments.

There is more evidence of recent natural and anthropogenic change than of that of the distant past. The extent of glaciation a million years ago is unknown, and the details of hominid evolution in Africa and subsequent migration are not well established. In contrast, the limits of the last three ice advances in Europe are known in detail, and there is considerable evidence of human–environment relationships in Europe following the last major ice advance of ten to twelve thousand years ago.

Natural Environmental Change

The longest records of environmental change over the past 3 million years are contained in marine sediments. Ocean basins receive millions of tons of sediments, and as they consolidate on the ocean floor they incorporate the remains of marine organisms. These sediments and the fossils they contain reflect the environmental conditions under which they were deposited. In particular, prevailing temperatures influence the isotopic mix of oxygen molecules in the calcium carbonate of the fossilized shells of marine organisms called foraminifera. Under cold conditions ocean water is enriched with the heavier oxygen isotope (O^{18}), because the lighter isotope (O^{16}) is evaporated preferentially. This water is used by marine organisms, so their body parts, including calcareous shells, reflect this isotopic signature. Thus, foraminifera shells have relatively high concentrations of O^{18} when cold stages or ice advances occur, and low concentrations during warm stages. The reverse occurs in polar ice sheets because it is to polar regions that water enriched with O^{16} is transported as atmospheric water vapor. Laboratory analysis of the oxygen-isotope characteristics of ocean-sediment cores from around the world and of polar ice cores has allowed scientists to estimate past global temperatures and ice volumes. Consequently, the major global environmental changes of the last 3 million years can be expressed in relation to numbered oxygen-isotope stages whose ages have been determined. It is to these stages that natural and anthropogenic change in Europe are referred whenever possible.

The overall pattern of environmental change involves over forty climatic cycles, each comprising a cold and warm stage. The duration of these cycles and the lengths of the cold and warm components have varied over the past 3 million years. Before 900,000 years ago, climatic cycles were approximately forty thousand years long. Thereafter they lengthened to approximately 120,000 years, the cold stages lasting 100,000 years, and the warm stages lasting a mere 20,000 years. Oxygen-isotope data from the Greenland ice core, which represents the last two climatic cycles, confirm this pattern. Thus Europe has alternated between warm and cold stages in tune with global patterns. This evidence shows that cold conditions have been more prevalent than warm, and that the switch from cold to warm and *vice versa* occurs relatively rapidly over just a few centuries.

Glacial deposits, peats, and lake sediments also provide evidence with which to reconstruct environmental history, but unlike marine sediments, none in Europe contain a complete record of the last 3 million years. However, these natural archives depict *local* and *regional* events over specific periods. Many contain organic materials such as pollen, plant parts, insect remains, algae, mollusc shells, and animal bones and teeth. These materials are valuable indicators of past environments and also present opportunities for radiocarbon dating. This technique relies on the fact that radioactive isotopes decay at a constant rate: comparing the amount of radiocarbon (C^{14} rather than the stable C^{12}) in a sample with that in the environment today, gives an approximate measure of the passage of time. This technique was developed in the late 1950s and it revolutionized archaeology and paleoenvironmental research. Although it can only be used on materials

under 50,000 years old, radiocarbon dating is the most widely used age-estimation technique.

The natural archives in continental Europe that contain the longest record are lake sediments in France, Italy, and Greece, the deepest of which spans the past million years. Such records provide evidence of environmental change in Mediterranean regions that never experienced direct glaciation. The fossil pollen from these sediments reflects past vegetation communities: during warm stages, forests of oak, elm, hornbeam, fir, beech, and hop hornbeam clothed the eastern Mediterranean; during the lengthier cold stages, forest steppe and desert steppe vegetation prevailed. In Scandinavia and in mountains such as the Alps, the Pyrenees, and the Pindus, ice caps and glaciers expanded during cold stages, and ice and snow replaced alpine vegetation communities. Sparse, low-growing vegetation communities, similar to those of northern Norway where herbaceous and shrub species (tundra communities) predominate, replaced the boreal forests which characterized the warm stages.

Similarly, as temperatures declined the temperate forests of western Europe were replaced with tundra and boreal species such as pine. The rise and fall of temperatures, involving shifts of approximately 10°C, also caused substantial changes in the composition of animal and insect communities. For example, sparse populations of woolly mammoth existed adjacent to ice caps, moving south and north as ice waxed and waned until the species became extinct at the beginning of the current interglacial period (the Holocene) some ten thousand years ago. Even during the warm stages, Europe's fauna was quite different from that of today: species of rhinoceros, straight-tusked elephant, horse, and hippopotamus roamed the temperate forests of western Europe which comprised mainly elm, oak, lime, alder, ash, and hazel.

The last ice age ended approximately twelve thousand years ago. Like the end of earlier ice ages, it brought rising sea levels, the colonization of deglaciated areas by herbs, shrubs, and eventually trees, and adjustments in animal populations. Many large animals, such as the mammoth, horse, and giant Irish elk, became extinct. It took between five and six thousand years for coastlines to reach their present configurations, and with average temperatures slightly higher than they are today, temperate forests reached their optimum extent as soils matured from mineral to organic-rich substrates. Subsequent increases in precipitation resulted in the spread of peatlands, especially in maritime regions. Thereafter the record of natural environmental change is obscured by human impact, including the adoption of agriculture and intensified resource use. Today, little natural vegetation remains in Europe and many of the animal species that survived the ice have not survived human activity.

Cultural Developments

Ancient Europe was influenced profoundly by human presence and resource exploitation, as the ancestors of modern humans migrated from their center of origin in eastern central Africa. It is believed that two waves of migration occurred: the first was about 2 million years ago by *Homo erectus* (upright hominids), and the second was approximately 300,000 years ago when *Homo sapiens* (early modern humans) arrived. The alternative, but less accepted theory is that European *H. erectus* populations independently evolved *in situ* to give rise to *H. sapiens*. There is little evidence from which to determine the subsistent strategies and resource-use patterns of these early Europeans. Until about seven thousand years ago, stone was the main material used for tool construction, so the long period from 2 million to seven thousand years ago is termed the Stone Age. It is subdivided into three phases: the Palaeolithic (Old Stone Age), Mesolithic (Middle Stone Age), and Neolithic (New Stone Age), which are not synchronous and not always represented throughout Europe. The Neolithic began about twelve thousand years ago in the Near East when permanent agriculture, a practice which gradually spread throughout Europe, began. Thereafter technological innovations lent their names to subsequent cultural periods, for example, the Bronze and Iron Ages, which were also asynchronous. By 4500 years ago the Greek civilization—itself a center of metallurgical innovation—was being founded. It was followed by the Roman Empire, which persisted until about 500 CE. Evidence of the environmental change wrought by these cultures derives from many sources.

The Palaeolithic

Having separated from ape-like ancestors between 6 and 7 million years ago, the range of early hominids was restricted to Africa. The first hominid to reach Europe was the large-brained *Homo erectus* that had evolved from small-brained Australopithecine species some 2 million years earlier. *H. erectus* was bipedal—which may have aided migration—and by about 1.6 million years ago the species was present in western

Asia, as evidenced by skeletal remains from Dmanisi in Georgia. One of the earliest records of *H. erectus* in Europe is that of Atapuerca, Spain, where skeletal remains are estimated to be almost 800,000 years old. *H. erectus* actively engaged in tool making, and the harnessing of fire enabled these early hominids to influence the carbon cycle at the local level. Tool making and controlled fire facilitated hunting, mainly through herding and trapping, which supplanted scavenging for obtaining animal protein. The tools from archaeological sites dating from this period are of stone or bone, but it is likely that wood was widely used to fashion tools and provide handles for holding wood and bone implements. The early hominids had become omnivores, unlike their vegetarian australopithecine ancestors, and were equally skilled in gathering plants and hunting animals.

Europe was subsequently occupied by descendants of *H. erectus*. Remains of *H. heidelbergensis* have been found in Germany and England. The latter are estimated to be 500,000 years old, and excavations at Boxgrove, Sussex, indicate that the species was an adept hunter and maker of stone tools and projectile points. The species originated in Africa and gave rise to Neanderthals (*H. sapiens neanderthalensis*) and early modern humans (*H. sapiens*), the immediate ancestors of modern humans (*H. sapiens sapiens*). Where Neanderthals originated has not been established, but the absence of Neanderthal remains from Africa indicates that the species evolved in Europe. It occupied central and southern Europe and western Asia from approximately 100,000 to 35,000 years ago. The reason for its extinction is unknown, but the species was an active hunter, used a wide range of tools, buried its dead, lived in social groups, and had larger brains than their probable *H. heidelbergensis* ancestors. They occupied caves as well as open sites and may have co-existed with modern humans. Certainly, their ranges overlapped but intermixing cannot be ascertained from the archaeological record.

Between 150,000 and 250,000 years ago modern humans evolved in Africa, migrating from there to Europe and elsewhere. Modern humans were hunter-gatherers who occupied caves, produced specialized tools, wore clothes, and communicated through language. This last capacity may be unique to *modern* humans, though the general understanding of language development is limited. Many cave dwellings bear witness to the ability to hunt and to depict their activities artistically. Cave paintings at Lascaux and Chauvet in France provide information on both the hunter and the hunted. The Chauvet paintings, approximately thirty-two thousand years old, represent the earliest cave art, and together with the Lascaux paintings they show that modern humans hunted aurochs and deer, and that horses and wolves were among Europe's cold-stage fauna. As ice retreated, modern humans spread from the areas where they were concentrated. Genetic analysis of modern Europeans has identified seven areas that contributed 70 percent of the modern European gene pool: the Mount Parnassus area (Greece), plains northwest of the Black Sea, southwestern France east of the Pyrenees, the Cantabria mountains of northern Spain, the Tuscany hills and the Venetian region of Italy, and the Euphrates basin of Syria. As Europe's last ice advance ended so did the Palaeolithic period.

The Mesolithic Period

The Mesolithic is a transition between the Palaeolithic and Neolithic periods. The material culture associated with it, notably small (microlithic) projectile points, blades, and scrapers, is not represented throughout Europe. Only northern, central, and western Europe experienced Mesolithic culture for approximately 6000 years of the Holocene; elsewhere a direct transition from Palaeolithic to Neolithic occurred.

The early Holocene experienced rapid climatic warming that stimulated major ecological changes, including the reforestation of the deglaciated boreal and temperate zones. Mesolithic communities operated in forested landscapes, while their Palaeolithic ancestors exploited the open rather than closed habitats of European forests in earlier interglacials. Microlithic tools represent an adaptation to the forest environment and enhanced hunting capabilities. Mammoth skeletons with embedded arrowheads from sites in Britain indicate that hunting might have killed off this and other large herbivores, such as the giant Irish elk. Archaeological sites in England and Denmark, such as Star Carr and Maglemose, reveal a society that was organized, resourceful, and skilled. People carved boats out of wood, covered wooden platforms with skins to provide shelter, hunted and fished to provide protein, and gathered wild foods such as hazelnuts. Fossil bones attest to the exploitation of badgers, foxes, deer, aurochs, boars, and elks; freshwater and marine fish and shellfish augmented animal protein, and the domestic dog probably helped with hunting.

The importance of fire to Mesolithic resource manipulation is reflected in European peats and lake sediments. The direct evidence comprises charcoal remains, while the indirect evidence comes from assemblages of pollen grains. The pollen record allows the reconstruction of vegetation change, and shows that variously sized forest clearings were created. Such openings encouraged the growth of grasses and various herbs that attracted animals, making them easier to trap and hunt. Fires were probably local and possibly regional in scale, and the resulting clearings were usually short-lived and subsequently recolonized by forest. Firing was widespread and was a major influence on forest extent and composition. Mesolithic communities were not far removed from agriculture: from sophisticated hunter-gatherer to agriculturalist was but a short step, though the environmental and cultural ramifications were profound.

The Neolithic Period

Neolithic cultures first emerged in the Near East, and the developments that occurred in this region in the first few millennia of a new interglacial period were momentous. The domestication of selected plants and animals and the introduction of agriculture represent significant alterations in human-environment relationships and the emergence of humans as a salient component of the global carbon cycle. Agriculture spread to Europe and Asia through the diffusion of ideas and human migration. Although there is considerable evidence as to where and when domestication occurred, why it occurred remains enigmatic.

Forests were cleared and, along with grasslands and shrublands, were modified to create pastures or replaced with arable land. Many early agricultural systems were ephemeral, and after a few years of cultivation, natural vegetation was allowed to recolonize. It took five thousand years for agriculture to spread throughout Europe, reaching its western and northern peripheries approximately six thousand years ago, coinciding with the optimum development of interglacial forest cover. First, elm populations were reduced, probably due to Dutch elm disease whose spread may have been facilitated by farmers clearing forests, then the populations of all deciduous species. Neolithic agriculturalists were responsible for the world's first culturally-driven deforestation episode—another factor influencing in the carbon cycle.

The first plants to be domesticated in the Near East were grasses and legumes such as wheat, barley, oats, rye, lentils, and broad beans. These were introduced throughout Europe and remain amongst the world's major crops. Similarly, the first animals to be domesticated in the Near East, notably, sheep, cattle, and swine, remain the world's major sources of animal protein.

Permanent settlement also emerged in the Neolithic. Although the earliest European settlements are not as well known as Jericho in modern-day Israel or Çatal Hüyük in Anatolia, people congregated in similar villages and towns throughout Europe. Various Neolithic cultures flourished, cultures such as the Karonovo of the Balkans and the Danubian (Bandkeramik) of central Europe. These agricultural communities used pottery vessels, pottery being another Neolithic technology that developed in different places at different times. Along Europe's western periphery agricultural communities were beginning to construct huge monuments and communal burial chambers. Amongst the most famous of these megaliths are Stonehenge, southern England, and New Grange in Ireland's Boyne Valley. Such constructions reflect social organization and stratification, a food production system that allowed part of the population to engage in non-food-production activities, and the technology to construct large edifices.

The Bronze Age

The Near East was one center where metalworking began. Hammered rather than smelted copper objects approximately 9500 years old have been discovered, but it was another five hundred years before metal smelting began, as evidenced by finds from Çatal Hüyük, Anatolia. Like agriculture, the technology spread east and west, though there were other centers of origin in Europe itself, and innovations in North Africa also influenced Europe because of its significance in the Mediterranean region. The copper age (Chalcolthic) was short lived, as copper is relatively soft and wears easily, but the production of bronze, an alloy of copper and tin or copper and arsenic, followed quickly. Perhaps bronze was accidentally discovered when the arsenic-rich, copper oxide ores of Anatolia were smelted. Bronze production broadened the resource base of prehistoric Europe, and bronze is ubiquitous in archaeological sites of the period—hence the term "Bronze Age." This "age" is time transgressive, because not all European cultures developed or adopted the technology simultaneously: Britain's Bronze Age began four thousand years ago, compared with eight thousand years ago in Anatolia and the Balkans, and six thousand years ago in Myceneae (where Greek civilization began to emerge). Both copper ores

and artifacts prompted trade and the exchange of ideas. Similarly, amber from the Baltic region was traded far and wide.

The Bronze Age witnessed population increase, growth and spread of settlement, establishment of trading centers, and continued megalith construction. Bronze Age burial mounds proliferated and their grave goods, notably bronze axes and pottery, attest to social hierarchy and a warrior tradition. Gold and silver were used for ornamental purposes, and the many hoards discovered indicate that jewelry was prized and widely used. Copper and bronze implements were themselves often icons rather than working tools, and the best-preserved specimens derive from burials. Furthermore, the establishment of value for these metals stimulated both trade and the exchange of ideas, enhancing links both within Europe and between Europe and its neighbors. Metal implements did not, however, supersede stone ones, though bronze tools were better for modifying the environment for agriculture. Smelting not only relied on the availability of wood fuel, but provided improved tools for obtaining it. The plough had become widespread by 4000 years ago. It facilitated the spread and intensification of agriculture; this accelerated the alteration of Europe's natural vegetation cover, and remaining woodlands were probably actively managed. Smelting technology, which may have developed from the attainment of high temperatures in enclosed pottery kilns, paved the way for the exploitation of iron, a more common metal than copper.

The Iron Age

By the time bronze production was beginning in Europe's western periphery, iron working was already underway in the Near East (about 4500 years ago). The technology probably developed in several places, but the earliest artifacts come from Anatolia in the Hittite empire. By 2500 years ago iron tools were already in wide use, because iron ores were more widespread than copper ores. Smelting and molding iron requires higher temperatures than does copper smelting, and carbon must be added to reduce brittleness and enhance durability. Use of iron led to improved agricultural tools, especially iron ploughs and axes, which exacerbated deforestation as agriculture expanded. Land subdivisions are evident in many areas, and in the Celtic field system fixed fields were separated by banks. Pressure on land resources may have increased the use of crop rotations and manuring to maintain productivity. Climatic deterioration, notably increasing precipitation some 3000 years ago, probably contributed to changes in the practice and distribution of agriculture and to the adoption of water deities.

European trade links strengthened as iron ores and artifacts were exchanged along with agricultural produce, precious metals, and jewelry. Trade generated wealth for sea-faring Greeks, the Phoenicians of modern day Lebanon, and the Etruscans of modern-day central Italy. The influential Hallstatt culture emerged in northern and central Europe. The Hallstatt traded via the Danube, Rhine, and Saône rivers and imported goods from Mediterranean regions. By 2500 years ago they gave way to the La Tène, a Celtic people. On Europe's western margins hill forts became commonplace, providing services for their catchments, including markets, centers of worship, and protection. Large settlements known as *oppida* also existed; these enclosed sites were often developed into cities by the Romans. Coinage was invented, new ceramic traditions were established, and grave goods attest to widespread trade. Iron Age Europe was controlled by tribal groups until the rise of the Romans.

The Greek Civilization

The wealth and expertise associated with bronze production underpinned Europe's first urban societies. These were the palace states of the Aegean, such as Minoan Crete and Mycenean Greece, which emerged as power bases approximately 4000 years ago and which persisted for some 800 years. Remains of ancient Crete's imposing architecture are evident at Knossos, Malia, and Phaistos, which were centers of between fifteen and fifty thousand people each. They survived earthquakes, thrived on agriculture and diversified trade, produced high-quality ceramics, invented scripts known as Linear A and B, and were skilled metallurgists, artisans, artists, and architects. By 3500 years ago Mycenae was gaining in stature. Differences in grave goods indicate a stratified society steeped in polytheism. Agricultural goods (such as barley, wheat, lentils, grapes, cattle, pigs, sheep, and goats), metal goods, and pottery, were traded with Egypt, the Near East, and the western Mediterranean. By approximately 3000 years ago the regional balance of power was upset, though the cause remains undetermined; war and drought are possibilities.

This upset did not end the influence of ancient Greece but merely shifted the power to city-states such as Sparta and Athens. As part of a *polis*—an economic and political unit—Athens united the urban and rural communities of Attica. It was important both commercially and intellectually, and is regarded as the source of western philosophy and science. By 2500 years ago Athens' population was approximately 275,000—a megalopolis by contemporary standards. Life in Athens and the other city-states on the Mediterranean was good for the elite, poor for the servant class, and worse for the slaves. Polytheism is evident from temple remains, and archaeological sites bear witness to a rich material culture. Trade and manufacturing were important, and agriculture provided goods for consumption and trade. The rural population was considerable even in the uplands, and olives, vines, pulses, and cereals were produced along with wool and milk from sheep and goats. Cereals were a major import and trade in them was regulated. Ship building and silver mining were other sources of wealth. The mines were owned by the rich and worked by slave gangs, and there may have been as many slaves as free people. Systems of law and order and political thought were established. Culturally, the Greeks were innovative: literature, theatre, philosophy, mathematics, and education all progressed, leaving a rich legacy of worldwide significance.

The Roman Empire

Even as the Greek city-states flourished a new Mediterranean power base was developing in Rome, a city founded in 753 BCE. Within 500 years Rome controlled the Italian peninsula and began to extend its influence into Europe. By 400 CE when it was at its largest—stretching from Britain to the Near East and encompassing the Iberian Peninsula and North Africa in the south—the Empire was beginning to disintegrate.

Roman wealth derived mainly from agriculture that relied heavily on the labor of slaves from conquered lands. Dry farming on agricultural estates known as *latifundia* dominated Italy with its Mediterranean climate of hot dry summers and warm wet winters. Lowland coastal regions mainly produced cereals, via a crop/fallow system yielding one crop every two years; slopes mainly produced grapes, olives, and citrus fruit, while upland pastures supported sheep. Some regions employed water-conservation measures and irrigation. The cool wet climate of the northern provinces favored mixed farming of cereal and legume cultivation and animal husbandry. The Romans also initiated drainage schemes to increase the extent of arable land, and examples are found in the Po Valley of northern Italy and in the Fens of East Anglia, England. The Romans generally encouraged agriculture in Iron Age Europe, seeking to improve productivity through engineering and improved implements such as ploughs, scythes, sickles, and water mills.

Characteristic Roman engineering feats reflect scientific advances. Road building improved communications, and aqueducts, bridges, and other public works were widespread. Roman cities flourished and grew in extent and population. Imposing public buildings had sculpted façades, and most cities had defensive walls and amphitheaters. The great demand for military equipment, agricultural and domestic implements, and coinage all fuelled metallurgical industries. Mining and smelting were widespread, generating both wealth and pollution. Roman-period iron, copper, and lead extraction and processing were sufficiently large in scale that their atmospheric impact is registered in Greenland ice cores. The large volume of charcoal required for smelting, construction, and domestic fuel meant that Europe's forests were heavily exploited and managed.

Intellectual developments also characterized the Roman era. Latin became the language of philosophers, scholars, playwrights, and authors whose works are still relevant. Science, mathematics, and engineering advanced considerably, education was common for the elite, and political systems based on law became increasingly sophisticated. The Roman Empire was eventually weakened by internal struggle and rivalry, and finally brought down by persistent barbarian invasions from the north and east.

A. M. Mannion

Further Reading

Cullen, T. (Ed.). (2001). *Aegean prehistory: A review.* Boston: Archaeological Institute of America.

Cunliffe, B. W. (Ed.). (1998). *Prehistoric Europe: An illustrated history.* Oxford, UK: Oxford University Press.

Fagan, B. M. (1999). *World prehistory: A brief introduction.* New York: Longman.

Gamble, C. (1999). *The palaeolithic societies of Europe.* Cambridge, UK: Cambridge University Press.

Harding, A. F. (2000). *European societies in the Bronze Age.* Cambridge, UK: Cambridge University Press.

Klein, J., & Takahata, N. (2002). *Where do we come from? Molecular evidence for human descent.* Berlin, Germany: Springer Verlag.

Klein, R. G., & Blake, E. (2002). *The dawn of human culture.* New York: John Wiley & Sons.

Lewin, R. (1999). *Human evolution: An illustrated introduction* (4th ed.). Oxford, UK: Blackwell.

Lowe, J. J., & Walker, M. J. C. (1997). *Reconstructing Quaternary environments.* Harlow, UK: Longman.

Mannion, A. M. (1999). *Natural environmental change.* London: Routledge.

Mannion, A. M. (2002). *Dynamic world: Land-cover and land-use change.* London: Arnold.

Price, T. D. (Ed.). (2000). *Europe's first farmers.* Cambridge, UK: Cambridge University Press.

Scarre, C. (1999). *Exploring prehistoric Europe.* Oxford, UK: Oxford University Press.

Sykes, B. (2001). *The seven daughters of Eve.* London: Transworld Publishers.

Wilson, R. C. L., Drury, S. A., & Chapman, J. L. (2000). *The great ice age: Climate change and life.* London: Routledge and the Open University.

Europe, Medieval

The sources for the environmental history of Europe increase considerably over the thousand years from 400 to 1492 CE, when Columbus landed in America. The written texts after about 1200 provide detailed records that indirectly include information about the environment. Archeology also provides important information; increasingly, this information has had added value as the means of dating sites have matured since the 1980s with refined typological (relating to types) sequences of ceramics, for example, and the greater use of dendrochronology (the science of dating events and variations in an environment by comparative study of growth rings in trees).

Climate

Episodes of climatic change played an important role in shaping the environmental history of medieval Europe. Data from a wide range of sources suggest that climatic changes have been in many cases dramatic with wide-ranging consequences. Ice core data from central Greenland indicate that from about 700 to 1200 CE—a period referred to as the "Medieval Warm Interval"—average temperatures were 1–2° C higher than at present. However, by the fourteenth century came an episode of cooler climatic conditions—widely known in Europe as the "Little Ice Age"—that would last until the end of the medieval period. The Little Ice

Age was characterized by markedly cooler summers, wetter winters, and a significant increase in storms, with average temperatures dropping by several degrees. The expansion of Arctic sea ice and the advance of several Alpine glaciers have been documented throughout the Little Ice Age. The exact causes are not well understood, although changes to a colder climate were likely to have been due to shifts in the main elements of global circulation. Some correlation between solar sunspot activity and glacier fluctuations may prove to be a major cause of short-term climatic change. The infusion into the atmosphere of large amounts of volcanic dust is also regarded as a likely cause of short-term variations in climate, and a cluster of volcanic eruptions is likely to reinforce a tendency already apparent in the global circulation. Local eruptions recorded within the Greenland ice sheet cores described by U.S. climatologist Gregory Zielinski and colleagues (1994), such as Oraefajokull, Iceland, in 1362, and intrahemispherically distributed eruptions such as that of Mount St. Helens, Washington, in 1479, may well have contributed to deteriorating climatic conditions throughout Europe.

In northwestern Europe the climatic optimum of the early medieval period allowed the extension of agriculture in the form of fields and cultivation ridges well beyond present altitudinal limits. In one of the areas of densest settlement, the central Rhineland of Germany, settlements began cultivating the uplands in the ninth century. Vineyards also extended three to five degrees of latitude farther north and 100–200 meters higher up hillsides. The Norman *Domesday Book* (1086 CE), which describes landlordings and resources of late eleventh century England, records thirty-eight vineyards in southern England. The excavation of Norse colony sites in Greenland has also demonstrated the presence of cereal pollen, suggesting the cultivation of these crops. At lower latitudes, the climate became wetter, with significant summer rainfalls, the result of the frequent displacement of the anticyclonic belt (which is characterized by the clockwise circulation of air in the upper atmosphere controlling the formation of weather systems) to the north. Evidence for the Medieval Warm Interval can be seen in the eastern Mediterranean and beyond in raised levels in the Dead Sea as well as precipitation maximums at the Nile headwaters. Alpine passes normally blocked with snow and ice also became traversable, opening trade and pilgrimage routes between France and Germany on the one hand and Italy on the other.

The effects of the first phases of the Little Ice Age manifested throughout Europe. After a minor period of cold winters during the period 1200–1220 CE, the first major episode of deteriorating conditions began in the 1280s, reaching a peak in 1305–1355. Cold periods are inherently linked to extreme weather episodes and increased risk from geomorphological (relating to relief features of the Earth) hazards. Deluges in particular led to dramatic local events, causing extensive soil erosion, gullying, and changes in river channels, floodplains, and deltas. November of 1333 brought widespread floods throughout middle Italy. The Ponte Vecchio in Florence replaced a bridge that was swept away in flooding at this time. Increased wetness during spring and summer appears to have led to widespread crop failure and poor pasture in many parts of medieval Europe. In England the growing season would have been reduced by one to two months compared to present-day values. In Tuscany and the south of France twenty-six seasons of "Dearth" or famine are recorded between 1282 and 1421.

The variations in tree-ring sequences from ancient trees and timber are widely used as proxy temperature and climatic indicators in paleoenvironmental reconstruction. Dendrochronological evidence from around the Aegean Sea has identified a number of periods of cooler climate, reaching a concentration during the sixteenth century, which corresponds to the second major peak of the Little Ice Age. Spanish pine trees have been found to respond strongly to summer rainfall and indicate that the Little Ice Age in Spain was characterized by increased wetness.

Settlement at higher latitudes and marginal areas is more susceptible to short-term climatic changes, which can have drastic effects on agricultural practices. Greenland, first settled by Norse communities in the tenth century, was abandoned by the fourteenth century, the climatic downturn being a major factor. In Iceland the growth of barley by Norse farmers declined significantly in the thirteenth century and had ceased by the sixteenth century. Several Norse farms were engulfed by expanding Icelandic glaciers, and in Norway agricultural land was also being overrun by expanding ice sheets. The effect of the Little Ice Age on Swiss farms was also severe. Within the cooler climate the parasite *Fusarium nivale*, which thrives under snow cover, devastated crops.

Sea-Level Change

Changes in sea level during the medieval period in Europe can be seen as fluctuations within the overall rising trend of the Holocene epoch, which covers the last ten thousand years. Many of the relative changes in sea level affecting northwestern Europe are linked to long-term isostatic (relating to equilibrium in the Earth's crust maintained by a yielding flow of rock material beneath the surface under gravitative stress) adjustments of land once heavily loaded with glacier ice, leading to small amounts of vertical displacement. Climatic changes also have an effect on relative sea level, seen in the expansion and contraction of the Arctic ice sheets. At lower latitudes within Europe, tectonic (relating to the Earth's crust) activity is the dominant cause of localized sea-level change. Subsidence of the ocean floor due to tectonic movement and increased sediment loading can also have an effect, seen clearly as an ongoing process in the North Sea region and the Mediterranean Sea basin.

Throughout Europe coastal areas with gentle relief are vulnerable to environmental change and short-term marine transgressive (the spreading or extension of the sea over land areas) and regressive (the retreat or withdrawal of water from land areas) episodes. Such changes are often the result of short- or medium-term climatic change, particularly increased storminess, and related changes in sediment input. In many areas changes in shoreline morphology are the result of increased sedimentary deposition from rivers, forming fertile coastal deltas, which continue to push shorelines seaward. Soil erosion from hillsides in many cases led to the choking and siltation of river mouths and the abandonment of former harbors.

In northwestern Europe low-lying coastal areas, often consisting of salt marsh, were reclaimed for agricultural use behind sea banks, a practice dating to the Roman period. In northern Holland, for example, large-scale dikes and drainage works began in the ninth century and became extensive in about 1100 CE. Localized marine transgressional phases often occurred, which seem to relate to a combination of sea-level fluctuations and increasing westerly and southwesterly winds. A greater frequency of such events seems to have occurred during periods of climatic deterioration, often affecting widely separated areas at the same time. Areas within the Severn Estuary of England and Wales were subject to a series of such transgression phases, inundating land previously reclaimed during the Roman period, cutting low cliffs into earlier sedimentary formations. Similar cycles of instability as a result of periodic episodes of marine inundation are found in areas of the Somerset Levels in England, where extensive fieldwork has revealed a pattern of Roman reclamation followed by post-Roman flooding.

Vegetation

The unfolding vegetational history of medieval Europe owes much to past cultural landscapes, inheriting many vegetational elements of different ages and origins. Environmental conditions related to changing climate often play a key role, especially in marginal areas where soils are poor and species are at the edge of their ecological niche. Changing population densities, agricultural practices, and the development of urban centers and industry in late medieval Europe also have an important impact.

After the decline of the Roman Empire, the regeneration of woodland around frontier zones of northwestern Europe, such as the Peak District of England, is often recorded. However, much spatial variability seems to exist within this generalized picture because in parts of Scotland and Ireland there is corresponding palynological (relating to the study of pollen and spores) evidence for continuity and increased clearance. Much of the old Roman Empire in the Mediterranean Sea basin experienced significant population decline after the sixth century with the subsequent abandonment of parts of the hills and more difficult lowlands, which, to judge from descriptions in the chronicles and land charters of the age, resulted in woodland regeneration. This has been seldom demonstrated archeologically.

By contrast, northwestern Europe tends to show a general continuity of agricultural practices throughout the early medieval period. However, regionally based variations are again evident, often the result of more localized environmental and socioeconomic conditions. Denmark, for example, was intensively cultivated from the seventh century onward. Studies of animal bones from eighth-century Hamwic, a large trading emporium, indicate the beginnings of livestock provisioning based upon intensified management of the countryside. Large-scale excavations of the Anglo-Saxon village at Raunds, Northamptonshire (England) show the introduction of a well-developed agricultural economy based upon crop rotation by the tenth century. In southern Sweden there is a marked increase in the clearance of woodland cover during the early Viking period. On Crete there is a sudden drop in tree pollen between 900 and 1100 CE, especially that of evergreen oak, which does not start to recover again until around 1300. It has been suggested that this may be attributable to a rise in population and prosperity in the early Venetian period, when innumerable chapels in western Crete were built.

Population increases in the twelfth and thirteenth centuries brought the expansion of cultivation in northern Europe toward limits set by altitude and soil during a period of favorable climatic conditions. A similar expansion is also recorded within areas of the Mediterranean. The growth of cities, often flourishing around shipbuilding and iron making, increased the demand for potentially large amounts of timber. Associated woodland management strategies are reflected in regional vegetation histories and palynological evidence. It is estimated that only 15 percent of *Domesday* England was wooded, less than 50 percent of the area was arable (suitable for cultivation) land, and by 1350 woodland cover had been reduced to around 10 percent. The subsequent survival or destruction of woodland lay almost entirely in the hands of the dominant social classes, notably as royal forests and deer parks.

Climatic changes associated with the Little Ice Age clearly impact the vegetational history of later medieval Europe. The large forests of *Pinus sylvestris*, a pine tree found in the Mediterranean, and those of the northern Sierra de Gredos in the middle of Meseta, eastern Spain, date back to at least the fourteenth century, at which time they were more extensive due to favorable climatic conditions brought about by the Little Ice Age. Such forests are documented as providing an important timber resource. Within the upland areas of northwestern Europe, the cooler, wetter climate led to the inevitable development of permanently wet pools dominated by *Sphagnum* moss, and a close correlation between phases of climate oscillation and peat development over the last millennium has been demonstrated.

Richard Hodges and David Bescoby

Further Reading

Allen, J. R. L., & Rae, J. E. (1987). Late Flandrian shoreline oscillations in the Severn Estuary; a geomorphological and stratigraphical reconnaissance. *Philosophical Transactions of the Royal Society of London, B315*, 185–230.

Barber, K. E. (1981). *Peat stratigraphy and climatic change.* Rotterdam, Netherlands: Balkema.

Bell, M. G., & Walker, M. J. C. (1992). *Late Quaternary environmental change.* New York: John Wiley & Sons.

Besteman, J. C. (1990). North Holland AD 400: Turning tide or tide turned? In J. C. Besteman, J. M. Bos, & H. A. Heidinga (Eds.), *Medieval archaeology in the Netherlands* (pp. 91–120). Assen, Netherlands: Van Gorcum.

Bourdillon, J. (1994). The animal provisioning of Saxon Southampton. In J. Rackham (Ed.), *Environment and economy in Anglo-Saxon England* (pp. 120–125). London: Council for British Archaeology.

Campbell, G. (1994). The preliminary archaeobotanical results from Anglo-Saxon west Cotton and Raunds. In J. Rackham (Ed.), *Environment and economy in Anglo-Saxon England* (pp. 65–82). London: Council for British Archaeology.

Crowley, T. J., & North, G. R. (1991). *Paleoclimatology.* New York: Oxford University Press.

Dark, S. P. (1996). Palaeoecological evidence for landscape continuity and change in Britain ca AD 400–800. In K. R. Dark (Ed.), *External contacts and the economy of late Roman and post-Roman Britain* (pp. 23–51). Rochester, NY: Boydell Press.

Dearing, J. A., Håkansson, H., Liedber-Jönsson, B., Persson, A., Skansjö, S., Widholm, D., & El-Daoushy, F. (1987). Lake sediments used to quantify the erosional response to land use changes in southern Sweden. *Oikos, 50*, 60–78.

Grove, A. T., & Rackham, O. (2001). *The nature of Mediterranean Europe, an ecological history.* New Haven, CT: Yale University Press.

Grove, J. M. (1988). *The Little Ice Age.* London: Methuen.

Guibal, F (1999). Some examples of climatic reconstruction in the Mediterranean using dendroclimatology. In P. Leveau, F. Trement, K. Walsh, & G. Barker (Eds.), *Environmental reconstruction in Mediterranean landscape archaeology* (Archaeology of Mediterranean Landscapes Series No. 2) (pp. 37–44). Oxford, UK: Oxbow.

Hassan, F. A. (1981). Historical Nile floods and their implications for climatic change. *Science, 212*, 1142–1145.

Hodges, R. (1991). *Wall-to-wall history.* London: Duckworth.

Hodges, R., & Whitehouse, D. (1983). *Mohammed, Charlemagne and the origins of Europe.* London: Duckworth.

Horden, P., & Purcell, N. (2000). *The corrupting sea: A study of Mediterranean history.* Oxford, UK: Blackwell.

Issar, A. S., Tsoar, H., & Levin, D. (1989). Climatic changes in Israel during historical times and their impact on hydrological, pedological and socioeconomic systems. In M. Leinen & M. Sarnthein (Eds.), *Paleoclimatology and paleometeorology: Modern and past patterns of global atmospheric transport* (pp. 535–541). Dordrecht, Netherlands: Kluwer Academic Publishers.

Kuniholm, P. I., & Striker, C. L. (1983). Dendrochronological investigations in the Aegean and neighbouring regions. *Journal of Field Archaeology, 10*(4), 411–420.

Lamb, H. H. (1977). *Climate: Present, past and future: Vol. 2.* London: Methuen.

Lamb, H. H. (1982). *Climate, history and the modern world.* London: Methuen.

Mann, M. E., Bradley, R. S., & Hughes, M. K. (1999). Northern Hemisphere temperatures during the past millennium: Inferences, uncertainties, and limitations. *Geophysical Research Letters, 26*(8), 759–762.

McCormick, M. (2001). *The origins of the medieval economy.* Cambridge, UK: Cambridge University Press.

McGovern, T. H. (1985). The Arctic frontier of Norse Greenland. In S. Green & S. Perlman (Eds.), *The archaeology of frontiers and boundaries* (pp. 275–323). New York: Academic Press.

Rackham, O. (1980). *Ancient woodland.* London: Edward Arnold.

Rackham, J. (1994). (Ed.). *Environment and economy in Anglo-Saxon England.* London: Council for British Archaeology.

Randsborg, K. (1980). *Denmark in the Viking age.* London: Duckworth.

Randsborg, K. (1990). *The first millenium AD in Europe and the Mediterranean.* Cambridge, UK: Cambridge University Press.

Rippon, S. (1997). *The Severn Estuary: Landscape evolution and wetland reclamation.* Leicester, UK: Leicester University Press.

Rippon, S. (2000). The Romano-British exploitation of coastal wetlands: Survey and excavation on the north Somerset Levels, 1993–7. *Britannia, 31,* 69–200.

Roberts, N. (1989). *The Holocene: An environmental history.* Oxford, UK: Blackwell.

Tessier, L. (1992). Dendroclimatic evidence from southwestern Europe and northwestern Africa. In R. S. Bradley & P. D. Jones (Eds.), *Climate since A.D. 1500* (pp. 349–365). New York: Routledge.

Tooley, M. J. (1985). Climate, sea-level and coastal changes. In M. J. Tooley & G. M. Sheail (Eds.), *The climatic scene* (pp. 206–234). London: Allen and Unwin.

Zielinski, G. A., Mayewski, P. A., Meeker, L. D., Whitlow, S. I., Twickler, M. S., Morrison, M. C., Meese, D., Alley, R., & Gow, A. J. (1994). A continuous record of volcanism (present–7000 BCE) and implications for the volcano-climate system. *Science, 264*(5159), 948–952.

European Starling

The European starling *(Sturnus vulgaris)* is a medium-sized (21–22 centimeters long) songbird; one of 114 species in the family Sturnidae. The plumage of adults is largely black but with white spotting on body feathers that is especially prominent in winter. These spots wear off in spring to reveal glossy iridescent sheens of purple, blue, and green during the breeding season. Juveniles are dun brown with a whiter chin. European starlings have strong legs and feet, and walk jauntily rather than hop. Their straight bill is dark brown most of the year but yellow in breeding season.

European starlings breed in holes, often in trees but also in man-made structures, within which they build bulky nests of dried vegetation with a lining of finer material such as mosses and feathers. During nest construction, which is undertaken mainly by the male, flowers and fresh green leaves are placed in the nest cup; these help attract females, and, as the plants selected have insecticidal properties, may also help to reduce numbers of parasites in the nest. European starlings lay from four to six clear blue eggs; some females lay eggs in other starlings' nests. Incubation, mainly by the female, lasts for eleven days. Chicks are usually fed by both parents and leave the nest at approximately twenty-two days old. Some males are polygynous, with up to five simultaneous mates recorded. Some females lay two clutches per year.

European starlings are highly social throughout year, breeding in colonies, feeding in flocks and roosting communally at night, sometimes in aggregations numbering millions of birds. They inhabit open land with scattered trees or other structures in which they can nest, and feed mainly on the ground where they are specially adapted, through head and bill structure, for taking invertebrates, especially insect larvae, from among grass roots or from the upper few centimeters of the soil. Their diet is broad, however, and also includes seeds and fruits.

Their natural range extends from western Europe, including the Azores, to central Asia as far east as Lake Baikal, or possibly to eastern Russia. However, their range has been considerably extended by human introduction. Starlings were taken to southeastern Australia and New Zealand by so-called Acclimatization Societies in the nineteenth century; these organizations aimed to provide human colonists with familiar plants and animals from "back home." Cecil Rhodes (1853–1902) brought the European starling to South Africa. They were then taken from England to the United States in the late nineteenth century by Eugene Schieffelin, a wealthy theater afficionado, who thought that all birds mentioned in the works of William Shakespeare should be allowed to colonize America. This fateful introduction led to the European starling's becoming one of North America's most numerous birds within a century.

In much of its natural range and in North America, the European starling is regarded as a serious agricultural pest because it consumes grapes, olives, cherries, germinating cereals, and cattle food. It is also considered an urban pest because it roosts at night in or near cities. It is thought to act as a focus for some diseases and as an aviation pest as a result of collisions with aircraft, sometimes with fatal results for passengers. In northern Eurasia and New Zealand, however, it is considered beneficial because of its consumption of insect pests.

Despite appearing to be one of the most successful birds in man's agricultural environments, the European starling has suffered a remarkable decline in numbers of more than 50 percent in the last quarter of the twentieth century in Britain and northern Europe. The decline is believed to be the result of various aspects of agricultural intensification and indicates that European starlings can be highly sensitive to environmental change. If the European Union does manage to change its Common Agricultural Policy, thereby making farming more environmentally-friendly, people in northwestern Europe may once again be amazed by synchronized swirling masses of European starlings as they go to roost, possibly one of the most spectacular sights in ornithology.

Chris Feare

Further Reading

Feare, C. (1984). *The starling*. Oxford, UK: Oxford University Press.

Feare, C., & Craig, A. (1998). *Starlings and mynas*. London: Helm (A & C Black).

Evolution and the Spread of Humans

Humans comprise one species, *Homo sapiens*, with a wide variety of body forms and other physical characteristics. More than 6 billion humans inhabit the Earth, and the population will continue to increase in the foreseeable future. Humans' closest living relatives among the nonhuman primates, the chimpanzees and gorillas, may succumb to the continued growth of humans. Humans differ from these primates in countless ways: in their manner of walking, their diets, their longevity, their social structure, their languages, and their manifest ability to manipulate their environments, to name a few. From the fossil record of ancient humans and extinct hominids, which were closer cousins to humans than are living apes, paleontologists have learned much about how human features arose and in what sequence. Hints of humans' past ways of life and behaviors remain as artifacts from which archeologists interpret the past. Also, geneticists have added to this knowledge by examining the genetic relationships and variation among living people and apes.

Early Hominids

The earliest known hominids lived in east Africa 6 million years ago and belonged to the species *Orrorin tugenensis*. Paleontologists can recognize these ancient animals as close human relatives because they share with humans a crucial adaptation: they walked on two legs. Although today's humans are distinguished from chimpanzees and other apes by many other anatomical and behavioral characteristics, bipedality was the first of these to arise. The hominid style of bipedality is unique among animals, and a combination of several skeletal adaptations allows it. Unlike those of other primates, human pelvic bones are short and broad to allow human muscles to keep humans upright; human legs are long compared to their trunk and arms to give them more efficient strides; human legs angle inward at the knee to keep a foot under their center of mass; and their spines insert beneath, rather than behind, their skulls. These characteristics set hominids apart, and although they enabled the great success of hominids, they also constrained the direction of later evolution.

Hominid bipedality probably arose because of a combination of factors. Living apes sometimes walk bipedally, commonly when they are carrying objects in their hands, when they are walking on branches balancing with or partially suspending from their arms, or when they are displaying their full height. These probably were among the factors influencing early hominids, especially if accompanied by changes in social structure that may have required bipedality, such as increased food sharing. A second early hominid characteristic, reduced canine teeth compared to those of apes, may indicate a change in the format of male competition or mate access, a change that might have involved bipedality. The earliest hominids were woodland creatures, as inferred from paleoenvironments where they have been found, meaning that the need to walk across open grassland probably played no important role in their early evolution. Likewise, stone tool manufacture arose much later than did the earliest hominids, who bear no sign of hand or wrist adaptations associated with toolmaking.

Over the next 5 million years a great diversity of hominid species arose. By 4 million years ago at least two forms of hominids had occupied East Africa. *Australopithecus anamensis* was mostly similar to earlier *Orrorin*, although with thicker molar teeth and stronger jaws, evidently as an adaptation to a rough low-energy diet for at least part of the year. In contrast, *Ardipithecus ramidus* had thin, chimpanzee-like molars, although the anatomy of this species remains mostly undescribed. These different forms have not been found together, and their anatomies may have been different adaptive solutions to different environments.

The period between 4 and 3 million years ago produced a similar range of variation. A large sample of hominids from Ethiopia and Tanzania details the evolution of a species with an increasing adaptation to powerful chewing and grinding teeth over a time span of a half-million years. This species, *Australopithecus afarensis*, is the best understood of the early hominids, with most of the skeleton preserved among the many fossils, including the famous "Lucy" skeleton. In this species males were 50 percent or more larger than females, with much more muscular bodies, but both sexes were far smaller than living humans, with males approximately the same size as chimpanzee males and females considerably smaller—standing slightly less than 1 meter in height. This basic body plan was shared by all early hominid species, none of whom varied substantially in body size, and together they are often called "australopithecines." The success of this small-bodied form with large grinding teeth is attested to by the recovery of such remains from north-central Africa and South Africa dating to 3.5 million years ago. Yet, at the same time, basically similar hominids with smaller teeth, *Kenyanthropus platyops*, existed in the midst of this range, in northern Kenya. Paleontologists do not know which of these early hominid species may be more closely related to later hominid forms.

Robust and Gracile Australopithecines

By around 2 million years ago three types of hominids had arisen. The first of these, often called the "robust" australopithecines, greatly elaborated the adaptation to powerful chewing. These hominids had molar teeth relatively larger than those of any other primate, and their premolar teeth also had a molar-like shape. The jaws of these hominids were massive and thick, and their jaw musculature extended to the very tops of their skulls, creating a distinctive crest. Despite their massive faces and jaws, these robust australopithecines were small like other early hominids, and neither chemical analysis of their bones nor microwear analysis of their teeth has yet revealed great differences between their diets and those of other australopithecines. It is likely that these hominids mostly ate the same broad range of foods, including fruit, seeds, insects, and possibly scavenged meat, with robust australopithecines able to exploit lower-energy foods during some parts of the year. There were several populations of robust australopithecines in Africa between 2.5 and 1.5 million years ago, and they probably represent at least two and possibly three species.

A second type of australopithecine maintained the same tooth sizes and cranial form as *A. afarensis*, although with slightly larger brains and slightly less-muscular skulls. These "gracile" australopithecines were quite variable, making the differences between and within their populations difficult to interpret. These generalized hominids fell into different lineages that may have shared different relationships with other hominid forms. In this group, relatively earlier forms, such as *Australopithecus africanus* from South Africa and *Australopithecus garhi* from East Africa, share some features with robust australopithecines. The gracile australopithecines persisted until after 1.6 million years ago in East Africa. The latest forms, which may represent one species or two, shared several features with early humans and may have descended from an australopithecine ancestor shared with humans. Sometimes called "*Homo habilis*," these hominids were basically australopithecine in body form and brain size, but with somewhat reduced teeth and larger brains in some individuals they present a closer appearance to ourselves than any other australopithecines.

Around 2.5 million years ago the earliest stone tools were manufactured. Living chimpanzees use a wide variety of tools, so it is likely that early hominids also could manipulate natural objects. But stone tool manufacture requires skeletal and muscular adaptations to strength and precision of grip that earlier hominids lacked. These characteristics are found in most later hominid remains, including those attributed to late robust and gracile australopithecines, and it is possible that all later hominids are descendants of the first toolmakers. However, the large accumulations of stone tools found shortly after 2 million years ago were likely the products of the third kind of hominid, the first humans.

The First Humans

The first humans were strikingly different from australopithecines in nearly every anatomical element. With statures approaching 1.8 meters, early humans were twice the height of australopithecine females, and female humans were nearly as large as males, unlike the great sexual differences of earlier hominids. Human teeth were actually smaller than even gracile australopithecine teeth, meaning that relative to body size the teeth were much reduced. At the same time, the brain had expanded from an australopithecine mean of 500 cubic centimeters or less to over 800.

These features reflect a markedly different interaction with the environment than in any earlier hominid. Although australopithecines had been restricted to areas near water sources, the long limbs of these larger hominids allowed them to range farther from water and allowed them more efficient dissipation of heat. This greater range of movement is substantiated by archeological traces, which appear farther in the paleoenvironment from ancient water sources and document increasing distances in the transport of materials from their sources. Because the limb proportions and trunk breadth of these hominids were like those of living Africans, these hominids were probably the first to sweat in a pattern like living humans, which proved to be a valuable adaptation to daytime activity in a hot, dry climate. The adaptation to sweating means that these hominids, like humans, were largely hairless.

The social lives of early humans also were greatly changed. The decrease in sexual dimorphism (the condition of having two forms) may reflect an increased investment in parenting by males. In fact, the division of labor in food acquisition between the sexes, which characterizes modern human-foraging groups, may have originated at this time. Hunting prey or scavenging of the prey of other carnivores may have been an important part of food acquisition. Still, as in living human foragers, gathered plant foods probably made up most of the diet.

These social changes may have gone hand in hand with a prolonged period of growth. Human children mature much more slowly than other primates, in part because of the need to develop their complex brains. Indeed, the brains of early humans were within the lower range of those of living people and are the first

to exhibit features, such as left-right asymmetry, that are common to humans. The increases in technology that are reflected by stone tools were certainly part of a trend toward larger brains. All of these changes are, in fact, the first signs of the development of culture. These hominids did not use a language quite like that of humans, but language had begun to evolve, as evidenced by changes in the vocal tract and brain structure. These hominids, the first that people would recognize as human, depended on each other in ways much as humans depend on each other today.

Nothing reflects this dependence more than the further changes in the birthing process. Although these long-legged early humans were even more efficient as bipeds than earlier hominids, the bipedal pelvis is not well suited for giving birth to large-brained infants. Because of the conflicting pressures of brain-size increase and efficient bipedalism, these early humans evolved the unusual birth process that humans still have today. Normal birth in humans requires the unborn baby to rotate within the birth canal, ultimately facing backward. This process is much more dangerous than that of other primates, and assistance is necessary both to comfort and protect the mother and to reduce infant mortality in difficult cases. Also, the amount to which the brain can develop within the womb is limited because the head must fit through the birth canal. Human infants compensate for this by conducting much of their brain development in the first year of life, a period during which they are effectively helpless. The reproduction of humans has therefore come to depend on culture, a dependence that was established nearly 2 million years ago.

Colonization of the Old World

Almost immediately after their origin, early humans moved out of Africa and spread across large parts of the Old World. The earliest sites documenting this spread are in the Caucasus, Java, China, and the Levant; most of the subtropical Old World appears to have been occupied by 1 million years ago. This spread appears to be directly associated with the new human features and ways of life because no australopithecines have yet been found outside Africa.

Despite their widespread distribution, humans were much more limited in behavioral variation than are today's humans. A few tool industries, with large-scale regional differences, existed between 1.8 million and 400,000 years ago. The most notable of these was the Acheulean industry, named after the site in France where it was first identified, although its origin lies in Africa about 1.4 million years ago. The Acheulean is known for its large, two-sided symmetrical tools, called "handaxes," and generally emphasized symmetry, standardization, and bifacial (having opposite sides or faces worked on to form an edge for cutting) flaking techniques much more than did earlier industries. This pattern spread widely through the Old World, which may indicate the substantial connections among ancient populations even after they dispersed from Africa. Populations in some regions never used this industry and used simpler chopping and flake tools throughout the lower and Middle Pleistocene epoch (1.6 million years ago). Such differences may reflect raw material availability, as in parts of east Asia, where the Acheulean did not appear at all, and these people may have used readily available bamboo, much as native peoples in these regions still do today. These techniques persisted over a long time, and it is clear that the rate of social and technological changes that characterizes living humans was almost nonexistent among early humans. This lack of change probably can be explained by a combination of lower biological capacity for culture, lower population size, and the frequent failure of small human groups.

Despite the spread of many people, Africa remained the center of the human population. It was in Africa that the first humans evolved and in Africa that they would remain at the highest density until recent times. Relatively large numbers of people meant that African populations contained more genetic diversity than other regions. With fewer people, populations in other parts of the Old World began to diversify from each other.

Explaining Human Differences

Upon a template of common features, regional variants began to appear. Many of the traits that differed from place to place were features of the skull, such as the relatively flat foreheads of Javan fossils, the projecting faces and noses of European skulls, and the flatter faces of east Asian fossil skulls. Most of the traits that varied in different regions have no obvious functional purpose, and it seems likely that one reason for their variation is the existence of social, or protocultural, differences in mating preferences within different ancient populations.

In the view of many scientists these regional variations proceeded so far that different species of humans began to appear. In this view the regions of the Old World became home to populations of humans who did not interbreed with each other. Only one of these ancient species was ancestral to today's humans, according to this view, and others became extinct during the late Pleistocene epoch as a result of competition from this ultimately successful human lineage. The persistence of regional differences over hundreds of thousands of years is one piece of evidence for this view.

A more significant piece of evidence is the great genetic similarity of living people. Humans today differ little between populations—among different continents, the level of genetic difference is only 15 percent of the average difference between two individuals in the same continent. And all individuals are similar to each other—varying only by one-tenth of 1 percent or less for most genes. Many geneticists interpret these similarities as a reflection of a population history in which all human direct ancestors numbered only a few thousand people during the past 2 million years, and today's populations began to diverge from this ancestral population only recently, within the past 100,000 years. If this were true, then most ancient human fossils could not represent the ancient ancestors of today's humans and must belong to a number of extinct species. Because of the relatively larger genetic variation of living Africans and the appearance of some human skeletal characteristics among ancient Africans, it appears likely that Africa was the original homeland of such an ancestral population, and this theory is often called the "Out of Africa" theory.

Other scientists interpret human genetic similarities differently. In their view human populations are similar to each other today because they share a long history of gene flow and possibly large migrations between them. With constant interchange of people, no population could become genetically very different from others. In this view the lack of large genetic differences between people is a consequence not of ancient population size, but rather of other evolutionary mechanisms, including natural selection. Such scientists note that human genetic variation is not low compared to that of other animal species and that it is unlikely that all species share the unusual mode of long-term isolation of small populations proposed by the Out of Africa theory. Without the long-term influence of geographic barriers to reproduction, today's humans would be unlikely to divide into reproductively isolated populations, and there are hints that this may have been true in the past. Evidence for this view includes the pattern of simultaneous evolutionary changes in different ancient populations and the apparent lack of major cultural or behavioral differences among ancient populations, as indicated by their archeological records.

Pleistocene Evolutionary Changes

From their initial spread out of Africa, humans across the world began to change. The most notable change was the increase in brain size: from a beginning size of around 800 milliliters to the worldwide average of around 1,350 milliliters today. As far as paleontologists can tell from fossil human skull sizes, this change happened continuously during the last 2 million years at a geometric rate of increase. One explanation for this change is the great complexity of the human brain. The evolution of different mental functions, involving many neural structures, probably involved small changes in many genes, an evolutionary pathway through which natural selection could navigate only over thousands of generations.

The changes in brain size triggered many related changes in the skull. As cranial size increased, the configuration of cranial muscles also changed. The height of the skull increased, and the face became relatively less prominent. Other changes, such as a reduction in tooth size, also reduced the size of the face, jaw, and cranial musculature. These changes all may be ultimately due to technological and social changes in food acquisition and preparation as cooking and other forms of food processing became more frequent.

Around 200,000 years ago technologies began to change. Whereas the Acheulean and earlier tool types are called the "lower Paleolithic" by archeologists, the new tool types are called "Middle Paleolithic." During the Middle Paleolithic period, regional variations in tool use became important for the first time. In different areas of Africa people experimented with a great diversity of tools, many of which were later discarded. Across Europe and western Asia new stone tools appeared and were created by what is called the "Levallois technique." This complex technique, which results in a well-formed tool created after a series of steps that seemingly has nothing to do with the tool's form, is thought by some psychologists to be a sign of a modern intelligence, because the structured sequence of toolmaking resembles mental activities like language. Starting sometime earlier than sixty thousand years ago, humans began to migrate to Australia, a voyage across 80 kilometers of open ocean. Brain size worldwide approached the average of that of living people,

and the first undoubted traces of art appeared around this time.

Latest Human Evolution

The Middle Paleolithic period began a complete reordering of the relationship between humans and their environments, a reordering that extended into the succeeding Upper Paleolithic period and up to the present day. The remains of hunted animals show that humans began to exploit a broader range of animal resources. Earlier humans generally hunted medium-size herbivores, such as sheep, deer, or gazelles, but during the late Pleistocene epoch, they increasingly added more dangerous or risky prey, such as cape buffalo and mammoths. Easily caught slow-growing animals, such as land tortoises and some shellfish, came under greater stress as indicated by the decreasing sizes of animals found by paleontologists and archeologists from this time period. In Australia there is evidence that humans systematically burned grasslands as early as fifty thousand years ago, a practice shared by many later peoples in order to attract animals to new growth. Also, across the Old World and later the New World, the Pleistocene megafauna—from the rhino-sized marsupials of Australia to the mammoths of Europe and ultimately the ancient American megafauna—began to disappear. All of these shifts probably were results of human population increases and consequent stress on other natural populations, and although there is no archeological record of plant use it is likely that other resources were coming under greater stress as well.

At the same time, humans increased their technological abilities to allow the greater exploitation of other resources. By twenty-five thousand years ago string was invented, and humans began to make nets and snares for fish and small animals. This change, which spread the ability to acquire animal protein to old and young alike, appears to have accompanied an increased sedentism (settled lifestyle) of human populations as population pressures began to prohibit the free movement of peoples and encourage the year-round exploitation of seasonal resources, as indicated by the increasing use of food storage pits. Larger populations may have caused increases in cultural differentiation and extended social networks beyond the numbers of people that any individual might know well. Cultural ornaments and artwork, which may have communicated status or other social information, became much more common during Upper Paleolithic times. Culminating in the fantastic art gracing the walls of European caves such as Lascaux in France, as well as Australian rock faces that are even older, the increasing use of persistent symbols reflects a concern with communicating with people who are distant, either in place or in time. These symbols, along with the increasingly elaborate human burials that characterized Middle as well as Upper Paleolithic peoples, are among the earliest signs of a human concern with the nonmaterial.

These vast behavioral changes were accompanied by substantial morphological (relating to form) changes. By twenty thousand years ago human populations in all regions of the world attained a form much more like that of their living descendants than like that of any humans earlier than fifty thousand years ago. Even so, substantial evolutionary changes occurred within this most recent time period, especially with the spread of agriculture to different regions of the world. Many geneticists believe that this spread was accompanied by the massive spread of human genes from the ancient agricultural centers, both because those populations were the first to attain civilization and its massive increases in population density, and because these populations were the first to attain resistance to the new epidemic diseases that civilized ways of life encouraged. In any event, the genetics of Europe, northeast Asia, and other peripheral regions appear to reflect great movements of peoples during the past ten thousand years. At the same, time agricultural peoples underwent waves of morphological changes, especially in the teeth, as a response to the history of food processing and dietary specialization.

Human evolution continues to occur. As humans alter their environments, they are placed in novel ecological circumstances that have reproductive and evolutionary consequences. Humans did not originate in social groups of thousands of people, nor did they in the past rely on a diet largely processed by machines. The large size of the current human population implies that some evolutionary changes, such as the natural selection that adapts humans to their environment, will occur only slowly in the future. Furthermore, human cultural practices, including medicine, environmental alteration, and economic systems, often reduce the genetic relationship between human behavior or physical form and their reproduction. However, other effects of the new human population structure may be accelerating. Today people move between populations around the world with increasing ease, and as a result human genes are mixing at an increasing rate. Large demographic differences between societies exist, with the rate of population growth different between re-

gions. These differences ensure that the human population of the future will have a genetic makeup that will be different from those in the world today.

John Hawks

See also Diseases, Human; Domestication, Plant and Animal

Further Reading

Cavalli-Sforza, L. L., & Cavalli-Sforza, F. (1995). *The great human diasporas: A history of diversity and evolution.* Reading, MA: Addison-Wesley.

Grine, F. E. (Ed.). (1988). *Evolutionary history of the "robust" australopithecines.* New York: Aldine de Gruyter.

Harpending, H. C., Batzer, M., Gurven, A. M., Jorde, L. B., Rogers, A. R., & Sherry, S. T. (1998). Genetic traces of ancient demography. *Proceedings of the National Academy of Sciences, USA, 95*(4), 1961–1967.

Hawks, J., Hunley, K., Lee, S.-H., & Wolpoff, M. H. (2000). Population bottlenecks and Pleistocene human evolution. *Molecular Biology and Evolution, 17*(1), 2–22.

Johanson, D. C., & Edey, M. A. (1981). *Lucy, the beginnings of humankind.* New York: Simon & Schuster.

Klein, R. (1999). *The human career.* Chicago: University of Chicago Press.

McBrearty, S., & Brooks, A. S. (2000). The revolution that wasn't: A new interpretation of the origin of modern human behavior. *Journal of Human Evolution, 39*(5), 453–563.

Pope, G. G., & Cronin, J. E. (1984). The Asian hominidae. *Journal of Human Evolution, 13*(5), 377–396.

Relethford, J. R. (2002). *Genetics and modern human origins.* New York: Wiley-Liss

Rosenberg, K. R., & Trevathan, W. R. (2001). The evolution of human birth. *Scientific American, 285*(5), 72–77.

Stiner, M. C., Munro, N. D., Surovell, T. A., Tchernov, E., & Bar-Yosef, O. (1999). Paleolithic population growth pulses evidenced by small animal exploitation. *Science, 283*(5399), 190–194.

Wheeler, P. E. (1993). The influence of stature and body form on hominid energy and water budgets: A comparison of *Australopithecus* and early *Homo* physiques. *Journal of Human Evolution, 24*(1), 13–28.

Wolpoff, M. H. (1999). *Paleoanthropology.* New York: McGraw-Hill.

Exotic Species

Life forms that originated somewhere else are variously known as "exotic," "nonindigenous," "nonnative," "immigrant," "introduced," "transplanted," "cosmopolitan," and "alien" species—with considerable debate among natural and social scientists over the appropriate terminology due to the human connotations of these terms. These exotics surround humankind. The majority of flowers and trees in British gardens and parks, for example, are of foreign origin. Olives, wheat, and grapes come from the Mediterranean region. But Italian food staples such as rice, maize (corn), and tomatoes hail from Asia and the Americas. Sunflowers, cranberries, pecans, tobacco, and maple syrup are the only major crops based on plants indigenous to North America. The U.S. livestock industry is also founded on exotic species.

Biotic (relating to living beings) interchange is a fundamental feature of Earth's history. When continental drift formed a land bridge between North and South America about 2.8 million years ago, the species of two hitherto-unrelated landmasses were thrown together. Whether in geological or historical times, flora and fauna have been dispersed by many natural methods, the most important being wind, water, and, in the case of plants, animal fur, feces, and feet. The fruits of the coconut palm drifted westward from Central America's Pacific Coast to Indian Ocean islands in prehistoric times. Species have also been moving around for as long as people have migrated. The Romans shipped carp from the Danube River back to Italy, from where they spread across Europe with Christianity and from monastery ponds into rivers and lakes. Norman invaders introduced the rabbit to the British Isles in the eleventh century. In the second half of the nineteenth century, however, acclimatization became a popular activity across the European settler colonies and the United States. Americans keen to rid urban shade trees of a caterpillar pest imported the European house sparrow (also known as house sparrow and English sparrow) in the 1860s (Canadians, Australians, and New Zealanders followed suit). Introductions have also been undertaken for sporting reasons and ornamental and sentimental reasons. The Chinese pheasant was introduced to Oregon in the 1870s to augment dwindling supplies of native game birds, while the American gray squirrel was imported to England to enrich the fauna of country estates. Meanwhile a homesick British settler shipped rabbits to Australia. The giant African land snail's advance around half the world between about 1800 and the 1940s began when the governor of Mauritius secured these 20-centimeter snails to ameliorate his wife's tuberculosis (snail soup was touted as a cure).

Unintended Consequences

Many well-intended introductions have brought unintended consequences. The house sparrow's impact was greater on native birds than on caterpillars. West Indian sugar planters in the 1870s hoped the "Indian" mongoose would protect their cane fields from rats. Instead, it ravaged native wildlife (and poultry). The giant African land snail will eat practically any plant material and reproduces at a staggering rate. Undeterred, Australian sugar planters brought the giant South American cane toad to Queensland to combat a beetle pest in 1935. The toads failed to eat the beetle, but, like the mongoose, ate almost everything else. Having left the checks and balances on their own expansion at home, populations of invasive exotics like the cane toad explode. In fact, many species that have not demonstrated invasive potential at home become invasive on relocation. The natural range of the Monterey pine—one of the most expansionist of trees in South Africa, Australia, and New Zealand, where it was introduced as a commercial plantation tree—is confined to a relatively few small areas of central California. As well as affecting native species through competition, predation, hybridization, and disease, invasive exotics can fundamentally transform ecosystems. A striking example of the "cascade" effect that can flow when an exotic is inserted into the food web is the opossum shrimp in northwestern Montana, where it was introduced in the late 1960s to enhance food supplies for rainbow trout. These large shrimps have preyed on native zooplankton, affecting local fish numbers, which, in turn, have had serious consequences for populations of eagle, otter, coyote, and bear. Scientists increasingly believe that the impact of invasive exotics is now second only to habitat loss as the major cause of the depletion and extinction of indigenous species.

Stowaways

Species also move around inadvertently in association with people. As Roman soldiers marched around Europe, North Africa, and the Middle East, they carried seeds stuck to the soles of their hobnailed sandals. Crockery from Europe often arrived in the North American colonies in straw packing riddled with seeds that, having been reused as stable bedding, frequently wound up on fields mixed with manure. Plants and animals (especially reptiles and insects) have also been redistributed via the proverbial bunch of bananas or as stowaways in the ballast material of cargo ships. A number of these unexpected visitors have become so-called nuisance species. Canadian waterweed, which arrived in Britain attached to imported logs, clogged Britain's waterways for a number of decades, even disrupting college rowing at Cambridge University in the 1840s. And since the late nineteenth century, European potato growers have feared the imminent arrival of the Colorado beetle, the major U.S. potato pest, which has showed up periodically.

The majority of exotics fail to establish themselves, despite notorious instances such as the chestnut blight (a plant disease agent that decimated the chestnut trees of the eastern United States in the early 1900s) and the brown tree snake, which hitched a ride on military transport planes during World War II from Papua New Guinea to previously snake-free Guam, where it has devastated the native bird population. Other exotic species become naturalized without significant impact on the host community. Some trees—such as the stately conifers that embellished many eighteenth-century English estates and California's eucalypts—are such an integral element of their landscapes that most Britons and Californians are unaware of their origins in western North America and Australia, respectively.

As globalization's rising volumes of trade and travel bring different parts of the world ever closer together, the last one hundred years have brought the highest rate of reshuffling since the era of European exploration and colonization (1492–1600), when European plants and animals were transplanted to re-create familiar worlds. Humans are sometimes dubbed the "ultimate exotic": Humans are generalists in their feeding habits, highly adaptable to a broad spectrum of climatic and environmental conditions, and able to breed year around. Whether humans are also a peerless *invasive* exotic is a matter for profound debate.

Peter Coates

Further Reading

Baskin, Y. (2000). *A plague of rats and rubbervines: The growing threat of species invasions*. Washington, DC: Island Press.

Bright, C. (1999). *Life out of bounds: Bio-invasions in a borderless world*. Washington, DC: Worldwatch Institute/Earthscan.

Crosby, A. (1986). *Ecological imperialism: The biological expansion of Europe, 900–1900*. New York: Cambridge University Press.

Elton, C. S. (2000). *The ecology of invasions by animals and plants*. Chicago: University of Chicago Press. (Original work published 1958)

McNeely, J. A. (Ed.). (2001). *The great reshuffling: Human dimensions of invasive alien species*. Cambridge, UK: International Union for Conservation of Nature.

U.S. Congress, Office of Technology Assessment. (1993). *Harmful non-indigenous species in the United States* (OTA-F–565). Washington, DC: U.S. Government Printing Office.

Exploration

The subject of exploration can be usefully divided into two categories, primary and secondary exploration. The first is the discovery and investigation of regions where humans are not living; the second is exploration of regions unfamiliar to the explorers but where humans are living.

Primary Exploration

The *Homo sapiens* species first appeared perhaps 200,000 years ago in Africa and from there migrated on foot to most of the habitable areas of the Old World. Humans were by 50,000 years ago probably the most widely distributed of all large land animals. When they next moved into Australia and then to and through the Americas they became unquestionably the most widespread.

Much of their primary exploration was undeliberate: for instance, entering North America by following herds of caribou across the Bering isthmus. In contrast, the speakers of the Austronesian languages, a people originally of Southeast Asia, were deliberate primary explorers. (One does not plod mindlessly across the Indian Ocean or the Pacific.) Some of them traveled east, discovered as yet unpopulated Madagascar, and settled there in the first millennium CE. Others, ancestors of the Polynesians, first appear in the archeological record in Melanesia, where they taught themselves to make ocean-going vessels, learned to negotiate eastward passage against the prevailing winds of the tropical Pacific, and devised techniques of oceanic navigation. Thus prepared, they migrated to what is now called central Polynesia: Fiji, Tonga, Samoa, and in time from there to other islands and to the extreme points of Polynesia—Hawaii to the north, Easter Island

---

A Swedish Traveler's Impression of the New World

Swedish botanist Peter Kalm traveled in eastern North America from 1748 to 1751. The following extract from his travel account shows that he did really see it as a "new world."

I found that I was now come into a new world. Whenever I looked to the ground I found everywhere such plants as I had never seen before. When I saw a tree, I was forced to stop an ask those who accompanied me, how it was called . . . I was seized with terror at the thought of ranging so many new and unknown parts of Natural History.

Source: Kalm, Peter. (1972). *Travels in North America* (John R. Forster, trans.). Barre, MA: The Imprint Society, p. 24.

---

to the east, and, most recently, New Zealand to the south around 1200 CE.

They may even have voyaged as far as America and back. The sweet potato, long one of their staples, is a plant of South American origin. The most reasonable explanation for its cultivation in the mid-Pacific is that Polynesian explorers sailed past Easter Island—why would they have stopped there, when for a thousand years of exploration there had always been more islands to the east?—and continued on to the New World, acquired the sweet potato there, and brought it home.

The Polynesians were the last major wave of pure frontiersmen and women: that is to say, they explored, with the sole possible exception of America, lands where no humans had preceded them.

Secondary Exploration

Since approximately 1000 CE exploration has been chiefly a matter of people from the relatively densely populated and often imperialistic societies coming upon and often invading the lands of other societies. There were, of course, men and women of the latter who traveled widely, but they left few written records or archeological evidence and had little influence in general. Squanto, a member of the Pawtuxet tribe of Massachusetts, is a good example of one of these individuals. As nearly as we can reconstruct his biography, he was captured by white slavers in 1614, sold in Spain, somehow got himself from there to England, then went to Newfoundland and thence home in 1619 in time to serve as interpreter for the Pilgrim settlers of Plym-

outh. His adventures are comparable to those of, for instance, John Smith of the Virginia colony, but he did not write a book and the Pawtuxet did not found an empire, and so he is not thought of as an explorer.

Secondary exploration defies easy definition. What is an explorer and what is a traveler? The Phoenicians who, according to one ancient text circumnavigated Africa in about 600 BCE (from east to west, the opposite of Vasco da Gama) would certainly qualify as explorers. Hanno, the Carthaginan who claimed to have sailed out of the Mediterranean and down the coast of West Africa in the fifth century BCE, would, presuming his truthfulness, qualify. On the other hand, Zheng He, the admiral of China's Ming dynasty, who in the early fifteenth century sent Chinese fleets to and across the Indian Ocean as far as East Africa, was more an imperialist than an explorer.

Marco Polo and Ibn Batutta, who ranged extensively between the Mediterranean and China Seas in the thirteenth and fourteenth centuries CE, were travelers rather than explorers. The claim that either discovered China seems a non sequitur.

In contrast, the Vikings who sailed west from Scandinavia in the last centuries of the first millennium CE were clearly explorers: they ventured to lands of which they knew nothing. They crossed the North Atlantic to Greenland, and, around 1000 CE, reached as far as America, specifically Newfoundland and possibly farther. All their colonies withered except Iceland, and the accounts of their explorations in their sagas went unread for many centuries outside of Iceland. Nevertheless, they were certainly explorers, though their historical influence was slight.

A half millennium later there were other and more influential European secondary explorers; indeed, these new explorers were the most colossally influential in history. They were the first to circumnavigate the world and to visit all the continents and major islands.

What tempted and drove them is not an easy question to answer. The desire for commerce directly with eastern Asia, rather than through Middle Eastern intermediaries, and the hope to find and enlist allies against the Muslims certainly were important. Christianity's missionary spirit and the rivalry between the European states for empire were other motives. All of these and others were influential, but we can't be sure of their strengths. We can be sure that Europeans went exploring because geography and prevailing winds made it possible, even attractive, for them to do so.

As far as Chinese, Japanese, and Southeast Asian sailors knew, the Pacific Ocean offered no prospect of contact with lands known, even by legend, to be rich. To the Muslim mariners of the societies bordering the Indian Ocean that body of water offered no more than it had offered for many centuries: opportunities to ride the monsoons back and forth between the ports of familiar and rich societies. Why sail out of its balmy latitudes into the cold and winds of the southern ocean, which led to no place they wanted to go to which they did not already have easy access?

The Atlantic west and south of Europe was, in contrast, tempting. Due west, as knowledgeable Europeans surmised, lay eastern Asia and its markets. South, then—if possible—east around Africa, and then north would lead to India. The prevailing wind patterns of the Atlantic in the lower latitudes made such dreams seem practical. In the fifteenth century it was already known that a voyage of a few hundred miles south of Iberia would bring you to the trade winds, providing, one might sensibly hope, quick passage to Asia or, with a bit of maneuvering, around Africa. And there were islands to serve as stepping stones and forward bases for explorers. Madeira and the Azores, discovered by or in the fifteenth century, were unpopulated. The Canaries, known to the Romans and rediscovered in the same general period, were populated, but by Stone Age people soon dislodged and available for enslavement. The tropical Atlantic was an invitation for European fishermen and merchant seamen to become explorers.

These explorers, most sailing for the Portuguese, spent the fifteenth century edging southward along the coast of Africa and improving their ship and rigging designs, seamanship, and navigation skills. In 1487 Bartolomeu Dias rounded the southern extreme of Africa and saw that the coast turned north. In 1497 Vasco da Gama confirmed that fact and continued on to India, initiating direct contact between western Europe and the advanced southern Asian societies.

In 1492 Christopher Columbus, sponsored by the Spanish and also searching for Asia, accomplished an even greater discovery. He dropped south to the Canaries, sidled into the trade wind belt, and a month later, on 12 October, landed in the Bahamas. As a demonstration of seamanship his achievement was inferior to many of those of the Polynesians, but theirs changed only their peoples' lives. His changed the lives of all peoples.

On this, his first voyage to America, Columbus visited the Bahamas, Cuba, and Española (also called Hispaniola, Santo Domingo, and, today, Haiti and the Dominican Republic). He was convinced that he was in Asian waters. He apparently maintained that belief through three additional trans-Atlantic voyages (1493, 1498, 1502) that, in total, took him through the Antilles and along the northern coasts of South America and of Central America. He was not a good geographer, but he was the most important explorer of all time.

The achievements of Vasco da Gama and Columbus inspired a great many exploratory voyages in the next century, of which we will only mention a few. In 1497 John Cabot sailed from England to Newfoundland and in 1500 Pedro Cabral sailed to India and incidentally discovered Brazil on the way. We might also mention Amerigo Vespucci's reconnaissance of the north coast of South America, if only because by an odd chance the entire New World was named after him.

Of the sixteenth-century exploratory voyages, the most important by far was that led by Ferdinand Magellan. In 1519 he embarked from Seville, crossed the Atlantic, coasted southward along South America looking for a passage through to the ocean washing Asian shores, found a way through the strait that bears his name, and named and crossed the almost indefatigably broad Pacific, completing the voyage to Asia that Columbus believed he had accomplished. Magellan died in a skirmish in the Philippines and Juan Sebastián Elcano led the few sailors who survived the hardships and quarrels on through the Indian Ocean, around Africa, and home in 1522. The log of the first circumnavigation of the globe was, when compared to the European calendar, off by one calendar day, which went unexplained for some time. The expedition had sailed west away from the rising sun all the way around the world and had thus gained one day.

Filling in the Blanks

Completion of the first circumnavigation brought the grandest age of secondary exploration to a close. After Magellan and Elcano, maps began to depict a world that resembles what our astronauts see from space. Of course, there were a myriad of details to fill in. For example, Dutch sailors stumbled upon Australia in the early seventeenth century, a discovery confirmed by Abel Tasman in the 1640s; Vitus Bering discovered that the Old and New Worlds were not connected by sailing the waters dividing them in 1725–1730 and 1733–1742; Willem Cornelis Schouten discovered Cape Horn, the southernmost tip of South America, in 1616; and so on and on.

Europeans had blundered up against the New World and now were obliged to find ways through or around it to Asia. Efforts to do so taught them a great deal about America's coasts, its northern and southern extremes and estuaries. In 1513, for example, Vasco Núñez de Balboa found his way across the Panamanian isthmus and sighted the Pacific Ocean years before Magellan. In 1524 Giovanni da Verrazano coasted from North Carolina to Newfoundland looking for a way through to the Pacific and Asia. He entertained the idea that the Outer Banks of North Carolina were an isthmus dividing the Atlantic from the Pacific. In 1534–1535 Jacques Cartier sailed into the Gulf of St. Lawrence and up the river as far as the site of Montreal. He was so optimistic about his supposed proximity to Asia that he named the rapids there *La Chine*, after China.

Other early explorers, most of them English or Dutch, learned a lot of geography in attempts, all in vain, to find passages to Asia northwest around Canada and, as well, northeast around Russia. The Northwest and Northeast Passages were not completed for three centuries more, when Nils Adolf Erik Nordenskiöld in 1878–1879 traversed the ice and water north of Russia and in 1903–1905 when Roald Amundsen did the same north of Canada and Alaska.

The Spanish conquistadors are not usually thought of as explorers because they were seeking gold, not geographical enlightenment, but they were explorers, if inadvertently. Hernán Cortés's invasion of the Aztec empire (1519–1521) and Francisco Pizarro's invasion of the Inca empire (1532–1533), were informative as well as wildly remunerative, and inspired others Euro-peans, especially Spaniards, to march off into the unknown in search for fortunes of their own. In 1541 Francisco de Orellana followed the course of the Amazon from the Andes to the Atlantic. In 1540–1542 Francisco Vásquez de Coronado led an expedition from Mexico north to look for the Seven Golden Cities of Cibola, penetrating the present-day United States as far as Kansas, and in 1539–1543 Hernando de Soto led another from Florida north and west as far as the Mississippi. Gonzalo Jiménez de Quesada in 1571 and Walter Raleigh in 1595 ventured deep into northern South America in search of the golden kingdom of El Dorado.

In the coming centuries greed, at first for precious metals and then for more mundane items, such as slaves and furs, would inspire dozens of lesser-known explorers, known collectively as the *coureurs de bois* of Canada, for example, or the *bandeira* of Brazil. When they were done, the locations of the chief physical features of the New World—the Rockies in North America, the Río de la Plata in South America, the llanos (wide plains in South America), the Mato Grosso Plateau in Brazil, and so forth—were widely known.

Exploration in time became less predatory and more scientific. In the eighteenth century the Pacific attracted a number of expeditions of the latter variety. Louis-Antoine de Bougainville, who sailed round the world in 1766–1769, visited Samoa, Tahiti, and other Pacific isles. Another French explorer, the Comte de La Perouse (Jean-François de Galaup), lost his life in the Pacific, dying in a shipwreck in the New Hebrides in 1788.

The greatest of the Pacific explorers, excepting only the Polynesians, was James Cook, who led three expeditions (1768–1771, 1772–1775, 1776–1779) into that ocean. He added considerably to European knowledge of that part of the world largely because he sailed not so much east-west, as the Spanish traders had many times between American and Asian entrepots, as north-south. He spent considerable time in the southern reaches of the Pacific and Indian Oceans looking for an answer to the greatest geographical question remaining. Was there an enormous southern continent, of which Australia was merely a peninsula, to balance Eurasia and North America on the other side of the Equator, as theorists had supposed for many generations? He didn't find it in weeks of sailing in the icy waters of the southern seas, pretty well dispatching that legend. On his third voyage, on which he became the first European to visit the Hawaiian Islands, he sailed far into the North Pacific to look for a passage around North America. He didn't find that either, and then returned to the Hawaiian Islands, where he was killed in a skirmish with the indigenes in 1778.

After Captain Cook there was still much to be learned about the geography of the major oceans, but only the details. The biggest blanks on European maps were in the interiors of continents. A lot of these were filled in by governmentally sponsored expeditions. Of these the most famous was the expedition of Meriwether Lewis and William Clark, better known simply as the Lewis and Clark expedition, dispatched by President Thomas Jefferson of the United States to journey across North America to the Pacific, 1804–1806, and to report methodically and scientifically on what they had seen. Their report covered the upper Missouri River, the Great Plains, the Rockies, the Columbia River, the Cascades, Douglas firs, grizzly bears, and indigenous tribes.

Samuel Hearne transected Canada in 1770–1771, opening that land's north for geographers to explicate and capitalists to exploit. He traveled overland from the south, specifically from mouth of the Churchill River to the Arctic Ocean, the first person, certainly the first European, ever to do so. Robert Burke did the same for Australia. It was in 1861 that he trekked from Melbourne, in the south of Australia, to the tropical waters of the Gulf of Carpentaria. He died of starvation and exhaustion on the return trip.

European exploration of the interior of Africa was hampered by Africa's fevers and the resistance of its kingdoms, which survived contact with outsiders much better than did America's. Not until the nineteenth, chiefly the late nineteenth, century did African continent give up its major geographical secrets to outsiders.

The idée fixe of its European explorers was to find the sources and trace the courses of Africa's greatest rivers: the Niger, the Congo, the Nile, and the Zambezi. Mungo Park, obsessed with the Niger, twice penetrated the interior in efforts to follow that river from its broad reaches near the Sahara to its mouth, drowning in 1806 before quite doing so. Richard Lander completed the full voyage of the Niger all the way to the Gulf of Guinea in 1830. The other rivers surrendered their secrets to the missionary, David Livingstone, the journalist, Henry Morton Stanley, and the like in the latter half of the nineteenth century. By 1875 there were no more than pockets of mystery in the map of Africa: the explorers had traced the courses of all its major rivers, and the continent's doors were wide open.

The last major event in the drama of secondary exploration opened in 1930 when gold-seeker Michael J. Leahy crossed the coastal mountains of Papua New Guinea to find himself not in uninhabited wilderness, as he expected, but among scores of thousands of Stone Age people, the last big population of such remaining. After that there were no new worlds, not whole ones, at least, left for secondary exploration.

The Return of Primary Exploration

The race for the North Pole, fueled by nationalistic and personal ambition as much as by scientific inquiry, took scientists and adventurers far out onto arctic ice where no sensible Inuit ever went. The rush north climaxed in 1909 when Robert Peary reached the North Pole (or at least came very close; there is controversy on the matter).

The North Pole was ice and water, not ice and land. The South Pole was in the middle of the one remaining uninhabited and, to this day, unconquered continent, Antarctica. Captain Cook saw the ice surrounding it, but never the land. A few sealers, whalers, and explorers probably sighted the actual land in the early and mid-nineteenth century, but it may have been as late as the end of the century before humans actually set foot on that continent. In 1895 a party of Norwegian whalers actually did so.

The continent was inhospitable in the extreme, but was catnip to adventurers. In 1911 Roald Amundsen won the race to the South Pole. Robert Falcon Scott came in second in 1912, but won greater fame by freezing to death in the effort. Exploration, as we have seen time and again, is a dangerous business.

Depths and Heights, New Chapters in Primary Exploration

Primary exploration continues, though not of the Earth's continents or islands. Most of the Earth's surface is under water and, therefore, subject exclusively to primary exploration. As of the middle of the nineteenth century we knew little more about the oceans per se and about what lies under them than Magellan did of the surface characteristics of the Pacific when he first sailed into that ocean.

The beginning of the science of oceanography can reasonably be associated with the voyage of *The Challenger*, dispatched in 1872 by the British government on a four-year circumnavigation of the world with the purpose of learning about its oceans. Since then the accumulation of data and analysis we call oceanography has been enormous, though still unimpressive when compared with what we do not know.

Oceanographic explorers have located the major geological features of the oceans. The tallest mountain in the world, top to bottom, turns out not to be Mount Everest but Hawaii's Mauna Kea, which rises 10,200 meters above the ocean floor. The greatest mountain ranges in the world are not the Andes or Himalayas but those that snake across the ocean bottom. The Mid-Atlantic Ridge stretches 16,000 kilometers from north of Iceland as far south as the southernmost tip of Africa.

All exploration into space is primary exploration. In the first years of the twentieth century scientists and dreamers were touting exploration of the heavens, but did not have the equipment to even try. Spacecraft, should someone ever invent them, would be so expensive that only governments could afford them, and so the motive to build them would have to be far more powerful and general than astronomical curiosity. The rage and fear engendered by wars, hot and cold, supplied that motive. The earliest long-range rocket, the German V–2, completed its first successful flight in 1942. Intercontinental ballistic missiles, children of that rocket and of the rivalry between the United States and the Union of Soviet Socialist Republics, were flying by the end of the 1950s. The technology for space exploration now existed.

On 20 July 1969 Neil Armstrong and Edwin Aldrin descended a ladder from the spacecraft that had ridden aloft in the tip of a Saturn V rocket and stepped down onto the surface of the Moon. Ten more humans have followed them to the Moon. Others will surely travel to Mars and elsewhere in space. In the meanwhile we content ourselves with unmanned space probes. Voyager 1, launched 5 September 1977, was on January 2001 as far from Earth as light travels in eleven hours. There is little likelihood that humans will ever forget that the urge to explore is one of their primary characteristics.

Alfred W. Crosby

See also Evolution and the Spread of Humans

Further Reading

Beaglehole, J. C. (1966). *The exploration of the Pacific* (3rd ed.). Stanford, CA: Stanford University Press.

Bellwood, P. (1987). *The Polynesians: Prehistory of an island people* (Rev. ed.). New York: Thames and Hudson.

Morison, S. E. (1971). *The European discovery of America: The northern voyages, A.D. 500–1600.* New York: Oxford University Press.

Morison, S. E. (1974). *The European discovery of America: The southern voyages, 1492–1616.* New York: Oxford University Press.

Parry, J. H. (1981). *The discovery of the sea.* Berkeley and Los Angeles: University of California Press.

Parry, J. H. (1982). *The age of reconnaissance: Discovery, exploration, and settlement, 1450–1650.* Berkeley and Los Angeles: University of California Press.

Perham, M., & Simmons, J. (Eds.). (1957). *African discovery* (2nd ed.). London: Faber.

Burrows, W. E. (1998). *This new ocean: The story of the first space age.* New York: Random House.

Extinction

Species extinction—the disappearance of all individuals of a species—has occurred throughout the 3.5 billion years of life on Earth, but the causes and rates of extinction have fluctuated dramatically. It is estimated that approximately 7 million species exist today, comprising approximately 2 percent of all species that have ever lived. The other species have thus gone extinct, after average lifespans of 5–10 million years. Part of this phenomenon is actually "pseudoextinction," caused by the fact that, as species evolve, individuals often come to look so different from their ancestors that a systematist seeing only specimens from periods separated by millennia, without specimens from intermediate periods, may classify them as separate species. However, even if the word "extinction" is restricted to the termination of a lineage, and change within a lineage is excluded, there have been millions of extinctions.

Mass extinctions of the distant past

Although most attention has been paid to very recent extinctions plus five historical "mass extinctions," during which the majority of then extant species went extinct, normal "background" extinction—the disappearance of species at a relatively slow, steady rate—probably accounts for 90–96 percent of all extinctions. The "big five" mass extinctions occurred in relatively short intervals at the ends of the Ordovician (490–433 million years ago), Devonian (417–354 million years ago), Permian (290–248 million years ago), Triassic

(248–206 million years ago), and Cretaceous (144–65 million years ago) periods. During all but the end-Permian extinction, 65–85 percent of marine animal species went extinct, while possibly 95 percent disappeared at the end of the Permian. In each of these mass extinctions, many species besides marine animals went extinct, but the fossil evidence is best for marine animals. The fact that these mass extinctions occurred at the ends of geological periods reflects the fact that geologists used major, abrupt faunal "breaks" to establish boundaries for the major time intervals. In addition to the big five, there are another 20–30 relatively short periods when extinction rates rose above background level but did not approach the levels of the big five. Many biologists believe that the Earth has recently embarked on a sixth major mass extinction, a claim addressed below.

The proposed causes of these mass extinctions are controversial. Although scientists generally prize hypotheses that explain many disparate phenomena, it is possible that the various mass extinctions do not all have the same cause. Most recent controversy has revolved around the contention by Luis Alvarez (1911–1988) and his colleagues that at least some mass extinctions were caused by large asteroids colliding with the Earth. The evidence for this proposition is most firmly established for the end-Cretaceous mass extinction, approximately 65 million years ago; this is the event during which dinosaurs largely disappeared, as did many other species of animals and plants. At several sites around the Earth, rocks of the Cretaceous-Tertiary border have high concentrations of rare-earth elements, especially iridium; these elements are also present in high concentrations in extraterrestrial objects, such as asteroids. Although some geologists believe this end-Cretaceous "iridium anomaly" could have been caused by volcanic eruptions, most believe it derives from an asteroid.

How could a collision between an asteroid and the Earth generate a mass extinction? From observed iridium concentrations at the Cretaceous-Tertiary boundary and in asteroids, the colliding asteroid is hypothesized to have been approximately 10 kilometers in diameter. The presence of a huge crater dated to the Cretaceous-Tertiary boundary and buried beneath sediments off the Yucatan coast of Mexico supports the hypothesis of an asteroid impact. The kinetic energy of such a large asteroid would have produced an explosion about 1,000 times greater than the eruption of Krakatoa in 1883. Loss of sunlight, increased temperature, and acid rain are but some of the possible consequences of such an explosion that could have caused many extinctions.

Raup and Sepkoski (1982) extended the asteroid-impact hypothesis to the other big five extinctions and several smaller mass extinctions. They suggest that the extinction dates corresponded to a quite regular cycle of approximately 26 million years, probably driven by solar system or galactic processes, such as passage of the solar system through the spiral arms of the Milky Way. This proposal has led to a flurry of activity by geologists and astronomers seeking supporting or conflicting evidence. Although the statistical support for the existence of such a cycle has been questioned, most observers see a degree of periodicity in the mass extinction dates. No proposed astronomical mechanism producing such periodicity is widely accepted. Smaller iridium anomalies than the one at the Cretaceous-Tertiary boundary have also been found corresponding to the times of several other mass extinctions; however, some researchers question whether any of these anomalies have extraterrestrial causes.

At least some mass extinctions could have been caused by terrestrial forces. For example, among the big five, the end-Ordovician extinction coincided with relatively rapid cooling. Changes in sea level, possibly associated with climate changes, are also associated with some mass extinctions. Among the big five, a drop in sea level (and therefore less continental area covered by sea) coincided with the end-Triassic and end-Cretaceous extinctions. It is also possible that changing shapes and degrees of connection among continents, as plate tectonic movement drove them apart or together, could have led to mass extinctions. For instance, at the end of the Permian, the time of the greatest mass extinction, the continental plates coalesced into the single supercontinent of Pangaea. This would have reduced the total length of continental perimeters, and many of the marine fossil species that went extinct then were invertebrates occupying near-shore shelves. Thus, the total area of their habitat decreased, and a general rule of ecology is that, all things being equal, number of species is roughly proportional to habitat area.

Aside from any decrease in habitat area, the simple mixing of formerly separate species that might have played similar ecological roles and occupied similar habitats (sometimes said to have occupied similar "ecological niches") could have caused extinction, as better adapted species outcompeted others formerly protected by isolation. A noteworthy potential example of such a process is the "Great American Interchange" of biota between North and South America (previously separated for over 50 million years) after the establishment of the Panamamian land bridge approximately 3 million years ago. In general, far more North American species successfully invaded South America than vice versa, and it is likely that at least some of them did so at the expense of ecologically similar South-American species that subsequently went extinct. The reasons for such general competitive superiority are disputed. One suggestion again relates to the relationship between area and number of species: it is possible that the larger North-American continent, harboring more species, forced all of them to lead a more competitive life, with the result that evolution produced species likely to be competitively superior. Other interactions than competition could have been at play. For example, brain size in North American mammals, both predators and prey species, increased greatly over the last 65 million years; a similar change did not occur in South American mammals. Harry J. Jerison (b. 1925) attributes this difference to greater competition between predators and prey on the larger, more species-rich continent. Similar explanations based on better competitive, predatory, or predator-resistant behavior of continental species have been proposed for the wave of recent extinctions of endemic island species in the wake of introduction of mainland species.

Extinctions in Historical Times

Scientists focussing on extinction in the geological past have de-emphasized background extinction in favor of mass extinctions. However, background extinction accounts for the great majority of all extinctions that have ever occurred, and its causes remain mysterious. Most biologists feel that the gradual, widespread extinction of marsupial mammals everywhere but Australia, where they remained isolated until very recently, and South America, where they were isolated until the Great American Interchange, arises from their general inferiority to placentals, probably resulting from the fact that the placentals carry their young internally until they are much more mature. However, the exact reasons for the replacement of marsupials by placentals are still controversial. It is small wonder, then, that the reasons so many species of formerly species-rich but less-studied groups such as brachiopods and bryozoans went extinct are poorly understood. Nevertheless, it is highly likely that, as either abiotic conditions (especially climate), the biota, or both change, various species become more poorly adapted than oth-

ers to their ambient environments, often to the point of extinction. The huge deer known as the Irish elk ranged east to Asia and south to northern Africa and evolved over the last few million years. Although it may have persisted longer on the continent, it disappeared from Ireland very rapidly after a brief warm spell from 10,000–9,000 BCE, apparently because it was adapted neither to the tundra that immediately followed nor to the forests that appeared after the glaciers retreated. One factor was probably that its massive antlers impeded its movement through these forests.

One would have expected a study of species extinction in the present and historical past to elucidate the nature of background extinction. However, such research suggests that the extinctions of the past few millennia are atypical of background extinctions throughout the history of life, as they are almost all attributed to the direct or indirect impact of humans. These impacts often appeared with surprising rapidity with the arrival of humans in a region.

Extinction of large endemic mammals on Mediterranean islands had long been attributed to climatic changes in the late Pleistocene, but an increasing amount of archeological evidence shows that humans caused almost all of them. When humans invaded Corsica and Sardinia in about 7,000 BCE, hunting quickly extinguished an endemic deer and dog. Other mammals lasted much longer but gradually succumbed to the combined effects of hunting, species introduced by humans, and vegetation changes associated with grazing and agriculture. The rabbit-like *Prolagus· sardous* persisted on the predator-free island of Tavolara near Sardinia until the eighteenth century. The fates of other Mediterranean island biotas were similar. For instance, Cyprus had dwarf elephants and hippopotami until shortly after the invasion of humans in about 10,000 BCE. Many birds went extinct on these islands over the same interval.

About 9,000 BCE, approximately two-thirds of North America's large mammals—mammoths, mastodons, large cats, and sloths—disappeared quite suddenly. Paul S. Martin (b. 1928) has advanced much evidence for the "Pleistocene overkill hypothesis"—the establishment of humans in North America was contemporaneous with the extinctions, and these species were probably simply hunted to death. The extinction of the moas, endemic giant flightless birds of New Zealand, was more recent and undoubtedly caused by forest clearance and hunting. There were about a dozen moa species, of which the largest was 3 meters tall when standing with neck erect. The first humans (Polynesians) arrived in New Zealand c. 800 CE. Archeological remains show that few moas of any species were left by the sixteenth century, and that probably none survived after 1700 CE. As with many other extinctions, extinction of the moas probably led to other extinctions. The New Zealand forest eagle (*Harpagornis moorei*), which preyed on large, ground-dwelling birds such as moas, disappeared c. 1,400 CE.

For many more recent extinctions, the role of hunting is confirmed by contemporary accounts. The destruction of the three dodo species of the Mascarenes by Europeans, the first humans to colonize these islands, was even more rapid, and it was so well documented that there is no doubt it was due to hunting plus introduced predators (especially pigs and macaques). The Portuguese discovered Mauritius c. 1507 CE, and the Mauritius dodo was extinct by 1680. As well as the Portuguese, the Dutch provisioned their ships with dodos beginning in 1598. The solitaire of La Réunion was eliminated by c. 1750, and that of Rodrigues by 1800. In the Pleistocene, Steller's sea cow occurred around the northern Pacific Rim from Japan to California, but hunting by primitive peoples gradually restricted it to the vicinity of the Commander Islands by 1741. It was common there at that time, but the discovery of this last population, numbering perhaps 2,000, by an expedition led by Captain Vitus Bering led to its demise through hunting within twenty-six years.

Extinction-proneness of Island Species

As the above examples suggest, island species are prominently represented among historic extinctions, and this fact highlights a grave threat to global biodiversity. If New Guinea is taken as the largest island, islands comprise approximately 3 percent of the global landmass, but over 15 percent of all plant, bird, and land snail species are restricted to islands. This high rate of island endemism is generated by isolation—in the absence of gene flow from conspecific species on the mainland or other islands, many island populations have evolved into distinct species. However, island species have proven to be extinction-prone in the face of various anthropogenic changes. For example, island plants are 2.5 times as likely as continental ones to be classified as endangered, and the analogous factor for birds is 2.7. Of known terrestrial vertebrate, mollusc, and insect extinctions since 1600 CE, 355 have occurred on islands and 95 on continents. Virtually all of these extinctions derived from human-activity. For birds, for example, only one or two of the ninety-seven

known island extinctions since 1600 CE can be attributed to natural causes, while over fifty are human-caused (the remainder are unexplained). Of 402 rare and declining island bird species, the rarity and decline are due to natural causes for only eleven species, and to unknown causes for another sixty-four; the remainder are all rare and declining because of human activity. For reptiles and mammals, the statistics are similar—disproportionate numbers of extinct and threatened species on islands, and most extinctions and threats anthropogenic.

There are two main reasons why island species are particularly prone to extinction: the isolation and small size of islands. The small size of islands means that any disaster befalling an island species is more likely to eliminate it than would a comparable event on the mainland. The Hawaiian Islands, the Mascarenes, and the West Indies all lie in cyclonic paths, and recent storms have eliminated or threatened bird species in all of these archipelagoes. A hurricane eliminated a bullfinch on St. Kitts, while Hurricane Hyacinthe in 1982 killed about half the individuals of several endemic bird species on La Réunion. Most remarkably, Hurricane Iniki in 1992 extinguished five endemic species and subspecies of birds on Kauai. It is instructive to compare the latter result to that of Hurricane Hugo in 1989 and Hurricane Andrew in 1992. Hurricane Hugo eliminated approximately half of all Puerto Rican parrots, which were all in one forest struck by the storm. The same hurricane then ravaged a national forest in South Carolina that housed the endangered red-cockaded woodpecker. However, unlike the parrot, the woodpecker existed in several populations, and the storm had minimal impact on the species as a whole. Hurricane Andrew, one of the largest and strongest to strike the United States in historical times, drove no bird species extinct or even into substantial decline. Unlike the Puerto Rican parrot and the birds of Kauai, all resident bird species of southern Florida are widespread, and the majority of their populations were unaffected by the hurricane.

Island isolation leads to a different sort of vulnerability. Because island species evolve in isolation, they lack adaptations to threats and stresses present on continents but not on islands. They are thus often at great risk from the ever-increasing wave of species introductions that began with the advent of fast steamboat travel and is powered by the accelerating rates of international trade and travel. Because most small oceanic islands lack ground-dwelling predators, many birds evolved on these islands to nest on the ground. Many even evolved flightlessness. Subsequent introduction of cats, rats, mongooses, and other carnivorous mammals led to many extinctions (some thirty-five of the ninety-seven island endemic bird extinctions known since 1600 CE). Island plants generally evolved without large grazers, and so lacked spines, thorns, chemical defenses, and rooting architecture that would have defended against the goats, sheep, pigs, cattle, rabbits, deer, reindeer, and other introduced grazers that have devastated island plant communities worldwide and generated myriad extinctions. Although there is no estimate of the total number of island plant extinctions caused by introduced grazers, it is surely enormous. For instance, on St. Helena, goats introduced in 1513 formed enormous herds within a century. It is believed that by the time botanists reached the island in 1805–1810, half the flora of approximately 100 endemic species was already extinct.

Current Extinction Rates

Though the extinction of unusual island species is the most striking feature of the loss of biodiversity over the last four centuries, there is a clear increase above previous background rates for continental species as well. Globally, for island and continental species combined, it is estimated that extinction rates over the last four centuries are between 100 and 1,000 times background rates, and about half of the extinctions recorded over the last four centuries have occurred within the last century. The major problem in assessing this increase is that some 80 percent of all species have not even been recognized or described by systematists, so estimating the rate at which they were and are being lost is highly speculative. Second, even for scientifically recognized species, the habitat requirements, biogeographic range, and status are poorly known for most groups. Finally, proving that no more individuals of a species exist is very difficult and often can be stated with assurance only decades after a species actually disappears. Nevertheless, by focussing on well-known taxa (such as birds and butterflies) and well-studied regions (such as Europe and parts of North America), a sense of the global rates of extinction and their causes can be gleaned.

Widely disputed claims in the 1970s that tens of thousands of species were disappearing annually were not supported by direct evidence and were extremely controversial, but subsequent research suggests they were not far off the mark—at least thousands and possibly tens of thousands of species go extinct each year.

For instance, in the case of birds, at least 103 species have been lost since 1800; careful examination of the range and biology of the survivors suggests that at least 1,186 (12 percent of all birds) are threatened, and that over 400 are unlikely to survive the century. This would constitute an extinction rate of about 0.04 percent per year. If there are 7,000,000 species in total, and birds are typical, then 2,800 species of all sorts could be disappearing each year. However, insects and plants make up a far greater fraction of biodiversity (perhaps two-thirds) and are likely to have much higher rates of threat and extinction than birds do because they tend to have much smaller geographic ranges. For molluscs and fish, fragmentary data also suggest even greater current extinction rates than that of birds.

As with birds, the general picture for other taxa is that many species have already gone extinct in historical times, and the prospect is for rapidly accelerating extinction in the current century. For example, in the United States, some groups have lost an appalling fraction of their species—freshwater mussels at least 10 percent, for example—and the total fractional loss for all species is believed to be approximately 1 percent. However, approximately 7 percent of the U.S. biota is believed to be critically imperiled, and most of these species will be extinct within a century. Another 24 percent is already of conservation concern but not apparently in imminent danger of extinction. For plants of the Mediterranean region, approximately 35 of some 23,000 species are known to have gone extinct in recent times, but approximately 15 percent of the species in this flora are believed to be threatened with extinction. A similar fraction holds for the other three regions with Mediterranean climates for which data exist—the Cape Province of South Africa, California, and western Australia.

An even more pessimistic prospect emerges when one considers the tabulated causes of current endangerment and recent extinction. All of these are anthropogenic, and most are increasing, often at a rate faster than human population growth. The greatest cause of endangerment and recent extinction worldwide is habitat destruction. For example, habitat destruction is at least part of the threat to 85 percent of all imperiled species in the United States. A key finding of ecological research is that many species are highly restricted in their ability to use habitats different from their original one. Unsurprisingly, massive habitat modification has led to great numbers of extinctions, and habitat destruction has been massive in many of the most species-rich habitats. For instance, in eastern North

America and Puerto Rico, 99 percent of primary forest has been destroyed over the last 400 years. In some regions (e.g., the eastern United States), there is much secondary forest, but many species found in primary forest cannot thrive in such forest. In many areas, an even higher fraction of wetlands has been lost than of forests. In the coterminous United States, 53 percent of wetlands were destroyed between 1780 and 1980, and similar wetland loss is recorded for many other regions. Unlike the case of forests, there is little replacement of original wetlands by other sorts of wetland.

The second greatest cause of recent species endangerment and extinction worldwide is the impact of introduced species. Of imperiled U.S. species, 49 percent are threatened at least partly by introduced species, a figure greater than the proportion threatened by pollution, harvest, and disease combined. Introduced species threaten and eliminate native species in many ways, but especially by modifying their habitat, preying on them, competing with them, transmitting new diseases to them, and hybridizing with them. This last phenomenon leads to a subtle sort of genetic extinction, as a lineage does not terminate, but the gene pool of a species changes inexorably until individuals differ greatly from those of the nominate species. This is no trivial mechanism. For example, twenty-four animal species listed under the United States Endangered Species Act (1973) are believed now to be extinct, and hybridization with an introduced species is believed to have been a key factor in three of these extinctions—those of the Tecopa pupfish (*Cyprinodon nevadensis calidae*), the Amistad gambusia (*Gambusia amistadensis*), and the longjaw cisco (*Coregonus alpenae*).

Worldwide, overexploitation by harvest and hunting is probably the third leading cause of endangerment and recent extinction. For example, of the 485 known animal extinctions over the last four centuries, causes have been assigned to 44 percent: 10 percent are believed to be due to hunting, which follows only habitat destruction and introduced species as a cause of extinction. However, among current threats to all species in the United States, pollution far outpaces overexploitation as a contributing factor (24 percent versus 17 percent). In the United States, in the seventeenth through nineteenth centuries, unregulated hunting for meat, eggs, fur, and feathers drastically affected many vertebrate species and led to several extinctions, such as that of the great auk (*Pinguinus impennis*), which disappeared in about 1800. In much of North America and Europe, the lessening reliance on game food and the passage of laws protecting wildlife

have reduced (but not eliminated) this threat. However, in many parts of the world, hunting of vertebrates for food remains a major cause of extinction. In the twentieth century, pollution from pesticides and various chemical by products became a key threat, although it is now regulated to a degree in some parts of the world and will probably decline substantially as a cause of extinction.

Finally, it is important to realize that various forces can combine to cause extinction, and it can be difficult to assign a single specific cause to an extinction even when the history of the decline and disappearance of a species is quite well documented. Consider the heath hen (*Tympanuchus cupido cupido*), a species in the eastern United States that disappeared in 1932 when the last bird died on the island of Martha's Vineyard. This extinction is typically ascribed to human habitat alteration plus hunting, though both hunting and habitat destruction in the bird's range had stopped well before 1932. A species found in sandy scrub-oak plains, heath hens were originally common from Maine to Virginia. Easily killed, they were quickly eliminated from accessible areas by hunting, disappearing by 1870 from all their last redoubts (in Long Island, New Jersey, and the foothills of the Pocono Mountains) save for Martha's Vineyard. By 1890 only 200 individuals survived, and by 1896, fewer than 100. A refuge was established for the last 50 birds on Martha's Vineyard in 1908; habitat was improved, and by 1915 approximately 2,000 heath hens foraged over the entire island. However, a fire during a gale in 1916 swept through the breeding area destroying birds, eggs, and habitat. An unusually severe winter followed, during which an unprecedented flight of goshawks reduced the population to fewer than 150, mostly males. It is believed that inbreeding depression ensued, and in 1920, a poultry disease brought to the island with domestic turkeys killed many heath hens. Only thirteen birds (eleven males) survived by 1927, and two individuals lasted until 1928. The last sighting of the lone survivor, a male that many ornithologists and birders flocked to see, was on 11 March 1932.

The lesson of this sad tale, which probably epitomizes the final disappearance of many species that have gone extinct, is that several factors probably combine to cause most extinctions, and once a species is greatly reduced in numbers and range, it is probably destined to decline inevitably to extinction short of extraordinary measures and good luck. It is this fact that leads conservation biologists, with knowledge of the population trajectories and current status of many species, to the pessimistic prediction of an even greater wave of extinction in the next few centuries than in the past few, and to the specter of a mass extinction.

Daniel Simberloff

Further Reading

Blondel, J., & Aronson, J. (1999). *Biology and wildlife of the Mediterranean region*. Oxford, UK: Oxford University Press.

Groombridge, B. (Ed.). (1991). *Global biodiversity: Status of the Earth's living resources*. London: Chapman & Hall.

Klein, R.G., & Martin, P.S. (Eds.). *Quaternary extinctions: A prehistoric revolution*. Tucson: University of Arizona Press.

Lawton, J. H., & May, R. M. (Eds.). (1995). *Extinction rates*. Oxford, UK: Oxford University Press.

Marshall, L. G., Webb, S. D., Sepkoski, J. J., Jr., & Raup, D. M. (1982). Mammalian evolution and the Great American Interchange. *Science, 215*, 1351–1357.

Martin, P. S. (1986). In D. K. Elliott (Ed.) *Dynamics of extinction* (pp. 107–130). New York: Wiley.

McMillan, M., & Wilcove, D. (1994). Why have species protected by the Endangered species Act become extinct? *Endangered species Update, 11*(11), 5–6.

Nitecki, M. H. (Ed.). (1984). *Extinctions*. Chicago: University of Chicago Press.

Raup, D. M. (1991). *Extinction: Bad genes or bad luck?* New York: Norton.

Raup, D. M., & Jablonski, D. (Eds.) (1986). *Patterns and processes in the history of life*. Berlin, Germany: Springer-Verlag.

Raup, D. M., & Sepkoski, J. J., Jr. (1982). Mass extinctions in the marine fossil record. *Science, 215*, 1501–1503.

Raven, P. H. (Ed.). (1999). *Nature and human society*. Washington, DC: National Academy Press.

Ridley, M. (1996). *Evolution* (2nd ed.). Cambridge, MA: Blackwell.

Simberloff, D. (1994). The ecology of extinction. *Acta palaeontologica polonica, 38*, 159–174.

Simberloff, D. (2000). Extinction-proneness of island species—causes and management implications. *Raffles bulletin of zoology, 48*, 1–9.

Stein, B. A., Kutner, L. S., & Adams, J. S. (Eds.). (2000). *Precious heritage*: The status of biodiversity in the United States. New York: Oxford University Press.

Whittaker, R. J. (1998). *Island biogeography*. Oxford, UK: Oxford University Press.